THE
LITERATURE OF AMERICA

THE
LITERATURE OF AMERICA

The
LITERATURE *of*
AMERICA

An ANTHOLOGY of PROSE and VERSE

VOLUME II From the Civil War to the Present

Edited by

ARTHUR HOBSON QUINN
Professor of English, University of Pennsylvania

ALBERT CROLL BAUGH
Professor of English, University of Pennsylvania

WILL DAVID HOWE
Formerly Professor of English, Indiana University

"88"

CHARLES SCRIBNER'S SONS
New York · Chicago · Boston

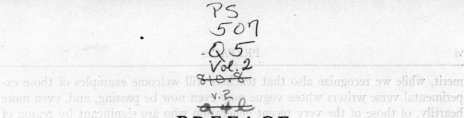

PREFACE

THE present anthology is intended to supply in compact form a reasonably extensive collection of material for the study of American literature. In the preparation of it the editors have been guided by the following considerations:

First, that the development of American literature in all its periods should be adequately represented,—that, while the large figures who established our literature at home and abroad during the first half of the nineteenth century should be properly emphasized, more complete recognition than has heretofore been given should be accorded to their predecessors in the Colonial and Revolutionary periods, to their successors in the later nineteenth century who, by their discovery of new fields in the South and West, made our literature truly national, and to the many original creative artists who during the twentieth century have widened the scope of poetry, the short story, the essay, and the drama in matter, form and spirit.

Second, that the literature selected should represent adequately the development of American thought and the distinctive aspects of American life,—both of which it not only reflects but in the past has often anticipated and at times profoundly influenced. Emphasis upon the national character of American literature does not imply that it need be parochial in theme. Art is greatest when it deals with universal motives, whether the scene be domestic or foreign, or, indeed, exist only in the imagination of a Poe or an O'Neill.

Third, that the selections should be representative of each author at his best, and should at the same time illustrate the various aspects of his work.

Fourth, that the selections should, with a few necessary exceptions, be complete texts or complete units of the works represented.

Practical considerations have forbidden the inclusion of passages from novels, which must usually be read in their entirety. Exceptions have been made only in the cases of the first important novelist, Charles Brockden Brown, and of Herman Melville, both of whom may be read in selection. Fortunately it has been found possible to represent nearly all the greater novelists by their short stories, and a list of novels suitable for supplementary reading will be found in the Notes. Five plays have been included, not as an adequate representation of American drama, but as illustrating certain phases of our literature which would otherwise be unrepresented. A list of representative plays has also been given in the Notes.

To meet the increasing demand for contemporary material, we have presented an unusually large number of selections from recent poetry, the short story, the essay, and the biography, to which at present so much attention is being paid. We have felt it most helpful to include a relatively large number of poems by those living poets whose work is generally acknowledged to be of permanent

v

merit, while we recognize also that teachers will welcome examples of those experimental verse writers whose vogue may even now be passing, and, even more heartily, of those of the very recent generation who are significant by reason of their promise.

The arrangement of material is chronological. In the later periods, however, because of the volume and variety of American literature, an attempt has been made to introduce a degree of order by grouping the poetry, the essay, fiction, and drama within the larger chronological scheme. Those who wish to study American poetry, fiction, or essays will welcome this arrangement. Those who prefer to treat individuals will readily assemble their work.

Each selection has been accompanied by a date indicating its chronological position. In the case of poetry the usual convention has been followed of printing the date of composition (if known) at the left and the date of publication at the right. More than one date indicates that the poem was subsequently revised. The dates of prose selections have been placed under the title. Unless otherwise stated, the date given is that of publication.

In preparing the Introductions and Notes the method has been varied in accordance with the material. Each section of the anthology is preceded by a brief introduction dealing with the period or the form of literature to which the section is devoted. At the end of the volume are all necessary notes, giving biographical accounts of the authors, more extended when adequate biographies are not easily procurable, but, in the cases of the greater writers, limited to a few of the more important events in their lives. Bibliographies follow and then explanations of individual works, obscure passages, or historical allusions. Throughout we have kept in mind the fact that this is not a history of literature and have provided the teacher with assistance rather than offered a substitute for him.

ACKNOWLEDGMENTS

The editors wish to express their indebtedness to the publishers and individuals who have permitted the use of material which is in copyright or of which they are the authorized publishers, as follows:

In volume II: To D. APPLETON AND COMPANY for Madison Cawein's "Happiness" and Joel Chandler Harris's "The Story of the Deluge" and "Mr. Rabbit Nibbles up the Butter." To DAVID BELASCO for "Madame Butterfly." To THE BOBBS-MERRILL COMPANY for the selections from Riley. To BRANDT AND BRANDT for the poems of Edna St. Vincent Millay. To THE CENTURY COMPANY for the selections from S. Weir Mitchell. To DODD, MEAD AND COMPANY for the poems of Dunbar and Hovey. To DOUBLEDAY, DORAN AND COMPANY for the selections from Stephen Vincent Benét, O. Henry, Joyce Kilmer, Booth Tarkington, Whitman, and for Lizette Woodworth Reese's "Betrayed," "Heroism," "Waiting," "Anne," and "April Weather." To E. P. DUTTON AND COMPANY for Cawein's "Aubade." To MRS. THEODOSIA GARRISON FAULKS and G. P. PUTNAM'S SONS for the selections from her poetry. To HAMLIN GARLAND for "The Return of a

Private." To HARCOURT, BRACE AND COMPANY for the poems of T. A. Daly, for
Carl Sandburg's "Washington Monument by Night" and the selection from his
"Abraham Lincoln: The Prairie Years," and for the story by W. D. Steele. To
HARPER AND BROTHERS for the selections from Margaret Deland, Mary Wilkins
Freeman, and Mark Twain. To JOSEPH HERGESHEIMER for "Charleston." To
HENRY HOLT AND COMPANY for the story by Dorothy Canfield, Sandburg's
"Chicago" and "Fog," and the selections from Robert Frost. To BRIAN HOOKER
for the selections from his poems. To the HOUGHTON, MIFFLIN COMPANY for the
selections from Henry Adams, Aldrich, Gamaliel Bradford, Burroughs, Crothers,
Gilder, Louise Imogen, Guiney, Bret Harte, John Hay, Sarah Orne, Jewett, Amy
Lowell, Moody, Josephine Preston Peabody, Bliss Perry, Agnes Repplier, Anne
Douglas Sedgwick, Sill, Stedman, and Woodrow Wilson. To MISS MILDRED
HOWELLS and JOHN MEAD HOWELLS for the selections from William Dean
Howells. To THOMAN S. JONES, JR., for the selections from his poetry. To ALFRED
A. KNOPF, Inc., for the stories by Willa Cather and Stephen Crane. To LITTLE,
BROWN AND COMPANY for the selections from Emily Dickinson, E. E. Hale, and
Louise Chandler Moulton. To F. A. LITZ for the poems of Father Tabb. To
HORACE LIVERIGHT for the selections from Dreiser and O'Neill. To JOHN N.
LODGE for the poems of George Cabot Lodge. To RICHARD J. MADDEN for the
release of "Lazarus Laughed," by Eugene O'Neill, prior to professional produc-
tion. To THE MACMILLAN COMPANY (New York) for the selections from James
Lane Allen, DuBose Heyward, Henry James, Vachel Lindsay, MacKaye, Nei-
hardt, Sara Teasdale, and for Robinson's "Flammonde," "Cassandra," "The
False Gods" and the passage from "Tristram." To THE MACMILLAN COMPANY
(London) for Henry James's "Emerson." To EDWIN MARKHAM for "The Man
with the Hoe" and "Lincoln, the Man of the People." To EDGAR LEE MASTERS
for the selections from his poems. To HOUSTON MIFFLIN and the OXFORD UNI-
VERSITY PRESS for the poems of Lloyd Mifflin. To MISS ABBIE LELAND MILLER
for the poems of Joaquin Miller. To JOHN P. MORTON AND COMPANY for Cawein's
"The Feud." To THOMAS BIRD MOSHER for Lizette Woodworth Reese's "To-
day," "Spinning Tops," "Tears," "Compensation," "The Thrush in the Orchard," and "At Last." To G. P. PUTNAM'S SONS for the story by F. Marion
Crawford. To MISS LIZETTE WOODWORTH REESE and the NORMAN REMINGTON
COMPANY for "The Common Lot." To CHARLES SCRIBNER'S SONS for the selec-
tions from Brownell, Cable, Olive Tilford Dargan, Field, Lanier, Page, Roosevelt,
Santayana, Seeger, Sherman, F. Hopkinson Smith, Stockton, Edith Wharton,
Wheelock, and for Joel Chandler Harris's "Free Joe and the Rest of the World"
and Robinson's "John Evereldown," "Luke Havergal," "Richard Cory," "Her
Eyes," "Calvary," "Dear Friends," "Amaryllis," "The Garden," "The Dead
Village," "Credo," "Sonnet," "L'Envoi," "Miniver Cheevy," "For a Dead
Lady," and "The Master." To the YALE UNIVERSITY PRESS for the poems of
William Alexander Percy.

The editors wish to acknowledge the personal interest and advice concerning
the selection of his poems given by Mr. Robert Frost.

the selection of the poems given by Mr. Robert Frost.

The editors wish to acknowledge the personal interest and advice concerning Mr...

CONTENTS

IX. LINCOLN AND THE CIVIL WAR

X. WALT WHITMAN

XI. THE COMEDY OF MANNERS

XII. THE POETRY OF THE LATER NINETEENTH CENTURY

CONTENTS

XIII. THE SHORT STORY OF THE LATER NINETEENTH CENTURY

XIV. THE MODERN ROMANTIC DRAMA

XV. THE MODERN ESSAY AND BIOGRAPHY

XVI. THE CONTEMPORARY SHORT STORY

XVII. CONTEMPORARY POETRY

XVIII. THE CONTEMPORARY DRAMA

THE
LITERATURE OF AMERICA

THE
LITERATURE OF AMERICA

IX. LINCOLN AND THE CIVIL WAR

ABRAHAM LINCOLN has become the chief representative of the prose of the Civil War, not only because his personality dominated that period, but also through the clarity and vigor of his style. These qualities become steadily more apparent, from the first of his utterances that rises into permanent value as literature, the speech at Springfield in 1858, in which he took his position that the United States could exist no longer "half slave and half free." His gift for compression is revealed in the Farewell Address at Springfield and the speech at Independence Hall, Philadelphia, with its note of prophecy. His skill in adaptation and his power of emotional appeal appear in the Inaugural Address and the Message to Congress, and his political philosophy, which was to save the Union, even if Abolition had to be postponed, is clearly expressed. The Letter to Horace Greeley illustrates his clear thinking and his rhetorical effectiveness. These qualities are seen in epitome in the Address at Gettysburg, with its unity and variety, its rhythmical cadence and the rise to a climax in which he turned an ordinary phrase into an immortal one.

If we would understand the spirit of the poetry growing out of the Civil War, we must follow it not from the point of view of individual authorship, but rather from that of the campaigns out of which it arose. The Civil War is best expressed as an attempt on the part of the Northern armies to break through a line drawn, roughly speaking, from Fortress Monroe, in Virginia, running through Chesapeake Bay and the Potomac River to the mountains, then across western Virginia and through Kentucky, Missouri, and Indian Territory to New Mexico.

In December 1860 South Carolina seceded, and on February 4, 1861, a convention established at Montgomery, Alabama, the Confederate States of America. The Northern reaction may be seen in Oliver Wendell Holmes' *Voice of the Loyal North* (see p. 375), read at his class dinner, January 3, 1861. In February 1861 Henry Timrod celebrated the birth of the Confederacy with his ode, *Ethnogenesis*, and James Ryder Randall was inspired by the first shedding of blood, April 19, 1861, in Baltimore, to write his stirring lyric, *My Maryland*. It has more literary quality than *Dixie*, which was first composed as a variety song by Dan D. Emmett in 1859. The words by General Albert Pike, while sung during the war, have never quite eclipsed the original version. The first forms of these war songs retained their hold even in the face of more ambitious efforts. Thus *The Bonnie Blue Flag*, by Annie Chambers Ketchum, while much better in quality, did not entirely supersede that written by Harry McCarthy for the Varieties Theatre in New Orleans, in 1861. *John Brown's Body* was the first of the Northern war songs to take hold of the soldiers' fancy. The version sung by them has an elemental quality and was never displaced by the more polished efforts of H. H. Brownell and others. It has been attributed to Charles Sprague Hall and to Frank E. Jerome, but the authorship has not been finally established.

The note of appeal to state pride expressed in *My Maryland*, which was one of the characteristics of Southern war poetry, is repeated by Francis Orray Ticknor's *The Virginians of the Valley*. Since the Confederates were defending their homes from attack, it is natural that the war poetry should at first reveal more inspiration on the Southern side. By September 1861, however, the regret for the losses occasioned by the early reverses of the Union armies found expression in such poems as *The Picket Guard*, by Ethel Lynn Beers. The Northern war sentiment rose to much greater heights in Mrs. Julia Ward Howe's *The Battle Hymn of the Republic*, which just filled the front page of *The Atlantic Monthly* in February 1862. In the same

717

issue of *The Atlantic Monthly* appeared Lowell's biting satire of *Jonathan to John* (see p. 389), representing the resentment of the North against the attitude of Great Britain at the time of the "Trent Affair." The national note was also struck with force and dignity in Boker's *Ode to America*, written March 7, 1862. Meanwhile Lincoln had called for more troops, and in response there appeared in the *New York Evening Post* for July 16, 1862, *We Are Coming, Father Abraham, Three Hundred Thousand More*, by James Sloan Gibbons.

General MacDowell's campaign against Richmond produced little significant verse except Ticknor's *Our Left*, celebrating the victory at Bull Run. General McClellan was placed in charge of the Army of the Potomac and advanced through the Peninsula. In preventing the junction of McClellan and MacDowell, Turner Ashby, a Southern cavalry leader, was killed, and in consequence Mrs. Preston wrote her touching *Dirge for Ashby*. This was paralleled on the Northern side a little later, after the second battle of Bull Run, by Boker's *Dirge for a Soldier*, written on the death of General Philip Kearny. McClellan, who had been superseded by General Pope, was restored to the command of the Army of the Potomac. He did not proceed rapidly enough, however, for the popular demand, which is reflected vigorously in Stedman's *Wanted—A Man*, published September 8, 1862, just nine days before McClellan defeated Lee at Antietam. Lincoln was so much impressed by this poem that he read it to his cabinet. This campaign also brought forth Whittier's *Barbara Frietchie* (see p. 339). General Hooker was put in command of the Army of the Potomac and advanced in April 1863. In the meantime, General John Pelham had been killed, giving occasion to Randall's fine requiem. The disastrous defeat of Chancellorsville was the result of Hooker's movement, but the Southern victory was counterbalanced by the loss of General Stonewall Jackson, who was killed through a mistake by his own men. There was a burst of lyric poetry on the Southern side occasioned by his death. The best of these lyrics are *The Dying Words of Stonewall Jackson*, by Sidney Lanier, *Under the Shade of the Trees*, by Mrs. Preston, Ticknor's *Our Great Captain*, and an anonymous poem, *The Brigade Must Not Know, Sir!* The invasion of the North by Lee in 1863, which culminated in the battle of Gettysburg, brought about a great deal of writing. On the Northern side the best poems were Bayard Taylor's *Gettysburg Ode*, and Bret Harte's *John Burns at Gettysburg*. On the Southern side, Will H. Thompson's *The High Tide at Gettysburg*, although it was not written until twenty-five years later, belongs to the poetry inspired directly by the Civil War, since Thompson was a Confederate soldier. From the later campaigns of the Army of the Potomac which culminated in the capture of Richmond, *Sheridan's Ride*, by Thomas Buchanan Read, still reflects the devotion to a leader, less frequent upon the Northern than upon the Southern side.

The war in the West, by which the Mississippi River was opened to the Union forces and the Confederate line turned back upon itself through Kentucky and Tennessee into Georgia, produced Ticknor's *The River*, George F. Root's *The Battle Cry of Freedom*, Boker's *The Black Regiment*, and one of the finest of all the war poems, Ticknor's *Little Giffen*.

During the entire war the Navy had as its greatest task the blockading of the Southern coast. The Southern note of defiance is represented best in the early stages of the war by Timrod's poem *Carolina* and later, in 1863, by his *Charleston*. The Confederate raider "Alabama" was the theme of Ticknor's vigorous lyric, *The Sword in the Sea*. On the Northern side the note of "Don't give up the ship" is struck even more insistently than that of victory. Among many verses inspired by the refusal of the "Cumberland" to surrender to the "Merrimac," Boker's *On Board the Cumberland* has something of the vigor of ballad poetry. The best of the Union poetry which celebrated the conflict on the sea is found in Henry Howard Brownell's *The River Fight* and *The Bay Fight*. *The Bay Fight*, describing Farragut's victory in Mobile

Bay, in which Brownell was present, is naturally more vigorous than *The River Fight*, since Brownell had only read reports of the earlier battle.

To the later period of the war belong the many lyrics which celebrated the return of the soldiers. Among the most moving of these is probably Kate Putnam Osgood's *Driving Home the Cows*, for it described an incident typical of thousands of similar occurrences in both North and South. Nora Perry's *Riding Down* emphasizes also the personal side of the war. Here belong the poems which lamented the "lost cause," such as Father Ryan's *The Conquered Banner* and *The Sword of Robert Lee*, Timrod's *Ode Sung at Magnolia Cemetery*, and Paul Hamilton Hayne's *South Carolina to the States of the North*, portraying the horrors of reconstruction. The note of reconciliation is best represented by Francis M. Finch's *The Blue and the Gray*. The lyrics here assembled suffer perhaps by comparison with that supreme utterance of the war, the *Harvard Commemoration Ode*, by Lowell (see p. 411), but they reveal the temper of a time when patriotic feeling ran high, and convey to us the emotional exaltation induced by the war which we cannot recover in any other way.

ABRAHAM LINCOLN (1809-1865)

SPEECH AT SPRINGFIELD, BEFORE THE REPUBLICAN STATE CONVENTION BY WHICH LINCOLN HAD BEEN NAMED AS CANDIDATE FOR UNITED STATES SENATOR

(June 16, 1858)

MR. PRESIDENT AND GENTLEMEN OF THE CONVENTION:

If we could first know where we are, and whither we are tending, we could better judge what to do, and how to do it. We are now far into the fifth year since a policy was initiated with the avowed object and confident promise of putting an end to slavery agitation. Under the operation of that policy, that agitation has not only not ceased but has constantly augmented. In my opinion, it will not cease until a crisis shall have been reached and passed. "A house divided against itself cannot stand." I believe this government cannot endure permanently half slave and half free. I do not expect the Union to be dissolved—I do not expect the house to fall—but I do expect it will cease to be divided. It will become all one thing, or all the other. Either the opponents of slavery will arrest the further spread of it, and place it where the public mind shall rest in the belief that it is in the course of ultimate extinction; or its advocates will push it forward till it shall become alike lawful in all the States, old as well as new, North as well as South.

Have we no tendency to the latter condition?

Let any one who doubts carefully contemplate that now almost complete legal combination—piece of machinery, so to speak—compounded of the Nebraska doctrine and the Dred Scott decision. Let him consider not only what work the machinery is adapted to do, and how well adapted; but also let him study the history of its construction, and trace, if he can, or rather fail, if he can, to trace the evidences of design and concert of action among its chief architects, from the beginning.

The new year of 1854 found slavery excluded from more than half the States by State constitutions, and from most of the national territory by congressional prohibition. Four days later commenced the struggle which ended in repealing that congressional prohibition. This opened all the national territory to slavery, and was the first point gained.

But, so far, Congress only had acted; and an indorsement by the people, real or apparent, was indispensable to save the point already gained and give chance for more.

This necessity had not been overlooked, but had been provided for, as well as might be, in the notable argument of "squatter sovereignty," otherwise called "sacred right of self-government," which latter phrase, though expressive of the only rightful basis of any government, was so perverted in this attempted use of it as to amount to just this: That if any one man choose to enslave another, not hird man shall be allowed to object. That argument was incorporated into the Nebraska bill itself, in the language which follows: "It being the true intent and meaning of this act not to legislate slavery into any Territory or State, nor to exclude it therefrom; but to leave the people thereof perfectly free to form and regulate their domestic institutions in their own way, subject only to the Constitution of the United States." Then opened the roar of loose declamation in favor of "squatter sovereignty" and "sacred right of self-government." "But," said opposition members, "let us amend the bill so as to expressly declare that the people of the Territory may exclude slavery." "Not we," said the friends of the measure; and down they voted the amendment.

While the Nebraska bill was passing through Congress, a law case involving the question of a negro's freedom, by reason of his owner having voluntarily taken him first into a free State and then into a Territory covered by the congressional prohibition, and held him as a slave for a long time in each, was passing through the United States Circuit Court for the District of Missouri; and both Nebraska bill and lawsuit were brought to a decision in the same month of May, 1854. The negro's name was Dred Scott, which name now designates the decision finally made in the case. Before the then next presidential election, the law case came to and was argued in the Supreme Court of the United States; but the decision of it was deferred until after the election. Still, before the election, Senator Trumbull, on the floor of the Senate, requested the leading advocate of the Nebraska bill to state his opinion whether the people of a Territory can constitutionally exclude slavery from their limits; and the latter answered: "That is a question for the Supreme Court."

The election came. Mr. Buchanan was elected, and the indorsement, such as it was, secured. That was the second point gained. The indorsement, however, fell short of a clear popular majority by nearly four hundred thousand votes, and so, perhaps, was not overwhelmingly reliable and satisfactory. The outgoing President, in his last annual message, as impressively as possible echoed back upon the people the weight and authority of the indorsement. The Supreme Court met again; did not announce their decision, but ordered a reargument. The presidential inauguration came, and still no decision of the court; but the incoming President in his inaugural address fervently exhorted the people to abide by the forthcoming decision, whatever it might be. Then, in a few days, came the decision.

The reputed author of the Nebraska bill finds an early occasion to make a speech at this capital indorsing the Dred Scott decision, and vehemently denouncing all opposition to it. The new President, too, seizes the early occasion of the Silliman letter to indorse and strongly construe that decision, and to express his astonishment that any different view had ever been entertained!

At length a squabble springs up between the President and the author of the Nebraska bill, on the mere question of fact, whether the Lecompton constitution was or was not, in any just sense, made by the people of Kansas; and in that quarrel the latter declares that all he wants is a fair vote for the people, and that he cares not whether slavery be voted down or voted up. I do not understand his declaration that he cares not whether slavery be voted down or voted up to be intended by him other than as an apt definition of the policy he would impress upon the public mind—the principle for which he declares he has suffered so much, and is ready to suffer to the end. And well may he cling to that principle. If he has any parental feeling, well may he cling to it. That principle is the only shred left of his original Nebraska doctrine. Under the Dred Scott decision "squatter sovereignty" squatted out of existence, tumbled down like temporary scaffolding,—like the mold at the foundry, served through one blast and fell back into loose sand,—helped to carry an election, and then was kicked to the winds. His late joint struggle with the Republicans against the Lecompton constitution involves nothing of the original Nebraska doctrine. That struggle was made on a point—the right of a people to make their own constitution—upon which he and the Republicans have never differed.

The several points of the Dred Scott decision, in connection with Senator Douglas's "care not" policy, constitute the piece of machinery in its present state of advancement. This was the third point gained. The working points of that machinery are:

(1) That no negro slave, imported as such from Africa, and no descendant of such slave, can ever be a citizen of any State, in the sense of that term as used in the Constitution of the United States. This point is made in order to deprive the negro in every possible event of the benefit of that provision of the United States Constitution which declares that "the citizens of each State shall be entitled to all the privileges and immunities of citizens in the several States."

(2) That, "subject to the Constitution of

the United States," neither Congress nor a territorial legislature can exclude slavery from any United States Territory. This point is made in order that individual men may fill up the Territories with slaves, without danger of losing them as property, and thus enhance the chances of permanency to the institution through all the future.

(3) That whether the holding a negro in actual slavery in a free State makes him free as against the holder, the United States courts will not decide, but will leave to be decided by the courts of any slave State the negro may be forced into by the master. This point is made not to be pressed immediately, but, if acquiesced in for a while, and apparently indorsed by the people at an election, then to sustain the logical conclusion that what Dred Scott's master might lawfully do with Dred Scott in the free State of Illinois, every other master may lawfully do with any other one or one thousand slaves in Illinois or in any other free State.

Auxiliary to all this, and working hand in hand with it, the Nebraska doctrine, or what is left of it, is to educate and mold public opinion, at least Northern public opinion, not to care whether slavery is voted down or voted up. This shows exactly where we now are, and partially, also, whither we are tending.

It will throw additional light on the latter, to go back and run the mind over the string of historical facts already stated. Several things will now appear less dark and mysterious than they did when they were transpiring. The people were to be left "perfectly free," "subject only to the Constitution." What the Constitution had to do with it outsiders could not then see. Plainly enough now, it was an exactly fitted niche for the Dred Scott decision to afterward come in, and declare the perfect freedom of the people to be just no freedom at all. Why was the amendment expressly declaring the right of the people voted down? Plainly enough now, the adoption of it would have spoiled the niche for the Dred Scott decision. Why was the court decision held up? Why even a senator's individual opinion withheld till after the presidential election? Plainly enough now, the speaking out then would have damaged the "perfectly free" argument upon which the election was to be carried. Why the outgoing President's felicitation on the indorsement? Why the delay of a reargument? Why the incoming President's advance exhortation in favor of the decision? These things look like the cautious patting and petting of a spirited horse preparatory to mounting him, when it is dreaded that he may give the rider a fall. And why the hasty after-endorsement of the decision by the President and others?

We cannot absolutely know that all these exact adaptations are the result of preconcert. But when we see a lot of framed timbers, different portions of which we know have been gotten out at different times and places and by different workmen,—Stephen, Franklin, Roger, and James, for instance,—and we see these timbers joined together, and see they exactly make the frame of a house or a mill, all the tenons and mortises exactly fitting, and all the lengths and proportions of the different pieces exactly adapted to their respective places, and not a piece too many or too few, not omitting even scaffolding—or, if a single piece be lacking, we see the place in the frame exactly fitted and prepared yet to bring such piece in—in such a case we find it impossible not to believe that Stephen and Franklin and Roger and James all understood one another from the beginning, and all worked upon a common plan or draft drawn up before the first blow was struck.

It should not be overlooked that, by the Nebraska bill, the people of a State as well as Territory were to be left "perfectly free," "subject only to the Constitution." Why mention a State? They were legislating for Territories, and not for or about States. Certainly the people of a State are and ought to be subject to the Constitution of the United States; but why is mention of this lugged into this merely territorial law? Why are the people of a Territory and the people of a State therein lumped together, and their relation to the Constitution therein treated as being precisely the same? While the opinion of the court, by Chief Justice Taney, in the Dred Scott case, and the separate opinions of all the concurring judges, expressly declare that the Constitution of the United States neither permits Congress nor a territorial legislature to exclude slavery from any United States Territory, they all omit to declare whether or not the same Constitution permits a State, or the people of a State, to exclude it. Possibly, this is a mere omission; but who can be quite sure, if McLean or Curtis had sought to get into the opinion a declaration of unlimited power in the people of a State to exclude slavery from their limits, just as Chase and Mace sought to get such declaration, in behalf of the people of a Territory, into the Nebraska bill—I ask, who can be quite sure that it would not have been voted down in the one case as it had been in the other? The nearest approach to the point of declaring the power of a State over slavery is made by Judge Nelson. He approaches it more than once, using the precise idea, and almost the language too, of the Nebraska act. On one occasion his exact language is: "Except in cases where the power is restrained by the Constitution of the United States, the law of the State is supreme over the subject of slavery within its jurisdiction." In what cases the power of the States is so restrained by the United States Constitution is left an open question, precisely as the same question as to the restraint on the power of the Territories was left open in the Nebraska act. Put this and that together, and we have another nice little niche, which we may, ere long, see filled with another Supreme Court decision declaring that the Constitution of the United States does not permit a State to exclude slavery from its limits. And this may especially be expected if the doctrine of "care not whether slavery be voted down or voted up" shall gain upon the public mind sufficiently to give promise that such a decision can be maintained when made.

Such a decision is all that slavery now lacks of being alike lawful in all the States. Welcome, or unwelcome, such decision is probably coming, and will soon be upon us, unless the power of the present political dynasty shall be met and overthrown. We shall lie down pleasantly dreaming that the people of Missouri are on the verge of making their State free, and we shall awake to the reality instead that the Supreme Court has made Illinois a slave State. To meet and overthrow the power of that dynasty is the work now before all those who would prevent that consummation. That is what we have to do. How can we best do it?

There are those who denounce us openly to their own friends, and yet whisper us softly that Senator Douglas is the aptest instrument there is with which to effect that object. They wish us to infer all from the fact that he now has a little quarrel with the present head of the dynasty; and that he has regularly voted with us on a single point upon which he and we have never differed. They remind us that he is a great man, and that the largest of us are very small ones. Let this be granted. But "a living dog is better than a dead lion." Judge Douglas, if not a dead lion for this work, is at least a caged and toothless one. How can he oppose the advances of slavery? He don't care anything about it. His avowed mission is impressing the "public heart" to care nothing about it. A leading Douglas Democratic newspaper thinks Douglas's superior talent will be needed to resist the revival of the African slave-trade. Does Douglas believe an effort to revive that trade is approaching? He has not said so. Does he really think so? But if it is, how can he resist it? For years he has labored to prove it a sacred right of white men to take negro slaves into the new Territories. Can he possibly show that it is less a sacred right to buy them where they can be bought cheapest? And unquestionably they can be bought cheaper in Africa than in Virginia. He has done all in his power to reduce the whole question of slavery to one of a mere right of property; and as such, how can he oppose the foreign slave-trade? How can he refuse that trade in that "property" shall be "perfectly free," unless he does it as a protection to the home production? And as the home producers will probably not ask the protection, he will be wholly without a ground of opposition.

Senator Douglas holds, we know, that a man may rightfully be wiser to-day than he was yesterday—that he may rightfully change when he finds himself wrong. But can we, for that reason, run ahead, and infer that he will make any particular change of which he, himself, has given no intimation? Can we safely base our action upon any such vague inference? Now, as ever, I wish not to misrepresent Judge Douglas's position, question his motives, or do aught that can be personally offensive to him. Whenever, if ever, he and we can come together on principle so that our great cause may have assistance from his great ability, I hope to have interposed no adventitious obstacle. But clearly, he is not now with us—he does not pretend to be—he does not promise ever to be.

Our cause, then, must be intrusted to, and conducted by, its own undoubted friends—those whose hands are free, whose hearts are in the work, who do care for the result. Two years ago the Republicans of the nation mustered over thirteen hundred thousand strong. We did this under the single impulse of resistance to a common danger, with every external circumstance against us. Of strange, discordant, and even hostile elements, we gathered from the four winds, and formed and fought the battle through, under the constant hot fire of a disciplined, proud, and pampered enemy. Did we brave all then to falter now?—now, when that same enemy is wavering, dissevered, and belligerent? The result is not doubtful. We shall not fail— if we stand firm, we shall not fail. Wise counsels may accelerate or mistakes delay it, but sooner or later, the victory is sure to come.

SPEECH AT COOPER UNION

(February 27, 1860)

MR. PRESIDENT AND FELLOW CITIZENS OF NEW YORK: The facts with which I shall deal this evening are mainly old and familiar; nor is there anything new in the general use I shall make of them. If there shall be any novelty, it will be in the mode of presenting the facts, and the inferences and observations following that presentation. In his speech last autumn at Columbus, Ohio, as reported in the New York *Times*, Senator Douglas said:

"Our fathers, when they framed the government under which we live, understood this question just as well, and even better, than we do now."

I fully indorse this, and I adopt it as a text for this discourse. I so adopt it because it furnishes a precise and an agreed starting-point for a discussion between Republicans and that wing of the Democracy headed by Senator Douglas. It simply leaves the inquiry: What was the understanding those fathers had of the question mentioned?

What is the frame of government under which we live? The answer must be, "The Constitution of the United States." That Constitution consists of the original, framed in 1787, and under which the present government first went into operation, and twelve subsequently framed amendments, the first ten of which were framed in 1789.

Who were our fathers that framed the Constitution? I suppose the "thirty-nine" who signed the original instrument may be fairly called our fathers who framed that part of the present government. It is almost exactly true to say they framed it, and it is altogether true to say they fairly represented the opinion and sentiment of the whole nation at that time. Their names, being familiar to nearly all, and accessible to quite all, need not now be repeated.

I take these "thirty-nine," for the present, as being "our fathers who framed the government under which we live." What is the question which, according to the text, those fathers understood "just as well, and even better, than we do now"?

It is this: Does the proper division of local from federal authority, or anything in the Constitution, forbid our federal government to control as to slavery in our federal territories?

Upon this, Senator Douglas holds the affirmative, and Republicans the negative. This affirmation and denial form an issue; and this issue—this question—is precisely what the text declares our fathers understood "better than we." Let us now inquire whether the "thirty-nine," or any of them, ever acted upon this question; and if they did, how they acted upon it—how they expressed that better understanding. In 1784, three years before the Constitution, the United States then owning the Northwestern Territory, and no other, the Congress of the Confederation had before them the question of prohibiting slavery in that territory; and four of the "thirty-nine" who afterward framed the Constitution were in that Congress, and voted on that question. Of these, Roger Sherman, Thomas Mifflin, and Hugh Williamson voted for the prohibition, thus showing that, in their understanding, no line dividing local from federal authority, nor anything else, properly forbade the federal government to control as to slavery in federal territory. The other of the four, James McHenry, voted against the prohibition, showing that for some cause he thought it improper to vote for it.

In 1787, still before the Constitution, but while the convention was in session framing it, and while the Northwestern Territory still was the only territory owned by the United States, the same question of prohibiting slavery in the territory again came before the Congress of the Confederation; and two more of the "thirty-nine" who afterward signed the Constitution were in that Congress, and voted on the question. They were William Blount and William Few; and they both voted for the prohibition—thus showing that in their understanding no line dividing local from federal authority, nor anything else, properly forbade the federal government to control as to slavery in federal territory. This time the prohibition became a law, being part of what is now well known as the Ordinance of '87.

The question of federal control of slavery in the territories seems not to have been directly before the convention which framed the original Constitution; and hence it is not recorded that the "thirty-nine," or any of them, while engaged on that instrument, expressed any opinion on that precise question.

In 1789, by the first Congress which sat under the Constitution, an act was passed to enforce the Ordinance of '87, including the prohibition of slavery in the Northwestern Territory. The bill for this act was reported by one of the "thirty-nine"—Thomas Fitzsimmons, then a member of the House of Representatives from Pennsylvania. It went through all its stages without a word of opposition, and finally passed both branches without ayes and nays, which is equivalent to a unanimous passage. In this Congress there were sixteen of the thirty-nine fathers who framed the original Constitution. They were John Langdon, Nicholas Gilman, William S. Johnson, Roger Sherman, Robert Morris, Thomas Fitzsimmons, William Few, Abraham Baldwin, Rufus King, William Paterson, George Clymer, Richard Bassett, George Read, Pierce Butler, Daniel Carroll, and James Madison.

This shows that, in their understanding, no line dividing local from federal authority, nor anything in the Constitution, properly forbade Congress to prohibit slavery in the federal territory; else both their fidelity to correct principle, and their oath to support the Constitution, would have constrained them to oppose the prohibition.

Again, George Washington, another of the "thirty-nine," was then President of the United States, and as such approved and signed the bill, thus completing its validity as a law, and thus showing that, in his understanding, no line dividing local from federal authority, nor anything in the Constitution, forbade the federal government to control as to slavery in federal territory.

No great while after the adoption of the original Constitution, North Carolina ceded to the federal government the country now constituting the state of Tennessee; and a few years later Georgia ceded that which now constitutes the states of Mississippi and Alabama. In both deeds of cession it was made a condition by the ceding states that the federal government should not prohibit slavery in the ceded country. Besides this, slavery was then actually in the ceded country. Under these circumstances, Congress, on taking charge of these countries, did not absolutely prohibit slavery within them. But they did interfere with it—take control of it—even there, to a certain extent. In 1798 Congress organized the Territory of Mississippi. In the act of organization they prohibited the bringing of slaves into the Territory from any place without the United States, by fine, and giving freedom to slaves so brought. This act passed both branches of Congress without yeas and nays. In that Congress were three of the "thirty-nine" who framed the original Constitution.

They were John Langdon, George Read, and Abraham Baldwin. They all probably voted for it. Certainly they would have placed their opposition to it upon record if, in their understanding, any line dividing local from federal authority, or anything in the Constitution, properly forbade the federal government to control as to slavery in federal territory.

In 1803 the federal government purchased the Louisiana country. Our former territorial acquisitions came from certain of our own states; but this Louisiana country was acquired from a foreign nation. In 1804 Congress gave a territorial organization to that part of it which now constitutes the state of Louisiana. New Orleans, lying within that part, was an old and comparatively large city. There were other considerable towns and settlements, and slavery was extensively and thoroughly intermingled with the people. Congress did not, in the Territorial Act, prohibit slavery; but they did interfere with it—take control of it—in a more marked and extensive way than they did in the case of Mississippi. The substance of the provision therein made in relation to slaves was:

1st. That no slave should be imported into the territory from foreign parts.

2d. That no slave should be carried into it who had been imported into the United States since the first day of May, 1798.

3d. That no slave should be carried into it, except by the owner, and for his own use as a settler; the penalty in all the cases being a fine upon the violator of the law, and freedom to the slave.

This act also was passed without ayes or nays. In the Congress which passed it there were two of the "thirty-nine." They were Abraham Baldwin and Jonathan Dayton. As stated in the case of Mississippi, it is probable they both voted for it. They would not have allowed it to pass without recording their opposition to it if, in their understanding, it violated either the line properly dividing local from federal authority, or any provision of the Constitution.

In 1819-20 came and passed the Missouri question. Many votes were taken, by yeas and nays, in both branches of Congress, upon the various phases of the general question. Two of the "thirty-nine"—Rufus King and Charles Pinckney—were members of that Congress. Mr. King steadily voted for slavery prohibition and against all compromises, while Mr, Pinckney as steadily voted against slavery prohibition and against all compromises. By this, Mr. King showed that, in his understanding, no line dividing local from federal authority, nor anything in the Constitution, was violated by Congress prohibiting slavery in federal territory; while Mr. Pinckney, by his votes, showed that, in his understanding, there was some sufficient reason for opposing such prohibition in that case.

The cases I have mentioned are the only acts of the "thirty-nine," or of any of them, upon the direct issue, which I have been able to discover.

To enumerate the persons who thus acted as being four in 1784, two in 1787, seventeen in 1789, three in 1798, two in 1804, and two in 1819-20, there would be thirty of them. But this would be counting John Langdon, Roger Sherman, William Few, Rufus King, and George Read each twice, and Abraham Baldwin three times. The true number of those of the "thirty-nine" whom I have shown to have acted upon the question which, by the text, they understood better than we, is twenty-three, leaving sixteen not shown to have acted upon it in any way.

Here, then, we have twenty-three out of our thirty-nine fathers "who framed the government under which we live," who have, upon their official responsibility and their corporal oaths, acted upon the very question which the text affirms they "understood just as well, and even better, than we do now"; and twenty-one of them—a clear majority of the whole "thirty-nine"—so acting upon it as to make them guilty of gross political impropriety and willful perjury if, in their understanding, any proper division between local and federal authority, or anything in the Constitution they had made themselves, and sworn to support, forbade the federal government to control as to slavery in the federal territories. Thus the twenty-one acted; and, as actions speak louder than words, so actions under such responsibility speak still louder.

Two of the twenty-three voted against congressional prohibition of slavery in the federal territories, in the instances in which they acted upon the question. But for what reasons they so voted is not known. They may have done so because they thought a proper division of local from federal authority, or some provision or principle of the Constitution, stood in the way; or they may, without any such question, have voted against the prohibition on what appeared to them to be sufficient grounds of expediency. No one who has sworn to support the Constitution can conscientiously vote for what he understands to be an unconstitutional measure, however expedient he may think it; but one may and ought to vote against a measure which he deems constitutional if, at the same time, he deems it inexpedient. It, therefore, would be unsafe to set down even the two who voted against the prohibition as having done so because, in their understanding, any proper division of local from federal authority, or anything in the Constitution, forbade the federal government to control as to slavery in federal territory.

The remaining sixteen of the "thirty-nine," so far as I have discovered, have left no record of their understanding upon the direct question of federal control of slavery in the federal territories. But there is much reason to believe that their understanding upon that question would not have appeared different from that of their twenty-three compeers, had it been manifested at all.

For the purpose of adhering rigidly to the text, I have purposely omitted whatever understanding may have been manifested by any person, however distinguished, other than the thirty-nine fathers who framed the original Constitution; and, for the same reason, I have also omitted whatever understanding may have been manifested by any of the "thirty-nine" even on any other phase of the general question of slavery. If we should look into their acts and declarations on those other phases, as the foreign slave-trade, and the morality and policy of slavery generally, it would appear to us that on the direct question of federal control of slavery in federal territories, the sixteen, if they had acted at all, would probably have acted just as the twenty-three did. Among that sixteen were several of the most noted anti-slavery men of those times,—as Dr. Franklin, Alexander Hamilton, and Gouverneur Morris,—while there was not one now known to have been otherwise, unless it may be John Rutledge, of South Carolina.

The sum of the whole is that of our thirty-nine fathers who framed the original Constitution, twenty-one—a clear majority of the whole—certainly understood that no proper division of local from federal authority, nor any part of the Constitution, forbade the federal government to control slavery in the federal territories; while all the rest had probably the same understanding. Such, unquestionably, was the understanding of our fathers who framed the original Constitution; and the text affirms that they understood the question "better than we."

But, so far, I have been considering the understanding of the question manifested by the framers of the original Constitution. In and by the original instrument, a mode was provided for amending it; and, as I have already stated, the present frame of "the government under which we live" consists of that original, and twelve amendatory articles framed and adopted since. Those who now insist that federal control of slavery in federal territories violates the Constitution, point us to the provisions which they suppose it thus violates; and, as I understand, they all fix upon provisions in these amendatory articles, and not in the original instrument. The Supreme Court, in the Dred Scott case, plant themselves upon the Fifth Amendment, which provides that no person shall be deprived of "life, liberty, or property without due process of law"; while Senator Douglas and his peculiar adherents plant themselves upon the Tenth Amendment, providing that "the powers not delegated to the United States by the Constitution" "are reserved to the states respectively, or to the people."

Now, it so happens that these amendments were framed by the first Congress which sat under the Constitution—the identical Congress which passed the act, already mentioned, enforcing the prohibition of slavery in the Northwestern Territory. Not only was it the same Congress, but they were the identical, same individual men who, at the same session, and at the same time within the session, had under consideration, and in progress toward maturity, these constitutional amendments, and this act prohibiting slavery in all the territory the nation then owned. The constitutional amendments were introduced before, and passed after, the act enforcing the Ordinance of '87; so that, during the whole pendency of the act to enforce the ordinance, the constitutional amendments were also pending.

The seventy-six members of that Congress, including sixteen of the framers of the original Constitution, as before stated, were preëminently our fathers who framed that part of "the government under which we live" which is now claimed as forbidding the federal government to control slavery in the federal territories.

Is it not a little presumptuous in anyone at this day to affirm that the two things which that Congress deliberately framed, and carried to maturity at the same time, are absolutely inconsistent with each other? And does not such affirmation become impudently absurd when coupled with the other affirmation, from the same mouth, that those who did the two things alleged to be inconsistent, understood whether they really were inconsistent better

than we—better than he who affirms that they are inconsistent?

It is surely safe to assume that the thirty-nine framers of the original Constitution, and the seventy-six members of the Congress which framed the amendments thereto, taken together, do certainly include those who may be fairly called "our fathers who framed the government under which we live." And so assuming, I defy any man to show that any one of them ever, in his whole life, declared that, in his understanding, any proper division of local from federal authority, or any part of the Constitution, forbade the federal government to control as to slavery in the federal territories. I go a step further. I defy any one to show that any living man in the whole world ever did, prior to the beginning of the present century (and I might almost say prior to the beginning of the last half of the present century), declare that, in his understanding, any proper division of local from federal authority, or any part of the Constitution, forbade the federal government to control as to slavery in the federal territories. To those who now so declare I give not only "our fathers who framed the government under which we live," but with them all other living men within the century in which it was framed, among whom to search, and they shall not be able to find the evidence of a single man agreeing with them.

Now, and here, let me guard a little against being misunderstood. I do not mean to say we are bound to follow implicitly in whatever our fathers did. To do so would be to discard all the lights of current experience—to reject all progress, all improvement. What I do say is that if we would supplant the opinions and policy of our fathers in any case, we should do so upon evidence so conclusive, and argument so clear, that even their great authority, fairly considered and weighed, cannot stand; and most surely not in a case whereof we ourselves declare they understood the question better than we.

If any man at this day sincerely believes that a proper division of local from federal authority, or any part of the Constitution, forbids the federal government to control as to slavery in the federal territories, he is right to say so, and to enforce his position by all truthful evidence and fair argument which he can. But he has no right to mislead others, who have less access to history, and less leisure to study it, into the false belief that "our fathers who framed the government under which we live" were of the same opinion—thus substituting falsehood and deception for truthful evidence and fair argument. If any man at this day sincerely believes "our fathers who framed the government under which we live" used and applied principles, in other cases, which ought to have led them to understand that a proper division of local from federal authority, or some part of the Constitution, forbids the federal government to control as to slavery in the federal territories, he is right to say so. But he should, at the same time, brave the responsibility of declaring that, in his opinion, he understands their principles better than they did themselves; and especially should he not shirk that responsibility by asserting that they "understood the question just as well, and even better, than we do now."

But enough! Let all who believe that "our fathers who framed the government under which we live understood this question just as well, and even better, than we do now," speak as they spoke, and act as they acted upon it. This is all Republicans ask—all Republicans desire—in relation to slavery. As those fathers marked it, so let it be again marked, as an evil not to be extended, but to be tolerated and protected only because of and so far as its actual presence among us makes that toleration and protection a necessity.. Let all the guaranties those fathers gave it be not grudgingly, but fully and fairly, maintained. For this Republicans contend, and with this, so far as I know or believe, they will be content.

And now, if they would listen,—as I suppose they will not,—I would address a few words to the Southern people.

I would say to them: You consider yourselves a reasonable and a just people; and I consider that in the general qualities of reason and justice you are not inferior to any other people. Still, when you speak of us Republicans, you do so only to denounce us as reptiles, or, at the best, as no better than outlaws. You will grant a hearing to pirates or murderers, but nothing like it to "Black Republicans." In all your contentions with one another, each of you deems an unconditional condemnation of "Black Republicanism" as the first thing to be attended to. Indeed, such condemnation of us seems to be an indispensable prerequisite —license, so to speak—among you to be admitted or permitted to speak at all. Now can you or not be prevailed upon to pause and to consider whether this is quite just to us, or even to yourselves? Bring forward your charges and specifications, and then be patient long enough to hear us deny or justify.

You say we are sectional. We deny it. That makes an issue; and the burden of proof is upon

you. You produce your proof; and what is it? Why, that our party has no existence in your section—gets no votes in your section. The fact is substantially true; but does it prove the issue? If it does, then in case we should, without change of principle, begin to get votes in your section, we should thereby cease to be sectional. You cannot escape this conclusion; and yet, are you willing to abide by it? If you are, you will probably soon find that we have ceased to be sectional, for we shall get votes in your section this very year. You will then begin to discover, as the truth plainly is, that your proof does not touch the issue. The fact that we get no votes in your section is a fact of your making, and not of ours. And if there be fault in that fact, that fault is primarily yours, and remains so until you show that we repel you by some wrong principle or practice. If we do repel you by any wrong principle or practice, the fault is ours; but this brings you to where you ought to have started—to a discussion of the right or wrong of our principle. If our principle, put in practice, would wrong your section for the benefit of ours, or for any other object, then our principle, and we with it, are sectional, and are justly opposed and denounced as such. Meet us, then, on the question of whether our principle, put in practice, would wrong your section; and so meet us as if it were possible that something may be said on our side. Do you accept the challenge? No! Then you really believe that the principle which "our fathers who framed the government under which we live" thought so clearly right as to adopt it, and indorse it again and again, upon their official oaths, is in fact so clearly wrong as to demand your condemnation without a moment's consideration.

Some of you delight to flaunt in our faces the warning against sectional parties given by Washington in his Farewell Address. Less than eight years before Washington gave that warning, he had, as President of the United States, approved and signed an act of Congress enforcing the prohibition of slavery in the Northwestern Territory, which act embodied the policy of the government upon that subject up to and at the very moment he penned that warning; and about one year after he penned it, he wrote Lafayette that he considered that prohibition a wise measure, expressing in the same connection his hope that we should at some time have a confederacy of free states.

Bearing this in mind, and seeing that sectionalism has since arisen upon this same subject, is that warning a weapon in your hands against us, or in our hands against you? Could

Washington himself speak, would he cast the blame of that sectionalism upon us, who sustain his policy, or upon you, who repudiate it? We respect that warning of Washington, and we commend it to you, together with his example pointing to the right application of it.

But you say you are conservative—eminently conservative—while we are revolutionary, destructive, or something of the sort. What is conservatism? Is it not adherence to the old and tried, against the new and untried? We stick to, contend for, the identical old policy on the point in controversy which was adopted by "our fathers who framed the government under which we live"; while you with one accord reject, and scout, and spit upon that old policy, and insist upon substituting something new. True, you disagree among yourselves as to what that substitute shall be. You are divided on new propositions and plans, but you are unanimous in rejecting and denouncing the old policy of the fathers. Some of you are for reviving the foreign slave-trade; some for a congressional slave-code for the territories; some for Congress forbidding the territories to prohibit slavery within their limits; some for maintaining slavery in the territories through the judiciary; some for the "gur-reat purrinciple" that "if one man would enslave another, no third man should object," fantastically called "popular sovereignty"; but never a a man among you is in favor of federal prohibition of slavery in federal territories, according to the practice of "our fathers who framed the government under which we live." Not one of all your various plans can show a precedent or an advocate in the century within which our government originated. Consider then, whether, your claim of conservatism for yourselves, and your charge of destructiveness against us, are based on the most clear and stable foundations.

Again, you say we have made the slavery question more prominent than it formerly was. We deny it. We admit that it is more prominent, but we deny that we made it so. It was not we, but you, who discarded the old policy of the fathers. We resisted, and still resist, your innovation; and thence comes the greater prominence of the question. Would you have that question reduced to its former proportions? Go back to that old policy. What has been will be again, under the same conditions. If you would have the peace of the old times, readopt the precepts and policy of the old times.

You charge that we stir up insurrections among your slaves. We deny it; and what is your proof? Harper's Ferry! John Brown!! John Brown was no Republican; and you have failed to implicate a single Republican in his Harper's Ferry enterprise. If any member of our party is guilty in that matter, you know it or you do not know it. If you do know it, you are inexcusable for not designating the man and proving the fact. If you do not know it, you are inexcusable for asserting it, and especially for persisting in the assertion after you have tried and failed to make the proof. You need not be told that persisting in a charge which one does not know to be true, is simply malicious slander.

Some of you admit that no Republican designedly aided or encouraged the Harper's Ferry affair, but still insist that our doctrines and declarations necessarily lead to such results. We do not believe it. We know we hold no doctrine, and make no declaration, which were not held to and made by "our fathers who framed the government under which we live." You never dealt fairly by us in relation to this affair. When it occurred, some important state elections were near at hand, and you were in evident glee with the belief that, by charging the blame upon us, you could get an advantage of us in those elections. The elections came, and your expectations were not quite fulfilled. Every Republican man knew that, as to himself at least, your charge was a slander, and he was not much inclined by it to cast his vote in your favor. Republican doctrines and declarations are accompanied with a continual protest against any interference with your slaves, or with you about your slaves. Surely, this does not encourage them to revolt. True, we do, in common with "our fathers who framed the government under which we live," declare our belief that slavery is wrong; but the slaves do not hear us declare even this. For anything we say or do, the slaves would scarcely know there is a Republican party. I believe they would not, in fact, generally know it but for your misrepresentations of us in their hearing. In your political contests among yourselves, each faction charges the other with sympathy with Black Republicanism; and then, to give point to the charge, defines Black Republicanism to simply be insurrection, blood, and thunder among the slaves.

Slave insurrections are no more common now than they were before the Republican party was organized. What induced the Southampton insurrection, twenty-eight years ago, in which at least three times as many lives were lost as at Harper's Ferry? You can scarcely stretch your very elastic fancy to the conclusion that Southampton was "got up by Black Republicanism." In the present state of things in the United States, I do not think a general, or even a very extensive, slave insurrection is possible. The indispensable concert of action cannot be attained. The slaves have no means of rapid communication; nor can incendiary freemen, black or white, supply it. The explosive materials are everywhere in parcels; but there neither are, nor can be supplied, the indispensable connecting trains.

Much is said by Southern people about the affection of slaves for their masters and mistresses; and a part of it, at least, is true. A plot for an uprising could scarcely be devised and communicated to twenty individuals before some one of them, to save the life of a favorite master or mistress, would divulge it. This is the rule; and the slave revolution in Haiti was not an exception to it, but a case occurring under peculiar circumstances. The gunpowder plot of British history, though not connected with slaves, was more in point. In that case, only about twenty were admitted to the secret; and yet one of them, in his anxiety to save a friend, betrayed the plot to that friend, and, by consequence, averted the calamity. Occasional poisonings from the kitchen, and open or stealthy assassinations in the field, and local revolts extending to a score or so, will continue to occur as the natural results of slavery; but no general insurrection of slaves, as I think, can happen in this country for a long time. Whoever much fears, or much hopes, for such an event, will be alike disappointed.

In the language of Mr. Jefferson, uttered many years ago, "It is still in our power to direct the process of emancipation and deportation peaceably, and in such slow degrees, as that the evil will wear off insensibly; and their places be, *pari passu*, filled up by free white laborers. If, on the contrary, it is left to force itself on, human nature must shudder at the prospect held up."

Mr. Jefferson did not mean to say, nor do I, that the power of emancipation is in the federal government. He spoke of Virginia; and, as to the power of emancipation, I speak of the slaveholding states only. The federal government, however, as we insist, has the power of restraining the extension of the institution—the power to insure that a slave insurrection shall never occur on any American soil which is now free from slavery.

John Brown's effort was peculiar. It was not a slave insurrection. It was an attempt by white men to get up a revolt among slaves, in which the slaves refused to participate. In fact, it was so absurd that the slaves, with all their ignorance, saw plainly enough it could not succeed. That affair, in its philosophy, corresponds with the many attemps, related in history, at the assassination of kings and emperors. An enthusiast broods over the oppression of a people till he fancies himself commissioned by Heaven to liberate them. He ventures the attempt, which ends in little else than his own execution. Orsini's attempt on Louis Napoleon, and John Brown's attempt at Harper's Ferry, were, in their philosophy, precisely the same. The eagerness to cast blame on old England in the one case, and on New England in the other, does not disprove the sameness of the two things.

And how much would it avail you, if you could, by the use of John Brown, Helper's book, and the like, break up the Republican organization? Human action can be modified to some extent, but human nature cannot be changed. There is a judgment and a feeling against slavery in this nation, which cast at least a million and a half of votes. You cannot destroy that judgment and feeling—that sentiment—by breaking up the political organization which rallies around it. You can scarcely scatter and disperse an army which has been formed into order in the face of your heaviest fire; but if you could, how much would you gain by forcing the sentiment which created it out of the peaceful channel of the ballot-box into some other channel? What would that other channel probably be? Would the number of John Browns be lessened or enlarged by the operation?

But you will break up the Union rather than submit to a denial of your constitutional rights.

That has a somewhat reckless sound; but it would be palliated, if not fully justified, were we proposing, by the mere force of numbers, to deprive you of some right plainly written down in the Constitution. But we are proposing no such thing.

When you make these declarations you have a specific and well-understood allusion to an assumed constitutional right of yours to take slaves into the federal territories, and to hold them there as property. But no such right is specifically written in the Constitution. That instrument is literally silent about any such right. We, on the contrary, deny that such a right has any existence in the Constitution, even by implication.

Your purpose, then, plainly stated, is that you will destroy the government, unless you be allowed to construe and force the Constitution as you please, on all points in dispute between you and us. You will rule or ruin in all events.

This, plainly stated, is your language. Perhaps you will say the Supreme Court has decided the disputed constitutional question in your favor. Not quite so. But waiving the lawyer's distinction between dictum and decision, the court has decided the question for you in a sort of way. The court has substantially said, it is your constitutional right to take slaves into the federal territories, and to hold them there as property. When I say the decision was made in a sort of way, I mean it was made in a divided court, by a bare majority of the judges, and they not quite agreeing with one another in the reasons for making it; that it is so made as that its avowed supporters disagree with one another about its meaning, and that it was mainly based upon a mistaken statement of fact—the statement in the opinion that "the right of property in a slave is distinctly and expressly affirmed in the Constitution."

An inspection of the Constitution will show that the right of property in a slave is not "distinctly and expressly affirmed" in it. Bear in mind, the judges do not pledge their judicial opinion that such right is impliedly affirmed in the Constitution; but they pledge their veracity that it is "distinctly and expressly" affirmed there—"distinctly," that is, not mingled with anything else—"expressly," that is, in words meaning just that, without the aid of any inference, and susceptible of no other meaning.

If they had only pledged their judicial opinion that such right is affirmed in the instrument by implication, it would be open to others to show that neither the word "slave" nor "slavery" is to be found in the Constitution, nor the word "property" even, in any connection with language alluding to the things slave, or slavery; and that wherever in that instrument the slave is alluded to, he is called a "person"; and whenever his master's legal right in relation to him is alluded to, it is spoken of as "service or labor which may be due"—as a debt payable in service or labor. Also it would be open to show, by contemporaneous history, that this mode of alluding to slaves and slavery, instead of speaking of them, was employed on purpose to exclude from the Constitution the idea that there could be property in man.

To show all this is easy and certain.

When this obvious mistake of the judges shall be brought to their notice, is it not reasonable to expect that they will withdraw the mistaken statement, and reconsider the conclusion based upon it?

And then it is to be remembered that "our fathers who framed the government under which we live"—the men who made the Constitution—decided this same constitutional question in our favor long ago: decided it without division among themselves when making the decision; without division among themselves about the meaning of it after it was made, and, so far as any evidence is left, without basing it upon any mistaken statement of facts.

Under all these circumstances, do you really feel yourselves justified to break up this government unless such a court decision as yours is shall be at once submitted to as a conclusive and final rule of political action? But you will not abide the election of a Republican President! In that supposed event, you say, you will destroy the Union; and then, you say, the great crime of having destroyed it will be upon us! That is cool. A highwayman holds a pistol to my ear, and mutters through his teeth, "Stand and deliver, or I shall kill you, and then you will be a murderer!"

To be sure, what the robber demanded of me—my money—was my own; and I had a clear right to keep it; but it was no more my own than my vote is my own; and the threat of death to me, to extort my money, and the threat of destruction to the Union, to extort my vote, can scarcely be distinguished in principle.

A few words now to Republicans. It is exceedingly desirable that all parts of this great confederacy shall be at peace, and in harmony one with another. Let us Republicans do our part to have it so. Even though much provoked, let us do nothing through passion and ill temper. Even though the Southern people will not so much as listen to us, let us calmly consider their demands, and yield to them if, in our deliberate view of our duty, we possibly can. Judging by all they say and do, and by the subject and nature of their controversy with us, let us determine, if we can, what will satisfy them.

Will they be satisfied if the territories be unconditionally surrendered to them? We know they will not. In all their present complaints against us, the territories are scarcely mentioned. Invasions and insurrections are the rage now. Will it satisfy them if, in the future, we have nothing to do with invasions and insurrections? We know it will not. We so know, because we know we never had anything to do with invasions and insurrections;

and yet this total abstaining does not exempt us from the charge and the denunciation.

The question recurs, What will satisfy them? Simply this: we must not only let them alone, but we must somehow convince them that we do let them alone. This, we know by experience, is no easy task. We have been so trying to convince them from the very beginning of our organization, but with no success. In all our platforms and speeches we have constantly protested our purpose to let them alone; but this has had no tendency to convince them. Alike unavailing to convince them is the fact that they have never detected a man of us in any attempt to disturb them.

These natural and apparently adequate means all failing, what will convince them? This, and this only: cease to call slavery wrong, and join them in calling it right. And this must be done thoroughly—done in acts as well as in words. Silence will not be tolerated—we must place ourselves avowedly with them. Senator Douglas's new sedition law must be enacted and enforced, suppressing all declarations that slavery is wrong, whether made in politics, in presses, in pulpits, or in private. We must arrest and return their fugitive slaves with greedy pleasure. We must pull down our free-state constitutions. The whole atmosphere must be disinfected from all taint of opposition to slavery, before they will cease to believe that all their troubles proceed from us.

I am quite aware they do not state their case precisely in this way. Most of them would probably say to us, "Let us alone; do nothing to us, and say what you please about slavery." But we do let them alone,—have never disturbed them,—so that, after all, it is what we say which dissatisfies them. They will continue to accuse us of doing, until we cease saying.

I am also aware they have not as yet in terms demanded the overthrow of our free-state constitutions. Yet those constitutions declare the wrong of slavery with more solemn emphasis than do all other sayings against it; and when all these other sayings shall have been silenced, the overthrow of these constitutions will be demanded, and nothing be left to resist the demand. It is nothing to the contrary that they do not demand the whole of this just now. Demanding what they do, and for the reason they do, they can voluntarily stop nowhere short of this consummation. Holding, as they do, that slavery is morally right and socially elevating, they cannot cease to demand a full national recognition of it as a legal right and a social blessing.

Nor can we justifiably withhold this on any ground save our conviction that slavery is wrong. If slavery is right, all words, acts, laws, and constitutions against it are themselves wrong, and should be silenced and swept away. If it is right, we cannot justly object to its nationality—its universality; if it is wrong, they cannot justly insist upon its extension—its enlargement. All they ask we could readily grant, if we thought slavery right; all we ask they could as readily grant, if they thought it wrong. Their thinking it right and our thinking it wrong is the precise fact upon which depends the whole controversy. Thinking it right, as they do, they are not to blame for desiring its full recognition as being right; but thinking it wrong, as we do, can we yield to them? Can we cast our votes with their view, and against our own? In view of our moral, social, and political responsibilities, can we do this?

Wrong as we think slavery is, we can yet afford to let it alone where it is, because that much is due to the necessity arising from its actual presence in the nation; but can we, while our votes will prevent it, allow it to spread into the national territories, and to overrun us here in these free states? If our sense of duty forbids this, then let us stand by our duty fearlessly and effectively. Let us be diverted by none of those sophistical contrivances wherewith we are so industriously plied and belabored—contrivances such as groping for some middle ground between the right and the wrong: vain as the search for a man who should be neither a living man nor a dead man; such as a policy of "don't care" on a question about which all true men do care; such as Union appeals beseeching true Union men to yield to Disunionists, reversing the divine rule, and calling, not the sinners, but the righteous to repentance; such as invocations to Washington, imploring men to unsay what Washington said and undo what Washington did.

Neither let us be slandered from our duty by false accusations against us, nor frightened from it by menaces of destruction to the government, nor of dungeons to ourselves. Let us have faith that right makes might, and in that faith let us to the end dare to do our duty as we understand it.

FAREWELL REMARKS AT SPRINGFIELD

(February 11, 1861)

MY FRIENDS: No one, not in my situation, can appreciate my feeling of sadness at this parting. To this place, and the kindness of these people, I owe everything. Here I have lived a quarter of a century, and have passed from a young to an old man. Here my children have been born, and one is buried. I now leave, not knowing when or whether ever I may return, with a task before me greater than that which rested upon Washington. Without the assistance of that Divine Being who ever attended him, I cannot succeed. With that assistance, I cannot fail. Trusting in Him who can go with me, and remain with you, and be everywhere for good, let us confidently hope that all will yet be well. To His care commending you, as I hope in your prayers you will commend me, I bid you an affectionate fare-well.

SPEECH IN INDEPENDENCE HALL, PHILADELPHIA

(February 22, 1861)

MR. CUYLER: I am filled with deep emotion at finding myself standing in this place, where were collected together the wisdom, the patriotism, the devotion to principle, from which sprang the institutions under which we live. You have kindly suggested to me that in my hands is the task of restoring peace to our distracted country. I can say in return, sir, that all the political sentiments I entertain have been drawn, so far as I have been able to draw them, from the sentiments which originated in and were given to the world from this hall. I have never had a feeling, politically, that did not spring from the sentiments embodied in the Declaration of Independence. I have often pondered over the dangers which were incurred by the men who assembled here and framed and adopted that Declaration. I have pondered over the toils that were endured by the officers and soldiers of the army who achieved that independence. I have often inquired of myself what great principle or idea it was that kept this Confederacy so long together. It was not the mere matter of separation of the colonies from the motherland, but that sentiment in the Declaration of Independence which gave liberty not alone to the people of this country, but hope to all the world, for all future time. It was that which gave promise that in due time the weight would be lifted from the shoulders of all men, and that all should have an equal chance. This is the sentiment embodied in the Declaration of Independence. Now, my friends, can this country be saved on that basis? If it can, I will consider myself one of the happiest men in the world if I can help to save it. If it cannot be saved upon that principle, it will be truly awful. But if this country cannot be saved without giving up that principle, I was about to say I would rather be assassinated on this spot than surrender it. Now, in my view of the present aspect of affairs, there is no need of bloodshed and war. There is no necessity for it. I am not in favor of such a course; and I may say in advance that there will be no bloodshed unless it be forced upon the government. The government will not use force, unless force is used against it.

My friends, this is wholly an unprepared speech. I did not expect to be called on to say a word when I came here. I supposed I was merely to do something toward raising a flag. I may, therefore, have said something indiscreet. [Cries of "No, no."] But I have said nothing but what I am willing to live by, and, if it be the pleasure of Almighty God, to die by.

FIRST INAUGURAL ADDRESS

(March 4, 1861)

FELLOW CITIZENS OF THE UNITED STATES: In compliance with a custom as old as the government itself, I appear before you to address you briefly, and to take in your presence the oath prescribed by the Constitution of the United States to be taken by the President "before he enters on the execution of his office."

I do not consider it necessary at present for me to discuss those matters of administration about which there is no special anxiety or excitement.

Apprehension seems to exist among the people of the Southern states that by the accession of a Republican administration their property and their peace and personal security are to be endangered. There has never been any reasonable cause for such apprehension. Indeed, the most ample evidence to the contrary has all the while existed and been open to their inspection. It is found in nearly all the published speeches of him who now addresses you. I do but quote from one of those speeches when I declare that "I have no purpose, directly or indirectly, to interfere with the institution of slavery in the states where it exists. I believe I have no lawful right to do so, and I have no inclination to do so." Those who nominated and elected me did so with full knowledge that I had made this and many similar declarations, and had never recanted them. And, more than this, they placed in the platform for my acceptance, and as a law to themselves and to me, the clear and emphatic resolution which I now read:

"*Resolved*, That the maintenance inviolate of the rights of the states, and especially the right of each state to order and control its own domestic institutions according to its own judgment exclusively, is essential to that balance of power on which the perfection and endurance of our political fabric depend, and we denounce the lawless invasion by armed force of the soil of any state or territory, no matter under what pretext, as among the gravest of crimes."

I now reiterate these sentiments; and, in doing so, I only press upon the public attention the most conclusive evidence of which the case is susceptible, that the property, peace, and security of no section are to be in any wise endangered by the now incoming administration. I add, too, that all the protection which, consistently with the Constitution and the laws, can be given, will be cheerfully given to all the states when lawfully demanded, for whatever cause—as cheerfully to one section as to another.

There is much controversy about the delivering up of fugitives from service or labor. The clause I now read is as plainly written in the Constitution as any other of its provisions:

"No person held to service or labor in one state, under the laws thereof, escaping into another, shall in consequence of any law or regulation therein be discharged from such service or labor, but shall be delivered up on claim of the party to whom, such service or labor may be due."

It is scarcely questioned that this provision was intended by those who made it for the reclaiming of what we call fugitive slaves; and the intention of the lawgiver is the law. All members of Congress swear their support to the whole Constitution—to this provision as much as to any other. To the proposition, then, that slaves whose cases come within the terms of this clause "shall be delivered up," their oaths are unanimous. Now, if they would make the effort in good temper, could they not with nearly equal unanimity frame and pass a law by means of which to keep good that unanimous oath?

There is some difference of opinion whether this clause should be enforced by national or by state authority; but surely that difference is not a very material one. If the slave is to be surrendered, it can be of but little consequence to him or to others by which authority it is done. And should any one in any case be content that his oath shall go unkept on a merely unsubstantial controversy as to how it shall be kept?

Again, in any law upon this subject, ought not all the safeguards of liberty known in civilized and humane jurisprudence to be introduced, so that a free man be not, in any case, surrendered as a slave? And might it not be well at the same time to provide by law for the enforcement of that clause in the Constitution which guarantees that "the citizen of each state shall be entitled to all privileges and immunities of citizens in the several states"?

I take the official oath today with no mental reservations, and with no purpose to construe the Constitution or laws by any hypercritical rules. And while I do not choose now to specify particular acts of Congress as proper to be enforced, I do suggest that it will be much safer for all, both in official and private stations, to conform to and abide by all those acts which stand unrepealed, than to violate any of them, trusting to find impunity in having them held to be unconstitutional.

It is seventy-two years since the first inauguration of a president under our national Constitution. During that period fifteen different and greatly distinguished citizens have, in succession, administered the executive branch of the government. They have conducted it through many perils, and generally with great success. Yet, with all this scope of precedent, I now enter upon the same task for the brief constitutional term of four years under great and peculiar difficulty. A disruption of the federal Union, heretofore only menaced, is now formidably attempted.

I hold that, in contemplation of universal law and of the Constitution, the union of these states is perpetual. Perpetuity is implied, if not expressed, in the fundamental law of all national governments. It is safe to assert that no government proper ever had a provision in its organic law for its own termination. Continue to execute all the express provisions of our national Constitution, and the Union will endure forever—it being impossible to destroy it except by some action not provided for in the instrument itself.

Again, if the United States be not a government proper, but an association of states in the nature of contract merely, can it, as a contract, be peaceably unmade by less than all the parties who made it? One party to a contract may violate it—break it, so to speak; but does it not require all to lawfully rescind it?

Descending from these general principles, we find the proposition that, in legal contemplation the Union is perpetual confirmed by the history of the Union itself. The Union is much older than the Constitution. It was formed, in fact, by the Articles of Association in 1774. It was matured and continued by the Declaration of Independence in 1776. It was further matured, and the faith of all the then thirteen states expressly plighted and engaged that it should be perpetual, by the Articles of Confederation in 1778. And, finally, in 1787 one of the declared objects for ordaining and establishing the Constitution was "to form a more perfect Union."

But if the destruction of the Union by one or by a part only of the states be lawfully possible, the Union is less perfect than before the Constitution, having lost the vital element of perpetuity.

It follows from these views that no state upon its own mere motion can lawfully get out of the Union; that resolves and ordinances to that effect are legally void; and that acts of violence, within any state or states, against the authority of the United States, are insurrectionary or revolutionary, according to circumstances.

I therefore consider that, in view of the Constitution and the laws, the Union is unbroken; and to the extent of my ability I shall take care, as the Constitution itself expressly enjoins upon me, that the laws of the Union be faithfully executed in all the states. Doing this I deem to be only a simple duty on my part; and I shall perform it so far as practicable, unless my rightful masters, the American people, shall withhold the requisite means, or in some authoritative manner direct the contrary. I trust this will not be regarded as a menace, but only as the declared purpose of the Union that it will constitutionally defend and maintain itself.

In doing this there needs to be no bloodshed or violence; and there shall be none, unless it be forced upon the national authority. The power confided to me will be used to hold, occupy, and possess the property and places belonging to the government, and to collect the duties and imposts; but beyond what may be necessary for these objects, there will be no invasion, no using of force against or among the people anywhere. Where hostility to the United States, in any interior locality, shall be so great and universal as to prevent competent resident citizens from holding the federal offices, there will be no attempt to force obnoxious strangers among the people for that object. While the strict legal right may exist in the government to enforce the exercise of these offices, the attempt to do so would be so irritating, and so nearly impracticable withal, that I deem it better to forego for the time the uses of such offices.

The mails, unless repelled, will continue to be furnished in all parts of the Union. So far as possible, the people everywhere shall have that sense of perfect security which is most favorable to calm thought and reflection. The course here indicated will be followed unless current events and experience shall show a modification or change to be proper, and in every case and exigency my best discretion will be exercised according to circumstances actually existing, and with a view and a hope of a peaceful solution of the national troubles and the restoration of fraternal sympathies and affections.

That there are persons in one section or another who seek to destroy the Union at all events, and are glad of any pretext to do it, I will neither affirm nor deny; but if there be such, I need address no word to them. To those, however, who really love the Union may I not speak?

Before entering upon so grave a matter as the destruction of our national fabric, with all its benefits, its memories, and its hopes, would it not be wise to ascertain precisely why we do it? Will you hazard so desperate a step while there is any possibility that any portion of the ills you fly from have no real existence? Will you, while the certain ills you fly to are greater than all the real ones you fly from—will you risk the commission of so fearful a mistake?

All profess to be content in the Union if all constitutional rights can be maintained. Is it true, then, that any right, plainly written in the Constitution, has been denied? I think not. Happily the human mind is so constituted that no party can reach to the audacity of doing this. Think, if you can, of a single instance in which a plainly written provision of the Constitution has ever been denied. If by the mere force of numbers a majority should deprive a minority of any clearly written constitutional right, it might, in a moral point of view, justify revolution—certainly would if such a right were a vital one. But such is not our case. All the vital rights of minorities and of individuals are so plainly assured to them by affirmations and negations, guarantees and prohibitions, in the Constitution, that controversies never arise concerning them. But no organic law can ever be framed with a provision specifically applicable to every question which may occur in practical administration. No foresight can anticipate, nor any document of reasonable length contain, express provisions for all possible questions. Shall fugitives from labor be surrendered by national or by state authority? The Constitution does not expressly say. *May* Congress prohibit slavery in the territories? The Constitution does not expressly say. *Must* Congress protect slavery in the territories? The Constitution does not expressly say.

From questions of this class spring all our constitutional controversies, and we divide upon them into majorities and minorities. If the minority will not acquiesce, the majority must, or the government must cease. There is no other alternative; for continuing the government is acquiescence on one side or the other.

If a minority in such case will secede rather than acquiesce, they make a precedent which in turn will divide and ruin them; for a minority of their own will secede from them whenever a majority refuses to be controlled by such minority. For instance, why may not any portion of a new confederacy a year or two hence arbitrarily secede again, precisely as portions of the present Union now claim to secede from it? All who cherish disunion sentiments are now being educated to the exact temper of doing this.

Is there such perfect identity of interests among the states to compose a new Union, as to produce harmony only, and prevent renewed secession?

Plainly, the central idea of secession is the essence of anarchy. A majority held in restraint by constitutional checks and limitations, and always changing easily with deliberate changes of popular opinions and sentiments, is the only true sovereign of a free people. Whoever rejects it does, of necessity, fly to anarchy or to despotism. Unanimity is impossible; the rule of a minority, as a permanent arrangement, is wholly inadmissible; so that, rejecting the majority principle, anarchy or despotism in some form is all that is left.

I do not forget the position, assumed by some, that constitutional questions are to be decided by the Supreme Court; nor do I deny that such decisions must be binding, in any case, upon the parties to a suit, as to the object of that suit, while they are also entitled to very high respect and consideration in all parallel cases by all other departments of the government. And while it is obviously possible that such decisions may be erroneous in any given case, still the evil effect following it, being limited to that particular case, with the chance that it may be overruled and never become a precedent for other cases, can better be borne than could the evils of a different practice. At the same time, the candid citizen must confess that if the policy of the government, upon vital questions affecting the whole people, is to be irrevocably fixed by decisions of the Supreme Court, the instant they are made, in ordinary litigation between parties in personal actions, the people will have ceased to be their own rulers, having to that extent practically resigned their government into the hands of that eminent tribunal. Nor is there in this view any assault upon the court or the judges. It is a duty from which they may not shrink to decide cases properly brought before them, and it is no fault of theirs if others seek to turn their decisions to political purposes.

One section of our country believes slavery is right, and ought to be extended, while the other believes it is wrong, and ought not be extended. This is the only substantial dispute. The fugitive-slave clause of the Constitution, and the law for the suppression of the foreign slave-trade, are each as well enforced, perhaps, as any law can ever be in a community where the moral sense of the people imperfectly supports the law itself. The great body of the people abide by the dry legal obligation in both cases, and a few break over in each. This, I think, cannot be perfectly cured; and it would be worse in both cases after the separation of the sections than before. The foreign slave-trade, now imperfectly suppressed, would be ultimately revived, without restriction, in one section, while fugitive slaves, now only partially surrendered, would not be surrendered at all by the other.

Physically speaking, we cannot separate. We cannot remove our respective sections from each other, nor build an impassable wall between them. A husband and wife may be divorced, and go out of the presence and beyond the reach of each other; but the different parts of our country cannot do this. They cannot but remain face to face, and intercourse, either amicable or hostile, must continue between them. Is it possible, then, to make that intercourse more advantageous or more satisfactory after separation than before? Can aliens make treaties easier than friends can make laws? Can treaties be more faithfully enforced between aliens than laws can among friends? Suppose you go to war, you cannot fight always; and when, after much loss on both sides, and no gain on either, you cease fighting, the identical old questions as to terms of intercourse are again upon you.

This country, with its institutions, belongs to the people who inhabit it. Whenever they shall grow weary of the existing government, they can exercise their constitutional right of amending it, or their revolutionary right to dismember or overthrow it. I cannot be ignorant of the fact that many worthy and patriotic citizens are desirous of having the national Constitution amended. While I make no recommendation of amendments, I fully recognize the rightful authority of the people over the whole subject, to be exercised in either of the modes prescribed in the instrument itself; and I should, under existing circumstances, favor rather than oppose a fair opportunity being afforded the people to act upon it. I will venture to add that to me the convention mode seems preferable, in that it allows amendments to originate with the people themselves, instead of only permitting them to take or reject propositions originated by others not especially chosen for the purpose, and which might not be precisely such as they would wish to either accept or refuse. I understand a proposed amendment to the Constitution—which amendment, however, I have not seen—has passed Congress, to the effect that the federal government shall never interfere with the domestic institutions of the states, including that of persons held to service. To avoid misconstruction of what I have said, I depart from my purpose not to speak of particular amendments so far as to say that, holding such a provision to now be implied constitutional law, I have no objections to its being made express and irrevocable.

The chief magistrate derives all his authority from the people, and they have conferred none upon him to fix terms for the separation of the states. The people themselves can do this also if they choose; but the executive, as such, has nothing to do with it. His duty is to administer the present government, as it came to his hands, and to transmit it, unimpaired by him, to his successor.

Why should there not be a patient confidence in the ultimate justice of the people? Is there any better or equal hope in the world? In our present differences is either party without faith of being in the right? If the Almighty Ruler of Nations, with His eternal truth and justice, be on your side of the North, or on yours of the South, that truth and that justice will surely prevail by the judgment of this great tribunal of the American people.

By the frame of the government under which we live, this same people have wisely given their public servants but little power for mischief; and have, with equal wisdom, provided for the return of that little to their own hands at very short intervals. While the people retain their virtue and vigilance, no administration, by any extreme of wickedness or folly, can very seriously injure the government in the short space of four years.

My countrymen, one and all, think calmly and well upon this whole subject. Nothing valuable can be lost by taking time. If there be an object to hurry any of you in hot haste to a step which you would never take deliberately, that object will be frustrated by taking time; but no good object can be frustrated by it. Such of you as are now dissatisfied, still have the old Constitution unimpaired, and, on the sensitive point, the laws of your own framing under it; while the new administration will have no immediate power, if it would, to change either. If it were admitted that you who are dissatisfied hold the right side in the dispute, there still is no single good reason for precipitate action. Intelligence, patriotism, Christianity, and a firm reliance on Him who has never yet forsaken this favored land, are still competent to adjust in the best way all our present difficulty.

In your hands, my dissatisfied fellow-countrymen, and not in mine, is the momentous issue of civil war. The government will not assail you. You can have no conflict without being yourselves the aggressors. You have no oath registered in heaven to destroy the government, while I shall have the most solemn one to "preserve, protect, and defend it."

I am loath to close. We are not enemies, but friends. We must not be enemies. Though passion may have strained, it must not break our bonds of affection. The mystic chords of memory, stretching from every battle-field and patriot grave to every living heart and hearth-stone all over this broad land, will yet swell the chorus of the Union when again touched, as surely they will be, by the better angels of our nature.

SPECIAL MESSAGE TO CONGRESS
(July 4, 1861)

FELLOW-CITIZENS OF THE SENATE AND HOUSE OF REPRESENTATIVES: Having been convened on an extraordinary occasion, as authorized by the Constitution, your attention is not called to any ordinary subject of legislation.

At the beginning of the present presidential term, four months ago, the functions of the Federal Government were found to be generally suspended within the several states of South Carolina, Georgia, Alabama, Mississippi, Louisiana, and Florida, excepting only those of the Post-office Department.

Within these states all the forts, arsenals, dockyards, custom-houses, and the like, including the movable and stationary property in and about them, had been seized, and were held in open hostility to this government, excepting only Forts Pickens, Taylor, and Jefferson, on and near the Florida coast, and Fort Sumter, in Charleston Harbor, South Carolina. The forts thus seized had been put in improved condition, new ones had been built, and armed forces had been organized and were organizing, all avowedly with the same hostile purpose.

The forts remaining in the possession of the Federal Government in and near these states were either besieged or menaced by warlike preparations, and especially Fort Sumter was nearly surrounded by well-protected hostile batteries, with guns equal in quality to the best of its own, and outnumbering the latter as perhaps ten to one. A disproportionate share of the Federal muskets and rifles had somehow found their way into these states, and had been seized to be used against the government. Accumulations of the public revenue lying within them had been seized for the same object. The navy was scattered in distant seas, leaving but a very small part of it within immediate reach of the government. Officers of the Federal army and navy resigned in great numbers; and of those resigning a large proportion had taken up arms against the government. Simultaneously, and in connection with all this, the purpose to sever the Federal Union was openly avowed. In accordance with this purpose, an ordinance had been adopted in each of these states, declaring the states respectively to be separated from the National Union. A formula for instituting a combined government of these states had been promulgated; and this illegal organization, in the character of confederate states, was already invoking recognition, aid, and intervention from foreign powers.

Finding this condition of things, and believing it to be an imperative duty upon the incoming executive to prevent, if possible, the consummation of such attempt to destroy the Federal Union, a choice of means to that end became indispensable. This choice was made and was declared in the inaugural address. The policy chosen looked to the exhaustion of all peaceful measures before a resort to any stronger ones. It sought only to hold the public places and property not already wrested from the government, and to collect the revenue, relying for the rest on time, discussion, and the ballot-box. It promised a continuance of the mails, at government expense, to the very people who were resisting the government; and it gave repeated pledges against any disturbance to any of the people, or any of their rights. Of all that which a President might constitutionally and justifiably do in such a case, everything was forborne without which it was believed possible to keep the government on foot.

On the 5th of March (the present incumbent's first full day in office), a letter of Major Anderson, commanding at Fort Sumter, written on the 28th day of February and received at the War Department on the 4th of March, was by that department placed in his hands. This letter expressed the professional opinion of the writer that reënforcements could not be thrown into that fort within the time for his relief, rendered necessary by the limited supply of provisions, and with a view of holding possession of the same, with a force of less than twenty thousand good and well-disciplined men. This opinion was concurred in by all the officers of his command, and their memoranda on the subject were made inclosures of Major Anderson's letter. The whole was immediately laid before Lieutenant-General Scott, who at once concurred with Major Anderson in opinion. On reflection, however, he took full time, consulting with other officers, both of the army and the navy, and at the end of four days came reluctantly but decidedly to the same conclusion as before. He also stated at the same time that no such sufficient force was then at the control of the government, or could be raised and brought to the ground within the time when the provisions in the fort would be exhausted. In a purely military point of view, this reduced the duty of the administration in the case to the mere matter of getting the garrison safely out of the fort.

It is believed, however, that to so abandon that position, under the circumstances, would be utterly ruinous; that the necessity under which it was to be done would not be fully understood; that by many it would be construed as a part of a voluntary policy; that at home it would discourage the friends of the Union, embolden its adversaries, and go far to insure to the latter a recognition abroad; that, in fact, it would be our national destruction consummated. This could not be allowed. Starvation was not yet upon the garrison, and ere it would be reached, Fort Pickens might be reënforced. This last would be a clear indication of policy, and would better enable the country to accept the evacuation of Fort Sumter as a military necessity. An order was at once directed to be sent for the landing of the troops from the steamship *Brooklyn* into Fort Pickens. This order could not go by land, but must take the longer and slower route by sea. The first return news from the order was received just one week before the fall of Fort Sumter. The news itself was that the officer commanding the *Sabine*, to which vessel the troops had been transferred from the *Brooklyn*, acting upon some *quasi* armistice of the late administration (and of the existence of which the present administration, up to the time the order was dispatched, had only too vague and uncertain rumors to fix attention), had refused to land the troops. To now reënforce Fort Pickens before a crisis would be reached at Fort Sumter was impossible—rendered so by the near exhaustion of provisions in the latter-named fort. In precaution against such a conjuncture, the government had, a few days before, commenced preparing an expedition as well adapted as might be to relieve Fort Sumter, which expedition was intended to be ultimately used, or not, according to circumstances. The strongest anticipated case for using it was now presented, and it was resolved to send it forward. As had been intended in this contingency, it was also resolved to notify the governor of South Carolina that he might expect an attempt would be made to provision the fort; and that, if the attempt should not be resisted, there would be no effort to throw in men, arms, or ammunition, without further notice, or in case of an attack upon the fort. This notice was accordingly given; whereupon the fort was attacked and bombarded to its fall, without even awaiting the arrival of the provisioning expedition.

It is thus seen that the assault upon and reduction of Fort Sumter was in no sense a matter of self-defense on the part of the assailants. They well knew that the garrison in the fort could by no possibility commit aggression upon them. They knew—they were expressly notified—that the giving of bread to a few brave and hungry men of the garrison was all which would on that occasion be attempted, unless themselves, by resisting so much, should provoke more. They knew that this government desired to keep the garrison in the fort, not to assail them, but merely to maintain visible possession, and thus to preserve the Union from actual and immediate dissolution—trusting, as hereinbefore stated, to time, discussion, and the ballot-box for final adjustment; and they assailed and reduced the fort for precisely the reverse object—to drive out the visible authority of the Federal Union, and thus force it to immediate dissolution. That this was their object the executive well understood; and having said to them in the inaugural address, "You can have no conflict without being yourselves the aggressors," he took pains not only to keep this declaration good, but also to keep the case so free from the power of ingenious sophistry that the world should not be able to misunderstand it. By the affair at Fort Sumter, with its surrounding circumstances, that point was reached. Then and thereby the assailants of the government began the conflict of arms, without a gun in sight or in expectancy to return their fire, save only the few in the fort sent to that harbor years before for their own protection, and still ready to give that protection in whatever was lawful. In this act, discarding all else, they have forced upon the country the distinct issue, "immediate dissolution or blood."

And this issue embraces more than the fate of these United States. It presents to the whole family of man the question whether a constitutional republic or democracy—a government of the people by the same people—can or cannot maintain its territorial integrity against its own domestic foes. It presents the question whether discontented individuals, too few in numbers to control administration according to organic law in any case, can always, by the pretenses made in this case, or on any other pretenses, or arbitrarily without any pretense, break up their government, and thus practically put an end to free government upon the earth. It forces us to ask: "Is there, in all republics, this inherent and fatal weakness?" "Must a government, of necessity, be too strong for the liberties of its own people, or too weak to maintain its own existence?"

So viewing the issue, no choice was left but to call out the war power of the government; and so to resist force employed for its destruction, by force for its preservation.

The call was made, and the response of the country was most gratifying, surpassing in unanimity and spirit the most sanguine expectation. Yet none of the states commonly called slave states, except Delaware, gave a regiment through regular state organization. A few regiments have been organized within some others of those states by individual enterprise, and received into the government service. Of course the seceded states, so called (and to which Texas had been joined about the time of the inauguration), gave no troops to the cause of the Union. The border states, so called, were not uniform in their action, some of them being almost for the Union, while in others—as Virginia, North Carolina, Tennessee, and Arkansas—the Union sentiment was nearly repressed and silenced. The course taken in Virginia was the most remarkable—perhaps the most important. A convention elected by the people of that state to consider the very question of disrupting the Federal Union was in session at the capital of Virginia when Fort Sumter fell. To this body the people had chosen a large majority of professed Union men. Almost immediately after the fall of Sumter, many members of that majority went over to the original disunion minority, and with them adopted an ordinance for withdrawing the state from the Union. Whether this change was wrought by their great approval of the assault upon Sumter, or their great resentment at the government's resistance to that assault, is not definitely known. Although they submitted the ordinance for ratification to a vote of the people, to be taken on a day then somewhat more than a month distant, the convention and the legislature (which was also in session at the same time and place), with leading men of the state not members of either, immediately commenced acting as if the state were already out of the Union. They pushed military preparations vigorously forward all over the state. They seized the United States armory at Harper's Ferry, and the navy-yard at Gosport, near Norfolk. They received—perhaps invited—into their state large bodies of troops with their warlike appointments, from the so-called seceded states. They formally entered into a treaty of temporary alliance and coöperation with the so-called "Confederate States," and sent members to their congress at Montgomery. And, finally, they permitted the insurrectionary government to be transferred to their capital at Richmond.

The people of Virginia have thus allowed this giant insurrection to make its nest within her borders; and this government has no choice left but to deal with it where it finds it. And it has the less regret as the loyal citizens have, in due form, claimed its protection. Those loyal citizens this government is bound to recognize and protect, as being Virginia.

In the border states, so called—in fact, the Middle States—there are those who favor a policy which they call "armed neutrality"; that is, an arming of those states to prevent the Union forces passing one way, or the disunion the other, over their soil. This would be disunion completed. Figuratively speaking, it would be the building of an impassable wall along the line of separation—and yet not quite an impassable one, for under the guise of neutrality it would tie the hands of Union men and freely pass supplies from among them to the insurrectionists, which it could not do as an open enemy. At a stroke it would take all the trouble off the hands of secession, except only what proceeds from the external blockade. It would do for the disunionists that which, of all things, they most desire—feed them well, and give them disunion without a struggle of their own. It recognizes no fidelity to the Constitution, no obligation to maintain the Union; and while very many who have favored it are doubtless loyal citizens, it is, nevertheless, very injurious in effect.

Recurring to the action of the government, it may be stated that at first a call was made for 75,000 militia; and, rapidly following this, a proclamation was issued for closing the ports of the insurrectionary districts by proceedings in the nature of blockade. So far all was believed to be strictly legal. At this point the insurrectionists announced their purpose to enter upon the practice of privateering.

Other calls were made for volunteers to serve

for three years, unless sooner discharged, and also for large additions to the regular army and navy. These measures, whether strictly legal or not, were ventured upon, under what appeared to be a popular demand and a public necessity; trusting then, as now, that Congress would readily ratify them. It is believed that nothing has been done beyond the constitutional competency of Congress.

Soon after the first call for militia, it was considered a duty to authorize the commanding general in proper cases, according to his discretion, to suspend the privilege of the writ of *habeas corpus*, or, in other words, to arrest and detain, without resort to the ordinary processes and forms of law, such individuals as he might deem dangerous to the public safety. This authority has purposely been exercised but very sparingly. Nevertheless, the legality and propriety of what has been done under it are questioned, and the attention of the country has been called to the proposition that one who has sworn to "take care that the laws be faithfully executed" should not himself violate them. Of course some consideration was given to the questions of power and propriety before this matter was acted upon. The whole of the laws which were required to be faithfully executed were being resisted and failing of execution in nearly one-third of the states. Must they be allowed to finally fail of execution, even had it been perfectly clear that by the use of the means necessary to their execution some single law, made in such extreme tenderness of the citizen's liberty that, practically, it relieves more of the guilty than of the innocent, should to a very limited extent be violated? To state the question more directly, are all the laws but one to go unexecuted, and the government itself go to pieces, lest that one be violated? Even in such a case, would not the official oath be broken if the government should be overthrown, when it was believed that disregarding the single law would tend to preserve it? But it was not believed that this question was presented. It was not believed that any law was violated. The provision of the Constitution that "the privilege of the writ of *habeas corpus* shall not be suspended, unless when, in cases of rebellion or invasion, the public safety may require it," is equivalent to a provision—is a provision—that such privilege may be suspended when, in case of rebellion or invasion, the public safety does require it. It was decided that we have a case of rebellion, and that the public safety does require the qualified suspension of the privilege of the writ which was authorized to be made. Now it is insisted that Con-

gress, and not the Executive, is vested with this power. But the Constitution itself is silent as to which or who is to exercise the power; and as the provision was plainly made for a dangerous emergency, it cannot be believed the framers of the instrument intended that in every case the danger should run its course until Congress could be called together, the very assembling of which might be prevented, as was intended in this case, by the rebellion.

No more extended argument is now offered, as an opinion at some length will probably be presented by the Attorney General. Whether there shall be any legislation upon the subject, and if any, what, is submitted entirely to the better judgment of Congress.

The forbearance of this government had been so extraordinary and so long continued as to lead some foreign nations to shape their action as if they supposed the early destruction of our National Union was probable. While this, on discovery, gave the Executive some concern, he is now happy to say that the sovereignty and rights of the United States are now everywhere practically respected by foreign powers; and a general sympathy with the country is manifested throughout the world.

The reports of the Secretaries of the Treasury, War, and the Navy will give the information in detail deemed necessary and convenient for your deliberation and action; while the Executive and all the departments will stand ready to supply omissions, or to communicate new facts considered important for you to know.

It is now recommended that you give the legal means for making this contest a short and decisive one: that you place at the control of the government for the work at least four hundred thousand men and $400,000,000. That number of men is about one-tenth of those of proper ages within the regions where, apparently, all are willing to engage; and the sum is less than a twenty-third part of the money value owned by the men who seem ready to devote the whole. A debt of $600,000,000 now is a less sum per head than was the debt of our Revolution when we came out of that struggle; and the money value in the country now bears even a greater proportion to what it was then than does the population. Surely each man has as strong a motive now to preserve our liberties as each had then to establish them.

A right result at this time will be worth more to the world than ten times the men and ten times the money. The evidence reaching us from the country leaves no doubt that the material for the work is abundant, and that it needs only the hand of legislation to give it legal sanction, and the hand of the Executive to give it practical shape and efficiency. One of the greatest perplexities of the government is to avoid receiving troops faster than it can provide for them. In a word, the people will save their government if the government itself will do its part only indifferently well.

It might seem, at first thought, to be of little difference whether the present movement at the South be called "secession" or "rebellion." The movers, however, will understand the difference. At the beginning they knew they could never raise their treason to any respectable magnitude by any name which implies violation of law. They knew their people possessed as much of moral sense, as much of devotion to law and order, and as much pride in and reverence for the history and government of their common country as any other civilized and patriotic people. They knew they could make no advancement directly in the teeth of these strong and noble sentiments. Accordingly, they commenced by an insidious debauching of the public mind. They invented an ingenious sophism which, if conceded, was followed by perfectly logical steps, through all the incidents, to the complete destruction of the Union. The sophism itself is that any state of the Union may consistently with the National Constitution, and therefore lawfully and peacefully, withdraw from the Union without the consent of the Union or of any other state. The little disguise that the supposed right is to be exercised only for just cause, themselves to be the sole judges of its justice, is too thin to merit any notice.

With rebellion thus sugar-coated they have been drugging the public mind of their section for more than thirty years, until at length they have brought many good men to a willingness to take up arms against the government the day after some assemblage of men have enacted the farcial pretense of taking their state out of the Union, who could have been brought to no such thing the day before.

This sophism derives much, perhaps the whole, of its currency from the assumption that there is some omnipotent and sacred supremacy pertaining to a state—to each state of our Federal Union. Our states have neither more nor less power than that reserved to them in the Union by the Constitution—no one of them ever having been a state out of the Union. The original ones passed into the Union even before they cast off their British colonial dependence; and the new ones each came into the Union directly from a condition of dependence, excepting Texas. And even Texas, in its temporary independence, was never designated a state. The new ones only took the designation of states on coming into the Union, while that name was first adopted for the old ones in and by the Declaration of Independence. Therein the "United Colonies" were declared to be "free and independent states"; but even then the object plainly was not to declare their independence of one another or of the Union, but directly the contrary, as their mutual pledge and their mutual action before, at the time and afterward, abundantly show. The express plighting of faith by each and all of the original thirteen in the Articles of Confederation, two years later, that the Union shall be perpetual, is most conclusive. Having never been states either in substance or in name outside of the Union, whence this magical omnipotence of "State Rights," asserting a claim of power to lawfully destroy the Union itself? Much is said about the "sovereignty" of the states; but the word even is not in the National Constitution, nor, as is believed, in any of the state constitutions. What is "sovereignty" in the political sense of the term? Would it be far wrong to define it "a political community without a political superior"? Tested by this, no one of our states except Texas ever was a sovereignty. And even Texas gave up the character on coming into the Union; by which act she acknowledged the Constitution of the United States, and the laws and treaties of the United States made in pursuance of the Constitution, to be for her the supreme law of the land. The states have their status in the Union, and they have no other legal status. If they break from this, they can only do so against law and by revolution. The Union, and not themselves separately, procured their independence and their liberty. By conquest or purchase the Union gave each of them whatever of independence or liberty it has. The Union is older than any of the states, and, in fact, it created them as states. Originally some dependent colonies made the Union, and, in turn, the Union threw off their old dependence for them, and made them states, such as they are. Not one of them ever had a state constitution independent of the Union. Of course, it is not forgotten that all the new states framed their constitutions before they entered the Union—nevertheless, dependent upon and preparatory to coming into the Union.

Unquestionably the states have the powers and rights reserved to them in and by the National Constitution; but among these surely are not included all conceivable powers, however mischievous or destructive, but, at most, such only as were known in the world at the time as governmental powers; and certainly a power to destroy the government itself had never been known as a governmental, as a merely administrative power. This relative matter of national power and state rights, as a principle, is no other than the principle of generality and locality. Whatever concerns the whole should be confided to the whole—to the General Government; while whatever concerns only the state should be left exclusively to the state. This is all there is of the original principle about it. Whether the National Constitution in defining boundaries between the two has applied the principle with exact accuracy, is not to be questioned. We are all bound by that defining, without question.

What is now combated is the position that secession is consistent with the Constitution—is lawful and peaceful. It is not contended that there is any express law for it; and nothing should ever be implied as law which leads to unjust or absurd consequences. The nation purchased with money the countries out of which several of these states were formed. Is it just that they shall go off without leave and without refunding? The nation paid very large sums (in the aggregate, I believe, nearly a hundred millions) to relieve Florida of the aboriginal tribes. Is it just that she shall now be off without consent or without making any return? The nation is now in debt for money applied to the benefit of these so-called seceding states in common with the rest. Is it just either that creditors shall go unpaid or the remaining states pay the whole? A part of the present national debt was contracted to pay the old debts of Texas. Is it just that she shall leave and pay no part of this herself?

Again, if one state may secede, so may another; and when all shall have seceded, none is left to pay the debts. Is this quite just to creditors? Did we notify them of this sage view of ours when we borrowed their money? If we now recognize this doctrine by allowing the seceders to go in peace, it is difficult to see what we can do if others choose to go or to extort terms upon which they will promise to remain.

The seceders insist that our Constitution admits of secession. They have assumed to make a national constitution of their own, in which of necessity they have either discarded or retained the right of secession as they insist it exists in ours. If they have discarded it, they thereby admit that on principle it ought not to be in ours. If they have retained it by their own construction of ours, they show that to be consistent they must secede from one another whenever they shall find it the easiest way of settling their debts, or effecting any other selfish or unjust object. The principle itself is one of disintegration, and upon which no government can possibly endure.

If all the states save one should assert the power to drive that one out of the Union, it is presumed the whole class of seceder politicians would at once deny the power and denounce the act as the greatest outrage upon state rights. But suppose that precisely the same act, instead of being called "driving the one out," should be called "the seceding of the others from that one," it would be exactly what the seceders claim to do, unless, indeed, they make the point that the one, because it is a minority, may rightfully do what the others, because they are a majority, may not rightfully do. These politicians are subtle and profound on the rights of minorities. They are not partial to that power which made the Constitution and speaks from the preamble, calling itself "We, the People."

It may well be questioned whether there is today a majority of the legally qualified voters of any state, except perhaps South Carolina, in favor of disunion. There is much reason to believe that the Union men are the majority in many, if not in every other one, of the so-called seceded states. The contrary has not been demonstrated in any one of them. It is ventured to affirm this even of Virginia and Tennessee; for the result of an election held in military camps, where the bayonets are all on one side of the question voted upon, can scarcely be considered as demonstrating popular sentiment. At such an election, all that large class who are at once for the Union and against coercion would be coerced to vote against the Union.

It may be affirmed without extravagance that the free institutions we enjoy have developed the powers and improved the condition of our whole people beyond any example in the world. Of this we now have a striking and an impressive illustration. So large an army as the government has now on foot was never before known, without a soldier in it but who has taken his place there of his own free choice. But more than this, there are many single regiments whose members, one and another, possess full practical knowledge of all the arts, sciences, professions, and whatever else, whether useful or elegant, is known in the world; and there is scarcely one from which there could not be selected a president, a cabinet, a congress, and perhaps a court, abundantly competent to administer the government itself. Nor do I say this is not true also in the army of our late friends, now adversaries in this contest; but if it is, so much better the reason why the government which has conferred such benefits on both them and us should not be broken up. Whoever in any section proposes to abandon such a government would do well to consider in deference to what principle it is that he does it—what better he is likely to get in its stead—whether the substitute will give, or be intended to give, so much of good to the people. There are some foreshadowings on this subject. Our adversaries have adopted some declarations of independence in which, unlike the good old one, penned by Jefferson, they omit the word "all men are created equal." Why? They have adopted a temporary national constitution, in the preamble of which, unlike our good old one, signed by Washington, they omit "We, the People," and substitute, "We, the deputies of the sovereign and independent states." Why? Why this deliberate pressing out of view the rights of men and the authority of the people?

This is essentially a people's contest. On the side of the Union it is a struggle for maintaining in the world that form and substance of government whose leading object is to elevate the condition of men—to lift artificial weights from all shoulders; to clear the paths of laudable pursuit for all; to afford all an unfettered start, and a fair chance in the race of life. Yielding to partial and temporary departures, from necessity, this is the leading object of the government for whose existence we contend.

I am most happy to believe that the plain people understand and appreciate this. It is worthy of note that while in this, the government's hour of trial, large numbers of those in the army and navy who have been favored with the offices have resigned and proved false to the hand which had pampered them, not one common soldier or common sailor is known to have deserted his flag.

Great honor is due to those officers who remained true, despite the example of their treacherous associates; but the greatest honor, and most important fact of all, is the unanimous firmness of the common soldiers and common sailors. To the last man, so far as known, they have successfully resisted the traitorous efforts of those whose commands, but an hour before, they obeyed as absolute law. This is the patriotic instinct of the plain people. They understand, without an argument, that the destroying of the government which was made by Washington means no good to them.

Our popular government has often been called an experiment. Two points in it our people have already settled—the successful establishing and the successful administering of it. One still remains—its successful maintenance against a formidable internal attempt to overthrow it. It is now for them to demonstrate to the world that those who can fairly carry an election can also suppress a rebellion; that ballots are the rightful and peaceful successors of bullets; and that when ballots have fairly and constitutionally decided, there can be no successful appeal back to bullets; that there can be no successful appeal, except to ballots themselves, at succeeding elections. Such will be a great lesson of peace: teaching men that what they cannot take by an election, neither can they take it by a war; teaching all the folly of being the beginners of a war.

Lest there be some uneasiness in the minds of candid men as to what is to be the course of the government toward the Southern states after the rebellion shall have been suppressed, the Executive deems it proper to say it will be his purpose then, as ever, to be guided by the Constitution and the laws; and that he probably will have no different understanding of the powers and duties of the Federal Government relatively to the rights of the states and the people, under the Constitution, than that expressed in the inaugural address.

He desires to preserve the government, that it may be administered for all as it was administered by the men who made it. Loyal citizens everywhere have the right to claim this of their government, and the government has no right to withhold or neglect it. It is not perceived that in giving it there is any coercion, any conquest, or any subjugation, in any just sense of those terms.

The Constitution provides, and all the states have accepted the provision, that "the United States shall guarantee to every state in this Union a republican form of government." But if a state may lawfully go out of the Union, having done so, it may also discard the republican form of government; so that to prevent its going out is an indispensable means to the end of maintaining the guarantee mentioned; and when an end is lawful and obligatory, the indispensable means to it are also lawful and obligatory.

It was with the deepest regret that the Executive found the duty of employing the war power in defense of the government forced upon him. He could but perform this duty or surrender the existence of the government. No compromise by public servants could, in this case, be a cure; not that compromises are not often proper, but that no popular government can long survive a marked precedent that those who carry an election can only save the government from immediate destruction by giving up the main point upon which the people gave the election. The people themselves, and not their servants, can safely reverse their own deliberate decisions.

As a private citizen the Executive could not have consented that these institutions shall perish; much less could he, in betrayal of so vast and so sacred a trust as the free people have confided to him. He felt that he had no moral right to shrink, nor even to count the chances of his own life in what might follow. In full view of his great responsibility he has, so far, done what he has deemed his duty. You will now, according to your own judgment, perform yours. He sincerely hopes that your views and your actions may so accord with his as to assure all faithful citizens who have been disturbed in their rights of a certain and speedy restoration to them, under the Constitution and the laws.

And having thus chosen our course, without guile and with pure purpose, let us renew our trust in God, and go forward without fear and with manly hearts.

OPEN LETTER TO HORACE GREELEY

Executive Mansion,
Washington, August 22, 1862

HON. HORACE GREELEY.

DEAR SIR: I have just read yours of the 19th, addressed to myself through the New York *Tribune*. If there be in it any statements or assumptions of fact which I may know to be erroneous, I do not, now and here, controvert them. If there be in it any inferences which I may believe to be falsely drawn, I do not, now and here, argue against them. If there be perceptible in it an impatient and dictatorial tone, I waive it in deference to an old friend whose heart I have always supposed to be right.

As to the policy I "seem to be pursuing," as you say, I have not meant to leave any one in doubt.

I would save the Union. I would save it the shortest way under the Constitution. The sooner the national authority can be restored, the nearer the Union will be "the Union as it was." If there be those who would not save the Union unless they could at the same time save slavery, I do not agree with them. If there be those who would not save the Union unless they could at the same time destroy slavery, I do not agree with them. My paramount object in this struggle is to save the Union, and is not either to save or to destroy slavery. If I could save the Union without freeing any slave, I would do it; and if I could save it by freeing all the slaves, I would do it; and if I could save it by freeing some and leaving others alone, I would also do that. What I do about slavery and the colored race, I do because I believe it helps to save the Union; and what I forbear, I forbear because I do not believe it would help to save the Union. I shall do less whenever I shall believe what I am doing hurts the cause, and I shall do more whenever I shall believe doing more will help the cause. I shall try to correct errors when shown to be errors, and I shall adopt new views so fast as they shall appear to be true views.

I have here stated my purpose according to my view of official duty; and I intend no modification of my oft-expressed personal wish that all men everywhere could be free.

Yours,
A. LINCOLN.

ADDRESS AT GETTYSBURG
(November 19, 1863)

Four score and seven years ago our fathers brought forth on this continent a new nation, conceived in liberty, and dedicated to the proposition that all men are created equal.

Now we are engaged in a great civil war; testing whether that nation, or any nation so conceived and so dedicated, can long endure. We are met on a great battle-field of that war.

We have come to dedicate a portion of that field as a final resting-place for those who here gave their lives that that nation might live. It is altogether fitting and proper that we should do this.

But, in a larger sense, we cannot dedicate—we cannot consecrate—we cannot hallow—this ground. The brave men, living and dead, who struggled here, have consecrated it far above our poor power to add or detract. The world will little note nor long remember what we say here, but it can never forget what they did here. It is for us the living, rather, to be dedicated here to the unfinished work which they who fought here have thus far so nobly advanced. It is rather for us to be here dedicated to the great task remaining before us—

that from these honored dead we take increased devotion to that cause for which they gave the last full measure of devotion; that we here highly resolve that these dead shall not have died in vain; that this nation, under God, shall have a new birth of freedom; and that government of the people, by the people, for the people, shall not perish from the earth.

TO MRS. BIXBY

Executive Mansion,
Washington, November 21, 1864.

DEAR MADAM: I have been shown in the files of the War Department a statement of the Adjutant-General of Massachusetts that you are the mother of five sons who have died gloriously on the field of battle. I feel how weak and fruitless must be any words of mine which should attempt to beguile you from the grief of a loss so overwhelming. But I cannot refrain

from tendering to you the consolation that may be found in the thanks of the Republic they died to save. I pray that our heavenly Father may assuage the anguish of your bereavement, and leave you only the cherished memory of the loved and lost, and the solemn pride that must be yours to have laid so costly a sacrifice upon the altar of freedom.

Yours very sincerely and respectfully,
ABRAHAM LINCOLN.

SECOND INAUGURAL ADDRESS
(March 4, 1865)

FELLOW COUNTRYMEN: At this second appearing to take the oath of the presidential office, there is less occasion for an extended address than there was at the first. Then a statement, somewhat in detail, of a course to be pursued, seemed fitting and proper. Now, at the expiration of four years, during which public declarations have been constantly called forth on every point and phase of the great contest which still absorbs the attention and engrosses the energies of the nation, little that is new could be presented. The progress of our arms, upon which all else chiefly depends, is as well known to the public as to myself; and it is, I trust, reasonably satisfactory and encouraging to all. With high hope for the future, no prediction in regard to it is ventured.

On the occasion corresponding to this four years ago, all thoughts were anxiously directed to an impending civil war. All dreaded it—all sought to avert it. While the inaugural address was being delivered from this place, devoted altogether to saving the Union without war, insurgent agents were in the city seeking to destroy it without war—seeking to dissolve the Union, and divide effects, by negotiation. Both parties deprecated war; but one of them would make war rather than let the nation survive; and the other would accept war rather than let it perish. And the war came.

One-eighth of the whole population were colored slaves, not distributed generally over the Union, but localized in the southern part of it. These slaves constituted a peculiar and powerful interest. All knew that this interest was, somehow, the cause of the war. To strengthen, perpetuate, and extend this interest was the object for which the insurgents would rend the Union, even by war; while the government claimed no right to do more than to restrict the territorial enlargement of it.

Neither party expected for the war the magnitude or the duration which it has already attained. Neither anticipated that the cause of the conflict might cease with, or even before, the conflict itself should cease. Each looked for an easier triumph, and a result less fundamental and astounding. Both read the same Bible, and pray to the same God; and each invokes His aid against the other. It may seem strange that any men should dare to ask a just God's assistance in wringing their bread from the sweat of other men's faces; but let us judge not, that we be not judged. The prayers of both could not be answered—that of neither has been answered fully.

The Almighty has his own purposes. "Woe unto the world because of offenses! for it must needs be that offenses come; but woe to that man by whom the offense cometh." If we shall suppose that American slavery is one of those offenses which, in the providence of God, must needs come, but which, having continued through His appointed time, He now wills to remove, and that He gives to both North and South this terrible war, as the woe due to those by whom the offense came, shall we discern therein any departure from those divine attributes which the believers in a living God always ascribe to Him? Fondly do we hope—fervently do we pray—that this mighty scourge of war may speedily pass away. Yet, if God wills that it continue until all the wealth piled by the bondman's two hundred and fifty years of unrequited toil shall be sunk, and until every drop of blood drawn with the lash shall be paid by another drawn with the sword, as was three thousand years ago, so still it must be said, "The judgments of the Lord are true and righteous altogether."

With malice toward none; with charity for all; with firmness in the right, as God gives us to see the right, let us strive on to finish the work we are in; to bind up the nation's wounds; to care for him who shall have borne the battle, and for his widow, and his orphan —to do all which may achieve and cherish a just and lasting peace among ourselves, and with all nations.

POETRY OF THE CIVIL WAR
The Call to Arms

ETHNOGENESIS

By Henry Timrod (1829–1867)

Written during the meeting of the First Southern Congress, at Montgomery, February, 1861.

I

Hath not the morning dawned with added
    light?
And shall not evening call another star
Out of the infinite regions of the night,
To mark this day in Heaven? At last, we are
A nation among nations; and the world
Shall soon behold in many a distant port
    Another flag unfurled!
Now, come what may, whose favor need we
    court?
And, under God, whose thunder need we fear?
    Thank Him who placed us here   10
Beneath so kind a sky—the very sun
Takes part with us; and on our errands run
All breezes of the ocean; dew and rain
Do noiseless battle for us; and the Year,
And all the gentle daughters in her train,
March in our ranks, and in our service wield
    Long spears of golden grain!
A yellow blossom as her fairy shield,
June flings her azure banner to the wind,
    While in the order of their birth   20
Her sisters pass, and many an ample field
Grows white beneath their steps, till now, be-
    hold,
    Its endless sheets unfold
The snow of Southern Summers! Let the
    earth

Rejoice! beneath those fleeces soft and warm
Our happy land shall sleep
In a repose as deep
As if we lay intrenched behind
Whole leagues of Russian ice and Arctic storm!

II

And what if, mad with wrongs themselves
    have wrought,   30
    In their own treachery caught,
    By their own fears made bold,
    And leagued with him of old,
Who long since in the limits of the North
Set up his evil throne, and warred with God—
What if, both mad and blinded in their rage,
Our foes should fling us down their mortal
    gage,
And with a hostile step profane our sod!
We shall not shrink, my brothers, but go forth
To meet them, marshalled by the Lord of
    Hosts,   40
And overshadowed by the mighty ghosts
Of Moultrie and of Eutaw—who shall foil
Auxiliars such as these? Nor these alone,
    But every stock and stone
    Shall help us; but the very soil,
And all the generous wealth it gives to toil,
And all for which we love our noble land,
Shall fight beside, and through us; sea and
    strand,
    The heart of woman, and her hand,
Tree, fruit, and flower, and every influence, 50
    Gentle, or grave, or grand;
    The winds in our defence
Shall seem to blow; to us the hills shall lend
    Their firmness and their calm;

And in our stiffened sinews we shall blend
  The strength of pine and palm!

III

Nor would we shun the battle-ground,
  Though weak as we are strong;
Call up the clashing elements around,
  And test the right and wrong!   60
On one side, creeds that dare to teach
What Christ and Paul refrained to preach;
Codes built upon a broken pledge,
And Charity that whets a poniard's edge;
Fair schemes that leave the neighboring poor
To starve and shiver at the schemer's door,
While in the world's most liberal ranks en-
    rolled,
He turns some vast philanthropy to gold;
Religion, taking every mortal form
But that a pure and Christian faith makes
    warm,   70
Where not to vile fanatic passion urged,
Or not in vague philosophies submerged,
Repulsive with all Pharisaic leaven,
And making laws to stay the laws of Heaven!
And on the other, scorn of sordid gain,
Unblemished honor, truth without a stain,
Faith, justice, reverence, charitable wealth,
And, for the poor and humble, laws which give,
Not the mean right to buy the right to live,
  But life, and home, and health!   80
To doubt the end were want of trust in God,
  Who, if he has decreed
That we must pass a redder sea
Than that which rang to Miriam's holy glee,
  Will surely raise at need
  A Moses with his rod!

IV

But let our fears—if fears we have—be still,
And turn us to the future! Could we climb
Some mighty Alp, and view the coming time,
The rapturous sight would fill   90
  Our eyes with happy tears!
Not only for the glories which the years
Shall bring us; not for lands from sea to sea,
And wealth, and power, and peace, though
    these shall be;
But for the distant peoples we shall bless,
And the hushed murmurs of a world's distress:
For, to give labor to the poor,
  The whole sad planet o'er,
And save from want and crime the humblest
    door,
Is one among the many ends for which   100
  God makes us great and rich!
The hour perchance is not yet wholly ripe
When all shall own it, but the type

Whereby we shall be known in every land
Is that vast gulf which lips our Southern
    strand,
And through the cold, untempered ocean pours
Its genial streams, that far off Arctic shores
May sometimes catch upon the softened breeze
Strange tropic warmth and hints of summer
    seas.

MARYLAND! MY MARYLAND!

By James Ryder Randall

(1839–1908)

Written at Pointe Coupée, La., April 26, 1861.

The despot's heel is on thy shore,
  Maryland!
His torch is at thy temple door,
  Maryland!
Avenge the patriotic gore
That flecked the streets of Baltimore,
And be the battle queen of yore,
  Maryland! My Maryland!

Hark to an exiled son's appeal,
  Maryland!   10
My mother State! to thee I kneel,
  Maryland!
For life and death, for woe and weal,
Thy peerless chivalry reveal,
And gird thy beauteous limbs with steel,
  Maryland! My Maryland!

Thou wilt not cower in the dust,
  Maryland!
Thy beaming sword shall never rust,
  Maryland!   20
Remember Carroll's sacred trust,
Remember Howard's warlike thrust,—
And all thy slumberers with the just,
  Maryland! My Maryland!

Come! 'tis the red dawn of the day,
  Maryland!
Come with thy panoplied array,
  Maryland!
With Ringgold's spirit for the fray,
With Watson's blood at Monterey,   30
With fearless Lowe and dashing May,
  Maryland! My Maryland!

Come! for thy shield is bright and strong,
  Maryland!
Come! for thy dalliance does thee wrong,
  Maryland!
Come to thine own heroic throng,

Stalking with Liberty along,
And chaunt thy dauntless slogan song,
  Maryland! My Maryland!   40

Dear Mother! burst the tyrant's chain,
  Maryland!
Virginia should not call in vain,
  Maryland!
She meets her sisters on the plain—
"*Sic semper!*" 'tis the proud refrain
That baffles minions back again,
  Maryland! My Maryland!

I see the blush upon thy cheek,
  Maryland!   50
For thou wast ever bravely meek,
  Maryland!
But lo! there surges forth a shriek
From hill to hill, from creek to creek—
Potomac calls to Chesapeake,
  Maryland! My Maryland!

Thou wilt not yield the Vandal toll,
  Maryland!
Thou wilt not crook to his control,
  Maryland!   60
Better the fire upon thee roll,
Better the blade, the shot, the bowl,
Than crucifixion of the soul,
  Maryland! My Maryland!

I hear the distant thunder-hum,
  Maryland!
The Old Line's bugle, fife, and drum,
  Maryland!
She is not dead, nor deaf, nor dumb—
Huzza! she spurns the Northern scum! 70
She breathes! she burns! she'll come! she'll
  come!
  Maryland! My Maryland!

DIXIE

By Albert H. Pike (1809–1891)

Southrons, hear your country call you!
Up, lest worse than death befall you!
  To arms! To arms! To arms, in Dixie!
Lo! all the beacon-fires are lighted—
Let all hearts be now united!
  To arms! To arms! To arms, in Dixie!
  Advance the flag of Dixie!
    Hurrah! hurrah!
  For Dixie's land we take our stand,
  And live or die for Dixie!   10
    To arms! To arms!
  And conquer peace for Dixie!

Hear the Northern thunders mutter!
Northern flags in South winds flutter!
  To arms!
Send them back your fierce defiance!
Stamp upon the accursed alliance!
  To arms!
  Advance the flag of Dixie!

Fear no danger! shun no labor!   20
Lift up rifle, pike, and sabre!
  To arms!
Shoulder pressing close to shoulder,
Let the odds make each heart bolder!
  To arms!
  Advance the flag of Dixie!

How the South's great heart rejoices
At your cannon's ringing voices!
  To arms!
For faith betrayed, and pledges broken, 30
Wrongs inflicted, insults spoken,
  To arms!
  Advance the flag of Dixie!

Strong as lions, swift as eagles,
Back to their kennels hunt these beagles!
  To arms!
Cut the unequal bond asunder!
Let them hence each other plunder!
  To arms!
  Advance the flag of Dixie!   40

Swear upon your country's altar
Never to submit or falter!
  To arms!
Till the spoilers are defeated,
Till the Lord's work is completed,
  To arms!
  Advance the flag of Dixie!

Halt not till our Federation
Secures among earth's powers its station!
  To arms!   50
Then at peace, and crowned with glory,
Hear your children tell the story!
  To arms!
  Advance the flag of Dixie!

If the loved ones weep in sadness,
Victory soon shall bring them gladness.
  To arms!
Exultant pride soon vanish sorrow;
Smiles chase tears away to-morrow.
    To arms! To arms! To arms, in Dixie! 60
    Advance the flag of Dixie!
      Hurrah! hurrah!
    For Dixie's land we take our stand,
    And live or die for Dixie!

To arms! To arms!
And conquer peace for Dixie!
To arms! To arms!
And conquer peace for Dixie!

THE BONNIE BLUE FLAG

By Annie Chambers Ketchum
(1824–1904)

Come, brothers! rally for the right!
  The bravest of the brave
Sends forth her ringing battle-cry
  Beside the Atlantic wave!
She leads the way in honor's path;
  Come, brothers, near and far,
Come rally round the Bonnie Blue Fag
  That bears a single star!

We've borne the Yankee trickery,
  The Yankee gibe and sneer,   10
Till Yankee insolence and pride
  Know neither shame nor fear;
But ready now with shot and steel
  Their brazen front to mar,
We hoist aloft the Bonnie Blue Flag
  That bears a single star.

Now Georgia marches to the front,
  And close beside her come
Her sisters by the Mexique Sea,
  With pealing trump and drum;   20
Till answering back from hill and glen
  The rallying cry afar,
A Nation hoists the Bonnie Blue Flag
  That bears a single star.

By every stone in Charleston Bay,
  By each beleaguered town,
We swear to rest not, night nor day,
  But hunt the tyrants down!
Till bathed in valor's holy blood
  The gazing world afar   30
Shall greet with shouts the Bonnie Blue Flag
  That bears the cross and star!

JOHN BROWN'S BODY

By Charles Sprague Hall?

John Brown's body lies a-mould'ring in the
  grave,
John Brown's body lies a-mould'ring in the
  grave,
John Brown's body lies a-mould'ring in the
  grave,
His soul is marching on!

CHORUS

Glory! Glory Hallelujah!
Glory! Glory Hallelujah!
Glory! Glory Hallelujah!
His soul is marching on.

He's gone to be a soldier in the army of the
  Lord!
He's gone to be a soldier in the army of the
  Lord!
He's gone to be a soldier in the army of the   10
  Lord!
His soul is marching on.—Cho.

John Brown's knapsack is strapped upon his
  back.
His soul is marching on.—Cho.

His pet lambs will meet him on the way,
And they'll go marching on.—Cho.

They'll hang Jeff Davis on a sour apple tree,
As they go marching on.—Cho.

Now for the Union let's give three rousing
  cheers,
  As we go marching on.   20
  Hip, hip, hip, hip, Hurrah!

THE VIRGINIANS OF THE VALLEY

By Francis Orray Ticknor
(1822–1874)

The knightliest of the knightly race
  That, since the days of old,
Have kept the lamp of chivalry
  Alight in hearts of gold;
The kindliest of the kindly band
  That, rarely hating ease,
Yet rode with Spotswood round the land,
  And Raleigh round the seas.

Who climbed the blue Virginia hills
  Against embattled foes,   10
And planted there, in valleys fair,
  The lily and the rose;
Whose fragrance lives in many lands,
  Whose beauty stars the earth,
And lights the hearths of happy homes
  With loveliness and worth.

We thought they slept!—the sons who kept
  The names of noble sires,
And slumbered while the darkness crept
  Around their vigil fires;   20

But, aye, the "Golden Horseshoe" Knights
   Their old Dominion keep,
Whose foes have found enchanted ground,
   But not a knight asleep!

THE PICKET–GUARD

By Ethel Lynn Beers (1827–1879)

"All quiet along the Potomac," they say,
   "Except now and then a stray picket
Is shot, as he walks on his beat to and fro,
   By a rifleman hid in the thicket.
'Tis nothing: a private or two, now and then,
   Will not count in the news of the battle;
Not an officer lost—only one of the men,
   Moaning out, all alone, the death rattle."

All quiet along the Potomac to-night,
   Where the soldiers lie peacefully dreaming;
Their tents in the rays of the clear autumn
     moon,   11
   Or the light of the watch-fire, are gleaming.
A tremulous sigh of the gentle night-wind
   Through the forest leaves softly is creeping,
While the stars up above, with their glittering
     eyes,
   Keep guard, for the army is sleeping.

There's only the sound of the lone sentry's
     tread
   As he tramps from the rock to the fountain,
And thinks of the two in the low trundle-bed
   Far away in the cot on the mountain.   20
His musket falls slack; his face, dark and grim,
   Grows gentle with memories tender,
As he mutters a prayer for the children
     asleep—
   For their mother—may Heaven defend her!

The moon seems to shine just as brightly as
     then,
   That night, when the love yet unspoken
Leaped up to his lips—when low-murmured
     vows
   Were pledged to be ever unbroken.
Then drawing his sleeve roughly over his eyes,
   He dashes off tears that are welling,   30
And gathers his gun closer up to its place
   As if to keep down the heart-swelling.

He passes the fountain, the blasted pine-tree;
   The footstep is lagging and weary;
Yet onward he goes, through the broad belt of
     light,
   Towards the shade of the forest so dreary.

Hark! was it the night-wind that rustled the
     leaves?
   Was it moonlight so wondrously flashing?
It looked like a rifle . . . "Ha! Mary, good-
     by!"
   The red life-blood is ebbing and plashing.   40

All quiet along the Potomac to-night—
   No sound save the rush of the river,
While soft falls the dew on the face of the
     dead—
   The picket's off duty forever!

BATTLE–HYMN OF THE REPUBLIC

By Julia Ward Howe (1819–1910)

Mine eyes have seen the glory of the coming
     of the Lord:
He is trampling out the vintage where the
     grapes of wrath are stored;
He hath loosed the fateful lightning of his
     terrible swift sword:
   His truth is marching on.

I have seen Him in the watch-fires of a hun-
     dred circling camps;
They have builded Him an altar in the evening
     dews and damps;
I can read his righteous sentence by the dim
     and flaring lamps.
   His day is marching on.

I have read a fiery gospel, writ in burnished
     rows of steel:
"As ye deal with my contemners, so with you
     my grace shall deal;   10
Let the Hero, born of woman, crush the ser-
     pent with his heel,
   Since God is marching on."

He has sounded forth the trumpet that shall
     never call retreat;
He is sifting out the hearts of men before his
     judgment-seat:
Oh! be swift, my soul, to answer Him! be jubi-
     lant, my feet!
   Our God is marching on.

In the beauty of the lilies Christ was born
     across the sea,
With a glory in his bosom that transfigures
     you and me:
As He died to make men holy, let us die to
     make men free,
   While God is marching on.   20

ODE TO AMERICA

March 7, 1862

By George Henry Boker

(1823–1890)

No more of girls and wine,
  No more of pastoral joys,
No after-sighing for some antique line
Of bearded kings, who, at their nation's birth,
  As children play with toys,
Made merry with our earth:
  No more, no more of these!
  The girls are pale;
The wine is drunken to the lees;
Still are the bleatings of the woolly fold; 10
The olden kings look thin and cold,
  Like dim belated ghosts
  That hurrying sail
Towards their dark graves,
  Along the brightening coasts,
And sapphire hollows of the crested waves,
  Chased by the golden lances hurled
From the young sun above his cloudy world.

My country, let me turn to thee,
  With love and pride that glow 20
  Pure as twin altar-fires which blow
Their flames together to one Deity.
  Look where I may,
  O land beneath the iron sway
Of the strong hand;—
O land gored through and through
  By thy own faithless brand;
Land of once happy homes,
  To whose now darkened doors
The hand of sorrow comes, 30
  Early and late, and pours,
With no soft prelude, or no warning beat,
Her urn of bitter tears before thy feet!
O suffering, patient land,
  Thou bearest thy awful woe
So grandly, with such high command
Of tears, that dare not flow
For the great godlike smile
  Which crowns thy lips the while,
And stills thy mighty heart to move 40
As calmly on as when the hand of love
  Guided thy peaceful realm,
And idly swung the almost useless helm;
  That I, who, in my erring thought,
  Have often wronged thy fame,
  By sneers and taunts of blame,
Bow down with penitence o'erfraught,
  And pangs of reverent shame.

Thy rulers put aside thy rights;
  Thou murmurest not: 50

They waste thy gold;
  Still thy great cause is not forgot.
Thy ancient foe grows loud, and bold
  To proffer counsel, jeers, and spurns;
  The swaggering coward burns
With new-found courage; England smites
Thy sensitive, proud cheek,—
Smites, like a craven, when she deems thee
  weak!
Thy pale, stern features blush,
  Thy passionate arteries gush 60
With hot rebellious blood:
But thou stillest the raging flood;
Thou seemest to listen, in a patient hush,
  To the audacious kings,
  As they prattle empty things.
Thy pale, stern features blush
From thy heart the churl is spurned;
  But thy ready sinews pause,
  Remembering thy holy cause,
And the blow is not returned! 70

Not yet, not yet! O, bear,
  As the lion in his lair,
Whetting his teeth and gathering all his
  strength,
  Bears the insulting cry
  Of hunters drawing nigh
The dreadful door of his invaded home:
Whence, with a roar and bound, at length—
With bristling hair, with mane that rolls
  Above his fiery eyes,
  Like the tumultuous vapors of the skies, 80
Above the piercing lightning—he shall come,
  The lordly beast, whose lifted paw controls
  The fatal ends of life, and, in his wrath,
  Sweep from his onward path
The awe-struck phalanx of his enemies!
I saw thy many squadrons file and form;
I saw them driving through a deadly storm
  Of shot and shell,
  Where thousands fell;
But who survived, ah! they, indeed, 90
Were soldiers true; a race to breed
Avenging warriors, ripening for the day
When thou shalt cast thy shame away.
I saw thy mail-clad fleets, whose ponderous
  arms
Laugh at the toys of Europe, daily grow
  By stream and silent lake.
I saw them glide and take
The sheltered waters, as the wild swan
  glides,
With scarce a ripple at their moulded sides,
  To mar the current in its onward flow. 100
Swiftly they gathered, by the rising walls
  Of arméd ports;
  Hither and thither at prodigious sports,

To try their watery wings, they sped;
  Then snuffed a welcome from the briny
    breeze,
And, with one will, away they fled
  To join their dusky sisters of the seas!
    I saw it all; and bending low,
    My lips against thy ear I set,
    With "Hist! a hope begins to grow! 110
    Bear on, bear on! Not yet, not yet!"

O glory of our race,
  Long suffering guardian of the free,
    Thou who canst dare to be,
For a great purpose, in a lowly place!—
Thou who canst stretch the olive o'er the
    wave,
  And smite the master of the slave,
    Yet wisely measure all
    That might and must befall
Ere the great end shall crown the thing to
  be!—   120
    How shall I honor thee?
    How shall I fitly speak,
    In song so faint and weak,
Of majesty and wisdom such as thine?
    For now the scales, so long
    Held on the side of wrong,
    To thee again incline;
  And thou mayst lift thy radiant head,
And bind thy ring of re-appearing stars
About thy forehead, and forget thy scars 139
  In joy at holding that for which they
    bled!

    Resume thy place, unchallenged now,
Nor bow thy glories to the haughtiest brow
    That wears a royal crown!
    False prophets scowled thee down,
And whispered darkly of thy coming fate:
    The cause, the way, the date,
They wrote for thee with the slow augur's
  hand.—
    Their lies were scrawled in sand!
    They perished utterly!   140
What is the splendor of the diadem,
The gilded throne, the broidered carpet-
  hem,
The purple robe, the sceptre, and the strain
    Of foregone kings, whose race
    Defies the herald's trace,
Before thy regal steps on land and main?
  There are some deeds so grand
  That their mighty doers stand
Ennobled, in a moment, more than kings;
    And such deeds, O land sublime,   150
    Need no sanctity from time;
    Their own epoch they create,
    Whence all meaner things take date;

Then exalt thee, for such noble deeds were
  thine!
  Envy nothing born of earth,
  Rank nor wealth nor ancient birth,
Nor the glittering sorrows of a crown.
  O Nation, take instead
  Thy measureless renown,
To wrap thy young limbs like a royal stole, 160
  And God's own flaming aureole,
  To settle on thy head!

WE ARE COMING, FATHER ABRAHAM, THREE HUNDRED THOUSAND MORE

By James Sloan Gibbons
(1810–1892)

We are coming, Father Abraham, three hun-
  dred thousand more,
From Mississippi's winding stream and from
  New England's shore;
We leave our ploughs and workshops, our
  wives and children dear,
With hearts too full for utterance, with but a
  silent tear;
We dare not look behind us, but steadfastly
  before:
We are coming, Father Abraham, three hun-
  dred thousand more!

If you look across the hill-tops that meet the
  northern sky,
Long moving lines of rising dust your vision
  may descry;
And now the wind, an instant, tears the cloudy
  veil aside,
And floats aloft our spangled flag in glory and
  in pride,   10
And bayonets in the sunlight gleam, and bands
  brave music pour:
We are coming, Father Abraham, three hundred thousand more!

If you look all up our valleys where the growing harvests shine,
You may see our sturdy farmer boys fast forming into line;
And children from their mother's knees are
  pulling at the weeds,
And learning how to reap and sow against their
  country's needs;
And a farewell group stands weeping at every
  cottage door:
We are coming, Father Abraham, three hundred thousand more!

You have called us, and we're coming, by
    Richmond's bloody tide
To lay us down, for Freedom's sake, our
    brother's bones beside,   20
Or from foul treason's savage grasp to wrench
    the murderous blade,

And in the face of foreign foes its fragments to
    parade.
Six hundred thousand loyal men and true have
    gone before:
We are coming, Father Abraham, three hun-
    dred thousand more!

The Campaigns Against Richmond

"OUR LEFT"

(FIRST MANASSAS)

BY FRANCIS ORRAY TICKNOR

From dawn to dark they stood
    That long midsummer day,
        While fierce and fast
        The battle blast
    Swept rank on rank away.

From dawn to dark they fought,
    With legions torn and cleft;
        And still the wide
        Black battle-tide
    Poured deadlier on "Our Left."   10

They closed each ghastly gap;
    They dressed each shattered rank;
        They knew—how well—
        That Freedom fell
    With that exhausted flank.

"Oh, for a thousand men
    Like these that melt away!"
        And down they came,
        With steel and flame,
    Four thousand to the fray!   20

They leaped the laggard train—
    The panting steam might stay—
        And down they came,
        With steel and flame—
    Four thousand to the fray.

Right through the blackest cloud
    Their lightning path they cleft;
        And triumph came—
        With deathless fame
    To "our" unconquered "Left."   30

Ye, of your sons secure,
    Ye, of your dead bereft,
        Honor the brave
        Who died to save
    Your *all* upon "Our Left."

DIRGE FOR ASHBY

BY MARGARET JUNKIN PRESTON

(1820–1897)

Heard ye that thrilling word—
    Accent of dread—
Flash like a thunderbolt,
    Bowing each head—
Crash through the battle dun,
Over the booming gun—
"Ashby, our bravest one,—
    Ashby is dead!"

Saw ye the veterans—
    Hearts that had known   10
Never a quail of fear,
    Never a groan—
Sob 'mid the fight they win,
—Tears their stern eyes within,—
"Ashby, our Paladin,
    Ashby is gone!"

Dash,—dash the tear away—
    Crush down the pain!
"Dulce et decus," be
    Fittest refrain!   20
Why should the dreary pall
Round him be flung at all?
Did not our hero fall
    Gallantly slain?

Catch the last word of cheer
    Dropt from his tongue;
Over the volley's din,
    Loud be it rung—
"Follow me! follow me!"—
Soldier, oh! could there be   30
Pæan or dirge for thee,
    Loftier sung!

Bold as the Lion-heart,
    Dauntless and brave;
Knightly as knightliest
    Bayard could crave;
Sweet with all Sidney's grace—
Tender as Hampden's face—

Who—who shall fill the space
    Void by his grave? 40

'Tis not *one* broken heart,
    Wild with dismay;
Crazed with her agony,
    Weeps o'er his clay:
Ah! from a thousand eyes
Flow the pure tears that rise;
Widowed Virginia lies
    Stricken to-day!

Yet—though that thrilling word—
    Accent of dread— 50
Falls like a thunderbolt,
    Bowing each head—
Heroes! be battle done
Bravelier every one,
Nerved by the thought alone—
    Ashby is dead!

DIRGE FOR A SOLDIER

IN MEMORY OF GEN. PHILIP KEARNY

BY GEORGE HENRY BOKER

Close his eyes; his work is done!
    What to him is friend or foeman,
Rise of moon, or set of sun,
    Hand of man, or kiss of woman?
      Lay him low, lay him low,
      In the clover or the snow!
      What cares he? he cannot know:
      Lay him low!

As man may, he fought his fight,
    Proved his truth by his endeavor; 10
Let him sleep in solemn night,
    Sleep forever and forever.
      Lay him low, lay him low,
      In the clover or the snow!
      What cares he? he cannot know:
      Lay him low!

Fold him in his country's stars,
    Roll the drum and fire the volley!
What to him are all our wars,
    What but death bemocking folly? 20
      Lay him low, lay him low,
      In the clover or the snow!
      What cares he? he cannot know:
      Lay him low!

Leave him to God's watching eye,
    Trust him to the hand that made him.
Mortal love weeps idly by:
    God alone has power to aid him.

      Lay him low, lay him low,
      In the clover or the snow! 30
      What cares he? he cannot know:
      Lay him low!

WANTED—A MAN

(September 8, 1862)

BY EDMUND CLARENCE STEDMAN

(1833–1908)

Back from the trebly crimsoned field
    Terrible words are thunder-tost;
Full of the wrath that will not yield,
    Full of revenge for battles lost!
Hark to their echo, as it crost
The Capital, making faces wan:
    "End this murderous holocaust;
Abraham Lincoln, give us a MAN!

"Give us a man of God's own mould,
    Born to marshal his fellow-men; 10
One whose fame is not bought and sold
    At the stroke of a politician's pen;
    Give us the man of thousands ten,
Fit to do as well as to plan;
    Give us a rallying-cry, and then,
Abraham Lincoln, give us a MAN!

"No leader to shirk the boasting foe,
    And to march and countermarch our brave,
Till they fall like ghosts in the marshes low,
    And swamp-grass covers each nameless
      grave; 20
    Nor another, whose fatal banners wave
Aye in Disaster's shameful van;
    Nor another, to bluster, and lie, and rave;—
Abraham Lincoln, give us a MAN!

"Hearts are mourning in the North,
    While the sister rivers seek the main,
Red with our life-blood flowing forth,—
    Who shall gather it up again?
    Though we march to the battle-plain
Firmly as when the strife began, 30
    Shall all our offering be in vain?—
Abraham Lincoln, give us a MAN!

"Is there never one in all the land,
    One on whose might the Cause may lean?
Are all the common ones so grand,
    And all the titled ones so mean?
    What if your failure may have been
In trying to make good bread from bran,
    From worthless metal a weapon keen?—
Abraham Lincoln, find us a MAN! 40

"O, we will follow him to the death,
  Where the foeman's fiercest columns are!
O, we will use our latest breath,
  Cheering for every sacred star!
His to marshal us high and far;
Ours to battle, as patriots can
  When a Hero leads the Holy War!—
Abraham Lincoln, give us a MAN!"

PELHAM
BY JAMES RYDER RANDALL

Just as the Spring came laughing through the
    strife,
  With all its gorgeous cheer;
In the bright April of historic life,
  Fell the great cannoneer.

The wondrous lulling of a hero's breath,
  His bleeding country weeps;
Hushed in the alabaster arms of Death,
  Our young Marcellus sleeps.

Nobler and grander than the Child of Rome,
  Curbing his chariot steeds,   10
The knightly scion of a Southern home
  Dazzled the land with deeds.

Gentlest and bravest in the battle's brunt,
  The Champion of the Truth;
He won his banner in the very front
  Of our immortal youth.

A clang of sabres 'mid Virginian snow,
  The fiery pang of shells—
And there's a wail of immemorial woe
  In Alabama dells.   20

The pennon droops that led the sacred band
  Along the crimson field;
The meteor blade sinks from the nerveless
    hand
  Over the spotless shield.

We gazed and gazed upon that beauteous face,
  While 'round the lips and eyes,
Couched in their marble slumber, flashed the
    grace
  Of a divine surprise.

O mother of a blesséd soul on high!
  Thy tears may soon be shed—   30
Think of thy boy with princes of the sky,
  Among the Southern Dead.

How must he smile on this dull world beneath,
  Favored with swift renown;

He with the martyr's amaranthine wreath
  Twining the victor's crown!

"THE BRIGADE MUST NOT KNOW, SIR!"
(ANONYMOUS)

"Who've ye got there?"—"Only a dying
    brother,
  Hurt in the front just now."
"Good boy! he'll do. Somebody tell his
    mother
  Where he was killed, and how."

"Whom have you there?"—"A crippled couri-
    er, Major,
  Shot by mistake, we hear.
He was with Stonewall." "Cruel work they've
    made here;
  Quick with him to the rear!"

"Well, who comes next?"—"Doctor, speak
    low, speak low, sir;
  Don't let the men find out!   10
It's Stonewall!" — "God!" — "The brigade
    must not know, sir,
  While there's a foe about!"

Whom have we here—shrouded in martial
    manner,
  Crowned with a martyr's charm?
A grand dead hero, in a living banner,
  Born of his heart and arm:

The heart whereon his cause hung—see how
    clingeth
  That banner to his bier!
The arm wherewith his cause struck—hark!
    how ringeth
  His trumpet in their rear!   20

What have we left? His glorious inspiration,
  His prayers in council met.
Living, he laid the first stones of a nation;
  And dead, he builds it yet.

THE HIGH TIDE AT GETTYSBURG
BY WILL HENRY THOMPSON
(1848–1918)

A cloud possessed the hollow field,
The gathering battle's smoky shield.
Athwart the gloom the lightning flashed,

And through the cloud some horsemen
   dashed,
And from the heights the thunder pealed.

Then at the brief command of Lee
Moved out that matchless infantry,
   With Pickett leading grandly down,
   To rush against the roaring crown
Of those dread heights of destiny.   10

Far heard above the angry guns
A cry across the tumult runs,—
   The voice that rang through Shiloh's woods
   And Chickamauga's solitudes,
The fierce South cheering on her sons!

Ah, how the withering tempest blew
Against the front of Pettigrew!
   A Khamsin wind that scorched and singed
   Like that infernal flame that fringed
The British squares at Waterloo!   20

A thousand fell where Kemper led;
A thousand died where Garnett bled:
   In blinding flame and strangling smoke
   The remnant through the batteries broke
And crossed the works wi h Armistead.

"Once more in Glory's van with me!"
Virginia cried to Tennessee;
   "We two together, come what may,
   Shall stand upon these works to-day!"
(The reddest day in history.)   30

Brave Tennessee! In reckless way
Virginia heard her comrade say:
   "Close round this rent and riddled rag!"
   What time she set her battle-flag
Amid the guns of Doubleday.

But who shall break the guards that wait
Before the awful face of Fate?
   The tattered standards of the South
   Were shriveled at the cannon's mouth,
And all her hopes were desolate.   40

In vain the Tennesseean set
His breast against the bayonet!
   In vain Virginia charged and raged,
   A tigress in her wrath uncaged,
Till all the hill was red and wet!

Above the bayonets, mixed and crossed,
Men saw a gray, gigantic ghost
   Receding through the battle-cloud,
   And heard across the tempest loud
The death-cry of a nation lost!   50

The brave went down! Without disgrace
They leaped to Ruin's red embrace.
   They only heard Fame's thunders wake,
   And saw the dazzling sun-burst break
In smiles on Glory's bloody face!

They fell, who lifted up a hand
And bade the sun in heaven to stand!
   They smote and fell, who set the bars
   Against the progress of the stars,
And stayed the march of Motherland!   60

They stood, who saw the future come
On through the fight's delirium!
   They smote and stood, who held the hope
   Of nations on that slippery slope,
Amid the cheers of Christendom.

God lives! He forged the iron will
That clutched and held that trembling hill.
   God lives and reigns! He built and lent
   The heights for Freedom's battlement
Where floats her flag in triumph still!   70

Fold up the banners! Smelt the guns!
Love rules. Her gentler purpose runs.
   A mighty mother turns in tears
   The pages of her battle years,
Lamenting all her fallen sons!

SHERIDAN'S RIDE
By Thomas Buchanan Read
(1822–1872)

Up from the South at break of day,
Bringing to Winchester fresh dismay,
The affrighted air with a shudder bore,
Like a herald in haste, to the chieftain's
   door,
The terrible grumble, and rumble, and roar,
Telling the battle was on once more,
And Sheridan twenty miles away.

And wider still those billows of war,
Thundered along the horizon's bar;
And louder yet into Winchester rolled   10
The roar of that red sea uncontrolled,
Making the blood of the listener cold,
As he thought of the stake in that fiery
   fray,
And Sheridan twenty miles away.

But there is a road from Winchester town,
A good broad highway leading down;
And there, through the flush of the morning
   light,

A steed as black as the steeds of night,
Was seen to pass, as with eagle flight,
As if he knew the terrible need: 20
He stretched away with his utmost speed;
Hills rose and fell; but his heart was gay,
With Sheridan fif een miles away.

Still sprung from those swift hoofs, thundering
    South,
The dust, like smoke from the cannon's
    mouth;
Or the trail of a comet, sweeping faster and
    faster,
Foreboding to traitors the doom of disaster.
The heart of the steed, and the heart of the
    master
Were beating like prisoners assaulting their
    walls,
Impatient to be where the battle-field calls;   30
Every nerve of the charger was strained to full
    play,
With Sheridan only ten miles away.

Under his spurning feet the road
Like an arrowy Alpine river flowed,
And the landscape sped away behind
Like an ocean flying before the wind,
And the steed, like a bark fed with furnace
    ire,
Swept on, with his wild eye full of fire.
But lo! he is nearing his heart's desire:

He is snuffing the smoke of the roaring fray,
With Sheridan only five miles away.   41

The first that the general saw were the groups
Of stragglers, and then the retreating troops,
What was done? what to do? a glance told him
    both,
Then striking his spurs, with a terrible oa h,
He dashed down the line, 'mid a storm of
    huzzas,
And the wave of retreat checked its course
    there, because
The sight of the master compelled it to pause.
With foam and with dust, the black charger
    was gray:
By the flash of his eye, and the red nostril's
    play,   50
He seemed to the whole great army to say,
"I have brought you Sheridan, all the way
From Winchester, down to save the day!"

Hurrah! hurrah for Sheridan!
Hurrah! hurrah for horse and man!
And when their statues are placed on high,
Under the dome of the Union sky,
The American soldiers' Temple of Fame;
There with the glorious general's name,
Be it said, in letters both bold and bright,   60
    "Here is the steed that saved the day,
By carrying Sheridan into the fight,
    From Winchester, twenty miles away!"

The War in the West

THE RIVER

By Francis Orray Ticknor

Hold to the giant river,
  Ye, with a giant claim!
Yours from the great All-Giver,
  Yours in Jehovah's name!
By fireside, field, and altar,
  By temple, by grove, by grave,
    By the smiles and tears
    Of a hundred years,
By the lifetime toil of your pioneers
And the life-blood of your braves.   10

De Soto sleeps in its bosom,
  Yet the dreamer's dream was truth,
And he left to your watch the waters
  Of the world's immortal youth;
Yours from the fount of story,
  Yours till oblivion's wave,
By the deed of your day of glory,
  By the seal of your Sidney's grave,

For yourselves, for your sons, forever,
  And ever, to hold and to have;   20
The broad and abounding river,
  Down to the salt sea wave;
    While the waters flow,
    While the grasses grow,
Till the last of your race lies cold and low,
  Or God forgets the brave!

THE BATTLE–CRY OF
FREEDOM

By George Frederick Root
(1820–1895)

Yes we'll rally 'round the flag, boys, we'll rally
    once again,
  Shouting the battle-cry of Freedom,
We will rally from the hillside, we'll gather
    from the plain,
  Shouting the battle-cry of Freedom.

Chorus.

The Union forever, hurrah, boys, Hurrah,
 Down with the traitor, up with the star,
While we rally 'round the flag, boys, rally once
  again,
 Shouting the battle-cry of Freedom.

We are springing to the call of our brothers
  gone before,
 Shouting the battle-cry of Freedom,   10
And we'll fill the vacant ranks with a million
  freemen more,
 Shouting the battle-cry of Freedom.—Cho.

We will welcome to our numbers the loyal,
  true, and brave,
 Shouting the battle-cry of Freedom,
And although they may be poor, not a man
  shall be a slave,
 Shouting the battle-cry of Freedom.—Cho.

So we're springing to the call from the East
  and from the West,
 Shouting the battle-cry of Freedom,
And we'll hurl the rebel crew from the land we
  love the best,   19
 Shouting the battle-cry of Freedom.—Cho.

THE BLACK REGIMENT
Port Hudson, May 27, 1863.

By George Henry Boker

Dark as the clouds of even,
Ranked in the western heaven,
Waiting the breath that lifts
All the dread mass, and drifts
Tempest and falling brand
Over a ruined land;—
So still and orderly,
Arm to arm, knee to knee,
Waiting the great event,
Stands the black regiment.   10

Down the long dusky line
Teeth gleam and eyeballs shine;
And the bright bayonet,
Bristling and firmly set,
Flashed with a purpose grand,
Long ere the sharp command
Of the fie ce rolling drum
Told them their time had come,
Told them what work was sent
For the black regiment.   20

"Now," the flag-sergeant cried,
"Though death and hell betide,

Let the whole nation see
If we are fit to be
Free in this land; or bound
Down, like the whining hound,—
Bound with red stripes of pain
In our old chains again!"
O, what a shout there went
From the black regiment!   30

"Charge!" Trump and drum awoke,
Onward the bondmen broke;
Bayonet and sabre-stroke
Vainly opposed their rush.
Through the wild battle's crush,
With but one thought aflush,
Driving their lords like chaff,
In the guns' mouths they augh;
Or at the slippery brands
Leaping with open hands,   40
Down they tear man and horse,
Down in their awful course;
Trampling with bloody heel
Over the crashing steel,
All their eyes forward bent,
Rushed the black regiment.

"Freedom!" their battle-cry,—
"Freedom! or leave to die!"
Ah! and they meant the word,
Not as with us 'tis heard,   50
Not a mere party shout:
They gave their spirits out;
Trusted the end to God,
And on the gory sod
Rolled in triumphant blood.
Glad to strike one free blow,
Whether for weal or woe;
Glad to breathe one free breath,
Though on the lips of death.
Praying—alas! in vain!—   60
That they might fall again,
So they could once more see
That burst to liberty!
This was what "freedom" lent
To the black regiment.

Hundreds on hundreds fell;
But they are resting well;
Scourges and shackles strong
Never shall do them wrong.
O, to the living few,   70
Soldiers, be just and true!
Hail them as comrades tried;
Fight with them side by side;
Never, in field or tent,
Scorn the black regiment!

LITTLE GIFFEN

By Francis Orray Ticknor

Out of the focal and foremost fire,
Out of the hospital walls as dire,
Smitten of grape-shot and gangrene,
(Eighteenth battle, and he sixteen!)
Spectre! such as you seldom see,
Little Giffen, of Tennessee!

"Take him and welcome!" the surgeons said:
Little the doctor can help the dead!
So we took him, and brought him where
The balm was sweet in the summer air;   10
And we laid him down on a wholesome bed—
Utter Lazarus, heel to head!

And we watched the war with abated breath,
Skeleton boy against skeleton death.
Months of torture, how many such?
Weary weeks of the stick and crutch;
And still a glint of the steel-blue eye
Told of a spirit that wouldn't die,

And didn't. Nay, more! in death's despite
The crippled skeleton learned to write.   20
Dear mother, at first, of course; and then
Dear captain, inquiring about the men.
Captain's answer: "Of eighty and five,
Giffen and I are left alive."

Word of gloom from the war, one day;
Johnson pressed at the front, they say.
Little Giffen was up and away;
A tear—his first—as he bade good-by,
Dimmed the glint of his steel-blue eye.
"I'll write, if spared!" There was news of the
    fight;
But none of Giffen. He did not write.

I sometimes fancy that, were I king
Of the princely Knights of the Golden Ring,
With the song of the minstrel in mine ear,
And the tender legend that trembles here,
I'd give the best on his bended knee,
The whitest soul of my chivalry,
For "Little Giffen," of Tennessee.

The Navy and the Blockade

CAROLINA

By Henry Timrod

I

The despot treads thy sacred sands,
Thy pines give shelter to his bands,
Thy sons stand by with idle hands,
    Carolina!
He breathes at ease thy airs of balm,
He scorns the lances of thy palm;
Oh! who shall break thy craven calm,
    Carolina!
Thy ancient fame is growing dim,
A spot is on thy garment's rim;
Give to the winds thy battle hymn,   10
    Carolina!

II

Call on thy children of the hill,
Wake swamp and river, coast and rill,
Rouse all thy strength and all thy skill,
    Carolina!
Cite wealth and science, trade and art,
Touch with thy fire the cautious mart,
And pour thee through the people's heart,
    Carolina!   20
Till even the coward spurns his fears,
And all thy fields and fens and meres
Shall bristle like thy palm with spears,
    Carolina!

III

Hold up the glories of thy dead;
Say how thy elder children bled,
And point to Eutaw's battle-bed,
    Carolina!
Tell how the patriot's soul was tried,
And what his dauntless breast defied;   30
How Rutledge ruled and Laurens died,
    Carolina!
Cry! till thy summons, heard at last,
Shall fall like Marion's bugle-blast
Re-echoed from the haunted past,
    Carolina!

IV

I hear a murmur as of waves
That grope their way through sunless caves,
Like bodies struggling in their graves,
    Carolina!   40
And now it deepens; slow and grand
It swells, as, rolling to the land,
An ocean broke upon thy strand,
    Carolina!
Shout! let it reach the startled Huns!
And roar with all thy festal guns!
It is the answer of thy sons,
    Carolina!

V

They will not wait to hear thee call;
From Sachem's Head to Sumter's wall   50

Resounds the voice of hut and hall,
    Carolina!
No! thou hast not a stain, they say,
Or none save what the battle-day
Shall wash in seas of blood away,
    Carolina!
Thy skirts indeed the foe may part,
Thy robe be pierced with sword and dart,
They shall not touch thy noble heart,
    Carolina!   60

VI

Ere thou shalt own the tyrant's thrall
Ten times ten thousand men must fall;
Thy corpse may hearken to his call,
    Carolina!
When, by thy bier, in mournful throngs
The women chant thy mortal wrongs,
'Twill be their own funereal songs,
    Carolina!
From thy dead breast by ruffians trod
No helpless child shall look to God;   70
All shall be safe beneath thy sod,
    Carolina!

VII

Girt with such wills to do and bear,
Assured in right, and mailed in prayer,
Thou wilt not bow thee to despair,
    Carolina!
Throw thy bold banner to the breeze!
Front with thy ranks the threatening seas
Like thine own proud armorial trees,
    Carolina!   80
Fling down thy gauntlet to the Huns,
And roar the challenge from thy guns;
Then leave the future to thy sons,
    Carolina!

ON BOARD THE CUMBERLAND

March 8, 1862

By George Henry Boker

"Stand to your guns, men!" Morris cried.
    Small need to pass the word;
Our men at quarters ranged themselves
    Before the drum was heard.

And then began the sailors' jests:
    "What thing is that, I say?"
"A long-shore meeting-house adrift
    Is stand ng down the bay!"

A frown came over Morris' face;
    The strange, dark craft he knew;   10

"That is the iron Merrimac,
    Manned by a rebel crew.

"So shot your guns, and point them straight;
    Before this day goes by,
We'll try of what her metal's made."
    A cheer was our reply.

"Remember, boys, this flag of ours
    Has seldom left ts place;
And where it falls, the deck it strikes
    Is covered with disgrace.   20

"I ask but this; or sink or swim,
    Or live or nobly die,
My last sight upon earth may be
    To see that ensign fly!"

Meanwhile the shapeless iron mass
    Came moving o'er the wave,
As gloomy as a passing hearse,
    As silent as the grave.

Her ports were closed; from stem to stern
    No sign of life appeared.   30
We wondered, questioned, strained our eyes,
    Joked,—everything but feared.

She reached our range. Our broadside rang,
    Our heavy pivots roared;
And shot and shell, a fire of hell,
    Against her sides we poured.

God's mercy! from her sloping roof
    The iron tempest glanced,
As hail bounds from a cottage thatch,
    And round her leaped and danced;   40

Or when against her dusky hull
    We struck a fair, full blow,
The mighty, solid iron globes
    Were crumbled up like snow.

On, on, with fa t increasing speed
    The silent monster came,
Though all our starboard battery
    Was one long line of flame.

She heeded not, no gun she fired,
    Straight on our bow she bore;   50
Through riving plank and crashing frame
    Her furious way she tore.

Alas! our beautiful, keen bow,
    That in the fiercest blast
So gently folded back the seas,
    They hardly felt we passed!

Alas! alas! my Cumberland,
That ne'er knew grief before,
To be so gored, to feel so deep
The tusk of that sea-boar!   60

Once more she backward drew a space,
Once more our side she rent;
Then, in the wantonness of hate,
Her broadside through us sent.

The dead and dying round us lay,
But our foeman lay abeam;
Her open port-holes maddened us;
We fired with shout and scream.

We felt our vessel settling fast,
We knew our time was brief,   70
"Ho! man the pumps!" But they who
worked,
And fought not, wept with grief.

"O keep us but an hour afloat!
O, give us only time
To mete unto yon rebel crew
The measure of their crime!"

From captain down to powder-boy
No hand was idle then;
Two soldiers, but by chance aboard,
Fought on like sailor men.   80

And when a gun's crew lost a hand,
Some bold marine stepped out,
And jerked his braided jacket off,
And hauled the gun about.

Our forward magazine was drowned;
And up from the sick bay
Crawled out the wounded, red with blood,
And round us gasping lay.

Yes, cheering, calling us by name,
Struggling with failing breath   90
To keep their shipmates at the post
Where glory strove with death.

With decks afloat, and powder gone,
The last broadside we gave
From the guns' heated iron lips
Burst out beneath the wave.

So sponges, rammers, and handspikes—
As men-of-war's-men should—
We placed within their proper racks,
And at our quarters stood.   100

"Up to the spar-deck! save yourselves!"
Cried Selfridge. "Up, my men!
God grant that some of us may live
To fight yon ship again!"

We turned,—we did not like to go;
Yet staying seemed but vain,
Knee-deep in water; so we left;
Some swore, some groaned with pain.

We reached the deck. There Randall stood:
"Another turn, men,—so!"   110
Calmly he aimed his pivot gun:
"Now, Tenny, let her go!"

It did our sore hearts good to hear
The song our pivot sang,
As, rushing on from wave to wave,
The whirring bomb-shell sprang.

Brave Randall leaped upon the gun,
And waved his cap in sport;
"Well done! well aimed! I saw that shell
Go through an open port."   120

It was our last, our deadliest shot;
The deck was overflown;
The poor ship staggered, lurched to port,
And gave a living groan.

Down, down, as headlong through the waves
Our gallant vessel rushed,
A thousand gurgling watery sounds
Around my senses gushed.

Then I remember little more.
One look to heaven I gave,   130
Where, like an angel's wing, I saw
Our spotless ensign wave.

I tried to cheer. I cannot say
Whether I swam or sank;
A blue mist closed around my eyes,
And everything was blank.

When I awoke, a soldier lad,
All dripping from the sea,
With two great tears upon his cheeks,
Was bending over me.   140

I tried to speak. He understood
The wish I could not speak.
He turned me. There, thank God! the flag
Still fluttered at the peak!

And there, while thread shall hang to thread,
O let that ensign fly!
The noblest constellation set
Against our northern sky.

A sign that we who live may claim
The peerage of the brave;   150
A monument, that needs no scroll,
For those beneath the wave.

CHARLESTON

BY HENRY TIMROD

Calm as that second summer which precedes
    The first fall of the snow,
In the broad sunlight of heroic deeds,
    The City bides the foe.

As yet, behind their ramparts stern and proud,
    Her bolted thunders sleep—
Dark Sumter, like a battlemented cloud,
    Looms o'er the solemn deep.

No Calpe frowns from lofty cliff or scar
    To guard the holy strand;   10
But Moultrie holds in leash her dogs of war
    Above the level sand.

And down the dunes a thousand guns lie
    couched,
    Unseen, beside the flood—
Like tigers in some Orient jungle crouched
    That wait and watch for blood.

Meanwhile, through streets still echoing with
    trade,
Walk grave and thoughtful men,
Whose hands may one day wield the patriot's
    blade
    As lightly as the pen.   20

And maidens, with such eyes as would grow
    dim
    Over a bleeding hound,
Seem each one to have caught the strength of
    him
    Whose sword she sadly bound.

Thus girt without and garrisoned at home,
    Day patient following day,
Old Charleston looks from roof, and spire, and
    dome,
    Across her tranquil bay.

Ships, through a hundred foes, from Saxon
    lands
And spicy Indian ports,   30
Bring Saxon steel and iron to her hands,
    And summer to her courts.

But still, along yon dim Atlantic line,
    The only hostile smoke
Creeps like a harmless mist above the brine,
    From some frail, floating oak.

Shall the Spring dawn, and she still clad in
    smiles,
    And with an unscathed brow,

Rest in the strong arms of her palm-crowned
    isles,
    As fair and free as now?   40

We know not; in the temple of the Fates
    God has inscribed her doom:
And, all untroubled in her faith, she waits
    The triumph or the tomb.

THE SWORD IN THE SEA

BY FRANCIS ORRAY TICKNOR

The billows plunge like steeds that bear
    The knights with snow-white crests;
The sea-winds blare like bugles where
    The Alabama rests.

Old glories from their splendor-mists
    Salute with trump and hail
The sword that held the ocean lists
    Against the world in mail.

And down from England's storied hills,
    From lyric slopes of France,   10
The old bright wine of valor fills
    The chalice of Romance.

For here was Glory's tourney-field,
    The tilt-yard of the sea;
The battle-path of kingly wrath,
    And kinglier courtesy.

And down the deeps, in sunless heaps,
    The gold, the gem, the pearl,
In one broad blaze of splendor belt
    Great England like an earl.   20

And there they rest, the princeliest
    Of earth's regalia gems,
The starlight of our Southern Cross,
    The Sword of Raphael Semmes.

Like that great glaive that Arthur gave
    In guerdon to the sea;
"Excalbur," that sleeps below,
    Until the great sea-bugles blow
    The summons of the Free.

THE BAY FIGHT

Mobile Bay, August 5, 1864

BY HENRY HOWARD BROWNELL
(1820–1872)

Three days through sapphire seas we sailed,
    The steady Trade blew strong and free,
The Northern Light his banners paled,

The Ocean Stream our channels wet,
We rounded low Canaveral's lee,
And passed the isles of emerald set
    In blue Bahama's turquoise sea.

By reef and shoal obscurely mapped,
    And hauntings of the gray sea-wolf,
The palmy Western Key lay lapped   10
    In the warm washing of the Gulf.

But weary to the hearts of all
    The burning glare, the barren reach
    Of Santa Rosa's weathered beach,
And Pensacola's ruined wall.

And weary was the long patrol,
    The thousand miles of shapeless strand,
From Brazos to San Blas that roll
    Their drifting dunes of desert sand.

Yet, coast-wise as we cruised or lay,   20
    The land-breeze still at nightfall bore,
By beach and fortress-guarded bay,
    Sweet odors from the enemy's shore,

Fresh from the forest solitudes,
    Unchallenged of his sentry lines—
The bursting of his cypress buds,
    And the warm fragrance of his pines.

Ah, never braver bark and crew,
    Nor bolder Flag a foe to dare,
Had left a wake on ocean blue   30
    Since Lion-Heart sailed *Trenc-le-mer!*

But little gain by that dark ground
    Was ours, save, sometime, freer breath
For friend or brother strangely found,
    'Scaped from the drear domain of death.

And little venture for the bold,
    Or laurel for our valiant Chief,
Save some blockaded British thief,
Full fraught with murder in his hold,

Caught unawares at ebb or flood—   40
    Or dull bombardment, day by day,
    With fort and earth-work, far away,
Low couched in sullen leagues of mud.

A weary time,—but to the strong
    The day at last, as ever, came;
And the volcano, laid so long,
    Leaped forth in thunder and in flame!

"Man your starboard battery!"
    Kimberly shouted—
The ship, with her hearts of oak,   50

Was going, mid roar and smoke,
    On to victory!
None of us doubted,
No, not our dying—
    Farragut's Flag was flying!

Gaines growled low on our left,
    Morgan roared on our right
Before us, gloomy and fell,
With breath like the fume of hell,
Lay the Dragon of iron shell,   60
    Driven at last to the fight!

Ha, old ship! do they thrill
    The brave two hundred scars
    You got in the River-Wars?
That were leeched with clamorous skill,
    (Surgery savage and hard,)
Splinted with bolt and beam,
    Probed in scarfing and seam,
    Rudely linted and tarred
With oakum and boiling pitch,   70
And sutured with splice and hitch,
    At the Brooklyn Navy-Yard!

Our lofty spars were down,
    To bide the battle's frown,
(Wont of old renown)—
But every ship was drest
In her bravest and her best,
    As if for a July day;
Sixty flags and three,
    As we floated up the bay—   80
Every peak and mast-head flew
The brave Red, White, and Blue—
    We were eighteen ships that day.

With hawsers strong and taut,
    The weaker lashed to port,
    On we sailed, two by two—
That if either a bolt should feel
Crash through caldron or wheel,
Fin or bronze or sinew of steel,
    Her mate might bear her through.   90

Steadily nearing the head,
    The great Flag-ship led,
    Grandest of sights!
On her lofty mizzen flew
Our Leader's dauntless Blue,
    That had waved o'er twenty fights—
So we went, with the first of the tide,
    Slowly, mid the roar
    Of the Rebel guns ashore
And the thunder of each full broadside. 100

Ah, how poor the prate
    Of statute and state
    We once held with these fellows—

Here, on the flood's pale-green,
  Hark how he bellows,
    Each bluff old Sea-Lawyer!
Talk to them, Dahlgren,
  Parrott, and Sawyer!

On, in the whirling shade
  Of the cannon's sulphury breath,   110
  We drew to the Line of Death
That our devilish Foe had laid—
  Meshed in a horrible net,
    And baited villanous well,
Right in our path were set
  Three hundred traps of hell!

And there, O sight forlorn!
  There, while the cannon
    Hurtled and thundered—
  (Ah, what ill raven   120
Flapped o'er the ship that morn!)—
  Caught by the under-death,
  In the drawing of a breath
    Down went dauntless Craven,
    He and his hundred!

A moment we saw her turret,
  A little heel she gave,
And a thin white spray went o'er her,
  Like the crest of a breaking wave—
In that great iron coffin,   130
  The channel for their grave,
  The fort their monument,
(Seen afar in the offing,)
Ten fathom deep lie Craven
  And the bravest of our brave.

Then, in that deadly track,
  A little the ships held back,
    Closing up in their stations—
There are minutes that fix the fate
  Of battles and of nations,   140
  (Christening the generations,)
When valor were all too late,
  If a moment's doubt be harbored—
From the main-top, bold and brief,
Came the word of our grand old Chief—
  "Go on!" 'twas all he said—
Our helm was put to starboard,
  And the Hartford passed ahead.

Ahead lay the Tennessee,
  On our starboard bow he lay,   150
With his mail-clad consorts three,
  (The rest had run up the Bay)—
There he was, belching flame from his bow,
And the steam from his throat's abyss
Was a Dragon's maddened hiss—
  In sooth a most curséd craft!—

In a sullen ring at bay
By the Middle Ground they lay,
  Raking us fore and aft.

  Trust me, our berth was hot,   160
  Ah, wickedly well they shot;
How their death-bolts howled and stung!
  And the water-batteries played
  With their deadly cannonade
Till the air around us rung;
So the battle raged and roared—
  Ah, had you been aboard
    To have seen the fight we made!

How they leaped, the tongues of flame,
  From the cannon's fiery lip!   170
How the broadsides, deck and frame,
  Shook the great ship!

And how the enemy's shell
  Came crashing, heavy and oft,
  Clouds of splinters flying aloft
And falling in oaken showers—
  But ah, the pluck of the crew!
Had you stood on that deck of ours,
  You had seen what men may do.

Still, as the fray grew louder,   180
  Boldly they worked and well;
Steadily came the powder,
  Steadily came the shell.
And if tackle or truck found hurt,
  Quickly they cleared the wreck;
And the dead were laid to port,
  All a-row, on our deck.

  Never a nerve that failed,
  Never a cheek that paled,
Not a tinge of gloom or pallor—   190
  There was bold Kentucky's grit,
And the old Virginian valor,
  And the daring Yankee wit.

There were blue eyes from turfy Shannon,
  There were black orbs from pal my Niger—
But there, alongside the cannon,
  Each man fought like a tiger!

A little, once, it looked ill,
  Our consort began to burn—
They quenched the flames with a will,   200
But our men were falling still,
  And still the fleet was astern.

Right abreast of the Fort
  In an awful shroud they lay,
  Broadsides thundering away,
And lightning from every port—
  Scene of glory and dread!

A storm-cloud all aglow
  With flashes of fiery red—
The thunder raging below,   210
  And the forest of flags o'erhead!

So grand the hurly and roar,
  So fiercely their broadsides blazed,
The regiments fighting ashore
  Forgot to fire as they gazed.

There, to silence the Foe,
  Moving grimly and slow,
They loomed in that deadly wreath,
  Where the darkest batteries frowned—
Death in the air all round,   220
And the black torpedoes beneath!

And now, as we looked ahead,
  All for'ard, the long white deck
Was growing a strange dull red;
  But soon, as once and agen
Fore and aft we sped,
  (The firing to guide or check,)
You could hardly choose but tread
  On the ghastly human wreck,
(Dreadful gobbet and shred   230
  That a minute ago were men!)

Red, from main-mast to bitts!
  Red, on bulwark and wale—
Red, by combing and hatch—
  Red, o'er netting and rail!

And ever, with steady con,
  The ship forged slowly by—
And ever the crew fought on,
  And their cheers rang loud and high.

Grand was the sight to see   240
  How by their guns they stood,
Right in front of our dead
  Fighting square abreast—
Each brawny arm and chest
All spotted with black and red,
  Chrism of fire and blood!

Worth our watch, dull and sterile,
  Worth all the weary time—
Worth the woe and the peril,
  To stand in that strait sublime! 250
Fear?   A forgotten form!
  Death?   A dream of the eyes!
We were atoms in God's great storm
  That roared through the angry skies.

One only doubt was ours,
  One only dread we knew—
Could the day that dawned so well

Go down for the Darker Powers?
  Would the fleet get through?
And ever the shot and shell   260
Came with the howl of hell,
The splinter-clouds rose and fell,
  And the long line of corpses grew—
  Would the fleet win through?

They are men that never will fail,
  (How aforetime they've fought!)
But Murder may yet prevail—
  They may sink as Craven sank.
Therewith one hard, fierce thought,
Burning on heart and lip,   270
Ran like fire through the ship—
  Fight her, to the last plank!

A dimmer Renown might strike
  If Death lay square alongside—
But the Old Flag has no like,
  She must fight, whatever betide—
When the War is a tale of old,
And this day's story is told,
  They shall hear how the Hartford died!

But as we ranged ahead,   280
  And the leading ships worked in,
  Losing their hope to win
The enemy turned and fled—
  And one seeks a shallow reach,
  And another, winged in her flight,
Our mate, brave Jouett, brings in—
  And one, all torn in the fight,
Runs for a wreck on the beach,
  Where her flames soon fire the night.

And the Ram, when well up the Bay, 290
  And we looked that our stems should meet,
(He had us fair for a prey,)
  Shifting his helm midway,
  Sheered off and ran for the fleet;
There, without skulking or sham,
  He fought them, gun for gun,
And ever he sought to ram,
  But could finish never a one.

From the first of the iron shower
  Till we sent our parting shell,
'Twas just one savage hour   300
  Of the roar and the rage of hell.

With the lessening smoke and thunder,
  Our glasses around we aim—
What is that burning yonder?
  Our Philippi,—aground and in flame!

Below, 'twas still all a-roar,
  As the ships went by the shore,
But the fire of the Fort had slacked,

(So fierce their volleys had been)—   310
And now, with a mighty din,
The whole fleet came grandly in,
   Though sorely battered and wracked.

So, up the Bay we ran,
   The Flag to port and ahead;
And a pitying rain began
   To wash the lips of our dead.

A league from the Fort we lay,
   And deemed that the end must lag;
When lo! looking down the Bay,   320
   There flaunted the Rebel Rag—
The Ram is again underway
   And heading dead for the Flag!

Steering up with the stream,
   Boldly his course he lay,
Though the fleet all answered his fire.
And, as he still drew nigher,
   Ever on bow and beam
      Our Monitors pounded away—
      How the Chicasaw hammered away!   330

Quickly breasting the wave,
   Eager the prize to win,
First of us all the brave
   Monongahela went in
Under full head of steam—
   Twice she struck him abeam,
Till her stem was a sorry work,
   (She might have run on a crag!)
The Lackawana hit fair,
   He flung her aside like a cork,   340
      And still he held for the Flag.

High in the mizzen shroud,
   (Lest the smoke his sight o'erwhelm,)
Our Admiral's voice rang loud,
   "Hard-a-starboard your helm!
Starboard! and run him down!"
      Starboard it was—and so,
Like a black squall's lifting frown,
Our mighty bow bore down
      On the iron beak of the Foe.   350

We stood on the deck together,
   Men that had looked on death
In battle and stormy weather—
   Yet a little we held our breath,
When, with the hush of death,
   The great ships drew together.

Our Captain strode to the bow,
   Drayton, courtly and wise,
Kindly cynic, and wise,
   (You hardly had known him now,   360
      The flame of fight in his eyes!)

His brave heart eager to feel
How the oak would tell on the steel!

   But, as the space grew short,
      A little he seemed to shun us,
Out peered a form grim and lanky,
   And a voice yelled—"Hard-a-port!
Hard-a-port!—here's the damned Yankee
      Coming right down on us!"

He sheered, but the ships ran foul   370
With a gnarring shudder and growl—
   He gave us a deadly gun;
But as he passed in his pride,
   (Rasping right alongside!)
The Old Flag, in thunder tones,
Poured in her port broadside,
Rattling his iron hide,
   And cracking his timber bones!

Just then, at speed on the Foe,
   With her bow all weathered and brown,   380
   The great Lackawana came down,
Full tilt, for another blow;
We were forging ahead,
   She reversed—but, for all our pains,
Rammed the old Hartford, instead,
   Just for'ard the mizzen chains!

Ah! how the masts did buckle and bend,
   And the stout hull ring and reel,
As she took us right on end!
   (Vain were engine and wheel,   390
   She was under full steam)—
With the roar of a thunder-stroke
Her two thousand tons of oak
   Brought up on us, right abeam!

A wreck, as it looked, we lay
(Rib and plankshear gave way
   To the stroke of that giant wedge!)
Here, after all, we go—
The old ship is gone!—ah, no,
   But cut to the water's edge.   400

Never mind, then—at him again!
   His flurry now can't last long;
He'll never again see land—
   Try that on him, Marchand!
      On him again, brave Strong!

Heading square at the hulk,
   Full on his beam we bore;
But the spine of the huge Sea-Hog
Lay on the tide like a log,
   He vomited flame no more.   410

By this, he had found it hot—
   Half the fleet, in an angry ring,

Closed round the hideous Thing,
Hammering with solid shot,
And bearing down, bow on bow—
   He has but a minute to choose;
Life or renown?—which now
   Will the Rebel Admiral lose?

Cruel, haughty, and cold,
He ever was strong and bold—   420
   Shall he shrink from a wooden stem?
He will think of that brave band
He sank in the Cumberland—
   Aye, he will sink like them.

Nothing left but to fight
Boldly his last sea-fight!
   Can he strike? By heaven, 'tis true!
Down comes the traitor Blue,
And up goes the captive White!

Up went the White! Ah then   430
The hurrahs that, once and agen,
Rang from three thousand men
   All flushed and savage with fight!
Our dead lay cold and stark,
But our dying, down in the dark,
   Answered as best they might—
Lifting their poor lost arms,
   And cheering for God and Right!

Ended the mighty noise,
   Thunder of forts and ships.   440
      Down we went to the hold—
O, our dear dying boys!
   How we pressed their poor brave lips,
      (Ah, so pallid and cold!)
And held their hands to the last,
   (Those that had hands to hold).

Still thee, O woman heart!
   (So strong an hour ago)—
If the idle tears must start,
   'Tis not in vain they flow.   450

They died, our children dear,
   On the drear berth deck they died;
Do not think of them here—
Even now their footsteps near
The immortal, tender sphere—
   (Land of love and cheer!
      Home of the Crucified!)

And the glorious deed survives,
   Our threescore, quiet and cold,
Lie thus, for a myriad lives   460
   And treasure-millions untold—
(Labor of poor men's lives,
Hunger of weans and wives,
   Such is war-wasted gold.)

Our ship and her fame to-day
   Shall float on the storied Stream,
When mast and shroud have crumbled away
   And her long white deck is a dream.

One daring leap in the dark,
   Three mortal hours, at the most—   470
And hell lies stiff and stark
   On a hundred leagues of coast.

For the mighty Gulf is ours—
   The Bay is lost and won,
An Empire is lost and won!
Land, if thou yet hast flowers,
Twine them in one more wreath
   Of tenderest white and red,
(Twin buds of glory and death!)
   For the brows of our brave dead—   480
      For thy Navy's noblest Son.

Joy, O Land, for thy sons,
   Victors by flood and field!
The traitor walls and guns
   Have nothing left but to yield—
   (Even now they surrender!)

And the ships shall sail once more,
   And the cloud of war sweep on
To break on the cruel shore—
   But Craven is gone,   490
   He and his hundred are gone.

The flags flutter up and down
   At sunrise and twilight dim,
The cannons menace and frown—
   But never again for him,
   Him and the hundred.

The Dahlgrens are dumb,
   Dumb are the mortars—
Never more shall the drum
   Beat to colors and quarters—   500
   The great guns are silent.

O brave heart and loyal!
   Let all your colors dip—
   Mourn him, proud Ship!
From main deck to royal.
   God rest our Captain,
   Rest our lost hundred.

Droop, flag and pennant!
   What is your pride for?
   Heaven, that he died for,   510
Rest our Lieutenant,
   Rest our brave threescore.

O Mother Land! this weary life
   We led, we lead, is 'long of thee;

Thine the strong agony of strife,
   And thine the lonely sea.

Thine the long decks all slaughter-sprent,
   The weary rows of cots that lie
With wrecks of strong men, marred and rent,
   'Neath Pensacola's sky.   520

And thine the iron caves and dens
   Wherein the flame our war-fleet drives;
The fiery vaults, whose breath is men's
   Most dear and precious lives.

Ah, ever, when with storm sublime
   Dread Nature clears our murky air,
Thus in the crash of falling crime
   Some lesser guilt must share.

Full red the furnace fires must glow
   That melt the ore of mortal kind: 530
The Mills of God are grinding slow,
   But ah, how close they grind!

To-day, the Dahlgren and the drum
   Are dread Apostles of his Name;

His Kingdom here can only come
   By chrism of blood and flame.

Be strong: already slants the gold
   Athwart these wild and stormy skies;
From out this blackened waste, behold,
   What happy homes shall rise!   540

But see thou well no traitor gloze,
   No striking hands with Death and Shame,
Betray the sacred blood that flows
   So freely for thy name.

And never fear a victor foe—
   Thy children's hearts are strong and high;
Nor mourn too fondly—well they know
   On deck or field to die.

Nor shalt thou want one willing breath,
   Though, ever smiling round the brave,   550
The blue sea bear us on to death,
   The green were one wide grave.

The Return of the Armies

DRIVING HOME THE COWS

By Kate Putnam Osgood
(1841–   )

Out of the clover and blue-eyed grass,
   He turned them into the river-lane;
One after another he let them pass,
   Then fastened the meadow-bars again.

Under the willows, and over the hill,
   He patiently followed their sober pace;
The merry whistle for once was still,
   And something shadowed the sunny face.

Only a boy! and his father had said
   He never could let his youngest go: 10
Two already were lying dead
   Under the feet of the trampling foe.

But after the evening work was done,
   And the frogs were loud in the meadow-
      swamp,
Over his shoulder he slung his gun,
   And stealthily followed the foot-path damp,

Across the clover, and through the wheat,
   With resolute heart and purpose grim,
Though cold was the dew on his hurrying feet,
   And the blind bat's flitting startled him.   20

Thrice since then had the lanes been white,
   And the orchards sweet with apple-bloom;
And now, when the cows came back at night,
   The feeble father drove them home.

For news had come to the lonely farm
   That three were lying where two had lain;
And the old man's tremulous, palsied arm
   Could never lean on a son's again.

The summer day grew cold and late.
   He went for the cows when the work was
      done;   30
But down the lane, as he opened the gate,
   He saw them coming, one by one,—

Brindle, Ebony, Speckle, and Bess,
   Shaking their horns in the evening wind;
Cropping the buttercups out of the grass,—
   But who was it following close behind?

Loosely swung in the idle air
   The empty sleeve of army blue;
And worn and pale, from the crisping hair,
   Looked out a face that the father knew.   40

For Southern prisons will sometimes yawn,
   And yield their dead unto life again;
And the day that comes with a cloudy dawn
   In golden glory at last may wane.

The great tears sprang to their meeting eyes;
   For the heart must speak when the lips are
      dumb;
And under the silent evening skies,
   Together they followed the cattle home.

RIDING DOWN

By Nora Perry (1832–1896)

O, did you see him riding down,
And riding down, while all the town
Came out to see, came out to see,
And all the bells rang mad with glee?

Oh, did you hear those bells ring out,
The bells ring out, the people shout,
And did you hear that cheer on cheer
That over all the bells rang clear?

And did you see the waving flags,
The fluttering flags, the tattered flags,   10
Red, white, and blue, shot through and through,
Baptized with battle's deadly dew?

And did you hear the drums' gay beat,
The drums' gay beat, the bugles sweet,
The cymbals clash, the cannons' crash,
That rent the sky with sound and flash?

And did you see me waiting there,
Just waiting there and watching there,
One little lass, amid the mass
That pressed to see the hero pass?   20

And did you see him smiling down,
And smiling down, as riding down
With slowest pace, with stately grace,
He caught the vision of a face,—

My face uplifted, red and white,
Turned red and white with sheer delight,
To meet the eyes, the smiling eyes,
Outflashing in their swift surprise?

O, did you see how swift it came,
How swift it came, like sudden flame,   30
That smile to me, to only me,
The little lass who blushed to see?

And at the windows all along,
O, all along, a lovely throng
Of faces fair, beyond compare,
Beamed out upon him riding there!

Each face was like a radiant gem,
A sparkling gem, and yet for them

No swift smile came, like sudden flame,
No arrowy glance took certain aim.   40

He turned away from all their grace,
From all that grace of perfect face,
He turned to me, to only me,
The little lass who blushed to see!

THE CONQUERED BANNER

By Abram Joseph Ryan
(1839–1888)

Furl that Banner, for 'tis weary;
Round its staff 'tis drooping dreary;
   Furl it, fold it, it is best;
For there's not a man to wave it,
And there's not a word to save it,
And there's not one left to lave it
In the blood which heroes gave it;
And its foes now scorn and brave it;
   Furl it, hide it—let it rest!

Take that Banner down! 'tis tattered;   10
Broken is its staff and shattered;
And the valiant hosts are scattered
   Over whom it floated high.
Oh! 'tis hard for us to fold it;
Hard to think there's none to hold it;
Hard that those who once unrolled it
   Now must furl it with a sigh.

Furl that Banner! furl it sadly!
Once ten thousands hailed it gladly,
And ten thousands wildly, madly,   20
   Swore it should forever wave;
Swore that foeman's sword should never
Hearts like theirs entwined dissever,
Till that flag should float forever
   O'er their freedom or their grave!

Furl it! for the hands that grasped it,
And the hearts that fondly clasped it,
   Cold and dead are lying low;
And that Banner—it is trailing!
While around it sounds the wailing   30
   Of its people in their woe.

For, though conquered, they adore it!
Love the cold, dead hands that bore it!
Weep for those who fell before it!
Pardon those who trailed and tore it!
But, oh! wildly they deplore it,
   Now must furl and fold it so.

Furl that Banner! True, 'tis gory,
Yet 'tis wreathed around with glory,

And 'twill live in song and story, 40
Though its folds are in the dust:
For its fame on brightest pages,
Penned by poets and by sages,
Shall go sounding down the ages—
Furl its folds though now we must.

Furl that Banner, softly, slowly!
Treat it gently—it is holy—
For it droops above the dead.
Touch it not—unfold it never,
Let it droop there, furled forever, 50
For its people's hopes are dead!

THE SWORD OF ROBERT LEE

By Abram Joseph Ryan

Forth from its scabbard, pure and bright,
Flashed the sword of Lee!
Far in the front of the deadly fight,
High o'er the brave in the cause of Right,
Its stainless sheen, like a beacon light,
Led us to Victory.

Out of its scabbard, where, full long,
It slumbered peacefully,
Roused from its rest by the battle's song,
Shielding the feeble, smiting the strong, 10
Guarding the right, avenging the wrong,
Gleamed the sword of Lee.

Forth from its scabbard, high in air
Beneath Virginia's sky—
And they who saw it gleaming there,
And knew who bore it, knelt to swear
That where that sword led they would dare
To follow—and to die.

Out of its scabbard! Never hand
Waved sword from stain as free, 20
Nor purer sword led braver band,
Nor braver bled for a brighter land,
Nor brighter land had a cause so grand,
Nor cause a chief like Lee!

Forth from its scabbard! How we prayed
That sword might victor be;
And when our triumph was delayed,
And many a heart grew sore afraid,
We still hoped on while gleamed the blade
Of noble Robert Lee. 30

Forth from its scabbard all in vain
Bright flashed the sword of Lee;
'Tis shrouded now in its sheath again,
It sleeps the sleep of our noble slain,
Defeated, yet without a stain,
Proudly and peacefully.

ODE

SUNG ON THE OCCASION OF DECORATING THE GRAVES OF THE CONFEDERATE DEAD, AT MAGNOLIA CEMETERY, CHARLESTON, S. C., 1867

By Henry Timrod

I

Sleep sweetly in your humble graves,
Sleep, martyrs of a fallen cause;
Though yet no marble column craves
The pilgrim here to pause.

II

In seeds of laurel in the earth
The blossom of your fame is blown,
And somewhere, waiting for its birth,
The shaft is in the stone!

III

Meanwhile, behalf the tardy years
Which keep in trust your storied tombs,
Behold! your sisters bring their tears, 11
And these memorial blooms.

IV

Small tributes! but your shades will smile
More proudly on these wreaths to-day,
Than when some cannon-moulded pile
Shall overlook this bay.

V

Stoop, angels, hither from the skies!
There is no holier spot of ground
Than where defeated valor lies,
By mourning beauty crowned! 20

SOUTH CAROLINA TO THE STATES OF THE NORTH

ESPECIALLY TO THOSE THAT FORMED A PART OF THE ORIGINAL THIRTEEN

By Paul Hamilton Hayne (1830–1886)

I lift these hands with iron fetters banded:
Beneath the scornful sunlight and cold stars
I rear my once imperial forehead branded
By alien shame's immedicable scars;
Like some pale captive, shunned by all the nations,
I crouch unpitied, quivering and apart—

Laden with countless woes and desolations,
The life-blood freezing round a broken heart!

About my feet, splashed red with blood of
    slaughters,
My children gathering in wild, mournful
    throngs;   10
Despairing sons, frail infants, stricken daugh-
    ters,
Rehearse the awful burden of their wrongs;
Vain is their cry, and worse than vain their
    pleading:
I turn from stormy breasts, from yearning
    eyes,
To mark where Freedom's outraged form re-
    ceding,
Wanes in chill shadow down the midnight
    skies!

I wooed her once in wild tempestuous places,
The purple vintage of my soul outpoured,
To win and keep her unrestrained embraces,
What time the olive-crown o'ertopped the
    sword;   20
O! northmen, with your gallant heroes blend-
    ing,
Mine, in old years, for this sweet goddess
    died;
But now—ah! shame, all other shame tran-
    scending!
Your pitiless hands have torn her from my
    side.

What! 'tis a tyrant-party's treacherous action—
Your hand is clean, your conscience clear, ye
    sigh;
Ay! but ere now your sires had throttled fac-
    tion,
Or, pealed o'er half the world their battle-
    cry;
Its voice outrung from solemn mountain-
    passes
Swept by wild storm-winds of the Atlantic
    strand,   30
To where the swart Sierras' sullen grasses,
Droop in low languors of the sunset-land!

Never, since earthly States began their story,
Hath any suffered, bided, borne like me:
At last, recalling all mine ancient glory,
I vowed my fettered commonwealth to free:
Even at the thought, beside the prostrate
    column
Of chartered rights, which blasted lay and
    dim—
Uprose my noblest son with purpose solemn,
While, host on host, his brethren followed
    him: 40

Wrong, grasped by *truth,* arraigned by *law,*
    (whose sober
Majestic mandates rule o'er change and
    · time)—
Smit by the *ballot,* like some flushed October,
Reeled in the autumn rankness of his crime;
Struck, tortured, pierced—but not a blow re-
    turning.
The steadfast phalanx of my honored braves
Planted their bloodless flag where sunrise
    burning,
Flashed a new splendor o'er our martyrs'
    graves!

What then? O, sister States! what welcome
    omen
Of love and concord crossed our brightening
    blue, ·   50
The foes we vanquished, are they not *your*
    foemen,
Our laws upheld, your sacred safeguards,
    too?
Yet scarce had victory crowned our grand en-
    deavor,
And peace crept out from shadowy glooms
    remote—
Than—as if bared to blast all hope forever,
Your tyrant's sword shone glittering at my
    throat!

Once more my bursting chains were reunited,
Once more barbarian plaudits wildly rung
O'er the last promise of deliverance blighted,
The prostrate purpose, and the palsied
    tongue: 60
Ah! faithless sisters, 'neath my swift undo-
    ing,
Peers the black presage of your wrath to
    come;
Above your heads are signal clouds of ruin,
Whose lightnings flash, whose thunders are
    not dumb!

There towers a judgment-seat beyond our
    seeing;
There lives a Judge, whom none can bribe
    or blind;
Before whose dread decree, your spirit flee-
    ing,
May reap the whirlwind, having sown the
    wind:
I, in that day of justice, fierce and torrid,
When blood—*your* blood—outpours like
    poisoned wine,   70
Pointing to these chained limbs, this blasted fore-
    head,
May mock your ruin, as ye mocked at mine!

THE BLUE AND THE GRAY

BY FRANCIS MILES FINCH
(1827–1907)

By the flow of the inland river,
  Whence the fleets of iron have fled,
Where the blades of the grave-grass quiver,
  Asleep are the ranks of the dead:—
    Under the sod and the dew,
      Waiting the Judgment Day:—
    Under the one, the Blue;
      Under the other, the Gray.

These in the robings of glory,
  Those in the gloom of defeat,   10
All with the battle-blood gory,
  In the dusk of eternity meet:—
    Under the sod and the dew,
      Waiting the Judgment Day:—
    Under the laurel, the Blue;
      Under the willow, the Gray.

From the silence of sorrowful hours,
  The desolate mourners go,
Lovingly laden with flowers,
  Alike for the friend and the foe:—
    Under the sod and the dew,
      Waiting the Judgment Day:—
    Under the roses, the Blue;
      Under the lilies, the Gray.

So, with an equal splendor
  The morning sun-rays fall,
With a touch impartially tender,
  On the blossoms blooming for all:—
    Under the sod and the dew,
      Waiting the Judgment Day:—   30
    Broidered with gold, the Blue;
      Mellowed with gold, the Gray.

So, when the summer calleth,
  On forest and field of grain,
With an equal murmur falleth
  The cooling drip of the rain:—
    Under the sod and the dew,
      Waiting the Judgment Day:—
    Wet with the rain, the Blue;
      Wet with the rain, the Gray.   40

Sadly, but not with upbraiding,
  The generous deed was done.
In the storms of the years that are fading
  No braver battle was won:—
    Under the sod and the dew,
      Waiting the Judgment Day:—
    Under the blossoms, the Blue;
      Under the garlands, the Gray.

No more shall the war-cry sever,
  Or the winding rivers be red: 50
They banish our anger forever
  When they laurel the graves of our dead!
    Under the sod and the dew,
      Waiting the Judgment Day:—
    Love and tears for the Blue;
      Tears and love for the Gray.

X. WALT WHITMAN

WHITMAN must be studied not as a departure from the development of our literature but as one element in its progression. In the poetry of Longfellow, Whittier, and Lowell, in the fiction and essays of Cooper, in the speeches of Lincoln, the principles of democracy were given lofty expression and received wide appreciation. With Whitman, these principles found an apostle, who has become identified with the social, political, and economic progress toward equality. Whitman was always a conscious artist; without his Preface to the *Leaves of Grass* in 1855 his work in verse cannot be understood. In this prose utterance and in his *Democratic Vistas*, he shows that his celebration of the levelling influence of democracy, his glorification of the average man, recognizes also that in America there is the greatest possibility for the development of the individual personality. The race and the individual are both to be free, from the shackles of convention, of intolerance, even of law itself, if that law runs counter to the liberty that belongs to every man and woman.

In his *Leaves of Grass* he strikes over and over again the notes of the love of humanity, the love of comrades, the joy of the open road, the equality of man and woman, the dignity of human and of animal life. These notes were, of course, not new; it was rather in their combination, and in the insistence upon their importance, and, to a certain degree, upon the manner of their expression that Whitman's contribution consisted. For some years after its first appearance, his work met with violent opposition. Unfortunately, Whitman declined the good advice which Emerson gave him and insisted upon the insertion of suggestive passages which distracted critical attention from his more important utterances. His peculiar form, which, as a matter of fact, was not original, repelled many, and Whitman had to wait for general recognition until the latter part of the century. Foreign appreciation of the breadth of his democratic vision, which was universal rather than parochial, reacted upon the critical judgments of his native land. The admiration of a small cult who had been stung by the comparative neglect of Whitman in America did him harm with the judicious. He is now regarded by the calmest criticism as a powerful thinker who expressed the aspirations of humanity in his own way, and made of himself a symbol of what he believed to be the longing of his land and time for a wider and freer life. Many poets and prose writers have been affected by him, and some, like Joaquin Miller, Moody, Hovey, and Lodge, who have understood his symbolism and have been wise enough to realize that his peculiar form is the least important element in his work, have profited by his example. A larger and much less significant group have spelled anarchy out of his experiments in rhythm and have sought to cover the poverty of their ideas by his mantle. For Whitman is at his best in passages like the memorial verses to Lincoln, in which the concreteness of his subject has helped him to achieve simplicity, especially in sections like *Come, lovely and soothing Death*, in which the power of imagination has fused his ideas into a rhythmic utterance in harmony with the poetic traditions of the race.

WALT WHITMAN (1819-1892)
PREFACE TO "LEAVES OF GRASS"
(1855)

America does not repel the past or what it has produced under its forms or amid other politics or the idea of castes or the old religions . . . accepts the lesson with calmness . . . is not so impatient as has been supposed that the slough still sticks to opinions and manners and literature while the life which served its requirements has passed into the new life of the new forms . . . perceives that the corpse is slowly borne from the eating and sleeping rooms of the house . . . perceives that it waits a little while in the door . . . that it was fittest for its days . . . that its action has descended to the stalwart and wellshaped heir who approaches . . . and that he shall be fittest for his days.

The Americans of all nations at any time upon the earth have probably the fullest poetical nature. The United States themselves are essentially the greatest poem. In the history of the earth hitherto the largest and most stirring appear tame and orderly to their ampler largeness and stir. Here at last is something in the doings of man that corresponds with the broadcast doings of the day and night. Here is not merely a nation but a teeming nation of nations. Here is action untied from strings necessarily blind to particulars and details magnificently moving in vast masses. Here is the hospitality which forever indicates heroes. . . . Here are the roughs and beards and space and ruggedness and nonchalance that the soul loves. Here the performance disdaining the trivial unapproached in the tremendous audacity of its crowds and groupings and the push of its perspective spreads with crampless and flowing breadth and showers its prolific and splendid extravagance. One sees it must indeed own the riches of the summer and winter, and need never be bankrupt while corn grows from the ground or the orchards drop apples or the bays contain fish or men beget children upon women.

Other states indicate themselves in their deputies . . . but the genius of the United States is not best or most in its executives or legislatures, nor in its ambassadors or authors or colleges or churches or parlors, nor even in its newspapers or inventors . . . but always most in the common people. Their manners, speech, dress, friendships—the freshness and candor of their physiognomy—the picturesque looseness of their carriage . . . their deathless attachment to freedom—their aversion to anything indecorous or soft or mean—the practical acknowledgment of the citizens of one state by the citizens of all other states—the fierceness of their roused resentment—their curiosity and susceptibility to a slight—the air they have of persons who never knew how it felt to stand in the presence of superiors—the fluency of their speech—their delight in music, the sure symptom of manly tenderness and native elegance of soul . . . their good temper and openhandedness—the terrible significance of their elections—the President's taking off his hat to them not they to him—these too are unrhymed poetry. It awaits the gigantic and generous treatment worthy of it.

The largeness of nature or the nation were monstrous without a corresponding largeness and generosity of the spirit of the citizen. Not nature nor swarming states nor streets and steamships nor prosperous business nor farms nor capital nor learning may suffice for the ideal of man . . . nor suffice the poet. No reminiscences may suffice either. A live nation can always cut a deep mark and can have the best authority the cheapest . . . namely from its own souls. This is the sum of the profitable uses of individuals or states and of present action and grandeur and of the subjects of poets.—As if it were necessary to trot back generation after generation to the eastern records! As if the beauty and sacredness of the demonstrable must fall behind that of the mythical! As if men do not make their mark out of any times! As if the opening of the western continent by discovery and what has transpired since in North and South America were less than the small theatre of the antique or the aimless sleepwalking of the middle ages! The pride of the United States leaves the wealth and finesse of the cities and all returns of commerce and agriculture and all the magnitude of geography or shows of exterior victory to enjoy the breed of full sized men or one full sized man unconquerable and simple.

The American poets are to enclose old and new for America is the race of races. Of them a bard is to be commensurate with a people.

To him the other continents arrive as contributions . . . he gives them reception for their sake and his own sake. His spirit responds to his country's spirit . . . he incarnates its geography and natural life and rivers and lakes. Mississippi with annual freshets and changing chutes, Missouri and Columbia and Ohio and Saint Lawrence with the falls and beautiful masculine Hudson, do not embouchure where they spend themselves more than they embouchure into him. The blue breadth over the inland sea of Virginia and Maryland and the sea off Massachusetts and Maine and over Manhattan bay and over Champlain and Erie and over Ontario and Huron and Michigan and Superior, and over the Texan and Mexican and Floridian and Cuban seas and over the seas off California and Oregon, is not tallied by the blue breadth of the waters below more than the breadth of above and below is tallied by him. When the long Atlantic coast stretches longer and the Pacific coast stretches longer he easily stretches with them north or south. He spans between them also from east to west and reflects what is between them. On him rise solid growths that offset the growths of pine and cedar and hemlock and liveoak and locust and chestnut and cypress and hickory and limetree and cottonwood and tuliptree and cactus and wildvine and tamarind and persimmon . . . and tangles as tangled as any canebrake or swamp . . . and forests coated with transparent ice and icicles hanging from the boughs and crackling in the wind . . . and sides and peaks of mountains . . . and pasturage sweet and free as savannah or upland or prairie . . . with flights and songs and screams that answer those of the wildpigeon and highhold and orchard-oriole and coot and surf-duck and redshouldered-hawk and fish-hawk and white-ibis and indian-hen and cat-owl and water-pheasant and qua-bird and pied sheldrake and blackbird and mockingbird and buzzard and condor and night-heron and eagle. To him the hereditary countenance descends both mother's and father's. To him enter the essences of the real things and past and present events—of the enormous diversity of temperature and agriculture and mines—the tribes of red aborigines —the weatherbeaten vessels entering new ports or making landings on rocky coasts—the first settlements north or south—the rapid stature and muscle—the haughty defiance of '76, and the war and peace and formation of the constitution . . . the union always surrounded by blatherers and always calm and impregnable —the perpetual coming of immigrants—the wharf-hem'd cities and superior marine—the unsurveyed interior—the loghouses and clearings and wild animals and hunters and trappers . . . the free commerce—the fisheries and whaling and gold-digging—the endless gestation of new states—the convening of Congress every December, the members duly coming up from all climates and the uttermost parts . . . the noble character of the young mechanics and of all free American workmen and workwomen . . . the general ardor and friendliness and enterprise—the perfect equality of the female with the male . . . the large amativeness—the fluid movement of the population—the factories and mercantile life and laborsaving machinery—the Yankee swap—the New-York firemen and the target excursion—the southern plantation life—the character of the northeast and of the northwest and southwest—slavery and the tremulous spreading of hands to protect it, and the stern opposition to it which shall never cease till it ceases or the speaking of tongues and the moving of lips cease. For such the expression of the American poet is to be transcendant and new. It is to be indirect and not direct or descriptive or epic. Its quality goes through these to much more. Let the age and wars of other nations be chanted and their eras and characters be illustrated and that finish the verse. Not so the great psalm of the republic. Here the theme is creative and has vista. Here comes one among the wellbeloved stonecutters and plans with decision and science and sees the solid and beautiful forms of the future where there are now no solid forms.

Of all nations the United States with veins full of poetical stuff most need poets and will doubtless have the greatest and use them the greatest. Their Presidents shall not be their common referee so much as their poets shall. Of all mankind the great poet is the equable man. Not in him but off from him things are grotesque or eccentric or fail of their sanity. Nothing out of its place is good and nothing in its place is bad. He bestows on every object or quality its fit proportions neither more nor less. He is the arbiter of the diverse and he is the key. He is the equalizer of his age and land . . . he supplies what wants supplying and checks what wants checking. If peace is the routine out of him speaks the spirit of peace, large, rich, thrifty, building vast and populous cities, encouraging agriculture and the arts and commerce—lighting the study of man, the soul, immortality—federal, state or municipal government, marriage, health, free trade, intertravel by land and sea . . . nothing too close, nothing too far off . . . the stars not too far off. In war he is the most deadly force of the war. Who recruits him recruits horse and foot . . . he fetches parks of artillery the best that engineer ever knew. If the time becomes slothful and heavy he knows how to arouse it . . . he can make every word he speaks draw blood. Whatever stagnates in the flat of custom or obedience or legislation he never stagnates. Obedience does not master him, he masters it. High up out of reach he stands turning a concentrated light . . . he turns the pivot with his finger . . . he baffles the swiftest runners as he stands and easily overtakes and envelops them. The time straying toward infidelity and confections and persiflage he withholds by his steady faith . . . he spreads out his dishes . . . he offers the sweet firmfibred meat that grows men and women. His brain is the ultimate brain. He is no arguer . . . he is judgment. He judges not as the judge judges but as the sun falling around a helpless thing. As he sees the farthest he has the most faith. His thoughts are the hymns of the praise of things. In the talk on the soul and eternity and God off of his equal plane he is silent. He sees eternity less like a play with a prologue and denouement . . . he sees eternity in men and women . . . he does not see men and women as dreams or dots. Faith is the antiseptic of the soul . . . it pervades the common people and preserves them . . . they never give up believing and expecting and trusting. There is that indescribable freshness and unconsciousness about an illiterate person that humbles and mocks the power of the noblest expressive genius. The poet sees for a certainty how one not a great artist may be just as sacred as the greatest artist. . . . The power to destroy or remould is freely used by him but never the power of attack. What is past is past. If he does not expose superior models and prove himself by every step he takes he is not what is wanted. The presence of the greatest poet conquers . . . not parleying or struggling or any prepared attempts. Now he has passed that way see after him! there is not left any vestige of despair or misanthropy or cunning or exclusiveness or the ignominy of a nativity or color or delusion of hell or the necessity of hell . . . and no man thenceforward shall be degraded for ignorance or weakness or sin.

The greatest poet hardly knows pettiness or triviality. If he breathes into any thing that was before thought small it dilates with the grandeur and life of the universe. He is a seer . . . he is individual . . . he is complete in himself . . . the others are as good as he, only he sees it and they do not. He is not one of the chorus . . . he does not stop for any regulations

. . . he is the president of regulation. What the eyesight does to the rest he does to the rest. Who knows the curious mystery of the eyesight? The other senses corroborate themselves, but this is removed from any proof but its own and foreruns the identities of the spiritual world. A single glance of it mocks all the investigations of man and all the instruments and books of the earth and all reasoning. What is marvelous? what is unlikely? what is impossible or baseless or vague? after you have once just opened the space of a peachpit and given audience to far and near and to the sunset and had all things enter with electric swiftness softly and duly without confusion or jostling or jam.

The land and sea, the animals fishes and birds, the sky of heaven and the orbs, the forests, mountains and rivers, are not small themes . . . but folks expect of the poet to indicate more than the beauty and dignity which always attach to dumb real objects . . . they expect him to indicate the path between reality and their souls. Men and women perceive the beauty well enough . . . probably as well as he. The passionate tenacity of hunters, woodmen, early risers, cultivators of gardens and orchards and fields, the love of healthy women for the manly form, seafaring persons, drivers of horses, the passion for light and the open air, all is an old varied sign of the unfailing perception of beauty and of a residence of the poetic in outdoor people. They can never be assisted by poets to perceive . . . some may but they never can. The poetic quality is not marshalled in rhyme or uniformity or abstract addresses to things nor in melancholy complaints or good precepts, but is the life of these and much else and is in the soul. The profit of rhyme is that it drops seeds of a sweeter and more luxuriant rhyme, and of uniformity that it conveys itself into its own roots in the ground out of sight. The rhyme and uniformity of perfect poems show the free growth of metrical laws and bud from them as unerringly and loosely as lilacs or roses on a bush, and take shapes as compact as the shapes of chestnuts and oranges and melons and pears, and shed the perfume impalpable to form. The fluency and ornaments of the finest poems or music or orations or recitations are not independent but dependent. All beauty comes from beautiful blood and a beautiful brain. If the greatnesses are in conjunction in a man or woman it is enough . . . the fact will prevail through the universe . . . but the gaggery and gilt of a million years will not prevail. Who troubles himself about his ornaments or fluency is lost. This is what you shall do: Love the earth and sun and the animals, despise riches, give alms to every one that asks, stand up for the stupid and crazy, devote your income and labor to others, hate tyrants, argue not concerning God, have patience and indulgence toward the people, take off your hat to nothing known or unknown or to any man or number of men, go freely with powerful uneducated persons and with the young and with the mothers of families, read these leaves in the open air every season of every year of your life, re-examine all you have been told at school or church or in any book, dismiss whatever insults your own soul, and your very flesh shall be a great poem and have the richest fluency not only in its words but in the silent lines of its lips and face and between the lashes of your eyes and in every motion and joint of your body. . . . The poet shall not spend his time in unneeded work. He shall know that the ground is always ready plowed and manured . . . others may not know it but he shall. He shall go directly to the creation. His trust shall master the trust of everything he touches . . . and shall master all attachment.

The known universe has one complete lover and that is the greatest poet. He consumes an eternal passion and is indifferent which chance happens and which possible contingency of fortune or misfortune and persuades daily and hourly his delicious pay. What balks or breaks others is fuel for his burning progress to contact and amorous joy. Other proportions of the reception of pleasure dwindle to nothing to his proportions. All expected from heaven or from the highest he is rapport with in the sight of the daybreak or a scene of the winterwoods or the presence of children playing or with his arm round the neck of a man or woman. His love above all love has leisure and expanse . . . he leaves room ahead of himself. He is no irresolute or suspicious lover . . . he is sure . . . he scorns intervals. His experience and the showers and thrills are not for nothing. Nothing can jar him . . . suffering and darkness cannot—death and fear cannot. To him complaint and jealousy and envy are corpses buried and rotten in the earth . . . he saw them buried. The sea is not surer of the shore or the shore of the sea than he is of the fruition of his love and of all perfection and beauty.

The fruition of beauty is no chance of hit or miss . . . it is inevitable as life . . . it is exact and plumb as gravitation. From the eyesight proceeds another eyesight and from the hearing proceeds another hearing and from the voice proceeds another voice eternally curious of the harmony of things with man. To these respond perfections not only in the committees that were supposed to stand for the rest but in the rest themselves just the same. These understand the law of perfection in masses and floods . . . that its finish is to each for itself and onward from itself . . . that it is profuse and impartial . . . that there is not a minute of the light or dark nor an acre of the earth or sea without it—nor any direction of the sky nor any trade or employment nor any turn of events. This is the reason that about the proper expression of beauty there is precision and balance . . . one part does not need to be thrust above another. The best singer is not the one who has the most lithe and powerful organ . . . the pleasure of poems is not in them that take the handsomest measure and similes and sound.

Without effort and without exposing in the least how it is done the greatest poet brings the spirit of any or all events and passions and scenes and persons some more and some less to bear on your individual character as you hear or read. To do this well is to compete with the laws that pursue and follow time. What is the purpose must surely be there and the clue of it must be there . . . and the faintest indication is the indication of the best and then becomes the clearest indication. Past and present and future are not disjoined but joined. The greatest poet forms the consistence of what is to be from what has been and is. He drags the dead out of their coffins and stands them again on their feet . . . he says to the past, Rise and walk before me that I may realize you. He learns the lesson . . . he places himself where the future becomes present. The greatest poet does not only dazzle his rays over character and scenes and passions . . . he finally ascends and finishes all . . . he exhibits the pinnacles that no man can tell what they are for or what is beyond . . . he glows a moment on the extremest verge. He is most wonderful in his last half-hidden smile or frown . . . by that flash of the moment of parting the one that sees it shall be encouraged or terrified afterwards for many years. The greatest poet does not moralize or make applications of morals . . . he knows the soul. The soul has that measureless pride which consists in never acknowledging any lessons but its own. But it has sympathy as measureless as its pride and the one balances the other and neither can stretch too far while it stretches in company with the other. The inmost secrets of art sleep with the twain. The greatest poet has lain close betwixt both and they are vital in his style and thought.

The art of art, the glory of expression and

the sunshine of the light of letters is simplicity. Nothing is better than simplicity . . . nothing can make up for excess or for the lack of definiteness. To carry on the heave of impulse and pierce intellectual depths and give all subjects their articulations are powers neither common nor very uncommon. But to speak in literature with the perfect rectitude and insousiance of the movements of animals and the unimpeachableness of the sentiment of trees in the woods and grass by the roadside is the flawless triumph of art. If you have looked on him who has achieved it you have looked on one of the masters of the artists of all nations and times. You shall not contemplate the flight of the graygull over the bay or the mettlesome action of the blood horse or the tall leaning of sunflowers on their stalk or the appearance of the sun journeying through heaven or the appearance of the moon afterward with any more satisfaction than you shall contemplate him. The greatest poet has less a marked style and is more the channel of thoughts and things without increase or diminution, and is the free channel of himself. He swears to his art, I will not be meddlesome, I will not have in my writing any elegance or effect or originality to hang in the way between me and the rest like curtains. I will have nothing hang in the way, not the richest curtains. What I tell I tell for precisely what it is. Let who may exalt or startle or fascinate or sooth I will have purposes as health or heat or snow has and be as regardless of observation. What I experience or portray shall go from my composition without a shred of my composition. You shall stand by my side and look in the mirror with me.

The old red blood and stainless gentility of great poets will be proved by their unconstraint. A heroic person walks at his ease through and out of that custom or precedent or authority that suits him not. Of the traits of the brotherhood of writers savans musicians inventors and artists nothing is finer than silent defiance advancing from new free forms. In the need of poems philosophy politics mechanism science behaviour, the craft of art, an appropriate native grand-opera, shipcraft, or any craft, he is greatest forever and forever who contributes the greatest original practical example. The cleanest expression is that which finds no sphere worthy of itself and makes one.

The messages of great poets to each man and woman are, Come to us on equal terms, Only then can you understand us, We are no better than you, What we enclose you enclose, What we enjoy you may enjoy. Did you suppose there could be only one Supreme? We affirm there can be unnumbered Supremes, and that one does not countervail another any more than one eyesight countervails another . . . and that men can be good or grand only of the consciousness of their supremacy within them. What do you think is the grandeur of storms and dismemberments and the deadliest battles and wrecks and the wildest fury of the elements and the power of the sea and the motion of nature and of the throes of human desires and dignity and hate and love? It is that something in the soul which says, Rage on, Whirl on, I tread master here and everywhere, Master of the spasms of the sky and of the shatter of the sea, Master of nature and passion and death, And of all terror and all pain.

The American bards shall be marked for generosity and affection and for encouraging competitors. . . . They shall be kosmos . . . without monopoly or secrecy . . . glad to pass any thing to any one . . . hungry for equals night and day. They shall not be careful of riches and privilege, they shall be riches and privilege . . . they shall perceive who the most affluent man is. The most affluent man is he that confronts all the shows he sees by equivalents out of the stronger wealth of himself. The American bard shall delineate no class of persons nor one or two out of the strata of interests nor love most nor truth most nor the soul most nor the body most . . . and not be for the eastern states more than the western or the northern states more than the southern.

Exact science and its practical movements are no checks on the greatest poet but always his encouragement and support. The outset and remembrance are there . . . there are the arms that lifted him first and brace him best . . . there he returns after all his goings and comings. The sailor and traveler . . . the atomist chemist astronomer geologist phrenologist spiritualist mathematician historian and lexicographer are not poets, but they are the lawgivers of poets and their construction underlies the structure of every perfect poem. No matter what rises or is uttered they sent the seed of the conception of it . . . of them and by them stand the visible proofs of souls . . . always of their fatherstuff must be begotten the sinewy races of bards. If there shall be love and content between the father and the son and if the greatness of the son is the exuding of the greatness of the father there shall be love between the poet and the man of demonstrable science. In the beauty of poems are the tuft and final applause of science.

Great is the faith of the flush of knowledge

and of the investigation of the depths of qualities and things. Cleaving and circling here swells the soul of the poet yet is president of itself always. The depths are fathomless and therefore calm. The innocence and nakedness are resumed . . . they are neither modest nor immodest. The whole theory of the special and supernatural and all that was twined with it or educed out of it departs as a dream. What has ever happened . . . what happens and whatever may or shall happen, the vital laws enclose all . . . they are sufficient for any case and for all cases . . . none to be hurried or retarded . . . any miracle of affairs or persons inadmissible in the vast clear scheme where every motion and every spear of grass and the frames and spirits of men and women and all that concerns them are unspeakably perfect miracles all referring to all and each distinct and in its place. It is also not consistent with the reality of the soul to admit that there is anything in the known universe more divine than men and women.

Men and women and the earth and all upon it are simply to be taken as they are, and the investigation of their past and present and future shall be unintermitted and shall be done with perfect candor. Upon this basis philosophy speculates ever looking toward the poet, ever regarding the eternal tendencies of all toward happiness never inconsistent with what is clear to the senses and to the soul. For the eternal tendencies of all toward happiness make the only point of sane philosophy. Whatever comprehends less than that . . . whatever is less than the laws of light and of astronomical motion . . . or less than the laws that follow the thief the liar the glutton and the drunkard through this life and doubtless afterward . . . or less than vast stretches of time or the slow formation of density or the patient upheaving of strata—if of no account. Whatever would put God in a poem or system of philosophy as contending against some being or influence, is also of no account. Sanity and ensemble characterise the great master . . . spoilt in one principle all is spoilt. The great master has nothing to do with miracles. He sees health for himself in being one of the mass . . . he sees the hiatus in singular eminence. To the perfect shape comes common ground. To be under the general law is great for that is to correspond with it. The master knows that he is unspeakably great and that all are unspeakably great . . . that nothing for instance is greater than to conceive children and bring them up well . . . that to be is just as great as to perceive or tell.

In the make of the great masters the idea of political liberty is indispensable. Liberty takes the adherence of heroes wherever men and women exist . . . but never takes any adherence or welcome from the rest more than from poets. They are the voice and exposition of liberty. They out of ages are worthy the grand idea . . . to them it is confided and they must sustain it. Nothing has precedence of it and nothing can warp or degrade it. The attitude of great poets is to cheer up slaves and horrify despots. The turn of their necks, the sound of their feet, the motions of their wrists, are full of hazard to the one and hope to the other. Come nigh them awhile and though they neither speak nor advise you shall learn the faithful American lesson. Liberty is poorly served by men whose good intent is quelled from one failure or two failures or any number of failures, or from the casual indifference or ingratitude of the people, or from the sharp show of the tushes of power, or the bringing to bear soldiers and cannon or any penal statutes. Liberty relies upon itself, invites no one, promises nothing, sits in calmness and light, is positive and composed, and knows no discouragement. The battle rages with many a loud alarm and frequent advance and retreat . . . the enemy triumphs . . . the prison, the handcuffs, the iron necklace and anklet, the scaffold, garrote and leadballs do their work . . . the cause is asleep . . . the strong throats are choked with their own blood . . . the young men drop their eyelashes toward the ground when they pass each other . . . and is liberty gone out of that place? No never. When liberty goes it is not the first to go nor the second nor third to go . . . it waits for all the rest to go . . . it is the last. . . . When the memories of the old martyrs are faded utterly away . . . when the large names of patriots are laughed at in the public halls from the lips of the orators . . . when the boys are no more christened after the same but christened after tyrants and traitors instead . . . when the laws of the free are grudgingly permitted and laws for informers and blood-money are sweet to the taste of the people . . . when I and you walk abroad upon the earth stung with compassion at the sight of numberless brothers answering our equal friendship and calling no man master —and when we are elated with noble joy at the sight of slaves . . . when the soul retires in the cool communion of the night and surveys its experience and has much extasy over the word and deed that put back a helpless innocent person into the gripe of the gripers or into any cruel inferiority . . . when those in all parts of these states who could easier realize the true American character but do not yet—when the swarms of cringers, suckers, doughfaces, lice of politics, planners of sly involutions for their own preferment to city offices or state legislatures or the judiciary or congress or the presidency, obtain a response of love and natural deference from the people whether they get the offices or no . . . when it is better to be a bound booby and rogue in office at a high salary than the poorest free mechanic or farmer with his hat unmoved from his head and firm eyes and a candid and generous heart . . . and when servility by town or state or the federal government or any oppression on a large scale or small scale can be tried on without its own punishment following duly after in exact proportion against the smallest chance of escape . . . or rather when all life and all the souls of men and women are discharged from any part of the earth—then only shall the instinct of liberty be discharged from that part of the earth.

As the attributes of the poets of the kosmos concentre in the real body and soul and in the pleasure of things they possess the superiority of genuineness over all fiction and romance. As they emit themselves facts are showered over with light . . . the daylight is lit with more volatile light . . . also the deep between the setting and rising sun goes deeper many fold. Each precise object or condition or combination or process exhibits a beauty . . . the multiplication table its—old age its—the carpenter's trade its—the grand-opera its . . . the hugehulled cleanshaped New-York clipper at sea under steam or full sail gleams with unmatched beauty . . . the American circles and large harmonies of government gleam with theirs . . . and the commonest definite intentions and actions with theirs. The poets of the kosmos advance through all interpositions and coverings and turmoils and stratagems to first principles. They are of use . . . they dissolve poverty from its need and riches from its conceit. You large proprietor they say shall not realize or perceive more than any one else. The owner of the library is not he who holds a legal title to it having bought and paid for it. Any one and every one is owner of the library who can read the same through all the varieties of tongues and subjects and styles, and in whom they enter with ease and take residence and force toward paternity and maternity, and make supple and powerful and rich and large. . . . These American states strong and healthy and accomplished shall receive no pleasure from violations of natural models and must not permit them. In paintings or mouldings or carvings in mineral or wood, or in the illustrations of books or newspapers, or in any comic or tragic prints, or in the patterns of woven stuffs or anything to beautify rooms or furniture or costumes, or to put upon cornices or monuments or on the prows or sterns of ships, or to put anywhere before the human eye indoors or out, that which distorts honest shapes or which creates unearthly beings or places or contingencies is a nuisance and revolt. Of the human form especially it is so great it must never be made ridiculous. Of ornaments to a work nothing outre can be allowed . . . but those ornaments can be allowed that conform to the perfect facts of the open air and that flow out of the nature of the work and come irrepressibly from it and are necessary to the completion of the work. Most works are most beautiful without ornament. . . . Exaggerations will be revenged in human physiology. Clean and vigorous children are jetted and conceived only in those communities where the models of natural forms are public every day. . . . Great genius and the people of these states must never be demeaned to romances. As soon as histories are properly told there is no more need of romances.

The great poets are also to be known by the absence in them of tricks and by the justification of perfect personal candor. Then folks echo a new cheap joy and a divine voice leaping from their brains: How beautiful is candor! All faults may be forgiven of him who has perfect candor. Henceforth let no man of us lie, for we have seen that openness wins the inner and outer world and that there is no single exception, and that never since our earth gathered itself in a mass have deceit or subterfuge or prevarication attracted its smallest particle or the faintest tinge of a shade—and that through the enveloping wealth and rank of a state or the whole republic of states a sneak or sly person shall be discovered and despised . . . and that the soul has never been once fooled and never can be fooled . . . and thrift without the loving nod of the soul is only a fœtid puff . . . and there never grew up in any of the continents of the globe nor upon any planet or satellite or star, nor upon the asteroids, nor in any part of ethereal space, nor in the midst of density, nor under the fluid wet of the sea, nor in the condition which precedes the birth of babes, nor at any time during the changes of life, nor in that condition that follows what we term death, nor in any stretch of abeyance or action afterward of vitality, nor in any process of formation or reformation anywhere, a being whose instinct hated the truth.

Extreme caution or prudence, the soundest organic health, large hope and comparison and fondness for women and children, large alimentiveness and destructiveness and causality, with a perfect sense of the oneness of nature and the propriety of the same spirit applied to human affairs . . . these are called up of the float of the brain of the world to be parts of the greatest poet from his birth out of his mother's womb and from her birth out of her mother's. Caution seldom goes far enough. It has been thought that the prudent citizen was the citizen who applied himself to solid gains and did well for himself and his family and completed a lawful life without debt or crime. The greatest poet sees and admits these economies as he sees the economies of food and sleep, but has higher notions of prudence than to think he gives much when he gives a few slight attentions at the latch of the gate. The premises of the prudence of life are not the hospitality of it or the ripeness and harvest of it. Beyond the independence of a little sum laid aside for burial-money, and of a few clapboards around and shingles overhead on a lot of American soil owned, and the easy dollars that supply the year's plain clothing and meals, the melancholy prudence of the abandonment of such a great being as a man is to the toss and pallor of years of moneymaking with all their scorching days and icy nights and all their stifling deceits and underhanded dodgings, or infinitesimals of parlors, or shameless stuffing while others starve . . . and all the loss of the bloom and odor of the earth and of the flowers and atmosphere and of the sea and of the true taste of the women and men you pass or have to do with in youth or middle age, and the issuing sickness and desperate revolt at the close of a life without elevation or naïveté, and the ghastly chatter of a death without serenity or majesty, is the great fraud upon modern civilization and forethought, blotching the surface and system which civilization undeniably drafts, and moistening with tears the immense features it spreads and spreads with such velocity before the reached kisses of the soul. . . . Still the right explanation remains to be made about prudence. The prudence of the mere wealth and respectability of the most esteemed life appears too faint for the eye to observe at all when little and large alike drop quietly aside at the thought of the prudence suitable for immortality. What is wisdom that fills the thinness of a year or seventy or eighty years to wisdom spaced out by ages and coming back at a certain time with strong reinforcements and rich presents and the clear faces of wedding-guests as far as you can look in every direction running gaily toward you? Only the soul is of itself . . . all else has reference to what ensues. All that a person does or thinks is of consequence. Not a move can a man or woman make that affects him or her in a day or a month or any part of the direct lifetime or the hour of death but the same affects him or her onward afterward through the indirect lifetime. The indirect is always as great and real as the direct. The spirit receives from the body just as much as it gives to the body. Not one name of word or deed . . . not of venereal sores or discolorations . . . not the privacy of the onanist . . . not of the putrid veins of gluttons or rum-drinkers . . . not peculation or cunning or betrayal or murder . . . no serpentine poison of those that seduce women . . . not the foolish yielding of women . . . not prostitution . . . not of any depravity of young men . . . not of the attainment of gain by discreditable means . . . not any nastiness of appetite . . . not any harshness of officers to men or judges to prisoners or fathers to sons or sons to fathers or husbands to wives or bosses to their boys . . . not of greedy looks or malignant wishes . . . nor any of the wiles practised by people upon themselves . . . ever is or ever can be stamped on the programme but it is duly realized and returned, and that returned in further performances . . . and they returned again. Nor can the push of charity or personal force ever be any thing else than the profoundest reason, whether it brings arguments to hand or no. No specification is necessary . . . to add or subtract or divide is in vain. Little or big, learned or unlearned, white or black, legal or illegal, sick or well, from the first inspiration down the windpipe to the last expiration out of it, all that a male or female does that is vigorous and benevolent and clean is so much sure profit to him or her in the unshakable order of the universe and through the whole scope of it forever. If the savage or felon is wise it is well . . . if the greatest poet or savan is wise it is simply the same . . . if the President or chief justice is wise it is the same . . . if the young mechanic or farmer is wise it is no more or less . . . if the prostitute is wise it is no more nor less. The interest will come round . . . all will come round. All the best actions of war and peace . . . all help given to relatives and strangers and the poor and old and sorrowful and young children and widows and the sick, and to all shunned persons . . . all furtherance of fugitives and of the escape of slaves . . . all the self-denial that stood steady and aloof on wrecks and saw others take the seats of the boats . . . all offering of substance or life for the good old cause, or for a friend's sake or opinion's sake . . . all pains of enthusiasts scoffed at by their neighbors . . . all the vast sweet love and precious suffering of mothers . . . all honest men baffled in strifes recorded or unrecorded . . . all the grandeur and goof of the few ancient nations whose fragments of annals we inherit . . . and all the good of the hundreds of far mightier and more ancient nations unknown to us by name or date or location . . . all that was ever manfully begun, whether it succeeded or not . . . all that has at any time been well suggested out of the divine heart of man or by the divinity of his mouth or by the shaping of his great hands . . . and all that is well thought or done this day on any part of the surface of the globe . . . or on any of the wandering stars or fixed stars by those there as we are here . . . or that is henceforth to be well thought or done by you whoever you are, or by any one—these singly and wholly inure at their time and inure now and will inure always to the identities from which they sprung or shall spring. . . . Did you guess any of them lived only its moment? The world does not so exist . . . no parts palpable or impalpable so exist . . . no result exists now without being from its long antecedent result, and that from its antecedent, and so backward without the farthest mentionable spot coming a bit nearer to the beginning than any other spot. . . . Whatever satisfies the soul is truth. The prudence of the greatest poet answers at last the craving and glut of the soul, is not contemptuous of less ways of prudence if they conform to its ways, puts off nothing, permits no let-up for its own case or any case, has no particular sabbath or judgment-day, divides not the living from the dead or the righteous from the unrighteous, is satisfied with the present, matches every thought or act by its correlative, knows no possible forgiveness or deputed atonement . . . knows that the young man who composedly periled his life and lost it has done exceeding well for himself, while the man who has not periled his life and retains it to old age in riches and ease has perhaps achieved nothing for himself worth mentioning . . . and that only that person has no great prudence to learn who has learnt to prefer real longlived things, and favors body and soul the same, and perceives the indirect assuredly following the direct, and what evil or good he does leaping onward and waiting to meet him again—and who in his spirit in any emergency whatever neither hurries or avoids death.

The direct trial of him who would be the greatest poet is today. If he does not flood himself with the immediate age as with vast oceanic tides . . . and if he does not attract his own land body and soul to himself and hang on its neck with incomparable love and plunge his semitic muscle into its merits and demerits . . . and if he be not himself the age transfigured . . . and if to him is not opened the eternity which gives similitude to all periods and locations and processes and animate and inanimate forms, and which is the bond of time, and rises up from its inconceivable vagueness and infiniteness in the swimming shape of today, and is held by the ductile anchors of life, and makes the present spot the passage from what was to what shall be, and commits itself to the representation of this wave of an hour and this one of the sixty beautiful children of the wave—let him merge in the general run and wait his development. . . . Still the final test of poems or any character or work remains. The prescient poet projects himself centuries ahead and judges performer or performance after the changes of time. Does it live through them? Does it still hold on untired? Will the same style and the direction of genius to similar points be satisfactory now? Has no new discovery in science or arrival at superior planes of thought and judgment and behaviour fixed him or his so that either can be looked down upon? Have the marches of tens and hundreds and thousands of years made willing detours to the right hand and the left hand for his sake? Is he beloved long and long after he is buried? Does the young man think often of him? and the young woman think often of him? and do the middle-aged and the old think of him?

A great poem is for ages and ages in common and for all degrees and complexions and all departments and sects and for a woman as much as a man and a man as much as a woman. A great poem is no finish to a man or woman but rather a beginning. Has any one fancied he could sit at last under some due authority and rest satisfied with explanations and realize and be content and full? To no such terminus does the greatest poet bring . . . he brings neither cessation or sheltered fatness and ease. The touch of him tells in action. Whom he takes with firm sure grasp into live regions previously unattained . . . thenceforward is no rest . . . they see the space and ineffable sheen that turn the old spots and lights into dead vacuums. The companion of him beholds the birth and progress of stars and learns one of the meanings. Now there shall be a man cohered out of tumult and chaos . . . the elder encourages the younger and shows him how . . . they two shall launch off fearlessly together till the new world fits an orbit for itself and looks unabashed on the lesser orbits of the stars and sweeps through the ceaseless rings and shall never be quiet again.

There will soon be no more priests. Their work is done. They may wait awhile . . . perhaps a generation or two . . . dropping off by degrees. A superior breed shall take their place . . . the gangs of kosmos and prophets en masse shall take their place. A new order shall arise and they shall be the priests of man, and every man shall be his own priest. The churches built under their umbrage shall be the churches of men and women. Through the divinity of themselves shall the kosmos and the new breed of poets be interpreters of men and women and of all events and things. They shall find their inspiration in real objects today, symptoms of the past and future. . . . They shall not deign to defend immortality or God or the perfection of things or liberty or the exquisite beauty and reality of the soul. They shall arise in America and be responded to from the remainder of the earth.

The English language befriends the grand American expression . . . it is brawny enough and limber and full enough. On the tough stock of a race who through all change of circumstances was never without the idea of political liberty, which is the animus of all liberty, it has attracted the terms of daintier and gayer and subtler and more elegant tongues. It is the powerful language of resistance . . . it is the dialect of common sense. It is the speech of the proud and melancholy races and of all who aspire. It is the chosen tongue to express growth faith self-esteem freedom justice equality friendliness amplitude prudence decision and courage. It is the medium that shall well nigh express the inexpressible.

No great literature nor any like style of behavior or oratory or social intercourse or household arrangements or public institutions or the treatment by bosses or employed people, nor executive detail or detail of the army or navy, nor spirit of legislation or courts or police or tuition or architecture or songs or amusements or the costumes of young men, can long elude the jealous and passionate instinct of American standards. Whether or no the sign appears from the mouths of the people, it throbs a live interrogation in every freeman's and freewoman's heart after that which passes by or this built to remain. Is it uniform with my country? Are its disposals without ignominious distinctions?

Is it for the evergrowing communes of brothers and lovers, large, well-united, proud beyond the old models, generous beyond all models? Is it something grown fresh out of the fields or drawn from the sea for use to me today here? I know that what answers for me an American must answer for any individual or nation that serves for a part of my materials. Does this answer? or is it without reference to universal needs? or sprung of the needs of the less developed society of special ranks? or old needs of pleasure overlaid by modern science and forms? Does this acknowledge liberty with audible and absolute acknowledgement, and set slavery at naught for life and death? Will it help breed one goodshaped and wellhung man, and a woman to be his perfect and independent mate? Does it improve manners? Is it for the nursing of the young of the republic? Does it solve readily with the sweet milk of the nipples of the breasts of the mother of many children? Has it too the old ever-fresh forbearance and impartiality? Does it look with the same love on the last born and those hardening toward stature, and on the errant, and on those who disdain all strength of assault outside of their own?

The poems distilled from other poems will probably pass away. The coward will surely pass away. The expectation of the vital and great can only be satisfied by the demeanor of the vital and great. The swarms of the polished deprecating and reflectors and the polite float off and leave no remembrance. America prepares with composure and goodwill for the visitors that have sent word. It is not intellect that is to be their warrant and welcome. The talented, the artist, the ingenious, the editor, the statesman, the erudite . . . they are not unappreciated . . . they fall in their place and do their work. The soul of the nation also does its work. No disguise can pass on it . . . no disguise can conceal from it. It rejects none, it permits all. Only toward as good as itself and toward the like of itself will it advance halfway. An individual is as superb as a nation when he has the qualities which make a superb nation. The soul of the largest and wealthiest and proudest nation may well go half-way to meet that of its poets. The signs are effectual. There is no fear of mistake. If the one is true the other is true. The proof of a poet is that his country absorbs him as affectionately as he has absorbed it.

From SONG OF MYSELF

1

I celebrate myself, and sing myself,
And what I assume you shall assume,
For every atom belonging to me as good belongs to you.

I loafe and invite my soul,
I lean and loafe at my ease observing a spear of summer grass.

My tongue, every atom of my blood, form'd from this soil, this air,
Born here of parents born here from parents the same, and their parents the same,
I, now thirty-seven years old in perfect health begin,
Hoping to cease not till death.

Creeds and schools in abeyance,   10
Retiring back a while sufficed at what they are, but never forgotten,
I harbor for good or bad, I permit to speak at every hazard,
Nature without check with original energy.

6

A child said *What is the grass?* fetching it to me with full hands,
How could I answer the child? I do not know what it is any more than he.

I guess it must be the flag of my disposition, out of hopeful green stuff woven.
Or I guess it is the handkerchief of the Lord,
A scented gift and remembrancer designedly dropt,
Bearing the owner's name someway in the corners, that we may see and remark, and say
    Whose?

Or I guess the grass is itself a child, the produced babe of the vegetation.   20

Or I guess it is a uniform hieroglyphic,
And it means, Sprouting alike in broad zones and narrow zones,
Growing among black folks as among white,
Kanuck, Tuckahoe, Congressman, Cuff, I give them the same, I receive them the same.

And now it seems to me the beautiful uncut hair of graves.

Tenderly will I use you curling grass,
It may be you transpire from the breasts of young men,
It may be if I had known them I would have loved them,
It may be you are from old people, or from offspring taken soon out of their mothers' laps,
And here you are the mothers' laps.   30

This grass is very dark to be from the white heads of old mothers,
Darker than the colorless beards of old men,
Dark to come from under the faint red roofs of mouths.

O I perceive after all so many uttering tongues,
And I perceive they do not come from the roofs of mouths for nothing.

I wish I could translate the hints about the dead young men and. women,
And the hints about old men and mothers, and the offspring taken soon out of their laps.

What do you think has become of the young and old men?
And what do you think has become of the women and children?

They are alive and well somewhere,   40
The smallest sprout shows there is really no death,
And if ever there was it led forward life, and does not wait at the end to arrest it,
And ceas'd the moment life appear'd.

All goes onward and outward, nothing collapses,
And to die is different from what any one supposed, and luckier.

17

These are really the thoughts of all men in all ages and lands, they are not original with me,
If they are not yours as much as mine they are nothing, or next to nothing,
If they are not the riddle and the untying of the riddle they are nothing,
If they are not just as close as they are distant they are nothing.

This is the grass that grows wherever the land is and the water is,   50
This the common air that bathes the globe.

18

With music strong I come, with my cornets and my drums,
I play not marches for accepted victors only, I play marches for conquer'd and slain persons.

Have you heard that it was good to gain the day?
I also say it is good to fall, battles are lost in the same spirit in which they are won.

I beat and pound for the dead,
I blow through my embouchures my loudest and gayest for them.

Vivas to those who have fail'd!
And to those whose war-vessels sank in the sea!
And to those themselves who sank in the sea!
And to all generals that lost engagements, and all overcome heroes!   60
And the numberless unknown heroes equal to the greatest heroes known!

21

I am the poet of the Body and I am the poet of the Soul,
The pleasures of heaven are with me and the pains of hell are with me,
The first I graft and increase upon myself, the latter I translate into a new tongue.

I am the poet of the woman the same as the man,
And I say it is as great to be a woman as to be a man,
And I say there is nothing greater than the mother of men.

I chant the chant of dilation or pride,
We have had ducking and deprecating about enough,   70
I show that size is only development.

Have you outstript the rest? are you the President?
It is a trifle, they will more than arrive there every one, and still pass on.

I am he that walks with the tender and growing night,
I call to the earth and sea half-held by the night.

Press close bare-bosom'd night—press close magnetic nourishing night!
Night of south winds—night of the large few stars!
Still nodding night—mad naked summer night.

Smile O voluptuous cool-breath'd earth!
Earth of the slumbering and liquid trees!   80

Earth of departed sunset—earth of the mountains misty-topt!
Earth of the vitreous pour of the full moon just tinged with blue!
Earth of shine and dark mottling the tide of the river!
Earth of the limpid gray of clouds brighter and clearer for my sake!
Far-swooping elbow'd earth—rich apple-blossom'd earth!
Smile, for your lover comes.

Prodigal, you have given me love—therefore I to you give love!
O unspeakable passionate love.

30

All truths wait in all things,
They neither hasten their own delivery nor resist it,
They do not need the obstetric forceps of the surgeon,
The insignificant is as big to me as any,
(What is less or more than a touch?)

Logic and sermons never convince,
The damp of the night drives deeper into my soul.

(Only what proves itself to every man and woman is so,
Only what nobody denies is so.)

A minute and a drop of me settle my brain,
I believe the soggy clods shall become lovers and lamps,
And a compend of compends is the meat of a man or woman,
And a summit and flower there is the feeling they have for each other,
And they are to branch boundlessly out of that lesson until it becomes omnific,
And until one and all shall delight us, and we them.

32

I think I could turn and live with animals, they're so placid and self-contain'd,
I stand and look at them long and long.

They do not sweat and whine about their condition,
They do not lie awake in the dark and weep for their sins,
They do not make me sick discussing their duty to God,
Not one is dissatisfied, not one is demented with the mania of owning things,
Not one kneels to another, nor to his kind that lived thousands of years ago,
Not one is respectable or unhappy over the whole earth.

So they show their relations to me and I accept them,
They bring me tokens of myself, they evince them plainly in their possession.

I wonder where they get those tokens,
Did I pass that way huge times ago and negligently drop them?

Myself moving forward then and now and forever,
Gathering and showing more always and with velocity,
Infinite and omnigenous, and the like of these among them,
Not too exclusive toward the reachers of my remembrancers,
Picking out here one that I love, and now go with him on brotherly terms.

A gigantic beauty of a stallion, fresh and responsive to my caresses,
Head high in the forehead, wide between the ears,
Limbs glossy and supple, tail dusting the ground,
Eyes full of sparkling wickedness, ears finely cut, flexibly moving.

His nostrils dilate as my heels embrace him,
His well-built limbs tremble with pleasure as we race around and return.
I but use you a minute, then I resign you, stallion,
Why do I need your paces when I myself out-gallop them?
Even as I stand or sit passing faster than you.

44

It is time to explain myself—let us stand up.   130

What is known I strip away,
I launch all men and women forward with me into the Unknown.

The clock indicates the moment—but what does eternity indicate?

We have thus far exhausted trillions of winters and summers,
There are trillions ahead, and trillions ahead of them.

Births have brought us richness and variety,
And other births will bring us richness and variety.

I do not call one greater and one smaller,
That which fills its period and place is equal to any.

Were mankind murderous or jealous upon you, my brother, my sister?   140
I am sorry for you, they are not murderous or jealous upon me,
All has been gentle with me, I keep no account with lamentation,
(What have I to do with lamentation?)

I am an acme of things accomplish'd, and I an encloser of things to be.

My feet strike an apex of the apices of the stairs,
On every step bunches of ages, and larger bunches between the steps,
All below duly travel'd, and still I mount and mount.

Rise after rise bow the phantoms behind me,
Afar down I see the huge first Nothing, I know I was even there,
I waited unseen and always, and slept through the lethargic mist,   150
And took my time, and took no hurt from the fetid carbon.

Long I was hugg'd close—long and long.

Immense have been the preparations for me,
Faithful and friendly the arms that have help'd me.

Cycles ferried my cradle, rowing and rowing like cheerful boatmen,
For room to me stars kept aside in their own rings,
They sent influences to look after what was to hold me.

Before I was born out of my mother generations guided me,
My embryo has never been torpid, nothing could overlay it.

For it the nebula cohered to an orb,   160
The long slow strata piled to rest it on,
Vast vegetables gave it sustenance,
Monstrous sauroids transported it in their mouths and deposited it with care.

All forces have been steadily employ'd to complete and delight me,
Now on this spot I stand with my robust soul.

46

I know I have the best of time and space, and was never measured and never will be measured.

I tramp a perpetual journey, (come listen all!)
My signs are a rain-proof coat, good shoes, and a staff cut from the woods,
No friend of mine takes his ease in my chair,
I have no chair, no church, no philosophy,   170
I lead no man to a dinner-table, library, exchange,
But each man and each woman of you I lead upon a knoll,
My left hand hooking you round the waist,
My right hand pointing to landscapes of continents and the public road.

Not I, not any one else can travel that road for you,
You must travel it for yourself.

It is not far, it is within reach,
Perhaps you have been on it since you were born and did not know,
Perhaps it is everywhere on water and on land.

Shoulder your duds dear son, and I will mine, and let us hasten forth,   180
Wonderful cities and free nations we shall fetch as we go.

If you tire, give me both burdens, and rest the chuff of your hand on my hip,
And in due time you shall repay the same service to me,
For after we start we never lie by again.

This day before dawn I ascended a hill and look'd at the crowded heaven,
And I said to my spirit *When we become the enfolders of those orbs, and the pleasure and knowl-
edge of every thing in them, shall we be fill'd and satisfied then?*
And my spirit said *No, we but level that lift to pass and continue beyond.*

You are also asking me questions and I hear you,
I answer that I cannot answer, you must find out for yourself.

Sit a while dear son,   190
Here are biscuits to eat and here is milk to drink,
But as soon as you sleep and renew yourself in sweet clothes, I kiss you with a good-by kiss
and open the gate for your egress hence.

Long enough have you dream'd contemptible dreams,
Now I wash the gum from your eyes,
You must habit yourself to the dazzle of the light and of every moment of your life.

Long have you timidly waded holding a plank by the shore,
Now I will you to be a bold swimmer,
To jump off in the midst of the sea, rise again, not to me, shout, and laughingly dash with
your hair.

48

I have said that the soul is not more than the body,
And I have said that the body is not more than the soul,
And nothing, not God, is greater to one than one's self is,   200
And whoever walks a furlong without sympathy walks to his own funeral drest in his shroud,
And I or you pocketless of a dime may purchase the pick of the earth,
And to glance with an eye or show a bean in its pod confounds the learning of all times,
And there is no trade or employment but the young man following it may become a hero,
And there is no object so soft but it makes a hub for the wheel'd universe,
And I say to any man or woman, Let your soul stand cool and composed before a million
universes.

And I say to mankind, Be not curious about God,
For I who am curious about each am not curious about God,
(No array of terms can say how much I am at peace about God and about death.)   210

I hear and behold God in every object, yet understand God not in the least.
Nor do I understand who there can be more wonderful than myself.

Why should I wish to see God better than this day?
I see something of God each hour of the twenty-four, and each moment then,
In the faces of men and women I see God, and in my own face in the glass,
I find letters from God dropt in the street, and every one is sign'd by God's name,
And I leave them where they are, for I know that wheresoe'er I go,
Others will punctually come for ever and ever.

51

The past and present wilt—I have fill'd them, emptied them,
And proceed to fill my next fold of the future.   220

Listener up there! what have you to confide to me?
Look in my face while I snuff the sidle of evening,
(Talk honestly, no one else hears you, and I stay only a minute longer.)

Do I contradict myself?
Very well then I contradict myself,
(I am large, I contain multitudes.)

I concentrate toward them that are nigh, I wait on the door-slab.

Who has done his day's work? who will soonest be through with his supper?
Who wishes to walk with me?

Will you speak before I am gone? will you prove already too late?   230

52

The spotted hawk swoops by and accuses me, he complains of my gab and my loitering.

I too am not a bit tamed, I too am untranslatable,
I sound my barbaric yawp over the roofs of the world.

The last scud of day holds back for me,
It flings my likeness after the rest and true as any on the shadow'd wilds,
It coaxes me to the vapor and the dusk.

I depart as air, I shake my white locks at the runaway sun,
I effuse my flesh in eddies, and drift it in lacy jags.

I bequeath myself to the dirt to grow from the grass I love,
If you want me again look for me under your boot-soles.   240

You will hardly know who I am or what I mean,
But I shall be good health to you nevertheless,
And filter and fibre your blood.

Failing to fetch me at first keep encouraged,
Missing me one place search another,
I stop somewhere waiting for you.

1855, 1881

SONG OF THE OPEN ROAD

1

Afoot and light-hearted I take to the open road,
Healthy, free, the world before me,
The long brown path before me leading wherever I choose.

Henceforth I ask not good-fortune, I myself am good-fortune,
Henceforth I whimper no more, postpone no more, need nothing,
Done with indoor complaints, libraries, querulous criticisms,
Strong and content I travel the open road.

The earth, that is sufficient,
I do not want the constellations any nearer,
I know they are very well where they are,   10
I know they suffice for those who belong to them.

(Still here I carry my old delicious burdens,
I carry them, men and women, I carry them with me wherever I go,
I swear it is impossible for me to get rid of them,
I am fill'd with them, and I will fill them in return.)

2

You road I enter upon and look around, I believe you are not all that is here,
I believe that much unseen is also here.

Here the profound lesson of reception, nor preference nor denial,
The black with his woolly head, the felon, the diseas'd, the illiterate person, are not denied;
The birth, the hasting after the physician, the beggar's tramp, the drunkard's stagger, the
    laughing party of mechanics,   20
The escaped youth, the rich person's carriage, the fop, the eloping couple,
The early market-man, the hearse, the moving of furniture into the town, the return back
    from the town,
They pass, I also pass, anything passes, none can be interdicted,
None but are accepted, none but shall be dear to me.

3

You air that serves me with breath to speak!
You objects that call from diffusion my meanings and give them shape!
You light that wraps me and all things in delicate equable showers!
You paths worn in the irregular hollows by the roadsides!
I believe you are latent with unseen existences, you are so dear to me.

You flagg'd walks of the cities! you strong curbs at the edges!   30
You ferries! you planks and posts of wharves! you timber-lined sides! you distant ships!
You rows of houses! you window-pierc'd façades! you roofs!
You porches and entrances! you copings and iron guards!
You windows whose transparent shells might expose so much!
You doors and ascending steps! you arches!
You gray stones of interminable pavements! you trodden crossings!
From all that has touch'd you I believe you have imparted to yourselves, and now would im-
    part the same secretly to me,
From the living and the dead you have peopled your impassive surfaces, and the spirits thereof
    would be evident and amicable with me.

4

The earth expanding right hand and left hand,
The picture alive, every part in its best light,
The music falling in where it is wanted, and stopping where it is not wanted,   40
The cheerful voice of the public road, the gay fresh sentiment of the road.

O highway I travel, do you say to me *Do not leave me?*
Do you say *Venture not—if you leave me you are lost?*
Do you say *I am already prepared, I am well-beaten and undenied, adhere to me?*

O public road, I say back I am not afraid to leave you, yet I love you,
You express me better than I can express myself,
You shall be more to me than my poem.

I think heroic deeds were all conceiv'd in the open air, and all free poems also,
I think I could stop here myself and do miracles,
I think whatever I shall meet on the road I shall like, and whoever beholds me shall like me,   50
I think whoever I see must be happy.

5

From this hour I ordain myself loos'd of limits and imaginary lines,
Going where I list, my own master total and absolute,
Listening to others, considering well what they say,
Pausing, searching, receiving, contemplating,
Gently, but with undeniable will, divesting myself of the holds that would hold me.

I inhale great draughts of space,
The east and the west are mine, and the north and the south are mine.

I am larger, better than I thought,   60
I did not know I held so much goodness.

All seems beautiful to me,
I can repeat over to men and women You have done such good to me I would do the same to
    you,
I will recruit for myself and you as I go,
I will scatter myself among men and women as I go,
I will toss a new gladness and roughness among them,
Whoever denies me it shall not trouble me,
Whoever accepts me he or she shall be blessed and shall bless me.

6

Now if a thousand perfect men were to appear it would not amaze me,
Now if a thousand beautiful forms of women appear'd it would not astonish me.   70

Now I see the secret of the making of the best persons,
It is to grow in the open air and to eat and sleep with the earth.

Here a great personal deed has room,
(Such a deed seizes upon the hearts of the whole race of men,
Its effusion of strength and will overwhelms law and mocks all authority and all argument
    against it.)

Here is the test of wisdom,
Wisdom is not finally tested in schools,
Wisdom cannot be pass'd from one having it to another not having it,
Wisdom is of the soul, is not susceptible of proof, is its own proof,

Applies to all stages and objects and qualities and is content,   80
Is the certainty of the reality and immortality of things, and the excellence of things;
Something there is in the float of the sight of things that provokes it out of the soul.

Now I re-examine philosophies and religions,
They may prove well in lecture-rooms, yet not prove at all under the spacious clouds and
     along the landscape and flowing currents.

Here is realization,
Here is a man tallied—he realizes here what he has in him,
The past, the future, majesty, love—if they are vacant of you, you are vacant of them.

Only the kernel of every object nourishes;
Where is he who tears off the husks for you and me?
Where is he that undoes stratagems and envelopes for you and me?   90

Here is adhesiveness, it is not previously fashion'd, it is apropos;
Do you know what it is as you pass to be loved by strangers?
Do you know the talk of those turning eye-balls?

7

Here is the efflux of the soul,
The efflux of the soul comes from within through embower'd gates, ever provoking questions,
These yearnings why are they? these thoughts in the darkness why are they?
Why are there men and women that while they are nigh me the sunlight expands my blood?
Why when they leave me do my pennants of joy sink flat and lank?
Why are there trees I never walk under but large and melodious thoughts descend upon me?
(I think they hang there winter and summer on those trees and always drop fruit as I pass;)
What is it I interchange so suddenly with strangers?   101
What with some driver as I ride on the seat by his side?
What with some fisherman drawing his seine by the shore as I walk by and pause?
What gives me to be free to a woman's and man's good-will? what gives them to be free to mine?

8

The efflux of the soul is happiness, here is happiness,
I think it pervades the open air, waiting at all times,
Now it flows unto us, we are rightly charged.

Here rises the fluid and attaching character,
The fluid and attaching character is the freshness and sweetness of man and woman,
(The herbs of the morning sprout no fresher and sweeter every day out of the roots of them-
     selves, than it sprouts fresh and sweet continually out of itself.)
Toward the fluid and attaching character exudes the sweat of the love of young and old,   110
From it falls distill'd the charm that mocks beauty and attainments,
Toward it heaves the shuddering longing ache of contact.

9

Allons! whoever you are come travel with me!
Traveling with me you find what never tires.

The earth never tires,
The earth is rude, silent, incomprehensible at first, Nature is rude and incomprehensible at first,
Be not discouraged, keep on, there are divine things well envelop'd,
I swear to you there are divine things more beautiful than words can tell.

Allons! we must not stop here,   120
However sweet these laid-up stores, however convenient this dwelling we cannot remain here,

However shelter'd this port and however calm these waters we must not anchor here,
However welcome the hospitality that surrounds us we are permitted to receive it but a little
  while.

10

Allons! the inducements shall be greater,
We will sail pathless and wild seas,
We will go where winds blow, waves dash, and the Yankee clipper speeds by under full sail.

Allons! with power, liberty, the earth, the elements,
Health, defiance, gayety, self-esteem, curiosity;
Allons! from all formules!
From your formules, O bat-eyed and materialistic priests.

The stale cadaver blocks up the passage—the burial waits no longer.

Allons! yet take warning!
He traveling with me needs the best blood, thews, endurance,
None may come to the trial till he or she bring courage and health,
Come not here if you have already spent the best of yourself,
Only those may come who come in sweet and determin'd bodies,
No diseas'd person, no rum-drinker or venereal taint is permitted here.

(I and mine do not convince by arguments, similes, rhymes,
We convince by our presence.)

11

Listen! I will be honest with you,
I do not offer the old smooth prizes, but offer rough new prizes,
These are the days that must happen to you:
You shall not heap up what is call'd riches,
You shall scatter with lavish hand all that you earn or achieve,
You but arrive at the city to which you were destin'd, you hardly settle yourself to satisfaction
  before you are call'd by an irresistible call to depart,
You shall be treated to the ironical smiles and mockings of those who remain behind you,
What beckonings of love you receive you shall only answer with passionate kisses of parting,
You shall not allow the hold of those who spread their reach'd hands toward you.

12

Allons! after the great Companions, and to belong to them!
They too are on the road—they are the swift and majestic men—they are the greatest women, 150
Enjoyers of calms of seas and storms of seas,
Sailors of many a ship, walkers of many a mile of land,
Habituès of many distant countries, habituès of far-distant dwellings,
Trusters of men and women, observers of cities, solitary toilers,
Pausers and contemplators of tufts, blossoms, shells of the shore,
Dancers at wedding-dances, kissers of brides, tender helpers of children, bearers of children,
Soldiers of revolts, standers by gaping graves, lowerers-down of coffins,
Journeyers over consecutive seasons, over the years, the curious years each emerging from that
  which preceded it,
Journeyers as with companions, namely their own diverse phases,
Forth-steppers from the latent unrealized baby-days,
Journeyers gayly with their own youth, journeyers with their bearded and well-grain'd manhood,
Journeyers with their womanhood, ample, unsurpass'd, content,
Journeyers with their own sublime old age of manhood or womanhood,
Old age, calm, expanded, broad with the haughty breadth of the universe,
Old age, flowing free with the delicious near-by freedom of death.

13

Allons! to that which is endless as it was beginningless,
To undergo much, tramps of days, rests of nights,
To merge all in the travel they tend to, and the days and nights they tend to,
Again to merge them in the start of superior journeys,
To see nothing anywhere but what you may reach it and pass it,
To conceive no time, however distant, but what you may reach it and pass it,
To look up or down no road but it stretches and waits for you, however long but it stretches
     and waits for you,
To see no being, not God's or any, but you also go thither,
To see no possession but you may possess it, enjoying all without labor or purchase, abstract-
     ing the feast yet not abstracting one particle of it,
To take the best of the farmer's farm and the rich man's elegant villa, and the chaste blessings
     of the well-married couple, and the fruits of orchards and flowers of gardens,
To take to your use out of the compact cities as you pass through,
To carry buildings and streets with you afterward wherever you go,
To gather the minds of men out of their brains as you encounter them, to gather the love out
     of their hearts,
To take your lovers on the road with you, for all that you leave them behind you,
To know the universe itself as a road, as many roads, as roads for traveling souls.

All parts away for the progress of souls,
All religion, all solid things, arts, governments—all that was or is apparent upon this globe or
     any globe, falls into niches and corners before the procession of souls along the grand roads
     of the universe.

Of the progress of the souls of men and women along the grand roads of the universe, all other
     progress is the needed emblem and sustenance.

Forever alive, forever forward,
Stately, solemn, sad, withdrawn, baffled, mad, turbulent, feeble, dissatisfied,
Desperate, proud, fond, sick, accepted by men, rejected by men,
They go! they go! I know that they go, but I know not where they go,
But I know that they go toward the best—toward something great.

Whoever you are, come forth! or man or woman come forth!
You must not stay sleeping and dallying there in the house, though you built it, or though it
     has been built for you.

Out of the dark confinement! out from behind the screen!
It is useless to protest, I know all and expose it.

Behold through you as bad as the rest,
Through the laughter, dancing, dining, supping, of people,
Inside of dresses and ornaments, inside of those wash'd and trimm'd faces,
Behold a secret silent loathing and despair.

No husband, no wife, no friend, trusted to hear the confession,
Another self, a duplicate of every one, skulking and hiding it goes,
Formless and wordless through the streets of the cities, polite and bland in the parlors,
In the cars of railroads, in steamboats, in the public assembly,
Home to the houses of men and women, at the table, in the bedroom, everywhere,
Smartly attired, countenance smiling, form upright, death under the breast-bones, hell under
     the skull-bones,
Under the broadcloth and gloves, under the ribbons and artificial flowers,
Keeping fair with the customs, speaking not a syllable of itself,
Speaking of any thing else but never of itself.

14

Allons! through struggles and wars!
The goal that was named cannot be countermanded.

Have the past struggles succeeded?
What has succeeded? yourself? your nation? Nature?
Now understand me well—it is provided in the essence of things that from any fruition of success, no matter what, shall come forth something to make a greater struggle necessary.   210

My call is the call of battle, I nourish active rebellion,
He going with me must go well arm'd,
He going with me goes often with spare diet, poverty, angry enemies, desertions.

15

Allons! the road is before us!
It is safe—I have tried it—my own feet have tried it well—be not detain'd!
Let the paper remain on the desk unwritten, and the book on the shelf unopen'd!
Let the tools remain in the workshop! let the money remain unearn'd!
Let the school stand! mind not the cry of the teacher!
Let the preacher preach in his pulpit! let the lawyer plead in the court, and the judge expound the law.

Camerado, I give you my hand!
I give you my love more precious than money,
I give you myself before preaching or law;
Will you give me yourself? will you come travel with me?
Shall we stick by each other as long as we live?   220

1856, 1881

OUT OF THE CRADLE ENDLESSLY ROCKING

Out of the cradle endlessly rocking,
Out of the mocking-bird's throat, the musical shuttle,
Out of the Ninth-month midnight,
Over the sterile sands and the fields beyond, where the child leaving his bed wander'd alone,
    bareheaded, barefoot,
Down from the shower'd halo,
Up from the mystic play of shadows twining and twisting as if they were alive,
Out from the patches of briers and blackberries,
From the memories of the bird that chanted to me,
From your memories sad brother, from the fitful risings and fallings I heard,
From under that yellow half-moon late-risen and swollen as if with tears,   10
From those beginning notes of yearning and love there in the mist,
From the thousand responses of my heart never to cease,
From the myriad thence-arous'd words,
From the word stronger and more delicious than any,
From such as now they start the scene revisiting,
As a flock, twittering, rising, or overhead passing,
Borne hither, ere all eludes me, hurriedly,
A man, yet by these tears a little boy again,
Throwing myself on the sand, confronting the waves,
I, chanter of pains and joys, uniter of here and hereafter,   20
Taking all hints to use them, but swiftly leaping beyond them,
A reminiscence sing.

Once Paumanok,
When the lilac-scent was in the air and Fifth-month grass was growing,
Up this seashore in some briers,

Two feather'd guests from Alabama, two together,
And their nest, and four light-green eggs spotted with brown,
And every day the he-bird to and fro near at hand,
And every day the she-bird crouch'd on her nest, silent, with bright eyes,
And every day I, a curious boy, never too close, never disturbing them,   30
Cautiously peering, absorbing, translating.

Shine! shine! shine!
Pour down your warmth, great sun!
While we bask, we two together.

Two together!
Winds blow south, or winds blow north,
Day come white, or night come black,
Home, or rivers and mountains from home,
Singing all time, minding no time,   40
While we two keep together.

Till of a sudden,
May-be kill'd, unknown to her mate,
One forenoon that she-bird crouch'd not on the nest,
Nor return'd that afternoon, nor the next,
Nor ever appear'd again.

And thenceforward all summer in the sound of the sea,
And at night under the full of the moon in calmer weather,
Over the hoarse surging of the sea,
Or flitting from brier to brier by day,
I saw, I heard at intervals the remaining one, the he-bird,   50
The solitary guest from Alabama.

Blow! blow! blow!
Blow up sea-winds along Paumanok's shore;
I wait and I wait till you blow my mate to me.

Yes, when the stars glisten'd,
All night long on the prong of a moss-scallop'd stake,
Down almost amid the slapping waves,
Sat the lone singer wonderful causing tears.

He call'd on his mate,
He pour'd forth the meanings which I of all men know.   60

Yes my brother I know,
The rest might not, but I have treasur'd every note,
For more than once dimly down to the beach gliding,
Silent, avoiding the moonbeams, blending myself with the shadows,
Recalling now the obscure shapes, the echoes, the sounds and sights after their sorts,
The white arms out in the breakers tirelessly tossing,
I, with bare feet, a child, the wind wafting my hair,
Listen'd long and long.

Listen'd to keep, to sing, now translating the notes,
Following you my brother.   70

Soothe! soothe! soothe!
Close on its wave soothes the wave behind,
And again another behind embracing and lapping, every one close,
But my love soothes not me, not me.

Low hangs the moon, it rose late,
It is lagging—O I think it is heavy with love, with love.

O madly the sea pushes upon the land,
With love, with love.

O night! do I not see my love fluttering out among the breakers?
What is that little black thing I see there in the white?   80

Loud! loud! loud!
Loud I call to you, my love!
High and clear, I shoot my voice over the waves,
Surely you must know who is here, is here,
You must know who I am, my love.

Low-hanging moon!
What is that dusky spot in your brown yellow?
O it is the shape, the shape of my mate!
O moon do not keep her from me any longer.

Land! land! O land!
Whichever way I turn, O I think you could give me my mate back again if you only would,   90
For I am almost sure I see her dimly whichever way I look.

O rising stars!
Perhaps the one I want so much will rise, will rise with one of you.

O throat! O trembling throat!
Sound clearer through the atmosphere!
Pierce the woods, the earth,
Somewhere listening to catch you must be the one I want.

Shake out carols!
Solitary here, the night's carols!   100
Carols of lonesome love! death's carols!
Carols under that lagging, yellow, waning moon!
O under that moon where she droops almost down into the sea!
O reckless despairing carols.

But soft, sink low!
Soft! let me just murmur,
And do you wait a moment you husky-nois'd sea,
For somewhere I believe I heard my mate responding to me,
So faint, I must be still, be still to listen,
But not altogether still, for then she might not come immediately to me.   110

Hither my love!
Here I am! here!
With this just-sustain'd note I announce myself to you,
This gentle call is for you my love, for you.

Do not be decoy'd elsewhere,
That is the whistle of the wind, it is not my voice,
That is the fluttering, the fluttering of the spray,
Those are the shadows of leaves.

O darkness! O in vain!
O I am very sick and sorrowful.   120

O brown halo in the sky near the moon, drooping upon the sea!
O troubled reflection in the sea!
O throat! O throbbing heart!
And I singing uselessly, uselessly all the night.

O past! O happy life! O songs of joy!
In the air, in the woods, over fields,
Loved! loved! loved! loved! loved!
But my mate no more, no more with me!
We two together no more.

The aria sinking,
All else continuing, the stars shining, 130
The winds blowing, the notes of the bird continuous echoing,
With angry moans the fierce old mother incessantly moaning,
On the sands of Paumanok's shore gray and rustling,
The yellow half-moon enlarged, sagging down, drooping, the face of the sea almost touching,
The boy ecstatic, with his bare feet the waves, with his hair the atmosphere dallying,
The love in the heart long pent, now loose, now at last tumultuously bursting,
The aria's meaning, the ears, the soul, swiftly depositing,
The strange tears down the cheeks coursing,
The colloquy there, the trio, each uttering, 140
The undertone, the savage old mother incessantly crying,
To the boy's soul's questions sullenly timing, some drown'd secret hissing,
To the outsetting bard.

Demon or bird! (said the boy's soul,)
Is it indeed toward your mate you sing? or is it really to me?
For I, that was a child, my tongue's use sleeping, now I have heard you,
Now in a moment I know what I am for, I awake,
And already a thousand singers, a thousand songs, clearer, louder and more sorrowful than yours,
A thousand warbling echoes have started to life within me, never to die.

O you singer solitary, singing by yourself, projecting me, 150
O solitary me listening, never more shall I cease perpetuating you,
Never more shall I escape, never more the reverberations,
Never more the cries of unsatisfied love be absent from me,
Never again leave me to be the peaceful child I was before what there in the night,
By the sea under the yellow and sagging moon,
The messenger there arous'd, the fire, the sweet hell within,
The unknown want, the destiny of me.

O give me the clew! (it lurks in the night here somewhere,)
O if I am to have so much, let me have more!

A word then, (for I will conquer it,) 160
The word final, superior to all,
Subtle, sent up—what is it?—I listen;
Are you whispering it, and have been all the time, you sea-waves?
Is that it from your liquid rims and wet sands?

Whereto answering, the sea,
Delaying not, hurrying not,
Whisper'd me through the night, and very plainly before daybreak,
Lisp'd to me the low and delicious word death,
And again death, death, death, death,
Hissing melodious, neither like the bird nor like my arous'd child's heart, 170
But edging near as privately for me rustling at my feet,

Creeping thence steadily up to my ears and laving me softly all over,
Death, death, death, death, death.

Which I do not forget,
But fuse the song of my dusky demon and brother,
That he sang to me in the moonlight on Paumanok's gray beach,
With the thousand responsive songs at random,
My own songs awaked from that hour,
And with them the key, the word up from the waves,
The word of the sweetest song and all songs,   180
That strong and delicious word which, creeping to my feet,
(Or like some old crone rocking the cradle, swathed in sweet garments, bending aside,)
The sea whisper'd me.

1859, 1881

ME IMPERTURBE

Me imperturbe, standing at ease in Nature,
Master of all or mistress of all, aplomb in the midst of irrational things,
Imbued as they, passive, receptive, silent as they,
Finding my occupation, poverty, notoriety, foibles, crimes, less important than I thought,
Me toward the Mexican Sea, or in the Mannahatta or the Tennessee, or far north or inland,
A river man, or a man of the woods or of any farm-life of these States or of the coast, or the
    lakes or Kanada,
Me wherever my life is lived, O to be self-balanced for contingencies,
To confront night, storms, hunger, ridicule, accidents, rebuffs, as the trees and animals do.

1860, 1881

POETS TO COME

Poets to come! orators, singers, musicians to come!
Not to-day is to justify me and answer what I am for,
But you, a new brood, native, athletic, continental, greater than before known,
Arouse! for you must justify me.

I myself but write one or two indicative words for the future,
I but advance a moment only to wheel and hurry back in the darkness.

I am a man who, sauntering along without fully stopping, turns a casual look upon you and
    then averts his face,
Leaving it to you to prove and define it,
Expecting the main things from you.

1860, 1867

FOR YOU O DEMOCRACY

Come, I will make the continent indissoluble,
I will make the most splendid race the sun ever yet shone upon,
I will make divine magnetic lands,
    With the love of comrades,
        With the life-long love of comrades.

I will plant companionship thick as trees along all the rivers of America, and along the shores
    of the great lakes, and all over the prairies,
I will make inseparable cities with their arms about each other's necks,
    By the love of comrades,
        By the manly love of comrades,

For you these from me, O Democracy, to serve you ma femme!
For you, for you I am trilling these songs.

1860, 1881

RECORDERS AGES HENCE

Recorders ages hence,
Come, I will take you down underneath this impassive exterior, I will tell you what to say of me,
Publish my name and hang up my picture as that of the tenderest lover,
The friend the lover's portrait, of whom his friend his lover was fondest,
Who was not proud of his songs, but of the measureless ocean of love within him, and freely
    pour'd it forth,
Who often walk'd lonesome walks thinking of his dear friends, his lovers,
Who pensive away from one he lov'd often lay sleepless and dissatisfied at night,
Who knew too well the sick, sick dread lest the one he lov'd might secretly be indifferent to him,
Whose happiest days were far away through fields, in woods, on hills, he and another wandering
    hand in hand, they twain apart from other men,
Who oft as he saunter'd the streets curv'd with his arm the shoulder of his friend, while the
    arm of his friend rested upon him also.   10

1860, 1867

FULL OF LIFE NOW

Full of life now, compact, visible,
I, forty years old the eighty-third year of the States,
To one a century hence or any number of centuries hence,
To you yet unborn these, seeking you.

When you read these I that was visible am become invisible,
Now it is you, compact, visible, realizing my poems, seeking me,
Fancying how happy you were if I could be with you and become your comrade;
Be it as if I were with you. (Be not too certain but I am now with you.)

1860, 1871

MYSELF AND MINE

Myself and mine gymnastic ever,
To stand the cold or heat, to make good aim with a gun, to sail a boat, to manage horses, to
    beget superb children,
To speak readily and clearly, to feel at home among common people,
And to hold our own in terrible positions on land and sea.

Not for an embroiderer,
(There will always be plenty of embroiderers, I welcome them also,)
But for the fibre of things and for inherent men and women.

Not to chisel ornaments,
But to chisel with free stroke the heads and limbs of plenteous supreme Gods, that the States
    may realize them walking and talking.

Let me have my own way,
Let others promulge the laws, I will make no account of the laws,   10
Let others praise eminent men and hold up peace, I hold up agitation and conflict,
I praise no eminent man, I rebuke to his face the one that was thought most worthy.

(Who are you? and what are you secretly guilty of all your life?
Will you turn aside all your life? will you grub and chatter all your life?
And who are you, blabbing by rote, years, pages, languages, reminiscences,
Unwitting to-day that you do not know how to speak properly a single word?)

Let others finish specimens, I never finish specimens,
I start them by exhaustless laws as Nature does, fresh and modern continually.

I give nothing as duties,   20
What others give as duties I give as living impulses,
(Shall I give the heart's action as a duty?)

Let others dispose of questions, I dispose of nothing, I arouse unanswerable questions,
Who are they I see and touch, and what about them?
What about these likes of myself that draw me so close by tender directions and indirections?

I call to the world to distrust the accounts of my friends, but listen to my enemies, as I myself do,
I charge you forever reject those who would expound me, for I cannot expound myself,
I charge that there be no theory or school founded out of me,
I charge you to leave all free, as I have left all free.

After me, vista!   30
O I see life is not short, but immeasurably long,
I henceforth tread the world chaste, temperate, an early riser, a steady grower,
Every hour the semen of centuries, and still of centuries.

I must follow up these continual lessons of the air, water, earth,
I perceive I have no time to lose.   1860, 1881

PIONEERS! O PIONEERS!

Come my tan-faced children,
Follow well in order, get your weapons ready,
Have you your pistols? have you your sharp-edged axes?
    Pioneers! O pioneers!

For we cannot tarry here,
We must march my darlings, we must bear the brunt of danger,
We the youthful sinewy races, all the rest on us depend,
    Pioneers! O pioneers!

O you youths, Western youths,
So impatient, full of action, full of manly pride and friendship,
Plain I see you Western youths, see you tramping with the foremost,   10
    Pioneers! O pioneers!

Have the elder races halted?
Do they droop and end their lesson, wearied over there beyond the seas?
We take up the task eternal, and the burden and the lesson,
    Pioneers! O pioneers!

All the past we leave behind,
We debouch upon a newer mightier world, varied world,
Fresh and strong the world we seize, world of labor and the march,
    Pioneers! O pioneers!   20

We detachments steady throwing,
Down the edges, through the passes, up the mountains steep,
Conquering, holding, daring, venturing as we go the unknown ways,
    Pioneers! O pioneers!

We primeval forests felling,
We the rivers stemming, vexing we and piercing deep the mines within,
We the surface broad surveying, we the virgin soil upheaving,
    Pioneers! O pioneers!

Colorado men are we,
From the peaks gigantic, from the great sierras and the high plateaus,   30
From the mine and from the gully, from the hunting trail we come,
Pioneers! O pioneers!

From Nebraska, from Arkansas,
Central inland race are we, from Missouri, with the continental blood interven'd,
All the hands of comrades clasping, all the Southern, all the Northern,
Pioneers! O pioneers!

O resistless restless race!
O beloved race in all! O my breast aches with tender love for all!
O I mourn and yet exult, I am rapt with love for all,
Pioneers! O pioneers!   40

Raise the mighty mother mistress,
Waving high the delicate mistress, over all the starry mistress, (bend your heads all,)
Raise the fang'd and warlike mistress, stern, impassive, weapon'd mistress,
Pioneers! O pioneers!

See my children, resolute children,
By those swarms upon our rear we must never yield or falter,
Ages back in ghostly millions frowning there behind us urging,
Pioneers! O pioneers!

On and on the compact ranks,
With accessions ever waiting, with the places of the dead quickly fill'd,   50
Through the battle, through defeat, moving yet and never stopping,
Pioneers! O pioneers!

O to die advancing on!
Are there some of us to droop and die? has the hour come?
Then upon the march we fittest die, soon and sure the gap is fill'd,
Pioneers! O pioneers!

All the pulses of the world,
Falling in they beat for us, with the Western movement beat,
Holding single or together, steady moving to the front, all for us,
Pioneers! O pioneers!   60

Life's involv'd and varied pageants,
All the forms and shows, all the workmen at their work,
All the seamen and the landsmen, all the masters with their slaves,
Pioneers! O pioneers!

All the hapless silent lovers,
All the prisoners in the prisons, all the righteous and the wicked,
All the joyous, all the sorrowing, all the living, all the dying,
Pioneers! O pioneers!

I too with my soul and body,
We, a curious trio, picking, wandering on our way,   70
Through these shores amid the shadows, with the apparitions pressing,
Pioneers! O pioneers!

Lo, the darting bowling orb!
Lo, the brother orbs around, all the clustering suns and planets,
All the dazzling days, all the mystic nights with dreams,
Pioneers! O pioneers!

These are of us, they are with us,
All for primal needed work, while the followers there in embryo wait behind,
We to-day's procession heading, we the route for travel clearing,
      Pioneers! O pioneers!   80

O you daughters of the West!
O you young and elder daughters! O you mothers and you wives!
Never must you be divided, in our ranks you move united,
      Pioneers! O pioneers!

Minstrels latent on the prairies!
(Shrouded bards of other lands, you may rest, you have done your work),
Soon I hear you coming warbling, soon you rise and tramp amid us,
      Pioneers! O pioneers!

Not for delectations sweet,
Not the cushion and the slipper, not the peaceful and the studious,   90
Not the riches safe and palling, not for us the tame enjoyment,
      Pioneers! O pioneers!

Do the feasters gluttonous feast?
Do the corpulent sleepers sleep? Have they lock'd and bolted doors?
Still be ours the diet hard, and the blanket on the ground,
      Pioneers! O pioneers!

Has the night descended?
Was the road of late so toilsome? did we stop discouraged nodding on our way?
Yet a passing hour I yield you in your tracks to pause oblivious,
      Pioneers! O pioneers!   100

Till with sound of trumpet,
Far, far off the daybreak call—hark! how loud and clear I hear it wind,
Swift! to the head of the army!—swift! spring to your places,
      Pioneers! O pioneers!

                   1865, 1881

WHEN I HEARD THE LEARN'D ASTRONOMER

When I heard the learn'd astronomer,
When the proofs, the figures, were ranged in columns before me,
When I was shown the charts and diagrams, to add, divide, and measure them,
When I sitting heard the astronomer where he lectured with much applause in the lecture-room,
How soon unaccountable I became tired and sick,
Till rising and gliding out I wander'd off by myself,
In the mystical moist night-air, and from time to time,
Look'd up in perfect silence at the stars.

                   1865, 1867

DRUM-TAPS

FIRST O SONGS FOR A PRELUDE

First O songs for a prelude,
Lightly strike on the stretch'd tympanum pride and joy in my city,
How she led the rest to arms, how she gave the cue,
How at once with lithe limbs unwaiting a moment she sprang,
(O superb! O Manhattan, my own, my peerless!
O strongest you in the hour of danger, in crisis! O truer than steel!)

How you sprang—how you threw off the costumes of peace with indifferent hand,
How your soft opera-music changed, and the drum and fife were heard in their stead,
How you led to the war, (that shall serve for our prelude, songs of soldiers,)
How Manhattan drum-taps led.   10

Forty years had I in my city seen soldiers parading,
Forty years as a pageant, till unawares the lady of this teeming and turbulent city,
Sleepless amid her ships, her houses, her incalculable wealth,
With her million children around her, suddenly,
At dead of night, at news from the south,
Incens'd struck with clench'd hand the pavement.

A shock electric, the night sustain'd it,
Till with ominous hum our hive at daybreak pour'd out its myriads.

From the houses then and the workshops, and through all the doorways,
Leapt they tumultuous, and lo! Manhattan arming.   20

To the drum-taps prompt,
The young men falling in and arming,
The mechanics arming, (the trowel, the jack-plane, the blacksmith's hammer, tost aside with
    precipitation,)
The lawyer leaving his office and arming, the judge leaving the court,
The driver deserting his wagon in the street, jumping down, throwing the reins abruptly down
    on the horses' backs,
The salesman leaving the store, the boss, book-keeper, porter, all leaving;
Squads gather everywhere by common consent and arm,
The new recruits, even boys, the old men show them how to wear their accoutrements, they
    buckle the straps carefully,
Outdoors arming, indoors arming, the flash of the musket-barrels,
The white tents cluster in camps, the arm'd sentries around, the sunrise cannon and again at
    sunset,   30
Arm'd regiments arrive every day, pass through the city, and embark from the wharves,
(How good they look as they tramp down to the river, sweaty, with their guns on their shoulders!
How I love them! how I could hug them, with their brown faces and their clothes and knap-
    sacks cover'd with dust!)
The blood of the city up—arm'd! arm'd! the cry everywhere,
The flags flung out from the steeples of churches and from all the public buildings and stores,
The tearful parting, the mother kisses her son, the son kisses his mother,
(Loth is the mother to part, yet not a word does she speak to detain him,)
The tumultuous escort, the ranks of policemen preceding, clearing the way,
The unpent enthusiasm, the wild cheers of the crowd for their favorites,
The artillery, the silent cannons bright as gold, drawn along, rumble lightly over the stones,
(Silent cannons, soon to cease your silence,   41
Soon unlimber'd to begin the red business;)
All the mutter of preparation, all the determin'd arming,
The hospital service, the lint, bandages and medicines,
The women volunteering for nurses, the work begun for in earnest, no mere parade now;
War! an arm'd race is advancing! the welcome for battle, no turning away;
War! be it weeks, months, or years, an arm'd race is advancing to welcome it.

Mannahatta a-march—and it's O to sing it well!
It's O for a manly life in the camp.

And the sturdy artillery,
The guns bright as gold, the work for giants, to serve well the guns,   50
Unlimber them! (no more as the past forty years for salutes or courtesies merely,
Put in something now besides powder and wadding.)

And you lady of ships, you Mannahatta,
Old matron of this proud, friendly, turbulent city,
Often in peace and wealth you were pensive or covertly frown'd amid all your children,
But now you smile with joy exulting old Mannahatta.

1865, 1867

GIVE ME THE SPLENDID SILENT SUN

1

Give me the splendid silent sun with all his beams full-dazzling,
Give me juicy autumnal fruit ripe and red from the orchard,
Give me a field where the unmow'd grass grows,
Give me an arbor, give me the trellis'd grape,
Give me fresh corn and wheat, give me serene-moving animals teaching content,
Give me nights perfectly quiet as on high plateaus west of the Mississippi, and I looking up
    at the stars,
Give me odorous at sunrise a garden of beautiful flowers where I can walk undisturb'd,
Give me for marriage a sweet-breath'd woman of whom I should never tire,
Give me a perfect child, give me away aside from the noise of the world a rural domestic life,
Give me to warble spontaneous songs recluse by myself, for my own ears only,   10
Give me solitude, give me Nature, give me again O Nature your primal sanities!

These demanding to have them, (tired with ceaseless excitement, and rack'd by the war-strife,)
These to procure incessantly asking, rising in cries from my heart,
While yet incessantly asking still I adhere to my city,
Day upon day and year upon year O city, walking your streets,
Where you hold me enchain'd a certain time refusing to give me up,
Yet giving to make me glutted, enrich'd of soul, you give me forever faces;
(O I see what I sought to escape, confronting, reversing my cries,
I see my own soul trampling down what it ask'd for.)

2

Keep you splendid silent sun   20
Keep your woods O Nature, and the quiet places by the woods,
Keep your fields of clover and timothy, and your corn-fields and orchards,
Keep the blossoming buckwheat fields where the Ninth-month bees hum;
Give me faces and streets—give me these phantoms incessant and endless along the trottoirs!
Give me interminable eyes—give me women—give me comrades and lovers by the thousand!
Let me see new ones every day—let me hold new ones by the hand every day!
Give me such shows—give me the streets of Manhattan!
Give me Broadway, with the soldiers marching—give me the sound of the trumpets and drums!
(The soldiers in companies or regiments—some starting away, flush'd and reckless,
Some, their time up, returning with thinn'd ranks, young, yet very old, worn, marching, notic-
    ing nothing;)   30
Give me the shores and wharves heavy-fringed with black ships!
O such for me! O an intense life, full to repletion and varied!
The life of the theatre, bar-room, huge hotel, for me!
The saloon of the steamer! the crowded excursion for me! the torchlight procession!
The dense brigade bound for the war, with high piled military wagons following;
People, endless, streaming, with strong voices, passions, pageants,
Manhattan streets with their powerful throbs, with beating drums as now,
The endless and noisy chorus, the rustle and clank of muskets, (even the sight of the wounded,)
Manhattan crowds, with their turbulent musical chorus!
Manhattan faces and eyes forever for me.   40

1865, 1867

DIRGE FOR TWO VETERANS

The last sunbeam
Lightly falls from the finish'd Sabbath,
On the pavement here, and there beyond it is looking,
  Down a new-made double grave.

Lo, the moon ascending,
Up from the east the silvery round moon,
Beautiful over the house-tops, ghastly, phantom moon,
  Immense and silent moon.

I see a sad procession,
And I hear the sound of coming full-key'd bugles,   10
All the channels of the city streets they're flooding,
  As with voices and with tears.

I hear the great drums pounding,
And the small drums steady whirring,
And every blow of the great convulsive drums,
  Strikes me through and through.

For the son is brought with the father,
(In the foremost ranks of the fierce assault they fell,
Two veterans son and father dropt together,
  And the double grave awaits them.)   20

Now nearer blow the bugles,
And the drums strike more convulsive,
And the daylight o'er the pavement quite has faded,
  And the strong dead-march enwraps me.

In the eastern sky up-buoying,
The sorrowful vast phantom moves illumin'd,
('Tis some mother's large transparent face,
  In heaven brighter growing.)

O strong dead-march you please me!   30
O moon immense with your silvery face you soothe me!
O my soldiers twain! O my veterans passing to burial!
  What I have I also give you.

The moon gives you light,
And the bugles and the drums give you music,
And my heart, O my soldiers, my veterans,
  My heart gives you love.

                                        1865, 1881

NOT YOUTH PERTAINS TO ME

Not youth pertains to me,
Nor delicatesse, I cannot beguile the time with talk,
Awkward in the parlor, neither a dancer nor elegant,
In the learn'd coterie sitting constrain'd and still, for learning inures not to me,
Beauty, knowledge, inure not to me—yet there are two or three things inure to me,
I have nourish'd the wounded and sooth'd many a dying soldier,
And at intervals waiting or in the midst of camp,
Composed these songs.

                                        1865, 1871

WHEN LILACS LAST IN THE DOORYARD BLOOM'D

1

When lilacs last in the dooryard bloom'd,
And the great star early droop'd in the western sky in the night,
I mourn'd, and yet shall mourn with ever-returning spring.

Ever-returning spring, trinity sure to me you bring,
Lilac blooming perennial and drooping star in the west,
And thought of him I love.

2

O powerful western fallen star!
O shades of night—O moody, tearful night!
O great star disappear'd—O the black murk that hides the star!
O cruel hands that hold me powerless—O helpless soul of me!   10
O harsh surrounding cloud that will not free my soul.

3

In the dooryard fronting an old farm-house near the white-wash'd palings,
Stands the lilac-bush tall-growing with heart-shaped leaves of rich green,
With many a pointed blossom rising delicate, with the perfume strong I love,
With every leaf a miracle—and from this bush in the dooryard,
With delicate-color'd blossoms and heart-shaped leaves of rich green,
A sprig with its flower I break.

4

In the swamp in secluded recesses,
A shy and hidden bird is warbling a song.

Solitary the thrush,
The hermit withdrawn to himself, avoiding the settlements,   20
Sings by himself a song.

Song of the bleeding throat,
Death's outlet song of life, (for well dear brother I know,
If thou wast not granted to sing thou would'st surely die.)

5

Over the breast of the spring, the land, amid cities,
Amid lanes and through old woods, where lately the violets peep'd from the ground, spotting the gray debris,
Amid the grass in the fields each side of the lanes, passing the endless grass,
Passing the yellow-spear'd wheat, every grain from its shroud in the dark-brown fields up-risen,
Passing the apple-tree blows of white and pink in the orchards,   30
Carrying a corpse to where it shall rest in the grave,
Night and day journeys a coffin.

6

Coffin that passes through lanes and streets,
Through day and night with the great cloud darkening the land,
With the pomp of the inloop'd flags with the cities draped in black,
With the show of the States themselves as of crape-veil'd women standing,
With processions long and winding and the flambeaus of the night,
With the countless torches lit, with the silent sea of faces and the unbared heads

With the waiting depot, the arriving coffin, and the sombre faces,
With dirges through the night, with the thousand voices rising strong and solemn,   40
With all the mournful voices of the dirges pour'd around the coffin,
The dim-lit churches and the shuddering organs—where amid these you journey,
With the tolling tolling bells' perpetual clang,
Here, coffin that slowly passes,
I give you my sprig of lilac.

7

(Nor for you, for one alone,
Blossoms and branches green to coffins all I bring,
For fresh as the morning, thus would I chant a song for you O sane and sacred death.

All over bouquets of roses,
O death, I cover you over with roses and early lilies,   50
But mostly and now the lilac that blooms the first,
Copious I break, I break the sprigs from the bushes,
With loaded arms I come, pouring for you,
For you and the coffins all of you O death.)

8

O western orb sailing the heaven,
Now I know what you must have meant as a month since I walk'd,
As I walk'd in silence the transparent shadowy night,
As I saw you had something to tell as you bent to me night after night,
As you droop'd from the sky low down as if to my side, (while the other stars all look'd on,)
As we wander'd together the solemn night, (for something I know not what kept me from sleep,)
As the night advanced, and I saw on the rim of the west how full you were of woe,   61
As I stood on the rising ground in the breeze in the cool transparent night,
As I watch'd where you pass'd and was lost in the netherward black of the night,
As my soul in its trouble dissatisfied sank, as where you sad orb,
Concluded, dropt in the night, and was gone.

9

Sing on there in the swamp,
O singer bashful and tender, I hear your notes, I hear your call,
I hear, I come presently, I understand you,
But a moment I linger, for the lustrous star has detain'd me,
The star my departing comrade holds and detains me.   70

10

O how shall I warble myself for the dead one there I loved?
And how shall I deck my song for the large sweet soul that has gone?
And what shall my perfume be for the grave of him I love?

Sea-winds blown from east and west,
Blown from the Eastern sea and blown from the Western sea, till there on the prairies meeting,
These and with these and the breath of my chant,
I'll perfume the grave of him I love.

11

O what shall I hang on the chamber walls?
And what shall the pictures be that I hang on the walls,
To adorn the burial-house of him I love?   80

Pictures of growing spring and farms and homes,
With the Fourth-month eve at sundown, and the gray smoke lucid and bright,

With floods of the yellow gold of the gorgeous, indolent, sinking sun, burning, expanding the air,
With the fresh sweet herbage under foot, and the pale green leaves of the trees prolific,
In the distance the flowing glaze, the breast of the river, with a wind-dapple here and there,
With ranging hills on the banks, with many a line against the sky, and shadows,
And the city at hand with dwellings so dense, and stacks of chimneys,
And all the scenes of life and the workshops, and the workmen homeward returning.

12

Lo, body and soul—this land,
My own Manhattan with spires, and the sparkling and hurrying tides, and the ships,   90
The varied and ample land, the South and the North in the light, Ohio's shores and flashing Missouri,
And ever the far-spreading prairies cover'd with grass and corn.

Lo, the most excellent sun so calm and haughty,
The violet and purple morn with just-felt breezes,
The gentle soft-born measureless light,
The miracle spreading bathing all, the fulfill'd noon,
The coming eve delicious, the welcome night and the stars,
Over my cities shining all, enveloping man and land.

13

Sing on, sing on you gray-brown bird,
Sing from the swamps, the recesses, pour your chant from the bushes,   100
Limitless out of the dusk, out of the cedars and pines.

Sing on dearest brother, warble your reedy song,
Loud human song, with voice of uttermost woe.

O liquid and free and tender!
O wild and loose to my soul—O wondrous singer!
You only I hear—yet the star holds me, (but will soon depart,)
Yet the lilac with mastering odor holds me.

14

Now while I sat in the day and look'd forth,
In the close of the day with its light and the fields of spring, and the farmers preparing their crops,
In the large unconscious scenery of my land with its lakes and forests,   110
In the heavenly aerial beauty, (after the perturb'd winds and the storms,)
Under the arching heavens of the afternoon swift passing, and the voices of children and women,
The many-moving sea-tides, and I saw the ships how they sail'd,
And the summer approaching with richness, and the fields all busy with labor,
And the infinite separate houses, how they all went on, each with its meals and minutia of daily usages,
And the streets how their throbbings throbb'd, and the cities pent—lo, then and there,
Falling upon them all and among them all, enveloping me with the rest,
Appear'd the cloud, appear'd the long black trail,
And I knew death, its thought, and the sacred knowledge of death.

Then with the knowledge of death as walking one side of me,   120
And the thought of death close-walking the other side of me,
And I in the middle as with companions, and as holding the hands of companions,
I fled forth to the hiding receiving night that talks not,
Down to the shores of the water, the path by the swamp in the dimness,
To the solemn shadowy cedars and ghostly pines so still.

And the singer so shy to the rest receiv'd me,
The gray-brown bird I know receiv'd us comrades three,
And he sang the carol of death, and a verse for him I love.

From deep secluded recesses,
From the fragrant cedars and the ghostly pines so still,   130
Came the carol of the bird.

And the charm of the carol rapt me,
As I held as if by their hands my comrades in the night,
And the voice of my spirit tallied the song of the bird.

Come lovely and soothing death,
Undulate round the world, serenely arriving, arriving,
In the day, in the night, to all, to each,
Sooner or later delicate death.

Prais'd be the fathomless universe,
For life and joy, and for objects and knowledge curious,   140
And for love, sweet love—but praise! praise! praise!
For the sure-enwinding arms of cool-enfolding death.

Dark mother always gliding near with soft feet,
Have none chanted for thee a chant of fullest welcome?
Then I chant it for thee, I glorify thee above all,
I bring thee a song that when thou must indeed come, come unfalteringly.

Approach strong deliveress,
When it is so, when thou hast taken them I joyously sing the dead,
Lost in the loving floating ocean of thee,
Laved in the flood of thy bliss O death.   150

From me to thee glad serenades,
Dances for thee I propose saluting thee, adornments and feastings for thee,
And the sights of the open landscape and the high-spread sky are fitting,
And life and the fields, and the huge and thoughtful night.

The night in silence under many a star,
The ocean shore and the husky whispering wave whose voice I know,
And the soul turning to thee O vast and well-veil'd death,
And the body gratefully nestling close to thee.

Over the tree-tops I float thee a song,
Over the rising and sinking waves, over the myriad fields and the prairies wide,   160
Over the dense-pack'd cities all and the teeming wharves and ways,
I float this carol with joy, with joy to thee O death.

15

To the tally of my soul,
Loud and strong kept up the gray-brown bird,
With pure deliberate notes spreading filling the night.
Loud in the pines and cedars dim,
Clear in the freshness moist and the swamp-perfume,
And I with my comrades there in the night.

While my sight that was bound in my eyes unclosed,
As to long panoramas of visions.   170

And I saw askant the armies,
I saw as in noiseless dreams hundreds of battle-flags,
Borne through the smoke of the battles and pierc'd with missiles I saw them,
And carried hither and yon through the smoke, and torn and bloody,

And at last but a few shreds left on the staffs, (and all in silence,)
And the staffs all splinter'd and broken.

I saw battle-corpses, myriads of them,
And the white skeletons of young men, I saw them,
I saw the debris and debris of all the slain soldiers of the war,
But I saw they were not as was thought,   180
They themselves were fully at rest, they suffer'd not,
The living remain'd and suffer'd, the mother suffer'd,
And the wife and the child and the musing comrade suffer'd,
And the armies that remain'd suffer'd.

16

Passing the visions, passing the night,
Passing, unloosing the hold of my comrades' hands,
Passing the song of the hermit bird and the tallying song of my soul,
Victorious song, death's outlet song, yet varying ever-altering song,
As low and wailing, yet clear the notes, rising and falling, flooding the night,
Sadly sinking and fainting, as warning and warning, and yet again bursting with joy,   190
Covering the earth and filling the spread of the heaven,
As that powerful psalm in the night I heard from recesses,
Passing, I leave thee lilac with heart-shaped leaves,
I leave thee there in the dooryard, blooming, returning with spring.

I cease from my song for thee,
From my gaze on thee in the west, fronting the west, communing with thee,
O comrade lustrous with silver face in the night.

Yet each to keep and all, retrievements out of the night,
The song, the wondrous chant of the gray-brown bird,
And the tallying chant, the echo arous'd in my soul,   200
With the lustrous and drooping star with the countenance full of woe,
With the holders holding my hand nearing the call of the bird,
Comrades mine and I in the midst, and their memory ever to keep, for the dead I loved so well,
For the sweetest, wisest soul of all my days and lands—and this for his dear sake,
Lilac and star and bird twined with the chant of my soul,
There in the fragrant pines and the cedars dusk and dim.

1865–6, 1881

O CAPTAIN! MY CAPTAIN!

O Captain! my Captain! our fearful trip is done,
 The ship has weather'd every rack, the prize we sought is won,
 The port is near, the bells I hear, the people all exulting,
 While follow eyes the steady keel, the vessel grim and daring;
   But O heart! heart! heart!
    O the bleeding drops of red,
     Where on the deck my Captain lies,
      Fallen cold and dead.

O Captain! my Captain! rise up and hear the bells;
 Rise up—for you the flag is flung—for you the bugle trills,   10
 For you bouquets and ribbon'd wreaths—for you the shores a-crowding,
 For you they call, the swaying mass, their eager faces turning;
   Here Captain! dear father!
    This arm beneath your head!
     It is some dream that on the deck,
      You've fallen cold and dead.

My Captain does not answer, his lips are pale and still,
My father does not feel my arm, he has no pulse nor will,
The ship is anchor'd safe and sound, its voyage closed and done,
From fearful trip the victor ship comes in with object won: 20
      Exult O shores, and ring O bells!
        But I with mournful tread,
        Walk the deck my Captain lies,
        Fallen cold and dead.

                    1865, 1871

HUSH'D BE THE CAMPS TO-DAY
(May 4, 1865)

Hush'd be the camps to-day,
And soldiers let us drape our war-worn weapons,
And each with musing soul retire to celebrate
Our dear commander's death.

No more for him life's stormy conflicts,
Nor victory, nor defeat—no more time's dark events,
Charging like ceaseless clouds across the sky.

But sing poet in our name,
Sing of the love we bore him—because you—dweller in camps, know it truly.

As they invault the coffin there,   10
Sing—as they close the doors of earth upon him—one verse,
For the heavy hearts of soldiers.

                    1865, 1871

ONE'S-SELF I SING

One's-self I sing, a simple separate person,
Yet utter the word Democratic, the word En-Masse.

Of physiology from top to toe I sing,
Not physiognomy alone nor brain alone is worthy for the Muse, I say the Form complete is
    worthier far,
The Female equally with the Male I sing.

Of Life immense in passion, pulse, and power,
Cheerful, for freest action form'd under the laws divine,
The Modern Man I sing.

                    1867, 1871

SHUT NOT YOUR DOORS

Shut not your doors to me proud libraries,
For that which was lacking on all your well-fill'd shelves, yet needed most, I bring,
Forth from the war emerging, a book I have made,
The words of my book nothing, the drift of it everything,
A book separate, not link'd with the rest nor felt by the intellect,
But you ye untold latencies will thrill to every page.

                    1865, 1881

WHISPERS OF HEAVENLY DEATH

Whispers of heavenly death murmur'd I hear,
Labial gossip of night, sibilant chorals,
Footsteps gently ascending, mystical breezes wafted soft and low,

Ripples of unseen rivers, tides of a current flowing, forever flowing,
(Or is it the plashing of tears? the measureless waters of human tears?)

I see, just see skyward, great cloud-masses,
Mournfully slowly they roll, silently swelling and mixing,
With at times a half-dimm'd sadden'd far-off star,
Appearing and disappearing.

(Some parturition rather, some solemn immortal birth;   10
On the frontiers to eyes impenetrable,
Some soul is passing over.)

                                                                    1868, 1871

THE LAST INVOCATION

At the last, tenderly,
From the walls of the powerful fortress'd house,
From the clasp of the knitted locks, from the keep of the well-closed doors,
Let me be wafted.

Let me glide noiselessly forth;
With the key of softness unlock the locks—with a whisper,
Set ope the doors O soul.

Tenderly—be not impatient,
(Strong is your hold O mortal flesh,
Strong is your hold O love.)   10

                                                                         1868

ETHIOPIA SALUTING THE COLORS
(A Reminiscence of 1864)

Who are you dusky woman, so ancient hardly human,
With your woolly-white and turban'd head, and bare bony feet?
Why rising by the roadside here, do you the colors greet?

('Tis while our army lines Carolina's sand and pines,
Forth from thy hovel door thou Ethiopia com'st to me,
As under doughty Sherman I march toward the sea.)

Me master years a hundred since from my parents sunder'd,
A little child, they caught me as the savage beast is caught,
Then hither me across the sea the cruel slaver brought.

No further does she say, but lingering all the day,   10
Her high-borne turban'd head she wags, and rolls her darkling eye,
And courtesies to the regiments, the guidons moving by.

What is it fateful woman, so blear, hardly human?
Why wag your head with turban bound, yellow, red and green?
Are the things so strange and marvelous you see or have seen?

                                                                         1871

THE MYSTIC TRUMPETER

I

Hark, some wild trumpeter, some strange musician,
Hovering unseen in air, vibrates capricious tunes to-night.

I hear thee trumpeter, listening alert I catch thy notes,
Now pouring, whirling like a tempest round me,
Now low, subdued, now in the distance lost.

2

Come nearer bodiless one, haply in thee resounds
Some dead composer, haply thy pensive life
Was fill'd with aspirations high, unform'd ideals,
Waves, oceans musical, chaotically surging,
That now ecstatic ghost, close to me bending, thy cornet echoing, pealing,   10
Gives out to no one's ears but mine, but freely gives to mine,
That I may thee translate.

3

Blow trumpeter free and clear, I follow thee,
While at thy liquid prelude, glad, serene,
The fretting world, the streets, the noisy hours of day withdraw,
A holy calm descends like dew upon me,
I walk in cool refreshing night the walks of Paradise,
I scent the grass, the moist air and the roses;
Thy song expands my numb'd imbonded spirit, thou freest, launchest me,
Floating and basking upon heaven's lake.   20

4

Blow again trumpeter! and for my sensuous eyes,
Bring the old pageants, show the feudal world.

What charm thy music works! thou makest pass before me,
Ladies and cavaliers long dead, barons are in their castle halls, the troubadours are singing,
Arm'd knights go forth to redress wrongs, some in quest of the holy Graal;
I see the tournament, I see the contestants incased in heavy armor seated on stately champing
   horses,
I hear the shouts, the sounds of blows and smiting steel;
I see the Crusaders' tumultuous armies—hark, how the cymbals clang,
Lo, where the monks walk in advance, bearing the cross on high.

5

Blow again trumpeter! and for thy theme,   30
Take now the enclosing theme of all, the solvent and the setting,
Love, that is pulse of all, the sustenance and the pang,
The heart of man and woman all for love,
No other theme but love—knitting, enclosing, all-diffusing love.

O how the immortal phantoms crowd around me!
I see the vast alembic ever working, I see and know the flames that heat the world,
The glow, the blush, the beating hearts of lovers,
So blissful happy some, and some so silent, dark, and nigh to death;
Love, that is all the earth to lovers—love, that mocks time and space,
Love, that is day and night—love, that is sun and moon and stars,   40
Love, that is crimson, sumptuous, sick with perfume,
No other words but words of love, no other thought but love.

6

Blow again trumpeter—conjure war's alarums.

Swift to thy spell a shuddering hum like distant thunder rolls,
Lo, where the arm'd men hasten—lo, mid the clouds of dust the glint of bayonets,
I see the grime-faced cannoneers, I mark the rosy flash amid the smoke, I hear the cracking of
   the guns;

Nor war alone—thy fearful music-song, wild player, brings every sight of fear,
The deeds of ruthless brigands, rapine, murder—I hear the cries for help!
I see ships foundering at sea, I behold on deck and below deck the terrible tableaus.

7

O trumpeter, methinks I am myself the instrument thou playest,   50
Thou melt'st my heart, my brain—thou movest, drawest, changest them at will;
And now thy sullen notes send darkness through me,
Thou takest away all cheering light, all hope,
I see the enslaved, the overthrown, the hurt, the opprest of the whole earth,
I feel the measureless shame and humiliation of my race, it becomes all mine,
Mine too the revenges of humanity, the wrongs of ages, baffled feuds and hatreds,
Utter defeat upon me weighs—all lost—the foe victorious,
(Yet 'mid the ruins Pride colossal stands unshaken to the last,
Endurance, resolution to the last.)

8

Now trumpeter for thy close,   60
Vouchsafe a higher strain than any yet,
Sing to my soul, renew its languishing faith and hope,
Rouse up my slow belief, give me some vision of the future,
Give me for once its prophecy and joy.

O glad, exulting, culminating song!
A vigor more than earth's is in thy notes,
Marches of victory—man disenthrall'd—the conqueror at last,
Hymns to the universal God from universal man—all joy!
A reborn race appears—a perfect world, all joy!
Women and men in wisdom innocence and health—all joy!   70
Riotous laughing bacchanals fill'd with joy!
War, sorrow, suffering gone—the rank earth purged—nothing but joy left!
The ocean fill'd with joy—the atmosphere all joy!
Joy! joy! in freedom, worship, love! joy in the ecstasy of life!
Enough to merely be! enough to breathe!
Joy! joy! all over joy!

1872, 1881

From DEMOCRATIC VISTAS
(1871)

First, let us see what we can make out of a brief general, sentimental consideration of political democracy, and whence it has arisen, with regard to some of its current features, as an aggregate, and as the basic structure of our future literature and authorship. We shall, it is true, quickly and continually find the origin-idea of the singleness of man, individualism, asserting itself, and cropping forth, even from the opposite ideas. But the mass, or lump character, for imperative reasons, is to be ever carefully weigh'd, borne in mind and provided for. Only from it, and from its proper regulation and potency, comes the other, comes the chance of individualism. The two are contradictory, but our task is to reconcile them.

The political history of the past may be summ'd up as having grown out of what underlies the words, order, safety, caste, and especially out of the need of some prompt authority, and of cohesion at all cost. Leaping time, we come to the period within the memory of people now living, when, as from some lair where they had slumber'd long, accumulating wrath, sprang up and are yet active (1790, and on even to the present, 1870), those noisy eructations, destructive iconoclasms, a fierce sense of wrongs, amid which moves the form, well known in modern history, in the Old World, stain'd with much blood, and mark'd by savage reactionary clamors and demands. These bear, mostly, as on one inclosing point of need.

For after the rest is said—after the many

time-honor'd and really true things for subor-
dination, experience, rights of property, etc.,
have been listen'd to and acquiesced in—after
the valuable and well-settled statement of our
duties and relations in society is thoroughly
conn'd over and exhausted—it remains to
bring forward and modify everything else with
the idea of that Something a man is (last precious consolation of the drudging poor), standing apart from all else, divine in his own right,
and a woman in hers, sole and untouchable by
any canons of authority, or any rule derived
from precedent, state-safety, the acts of legislatures, or even from what is called religion,
modesty, or art. The radiation of this truth is
the key of the most significant doings of our
immediately preceding three centuries, and has
been the political genesis and life of America.
Advancing visibly, it still more advances in-
visibly. Underneath the fluctuations of the expressions of society, as well as the movements
of the politics of the leading nations of the
world, we see steadily pressing ahead and
strengthening itself, even in the midst of immense tendencies toward aggregation, this
image of completeness in separatism, of individual personal dignity, of a single person,
either male or female, characterized in the
main, not from extrinsic acquirements or position, but in the pride of himself or herself
alone; and, as an eventual conclusion and summing up (or else the entire scheme of things is
aimless, a cheat, a crash), the simple idea that
the last, best dependence is to be upon humanity itself, and its own inherent, normal,
full-grown qualities, without any superstitious
support whatever. This idea of perfect individualism it is indeed that deepest tinges and
gives character to the idea of the aggregate.
For it is mainly or altogether to serve independent separatism that we favor a strong generalization, consolidation. As it is to give the
best vitality and freedom to the rights of the
States (every bit as important as the right of
nationality, the union), that we insist on the
identity of the Union at all hazards.

The purpose of democracy—supplanting old
belief in the necessary absoluteness of establish'd dynastic rulership, temporal, ecclesiastical, and scholastic, as furnishing the only security against chaos, crime, and ignorance—
is, through many transmigrations, and amid
endless ridicules, arguments, and ostensible
failures, to illustrate, at all hazards, this doctrine or theory that man, properly train'd in
sanest, highest freedom, may and must become
a law, and series of laws, unto himself, surrounding and providing for, not only his own

personal control, but all his relations to other
individuals, and to the State; and that, while
other theories, as in the past histories of nations, have proved wise enough, and indispensable perhaps for their conditions, *this*, as matters now stand in our civilized world, is the
only scheme worth working from, as warrant-
ing results like those of Nature's laws, reliable,
when once establish'd, to carry on themselves.

The argument of the matter is extensive,
and, we admit, by no means all on one side.
What we shall offer will be far, far from sufficient. But while leaving unsaid much that
should properly even prepare the way for the
treatment of this many-sided question of political liberty, equality, or republicanism—leaving the whole history and consideration of the
feudal plan and its products, embodying humanity, its politics and civilization, through
the retrospect of past time (which plan and
products, indeed, make up all of the past, and
a large past of the present)—leaving unan-
swer'd, at least by any specific and local answer, many a well-wrought argument and instance, and many a conscientious declamatory
cry and warning—as, very lately, from an eminent and venerable person abroad—things,
problems, full of doubt, dread, suspense (not
new to me, but old occupiers of many an anxious hour in city's din, or night's silence), we
still may give a page or so, whose drift is oppor-
tune. Time alone can finally answer these
things. But as a substitute in passing, let us,
even if fragmentarily, throw forth a short direct or indirect suggestion of the premises of
that other plan, in the new spirit, under the
new forms, started here in our America.

As to the political section of Democracy,
which introduces and breaks ground for further and vaster sections, few probably are the
minds, even in these republican States, that
fully comprehend the aptness of that phrase,
"THE GOVERNMENT OF THE PEOPLE, BY THE
PEOPLE, FOR THE PEOPLE" which we inherit
from the lips of Abraham Lincoln; a formula
whose verbal shape is homely wit, but whose
scope includes both the totality and all minutiæ
of the lesson.

The People! Like our huge earth itself,
which, to ordinary scansion, is full of vulgar
contradictions and offense, man, viewed in the
lump, displeases, and is a constant puzzle and
affront to the merely educated classes. The
rare, cosmical, artist mind, lit with the Infinite,
alone confronts his manifold and oceanic qualities—but taste, intelligence, and culture (so
called) have been against the masses, and remain so. There is plenty of glamor about the

most damnable crimes and hoggish meannesses, special and general, of the feudal and dynastic world over there, with its *personnel* of lords and queens and courts, so well-dress'd and so handsome. But the People are ungrammatical, untidy, and their sins gaunt and ill-bred.

Literature, strictly consider'd, has never recognized the People, and, whatever may be said, does not to-day. Speaking generally, the tendencies of literature, as hitherto pursued, have been to make mostly critical and querulous men. It seems as if, so far, there were some natural repugnance between a literary and professional life and the rude rank spirit of the democracies. There is, in later literature, a treatment of benevolence, a charity business, rife enough it is true; but I know nothing more rare, even in this country, than a fit scientific estimate and reverent appreciation of the People—of their measureless wealth of latent power and capacity, their vast, artistic contrasts of lights and shades—with, in America, their entire reliability in emergencies, and a certain breadth of historic grandeur, of peace or war, far surpassing all the vaunted samples of book-heroes, or any *haut ton* coteries, in all the records of the world.

The movements of the late secession war, and their results, to any sense that studies well and comprehends them, show that popular democracy, whatever its faults and dangers, practically justifies itself beyond the proudest claims and wildest hopes of its enthusiasts. Probably no future age can know, but I well know, how the gist of this fiercest and most resolute of the world's war-like contentions resided exclusively in the unnamed, unknown rank and file; and how the brunt of its labor of death was, to all essential purposes, volunteer'd. The People, of their own choice, fighting, dying for their own idea, insolently attack'd by the secession-slave-power, and its very existence imperil'd. Descending to detail, entering any of the armies, and mixing with the private soldiers, we see and have seen august spectacles. We have seen the alacrity with which the American-born populace, the peaceablest and most good-natured race in the world, and the most personally independent and intelligent, and the least fitted to submit to the irksomeness and exasperation of regimental discipline, sprang, at the first tap of the drum, to arms—not for gain, nor even glory, nor to repel invasion—but for an emblem, a mere abstraction—for the life, the *safety of the flag.* We have seen the unequal'd docility and obedience of these soldiers. We

have seen them tried long and long by hopelessness, mismanagement, and by defeat; have seen the incredible slaughter toward or through which the armies (as at first Fredericksburg, and afterward at the Wilderness) still unhesitatingly obey'd orders to advance. We have seen them in trench, or crouching behind breastwork, or tramping in deep mud, or amid pouring rain or thick-falling snow, or under forced marches in hottest summer (as on the road to get to Gettysburg)—vast suffocating swarms, divisions, corps, with every single man so grimed and black with sweat and dust, his own mother would not have known him—his clothes all dirty, stain'd and torn, with sour, accumulated sweat for perfume—many a comrade, perhaps a brother, sun-struck, staggering out, dying, by the roadside, of exhaustion—yet the great bulk bearing steadily on, cheery enough, hollow-bellied from hunger, but sinewy with unconquerable resolution.

We have seen this race proved by wholesale by drearier, yet more fearful tests—the wound, the amputation, the shatter'd face or limb, the slow hot fever, long impatient anchorage in bed, and all the forms of maiming, operation and disease. Alas! America have we seen, though only in her early youth, already to hospital brought. There have we watch'd these soldiers, many of them only boys in years—mark'd their decorum, their religious nature and fortitude, and their sweet affection. Wholesale, truly. For at the front, and through the camps, in countless tents, stood the regimental, brigade, and division hospitals; while everywhere amid the land, in or near cities, rose clusters of huge, white-wash'd, crowded, one-story wooden barracks; and there ruled agony with bitter scourge, yet seldom brought a cry; and there stalk'd death by day and night along the narrow aisles between the rows of cots, or by the blankets on the ground, and touch'd lightly many a poor sufferer, often with blessed, welcome touch.

I know not whether I shall be understood, but I realize that it is finally from what I learn'd personally mixing in such scenes that I am now penning these pages. One night in the gloomiest period of the war, in the Patent-office hospital in Washington city, as I stood by the bedside of a Pennsylvania soldier, who lay, conscious of quick approaching death, yet perfectly calm, and with noble, spiritual manner, the veteran surgeon, turning aside, said to me, that though he had witness'd many, many deaths of soldiers, and had been a worker at Bull Run, Antietam, Fredericksburg, etc., he had not seen yet the first case of a man or boy that met the approach of dissolution with cowardly qualms or terror. My own observation fully bears out the remark.

What have we here, if not, towering above all talk and argument, the plentifully-supplied, last-needed proof of democracy, in its personalities? Curiously enough, too, the proof on this point comes, I should say, every bit as much from the South, as from the North. Although I have spoken only of the latter, yet I deliberately include all. Grand, common stock! to me the accomplish'd and convincing growth, prophetic of the future; proof undeniable to sharpest sense, of perfect beauty, tenderness and pluck, that never feudal lord, nor Greek, nor Roman breed, yet rival'd. Let no tongue ever speak in disparagement of the American races, North or South, to one who has been through the war in the great army hospitals.

Meantime, general humanity (for to that we return, as, for our purposes, what it really is, to bear in mind) has always, in every department, been full of perverse maleficence, and is so yet. In downcast hours the soul thinks it always will be—but soon recovers from such sickly moods. I myself see clearly enough the crude, defective streaks in all the strata of the common people; the specimens and vast collections of the ignorant, the credulous, the unfit and uncouth, the incapable, and the very low and poor. The eminent person just mention'd sneeringly asks whether we expect to elevate and improve a nation's politics by absorbing such morbid collections and qualities therein. The point is a formidable one, and there will doubtless always be numbers of solid and reflective citizens who will never get over it. Our answer is general, and is involved in the scope and letter of this essay. We believe the ulterior object of political and all other government (having, of course, provided for the police, the safety of life, property, and for the basic statute and common law, and their administration, always first in order) to be among the rest, not merely to rule, to repress disorder, etc., but to develop, to open up to cultivation, to encourage the possibilities of all beneficent and manly outcroppage, and of that aspiration for independence, and the pride and self-respect latent in all characters. (Or, if there be exceptions, we cannot, fixing our eyes on them alone, make theirs the rule for all.)

I say the mission of government, henceforth, in civilized lands, is not repression alone, and not authority alone, not even of law, nor by that favorite standard of the eminent writer, the rule of the best men, the born heroes and captains of the race (as if such ever, or one time out of a hundred, get into the big places, elective or dynastic), but higher than the highest arbitrary rule, to train communities through all their grades, beginning with individuals and ending there again, to rule themselves. What Christ appear'd for in the moral-spiritual field for human-kind, namely, that in respect to the absolute soul, there is in the possession of such by each single individual, something so transcendent, so incapable of gradations (like life), that, to that extent, it places all beings on a common level, utterly regardless of the distinctions of intellect, virtue, station, or any height or lowliness whatever—is tallied in like manner, [in this other field, by democracy's rule that men, the nation, as a common aggregate of living identities, affording in each a separate and complete subject for freedom, worldly thrift and happiness, and for a fair chance for growth, and for protection in citizenship, etc., must, to the political extent of the suffrage or vote, if no further, be placed, in each and in the whole, on one broad, primary, universal, common platform. . . .

So much contributed, to be conn'd well, to help prepare and brace our edifice, our plann'd Idea—we still proceed to give it in another of its aspects—perhaps the main, the high façade of all. For to democracy, the leveler, the unyielding principle of the average, is surely join'd another principle, equally unyielding, closely tracking the first, indispensable to it, opposite (as the sexes are opposite), and whose existence, confronting and ever modifying the other, often clashing, paradoxical, yet neither of highest avail without the other, plainly supplies to these grand cosmic politics of ours, and to the launch'd-forth mortal dangers of republicanism, to-day or any day, the counterpart and offset whereby Nature restrains the deadly relentlessness of all her first-class laws. This second principle is individuality, the pride and centripetal isolation of a human being in himself—identity—personalism. Whatever the name, its acceptance and thorough infusion through the organizations of political commonality now shooting Aurora-like about the world, are of utmost importance, as the principle itself is needed for very life's sake. It forms, in a sort, or is to form, the compensating balance-wheel of the successful working machinery of aggregate America.

XI. THE COMEDY OF MANNERS

SINCE it is impossible to reprint a novel of William Dean Howells and since his few short stories are not among his most significant contributions, he is represented in the present volume by the two departments of literature in which he equalled or surpassed his contemporaries. His criticism is dealt with elsewhere. There he led and others followed, but in the field of farce-comedy he remained unrivalled. To do one thing supremely well is sufficient perhaps for any writer, and the comedies of manners which Howells created from 1876 to 1916 form a body of literature unique in quality and effect. They were not only read; they were played by thousands of amateur groups and some of them had professional production both in the United States and in England, where actresses like Ellen Terry and Mrs. Kendal performed them with success. Theatrical conditions in the United States, which provided little market for the one-act play, alone prevented their wider production, for they are distinctly not closet drama but practical stage plays.

It is as literature, however, that they achieve their permanent importance. They were one of the most effective methods of spreading the gospel of realism, and they meet the supreme test, that of the creation of character. The four personages who appear in the best of the farces, Edward and Agnes Roberts, Amy Somers and Willis Campbell, are not mere caricature; they are subtly drawn and they develop in the ten years in which the best work of Howells was done. From the purely farcical *Parlor Car* in 1876 he progressed through *The Elevator* (1885), *The Garroters* (1886), *The Mouse Trap* (1889) and others, to the finer art of the comedy of manners in *A Letter of Introduction* (1892) and *The Unexpected Guests* (1893). In the earlier farces the situation is all important, but in the later comedies the characters dominate the situation. In *The Unexpected Guests*, Amy Somers' triumph over the complications, for which she herself is responsible, is won by the use of weapons wielded by a gentlewoman conscious at all times of social values and remaining mistress of the scene.

WILLIAM DEAN HOWELLS (1837-1920)

THE UNEXPECTED GUESTS[1]
(1893)

CAST

WILLIS CAMPBELL
DR. LAWTON
EDWARD ROBERTS
MR. BEMIS
MR. CURWEN
YOUNG MR. BEMIS
MR. BELFORT
MRS. CAMPBELL
MRS. CRASHAW
MRS. CURWEN
YOUNG MRS. BEMIS
MISS REYNOLDS
MRS. BELFORT

SCENE: *A drawing-room.*
TIME: *The present.*

MRS. WILLIS CAMPBELL's *drawing-room.*

I

(MRS. CAMPBELL, CAMPBELL, DR. LAWTON.)

Dr. Lawton. Then truth, as I understand you, Mrs. Campbell, is a female virtue.

Mrs. Campbell. It is one of them.

Dr. Lawton. Oh! You have several?

Mrs. Campbell. Legions, Dr. Lawton.

Dr. Lawton. What do you do with them all?

Mrs. Campbell. Oh, we just keep them. You may be sure we don't waste them on *men.* What would be the use, for instance, of always telling Willis the truth? He wouldn't believe it, to begin with.

Campbell. You had better try me once, Amy. My impression is that it's the other thing I can't get away with. And yet I'm a great deal more accustomed to it!

Mrs. Campbell. That is neither here nor there. But what I say, and what I insist, is that the conventional lies that people tell are just as much lies as any—just as wicked, and altogether unnecessary. Why should I send word to the door that I'm not at home, or that I'm engaged, when I'm not, merely to get out of seeing a person?

Campbell. Because you are such a liar, my love.

Dr. Lawton. No! Excuse me, Campbell! I don't wish to intercept any little endearments, but really I think that in this case Mrs. Campbell's sacrifice of the truth is a piece of altruism. She knows how it is herself; she wouldn't like to be in the place of the person she wants to get out of seeing. So she sends word that she is not at home, or that she's engaged.

Mrs. Campbell. Of course I do. Willis's idea of *truth* would be to send word that he didn't want to see them.

Dr. Lawton. (*Laughing*) I haven't the least doubt of it.

Campbell. Well, you hoary-headed imposter, what would yours be?

Dr. Lawton. Mine? I have none! I have been a general practitioner for forty years. But what time did you ask me for, Mrs. Campbell?

Mrs. Campbell. Seven. I don't see what's keeping them all.

Campbell. The women are not coming.

Mrs. Campbell. Why?

Campbell. Because they said they were. Truth is a female virtue.

Mrs. Campbell. I must say, I don't see why they're so late. I can't understand, when every woman knows the anxiety of a hostess, how any one can be late. It's very heartless, I think. (MRS. CAMPBELL *is in dinner dress; she remains tranquilly seated on the sofa while she speaks, but the movement of her alternately folded and expanded fan betrays the agitation of her spirits.* DR. LAWTON, *lounging at large ease in a low chair, regards her with a mixture of admiration and scientific interest. Her husband walks up and down with a surcharge of nervous energy which the husband of a dinner-giver naturally expends when the guests are a little late.*)

Campbell. They will probably come in a lump—if they come at all. Don't be discouraged, Amy. If they don't come, I shall be hungry enough, by-and-by, to eat the whole dinner myself.

Mrs. Campbell. That is a man's idea; you think that the great thing about a dinner is to get it eaten.

Dr. Lawton. Oh, not *all* of us, Mrs. Campbell!

Mrs. Campbell. Well, I will except you, Dr. Lawton.

Campbell. And what is a woman's idea of a dinner, I should like to know?

Mrs. Campbell. To get it over.

Campbell. In this instance, then, I think you're going to fail. I see no prospect of your getting it over. The people are not coming. I guess you wrote Thursday when you meant Tuesday; didn't you, Amy? Your Tuesdays always look like Thursdays, anyway.

Mrs. Campbell. Now, Willis, if you begin your teasing!

Campbell. Well, what I want you to do is to tell them what you really think of them when they do come. I don't want any hollow-hearted pretense that it isn't at all late, and that you did not expect them before, and all that kind of thing. You just say, *Yes, you are rather behind time;* and, *No, I didn't write half-past seven; I wrote seven.* With all your devotion to truth, I'll bet you wouldn't dare to speak it once.

Mrs. Campbell. What will you bet? Come, now! Dr. Lawton will hold the stakes.

Campbell. Ah, *I* should have to pay, whichever lost, and Lawton would pocket the stakes.

Dr. Lawton. Try me!

Campbell. I'd rather not. It would be too expensive. (*A ring is heard; and then voices below and on the stairs.*) The spell is broken! I hear the stentorian tones of my sister Agnes.

Mrs. Campbell. Yes, it *is* Agnes; and now they'll all come. (*She runs out to the space at the top of the stairs which forms a sort of passageway between the drawing-room and library.*) Oh, Agnes! I'm *so* glad to see you! And Mr. Robets! (*She says this without, and the shock of kisses penetrates to the drawing-room, where* CAMPBELL *and* DR. LAWTON *remain.*)

Mrs. Roberts. (*Without*) Amy, I'm quite ashamed of myself! I'm afraid we're late. I think Edward's watch must be slow.

Mrs. Campbell. (*Without*) Not at all! I don't believe it's seven yet. I've only just got into my gown.

Campbell. It *is* a female virtue, Doctor!

Dr. Lawton. Oh, there's no doubt of its sex.

Mrs. Campbell. (*Without*) You'll find Willis in the drawing-room with Dr. Lawton, Mr. Roberts.

II

(ROBERTS, CAMPBELL, DR. LAWTON.)

Campbell. (*As* ROBERTS *meekly appears*) Hello, Roberts! You're late, old fellow. You ought to start Agnes dressing just after lunch.

Roberts. No, I'm afraid it's my fault. How do you do, Dr. Lawton? I think my watch is losing time.

Campbell. You didn't come your old dodge of stealing a garroter's watch on your way through the Common? That was a tremendous exploit of yours, Roberts.

Dr. Lawton. And you were at your best that night, Campbell. For a little while I wasn't sure but truth was a boy.

Campbell. I don't believe old Bemis has quite forgiven Roberts to this day. By-the-way, Bemis is late, too. Wouldn't have helped much to grab his watch to-night, Roberts. Hold on! That's his voice, now! (*As* MR. BEMIS *enters*) Good evening, Mr. Bemis. Roberts and I were just talking of that night when you tried to garrote him in the Common, and he got away with your watch.

III

(MR. BEMIS *and the* OTHERS.)

Mr. Bemis. (*Reluctantly*) Oh! very good. Ha, ha, ha!

Roberts. (*Cringingly*) Ha, ha, ha! Capital!

Mr. Bemis. Talking of watches, I hope I'm not late.

Campbell. About half an hour.

Mrs. Campbell. (*Re-entering and giving her hand.*) Don't believe a word of it, Mr. Bemis. You're just in time. Why, even Aunt Mary is not here yet!

Aunt Mary Crashaw. (*Without*) Yes, I am, my dear—half-way up your ridiculous stairs.

Mrs. Campbell. Oh, Aunt Mary! (*She runs out to meet her.*)

Campbell. (*To* DR. LAWTON) You see! she can't tell the truth even by accident.

Roberts. What in the world do you mean, Willis?

Campbell. 'Sh! It's a bet. (*To* Mrs. CRASHAW, *coming in with his wife.*) You *are* pretty well blown, Aunt Mary.

IV

(MRS. CRASHAW, MRS. CAMPBELL, *and the* OTHERS.)

Mrs. Crashaw. Blown? I wonder I'm alive to reproach Amy for these stairs. Why don't you live in a flat?

Campbell. I am going to put in an elevator here, and you can get stuck in it.

Mrs. Crashaw. I dare say I shall, if *you* put it in. What a frightful experience! I shall

never forget that night. How d'ye do, Edward? (*She shakes hands with* ROBERTS *and* MR. BEMIS.) How do you do, Mr. Bemis? I *know* how Dr. Lawton does, without asking.

Dr. Lawton. (*Gallantly*) All the better for——

Mrs. Crashaw. Don't say, for seeing me! We may *be* chestnuts, doctor, but we needn't speak them. (*To* MRS. CAMPBELL) Are you going to have the whole elevator company, as usual?

Mrs. Campbell. Yes—all but Mr. and Mrs. Miller. I asked them, but they had an engagement.

Mrs. Crashaw. So much the worse for them. Mrs. Curwen will be very much disappointed not to see—Mrs. Miller. (*The men laugh. She shakes her fan at them.*) You ought to be ashamed to provoke me to say such things. Well, now, since I'm here, I wish the others would come. I'm rather hungry, and it's late, isn't it?

Mrs. Campbell. Not at all! I don't see why you all think it's late. I'm sure it's very early. Ah, Mrs. Curwen! (*She advances upon this lady, who enters with her husband behind her.*) So glad you could come. And Mr. Curwen! I didn't hear you coming!

V

(MR. *and* MRS. CURWEN *and the* OTHERS.)

Mrs. Curwen. That proves you didn't eavesdrop at the head of the stairs, my dear. We were quarrelling all the way up to this threshold. After I'd answered it, I mislaid your invitation, and Mr. Curwen was sure we were asked for Wednesday. But I knew better. As it is, I'm afraid we're rather late.

Mrs. Campbell. (*Forcing a laugh*) We rarely sit down before eight. Oh, Mrs. Bemis! How do you do, Mr. Bemis? (*She greets young* MR. *and* MRS. BEMIS *with effusion, as they come in with an air of haste.*)

VI

(YOUNG MR. *and* MRS. BEMIS *and the* OTHERS.)

Mrs. Bemis. Oh, I *know* we're frightfully late!

Bemis. Yes, it's quite shocking——

Mrs. Campbell. Not at all! Really, I think it must be a conspiracy. Everybody says they are late, and I don't know why.

Campbell. I do; but I don't like to tell.

Dr. Lawton. Much safer, my dear boy! Much!

Mrs. Campbell. (*Ignoring this passage*) If I should make you wait, just to *show* you that it was early, I don't think it would be more than you deserve.

Campbell. Probably, if you did that, Miss Reynolds would get here too soon.

Mrs. Campbell. Yes; and she's usually so prompt.

Mrs. Curwen. I'm beginning to have the courage of my convictions, Mrs. Campbell. Are you *sure* you didn't say half-past?

Mrs. Campbell. I'm sure I can't say. Very likely I may have done so in your note. But I don't see why we are so inflexible about dinner engagements. I think we ought to give people at least three-quarters of an hour's grace, instead of that wretched fifteen minutes that keeps everybody's heart in their mouth. (*The door-bell sounds.*) Ah! That's Miss Reynolds' ring, and——

Campbell. We are saved! I was afraid we were going to be thirteen at table.

Mrs. Roberts. Thirteen! What do you mean, Willis?

Campbell. Why, one from twelve, you know.

Mrs. Campbell. Oh, yes. (*The* OTHERS *laugh.*)

Mrs. Campbell. Don't notice him, Agnes. He's in one of his very worst ways to-night.

Mrs. Roberts. But I don't see what the joke is!

Mrs. Campbell. Neither do I, Agnes. I——

A Ghostly Voice. (*As of an asthmatic spectre speaking through an imperfectly attached set of artificial teeth, makes itself heard from the library*) Truth crushed to earth will rise again. For God's eternal years are hers—er—r—r—ck—ck—cr—cr—cr—ee—ck——

Mrs. Crashaw. Good heavens, Willis, what in the world is that?

The Voice. This is the North America Company's perfected phonograph, invented by Thomas A.—cr—cr—cr—ee—ee—ck—ck —ck—New Jersey. This cylinder was cr—cr—elocutionist—ee—ee—ck—Cullen Bryant—— Truth crushed to—cr—cr—ck—ck——

Campbell. Don't be alarmed, Aunt Mary. It's just a phonograph that I had got in to amuse you after dinner. It don't seem to be exactly in order. Perhaps the cylinder's got dry, or Jim hasn't got quite the right pressure on——

Mrs. Crashaw. Is Jim in there?

Mrs. Campbell. Yes; Agnes has lent him to us to-day. I adore boys, and Jim has been angelic the whole afternoon.

Mrs. Roberts. Oh, you're *too* good, Amy!

Mrs. Crashaw. I don't wonder he's been angelic, with a thing like that to play with. I should be angelic myself. Why can't we go and be amused with it a little before dinner, Willis?

The Others. (*Respectively*) Oh, yes. Do. By all means. I never heard one before. We really can't wait. Let us hear it now, Mr. Campbell! Do make him, Mrs. Campbell.

Campbell. Well, all right. I'll go with you—— (*He stops, feeling himself significantly clutched by the wrist, and arrested in mid-career, by* MRS. CAMPBELL.) Or, Jim can show it off. It'll do him so much good. I'll let Jim. (*The guests follow one another out with cries of real and simulated interest, and* CAMPBELL *turns to his wife.*) What in the world is it, Amy?

VII

(MR. *and* MRS. CAMPBELL.)

Mrs. Campbell. What is it? I shall die, Willis!

Campbell. Well, speak first.

MRS. CAMPBELL. Something's happened to the dinner, I know. And I'm afraid to go and see. The cook's so cross!

Campbell. Well, shall *I* go?

Mrs. Campbell. And if you keep up this teasing of yours, you'll simply kill me.

Campbell. Well, I won't, then. But it's very lucky your guests are belated, too, Amy. Now, if you *could* get the dinner on in about ten minutes, we should be just right. But you've told them all they were so early that they'll believe the delay is all yours.

Mrs. Campbell. They won't believe anything of the kind! They know better. But I don't dare——

Jane. (*The waitress, appearing through the portière of the drawing-room*) Dinner is ready, Mrs. Campbell.

Mrs. Campbell. Oh, well, then, do get them started, Willis! Don't forget, it's young Mrs. Bemis you're to take down—*not* Mrs. Curwen.

Campbell. Oh, no! I sha'n't forget that. I hope Mrs. Curwen won't. Hello! There's another ring. Who in the world is that?

Mrs. Campbell. 'Sh! If that horrid, squeaking phonograph——

The Phonograph. (*From the library*) Truth crushed to earth will——

Mrs. Campbell. Good gracious! I can't hear a word. Hark! It's Miss Reynolds talking with some one in the reception-room, and it sounds like—but it can't be—no, it can't—it—it—it—*is*—yes! And that's *his* voice, too,

Willis! What does it mean? Am I losing my five senses? Or am I simply going stark, staring mad?

Campbell. You don't say the Millers have come?

Mrs. Campbell. The Millers? No! Who cares anything about the Millers? 'Sh!
(*She listens.*)

Campbell. (*Listening*) Why, it's the Belforts!

Mrs. Campbell. How can you *dare* to say it, Willis? Of course it's the Belforts. Hark!
(*She listens.*)

Campbell. (*Listening*) But I thought you said they declined, too.

Mrs. Campbell. They did. It's some frightful mystery. Be still, do, Willis!

Campbell. Why, I'm not making any noise. It's the froufrou of that dress of yours.

Mrs. Campbell. It's your shirt bosom. You always *will* have them so stiff; and you keep breathing so.

Campbell. Oh, well, if you don't want me to breathe!

Mrs. Campbell. (*Desperately*) It doesn't matter. It wouldn't help now if you *never* breathed again. Don't joke, Willis! I can't bear it. If you do, I shall scream.

Campbell. I wasn't going to joke. It's too serious. What are you going to do?

Mrs. Campbell. I don't know. We must do anything to keep them from finding out that they weren't expected.

Campbell. But how do you suppose it's happened, Amy?

Mrs. Campbell. I don't know. They meant to decline somewhere else and accept here, and they mixed the letters. It's always happening. But be still now! They're coming up, and all we can do is to keep them in the dark as well as we can. You must help me, Willis.

Campbell. Oh, there's nothing I like better than throwing dust in people's eyes. It's my native element.

Mrs. Campbell. Of course it puts the table all out, and we've got to rearrange the places, and think who is going to take out who again as soon as we can get rid of them. Be making up some pretext, Willis. We've got to consult together, or else we are completely lost. You'll have to stay and keep talking, while I run down and make them put another leaf into the table. I don't believe there's room enough now, and I'm not certain about the quails. The cook said she didn't believe they were all nice. How can people be so careless about notes? I think it's really criminal. There ought to be something done about it. If people

won't read their notes over they ought to be told about it, and I've the greatest mind to say at once that they sent a refusal, and I wasn't expecting them. It would serve them right.

Campbell. Yes, and it would be such a relief to your feelings. I wish you *would* do it, Amy. Just for once.

Mrs. Campbell. I shall have to take the tablecloth off if I put another leaf in, and the whole thing has got to be rearranged, decorations and everything; and I'd got the violets scattered so carelessly. Now I shall just *fling* them on. I don't care how they look. I'm completely discouraged, and I shall just go through it all like a stone.

Campbell. Like a precious stone. You *are* such a perfect little brick, Amy.

Mrs. Campbell. I guess you wouldn't like it yourself, Willis. And the Belforts are just the people I should have liked to do my best before, and now their being here spoils everything.

Campbell. (*Smiling*) It *is* a complication!

Mrs. Campbell. Oh, yes, giggle, do! I suppose you'd expect me to be logical, as you call it, with my dying breath.

Campbell. No, I shouldn't, Amy; but I know you'd be delightful under any circumstances. You always get there just the same, whether you take the steps or not. But brace up now, dear, and you'll come out all right. Tell them the truth and I'll stand by you. I don't want any better fun. (*He slips behind his wife, who gives him a ghastly glance over her shoulder as the* BELFORTS *enter the room with* MISS REYNOLDS.)

VIII

(*The* BELFORTS, MISS REYNOLDS, *and the* CAMPBELLS.)

Mrs. Campbell. Oh, how do you do, Maria? (*She kisses* MISS REYNOLDS, *and then, with gay cordiality, gives her hand to* MRS. BELFORT.) I'm *so* glad to see you! (*She shakes hands with* BELFORT.) So kind of you to come.

MISS REYNOLDS. I'm sorry to be a little late, Amy; but better late than never, I suppose.

MRS. BELFORT. I'm not so sure of that. Dear Mrs. Campbell! I wish you would be quite frank with me!

Mrs. Campbell. Late? Frank? What do you mean, both of you? You know you're never late, Maria; and why should I be frank with you, Mrs. Belfort?

Campbell. What do you take us for?

Mrs. Belfort. (*Holding* MRS. CAMPBELL'S *hand clasped between both of hers.*) For the very nicest and kindest people in the world, who wouldn't let me have the mortification of deranging them on any account. Did you expect us this evening?

Mrs. Campbell. Expect you? What a strange question! Why in the world shouldn't we expect you?

Campbell. What an extraordinary idea!

Mrs. Belfort. Because I had to hurry away from Mrs. Miller's tea when I went home to dress, and when I told her we were coming here to dinner, she said, "Oh, you are *going,* then?" in such a way that, though she covered it up afterwards, and said she didn't mean anything, and she didn't know why she had spoken, I felt sure there must be some misunderstanding, and I've come quite ready to be sent away again if there is. Didn't you get my note?

Mrs. Campbell. Your note? Why, of course I did!

Mrs. Belfort. Then it's all right. *Such* a relief! Now I feel that I can breathe freely again.

Mr. Belfort. I assure you, Mrs. Campbell, it's a relief to me, too. I've never seen my wife of quite so many minds as she's been for the last hour and a half. She was quite encyclopedic.

Campbell. Oh, I know how that is, my dear boy. I've known Mrs. Campbell change hers as often as an unabridged dictionary in great emergencies.

Mrs. Belfort. But really, the only thing for us to do was to come, as I felt from the beginning, in spite of my doubts what to do. I thought I could depend upon you to send us away if we weren't wanted; but if we were, and didn't come, you couldn't very well have sent for us.

Mrs. Campbell. (*Gayly*) Indeed I should!

Campbell. (*Gallantly*) The dinner would have been nothing without you.

Mrs. Belfort. I don't know about that, but I'm sure we should have been nothing without the dinner. We were *so* glad to come. I waited a little while about answering, till I could see whether we could be free of a sort of provisional engagement we had hanging over us. Even after we got here, though, I'd half a mind to run away, and we've been catechising poor Miss Reynolds down in the reception-room till she wouldn't stand it any longer, and so here we are.

Mrs. Campbell. And I'm perfectly delighted. If you had yielded to any such ridiculous misgiving, I should never have forgiven you. I'm sure I don't know what Mrs. Miller could have——

The Phonograph. (*In the library*) Truth crushed to earth will cr—cr-r-r—ck—ck—cr——

Mrs. Belfort. A phonograph! Oh, have you got one? I *must* hear it!

Campbell. Well, won't you come into the library? My nephew is in there, driving everybody mad with it. He'll be perfectly delighted with a fresh victim.

Mrs. Belfort. And I shall be charmed to offer myself up. Come, Miss Reynolds. Come, Roger.

Campbell. Yes, come along, Belfort. (*He leads the way to the door, and then adroitly slips back to his wife, who has abandoned herself wildly upon the sofa.*)

IX

(CAMPBELL *and* MRS. CAMPBELL.)

Mrs. Campbell. Well, now, what are you going to do, Willis?

Campbell. I'm not going to do anything. I haven't been flying in the face of Providence. If ever there was a woman offered a clean and safe way out! But since you preferred to remain in this labyrinth—this Black Forest of improbabilities——

Mrs. Campbell. Oh, don't torment me, Willis! Don't you see that her taking it that way made it all the more impossible for me to tell her of the blunder she had committed? I simply couldn't do it, then.

Campbell. I don't see how you could help doing it then.

Mrs. Campbell. When she behaved so magnanimously about it, and put herself in my power? I would sooner have died, and she knew it perfectly well. That's the reason she *was* so magnanimous. You wouldn't have done it yourself after that. But it's no use talking about that now. We've got to do something, and you've got to think what we shall do. Now think!

Campbell. What about?

Mrs. Campbell. Oh, don't tease, dearest! About the trouble—and who shall take out who—and the quails. You know what!

Campbell. Well, I think if we leave those people alone much longer, they'll all come out here and ask if they weren't mistaken in supposing they were expected.

Mrs. Campbell. (*Whimpering*) Oh, there you go! How perfectly heartless!

X

(MRS. ROBERTS *and the* CAMPBELLS.)

Mrs. Roberts. (*Showing herself at the door*) Amy, dear, what *is* the matter? Didn't you tell me the Belforts were not coming? Is that what's keeping you out here? I just knew it was!

Mrs. Campbell. Yes, Agnes; but do go back to them, and keep them amused. Willis and I are trying to think what to do. I've got to re-arrange the whole table, you know, and I'm not sure whether there'll be quails enough to go round.

Mrs. Roberts. Don't worry about that, Amy. I won't take any, and I'll give Edward a hint about them.

Campbell. And Roberts is capable of asking you before the whole company why you don't want him to take quail. There's nothing like Roberts for presence of mind and any little bit of *finesse* like that. No, it won't do for the en-tire connection to fight shy of quail. Mrs. Bel-fort has got her suspicions roused, and she'd be on to a thing of that kind like lightning. She's got the notion that she wasn't expected, some-how, and she's been making it hot for Amy— trying to get her to own up, and all that. If it hadn't been for me, Amy *would* have owned up, too. But I kept my eye on her, and she lied out of it like a little man.

Mrs. Campbell. It isn't so, Agnes. He *wanted* me to tell the truth about it, as he calls it——

Mrs. Roberts. What an idea! You might as well have died at once. I don't see what you could have been thinking of, Willis!

Mrs. Campbell. Yes, he can't understand yet why I shouldn't, when Mrs. Belfort asked me if there wasn't some mistake, and literally threw herself on my mercy. She had no busi-ness to do it, and I shall always think it was taking a mean advantage; but I wasn't going to let myself be outdone in magnanimity. I shouldn't have thought she would be capable of it.

Mrs. Roberts. It wasn't very nice, but I suppose she was excited. We mustn't blame her, and you did the only thing that any hu-man creature could do. I'm surprised at Wil-lis; or, rather, I'm *not* surprised.

Campbell. Well, don't let it keep you away from our other guests, Agnes.

Mrs. Campbell. Oh, yes; *do* go back to them, Agnes, dear! I have got to arrange all over again now, about who's to go out with who, you know. I shall want you to let Ed-ward take Mrs. Curwen, and——

Mrs. Roberts. Oh, Amy, you know I'd do anything for you, especially in a case like this; but I *can't* let Edward take Mrs. Curwen out. I don't mind her flirting; she does that with every one; but she always gets Edward to

laughing so that it attracts the attention of the whole table, and——

Campbell. That's a very insignificant mat-ter. I'll take out Mrs. Curwen, myself——

Mrs. Campbell. No, indeed you won't! You always get *her* laughing, and that's a great deal worse.

Campbell. Well, well, I won't, then. But we can arrange that afterwards.

Mrs. Campbell. No, we'll settle it now, if you please; and I don't want you to go *near* Mrs. Curwen. She'll be sure to see that there's something wrong from the delay, and she'll try to find it out, and if she should I shall simply perish on the spot. She'll try to get round you and make you tell, and I want you to promise me, Willis, on your bended knees, that you won't let it out. She's insufferable enough as it is, but if she got to sympathizing with me, or patronizing me about such a thing, as she'd be sure to do, I don't know what I *should* do. Will you promise?

Campbell. Oh, I promise. Look out you don't tell her yourself, Amy! But now I've got to see that there's enough to eat, under this new deal, and the great question is about the quail. I'll just run down to the telephone, and send to the club for them. We can have them here in-side of a half-hour, and never turn a feather.

Mrs. Campbell. Oh, Willis, you *are* inspired. Well, I shall always say that when there is any real thinking to be done—— But hurry back, do, dear, and Agnes and I will be trying to set-tle who shall take out—— Oh, I'm afraid you won't get back in time to help us! It takes so long to telephone the simplest thing.

Campbell. I'll be back in one-quarter of a second. (*He rushes out, brushing by* MRS. CRASHAW, *who enters at the same moment from the library.*)

XI

(MRS. CRASHAW *and the other ladies; then* CAMPBELL.)

Mrs. Crashaw. Amy, child, what in the world has happened? What are you staying out here away from your company for? Where's Willis going? What's Agnes doing here? It's perfectly scandalous to leave all those people alone!

Mrs. Campbell. Oh, Aunt Mary, if you only knew, you wouldn't scold us! Don't you see the Belforts have come?

Mrs. Crashaw. Yes, of course, they've come, and after they declined; I understand that. But it's only a matter of two plates more at the table——

Mrs. Campbell. Oh, is it? And am I to let *him* go down with *her?* The whole affair has got to be planned over, and another leaf put in, and the table rearranged, and I don't know what all.

Mrs. Roberts. And Willis has gone down to telephone to the club for more quails.

Mrs. Crashaw. (*To* Mrs. CAMPBELL) You don't mean that you only got just quails enough?

Mrs. Campbell. (*Indignantly*) A dinner for ten is not a dinner for twelve. I may not have kept house so long as you, Aunt Mary, but I'm not *quite* a child! (*At this critical moment* CAMPBELL *returns.*) Well, will they send them?

Campbell. Yes, yes. It's all right. I couldn't get the club, just now; Central was busy; but I've primed Green's man, down below, and he'll call them up in a minute. He understands it. I thought I'd hurry back and see if I could be of use. Well, have you got things all straight?

Mrs. Crashaw. No; we've spent the time in getting them crookeder, if possible. I've insinuated that Amy didn't know how to order her dinner, and she's told me I'm an old woman. I *am* an old woman, Amy, and you mustn't regard me. I think my mind's going. (*She kisses* Mrs. CAMPBELL, *who clasps her in a forgiving embrace.*)

Mrs. Campbell. Mine's *gone*, Aunt Mary, or I could have taken anything amiss from *you!* I don't see how I shall live through it. I don't know what to do; it seems to get worse every moment.

Mrs. Crashaw. Why, you don't suppose the Belforts *suspect* anything, do you?

Mrs. Campbell. That's the worst of it. I thought I ought to let the Millers know who had failed when I asked them so late; and the Belforts were there at tea this afternoon, and Mrs. Miller let out her surprise that they were coming. So, of course, I had a double duty.

Campbell. But, thank goodness, she was equal to it, Aunt Mary. I've had to do some tall lying in my time, but I never soared to the heights that Amy reached with the Belforts, in my palmiest days.

Mrs. Crashaw. Well, then, if she convinced them that their suspicions were wrong, it's all right; and if the quails are coming from the club, I don't see what there is to worry about. We must be thankful that you could get out of it so easily.

Mrs. Campbell. But we're *not* out of it. The table has to be rearranged, but I can have that done now somehow, while we're waiting

for the quails. The great thing is to manage about the going out. It happens very fortunately that if I tell all the other men whom they're to take out, Mr. Belfort can't suppose that he was an after-thought. But I can't seem to make a start with a new arrangement, in my own mind.

Campbell. You've used up all your invention in convincing the Belforts that they were expected. Good gracious, here's Dr. Lawton! What do you want here, you venerable opprobrium of science?

XI

(DR. LAWTON *and the* OTHERS.)

Dr. Lawton. (*Standing at ease on the threshold of the drawing-room.* Nothing. I merely got tired of hearing the praises of truth chanted in there, and came out here for—a little change.

Campbell. Well, you can't stay. You've got to go back, and help keep the Belforts from supposing they weren't expected, if it takes all your hoarded wisdom as a general practitioner for forty years.

Mrs. Campbell. Oh, yes; do go back, doctor!

Dr. Lawton. What has been the treatment up to the present time?

Campbell. The most heroic kind. Amy has spared neither age nor sex, in the use of whoppers. You know what she is, doctor, when she has a duty to perform.

Dr. Lawton. But whoppers, as I understand, are always of one sex. They may be old; they often are, I believe; but they are invariably masculine.

Campbell. Oh, that doesn't prevent women's using them. They use all of us.

Dr. Lawton. Well, then, there's no need of my going back on that account. In fact, I may congratulate Mrs. Campbell on the most complete success. The Belforts are thoroughly deceived.

Mrs. Campbell. (*With tremulous eagerness*) Oh, do you *think* so, doctor? If I could only believe that, how happy I should be!

Dr. Lawton. You may be sure of it, Mrs. Campbell. Belfort doesn't count, of course?

Mrs. Crashaw. Of course not; men will believe anything that's told them.

Dr. Lawton. And I don't allude to *him*. But Mrs. Belfort got me to one side as soon as she saw me, and told me she had been afraid there was something wrong, but Mrs. Campbell had assured her that she had got her note of acceptance, and now she was going to give her whole mind to the phonograph's beautiful rendering of Bryant's poem on truth.

Mrs. Roberts. There, Amy, you see there's no reason to worry about that!

Mrs. Crashaw. No; the only thing now is to get your dinner on the table, child, and let us eat it as soon as possible.

Campbell. Yes, if Lawton's telling the truth.

The Ladies. Willis!

Dr. Lawton. Don't mind him, ladies! The experiences of his early life in California, you know, must have been very unfavorable to a habit of confidence in his fellow-men. I pity him.

XIII

(MRS. CURWEN *and the* OTHERS.)

Mrs. Curwen. (*Appearing with young* MR. BEMIS) Dr. Lawton, I wish you would go and bring your daughter here. She's flirting outrageously with my husband. (*In making this accusation,* MRS. CURWEN *casts the eye of experienced coquetry at young* MR. BEMIS, *who laughs foolishly.*)

Dr. Lawton. Oh, I dare say he won't mind; he must be so used to it.

Mrs. Curwen. What do you mean, Dr. Lawton? What does he mean, Mr. Campbell?

Campbell. I couldn't imagine, for the life of me.

Mrs. Curwen. Can *you* tell me, Mrs. Campbell?

Mrs. Campbell. Oh, I *never* tell—such things.

Mrs. Curwen. What mysteries! Well, can you tell me what makes Mrs. Belfort so uncommonly gay, this evening? She seems to be in the greatest spirits, laughing with everybody—Mr. Bemis *père*, and Mr. Roberts.

Mrs. Campbell. Mrs. Belfort?

Mrs. Curwen. Yes. She seems a little hysterical. I wonder if anything's happened?

Mrs. Campbell. (*Sweeping the circle of her confidants with a look of misery.*) What could have happened?

Dr. Lawton. It's merely the pleasure of finding herself in your company, Mrs. Curwen.

Mrs. Curwen. Oh, thank you, Dr. Lawton. I know that I scatter sunshine in my path, but not to that extent, I think. (*With winning appeal.*) Oh, what *is* the cat in the meal, doctor? (*To young* MR. BEMIS, *archly.*) *Do* make them tell me, Mr. Bemis!

Young Mr. Bemis. (*With the air of epigram*) I'm sure *I* don't know. (*He chokes with flattered laughter.*)

Mrs. Curwen. How cruel of you not even to try! (*She makes eyes at young* MR. BEMIS, *and then transfers them rapidly to* CAMPBELL.)

Won't you just whisper it in my ear, Mr. Campbell? Mrs. Roberts, you can't imagine what nice things your husband's been saying to me! I didn't know he paid compliments. And now I suppose he's devoting himself to Mrs. Belfort. Perhaps it was that made her so lively. He began at once. He's *so* amusing. I envy you having such a husband always about.

Young Mr. Bemis. (*In the belief that he is saying something gallant*) I'm sure we're none of us so hard-hearted as to envy *you*, Mrs. Curwen.

Mrs. Curwen. Oh, *thank* you, Mr. Bemis! I shall really be afraid to tell Mr. Curwen *all* you say. (*She laughs, and* CAMPBELL *joins her, even under the reproachful gaze of his wife and sister.* MRS. CURWEN *turns coaxingly to him.*) Do tell!

Campbell. Tell what?

Mrs. Curwen. Well—— (*She pauses thoughtfully, and then suddenly adds.*) Who's going to take me out to dinner?

Mrs. Campbell. (*Surprised into saying it*) Why, it's all disarranged now by the Belforts—— (*She stops, and a thrill of dismay at her self-betrayal makes itself apparent to the spectators.*)

Mrs. Curwen. (*With clasped hands*) Don't say by the Belforts coming unexpectedly! Oh, *dear* Mrs. Campbell, I know how to pity you! That very thing happened to me last winter. Only, it was Mrs. Miller who came after she'd declined; she said Mr. Miller wouldn't come without her. But why do you mind it? *We* all went out pell-mell. Such fun! But it must have taken all Mr. Campbell's ingenuity to keep them from suspecting.

Campbell. More, too. I was nowhere.

Mrs. Curwen. (*With caressing deference to* MRS. CAMPBELL) Of course you were not needed. But isn't it shocking how one has to manage in such an emergency? I really believe it would be better to tell the truth sometimes. Don't you?

Mrs. Campbell. It's all very well telling the truth if they don't suspect anything. But when people tax you with their mistakes, and try to make you own up that they've blundered, then of course you *have* to deny it.

Mrs. Roberts. You simply *have* to.

Mrs. Crashaw. There's no other way, in that case, even if you'd prefer to tell the truth.

Mrs. Curwen. Oh, in that case, yes, indeed. Poor Mrs. Campbell! I can imagine how annoying it must have been; but I *should* have liked to hear you getting out of it! What *did* you say? *I'm* so transparent, people see through me at once.

Campbell. Are you?

Dr. Lawton. Don't you think you're a little hard on yourself, Mrs. Curwen?

Mrs. Curwen. (*With burlesque meekness and sincerity*) No, not the least. It's simple justice. (MR. CURWEN *enters with* ROBERTS.) You can ask my husband if you don't believe *me*. Or no, I'll put the case to him myself. Fred, dear, if people whom I didn't expect to dinner, came, *could* I keep them from discovering that they weren't expected? You know how awkward I am about such things—little fibs, and all that?

XIV

(ROBERTS, CURWEN, *and the* OTHERS; *then the* BELFORTS.)

Curwen. Well, I don't know——

Mrs. Curwen. (*Shaking her fan at him during the general laughing*) Oh, what a wicked husband! *You* don't believe I could fib out of such a thing, *do* you, Mr. Roberts?

Roberts. (*Gallantly*) If I knew what the thing was?

Mrs. Curwen. Why, like the Belforts—— Oh, *poor* Mrs. Campbell! I *didn't* mean to let it out!

Mrs. Campbell. Oh, it doesn't matter. Would you like to go and tell the Belforts themselves? Or, you needn't go; they're coming here.

Mrs. Belfort. (*Returning from the library, followed by her husband and the elder* MR. BEMIS) How perfectly the phonograph renders that piece, Mr. Campbell! I've never heard anything like it.

Campbell. It's all in practice. You wouldn't hear anything else here, Mrs. Belfort. It's my favorite poem. And I'm happy to find that Mrs. Curwen likes it as much as I do.

Mrs. Curwen. I adore it!

The Phonograph. (*Within*) Truth crushed to earth will rise again.

Campbell. Every time! But I wish Jim would change the cylinder. I like a little vari——

A Sound. (*From the regions below, something like this*) Woor, roor, roor; woor, roor, roor! (*And then a voice*) Hello! Is that you, Central? Well, give me two hundred and forty-one, please! Yes, two, four, one: Iroquois Club. Yes! What? Yes, Iroquois Club —two forty-one. Well, hurry up! Is that you, Iroquois? Yes? Busy? Well, that won't work. I don't care if you *are* busy. You've got to take my message, and take it right away. Hear that?

Campbell. Hear it? I should think they could! That confounded fool has left the closet-door open! (*He rushes out and down the stairs, while the* OTHERS *assume various attitudes of sympathy and dismay, and* MRS. CURWEN *bows herself into her fan, and the voice below continues.*)

The Voice. Well, why don't you send them quails you promised half an hour ago? What? Who is it? It's Mr. Campbell. C, a, m, Cam, m, e, l, mel, Campbell. One hump! What? Oh, hump yourself! It's Mr. Cam——

Campbell's Voice. (*From below*) Why the deuce don't you shut that closet-door? Shut it! Shut it! We can hear you all over the house, the way you yell. Don't you know how to use a telephone? Shut that door, anyway!

The Voice. Oh, I beg your pardon, sir, I didn't think about the door. I didn't know it was open. All right, sir. (*There is the sound of a closing door, and then, as* CAMPBELL *rejoins his guests with a flushed face, the woor-roor-rooring of the electric bell begins again.*) Iroquois! Is this Iroquois? No, I don't want you; I want Iroquois. Well, is that Iroquois now? (*The words are at first muffled; then they grow more and more distinct, in spite of the intervening door.*) Yes, quails! A dozen roast quails. You got the order half an hour ago. There's a lot of folks come that they didn't expect, and they got to have some more birds. Well, hurry up, then! Good-by! Woor-roor!

Campbell. (*Amid the consternation of the company, while* MR. BELFORT *fixes his wife with an eye of mute reproach*) Now, my dear, this is so awful that nothing can be done about it on the old lines.

Mrs. Campbell. Yes; I give it up. Mrs. Belfort, I tried my very best to keep you from suspecting, and even when you did suspect, I'm sure you must say that I did all I could. But fate was against me.

Mrs. Curwen. Oh, *poor* Mrs. Campbell! Must you own up?

Mrs. Belfort. But I don't understand. You got my note of acceptance, didn't you?

Mrs. Campbell. But it *wasn't* a note of acceptance: it was a note of regret!

Mrs. Belfort. Indeed it was not!

Mrs. Campbell. I knew just how it had happened as soon as I saw you this evening, and I determined that wild horses should not get the truth out of me. (CAMPBELL *and* DR. LAWTON *exchange signals of admiration.*) You must have been writing two notes, declining somewhere else, and then got them mixed. It's always happening.

Campbell. It's one of the commonest things

in the world—on the stage; and ever since a case of the kind happened to Mrs. Campbell down at the Shore, one summer, she's known how to deal with it.

Mrs. Belfort. But I *didn't* write two notes and get them mixed. I wrote but one, to tell Mrs. Campbell how very glad I was to come. Do you happen to have kept my note?

Mrs. Campbell. They are all here in this desk, and— (*Running to it, and pulling it open.*) —here is yours. (*She reads.*) "*Dear Mrs. Campbell, I am very sorry to be so late in answering. An out-of-town engagement for the tenth, which has been hanging over us in a threatening way for the past fortnight——*" (MRS. CAMPBELL *turns the leaf, and continues reading in a murmur that finally fades into the silence of utter dismay.*)

Campbell. Well, my dear?

Mrs. Crashaw. What in the world is it, child?

Mrs. Roberts. Amy!

Mrs. Curwen. Oh, not *another* mystery, I hope!

Campbell. Go on, Amy, or shall I——

Mrs. Campbell. (*Reading desperately on*) "*—for the past fortnight, is happily off at last, and I am very glad indeed to accept your kind invitation for dinner at seven on that day, for Mr. Belfort and myself—*" (*She lets her hands, with the letter stretched between them, fall dramatically before her.*)

Campbell. Well, my dear, there seems to be a pretty clear case against you, and unless you can plead mind-transference, or something like that——

Mrs. Roberts. I'm sure it's mind-transference, Amy! I've often been through the same experience myself. Just take the opposite of what's said.

Mrs. Campbell. (*In a daze*) But I don't see —— Yes, now I begin to remember how it must have been—how it was. I know now, but

I don't know how I can ever forgive myself for such carelessness, when I'm always so particular about notes——

Campbell. Yes, I've even heard you say it was criminal to read them carelessly. I can bear witness for you there.

Mrs. Roberts. I'm sure I could, too, Amy, in a court of justice.

Mrs. Campbell. Yes, I was just going out when your note came, Mrs. Belfort, and I read the first page—down to "*for the past fortnight*" —and I took it for granted that the opening regret meant a refusal, and just dropped it into my desk and gave you up. It's inexcusable, perfectly inexcusable! I'm quite at your feet, Mrs. Belfort, and I shall not blame you at all if you can't forgive me. What shall I say to you?

Mrs. Belfort. (*Amiably*) Nothing, my dear, except that you will let me stay, now I'm here!

Mrs. Campbell. How sweet you are! You shall *live* with us!

Campbell. Truth crushed to earth! It's perfectly wonderful! Mrs. Campbell can't get away from it when she tries her best. She tells it in spite of herself. She supposed she wasn't telling it when she said there was no mistake on your part; but she *was*. Well, it *is* a feminine virtue, doctor.

Dr. Lawton. Unquestionably, I think that it came into the world with woman.

Mrs. Campbell. (*With mounting courage*) Yes, a pretty predicament I should have been in, Willis, if I had taken your advice, and told the truth, as you call it, in the beginning. But now we won't wait any longer. The quails will come in their own good time. My dear, will you give Mrs. Belfort your arm? And, Mr. Belfort, will you give me yours?

Mrs. Curwen. And all the rest of us?

Mrs. Campbell. Oh, you can come out pell-mell.

Mrs. Curwen. Oh, *dear* Mrs. Campbell!

XII. THE·POETRY OF THE LATER NINETEENTH CENTURY

THE most obvious classification of the poets of the last half of the nineteenth century follows the geographical division into the Eastern, the Southern, and the Western groups. Yet at the outset we are reminded that one test of a poet's significance lies in his refusal to be neatly classified. Emily Dickinson is of New England, yet her poetry is tied to no locality and deals with themes of universal appeal. It is, however, through her intense individuality rather than through her lack of provincialism that Emily Dickinson remains somewhat remote from the other poets of the East. To a certain degree this universal quality is true of all the group. Geographically, they were Eastern: Thomas Bailey Aldrich and Louise Imogen Guiney being born in Massachusetts; Edmund Clarence Stedman, Edward Rowland Sill, and Louise Chandler Moulton, in Connecticut; Weir Mitchell and Lloyd Mifflin, in Pennsylvania; and Richard Watson Gilder, in New Jersey. But they did not confine themselves to the life of their section, and they are connected rather by a similarity of tone and metrical impulse, by a likeness of poetic ancestry, and frequently by personal friendship and even relationship. They are the heirs of the tradition which Tennyson and Longfellow had established, but it would be a mistake to give the impression that these poets are essentially imitative. They all have distinct notes, but they had learned their art of writing at a good school. Nearly all of them began to read poetry in the forties or fifties, and the great message which that age brought to them was the necessity for clarity of thought and care in expression. They believed, too, in the right of an American poet to choose his theme from any place or time.

The poetry of the Western group presents a sharp contrast to that of the East. Much more definitely reflective of locality and period, Bret Harte, John Hay, "Joaquin" Miller, James Whitcomb Riley, and Eugene Field belong together through a deliberate attempt at the portrayal of native conditions and the stress upon force and vigor rather than the serene beauty sought for in the Eastern group. Harte and Miller came from the East and the Middle West, but it was the Far West which formed the material for their verse. They won Eastern and foreign admiration partly through the vivid contrasts they presented to the familiar life of more settled countries and through their celebration of a life made picturesque by the varied elements which composed it. Miller stood for the West in dead earnest, while Harte lightened his attack upon the menace of the Chinese immigration or the growing arrogance of science by a humor which perhaps constitutes the chief claim of his verse to remembrance. Field and Riley were of the Middle West, but Field's humorous verse described the West of the frontier, which his stay at Denver revealed to him, while Riley remained in Indiana. Riley became the laureate of the American village and small town. Both of them have an important place in the poetry of child life, and Field has a scholarly side to which Riley is a stranger. All of this group except Miller wrote in dialect, but dialect is, after all, an artificial medium to them, and except for humorous effects, it is to be doubted whether their dialect verse will be remembered as long as their poetry written in normal English. Much of it is really not dialect but simply colloquial language, which is destructive rather than preservative. Unrelated to the poetry of the other writers of the Middle West, the work of Paul Laurence Dunbar is significant as heralding a native negro expression which substituted for the conventional picture of the colored race a sincere attempt at racial self-revelation.

The qualities which the Southern poets possess in common are a love of nature, a tendency to symbolism, and a fondness for classical themes. The most marked characteristic, however, is a certain enthusiasm, a rapturous quality, rising at times into inspiration of a high order, at times achieving only a rhetorical stress that seeks to take the place of inspiration. This rhetorical stress is surely a characteristic note. The great age of Southern oratory passed, it would seem, into another field and the declamatory, at times interjectional, nature of some of the poetry of this group may be accounted for on this hypothesis. The influence of Poe is apparent in nearly all of them. But as was the case with Emily Dickinson, the two greatest, Sidney Lanier and John Banister Tabb, are fitted with difficulty into a group. Both have a spiritual quality that is rare, a delicacy of touch, and a gift of phrasing that is unusual. Yet there is a marked distinction in their form, and in the restraint and compression of his verse, Father Tabb is more akin to Emily Dickinson than to any of the Southern poets.

THE EASTERN GROUP
THOMAS BAILEY ALDRICH (1836-1907)

PALABRAS CARIÑOSAS

(SPANISH AIR)

Good-night! I have to say good-night
To such a host of peerless things!
Good-night unto the slender hand
All queenly with its weight of rings!
Good-night to fond, uplifted eyes,
Good-night to chestnut braids of hair,
Good-night unto the perfect mouth,
And all the sweetness nestled there—
    The snowy hand detains me, then
    I'll have to say Good-night again!   10

But there will come a time, my love,
When, if I read our stars aright,
I shall not linger by this porch
With my farewells. Till then, good-night!
You wish the time were now? And I.
You do not blush to wish it so?
You would have blushed yourself to death
To own so much a year ago—
    What, both these snowy hands! ah, then,
    I'll have to say Good-night again!   20
                              1859, 1882, 1897

WHEN THE SULTAN GOES TO ISPAHAN

When the Sultan Shah-Zaman
Goes to the city Ispahan,
Even before he gets so far
As the place where the clustered palm-trees are,
At the last of the thirty palace-gates,
The flower of the harem, Rose-in-Bloom,
Orders a feast in his favorite room—
Glittering squares of colored ice,
Sweetened with syrop, tinctured with spice,
Creams, and cordials, and sugared dates,   10
Syrian apples, Othmanee quinces,
Limes, and citrons, and apricots,

And wines that are known to Eastern princes:
And Nubian slaves, with smoking pots
Of spicèd meats and costliest fish
And all that the curious palate could wish,
Pass in and out of the cedern doors;
Scattered over mosaic floors
Are anemones, myrtles, and violets,
And a musical fountain throws its jets   20
Of an hundred colors into the air.
The dusk Sultana loosens her hair,
And stains with the henna-plant the tips
Of her pointed nails, and bites her lips
Till they bloom again; but, alas, *that* rose
Not for the Sultan buds and blows,
Not for the Sultan Shah-Zaman,
When he goes to the city Ispahan.

Then at a wave of her sunny hand,
The dancing-girls of Samarcand   30
Glide in like shapes from fairy-land,
Making a sudden mist in air
Of fleecy veils and floating hair
And white arms lifted. Orient blood
Runs in their veins, shines in their eyes.
And there, in this Eastern Paradise,
Filled with the breath of sandal-wood,
And Khoten musk, and aloes and myrrh,
Sits Rose-in-Bloom on a silk divan,
Sipping the wines of Astrakhan;   40
And her Arab lover sits with her.
That's when the Sultan Shah-Zaman
Goes to the city of Ispahan!

Now, when I see an extra light,
Flaming, flickering on the night
From my neighbor's casement opposite,
I know as well as I know to pray,
I know as well as a tongue can say,
That the innocent Sultan Shah-Zaman
Has gone to the city Ispahan!   50
                              1859, 1882

FRIAR JEROME'S BEAUTIFUL BOOK

A. D. 1200

The Friar Jerome, for some slight sin,
Done in his youth, was struck with woe.
"When I am dead," quoth Friar Jerome,
"Surely, I think my soul will go
Shuddering through the darkened spheres,
Down to eternal fires below!
I shall not dare from that dread place
To lift mine eyes to Jesus' face,
Nor Mary's, as she sits adored
At the feet of Christ the Lord.   10
Alas! December's all too brief
For me to hope to wipe away
The memory of my sinful May!"
And Friar Jerome was full of grief,
That April evening, as he lay
On the straw pallet in his cell.
He scarcely heard the curfew-bell
Calling the brotherhood to prayer;
But he arose, for 'twas his care
Nightly to feed the hungry poor   20
That crowded to the Convent door.

His choicest duty it had been:
But this one night it weighed him down.
"What work for an immortal soul,
To feed and clothe some lazy clown?
Is there no action worth my mood,
No deed of daring, high and pure,
That shall, when I am dead, endure,
A well-spring of perpetual good?"

And straight he thought of those great
    tomes   30
With clamps of gold,—the Convent's boast,—
How they endured, while kings and realms
Past into darkness and were lost;
How they had stood from age to age,
Clad in their yellow vellum-mail,
'Gainst which the Paynim's godless rage,
The Vandal's fire, could naught avail:
Though heathen sword-blows fell like hail,
Though cities ran with Christian blood,
Imperishable they had stood!   40
They did not seem like books to him,
But Heroes, Martyrs, Saints—themselves
The things they told of, not mere books
Ranged grimly on the oaken shelves.

To those dim alcoves, far withdrawn,
He turned with measured steps and slow,
Trimming his lantern as he went;
And there, among the shadows, bent
Above one ponderous folio,

With whose miraculous text were blent   50
Seraphic faces: Angels, crowned
With rings of melting amethyst;
Mute, patient Martyrs, cruelly bound
To blazing fagots; here and there,
Some bold, serene Evangelist,
Or Mary in her sunny hair;
And here and there from out the words
A brilliant tropic bird took flight;
And through the margins many a vine
Went wandering—roses, red and white,   60
Tulip, wind-flower, and columbine
Blossomed. To his believing mind
These things were real, and the wind,
Blown through the mullioned window, took
Scent from the lilies in the book.

"Santa Maria!" cried Friar Jerome,
"Whatever man illumined this,
Though he were steeped heart-deep in sin,
Was worthy of unending bliss,
And no doubt hath it! Ah! dear Lord,   70
Might I so beautify Thy Word!
What sacristan, the convents through,
Transcribes with such precision? who
Does such initials as I do?
Lo! I will gird me to this work,
And save me, ere the one chance slips.
On smooth, clean parchment I'll engross
The Prophet's fell Apocalypse;
And as I write from day to day,
Perchance my sins will pass away."   80

So Friar Jerome began his Book.
From break of dawn till curfew-chime
He bent above the lengthening page,
Like some rapt poet o'er his rhyme.
He scarcely paused to tell his beads,
Except at night; and then he lay
And tossed, unrestful, on the straw,
Impatient for the coming day—
Working like one who feels, perchance,
That, ere the longed-for goal be won,   90
Ere Beauty bare her perfect breast,
Black Death may pluck him from the sun.
At intervals the busy brook,
Turning the mill-wheel, caught his ear;
And through the grating of the cell
He saw the honeysuckles peer,
And knew 'twas summer, that the sheep
In fragrant pastures lay asleep,
And felt, that, somehow, God was near.
In his green pulpit on the elm,   100

The robin, abbot of that wood,
Held forth by times; and Friar Jerome
Listened, and smiled, and understood.

While summer wrapt the blissful land
What joy it was to labor so,
To see the long-tressed Angels grow
Beneath the cunning of his hand,
Vignette and tail-piece subtly wrought!
And little recked he of the poor
That missed him at the Convent door;   110
Or, thinking of them, put the thought
Aside. "I feed the souls of men
Henceforth, and not their bodies!"—yet
Their sharp, pinched features, now and then,
Stole in between him and his Book,
And filled him with a vague regret.

Now on that region fell a blight:
The grain grew cankered in its sheath;
And from the verdurous uplands rolled
A sultry vapor fraught with death,—   120
A poisonous mist, that, like a pall,
Hung black and stagnant over all.
Then came the sickness—the malign
Green-spotted terror called the Pest,
That took the light from loving eyes,
And made the young bride's gentle breast
A fatal pillow. Ah! the woe,
The crime, the madness that befell!
In one short night that vale became
More foul than Dante's inmost hell.   130
Men cursed their wives; and mothers left
Their nursing babes alone to die,
And wantoned, singing, through the streets,
With shameless brow and frenzied eye;
And senseless clowns, not fearing God—
Such power the spotted fever had—
Razed Cragwood Castle on the hill,
Pillaged the wine-bins, and went mad.
And evermore that dreadful pall
Of mist hung stagnant over all: 140
By day, a sickly light broke through
The heated fog, on town and field;
By night, the moon, in anger, turned
Against the earth its mottled shield.

Then from the Convent, two and two,
The Prior chanting at their head,
The monks went forth to shrive the sick,
And give the hungry grave its dead—
Only Jerome, he went not forth,
But muttered in his dusty nook,   150
"Let come what will, I must illume
The last ten pages of my Book!"
He drew his stool before the desk,
And sat him down, distraught and wan,
To paint his darling masterpiece,

The stately figure of Saint John.
He sketched the head with pious care,
Laid in the tint, when, powers of Grace!
He found a grinning Death's-head there,
And not the grand Apostle's face!   160

Then up he rose with one long cry:
"'Tis Satan's self does this," cried he,
"Because I shut and barred my heart
When Thou didst loudest call to me!
O Lord, Thou know'st the thoughts of men,
Thou know'st that I did yearn to make
Thy Word more lovely to the eyes
Of sinful souls, for Christ his sake!
Nathless, I leave the task undone:
I give up all to follow Thee—   170
Even like him who gave his nets
To winds and waves by Galilee!"

Which said, he closed the precious Book
In silence, with a reverent hand;
And, drawing his cowl about his face
Went forth into the stricken land.
And there was joy in Heaven that day—
More joy o'er this forlorn old friar
Than over fifty sinless men
Who never struggled with desire!   180

What deeds he did in that dark town,
What hearts he soothed with anguish torn,
What weary ways of woe he trod,
Are written in the Book of God,
And shall be read at Judgment Morn.
The weeks crept on, when, one still day,
God's awful presence filled the sky,
And that black vapor floated by,
And, lo! the sickness past away.
With silvery clang, by thorp and town,   190
The bells made merry in their spires:
Men kissed each other on the street,
And music piped to dancing feet
The livelong night, by roaring fires!

Then Friar Jerome, a wasted shape—
For he had taken the Plague at last—
Rose up, and through the happy town,
And through the wintry woodlands, past
Into the Convent. What a gloom
Sat brooding in each desolate room!   200
What silence in the corridor!
For of that long, innumerous train
Which issued forth a month before,
Scarce twenty had come back again!

Counting his rosary step by step,
With a forlorn and vacant air,
Like some unshriven churchyard thing,
The Friar crawled up the mouldy stair

To his damp cell, that he might look
Once more on his belovèd Book.   210

And there it lay upon the stand,
Open!—he had not left it so.
He grasped it, with a cry; for, lo!
He saw that some angelic hand,
While he was gone, had finished it!
There 'twas complete, as he had planned;
There, at the end, stood 𝔉𝔦𝔫𝔦𝔰, writ
And gilded as no man could do—
Not even that pious anchoret,
Bilfrid, the wonderful, nor yet   220
The miniatore Ethelwold,—
Nor Durham's Bishop, who of old
(England still hoards the priceless leaves)
Did the Four Gospels all in gold.
And Friar Jerome nor spoke nor stirred,
But, with his eyes fixed on that word,
He past from sin and want and scorn;
And suddenly the chapel-bells
Rang in the holy Christmas-Morn!

In those wild wars which racked the land
Since then, and kingdoms rent in twain,   231
The Friar's Beautiful Book was lost—
That miracle of hand and brain:
Yet, though its leaves were torn and tossed,
The volume was not writ in vain!

                          1864, 1882

THE GUERDON

Alain, the poet, fell asleep one day
  In the lords' chamber, when it chanced the
      Queen
With her twelve maids of honor passed that
      way,—
  She like a slim white lily set between
  Twelve glossy leaves, for they were robed
      in green.

A forest of gold pillars propped the roof,
  And from the heavy corbels of carved stone
Yawned drowsy dwarfs, with satyr's face and
      hoof:
  Like one of those bright pillars overthrown,
  The slanted sunlight through the casement
      shone,   10

Gleaming across the body of Alain,—
  As if the airy column in its fall
Had caught and crushed him. So the laugh-
      ing train
  Came on him suddenly, and one and all
  Drew back, affrighted, midway in the hall.

Like some huge beetle curled up in the sun
  Was this man lying in the noontide glare,

Deformed, and hideous to look upon,
  With sunken eyes and masses of coarse hair,
  And sallow cheeks deep seamed with time
      and care.   20

Forth from her maidens stood Queen Mar-
      garet:
  The royal blood up to her temples crept
Like a wild vine with faint red roses set,
  As she across the pillared chamber swept,
  And, kneeling, kissed the poet while he
      slept.

Then from her knees uprose the stately Queen,
  And, seeing her ladies titter, 'gan to frown
With those great eyes wherein methinks were
      seen
  Lights that outflashed the lustres in her
      crown,—
  Great eyes that looked the shallow women
      down.   30

"Nay, not for love,"—'twas like a sudden
      bliss,
  The full sweet measured music of her
      tongue,—
"Nay, not for love's sake did I give the kiss,
  Not for his beauty who's nor fair nor young,
  But for the songs which those mute lips
      have sung!"

                                1867

DESTINY

Three roses, wan as moonlight and weighed
      down
Each with its loveliness as with a crown,
Drooped in a florist's window in a town.

The first a lover bought. It lay at rest,
Like flower on flower, that night, on Beauty's
      breast.

The second rose, as virginal and fair,
Shrunk in the tangles of a harlot's hair.

The third, a widow, with new grief made wild,
Shut in the icy palm of her dead child.

                                1872

AN UNTIMELY THOUGHT

I wonder what day of the week,
I wonder what month of the year—
Will it be midnight, or morning,
And who will bend over my bier? . . .

—What a hideous fancy to come
As I wait at the foot of the stair,

While Lilian gives the last touch
To her robe, or the rose in her hair.

Do I like your new dress—pompadour?
And do I like *you?* On my life,
You are eighteen, and not a day more,
And have not been six years my wife.

Those two rosy boys in the crib
Up-stairs are not ours, to be sure!—
You are just a sweet bride in her bloom,
All sunshine, and snowy, and pure.

As the carriage rolls down the dark street,
The little wife laughs and makes cheer—
But . . . I wonder what day of the week,
I wonder what month of the year.

1873

IN AN ATELIER

I pray you, do not turn your head;
And let your hands lie folded, so.
It was a dress like this, wine-red,
That troubled Dante, long ago.
You don't know Dante? Never mind.
He loved a lady wondrous fair—
His model? Something of the kind.
I wonder if she had your hair!

I wonder if she looked so meek,
And was not meek at all (my dear,
I want that side light on your cheek).
He loved her, it is very clear,
And painted her, as I paint you,
But rather better, on the whole
(Depress your chin; yes, that will do):
He was a painter of the soul!

(And painted portraits, too, I think,
In the INFERNO—devilish good!
I'd make some certain critics blink
Had I his method and his mood.)
Her name was (Fanny, let your glance
Rest there, by that majolica tray)—
Was Beatrice; they met by chance—
They met by chance, the usual way.

(As you and I met, months ago,
Do you remember? How your feet
Went crinkle-crinkle on the snow
Along the bleak gas-lighted street!
An instant in the drug-store's glare
You stood as in a golden frame,
And then I swore it, then and there,
To hand your sweetness down to fame.)

They met, and loved, and never wed
(All this was long before our time),
And though they died, they are not dead—
Such endless youth gives mortal rhyme!
Still walks the earth, with haughty mien,
Pale Dante, in his soul's distress;
And still the lovely Florentine
Goes lovely in her wine-red dress.

You do not understand at all?
He was a poet; on his page
He drew her; and, though kingdoms fall,
This lady lives from age to age.
A poet—that means painter too,
For words are colors, rightly laid;
And they outlast our brightest hue,
For varnish cracks and crimsons fade.

The poets—they are lucky ones!
When *we* are thrust upon the shelves,
Our works turn into skeletons
Almost as quickly as ourselves;
For our poor canvas peels at length,
At length is prized—when all is bare:
"What grace!" the critics cry, "what
strength!"
When neither strength nor grace is there.

Ah, Fanny, I am sick at heart,
It is so little one can do;
We talk our jargon—live for Art!
I'd much prefer to live for you.
How dull and lifeless colors are!
You smile, and all my picture lies:
I wish that I could crush a star
To make a pigment for your eyes.

Yes, child, I know, I'm out of tune;
The light is bad; the sky is gray:
I paint no more this afternoon,
So lay your royal gear away.
Besides, you're moody—chin on hand—
I know not what—not in the vein—
Not like Anne Bullen, sweet and bland:
You sit there smiling in disdain.

Not like the Tudor's radiant Queen,
Unconscious of the coming woe,
But rather as she might have been,
Preparing for the headsman's blow.
So, I have put you in a miff—
Sitting bolt-upright, wrist on wrist.
How *should* you look? Why, dear, as if—
Somehow—as if you'd just been kissed!

1875

PAULINE PAVLOVNA

SCENE: St. Petersburg. Period: the present time.
A ballroom in the winter palace of the Prince —.
The ladies in character costumes and masks. The
gentlemen in official dress and unmasked, with the
exception of six tall figures in scarlet kaftans, who
are treated with marked distinction as they move
here and there among the promenaders. Quadrille
music throughout the dialogue.

COUNT SERGIUS PAVLOVICH PANSHINE, who has
just arrived, is standing anxiously in the doorway
of an antechamber with his eyes fixed upon a lady
in the costume of a maid of honor in the time of
Catharine II. The lady presently disengages herself from the crowd, and passes near COUNT PAN-
SHINE, who impulsively takes her by the hand and
leads her across the threshold of the inner apartment, which is unoccupied.

He.   Pauline!
She.   You knew me?
He.   How could I have failed?
A mask may hide your features, not your soul.
There is an air about you like the air
That holds a star. A blind man knows the
       night,
And feels the constellations. No coarse sense
Of eye or ear had made you plain to me.
Through these I had not found you; for your
       eyes,
As blue as violets of our Novgorod,
Look black behind your mask there, and your
       voice—
I had not known that either. My heart said,
"Pauline Pavlovna."   10
She.   Ah! Your heart said that?
You trust your heart, then! 'Tis a serious
       risk!—
How is it you and others wear no mask?
He.   The Emperor's orders.
She.   Is the Emperor here?
I have not seen him.
He.   He is one of the six
In scarlet kaftans and all masked alike.
Watch—you will note how every one bows
       down
Before those figures, thinking each by chance
May be the Tsar; yet none knows which is he.
Even his counterparts are left in doubt.   20
Unhappy Russia! No serf ever wore
Such chains as gall our Emperor these sad
       days.
He dare trust no man.
She.   All men are so false.
He.   Save one, Pauline Pavlovna.
She.   No; all, all!
I think there is no truth left in the world,
In man or woman. Once were noble souls.—

Count Sergius, is Nastasia here to-night?
He.   Ah! then you know! I thought to tell
       you first.
Not here, beneath these hundred curious eyes,
In all this glare of light; but in some place   30
Where I could throw me at your feet and weep.
In what shape came the story to your ear?
Decked in the teller's colors, I'll be sworn;
The truth, but in the livery of a lie,
And so must wrong me. Only this is true:
The Tsar, because I risked my wretched life
To shield a life as wretched as my own,
Bestows upon me, as supreme reward—
O irony!—the hand of this poor girl.
He stayed me at the bottom of a stair,   40
And said, *We have the pearl of pearls for you,*
Such as from out the sea was never plucked
By Indian diver, for a Sultan's crown.
Your joy's decreed, and stabbed me with a
       smile.
She.   And she—she loves you?
He.   I much question that.
Likes me, perhaps. What matters it?—her
       love!
The guardian, Sidor Yurievich, consents,
And she consents. Love weighs not in such
       scales—
A mere caprice, a young girl's springtide
       dream.
Sick of her ear-rings, weary of her mare,   50
She'll have a lover, something ready-made,
Or improvised between two cups of tea—
A lover by imperial ukase!
Fate said her word—I chanced to be the man!
If that grenade the crazy student threw
Had not spared me, as well as spared the Tsar,
All this would not have happened. I'd have
       been
A hero, but quite safe from her romance.
She takes me for a hero—think of that!
Now by our holy Lady of Kazan,   60
When I have finished pitying myself,
I'll pity her.
She.   Oh no; begin with her;
She needs it most.
He.   At her door lies the blame,
Whatever falls. She, with a single word,
With half a tear, had stopped it at the first,
This cruel juggling with poor human hearts.
She.   The Tsar commanded it—you said
       the Tsar.
He.   The Tsar does what she wishes—God
       knows why.
Were she his mistress, now! but there's no
       snow

Whiter within the bosom of a cloud,   70
No colder either. She is very haughty,
For all her fragile air of gentleness;
With something vital in her, like those flowers
That on our desolate steppes outlast the year.
Resembles you in some things. It was that
First made us friends. I do her justice, mark.
For we were friends in that smooth surface
    way
We Russians have imported out of France—
Forgetting Alma and Sevastopol.   79
Alas! from what a blue and tranquil heaven
This bolt fell on me! After these two years,
My suit with Alexandrovitch at end,
The old wrong righted, the estates restored,
And my promotion, with the ink not dry!
Those fairies which neglected me at birth
Seemed now to lavish all good gifts on me—
Gold roubles, office, sudden dearest friends.
The whole world smiled; then, as I stooped to
    taste
The sweetest cup, freak dashed it from my lip.
This very night—just think, this very night—
I planned to come and beg of you the alms   91
I dared not ask for in my poverty.
I thought me poor then. How stripped am I
    now!
There's not a ragged mendicant one meets
Along the Nevski Prospekt but has leave
To tell his love, and I have not that right!
Pauline Pavlovna, why do you stand there
Stark as a statue, with no word to say?

She. Because this thing has frozen up my
    heart.
I think that there is something killed in me,   100
A dream that would have mocked all other
    bliss.
What shall I say? What would you have me
    say?

He. If it be possible, the word of words!

She (*Very slowly*) Well, then—I love you. I
    may tell you so
This once, . . . and then for ever hold my peace.
We cannot longer stay here unobserved.
No—do not touch me! but stand farther off,
And seem to laugh, as if we talked in jest,
Should we be watched. Now turn your face
    away.
I love you.

He.   With such music in my ears   110
I would death found me. It were sweet to die
Listening! You love me—prove it.

She.   Prove it—how?

I prove it saying it. How else?

He.   Pauline,

I have three things to choose from; you shall
    choose:
This marriage, or Siberia, or France.

The first means hell; the second, purgatory;
The third—with you—were nothing less than
    heaven!

She. (*Starting*) How dared you even dream
    it!

He. I was mad.
This business has touched me in the brain.
Have patience! the calamity is new. (*Pauses*)
There is a fourth way; but that gate is shut   121
To brave men who hold life a thing of God.

She. Yourself spoke there; the rest was not
    of you.

He. Oh, lift me to your level! Where you
    move
The air is temperate, and no pulses beat.
What's to be done?

She.   I lack invention—stay,
Perhaps the Emperor—

He.   Not a shred of hope!
His mind is set on this with that insistence
Which seems to seize on all match-making folk.
The fancy bites them, and they straight go
    mad.   130

She. Your father's friend, the Metropoli-
    tan—
A word from him. . . .

He.   Alas, he too is bitten!
Gray-haired, gray-hearted, worldly wise, he
    sees
This marriage makes me the Tsar's protégé,
And opens every door to preference.

She. Then let him be. There surely is some
    way
Out of the labyrinth, could we but find it.
Nastasia!

He.   What! beg life of her? Not I.

She. Beg love. She is a woman, young,
    perhaps
Untouched as yet of this too poisonous air.   140
Were she told all, would she not pity us?
For if she love you, as I think she must,
Would not some generous impulse stir in her,
Some latent, unsuspected spark illume?
How love thrills even commonest girl-clay,
Ennobling it an instant, if no more!
You said that she is proud; then touch her
    pride,
And turn her into marble with the touch.
But yet the gentler passion is the stronger.
Go to her, tell her, in some tenderest phrase   150
That will not hurt too much—ah, but 'twill
    hurt!—
Just how your happiness lies in her hand
To make or mar for all time; hint, not say,
Your heart is gone from you, and you may
    find—

He. A casemate in St. Peter and St. Paul
For, say, a month; then some Siberian town.

Not this way lies escape. At my first word
That sluggish Tartar blood would turn to fire
In every vein.
   She.   How blindly you read her,
Or any woman! Yes, I know. I grant   160
How small we often seem in our small world
Of trivial cares and narrow precedents—
Lacking that wide horizon stretched for men—
Capricious, spiteful, frightened at a mouse;
But when it comes to suffering mortal pangs,
The weakest of us measures pulse with you.
   He.   Yes, you, not she. If she were at your
      height!
But there's no martyr wrapped in *her* rose flesh.
There should have been; for Nature gave you
      both
The self-same purple for your eyes and hair, 170
The self-same Southern music to your lips,
Fashioned you both, as 'twere, in the same
      mould,
Yet failed to put the soul in one of you!
I know her wilful—her light head quite turned

In this court atmosphere of flatteries;
A Moscow beauty, petted and spoiled there,
And since spoiled here; as soft as swan's-down
      now,
With words like honey melting from the comb,
But being crossed, vindictive, cruel, cold.
I fancy her, between two languid smiles, 180
Saying, "Poor fellow, in the Nertchinsk
      mines!"
I know her pitiless.
   She.   You know her not.
Count Sergius Pavlovich, you said no mask
Could hide the soul, yet how you have mis-
      taken
The soul these two months—and the face to-
      night!   (*Removes her mask*)
   He.   You!—it was *you!*
   She.   Count Sergius Pavlovich,
Go find Pauline Pavlovna—she is here—
And tell her that the Tsar has set you free.
   (*She goes out hurriedly, replacing her mask.*)
                         1887

LOUISE CHANDLER MOULTON (1835–1908)

THE HOUSE OF DEATH

Not a hand has lifted the latchet
  Since she went out of the door,—
No footstep shall cross the threshold,
  Since she can come in no more.

There is rust upon locks and hinges,
  And mold and blight on the walls,
And silence faints in the chambers,
  And darkness waits in the halls,—

Waits, as all things have waited,
  Since she went, that day of spring,   10
Borne in her pallid splendor,
  To dwell in the Court of the King:

With lilies on brow and bosom,
  With robes of silken sheen,
And her wonderful frozen beauty
  The lilies and silk between.

Red roses she left behind her,
  But they died long, long ago,—
'Twas the odorous ghost of a blossom   19
  That seemed through the dusk to glow.

The garments she left mock the shadows
  With hints of womanly grace,
And her image swims in the mirror
  That was so used to her face.

The birds make insolent music
  Where the sunshine riots outside;
And the winds are merry and wanton,
  With the summer's pomp and pride.

But into this desolate mansion,
  Where Love has closed the door,   30
Nor sunshine nor summer shall enter,
  Since she can come in no more.
                      1877

LAUS VENERIS

A PICTURE BY BURNE JONES

Pallid with too much longing,
  White with passion and prayer,
Goddess of love and beauty,
  She sits in the picture there,—

Sits with her dark eyes seeking
  Something more subtle still
Than the old delights of loving
  Her measureless days to fill.

She has loved and been loved so often
  In her long, immortal years,   10
That she tires of the worn-out rapture,
  Sickens of hopes and fears.

No joys or sorrows move her,
  Done with her ancient pride;
For her head she found too heavy
  The crown she has cast aside.

Clothed in her scarlet splendor,
  Bright with her glory of hair,
Sad that she is not mortal,—
  Eternally sad and fair,   20
Longing for joys she knows not,
  Athirst with a vain desire,
There she sits in the picture,
  Daughter of foam and fire.
      1878

EDMUND CLARENCE STEDMAN (1833-1908)

HOW OLD BROWN TOOK HARPER'S FERRY

John Brown in Kansas settled, like a steadfast Yankee farmer,
  Brave and godly, with four sons, all stalwart men of might.
There he spoke aloud for freedom, and the Border-strife grew warmer,
  Till the Rangers fired his dwelling, in his absence, in the night;
        And Old Brown,
        Osawatomie Brown,
Came homeward in the morning—to find his house burned down.

Then he grasped his trusty rifle and boldly fought for freedom;
  Smote from border unto border the fierce, invading band;
And he and his brave boys vowed—so might Heaven help and speed 'em!—   10
  They would save those grand old prairies from the curse that blights the land;
        And Old Brown,
        Osawatomie Brown,
Said, "Boys, the Lord will aid us!" and he shoved his ramrod down.

And the Lord *did* aid these men, and they labored day and even,
  Saving Kansas from its peril; and their very lives seemed charmed,
Till the ruffians killed one son, in the blessed light of Heaven,—
  In cold blood the fellows slew him, as he journeyed all unarmed;
        Then Old Brown,
        Osawatomie Brown,   20
Shed not a tear, but shut his teeth, and frowned a terrible frown!

Then they seized another brave boy,—not amid the heat of battle,
  But in peace, behind his ploughshare,—and they loaded him with chains,
And with pikes, before their horses, even as they goad their cattle,
  Drove him cruelly, for their sport, and at last blew out his brains;
        Then Old Brown,
        Osawatomie Brown,
Raised his right hand up to Heaven, calling Heaven's vengeance down.

And he swore a fearful oath, by the name of the Almighty,
  He would hunt this ravening evil that had scathed and torn him so;   30
He would seize it by the vitals; he would crush it day and night; he
  Would so pursue its footsteps, so return it blow for blow,
        That Old Brown,
        Osawatomie Brown,
Should be a name to swear by, in backwoods or in town!

Then his beard became more grizzled, and his wild blue eye grew wilder,
  And more sharply curved his hawk's-nose, snuffing battle from afar;
And he and the two boys left, though the Kansas strife waxed milder,
  Grew more sullen, till was over the bloody Border War,
        And Old Brown,   40
        Osawatomie Brown,
Had gone crazy, as they reckoned by his fearful glare and frown.

So he left the plains of Kansas and their bitter woes behind him,
  Slipt off into Virginia, where the statesmen all are born,

Hired a farm by Harper's Ferry, and no one knew where to find him,
  Or whether he'd turned parson, or was jacketed and shorn;
        For Old Brown,
        Osawatomie Brown,
Mad as he was, knew texts enough to wear a parson's gown.

He bought no ploughs and harrows, spades and shovels, and such trifles;   50
  But quietly to his rancho there came, by every train,
Boxes full of pikes and pistols, and his well-beloved Sharp's rifles;
  And eighteen other madmen joined their leader there again.
        Says Old Brown,
        Osawatomie Brown,
"Boys, we've got an army large enough to march and take the town!

"Take the town, and seize the muskets, free the negroes and then arm them;
  Carry the County and the State, ay, and all the potent South.
On their own heads be the slaughter, if their victims rise to harm them—
  These Virginians! who believed not, nor would heed the warning mouth."   60
        Says Old Brown,
        Osawatomie Brown,
"The world shall see a Republic, or my name is not John Brown."

'Twas the sixteenth of October, on the evening of a Sunday:
  "This good work," declared the captain, "shall be on a holy night!"
It was on a Sunday evening, and before the noon of Monday,
  With two sons, and Captain Stephens, fifteen privates—black and white,
        Captain Brown,
        Osawatomie Brown,
Marched across the bridged Potomac, and knocked the sentry down;   70

Took the guarded armory-building, and the muskets and the cannon;
  Captured all the county majors and the colonels, one by one;
Scared to death each gallant scion of Virginia they ran on,
  And before the noon of Monday, I say, the deed was done.
        Mad Old Brown,
        Osawatomie Brown,
With his eighteen other crazy men, went in and took the town.

Very little noise and bluster, little smell of powder made he;
  It was all done in the midnight, like the Emperor's *coup d'état*.
"Cut the wires! Stop the rail-cars! Hold the streets and bridges!" said he,   80
  Then declared the new Republic, with himself for guiding star,—
        This Old Brown,
        Osawatomie Brown,
And the bold two thousand citizens ran off and left the town.

Then was riding and railroading and expressing here and thither;
  And the Martinsburg Sharpshooters and the Charlestown Volunteers,
And the Shepherdstown and Winchester Militia hastened whither
  Old Brown was said to muster his ten thousand granadiers.
        General Brown,
        Osawatomie Brown!   90
Behind whose rampant banner all the North was pouring down.

But at last, 'tis said, some prisoners escaped from Old Brown's durance,
  And the effervescent valor of the Chivalry broke out,
When they learned that nineteen madmen had the marvellous assurance—
  Only nineteen—thus to seize the place and drive them straight about;
        And Old Brown,
        Osawatomie Brown,
Found an army come to take him, encamped around the town.

But to storm, with all the forces I have mentioned, was too risky;
  So they hurried off to Richmond for the Government Marines,   100
Tore them from their weeping matrons, fired their souls with Bourbon whiskey,
  Till they battered down Brown's castle with their ladders and machines;
      And Old Brown,
      Osawatomie Brown,
Received three bayonet stabs, and a cut on his brave old crown.

Tallyho! the old Virginian gentry gather to the baying!
  In they rushed and killed the game, shooting lustily away;
And whene'er they slew a rebel, those who came too late for slaying,
  Not to lose a share of glory, fired their bullets in his clay;
      And Old Brown,   110
      Osawatomie Brown,
Saw his sons fall dead beside him, and between them laid him down.

How the conquerors wore their laurels; how they hastened on the trial;
  How Old Brown was placed, half dying, on the Charlestown court-house floor;
How he spoke his grand oration, in the scorn of all denial;
  What the brave old madman told them,—these are known the country o'er.
      "Hang Old Brown,
      Osawatomie Brown,"
Said the judge, "and all such rebels!" with his most judicial frown.

But, Virginians, don't do it! for I tell you that the flagon,   120
  Filled with blood of Old Brown's offspring, was first poured by Southern hands;
And each drop from Old Brown's life-veins, like the red gore of the dragon,
  May spring up a vengeful Fury, hissing through your slave-worn lands!
      And Old Brown,
      Osawatomie Brown,
May trouble you more than ever, when you've nailed his coffin down!

                    1859
November, 1859.

"THE UNDISCOVERED COUNTRY"

Could we but know
The land that ends our dark, uncertain travel,
Where lie those happier hills and meadows
  low,—
Ah, if beyond the spirit's inmost cavil,
Aught of that country could we surely know,
  Who would not go?

Might we but hear
The hovering angels' high imagined chorus,
Or catch, betimes, with wakeful eyes and
  clear,

One radiant vista of the realm before us,—   10
With one rapt moment given to see and
  hear,
  Ah, who would fear?
    Were we quite sure
To find the peerless friend who left us lonely,
Or there, by some celestial stream as pure,
To gaze in eyes that here were lovelit only,—
This weary mortal coil, were we quite sure,
  Who would endure?
February, 1865   1866

PAN IN WALL STREET

Just where the Treasury's marble front
  Looks over Wall Street's mingled nations;
Where Jews and Gentiles most are wont
  To throng for trade and last quotations;
Where, hour by hour, the rates of gold
  Outrival, in the ears of people,

The quarter-chimes, serenely told
  From Trinity's undaunted steeple,—

Even then I heard a strange, wild strain
  Sound high above the modern clamor,   10
Above the cries of greed and gain,

The curbstone war, the auction's hammer;
And swift, on Music's misty ways,
  It led, from all this strife for millions,
To ancient, sweet-do-nothing days
  Among the kirtle-robed Sicilians.

And as it stilled the multitude,
  And yet more joyous rose, and shriller,
I saw the minstrel, where he stood
  At ease against a Doric pillar: 20
One hand a droning organ played,
  The other held a Pan's-pipe (fashioned
Like those of old) to lips that made
  The reeds give out that strain impassioned.

'T was Pan himself had wandered here
  A-strolling through this sordid city,
And piping to the civic ear
  The prelude of some pastoral ditty!
The demigod had crossed the seas,—
  From haunts of shepherd, nymph, and
    satyr,   30
And Syracusan times,—to these
  Far shores and twenty centuries later.

A ragged cap was on his head;
  But—hidden thus—there was no doubting
That, all with crispy locks o'erspread,
  His gnarléd horns were somewhere sprout-
    ing;
His club-feet, cased in rusty shoes,
  Were crossed, as in some frieze you see them,
And trousers, patched of divers hues,   39
  Concealed his crooked shanks beneath them.

He filled the quivering reeds with sound,
  And o'er his mouth their changes shifted,
And with his goat's-eyes looked around
  Where'er the passing current drifted;
And soon, as on Trinacrian hills
  The nymphs and herdsmen ran to hear him,
Even now the tradesmen from their tills,
  With clerks and porters, crowded near him.

The bulls and bears together drew
  From Jauncey Court and New Street Alley,
As erst, if pastorals be true,   51
  Came beasts from every wooded valley;
The random passers stayed to list,—
  A boxer Ægon, rough and merry,
A Broadway Daphnis, on his tryst
  With Nais at the Brooklyn Ferry.

A one-eyed Cyclops halted long
  In tattered cloak of army pattern,
And Galatea joined the throng,—
  A blowsy, apple-vending slattern;   60
While old Silenus staggered out
  From some new-fangled lunch-house handy,

And bade the piper, with a shout,
  To strike up Yankee Doodle Dandy!

A newsboy and a peanut-girl
  Like little Fauns began to caper:
His hair was all in tangled curl,
  Her tawny legs were bare and taper;
And still the gathering larger grew,
  And gave its pence and crowded nigher,   70
While aye the shepherd-minstrel blew
  His pipe, and struck the gamut higher.

O heart of Nature, beating still
  With throbs her vernal passion taught
    her,—
Even here, as on the vine-clad hill,
  Or by the Arethusan water!
New forms may fold the speech, new lands
  Arise within these ocean-portals,
But Music waves eternal wands,—
  Enchantress of the souls of mortals!   80

So thought I,—but among us trod
  A man in blue, with legal baton,
And scoffed the vagrant demigod,
  And pushed him from the step I sat on.
Doubting I mused upon the cry,
  "Great Pan is dead!"—and all the people
Went on their ways:—and clear and high
  The quarter sounded from the steeple.
                                       1867

STANZAS FOR MUSIC

Thou art mine, thou hast given thy word;
  Close, close in my arms thou art clinging;
  Alone for my ear thou art singing
A song which no stranger hath heard:
But afar from me yet, like a bird,
Thy soul, in some region unstirred,
  On its mystical circuit is winging.

Thou art mine, I have made thee mine own;
  Henceforth we are mingled forever:
  But in vain, all in vain, I endeavor—   10
Though round thee my garlands are thrown,
And thou yieldest thy lips and thy zone—
To master the spell that alone
  My hold on thy being can sever.

Thou art mine, thou hast come unto me!
  But thy soul, when I strive to be near it—
  The innermost fold of thy spirit—
Is as far from my grasp, is as free,
As the stars from the mountain-tops be,
  As the pearl, in the depths of the sea, 20
  From the portionless king that would wear
    it.
                                       1873

SISTER BEATRICE

A LEGEND FROM THE "SERMONES DISCIPULI" OF JEAN HEROLT, THE DOMINICAN, A. D. 1518

A cloister tale,—a strange and ancient thing
  Long since on vellum writ in gules and or:
And why should Chance to me this trover
    bring
From the grim dust-heap of forgotten lore,
  And not to that gray bard still measuring
His laurelled years by music's golden score,
Nor to some comrade who like him has caught
The charm of lands by me too long unsought?

Why not to one who, with a steadfast eye,
  Ingathering her shadow and her sheen,   10
Saw Venice as she is, and, standing nigh,
  Drew from the life that old, dismantled
    queen?
Or to the poet through whom I well descry
  Castile, and the Campeador's demesne?
Or to that eager one whose quest has found
Each place of long renown, the world around;

Whose foot has rested firm on either hill,—
  The sea-girt height where glows the mid-
    night sun,
And wild Parnassus; whose melodious skill 19
  Has left no song untried, no wreath unwon?
Why not to these? Yet, since by Fortune's
    will
This quaint task given me I must not shun,
My verse shall render, fitly as it may,
An old church legend, meet for Christmas
  Day.

Once on a time (so read the monkish pages),
  Within a convent—that doth still abide
Even as it stood in those devouter ages,
  Near a fair city, by the highway's side—
There dwelt a sisterhood of them whose wages
  Are stored in heaven: each a virgin bride 30
Of Christ, and bounden meekly to endure
In faith, and works, and chastity most pure.

A convent, and within a summer-land,
  Like that of Browning and Boccaccio!
Years since, my greener fancy would have
    planned
  Its station thus: it should have had, I trow,
A square and flattened bell-tower, that might
    stand
  Above deep-windowed buildings long and
    low,
Closed all securely by a vine-clung wall,
And shadowed on one side by cypress tall. 40

Within the gate, a garden set with care:
  Box-bordered plots, where peach and al-
    mond trees
Rained blossoms on the maidens walking
    there,
  Or rustled softly in the summer breeze;
Here were sweet jessamine and jonquil rare,
  And arbors meet for pious talk at ease;
There must have been a dove-cote too, I know,
Where white-winged birds like spirits come
  and go.

Outside, the thrush and lark their music made
  Beyond the olive-grove at dewy morn;   50
By noon, cicalas, shrilling in the shade
  Of oak and ilex, woke the peasant's horn;
And, at the time when into darkness fade
  The vineyards, from their purple depths
    were borne
The nightingale's responses to the prayer
Of those sweet saints at vespers, meek and fair.

Such is the place that, with the hand and eye
  Which are the joy of youth, I should have
    painted.
Say not, who look thereon, that 't is awry—
  Like nothing real, by rhymesters' use at-
    tainted.   60
Ah well! then put the faulty picture by,
  And help me draw an abbess long since
    sainted.
Think of your love, each one, and thereby
    guess
The fashion of this lady's beauteousness.

For in this convent Sister Beatrice,
  Of all her nuns the fairest and most young,
Became, through grace and special holiness,
  Their sacred head, and moved, her brood
    among,
Dévote d'âme et fervente au service;
  And thrice each day, their hymns and Aves
    sung,   70
At Mary's altar would before them kneel,
Keeping her vows with chaste and pious zeal.

Now in the Holy Church there was a clerk,
  A godly-seeming man (as such there be
Whose selfish hearts with craft and guile are
    dark),
  Young, gentle-phrased, of handsome mien
    and free.

His passion chose this maiden for its mark,
  Begrudging heaven her white chastity,
And with most sacrilegious art the while
He sought her trustful nature to beguile. 80

Oft as they met, with subtle hardihood
  He still more archly played the traitor's
    part,
And strove to wake that murmur in her blood
  That times the pulses of a woman's heart;
And in her innocence she long withstood
  The secret tempter, but at last his art
Changed all her tranquil thoughts to love's
    desire,
Her vestal flame to earth's unhallowed fire.

So the fair governess, o'ermastered, gave
  Herself to the destroyer, yet as one 90
That slays, in pity, her sweet self, to save
  Another from some wretched deed undone;
But when she found her heart was folly's
    slave,
  She sought the altar which her steps must
    shun
Thenceforth, and yielded up her sacred trust,
Ere tasting that false fruit which turns to
    dust.

One eve the nuns beheld her entering
  Alone, as if for prayer beneath the rood,
Their chapel-shrine, wherein the offering
  And masterpiece of some great painter
    stood,— 100
The Virgin Mother, without plume or wing
  Ascending, poised in rapt beatitude,
With hands crosswise, and intercession mild
For all who crave her mercy undefiled.

There Beatrice—poor, guilty, desperate maid—
  Took from her belt the convent's blessed
    keys,
.And with them on the altar humbly laid
  Her missal, uttering such words as these
(Her eyes cast down, and all her soul afraid):
  "O dearest mistress, hear me on my knees
Confess to thee, in helplessness and shame,
I am no longer fit to speak thy name. 112

"Take back the keys wherewith in constancy
  Thy house and altar I have guarded well!
No more may Beatrice thy servant be,
  For earthly love her steps must needs com-
    pel.
Forget me in this sore infirmity
  When my successor here her beads shall
    tell."
This said, the girl withdrew her as she might,
And with her lover fled that selfsame night; 120

Fled out, and into the relentless world
  Where Love abides, but Love that breedeth
    Sorrow,
Where Purity still weeps with pinions furled,
  And Passion lies in wait her all to borrow.
From such a height to such abasement whirled
  She fled that night, and many a day and
    morrow
Abode indeed with him for whose embrace
She bartered heaven and her hope of grace.

O fickle will and pitiless desire, 129
  Twin wolves, that raven in a lustful heart
And spare not innocence, nor yield, nor tire,
  But youth from joy and life from goodness
    part;
That drag an unstained victim to the mire,
  Then cast it soiled and hopeless on the
    mart!
Even so the clerk, once having dulled his
    longing,
A worse thing did than that first bitter wrong-
    ing.

The base hind left her, ruined and alone,
  Unknowing by what craft to gain her bread
In the hard world that gives to Want a stone.
  What marvel that she drifted whither led 140
The current, that with none to heed her moan
  She reached the shore where life on husks is
    fed,
Sank down, and, in the strangeness of her fall,
Among her fellows was the worst of all!

Thus stranded, her fair body, consecrate
  To holiness, was smutched by spoilers rude,
And entered all the seven fiends where late
  Abode a seeming angel, pure and good.
What paths she followed in such woful state,
  By want, remorse, and the world's hate
    pursued, 150
Were known alone to them whose spacious ken
O'erlooks not even the poor Magdalen.

After black years their dismal change had
    wrought
  Upon her beauty, and there was no stay
By which to hold, some chance or yearning
    brought
  Her vagrant feet along the convent-way;
And half as in a dream there came a thought
  (For years she had not dared to think or
    pray)
That moved her there to bow her in the dust
And bear no more, but perish as she must. 160

Crouched by the gate she waited, it is told,
  Brooding the past and all of life forlorn,

Nor dared to lift her pallid face and old
  Against the passer's pity or his scorn;
And there perchance had ere another morn
  Died of her shame and sorrows manifold,
But that a portress bade her pass within
For solace of her wretchedness or sin.

To whom the lost one, drinking now her fill
  Of woe that wakened memories made more
    drear,   170
Said, "Was there not one Beatrice, until
  Some time now gone, that was an abbess
    here?"
"That was?" the other said. "Is she not still
  The convent's head, and still our mistress
    dear?
Look! even now she comes with open hand,
The purest, saintliest lady in the land!"

And Beatrice, uplifting then her eyes,
  Saw her own self (in womanhood divine,
It seemed) draw nigh, with holy look and
    wise,
  The aged portress leaving at a sign.   180
Even while she marvelled at that strange dis-
    guise,

There stood before her, radiant, benign,
The blessed Mother of Mercy, all aflame
With light, as if from Paradise she came!

From her most sacred lips, upon the ears
  Of Beatrice, these words of wonder fell:
"Daughter, thy sins are pardoned; dry thy
    tears,
  And in this house again my mercies tell,
For, in thy stead, myself these woful years
  Have governed here and borne thine office
    well.   190
Take back the keys: save thee and me alone
No one thy fall and penance yet hath known!"

Even then, as faded out that loveliness,
  The abbess, looking down, herself descried
Clean-robed and spotless, such as all confess
  To be a saint and fit for Heaven's bride.
So ends the legend, and ye well may guess
  (Who, being untempted, walk in thought-
    less pride)
God of his grace can make the sinful pure,
And while earth lasts shall mercy still en-
    dure.   200
                                              1877

EMILY DICKINSON (1830-1886)

THIS IS MY LETTER TO THE WORLD

This is my letter to the world,
  That never wrote to me,—
The simple news that Nature told,
  With tender majesty.

Her message is committed
  To hands I cannot see;
For love of her, sweet countrymen,
  Judge tenderly of me!
                              1890

SUCCESS IS COUNTED SWEETEST

Success is counted sweetest
By those who ne'er succeed.
To comprehend a nectar
Requires sorest need.

Not one of all the purple host
Who took the flag to-day
Can tell the definition,
So clear, of victory,

As he, defeated, dying,
On whose forbidden ear   10

The distant strains of triumph
Break, agonized and clear.
                              1890

I HAD NO TIME TO HATE

I had no time to hate, because
  The grave would hinder me,
And life was not so ample I
  Could finish enmity.

Nor had I time to love; but since
  Some industry must be,
The little toil of love, I thought,
  Was large enough for me.
                              1890

I NEVER SAW A MOOR

I never saw a moor,
I never saw the sea;
Yet know I how the heather looks,
And what a wave must be.

I never spoke with God,
Nor visited in heaven;
Yet certain am I of the spot
As if the chart were given.
                              1890

THE BUSTLE IN A HOUSE

The bustle in a house
The morning after death
Is solemnest of industries
Enacted upon earth,—

The sweeping up the heart,
And putting love away
We shall not want to use again
Until eternity.

1890

AS IMPERCEPTIBLY AS GRIEF

As imperceptibly as grief
The summer lapsed away,—
Too imperceptible, at last,
To seem like perfidy.

A quietness distilled,
As twilight long begun,
Or Nature, spending with herself
Sequestered afternoon.

The dusk drew earlier in,
The morning foreign shone,—   10
A courteous, yet harrowing grace,
As guest who would be gone.

And thus, without a wing,
Or service of a keel,
Our summer made her light escape
Into the beautiful.

1891

MY LIFE CLOSED TWICE

My life closed twice before its close;
It yet remains to see
If Immortality unveil
A third event to me,

So huge, so hopeless to conceive,
As these that twice befell.
Parting is all we know of heaven,
And all we need of hell.

1896

HEART, WE WILL FORGET HIM

Heart, we will forget him!
You and I, tonight!
You may forget the warmth he gave,
I will forget the light.

When you have done, pray tell me,
That I my thoughts may dim;
Haste! lest while you're lagging,
I may remember him!

1896

EDWARD ROWLAND SILL (1841–1887)

THE FOOL'S PRAYER

The royal feast was done; the King
  Sought some new sport to banish care,
And to his jester cried: "Sir Fool,
  Kneel now, and make for us a prayer!"

The jester doffed his cap and bells,
  And stood the mocking court before;
They could not see the bitter smile
  Behind the painted grin he wore.

He bowed his head, and bent his knee
  Upon the monarch's silken stool;   10
His pleading voice arose: "O Lord,
  Be merciful to me, a fool!

"No pity, Lord, could change the heart
  From red with wrong to white as wool;
The rod must heal the sin: but Lord,
  Be merciful to me, a fool!

"'T is not by guilt the onward sweep
  Of truth and right, O Lord, we stay;
'T is by our follies that so long
  We hold the earth from heaven away.   20

"These clumsy feet, still in the mire,
  Go crushing blossoms without end;
These hard, well-meaning hands we thrust
  Among the heart-strings of a friend.

"The ill-timed truth we might have kept—
  Who knows how sharp it pierced and stung?
The word we had not sense to say—
  Who knows how grandly it had rung?

"Our faults no tenderness should ask,
  The chastening stripes must cleanse them all;   30
But for our blunders—oh, in shame
  Before the eyes of heaven we fall.

"Earth bears no balsam for mistakes;
  Men crown the knave, and scourge the tool
That did his will; but Thou, O Lord,
  Be merciful to me, a fool!"

The room was hushed; in silence rose
  The King, and sought his gardens cool,
And walked apart, and murmured low,
  "Be merciful to me, a fool!"   40

1879

TEMPTED

Yes, I know what you say:
  Since it cannot be soul to soul,
Be it flesh to flesh, as it may;
  But is Earth the whole?

Shall a man betray the Past
  For all Earth gives?
"But the Past is dead?" At last,
  It is all that lives.

Which were the nobler goal—
  To snatch at the moment's bliss,   10

Or to swear I will keep my soul
  Clean for her kiss?   1885

ON SECOND THOUGHT

The end's so near,
  It is all one
What track I steer,
  What work's begun.
It is all one
  If *nothing's* done,
The end's so near!

The end's so near,
  It is all one
What track thou steer,   10
  What work's begun—
Some deed, *some* plan,
  As thou 'rt a man!
The end 's so near!   1899

SILAS WEIR MITCHELL (1829-1914)

THE MOTHER

"I will incline mine ear to the parable, and show my dark speech upon the harp."

Christmas! Christmas! merry Christmas! rang the bells. O God of grace!
In the stillness of the death-room motionless I kept my place,
While beneath my eyes a wanness came upon the little face,
And an empty smile that stung me, as the pallor grew apace.
Then, as if from some far distance, spake a voice: "The child is dead!"
"Dead?" I cried. "Is God not good? What thing accursed is that you said?"
Swift I searched their eyes of pity, swaying, bowed, and all my soul,
Shrunken as a hand had crushed it, crumpled like a useless scroll
Read and done with, passed from sorrows; only with me lingered yet
Some dim sense of easeful comfort in the glad leave to forget.   10
But again life's scattered fragments, memories of joy and woe,
Tremulously came to oneness, as a storm-torn lake may grow
Quiet, winning back its pictures, when the wild winds cease to blow.
As if called for God's great audit came a vision of my years,
Broken gleams of youth and girlhood, all the woman's love and tears.
Marvelling, myself I saw as one another sees, and smiles,
Crooning o'er my baby dolls,—part a mother, part a child;
Then, half sorry, ceased to wonder why I left my silent brood,
Till the lessoning years went by me, and the instinct, love-renewed,
Stirred again life's stronger fibre, and were mine twain living things;   20
Bone of my bone! flesh of my flesh! Who on earth a title brings
Flawless as this mother-title, free from aught of mortal stain,
Innocent and pure possession, double-born of joy and pain?
Oh, what wonder these could help me, set me laughing, though I sobbed
As they drew my very heart out, and the laden breasts were robbed!
Tender buds of changeful pleasure came as come the buds of May,
Trivial, wondrous, unexpected, blossoming from day to day.
Ah! the clutch of tendril-fingers, that with nature's cunning knew
So to coil in sturdy grapple round the stem from which they grew.

Shall a man this joy discover? How the heart-wine to the brain 30
Rushed with shock of bliss when, startled, first I won this simple gain!
How I mocked those seeking fingers, eager for their earliest toy,
Telling none my new-found treasure! Miser of the mother's joy,
Quick I caught the first faint ripple, answering me with lip and eyes,
As I stooped with mirthful purpose, keen to capture fresh replies;
Oh, the pretty wonder of it, when was born the art to smile,
Or the new, gay trick of laughter filled my eyes with tears the while,—
Helpful tears, love's final language, when the lips no more can say,
Tears, like kindly prophets, warning of another, darker day.
Thus my vision lost its gladness, and I stood on life's dim strand, 40
Watching where a little love-bark drifted slowly from the land;
For again the bells seemed ringing Christmas o'er the snow of dawn,
And my dreaming memory hurt me with a hot face, gray and drawn,
And with small hands locked in anguish. Ah! those days of helpless pain!
Mine the mother's wrathful sorrow. Ah! my child, hadst thou been Cain,
Father of the primal murder, black with every hideous thought,
Cruel were the retribution; for, alas! what good is wrought
When the very torture ruins all the fine machine of thought?
So, with reeling brain I questioned, while the fevered cheek grew white,
And at last I seemed to pass with him, released, to death's dark night. 50
Seraph voices whispered round me. "God," they said, "hath set our task,—
Thou to question, we to answer: fear not; ask what thou wouldst ask."
Wildly beat my heart. Thought only, regnant, held its sober pace,
Whilst, a wingèd mind, I wandered in the bleak domain of space.
Then I sought and seeing marvelled at the mystery of time,
Where beneath me rolled the earth-star in its first chaotic slime,
As bewildering ages passing with their cyclic changes came,
Heaving land and 'whelming waters, ice and fierce volcanic flame,
Sway and shock of tireless atoms, pulsing with the throb of force,
Whilst the planet, rent and shaken, fled upon its mighty course, 60
Last, with calm of wonder hushed, I saw amid the surging strife
Rise the first faint stir of being and the tardy morn of life,—
Life in countless generations. Speechless, mercilessly dumb,
Swept by ravage of disaster, tribe on tribe in silence come,
Till the yearning sense found voices, and on hill, and shore, and plain,
Dreary from the battling myriads rose the birthright wail of pain.
God of pity! Son of sorrows! Wherefore should a power unseen
Launch on years of needless anguish this great agonized machine?
Was Himself who willed this torment but a slave to law self-made?
Or had some mad angel-demon here, unchecked and undismayed, 70
Leave to make of earth a Job; until the cruel game was played
Free to whirl the spinning earth-toy where his despot forces wrought,
While he watched each sense grow keener as the lifted creature bought
With the love-gift added sorrow, and there came to man's estate
Will, the helpless; thought, the bootless; all the deathward war with fate?
Had this lord of trampled millions joy or grief, when first the mind,
Awful prize of contests endless, rose its giant foes to bind;
When his puppet tamed the forces that had helped its birth to breed,
And with growth of wisdom master, trained them to its growing need;
Last, upon the monster turning, on the serpent form of Pain, 80
Cried, "Bring forth no more in anguish;" with the arrows of the brain
Smote this brute thing that no use had save to teach him to refrain
When earth's baser instincts tempted, and the better thought was vain?
Then my soul one harshly answered, "Thou hast seen the whole of earth,
All its boundless years of misery, yea, its gladness and its mirth,
Yet thou hast a life created! Hadst thou not a choice? Why cast
Purity to life's mad chances, where defeat is sure at last?"

Low I moaned, "My tortured baby," and a gentler voice replied,
"One alone thy soul can answer,—this, this only, is denied.
Yet take counsel of thy sadness. Should God give thy will a star 90
Freighted with eternal pleasure, free from agony and war,
Wouldst thou wish it? Think! Time is not for the souls who roam in space.
Speak! Thy will shall have its way. Be mother of one joyous race.
Choose! Yon time-worn world beneath thee thou shalt people free from guilt.
There nor pain nor death shall ruin, never there shall blood be spilt."
Then I trembled, hesitating, for I saw its beauty born,
Saw a Christ-like world of beings where no beast by beast was torn,
Where the morrows bred no sorrows, and the gentle knew not scorn,
"Yes," I said, "if life have meaning, and man must be, what shall lift
These but born for joy's inaction, these who crave no added gift? 100
Let the world you bid me people hurl forever through the gloom,
Tenantless, a blasted record of some huge funereal doom,
Sad with unremembered slaughter, but a cold and lonely tomb."

Deep and deeper grew the stillness, and I knew how vain my quest.
Not by God's supremest angel is that awful secret guessed.
Yet with dull reiteration, like the pendulum's dead throb,
Beat my heart; a moaning infant, all my body seemed to sob,
And a voice like to my baby's called to me across the night
As the darkness fell asunder, and I saw a wall of light
Barred with crucificial shadows, whence a weary wind did blow 110
Shuddering. I felt it pass me heavy with its freight of woe.
Said a voice, "Behold God's dearest; also these no answer know.
These be they who paid in sorrow for the right to bid thee hear.
Had their lives in ease been cradled, had they never known a tear,
Feebly had their psalms of warning fallen upon the listening ear.
God the sun is God the shadow; and where pain is, God is near.
Take again thy life and use it with a sweetened sense of fear;
God is Father! God is Mother! Regent of a growing soul,
Free art thou to grant mere pleasure, free to teach it uncontrol.
Time is childhood! larger manhood bides beyond life's sunset hour, 120
Where far other foes are waiting; and with ever gladder power,
Still the lord of awful choice, O striving creature of the sod,
Thou shalt learn that imperfection is the noblest gift of God!
For they mock his ample purpose who but dream, beyond the sky,
Of a heaven where will may slumber, and the trained decision die
In the competence of answer found in death's immense reply."
Then my vision passed, and weeping, lo! I woke, of death bereft;
At my breast the baby brother, yonder there the dead I left.
For my heart two worlds divided: his, my lost one's; his, who pressed
Closer, waking all the mother, as he drew the aching breast, 130
While twain spirits, joy and sorrow, hovered o'er my plundered nest.

Newport, *October*, 1891.   1893

GUIDARELLO GUIDARELLI

RAVENNA WARRIOR (1502)

What was said to the Duke by the sculptor concerning Guidarello Guidarelli, and of the monument he made of his friend.[1]

I

"Guidarello Guidarelli!"
Ran a murmur low or loud,
As he rode with lifted vizor,
Smiling on the anxious crowd.

"Guidarello Guidarelli!"
Rang the cry from street and tower,
As our Guido rode to battle
In Ravenna's darkest hour.

[1] This monumental recumbent statue is now in the museum at Ravenna. (*Author's note*)

"Guidarello Guidarelli!"
  Little thought we of his doom   10
When a love-cast rain of roses
  Fell on saddle, mail, and plume.

Low he bowed, and laughing gaily
  Set one red rose in his crest,
All his mail a scarlet splendor
  From the red sun of the west.

"Guidarello Guidarelli!"
  So, he passed to meet his fate,
With the cry of "Guidarelli!"
  And the clangor of the gate.   20

II

Well, at eve we bore him homeward,
  Lying on our burdened spears.
Ah! defeat had been less bitter,
  And had cost us fewer tears.

At her feet we laid her soldier,
  While men saw her with amaze—
Fearless, tearless, waiting patient,
  Some wild challenge in her gaze.

Then the hand that rained the roses
  Fell upon his forehead cold.   30
"Go!" she cried, "ye faltering cravens!
  One that fled, your shame has told.

"Go! How dare ye look upon him—
  Ye who failed him in the fight?
Off! ye beaten hounds, and leave me
  With my lonely dead to-night!"

No man answered, and they left us
  Where our darling Guido lay.
I alone, who stood beside him
  In the fight, make bold to stay.   40

"Shut the Gate!" she cried. I closed it.
  "Lay your hand upon his breast;
Were you true to him?" "Ay, surely,
  As I hope for Jesu's rest!"

Then I saw her staring past me,
  As to watch a bird that flies,
All the light of youthful courage
  Fading from her valiant eyes.

And with one hoarse cry of anguish
  On the courtyard stones she fell,   50
Crying, "Guido Guidarelli!"
  Like the harsh notes of a bell.

Breaking with its stress of sweetness,
  Hence to know a voiceless pain.
"Guidarello Guidarelli!"
  Never did she speak again:

Save, 't is said, she wins, when dreaming,
  Tender memories of delight;
"Guidarello Guidarelli!"
  Crying through the quiet night.   60

III

Ah! you like it? Well, I made it
  Ere death aged upon his face.
See, I caught the parted lip-lines
  And the lashes' living grace:

For the gentle soul within him,
  Freed by death, had lingered here,
Kissing his dead face to beauty,
  As to bless a home grown dear.

He, my lord, was pure as woman,
  Past the thought of man's belief;   70
Truth and honor here are written,
  And some strangeness of relief

Born beneath my eager chisel
  As a child is born—a birth
To my parent-skill mysterious,
  Of, and yet not all of, earth.

Still one hears our women singing,—
  For a love-charm, so 'tis said,—
"Guidarello Guidarelli!"
  Like a love-mass for the dead.   80

In caressing iteration
  With his name their voices play—
"Elli, Nelli, Guidarelli,"
  Through some busy market-day.

Ah, my lord, I have the fancy
  That through many a year to come
This I wrought shall make the stranger
  Share our grief when mine is dumb.

Venice, *June*, 1897.   1899

TO A MAGNOLIA FLOWER

IN THE GARDEN OF THE ARMENIAN CONVENT AT VENICE

I saw thy beauty in its high estate
    Of perfect empire, where at set of sun
In the cool twilight of thy lucent leaves
    The dewy freshness told that day was done.
Hast thou no gift beyond thine ivory cone's
    Surpassing loveliness? Art thou not near—
More near than we—to nature's silentness;
    Is it not voiceful to thy finer ear?

Thy folded secrecy doth like a charm
    Compel to thought. What spring-born
        yearning lies   10
Within the quiet of thy stainless breast
    That doth with languorous passion seem to
        rise?

The soul doth truant angels entertain
    Who with reluctant joy their thoughts con-
        fess:
Low-breathing, to these sister spirits give
    The virgin mysteries of thy heart to guess.

What whispers hast thou from yon childlike
        sea
    That sobs all night beside these garden
        walls?
Canst thou interpret what the lark hath sung
    When from the choir of heaven her music
        falls?   20

If for companionship of purity
    The equal pallor of the risen moon
Disturb thy dreams, dost know to read aright
    Her silver tracery on the dark lagoon?

The mischief-making fruitfulness of May
    Stirs all the garden folk with vague desires.
Doth there not reach thine apprehensive ear
    The faded longing of these dark-robed friars,

When, in the evening hour to memories given,
    Some gray-haired man amid the gathering
        gloom   30

For one delirious moment sees again
    The gleam of eyes and white-walled Er-
        zeroum?
Hast thou not loved him for this human
        dream?
    Or sighed with him who yesterevening sat
Upon the low sea-wall, and saw through tears
    His ruined home and snow-clad Ararat?

If thou art dowered with some refinèd sense
    That shares the counsels of the nesting bird,
Canst hear the mighty laughter of the earth,
    And all that ear of man hath never heard,

If the abysmal stillness of the night   41
    Be eloquent for thee, if thou canst read
The glowing rubric of the morning song,
    Doth each new day no gentle warning
        breed?

Shall not the gossip of the maudlin bee,
    The fragrant history of the fallen rose,
Unto the prescience of instinctive love
    Some humbler prophecy of joy disclose?

Cold vestal of the leafy convent cell,
    The traitor days have thy calm trust be-
        trayed;   50
The sea-wind boldly parts thy shining leaves
    To let the angel in. Be not afraid!

The gold-winged sun, divinely penetrant,
    The pure annunciation of the morn
Breathes o'er thy chastity, and to thy soul
    The tender thrill of motherhood is borne.

Set wide the glory of thy radiant bloom!
    Call every wind to share thy scented breaths!
No life is brief that doth perfection win.
    To-day is thine—to-morrow thou art
        death's!   60
Cortino d'Ampezzo, July 1897   1899

ODE ON A LYCIAN TOMB[1]

I

What gracious nunnery of grief is here!
One woman garbed in sorrow's every mood;
Each sad presentment celled apart, in fear

Lest that herself upon herself intrude
And break some tender dream of sorrow's day,
Here cloistered lonely, set in marble gray.

Oh, pale procession of immortal love
Forever married to immortal grief!
All life's high-passioned sorrow far above,
Past help of time's compassionate relief;   10

[1] On this famous monument, known as Les Pleureuses, and now in the museum at Constantinople, one and the same mourning woman is carved in many attitudes of grief. These eighteen figures stand niched between Doric columns. Above and below are funeral scenes—battle and the chase. (*Author's note*)

These changeless stones are treasures of regret
And mock the term by time for sorrow set.

Ah me! What tired hearts have hither come
To weep with thee, and give thy grief a voice;
And such as have not added to life's sum
The count of loss, they who do still rejoice
In love which time yet leaveth unassailed,
Here tremble, by prophetic sadness paled.

Thou who hast wept for many, weep for me,
For surely I, who deepest grief have known,
Share thy stilled sadness, which must ever
   be   21
Too changeless, and unending like my own,
Since thine is woe that knows not time's re-
   lease,
And sorrow that can never compass peace.

He too who wrought this antique poetry,
Which wakes sad rhythms in the human heart,
Must oft with thee have wondered silently,
Touched by the strange revealments of his
   art,
When at his side you watched the chisel's
   grace
Foretell what time would carve upon thy
   face.   30

If to thy yearning silence, which in vain
Suggests its speechless plea in marbles old,
We add the anguish of an equal pain,
Shall not the sorrow of these statues cold
Inherit memories of our tears, and keep
Record of grief long time in death asleep?

Ah me! In death asleep; how pitiful,
If, in that timeless time the soul should wake
To wander heart-blind where no years may
   dull
Remembrance, with a heart forbid to break. 40
—Dove of my home, that fled life's stranded
   ark,
The sea of death is shelterless and dark.—

Cold mourner set in stone so long ago,
Too much my thoughts have dwelt with thee
   apart;
Again my grief is young: full well I know
The pang re-born, that mocked my feeble art
With that too human wail in pain expressed,
The parent cry above the empty nest!

Come back, I cried. "I may not come again,
Not islandless is this uncharted sea;   50
Here is no death, nor any creature's pain,
Nor any terror of what is to be.

'Tis but to trust one pilot; soon are seen
The sunlit peaks of thought and peace serene."

II

Fair worshipper of many gods, whom I
In one God worship, very surely He
Will for thy tears and mine have some reply,
When death assumes the trust of life, and we
Hear once again the voices of our dead,
And on a newer earth contented tread.   60

Doubtless for thee thy Lycian fields were
   sweet,
Thy dream of heaven no wiser than my own;
Nature and love, the sound of children's feet,
Home, husbands, friends; what better hast
   thou known?
What of the gods could ask thy longing prayer
Except again this earth and love to share?

For all in vain with vexed imaginings,
We build of dreams another earth than ours,
And high in thought's thinned atmosphere,
   with wings
That helpless beat, and mock our futile
   powers,   70
Falter and flutter, seeing naught above,
And naught below except the earth we love.

Enough it were to find our own old earth
With death's dark riddle answered, and un-
   spoiled
By fear, or sin, or pain; where joy and mirth
Have no sad shadows, and love is not foiled,
And where, companioned by the mighty dead,
The dateless books of time and fate are read.

III

What stately melancholy doth possess
This innocent marble with eternal doom!   80
What most imperious grief doth here oppress
The one sad soul which haunts this peopled
   tomb
In many forms that all these years have worn
One thought, for time's long comment more
   forlorn!

Lo grief, through love instinct with silentness,
Reluctant, in these marbles eloquent,
The ancient tale of loss doth here confess
The first confusing, mad bewilderment,
Life's unbelief in death, in love fore-spent,
Thought without issue, child-like discon-
   tent.   90

Time, that for thee awhile did moveless seem,
Again his glass hath turned: I see thee stand

Thought-netted, or, like one who in a dream
Self-wildered, in some alien forest land
Lone-wandering, in endless mazes lost,
Wearily stumbles over tracks re-crossed.

Oft didst thou come in after days to leave
Roses and laurel on thy warrior's grave,
And with thy marble self again to grieve,
Glad of what genius unto sorrow gave,   100
Interpreting what had been and would be,
Love, tears, despair, attained serenity.

There are whom sorrow leaves full-wrecked.
    The great

Grow in the urgent anguish of defeat,
And with mysterious confidence await
The silent coming of the bearer's feet;
Wherefore this quiet face so proudly set
To front life's duties, but naught to forget.

For life is but a tender instrument
Whereon the master hand of grief doth fall,
Leaving love's vibrant tissue resonant   112
With echoes, ever waking at the call
Of every kindred tone: so grief doth change
The instrument o'er which his fateful fingers
    range.
1899   1901

RICHARD WATSON GILDER (1844-1909)

A WOMAN'S THOUGHT

I am a woman—therefore I may not
Call to him, cry to him,
Fly to him,
Bid him delay not!

Then when he comes to me, I must sit quiet;
Still as a stone—
All silent and cold.
If my heart riot—
Crush and defy it!
Should I grow bold,   10
Say one dear thing to him,
All my life fling to him,
Cling to him—
What to atone
Is enough for my sinning!
This were the cost to me,
This were my winning—
That he were lost to me.

Not as a lover
At last if he part from me,   20
Tearing my heart from me,
Hurt beyond cure—
Calm and demure
Then must I hold me,
In myself fold me,
Lest he discover;
Showing no sign to him
By look of mine to him
What he has been to me—
How my heart turns to him,   30
Follows him, yearns to him,
Prays him to love me.

Pity me, lean to me,
Thou God above me!
                                        1885

THE PASSING OF CHRIST

O Man of light and lore!
Do you mean that in our day
The Christ hath past away;
That nothing now is divine
In the fierce rays that shine
Through every cranny and thought;
That Christ as he once was taught
Shall be the Christ no more?
That the Hope and Savior of men
Shall be seen no more again;   10
That, miracles being done,
Gone is the Holy One?
And thus, you hold, this Christ

For the past alone sufficed;
From the throne of the hearts of the world
The Son of God shall be hurled,
And henceforth must be sought
New prophets and kings of thought;
That the tenderest, truest word
The heart of sorrow hath heard   20
Shall sound no more upon earth;
That he who hath made of birth
A dread and sacred rite,
Who hath brought to the eyes of death
A vision of heavenly light,
Shall fade with our failing faith;—

He who saw in children's eyes
Eternal paradise;
Who made the poor man's lowly
Labor a service holy,   30
And sweat of work more sweet
Than incense at God's feet;
Who turned the God of Fear
To a father, bending near;
Who looked through shame and sin
At the sanctity within;
Whose memory, since he died,
The earth hath sanctified—
Hath been the stay and the hold
Of millions of lives untold,   40
And the world on its upward path
Hath led from crime and wrath;—
You say that this Christ hath past
And we cannot hold him fast?

II

Ah, no! If the Christ you mean
Shall pass from this time, this scene,
These hearts, these lives of ours,
'T is but as the summer flowers
Pass, but return again,
To gladden a world of men.   50
For he,—the only, the true,—
In each age, in each waiting heart,
Leaps into life anew;
Tho' he pass, he shall not depart.

Behold him now where he comes!
Not the Christ of our subtile creeds,

But the lord of our hearts, of our homes,
Of our hopes, our prayers, our needs;
The brother of want and blame,
The lover of women and men,   60
With a love that puts to shame
All passions of mortal ken;—
Yet of all of woman born
His is the scorn of scorn;
Before whose face do fly
Lies, and the love of a lie;
Who from the temple of God
And the sacred place of laws
Drives forth, with smiting rod,
The herds of ravening maws.   70

'Tis he, as none other can,
Makes free the spirit of man,
And speaks, in darkest night,
One word of awful light
That strikes through the dreadful pain
Of life, a reason sane—
That word divine which brought
The universe from naught.

Ah, no, thou life of the heart,
Never shalt thou depart!   80
Not till the leaven of God
Shall lighten each human clod;
Not till the world shall climb
To thy height serene, sublime,
Shall the Christ who enters our door
Pass to return no more.

                                        1891

LLOYD MIFFLIN (1846-1921)

SESOSTRIS

Sole Lord of Lords and very King of Kings,
He sits within the desert, carved in stone;
Inscrutable, colossal, and alone,
And ancienter than memory of things.
Graved on his front the sacred beetle clings;
Disdain sits on his lips; and in a frown
Scorn lives upon his forehead for a crown.
The affrighted ostrich dare not dust her wings
Anear this Presence. The long caravan's
Dazed camels pause, and mute the Bedouins
    stare.   10
This symbol of past power more than man's
Presages doom. Kings look—and Kings de-
    spair;
Their sceptres tremble in their jewelled hands,
And dark thrones totter in the baleful air!
1885   1897

THE FLIGHT

Upon a cloud among the stars we stood:
The angel raised his hand, and looked, and said,
"Which world of all yon starry myriad
Shall we make wing to?" The still solitude
Became a harp whereon his voice and mood
Made spheral music round his haloed head.
I spake—for then I had not long been dead—
"Let me look round upon the vasts, and brood
A moment on these orbs ere I decide . . .
What is yon lower star that beauteous shines,
And with soft splendor now incarnadines   11
Our wings?— *There* would I go, and there
    abide."
Then he, as one who some child's thought
    divines:
"That is the world where yesternight you died."
1886   1897

LOUISE IMOGEN GUINEY (1861-1920)

THE WILD RIDE

I hear in my heart, I hear in its ominous pulses
All day, on the road, the hoofs of invisible
    horses,
All night, from their stalls, the importunate
    pawing and neighing.

Let cowards and laggards fall back! but alert
    to the saddle
Weather-worn and abreast, go men of our
    galloping legion,
With a stirrup-cup each to the lily of women
    that loves him.

The trail is through dolour and dread, over
    crags and morasses;
There are shapes by the way, there are things
    that appal or entice us:
What odds? We are Knights of the Grail, we
    are vowed to the riding.

Thought's self is a vanishing wing, and joy is
    a cobweb,   10
And friendship a flower in the dust, and glory
    a sunbeam:
Not here is our prize, nor, alas! after these
    our pursuing.

A dipping of plumes, a tear, a shake of the
    bridle,
A passing salute to this world and her pitiful
    beauty:
We hurry with never a word in the track of
    our fathers.

(I hear in my heart, I hear in its ominous
    pulses
All day, on the road, the hoofs of invisible
    horses,
All night, from their stalls, the importunate
    pawing and neighing.)

We spur to a land of no name, out-racing the
    stormwind;
We leap to the infinite dark like sparks from
    the anvil.   20
Thou leadest, O God! All's well with Thy
    troopers that follow.

                              1887, 1909

THE KINGS

A man said unto his Angel:
"My spirits are fallen low,
And I cannot carry this battle:
O brother! where might I go?

"The terrible Kings are on me
With spears that are deadly bright;
Against me so from the cradle
Do fate and my fathers fight."

Then said to the man his Angel:
"Thou wavering witless soul,   10
Back to the ranks! What matter
To win or to lose the whole,

"As judged by the little judges
Who hearken not well, nor see?
Not thus, by the outer issue,
The Wise shall interpret thee.

"Thy will is the sovereign measure
And only event of things:
The puniest heart, defying,
Were stronger than all these Kings.   20

"Though out of the past they gather,
Mind's Doubt, and Bodily Pain,
And pallid Thirst of the Spirit
That is kin to the other twain,

"And Grief, in a cloud of banners,
And ringletted Vain Desires,
And Vice, with the spoils upon him
Of thee and thy beaten sires,—

"While Kings of eternal evil
Yet darken the hills about,   30
Thy part is with broken sabre
To rise on the last redoubt;

"To fear not sensible failure,
Nor covet the game at all,
But fighting, fighting, fighting,
Die, driven against the wall."
                              1893, 1909

IRISH PEASANT SONG

IN LEINSTER

I try to knead and spin, but my life is low the
    while.
Oh, I long to be alone, and walk abroad a
    mile;
Yet if I walk alone, and think of naught at all,
Why from me that's young should the wild
    tears fall?

The shower-sodden earth, the earth-coloured
    streams,
They breathe on me awake, and moan to me
    in dreams,

And yonder ivy fondling the broke castle-wall,
It pulls upon my heart till the wild tears fall.

The cabin-door looks down a furze-lighted hill,
And far as Leighlin Cross the fields are green
    and still;   10

But once I hear the blackbird in Leighlin
    hedges call,
The foolishness is on me, and the wild tears
    fall!

                  1893, 1909

THE WESTERN GROUP

FRANCIS BRET HARTE (1836-1902)

IN THE TUNNEL

Didn't know Flynn,—
Flynn of Virginia,—
Long as he's been 'yar?
Look 'ee here, stranger,
Whar *hev* you been?

Here in this tunnel
He was my pardner,
That same Tom Flynn,—
    Working together,
    In wind and weather,   10
Day out and in.

Didn't know Flynn!
Well, that *is* queer;
Why, it's a sin
To think of Tom Flynn,—
    Tom with his cheer,
    Tom without fear,—
Stranger, look 'yar!

Thar in the drift,
    Back to the wall,   20
He held the timbers
    Ready to fall;
Then in the darkness
I heard him call:

"Run for your life, Jake!
Run for your wife's sake!
Don't wait for me."

And that was all
    Heard in the din,
    Heard of Tom Flynn,—   30
Flynn of Virginia.

That's all about
    Flynn of Virginia.
That lets me out.
    Here in the damp,—
    Out of the sun,—
That 'ar derned lamp
Makes my eyes run.
Well, there,—I'm done!

But, sir, when you'll   40
Hear the next fool
    Asking of Flynn,—
Flynn of Virginia,—
    Just you chip in,
    Say you knew Flynn;
Say that you've been 'yar.
                  1869

HER LETTER

I'm sitting alone by the fire,
    Dressed just as I came from the dance,
In a robe even *you* would admire,—
    It cost a cool thousand in France;
I'm be-diamonded out of all reason,
    My hair is done up in a cue:
In short, sir, "the belle of the season"
    Is wasting an hour upon you.

A dozen engagements I've broken;
    I left in the midst of a set;   10
Likewise a proposal, half spoken,
    That waits—on the stairs—for me yet.
They say he'll be rich,—when he grows up,—
    And then he adores me indeed;

And you, sir, are turning your nose up,
    Three thousand miles off, as you read.

"And how do I like my position?"
    "And what do I think of New York?"
"And now, in my higher ambition,
    With whom do I waltz, flirt, or talk?"   20
"And isn't it nice to have riches,
    And diamonds and silks, and all that?"
"And aren't they a change to the ditches
    And tunnels of Poverty Flat?"

Well, yes,—if you saw us out driving
    Each day in the Park, four-in-hand,
If you saw poor dear mamma contriving

To look supernaturally grand,—
  If you saw papa's picture, as taken
By Brady, and tinted at that,—   30
  You'd never suspect he sold bacon
And flour at Poverty Flat.

And yet, just this moment, when sitting
  In the glare of the grand chandelier,—
In the bustle and glitter befitting
  The "finest *soirée* of the year,"—
In the mists of a *gaze de Chambéry*,
  And the hum of the smallest of talk,—
Somehow, Joe, I thought of the "Ferry," 39
  And the dance that we had on "The Fork;"

Of Harrison's barn, with its muster
  Of flags festooned over the wall;
Of the candles that shed their soft lustre
  And tallow on head-dress and shawl;
Of the steps that we took to one fiddle,
  Of the dress of my queer *vis-à-vis ;*
And how I once went down the middle
  With the man that shot Sandy McGee;

Of the moon that was quietly sleeping
  On the hill, when the time came to go; 50
Of the few baby peaks that were peeping
  From under their bedclothes of snow;
Of that ride,—that to me was the rarest;
  Of—the something you said at the gate.

Ah! Joe, then I wasn't an heiress
  To "the best-paying lead in the State."

Well, well, it's all past; yet it's funny
  To think, as I stood in the glare
Of fashion and beauty and money,
  That I should be thinking, right there, 60
Of some one who breasted high water,
  And swam the North Fork, and all that,
Just to dance with old Folinsbee's daughter,
  The Lily of Poverty Flat.

But goodness! what nonsense I'm writing!
  (Mamma says my taste still is low),
Instead of my triumphs reciting,
  I'm spooning on Joseph,—heigh-ho!
And I'm to be "finished" by travel,—
  Whatever's the meaning of that. 70
Oh, why did papa strike pay gravel
  In drifting on Poverty Flat?

Good-night!—here's the end of my paper;
  Good-night!—if the longitude please,—
For maybe, while wasting my taper,
  Your sun's climbing over the trees.
But know, if you haven't got riches,
  And are poor, dearest Joe, and all that,
That my heart's somewhere there in the ditches,
  And you've struck it,—on Poverty Flat. 80
1869

PLAIN LANGUAGE FROM TRUTHFUL JAMES

Which I wish to remark,
  And my language is plain,
That for ways that are dark
  And for tricks that are vain,
The heathen Chinee is peculiar,
  Which the same I would rise to explain.

Ah Sin was his name;
  And I shall not deny,
In regard to the same,
  What that name might imply; 10
But his smile, it was pensive and childlike,
  As I frequent remarked to Bill Nye.

It was August the third,
  And quite soft was the skies;
Which it might be inferred
  That Ah Sin was likewise;
Yet he played it that day upon William
  And me in a way I despise.

Which we had a small game,
  And Ah Sin took a hand: 20

It was Euchre. The same
  He did not understand;
But he smiled as he sat by the table,
  With a smile that was childlike and bland.

Yet the cards they were stocked
  In a way that I grieve,
And my feelings were shocked
  At the state of Nye's sleeve,
Which was stuffed full of aces and bowers,
  And the same with intent to deceive. 30

But the hands that were played
  By that heathen Chinee,
And the points that he made,
  Were quite frightful to see,—
Till at last he put down a right bower
  Which the same Nye had dealt unto me.

Then I looked up at Nye,
  And he gazed upon me;
And he rose with a sigh,
  And said, "Can this be? 40

We are ruined by Chinese cheap labor,"—
  And he went for that heathen Chinee.

In the scene that ensued
  I did not take a hand,
But the floor it was strewed
  Like the leaves on the strand
With the cards that Ah Sin had been hiding,
  In the game "he did not understand."

In his sleeves, which were long,
  He had twenty-four jacks,—   50

Which was coming it strong,
  Yet I state but the facts;
And we found on his nails, which were taper,
  What is frequent in tapers,—that's wax.

Which is why I remark,
  And my language is plain,
That for ways that are dark
  And for tricks that are vain,
The heathen Chinee is peculiar,—
  Which the same I am free to maintain. 60

Table Mountain, 1870   1870

THE SOCIETY UPON THE STANISLAUS

I reside at Table Mountain, and my name is Truthful James;
I am not up to small deceit or any sinful games;
And I'll tell in simple language what I know about the row
That broke up our Society upon the Stanislow.

But first I would remark, that it is not a proper plan
For any scientific gent to whale his fellow-man,
And, if a member don't agree with his peculiar whim,
To lay for that same member for to "put a head" on him.

Now nothing could be finer or more beautiful to see
Than the first six months' proceedings of that same Society, 10
Till Brown of Calaveras brought a lot of fossil bones
That he found within a tunnel near the tenement of Jones.

Then Brown he read a paper, and he reconstructed there,
From those same bones, an animal that was extremely rare;
And Jones then asked the Chair for a suspension of the rules,
Till he could prove that those same bones was one of his lost mules.

Then Brown he smiled a bitter smile, and said he was at fault.
It seemed he had been trespassing on Jones's family vault;
He was a most sarcastic man, this quiet Mr. Brown,
And on several occasions he had cleaned out the town. 20

Now I hold it is not decent for a scientific gent
To say another is an ass,—at least, to all intent;
Nor should the individual who happens to be meant
Reply by heaving rocks at him, to any great extent.

Then Abner Dean of Angel's raised a point of order, when
A chunk of old red sandstone took him in the abdomen,
And he smiled a kind of sickly smile, and curled up on the floor,
And the subsequent proceedings interested him no more.

For, in less time than I write it, every member did engage
In a warfare with the remnants of a palæozoic age; 30
And the way they heaved those fossils in their anger was a sin,
Till the skull of an old mammoth caved the head of Thompson in.

And this is all I have to say of these improper games,
For I live at Table Mountain, and my name is Truthful James;
And I've told in simple language what I know about the row
That broke up our Society upon the Stanislow.

1871

OFF SCARBOROUGH

(September, 1779)

I

"Have a care!" the bailiffs cried
From their cockleshell that lay
Off the frigate's yellow side,
Tossing on Scarborough Bay,
While the forty sail it convoyed on a bowline stretched away.
"Take your chicks beneath your wings,
And your claws and feathers spread,
Ere the hawk upon them springs,—
Ere around Flamborough Head
Swoops Paul Jones, the Yankee falcon, with his beak and talons red."   10

II

How we laughed!—my mate and I,—
On the "Bon Homme Richard's" deck,
As we saw that convoy fly
Like a snow-squall, till each fleck
Melted in the twilight shadows of the coast-line, speck by speck;
And scuffling back to shore
The Scarborough bailiffs sped,
As the "Richard," with a roar
Of her cannon round the Head,
Crossed her royal yards and signaled to her consort: "Chase ahead!"   20

III

But the devil seize Landais
In that consort ship of France!
For the shabby, lubber way
That he worked the "Alliance"
In the offing,—nor a broadside fired save to our mischance!—
When tumbling to the van,
With his battle-lanterns set,
Rose the burly Englishman
'Gainst our hull as black as jet,—
Rode the yellow-sided "Serapis," and all alone we met!   30

IV

All alone, though far at sea
Hung his consort, rounding to;
All alone, though on our lee
Fought our "Pallas," stanch and true!
For the first broadside around us both a smoky circle drew:
And, like champions in a ring,
There was cleared a little space—
Scarce a cable's length to swing—
Ere we grappled in embrace,
All the world shut out around us, and we only face to face!   40

V

Then awoke all hell below
From that broadside, doubly curst,
For our long eighteens in row

Leaped the first discharge and burst!
And on deck our men came pouring, fearing their own guns the worst.
    And as dumb we lay, till, through
      Smoke and flame and bitter cry,
    Hailed the "Serapis": "Have you
      Struck your colors?" Our reply,
"We have not yet begun to fight!" went shouting to the sky!   50

VI

    Roux of Brest, old fisher, lay
      Like a he ring gasping here;
    Bunker of Nantucket Bay,
      Blown from out the port, dropped sheer
Half a cable's length to leeward; yet we faintly raised a cheer
    As with his own right hand
      Our Commodore made fast
    The foeman's head-gear and
      The "Richard's" mizzen-mast,
And in that death-lock clinging held us there from first to last!   60

VII

    Yet the foeman, gun on gun,
      Through the "Richard" tore a road,
    With his gunners' rammers run
      Through our ports at every load,
Till clear the blue beyond us through our yawning timbers showed.
    Yet with entrails torn we clung
      Like the Spartan to our fox,
    And on deck no coward tongue
      Wailed the enemy's hard knocks,
Nor that all below us trembled like a wreck upon the rocks.   70

VIII

    Then a thought rose in my brain,
      As through Channel mists the sun,
    From our tops a fire like rain
      Drove below decks every one
Of the enemy's ship's company to hide or work a gun:
    And that thought took shape as I
      On the "Richard's" yard lay out,
    That a man might do and die,
      If the doing brought about
Freedom for his home and country, and his messmates' cheering shout!   80

IX

    Then I crept out in the dark
      Till I hung above the hatch
    Of the "Serapis,"—a mark
      For her marksmen!—with a match
And a hand-grenade, but lingered just a moment more to snatch
    One last look at sea and sky!
      At the lighthouse on the hill!
    At the harvest-moon on high!
      And our pine flag fluttering still!
Then turned and down her yawning throat I launched that devil's pill!   90

X

Then a blank was all between
As the flames around me spun!
Had I fired the magazine?
Was the victory lost or won?
Nor knew I till the fight was o'er but half my work was done:
For I lay among the dead
In the cockpit of our foe,
With a roar above my head,—
Till a trampling to and fro,
And a lantern showed my mate's face, and I knew what now you know.   100

1878

"CROTALUS"

(RATTLESNAKE BAR, SIERRAS)

No life in earth, or air, or sky;
The sunbeams, broken silently,
On the bared rocks around me lie,—

Cold rocks with half-warmed lichens scarred,
And scales of moss; and scarce a yard
Away, one long strip, yellow-barred.

Lost in a cleft! 'Tis but a stride
To reach it, thrust its roots aside,
And lift it on thy stick astride!

Yet stay! That moment is thy grace!   10
For round thee, thrilling air and space,
A chattering terror fills the place!

A sound as of dry bones that stir
In the Dead Valley! By yon fir
The locust stops its noonday whir!

The wild bird hears; smote with the sound,
As if by bullet brought to ground,
On broken wing, dips, wheeling round!

The hare, transfixed, with trembling lip,
Halts, breathless, on pulsating hip,   20
And palsied tread, and heels that slip.

. . . .

Enough, old friend! 'tis thou. Forget
My heedless foot, nor longer fret
The peace with thy grim castanet!

I know thee! Yes! Thou mayst forego
That lifted crest; the measured blow
Beyond which thy pride scorns to go,

Or yet retract! For me no spell
Lights those slit orbs, where, some think, swell
Machicolated fires of hell!   30

I only know thee humble, bold,
Haughty, with miseries untold,
And the old Curse that left thee cold,

And drove thee ever to the sun,
On blistering rocks; nor made thee shun
Our cabin's hearth, when day was done,

And the spent ashes warmed thee best;
We knew thee,—silent, joyless guest
Of our rude ingle. E'en thy quest

Of the rare milk-bowl seemed te be   40
Naught but a brother's poverty,
And Spartan taste that kept thee free

From lust and rapine. Thou! whose fame
Searchest the grass with tongue of flame,
Making all creatures seem thy game;

When the whole woods before thee run,
Asked but—when all was said and done—
To lie, untrodden, in the sun!

JOHN HAY (1838-1905)

JIM BLUDSO

(OF THE PRAIRIE BELLE)

Wall, no! I can't tell whar he lives,
Because he don't live, you see;
Leastways, he's got out of the habit
Of livin' like you and me.
Whar have you been for the last three year
That you haven't heard folks tell

How Jimmy Bludso passed in his checks,
The night of the Prairie Belle?

He weren't no saint—them engineers
Is all pretty much alike—   10
One wife in Natchez-under-the-Hill

And another here, in Pike;
A keerless man in his talk was Jim,
And an awkward man in a row,
But he never flunked, and he never lied,—
    I reckon he never knowed how.

And this was all the religion he had,—
    To treat his engine well;
Never be passed on the river;
    To mind the Pilot's bell;   20
And if ever the Prairie Belle took fire,—
    A thousand times he swore,
He'd hold her nozzle agin the bank
    Till the last soul got ashore.

All boats has their day on the Mississip,
    And her day come at last,—
The Movastar was a better boat,
    But the Belle she *wouldn't* be passed.
And so she come tearin' along that night—
    The oldest craft on the line—   30
With a nigger squat on her safety valve,
    And her furnace crammed, rosin and pine.

The fire bust out as she clared the bar,
    And burnt a hole in the night,

And quick as a flash she turned, and made
    For that willer-bank on the right.
There was runnin' and cursin', but Jim yelled
        out,
    Over all the infernal roar,
"I'll hold her nozzle agin the bank
    Till the last galoot's ashore."   40

Through the hot, black breath of the burnin'
        boat
    Jim Bludso's voice was heard,
And they all had trust in his cussedness,
    And knowed he would keep his word.
And, sure's you're born, they all got off
    Afore the smokestacks fell,—
And Bludso's ghost went up alone
    In the smoke of the Prairie Belle.

He weren't no saint—but at jedgment
    I'd run my chance with Jim,   50
'Longside of some pious gentlemen
    That wouldn't shook hands with him.
He seen his duty, a dead-sure thing,—
    And went for it thar and then;
And Christ ain't a goin' to be too hard
    On a man that died for men.

                                                    1871

JOAQUIN MILLER (1841-1913)

KIT CARSON'S RIDE

Room! room to turn round in, to breathe and be free,
To grow to be giant, to sail as at sea
With the speed of the wind on a steed with his mane
To the wind, without pathway or route or a rein.
Room! room to be free where the white border'd sea
Blows a kiss to a brother as boundless as he;
Where the buffalo come like a cloud on the plain,
Pouring on like the tide of a storm-driven main,
And the lodge of the hunter to friend or to foe
Offers rest; and unquestion'd you come or you go.   10
My plains of America! Seas of wild lands!
From a land in the seas in a raiment of foam,
That has reached to a stranger the welcome of home,
I turn to you, lean to you, lift you my hands.

    Run? Run? See this flank, sir, and I do love him so!
But he's blind, badger blind. Whoa, Pache, boy, whoa.
No, you wouldn't believe it to look at his eyes,
But he's blind, badger blind, and it happen'd this wise:

'We lay in the grass and the sunburnt clover
    That spread on the ground like a great brown cover   20
Northward and southward, and west and away
To the Brazos, where our lodges lay,
    One broad and unbroken level of brown.
We were waiting the curtains of night to come down

To cover us trio and conceal our flight
With my brown bride, won from an Indian town
That lay in the rear the full ride of a night.

'We lounged in the grass—her eyes were in mine,
And her hands on my knee, and her hair was as wine
In its wealth and its flood, pouring on and all over
Her bosom wine red, and press'd never by one.
Her touch was as warm as the tinge of the clover
Burnt brown as it reach'd to the kiss of the sun.
Her words they were low as the lute-throated dove,
And as laden with love as the heart when it beats
In its hot, eager answer to earliest love.
Or the bee hurried home by its burthen of sweets.

'We lay low in the grass on the broad plain levels,
Old Revels and I, and my stolen brown bride;
"Forty full miles if a foot to ride!
Forty full miles if a foot, and the devils
Of red Comanches are hot on the track
When once they strike it. Let the sun go down
Soon, very soon," muttered bearded old Revels
As he peer'd at the sun, lying low on his back,
Holding fast to his lasso. Then he jerk'd at his steed
And he sprang to his feet, and glanced swiftly around,
And then dropp'd, as if shot, with an ear to the ground;
Then again to his feet, and to me, to my bride,
While his eyes were like flame, his face like a shroud,
His form like a king, and his beard like a cloud,
And his voice loud and shrill, as both trumpet and reed,—
"Pull, pull in your lassoes, and bridle to steed,
And speed you if ever for life you would speed.
Aye, ride for your lives, for your lives you must ride!
For the plain is aflame, the prairie on fire,
And the feet of wild horses hard flying before
I heard like a sea breaking high on the shore,
While the buffalo come like a surge of the sea,
Driven far by the flame, driving fast on us three
As a hurricane comes, crushing palms in his ire."

'We drew in the lassoes, seized the saddle and rein,
Threw them on, cinched them on, cinched them over again,
And again drew the girth; and spring we to horse,
With head to Brazos, with a sound in the air
Like the surge of a sea, with a flash in the eye,
From that red wall of flame reaching up to the sky;
A red wall of flame and a black rolling sea
Rushing fast upon us, as the wind sweeping free
And afar from the desert blown hollow and hoarse.

'Not a word, not a wail from a lip was let fall,
We broke not a whisper, we breathed not a prayer,
There was work to be done, there was death in the air,
And the chance was as one to a thousand for all.

'Twenty miles! . . . thirty miles! . . . a dim distant speck
Then a long reaching line, and the Brazos in sight!

30

40

50

60

70

And I rose in my seat with a shout of delight.
I stood in my stirrup, and look'd to my right—
But Revels was gone; I glanced by my shoulder
And saw his horse stagger; I saw his head drooping   80
Hard down on his breast, and his naked breast stooping
Low down to the mane, as so swifter and bolder
Ran reaching out for us the red-footed fire.
He rode neck to neck with a buffalo bull,
That made the earth shake where he came in his course,
The monarch of millions, with shaggy mane full
Of smoke and of dust, and it shook with desire
Of battle, with rage and with bellowings hoarse.
His keen, crooked horns, through the storm of his mane,
Like black lances lifted and lifted again;   90
And I looked but this once, for the fire licked through,
And Revels was gone, as we rode two and two.

'I look'd to my left then—and nose, neck, and shoulder
Sank slowly, sank surely, till back to my thighs,
And up through the black blowing veil of her hair
Did beam full in mine her two marvelous eyes,
With a longing and love yet a look of despair
And of pity for me, as she felt the smoke fold her,
And flames leaping far for her glorious hair.
Her sinking horse falter'd, plunged, fell and was gone   100
As I reach'd through the flame and I bore her still on.
On! into the Brazos, she, Pache and I—
Poor, burnt, blinded Pache. I love him . . .
That's why.'

1871, 1909

COLUMBUS

Behind him lay the gray Azores,
  Behind the Gates of Hercules;
Before him not the ghost of shores,
  Before him only shoreless seas.
The good mate said: "Now must we pray,
  For lo! the very stars are gone.
Brave Adm'r'l, speak; what shall I say?"
  "Why, say: 'Sail on! sail on! and on!'"

"My men grow mutinous day by day;
  My men grow ghastly, wan and weak,"   10
The stout mate thought of home; a spray
  Of salt wave washed his swarthy cheek.
"What shall I say, brave Adm'r'l, say,
  If we sight naught but seas at dawn?"
"Why, you shall say at break of day:
  'Sail on! sail on! sail on! and on!'"

They sailed and sailed, as winds might blow,
  Until at last the blanched mate said:
"Why, now not even God would know
  Should I and all my men fall dead.   20
These very winds forget their way,
  For God from these dread seas is gone.

Now speak, brave Adm'r'l, speak and say—"
  He said: "Sail on! sail on! and on!"

They sailed. They sailed. Then spake the
    mate:
  "This mad sea shows his teeth to-night.
He curls his lip, he lies in wait,
  He lifts his teeth, as if to bite!
Brave Adm'r'l, say but one good word:
  "What shall we do when hope is gone?"
The words leapt like a leaping sword: 31
  "Sail on! sail on! sail on! and on!"

Then pale and worn, he paced his deck,
  And peered through darkness. Ah, that
    night
Of all dark nights! And then a speck—
  A light! A light! At last a light!
It grew, a starlit flag unfurled!
  It grew to be Time's burst of dawn.
He gained a world; he gave that world
  Its grandest lesson: "On! sail on!"   40
1896

JAMES WHITCOMB RILEY (1849-1916)

IKE WALTON'S PRAYER

I crave, dear Lord,
No boundless hoard
  Of gold and gear,
    Not jewels fine,
    Nor lands, nor kine,
Nor treasure-heaps of anything.—
    Let but a little hut be mine
Where at the hearthstone I may hear
    The cricket sing,
    And have the shine   10
Of one glad woman's eyes to make,
For my poor sake,
    Our simple home a place divine;—
Just the wee cot—the cricket's chirr—
Love, and the smiling face of her.

  I pray not for
  Great riches, nor
For vast estates and castle halls,—
Give me to hear the bare footfalls
    Of children o'er   20
An oaken floor
New-rinsed with sunshine, or bespread
With but the tiny coverlet
And pillow for the baby's head;
And, pray Thou, may
The door stand open and the day
    Send ever in a gentle breeze,
    With fragrance from the locust trees,
      And drowsy moan of doves, and blur

Of robin-chirps, and drone of bees,   30
    With after-hushes of the stir
Of intermingling sounds, and then
    The goodwife and the smile of her
Filling the silences again—
    The cricket's call
    And the wee cot,
Dear Lord of all,
    Deny me not!

I pray not that
Men tremble at   40
    My power of place
    And lordly sway,—
  I only pray for simple grace
To look my neighbor in the face
    Full honestly from day to day—
  Yield me his horny palm to hold,
    And I'll not pray
      For gold;—
The tanned face, garlanded with mirth,
It hath the kingliest smile on earth;   50
The swart brow, diamonded with sweat,
Hath never need of coronet.
    And so I reach,
      Dear Lord, to Thee,
      And do beseech
    Thou givest me
The wee cot, and the cricket's chirr,
Love, and the glad sweet face of her!
                                      1887

A LIFE–LESSON

There! little girl; don't cry!
  They have broken your doll, I know;
    And your tea-set blue,
    And your play-house, too,
  Are things of the long ago;
    But childish troubles will soon pass by.—
    There! little girl; don't cry!

There! little girl; don't cry!
  They have broken your slate, I know;
    And the glad, wild ways   10
    Of your schoolgirl days

Are things of the long ago;
  But life and love will soon come by.—
    There! little girl; don't cry!

There! little girl; don't cry!
  They have broken your heart, I know;
    And the rainbow gleams
    Of your youthful dreams
  Are things of the long ago;
    But Heaven holds all for which you sigh.—
    There! little girl; don't cry!   21
                                      1887

KNEE–DEEP IN JUNE

I

Tell you what I like the best—
  'Long about knee-deep in June,
    'Bout the time strawberries melts

On the vine,—some afternoon
Like to jes' git out and rest,
    And not work at nothin' else!

II

Orchard's where I'd ruther be—
Needn't fence it in fer me!—
Jes' the whole sky overhead,
And the whole airth underneath—
Sort o' so's a man kin breathe
  Like he ort, and kind o' has
  Elbow-room to keerlessly
    Sprawl out len'thways on the grass
    Where the shadders thick and soft
  As the kivvers on the bed
  Mother fixes in the loft
Allus, when they's company!

III

Jes' a-sort o' lazin' there—
  S'lazy, 'at you peek and peer
    Through the wavin' leaves above,
    Like a feller 'ats in love
And don't know it, ner don't keer!
Ever'thing you hear and see
  Got some sort o' interest—
  Maybe find a bluebird's nest
Tucked up there conveenently
Fer the boy 'at 's ap' to be
Up some other apple-tree!
Watch the swallers skootin' past
'Bout as peert as you could ast;
  Er the Bob-white raise and whiz
  Where some other's whistle is.

IV

Ketch a shadder down below,
And look up to find the crow—
Er a hawk,—away up there,
'Pearantly *froze* in the air!—
  Hear the old hen squawk, and squat
  Over ever' chick she's got,
Suddent-like!—and she knows where
  That-air hawk is, well as you!—
  You jes' bet yer life she do!—
    Eyes a-glitterin' like glass,
    Waitin' till he makes a pass!

V

Pee-wees' singin', to express
  My opinion, 's second class,
Yit you'll hear 'em more er less;
Sapsucks gittin' down to biz,
Weedin' out the lonesomeness;
  Mr. Bluejay, full o' sass,
    In them baseball clothes o' his,
Sportin' round the orchard jes'

Like he owned the premises!
  Sun out in the fields kin sizz,
But flat on yer back, I guess,
  In the shade's where glory is!
That's jes' what I'd like to do
Stiddy fer a year er two!

VI

Plague! ef they ain't somepin' in
Work 'at kind o' goes ag'in'
  My convictions!—'long about
  Here in June especially!—
    Under some old apple tree,
    Jes' a-restin' through and through,
I could git along without
    Nothin' else at all to do
    Only jes' a-wishin' you
Wuz a-gittin' there like me,
And June was eternity!

VII

Lay out there and try to see
Jes' how lazy you kin be!—
Tumble round and souse yer head
In the clover-bloom, er pull
  Yer straw hat acrost yer eyes
  And peek through it at the skies,
  Thinkin' of old chums 'at's dead,
  Maybe, smilin' back at you
In betwixt the beautiful
  Clouds o' gold and white and blue!—
Month a man kin railly love—
June, you know, I'm talkin' of!

VIII

March ain't never nothin' new!—
April's altogether too
  Brash fer me! and May—I jes'
  'Bominate its promises,—
Little hints o' sunshine and
Green around the timber-land—
  A few blossoms, and a few
  Chip-birds, and a sprout er two,—
  Drap asleep, and it turns in
  'Fore daylight and *snows* ag'in!—
But when *June* comes—Clear my th'oat
  With wild honey!—Rench my hair
In the dew! and hold my coat!
  Whoop out loud! and th'ow my hat!—
June wants me, and I'm to spare!
Spread them shadders anywhere,
I'll git down and waller there,
  And obleeged to you at that!   1887

THE OLD MAN AND JIM

Old man never had much to say—
    'Ceptin' to Jim,—
And Jim was the wildest boy he had—
    And the old man jes' wrapped up in him!
Never heerd him speak but once
Er twice in my life,—and first time was
When the army broke out, and Jim he went,
The old man backin' him, fer three months;
And all 'at I heerd the old man say
Was, jes' as we turned to start away,—   10
    "Well, good-by, Jim:
    Take keer of yourse'f!"

'Peared-like he was more satisfied
    Jes *lookin'* at Jim
And likin' him all to hisse'f-like, see?
    'Cause he was jes' wrapped up in him!
And over and over I mind the day
The old man come and stood round in the way
While we was drillin', a-watchin' Jim—
And down at the deepot a-heerin' him say,
    "Well, good-by, Jim: 21
    Take keer of yourse'f!"

Never was nothin' about the *farm*
    Disting'ished Jim;
Neighbors all uset to wonder why
    The old man 'peared wrapped up in him:
But when Cap. Biggler, he writ back
'At Jim was the bravest boy we had
In the whole dern rigiment, white er black,
And his fightin' good as his farmin' bad—   30
'At he had led, with a bullet clean
Bored through his thigh, and carried the flag
Through the bloodiest battle you ever seen,—
The old man wound up a letter to him
'At Cap. read to us, 'at said,—"Tell Jim
    Good-by,
    And take keer of hisse'f!"

Jim come home jes' long enough
    To take the whim
'At he'd like to go back in the calvery—   40
    And the old man jes' wrapped up in him!
Jim 'lowed 'at he'd had sich luck afore,
Guessed he'd tackle her three years more.
And the old man give him a colt he'd raised,
And follered him over to Camp Ben Wade,
And laid around fer a week er so,
Watchin' Jim on dress-parade—
'Tel finally he rid away,
And last he heerd was the old man say,—   50
    "Well, good-by, Jim:
    Take keer of yourse'f!"

Tuk the papers, the old man did,
    A-watchin' fer Jim—
Fully believin' he'd make his mark
    Some way—jes' wrapped up in him!—
And many a time the word 'u'd come
'At stirred him up like the tap of a drum—
At Petersburg, fer instunce, where
Jim rid right into their cannons ther,
And *tuk* 'em, and p'inted 'em t'other way,   60
And socked it home to the boys in gray,
As they scooted fer timber, and on and on—
Jim a lieutenant,—and one arm gone,—
And the old man's words in his mind all day,—
    "Well, good-by, Jim:
    Take keer of yourse'f!"

Think of a private, now, perhaps,
    We'll say like Jim,
'At's clumb clean up to the shoulder-straps—
    And the old man jes' wrapped up in him!   70
Think of him—with the war plum' through,
And the glorious old Red-White-and-Blue
A-laughin' the news down over Jim,
And the old man, bendin' over him—
The surgeon turnin' away with tears
'At hadn't leaked fer years and years,
As the hand of the dyin' boy clung to
His father's, the old voice in his ears,—
    "Well, good-by, Jim:
    Take keer of yourse'f!"
                   1888

BEREAVED

Let me come in where you sit weeping,—ay,
Let me, who have not any child to die,
Weep with you for the little one whose love
    I have known nothing of.

The little arms that slowly, slowly loosed
Their pressure round your neck; the hands
    you used
To kiss.—Such arms—such hands I never
    knew.
    May I not weep with you?

Fain would I be of service—say something,
Between the tears, that would be comfort-
    ing,—   10
But ah! so sadder than yourselves am I,
    Who have no child to die.
                   1890

EUGENE FIELD (1850-1895)

LITTLE BOY BLUE

The little toy dog is covered with dust,
  But sturdy and stanch he stands;
And the little toy soldier is red with rust,
  And his musket moulds in his hands.
Time was when the little toy dog was new
  And the soldier was passing fair,
And that was the time when our Little Boy
    Blue
  Kissed them and put them there.

"Now, don't you go till I come," he said,
  "And don't you make any noise!"   10
So toddling off to his trundle-bed
  He dreamt of the pretty toys.

And, as he was dreaming, an angel song
  Awakened our Little Boy Blue,—
Oh! the years are many, the years are long,
  But the little toy friends are true.

Ay, faithful to Little Boy Blue they stand,
  Each in the same old place,
Awaiting the touch of a little hand,
  The smile of a little face.   20
And they wonder, as waiting the long years
    through,
  In the dust of that little chair,
What has become of our Little Boy Blue
  Since he kissed them and put them there.
                                        1888

CASEY'S TABLE D'HÔTE

Oh, them days on Red Hoss Mountain, when the skies wuz fair 'nd blue,
When the money flowed like likker, 'nd the folks wuz brave 'nd true!
When the nights wuz crisp 'nd balmy, 'nd the camp wuz all astir,
With the joints all throwed wide open 'nd no sheriff to demur!
Oh, them times on Red Hoss Mountain in the Rockies fur away,—
There's no sich place nor times like them as I kin find to-day!
What though the camp *hez* busted? I seem to see it still
A-lyin', like it loved it, on that big 'nd warty hill;
And I feel a sort of yearnin' 'nd a chokin' in my throat
When I think of Red Hoss Mountain 'nd of Casey's tabble dote!   10

Wal, yes; it's true I struck it rich, but that don't cut a show
When one is old 'nd feeble 'nd it's nigh his time to go;
The money that he's got in bonds or carries to invest
Don't figger with a codger who has lived a life out West;
Us old chaps like to set around, away from folks 'nd noise,
'Nd think about the sights we seen and things we done when boys;
The which is why *I* love to set 'nd think of them old days
When all us Western fellers got the Colorado craze,—
And *that* is why I love to set around all day 'nd gloat
On thoughts of Red Hoss Mountain 'nd of Casey's tabble dote.   20

This Casey wuz an Irishman,—you'd know it by his name
And by the facial features appertainin' to the same.
He'd lived in many places 'nd had done a thousand things,
From the noble art of actin' to the work of dealin' kings,
But, somehow, hadn't caught on; so, driftin' with the rest,
He drifted for a fortune to the undeveloped West,
And he come to Red Hoss Mountain when the little camp wuz new,
When the money flowed like likker, 'nd the folks wuz brave 'nd true;
And, havin' been a stewart on a Mississippi boat,   30
He opened up a caffy 'nd he run a tabble dote.

The bar wuz long 'nd rangey, with a mirrer on the shelf,
'Nd a pistol, so that Casey, when required, could help himself;
Down underneath there wuz a row of bottled beer 'nd wine,
'Nd a kag of Burbun whiskey of the run of '59;

Upon the walls wuz pictures of hosses 'nd of girls,—
Not much on dress, perhaps, but strong on records 'nd on curls!
The which had been identified with Casey in the past,—
The hosses 'nd the girls, I mean,—and both wuz mighty fast!
But all these fine attractions wuz of precious little note
By the side of what wuz offered at Casey's tabble dote.   40

There wuz half-a-dozen tables altogether in the place,
And the tax you had to pay upon your vittles wuz a case;
The boardin'-houses in the camp protested 't wuz a shame
To patronize a robber, which this Casey wuz the same!
They said a case was robbery to tax for ary meal;
But Casey tended strictly to his biz, 'nd let 'em squeal;
And presently the boardin'-houses all began to bust,
While Casey kept on sawin' wood 'nd layin' in the dust;
And oncet a trav'lin' editor from Denver City wrote
A piece back to his paper, puffin' Casey's tabble dote.   50

A tabble dote is different from orderin' aller cart:
In *one* case you git all there is, in *t'other*, only *part!*
And Casey's tabble dote began in French,—as all begin,—
And Casey's ended with the same, which is to say, with "vin";
But in between wuz every kind of reptile, bird, 'nd beast,
The same like you can git in high-toned restauraws down east;
'Nd windin' up wuz cake or pie, with coffee demy tass,
Or, sometimes, floatin' Ireland in a soothin' kind of sass
That left a sort of pleasant ticklin' in a feller's throat,
'Nd made him hanker after more of Casey's tabble dote.   60

The very recollection of them puddin's 'nd them pies
Brings a yearnin' to my buzzum 'nd the water to my eyes;
'Nd seems like cookin' nowadays aint what it used to be
In camp on Red Hoss Mountain in that year of '63;
But, maybe, it is better, 'nd, maybe, I'm to blame—
I'd like to be a-livin' in the mountains jest the same—
I'd like to live that life again when skies wuz fair 'nd blue,
When things wuz run wide open 'nd men wuz brave 'nd true;
When brawny arms the flinty ribs of Red Hoss Mountain smote
For wherewithal to pay the price of Casey's tabble dote.   70

And you, O cherished brother, a-sleepin' way out west,
With Red Hoss Mountain huggin' you close to its lovin' breast,—
Oh, do you dream in your last sleep of how we used to do,
Of how we worked our little claims together, me 'nd you?
Why, when I saw you last a smile wuz restin' on your face,
Like you wuz glad to sleep forever in that lonely place;
And so you wuz, 'nd I'd be, too, if I wuz sleepin' so.
But, bein' how a brother's love aint for the world to know,
Whenever I've this heartache 'nd this chokin' in my throat,
I lay it all to thinkin' of Casey's tabble dote.   80

1889

THE TRUTH ABOUT HORACE

It is very aggravating
To hear the solemn prating
Of the fossils who are stating
That old Horace was a prude;
When we know that with the ladies
He was always raising Hades,
And with many an escapade his
Best productions are imbued.

There's really not much harm in a
Large number of his carmina,   10
But these people find alarm in a

Few records of his acts;
So they'd squelch the muse caloric,
And to students sophomoric
They'd present as metaphoric
What old Horace meant for facts.

We have always thought 'em lazy;
Now we adjudge 'em crazy!
Why, Horace was a daisy
That was very much alive!　　20
And the wisest of us know him
As his Lydia verses show him,—
Go, read that virile poem,—
It is No. 25.

He was a very owl, sir,
And starting out to prowl, sir,
You bet he made Rome howl, sir,
Until he filled his date;
With a massic-laden ditty
And a classic maiden pretty　　30
He painted up the city,
And Mæcenas paid the freight!
　　　　　　　　1889

TO THE PASSING SAINT

As to-night you came your way,
Bearing earthward heavenly joy,
Tell me, O dear saint, I pray,
Did you see my little boy?

By some fairer voice beguiled,
Once he wandered from my sight;

He is such a little child,
He should have my love this night.

It has been so many a year,—　　10
Oh, so many a year since then!
Yet he was so very dear,
Surely he will come again.

If upon your way you see
One whose beauty is divine,
Will you send him back to me?
He is lost, and he is mine.

Tell him that his little chair
Nestles where the sunbeams meet,
That the shoes he used to wear
Yearn to kiss his dimpled feet.　　20

Tell him of each pretty toy
That was wont to share his glee;
Maybe that will bring my boy
Back to them and back to me.

O dear saint, as on you go
Through the glad and sparkling frost,
Bid those bells ring high and low
For a little child that's lost!

O dear saint, that blessest men
With the grace of Christmas joy,　　30
Soothe this heart with love again,—
Give me back my little boy!
　　　　　　　　1892

PAUL LAURENCE DUNBAR (1872-1906)

HARRIET BEECHER STOWE

She told the story, and the whole world wept
At wrongs and cruelties it had not known
But for this fearless woman's voice alone.
She spoke to consciences that long had slept:
Her message, Freedom's clear reveille, swept
From heedless hovel to complacent throne.
Command and prophecy were in the tone
And from its sheath the sword of justice leapt.
Around two peoples swelled a fiery wave,
But both came forth transfigured from the
　　flame.　　10
Blest be the hand that dared be strong to save,
And blest be she who in our weakness came—
Prophet and priestess! At one stroke she gave
A race to freedom and herself to fame.
　　　　　　　　1898

MORTALITY

Ashes to ashes, dust unto dust,
What of his loving, what of his lust?
What of his passion, what of his pain?
What of his poverty, what of his pride?
Earth, the great mother, has called him again:
Deeply he sleeps, the world's verdict de-
fied.
Shall he be tried again? Shall he go free?
Who shall the court convene? Where shall it
be?
No answer on the land, none from the sea.
Only we know that as he did, we must:　　10
You with your theories, you with your trust,—
Ashes to ashes, dust unto dust!
　　　　　　　　1899

ANGELINA

When de fiddle gits to singin' out a ol' Vahginny reel,
An' you 'mence to feel a ticklin' in yo' toe an' in yo' heel;
Ef you t'ink you got 'uligion an' you wants to keep it, too,
You jes' bettah tek a hint an' git yo'self clean out o' view.
Case de time is mighty temptin' when de chune is in de swing,
Fu' a darky, saint or sinner man, to cut de pigeon-wing.
An' you couldn't he'p f'om dancin' ef yo' feet was boun' wif twine,
When Angelina Johnson comes a-swingin' down de line.

Don't you know Miss Angelina? She's de da'lin' of de place.
W'y, dey ain't no high-toned lady wif sich mannahs an' sich grace.   10
She kin move across de cabin, wif its planks all rough an' wo';
Jes' de same's ef she was dancin' on ol' mistus' ball-room flo'.
Fact is, you do' see no cabin—evaht'ing you see look grand,
An' dat one ol' squeaky fiddle soun' to you jes' lak a ban';
Cotton britches look lak broadclof an' a linsey dress look fine,
When Angelina Johnson comes a-swingin' down de line.

Some folks say dat dancin's sinful, an' de blessed Lawd, dey say,
Gwine to purnish us fu' steppin' w'en we hyeah de music play.
But I tell you I don' b'lieve it, fu' de Lawd is wise and good,
An' he made de banjo's metal an' he made de fiddle's wood,   20
An' he made de music in dem, so I don't quite t'ink he'll keer
Ef our feet keeps time a little to de melodies we hyeah.
W'y, dey's somep'n' downright holy in de way our faces shine,
When Angelina Johnson comes a-swingin' down de line.

Angelina steps so gentle, Angelina bows so low,
An' she lif' huh sku't so dainty dat huh shoetop skacely show:
An' dem teef o' huh'n a-shinin', ez she tek you by de han'—
Go 'way, people, d'ain't anothah sich a lady in de lan'!
When she's movin' thoo de figgers er a-dancin' by huhse'f,
Folks jes' stan' stock-still a-sta'in', an' dey mos' nigh hol's dey bref;   30
An' de young mens, dey's a-sayin', "I's gwine mek dat damsel mine,"
When Angelina Johnson comes a-swingin' down de line.

                                                                1899

THE SOUTHERN GROUP

HENRY TIMROD (1829-1867)

TWO PORTRAITS

I

You say, as one who shapes a life,
That you will never be a wife,

And, laughing lightly, ask my aid
To paint your future as a maid.

This is the portrait; and I take
The softest colors for your sake:

The springtime of your soul is dead,
And forty years have bent your head;

The lines are firmer round your mouth,
But still its smile is like the South.   10

Your eyes, grown deeper, are not sad,
Yet never more than gravely glad;

And the old charm still lurks within
The cloven dimple of your chin.

Some share, perhaps, of youthful gloss
Your cheek hath shed; but still across

The delicate ear are folded down
Those silken locks of chestnut brown;

Though here and there a thread of gray
Steals through them like a lunar ray.   20

One might suppose your life had passed
Unvexed by any troubling blast;

And such—for all that I foreknow—
May be the truth! The deeper woe!

A loveless heart is seldom stirred;
And sorrow shuns the mateless bird;

But ah! through cares alone we reach
The happiness which mocketh speech;

In the white courts beyond the stars
The noblest brow is seamed with scars;   30

And they on earth who've wept the most
Sit highest of the heavenly host.

Grant that your maiden life hath sped
In music o'er a golden bed,

With rocks, and winds, and storms at truce,
And not without a noble use;

Yet are you happy? In your air
I see a nameless want appear,

And a faint shadow on your cheek
Tells what the lips refuse to speak.   40

You have had all a maid could hope
In the most cloudless horoscope:

The strength that cometh from above;
A Christian mother's holy love;

And always at your soul's demand
A brother's, sister's heart and hand.

Small need your heart hath had to roam
Beyond the circle of your home;

And yet upon your wish attends
A loving throng of genial friends.   50

What, in a lot so sweet as this,
Is wanting to complete your bliss?

And to what secret shall I trace
The clouds that sometimes cross your face,

And that sad look which now and then
Comes, disappears, and comes again,

And dies reluctantly away
In those clear eyes of azure gray?

At best, and after all, the place
You fill with such a serious grace,   60

Hath much to try a woman's heart,
And you but play a painful part.

The world around, with little ruth,
Still laughs at maids who have not youth,

And, right or wrong, the old maid rests
The victim of its paltry jests,

And still is doomed to meet and bear
Its pitying smile or furtive sneer.

These are indeed but petty things,   69
And yet they touch some hearts like stings.

But I acquit you of the shame
Of being unresisting game;

For you are of such tempered clay
As turns far stronger shafts away,

And all that foes or fools could guide
Would only curl that lip of pride.

How then, O weary one! explain
The sources of that hidden pain?

Alas! you have divined at length
How little you have used your strength,   80

Which, with who knows what human good,
Lies buried in that maidenhood,

Where, as amid a field of flowers,
You have but played with April showers.

Ah! we would wish the world less fair,
If Spring alone adorned the year,

And Autumn came not with its fruit,
And Autumn hymns were ever mute.

So I remark without surprise
That, as the unvarying season flies,   90

From day to night and night to day,
You sicken of your endless May.

In this poor life we may not cross
One virtuous instinct without loss,

And the soul grows not to its height
Till love calls forth its utmost might.

Not blind to all you might have been,
And with some consciousness of sin—

Because with love you sometimes played, 99
And choice, not fate, hath kept you maid—

You feel that you must pass from earth
But half-acquainted with its worth,

And that within your heart are deeps
In which a nobler woman sleeps;

That not the maiden, but the wife
Grasps the whole lesson of a life,

While such as you but sit and dream
Along the surface of its stream.

And doubtless sometimes, all unsought,
There comes upon your hour of thought, 110

Despite the struggles of your will,
A sense of something absent still;

And then you cannot help but yearn
To love and be beloved in turn,

As they are loved, and love, who live
As love were all that life could give;

And in a transient clasp or kiss
Crowd an eternity of bliss;

They who of every mortal joy
Taste always twice, nor feel them cloy, 120

Or, if woes come, in Sorrow's hour
Are strengthened by a double power.

II

Here ends my feeble sketch of what
Might, but will never be your lot;

And I foresee how oft these rhymes
Shall make you smile in after-times.

If I have read your nature right,
It only waits a spark of light;

And when that comes, as come it must,
It will not fall on arid dust, 130

Nor yet on that which breaks to flame
In the first blush of maiden shame;

But on a heart which, even at rest,
Is warmer than an April nest,

Where, settling soft, that spark shall creep
About as gently as a sleep;

Still stealing on with pace so slow
Yourself will scarcely feel the glow,

Till after many and many a day,
Although no gleam its course betray, 140

It shall attain the inmost shrine,
And wrap it in a fire divine!

I know not when or whence indeed
Shall fall and burst the burning seed,

But oh! once kindled, it will blaze,
I know, forever! By its rays

You will perceive, with subtler eyes,
The meaning in the earth and skies,

Which, with their animated chain
Of grass and flowers, and sun and rain, 150

Of green below, and blue above,
Are but a type of married love.

You will perceive that in the breast
The germs of many virtues rest,

Which, ere they feel a lover's breath,
Lie in a temporary death;

And till the heart is wooed and won
It is an earth without a sun.

III

But now, stand forth as sweet as life!
And let me paint you as a wife. 160

I note some changes in your face,
And in your mien a graver grace;

Yet the calm forehead lightly bears
Its weight of twice a score of years;

And that one love which on this earth
Can wake the heart to all its worth,

And to their height can lift and bind
The powers of soul, and sense, and mind,

Hath not allowed a charm to fade—
And the wife's lovelier than the maid. 170

An air of still, though bright repose
Tells that a tender hand bestows

All that a generous manhood may
To make your life one bridal day,

While the kind eyes betray no less,
In their blue depths of tenderness,

That you have learned the truths which lie
Behind that holy mystery,

Which, with its blisses and its woes,
Nor man nor maiden ever knows.   180

If now, as to the eyes of one
Whose glance not even thought can shun,

Your soul lay open to my view,
I, looking all its nature through,

Could see no incompleted part,
For the whole woman warms your heart.

I cannot tell how many dead
You number in the cycles fled,

And you but look the more serene
For all the griefs you may have seen,   190

As you had gathered from the dust
The flowers of Peace, and Hope, and Trust.

Your smile is even sweeter now
That when it lit your maiden brow,

And that which wakes this gentler charm
Coos at this moment on your arm.

Your voice was always soft in youth,
And had the very sound of truth,

But never were its tones so mild
Until you blessed your earliest child;   200

And when to soothe some little wrong
It melts into a mother's song,

The same strange sweetness which in years
Long vanished filled the eyes with tears,

And (even when mirthful) gave always
A pathos to your girlish lays,

Falls, with perchance a deeper thrill,
Upon the breathless listener still.

I cannot guess in what fair spot
The chance of Time hath fixed your lot, 210

Nor can I name what manly breast
Gives to that head a welcome rest;

I cannot tell if partial Fate
Hath made you poor, or rich, or great;

But oh! whatever be your place,
I never saw a form or face

To which more plainly hath been lent
The blessing of a full content!
                                        1860

SPRING

Spring, with that nameless pathos in the air
Which dwells with all things fair,
Spring, with her golden suns and silver rain,
Is with us once again.

Out in the lonely woods the jasmine burns
Its fragrant lamps, and turns
Into a royal court with green festoons
The banks of dark lagoons.

In the deep heart of every forest tree
The blood is all aglee,   10
And there's a look about the leafless bowers
As if they dreamed of flowers.

Yet still on every side we trace the hand
Of Winter in the land,
Save where the maple reddens on the lawn,
Flushed by the season's dawn;

Or where, like those strange semblances we find
That age to childhood bind,

The elm puts on, as if in Nature's scorn,
The brown of Autumn corn.   20

As yet the turf is dark, although you know
That, not a span below,
A thousand germs are groping through the
      gloom,
And soon will burst their tomb.

Already, here and there, on frailest stems
Appear some azure gems,
Small as might deck, upon a gala day,
The forehead of a fay.

In gardens you may note amid the dearth
The crocus breaking earth;   30
And near the snowdrop's tender white and
      green,
The violet in its screen.

But many gleams and shadows need must pass
Along the budding grass,

And weeks go by, before the enamored South
Shall kiss the rose's mouth.

Still there's a sense of blossoms yet unborn
In the sweet airs of morn;
One almost looks to see the very street
Grow purple at his feet.   40

At times a fragrant breeze comes floating by,
And brings, you know not why,
A feeling as when eager crowds await
Before a palace gate.

Some wondrous pageant; and you scarce would start,
If from a beech's heart,
A blue-eyed Dryad, stepping forth, should say,
"Behold me! I am May!"

Ah! who would couple thoughts of war and crime
With such a blessëd time!   50

Who in the west wind's aromatic breath
Could hear the call of Death!

Yet not more surely shall the Spring awake
The voice of wood and brake,
Than she shall rouse, for all her tranquil charms,
A million men to arms.

There shall be deeper hues upon her plains
Than all her sunlit rains,
And every gladdening influence around,
Can summon from the ground.   60

Oh! standing on this desecrated mould,
Methinks that I behold,
Lifting her bloody daisies up to God,
Spring kneeling on the sod,

And calling, with the voice of all her rills,
Upon the ancient hills
To fall and crush the tyrants and the slaves
Who turn her meads to graves.
    1862?

THE COTTON BOLL

While I recline
At ease beneath
This immemorial pine,
Small sphere!
(By dusky fingers brought this morning here
And shown with boastful smiles),
I turn thy cloven sheath,
Through which the soft white fibres peer,
That, with their gossamer bands,
Unite, like love, the sea-divided lands,   10
And slowly, thread by thread,
Draw forth the folded strands,
Than which the trembling line,
By whose frail help yon startled spider fled
Down the tall spear-grass from his swinging bed,
Is scarce more fine;
And as the tangled skein
Unravels in my hands,
Betwixt me and the noonday light,
A veil seems lifted, and for miles and miles
The landscape broadens on my sight,   20
As, in the little boll, there lurked a spell
Like that which, in the ocean shell,
With mystic sound,
Breaks down the narrow walls that hem us round,
And turns some city lane
Into the restless main,
With all his capes and isles!

Yonder bird,
Which floats, as if at rest,
In those blue tracts above the thunder, where   29
No vapors cloud the stainless air,
And never sound is heard,
Unless at such rare time
When, from the City of the Blest,
Rings down some golden chime,
Sees not from his high place
So vast a cirque of summer space
As widens round me in one mighty field,
Which, rimmed by seas and sands,
Doth hail its earliest daylight in the beams
Of gray Atlantic dawns;   41
And, broad as realms made up of many lands,
Is lost afar
Behind the crimson hills and purple lawns
Of sunset, among plains which roll their streams
Against the Evening Star!
And lo!
To the remotest point of sight,
Although I gaze upon no waste of snow,   50
The endless field is white;
And the whole landscape glows,
For many a shining league away,
With such accumulated light
As Polar lands would flash beneath a tropic day!
Nor lack there (for the vision grows,

And the small charm within my hands—
More potent even than the fabled one,
Which oped whatever golden mystery
Lay hid in fairy wood or magic vale, 60
The curious ointment of the Arabian tale—
Beyond all mortal sense
Doth stretch my sight's horizon, and I see,
Beneath its simple influence,
As if with Uriel's crown,
I stood in some great temple of the Sun,
And looked, as Uriel, down!)
Nor lack there pastures rich and fields all
green
With all the common gifts of God,
For temperate airs and torrid sheen 70
Weave Edens of the sod;
Through lands which look one sea of billowy
gold
Broad rivers wind their devious ways;
A hundred isles in their embraces fold
A hundred luminous bays;
And through yon purple haze
Vast mountains lift their plumed peaks cloud-
crowned;
And, save where up their sides the plowman
creeps,
An unhewn forest girds them grandly round,
In whose dark shades a future navy sleeps!
Ye Stars, which, though unseen, yet with me
gaze 81
Upon this loveliest fragment of the earth!
Thou Sun, that kindlest all thy gentlest rays
Above it, as to light a favorite hearth!
Ye Clouds, that in your temples in the West
See nothing brighter than its humblest flowers!
And you, ye Winds, that on the ocean's breast
Are kissed to coolness ere ye reach its bowers!
Bear witness with me in my song of praise,
And tell the world that, since the world began,
No fairer land hath fired a poet's lays, 91
Or given a home to man!

But these are charms already widely blown!
His be the meed whose pencil's trace
Hath touched our very swamps with grace,
And round whose tuneful way
All Southern laurels bloom;
The Poet of "The Woodlands," unto whom
Alike are known
The flute's low breathing and the trumpet's
tone 100
And the soft west wind's sighs;
But who shall utter all the debt,
O Land wherein all powers are met
That bind a people's heart,
The world doth owe thee at this day,
And which it never can repay,
Yet scarcely deigns to own!

Where sleeps the poet who shall fitly sing
The source wherefrom doth spring
That mighty commerce which, confined 110
To the mean channels of no selfish mart,
Goes out to every shore
Of this broad earth, and throngs the sea with
ships
That bear no thunders; hushes hungry lips
In alien lands;
Joins with a delicate web remotest strands;
And gladdening rich and poor,
Doth gild Parisian domes,
Or feed the cottage-smoke of English homes,
And only bounds its blessings by mankind!
In offices like these, thy mission lies, 121
My Country! and it shall not end
As long as rain shall fall and Heaven bend
In blue above thee; though thy foes be hard
And cruel as their weapons, it shall guard
Thy hearth-stones as a bulwark; make thee
great
In white and bloodless state;
And haply, as the years increase—
Still working through its humbler reach
With that large wisdom which the ages
teach— 130
Revive the half-dead stream of universal
peace!
As men who labor in that mine
Of Cornwall, hollowed out beneath the bed
Of ocean, when a storm rolls overhead,
Hear the dull booming of the world of brine
Above them, and a mighty muffled roar
Of winds and waters, yet toil calmly on,
And split the rock, and pile the massive ore,
Or carve a niche, or shape the archèd roof;
So I, as calmly, weave my woof 140
Of song, chanting the days to come,
Unsilenced, though the quiet summer air
Stirs with the bruit of battles, and each dawn
Wakes from its starry silence to the hum
Of many gathering armies. Still,
In that we sometimes hear,
Upon the Northern winds, the voice of woe
Not wholly drowned in triumph, though I
know
The end must crown us, and a few brief years
Dry all our tears, 150
I may not sing too gladly. To Thy will
Resigned, O Lord! we cannot all forget
That there is much even Victory must regret.
And, therefore, not too long
From the great burthen of our country's wrong
Delay our just release!
And, if it may be, save
These sacred fields of peace
From stain of patriot or of hostile blood!
Oh, help us, Lord! to roll the crimson flood 160

Back on its course, and while our banners wing
Northward, strike with us! till the Goth shall cling
To his own blasted altar-stones, and crave
Mercy; and we shall grant it, and dictate

The lenient future of his fate
There, where some rotting ships and crumbling quays
Shall one day mark the Port which ruled the Western seas.
1862?

PAUL H. HAYNE (1830-1886)

MARGUERITE

She was a child of gentlest air,
Of deep-dark eyes, but golden hair,
And, ah! I loved her unaware,
      Marguerite!

She spelled me with those midnight eyes,
The sweetness of her naïve replies,
And all her innocent sorceries,
      Marguerite!

The fever of my soul grew calm
Beneath her smile that healed like balm, 10
Her words were holier than a psalm,
      Marguerite!

But 'twixt us yawned a gulf of fate,
Whose blackness I beheld,—too late.
O Christ! that love should smite like hate.
      Marguerite!

She did not wither to the tomb,
But round her crept a tender gloom
More touching than her earliest bloom,
      Marguerite!   20

The sun of one fair hope had set,
A hope she dared not all forget,
Its twilight glory kissed her yet,—
      Marguerite!

And ever in the twilight fair
Moves with deep eyes and golden hair
The child who loved me unaware!
      Marguerite!
            1872

THE SPIREA

This exquisite plant blooms in the Southern States as early as the middle of February.

Of all the subtle fires of earth
      Which rise in form of spring-time flowers,
Oh, say if aught of purer birth
      Is nursed by suns and showers

Than this fair plant, whose stems are bowed
      In such lithe curves of maiden grace,
Veiled in white blossoms like a cloud
      Of daintiest bridal lace?

So rare, so soft, its blossoms seem
      Half woven of moonshine's misty bars, 10
And tremulous as the tender gleam
      Of the far Southland stars.

Perchance—who knows?—some virgin bright,
      Some loveliest of the Dryad race,
Pours through these flowers the kindling light
      Of her Arcadian face.

Nor would I marvel overmuch
      If from yon pines a wood-god came,
And with a bridegroom's lips should touch
      Her conscious heart to flame;   20

While she, revealed at that strange tryst,
      In all her mystic beauty glows,
Lifting the cheek her Love had kissed,
      Paled like a bridal rose.
                  1882

SIDNEY LANIER (1842-1881)

MY SPRINGS

In the heart of the Hills of Life, I know
Two springs that with unbroken flow
Forever pour their lucent streams
Into my soul's far Lake of Dreams.

Not larger than two eyes, they lie
Beneath the many-changing sky

And mirror all of life and time,
—Serene and dainty pantomime.

Shot through with lights of stars and dawns,
And shadowed sweet by ferns and fawns,   10
—Thus heaven and earth together vie
Their shining depths to sanctify.

Always when the large Form of Love
Is hid by storms that rage above,
I gaze in my two springs and see
Love in his very verity.

Always when Faith with stifling stress
Of grief hath died in bitterness,
I gaze in my two springs and see
A Faith that smiles immortally.   20

Always when Charity and Hope,
In darkness bounden, feebly grope,
I gaze in my two springs and see
A Light that sets my captives free.

Always, when Art on perverse wing
Flies where I cannot hear him sing,
I gaze in my two springs and see
A charm that brings him back to me.

When Labor faints, and Glory fails,
And coy Reward in sighs exhales,   30
I gaze in my two springs and see
Attainment full and heavenly.

O Love, O Wife, thine eyes are they,
—My springs from out whose shining gray

Issue the sweet celestial streams
That feed my life's bright Lake of Dreams.

Oval and large and passion-pure
And gray and wise and honor-sure;
Soft as a dying violet-breath
Yet calmly unafraid of death;   40

Thronged, like two dove-cotes of gray doves,
With wife's and mother's and poor-folk's loves,
And home-loves and high glory-loves
And science-loves and story-loves,

And loves for all that God and man
In art and nature make or plan,
And lady-loves for spidery lace
And broideries and supple grace

And diamonds and the whole sweet round
Of littles that large life compound,   50
And loves for God and God's bare truth,
And loves for Magdalen and Ruth,

Dear eyes, dear eyes and rare complete—
Being heavenly-sweet and earthly-sweet,
—I marvel that God made you mine,
For when He frowns, 'tis then ye shine!
Baltimore, 1874   1882

THE SYMPHONY

"O Trade! O Trade! would thou wert dead!
The Time needs heart—'tis tired of head:
We're all for love," the violins said.
"Of what avail the rigorous tale
Of bill for coin and box for bale?
Grant thee, O Trade! thine uttermost hope:
Level red gold with blue sky-slope,
And base it deep as devils grope:
When all's done, what hast thou won
Of the only sweet that's under the sun?   10
Ay, canst thou buy a single sigh
Of true love's least, least ecstasy?"
Then, with a bridegroom's heart-beats trem-
bling,
All the mightier strings assembling
Ranged them on the violins' side
As when the bridegroom leads the bride,
And, heart in voice, together cried:
"Yea, what avail the endless tale
Of gain by cunning and plus by sale?
Look up the land, look down the land   20
The poor, the poor, the poor, they stand
Wedged by the pressing of Trade's hand
Against an inward-opening door
That pressure tightens evermore:
They sigh a monstrous foul-air sigh
For the outside leagues of liberty,

Where Art, sweet lark, translates the sky
Into a heavenly melody.
'Each day, all day' (these poor folks say),
'In the same old year-long, drear-long way,   30
We weave in the mills and heave in the kilns,
We sieve mine-meshes under the hills,
And thieve much gold from the Devil's bank
tills,—
To relieve, O God, what manner of ills?—
The beasts, they hunger, and eat, and die;
And so do we, and the world's a sty;
Hush, fellow-swine: why nuzzle and cry?
Swinehood hath no remedy
Say many men, and hasten by,
Clamping the nose and blinking the eye.   40
But who said once, in the lordly tone,
Man shall not live by bread alone
But all that cometh from the Throne?
          Hath God said so?
          But Trade saith *No*:
And the kilns and the curt-tongued mills say
          Go!
There's plenty that can, if you can't: we know.
Move out, if you think you're underpaid.
The poor are prolific; we're not afraid;
          Trade is trade.'"   50
Thereat this passionate protesting

Meekly changed, and softened till
It sank to sad requesting
And suggesting sadder still:
"And oh, if men might some time see
How piteous-false the poor decree
That trade no more than trade must be!
Does business mean, *Die, you—live, I?*
Then "Trade is trade" but sings a lie:
'Tis only war grown miserly.   60
If business is battle, name it so:
War-crimes less will shame it so,
And widows less will blame it so.
Alas, for the poor to have some part
In yon sweet living lands of Art,
Makes problem not for head, but heart.
Vainly might Plato's brain revolve it:
Plainly the heart of a child could solve it."

And then, as when from words that seem but
   rude
We pass to silent pain that sits abroad   70
Back in our heart's great dark and solitude,
So sank the strings to gentle throbbing
Of long chords change-marked with sobbing—
Motherly sobbing, not distinctlier heard
Than half wing-openings of the sleeping bird,
Some dream of danger to her young hath
   stirred.
Then stirring and demurring ceased, and lo!
Every least ripple of the string's song-flow
Died to a level with each level bow   79
And made a great chord tranquil-surfaced so,
As a brook beneath his curving bank doth go
To linger in the sacred dark and green
Where many boughs the still pool overlean
And many leaves make shadow with their
   sheen.
   But presently
A velvet flute-note fell down pleasantly
Upon the bosom of that harmony,
And sailed and sailed incessantly,
As if a petal from a wild-rose blown
Had fluttered down upon that pool of tone   90
And boatwise dropped o' the convex side
And floated down the glassy tide
And clarified and glorified
The solemn spaces where the shadows bide.
From the warm concave of that fluted note
Somewhat, half song, half odor, forth did float,
As if a rose might somehow be a throat:
"When Nature from her far-off glen
Flutes her soft messages to men,
   The flute can say them o'er again;   100
   Yea, Nature, singing sweet and lone,
Breathes through life's strident polyphone
The flute-voice in the world of tone.
   Sweet friends,
   Man's love ascends

To finer and diviner ends
Than man's mere thought e'er comprehends
For I, e'en I,
As here I lie,
A petal on a harmony,   110
Demand of Science whence and why
Man's tender pain, man's inward cry,
When he doth gaze on earth and sky?
I am not overbold:
   I hold
Full powers from Nature manifold.
I speak for each no-tonguèd tree
That, spring by spring, doth nobler be,
And dumbly and most wistfully
His mighty prayerful arms outspreads   120
Above men's oft-unheeding heads,
And his big blessing downward sheds.
I speak for all-shaped blooms and leaves,
Lichens on stones and moss on eaves,
Grasses and grains in ranks and sheaves;
Broad-fronded ferns and keen-leaved canes,
And briery mazes bounding lanes,
And marsh-plants, thirsty-cupped for rains,
And milky stems and sugary veins;
For every long-armed woman-vine   130
That round a piteous tree doth twine;
For passionate odors, and divine
Pistils, and petals crystalline;
All purities of shady springs,
All shynesses of film-winged things
That fly from tree-trunks and bark-rings;
All modesties of mountain-fawns
That leap to covert from wild lawns,
And tremble if the day but dawns;
All sparklings of small beady eyes   140
Of birds, and sidelong glances wise
Wherewith the jay hints tragedies;
All piquancies of prickly burs,
And smoothnesses of downs and furs,
Of eiders and of minevers;
All limpid honeys that do lie
At stamen-bases, nor deny
The humming-birds' fine roguery,
Bee-thighs, nor any butterfly;
All gracious curves of slender wings,   150
Bark-mottlings, fibre-spiralings,
Fern-wavings and leaf-flickerings;
Each dial-marked leaf and flower-bell
Wherewith in every lonesome dell
Time to himself his hours doth tell;
All tree-sounds, rustlings of pinecones,
Wind-sighings, doves' melodious moans,
And night's unearthly under-tones;
All placid lakes and waveless deeps,
All cool reposing mountain-steeps,   160
Vale-calms and tranquil lotos-sleeps;—
Yea, all fair forms, and sounds, and lights,
And warmths, and mysteries, and mights,

Of Nature's utmost depths and heights,
—These doth my timid tongue present,
Their mouthpiece and leal instrument
And servant, all love-eloquent.
I heard, when "*All for love*" the violins cried:
So, Nature calls through all her system wide,
Give me thy love, O man, so long denied. 170
Much time is run, and man hath changed his
     ways,
Since Nature, in the antique fable-days,
Was hid from man's true love by proxy fays,
False fauns and rascal gods that stole her
     praise.
The nymphs, cold creatures of man's colder
     brain;
Chilled Nature's streams till man's warm heart
     was fain
Never to lave its love in them again.
Later, a sweet Voice *Love thy neighbor* said;
Then first the bounds of neighborhood out-
     spread
Beyond all confines of old ethnic dread. 180
Vainly the Jew might wag his covenant head:
"*All men are neighbors,*" so the sweet Voice
     said.
So, when man's arms had circled all man's
     race,
The liberal compass of his warm embrace
Stretched bigger yet in the dark bounds of
     space;
With hands a-grope he felt smooth Nature's
     grace,
Drew her to breast and kissed her sweetheart
     face:
Yea, man found neighbors in great hills and
     trees
And streams and clouds and suns and birds
     and bees,
And throbbed with neighbor-loves in loving
     these. 190
But oh, the poor! the poor! the poor!
That stand by the inward-opening door
Trade's hand doth tighten ever more,
And sigh their monstrous foul-air sigh
For the outside hills of liberty,
Where Nature spreads her wild blue sky
For Art to make into melody!
Thou Trade! thou king of the modern days!
     Change thy ways,   •
     Change thy ways; 200
Let the sweaty laborers file
     A little while,
     A little while,
Where Art and Nature sing and smile.
Trade! is thy heart all dead, all dead?
And hast thou nothing but a head?
"I'm all for heart," the flute-voice said,
And into sudden silence fled,

Like as a blush that while 'tis red
Dies to a still, still white instead. 210

     Thereto a thrilling calm succeeds,
Till presently the silence breeds
A little breeze among the reeds
That seems to blow by sea-marsh weeds:
Then from the gentle stir and fret
Sings out the melting clarionet,
Like as a lady sings while yet
Her eyes with salty tears are wet.
"O Trade! O Trade!" the Lady said,
"I too will wish thee utterly dead 220
If all thy heart is in thy head.
For O my God! and O my God!
What shameful ways have women trod
At beckoning of Trade's golden rod!
Alas when sighs are traders' lies,
And heart's-ease eyes and violet eyes
     Are merchandise!
O purchased lips that kiss with pain!
O cheeks coin-spotted with smirch and stain!
O trafficked hearts that break in twain! 230
—And yet what wonder at my sisters' crime?
So hath Trade withered up Love's sinewy
     prime,
Men love not women as in olden time.
Ah, not in these cold merchantable days
Deem men their life an opal gray, where plays
The one red Sweet of gracious ladies'-praise.
Now, comes a suitor with sharp prying eye—
Says, *Here, you Lady, if you'll sell, I'll buy:
Come, heart for heart—a trade? What! weep-
     ing? why?*
Shame on such wooers' dapper mercery! 240
I would my lover kneeling at my feet
In humble manliness should cry, *O sweet!
I know not if thy heart my heart will greet:
I ask not if thy love my love can meet:
Whate'er thy worshipful soft tongue shall say,
I'll kiss thine answer, be it yea or nay:
I do but know I love thee, and I pray
To be thy knight until my dying day.*
Woe him that cunning trades in hearts con-
     trives!
Base love good women to base loving drives.
If men loved larger, larger were our lives; 251
And wooed they nobler, won they nobler
     wives."

There thrust the bold straightforward horn
To battle for that lady lorn,
With heartsome voice of mellow scorn,
Like any knight in knighthood's morn.
     "Now comfort thee," said he,
          "Fair Lady.
For God shall right thy grievous wrong,
And man shall sing thee a true-love song, 260

Voiced in act his whole life long,
    Yea, all thy sweet life long,
        Fair Lady.
Where's he that craftily hath said,
The day of chivalry is dead?
I'll prove that lie upon his head,
    Or I will die instead,
        Fair Lady.
Is Honor gone into his grave?
Hath Faith become a caitiff knave,   270
And Selfhood turned into a slave
    To work in Mammon's cave,
        Fair Lady?
Will Truth's long blade ne'er gleam again?
Hath Giant Trade in dungeons slain
All great contempts of mean-got gain
    And hates of inward stain,
        Fair Lady?
For aye shall name and fame be sold,
And place be hugged for the sake of gold,   280
And smirch-robed Justice feebly scold
    At Crime all money-bold,
        Fair Lady?
Shall self-wrapt husbands aye forget
Kiss-pardons for the daily fret
Wherewith sweet wifely eyes are wet—
    Blind to lips kiss-wise set—
        Fair Lady?
Shall lovers higgle, heart for heart,
Till wooing grows a trading mart   290
Where much for little, and all for part,
    Make love a cheapening art,
        Fair Lady?
Shall woman scorch for a single sin
That her betrayer may revel in,
And she be burnt, and he but grin
    When that the flames begin,
        Fair Lady?
Shall ne'er prevail the woman's plea,
We maids would far, far whiter be   300
If that our eyes might sometimes see
    Men maids in purity,
        Fair Lady?
Shall Trade aye salve his conscience-aches
With jibes at Chivalry's old mistakes—
The wars that o'erhot knighthood makes
    For Christ's and ladies' sakes,
        Fair Lady?
Now by each knight that e'er hath prayed
To fight like a man and love like a maid,   310
Since Pembroke's life, as Pembroke's blade,
    I' the scabbard, death, was laid,
        Fair Lady,
I dare avouch my faith is bright
That God doth right and God hath might.
Nor time hath changed His hair to white,
    Nor His dear love to spite,
        Fair Lady.

I doubt no doubts: I strive, and shrive my
    clay,   319
And fight my fight in the patient modern way
For true love and for thee—ah me! and pray
    To be thy knight until my dying day,
        Fair Lady."
Made end that knightly horn, and spurred
    away
Into the thick of the melodious fray.

And then the hautboy played and smiled,
And sang like any large-eyed child,
Cool-hearted and all undefiled.
    "Huge Trade!" he said.
"Would thou wouldst lift me on thy head   330
And run where'er my finger led!
Once said a Man—and wise was He—
Never shalt thou the heavens see,
Save as a little child thou be."
Then o'er sea-lashings of commingling tunes
The ancient wise bassoons;
    Like weird
    Gray-beard
Old harpers sitting on the high sea-dunes,
    Chanted runes: 340
"Bright-waved gain, gray-waved loss,
The sea of all doth lash and toss,
One wave forward and one across:
But now 'twas trough, now 'tis crest,
And worst doth foam and flash to best,
    And curst to blest.

"Life! Life! thou sea-fugue, writ from east
    to west,
    Love, Love alone can pore
    On thy dissolving score
    Of harsh half-phrasings,   350
    Blotted ere writ,
    And double erasings
    Of chords most fit.
Yea, Love, sole music-master blest,
May read thy weltering palimpsest.
To follow Time's dying melodies through,
And never to lose the old in the new,
And ever to solve the discords true—
    Love alone can do.   359
And ever Love hears the poor-folks' crying,
And ever Love hears the women's sighing,
And ever sweet knighthood's death-defying,
And ever wise childhood's deep implying,
But never a trader's glozing and lying.

"And yet shall Love himself be heard,
Though long deferred, though long deferred:
O'er the modern waste a dove hath whirred:
Music is Love in search of a word."
    Baltimore, 1875   **1875**

EVENING SONG

Look off, dear Love, across the sallow sands,
  And mark yon meeting of the sun and sea,
How long they kiss in sight of all the lands.
    Ah! longer, longer, we.

Now in the sea's red vintage melts the sun,
  As Egypt's pearl dissolved in rosy wine,
And Cleopatra night drinks all. 'Tis done,
    Love, lay thine hand in mine.

Come forth, sweet stars, and comfort heaven's
    heart;
  Glimmer, ye waves, round else unlighted
    sands.   10
O night! divorce our sun and sky apart
    Never our lips, our hands.
1876   1877

SONG OF THE CHATTAHOOCHE

Out of the hills of Habersham,
  Down the valleys of Hall,
I hurry amain to reach the plain,
Run the rapid and leap the fall,
Split at the rock and together again,
Accept my bed, or narrow or wide,
And flee from folly on every side
With a lover's pain to attain the plain
    Far from the hills of Habersham,
    Far from the valleys of Hall.   10

All down the hills of Habersham,
  All through the valleys of Hall,
The rushes cried, *Abide, abide*,
The willful waterweeds held me thrall,
The laving laurel turned my tide,
The ferns and the fondling grass said, *Stay*,

The dewberry dipped for to work delay,
And the little reeds sighed, *Abide, abide,
  Here in the hills of Habersham,
  Here in the valleys of Hall.*   20

High o'er the hills of Habersham,
  Veiling the valleys of Hall,
The hickory told me manifold
Fair tales of shade, the poplar tall
Wrought me her shadowy self to hold,
The chestnut, the oak, the walnut, the pine,
Overleaning, with flickering meaning and sign,
Said, *Pass not, so cold, these manifold
  Deep shades of the hills of Habersham,
  These glades in the valleys of Hall.*   30

And oft in the hills of Habersham,
  And oft in the valleys of Hall,
The white quartz shone, and the smooth
    brook-stone
Did bar me of passage with friendly brawl,
And many a luminous jewel lone
—Crystals clear or a-cloud with mist,
Ruby, garnet, and amethyst—
Made lures with the lights of streaming stone
    In the clefts of the hills of Habersham,
    In the beds of the valleys of Hall.   40

But oh, not the hills of Habersham,
  And oh, not the valleys of Hall
Avail: I am fain for to water the plain.
Downward the voices of Duty call—
Downward, to toil and be mixed with the
    main,
The dry fields burn, and the mills are to turn,
And a myriad flowers mortally yearn,
And the lordly main from beyond the plain
    Calls o'er the hills of Habersham,
    Calls through the valleys of Hall.   50
1877   1877

THE REVENGE OF HAMISH

It was three slim does and a ten-tined buck in the bracken lay;
  And all of a sudden the sinister smell of a man,
  Awaft on a wind-shift, wavered and ran
Down the hill-side and sifted along through the bracken and passed that way.

Then Nan got a-tremble at nostril; she was the daintiest doe;
  In the print of her velvet flank on the velvet fern
  She reared, and rounded her ears in turn.
Then the buck leapt up, and his head as a king's to a crown did go

Full high in the breeze, and he stood as if Death had the form of a deer;
  And the two slim does long lazily stretching arose,   10
  For their day-dream slowlier came to a close,
Till they woke and were still, breath-bound with waiting and wonder and fear.

Then Alan the huntsman sprang over the hillock, the hounds shot by,
  The does and the ten-tined buck made a marvellous bound,
  The hounds swept after with never a sound,
But Alan loud winded his horn in sign that the quarry was nigh.

For at dawn of that day proud Maclean of Lochbuy to the hunt had waxed wild,
  And he cursed at old Alan till Alan fared off with the hounds
  For to drive him the deer to the lower glen-grounds:
"I will kill a red deer," quoth Maclean, "in the sight of the wife and the child."   20

So gayly he paced with the wife and the child to his chosen stand;
  But he hurried tall Hamish the henchman ahead: "Go turn,"—
  Cried Maclean,—"if the deer seek to cross to the burn,
Do thou turn them to me: nor fail, lest thy back be red as thy hand."

Now hard-fortuned Hamish, half blown of his breath with the height of the hill,
  Was white in the face when the ten-tined buck and the does
  Drew leaping to burn-ward; huskily rose
His shouts, and his nether lip twitched and his legs were o'er-weak for his will.

So the deer darted lightly by Hamish and bounded away to the burn.
  But Maclean never bating his watch tarried waiting below;   30
  Still Hamish hung heavy with fear for to go
All the space of an hour; then he went, and his face was greenish and stern,

And his eye sat back in the socket, and shrunken the eye-balls shone,
  As withdrawn from a vision of deeds it were shame to see.
  "Now, now, grim henchman, what is't with thee?"
Brake Maclean, and his wrath rose red as a beacon the wind hath upblown.

"Three does and a ten-tined buck made out," spoke Hamish, full mild,
  "And I ran for to turn, but my breath it was blown, and they passed;
  I was weak, for ye called ere I broke me my fast."
Cried Maclean: "Now a ten-tined buck in the sight of the wife and the child   40

I had killed if the gluttonous kern had not wrought me a snail's own wrong!"
  Then he sounded, and down came kinsmen and clansmen all:
  "Ten blows, for ten tine, on his back let fall,
And reckon no stroke if the blood follow not at the bite of thong!"

So Hamish made bare, and took him his strokes; at the last he smiled.
  "Now I'll to the burn," quoth Maclean, "for it still may be,
  If a slimmer-paunched henchman will hurry with me,
I shall kill me the ten-tined buck for a gift to the wife and the child!"

Then the clansmen departed, by this path and that; and over the hill
  Sped Maclean with an outward wrath for an inward shame;   50
  And that place of the lashing full quiet became;
And the wife and the child stood sad; and bloody-backed Hamish sat still.

But look! red Hamish has risen; quick about and about turns he.
  "There is none betwixt me and the crag-top!" he screams under breath.
  Then, livid as Lazarus lately from death,
He snatches the child from the mother, and clambers the crag toward the sea.

Now the mother drops breath; she is dumb, and her heart goes dead for a space,
  Till the motherhood, mistress of death, shrieks, shrieks through the glen,
  And that place of the lashing is live with men,
And Maclean, and the gillie that told him, dash up in a desperate race.   60

Not a breath's time for asking; an eye-glance reveals all the tale untold.
  They follow mad Hamish afar up the crag toward the sea,
  And the lady cries: "Clansmen, run for a fee!—
Yon castle and lands to the two first hands that shall hook him and hold

"Fast Hamish back from the brink!"—and ever she flies up the steep,
  And the clansmen pant, and they sweat, and they jostle and strain.
  But, mother, 'tis vain; but, father, 'tis vain;
Stern Hamish stands bold on the brink, and dangles the child o'er the deep.

Now a faintness falls on the men that run, and they all stand still.
  And the wife prays Hamish as if he were God, on her knees,   70
  Crying: "Hamish! O Hamish! but please, but please
For to spare him!" and Hamish still dangles the child, with a wavering will.

On a sudden he turns; with a sea-hawk scream, and a gibe, and a song,
  Cries: "So; I will spare ye the child if, in sight of ye all,
  Ten blows on Maclean's bare back shall fall,
And ye reckon no stroke if the blood follow not at the bite of the thong!"

Then Maclean he set hardly his tooth to his lip that his tooth was red,
  Breathed short for a space, said: "Nay, but it never shall be!
  Let me hurl off the damnable hound in the sea!"
But the wife: "Can Hamish go fish us the child from the sea, if dead?   80

"Say yea!—Let them lash me, Hamish?"—"Nay!"—"Husband, the lashing will heal;
  But, oh, who will heal me the bonny sweet bairn in his grave?
  Could ye cure me my heart with the death of a knave?
Quick! Love! I will bare thee—so—kneel!" Then Maclean 'gan slowly to kneel.

With never a word, till presently downward he jerked to the earth.
  Then the henchman—he that smote Hamish—would tremble and lag;
  "Strike, hard!" quoth Hamish, full stern, from the crag;
Then he struck him, and "One" sang Hamish, and danced with the child in his mirth.

And no man spake beside Hamish; he counted each stroke with a song.
  When the last stroke fell, then he moved him a pace down the height,   90
  And he held forth the child in the heartaching sight
Of the mother, and looked all pitiful grave, as repenting a wrong.

And there as the motherly arms stretched out with the thanksgiving prayer—
  And there as the mother crept up with a fearful swift pace,
  Till her finger nigh felt of the bairnie's face—
In a flash fierce Hamish turned round and lifted the child in the air,

And sprang with the child in his arms from the horrible height in the sea,
  Shrill screeching, "Revenge!" in the wind-rush; and pallid Maclean,
  Age-feeble with anger and impotent pain,
Crawled up on the crag, and lay flat, and locked hold of dead roots of a tree.   100

And gazed hungrily o'er, and the blood from his back drip-dripped in the brine,
  And a sea-hawk flung down a skeleton fish as he flew,
  And the mother stared white on the waste of blue,
And the wind drove a cloud to seaward, and the sun began to shine.
    Baltimore, 1878   1878

THE MARSHES OF GLYNN

Glooms of the live-oaks, beautiful-braided and woven
With intricate shades of the vines that myriad-cloven
   Clamber the forks of the multiform boughs,—
      Emerald twilights,—
      Virginal shy lights,
Wrought of the leaves to allure to the whisper of vows,
When lovers pace timidly down through the green colonnades
Of the dim sweet woods, of the dear dark woods,
   Of the heavenly woods and glades,
That run to the radiant marginal sand-beach within   **10**
      The wide sea-marshes of Glynn;—

Beautiful glooms, soft dusks in the noon-day fire,—
Wildwood privacies, closets of lone desire,
Chamber from chamber parted with wavering arras of leaves,—
Cells for the passionate pleasure of prayer to the soul that grieves,
Pure with a sense of the passing of saints through the wood,
Cool for the dutiful weighing of ill with good;—

O braided dusks of the oak and woven shades of the vine,
While the riotous noon-day sun of the June-day long did shine
Ye held me fast in your heart and I held you fast in mine;   **20**
But now when the noon is no more, and riot is rest,
And the sun is a-wait at the ponderous gate of the West,
And the slant yellow beam down the wood-aisle doth seem
Like a lane into heaven that leads from a dream,—
Ay, now, when my soul all day hath drunken the soul of the oak,
And my heart is at ease from men, and the wearisome sound of the stroke
   Of the scythe of time and the trowel of trade is low,
     And belief overmasters doubt, and I know that I know,
     And my spirit is grown to a lordly great compass within,
That the length and the breadth and the sweep of the marshes of Glynn   **30**
Will work me no fear like the fear they have wrought me of yore
When length was fatigue, and when breadth was but bitterness sore,
And when terror and shrinking and dreary unnamable pain
Drew over me out of the merciless miles of the plain,—

Oh, now, unafraid, I am fain to face
   The vast sweet visage of space.
To the edge of the wood I am drawn, I am drawn,
Where the gray beach glimmering runs, as a belt of the dawn,
   For a mete and a mark
     To the forest-dark:—   **40**
      So:
Affable live-oak, leaning low,—
Thus—with your favor—soft, with a reverent hand,
(Not lightly touching your person, Lord of the land!)
Bending your beauty aside, with a step I stand
On the firm-packed sand,
     Free
By a world of marsh that borders a world of sea.
   Sinuous southward and sinuous northward the shimmering band
   Of the sand-beach fastens the fringe of the marsh to the folds of the land.   **50**
Inward and outward to northward and southward the beach-lines linger and curl

As a silver-wrought garment that clings to and follows the firm sweet limbs of a girl.
Vanishing, swerving, evermore curving again into sight,
Softly the sand-beach wavers away to a dim gray looping of light.
And what if behind me to westward the wall of the woods stands high?
The world lies east: how ample, the marsh and the sea and the sky!
A league and a league of marsh-grass, waist-high broad in the blade,
Green, and all of a height, and unflecked with a light or a shade,
Stretch leisurely off, in a pleasant plain,
To the terminal blue of the main.   60

Oh, what is abroad in the marsh and the terminal sea?
    Somehow my soul seems suddenly free
From the weighing of fate and the sad discussion of sin,
By the length and the breadth and the sweep of the marshes of Glynn.

Ye marshes, how candid and simple and nothing-withholding and free
Ye publish yourselves to the sky and offer yourselves to the sea!
Tolerant plains, that suffer the sea and the rains and the sun,
Ye spread and span like the catholic man who hath mightily won
God out of knowledge and good out of infinite pain
And sight out of blindness and purity out of a stain.   70

As the marsh-hen secretly builds on the watery sod,
Behold I will build me a nest on the greatness of God:
I will fly in the greatness of God as the marsh-hen flies
In the freedom that fills all the space 'twixt the marsh and the skies:
By so many roots as the marsh-grass sends in the sod
I will heartily lay me a-hold on the greatness of God:
Oh, like to the greatness of God is the greatness within
The range of the marshes, the liberal marshes of Glynn.

And the sea lends large, as the marsh: lo, out of his plenty the sea
Pours fast: full soon the time of the flood-tide must be: 80
Look how the grace of the sea doth go
About and about through the intricate channels that flow
    Here and there,
        Everywhere,
Till his waters have flooded the uttermost creeks and the low-lying lanes,
And the marsh is meshed with a million veins,
That like as with rosy and silvery essences flow
In the rose-and-silver evening glow.
        Farewell, my lord Sun!
The creeks overflow: a thousand rivulets run   90
'Twixt the roots of the sod; the blades of the marsh-grass stir;
Passeth a hurrying sound of wings that westward whirr;
Passeth, and all is still; and the currents cease to run;
And the sea and the marsh are one.

How still the plains of the waters be!
The tide is in his ecstasy.
The tide is at his highest height:
    And it is night.

And now from the Vast of the Lord will the waters of sleep
Roll in on the souls of men,   100
But who will reveal to our waking ken
The forms that swim and the shapes that creep
    Under the waters of sleep?

And I would I could know what swimmeth below when the tide comes in
On the length and the breadth of the marvelous marshes of Glynn.
      Baltimore, 1878   1879

A BALLAD OF TREES AND THE MASTER

Into the woods my Master went,
Clean forspent, forspent.
Into the woods my Master came,
Forspent with love and shame.
But the olives they were not blind to Him,
The little gray leaves were kind to Him:
The thorn-tree had a mind to Him
When into the woods He came.

Out of the woods my Master went,
And He was well content.   10
Out of the woods my Master came,
Content with death and shame.
When Death and Shame would woo Him last,
From under the trees they drew Him last:
'Twas on a tree they slew Him—last
When out of the woods He came.

      Baltimore, November, 1880   1880

MAURICE THOMPSON (1844–1901)

TO AN ENGLISH SKYLARK

Oh,
  How I long to go,
On a seaward-blowing breeze,
To the garden of the seas—
To brave King Arthur's land,
To that fair island Alfred made so free,
  To the haunt of chivalry,
Where master-birds sang (in the days of song)
  So long
  And strong!   10
Oh let me dwell a space by Avon's tide,
  Or hide
In some old grove, where still a note may
  linger
    Of Herrick's flute,
    Of Sidney's lute,
Or of some precious rondel voiced by a for-
  gotten singer.

Hark!
  Even now I hear a lark,
The lark of England's ripe and mellow story,
The lark of England's fallow fields of glory,
    Springing,   21
    Singing,
Far and high in heaven's remotest blue,
  His wings still cool with dew,
His voice (of which one song-god fair and
  young
A lyric of immortal fervor sung)
  Still firm and true,
Still rich with exultation, rising higher,
  And brimming with desire,
To fill ethereal vastness with its fire;   30
Forgetting love and sympathy and that law
  Of human harmony

And rhythmic destiny,
Which darkly through a glass the seers and
  prophets saw!

  O bird,
  Whom gods and heroes heard
Sing in the far dim twilight hours of Time,
  Whose rapture stirred
Through many a new sweet rhyme
  Whilst thou didst rise   40
  Into the skies
To purify thy song in empyrean fire!
  Say where
  In upper air
Dost hope to find fulfillment of thy dream?
On what far peak seest thou a morning-gleam?
Why shall the stars still blind thee unaware?
  Why needst thou mount to sing?
Why seek the sun's fierce-tempered glow and
  glare?   49
Why shall a soulless impulse prompt thy wing?
Why are thy meadows and thy groves bereft
Of Freedom's inspiration, and so left
    To silence in mid-spring?

  O lark!
  I mark,
Since Shelley died, thy wings have somewhat
  failed.
A precious note has faded from thy hymn,
Thy lyric fire has smouldered low and dim!
Nor ever have thy cloud-wrapt strains availed
Against the will of tyrants and the dark,   60
  Strong doors of prisons grim,
    And shackles manifold,
    And dungeons cold,

Wherein sweet Freedom lies
With hopeless longing in her starry eyes
And lifeless languor on her splendid wings!
    I hold
    This truth as gold:
The grandest life is lowliest; he who sings
To fill the highest purpose need not soar   70
Above the lintel of the peasant's door,
And must not hunger for the praise of kings,
Or quench his thirst at too ethereal springs.

    As for me
    My life is liberty,
And close to earth's bloom-scented, fragrant
    floor
    I gather more and more
    The larger elements,
The fine suggestions of Time's last events;
    I strive to know   80
Whither all currents flow;
    I sing
On branches that the newest breezes swing;
    I overreach
The limit of the present, day by day;
    I teach
By shrewd anticipation, and foresay
    What wider life is coming,
    What joys are humming,
Like Hybla's bees, around the Future's comb;
    My home   91
Is where all wind-tides and all perfumes meet;
    Cool and clean and sweet
The young leaves rustle round my sensitive feet,
    Whilst my enraptured tongue
    Rolls under it
Morsels of all the songs the world's best bards
    have sung!

    Lo! Homer's strength is mine,
    And Sappho's fire divine.
And old Anacreon's flask of purple wine   100
    Stains every note
Blown from the silvery labyrinth of my
    charmèd throat!
    And yet the past
Has nothing in it glorious as the vast
    Hope that the future holds,
    Of life whose flame enfolds
    The final focal thought—
The meed for which the grandest souls from
    Time's first dawn have wrought.

    Erewhile I lived   110
    Where Liberty pined and grieved,
Under the sunniest of all sunny skies,
In a rich-fruited, dreamy, slumbrous paradise;
    Low
    And slow

The tide of human sympathy did ebb and
    flow.
    At length, one day,
I heard a bloodhound bay;
The swamps were Freedom's sanctuary then;
    Year after year   120
    I sang the slave to cheer,
And sang to fire the hearts of earnest, freeborn
    men,
    Until the new day broke,
    With the lifting of the yoke,
And in broad floods of sudden light divine,
I saw the slave to manhood's summit rise,
    His vision set on farthest destinies,
And the slave cabin like a palace shine.

    Oh, what a bliss
    This love of Freedom is!   130
    And what delight
    To feel, by day and night,
    Its ecstasy run deeper in my blood
While life's strong tide swells toward its
    highest flood!
    Not in the sky
    Where wastes of grandeur lie,
May genius find wherewith to slake its thirst;
    The rainbow is not first
    On Beauty's list;
Nor is the enchantment of heaven's highest
    mist   140
    The master maker's aim!
    The lowliest hearth-stone flame
Is worthier of worship than the sun!
The patter of bare brown feet that dance and
    run
With childish grace on the roughest cabin
    floor,
And the poor mother's happy smile, are more
    Than starry hosts
    And lofty ghosts
And awful phantoms born of overwrought   149
And soulless travail on the heights of thought!

    Come down, O Lark, to earth,
    And give a new song birth—
The song of life that grants its sweets to all,
    In hut and lofty hall;
    Forsake the sky,
    And sky-born melody;
Fill thy meadow and thy grove
With a strain of human love—
With a wide strong pulse of music for the wait-
    ing ears of men,
    Who, to be born again,   160
And live the life of freedom that I live,
    More than their lives would give;
    Yea,
    Would slay,

And heap vast hecatombs, and flood
  The world with blood,
    And jar
  Heaven with the thunder,
    And the wonder
And the awful weltering whirlwind of the
  storm of war!   170

      Oh, ere it is too late,
      Take heed, and contemplate
        What tempests sleep,
        That yet will wake and leap
Across thy starry fields and blot them out,
And drown thy voice in their uproarious
  shout!
        Thou art too high;
        No longing ear or eye
May follow thee, nor is thy sweetest note
      Echoed by mortal throat;   180
But ever it goes forth with none to hear
      And none to catch its cheer!
      Come sit beside me now,
      Here on my orange-bough;
    Forsake the legendary lights,
Forget the old hereditary heights,
And we will pipe one lusty score together
      Wing by wing,
      In this land of spring,
While all the world comes out to feel the
  weather   190
Throb with the fire of Freedom as we sing!
                                          1892

JOHN BANISTER TABB (1845-1909)

St. MARY OF EGYPT

Strong to suffer, strong to sin,
  Loving much, and much forgiven,
In the desert realm a queen,
  Penance-crowned, to cope with Heaven,
Solitude alone could be
Room enough for God and thee.

Long the vigil, stern the fast;
  Morn, with night's anointing, chill;
Noon with passion overcast;
  Night with phantoms fouler still;   10
Prayer and penitential tears
Battling with the lust of years.

Low upon the parching sand,
  Shrivelled in the blight of day,
As beneath a throbbing brand
  Prone thy ghastly shadow lay,
Till the manacles of hell
From thy fevered spirit fell.

MORNING DEW

When germs were quickening in the mould,
  And sap was rich and leaves were young,
Deep in the fragrant wood a lute,
  As old as Time, was newly strung.

Some swift, divine, invisible hand,
  From fret to fret, tried all the chords,
Until a tune, supremely sweet,
  Was set to immemorial words.

And then the wild bird sought its mate;
  The lusty bee a-booming came;   10
The maples, filled with racy pangs,
  Let go their buds' imprisoned flame;

A dreamy mystery veiled the sun;
Keen perfumes stole through glade and grove,
And all the founts of Nature burst
  With sudden bubbling steams of love!

Ah! passion, pure as morning dew,
  And fresh as breath of mint and thyme!
Impulse of Spring, so new and true!
  Essence of innocence and prime!   20

I bowed my head and stilled my breath
  (For it was May and I was young),
While to a tune supremely sweet
  Those immemorial words were sung.
                                          1892

Then, O queen of solitude!
  Silence led thee as a bride,   20
Clothed anew in maidenhood,
  To an altar purified,
Lit with holy fires, to prove
Self the sacrifice of love.
                                          1882

THE HOSPITAL BIRD

A breath of joy, sweet bird,
  A solace to each prisoner of pain,
  A pledge of hope returning, is thy strain
Through the long watches heard.

The soul in sleepless sighs,
  Or else in dreams, through panting hours,
    the prey,
  Hails in thy voice a prophecy of day
Ere yet the darkness flies.

The tender babe, new-born,
  The dying mother startled by its wail,   10

The fevered brow, the cheek of madness
    pale,
The bosom rest-forlorn,

Each, with emotion strong,
    Heaves through the billowed agonies of
    night,
    Whilst over them, a glittering foam of light,
Drifts thy unshadowed song.

How vast its influence sweet!
    How small the voiceful compass of thy
    throat,
    Whereof each silver scintillating note
A thousand blessings greet!   20

Teach me the power divine
    Some light o'er dark humanity to fling,
    Some song of hope celestial to sing,
Dear to all hearts as thine.
                 1882

TO THE WOOD-ROBIN

The wooing air is jubilant with song,
    And blossoms swell
As leaps thy liquid melody along
    The dusky dell,
Where silence, late supreme, foregoes her
    wonted spell.

Ah, whence, in sylvan solitudes remote,
    Hast learned the lore
That breeds delight in every echoing note,
    The woodlands o'er;
As when through slanting sun descends the
    quickening shower?   10

Thy hermitage is peopled with the dreams
    That gladden sleep;
Here fancy dallies with delirious themes
    'Mid shadows deep,
Till eyes, unused to tears, with wild emotion
    weep.

We rise, alas, to find our visions fled!
    But thine remain.
Night weaves of golden harmonies the
    thread,
    And fills thy brain
With joys that overflow in love's awakening
    strain.   20

Yet thou, from mortal influence apart,
    Seek'st naught of praise;
The empty plaudits of the emptier heart
    Taint not thy lays:

Thy Maker's smile alone thy tuneful bosom
    sways.

Teach me, thou warbling eremite, to sing
    Thy rhapsody;
Nor borne on vain ambition's vaunting
    wing,
    But led of thee   29
To rise from earthly dreams to hymn eternity.
    June, 1889   1902

EVOLUTION

Out of the dusk a shadow,
    Then a spark;
Out of the cloud a silence,
    Then a lark;

Out of the heart a rapture,
    Then a pain;
Out of the dead, cold ashes,
    Life again.
                 1894

FAITH

In every seed to breathe the flower,
    In every drop of dew
To reverence a cloistered star
    Within the distant blue;
To wait the promise of the bow,
    Despite the cloud between,
Is Faith—the fervid evidence
    Of loveliness unseen.
    Aug. 5, 1895

ANONYMOUS

Anonymous—nor needs a name
To tell the secret whence the flame,
With light and warmth and incense, came
A new creation to proclaim.

So was it when, His labor done,
God saw His work and smiled thereon:
His glory in the picture shone,
But name upon the canvas none.
                 1897

SHELL-TINTS

Sea-shell, whence the rainbow dyes,
Flashing in thy sunset skies?
Thou wast in the penal brine
When appeared the saving sign.
"Yea, but when the bow was bended,
Hope, that hung it in the sky,
Down into the deep descended

Where the starless shadows lie;
And with tender touch of glory
Traced in living lines of love,   10
On my lowly walls, the story
Written in the heavens above."

1897

THE SHELL

Silence—a deeper sea—
Now sunders thee
Save from the primal tone—
Thy mother's moan.

Within her waves, hadst thou
No voice as now;
A life of exile long
Hath taught thee song.

1902

BEREFT

As when her calf is taken, far and near
  The restless mother roves,
So now my heart lows, wandering everywhere,
  To wake the voice it loves.
O Distance, are the echoes backward thrown
  In mockery of pain?
Or doth remembered anguish of thine own
  Bring them to birth again?

1902

OVERFLOW

Hush!
With sudden gush
As from a fountain sings in yonder bush
The hermit thrush.

Hark!
Did ever lark
With swifter scintillations fling the spark
That fires the dark?

Again,
Like April rain   10
Of mist and sunshine mingled, moves the
    strain
O'er hill and plain.

Strong
As love, O Song,
In flame or torrent sweep through life along
O'er grief and wrong.

1902

RACERS

The winds from many a cloudy mane
Shake off the sweat of gathering rain
    And whicker with delight;
No slope of pasture-lands they need,
Whereon to rest or drink or feed,
Their life the rapture of the speed,
    The frenzy of the flight.

1903

THE TEST

The dead there are, who live;
  The living, who are dead;
The poor, who still can give;
  The rich, who lack for bread;
To love it is and love alone
That life or luxury is known.

1904

IN AUTUMN

Now that the birds are gone
  That sang the summer through,
And now that, one by one,
  The leaves are going too,
Is all their beauty but a show
To fade forever when they go?

Nay, what is heard and seen,
  In time must pass away;
But beauty, born within,
  The blossom of a day,   10
Unto its hiding place again
Returns forever to remain

1904

WINTER RAIN

Rain on the roof and rain
On the burial-place of grain;
To one a voice in vain;
To one o'er hill and plain
The pledge of life again.

Rain on the sterile sea,
That hath no need of thee,
Nor keeps thy memory—
'Tis thou that teachest me
The range of charity.   10

1905

IN AETERNUM

If Life and Death be things that seem,
If Death be sleep, and Life a dream,

May not the everlasting sleep
The dream of life eternal keep?

1906

BEAUTY

She sleeps, her hiding-place unknown
  To other worshippers,
Till Art, her lover, comes alone
  To press his lips to hers.

1910

FIAT LUX

"Give us this day our daily bread," and *light;*
For more to me, O Lord, than food is sight:
    And I at noon have been
In twilight, where my fellow-men were seen
  "As trees" that walked before me. E'en
to-day

From time to time there falls upon my way
  A feather of the darkness. But again
It passes; and amid the falling rain
  Of tears, I lift, O Lord, mine eyes to Thee,
    For, lo! I *see!*   10

1910

LOVE IMMORTAL

The soul that sees no hell below,
    No heaven above,
All other mysteries may know,
    But never love.

If from the prison-walls of time
    No life may fly,
Then love and innocence and crime
    Alike must die.

1910

MADISON CAWEIN (1865-1914)

AUBADE

Awake! the Dawn is on the hills!
  Behold, at her cool throat a rose,
  Blue-eyed and beautiful she goes,
Leaving her steps in daffodils.—
Awake! arise! and let me see
  Thine eyes, whose deeps epitomize
All dawns that were or are to be,
  O love, all Heaven in thine eyes!—
Awake! arise! come down to me!

Behold! the Dawn is up: behold!   10
  How all the birds around her float,
  Wild rills of music, note on note,
Spilling the air with mellow gold.—
Arise! awake! and, drawing near,
  Let me but hear thee and rejoice!
Thou, who keep'st captive, sweet and clear,
  All song, O love, within thy voice!
Arise! awake! and let me hear!

See, where she comes, with limbs of day,
  The Dawn! with wild-rose hands and feet,
  Within whose veins the sunbeams beat, 21
And laughters meet of wind and ray.
Arise! come down! and, heart to heart,
  Love, let me clasp in thee all these—
The sunbeam, of which thou art part,
  And all the rapture of the breeze!—
Arise! come down! loved that thou art!

1905

THE FEUD

Rocks, trees and rocks; and down a mossy
    stone
  The murmuring ooze and trickle of a stream
Though brambles, where the mountain spring
    lies lone,—
  A gleaming cairngorm where the shadows
    dream,—
And one wild road winds like a saffron seam.

Here sang the thrush, whose pure, mellifluous
    note
  Dropped golden sweetness on the fragrant
    June;
Here cat- and blue-bird and wood-sparrow
    wrote
  There presence on the silence with a tune;
And here the fox drank 'neath the mountain
    moon.   10

Frail ferns and dewy mosses and dark brush,—
  Impenetrable briers, deep and dense,
And wiry bushes;—brush, that seemed to
    crush
  The struggling saplings with its tangle,
    whence
Sprawled out the ramble of an old rail-fence.

A wasp buzzed by; and then a butterfly
  In orange and amber, like a floating flame;
And then a man, hard-eyed and very sly,

Gaunt-cheeked and haggard and a little
  lame,   19
With an old rifle, down the mountain came.

He listened, drinking from a flask he took
  Out of the ragged pocket of his coat;
Then all around him cast a stealthy look;
  Lay down; and watched an eagle soar and
    float,
His fingers twitching at his hairy throat.

The shades grew longer; and each Cumberland height
Loomed, framed in splendors of the dolphin
  dusk.

Around the road a horseman rode in sight;
  Young, tall, blond-bearded. Silent, grim,
    and brusque,
He in the thicket aimed— Quick, harsh, then
  husk.   30

The echoes barked among the hills and made
  Repeated instants of the shot's distress.—
Then silence—and the trampled bushes
  swayed:—
Then silence, packed with murder and the
  press
Of distant hoofs that galloped riderless.
                          1894

HAPPINESS

There is a voice that calls to me; a voice that cries deep down;
  That calls within my heart of hearts when Summer doffs her crown:
When Summer doffs her crown, my dear, and by the hills and streams
The spirit of September walks through gold and purple gleams:
It calls my heart beyond the mart, beyond the street and town,
To take again, in sun or rain, the oldtime trail of dreams.

Oh, it is long ago, my dear, a weary time since we
Trod back the way we used to know by wildwood rock and tree:
By mossy rock and tree, dear Heart, and sat below the hill,
And watched the wheel, the old mill-wheel, turn round on Babbitts mill: 10
Or in the Brook, with line and hook, to dronings of the bee,
Waded or swam, above the dam, and drank of joy our fill.

The ironweed is purple now; the blackeyed-Susans nod;
And by its banks, weighed down with wet, blooms bright the goldenrod:
Blooms bright the goldenrod, my dear, and in the mist of morn
The gray hawk soars and screams and soars above the dripping corn:
And by the pool, cerulean cool, the milkweed bursts its pod,
As through the air the wild fanfare rings of the hunter's horn.

The hunter's horn we heard, my dear, that echoed 'mid the rocks,
And cheered the hounds whose belling bay trailed far behind the fox: 20
Trailed far behind the fox, dear Heart, whose den we oft had seen,
A cave-like place within the woods wild-hid in trailing green:
Old Owlet's Roost, wherein we used to search, with tangled locks,
For buried gold, where, we were told, the bandit's lair had been.

O gladness of the long-gone years! O boyhood's days and dreams!
Again my soul would trace with you the oldtime woods and streams;
The oldtime woods and streams, dear Heart, and seek again, I guess,
The buried gold, we sought of old, and find it none the less
Still in the ground, fast sealed and bound, among the glooms and gleams,
As long ago we left it so, the gold of Happiness.   30

                          1913

XIII. THE SHORT STORY OF THE LATER NINETEENTH CENTURY

THE development of the short story in America since the Civil War is one of the most significant phases of our literary history. Not only are the stories important in themselves, but, since practically all the great novelists of this period, with the exception of Howells, won distinction also through their short stories, it becomes possible to illustrate by selection from among them the progress of our fiction. This development falls into two periods, the first including those writers whose work began before the later eighties. It was still tinged with romance and was concerned frequently with the depiction of local scenes. As the authors were often pioneers in their fields, they naturally used the method of selection and, in a period so acutely conscious of national and sectional progress and achievement, it was natural that writers of fiction should portray special phases of American life.

Edward Everett Hale represents the patriotic ideal of the Civil War, but *The Man Without a Country* is significant in theme rather than in method. With the work of Thomas Bailey Aldrich, however, the short story of situation achieved a unity of form, charm, and an element of climax which has been the inspiration of many writers since his day. With an even wider choice of material, Stockton developed the humorous aspects of a life largely the product of his fancy, shot through with a delightful humor, which has not been remembered as well as it deserves. Henry James, in his early period, rivalled the charm of Aldrich and penetrated more deeply into the depths of character. More of a realist than Aldrich or Bret Harte, he has had a great influence upon later writers, but his vogue was not as immediate as that of Harte. The latter claimed that he made the short story American and modern. He was of course mistaken, but he did initiate the story of local color in which this period was so rich. In his great moment, that of his earliest stories, he added however to his background a study of the moral contrast, a fictional theme which has lifted such a story as *The Outcasts of Poker Flat* to a high level of art.

Harte's treatment of the West was rivalled in the South by the Creole stories of Cable and the studies of the Virginia patricians of Page and Smith. Among hosts of imitators their stories still remain secure, for their material, picturesque as it is, is only the background for characters who represent the dignity of sacrifice and the loyalty of both the white and black races to their own standards of conduct. In Harris the story of folklore found its first great interpreter, and with Bret Harte he became an international figure. While the South was being rediscovered, Miss Jewett portrayed with a delicate artistry the decaying grandeur of New England.

While Crawford's short stories cannot represent his most important contribution to fiction, the cosmopolitan novel, his stories of the supernatural possess his salient characteristic, the desire to entertain. Ghost stories are most effective when the illusion is most perfect, and Crawford by securing the reaction of three senses produced a striking result. Unusual, in another fashion, Dr. Mitchell's *Little Stories*, marvels of compression, reveal the response of the scientific mind to the prompting of the story teller's art.

EDWARD EVERETT HALE (1822-1909)

THE MAN WITHOUT A COUNTRY

(1863)

I suppose that very few casual readers of the *New York Herald* of August 13th observed, in an obscure corner, among the "Deaths," the announcement,—

"NOLAN. Died, on board U. S. Corvette *Levant*, Lat. 2° 11′ S., Long. 131° W., on the 11th May, PHILIP NOLAN."

I happened to observe it, because I was stranded at the old Mission-House in Mackinaw, waiting for a Lake Superior steamer which did not choose to come, and I was devouring to the very stubble all the current literature I could get hold of, even down to the deaths and marriages in the *Herald*. My memory for names and people is good, and the reader will see, as he goes on, that I had reason enough to remember Philip Nolan. There are hundreds of readers who would have paused at that announcement, if the officer of the *Levant* who reported it had chosen to make it thus:— "Died, May 11th, THE MAN WITHOUT A COUNTRY." For it was as "The Man without a Country" that poor Philip Nolan had generally been known by the officers who had him in charge during some fifty years, as, indeed, by all the men who sailed under them. I dare say there is many a man who has taken wine with him once a fortnight, in a three years' cruise, who never knew that his name was "Nolan," or whether the poor wretch had any name at all.

There can now be no possible harm in telling this poor creature's story. Reason enough there has been till now, ever since Madison's administration went out in 1817, for very strict secrecy, the secrecy of honor itself, among the gentlemen of the navy who have had Nolan in successive charge. And certainly it speaks well for the *esprit de corps* of the profession, and the personal honor of its members, that to the press this man's story has been wholly unknown,—and, I think, to the country at large also. I have reason to think, from some investigations I made in the Naval Archives when I was attached to the Bureau of Construction, that every official report relating to him was burned when Ross burned the public buildings at Washington. One of the Tuckers, or possibly one of the Watsons, had Nolan in charge at the end of the war; and

when, on returning from his cruise, he reported at Washington to one of the Crowninshields,— who was in the Navy Department when he came home,—he found that the Department ignored the whole business. Whether they really knew nothing about it, or whether it was a *"Non mi ricordo"* determined on as a piece of policy, I do not know. But this I do know, that since 1817, and possibly before, no naval officer has mentioned Nolan in his report of a cruise.

But, as I say, there is no need for secrecy any longer. And now the poor creature is dead, it seems to me worth while to tell a little of his story, by way of showing young Americans of to-day what it is to be a man without a country.

Philip Nolan was as fine a young officer as there was in the "Legion of the West," as the Western division of our army was then called. When Aaron Burr made his first dashing expedition down to New Orleans in 1805, at Fort Massac, or somewhere above on the river, he met, as the Devil would have it, this gay, dashing, bright young fellow, at some dinner-party, I think. Burr marked him, talked to him, walked with him, took him a day or two's voyage in his flat-boat, and, in short, fascinated him. For the next year barrack-life was very tame to poor Nolan. He occasionally availed himself of the permission the great man had given him to write to him. Long, high-worded, stilted letters the poor boy wrote and rewrote and copied. But never a line did he have in reply from the gay deceiver. The other boys in the garrison sneered at him, because he sacrificed in this unrequited affection for a politician the time which they devoted to Monongahela, sledge, and high-low-jack. Bourbon, euchre, and poker were still unknown. But one day Nolan had his revenge. This time Burr came down the river, not as an attorney seeking a place for his office, but as a disguised conqueror. He had defeated I know not how many district-attorneys; he had dined at I know not how many public dinners; he had been heralded in I know not how many *Weekly Arguses*, and it was rumored that he had an army behind him and an empire before him. It was a great day—his arrival—to poor

Nolan. Burr had not been at the fort an hour before he sent for him. That evening he asked Nolan to take him out in his skiff, to show him a canebrake or a cotton-wood tree, as he said, —really to seduce him; and by the time the sail was over Nolan was enlisted body and soul. From that time, though he did not yet know it, he lived as a man without a country.

What Burr meant to do I know no more than you, dear reader. It is none of our business just now. Only, when the grand catastrophe came, and Jefferson and the House of Virginia of that day undertook to break on the wheel all the possible Clarences of the then House of York, by the great treason-trial at Richmond, some of the lesser fry in that distant Mississippi Valley, which was farther from us than Puget's Sound is to-day, introduced the like novelty on their provincial stage, and, to while away the monotony of the summer at Fort Adams, got up, for *spectacles*, a string of court-martials on the officers there. One and another of the colonels and majors were tried, and, to fill out the list, little Nolan, against whom, Heaven knows, there was evidence enough,—that he was sick of the service, had been willing to be false to it, and would have obeyed any order to march any-whither with any one who would follow him, had the order only been signed, "By command of His Exc. A. Burr." The courts dragged on. The big flies escaped,—rightly for all I know. Nolan was proved guilty enough, as I say; yet you and I would never have heard of him, reader, but that, when the president of the court asked him at the close whether he wished to say anything to show that he had always been faithful to the United States, he cried out, in a fit of frenzy,—

"D—n the United States! I wish I may never hear of the United States again!"

I suppose he did not know how the words shocked old Colonel Morgan, who was holding the court. Half the officers who sat in it had served through the Revolution, and their lives, not to say their necks, had been risked for the very idea which he so cavalierly cursed in his madness. He, on his part, had grown up in the West of those days, in the midst of "Spanish plot," "Orleans plot," and all the rest. He had been educated on a plantation where the finest company was a Spanish officer or a French merchant from Orleans. His education, such as it was, had been perfected in commercial expeditions to Vera Cruz, and I think he told me his father once hired an Englishman to be a private tutor for a winter on the plantation. He had spent half his youth with an older brother, hunting horses in Texas; and, in a word, to him "United States" was scarcely a reality. Yet he had been fed by "United States" for all the years since he had been in the army. He had sworn on his faith as a Christian to be true to "United States." It was "United States" which gave him the uniform he wore, and the sword by his side. Nay, my poor Nolan, it was only because "United States" had picked you out first as one of her own confidential men of honor that "A. Burr" cared for you a straw more than for the flat-boat men who sailed his ark for him. I do not excuse Nolan; I only explain to the reader why he damned his country, and wished he might never hear her name again.

He never did hear her name but once again. From that moment, September 23, 1807, till the day he died, May 11, 1863, he never heard her name again. For that half-century and more he was a man without a country.

Old Morgan, as I said, was terribly shocked. If Nolan had compared George Washington to Benedict Arnold, or had cried, "God save King George," Morgan would not have felt worse. He called the court into his private room, and returned in fifteen minutes, with a face like a sheet, to say,—

"Prisoner, hear the sentence of the Court! The Court decides, subject to the approval of the President, that you never hear the name of the United States again."

Nolan laughed. But nobody else laughed. Old Morgan was too solemn, and the whole room was hushed dead as night for a minute. Even Nolan lost his swagger in a moment. Then Morgan added,—

"Mr. Marshal, take the prisoner to Orleans in an armed boat, and deliver him to the naval commander there."

The Marshal gave his orders and the prisoner was taken out of court.

"Mr. Marshal," continued old Morgan, "see that no one mentions the United States to the prisoner. Mr. Marshal, make my respects to Lieutenant Mitchell at Orleans, and request him to order that no one shall mention the United States to the prisoner while he is on board ship. You will receive your written orders from the officer on duty here this evening. The court is adjourned without day."

I have always supposed that Colonel Morgan himself took the proceedings of the court to Washington City, and explained them to Mr. Jefferson. Certain it is that the President approved them,—certain it is, that is, if I may believe the men who say they have seen his signature. Before the Nautilis got round from New Orleans to the Northern Atlantic coast with the prisoner on board, the sentence had been approved, and he was a man without a country.

The plan then adopted was substantially the same which was necessarily followed ever after. Perhaps it was suggested by the necessity of sending him by water from Fort Adams and Orleans. The Secretary of the Navy—it must have been the first Crowninshield, though he is a man I do not remember—was requested to put Nolan on board a government vessel bound on a long cruise, and to direct that he should be only so far confined there as to make it certain that he never saw or heard of the country. We had few long cruises then, and the navy was very much out of favor; and as almost all of this story is traditional, as I have explained, I do not know certainly what his first cruise was. But the commander to whom he was intrusted,—perhaps it was Tingey or Shaw, though I think it was one of the younger men,—we are all old enough now,—regulated the etiquette and the precautions of the affair, and according to his scheme they were carried out, I suppose, till Nolan died.

When I was second officer of the *Intrepid*, some thirty years after, I saw the original paper of instructions. I have been sorry ever since that I did not copy the whole of it. It ran, however, much in this way:—

"WASHINGTON" (with a date, which must have been late in 1807).

"SIR,—You will receive from Lieutenant Neale the person of Philip Nolan, late a lieutenant in the United States Army.

"This person on his trial by court-martial expressed with an oath the wish that he might 'never hear of the United States again.'

"The Court sentenced him to have his wish fulfilled.

"For the present, the execution of the order is intrusted by the President to this Department.

"You will take the prisoner on board your ship, and keep him there with such precautions as shall prevent his escape.

"You will provide him with such quarters, rations, and clothing as would be proper for an officer of his late rank, if he were a passenger on your vessel on the business of his government.

"The gentlemen on board will make any arrangements agreeable to themselves regarding his society. He is to be exposed to no indignity

of any kind, nor is he ever unnecessarily to be reminded that he is a prisoner.

"But under no circumstances is he ever to hear of his country or to see any information regarding it; and you will specially caution all the officers under your command to take care, that in the various indulgences which may be granted, this rule, in which his punishment is involved, shall not be broken.

"It is the intention of the government that he shall never again see the country which he has disowned. Before the end of your cruise you will receive orders which will give effect to this intention.

"Respectfully yours,
"W. SOUTHARD, for the
Secretary of the Navy."

If I had only preserved the whole of this paper, there would be no break in the beginning of my sketch of this story. For Captain Shaw, if it was he, handed it to his successor in the charge, and he to his, and I suppose the commander of the *Levant* has it to-day as his authority for keeping this man in this mild custody.

The rule adopted on board the ships on which I have met "the man without a country" was, I think, transmitted from the beginning. No mess liked to have him permanently, because his presence cut off all talk of home or of the prospect of return, of politics or letters, of peace or of war,—cut off more than half the talk men like to have at sea. But it was always thought too hard that he should never meet the rest of us, except to touch hats, and we finally sank into one system. He was not permitted to talk with the men, unless an officer was by. With officers he had unrestrained intercourse, as far as they and he chose. But he grew shy, though he had favorites; I was one. Then the captain always asked him to dinner on Monday. Every mess in succession took up the invitation in its turn. According to the size of the ship, you had him at your mess more or less often at dinner. His breakfast he ate in his own state-room,—he always had a state-room,—which was where a sentinel or somebody on the watch could see the door. And whatever else he ate or drank, he ate or drank alone. Sometimes, when the marines or sailors had any special jollification, they were permitted to invite "Plain-Buttons," as they called him. Then Nolan was sent with some officer, and the men were forbidden to speak of home while he was there. I believe the theory was that the sight of his punishment did them good. They called him "Plain-Buttons" because, while he always chose to wear a regulation army-uniform, he was not permitted to wear the army-button, for the reason that it bore either the initials or the insignia of the country he had disowned.

I remember, soon after I joined the navy, I was on shore with some of the older officers from our ship and from the *Brandywine*, which we had met at Alexandria. We had leave to make a party and go up to Cairo and the pyramids. As we jogged along (you went on donkeys then), some of the gentlemen (we boys called them "Dons," but the phrase was long since changed) fell to talking about Nolan, and some one told the system which was adopted from the first about his books and other reading. As he was almost never permitted to go on shore, even though the vessel lay in port for months, his time, at the best, hung heavy; and everybody was permitted to lend him books, if they were not published in America and made no allusion to it. These were common enough in the old days, when people in the other hemisphere talked of the United States as little as we do of Paraguay. He had almost all the foreign papers that came into the ship, sooner or later; only somebody must go over them first, and cut out any advertisement or stray paragraph that alluded to America. This was a little cruel sometimes, when the back of what was cut out might be as innocent as Hesiod. Right in the midst of one of Napoleon's battles, or one of Canning's speeches, poor Nolan would find a great hole, because on the back of the page of that paper there had been an advertisement of a packet for New York, or a scrap from the President's message. I say this was the first time I ever heard of this plan, which afterwards I had enough, and more than enough to do with. I remember it, because poor Phillips, who was of the party, as soon as the allusion to reading was made, told a story of something which happened at the Cape of Good Hope on Nolan's first voyage; and it is the only thing I ever knew of that voyage. They had touched at the Cape, and had done the civil thing with the English Admiral and the fleet; and then, leaving for a long cruise up the Indian Ocean, Phillips had borrowed a lot of English books from an officer, which, in those days, as indeed in these, was quite a windfall. Among them, as the Devil would order, was the "Lay of the Last Minstrel," which they had all of them heard of, but which most of them had never seen. I think it could not have been published long. Well, nobody thought there could be any risk of anything national in that, though Phillips swore

old Shaw had cut out the "Tempest" from Shakespeare before he let Nolan have it, because he said "the Bermudas ought to be ours, and, by Jove, should be one day." So Nolan was permitted to join the circle one afternoon when a lot of them sat on deck smoking and reading aloud. People do not do such things so often now; but when I was young we got rid of a great deal of time so. Well, so it happened that in his turn Nolan took the book and read to the others; and he read very well, as I know. Nobody in the circle knew a line of the poem, only it was all magic and Border chivalry, and was ten thousand years ago. Poor Nolan read steadily through the fifth canto, stopped a minute and drank something, and then began, without a thought of what was coming,—

> "Breathes there the man, with soul so dead,
> Who never to himself hath said,—"

It seems impossible to us that anybody ever heard this for the first time; but all these fellows did then, and poor Nolan himself went on, still unconsciously or mechanically,—

> "This is my own, my native land!"

Then they all saw something was to pay; but he expected to get through, I suppose, turned a little pale, but plunged on,—

> "Whose heart hath ne'er within him burned,
> As home his footsteps he hath turned
> From wandering on a foreign strand?—
> If such there breathe, go, mark him well,"—

By this time the men were all beside themselves, wishing there was any way to make him turn over two pages; but he had not quite presence of mind for that; he gagged a little, colored crimson, and staggered on,—

> "For him no minstrel raptures swell;
> High though his titles, proud his name,
> Boundless his wealth as wish can claim,
> Despite these titles, power, and pelf,
> The wretch, concentred all in self—"

and here the poor fellow choked, could not go on, but started up, swung the book into the sea, vanished into his state-room, "And by Jove," said Phillips, "we did not see him for two months again. And I had to make up some beggarly story to that English surgeon why I did not return his Walter Scott to him."

That story shows about the time when Nolan's braggadocio must have broken down. At first, they said, he took a very high tone, considered his imprisonment a mere farce, af fected to enjoy the voyage, and all that; but Phillips said that after he came out of his state-room he never was the same man again. He never read aloud again, unless it was the Bible or Shakespeare, or something else he was sure of. But it was not that merely. He never entered in with the other young men exactly as a companion again. He was always shy afterwards, when I knew him,—very seldom spoke, unless he was spoken to, except to a very few friends. He lighted up occasionally,—I remember late in his life hearing him fairly eloquent on something which had been suggested to him by one of Fléchier's sermons,—but generally he had the nervous, tired look of a heart-wounded man.

When Captain Shaw was coming home,—if, as I say, it was Shaw,—rather to the surprise of everybody they made one of the Windward Islands, and lay off and on for nearly a week. The boys said the officers were sick of salt-junk, and meant to have turtle-soup before they came home. But after several days the *Warren* came to the same rendezvous; they exchanged signals; she sent to Phillips and these homeward-bound men letters and papers, and told them she was outward-bound, perhaps to the Mediterranean, and took poor Nolan and his traps on the boat back to try his second cruise. He looked very blank when he was told to get ready to join her. He had known enough of the signs of the sky to know that till that moment he was going "home." But this was a distinct evidence of something he had not thought of, perhaps,—that there was no going home for him, even to a prison. And this was the first of some twenty such transfers, which brought him sooner or later into half our best vessels, but which kept him all his life at least some hundred miles from the country he had hoped he might never hear of again.

It may have been on that second cruise—it was once when he was up the Mediterranean —that Mrs. Graff, the celebrated Southern beauty of those days, danced with him. They had been lying a long time in the Bay of Naples, and the officers were very intimate in the English fleet, and there had been great festivities, and our men thought they must give a great ball on board the ship. How they ever did it on board the *Warren* I am sure I do not know. Perhaps it was not the *Warren*, or perhaps ladies did not take up so much room as they do now. They wanted to use Nolan's state-room for something, and they hated to do it without asking him to the ball; so the captain said they might ask him, if they would

be responsible that he did not talk with the wrong people, "who would give him intelligence." So the dance went on, the finest party that had ever been known, I dare say; for I never heard of a man-of-war ball that was not. For ladies they had the family of the American consul, one or two travellers who had adventured so far, and a nice bevy of English girls and matrons, perhaps Lady Hamilton herself.

Well, different officers relieved each other in standing and talking with Nolan in a friendly way, so as to be sure that nobody else spoke to him. The dancing went on with spirit, and after a while even the fellows who took this honorary guard of Nolan ceased to fear any *contretemps*. Only when some English lady— Lady Hamilton, as I said, perhaps—called for a set of "American dances," an odd thing happened. Everybody then danced contra-dances. The black band, nothing loath, conferred as to what "American dances" were, and started off with "Virginia Reel," which they followed with "Money-Musk," which in its turn in those days should have been followed by "The Old Thirteen." But just as Dick, the leader tapped for his fiddle to begin, and bent forward, about to say in true negro state, " 'The Old Thirteen,' gentlemen and ladies!" as he had said " 'Virginny Reel,' if you please!" and " 'Money-Musk,' if you please!" the captain's boy tapped him on the shoulder, whispered to him, and he did not announce the name of the dance; he merely bowed, began on the air, and they all fell to,—the officers teaching the English girls the figure, but not telling them why it had no name.

But that is not the story I started to tell. As the dancing went on, Nolan and our fellows all got at ease, as I said,—so much so, that it seemed quite natural for him to bow to that splendid Mrs. Graff, and say,—

"I hope you have not forgotten me, Miss Rutledge. Shall I have the honor of dancing?"

He did it so quickly that Fellows, who was by him, could not hinder him. She laughed, and said,—

"I am not Miss Rutledge any longer, Mr. Nolan; but I will dance all the same," just nodded to Fellows, as if to say he must leave Mr. Nolan to her, and led him off to the place where the dance was forming.

Nolan thought he had got his chance. He had known her at Philadelphia, and at other places had met her, and this was a godsend. You could not talk in contra-dances, as you do in cotillions, or even in the pauses of waltzing; but there were chances for tongues and sounds, as well as for eyes and blushes. He began with her travels, and Europe, and Vesuvius, and the French; and then, when they had worked down, and had that long talking-time at the bottom of the set, he said boldly,—a little pale, she said, as she told me the story, years after,—

"And what do you hear from home, Mrs. Graff?"

And that splendid creature looked through him. Jove! how she must have looked through him!

"Home!! Mr. Nolan!!! I thought you were the man who never wanted to hear of home again!"—And she walked directly up the deck to her husband, and left poor Nolan alone, as he always was. He did not dance again.

I cannot give any history of him in order; nobody can now; and, indeed, I am not trying to. These are the traditions, which I sort out, as I believe them, from the myths which have been told about this man for forty years. The lies that have been told about him are legion. The fellows used to say he was the "Iron Mask"; and poor George Pons went to his grave in the belief that this was the author of "Junius," who was being punished for his celebrated libel on Thomas Jefferson. Pons was not very strong in the historical line. A happier story than either of these I have told is of the war. That came along soon after. I have heard this affair told in three or four ways,—and indeed it may have happened more than once. But which ship it was on I cannot tell. However, in one, at least, of the great frigate-duels with the English, in which the navy was really baptized, it happened that a round-shot from the enemy entered one of our ports square, and took right down the officer of the gun himself, and almost every man of the gun's crew. Now you may say what you choose about courage, but that is not a nice thing to see. But, as the men who were not killed picked themselves up, and as they and the surgeon's people were carrying off the bodies, there appeared Nolan, in his shirt-sleeves, with the rammer in his hand, and, just as if he had been the officer, told them off with authority,—who should go to the cockpit with the wounded men, who should stay with him, —perfectly cheery, and with that way which makes men feel sure all is right and is going to be right. And he finished loading the gun with his own hands, aimed it, and bade the men fire. And there he stayed, captain of that gun, keeping those fellows in spirits, till the enemy struck,—sitting on the carriage while the gun was cooling, though he was exposed all the time,—showing them easier ways to handle heavy shot,—making the raw hands laugh at their own blunders,—and when the gun cooled again, getting it loaded and fired twice as often as any other gun on the ship. The captain walked forward by way of encouraging the men, and Nolan touched his hat and said,—

"I am showing them how we do this in the artillery, sir."

And this is the part of the story where all the legends agree; that the Commodore said,—

"I see you do, and I thank you, sir; and I shall never forget this day, sir, and you never shall, sir."

And after the whole thing was over, and he had the Englishman's sword, in the midst of the state and ceremony of the quarter-deck, he said,—

"Where is Mr. Nolan? Ask Mr. Nolan to come here."

And when Nolan came the captain said,—

"Mr. Nolan, we are all very grateful to you to-day; you are one of us to-day; you will be named in the despatches."

And then the old man took off his own sword of ceremony, and gave it to Nolan, and made him put it on. The man told me this who saw it. Nolan cried like a baby, and well he might. He had not worn a sword since that infernal day at Fort Adams. But always afterwards, on occasions of ceremony, he wore that quaint old French sword of the Commodore's.

The captain did mention him in the despatches. It was always said he asked that he might be pardoned. He wrote a special letter to the Secretary of War. But nothing ever came of it. As I said, that was about the time when they began to ignore the whole transaction at Washington, and when Nolan's imprisonment began to carry itself on because there was nobody to stop it without any new orders from home.

I have heard it said that he was with Porter when he took possession of the Nukahiwa Islands. Not this Porter, you know, but old Porter, his father, Essex Porter,—that is, the old Essex Porter, not this Essex. As an artillery officer, who had seen service in the West, Nolan knew more about fortifications, embrasures, ravelins, stockades, and all that, than any of them did; and he worked with a right good-will in fixing that battery all right. I have always thought it was a pity Porter did not leave him in command there with Gamble. That would have settled all the question about his punishment. We should have kept the islands, and at this moment we should have one station in the Pacific Ocean. Our French friends, too, when they wanted this little watering-place, would have found it was pre-occupied. But Madison and the Virginians, of course, flung all that away.

All that was near fifty years ago. If Nolan was thirty then, he must have been near eighty when he died. He looked sixty when he was forty. But he never seemed to me to change a hair afterwards. As I imagine his life, from what I have seen and heard of it, he must have been in every sea, and yet almost never on land. He must have known, in a formal way, more officers in our service than any man living knows. He told me once, with a grave smile, that no man in the world lived so methodical a life as he. "You know the boys say I am the Iron Mask, and you know how busy he was." He said it did not do for any one to try to read all the time, more than to do anything else all the time; but that he read just five hours a day. "Then," he said, "I keep up my note-books, writing in them at such and such hours from what I have been reading; and I include in these my scrap-books." These were very curious indeed. He had six or eight, of different subjects. There was one of History, one of Natural Science, one which he called "Odds and Ends." But they were not merely books of extracts from newspapers. They had bits of plants and ribbons, shells tied on, and carved scraps of bone and wood, which he had taught the men to cut for him, and they were beautifully illustrated. He drew admirably. He had some of the funniest drawings there, and some of the most pathetic, that I have ever seen in my life. I wonder who will have Nolan's scrap-books.

Well, he said his reading and his notes were his profession, and that they took five hours and two hours respectively of each day. "Then," said he, "every man should have a diversion as well as a profession. My Natural History is my diversion." That took two hours a day more. The men used to bring him birds and fish, but on a long cruise he had to satisfy himself with centipedes and cock-roaches and such small game. He was the only naturalist I ever met who knew anything about the habits of the house-fly and the mos-quito. All those people can tell you whether they are *Lepidoptera* or *Steptopotera ;* but as for telling how you can get rid of them, or how they get away from you when you strike them, —why, Linnæus knew as little of that as John Foy the idiot did. These nine hours made Nolan's regular daily "occupation." The rest of the time he talked or walked. Till he grew very old, he went aloft a great deal. He always

kept up his exercise; and I never heard that he was ill. If any other man was ill, he was the kindest nurse in the world; and he knew more than half the surgeons do. Then if anybody was sick or died, or if the captain wanted him to on any other occasion, he was always ready to read prayers. I have said that he read beautifully.

My own acquaintance with Philip Nolan began six or eight years after the War, on my first voyage after I was appointed a midshipman. It was in the first days after our Slave-Trade treaty, while the reigning House, which was still the House of Virginia, had still a sort of sentimentalism about the suppression of the horrors of the Middle Passage, and something was sometimes done that way. We were in the South Atlantic on that business. From the time I joined, I believe I thought Nolan was a sort of lay chaplain,—a chaplain with a blue coat. I never asked about him. Everything in the ship was strange to me. I knew it was green to ask questions, and I suppose I thought there was a "Plain Buttons" on every ship. We had him to dine in our mess once a week, and the caution was given that on that day nothing was to be said about home. But if they had told us not to say anything about the planet Mars or the Book of Deuteronomy, I should not have asked why; there were a great many things which seemed to me to have as little reason. I first came to understand any-thing about "the man without a country" one day when we overhauled a dirty little schooner which had slaves on board. An officer was sent to take charge of her, and, after a few minutes, he sent back his boat to ask that some one might be sent him who could speak Portuguese. We were all looking over the rail when the message came, and we all wished we could interpret, when the captain asked who spoke Portuguese. But none of the officers did; and just as the captain was sending forward to ask if any of the people could, Nolan stepped out and said he should be glad to interpret, if the captain wished, as he understood the lan-guage. The captain thanked him, fitted out another boat with him, and in this boat it was my luck to go.

When we got there, it was such a scene as you seldom see, and never want to. Nastiness beyond account, and chaos run loose in the midst of the nastiness. There were not a great many of the negroes; but by way of making what there were understand that they were free, Vaughan had had their hand-cuffs and ankle-cuffs knocked off, and, for convenience' sake, was putting them upon the rascals of the schooner's crew. The negroes were, most of them, out of the hold, and swarming all round the dirty deck, with a central throng surrounding Vaughan and addressing him in every dialect and *patois* of a dialect, from the Zulu click up to the Parisian of Beledeljereed.

As we came on deck, Vaughan looked down from a hogshead, on which he had mounted in desperation, and said,—

"For God's love, is there anybody who can make these wretches understand something? The men gave them rum, and that did not quiet them. I knocked that big fellow down twice, and that did not soothe him. And then I talked Choctaw to all of them together; and I'll be hanged if they understood that as well as they understood the English."

Nolan said he could speak Portuguese, and one or two fine-looking Kroomen were dragged out, who, as it had been found already, had worked for the Portuguese on the coast at Fernando Po.

"Tell them they are free," said Vaughan; "and tell them that these rascals are to be hanged as soon as we can get rope enough."

Nolan "put that into Spanish,"—that is, he explained it in such Portuguese as the Kroomen could understand, and they in turn to such of the negroes as could understand them. Then there was such a yell of delight, clinching of fists, leaping and dancing, kissing of Nolan's feet, and a general rush made to the hogshead by way of spontaneous worship of Vaughan, as the *deus ex machina* of the occasion.

"Tell them," said Vaughan, well pleased, "that I will take them all to Cape Palmas."

This did not answer so well. Cape Palmas was practically as far from the homes of most of them as New Orleans or Rio Janeiro was; that is, they would be eternally separated from home there. And their interpreters, as we could understand, instantly said, "*Ah, non Palmas,*" and began to propose infinite other expedients in most voluble language. Vaughan was rather disappointed at this result of his liberality, and asked Nolan eagerly what they said. The drops stood on poor Nolan's white forehead, as he hushed the men down, and said,—

"He says, 'Not Palmas.' He says, 'Take us home, take us to our own country, take us to our own house, take us to our own pickaninnies and our own women.' He says he has an old father and mother who will die if they do not see him. And this one says he left his people all sick, and paddled down to Fernando to beg the white doctor to come and help them, and

that these devils caught him in the bay just in sight of home, and that he has never seen anybody from home since then. And this one says," choked out Nolan, "that he has not heard a word from his home in six months, while he has been locked up in an infernal barracoon."

Vaughan always said he grew gray himself while Nolan struggled through this interpretation. I, who did not understand anything of the passion involved in it, saw that the very elements were melting with fervent heat, and that something was to pay somewhere. Even the negroes themselves stopped howling, as they saw Nolan's agony, and Vaughan's almost equal agony of sympathy. As quick as he could get words he said,—

"Tell them yes, yes, yes; tell them they shall go to the Mountains of the Moon, if they will. If I sail the schooner through the Great White Desert, they shall go home!"

And after some fashion Nolan said so. And then they all fell to kissing him again, and wanted to rub his nose with theirs.

But he could not stand it long; and getting Vaughan to say he might go back, he beckoned me down into our boat. As we lay back in the stern-sheets and the men gave way, he said to me, "Youngster, let that show you what it is to be without a family, without a home, and without a country. And if you are ever tempted to say a word or to do a thing that shall put a bar between you and your family, your home, and your country, pray God in his mercy to take you that instant home to his own heaven. Stick by your family, boy; forget you have a self, while you do everything for them. Think of your home, boy; write and send, and talk about it. Let it be nearer and nearer to your thought, the farther you have to travel from it; and rush back to it, when you are free, as that poor black slave is doing now. And for your country, boy," and the words rattled in his throat, "and for that flag," and he pointed to the ship, "never dream a dream but of serving her as she bids you, though the service carry you through a thousand hells. No matter what happens to you, no matter who flatters you or who abuses you, never look at another flag, never let a night pass but you pray God to bless that flag. Remember, boy, that behind all these men you have to do with, behind officers, and government, and people even, there is the Country Herself, your Country, and that you belong to Her as you belong to your own mother. Stand by Her, boy, as you would stand by your mother, if those devils there had got hold of her to-day!"

I was frightened to death by his calm, hard passion; but I blundered out, that I would, by all that was holy, and that I had never thought of doing anything else. He hardly seemed to hear me; but he did, almost in a whisper, say "Oh, if anybody had said so to me when I was of your age!"

I think it was this half-confidence of his, which I never abused, for I never told this story till now, which afterward made us great friends. He was very kind to me. Often he sat up, or even got up, at night, to walk the deck with me, when it was my watch. He explained to me a great deal of my mathematics, and I owe to him my taste for mathematics. He lent me books, and helped me about my reading. He never alluded so directly to his story again; but from one and another officer I have learned, in thirty years, what I am telling. When we parted from him in St. Thomas Harbor, at the end of our cruise, I was more sorry than I can tell. I was very glad to meet him again in 1830; and later in life, when I thought I had some influence in Washington, I moved heaven and earth to have him discharged. But it was like getting a ghost out of prison. They pretended there was no such man, and never was such a man. They will say so at the Department now! Perhaps they do not know. It will not be the first thing in the service of which the Department appears to know nothing!

There is a story that Nolan met Burr, once on one of our vessels, when a party of Americans came on board in the Mediterranean. But this I believe to be a lie; or, rather, it is a myth, *ben trovato*, involving a tremendous blowing-up with which he sunk Burr,—asking him how he liked to be "without a country." But it is clear, from Burr's life, that nothing of the sort could have happened; and I mention this only as an illustration of the stories which get a-going where there is the least mystery at bottom.

So poor Philip Nolan had his wish fulfilled. I know but one fate more dreadful: it is the fate reserved for those men who shall have one day to exile themselves from their country because they have attempted her ruin, and shall have at the same time to see the prosperity and honor to which she rises when she has rid herself of them and their iniquities. The wish of poor Nolan, as we all learned to call him, not because his punishment was too great, but because his repentance was so clear, was precisely the wish of every Bragg and Beauregard who broke a soldier's oath two years ago, and of

every Maury and Barron who broke a sailor's. I do not know how often they have repented. I do know that they have done all that in them lay that they might have no country,—that all the honors, associations, memories, and hopes which belong to "country" might be broken up into little shreds and distributed to the winds. I know, too, that their punishment, as they vegetate through what is left of life to them in wretched Boulognes and Leicester Squares, where they are destined to upbraid each other till they die, will have all the agony of Nolan's, with the added pang that every one who sees them will see them to despise and to execrate them. They will have their wish, like him.

For him, poor fellow, he repented of his folly, and then, like a man, submitted to the fate he had asked for. He never intentionally added to the difficulty or delicacy of the charge of those who had him in hold. Accidents would happen; but they never happened from his fault. Lieutenant Truxton told me that, when Texas was annexed, there was a careful discussion among the officers, whether they should get hold of Nolan's handsome set of maps and cut Texas out of it,—from the map of the world and the map of Mexico. The United States had been cut out when the atlas was bought for him. But it was voted rightly enough, that to do this would be virtually to reveal to him what had happened, or, as Harry Cole said, to make him think old Burr had succeeded. So it was from no fault of Nolan's that a great botch happened at my own table, when, for a short time, I was in command of the *George Washington* corvette, on the South American station. We were lying in the La Plata, and some of the officers, who had been on shore, and had just joined again, were entertaining us with accounts of their misadventures in riding the half-wild horses of Buenos Ayres. Nolan was at table, and was in an unusually bright and talkative mood. Some story of a tumble reminded him of an adventure of his own, when he was catching wild horses in Texas with his brother Stephen, at a time when he must have been quite a boy. He told the story with a good deal of spirit,—so much so, that the silence which often follows a good story hung over the table for an instant, to be broken by Nolan himself. For he asked, perfectly unconsciously,—

"Pray, what has become of Texas? After the Mexicans got their independence, I thought that province of Texas would come forward very fast. It is really one of the finest regions on earth; it is the Italy of this continent. But I have not seen or heard a word of Texas for near twenty years."

There were two Texan officers at the table. The reason he had never heard of Texas was that Texas and her affairs had been painfully cut out of his newspapers since Austin began his settlements; so that, while he read of Honduras and Tamaulipas, and till quite lately, of California, this virgin province, in which his brother had travelled so far, and, I believe, had died, had ceased to be to him. Waters and Williams, the two Texas men, looked grimly at each other, and tried not to laugh. Edward Morris had his attention attracted by the third link in the chain of the captain's chandelier. Watrous was seized with a convulsion of sneezing. Nolan himself saw that something was to pay, he did not know what. And I, as master of the feast, had to say,—

"Texas is out of the map, Mr. Nolan. Have you seen Captain Back's curious account of Sir Thomas Roe's Welcome?"

After that cruise I never saw Nolan again. I wrote to him at least twice a year, for in that voyage we became even confidentially intimate; but he never wrote to me. The other men tell me that in those fifteen years he *aged* very fast, as well he might indeed, but that he was still the same gentle, uncomplaining, silent sufferer that he ever was, bearing as best he could his self-appointed punishment,—rather less social, perhaps, with new men whom he did not know, but more anxious, apparently, than ever to serve and befriend and teach the boys, some of whom fairly seemed to worship him. And now, it seems, the dear old fellow is dead. He has found a home at last, and a country.

Since writing this, and while considering whether or no I would print it, as a warning to the young Nolans and Vallandighams and Tatnalls of to-day of what it is to throw away a country, I have received from Danforth, who is on board the *Levant*, a letter which gives an account of Nolan's last hours. It removes all my doubts about telling this story.

To understand the first words of the letter, the non-professional reader should remember that after 1817, the position of every officer who had Nolan in charge was one of the greatest delicacy. The government had failed to renew the order of 1807 regarding him. What was a man to do? Should he let him go? What, then, if he were called to account by the Department for violating the order of 1807? Should he keep him? What, then, if Nolan should be liberated some day, and should bring an action for false imprisonment

or kidnapping against every man who had had him in charge? I urged and pressed this upon Southard, and I have reason to think that other officers did the same thing. But the Secretary always said, as they so often do at Washington, that there were no special orders to give, and that we must act on our own judgment. That means, "If you succeed, you will be sustained; if you fail, you will be disavowed." Well, as Danforth says, all that is over now, though I do not know but I expose myself to a criminal prosecution on the evidence of the very revelation I am making.

Here is the letter:—

LEVANT, 2° 2′ S. @ 131° W.

"DEAR FRED,—I try to find heart and life to tell you that it is all over with dear old Nolan. I have been with him on this voyage more than I ever was, and I can understand wholly now the way in which you used to speak of the dear old fellow. I could see that he was not strong, but I had no idea the end was so near. The doctor has been watching him very carefully, and yesterday morning came to me and told me that Nolan was not so well, and had not left his state-room,—a thing I never remember before. He had let the doctor come and see him as he lay there,—the first time the doctor had been in the state-room,—and he said he should like to see me. O dear! do you remember the mysteries we boys used to invent about his room, in the old *Intrepid* days? Well, I went in, and there, to be sure, the poor fellow lay in his berth, smiling pleasantly as he gave me his hand, but looking very frail. I could not help a glance round, which showed me what a little shrine he had made of the box he was lying in. The stars and stripes were triced up above and around a picture of Washington, and he had painted a majestic eagle, with lightnings blazing from his beak and his foot just clasping the whole globe, which his wings overshadowed. The dear old boy saw my glance, and said, with a sad smile, 'Here, you see, I have a country!' And then he pointed to the foot of his bed, where I had not seen before a great map of the United States, as he had drawn it from memory, and which he had there to look upon as he lay. Quaint, queer old names were on it, in large letters: 'Indiana Territory,' 'Mississippi Territory,' and 'Louisiana Territory,' as I suppose our fathers learned such things: but the old fellow had patched in Texas, too; he had carried his western boundary all the way to the Pacific, but on that shore he had defined nothing.

" 'O Danforth,' he said, 'I know I am dying.

I cannot get home. Surely you will tell me something now? Stop! stop! Do not speak till I say what I am sure you know, that there is not in this ship, that there is not in America, —God bless her!—a more loyal man than I. There cannot be a man who loves the old flag as I do, or prays for it as I do, or hopes for it as I do. There are thirty-four stars in it now, Danforth. I thank God for that, though I do not know what their names are. There has never been one taken away: I thank God for that. I know by that, that there has never been any successful Burr. O Danforth, Danforth,' he sighed out, 'how like a wretched night's dream a boy's idea of personal fame or of separate sovereignty seems, when one looks back on it after such a life as mine! But tell me,—tell me something,—tell me everything, Danforth, before I die!'

"Ingham, I swear to you that I felt like a monster that I had not told him everything before. Danger or no danger, delicacy or no delicacy, who was I, that I should have been acting the tyrant all this time over this dear, sainted old man, who had years ago expiated, in his whole manhood's life, the madness of a boy's treason? 'Mr. Nolan,' said I, 'I will tell you everything you ask about. Only, where shall I begin?'

"O the blessed smile that crept over his white face! and he pressed my hand and said, 'God bless you!' 'Tell me their names,' he said, and he pointed to the stars on the flag. 'The last I know is Ohio. My father lived in Kentucky. But I have guessed Michigan and Indiana and Mississippi,—that was where Fort Adams is,—they make twenty. But where are your other fourteen? You have not cut up any of the old ones, I hope?'

"Well, that was not a bad text, and I told him the names in as good order as I could, and he bade me take down his beautiful map and draw them in as I best could with my pencil. He was wild with delight about Texas, told me how his brother died there; he had marked a gold cross where he supposed his brother's grave was; and he had guessed at Texas. Then he was delighted as he saw California and Oregon;—that, he said, he had suspected partly, because he had never been permitted to land on that shore, though the ships were there so much. 'And the men,' said he, laughing, 'brought off a good deal beside furs.' Then he went back—heavens, how far!—to ask about the *Chesapeake*, and what was done to Barron for surrendering her to the *Leopard*, and whether Burr ever tried again,—and he ground his teeth with the only passion he

showed. But in a moment that was over, and he said, 'God forgive me, for I am sure I forgive him.' Then he asked about the old war,— told me the true story of his serving the gun the day we took the Java,—asked about dear old David Porter, as he called him. Then he settled down more quietly, and very happily, to hear me tell in an hour the history of fifty years.

"How I wished it had been somebody who knew something! But I did as well as I could. I told him of the English war. I told him about Fulton and the steamboat beginning. I told him about old Scott, and Jackson; told him all I could think about the Mississippi, and New Orleans, and Texas, and his own old Kentucky. And do you think, he asked, who was in command of the 'Legion of the West.' I told him it was a very gallant officer named Grant, and that, by our last news, he was about to establish his head-quarters at Vicksburg. Then, 'Where was Vicksburg?' I worked that out on the map; it was about a hundred miles, more or less, above his old Fort Adams; and I thought Fort Adams must be a ruin now. 'It must be at old Vick's plantation,' said he; 'well, that is a change!'

"I tell you, Ingham, it was a hard thing to condense the history of half a century into that talk with a sick man. And I do not know what I told him,—of emigration, and the means of it,—of steamboats, and railroads, and telegraphs,—of inventions, and books, and literature,—of the colleges, and West Point, and the Naval School,—but with the queerest interruptions that ever you heard. You see it was Robinson Crusoe asking all the accumulated questions of fifty-six years!

"I remember he asked, all of a sudden, who was President now; and when I told him, he asked if Old Abe was General Benjamin Lincoln's son. He said he met old General Lincoln, when he was quite a boy himself, at some Indian treaty. I said no, that Old Abe was a Kentuckian like himself, but I could not tell him of what family; he had worked up from the ranks. 'Good for him!' cried Nolan; 'I am glad of that. As I have brooded and wondered, I have thought our danger was in keeping up those regular successions in the first families.' Then I got talking about my visit to Washington. I told him of meeting the Oregon Congressman, Harding; I told him about the Smithsonian, and the Exploring Expedition; I told him about the Capitol, and the statues for the pediment, and Crawford's *Liberty*, and Greenough's *Washington*: Ingham, I told him everything I could think of that would show the grandeur of his country and its prosperity; but I could not make up my mouth to tell him a word about this infernal Rebellion!

"And he drank it in, and enjoyed it as I cannot tell you. He grew more and more silent, yet I never thought he was tired or faint. I gave him a glass of water, but he just wet his lips, and told me not to go away. Then he asked me to bring the Presbyterian 'Book of Public Prayer,' which lay there, and said, with a smile, that it would open at the right place, —and so it did. There was his double red mark down the page; and I knelt down and read, and he repeated with me, 'For ourselves and our country, O gracious God, we thank Thee, that notwithstanding our manifold transgressions of Thy holy laws, Thou hast continued to us Thy marvellous kindness,'—and so to the end of that thanksgiving. Then he turned to the end of the same book, and I read the words more familiar to me,—'Most heartily we beseech Thee with Thy favor to behold and bless Thy servant, the President of the United States, and all others in authority,'—and the rest of the Episcopal Collect. 'Danforth,' said he, 'I have repeated those prayers night and morning, it is now fifty-five years.' And then he said he would go to sleep. He bent me down over him and kissed me; and he said, 'Look in my Bible, Danforth, when I am gone.' And I went away.

"But I had no thought it was the end. I thought he was tired and would sleep. I knew he was happy and I wanted him to be alone.

"But in an hour, when the doctor went in gently, he found Nolan had breathed his life away with a smile. He had something pressed close to his lips. It was his father's badge of the Order of Cincinnati.

"We looked in his Bible, and there was a slip of paper, at the place where he had marked the text:—

"'They desire a country, even a heavenly: wherefore God is not ashamed to be called their God: for he hath prepared for them a city.'

"On this slip of paper he had written:—

"Bury me in the sea; it has been my home, and I love it. But will not some one set up a stone for my memory at Fort Adams or at Orleans, that my disgrace may not be more than I ought to bear? Say on it:—

In Memory of

PHILIP NOLAN,

Lieutenant in the Army of the United States.

He loved his country as no other man has loved her; but no man deserved less at her hands."

HENRY JAMES (1843-1916)

THE ROMANCE OF CERTAIN OLD CLOTHES

(1868)

Toward the middle of the eighteenth century there lived in the Province of Massachusetts a widowed gentlewoman, the mother of three children. Her name is of little account: I shall take the liberty of calling her Mrs. Willoughby,—a name, like her own, of a highly respectable sound. She had been left a widow after some six years of marriage, and had devoted herself to the care of her children. These latter grew up in a manner to reward her tender care and to gratify her fondest hopes. The first-born was a son, whom she had called Bernard, after his father. The others were daughters,—born at an interval of three years apart. Good looks were traditional in the family, and these young persons were not likely to allow the tradition to perish. The boy was of that fair and ruddy complexion and of that athletic mould which in those days (as in

these) were the sign of genuine English blood, —a frank, affectionate young fellow, a capital son and brother, and a steadfast friend. Clever, however, he was not; the wit of the family had been apportioned chiefly to his sisters. Mr. Willoughby had been a great reader of Shakespeare, at a time when this pursuit implied more penetration of mind than at the present day, and in a community where it required much courage to patronize the drama even in the closet; and he had wished to record his admiration of the great poet by calling his daughters out of his favorite plays. Upon the elder he had bestowed the romantic name of Viola; and upon the younger, the more serious one of Perdita, in memory of a little girl born between them, who had lived but a few weeks.

When Bernard Willoughby came to his sixteenth year, his mother put a brave face upon it, and prepared to execute her husband's last request. This had been an earnest entreaty that, at the proper age, his son should be sent out to England, there to complete his education at the University of Oxford, which had been the seat of his own studies. Mrs. Willoughby valued her son three times as much as she did her two daughters together; but she valued her husband's wishes more. So she swallowed her sobs, and made up her boy's trunk and his simple provincial outfit, and sent him on his way across the seas. Bernard was entered at his father's college, and spent five years in England, without great honor, indeed, but with a vast deal of pleasure and no discredit. On leaving the University he made the journey to France. In his twenty-third year he took ship for home, prepared to find poor little New England (New England was very small in those days) an utterly intolerable place of abode. But there had been changes at home, as well as in Mr. Bernard's opinions. He found his mother's house quite habitable, and his sisters grown into two very charming young ladies, with all the accomplishments and graces of the young women of Britain, and a certain native-grown gentle *brusquerie* and wildness, which, if it was not an accomplishment, was certainly a grace the more. Bernard privately assured his mother that his sisters were fully a match for the most genteel young women in England; whereupon poor Mrs. Willoughby quite came into conceit of her daughters. Such was Bernard's opinion, and such, in a tenfold higher degree, was the opinion of Mr. Arthur Lloyd. This gentleman, I hasten to add, was a college-mate of Mr. Bernard, a young man of reputable family, of a good person and a handsome inheritance; which latter appurtenance he prepared to invest in trade in this country. He and Bernard were warm friends; they had crossed the ocean together, and the young American had lost no time in presenting him at his mother's house, where he had made quite as good an impression as that which he had received, and of which I have just given a hint.

The two sisters were at this time in all the freshness of their youthful bloom; each wearing, of course, this natural brilliancy in the manner that became her best. They were equally dissimilar in appearance and character. Viola, the elder,—now in her twenty-second year,—was tall and fair, with calm gray eyes and auburn tresses; a very faint likeness to the Viola of Shakespeare's comedy, whom I imagine as a brunette (if you will), but a slender, airy creature, full of the softest and finest emotions. Miss Willoughby, with her rich, fair skin, her fine arms, her majestic height, and her slow utterance, was not cut out for adventures. She would never have put on a man's jacket and hose; and, indeed, being a very plump beauty, it is perhaps as well that she wouldn't. Perdita, too, might very well have exchanged the sweet melancholy of her name against something more in consonance with her aspect and disposition. She was a positive brunette, short of stature, light of foot, with dark brown eyes full of fire and animation. She had been from her childhood a creature of smiles and gayety; and so far from making you wait for an answer to your speech, as her handsome sister was wont to do (while she gazed at you with her somewhat cold gray eyes), she had given you the choice of half a dozen, suggested by the successive clauses of your proposition, before you had got to the end of it.

The young girls were very glad to see their brother once more; but they found themselves quite able to maintain a reserve of good-will for their brother's friend. Among the young men their friends and neighbors, the *belle jeunesse* of the Colony, there were many excellent fellows, several devoted swains, and some two or three who enjoyed the reputation of universal charmers and conquerors. But the home-bred arts and the somewhat boisterous gallantry of those honest young colonists were completely eclipsed by the good looks, the fine clothes, the respectful *empressement*, the perfect elegance, the immense information, of Mr. Arthur Lloyd. He was in reality no paragon; he was an honest, resolute, intelligent young man, rich in pounds sterling, in his health and comfortable hopes, and his little capital of uninvested affections. But he was a gentleman; he had a handsome face; he had studied and travelled; he spoke French, he played on the flute, and he read verses aloud with very great taste. There were a dozen reasons why Miss Willoughby and her sister should forthwith have been rendered fastidious in the choice of their male acquaintance. The imagination of woman is especially adapted to the various little conventions and mysteries of polite society. Mr. Lloyd's talk told our little New England maidens a vast deal more of the ways and means of people of fashion in European capitals than he had any idea of doing. It was delightful to sit by and hear him and Bernard discourse upon the fine people and fine things they had seen. They would all gather round the fire after tea, in the little wainscoted parlor,—quite innocent then of any intention of being picturesque or of being anything else, indeed, than economical, and saving the expense of stamped papers and tapestries,—and the two young men would remind each other, across the rug, of this, that, and the other adventure. Viola and Perdita would often have given theirs ears to know exactly what adventure it was, and where it happened, and who was there, and what the ladies had on; but in those days a well-bred young woman was not expected to break into the conversation of her own movement or to ask too many questions; and the poor girls used therefore to sit fluttering behind the more languid—or more discreet —curiosity of their mother.

That they were both very nice girls Arthur Lloyd was not slow to discover; but it took him some time to satisfy himself as to the balance of their charms. He had a strong presentiment—an emotion of a nature entirely too cheerful to be called a foreboding—that he was destined to marry one of them; yet he was unable to arrive at a preference, and for such a consummation a preference was certainly indispensable, inasmuch as Lloyd was quite too much of a young man to reconcile himself to the idea of making a choice by lot and being cheated of the heavenly delight of falling in love. He resolved to take things easily, and to let his heart speak. Meanwhile, he was on a very pleasant footing. Mrs. Willoughby showed a dignified indifference to his "intentions," equally remote from a carelessness of her daughters' honor and from that hideous alacrity to make him commit himself, which, in his quality of a young man of property, he had but too often encountered in the venerable dames of his native islands. As for Bernard, all that he asked was that his friend should take his sisters as his own; and as for the fair creatures themselves, however each may have secretly longed for the monopoly of Mr. Lloyd's attentions, they observed a very decent and modest and contented demeanor.

Towards each other, however, they were somewhat more on the offensive. They were good sisterly friends, betwixt whom it would take more than a day for the seeds of jealousy to sprout and bear fruit; but the young girls felt that the seeds had been sown on the day that Mr. Lloyd came into the house. Each made up her mind that, if she should be slighted, she would bear her grief in silence, and that no one should be any the wiser; for if they had a great deal of love, they had also a great deal of pride. But each prayed in secret, nevertheless, that upon *her* the glory might fall. They had need of a vast deal of

patience, of self-control, and of dissimulation. In those days a young girl of decent breeding could make no advances whatever, and barely respond, indeed, to those that were made. She was expected to sit still in her chair with her eyes on the carpet, watching the spot where the mystic handkerchief should fall. Poor Arthur Lloyd was obliged to undertake his wooing in the little wainscoted parlor, before the eyes of Mrs. Willoughby, her son, and his prospective sister-in-law. But youth and love are so cunning that a hundred little signs and tokens might travel to and fro, and not one of these three pair of eyes detect them in their passage. The young girls had but one chamber and one bed between them, and for long hours together they were under each other's direct inspection. That each knew that she was being watched, however, made not a grain of difference in those little offices which they mutually rendered, or in the various household tasks which they performed in common. Neither flinched nor fluttered beneath the silent batteries of her sister's eyes. The only apparent change in their habits was that they had less to say to each other. It was impossible to talk about Mr. Lloyd, and it was ridiculous to talk about anything else. By tacit agreement they began to wear all their choice finery, and to devise such little implements of coquetry, in the way of ribbons and top-knots and furbelows as were sanctioned by indubitable modesty. They executed in the same inarticulate fashion a little agreement of sincerity on these delicate matters. "Is it better so?" Viola would ask, tying a bunch of ribbons on her bosom, and turning about from her glass to her sister. Perdita would look up gravely from her work, and examine the decoration. "I think you had better give it another loop," she would say, with great solemnity, looking hard at her sister with eyes that added, "upon my honor." So they were forever stitching and trimming their petticoats, and pressing out their muslins, and contriving washes and ointments and cosmetics, like the ladies in the household of the Vicar of Wakefield. Some three or four months went by; it grew to be midwinter, and as yet Viola knew that if Perdita had nothing more to boast of than she, there was not much to be feared from her rivalry. But Perdita by this time, the charming Perdita, felt that her secret had grown to be tenfold more precious than her sister's.

One afternoon Miss Willoughby sat alone before her toilet-glass, combing out her long hair. It was getting too dark to see; she lit the two candles in their sockets on the frame of her mirror, and then went to the window to draw her curtains. It was a gray December evening; the landscape was bare and bleak, and the sky heavy with snow-clouds. At the end of the long garden into which her window looked was a wall with a little postern door, opening into a lane. The door stood ajar, as she could vaguely see in the gathering darkness, and moved slowly to and fro, as if some one were swaying it from the lane without. It was doubtless a servant-maid. But as she was about to drop her curtain, Viola saw her sister step within the garden, and hurry along the path toward the house. She dropped the curtain, all save a little crevice for her eyes. As Perdita came up the path, she seemed to be examining something in her hand, holding it close to her eyes. When she reached the house she stopped a moment, looked intently at the object, and pressed it to her lips.

Poor Viola slowly came back to her chair, and sat down before her glass, where, if she had looked at it less abstractedly, she would have seen her handsome features sadly disfigured by jealousy. A moment afterwards, the door opened behind her, and her sister came into the room, out of breath, and her cheeks aglow with the chilly air.

Perdita started. "Ah," said she, "I thought you were with mamma." The ladies were to go to a tea-party, and on such occasions it was the habit of one of the young girls to help their mother to dress. Instead of coming in, Perdita lingered at the door.

"Come in, come in," said Viola. "We've more than an hour yet. I should like you very much to give a few strokes to my hair." She knew that her sister wished to retreat, and that she could see in the glass all her movements in the room. "Nay, just help me with my hair," she said, "and I'll go to mamma."

Perdita came reluctantly, and took the brush. She saw her sister's eyes, in the glass, fastened hard upon her hands. She had not made three passes, when Viola clapped her own right hand upon her sister's left, and started out of her chair. "Whose ring is that?" she cried, passionately, drawing her towards the light.

On the young girl's third finger glistened a little gold ring, adorned with a couple of small rubies. Perdita felt that she need no longer keep her secret, yet that she must put a bold face on her avowal. "It's mine," she said proudly.

"Who gave it to you?" cried the other.

Perdita hesitated a moment. "Mr. Lloyd."

"Mr. Lloyd is generous, all of a sudden."

"Ah no," cried Perdita, with spirit, "not all of a sudden. He offered it to me a month ago."

"And you needed a month's begging to take it?" said Viola, looking at the little trinket; which indeed was not especially elegant, although it was the best that the jeweller of the Province could furnish. "I shouldn't have taken it in less than two."

"It isn't the ring," said Perdita, "it's what it means!"

"It means that you're not a modest girl," cried Viola. "Pray does mamma know of your conduct? does Bernard?"

"Mamma has approved my 'conduct,' as you call it. Mr. Lloyd has asked my hand, and mamma has given it. Would you have had him apply to you, sister?"

Viola gave her sister a long look, full of passionate envy and sorrow. Then she dropped her lashes on her pale cheeks, and turned away. Perdita felt that it had not been a pretty scene; but it was her sister's fault. But the elder girl rapidly called back her pride, and turned herself about again. "You have my very best wishes," she said with a low courtesy. "I wish you every happiness, and a very long life."

Perdita gave a bitter laugh. "Don't speak in that tone," she cried. "I'd rather you cursed me outright. Come, sister," she added, "he couldn't marry both of us."

"I wish you very great joy," Viola repeated mechanically, sitting down to her glass again, "and a very long life, and plenty of children."

There was something in the sound of these words not at all to Perdita's taste. "Will you give me a year, at least?" she said. "In a year I can have one little boy,—or one little girl at least. If you'll give me your brush again, I'll do your hair."

"Thank you," said Viola. "You had better go to mamma. It isn't proper that a young lady with a promised husband should wait on a girl with none."

"Nay," said Perdita, good-humoredly, "I have Arthur to wait upon me. You need my service more than I need yours."

But her sister motioned her away, and she left the room. When she had gone, poor Viola fell on her knees before her dressing-table, buried her head in her arms, and poured out a flood of tears and sobs. She felt very much the better for this effusion of sorrow. When her sister came back, she insisted upon helping her to dress, and upon her wearing her prettiest things. She forced upon her acceptance a bit of lace of her own, and declared that now that she was to be married she should do her best to appear worthy of her lover's choice. She discharged these offices in stern silence; but, such as they were, they had to do duty as an apology and an atonement; she never made any other.

Now that Lloyd was received by the family as an accepted suitor, nothing remained but to fix the wedding-day. It was appointed for the following April, and in the interval preparations were diligently made for the marriage. Lloyd, on his side, was busy with his commercial arrangements, and with establishing a correspondence with the great mercantile house to which he had attached himself in England. He was therefore not so frequent a visitor at Mrs. Willoughby's as during the months of his diffidence and irresolution, and poor Viola had less to suffer than she had feared from the sight of the mutual endearments of the young lovers. Touching his future sister-in-law Lloyd had a perfectly clear conscience. There had not been a particle of sentiment uttered between them, and he had not the slightest suspicion that she coveted anything more than his fraternal regard. He was quite at his ease; life promised so well, both domestically and financially. The lurid clouds of revolution were as yet twenty years beneath the horizon, and that his connubial felicity should take a tragic turn it was absurd, it was blasphemous, to apprehend. Meanwhile at Mrs. Willoughby's there was a greater rustling of silks, a more rapid clicking of scissors, and flying of needles than ever. Mrs. Willoughby had determined that her daughter should carry from home the most elegant outfit that her money could buy, or that the country could furnish. All the sage women in the county were convened, and their united taste was brought to bear on Perdita's wardrobe. Viola's situation, at this moment, was assuredly not to be envied. The poor girl had an inordinate love of dress, and the very best taste in the world, as her sister perfectly well knew. Viola was tall, she was full and stately, she was made to carry stiff brocade and masses of heavy lace, such as belong to the toilet of a rich man's wife. But Viola sat aloof, with her beautiful arms folded and her head averted, while her mother and sister and the venerable women aforesaid worried and wondered over their materials, oppressed by the multitude of their resources. One day there came in a beautiful piece of white silk, brocaded with heavenly blue and silver, sent by the bridegroom himself,—it not being thought amiss in those days that the husband elect should contribute to the bride's

trousseau. Perdita was quite at loss to imagine a pattern and trimmings which should do sufficient honor to the splendor of the material.

"Blue's your color, sister, more than mine," she said with appealing eyes. "It's a pity it's not for you. You'd know what to do with it."

Viola got up from her place and looked at the great shining fabric as it lay spread over the back of a chair. Then she took it up in her hands and felt it,—lovingly, as Perdita could see,—and turned about toward the mirror with it. She let it roll down to her feet, and flung the other end over her shoulder, gathering it in about her waist with her white arm bare to the elbow. She threw back her head, and looked at her image, and a hanging tress of her auburn hair fell upon the gorgeous surface of the silk. It made a dazzling picture. The women standing about uttered a little "Ah!" of admiration. "Yes, indeed," said Viola, quietly, "blue is my color." But Perdita could see that her fancy had been stirred, and that she would now fall to work and solve all their silken riddles. And indeed she behaved very well, as Perdita, knowing her insatiable love of millinery, was quite ready to declare. Yards and yards of lovely silks and satins, of muslins, velvets, and laces, passed through her cunning hands, without a word of envy coming from her lips. Thanks to her efforts, when the wedding-day came Perdita was prepared to espouse more of the vanities of life than any fluttering young bride who had yet challenged the sacramental blessing of a New England divine.

It had been arranged that the young couple should go out and spend the first days of their wedded life at the country house of an English gentleman,—a man of rank, and a very kind friend to Lloyd. He was an unmarried man; he professed himself delighted to withdraw and leave them for a week to their billing and cooing. After the ceremony at church,—it had been performed by an English priest,—young Mrs. Lloyd hastened back to her mother's house to change her wedding gear for a riding-dress. Viola helped her to effect the change, in the little old room in which they had been fond sisters together. Perdita then hurried off to bid farewell to her mother, leaving Viola to follow. The parting was short; the horses were at the door, and Arthur impatient to start. But Viola had not followed, and Perdita hastened back to her room, opening the door abruptly. Viola, as usual, was before the glass, but in a position which caused the other to stand still, amazed. She had dressed herself in Perdita's cast-off wedding veil and wreath, and on her neck she had hung the heavy string of pearls which the young girl had received from her husband as a wedding-gift. These things had been hastily laid aside, to await their possessor's disposal on her return from the country. Bedizened in this unnatural garb, Viola stood at the mirror, plunging a long look into its depths, and reading Heaven knows what audacious visions. Perdita was shocked and pained. It was a hideous image of their old rivalry come to life again. She made a step toward her sister, as if to pull off the veil and the flowers. But catching her eyes in the glass, she stopped.

"Farewell, Viola," she said. "You might at least have waited till I had got out of the house." And she hurried away from the room.

Mr. Lloyd had purchased in Boston a house which, in the taste of those days, was considered a marvel of elegance and comfort; and here he very soon established himself with his young wife. He was thus separated by a distance of twenty miles from the residence of his mother-in-law. Twenty miles in that primitive era of roads and conveyances were as good a hundred at the present day, and Mrs. Willoughby saw but little of her daughter during the first twelvemonth of her marriage. She suffered in no small degree from her absence; and her affliction was not diminished by the fact that Viola had fallen into a spiritless and languid state, which made change of scene and of air essential to her restoration. The real cause of the young girl's dejection the reader will not be slow to suspect. Mrs. Willoughby and her gossips, however, deemed her complaint a purely physical one, and doubted not that she would obtain relief from the remedy just mentioned. Her mother accordingly proposed on her behalf a visit to certain relatives on the paternal side, established in New York, who had long complained that they were able to see so little of their New England cousins. Viola was despatched to these good people, under a suitable escort, and remained with them for several months. In the interval her brother Bernard, who had begun the practice of the law, made up his mind to take a wife. Viola came home to the wedding, apparently cured of her heartache, with honest roses and lilies in her face, and a proud smile on her lips. Arthur Lloyd came over from Boston to see his brother-in-law married, but without his wife, who was expecting shortly to be confined. It was nearly a year since Viola had seen him. She was glad—she hardly knew why—that Perdita had stayed at home. Arthur looked happy, but he was more grave and solemn than before his marriage. She thought he looked "interesting,"—for although the word in its modern sense was not then invented, we may be sure that the idea was. The truth is, he was simply preoccupied with his wife's condition. Nevertheless he by no means failed to observe Viola's beauty and splendor, and how she quite effaced the poor little bride. The allowance that Perdita had enjoyed for her dress had now been transferred to her sister, who certainly made the most of it. On the morning after the wedding, he had a lady's saddle put on the horse of the servant who had come with him from town, and went out with the young girl for a ride. It was a keen, clear morning in January; the ground was bare and hard, and the horses in good condition,—to say nothing of Viola, who was charming in her hat and plume, and her dark blue riding-coat, trimmed with fur. They rode all the morning, they lost their way, and were obliged to stop for dinner at a farm-house. The early winter dusk had fallen when they got home. Mrs. Willoughby met them with a long face. A messenger had arrived at noon from Mrs. Lloyd; she was beginning to be ill, and desired her husband's immediate return. The young man swore at the thought that he had lost several hours, and that by hard riding he might already have been with his wife. He barely consented to stop for a mouthful of supper, but mounted the messenger's horse and started off at a gallop.

He reached home at midnight. His wife had been delivered of a little girl. "Ah, why weren't you with me?" she said, as he came to her bedside.

"I was out of the house when the man came. I was with Viola," said Lloyd, innocently.

Mrs. Lloyd made a little moan, and turned about. But she continued to do very well, and for a week her improvement was uninterrupted. Finally, however, through some excess of diet or of exposure, it was checked, and the poor lady grew rapidly worse. Lloyd was in despair. It very soon became evident that the relapse was fatal. Mrs. Lloyd came to a sense of her approaching end, and declared that she was reconciled with death. On the third evening after the change took place she told her husband that she felt she would not outlast the night. She dismissed her servants, and also requested her mother to withdraw,—Mrs. Willoughby having arrived on the preceding day. She had had her infant placed on the bed beside her, and she lay on her side, with the child against her breast, holding her husband's hands. The night-lamp was hidden behind the heavy curtains of the bed, but the room was illumined with a red glow from the immense fire of logs on the hearth.

"It seems strange to die by such a fire as that," the young woman said, feebly trying to smile. "If I had but a little of such fire in my veins! But I've given it all to this little spark of mortality." And she dropped her eyes on her child. Then raising them she looked at her husband with a long penetrating gaze. The last feeling which lingered in her heart was one of mistrust. She had not recovered from the shock which Arthur had given her by telling her that in the hour of her agony he had been with Viola. She trusted her husband very nearly as well as she loved him; but now that she was called away forever, she felt a cold horror of her sister. She felt in her soul that Viola had never ceased to envy her good fortune; and a year of happy security had not effaced the young girl's image, dressed in her wedding garments, and smiling with fancied triumph. Now that Arthur was to be alone, what might not Viola do? She was beautiful, she was engaging; what arts might she not use, what impression might she not make upon the young man's melancholy heart? Mrs. Lloyd looked at her husband in silence. It seemed hard, after all, to doubt of his constancy. His fine eyes were filled with tears; his face was convulsed with weeping; the clasp of his hands was warm and passionate. How noble he looked, how tender, how faithful and devoted! "Nay," thought Perdita, "he's not for such as Viola. He'll never forget me. Nor does Viola truly care for him; she cares only for vanities and finery and jewels." And she dropped her eyes on her white hands, which her husband's liberality had covered with rings, and on the lace ruffles which trimmed the edge of her night-dress. "She covets my rings and my laces more than she covets my husband."

At this moment the thought of her sister's rapacity seemed to cast a dark shadow between her and the helpless figure of her little girl. "Arthur," she said, "you must take off my rings. I shall not be buried in them. One of these days my daughter shall wear them,—my rings and my laces and silks. I had them all brought out and shown me to-day. It's a great wardrobe,—there's not such another in the Province; I can say it without vanity now that I've done with it. It will be a great inheritance for my daughter, when she grows into a young woman. There are things there that a man never buys twice, and if they're lost you'll never again see the like. So you'll watch them well. Some dozen things I've left

to Viola; I've named them to my mother. I've given her that blue and silver; it was meant for her; I wore it only once, I looked ill in it. But the rest are to be sacredly kept for this little innocent. It's such a providence that she should be my color; she can wear my gowns; she has her mother's eyes. You know the same fashions come back every twenty years. She can wear my gowns as they are. They'll lie there quietly waiting till she grows into them, —wrapped in camphor and rose-leaves, and keeping their colors in the sweet-scented darkness. She shall have black hair, she shall wear my carnation satin. Do you promise me, Arthur?"

"Promise you what, dearest?"

"Promise me to keep your poor little wife's old gowns."

"Are you afraid I'll sell them?"

"No, but that they may get scattered. My mother will have them properly wrapped up, and you shall lay them away under a double-lock. Do you know the great chest in the attic, with the iron bands? There's no end to what it will hold. You can lay them all there. My mother and the housekeeper will do it, and give you the key. And you'll keep the key in your secretary, and never give it to any one but your child. Do you promise me?"

"Ah, yes; I promise you," said Lloyd, puzzled at the intensity with which his wife appeared to cling to this idea.

"Will you swear?" repeated Perdita.

"Yes, I swear."

"Well—I trust you—I trust you," said the poor lady, looking into his eyes with eyes in which, if he had suspected her vague apprehensions, he might have read an appeal quite as much as an assurance.

Lloyd bore his bereavement soberly and manfully. A month after his wife's death, in the course of commerce, circumstances arose which offered him an opportunity of going to England. He embraced it as an alleviation to his sadness. He was absent nearly a year; during which his little girl was tenderly nursed and cherished by her grandmother. On his return he had his house again thrown open, and announced his intention of keeping the same state as during his wife's lifetime. It very soon came to be predicted that he would marry again, and there were at least a dozen young women of whom one may say that it was by no fault of theirs that, for six months after his return, the prediction did not come true. During this interval he still left his little daughter in Mrs. Willoughby's hands, the latter assuring him that a change of residence at so tender an age was perilous to her health. Finally, however, he declared that his heart longed for the little creature's presence, and that she must be brought up to town. He sent his coach and his housekeeper to fetch her home. Mrs. Willoughby was in terror lest something should befall her on the road; and, in accordance with this feeling, Viola offered to ride along with her. She could return the next day. So she went up to town with her little niece, and Mr. Lloyd met her on the threshold of his house, overcome with her kindness and with gratitude. Instead of returning the next day, Viola stayed out the week; and when at last she reappeared, she had only come for her clothes. Arthur would not hear of her coming home, nor would the baby. She cried and moaned if Viola left her; and at the sight of her grief Arthur lost his wits, and swore that she was going to die. In fine, nothing would suit them but that Viola should remain until the little thing had grown used to strange faces.

It took two months for this consummation to be brought about; for it was not until this period had elapsed that Viola took leave of her brother-in-law. Mrs. Willoughby had fretted and fumed over her daughter's absence; she had declared that it was not becoming, and that it was the talk of the town. She had reconciled herself to it only because, during the young girl's visit, the household enjoyed an unwonted term of peace. Bernard Willoughby had brought his wife home to live, between whom and her sister-in-law there existed a bitter hostility. Viola was perhaps no angel; but in the daily practice of life she was a sufficiently good-natured girl, and if she quarrelled with Mrs. Bernard, it was not without provocation. Quarrel, however, she did, to the great annoyance not only of her antagonist, but of the two spectators of these constant altercations. Her stay in the household of her brother-in-law, therefore, would have been delightful, if only because it removed her from contact with the object of her antipathy at home. It was doubly—it was ten times—delightful, inasmuch as it kept her near the object of her old passion. Mrs. Lloyd's conjectures had fallen very far short of the truth touching Viola's feeling for her husband. It had been a passion at first, and a passion it remained,—a passion of whose radiant heat, tempered to the delicate state of his feelings, Mr. Lloyd very soon felt the influence. Lloyd, as I have said, was no paragon; it was not in his nature to practise an ideal constancy. He had not been many days in the house with his sister-in-law before he began to assure himself

that she was, in the language of that day, a devilish fine woman. Whether Viola really practised those insidious arts that her sister had been tempted to impute to her it is needless to inquire. It is enough to say that she found means to appear to the very best advantage. She used to seat herself every morning before the great fireplace in the dining-room, at work upon a piece of tapestry, with her little niece disporting herself on the carpet at her feet, or on the train of her dress, and playing with her woollen balls. Lloyd would have been a very stupid fellow if he had remained insensible to the rich suggestions of this charming picture. He was prodigiously fond of his little girl, and was never weary of taking her in his arms and tossing her up and down, and making her crow with delight. Very often, however, he would venture upon greater liberties than the little creature was yet prepared to allow, and she would suddenly vociferate her displeasure. Viola would then drop her tapestry, and put out her handsome hands with the serious smile of the young girl whose virgin fancy has revealed to her all a mother's healing arts. Lloyd would give up the child, their eyes would meet, their hands would touch, and Viola would extinguish the little girl's sobs upon the snowy folds of the kerchief that crossed her bosom. Her dignity was perfect, and nothing could be less obtrusive than the manner in which she accepted her brother-in-law's hospitality. It may be almost said, perhaps, that there was something harsh in her reserve. Lloyd had a provoking feeling that she was in the house, and yet that she was unapproachable. Half an hour after supper, at the very outset of the long winter evenings, she would light her candle, and make the young man a most respectful courtesy, and march off to bed. If these were arts, Viola was a great artist. But their effect was so gentle, so gradual, they were calculated to work upon the young widower's fancy with such a finely shaded *crescendo*, that, as the reader has seen, several weeks elapsed before Viola began to feel sure that her return would cover her outlay. When this became morally certain, she packed up her trunk, and returned to her mother's house. For three days she waited; on the fourth Mr. Lloyd made his appearance, a respectful but ardent suitor. Viola heard him out with great humility, and accepted him with infinite modesty. It is hard to imagine that Mrs. Lloyd should have forgiven her husband; but if anything might have disarmed her resentment, it would have been the ceremonious continence of this interview. Viola imposed upon her lover but a short probation. They were married, as was becoming, with great privacy,—almost with secrecy,—in the hope perhaps, as was waggishly remarked at the time, that the late Mrs. Lloyd wouldn't hear of it.

The marriage was to all appearance a happy one, and each party obtained what each had desired,—Lloyd "a devilish fine woman," and Viola—but Viola's desires, as the reader will have observed, have remained a good deal of a mystery. There were, indeed, two blots upon their felicity; but time would perhaps, efface them. During the three first years of her marriage Mrs. Lloyd failed to become a mother, and her husband on his side suffered heavy losses of money. This latter circumstance compelled a material retrenchment in his expenditure, and Viola was perforce less of a great lady than her sister had been. She contrived, however, to sustain with unbroken consistency the part of an elegant woman, although it must be confessed that it required the exercise of more ingenuity than belongs to your real aristocratic repose. She had long since ascertained that her sister's immense wardrobe had been sequestrated for the benefit of her daughter, and that it lay languishing in thankless gloom in the dusty attic. It was a revolting thought that these glorious fabrics should wait on the bidding of a little girl who sat in a high chair, and ate bread-and-milk with a wooden spoon. Viola had the good taste, however, to say nothing about the matter until several months had expired. Then, at last, she timidly broached it to her husband. Was it not a pity that so much finery should be lost?—for lost it would be, what with colors fading, and moths eating it up, and the change of fashions. But Lloyd gave so abrupt and peremptory a negative to her inquiry, that she saw that for the present her attempt was vain. Six months went by, however, and brought with them new needs and new fancies. Viola's thoughts hovered lovingly about her sister's relics. She went up and looked at the chest in which they lay imprisoned. There was a sullen defiance in its three great padlocks and its iron bands, which only quickened her desires. There was something exasperating in its incorruptible immobility. It was like a grim and grizzled old household servant, who locks his jaws over a family secret. And then there was a look of capacity in its vast extent, and a sound as of dense fulness, when Viola knocked its side with the toe of her little slipper, which caused her to flush with baffled longing. "It's absurd," she cried; "it's improper, it's wicked,"

and she forthwith resolved upon another attack upon her husband. On the following day, after dinner, when he had had his wine, she bravely began it. But he cut her short with great sternness.

"Once for all, Viola," said he, "it's out of the question. I shall be gravely displeased if you return to the matter."

"Very good," said Viola. "I'm glad to learn the value at which I'm held. Great Heaven!" she cried, "I'm a happy woman. It's a delightful thing to feel one's self sacrificed to a caprice!" And her eyes filled with tears of anger and disappointment.

Lloyd had a good-natured man's horror of a woman's sobs, and he attempted—I may say he condescended—to explain. "It's not a caprice, dear, it's a promise," he said,—"an oath."

"An oath? It's a pretty matter for oaths! and to whom, pray?"

"To Perdita," said the young man, raising his eyes for an instant, but immediately dropping them.

"Perdita,—ah, Perdita!" and Viola's tears broke forth. Her bosom heaved with stormy sobs,—sobs which were the long-deferred counterpart of the violent fit of weeping in which she had indulged herself on the night when she discovered her sister's betrothal. She had hoped, in her better moments, that she had done with her jealousy; but here it raged again as fierce as ever. "And pray what right," she cried, "had Perdita to dispose of my future? What right had she to bind you to meanness and cruelty? Ah, I occupy a dignified place, and I make a very fine figure! I'm welcome to what Perdita has left! And what has she left? I never knew till now how little! Nothing, nothing, nothing!"

This was very poor logic, but it was very good passion. Lloyd put his arm around his wife's waist and tried to kiss her, but she shook him off with magnificent scorn. Poor fellow! he had coveted a "devilish fine woman," and he had got one. Her scorn was intolerable. He walked away with his ears tingling,—irresolute, distracted. Before him was his secretary, and in it the sacred key which with his own hand he had turned in the triple lock. He marched up and opened it, and took the key from a secret drawer, wrapped in a little packet which he had sealed with his own honest bit of blazonry. *Teneo*, said the motto,—"I hold." But he was ashamed to put it back. He flung it upon the table beside his wife.

"Keep it!" she cried. "I want it not. I hate it!"

"I wash my hands of it," cried her husband. "God forgive me!"

Mrs. Lloyd gave an indignant shrug of her shoulders, and swept out of the room, while the young man retreated by another door. Ten minutes later Mrs. Lloyd returned, and found the room occupied by her little step-daughter and the nursery-maid. The key was not on the table. She glanced at the child. The child was perched on a chair with the packet in her hands. She had broken the seal with her own little fingers. Mrs. Lloyd hastily took possession of the key.

At the habitual supper-hour Arthur Lloyd came back from his counting-room. It was the month of June, and supper was served by daylight. The meal was placed on the table, but Mrs. Lloyd failed to make her appearance. The servant whom his master sent to call her came back with the assurance that her room was empty, and that the women informed him that she had not been seen since dinner. They had in truth observed her to have been in tears, and, supposing her to be shut up in her chamber, had not disturbed her. Her husband called her name in various parts of the house, but without response. At last it occurred to him that he might find her by taking the way to the attic. The thought gave him a strange feeling of discomfort, and he bade his servants remain behind, wishing no witness in his quest. He reached the foot of the staircase leading to the topmost flat, and stood with his hand on the banisters, pronouncing his wife's name. His voice trembled. He called again, louder and more firmly. The only sound which disturbed the absolute silence was a faint echo of his own voice, repeating his question under the great eaves. He nevertheless felt irresistibly moved to ascend the staircase. It opened upon a wide hall, lined with wooden closets, and terminating in a window which looked westward, and admitted the last rays of the sun. Before the window stood the great chest. Before the chest, on her knees, the young man saw with amazement and horror the figure of his wife. In an instant he crossed the interval between them, bereft of utterance. The lid of the chest stood open, exposing, amid their perfumed napkins, its treasure of stuffs and jewels. Viola had fallen backward from a kneeling posture, with one hand supporting her on the floor and the other pressed to her heart. On her limbs was the stiffness of death, and on her face, in the fading light of the sun, the terror of something more than death. Her lips were parted in entreaty, in dismay, in agony; and on her bloodless brow and cheeks there glowed the marks of ten hideous wounds from two vengeful ghostly hands.

FRANCIS BRET HARTE (1836-1902)

THE LUCK OF ROARING CAMP

(1868)

There was commotion in Roaring Camp. It could not have been a fight, for in 1850 that was not novel enough to have called together the entire settlement. The ditches and claims were not only deserted, but "Tuttle's grocery" had contributed its gamblers, who, it will be remembered, calmly continued their game the day that French Pete and Kanaka Joe shot each other to death over the bar in the front room. The whole camp was collected before a rude cabin on the outer edge of the clearing. Conversation was carried on in a low tone, but the name of a woman was frequently repeated. It was a name familiar enough in the camp,— "Cherokee Sal."

Perhaps the less said of her the better. She was a coarse and, it is to be feared, a very sinful woman. But at that time she was the only woman in Roaring Camp, and was just then lying in sore extremity, when she most needed the ministration of her own sex. Dissolute, abandoned, and irreclaimable, she was yet suffering a martyrdom hard enough to bear even when veiled by sympathizing womanhood, but now terrible in her loneliness. The primal curse had come to her in that original isolation which must have made the punishment of the first transgression so dreadful. It was, perhaps, part of the expiation of her sin that, at a moment when she most lacked her sex's intuitive tenderness and care, she met only the half-contemptuous faces of her masculine associates. Yet a few of the spectators were, I think, touched by her sufferings. Sandy Tipton thought it was "rough on Sal," and, in the contemplation of her condition, for a moment rose superior to the fact that he had an ace and two bowers in his sleeve.

It will be seen also that the situation was novel. Deaths were by no means uncommon in Roaring Camp, but a birth was a new thing. People had been dismissed the camp effectively, finally, and with no possibility of return; but this was the first time that anybody had been introduced *ab initio*. Hence the excitement.

"You go in there, Stumpy," said a prominent citizen known as "Kentuck," addressing one of the loungers. "Go in there, and see what you kin do. You've had experience in them things."

Perhaps there was a fitness in the selection. Stumpy, in other climes, had been the putative head of two families; in fact, it was owing to some legal informality in these proceedings that Roaring Camp—a city of refuge—was indebted to his company. The crowd approved the choice, and Stumpy was wise enough to bow to the majority. The door closed on the extempore surgeon and midwife, and Roaring Camp sat down outside, smoked its pipe, and awaited the issue.

The assemblage numbered about a hundred men. One or two of these were actual fugitives from justice, some were criminal, and all were reckless. Physically they exhibited no indication of their past lives and character. The greatest scamp had a Raphael face, with a profusion of blonde hair; Oakhurst, a gambler, had the melancholy air and intellectual abstraction of a Hamlet; the coolest and most courageous man was scarcely over five feet in height, with a soft voice and an embarrassed, timid manner. The term "roughs" applied to them was a distinction rather than a definition. Perhaps in the minor details of fingers, toes, ears, etc., the camp may have been deficient, but these slight omissions did not detract from their aggregate force. The strongest man had but three fingers on his right hand; the best shot had but one eye.

Such was the physical aspect of the men that were dispersed around the cabin. The camp lay in a triangular valley between two hills and a river. The only outlet was a steep trail over the summit of a hill that faced the cabin, now illuminated by the rising moon. The suffering woman might have seen it from the rude bunk whereon she lay,—seen it winding like a silver thread until it was lost in the stars above.

A fire of withered pine boughs added sociability to the gathering. By degrees the natural levity of Roaring Camp returned. Bets were freely offered and taken regarding the result. Three to five that "Sal would get through with it;" even that the child would survive; side bets as to the sex and complexion

of the coming stranger. In the midst of an excited discussion an exclamation came from those nearest the door, and the camp stopped to listen. Above the swaying and moaning of the pines, the swift rush of the river, and the crackling of the fire rose a sharp, querulous cry,—a cry unlike anything heard before in the camp. The pines stopped moaning, the river ceased to rush, and the fire to crackle. It seemed as if Nature had stopped to listen too.

The camp rose to its feet as one man! It was proposed to explode a barrel of gunpowder; but in consideration of the situation of the mother, better counsels prevailed, and only a few revolvers were discharged; for whether owing to the rude surgery of the camp, or some other reason, Cherokee Sal was sinking fast. Within an hour she had climbed, as it were, that rugged road that led to the stars, and so passed out of Roaring Camp, its sin and shame, forever. I do not think that the announcement disturbed them much, except in speculation as to the fate of the child. "Can he live now?" was asked of Stumpy. The answer was doubtful. The only other being of Cherokee Sal's sex and maternal condition in the settlement was an ass. There was some conjecture as to fitness, but the experiment was tried. It was less problematical than the ancient treatment of Romulus and Remus, and apparently as successful.

When these details were completed, which exhausted another hour, the door was opened, and the anxious crowd of men, who had already formed themselves into a queue, entered in single file. Beside the low bunk or shelf, on which the figure of the mother was starkly outlined below the blankets, stood a pine table. On this a candle-box was placed, and within it, swathed in staring red flannel, lay the last arrival at Roaring Camp. Beside the candle-box was placed a hat. Its use was soon indicated. "Gentlemen," said Stumpy, with a singular mixture of authority and *ex officio* complacency,—"gentlemen will please pass in at the front door, round the table, and out at the back door. Them as wishes to contribute anything toward the orphan will find a hat handy." The first man entered with his hat on; he uncovered, however, as he looked about him, and so unconsciously set an example to the next. In such communities good and bad actions are catching. As the procession filed in comments were audible,—criticisms addressed perhaps rather to Stumpy in the character of showman: "Is that him?" "Mighty small specimen;" "Hasn't more'n got the color;" "Ain't bigger nor a derringer." The contributions were as characteristic: A silver tobacco box; a doubloon; a navy revolver, silver mounted; a gold specimen; a very beautifully embroidered lady's handkerchief (from Oakhurst the gambler); a diamond breastpin; a diamond ring (suggested by the pin, with the remark from the giver that he "saw that pin and went two diamonds better"); a slungshot; a Bible (contributor not detected); a golden spur; a silver teaspoon (the initials, I regret to say, were not the giver's); a pair of surgeon's shears; a lancet; a Bank of England note for £5; and about $200 in loose gold and silver coin. During these proceedings Stumpy maintained a silence as impassive as the dead on his left, a gravity as inscrutable as that of the newly born on his right. Only one incident occurred to break the monotony of the curious procession. As Kentuck bent over the candle-box half curiously, the child turned, and, in a spasm of pain, caught at his groping finger, and held it fast for a moment. Kentuck looked foolish and embarrassed. Something like a blush tried to assert itself in his weather-beaten cheek. "The d—d little cuss!" he said, as he extricated his finger, with perhaps more tenderness and care than he might have been deemed capable of showing. He held that finger a little apart from its fellows as he went out, and examined it curiously. The examination provoked the same original remark in regard to the child. In fact, he seemed to enjoy repeating it. "He rastled with my finger," he remarked to Tipton, holding up the member, "the d—d little cuss!"

It was four o'clock before the camp sought repose. A light burnt in the cabin where the watchers sat, for Stumpy did not go to bed that night. Nor did Kentuck. He drank quite freely, and related with great gusto his experience, invariably ending with his characteristic condemnation of the newcomer. It seemed to relieve him of any unjust implication of sentiment, and Kentuck had the weakness of the nobler sex. When everybody else had gone to bed, he walked down to the river and whistled reflectively. Then he walked up the gulch past the cabin, still whistling with demonstrative unconcern. At a large redwood-tree he paused and retraced his steps, and again passed the cabin. Halfway down to the river's bank he again paused, and then returned and knocked at the door. It was opened by Stumpy. "How goes it?" said Kentuck, looking past Stumpy toward the candle-box. "All serene!" replied Stumpy. "Anything up?" "Nothing." There was a pause—an embarrassing one—Stumpy still holding the door. Then Kentuck had re-

course to his finger, which he held up to Stumpy. "Rastled with it,—the d—d little cuss," he said, and retired.

The next day Cherokee Sal had such rude sepulture as Roaring Camp afforded. After her body had been committed to the hillside, there was a formal meeting of the camp to discuss what should be done with her infant. A resolution to adopt it was unanimous and enthusiastic. But an animated discussion in regard to the manner and feasibility of providing for its wants at once sprang up. It was remarkable that the argument partook of none of those fierce personalities with which discussions were usually conducted at Roaring Camp. Tipton proposed that they should send the child to Red Dog,—a distance of forty miles, —where female attention could be procured. But the unlucky suggestion met with fierce and unanimous opposition. It was evident that no plan which entailed parting from their new acquisition would for a moment be entertained. "Besides," said Tom Ryder, "them fellows at Red Dog would swap it, and ring in somebody else on us." A disbelief in the honesty of other camps prevailed at Roaring Camp, as in other places.

The introduction of a female nurse in the camp also met with objection. It was argued that no decent woman could be prevailed to accept Roaring Camp as her home, and the speaker urged that "they didn't want any more of the other kind." This unkind allusion to the defunct mother, harsh as it may seem, was the first spasm of propriety,—the first symptom of the camp's regeneration. Stumpy advanced nothing. Perhaps he felt a certain delicacy in interfering with the selection of a possible successor in office. But when questioned, he averred stoutly that he and "Jinny" —the mammal before alluded to—could manage to rear the child. There was something original, independent, and heroic about the plan that pleased the camp. Stumpy was retained. Certain articles were sent for to Sacramento. "Mind," said the treasurer, as he pressed a bag of gold-dust into the express-man's hand, "the best that can be got,—lace, you know, and filigree-work and frills,—d—n the cost!"

Strange to say, the child thrived. Perhaps the invigorating climate of the mountain camp was compensation for material deficiencies. Nature took the foundling to her broader breast. In that rare atmosphere of the Sierra foothills,—that air pungent with balsamic odor, that ethereal cordial at once bracing and exhilarating,—he may have found food and nourishment, or a subtle chemistry that transmuted ass's milk to lime and phosphorus. Stumpy inclined to the belief that it was the latter and good nursing. "Me and that ass," he would say, "has been father and mother to him! Don't you," he would add, apostrophizing the helpless bundle before him, "never go back on us."

By the time he was a month old the necessity of giving him a name became apparent. He had generally been known as "The Kid," "Stumpy's Boy," "The Coyote" (an allusion to his vocal powers), and even by Kentuck's endearing diminutive of "The d—d little cuss." But these were felt to be vague and unsatisfactory, and were at last dismissed under another influence. Gamblers and adventurers are generally superstitious, and Oakhurst one day declared that the baby had brought "the luck" to Roaring Camp. It was certain that of late they had been successful. "Luck" was the name agreed upon, with the prefix of Tommy for greater convenience. No allusion was made to the mother, and the father was unknown. "It's better," said the philosophical Oakhurst, "to take a fresh deal all round. Call him Luck, and start him fair." A day was accordingly set apart for the christening. What was meant by this ceremony the reader may imagine who has already gathered some idea of the reckless irreverence of Roaring Camp. The master of ceremonies was one "Boston," a noted wag, and the occasion seemed to promise the greatest facetiousness. This ingenious satirist had spent two days in preparing a burlesque of the Church service, with pointed local allusions. The choir was properly trained, and Sandy Tipton was to stand godfather. But after the procession had marched to the grove with music and banners, and the child had been deposited before a mock altar, Stumpy stepped before the expectant crowd. "It ain't my style to spoil fun, boys," said the little man, stoutly eyeing the faces around him, "but it strikes me that this thing ain't exactly on the squar. It's playing it pretty low down on this yer baby to ring in fun on him that he ain't goin' to understand. And ef there's goin' to be any godfathers round, I'd like to see who's got any better rights than me." A silence followed Stumpy's speech. To the credit of all humorists be it said that the first man to acknowledge its justice was the satirist thus stopped of his fun. "But," said Stumpy, quickly following up his advantage, "we're here for a christening, and we'll have it. I proclaim you Thomas Luck, according to the laws of the United States and the State of California, so help me God." It was the first time that the name of the Deity had been otherwise uttered than profanely in the camp. The form of christening was perhaps even more ludicrous than the satirist had conceived; but strangely enough, nobody saw it and nobody laughed. "Tommy" was christened as seriously as he would have been under a Christian roof, and cried and was comforted in as orthodox fashion.

And so the work of regeneration began in Roaring Camp. Almost imperceptibly a change came over the settlement. The cabin assigned to "Tommy Luck"—or "The Luck," as he was more frequently called—first showed signs of improvement. It was kept scrupulously clean and whitewashed. Then it was boarded, clothed, and papered. The rosewood cradle, packed eighty miles by mule, had in Stumpy's way of putting it, "sorter killed the rest of the furniture." So the rehabilitation of the cabin became a necessity. The men who were in the habit of lounging in at Stumpy's to see "how 'The Luck' got on" seemed to appreciate the change, and in self-defense the rival establishment of "Tuttle's grocery" bestirred itself and imported a carpet and mirrors. The reflections of the latter on the appearance of Roaring Camp tended to produce stricter habits of personal cleanliness. Again Stumpy imposed a kind of quarantine upon those who aspired to the honor and privilege of holding The Luck. It was a cruel mortification to Kentuck—who, in the carelessness of a large nature and the habits of frontier life, had begun to regard all garments as a second cuticle, which, like a snake's, only sloughed off through decay—to be debarred this privilege from certain prudential reasons. Yet such was the subtle influence of innovation that he thereafter appeared regularly every afternoon in a clean shirt and face still shining from his ablutions. Nor were moral and social sanitary laws neglected. "Tommy," who was supposed to spend his whole existence in a persistent attempt to repose, must not be disturbed by noise. The shouting and yelling, which had gained the camp its infelicitous title, were not permitted within hearing distance of Stumpy's. The men conversed in whispers or smoked with Indian gravity. Profanity was tacitly given up in these sacred precincts, and throughout the camp a popular form of expletive, known as "D—n the luck!" and "Curse the luck!" was abandoned, as having a new personal bearing. Vocal music was not interdicted, being supposed to have a soothing, tranquilizing quality; and one song, sung by "Man-o'-War

Jack," an English sailor from her Majesty's Australian colonies, was quite popular as a lullaby. It was a lugubrious recital of the exploits of "the Arethusa, Seventy-four," in a muffled minor, ending with a prolonged dying fall at the burden of each verse, "On b-oo-o-ard of the Arethusa." It was a fine sight to see Jack holding The Luck, rocking from side to side as if with the motion of a ship, and crooning forth this naval ditty. Either through the peculiar rocking of Jack or the length of his song,—it contained ninety stanzas, and was continued with conscientious deliberation to the bitter end,—the lullaby generally had the desired effect. At such times the men would lie at full length under the trees in the soft summer twilight, smoking their pipes and drinking in the melodious utterances. An indistinct idea that this was pastoral happiness pervaded the camp. "This 'ere kind o' think," said the Cockney Simmons, meditatively reclining on his elbow, "is 'evingly." It reminded him of Greenwich.

On the long summer days The Luck was usually carried to the gulch from whence the golden store of Roaring Camp was taken. There, on a blanket spread over pine boughs, he would lie while the men were working in the ditches below. Latterly there was a rude attempt to decorate this bower with flowers and sweet-smelling shrubs, and generally some one would bring him a cluster of wild honeysuckles, azaleas, or the painted blossoms of Las Mariposas. The men had suddenly awakened to the fact that there were beauty and significance in these trifles, which they had so long trodden carelessly beneath their feet. A flake of glittering mica, a fragment of variegated quartz, a bright pebble from the bed of the creek, became beautiful to eyes thus cleared and strengthened, and were invariably put aside for The Luck. It was wonderful how many treasures the woods and hillsides yielded that "would do for Tommy." Surrounded by playthings such as never child out of fairy-land had before, it is to be hoped that Tommy was content. He appeared to be serenely happy, albeit there was an infantine gravity about him, a contemplative light in his round gray eyes, that sometimes worried Stumpy. He was always tractable and quiet, and it is recorded that once, having crept beyond his "corral,"— a hedge of tessellated pine boughs, which surrounded his bed,—he dropped over the bank on his head in the soft earth, and remained with his mottled legs in the air in that position for at least five minutes with unflinching gravity. He was extricated without a murmur. I hesitate to record the many other instances of his sagacity, which rest, unfortunately, upon the statements of prejudiced friends. Some of them were not without a tinge of superstition. "I crep' up the bank just now," said Kentuck one day, in a breathless state of excitement, "and dern my skin if he wasn't a-talking to a jaybird as was a-sittin' on his lap. There they was, just as free and sociable as anything you please, a-jawin' at each other just like two cherrybums." Howbeit, whether creeping over the pine boughs or lying lazily on his back blinking at the leaves above him, to him the birds sang, the squirrels chattered, and the flowers bloomed. Nature was his nurse and playfellow. For him she would let slip between the leaves golden shafts of sunlight that fell just within his grasp; she would send wandering breezes to visit him with the balm of bay and resinous gum; to him the tall redwoods nodded familiarly and sleepily, the bumble-bees buzzed, and the rooks cawed a slumbrous accompaniment.

Such was the golden summer of Roaring Camp. They were "flush times," and the luck was with them. The claims had yielded enormously. The camp was jealous of its privileges and looked suspiciously on strangers. No encouragement was given to immigration, and, to make their seclusion more perfect, the land on either side of the mountain wall that surrounded the camp they duly preëmpted. This, and a reputation for singular proficiency with the revolver, kept the reserve of Roaring Camp inviolate. The expressman—their only connecting link with the surrounding world—sometimes told wonderful stories of the camp. He would say, "They've a street up there in 'Roaring' that would lay over any street in Red Dog. They've got vines and flowers round their houses, and they wash themselves twice a day. But they're mighty rough on strangers, and they worship an Ingin baby."

With the prosperity of the camp came a desire for further improvement. It was proposed to build a hotel in the following spring, and to invite one or two decent families to reside there for the sake of The Luck, who might perhaps profit by female companionship. The sacrifice that this concession to the sex cost these men, who were fiercely skeptical in regard to its general virtue and usefulness, can only be accounted for by their affection for Tommy. A few still held out. But the resolve could not be carried into effect for three months, and the minority meekly yielded in the hope that something might turn up to prevent it. And it did.

The winter of 1851 will long be remembered in the foothills. The snow lay deep on the Sierras, and every mountain creek became a river, and every river a lake. Each gorge and gulch was transformed into a tumultuous watercourse that descended the hillsides, tearing down giant trees and scattering its drift and débris along the plain. Red Dog had been twice under water, and Roaring Camp had been forewarned. "Water put the gold into them gulches," said Stumpy. "It's been here once and will be here again!" And that night the North Fork suddenly leaped over its banks and swept up the triangular valley of Roaring Camp.

In the confusion of rushing water, crashing trees, and crackling timber, and the darkness which seemed to flow with the water and blot out the fair valley, but little could be done to collect the scattered camp. When the morning broke, the cabin of Stumpy, nearest the riverbank, was gone. Higher up the gulch they found the body of its unlucky owner; but the pride, the hope, the joy, The Luck, of Roaring Camp had disappeared. They were returning with sad hearts when a shout from the bank recalled them.

It was a relief-boat from down the river. They had picked up, they said, a man and an infant, nearly exhausted, about two miles below. Did anybody know them, and did they belong here?

It needed but a glance to show them Kentuck lying there, cruelly crushed and bruised, but still holding The Luck of Roaring Camp in his arms. As they bent over the strangely assorted pair, they saw that the child was cold and pulseless. "He is dead," said one. Kentuck opened his eyes. "Dead?" he repeated feebly. "Yes, my man, and you are dying too." A smile lit the eyes of the expiring Kentuck. "Dying!" he repeated; "he's a-taking me with him. Tell the boys I've got The Luck with me now;" and the strong man, clinging to the frail babe as a drowning man is said to cling to a straw, drifted away into the shadowy river that flows forever to the unknown sea.

THE OUTCASTS OF POKER FLAT

(1869)

As Mr. John Oakhurst, gambler, stepped into the main street of Poker Flat on the morning of the 23d of November, 1850, he was conscious of a change in its moral atmosphere since the preceding night. Two or three men, conversing earnestly together, ceased as he approached, and exchanged significant glances. There was a Sabbath lull in the air, which, in a settlement unused to Sabbath influences, looked ominous.

Mr. Oakhurst's calm, handsome face betrayed small concern in these indications. Whether he was conscious of any predisposing cause was another question. "I reckon they're after somebody," he reflected; "likely it's me." He returned to his pocket the handkerchief with which he had been whipping away the red dust of Poker Flat from his neat boots, and quietly discharged his mind of any further conjecture.

In point of fact, Poker Flat was "after somebody." It had lately suffered the loss of several thousand dollars, two valuable horses, and a prominent citizen. It was experiencing a spasm of virtuous reaction, quite as lawless and ungovernable as any of the acts that had provoked it. A secret committee had determined to rid the town of all improper persons. This was done permanently in regard of two men who were then hanging from the boughs of a sycamore in the gulch, and temporarily in the banishment of certain other objectionable characters. I regret to say that some of these were ladies. It is but due to the sex, however, to state that their impropriety was professional, and it was only in such easily established standards of evil that Poker Flat ventured to sit in judgment.

Mr. Oakhurst was right in supposing that he was included in this category. A few of the committee had urged hanging him as a possible example and a sure method of reimbursing themselves from his pockets of the sums he had won from them. "It's agin justice," said Jim Wheeler, "to let this yer young man from Roaring Camp—an entire stranger—carry away our money." But a crude sentiment of equity residing in the breasts of those who had been fortunate enough to win from Mr. Oakhurst overruled this narrower local prejudice.

Mr. Oakhurst received his sentence with philosophic calmness, none the less coolly that he was aware of the hesitation of his judges. He was too much of a gambler not to accept fate. With him life was at best an uncertain game, and he recognized the usual percentage in favor of the dealer.

A body of armed men accompanied the deported wickedness of Poker Flat to the outskirts of the settlement. Besides Mr. Oakhurst, who was known to be a coolly desperate man, and for whose intimidation the armed escort was intended, the expatriated party consisted of a young woman familiarly known as "The Duchess;" another who had won the title of "Mother Shipton;" and "Uncle Billy," a suspected sluice-robber and confirmed drunkard. The cavalcade provoked no comments from the spectators, nor was any word uttered by the escort. Only when the gulch which marked the uttermost limit of Poker Flat was reached, the leader spoke briefly and to the point. The exiles were forbidden to return at the peril of their lives.

As the escort disappeared, their pent-up feelings found vent in a few hysterical tears from the Duchess, some bad language from Mother Shipton, and a Parthian volley of expletives from Uncle Billy. The philosophic Oakhurst alone remained silent. He listened calmly to Mother Shipton's desire to cut somebody's heart out, to the repeated statements of the Duchess that she would die in the road, and to the alarming oaths that seemed to be bumped out of Uncle Billy as he rode forward. With the easy good humor characteristic of his class, he insisted upon exchanging his own riding-horse, "Five-Spot," for the sorry mule which the Duchess rode. But even this act did not draw the party into any closer sympathy. The young woman readjusted her somewhat draggled plumes with a feeble, faded coquetry; Mother Shipton eyed the possessor of "Five-Spot" with malevolence, and Uncle Billy included the whole party in one sweeping anathema.

The road to Sandy Bar—a camp that, not having as yet experienced the regenerating influences of Poker Flat, consequently seemed to offer some invitation to the emigrants—lay over a steep mountain range. It was distant a day's severe travel. In that advanced season the party soon passed out of the moist, temperate regions of the foothills into the dry, cold, bracing air of the Sierras. The trail was narrow and difficult. At noon the Duchess, rolling out of her saddle upon the ground, declared her intention of going no farther, and the party halted.

The spot was singularly wild and impressive. A wooded amphitheatre, surrounded on three sides by precipitous cliffs of naked granite, sloped gently toward the crest of another precipice that overlooked the valley. It was, undoubtedly, the most suitable spot for a camp, had camping been advisable. But Mr. Oakhurst knew that scarcely half the journey to Sandy Bar was accomplished, and the party were not equipped or provisioned for delay. This fact he pointed out to his companions curtly, with a philosophic commentary on the folly of "throwing up their hand before the game was played out." But they were furnished with liquor, which in this emergency stood them in place of food, fuel, rest, and prescience. In spite of his remonstrances, it was not long before they were more or less under its influence. Uncle Billy passed rapidly from a bellicose state into one of stupor, the Duchess became maudlin, and Mother Shipton snored. Mr. Oakhurst alone remained erect, leaning against a rock, calmly surveying them.

Mr. Oakhurst did not drink. It interfered with a profession which required coolness, impassiveness, and presence of mind, and, in his own language, he "couldn't afford it." As he gazed at his recumbent fellow exiles, the loneliness begotten of his pariah trade, his habits of life, his very vices, for the first time seriously oppressed him. He bestirred himself in dusting his black clothes, washing his hands and face, and other acts characteristic of his studiously neat habits, and for a moment forgot his annoyance. The thought of deserting his weaker and more pitiable companions never perhaps occurred to him. Yet he could not help feeling the want of that excitement which, singularly enough, was most conducive to that calm equanimity for which he was notorious. He looked at the gloomy walls that rose a thousand feet sheer above the circling pines around him, at the sky ominously clouded, at the valley below, already deepening into shadow; and, doing so, suddenly he heard his own name called.

A horseman slowly ascended the trail. In the fresh, open face of the newcomer Mr. Oakhurst recognized Tom Simson, otherwise known as "The Innocent," of Sandy Bar. He had met him some months before over a "little game," and had, with perfect equanimity, won the entire fortune—amounting to some forty dollars—of that guileless youth. After the game was finished, Mr. Oakhurst drew the youthful speculator behind the door and thus addressed him: "Tommy, you're a good little man, but you can't gamble worth a cent. Don't try it over again." He then handed him his money back, pushed him gently from the room, and so made a devoted slave of Tom Simson.

There was a remembrance of this in his boyish and enthusiastic greeting of Mr. Oakhurst. He had started, he said, to go to Poker Flat to seek his fortune. "Alone?" No, not exactly alone; in fact (a giggle), he had run away with Piney Woods. Didn't Mr. Oakhurst remember Piney? She that used to wait on the table at the Temperance House? They had been engaged a long time, but old Jake Woods had objected, and so they had run away, and were going to Poker Flat to be married, and here they were. And they were tired out, and how lucky it was they had found a place to camp, and company. All this the Innocent delivered rapidly, while Piney, a stout, comely damsel of fifteen, emerged from behind the pine-tree, where she had been blushing unseen, and rode to the side of her lover.

Mr. Oakhurst seldom troubled himself with sentiment, still less with propriety; but he had a vague idea that the situation was not fortunate. He retained, however, his presence of mind sufficiently to kick Uncle Billy, who was about to say something, and Uncle Billy was sober enough to recognize in Mr. Oakhurst's kick a superior power that would not bear trifling. He then endeavored to dissuade Tom Simson from delaying further, but in vain. He even pointed out the fact that there was no provision, nor means of making a camp. But, unluckily, the Innocent met this objection by assuring the party that he was provided with an extra mule loaded with provisions, and by the discovery of a rude attempt at a log house near the trail. "Piney can stay with Mrs. Oakhurst," said the Innocent, pointing to the Duchess, "and I can shift for myself."

Nothing but Mr. Oakhurst's admonishing foot saved Uncle Billy from bursting into a roar of laughter. As it was, he felt compelled to retire up the cañon until he could recover his gravity. There he confided the joke to the tall pine-trees, with many slaps of his leg, contortions of his face, and the usual profanity. But when he returned to the party, he found them seated by a fire—for the air had grown strangely chill and the sky overcast—in apparently amicable conversation. Piney was actually talking in an impulsive girlish fashion to the Duchess, who was listening with an interest and animation she had not shown for many days. The Innocent was holding forth, apparently with equal effect, to Mr. Oakhurst and Mother Shipton, who was actually relaxing into amiability. "Is this yer a d—d picnic?" said Uncle Billy, with inward scorn, as he surveyed the sylvan group, the glancing firelight, and the tethered animals in the foreground. Suddenly an idea mingled with the alcoholic fumes that disturbed his brain. It was apparently of a jocular nature, for he felt impelled to slap his leg again and cram his fist into his mouth.

As the shadows crept slowly up the mountain, a slight breeze rocked the tops of the pine-trees and moaned through their long and gloomy aisles. The ruined cabin, patched and covered with pine boughs, was set apart for the ladies. As the lovers parted, they unaffectedly exchanged a kiss, so honest and sincere that it might have been heard above the swaying pines. The frail Duchess and the malevolent Mother Shipton were probably too stunned to remark upon this last evidence of simplicity, and so turned without a word to the hut. The fire was replenished, the men lay down before the door, and in a few minutes were asleep.

Mr. Oakhurst was a light sleeper. Toward morning he awoke benumbed and cold. As he stirred the dying fire, the wind, which was now blowing strongly, brought to his cheek that which caused the blood to leave it,—snow!

He started to his feet with the intention of awakening the sleepers, for there was no time to lose. But turning to where Uncle Billy had been lying, he found him gone. A suspicion leaped to his brain, and a curse to his lips. He ran to the spot where the mules had been tethered—they were no longer there. The tracks were already rapidly disappearing in the snow.

The momentary excitement brought Mr. Oakhurst back to the fire with his usual calm. He did not waken the sleepers. The Innocent slumbered peacefully, with a smile on his good-humored, freckled face; the virgin Piney slept beside her frailer sisters as sweetly as though attended by celestial guardians; and Mr. Oakhurst, drawing his blanket over his shoulders, stroked his mustaches and waited for the dawn. It came slowly in a whirling mist of snowflakes that dazzled and confused the eye. What could be seen of the landscape appeared magically changed. He looked over the valley, and summed up the present and future in two words, "Snowed in!"

A careful inventory of the provisions, which, fortunately for the party, had been stored within the hut, and so escaped the felonious fingers of Uncle Billy, disclosed the fact that with care and prudence they might last ten days longer. "That is," said Mr. Oakhurst *sotto voce* to the Innocent, "if you're willing to board us. If you ain't—and perhaps you'd better not—you can wait till Uncle Billy gets back with provisions." For some occult reason, Mr. Oakhurst could not bring himself to disclose Uncle Billy's rascality, and so offered the hypothesis that he had wandered from the camp and had accidentally stampeded the animals. He dropped a warning to the Duchess and Mother Shipton, who of course knew the facts of their associate's defection. "They'll find out the truth about us *all* when they find out anything," he added significantly, "and there's no good frightening them now."

Tom Simson not only put all his worldly store at the disposal of Mr. Oakhurst, but seemed to enjoy the prospect of their enforced seclusion. "We'll have a good camp for a week, and then the snow'll melt, and we'll all go back together." The cheerful gayety of the young man and Mr. Oakhurst's calm infected the others. The Innocent, with the aid of pine boughs, extemporized a thatch for the roofless cabin, and the Duchess directed Piney in the rearrangement of the interior with a taste and tact that opened the blue eyes of that provincial maiden to their fullest extent. "I reckon now you're used to fine things at Poker Flat," said Piney. The Duchess turned away sharply to conceal something that reddened her cheeks through their professional tint, and Mother Shipton requested Piney not to "chatter." But when Mr. Oakhurst returned from a weary search for the trail, he heard the sound of happy laughter echoed from the rocks. He stopped in some alarm, and his thoughts first naturally reverted to the whiskey, which he had prudently cachéd. "And yet it don't somehow sound like whiskey," said the gambler. It was not until he caught sight of the blazing fire through the still blinding storm, and the group around it, that he settled to the conviction that it was "square fun."

Whether Mr. Oakhurst had cachéd his cards with the whiskey as something debarred the free access of the community, I cannot say. It was certain that, in Mother Shipton's words, he "didn't say 'cards' once" during that evening. Haply the time was beguiled by an accordion, produced somewhat ostentatiously by Tom Simson from his pack. Notwithstanding some difficulties attending the manipulation of this instrument, Piney Woods managed to pluck several reluctant melodies from its keys, to an accompaniment by the Innocent on a pair of bone castanets. But the crowning festivity of the evening was reached in a rude camp-meeting hymn, which the lovers, joining hands, sang with great earnestness and vocif-

eration. I fear that a certain defiant tone and Covenanter's swing to its chorus, rather than any devotional quality, caused it speedily to infect the others, who at last joined in the refrain:—

"I'm proud to live in the service of the Lord,
    And I'm bound to die in His army."

The pines rocked, the storm eddied and whirled above the miserable group, and the flames of their altar leaped heavenward, as if in token of the vow.

At midnight the storm abated, the rolling clouds parted, and the stars glittered keenly above the sleeping camp. Mr. Oakhurst, whose professional habits had enabled him to live on the smallest possible amount of sleep, in dividing the watch with Tom Simson somehow managed to take upon himself the greater part of that duty. He excused himself to the Innocent by saying that he had "often been a week without sleep." "Doing what?" asked Tom. "Poker!" replied Oakhurst sententiously. "When a man gets a streak of luck, —nigger-luck,—he don't get tired. The luck gives in first. Luck," continued the gambler reflectively, "is a mighty queer thing. All you know about it for certain is that it's bound to change. And it's finding out when it's going to change that makes you. We've had a streak of back luck since we left Poker Flat,—you come along, and slap you get into it, too. If you can hold your cards right along you're all right. For," added the gambler, with cheerful irrelevance—

"'I'm proud to live in the service of the Lord,
    And I'm bound to die in His army.'"

The third day came, and the sun, looking through the white-curtained valley, saw the outcasts divide their slowly decreasing store of provisions for the morning meal. It was one of the peculiarities of that mountain climate that its rays diffused a kindly warmth over the wintry landscape, as if in regretful commiseration of the past. But it revealed drift on drift of snow piled high around the hut,—a hopeless, uncharted, trackless sea of white lying below the rocky shores to which the castaways still clung. Through the marvelously clear air the smoke of the pastoral village of Poker Flat rose miles away. Mother Shipton saw it, and from a remote pinnacle of her rocky fastness hurled in that direction a final malediction. It was her last vituperative attempt, and perhaps for that reason was invested with a certain degree of sublimity. It did her good, she privately informed the Duchess. "Just you go out there and cuss, and see." She then set herself to the task of amusing "the child," as she and the Duchess were pleased to call Piney. Piney was no chicken, but it was a soothing and original theory of the pair thus to account for the fact that she didn't swear and wasn't improper.

When night crept up again through the gorges, the reedy notes of the accordion rose and fell in fitful spasms and long-drawn gasps by the flickering campfire. But music failed to fill entirely the aching void left by insufficient food, and a new diversion was proposed by Piney,—story-telling. Neither Mr. Oakhurst nor his female companions caring to relate their personal experiences, this plan would have failed too, but for the Innocent. Some months before he had chanced upon a stray copy of Mr. Pope's ingenious translation of the Iliad. He now proposed to narrate the principal incidents of that poem—having thoroughly mastered the argument and fairly forgotten the words—in the current vernacular of Sandy Bar. And so for the rest of that night the Homeric demigods again walked the earth. Trojan bully and wily Greek wrestled in the winds, and the great pines in the cañon seemed to bow to the wrath of the son of Peleus. Mr. Oakhurst listened with quiet satisfaction. Most especially was he interested in the fate of "Ash-heels," as the Innocent persisted in denominating the "swift-footed Achilles."

So, with small food and much of Homer and the accordion, a week passed over the heads of the outcasts. The sun again forsook them, and again from leaden skies the snowflakes were sifted over the land. Day by day closer around them drew the snowy circle, until at last they looked from their prison over drifted walls of dazzling white, that towered twenty feet above their heads. It became more and more difficult to replenish their fires, even from the fallen trees beside them, now half hidden in the drifts. And yet no one complained. The lovers turned from the dreary prospect and looked into each other's eyes, and were happy. Mr. Oakhurst settled himself coolly to the losing game before him. The Duchess, more cheerful than she had been, assumed the care of Piney. Only Mother Shipton—once the strongest of the party—seemed to sicken and fade. At midnight on the tenth day she called Oakhurst to her side. "I'm going," she said, in a voice of querulous weakness, "but don't say anything about it. Don't waken the kids. Take the bundle from under my head, and open it." Mr. Oakhurst did so. It contained Mother Shipton's rations for the last week, untouched. "Give 'em to the child," she said, pointing to the sleeping Piney. "You've starved yourself," said the gambler. "That's what they call it," said the woman querulously, as she lay down again, and, turning her face to the wall, passed quietly away.

The accordion and the bones were put aside that day, and Homer was forgotten. When the body of Mother Shipton had been committed to the snow, Mr. Oakhurst took the Innocent aside, and showed him a pair of snowshoes, which he had fashioned from the old pack-saddle. "There's one chance in a hundred to save her yet," he said, pointing to Piney; "but it's there," he added, pointing toward Poker Flat. "If you can reach there in two days she's safe." "And you?" asked Tom Simson. "I'll stay here," was the curt reply.

The lovers parted with a long embrace. "You are not going, too?" said the Duchess, as she saw Mr. Oakhurst apparently waiting to accompany him. "As far as the cañon," he replied. He turned suddenly and kissed the Duchess, leaving her pallid face aflame, and her trembling limbs rigid with amazement.

Night came, but not Mr. Oakhurst. It brought the storm again and the whirling snow. Then the Duchess, feeding the fire, found that some one had quietly piled beside the hut enough fuel to last a few days longer. The tears rose to her eyes, but she hid them from Piney.

The women slept but little. In the morning, looking into each other's faces, they read their fate. Neither spoke, but Piney, accepting the position of the stronger, drew near and placed her arm around the Duchess's waist. They kept this attitude for the rest of the day. That night the storm reached its greatest fury, and, rending asunder the protecting vines, invaded the very hut.

Toward morning they found themselves unable to feed the fire, which gradually died away. As the embers slowly blackened, the Duchess crept closer to Piney, and broke the silence of many hours: "Piney, can you pray?" "No, dear," said Piney simply. The Duchess, without knowing exactly why, felt relieved, and, putting her head upon Piney's shoulder, spoke no more. And so reclining, the younger and purer pillowing the head of her soiled sister upon her virgin breast, they fell asleep.

The wind lulled as if it feared to waken them. Feathery drifts of snow, shaken from the long pine boughs, flew like white winged birds, and settled about them as they slept. The moon through the rifted clouds looked down upon what had been the camp. But all human stain, all trace of earthly travail, was hidden beneath the spotless mantle mercifully flung from above.

They slept all that day and the next, nor did they waken when voices and footsteps broke the silence of the camp. And when pitying fingers brushed the snow from their wan faces, you could scarcely have told from the equal peace that dwelt upon them which was she that had sinned. Even the law of Poker Flat recognized this, and turned away, leaving them still locked in each other's arms.

But at the head of the gulch, one of the largest pine-trees, they found the deuce of clubs pinned to the bark with a bowie-knife.

It bore the following, written in pencil in a firm hand:—

†

BENEATH THIS TREE
LIES THE BODY
OF
JOHN OAKHURST,
WHO STRUCK A STREAK OF BAD LUCK
ON THE 23D OF NOVEMBER 1850,
AND
HANDED IN HIS CHECKS
ON THE 7TH DECEMBER, 1850.

↓

And pulseless and cold, with a Derringer by his side and a bullet in his heart, though still calm as in life, beneath the snow lay he who was at once the strongest and yet the weakest of the outcasts of Poker Flat.

THOMAS BAILEY ALDRICH (1836-1907)

MARJORIE DAW
(1873)

I

DR. DILLON TO EDWARD DELANEY, ESQ., AT THE PINES, NEAR RYE, N. H.

August 8, 187—.

MY DEAR SIR: I am happy to assure you that your anxiety is without reason. Flemming will be confined to the sofa for three or four weeks, and will have to be careful at first how he uses his leg. A fracture of this kind is always a tedious affair. Fortunately, the bone was very skilfully set by the surgeon who chanced to be in the drug-store where Flemming was brought after his fall, and I apprehend no permanent inconvenience from the accident. *Flemming is doing perfectly well physically;* but I must confess that the irritable and morbid state of mind into which he has fallen causes me a great deal of uneasiness. He is the last man in the world who ought to break his leg. You know how impetuous our friend is ordinarily, what a soul of restlessness and energy, never content unless he is rushing at some object, like a sportive bull at a red shawl; but amiable withal. He is no longer amiable. His temper has become something frightful. Miss Fanny Flemming came up from Newport, where the family are staying for the summer, to nurse him; but he packed her off the next morning in tears. He has a complete set of Balzac's works, twenty-seven volumes, piled up near his sofa, to throw at Watkins whenever that exemplary serving-man appears with his meals. Yesterday I very innocently brought Flemming a small basket of lemons. You know it was a strip of lemon-peel on the curbstone that caused our friend's mischance. Well, he no sooner set his eyes upon these lemons than he fell into such a rage as I cannot adequately describe. This is only one of his moods, and the least distressing. At other times he sits with bowed head regarding his splintered limb, silent, sullen, despairing. When this fit is on him—and it sometimes lasts all day—nothing can distract his melancholy. He refuses to eat, does not even read the newspapers; books, except as projectiles for Watkins, have no charms for him. His state is truly pitiable.

Now, if he were a poor man, with a family depending on his daily labor, this irritability and despondency would be natural enough. But in a young fellow of twenty-four, with plenty of money and seemingly not a care in the world, the thing is monstrous. If he continues to give way to his vagaries in this manner, he will end by bringing on an inflammation of the fibula. It was the fibula he broke. I am at my wits' end to know what to prescribe for him. I have anæsthetics and lotions, to make people sleep and to soothe pain; but I've no medicine that will make a man have a little common-sense. That is beyond my skill, but maybe it is not beyond yours. You are Flemming's intimate friend, his *fidus Achates.* Write to him, write to him frequently, distract his mind, cheer him up, and prevent him from becoming a confirmed case of melancholia. Perhaps he has some important plans disarranged by his present confinement. If he has you will know, and will know how to advise him judiciously. I trust your father finds the change beneficial? I am, my dear sir, with great respect, etc.

II

EDWARD DELANEY TO JOHN FLEMMING, WEST 38TH STREET, NEW YORK

Aug 9,—.

MY DEAR JACK: I had a line from Dillon this morning, and was rejoiced to learn that your hurt is not so bad as reported. Like a certain personage, you are not so black and blue as you are painted. Dillon will put you on your pins again in two or three weeks, if you will only have patience and follow his counsels. Did you get my note of last Wednesday? I was greatly troubled when I heard of the accident.

I can imagine how tranquil and saintly you are with your leg in a trough! It is deuced awkward, to be sure, just as we had promised ourselves a glorious month together at the seaside; but we must make the best of it. It is unfortunate, too, that my father's health renders it impossible for me to leave him. I think he has much improved; the sea air is his native element; but he still needs my arm to lean upon in his walks, and requires some one more careful than a servant to look after him. I cannot come to you, dear Jack, but I have hours of unemployed time on hand, and I will write you a whole post-office full of letters if that will divert you. Heaven knows, I haven't anything to write about. It isn't as if we were living at one of the beach houses; then I could do you some character studies, and fill your imagination with groups of sea-goddesses, with their (or somebody else's) raven and blond manes hanging down their shoulders. You should have Aphrodite in morning wrapper, in evening costume, and in her prettiest bathing suit. But we are far from all that here. We have rooms in a farm-house, on a cross-road, two miles from the hotels, and lead the quietest of lives.

I wish I were a novelist. This old house, with its sanded floors and high wainscots, and its narrow windows looking out upon a cluster of pines that turn themselves into æolian-harps every time the wind blows, would be the place in which to write a summer romance. It should be a story with the odors of the forest and the breath of the sea in it. It should be a

novel like one of that Russian fellow's,—what's his name?—Tourguénieff, Turguenef, Turgenif, Toorguniff, Turgénjew,—nobody knows how to spell him. Yet I wonder if even a Liza or an Alexandra Paulovna could stir the heart of a man who has constant twinges in his leg. I wonder if one of our own Yankee girls of the best type, haughty and *spirituelle*, would be of any comfort to you in your present deplorable condition. If I thought so, I would hasten down to the Surf House and catch one for you; or, better still, I would find you one over the way.

Picture to yourself a large white house just across the road, nearly opposite our cottage. It is not a house, but a mansion, built, perhaps, in the colonial period, with rambling extensions, and gambrel roof, and a wide piazza on three sides,—a self-possessed, high-bred piece of architecture, with its nose in the air. It stands back from the road, and has an obsequious retinue of fringed elms and oaks and weeping willows. Sometimes in the morning, and oftener in the afternoon, when the sun has withdrawn from that part of the mansion, a young woman appears on the piazza with some mysterious Penelope web of embroidery in her hand, or a book. There is a hammock over there,—of pineapple fibre, it looks from here. A hammock is very becoming when one is eighteen, and has golden hair, and dark eyes, and an emerald-colored illusion dress looped up after the fashion of a Dresden china shepherdess, and is *chaussée* like a belle of the time of Louis Quatorze. All this splendor goes into that hammock, and sways there like a pond-lily in the golden afternoon. The window of my bedroom looks down on that piazza,—and so do I.

But enough of this nonsense, which ill becomes a sedate young attorney taking his vacation with an invalid father. Drop me a line, dear Jack, and tell me how you really are. State your case. Write me a long, quiet letter. If you are violent or abusive, I'll take the law to you.

III

JOHN FLEMMING TO EDWARD DELANEY

August 11,—.

Your letter, dear Ned, was a godsend. Fancy what a fix I am in,—I, who never had a day's sickness since I was born. My left leg weighs three tons. It is embalmed in spices and smothered in layers of fine linen, like a mummy. I can't move. I haven't moved for five thousand years. I'm of the time of Pharaoh.

I lie from morning till night on a lounge,

staring into the hot street. Everybody is out of town enjoying himself. The brown-stone-front houses across the street resemble a row of particularly ugly coffins set up on end. A green mould is settling on the names of the deceased, carved on the silver door-plates. Sardonic spiders have sewed up the key-holes. All is silence and dust and desolation.—I interrupt this a moment, to take a shy at Watkins with the second volume of César Birotteau. Missed him! I think I could bring him down with a copy of Sainte-Beuve or the Dictionnaire Universel, if I had it. These small Balzac books somehow don't quite fit my hand; but I shall fetch him yet. I've an idea Watkins is tapping the old gentleman's Château Yquem. Duplicate key of the wine-cellar. Hibernian swarries in the front basement. Young Cheops upstairs, snug in his cerements. Watkins glides into my chamber, with that colorless, hypocritical face of his drawn out long like an accordion; but I know he grins all the way down stairs, and is glad I have broken my leg. Was not my evil star in the very zenith when I ran up to town to attend that dinner at Delmonico's? I didn't come up altogether for that. It was partly to buy Frank Livingstone's roan mare Margot. And now I shall not be able to sit in the saddle these two months. I'll send the mare down to you at The Pines,—is that the name of the place?

Old Dillon fancies that I have something on my mind. He drives me wild with lemons. Lemons for a mind diseased! Nonsense. I am only as restless as the devil under this confinement,—a thing I'm not used to. Take a man who has never had so much as a headache or a toothache in his life, strap one of his legs in a section of water-spout, keep him in a room in the city for weeks, with the hot weather turned on, and then expect him to smile and purr and be happy! It is preposterous. I can't be cheerful or calm.

Your letter is the first consoling thing I have had since my disaster, ten days ago. It really cheered me up for half an hour. Send me a screed, Ned, as often as you can, if you love me. Anything will do. Write me more about that little girl in the hammock. That was very pretty, all that about the Dresden china shepherdess and the pond-lily; the imagery a little mixed, perhaps, but very pretty. I didn't suppose you had so much sentimental furniture in your upper story. It shows how one may be familiar for years with the reception-room of his neighbor, and never suspect what is directly under his mansard. I supposed your loft stuffed with dry legal parchments, mortgages and affidavits; you take down a package of manuscript, and lo! there are lyrics and sonnets and canzonettas. You really have a graphic descriptive touch, Edward Delaney, and I suspect you of anonymous love-tales in the magazines.

I shall be a bear until I hear from you again. Tell me all about your pretty *inconnue* across the road. What is her name? Who is she? Who's her father? Where's her mother? Who's her lover? You cannot imagine how this will occupy me. The more trifling the better. My imprisonment has weakened me intellectually to such a degree that I find your epistolary gifts quite considerable. I am passing into my second childhood. In a week or two I shall take to India-rubber rings and prongs of coral. A silver cup, with an appropriate inscription, would be a delicate attention on your part. In the meantime, write!

IV

EDWARD DELANEY TO JOHN FLEMMING

August 12,—.

The sick pasha shall be amused. *Bismillah!* he wills it so. If the story-teller becomes prolix and tedious,—the bow-string and the sack, and two Nubians to drop him into the Piscataqua! But, truly, Jack, I have a hard task. There is literally nothing here,—except the little girl over the way. She is swinging in the hammock at this moment. It is to me compensation for many of the ills of life to see her now and then put out a small kid boot, which fits like a glove, and set herself going. Who is she, and what is her name? Her name is Daw. Only daughter of Mr. Richard W. Daw, ex-colonel and banker. Mother dead. One brother at Harvard, elder brother killed at the battle of Fair Oaks, nine years ago. Old, rich family, the Daws. This is the homestead, and where father and daughter pass eight months of the twelve; the rest of the year in Baltimore and Washington. The New England winter too many for the old gentleman. The daughter is called Marjorie,—Marjorie Daw. Sounds odd at first, doesn't it? But after you say it over to yourself half a dozen times, you like it. There's a pleasing quaintness to it, something prim and violet-like. Must be a nice sort of girl to be called Marjorie Daw.

I had mine host of The Pines in the witness-box last night, and drew the foregoing testimony from him. He has charge of Mr. Daw's vegetable-garden, and has known the family these thirty years. Of course I shall make the acquaintance of my neighbors before many days. It will be next to impossible for me not to meet Mr. Daw or Miss Daw in some of my walks. The young lady has a favorite path to the sea-beach. I shall intercept her some morning, and touch my hat to her. Then the princess will bend her fair head to me with courteous surprise not unmixed with haughtiness. Will snub me, in fact. All this for thy sake, O Pasha of the Snapt Axle-tree ! . . . . How oddly things fall out ! Ten minutes ago I was called down to the parlor,—you know the kind of parlors in farm-houses on the coast, a sort of amphibious parlor, with sea-shells on the mantel-piece and spruce branches in the chimney-place,—where I found my father and Mr. Daw doing the antique polite to each other. He had come to pay his respects to his new neighbors. Mr. Daw is a tall, slim gentleman of fifty-five, with a florid face and snow-white mustache and side-whiskers. Looks like Mr. Dombey, or as Mr. Dombey would have looked if he had served a few years in the British Army. Mr. Daw was a colonel in the late war, commanding the regiment in which his son was a lieutenant. Plucky old boy, backbone of New Hampshire granite. Before taking his leave, the colonel delivered himself of an invitation as if he were issuing a general order. Miss Daw has a few friends coming, at 4 P. M., to play croquet on the lawn (parade-ground) and have tea (cold rations) on the piazza. Will we honor them with our company? (or be sent to the guard-house.) My father declines on the plea of ill-health. My father's son bows with as much suavity as he knows, and accepts.

In my next I shall have something to tell you. I shall have seen the little beauty face to face. I have a presentiment, Jack, that this Daw is a *rara avis!* Keep up your spirits, my boy, until I write you another letter,—and send me along word how's your leg.

V

EDWARD DELANEY TO JOHN FLEMMING

August 13,—.

The party, my dear Jack, was as dreary as possible. A lieutenant of the navy, the rector of the Episcopal church at Stillwater, and a society swell from Nahant. The lieutenant looked as if he had swallowed a couple of his buttons, and found the bullion rather indigestible; the rector was a pensive youth, of the daffydowndilly sort; and the swell from Nahant was a very weak tidal wave indeed. The women were much better, as they always are; the two Miss Kingsburys of Philadelphia, stay-ing at the Sea-shell House, two bright and engaging girls. But Marjorie Daw !

The company broke up soon after tea, and I remained to smoke a cigar with the colonel on the piazza. It was like seeing a picture to see Miss Marjorie hovering around the old soldier, and doing a hundred gracious little things for him. She brought the cigars and lighted the tapers with her own delicate fingers, in the most enchanting fashion. As we sat there, she came and went in the summer twilight, and seemed, with her white dress and pale gold hair, like some lovely phantom that had sprung into existence out of the smoke-wreaths. If she had melted into air, like the statue of Galatea in the play, I should have been more sorry than surprised.

It was easy to perceive that the old colonel worshipped her, and she him. I think the relation between an elderly father and a daughter just blooming into womanhood the most beautiful possible. There is in it a subtile sentiment that cannot exist in the case of mother and daughter, or that of son and mother. But this is getting into deep water.

I sat with the Daws until half past ten, and saw the moon rise on the sea. The ocean, that had stretched motionless and black against the horizon, was changed by magic into a broken field of glittering ice, interspersed with marvellous silvery fjords. In the far distance the Isles of Shoals loomed up like a group of huge bergs drifting down on us. The Polar Regions in a June thaw ! It was exceedingly fine. What did we talk about? We talked about the weather —and *you!* The weather has been disagreeable for several days past,—and so have you. I glided from one topic to the other very naturally. I told my friends of your accident; how it had frustrated all our summer plans, and what our plans were. I played quite a spirited solo on the fibula. Then I described you; or, rather, I didn't. I spoke of your amiability, of your patience under this severe affliction; of your touching gratitude when Dillon brings you little presents of fruit; of your tenderness to your sister Fanny, whom you would not allow to stay in town to nurse you, and how you heroically sent her back to Newport, preferring to remain alone with Mary, the cook, and your man Watkins, to whom, by the way, you were devotedly attached. If you had been there, Jack, you wouldn't have known yourself. I should have excelled as a criminal lawyer, if I had not turned my attention to a different branch of jurisprudence.

Miss Marjorie asked all manner of leading questions concerning you. It did not occur to me then, but it struck me forcibly afterwards, that she evinced a singular interest in the conversation. When I got back to my room, I recalled how eagerly she leaned forward, with her full, snowy throat in strong moonlight, listening to what I said. Positively, I think I made her like you!

Miss Daw is a girl whom you would like immensely, I can tell you that. A beauty without affectation, a high and tender nature,—if one can read the soul in the face. And the old colonel is a noble character, too.

I am glad the Daws are such pleasant people. The Pines is an isolated spot, and my resources are few. I fear I should have found life here somewhat monotonous before long, with no other society than that of my excellent sire. It is true, I might have made a target of the defenceless invalid; but I haven't a taste for artillery, *moi*.

VI

JOHN FLEMMING TO EDWARD DELANEY

August 17,—.

For a man who hasn't a taste for artillery, it occurs to me, my friend, you are keeping up a pretty lively fire on my inner works. But go on. Cynicism is a small brass field-piece that eventually bursts and kills the artilleryman.

You may abuse me as much as you like, and I'll not complain; for I don't know what I should do without your letters. They are curing me. I haven't hurled anything at Watkins since last Sunday, partly because I have grown more amiable under your teaching, and partly because Watkins captured my ammunition one night, and carried it off to the library. He is rapidly losing the habit he had acquired of dodging whenever I rub my ear, or make any slight motion with my right arm. He is still suggestive of the wine-cellar, however. You may break, you may shatter Watkins, if you will, but the scent of the Roederer will hang round him still.

Ned, that Miss Daw must be a charming person. I should certainly like her. I like her already. When you spoke in your first letter of seeing a young girl swinging in a hammock under your chamber window, I was somehow strangely drawn to her. I cannot account for it in the least. What you have subsequently written of Miss Daw has strengthened the impression. You seem to be describing a woman I have known in some previous state of existence, or dreamed of in this. Upon my word, if you were to send me her photograph, I believe I should recognize her at a glance. Her manner, that listening attitude, her traits of char-

acter, as you indicate them, the light hair and the dark eyes,—they are all familiar things to me. Asked a lot of questions, did she? Curious about me? That is strange.

You would laugh in your sleeve, you wretched old cynic, if you knew how I lie awake nights, with my gas turned down to a star, thinking of The Pines and the house across the road. How cool it must be down there! I long for the salt smell of the air. I picture the colonel smoking his cheroot on the piazza. I send you and Miss Daw off on afternoon rambles along the beach. Sometimes I let you stroll with her under the elms in the moonlight, for you are great friends by this time, I take it, and see each other every day. I know your ways and your manners! Then I fall into a truculent mood, and would like to destroy somebody. Have you noticed anything in the shape of a lover hanging around the colonial Lares and Penates? Does that lieutenant of the horse-marines or that young Stillwater parson visit the house much? Not that I am pining for news of them, but any gossip of the kind would be in order. I wonder, Ned, you don't fall in love with Miss Daw. I am ripe to do it myself. Speaking of photographs, couldn't you manage to slip one of her *cartes-de-visite* from her album,—she must have an album, you know,—and send it to me? I will return it before it could be missed. That's a good fellow! Did the mare arrive safe and sound? It will be a capital animal this autumn for Central Park.

O—my leg? I forgot about my leg. It's better.

VII

EDWARD DELANEY TO JOHN FLEMMING

August 20,—.

You are correct in your surmises. I am on the most friendly terms with our neighbors. The colonel and my father smoke their afternoon cigar together in our sitting-room or on the piazza opposite, and I pass an hour or two of the day or the evening with the daughter. I am more and more struck by the beauty, modesty, and intelligence of Miss Daw.

You ask me why I did not fall in love with her. I will be frank, Jack: I have thought of that. She is young, rich, accomplished, uniting in herself more attractions, mental and personal, than I can recall in any girl of my acquaintance; but she lacks the something that would be necessary to inspire in me that kind of interest. Possessing this unknown quantity, a woman neither beautiful nor wealthy nor very young could bring me to her feet. But not Miss Daw. If we were shipwrecked together on an uninhabited island,—let me suggest a tropical island, for it costs no more to be picturesque,—I would build her a bamboo hut, I would fetch her bread-fruit and cocoanuts, I would fry yams for her, I would lure the ingenuous turtle and make her nourishing soups, but I wouldn't make love to her,—not under eighteen months. I would like to have her for a sister, that I might shield her and counsel her, and spend half my income on thread-laces and camel's-hair shawls. (We are off the island now.) If such were not my feeling, there would still be an obstacle to my loving Miss Daw. A greater misfortune could scarcely befall me than to love her. Flemming, I am about to make a revelation that will astonish you. I may be all wrong in my premises and consequently in my conclusions; but you shall judge.

That night when I returned to my room after the croquet party at the Daw's, and was thinking over the trivial events of the evening, I was suddenly impressed by the air of eager attention with which Miss Daw had followed my account of your accident. I think I mentioned this to you. Well, the next morning, as I went to mail my letter, I overtook Miss Daw on the road to Rye, where the post-office is, and accompanied her thither and back, an hour's walk. The conversation again turned on you, and again I remarked that inexplicable look of interest which had lighted up her face the previous evening. Since then, I have seen Miss Daw perhaps ten times, perhaps oftener, and on each occasion I found that when I was not speaking of you, or your sister, or some person or place associated with you, I was not holding her attention. She would be absent-minded, her eyes would wander away from me to the sea, or to some distant object in the landscape; her fingers would play with the leaves of a book in a way that convinced me she was not listening. At these moments if I abruptly changed the theme,—I did it several times as an experiment,—and dropped some remark about my friend Flemming, then the sombre blue eyes would come back to me instantly.

Now, is not this the oddest thing in the world? No, not the oddest. The effect which you tell me was produced on you by my casual mention of an unknown girl swinging in a hammock is certainly as strange. You can conjecture how that passage in your letter of Friday startled me. Is it possible, then, that two people who have never met, and who are hundreds of miles apart, can exert a magnetic influence on each other? I have read of such psychological phenomena, but never credited them. I leave the solution of the problem to you. As for myself, all other things being favorable, it would be impossible for me to fall in love with a woman who listens to me only when I am talking of my friend!

I am not aware that any one is paying marked attention to my fair neighbor. The lieutenant of the navy—he is stationed at Rivermouth—sometimes drops in of an evening, and sometimes the rector from Stillwater; the lieutenant the oftener. He was there last night. I would not be surprised if he had an eye to the heiress; but he is not formidable. Mistress Daw carries a neat little spear of irony, and the honest lieutenant seems to have a particular facility for impaling himself on the point of it. He is not dangerous, I should say; though I have known a woman to satirize a man for years, and marry him after all. Decidedly, the lowly rector is not dangerous; yet, again, who has not seen Cloth of Frieze victorious in the lists where Cloth of Gold went down?

As to the photograph. There is an exquisite ivorytype of Marjorie, in passe-partout, on the drawing-room mantel-piece. It would be missed at once, if taken. I would do anything reasonable for you, Jack; but I've no burning desire to be hauled up before the local justice of the peace, on a charge of petty larceny.

P. S.—Enclosed is a spray of mignonette, which I advise you to treat tenderly. Yes, we talked of you again last night, as usual. It is becoming a little dreary for me.

VIII

EDWARD DELANEY TO JOHN FLEMMING
August 22,—

Your letter in reply to my last has occupied my thoughts all the morning. I do not know what to think. Do you mean to say that you are seriously half in love with a woman whom you have never seen,—with a shadow, a chimera? for what else can Miss Daw be to you? I do not understand it at all. I understand neither you nor her. You are a couple of ethereal beings moving in finer air than I can breathe with my commonplace lungs. Such delicacy of sentiment is something I admire without comprehending. I am bewildered. I am of the earth earthy, and I find myself in the incongruous position of having to do with mere souls, with natures so finely tempered that I run some risk of shattering them in my awkwardness. I am as Caliban among the spirits!

Reflecting on your letter, I am not sure it is wise in me to continue this correspondence. But no, Jack; I do wrong to doubt the good sense that forms the basis of your character. You are deeply interested in Miss Daw; you feel that she is a person whom you may perhaps greatly admire when you know her: at the same time you bear in mind that the chances are ten to five that, when you do come to know her, she will fall far short of your ideal, and you will not care for her in the least. Look at it in this sensible light, and I will hold back nothing from you.

Yesterday afternoon my father and myself rode over to Rivermouth with the Daws. A heavy rain in the morning had cooled the atmosphere and laid the dust. To Rivermouth is a drive of eight miles, along a winding road lined all the way with wild barberry-bushes. I never saw anything more brilliant than these bushes, the green of the foliage and the pink of the coral berries intensified by the rain. The colonel drove, with my father in front, Miss Daw and I on the back seat. I resolved that for the first five miles your name should not pass my lips. I was amused by the artful attempts she made, at the start, to break through my reticence. Then a silence fell upon her; and then she became suddenly gay. That keenness which I enjoyed so much when it was exercised on the lieutenant was not so satisfactory directed against myself. Miss Daw has great sweetness of disposition, but she can be disagreeable. She is like the young lady in the rhyme, with the curl on her forehead,

"When she is good,
She is very, very good,
And when she is bad, she is horrid!"

I kept to my resolution, however; but on the return home I relented, and talked of your mare! Miss Daw is going to try a side-saddle on Margot some morning. The animal is a trifle too light for my weight. By the by, I nearly forgot to say Miss Daw sat for a picture yesterday to a Rivermouth artist. If the negative turns out well, I am to have a copy. So our ends will be accomplished without crime. I wish, though, I could send you the ivorytype in the drawing-room; it is cleverly colored, and would give you an idea of her hair and eyes, which of course the other will not.

No, Jack, the spray of mignonette did not come from me. A man of twenty-eight doesn't enclose flowers in his letters—to another man. But don't attach too much significance to the circumstance. She gives sprays of mignonette to the rector, sprays to the lieutenant. She has even given a rose from her bosom to your slave. It is her jocund nature to scatter flowers, like Spring.

If my letters sometimes read disjointedly, you must understand that I never finish one at a sitting, but write at intervals, when the mood is on me.

The mood is not on me now.

IX

EDWARD DELANEY TO JOHN FLEMMING
August 23,—

I have just returned from the strangest interview with Marjorie. She has all but confessed to me her interest in you. But with what modesty and dignity! Her words elude my pen as I attempt to put them on paper; and, indeed, it was not so much what she said as her manner; and that I cannot reproduce. Perhaps it was of a piece with the strangeness of this whole business, that she should tacitly acknowledge to a third party the love she feels for a man she has never beheld! But I have lost, through your aid, the faculty of being surprised. I accept things as people do in dreams. Now that I am again in my room, it all appears like an illusion,—the black masses of Rembrandtish shadow under the trees, the fire-flies whirling in Pyrrhic dances among the shrubbery, the sea over there, Marjorie sitting on the hammock!

It is past midnight, and I am too sleepy to write more.

Thursday Morning.

My father has suddenly taken it into his head to spend a few days at the Shoals. In the mean while you will not hear from me. I see Marjorie walking in the garden with the colonel. I wish I could speak to her alone, but shall probably not have an opportunity before we leave.

X

EDWARD DELANEY TO JOHN FLEMMING
August 28,—

You were passing into your second childhood, were you? Your intellect was so reduced that my epistolary gifts seemed quite considerable to you, did they? I rise superior to the sarcasm in your favor of the 11th instant,when I notice that five days' silence on my part is sufficient to throw you into the depths of despondency.

We returned only this morning from Appledore, that enchanted island,—at four dollars per day. I find on my desk three letters from you! Evidently there is no lingering doubt in *your* mind as to the pleasure I derive from your correspondence. These letters are undated, but in what I take to be the latest are two passages that require my consideration. You will pardon my candor, dear Flemming, but the conviction forces itself upon me that as your leg grows stronger your head becomes weaker. You ask my advice on a certain point. I will give it. In my opinion you could do nothing more unwise than to address a note to Miss Daw, thanking her for the flower. It would, I am sure, offend her delicacy beyond pardon. She knows you only through me; you are to her an abstraction, a figure in a dream,—a dream from which the faintest shock would awaken her. Of course, if you enclose a note to me and insist on its delivery, I shall deliver it; but I advise you not to do so.

You say you are able, with the aid of a cane, to walk about your chamber, and that your purpose to come to The Pines the instant Dillon thinks you strong enough to stand the journey. Again I advise you not to. Do you not see that, every hour you remain away, Marjorie's glamour deepens, and your influence over her increases? You will ruin everything by precipitancy. Wait until you are entirely recovered; in any case, do not come without giving me warning. I fear the effect of your abrupt advent here—under the circumstances.

Miss Daw was evidently glad to see us back again, and gave me both hands in the frankest way. She stopped at the door a moment, this afternoon, in the carriage; she had been over to Rivermouth for her pictures. Unluckily the photographer had spilt some acid on the plate, and she was obliged to give him another sitting. I have an intuition that something is troubling Marjorie. She had an abstracted air not usual with her. However, it may be only my fancy. . . . I end this, leaving several things unsaid, to accompany my father on one of those long walks which are now his chief medicine,—and mine!

XI

EDWARD DELANEY TO JOHN FLEMMING

August 29,—

I write in great haste to tell you what has taken place here since my letter of last night. I am in the utmost perplexity. Only one thing is plain,—*you* must not dream of coming to The Pines. Marjorie has told her father everything! I saw her for a few minutes, an hour ago, in the garden; and, as near as I could gather from her confused statement, the facts

are these: Lieutenant Bradly—that's the naval officer stationed at Rivermouth—has been paying court to Miss Daw for some time past, but not so much to her liking as to that of the colonel, who it seems is an old friend of the young gentleman's father. Yesterday (I knew she was in some trouble when she drove up to our gate) the colonel spoke to Marjorie of Bradly,—urged his suit, I infer. Marjorie expressed her dislike for the lieutenant with characteristic frankness, and finally confessed to her father—well, I really do not know what she confessed. It must have been the vaguest of confessions, and must have sufficiently puzzled the colonel. At any rate, it exasperated him. I suppose I am implicated in the matter, and that the colonel feels bitterly towards me. I do not see why: I have carried no messages between you and Miss Daw; I have behaved with the greatest discretion. I can find no flaw anywhere in my proceeding. I do not see that anybody has done anything,—except the colonel himself.

It is probable, nevertheless, that the friendly relations between the two houses will be broken off. "A plague o' both your houses," say you. I will keep you informed, as well as I can, of what occurs over the way. We shall remain here until the second week in September. Stay where you are, or, at all events, do not dream of joining me. . . . Colonel Daw is sitting on the piazza looking rather wicked. I have not seen Marjorie since I parted with her in the garden.

XII

EDWARD DELANEY TO THOMAS DILLON, M.D., MADISON SQUARE, NEW YORK

August 30,—

MY DEAR DOCTOR: If you have any influence over Flemming, I beg of you to exert it to prevent his coming to this place at present. There are circumstances, which I will explain to you before long, that make it of the first importance that he should not come into this neighborhood. His appearance here, I speak advisedly, would be disastrous to him. In urging him to remain in New York, or to go to some inland resort, you will be doing him and me a real service. Of course you will not mention my name in this connection. You know me well enough, my dear doctor, to be assured that, in begging your secret co-operation, I have reasons that will meet your entire approval when they are made plain to you. We shall return to town on the 15th of next month, and my first duty will be to present myself at your hospitable door and satisfy your curiosity, if I have excited it, My father, I am glad to state, has so greatly improved that he can no longer be regarded as an invalid. With great esteem, I am, etc., etc.

XIII

EDWARD DELANEY TO JOHN FLEMMING
August 31,—

Your letter, announcing your mad determination to come here, has just reached me. I beseech you to reflect a moment. The step would be fatal to your interests and hers. You would furnish just cause for irritation to R. W. D.; and, though he loves Marjorie tenderly, he is capable of going to any lengths if opposed. You would not like, I am convinced, to be the means of causing him to treat *her* with severity. That would be the result of your presence at The Pines at this juncture. I am annoyed to be obliged to point out these things to you. We are on very delicate ground, Jack; the situation is critical, and the slightest mistake in a move would cost us the game. If you consider it worth the winning, be patient. Trust a little to my sagacity. Wait and see what happens. Moreover, I understand from Dillon that you are in no condition to take so long a journey. He thinks the air of the coast would be the worst thing possible for you; that you ought to go inland, if anywhere. Be advised by me. Be advised by Dillon.

XIV

TELEGRAMS
September 1,—

1.—TO EDWARD DELANEY

Letter received. Dillon be hanged. I think I ought to be on the ground.　　　　　J. F.

2.—TO JOHN FLEMMING

Stay where you are. You would only complicate matters. Do not move until you hear from me.　　　　　E. D.

3.—TO EDWARD DELANEY

My being at The Pines could be kept secret. I must see her.　　　　　J. F.

4.—TO JOHN FLEMMING

Do not think of it. It would be useless. R. W. D. has locked M. in her room. You would not be able to effect an interview.　　　　　E. D.

5.—TO EDWARD DELANEY

Locked her in her room. Good God. That settles the question. I shall leave by the twelve-fifteen express.　　　　　J. F.

XV

THE ARRIVAL

On the second of September, 187-, as the down express due at 3.40 left the station at Hampton, a young man, leaning on the shoulder of a servant, whom he addressed as Watkins, stepped from the platform into a hack, and requested to be driven to "The Pines." On arriving at the gate of a modest farmhouse, a few miles from the station, the young man descended with difficulty from the carriage, and, casting a hasty glance across the road, seemed much impressed by some peculiarity in the landscape. Again leaning on the shoulder of the person Watkins, he walked to the door of the farm-house and inquired for Mr. Edward Delaney. He was informed by the aged man who answered his knock, that Mr. Edward Delaney had gone to Boston the day before, but that Mr. Jonas Delaney was within. This information did not appear satisfactory to the stranger, who inquired if Mr. Edward Delaney had left any message for Mr. John Flemming. There *was* a letter for Mr. Flemming, if he were that person. After a brief absence the aged man reappeared with a Letter.

XVI

EDWARD DELANEY TO JOHN FLEMMING
September 1,—

I am horror-stricken at what I have done! When I began this correspondence I had no other purpose than to relieve the tedium of your sick-chamber. Dillon told me to cheer you up. I tried to. I thought you entered into the spirit of the thing. I had no idea, until within a few days, that you were taking matters *au serieux*.

What can I say? I am in sackcloth and ashes. I am a pariah, a dog of an outcast. I tried to make a little romance to interest you, something soothing and idyllic, and, by Jove! I have done it only too well! My father doesn't know a word of this, so don't jar the old gentleman any more than you can help. I fly from the wrath to come—when you arrive! For O, dear Jack, there isn't any colonial mansion on the other side of the road, there isn't any piazza, there isn't any hammock,—there isn't any Marjorie Daw!!

GEORGE WASHINGTON CABLE (1844-1925)

"POSSON JONE' "

(1876)

To Jules St.-Ange—elegant little heathen —there yet remained at manhood a remembrance of having been sent to school, and of having been taught by a stony-headed Capuchin that the world is round—for example, like a cheese. This round world is a cheese to be eaten through, and Jules had nibbled quite into his cheese-world already at twenty-two.

He realized this as he idled about one Sunday morning where the intersection of Royal and Conti streets some seventy years ago formed a central corner of New Orleans. Yes, yes, the trouble was he had been wasteful and honest. He discussed the matter with that faithful friend and confidant, Baptiste, his yellow body-servant. They concluded that, papa's patience and *tante's* pin-money having been gnawed away quite to the rind, there were left open only these few easily enumerated resorts: to go to work—they shuddered; to join Major Innerarity's filibustering expedition; or else—why not?—to try some games of confidence. At twenty-two one must begin to be something. Nothing else tempted; could that avail? One could but try. It is noble to try; and, besides, they were hungry. If one could "make the friendship" of some person from the country, for instance, with money, not expert at cards or dice, but, as one would say, willing to learn, one might find cause to say some "Hail Marys."

The sun broke through a clearing sky, and Baptiste pronounced it good for luck. There had been a hurricane in the night. The weed-grown tile-roofs were still dripping, and from lofty brick and low adobe walls a rising steam responded to the summer sunlight. Up-street, and across the Rue du Canal, one could get glimpses of the gardens in Faubourg Ste.-Marie standing in silent wretchedness, so many tearful Lucretias, tattered victims of the storm. Short remnants of the wind now and then came down the narrow street in erratic puffs heavily laden with odors of broken boughs and torn flowers, skimmed the little pools of rain-water in the deep ruts of the unpaved street, and suddenly went away to nothing, like a juggler's butterflies or a young man's money.

It was very picturesque, the Rue Royale. The rich and poor met together. The locksmith's swinging key creaked next door to the bank; across the way, crouching mendicant-like in the shadow of a great importing house, was the mud laboratory of the mender of broken combs. Light balconies overhung the rows of showy shops and stores open for trade this Sunday morning, and pretty Latin faces of the higher class glanced over their savagely pronged railings upon the passers below. At some windows hung lace curtains, flannel duds at some, and at others only the scraping and sighing one-hinged shutter groaning toward Paris after its neglectful master.

M. St.-Ange stood looking up and down the street for nearly an hour. But few ladies, only the inveterate mass-goers, were out. About the entrances of the frequent *cafés* the masculine gentility stood leaning on canes, with which now one and now another beckoned to Jules, some even adding pantomimic hints of the social cup.

M. St.-Ange remarked to his servant without turning his head that somehow he felt sure he should soon return those *bons* that the mulatto had lent him.

"What will you do with them?"

"Me!" said Baptiste, quickly; "I will go and see the bull-fight in the Place Congo."

"There is to be a bull-fight? But where is M. Cayetano?"

"Ah, got all his affairs wet in the tornado. Instead of his circus, they are to have a bull-fight—not an ordinary bull-fight with sick horses, but a buffalo-and-tiger fight. I would not miss it——"

Two or three persons ran to the opposite corner, and commenced striking at something with their canes. Others followed. Can M. St.-Ange and servant, who hasten forward—can the Creoles, Cubans, Spaniards, San Domingo refugees, and other loungers—can they hope it is a fight? They hurry forward. Is a man in a fit? The crowd pours in from the side-streets. Have they killed a so-long snake? Bareheaded shopmen leave their wives, who stand upon chairs. The crowd huddles and packs. Those on the outside make little leaps into the air, trying to be tall.

"What is the matter?"

"Have they caught a real live rat?"

"Who is hurt?" asks some one in English.

"*Personne*," replies a shopkeeper; "a man's hat blow' in the gutter; but he has it now. Jules pick it. See, that is the man, head and shoulders on top of the res'."

"He in the homespun?" asks a second shopkeeper. "Humph! an *Américain*—a West-Floridian; bah!"

"But wait; 'st! he is speaking; listen!"

"To who 'is he speak——?"

"Sh-sh-sh! to Jules."

"Jules who?"

"Silence, you! To Jules St.-Ange, what h-owe me a bill since long time. Sh-sh-sh!"

Then the voice was heard.

Its owner was a man of giant stature, with a slight stoop in his shoulders, as if he was making a constant, good-natured attempt to accommodate himself to ordinary doors and ceilings. His bones were those of an ox. His face was marked more by weather than age, and his narrow brow was bald and smooth. He had instantaneously formed an opinion of Jules St.-Ange, and the multitude of words, most of them lingual curiosities, with which he was rasping the wide-open ears of his listeners, signified, in short, that, as sure as his name was Parson Jones, the little Creole was a "plumb gentleman."

M. St.-Ange bowed and smiled, and was about to call attention, by both gesture and speech, to a singular object on top of the still uncovered head, when the nervous motion of the *Américain* anticipated him, as, throwing up an immense hand, he drew down a large roll of bank-notes. The crowd laughed, the West-Floridian joining, and began to disperse.

"Why, that money belongs to Smyrny Church," said the giant.

"You are very dengerous to make your money expose like that, Misty Posson Jone'," said St.-Ange, counting it with his eyes.

The countryman gave a start and smile of surprise.

"How d'dyou know my name was Jones?" he asked; but, without pausing for the Creole's answer, furnished in his reckless way some further specimens of West-Floridian English; and the conciseness with which he presented full intelligence of his home, family, calling, lodging-house, and present and future plans, might have passed for consummate art, had it not been the most run-wild nature. "And I've done been to Mobile, you know, on busi*ness* for Bethesdy Church. It's the on'yest time I ever been from home; now you wouldn't of believed that, would you? But I admire to have saw you, that's so. You've got to come and eat with me. Me and my boy ain't been fed yit.

What might one call yo' name? Jools? Come on, Jools. Come on, Colossus. That's my niggah—his name's Colossus of Rhodes. Is that yo' yallah boy, Jools? Fetch him along, Colossus. It seems like a special provi*dence*.— Jools, do you believe in a special provi*dence*?"

Jules remembered the roll of bank-notes and said he did.

The new-made friends moved briskly off, followed by Baptiste and a short, square, old negro, very black and grotesque, who had introduced himself to the mulatto, with many glittering and cavernous smiles, as "d'body-sarvant of d'Rev'n Mr. Jones."

Both pairs enlivened their walk with conversation. Parson Jones descanted upon the doctrine he had mentioned, as illustrated in the perplexities of cotton-growing, and concluded that there would always be "a special provi*dence* again' cotton untell folks quits a-pressin' of it and haulin' of it on Sundays!"

"*Je dis*," said St.-Ange, in response, "I thing you is juz right. I believe, me, strong-strong in the improvidence, yes. You know my papa he h-own a sugah-plantation, you know. 'Jules, my son,' he say one time to me, 'I goin' to make one baril sugah to fedge the moze high price in New Orleans.' Well, he take his bez baril sugah—I nevah see a so careful man like my papa always to make a so beautiful sugah *et sirop*. 'Jules, go at Father Pierre, an' ged this lill pitcher fill with holy-water, an' tell him sen' his tin bucket, and I will make it fill with *quitte*.' I ged the holy-water; my papa sprinkle it over the baril, an' make one cross on the 'ead of the baril."

"Why, Jools," said Parson Jones, "that didn't do no good."

"Din do no good! Id broughd the so great value! You can strike me dead if thad baril sugah din fedge the more high cost than any other in the city. *Parceque*, the man what buy that baril sugah he make a mistake of one hundred pound"—falling back—"*Mais* certain-lee!"

"And you think that was growin' out of the holy-water?" asked the parson.

"*Mais*, what could make it else? Id could not be the *quitte*, because my papa keep the bucket, an' forget to sen' the *quitte* to Father Pierre."

Parson Jones was disappointed.

"Well, now, Jools, you know, I don't think that was right. I reckon you must be a plumb Catholic."

M. St.-Ange shrugged. He would not deny his faith.

"I am a *Catholique, mais*"—brightening as

he hoped to recommend himself anew—"not a good one."

"Well, you know," said Jones—"where's Colossus? Oh! all right. Colossus strayed off a minute in Mobile, and I plumb lost him for two days. Here's the place; come in. Colossus and this boy can go to the kitchen.—Now, Colossus, what *air* you a-beckonin at me faw?"

He let his servant draw him aside and address him in a whisper.

"Oh, go 'way!" said the parson with a jerk. "Who's goin' to throw me? What? Speak louder. Why, Colossus, you shayn't talk so, saw. 'Pon my soul, yo're the mightiest fool I ever taken up with. Jest you go down that alley-way with this yallah boy, and don't show yo' face untell yo' called!"

The negro begged; the master wrathily insisted.

"Colossus, will you do ez I tell you, or shell I hev to strike you, saw?"

"O Mahs Jimmy, I—I's gwine; but"—he ventured nearer—"don't on no account drink nothin', Mahs Jimmy."

Such was the negro's earnestness that he put one foot in the gutter, and fell heavily against his master. The parson threw him off angrily.

"Thar, now! Why, Colossus, you must of been dosted with sumthin'; yo' plumb crazy.—Humph, come on, Jools, let's eat! Humph! to tell me that when I never taken a drop, exceptin' for chills, in my life—which he knows so as well as me!"

The two masters began to ascend a stair.

"*Mais*, he is a sassy; I would sell him, me," said the young Creole.

"No, I wouldn't do that," replied the parson; "though there is people in Bethesdy who says he is a roscal. He's a powerful smart fool. Why, that boy's got money, Jools; more money than religion, I reckon. I'm shore he fallen into mighty bad company"—they passed beyond earshot.

Baptiste and Colossus, instead of going to the tavern kitchen, went on to the next door and entered the dark rear corner of a low grocery, where, the law notwithstanding, liquor was covertly sold to slaves. There, in the quiet company of Baptiste and the grocer, the colloquial powers of Colossus, which were simply prodigious, began very soon to show themselves.

"For whilst," said he, "Mahs Jimmy has eddication, you know—whilst he has eddication, I has 'scretion. He has eddication and I has 'scretion, an' so we gits along."

He drew a black bottle down the counter,

and, laying half his length upon the damp board, continued:

"As a p'inciple I discredits de imbimin' of awjus liquors. De imbimin' of awjus liquors, de wiolution of de Sabbaf, de playin' of de fiddle, and de usin' of by-words, dey is de fo' sins of de conscience; an' if any man sin de fo' sins of de conscience, de debble done sharp his fork fo' dat man.—Ain't dat so, boss?"

The grocer was sure it was so.

"Neberdeless, mind you"—here the orator brimmed his glass from the bottle and swallowed the contents with a dry eye—"mind you, a roytious man, sech as ministers of de gospel and deir body-sarvants, can take a *leetle* for de weak stomach."

But the fascinations of Colossus's eloquence must not mislead us; this is the story of a true Christian; to wit, Parson Jones.

The parson and his new friend ate. But the coffee M. St.-Ange declared he could not touch; it was too wretchedly bad. At the French Market, near by, there was some noble coffee. This, however, would have to be bought, and Parson Jones had scruples.

"You see, Jools, every man has his conscience to guide him, which it does so in——"

"Oh, yes!" cried St.-Ange, "conscien'; thad is the bez, Posson Jone'. Certainlee! I am a *Catholique*, you is a *schismatique*; you thing it is wrong to dring some coffee—well, then it *is* wrong; you thing it is wrong to make the sugah to ged the so large price—well, then it *is* wrong; I thing it is right—well, then, it *is* right; it is all 'abit; *c'est tout*. What a man thing is right, *is right;* 'tis all 'abit. A man muz nod go again' his conscien'. My faith! do you thing I would go again' my conscien'? *Mais allons*, led us go and ged some coffee."

"Jools."

"W'at?"

"Jools, it ain't the drinkin' of coffee, but the buyin' of it on a Sabbath. You must really excuse me, Jools, it's again' conscience, you know."

"Ah!" said St.-Agne, "*c'est* very true. For you it would be a sin, *mais* for me it is only 'abit. Rilligion is a very strange; I know a man one time, he thing it was wrong to go to cock-fight Sunday evening. I thing it is all 'abit. *Mais*, come, Posson Jone'; I have got one friend, Miguel; led us go at his house and ged some coffee. Come; Miguel have no familie; only him and Joe—always like to see friend; *allons*, led us come yonder."

"Why, Jools, my dear friend, you know," said the shamefaced parson, "I never visit on Sundays."

"Never w'at?" asked the astounded Creole.

"No," said Jones, smiling awkwardly.

"Never visite?"

"Exceptin' sometimes amongst church-members," said Parson Jones.

"*Mais*," said the seductive St.-Ange, "Miguel and Joe is church-member'—certainlee! They love to talk about rilligion. Come at Miguel and talk about some rilligion. I am nearly expire for my coffee."

Parson Jones took his hat from beneath his chair and rose up.

"Jools," said the weak giant, "I ought to be in church right now."

"*Mais*, the church is right yond' at Miguel, yes. Ah!" continued St.-Ange, as they descended the stairs, "I thing every man muz have the rilligion he like the bez—me, I like the *Catholique* rilligion the bez—for me it *is* the bez. Every man will sure go to heaven if he like his rilligion the bez."

"Jools," said the West-Floridian, laying his great hand tenderly upon the Creole's shoulder, as they stepped out upon the *banquette*, "do you think you have any shore hopes of heaven?"

"Yass!" replied St.-Ange; "I am sure-sure. I thing everybody will go to heaven. I thing you will go, *et* I thing Miguel will go, *et* Joe—everybody, I thing—*mais*, h'of course, not if they not have been christen'. Even I thing some niggers will go."

"Jools," said the parson, stopping in his walk—"Jools, I *don't* want to lose my niggah."

"You will not loose him. With Baptiste he *cannot* ged loose."

But Colossus's master was not reassured.

"Now," said he, still tarrying, "this is jest the way; had I of gone to church——"

"Posson Jone'," said Jules.

"What?"

"I tell you. We goin' to church!"

"Will you?" asked Jones, joyously.

"*Allons*, come along," said Jules, taking his elbow.

They walked down the Rue Chartres, passed several corners, and by and by turned into a cross street. The parson stopped an instant as they were turning, and looked back up the street.

"W'at you lookin'?" asked his companion.

"I thought I saw Colossus," answered the parson, with an anxious face; "I reckon 'twa'n't him, though." And they went on.

The street they now entered was a very quiet one. The eye of any chance passer would have been at once drawn to a broad, heavy, white brick edifice on the lower side of the way, with a flag-pole standing out like a bowsprit from one of its great windows, and a pair of lamps hanging before a large closed entrance. It was a theatre, sub-let to gamblers. At this morning hour all was still, and the only sign of life was a knot of little barefoot girls gathered within its narrow shade, and each carrying an infant relative. Into this place the parson and M. St.-Ange entered, the little nurses jumping up from the sills to let them pass in.

A half-hour may have passed. At the end of that time the whole juvenile company were laying alternate eyes and ears to the chinks, to gather what they could of an interesting quarrel going on within.

"I did not, saw! I given you no cause of offence, saw! It's not so, saw! Mister Jools simply mistaken the house, thinkin' it was a Sabbath-school! No such thing, saw; I *ain't* bound to bet! Yes, I kin git out! Yes, without bettin'! I hev a right to my opinion; I reckon I'm a *white man*, saw! No, saw! I on'y said I didn't think you could get the game on them cards. 'Sno such thing, saw! I do *not* know how to play! I wouldn't hev a roscal's money ef I should win it! Shoot, ef you dare! You can kill me, but you can't scare me! No, I shayn't bet! I'll die first! Yes, saw; Mr. Jools can bet for me if he admires to; I ain't his mostah."

Here the speaker seemed to direct his words to St.-Ange.

"Saw, I don't understand you, saw. I never said I'd loan you money to bet on me. I didn't suspicion this from you, saw. No, I won't take any mo' lemonade; it's the most notorious stuff I ever drank, saw!"

M. St.-Ange's replies were in *falsetto* and not without effect; for presently the parson's indignation and anger began to melt. "Don't ask me, Jools, I can't help you. It's no use; it's a matter of conscience with me, Jools."

"*Mais oui!* 'tis a matt' of conscien' wid me, the same."

"But, Jools, the money's none o' mine, nohow; it belongs to Smyrny, you know."

"If I could make juz *one* bet," said the persuasive St.-Ange, "I would leave this place, fas'-fas', yes. If I had thing—*mais* I did not soupsicion this from you, Posson Jone'——"

"Don't, Jools, don't!"

"No! Posson Jone'."

"You're bound to win?" said the parson, wavering.

"*Mais certainement!* But it is not to win that I want; 'tis my conscien'—my honor!"

"Well, Jools, I hope I'm not a-doin' no wrong. I'll loan you some of this money if you say you'll come right out 'thout takin' your winnin's."

All was still. The peeping children could see the parson as he lifted his hand to his breast-pocket. There it paused a moment in bewilderment, then plunged to the bottom. It came back empty, and fell lifelessly at his side. His head dropped upon his breast, his eyes were for a moment closed, his broad palms were lifted and pressed against his forehead, a tremor seized him, and he fell all in a lump to the floor. The children ran off with their infant loads, leaving Jules St.-Ange swearing by all his deceased relatives, first to Miguel and Joe, and then to the lifted parson, that he did not know what had become of the money "except if" the black man had got it.

In the rear of ancient New Orleans, beyond the sites of the old rampart, (a trio of Spanish forts,) where the town has since sprung up and grown old, green with all the luxuriance of the wild Creole summer, lay the Congo Plains. Here stretched the canvas of the historic Cayetano, who Sunday after Sunday sowed the sawdust for his circus-ring.

But to-day the great showman had fallen short of his printed promise. The hurricane had come by night, and with one fell swash had made an irretrievable sop of everything. The circus trailed away its bedraggled magnificence, and the ring was cleared for the bull. Then the sun seemed to come out and work for the people. "See," said the Spaniards, looking up at the glorious sky with its great white fleets drawn off upon the horizon—"see —heaven smiles upon the bull-fight!"

In the high upper seats of the rude amphitheatre sat the gayly decked wives and daughters of the Gascons, from the *métairies* along the Ridge, and the chattering Spanish women of the Market, their shining hair unbonneted to the sun. Next below were their husbands and lovers in Sunday blouses, milkmen, butchers, bakers, black-bearded fishermen, Sicilian fruiterers, swarthy Portuguese sailors in little woollen caps, and strangers of the graver sort; mariners of England, Germany, and Holland. The lowest seats were full of trappers, smugglers, Canadian *voyageurs*, drinking and singing; *Américains*, too—more's the shame— from the upper rivers—who will not keep their seats, who ply the bottle, and who will get home by and by and tell how wicked Sodom is; broad-brimmed, silver-braided Mexicans, also, with their copper cheeks, and bat's eyes, and their tinkling spurred heels. Yonder, in that quieter section, are the quadroon women in

their black lace shawls—and there is Baptiste; and below them are the turbaned black women, and there is—but he vanishes—Colossus.

The afternoon is advancing, yet the sport, though loudly demanded, does not begin. The, *Américains* grow derisive and find pastime in gibes and raillery. They mock the various Latins with their national inflections, and answer their scowls with laughter. Some of the more aggressive shout pretty French greetings to the women of Gascony, and one bargeman, amid peals of applause, stands on a seat and hurls a kiss to the quadroons. The mariners of England, Germany, and Holland, as spectators, like the fun, while the Spaniards look black and cast defiant imprecations upon their persecutors. Some Gascons, with timely caution, pick their women out and depart, running a terrible fire of gallantries.

In hope of truce, a new call is raised for the bull: "The bull, the bull!—hush!"

In a tier near the ground a man is standing and calling—standing head and shoulders above the rest—calling in the *Américaine* tongue. Another man, big and red, named Joe, and a handsome little Creole, in elegant dress and full of laughter, wish to stop him, but the flat-boatmen, ha-ha-ing and cheering, will not suffer it. Ah, through some shameful knavery of the men, into whose hands he has fallen, he is drunk! Even the women can see that; and now he throws his arms wildly and raises his voice until the whole great circle hears it. He is preaching!

Ah! kind Lord, for a special providence now! The men of his own nation—men from the land of the open English Bible and temperance cup and song are cheering him on to mad disgrace. And now another call for the appointed sport is drowned by the flat-boatmen singing the ancient tune of Mear. You can hear the words—

"Old Grimes is dead, that good old soul"

—From ribald lips and throats turned brazen with laughter, from singers who toss their hats aloft and roll in their seats the chorus swells to the accompaniment of a thousand brogans—

"He used to wear an old gray coat
    All buttoned down before."

A ribboned man in the arena is trying to be heard, and the Latins raise one mighty cry for silence. The big red man gets a hand over the parson's mouth, and the ribboned man seizes his moment.

"They have been endeavoring for hours," he says, "to draw the terrible animals from their dens, but such is their strength and fierceness, that——"

His voice is drowned. Enough has been heard to warrant the inference that the beasts cannot be whipped out of the storm-drenched cages to which menagerie life and long starvation have attached them, and from the roar of indignation the man of ribbons flies. The noise increases. Men are standing up by hundreds, and women are imploring to be let out of the turmoil. All at once, like the bursting of a dam, the whole mass pours down into the ring. They sweep across the arena and over the showman's barriers. Miguel gets a frightful trampling. Who cares for gates or doors? They tear the beasts' houses bar from bar, and, laying hold of the gaunt buffalo, drag him forth by feet, ears, and tail; and in the midst of the *mêlée*, still head and shoulders above all, wilder, with the cup of the wicked, than any beast, is the man of God from the Florida parishes!

In his arms he bore—and all the people shouted at once when they saw it—the tiger. He had lifted it high up with its back to his breast, his arms clasped under its shoulders; the wretched brute had curled up caterpillar-wise, with its long tail against its belly, and through its filed teeth grinned a fixed and impotent wrath. And Parson Jones was shouting:

"The tiger and the buffler *shell* lay down together! You dah to say they shayn't, and I'll comb you with this varmint from head to foot! The tiger and the buffler *shell* lay down together. They *shell*. Now, you, Joe! Behold! I am here to see it done. The lion and the buffler *shell* lay down together!"

Mouthing these words again and again, the parson forced his way through the surge in the wake of the buffalo. This creature the Latins had secured by a lariat over his head, and were dragging across the old rampart and into a street of the city.

The northern races were trying to prevent, and there was pommelling and knocking down, cursing and knife-drawing, until Jules St.-Ange was quite carried away with the fun, laughed, clapped his hands, and swore with delight, and ever kept close to the gallant parson.

Joe, contrariwise, counted all this child's-play an interruption. He had come to find Colossus and the money. In an unlucky moment he made bold to lay hold of the parson, but a piece of the broken barriers in the hands of a flat-boatman felled him to the sod, the terrible crowd swept over him, the lariat was cut, and the giant parson hurled the tiger upon the buffalo's back. In another instant both brutes were dead at the hands of the mob; Jones was lifted from his feet, and prating of Scripture and the millennium, of Paul at Ephesus and Daniel in the "buffler's" den, was borne aloft upon the shoulders of the huzzaing *Américains*. Half an hour later he was sleeping heavily on the floor of a cell in the *calaboza*.

When Parson Jones awoke, a bell was somewhere tolling for midnight. Somebody was at the door of his cell with a key. The lock grated, the door swung, the turnkey looked in and stepped back, and a ray of moonlight fell upon M. Jules St.-Ange. The prisoner sat upon the empty shackles and ring-bolt in the centre of the floor.

"Misty Posson Jone'," said the visitor, softly.

"O Jools!"

"*Mais*, w'at de matter, Posson Jone'?"

"My sins, Jools, my sins!"

"Ah! Posson Jone', is that something to cry, because a man get sometime a litt' bit intoxicate? *Mais*, if a man keep *all the time* intoxicate, I think that is again' the conscien'."

"Jools, Jools, your eyes is darkened—oh! Jools, where's my pore old niggah?"

"Posson Jone', never mine; he is wid Baptiste."

"Where?"

"I don't know w'ere—*mais* he is wid Baptiste. Baptiste is a beautiful to take care of somebody."

"Is he as good as you, Jools?" asked Parson Jones, sincerely.

Jules was slightly staggered.

"You know, Posson Jone', you know, a nigger cannot be good as a w'ite man—*mais* Baptiste is a good nigger."

The parson moaned and dropped his chin into his hands.

"I was to of left for home to-morrow, sun up, on the *Isabella* schooner. Pore Smyrny!" He deeply sighed.

"Posson Jone'," said Jules, leaning against the wall and smiling. "I swear you is the moz funny man what I never see. If I was you I would say, me, 'Ah! 'ow I am lucky! the money I los', it was not mine, anyhow!' My faith! shall a man make hisse'f to be the more sorry because the money he los' is not his? Me, I would say, 'it is a specious providence.' "Ah! Misty Posson Jone'," he continued, "you make a so droll sermon ad the bull-ring. Ha! ha! I swear I think you can make money to preach thad sermon many time ad the theatre St. Philippe. Hah! you is the moz brave dat I never see, *mais* ad the same time the moz rilligious man. Where I'm goin' to fin' one priest to make like dat? *Mais*, why you can't cheer up an' be 'appy? Me, if I should be miserabl' like dat I would kill meself."

The countryman only shook his head.

"*Bien*, Posson Jone', I have the so good news for you."

The prisoner looked up with eager inquiry.

"Laz' evening when they lock' you, I come right off at M. De Blanc's house to get you let out of the calaboose; M. De Blanc he is the judge. So soon I was entering—'Ah! Jules, me boy, juz the man to make complete the game!' Posson Jone', it was a specious providence! I win in t'ree hours more dan six hundred dollah! Look." He produced a mass of bank-notes, *bons*, and due-bills.

"And you got the pass?" asked the parson, regarding the money with a strange sadness.

"It is here; it take the effect so soon the daylight."

"Jools, my friend, your kindness is in vain."

The Creole's face became a perfect blank.

"Because," said the parson, "for two reasons: firstly, I have broken the laws, and ought to stand the penalty; and secondly—you must really excuse me, Jools, you know, but the pass has been got onfairly, I'm afeerd. You told the judge I was innocent; and in neither case it don't become a Christian (which I hope I can still say I am one) to 'do evil that good may come.' I muss stay."

M. St.-Ange stood up aghast, and for a moment speechless, at this exhibition of moral heroism: but an artifice was presently hit upon. "*Mais*, Posson Jone'!"—in his old *falsetto*— "de order—you cannot read it, it is in French —compel you to go h-out, sir!"

"Is that so?" cried the parson, bounding up with radiant face—"is that so, Jools?"

The young man nodded, smiling; but, though he smiled, the fountain of his tenderness was opened. He made the sign of the cross as the parson knelt in prayer, and even whispered "Hail Mary," etc., quite through, twice over.

Morning broke in summer glory upon a cluster of villas behind the city, nestled under live-oaks and magnolias on the banks of a deep bayou, and known as Suburb St. Jean.

With the first beam came the West-Floridian and the Creole out upon the bank below the village. Upon the parson's arm hung a pair of antique saddle-bags. Baptiste limped wearily behind; both his eyes were encircled with broad blue rings, and one cheek-bone bore the official impress of every knuckle of Colossus's left hand. The "beautiful to take care of somebody" had lost his charge. At mention of the negro he became wild, and, half in English, half in the "gumbo" dialect, said murderous things. Intimidated by Jules to calmness, he became able to speak confidently on one point; he could, would, and did swear that Colossus had gone home to the Florida parishes; he was almost certain; in fact, he thought so.

There was a clicking of pulleys as the three appeared upon the bayou's margin, and Baptiste pointed out, in the deep shadow of a great oak, the *Isabella*, moored among the bulrushes, and just spreading her sails for departure. Moving down to where she lay, the parson and his friend paused on the bank, loath to say farewell.

"O Jools!" said the parson, "supposin' Colossus ain't gone home! O Jools, if you'll look him out for me, I'll never forget you—I'll never forget you, nohow, Jools. No, Jools, I never will believe he taken that money. Yes, I know all niggahs will steal"—he set foot upon the gang-plank—"but Colossus wouldn't steal from me. Good-by."

"Misty Posson Jone'," said St.-Ange, putting his hand on the parson's arm with genuine affection, "hol' on. You see dis money—w'at I win las' night? Well, I win' it by a specious providence, ain't it?"

"There's no tellin'," said the humbled Jones. "Providence

"'Moves in a mysterious way
His wonders to perform.'"

"Ah!" cried the Creole, "*c'est* very true. I ged this money in the mysterieuze way. *Mais*, if I keep dis money, you know where it goin' be to-night?"

"I really can't say," replied the parson.

"Goin' to de dev'," said the sweetly smiling young man.

The schooner-captain, leaning against the shrouds, and even Baptiste, laughed outright.

"O Jools, you mustn't!"

"Well, den, w'at I shall do wid *it*?"

"Any thing!" answered the parson; "better donate it away to some poor man——"

"Ah! Misty Posson Jone', dat is w'at I want. You los' five hundred dollah'—'twas my fault."

"No, it wa'n't, Jools."

"*Mais*, it was!"

"No!"

"It *was* my fault! I *swear* it was my fault! *Mais*, here is five hondred dollah'; I wish you shall take it. Here! I don't got no use for money.—Oh, my faith! Posson Jone', you must not begin to cry some more."

Parson Jones was choked with tears. When he found voice he said:

"O Jools, Jools, Jools! my pore, noble, dear, misguidened friend! ef you hed of hed a Christian raisin'! May the Lord show you your errors, better'n I kin, and bless you for your good intentions—oh, no! I cayn't touch that money with a ten-foot pole; it wa'n't rightly got; you must really excuse me, my dear friend, but I cayn't touch it."

St.-Ange was petrified.

"Good-by, dear Jools," continued the parson. "I'm in the Lord's haynds, and he's very merciful, which I hope and trust you'll find it out. Good-by!"—the schooner swung slowly off before the breeze—"good-by!"

St.-Ange roused himself.

"Posson Jone'! make me hany'ow *dis* promise: you never, never, *never* will come back to New Orleans."

"Ah, Jools, the Lord willin', I'll never leave home again!"

"All right!" cried the Creole; "I thing He's willin'. Adieu, Posson Jone'. My faith'! you are the so fighting an' moz rilligious man as I never saw! Adieu! Adieu!"

Baptiste uttered a cry and presently ran by his master toward the schooner, his hands full of clods.

St.-Ange looked just in time to see the sable form of Colossus of Rhodes emerge from the vessel's hold, and the pastor of Smyrna and Bethesda seize him in his embrace.

"O Colossus! you outlandish old niggah! Thank the Lord! Thank the Lord!"

The little Creole almost wept. He ran down the tow-path, laughing and swearing, and making confused allusion to the entire *personnel* and furniture of the lower regions.

By odd fortune, at the moment that St.-Ange further demonstrated his delight by tripping his mulatto into a bog, the schooner came brushing along the reedy bank with a graceful curve, the sails flapped, and the crew fell to poling her slowly along.

Parson Jones was on the deck, kneeling once more in prayer. His hat had fallen before him; behind him knelt his slave. In thundering tones he was confessing himself "a plumb fool," from whom "the conceit had been jolted out," and who had been made to see that even his "nigger had the longest head of the two."

Colossus clasped his hands and groaned.

The parson prayed for a contrite heart.

"Oh, yes!" cried Colossus.

The master acknowledged countless mercies.

"Dat's so!" cried the slave.

The master prayed that they might still be "piied on."

"Glory!" cried the black man, clapping his hands; "pile on!"

"An' now," continued the parson, "bring this pore, backslidin' jackace of a parson and this pore ole fool niggah back to thar home in peace!"

"Pray fo' de money!" called Colossus.

But the parson prayed for Jules.

"Pray fo' de *money!*" repeated the negro.

"And oh, give thy servant back that there lost money!"

Colossus rose stealthily, and tiptoed by his still shouting master. St.-Ange, the captain, the crew, gazed in silent wonder at the strategist. Pausing but an instant over the master's hat to grin an acknowledgment of his beholders' speechless interest, he softly placed in it the faithfully mourned and honestly prayed-for Smyrna fund; then, saluted by the gesticulative, silent applause of St.-Ange and the schooner men, he resumed his first attitude behind his roaring master.

"Amen!" cried Collossus, meaning to bring him to a close.

"Onworthy though I be—" cried Jones.

"*Amen!*" reiterated the negro.

"A-a-amen!" said Parson Jones.

He rose to his feet, and, stooping to take up his hat, beheld the well-known roll. As one stunned he gazed for a moment upon his slave, who still knelt with clasped hands and rolling eyeballs; but when he became aware of the laughter and cheers that greeted him from both deck and shore, he lifted eyes and hands to heaven, and cried like the veriest babe. And when he looked at the roll again, and hugged and kissed it, St.-Ange tried to raise a second shout, but choked, and the crew fell to their poles.

And now up runs Baptiste, covered with slime, and prepares to cast his projectiles. The first one fell wide of the mark; the schooner swung round into a long reach of water, where the breeze was in her favor; another shout of laughter drowned the maledictions of the muddy man; the sails filled; Colossus of Rhodes, smiling and bowing as hero of the moment, ducked as the main boom swept round, and the schooner, leaning slightly to the pleasant influence, rustled a moment over the bulrushes, and then sped far away down the rippling bayou.

M. Jules St.-Ange stood long, gazing at the receding vessel as it now disappeared, now reappeared beyond the tops of the high undergrowth; but, when an arm of the forest hid it finally from sight, he turned townward, followed by that fagged-out spaniel, his servant, saying, as he turned, "Baptiste."

"*Miché?*"

"You know w'at I goin' do wid dis money?"

"*Non, miché.*"

"Well, you can strike me dead if I don't goin' to pay hall my debts! *Allons!*"

He began a merry little song to the effect that his sweetheart was a wine-bottle, and master and man, leaving care behind, returned to the picturesque Rue Royale. The ways of Providence are indeed strange. In all Parson Jones's after-life, amid the many painful reminiscences of his visit to the City of the Plain, the sweet knowledge was withheld from him that by the light of the Christian virtue that shone from him even in his great fall, Jules St.-Ange arose, and went to his father an honest man.

JOEL CHANDLER HARRIS (1848–1908)

From UNCLE REMUS: HIS SONGS AND HIS SAYINGS
(1880)

THE STORY OF THE DELUGE AND HOW IT CAME ABOUT

"One time," said Uncle Remus—adjusting his spectacles so as to be able to see how to thread a large darning-needle with which he was patching his coat—"one time, way back yander, 'fo' you wuz borned, honey, en 'fo' Mars John er Miss Sally wuz borned—way back yonder 'fo' enny un us wuz borned, de anemils en de creeturs sorter 'lecshuneer roun' 'mong deyselves, twel at las' day 'greed fer ter have a 'sembly. In dem days," continued the old man, observing a look of incredulity on the little boy's face, "in dem days creeturs had lots mo' sense dan dey got now; let 'lone dat, dey had sense same like folks. Hit wuz tech en go wid um, too, mon, en w'en dey make up der mines w'at hatter be done, 'twant mo'n menshun'd 'fo' hit wuz done. Well, dey 'lected dat dey hatter hole er 'sembly fer ter sorter straighten out marters en hear de complaints, en w'en de day come dey wuz on han'. De Lion, he wuz dar, kase he wuz de king, en he hatter be dar. De Rhynosyhoss, he wuz dar, en de Elephent, he wuz dar, en de Cammils, en de Cows, en plum down ter de Crawfishes, dey wuz dar. Dey wuz all dar. En w'en de Lion shuck his mane, en tuck his seat in de big cheer, den de sesshun begun fer ter commence."

"What did they do, Uncle Remus?" asked the little boy.

"I can't skacely call to mine 'zackly w'at dey did do, but dey spoke speeches, en hollered, en cusst, en flung der langwidge 'roun' des like w'en yo' daddy wuz gwineter run fer de legislater en got lef'. Howsomever, dey 'ranged der 'fairs, en splained der bizness.

Bimeby, w'ile dey wuz 'sputin' 'longer one er nudder, de Elephent trompled on one er de Crawfishes. Co'se w'en dat creetur put his foot down, w'atsumever's under dar wuz boun' fer ter be squshed, en dey wa'n't nuff er dat Crawfish lef' fer ter tell dat he'd bin dar.

"Dis make de udder Crawfishes mighty mad, en dey sorter swarmed tergedder en draw'd up a kinder peramble wid some warfo'es in it, en read her out in de 'sembly. But, bless grashus! sech a racket wuz a gwine on dat nobody ain't hear it, 'ceppin may be de Mud Turkle en de Spring Lizzud, en dere enfloons wuz pow'ful lackin'.

"Bimeby, w'iles de Nunicorn wuz 'sputin' wid de Lion, en w'ile de Hyener wuz a laughin' ter hisse'f, de Elephent squshed anudder one er de Crawfishes, en a little mo'n he'd er ruint de Mud Turkle. Den de Crawfishes, w'at dey wuz lef' un um, swarmed tergedder en draw'd up annuder peramble wid sum mo' wharfo'es; but dey might ez well er sung Ole Dan Tucker ter a harrycane. De udder creeturs wuz too busy wid der fussin' fer ter 'spon' unto de Crawfishes. So dar dey wuz, de Crawfishes, en dey didn't know w'at minnit wuz gwineter be de nex'; en dey kep' on gittin madder en madder en skeerder en skeerder, twel bimeby dey gun de wink ter de Mud Turkle en de Spring Lizzud, en den dey bo'd little holes in de groun' en went down outer sight."

"Who did, Uncle Remus?" asked the little boy.

"De Crawfishes, honey. Dey bo'd inter de groun' en kep' on bo'in twel dey onloost de fountains er de earf; en de waters squirt out, en riz higher en higher twel de hills wuz kivered, en de creeturs wuz all drownded; en all bekaze dey let on 'mong deyselves dat dey wuz bigger dan de Crawfishes."

Then the old man blew the ashes from a smoking yam, and proceeded to remove the peeling.

"Where was the ark, Uncle Remus?" the little boy inquired, presently.

"W'ich ark's dat?" asked the old man, in a tone of well-feigned curiosity.

"Noah's ark," replied the child.

"Don't you pester wid ole man Noah, honey. I boun' he tuck keer er dat ark. Dat's w'at he wuz dar fer, en dat's w'at he done. Leas'ways, dat's w'at dey tells me. But don't you bodder longer dat ark, 'ceppin' your mammy fetches it up. Dey mout er bin two deloojes, en den agin dey moutent. Ef dey wuz enny ark in dish yer w'at de Crawfishes brung on, I ain't heern tell un it, en w'en dey ain't no arks 'roun', I ain't got no time fer ter make um en put um in dar. Hit's gittin' yo' bedtime, honey."

MR. RABBIT NIBBLES UP THE BUTTER

"De animils en de creeturs," said Uncle Remus, shaking his coffee around in the bottom of his tin-cup, in order to gather up all the sugar, "dey kep' on gittin' mo' en mo' familious wid wunner nudder, twel bimeby, 'twan't long 'fo' Brer Rabbit, en Brer Fox, en Brer Possum got ter sorter bunchin' der perwishuns tergedder in de same shanty. Atter w'ile de roof sorter 'gun ter leak, en one day Brer Rabbit, en Brer Fox, en Brer Possum, 'semble fer ter see ef dey can't kinder patch her up. Dey had a big day's work in front un um, en dey fotch der dinner wid um. Dey lump de vittles up in one pile, en de butter w'at Brer Fox brung, dey goes en puts in de spring-'ouse fer ter keep cool, en den dey went ter wuk, en 'twan't long 'fo' Brer Rabbit stummuck 'gun ter sorter growl en pester 'im. Dat butter er Brer Fox sot heavy on his mine, en his mouf water eve'y time he 'member 'bout it. Present'y he say ter hisse'f dat he bleedzd ter have a nip at dat butter, en den he lay his plans, he did. Fus' news you know, w'ile dey wuz all wukkin' 'long, Brer Rabbit raise his head quick en fling his years forrerd en holler out:

"'Here I is. W'at you want wid me?' en off he put like sump'n wuz atter 'im.

"He sallied 'roun', ole Brer Rabbit did, en atter he make sho dat nobody ain't foller'n un 'im, inter de spring-'ouse he bounces, en dar he stays twel he git a bait er butter. Den he santer on back en go to wuk.

"'Whar you bin?' sez Brer Fox, sezee.

"'I hear my chilluns callin' me,' sez Brer Rabbit, sezee, 'en I hatter go see w'at dey want. My ole 'oman done gone en tuck mighty sick,' sezee.

"Dey wuk on twel bimeby de butter tas'e so good dat ole Brer Rabbit want some mo'. Den he raise up his head, he did, en holler out:

"'Heyo! Hole on! I'm a comin'! 'en off he put.

"Dis time he stay right smart w'ile, en w'en he git back Brer Fox ax him whar he bin.

"'I been ter see my ole 'oman, en she's a sinkin',' sezee.

"Dreckly Brer Rabbit hear um callin' 'im ag'in en off he goes, en dis time, bless yo' soul, he gits de butter out so clean dat he kin see hisse'f in de bottom er de bucket. He scrape it clean en lick it dry, en den he go back ter wuk lookin' mo' samer dan a nigger w'at de patter-rollers bin had holt un.

"'How's yo' ole 'oman dis time?' sez Brer Fox, sezee.

"'I'm oblije ter you, Brer Fox,' sez Brer Rabbit, sezee, 'but I'm fear'd she's done gone by now,' en dat sorter make Brer Fox en Brer Possum feel in moanin' wid Brer Rabbit.

"Bimeby, w'en dinner-time come, dey all got out der vittles, but Brer Rabbit keep on lookin' lonesome, en Brer Fox en Brer Possum dey sorter rustle roun' fer ter see ef dey can't make Brer Rabbit feel sorter splimmy."

"What is that, Uncle Remus?" asked the little boy.

"Sorter splimmy-splammy, honey—sorter like he in a crowd—sorter like his ole 'oman ain't dead ez she mout be. You know how fokes duz w'en dey gits whar people's a moanin'."

The little boy didn't know, fortunately for him, and Uncle Remus went on:

"Brer Fox en Brer Possum rustle roun', dey did, gittin out de vittles, en bimeby Brer Fox, he say, sezee:

"'Brer Possum, you run down ter de spring en fetch de butter, en I'll sail 'roun' yer en set de table,' sezee.

"Brer Possum, he lope off atter de butter, en dreckly here he come lopin' back wid his years a trimblin' en his tongue a hangin' out. Brer Fox, he holler out:

"'W'at de matter now, Brer Possum?' sezee.

"'You all better run yer, fokes,' sez Brer Possum, sezee. 'De las' drap er dat butter done gone!'

" 'Whar she gone?' sez Brer Fox, sezee.

" 'Look like she dry up,' sez Brer Possum, sezee.

"Den Brer Rabbit, he look sorter sollum, he did, en he up'n say, sezee.

" 'I speck dat butter melt in somebody mouf,' sezee.

"Den dey went down ter de spring wid Brer Possum, en sho nuff de butter done gone. W'iles dey wuz sputin' over der wunderment, Brer Rabbit say he see tracks all 'roun' dar, en he p'int out dat ef dey'll all go ter sleep, he kin ketch de chap w'at stole de butter. Den dey all lie down en Brer Fox en Brer Possum dey soon drapt off ter sleep, but Brer Rabbit he stay 'wake, en w'en de time come he raise up easy en smear Brer Possum mouf wid de butter on his paws, en den he run off en nibble up de bes' er de dinner w'at dey lef' layin' out, en den he come back en wake up Brer Fox, en show 'im de butter on Brer Possum mouf. Den dey wake up Brer Possum, en tell 'im 'bout it, but c'ose Brer Possum 'ny it ter de las'. Brer Fox, dough, he's a kinder lawyer, en he argafy dis way—dat Brer Possum wuz de fus one at de butter, en de fus one fer ter miss it, en mo'n dat, dar hang de signs on his mouf. Brer Possum see dat dey got 'im jammed up in a cornder, en den he up en say dat de way fer ter ketch de man w'at stole de butter is ter b'il' a big bresh-heap en set her afier, en all han's try ter jump over, en de one w'at fall in, den he de chap w'at stole de butter. Brer Rabbit en Brer Fox dey bofe 'gree, dey did, en dey whirl in en b'il' de bresh-heap, en dey b'il' her

high en dey b'il' her wide, en den dey totch her off. W'en she got ter blazin' up good, Brer Rabbit, he tuck de fus turn. He sorter step back, en look 'roun' en giggle, en over he went mo' samer dan a bird flyin'. Den come Brer Fox. He got back little fudder, en spit on his han's, en lit out en made de jump, en he come so nigh gittin' in dat de een' er his tail kotch afier. Ain't you never see no fox, honey?" inquired Uncle Remus, in a tone that implied both conciliation and information.

The little boy thought probably he had, but he wouldn't commit himself.

"Well, den," continued the old man, "nex' time you see one un um, you look right close en see ef de een' er his tail ain't w'ite. Hit's des like I tell you. Dey b'ars de skyar er dat bresh-heap down ter dis day. Dey er marked —dat's w'at dey is—dey er marked."

"And what about Brother Possum?" asked the little boy.

"Ole Brer Possum, he tuck a runnin' start, he did, en he come lumberin' 'long, en de lit—kerblam!—right in de middle er de fier, en dat wuz de las' er ole Brer Possum."

"But, Uncle Remus, Brother Possum didn't steal the butter after all," said the little boy, who was not at all satisfied with such summary injustice.

"Dat w'at make I say w'at I duz, honey. In dis worril, lots er fokes is gotter suffer fer udder fokes sins. Look like hit's mighty onwrong; but hit's des dat away. Tribbalashun seem like she's a waitin' roun' de cornder fer ter ketch one en all un us, honey."

FREE JOE AND THE REST OF THE WORLD
(1884)

The name of Free Joe strikes humorously upon the ear of memory. It is impossible to say why, for he was the humblest, the simplest, and the most serious of all God's living creatures, sadly lacking in all those elements that suggest the humorous. It is certain, moreover, that in 1850 the sober-minded citizens of the little Georgian village of Hillsborough were not inclined to take a humorous view of Free Joe, and neither his name nor his presence provoked a smile. He was a black atom, drifting hither and thither without an owner, blown about by all the winds of circumstance, and given over to shiftlessness.

The problems of one generation are the paradoxes of a succeeding one, particularly if war, or some such incident, intervenes to clarify the atmosphere and strengthen the under-

standing. Thus, in 1850, Free Joe represented not only a problem of large concern, but, in the watchful eyes of Hillsborough, he was the embodiment of that vague and mysterious danger that seemed to be forever lurking on the outskirts of slavery, ready to sound a shrill and ghostly signal in the impenetrable swamps, and steal forth under the midnight stars to murder, rapine, and pillage,—a danger always threatening, and yet never assuming shape; intangible, and yet real; impossible, and yet not improbable. Across the serene and smiling front of safety, the pale outlines of the awful shadow of insurrection sometimes fell. With this invisible panorama as a background, it was natural that the figure of Free Joe, simple and humble as it was, should assume undue proportions. Go where he would, do what he might, he could not escape the finger of observation and the kindling eye of suspicion. His lightest words were noted, his slightest actions marked.

Under all the circumstances it was natural that his peculiar condition should reflect itself in his habits and manners. The slaves laughed loudly day by day, but Free Joe rarely laughed. The slaves sang at their work and danced at their frolics, but no one ever heard Free Joe sing or saw him dance. There was something painfully plaintive and appealing in his attitude, something touching in his anxiety to please. He was of the friendliest nature, and seemed to be delighed when he could amuse the little children who had made a playground of the public square. At times he would please them by making his little dog Dan perform all sorts of curious tricks, or he would tell them quaint stories of the beasts of the field and birds of the air; and frequently he was coaxed into relating the story of his own freedom. That story was brief, but tragical.

In the year of our Lord 1840, when a negro speculator of a sportive turn of mind reached the little village of Hillsborough on his way to the Mississippi region, with a caravan of likely negroes of both sexes, he found much to interest him. In that day and at that time there were a number of young men in the village who had not bound themselves over to repentance for the various misdeeds of the flesh. To these young men the negro speculator (Major Frampton was his name) proceeded to address himself. He was a Virginian, he declared; and, to prove the statement, he referred all the festively inclined young men of Hillsborough to a barrel of peach-brandy in one of his covered wagons. In the minds of these young men there was less doubt in regard to the age and quality of the brandy than there was in regard to the negro trader's birthplace. Major Frampton might or might not have been born in the Old Dominion—that was a matter for consideration and inquiry—but there could be no question as to the mellow pungency of the peach-brandy.

In his own estimation, Major Frampton was one of the most accomplished of men. He had summered at the Virginia Springs; he had been to Philadelphia, to Washington, to Richmond, to Lynchburg, and to Charleston, and had accumulated a great deal of experience which he found useful. Hillsborough was hid in the woods of Middle Georgia, and its general aspect of innocence impressed him. He looked on the young men who had shown their readiness to test his peach-brandy as overgrown country boys who needed to be introduced to some of the arts and sciences he had at his command. Thereupon the major pitched his tents, figuratively speaking, and became, for the time being, a part and parcel of the innocence that characterized Hillsborough. A wiser man would doubtless have made the same mistake.

The little village possessed advantages that seemed to be providentially arranged to fit the various enterprises that Major Frampton had in view. There was the auction block in front of the stuccoed court-house, if he desired to dispose of a few of his negroes; there was a quarter-track, laid out to his hand and in excellent order, if he chose to enjoy the pleasures of horse-racing; there were secluded pine thickets within easy reach, if he desired to indulge in the exciting pastime of cock-fighting; and various lonely and unoccupied rooms in the second story of the tavern, if he cared to challenge the chances of dice or cards.

Major Frampton tried them all with varying luck, until he began his famous game of poker with Judge Alfred Wellington, a stately gentleman with a flowing white beard and mild blue eyes that gave him the appearance of a benevolent patriarch. The history of the game in which Major Frampton and Judge Alfred Wellington took part is something more than a tradition in Hillsborough, for there are still living three or four men who sat around the table and watched its progress. It is said that at various stages of the game Major Frampton would destroy the cards with which they were playing, and send for a new pack, but the result was always the same. The mild blue eyes of Judge Wellington, with few exceptions, continued to overlook "hands" that were invincible—a habit they had acquired during a long and arduous course of training from Saratoga to New Orleans. Major Frampton lost his money, his horses, his wagons, and all his negroes but one, his body-servant. When his misfortune had reached this limit, the major adjourned the game. The sun was shining brightly, and all nature was cheerful. It is said that the major also seemed to be cheerful. However this may be, he visited the court-house, and executed the papers that gave his body-servant his freedom. This being done, Major Frampton sauntered into a convenient pine thicket, and blew out his brains.

The negro thus freed came to be known as Free Joe. Compelled, under the law, to choose a guardian, he chose Judge Wellington, chiefly because his wife Lucinda was among the negroes won from Major Frampton. For several years Free Joe had what may be called a jovial time. His wife Lucinda was well provided for, and he found it a comparatively easy matter to provide for himself; so that, taking all the circumstances into consideration, it is not matter for astonishment that he became somewhat shiftless.

When Judge Wellington died, Free Joe's troubles began. The Judge's negroes, including Lucinda, went to his half-brother, a man named Calderwood, who was a hard master and a rough customer generally—a man of many eccentricities of mind and character. His neighbors had a habit of alluding to him as "Old Spite"; and the name seemed to fit him so completely that he was known far and near as "Spite" Calderwood. He probably enjoyed the distinction the name gave him; at any rate he never resented it, and it was not often that he missed an opportunity to show that he deserved it. Calderwood's place was two or three miles from the village of Hillsborough, and Free Joe visited his wife twice a week, Wednesday and Saturday nights.

One Sunday he was sitting in front of Lucinda's cabin, when Calderwood happened to pass that way.

"Howdy, marster?" said Free Joe, taking off his hat.

"Who are you?" exclaimed Calderwood abruptly, halting and staring at the negro.

"I'm name' Joe, marster. I'm Lucindy's ole man."

"Who do you belong to?"

"Marse John Evans is my gyardeen, marster."

"Big name—gyardeen. Show your pass."

Free Joe produced that document, and Calderwood read it aloud slowly, as if he found it difficult to get at the meaning:

"To whom it may concern: This is to certify that the boy Joe Frampton has my permission to visit his wife Lucinda."

This was dated at Hillsborough, and signed "John W. Evans."

Calderwood read it twice, and then looked at Free Joe, elevating his eyebrows, and showing his discolored teeth.

"Some mighty big words in that there. Evans owns this place, I reckon. When's he comin' down to take hold?"

Free Joe fumbled with his hat. He was badly frightened.

"Lucindy say she speck you wouldn't min' my comin', long ez I behave, marster."

Calderwood tore the pass in pieces and flung it away.

"Don't want no free niggers 'round here," he exclaimed. "There's the big road. It'll

carry you to town. Don't let me catch you here no more. Now, mind what I tell you."

Free Joe presented a shabby spectacle as he moved off with his little dog Dan slinking at his heels. It should be said in behalf of Dan, however, that his bristles were up, and that he looked back and growled. It may be that the dog had the advantage of insignificance, but it is difficult to conceive how a dog bold enough to raise his bristles under Calderwood's very eyes could be as insignificant as Free Joe. But both the negro and his little dog seemed to give a new and more dismal aspect to forlornness as they turned into the road and went toward Hillsborough.

After this incident Free Joe appeared to have clearer ideas concerning his peculiar condition. He realized the fact that though he was free he was more helpless than any slave. Having no owner, every man was his master. He knew that he was the object of suspicion, and therefore all his slender resources (ah! how pitifully slender they were!) were devoted to winning, not kindness and appreciation, but toleration; all his efforts were in the direction of mitigating the circumstances that tended to make his condition so much worse than that of the negroes around him—negroes who had friends because they had masters.

So far as his own race was concerned, Free Joe was an exile. If the slaves secretly envied him his freedom (which is to be doubted, considering his miserable condition), they openly despised him, and lost no opportunity to treat him with contumely. Perhaps this was in some measure the result of the attitude which Free Joe chose to maintain toward them. No doubt his instinct taught him that to hold himself aloof from the slaves would be to invite from the whites the toleration which he coveted, and without which even his miserable condition would be rendered more miserable still.

His greatest trouble was the fact that he was not allowed to visit his wife; but he soon found a way out of his difficulty. After he had been ordered away from the Calderwood place, he was in the habit of wandering as far in that direction as prudence would permit. Near the Calderwood place, but not on Calderwood's land, lived an old man named Micajah Staley and his sister Becky Staley. These people were old and very poor. Old Micajah had a palsied arm and hand; but, in spite of this, he managed to earn a precarious living with his turning-lathe.

When he was a slave Free Joe would have scorned these representatives of a class known as poor white trash, but now he found them sympathetic and helpful in various ways. From the back door of their cabin he could hear the Calderwood negroes singing at night, and he sometimes fancied he could distinguish Lucinda's shrill treble rising above the other voices. A large poplar grew in the woods some distance from the Staley cabin, and at the foot of this tree Free Joe would sit for hours with his face turned toward Calderwood's. His little dog Dan would curl up in the leaves near by, and the two seemed to be as comfortable as possible.

One Saturday afternoon Free Joe, sitting at the foot of this friendly poplar, fell asleep. How long he slept, he could not tell; but when he awoke little Dan was licking his face, the moon was shining brightly, and Lucinda his wife stood before him laughing. The dog, seeing that Free Joe was asleep had grown somewhat impatient, and he concluded to make an excursion to the Calderwood place on his own account. Lucinda was inclined to give the incident a twist in the direction of superstition. "I 'uz settin' down front er de fireplace," she said, "cookin' me some meat, w'en all of a sudden I year sumpin at de do'—scratch, scratch. I tuck'n tu'n de meat over, en make out I ain't year it. Bimeby it come dar 'gin— scratch, scratch. I up en open de do', I did, en, bless de Lord! dar wuz little Dan, en it look like ter me dat his ribs done grow terge'er. I gin 'im some bread, en den, w'en he start out, I tuck'n foller 'im, kaze, I say ter myse'f, maybe my nigger man mought be some'rs 'roun'. Dat ar little dog got sense, mon."

Free Joe laughed and dropped his hand lightly on Dan's head. For a long time after that he had no difficulty in seeing his wife. He had only to sit by the poplar tree until little Dan could run and fetch her. But after a while the other negroes discovered that Lucinda was meeting Free Joe in the woods, and information of the fact soon reached Calderwood's ears. Calderwood was what is called a man of action. He said nothing; but one day he put Lucinda in his buggy, and carried her to Macon, sixty miles away. He carried her to Macon, and came back without her; and nobody in or around Hillsborough, or in that section, ever saw her again.

For many a night after that Free Joe sat in the woods and waited. Little Dan would run merrily off and be gone a long time, but he always came back without Lucinda. This happened over and over again. The "willis-whistlers" would call and call, like phantom huntsmen wandering on a far-off shore; the screech-owl would shake and shiver in the depths of

the woods; the night-hawks, sweeping by on noiseless wings, would snap their beaks as though they enjoyed the huge joke of which Free Joe and little Dan were the victims; and the whip-poor-wills would cry to each other through the gloom. Each night seemed to be lonelier than the preceding, but Free Joe's patience was proof against loneliness. There came a time, however, when little Dan refused to go after Lucinda. When Free Joe motioned him in the direction of the Calderwood place, he would simply move about uneasily and whine; then he would curl up in the leaves and make himself comfortable.

One night, instead of going to the poplar-tree to wait for Lucinda, Free Joe went to the Staley cabin, and, in order to make his welcome good, as he expressed it, he carried with him an armful of fat-pine splinters. Miss Becky Staley had a great reputation in those parts as a fortune-teller, and the schoolgirls, as well as older people, often tested her powers in this direction, some in jest and some in earnest. Free Joe placed his humble offering of lightwood in the chimney corner, and then seated himself on the steps, dropping his hat on the ground outside.

"Miss Becky," he said presently, 'whar in de name er gracious you reckon Lucindy is?"

"Well, the Lord he'p the nigger!" exclaimed Miss Becky, in a tone that seemed to reproduce, by some curious agreement of sight with sound, her general aspect of peakedness. "Well, the Lord he'p the nigger! hain't you been a-seein' her all this blessed time? She's over at old Spite Calderwood's, if she's anywheres, I reckon."

"No'm, dat I ain't, Miss Becky. I ain't seen Lucindy is now gwine on mighty nigh a mont'."

"Well, it hain't a-gwine to hurt you," said Miss Becky, somewhat sharply. "In my day an' time it wuz allers took to be a bad sign when niggers got to honeyin' 'round an' gwine on."

"Yessum," said Free Joe, cheerfully assenting to the proposition—"yessum, dat's so, but me an' my ole 'oman, we 'uz raise terge'er, en dey ain't bin many days w'en we 'uz 'way fum one 'n'er like we is now."

"Maybe she's up an' took up wi' some un else," said Micajah Staley from the corner. "You know what the sayin' is, 'New master, new nigger.'"

"Dat's so, dat's de sayin', but tain't wid my ole 'oman like 'tis wid yuther niggers. Me en her wuz des natally raise up terge'er. Dey's lots likelier niggers dan w'at I is," said Free

Joe, viewing his shabbiness with a critical eye, "but I knows Lucindy mos' good ez I does little Dan dar—dat I does."

There was no reply to this, and Free Joe continued:

"Miss Becky, I wish you please, ma'am, take en run yo' kyards en see sump'n n'er 'bout Lucindy; kaze ef she sick, I'm gwine dar. Dey ken take en take me up en gimme a stroppin', but I'm gwine dar."

Miss Becky got her cards, but first she picked up a cup, in the bottom of which were some coffee-grounds. These she whirled slowly round and round, ending finally by turning the cup upside down on the hearth and allowing it to remain in that position.

"I'll turn the cup first," said Miss Becky, "and then I'll run the cards and see what they say."

As she shuffled the cards the fire on the hearth burned low, and in its fitful light the gray-haired, thin-featured woman seemed to deserve the weird reputation which rumor and gossip had given her. She shuffled the cards for some moments, gazing intently in the dying fire; then, throwing a piece of pine on the coals, she made three divisions of the pack, disposing them about in her lap. Then she took the first pile, ran the cards slowly through her fingers, and studied them carefully. To the first she added the second pile. The study of these was evidently not satisfactory. She said nothing, but frowned heavily; and the frown deepened as she added the rest of the cards until the entire fifty-two had passed in review before her. Though she frowned, she seemed to be deeply interested. Without changing the relative position of the cards, she ran them all over again. Then she threw a larger piece of pine on the fire, shuffled the cards afresh, divided them into three piles, and subjected them to the same careful and critical examination.

"I can't tell the day when I've seed the cards run this a-way," she said after a while. "What is an' what ain't, I'll never tell you; but I know what the cards sez."

"W'at does dey say, Miss Becky?" the negro inquired, in a tone the solemnity of which was heightened by its eagerness.

"They er runnin' quare. These here that I'm a-look-in' at," said Miss Becky, "they stan' for the past. Them there, they er the present; and the t'others, they er the future. Here's a bundle"—tapping the ace of clubs with her thumb—"an' here's a journey as plain as the nose on a man's face. Here's Lucinda"——

"Whar she, Miss Becky?"

"Here she is—the queen of spades."

Free Joe grinned. The idea seemed to please him immensely.

"Well, well, well!" he exclaimed. "Ef dat don't beat my time! De queen er spades! W'en Lucindy year dat hit'll tickle 'er sho'!"

Miss Becky continued to run the cards back and forth through her fingers.

"Here's a bundle an' a journey, and here's Lucinda. An' here's ole Spite Calderwood." She held the cards toward the negro and touched the king of clubs.

"De Lord he'p my soul!" exclaimed Free Joe with a chuckle. "De faver's dar. Yessir, dat's him! W'at de matter 'long wid all un um, Miss Becky?"

The old woman added the second pile of cards to the first, and then the third, still running them through her fingers slowly and critically. By this time the piece of pine in the fireplace had wrapped itself in a mantle of flame, illuminating the cabin and throwing into strange relief the figure of Miss Becky as she sat studying the cards. She frowned ominously at the cards and mumbled a few words to herself. Then she dropped her hands in her lap and gazed once more into the fire. Her shadow danced and capered on the wall and floor behind her, as if, looking over her shoulder into the future, it could behold a rare spectacle. After a while she picked up the cup that had been turned on the hearth. The coffee-grounds, shaken around, presented what seemed to be a most intricate map.

"Here's the journey," said Miss Becky, presently; "here's the big road, here's rivers to cross, here's the bundle to tote." She paused and sighed. "They hain't no names writ here, an' what it all means I'll never tell you. Cajy, I wish you'd be so good as to han' me my pipe."

"I hain't no hand wi' the kyards," said Cajy, as he handed the pipe, "but I reckon I can patch out your misinformation, Becky, bekaze the other day, whiles I was a-finishin' up Mizzers Perdue's rollin'-pin, I hearn a rattlin' in the road. I looked out, an' Spite Calderwood was a-drivin' by in his buggy, an' that sot Lucinda by him. It'd in-about drapt out er my min'."

Free Joe sat on the door-sill and fumbled at his hat, flinging it from one hand to the other.

"You ain't see um gwine back, is you, Mars Cajy?" he asked after a while.

"Ef they went back by this road," said Mr. Staley, with the air of one who is accustomed

to weigh well his words, "it must 'a' bin en-
durin' of the time whiles I was asleep, bekaze I
hain't bin no furder from my shop than to yon
bed."

"Well, sir!" exclaimed Free Joe in an awed
tone, which Mr. Staley seemed to regard as a
tribute to his extraordinary powers of statement.

"Ef it's my beliefs you want," continued the
old man, "I'll pitch 'em at you fair and free.
My beliefs is that Spite Calderwood is gone an'
took Lucindy outen the county. Bless your
heart and soul! when Spite Calderwood meets
the Old Boy in the road they'll be a turrible
scuffle. You mark what I tell you."

Free Joe, still fumbling with his hat, rose
and leaned against the door-facing. He seemed
to be embarrassed. Presently he said:

"I speck I better be gittin' 'long. Nex' time
I see Lucindy, I'm gwine tell 'er w'at Miss
Becky say 'bout de queen er spades—dat I is.
Ef dat don't tickle 'er, dey ain't no nigger
'oman never bin tickle'."

He paused a moment, as though waiting for
some remark or comment, some confirmation
of misfortune, or, at the very least, some en-
dorsement of his suggestion that Lucinda
would be greatly pleased to know that she had
figured as the queen of spades; but neither
Miss Becky nor her brother said anything.

"One minnit ridin' in the buggy 'longside er
Mars Spite, en de nex' highfalutin' 'roun' playin' de queen er spades. Mon, deze yer nigger
gals gittin' up in de pictur's; dey sholy is."

With a brief "Good-night, Miss Becky,
Mars Cajy," Free Joe went out into the darkness, followed by little Dan. He made his way
to the poplar, where Lucinda had been in the
habit of meeting him, and sat down. He sat
there a long time; he sat there until little Dan,
growing restless, trotted off in the direction of
the Calderwood place. Dozing against the
poplar, in the gray dawn of the morning, Free
Joe heard Spite Calderwood's fox-hounds in
full cry a mile away.

"Shoo!" he exclaimed, scratching his head,
and laughing to himself, "dem ar dogs is des
a-warmin' dat old fox up."

But it was Dan the hounds were after, and
the little dog came back no more. Free Joe
waited and waited, until he grew tired of waiting. He went back the next night and waited,
and for many nights thereafter. His waiting
was in vain, and yet he never regarded it as in
vain. Careless and shabby as he was, Free Joe
was thoughtful enough to have his theory. He
was convinced that little Dan had found Lucinda, and that some night when the moon was

shining brightly through the trees, the dog
would rouse him from his dreams as he sat
sleeping at the foot of the poplar-tree, and he
would open his eyes and behold Lucinda standing over him, laughing merrily as of old; and
then he thought what fun they would have
about the queen of spades.

How many long nights Free Joe waited at
the foot of the poplar tree for Lucinda and
little Dan no one can ever know. He kept no
account of them, and they were not recorded
by Micajah Staley nor by Miss Becky. The season ran into summer and then into fall. One
night he went to the Staley cabin, cut the two
old people an armful of wood, and seated himself on the door-steps, where he rested. He was
always thankful—and proud, as it seemed—
when Miss Becky gave him a cup of coffee,
which she was sometimes thoughtful enough
to do. He was especially thankful on this particular night.

"You er still layin' off for to strike up wi'
Lucindy out thar in the woods, I reckon," said
Micajah Staley, smiling grimly. The situation
was not without its humorous aspects.

"Oh, dey er comin', Mars Cajy, dey er comin', sho," Free Joe replied. "I boun' you dey'll
come; en w'en dey does come, I'll des taken en
fetch um yer, whar you kin see um wid you
own eyes, you en Miss Becky."

"No," said Mr. Staley, with a quick and emphatic gesture of disapproval. "Don't! don't
fetch 'em anywheres. Stay right wi' 'em as
long as may be."

Free Joe chuckled, and slipped away into
the night, while the two old people sat gazing
in the fire. Finally Micajah spoke.

"Look at that nigger; look at 'im. He's
pine-blank as happy now as a killdee by a mill-
race. You can't faze 'em. I'd in-about give
up my t'other hand ef I could stan' flat-footed,
an' grin at trouble like that there nigger."

"Niggers is niggers," said Miss Becky, smiling grimly, "an' you can't rub it out; yit I lay
I've seed a heap of white people lots meaner'n
Free Joe. He grins—an' that's nigger—but
I've ketched his under jaw a-tremblin' when
Lucindy's name uz brung up. An' I tell you,"
she went on, bridling up a little, and speaking
with almost fierce emphasis, "the Old Boy's
done sharpened his claws for Spite Calderwood. You'll see it."

"Me, Rebecca?" said Mr. Staley, hugging
his palsied arm; "me? I hope not."

"Well, you'll know it then," said Miss
Becky, laughing heartily at her brother's look
of alarm.

The next morning Micajah Staley had occasion to go into the woods after a piece of timber. He saw Free Joe sitting at the foot of the poplar, and the sight vexed him somewhat.

"Git up from there," he cried, "an' go an' arn your livin'. A mighty purty pass it's come to, when great big buck niggers can lie a-snorin' in the woods all day, when t'other folks is got to be up and a-gwine. Git up from there!"

Receiving no response, Mr. Staley went to Free Joe, and shook him by the shoulder; but the negro made no response. He was dead. His hat was off, his head was bent, and a smile was on his face. It was as if he had bowed and smiled when death stood before him, humble to the last. His clothes were ragged; his hands were rough and callous; his shoes were literally tied together with strings; he was shabby in the extreme. A passer-by, glancing at him, could have no idea that such a humble creature had been summoned as a witness before the Lord God of Hosts.

FRANK R. STOCKTON (1834-1902)

THE LADY OR THE TIGER?

(1882)

In the very olden time, there lived a semi-barbaric king, whose ideas, though somewhat polished and sharpened by the progressiveness of distant Latin neighbors, were still large, florid, and untrammelled, as became the half of him which was barbaric. He was a man of exuberant fancy, and, withal, of an authority so irresistible that, at his will, he turned his varied fancies into facts. He was greatly given to self-communing; and when he and himself agreed upon anything, the thing was done. When every member of his domestic and political systems moved smoothly in its appointed course, his nature was bland and genial; but whenever there was a little hitch, and some of his orbs got out of their orbits, he was blander and more genial still, for nothing pleased him so much as to make the crooked straight, and crush down uneven places.

Among the borrowed notions by which his barbarism had become semified was that of the public arena, in which, by exhibitions of manly and beastly valor, the minds of his subjects were refined and cultured.

But even here the exuberant and barbaric fancy asserted itself. The arena of the king was built, not to give the people an opportunity of hearing the rhapsodies of dying gladiators, nor to enable them to view the inevitable conclusion of a conflict between religious opinions and hungry jaws, but for purposes far better adapted to widen and develop the mental energies of the people. This vast amphitheatre, with its encircling galleries, its mysterious vaults, and its unseen passages, was an agent of poetic justice, in which crime was punished, or virtue rewarded, by the decrees of an impartial and incorruptible chance.

When a subject was accused of a crime of sufficient importance to interest the king, public notice was given that on an appointed day the fate of the accused person would be decided in the king's arena—a structure which well deserved its name; for, although its form and plan were borrowed from afar, its purpose emanated solely from the brain of this man, who, every barleycorn a king, knew no tradition to which he owed more allegiance than pleased his fancy, and who ingrafted on every adopted form of human thought and action the rich growth of his barbaric idealism.

When all the people had assembled in the galleries, and the king, surrounded by his court, sat high up on his throne of royal state on one side of the arena, he gave a signal, a door beneath him opened, and the accused subject stepped out into the amphitheatre. Directly opposite him, on the other side of the enclosed space, were two doors, exactly alike and side by side. It was the duty and the privilege of the person on trial to walk directly to these doors and open one of them. He could open either door he pleased. He was subject to no guidance or influence but that of the aforementioned impartial and incorruptible chance. If he opened the one, there came out of it a hungry tiger, the fiercest and most cruel that could be procured, which immediately sprang upon him, and tore him to pieces, as a punishment for his guilt. The moment that the case of the criminal was thus decided, doleful iron bells were clanged, great wails went up from the hired mourners posted on the outer rim of the arena, and the vast audience, with bowed heads and downcast hearts, wended slowly their homeward way, mourning greatly that one so young and fair, or so old and respected, should have merited so dire a fate.

But if the accused person opened the other door, there came forth from it a lady, the most suitable to his years and station that his Majesty could select among his fair subjects; and to his lady he was immediately married, as a reward of his innocence. It mattered not that he might already possess a wife and family, or that his affections might be engaged upon an object of his own selection. The king allowed no such subordinate arrangements to interfere with his great scheme of retribution and reward. The exercises, as in the other instance, took place immediately, and in the arena. Another door opened beneath the king, and a priest, followed by a band of choristers, and dancing maidens blowing joyous airs on golden horns and treading an epithalamic measure, advanced to where the pair stood side by side, and the wedding was promptly and cheerily solemnized. Then the gay brass bells rang forth their merry peals, the people shouted glad hurrahs, and the innocent man, preceded by children strewing flowers on his path, led his bride to his home.

This was the king's semi-barbaric method of administering justice. Its perfect fairness is obvious. The criminal could not know out of which door would come the lady. He opened either he pleased, without having the slightest idea whether, in the next instant, he was to be devoured or married. On some occasions the tiger came out of one door, and on some out of the other. The decisions of this tribunal were not only fair—they were positively determinate. The accused person was instantly punished if he found himself guilty, and if innocent he was rewarded on the spot, whether he liked it or not. There was no escape from the judgments of the king's arena.

The institution was a very popular one. When the people gathered together on one of the great trial days, they never knew whether they were to witness a bloody slaughter or a hilarious wedding. This element of uncertainty lent an interest to the occasion which it could not otherwise have attained. Thus the masses were entertained and pleased, and the thinking part of the community could bring no charge of unfairness against this plan; for did not the accused person have the whole matter in his own hands?

This semi-barbaric king had a daughter as blooming as his most florid fancies, and with a soul as fervent and imperious as his own. As is usual in such cases, she was the apple of his eye, and was loved by him above all humanity. Among his courtiers was a young man of that fineness of blood and lowness of station common to the conventional heroes of romance who love royal maidens. This royal maiden was well satisfied with her lover, for he was handsome and brave to a degree unsurpassed in all this kingdom, and she loved him with an ardor that had enough of barbarism in it to make it exceedingly warm and strong. This love affair moved on happily for many months, until, one day, the king happened to discover its existence. He did not hesitate nor waver in regard to his duty in the premises. The youth was immediately cast into prison, and a day was appointed for his trial in the king's arena. This, of course, was an especially important occasion, and his Majesty, as well as all the people, was greatly interested in the workings and development of this trial. Never before had such a case occurred—never before had a subject dared to love the daughter of a king. In after years such things became commonplace enough, but then they were, in no slight degree, novel and startling.

The tiger cages of the kingdom were searched for the most savage and relentless beasts, from which the fiercest monster might be selected for the arena, and the ranks of maiden youth and beauty throughout the land were carefully surveyed by competent judges, in order that the young man might have a fitting bride in case fate did not determine for him a different destiny. Of course, everybody knew that the deed with which the accused was charged had been done. He had loved the princess, and neither he, she, nor any one else thought of denying the fact. But the king would not think of allowing any fact of this kind to interfere with the workings of the tribunal, in which he took such great delight and satisfaction. No matter how the affair turned out, the youth would be disposed of, and the king would take an æsthetic pleasure in watching the course of events which would determine whether or not the young man had done wrong in allowing himself to love the princess.

The appointed day arrived. From far and near the people gathered, and thronged the great galleries of the arena, while crowds, unable to gain admittance, massed themselves against its outside walls. The king and his court were in their places, opposite the twin doors—those fateful portals, so terrible in their similarity!

All was ready. The signal was given. A door beneath the royal party opened, and the lover of the princess walked into the arena. Tall, beautiful, fair, his appearance was greeted with a low hum of admiration and anxiety. Half the audience had not known so grand a youth had lived among them. No wonder the princess loved him! What a terrible thing for him to be there!

As the youth advanced into the arena, he turned, as the custom was, to bow to the king. But he did not think at all of that royal personage; his eyes were fixed upon the princess, who sat to the right of her father. Had it not been for the moiety of barbarism in her nature, it is probable that lady would not have been there. But her intense and fervid soul would not allow her to be absent on an occasion in which she was so terribly interested. From the moment that the decree had gone forth that her lover should decide his fate in the king's arena, she had thought of nothing, night or day, but this great event and the various subjects connected with it. Possessed of more power, influence, and force of character than any one who had ever before been interested in such a case, she had done what no other person had done— she had possessed herself of the secret of the doors. She knew in which of the two rooms behind those doors stood the cage of the tiger, with its open front, and in which waited the lady. Through these thick doors, heavily curtained with skins on the inside, it was impossible that any noise or suggestion should come from within to the person who should approach to raise the latch of one of them. But gold, and the power of a woman's will, had brought the secret to the princess.

And not only did she know in which room stood the lady, ready to emerge, all blushing and radiant, should her door be opened, but she knew who the lady was. It was one of the fairest and loveliest of the damsels of the court who had been selected as the reward of the accused youth, should he be proved innocent of the crime of aspiring to one so far above him; and the princess hated her. Often had she seen, or imagined that she had seen, this fair creature throwing glances of admiration upon the person of her lover, and sometimes she thought these glances were perceived and even returned. Now and then she had seen them talking together. It was but for a moment or two, but much can be said in a brief space. It may have been on most unimportant topics, but how could she know that? The girl was lovely, but she had dared to raise her eyes to the loved one of the princess, and, with all the intensity of the savage blood transmitted to her through long lines of wholly barbaric ancestors, she hated the woman who blushed and trembled behind that silent door.

When her lover turned and looked at her, and his eye met hers as she sat there paler and whiter than any one in the vast ocean of anxious faces about her, he saw, by that power of quick perception which is given to those whose souls are one, that she knew behind which door crouched the tiger, and behind which door stood the lady. He had expected her to know it. He understood her nature, and his soul was assured that she would never rest until she had made plain to herself this thing, hidden to all other lookers-on, even to the king. The only hope for the youth in which there was any element of certainty was based upon the success of the princess in discovering this mystery, and the moment he looked upon her, he saw she had succeeded.

Then it was that his quick and anxious glance asked the question, "Which?" It was as plain to her as if he shouted it from where he stood. There was not an instant to be lost. The question was asked in a flash; it must be answered in another.

Her right arm lay on the cushioned parapet before her. She raised her hand, and made a slight, quick movement toward the right. No one but her lover saw her. Every eye but his was fixed on the man in the arena.

He turned, and with a firm and rapid step he walked across the empty space. Every heart stopped beating, every breath was held, every eye was fixed immovably upon that man. Without the slightest hesitation, he went to the door on the right, and opened it.

Now, the point of the story is this: Did the tiger come out of that door, or did the lady?

The more we reflect upon this question, the harder it is to answer. It involves a study of the human heart which leads us through devious mazes of passion, out of which it is difficult to find our way. Think of it, fair reader, not as if the decision of the question depended upon yourself, but upon that hot-blooded, semi-barbaric princess, her soul at a white heat beneath the combined fires of despair and jealousy. She had lost him, but who should have him?

How often, in her waking hours and in her dreams, had she started in wild horror and covered her face with her hands as she thought of her lover opening the door on the other side of which waited the cruel fangs of the tiger!

But how much oftener had she seen him at the other door! How in her grievous reveries had she gnashed her teeth and torn her hair when she saw his start of rapturous delight as he opened the door of the lady! How her soul had burned in agony when she had seen him rush to meet that woman, with her flushing cheek and sparkling eye of triumph; when she had seen him lead her forth, his whole frame kindled with the joy of recovered life; when she had heard the glad shouts from the multitude, and the wild ringing of the happy bells; when she had seen the priest, with his joyous followers, advance to the couple, and make them man and wife before her very eyes; and when she had seen them walk away together upon their path of flowers, followed by the tremendous shouts of the hilarious multitude, in which her one despairing shriek was lost and drowned!

Would it not be better for him to die at once, and go to wait for her in the blessed regions of semi-barbaric futurity?

And yet, that awful tiger, those shrieks, that blood!

Her decision had been indicated in an instant, but it had been made after days and nights of anguished deliberation. She had known she would be asked, she had decided what she would answer, and, without the slightest hesitation, she had moved her hand to the right.

The question of her decision is one not to be lightly considered, and it is not for me to presume to set myself up as the one person able to answer it. And so I leave it with all of you: Which came out of the opened door—the lady or the tiger?

THOMAS NELSON PAGE (1853-1922)

MARSE CHAN

A Tale of Old Virginia

(1884)

One afternoon, in the autumn of 1872, I was riding leisurely down the sandy road that winds along the top of the water-shed between two of the smaller rivers of eastern Virginia. The road I was travelling, following "the ridge" for miles, had just struck me as most significant of the character of the race which had dwelt upon it and whose only avenue of communication with the outside world it had formerly been. Their once splendid mansions, now fast falling to decay, appeared to view from time to time, set back far from the road, in proud seclusion, among groves of oak and hickory, now scarlet and gold with the early frost. Distance was nothing to this people; time was of no consequence to them. They desired but a level path in life, and that they had, though the way was longer, and the outer world strode by them as they dreamed.

I was aroused from my reflections by hearing some one ahead of me calling, "Heah!—heah—whoo-oop, heah!"

Turning the curve in the road, I saw just before me a negro standing, with a hoe and a watering-pot in his hand. He had evidently just gotten over the "worm-fence" into the road, out of the path which led zigzag across the "old field" and was lost to sight in the dense growth of sassafras. When I rode up, he was looking anxiously back down this path for his dog. So engrossed was he that he did not even hear my horse and I reined in to wait until he should turn around and satisfy my curiosity as to the handsome old place half a mile off from the road.

The numerous out-buildings and the large barns and stables told that it had once been the seat of wealth, and the wild waste of sassafras that covered the broad fields gave it an air of desolation which greatly excited my interest.

Entirely oblivious of my proximity, the negro went on calling "Whoo-oop, heah!" until along the path, walking very slowly and with great dignity, appeared a noble-looking old orange and white setter, gray with age, and corpulent with excessive feeding. As soon as he came in sight, his master began:

"Yes, dat you! You gittin' deaf as well as bline, I s'pose! Kyarnt heah me callin', I reckon? Whyn't yo' come on, dawg?"

The setter sauntered slowly up to the fence and stopped, without even deigning a look at the speaker, who immediately proceeded to take the rails down, talking meanwhile:

"Now, I got to pull down de gap, I s'pose! Yo' so sp'ilt yo' kyahn hardly walk. Jes' ez able to git over it as I is! Jes' like white folks—think 'cuz you's white and I's black, I got to wait on yo' all de time. Ne'm mine, I ain' gwine do it!"

The fence having been pulled down sufficiently low to suit his dogship, he marched sedately through, and, with a hardly perceptible lateral movement of his tail, walked on down the road. Putting up the rails carefully, the negro turned and saw me.

"Sarvent, marster," he said, taking his hat off. Then, as if apologetically for having permitted a stranger to witness what was merely a family affair, he added: "He know I don' mean nothin' by what I sez. He's Marse Chan's dawg, an' he's so ole he kyahn git long no pearter. He know I'se jes' prodjickin' wid 'im."

"Who is Marse Chan?" I asked; "and whose place is that over there, and the one a mile or two back—the place with the big gate and the carved stone pillars?"

"Marse Chan," said the darky, "he's Marse Channin'—my young marster; an' dem places —dis one's Weall's, an' de one back dyar wid de rock gatepos's is ole Cun'l Chahmb'lin's. Dey don' nobody live dyar now, 'cep' niggers. Arfter de war some one or nurr buyed our place, but his name done kind o' slipped me. I nuver hearn on him befo'; I think dey's half-strainers. I don' ax none on 'em no odds. I lives down de road heah, a little piece, an' I jes' steps down of a evenin' and looks arfter de graves."

"Well, where is Marse Chan?" I asked.

"Hi! don' you know? Marse Chan, he went in de army. I was wid 'im. Yo' know he warn' gwine an' lef' Sam."

"Will you tell me all about it?" I said, dismounting.

Instantly, and as if by instinct, the negro stepped forward and took my bridle. I demurred a little; but with a bow that would have honored old Sir Roger, he shortened the reins, and taking my horse from me, led him along.

"Now tell me about Marse Chan," I said.

"Lawd, marster, hit's so long ago, I'd a'most forgit all about it, ef I hedn' been wid him ever sence he wuz born. Ez 'tis, I remembers it jes' like 'twuz yistiddy. Yo' know Marse Chan an' me—we wuz boys togerr. I wuz older'n he wuz, jes' de same ez he wuz whiter'n me. I wuz born like plantin' corn time, de spring arfter big Jim an' de six steers got washed away at de upper ford right down dyar b'low de quarters ez he wuz a-bringin' de Chris'mas things home; an' Marse Chan, he warn' born tell mos' to de harves' de year arfter my sister Nancy married Cun'l Chahmb'lin's Torm, 'bout eight years arfterwoods.

"Well, when Marse Chan wuz born, dey wuz de grettes' doin's at home you ever did see. De folks all hed holiday, jes' like in de Chris'mas. Ole marster (we didn't call 'im *ole* marster tell arfter Marse Chan wuz born— befo' dat he wuz jes' de marster, so)—well, de marster, his face fyar shine wid pleasure, an' all de folks wuz mighty glad, too, 'cause dey all loved ole marster, and aldo' dey did step aroun' right peart when de marster was lookin' at 'em, dyar warn' nyar han' on de place but what, ef he wanted anythin', would walk up to de back poach, an' say he warn' to see de marster. An' ev'ybody wuz talkin' 'bout de young marster, an' de maids an' de wimmens 'bout de kitchen wuz sayin' how 'twuz de purties' chile dey ever see; an' at dinner-time de mens (all on 'em hed holiday) come roun' de poach an' ax how de missis an' de young marster wuz, an' marster come out on de poach an' smile wus'n a 'possum, an' sez, 'Thankee! Bofe doin' fust rate, boys;' an' den he stepped back in de house, sort o' laughin' to hisse'f, an' in a minute he come out ag'in wid de baby in he arms, all wropped up in flannens an' things, an' sez, 'Heah he, boys.' All de folks den, dey went up on de poach to look at 'im, drappin' dey hats on de steps an' scrapin' dey feets ez dey went up. An' pres'n'y marster, lookin' down at we all chil'en all packed togerr down dyah like a parecel o' sheep-burrs, cotch sight o' *me* (he knowed my name, 'cause I use' to hole he hoss fur 'im sometimes; but he didn' know all de chil'en by name, dey wuz so many on 'em), an' he sez, 'Come up heah.' So up I goes tippin', skeered like, an' de marster sez, 'Ain' you Mymie's son?' 'Yass, seh,' sez I. 'Well,' sez he, 'I'm gwine to give you to yo' young Marse Channin' to be his body-servant,' an' he put de baby right in my arms (it's de truth I'm tellin' yo'!), an' yo' jes' ought to a-heard de folks sayin', 'Lawd! marster, dat boy'll drap dat chile!' 'Naw, he won't,' sez marster; 'I kin trust 'im.' And den he sez: 'Now, Sam, from dis time you belong to yo' young Marse Channin'; I wan' you to tek keer on 'im ez long ez he lives. You are to be his boy from dis time. An' now,' he sez, 'carry 'im in de house.' An' he walks arfter me an' opens de do's fur me, an' I kyars 'im in in my arms, an' lays 'im down on de bed. An' from dat time I was tooken in de house to be Marse Channin's body-servant.

"Well, you nuver see a chile grow so!

"Pres'n'y he growed up right big, an' ole marster sez he must have some edication. So he sont 'im to school to ole Miss Lawry down dyar, dis side o' Cun'l Chahmb'lin's, an' I use' to go 'long wid 'im an' tote he books an' we all's snacks; an' when he larnt to read an' spell right good, an' got 'bout so-o big (measuring with his hand a height of some three feet), ole

Miss Lawry she died, an' ole marster said he mus' have a man to teach 'im an' trounce 'im. So we all went to Mr. Hall, whar kep' de school-house beyant de creek, an' dyar we went ev'y day,—'cep Sat'd'ys of co'se, an' sich days ez Marse Chan din' warn' go, an' ole missis begged 'im off.

"Hit wuz down dyar Marse Chan fust took noticement o' Miss Anne.

"Mr. Hall, he teach gals ez well ez boys, an' Cun'l Chahmb'lin he sont his daughter (dat's Miss Anne I'm talkin' about). She wuz a leetle bit o' gal when she fust come. Yo' see, her ma wuz dead, an' ole Miss Lucy Chahmb'-lin, she lived wid her brurr an' keep' house for 'im; an' he wuz so busy wid politics, he didn' have much time to spyar, so he sont Miss Anne to Mr. Hall's by a 'ooman wid a note.

"When she come dat day in de school-house, an' all de chil'en looked at her so hard, she tu'n right red, an' tried to pull her long curls over her eyes, an' den put bofe de backs of her little han's in her two eyes, an' begin to cry to herse'f. Marse Chan he was settin' on de een' o' de bench nigh de do', an' he jes' retched out an' put he arm roun' her an' drawed her up to 'im. An' he kep' whisperin' to her, an' callin' her name, an' coddlin' her; an' pres'n'y she teck her han's down an' begin to laugh.

"Well, dey 'peared to tek' a gre't fancy to each urr from dat time. Miss Anne she warn' nuttin' but a baby hardly, an' Marse Chan he wuz a good big boy 'bout mos' thirteen year ole, I reckon. Hows'ever, dey sut'n'y wuz sot on each urr an' (yo' heah me!) ole marster an' Cun'l Chahmb'lin dey 'peared to like it 'bout well ez de chil'en. Yo' see, Cun'l Chahmb'lin place j'ined ourn, an' it looked jes' ez nat'chal fur dem two chil'en to marry an' mek it one plantation, ez it did fur de creek to run down de bottom from our place into Cun'l Chahmb'lin's. I don' rightly think de chil'en thought 'bout gittin' mar'ied, not den, no mo'n I thought 'bout mar'yin Judy when she wuz a little gal at Cun'l Chahmb'lin's, runnin' 'bout de house, huntin' fur Miss Lucy's spectacles; but dey wuz good frien's from de start. Marse Chan he use' to kyar Miss Anne's books fur her ev'y day, an' ef de road wuz muddy or she wuz tired, he use' to tote her; an' 'twarn' hard-ly a day passed dat he didn' kyar her some'n' to school—apples or hick'y nuts, or some'n'. He wouldn' let none o' de chil'en tease her, nurr. Heh! One day, one o' de boys poke' he finger at Miss Anne, and arfter school Marse Chan he axed 'im out 'roun' hine de school-house out o' sight, an' ef he didn' whup 'im!

"(Marse Chan, he wuz de peartes' scholar ole Mr. Hall hed, an' Mr. Hall he wuz mighty proud on 'im. I don' think he use' to beat 'im ez much ez he did de urrs, aldo' he wuz de head in all debilment dat went on, jes' ez he wuz in sayin' he lessons.)

"Heh! one day in summer, jes' fo' de school broke up, dyah come up a storm right sudden, an' riz de creek (dat one yo' cross' back yon-der), an' Marse Chan he toted Miss Anne home on he back. He ve'y off'n did dat when de parf wuz muddy. But dis day when dey come to de creek, it had done washed all de lawgs 'way. 'Twuz still mighty high, so Marse Chan he put Miss Anne down, an' he took a pole an' waded right in. Hit took 'im long up to de shoulders. Den he waded back, an' took Miss Anne up on his head an' kyared her right over. At fust she was skeered; but he tol' her he could swim an' wouldn' let her git hu't, an' den she let 'im kyar her 'cross, she hol'in' his han's. I warn' 'long dat day, but he sut'n'y did dat thing!

"Ole marster he wuz so pleased 'bout it, he giv' Marse Chan a pony; an' Marse Chan rid 'im to school de day arfter he come, so proud, an' sayin' how he wuz gwine to let Anne ride behine 'im. When he come home dat evenin' he wuz walkin'. 'Hi! where's yo' pony?' said ole marster. 'Did he fling you?' 'I give 'im to Anne,' says Marse Chan. 'She liked 'im, an'—I kin walk.' 'Yes,' sez ole marster, laugh-in', 'I s'pose you's already done giv' her yo'-se'f, an' nex' thing I know you'll be givin' her this plantation and all my niggers.'

"Well, about a fortnight or sich a matter arfter dat, Cun'l Chahmb'lin sont over an' in-vited all o' we all over to dinner, an' Marse Chan wuz 'spressaly named in de note whar Ned brought; an' arfter dinner he made ole Phil, whar wuz his ker'ige-driver, bring roun' Marse Chan's pony wid a little side-saddle on 'im, an' a beautiful little haws wid a bran'-new saddle an' bridle on him; an' he gits up an' meks Marse Chan a gre't speech, an' presents 'im de little haws; an' den he calls Miss Anne, an' she comes out on de poach in a little ridin' frock, an' dey puts her on her pony, an' Marse Chan mounts his haws, an' dey goes to ride, while de grown folks is a-settin' on de poach an' a-laughin' an' chattin' an' smokin' dey cigars.

"Dem wuz good ole times, marster—de bes' Sam uver see! Dey wuz, in fac'! Niggers didn't hed nothin' 't all to do—jes' hed to 'ten' to de feedin' an' cleanin' de hawses, an' doin' what de marster tell 'em to do; an' when dey wuz sick, dey had things sont 'em out de house, an' de same doctor come to see 'em whar 'ten' to de white folks when dey wuz po'ly, an' all. Dyar warn' no trouble nor nuttin'.

"Well, things tuk a change arfter dat. Marse Chan he went to de bo'din' school, whar he use' to write to me constant. Ole missis use' to read me de letters, an' den I'd git Miss Anne to read 'em ag'in to me when I'd see her. He use' to write to her too, an' she use' to write to him too! Den Miss Anne she wuz sont off to school too. An' in de summer time dey'd bofe come home, an' yo' hardly know wherr Marse Chan lived at home or over at Cun'l Chahmb'lin's! He wuz over dyah constant! 'Twuz al'ays ridin' or fishin' down dyah in de river; or sometimes he'd go over dyah, an' 'im an' she'd go out an' set in de yard onder de trees; she settin' up mekin' out she wuz knittin' some sort o' bright-cullored some'n', wid de grarss growin' all up 'g'inst her, an' her hat th'owed back on her neck, an' he readin' to her out books; an' sometimes dey'd bofe read out de same book, fust one an' den turr. I use' to see 'em! Dat wuz when dey wuz growin' up like.

"Den ole marster he run for Congress, an' ole Cun'l Chahmb'lin he wuz put up to run 'g'inst ole marster by de Dimicrats; but ole marster he beat 'im. Yo' know he wuz gwine do dat! Co'se he wuz! Dat made ole Cun'l Chahmb'lin mighty mad, and dey stopt visit-in' each urr reg'lar, like dey had been doin' all 'long. Den Cun'l Chahmb'lin he sort o' got in debt, an' sell some o' he niggers, an' dat's de way de fuss begun. Dat's whar de lawsuit come from. Ole marster he didn' like nobody to sell niggers, an' knowin' dat Cun'l Chahmb'lin wuz sellin' o' his, he writ an' of-fered to buy his M'ria an' all her chil'en, 'cause she hed mar'ied our Zeek'yel. An' don' yo' think, Cun'l Chahmb'lin axed ole marster mo' 'n th'ee niggers wuz wuth fur M'ria! Befo' old marster buy her, dough, de sheriff come an' levelled on M'ria an' a whole parecel o' urr niggers. Ole marster he went to de sale, an' bid for 'em; but Cun'l Chahmb'lin he got some one to bid 'g'inst ole marster. Dey wuz knocked out to ole marster dough, an' den dey hed a big lawsuit, an' ole marster was agwine to co't, off an' on, fur some years, till at lars' de co't decided dat M'ria belongst to ole mars-ter. Ole Cun'l Chahmb'lin den wuz so mad he sued ole marster for a little slipe o' lan' down dyah on de line fence, whar he said belongst to him. Evy'body knowed hit belongst to ole marster. Ef yo' go down dyah now, I kin show it to yo', inside de line fence, whar it hed done been uver sence long befo' Cun'l Chahmb'lin wuz born. But Cun'l Chahmb'lin was a

mons'us perseverin' man, an' ole marster he wouldn' let nobody run over 'im. No, dat he wouldn'! So dey wuz agwine down to co't about dat, fur I don' know how long, till ole marster beat 'im agin.

"All dis time, yo' know, Marse Chan wuz agoin' back'ads and for'ads to college, an' wuz growed' up a ve'y fine young man. He wuz a ve'y likely gent'man! Miss Anne she hed done mos' growed up too—wuz puttin' her hyar up like ole missis use' to put hern up, an' 'twuz jes' ez bright ez de sorrel's mane when de sun cotch on it, an' her eyes wuz gre't big dark eyes, like her pa's, on'y bigger an' not so fierce, an' 'twarn' none o' de young ladies ez purty ez she wuz. She an' Marse Chan still set a heap o' sto' by one 'nurr, but I don't think dey wuz easy wid each urr ez when he used to tote her home from school on he back. Marse Chan he use' to love de ve'y groun' she walked on, dough, is my 'pinion. Heh! His face 'twould light up whenever she come into chu'ch, or anywhere, jes' like de sun hed come th'oo a chink on it sudden'y.

"Den ole marster los' he eyes. D' yo' ever heah 'bout dat? Heish! Didn' yo'?

"Well, one night de big barn cotch fire. De stables, yo' know, wuz onder de big barn, an' all de hawses wuz in dyah. Hit 'peared to me like 'twarn' no time befo' all de folks an' de neighbors dey come, an' dey wuz a-totin' water, an' a-tryin' to save de po' critters, an' dey got a heap on 'em out; but de ker'ige-hawses dey wouldn' come out, an' dey wuz a-runnin' back'ads an' for'ads inside de stalls, a-nikerin' an' a-screamin', like dey knowed dey time hed come. Yo' could heah 'em in dyah so pitiful, an' pres'n'y ole marster said to Ham Fisher (he wuz de ker'ige-driver), 'Go in dyah, Ham, an' try to save 'em; don' let 'em bu'n to death.'

"An' Ham he went right in.

"An' jes' arfter he got in, de shed whar it hed fus' cotch fell in, an' de sparks shot 'way up in de air; an' Ham didn' come back; an' de fire begin to lick out onder de eaves over whar de ker'ige-hawses' stalls wuz. An' all of a sud-den ole marster tu'ned an' kissed ole missis, who wuz standin' dyah nigh him, wid her face jes' ez white ez a sperit's, an', befo' anybody knowed what he wuz gwine do, jumped right in de do', an' de smoke come po'in' out behine 'im. Well, seh! I nuver 'spects to heah tell Jedgment sich a soun' ez de folks set up! Ole missis—she jes' drapt down on her knees in de mud an' prayed out loud.

"Hit 'peared like her pra'r wuz heard; for in a minit, right out de same do', kyain' Ham

Fisher in his arms, come ole marster, wid his clo's all blazin'. Dey fling water on 'im, an' put 'im out; an', ef you b'lieve me, yo' wouldn' a-knowed 'twuz ole marster.

"Yo' see, he hed done find Ham Fisher done fall down in de smoke right by de ker'ige-haws' stalls, whar he sont him, an' he hed to tote 'im back in his arms th'oo de fire what hed done cotch de front part o' de stable, an' to keep de flame from gittin' dcwn Ham Fisher' th'ote he hed teck off his own hat and mashed it all over Ham Fisher' face, an' he hed kep' Ham Fisher from bein' so much bu'nt; but *he* wuz bu'nt dreadful! He beard an' hyar wuz all nyawed off, an' he face an' han's an' neck wuz scorified turrible. Well, he jes' laid Ham Fisher down, an' then he kind o' staggered for-'ad, an' ole missis ketch' 'im in her arms.

"Ham Fisher, he warn't bu'nt so bad, an' he got out in a month or two; an' arfter a long time, ole marster he got well, too; but he wuz always stone blind arfter that. He nuver could see none from dat night.

"Marse Chan he comed home from college toreckly, an' he sut'n'y did nuss ole marster faithful—jes' like a 'ooman.

"Den he teck charge of de plantation arfter dat; an' I use' to wait on 'im jes' like when we wuz boys togerr; an' sometimes we'd slip off an' have a fox-hunt, an' he'd be jes' like he wuz in ole times, befo' ole marster got bline, an' Miss Anne Chahmb'lin stopt comin' over to our house, an' settin' onder de trees, readin' out de same book.

"He sut'n'y wuz good to me. Nuttin nuver made no diffunce 'bout dat! He nuver hit me a lick in his life—an' nuver let nobody else do it, nurr.

"I 'members one day, when he wuz a leetle bit o' boy, ole marster hed done tole we all chil'en not to slide on de straw-stacks; an' one day me an' Marse Chan thought ole marster hed done gone 'way from home. We watched him git on he haws an' ride up de road out o' sight, an' we wuz out in de field a-slidin' an' a-slidin', when up comes ole marster. We start to run; but he hed done see us, an' he called us to come back; an' sich a whuppin' ez he did gi' us!

"Fust he teck Marse Chan, an' den heg teched me up. He nuver hu't me, but in co'se I wuz a-hollerin' ez hard ez I could stave it, 'cause I knowed dat wuz gwine mek him stop. Marse Chan he hed'n open he mouf long ez ole marster was tunin' 'im; but soon ez he commence warmin' me an' I begin to holler, Marse Chan he bu'st out cryin', an' stept right in befo' ole marster, an' ketchin' de whup, said:

"'Stop, seh! Yo' sha'n't whup 'im; he b'-longs to me, an' ef you hit 'im another lick I'll set 'im free!'

"I wish yo' hed see ole marster! Marse Chan he warn' mo'n eight years ole, an' dyah dey wuz—ole marster stan'in' wid he whup raised up, an' Marse Chan red an' cryin', hol'in' on to it, an' sayin' I b'longst to 'im.

"Ole marster, he raise' de whup, an' den he drapt it, an' breke out in a smile over he face, an' he chuck' Marse Chan onder de chin, an' tu'n right roun' an' went away, laughin' to his-s'f, an' I heah 'im tellin' ole missis 'bout it dat evenin', an' laughin' 'bout it.

"'Twan' so mighty long arfter dat when dey fust got to talkin' 'bout de war. Dey wuz a-dictatin' back'ads an' for'ds 'bout it fur two or th'ee years, 'fo' it come sho' nuff, you know. Ole marster, he wuz a Whig, an' co'se Marse Chan he teck after he pa. Cun'l Chahmb'lin, he wuz a Dimicrat. He wuz in favor of de war, an' ole marster and Marse Chan dey wuz agin' it. Dey wuz a-talkin' 'bout it all de time, an' purty soon Cun'l Chahmb'lin he went about ev'vywhar speakin' an' noratin' 'bout Ferginia ought to secede; an' Marse Chan he wuz picked up to talk agin' 'im. Dat wuz de way dey come to fight de duil. I sut'n'y wuz skeered fur Marse Chan dat mawnin', an' he was jes' ez cool!

"Yo' see, it happen so: Marse Chan he wuz a-speakin' down at de Deep Creek Tavern, an' he kind o' got de bes' of ole Cun'l Chahmb'lin. All de white folks laughed an' hoorawed, an' ole Cun'l Chahmb'lin—my Lawd! I t'ought he'd 'a' bu'st, he was so mad. Well, when it come to his tu'n to speak, he jes' light into Marse Chan. He call 'im a traitor, an' a ab'li-tionis', an' I don' know what all. Marse Chan, he jes' kep' cool till de ole Cun'l light into he pa. Ez soon ez he name ole marster, I seen Marse Chan sort o' lif' up he head. D' yo' ever see a haws rar he head up right sudden at night when he see somethin' comin' to'ds 'im from de side an' he don' know what 'tis? Ole Cun'l Chahmb'lin he went right on. He say ole marster hed teach Marse Chan; dat ole marster wuz a wuss ab'litionis' dan he son. I looked at Marse Chan, an' sez to myse'f: 'Fo' Gord! old Cun'l Chahmb'lin better min'!' an' I hedn' got de wuds out, when ole Cun'l Chahmb'lin scuse' ole marster o' cheatin' 'im out o' he niggers, an' stealin' piece o' he lan'— dat's de lan' I tole you 'bout. Well, seh, nex' thing I knowed, I heahed Marse Chan—hit all happen right 'long togerr, jis' like lightnin' and thunder when they hit right at you!—I heab 'im say:

"'Cun'l Chahmb'lin, what you says is false, an' yo' knows it to be so. You have wilfully slandered one of de pures' an' nobles' men Gord ever made, an' nuttin' but yo' gray hyars protects you.'

"Well, ole Cun'l Chahmb'lin, he ra'ed an' he pitch'd! He say he wan' too ole, an' he'd show 'im so.

"'Ve'y well,' says Marse Chan.

"De meetin' breke up den. I wuz hol'in' de hawses out dyar in de road by de een' o' de poach, an' I see Marse Chan talkin' an' talkin' to Mr. Gordon an' anurr gent'man, an' den he come out an' got on de sorrel an' galloped off. Soon ez he got out o' sight he pulled up, an' we walked along tell we come to de road whar leads off to'ds Mr. Barbour's. He wuz de big lawyer o' de country. Dyar he tu'ned off. All dis time he hedn' said a wud, 'cep' to kind o' mumble to hisse'f now an' den. When we got to Mr. Barbour's, he got down an' went in. (Dat wuz in de late winter; de folks wuz jes' beginnin' to plough fur corn.) He stayed dyar 'bout two hours, an' when he come out Mr. Barbour come out to de gate wid 'im an' shake han's arfter he got up in de saddle. Den we all rode off.

"'Twuz late den—good dark; an' we rid ez hard ez we could, tell we come to de ole school-house at ole Cun'l Chahmb'lin's gate. When we got deah, Marse Chan got down an' walked right slow 'roun' de house. Arfter lookin' roun' a little while an' tryin' de do' to see ef 'twuz shet, he walked down de road tell he got to de creek. He stop' dyar a little while an' picked up two or three little rocks an' frowed 'em in, an' pres'n'y he got up an' we come on home. Ez he got down, he tu'ned to me, an', rubbin' de sorrel's nose, he said: 'Have 'em well fed, Sam; I'll want 'em early in de mawnin'.'

"Dat night at supper he laugh an' talk, an' he set at de table a long time. Arfter ole marster went to bed, he went in de charmber an' set on de bed by 'im talkin' to 'im an' tellin' 'im 'bout de meetin' an' e'vything; but he ain' nuver mention ole Cun'l Chahmb'lin's name. When he got up to come out to de office in de yard, whar he slept, he stooped down an' kissed 'im jes' like he wuz a baby layin' dyah in de bed, an' he'd hardly let ole misses go at all.

"I knowed some'n wuz up, an' nex mawnin' I called 'im early befo' light, like he tole me, an' he dressed an' come out pres'n'y jes' like he wuz gwine to church. I had de hawses ready, an' we went out de back way to'ds de river.

"Ez we rid along, he said:

"'Sam, you an' I wuz boys togerr, wa'n't we?'

"'Yes,' sez I, 'Marse Chan, dat we wuz.'

"'You have been ve'ry faithful 'to me,' sez he, 'an' I have seen to it that you are well provided fur. You want to marry Judy, I know, an' you'll be able to buy her ef yo' want to.'

"Den he tole me he wuz gwoine to fight a duil, an' in case he should git shot, he had set me free an' giv' me nuff to tek keer o' me an' my wife when I git her ez long ez we lived. He said he'd like me to stay an' tek keer o' ole marster an' ole missis ez long ez dey lived, an' he said it wouldn' be ve'y long, he reckoned. Dat wuz de on'y time he voice broke—when he said dat; an' I couldn' speak a wud, my th'oat choked me so.

"When we come to de river, we tu'ned right up de bank, an' arfter ridin' 'bout a mile or sich a motter, we stopped whar dey wuz a little clearin' wid elder bushes on one side an' two big gum-trees on de urr, an' de sky wuz all red, an' de water down tow'ds whar de sun wuz comin' wuz jes' like de sky.

"Pres'n'y Mr. Gordon he come, wid a 'hog-any box, 'bout so big, 'fore 'im, an' he got down, an' Marse Chan tole me to tek all de hawses an' go 'roun' behine de bushes whar I tell you 'bout—off to one side; an' 'fore I got 'roun' dyah, ole Cun'l Chahmb'lin an' Mr. Hennin an' Dr. Call come ridin' from t'urr way, to'ds ole Cun'l Chahmb'lin's. When dey hed tied dey hosses, de urr gent'mens went up to whar Mr. Gordon wuz, an' arfter some chattin' Mr. Hennin step' off 'bout fur ez' cross dis road, or mebbe it mout be a little fur'er; an' den I see 'em th'oo de bushes loadin' de pistils, an' talk a little while; an' den Marse Chan an' ole Cun'l Chahmb'lin walked up an' dey gin' 'em de pistils in dey han's, an' Marse Chan he stand wid his face right tow'ds de sun. I seen it shine on him jes' ez it come up over de low groun's, an' he look' like he do sometimes when he come out of church.

"I wuz so skeered I couldn' say nuttin'. Ole Cun'l Chahmb'lin could shoot fust rate, an' Marse Chan he nuver missed.

"Den I heahed Mr. Gordon say, 'Gent'mens, is yo' ready?' and bofe on 'em sez, 'Ready,' jes' so.

"An' he sez, 'Fire, one, two'—an' ez he sez 'one,' ole Cun'l Chahmb'lin raised he pistil an' shoot right at Marse Chan. De ball went th'oo his hat: I seen he hat sort o' settle on he head ez de bullit hit it! an' he jes' tilted his pistil up in de a'r an' shot—bang; an' ez de pistil went 'bang,' he sez to Cun'l Chahmb'lin, 'I mek you a present to yo' fam'ly, seh!'

"Well, dey had some talkin' arfter dat. I didn' git rightly what 't wuz; but it 'peared like Cun'l Chahmb'lin he warn't satisfied, an' wanted to have anurr shot. De seconds dey wuz talkin', an' pres'n'y dey put de pistils up, an' Marse Chan an' Mr. Gordon shook han's wid Mr. Hennin an' Dr. Call, an' come an' got on dey hawses. An' Cun'l Chahmb'lin he got on his hawse an' rode away wid de urr gent'-mens, lookin' like he did de day befo' when all de people laughed at 'im.

"I b'lieve ole Cun'l Chahmb'lin wan' to shoot Marse Chan, anyways!

"We come on home to breakfast, I totin' de box wid de pistils befo' me on de roan. Would you b'lieve me, seh, Marse Chan he ain' nuver said a wud 'bout it to ole marster or nobody! Ole missis didn' fin' out 'bout it for mo'n a month, an' den, Lawd! how she did cry and kiss Marse Chan; an' ole marster, aldo' he nuver say much, he wuz jes' ez please' ez ole missis: he call' me in de room an' made me lock de do' an' tole 'im all 'bout it, an' when I got th'oo he gi' me five dollars an' a pyar of breeches.

"But ole Cun'l Chahmb'lin he nuver did furgive Marse Chan, an' Miss Anne she got mad too. Wimmens is mons'us onreasonable nohow. Dey's jes' like a catfish: you can n' tek hole on 'em like urr folks, an' when you gits 'm yo' can n' always hole 'em.

"What meks me think so? Heap o' things —dis: Marse Chan he done gi' Miss Anne her pa jes' ez good ez I gi' Marse Chan's dawg sweet 'taters, an' she git mad wid 'im ez if he hed kill 'im stid o' sen'in 'im back to her dat mawnin' whole an' soun'. B'lieve me! she wouldn' even speak to him arfter dat.

"Don' I 'member dat mawnin'!

"We wuz gwine fox-huntin', 'bout six weeks or sich a matter arfter de duil, an' we meet Miss Anne ridin' 'long wid anurr lady an' two gent'mens whar wuz stayin' at her house. Dyah wuz always some one or nurr dyah co't-in' her. Well, dat mawnin' we meet 'em right in de road. 'Twuz de fust time Marse Chan had see her sence de duil, an' he raises he hat ez he pahss, an' she looks right at 'im wid her head up in de yair like she nuver see 'im befo' in her born days; an' when she comes by me, she sez, 'Good-mawnin', Sam!' Gord! I nuver see nuttin' like de look dat come on Marse Chan's face when she pahss 'im like dat. He gi' de sorrel a pull dat fotch 'im back settin down in de san' on he hanches. He ve'y lips wuz white. I tried to keep up wid 'im, but 'twarn no use. He sont me back home pres'-n'y, an' he rid on. I sez to myself, 'Cun'l Chahmb'lin, don' yo' meet Marse Chan dis mawnin'. He ain' bin lookin' roun' de ole

school-house, whar he an' Miss Anne use' to go to school to ole Mr. Hall togerr, to-day. He won' stan' no prodjickin' to-day.'

"He nuver come home dat night tell 'way late, an' ef he'd been fox-huntin' it mus' ha' been de ole red whar lives down in de green-scum mashes he'd been chasin'. De way de sorrel wuz gormed up wid sweat an' mire sut'-n'y did hu't me. He walked up to de stable wid he head down all de way, an' I'se seen 'im go eighty miles of a winter day, an' prance into de stable at night jes' ez fresh ez ef he hed jes' cantered over to ole Cun'l Chahmb'lin's to supper. I nuver see a haws beat so sence I knowed de fetlock from de fo'lock, an' bad ez he wuz he want ez bad ez Marse Chan.

"Whew! he didn' git over dat thing, seh— he nuver did git over it!

"De war come on jes' den, an' Marse Chan wuz elected cap'n; but he wouldn' tek it. He said Firginia hadn' seceded, an' he wuz gwine stan' by her. Den dey 'lected Mr. Gordon cap'n.

"I sut'n'y did wan' Marse Chan to tek de place, cuz I knowed he wuz gwine tek me wid 'im. He wan' gwine widout Sam. An' beside, he look so po' an' thin, I thought he wuz gwine die.

"Of co'se, ole missis she heared 'bout it, an' she meet Miss Anne in de road, an' cut her jes' like Miss Anne cut Marse Chan. Ole missis, she wuz proud ez anybody!

"So we wuz mo' strangers dan ef we hadn' live' in a hunderd miles of each urr. An' Marse Chan he wuz gittin' thinner an' thinner, an' Firginia she come out, an' den Marse Chan he went to Richmond an' listed, an' come back an' sey he wuz a private, an' he didn' know whe'r he could tek me or not. He writ to Mr. Gordon, hows'ever, an' 'twuz 'cided dat when he went I wuz to go 'long an' wait on him an' de cap'n too. I didn' min' dat, yo' know, long ez I could go wid Marse Chan, an' I like' Mr. Gordon, anyways.

"Well, one night Marse Chan come back from de offis wid a telegram dat say, 'Come at once,' so he wuz to start nex' mawnin'. His uniform wuz all ready, gray wid yaller trim-min's, an' mine wuz ready too, an' he had ole marster's sword, whar de State gi' 'im in de Mexikin war; an' he trunks wuz all packed wid ev'rything in 'em, an' my chist was packed too, an' Jim Rasher he druv 'em over to de depo' in de waggin, an' we wuz to start nex' mawnin' 'bout light. Dis wuz 'bout de las' o' spring, you know.

"Dat night ole missis made Marse Chan dress up in he uniform, an' he sut'n'y did look splendid, wid he long mustache an' he wavin' hyah an' he tall figger.

"Arfter supper he come down an' sez: 'Sam, I wan' you to tek dis note an' kyar it over to Cun'l Chahmb'lin's, an' gi' it to Miss Anne wid yo' own han's, an' bring me wud what she sez. Don' let any one know 'bout it, or know why you've gone.' 'Yes, seh,' sez I.

"Yo' see, I knowed Miss Anne's maid over at ole Cun'l Chahmb'lin's—dat wuz Judy,— an' I knowed I could wuk it. So I tuk de roan an' rid over, an' tied 'im down de hill in de cedars, an' I wen' 'roun' to de back yard. 'Twuz a right blowy sort o' night; de moon wuz jes' risin', but de clouds wuz so big it didn' shine 'cep th'oo a crack now an' den. I soon foun' my gal, an' arfter tellin' her two or three lies 'bout herse'f, I got her to go in an' ax Miss Anne to come to de do'. When she come, I gi' her de note, an' arfter a little while she bro't me anurr, an' I tole her good-by, an' she gi' me a dollar, an' I come home an' gi' de letter to Marse Chan. He read it, an' tole me to have de hawses ready at twenty minits to twelve at de corner of de garden. An' jes' befo' dat he come out ez he wuz gwine to bed, but instid he come, an' we all struck out to'ds Cun'l Chahmb'lin's. When we got mos' to de gate, de hawses got sort o' skeered, an' I see dey wuz some'n or somebody standin' jes' inside; an' Marse Chan he jumpt off de sorrel an' flung me de bridle and he walked up.

"She spoke fust. 'Twuz Miss Anne had done come out dyah to meet Marse Chan, an' she sez, jes' ez cold ez a chill, 'Well, seh, I granted your favor. I wished to reliebe myse'f of de obligations you placed me under a few months ago, when you made me a present of my father, whom you fust insulted an' then prevented from gittin' satisfaction.'

"Marse Chan he didn' speak fur a minit, an' den he said: 'Who is wid you' (Dat wuz ev'y wud.)

"'No one,' sez she; 'I came alone.'

"'My God!' sez he, 'you didn' come all through those woods by yourse'f at this time o' night?'

"'Yes, I'm not afraid,' sez she. (An' heah dis nigger! I don' b'lieve she wuz.)

"De moon come' out, an' I cotch sight on her stan'in dyah in her white dress, wid de cloak she done wrapped herse'f up in drapped off on de groun', an' she didn't look like she wuz 'feared o' nuttin'. She wuz mons'us purty ez she stood dyah wid de green bushes behine her, an' she hed jes' a few flowers in her breas' —right heah—and some leaves in her sorrel

hyah; an' de moon come' out an' shined down on her hyah an' her frock, an' peared like de light wuz jes' stan'in off it ez she stood dyah lookin' at Marse Chan wid her head tho'd back, jes' like dat mawnin' when she pahss Marse Chan in de road widout speakin' to 'im, an' sez to me, 'Good-mawnin', Sam.'

"Marse Chan, he den tole her he hed come to say good-by to her, ez he wuz gwine 'way to de war nex' mawnin'. I wuz watchin' on her, an' I thought, when Marse Chan tole her dat, she sort o' started an' looked up at 'im like she wuz mighty sorry, an' 'peared like she didn' stan' quite so straight arfter dat. Den Marse Chan he went on talkin' right fars' to her; an' he tole her how he had loved her ever sence she wuz a little bit o' baby mos', an' how he nuver 'membered de time when he hedn' hope' to marry her. He tole her it wuz his love for her dat hed made 'im stan' fust at school an' college, an' hed kep' 'im good an' pure; an' now he was gwine 'way, wouldn' she let it be like 'twuz in ole times, an' ef he come back from de war wouldn' she try to think on him ez she use' to when she wuz a little guirl?

"Marse Chan he had done been talkin' so serious, he hed done tek Miss Anne' han', an' wuz lookin' down in her face like he wuz list'nin' wid he eyes.

"Arfter a minit Miss Anne she said somethin', an' Marse Chan he cotch her urr han' an' sez:

"'But if you love me, Anne?'

"When he said dat, she tu'ned her head 'way from 'im, an' wait' a minit, an' den she said— right clear:

"'But I don' love yo'. (Jes' dem th'ee wuds!) De wuds fall right slow—like dirt falls out a spade on a coffin when yo' 's buryin' anybody, an' seys, 'Uth to uth.' Marse Chan he jes' let her hand drap, an' he stiddy hisse'f g'inst de gate-pos' an' he didn' speak torekly. When he did speak, all he sez wuz:

"'I mus' see yo' home safe.'

"I 'clar, marster, I didn' know 'twuz Marse Chan's voice tell I look at 'im right good. Well, she wouldn' let 'im go wid her. She jes' wrap' her cloak roun' her shoulders, an' wen' 'long back by herse'f, widout doin' more'n jes' to look up once at Marse Chan leanin' dyah 'g'inst de gate-pos' in he sowger clo's, wid he eyes on de groun'. She said 'Good-by' sort o' sorf, an' Marse Chan, widout lookin' up, shake han's wid her, an' she wuz done gone down de road. Soon ez she got 'mos' 'roun de curve, Marse Chan he followed her, keepin' onder de trees so ez not to be seen, an' I led de hawses on down de road behine 'im. He kep' 'long behine her tell she wuz safe in de house, an' den he come an' got on he haws, an' we all come home.

"Nex' mawnin' we all went off to j'ine de army. An' dey wuz a-drillin' an' a-drillin' all 'bout for a while an' we went 'long wid all de res' o' de army, an' I went wid Marse Chan an' clean he boots an' look arfter de tent, an' tek keer o' him an' de hawses. An' Marse Chan, he wan't a bit like he use' to be, at leas' 'cep' when dyah wuz gwine to be a fight. Den he'd peart-in' up, an' he alwuz rid at de head o' de company, 'cause he wuz tall; an' hit wan' on'y in battles whar all his company wuz dat he went, but he use' to volunteer whenever de cun'l wanted anybody to fine out anythin', an' 'twuz so dangersome he didn' like to mek one man go no sooner'n anurr, yo' know, an' ax'd who'd volunteer. He 'peared to like to go prowlin' aroun' 'mong dem Yankees, an' he use' to tek me wid 'im whenever he could. Yes, seh, he sut'n'y wuz a good sowger! He didn' mine bullets no more'n he did so many draps o' rain. But I tell you Sam use' to be pow'ful skeered sometimes. It jes' use' to 'pear like fun to him. In camp he use' to be so sorreful he'd hardly open he mouf. You'd a' tho't he wuz seekin', he used to look so moanful; but jes' le' 'im git into danger, an' he use' to be like old times—jolly an' laughin' like when he wuz a boy.

"When Cap'n Gordon got he leg shoot off, dey mek Marse Chan cap'n on de spot, 'cause one o' de lieutenants got kilt de same day, an' turr one (named Mr. Ronny) wan' no 'count, an' all de company said Marse Chan wuz de man.

"An' Marse Chan he wuz jes' de same. He didn't nuver mention Miss Anne's name, but I knowed he wuz thinkin' on her constant. One night he wuz settin' by de fire in camp, an' Mr. Ronny—he wuz de secon' lieutenant—got to talkin' 'bout ladies, an' he say all sorts o' things 'bout 'em, an' I see Marse Chan kinder lookin' mad; an' de lieutenant mention Miss Anne's name. He hed been courtin' Miss Anne 'bout de time Marse Chan fit de duil wid her pa, an' Miss Anne hed kicked 'im, dough he wuz mighty rich, 'cause he warn' nuttin' but a half-strainer, an' 'cause she like Marse Chan, I believe, dough she didn't speak to 'im; an' Mr. Ronny he got drunk, an' 'cause Cun'l Chahmb'lin tole 'im not to come dyah no more, he got mighty mad. An' dat evenin' I'se tellin' yo' 'bout, he wuz talkin' by de camp-fire, an' he mention Miss Anne's name. I see Marse Chan tu'n he eye 'roun' on 'im an' keep it on he face, an' pres'n'y Mr. Ronny said he

wuz gwine git even dyah yit. He didn' men-tion her name dat time; but he said dey wuz all on 'em a parecel of stuck-up 'risticrats, an' her pa wan' no gent'man anyway, an'——I don' know what he wuz gwine say (he nuver said it); fur ez he got dat far Marse Chan riz up an' hit 'im a crack, an' he fall like he hed been hit wid a fence-rail. He challenged Marse Chan to fight a duil, an' Marse Chan he excepted de challenge, an' dey wuz gwine fight; but some on 'em tole 'im Marse Chan wan' gwine mek a present o' 'im to his fam'ly, an' he got some-body to bre'k up de duil; twan' nuttin' dough, but he wuz 'fred to fight Marse Chan. An' purty soon he lef' de comp'ny.

"Well, I got one o' de gent'mens to write Judy a letter for me, an' I tole her all 'bout de fight, an' how Marse Chan knock' Mr. Ronny over fur speakin' discontemptuous o' Cun'l Chahmb'lin, an' I tole her how Marse Chan wuz a-dyin' fur love o' Miss Anne. An Judy she couldn' read an' she had to git Miss Anne to read de letter fur her. Den Miss Anne she tells her pa, an'—you mind, Judy tells me all dis arfterwards, an' she say when Cun'l Chahmb'lin hear 'bout it, he wuz settin' on de poach, an' he set still a good while, an' den he sey to his-se'f:

"'Well, he carn' he'p bein' a Whig.'

"An' den he gits up an' walks up to Miss Anne an' looks at her right hard; an' Miss Anne she hed done tu'n away her haid an' wuz makin' out like she wuz fixin' a rose-bush 'g'inst de poach; an' when her pa kep' lookin' at her, her face, Judy say, got jes' de color o' de roses on de bush, an' pres'n'y her pa sez:

"'Anne!'

"An' she tu'ned roun', an' sez: 'Sir?'

"An' he sez, 'Do yo' want 'im?'

"An' she sez, 'Yes,' an' put her head on he shoulder an' begin to cry; an' he sez:

"'Well, I won't stan' between yo' no longer. Write to 'im an' say so.'

"We didn' know nuttin' 'bout dis not den. We wuz a-fightin' an' a-fightin' all dat time: an' come one day a letter to Marse Chan, an' I see 'im start to read it in his tent onder de cedar tree, an' he face hit look so cu'iousome, an' he han's trembled so I couldn' mek out what wuz de motter wid 'im. An' he fol' de letter up an' wen' out an' wen' 'way down 'hine de camp, an' stayed dyah 'bout nigh a hour. Well, seh, I wuz on de lookout for 'im when he come back, an', fo' Gord! ef he face didn' shine like a angel'! I say to myse'f, 'Um'm! ef de glory o' Gord ain' done shine on 'im!' An' what yo' 'spose 'twuz?

"He tuk me wid 'im dat evenin', an' he tell

me he hed done git a letter from Miss Anne, an' Marse Chan he eyes look' like gre't big stars, an' he face wuz jes' like 'twuz dat mawnin' when de sun riz up over de low groun', an' I see 'im stan'in' dyah wid de pistil in he han', lookin' at it, an' not knowin' but what it mout be de lars' time, an' he done mek up his mine not to shoot ole Cun'l Chahmb'lin fur Miss Anne's sake, whah writ 'im de letter.

"He fol' de letter wha' was in his han' up, an' put it in he inside pocket—right dyah on de lef' side; an' den he tole me he tho't mebbe we wuz gwine hev some warm wuk in de nex' two or th'ee days, an' arfter dat ef Gord speared 'im he'd git a leave o' absence fur a few days, an' we'd go home.

"Well, dat night de orders come, an' we all hed to git over to'ds Romney; an' we rid all night till 'bout light; an' we halted right on a little creek, an' we stayed dyah till mos' breakfas' time,—but we didn' had no breakfast,—an' I see Marse Chan set down on de groun' 'hine a bush an' read dat letter over an' over. I watch 'im, an' de battle wuz a-goin' on, but we had orders to stay 'hine de hill, an' ev'y now an' den de bullets would clip de limbs o' de trees right over us, an' one o' dem big shells what goes '*Awhar—awhar—awhar is you!*' would fall right 'mong us; but Marse Chan he didn' mine it no mo'n nuttin'! Den it 'peared to git closer an' thicker, an' Marse Chan he calls me, an' I crep' up, an' he sez:

"'Sam, we'se goin' to win in dis battle, an' den we'll go home an' git married; an' I'm goin' home wid a star on my collar.' An' den he sez, 'Ef I'm wounded, kyah me home, yo' hear?' An' I sez, 'Yes, Marse Chan.'

"Well, jes' den dey blowed 'boots an' saddles,' an' we mounted; an' de orders come to ride 'roun' de slope, an' Marse Chan's comp'ny wuz de secon', an' when we got 'roun' dyah, we wuz right in it. Hit wuz de wust place uver dis nigger got in! An' dey said, 'Charge 'em!' an' my king! ef uver you see bullets fly, dey did dat day. Hit wuz jes' like hail; an' we wen' down de slope (I 'long wid de res') an' up de hill right to'ds de cannons, an' de fire wuz so strong dyah (deh hed a whole rigiment o' infintrys layin' down dyah onder de guns) our lines sort o' broke an' stop; an' de cun'l was kilt, an' I b'lieve dey wuz jes' 'bout to bre'k all to pieces, when Marse Chan rid up 'an cotch holt de fleg and hollers, 'Foller me!' an' rid strainin' up de hill 'mong de cannons. I seen 'im when he went, de sorrel four good lengths ahead o' ev'y urr hoss, jes' like he use' to be in a fox-hunt, an' de whole rigiment clamorin' right arfter 'im. Yo' ain' nuver heah

thunder! Fust thing I knowed, de roan roll' head over heels an' flung me up 'g'inst de bank like yo' chuck a nubbin over 'g'inst de foot o' de corn pile. An dat's what kep' me from bein' kilt, I 'spects. Judy she say she thinks 'twuz Providence, but I thinks 'twuz de bank. In co'se, Providence put de bank dyah, but how come Providence nuver saved Marse Chan? When I look 'roun', de roan wuz layin' dyah by me, stone dead, wid a cannon-ball gone 'mos' th'oo him, an' our men hed done swep' dem on t'urr side from de top o' de hill. 'Twan mo'n a minit, de sorrel come gallupin' back wid his mane flyin', an' de rein hangin' down on one side to his knee. 'Dyah!' says I, 'fo' Gord! I 'specks dey done kill Marse Chan, an' I promised to tek care on him.'

"I jumped up an' run over de bank, an' dyah, wid a whole lot o' dead mens, an' some not dead yit, onder one o' de guns wid de fleg still in he han', an' a bullet right th'oo he body, lay Marse Chan. I tu'n 'im over an' all 'im, 'Marse Chan!' but 'twan' no use, he wuz done gone home, sho' 'nuff.

"I pick' 'im up in my arms wid de fleg still in he han', an' toted 'im back jes' like I did dat day when he wuz a baby, an' ole marster gin' 'im to me in my arms, an' sey he could trus' me, an' tell me to tek keer on 'im long ez he lived. I kyah'd 'im 'way off de battlefiel' out de way o' de balls, an' I laid 'im down onder a big tree till I could git somebody to ketch de sorrel for me. He was cotched arfter a while, an' I hed some money, so I got some pine plank an' made a coffin dat evenin', an' wrapt Marse Chan's body up in de fleg, an' put 'im in de coffin; but I didn' nail de top on strong, 'cause I knowed ole missis' wan' see 'im; an' I got a' ambulance an' set out for home dat night. We reached dyah de nex' evein', arfter travellin' all dat night an' all nex' day.

"Hit 'peared like somethin' hed tole ole missis we wuz comin' so; for when we got home she wuz waitin' for us—done drest up in her best Sunday-clo'es, an' stan'n' at de head o' de big steps, an' ole marster settin' dyah bline in his big cheer—ez we druv up de hill to'ds de house, I drivin' de ambulance an' de sorrel leadin' long behine wid de stirrups crost over de saddle.

"She come down to de gate to meet us. We took de coffin out de ambulance an' kyah'd it right into de big parlor wid de pictures in it, whar dey use' to dance in ole times when Marse Chan wuz a schoolboy, an' Miss Anne Chahmb'lin use' to come over, an' go wid ole missis into her chamber an' tek her things off. In dyah we laid de coffin on two o' de cheers, an' ole missis nuver said a wud; she jes' looked so ole an' white.

"When I had tell 'em all 'bout it, I tu'ned right 'roun' an' rid over to Cun'l Chahmb'lin's, 'cause I knowed dat wuz what Marse Chan he'd 'a' wanted me to do. I didn' tell nobody whar I was gwine, 'cause yo' know, none on 'em hadn' nuver speak to Miss Anne, not sence de duil, an' dey didn't know 'bout de letter.

"When I rid up in de yard, dyah wuz Miss Anne a-stan'in' on de poach watchin' me ez I rid up. I tied my hoss to de fence, an' walked up de parf. She knowed by de way I walked dyah wuz som'thin' de motter, an' she wuz mighty pale. I drapt my cap down on de een' o' de steps an' went up. She nuver opened her mouf; jes' stan' right still an' keep her eyes on my face. Fust, I couldn' speak; den I cotch my voice, an' I say, 'Marse Chan, he done got he furlough.'

"Her face was mighty ashy, an' she sort o' shook, but she didn't fall. She tu'ned roun' an' said, 'Git me de ker'ige!' Dat wuz all.

"When de ker'ige come roun' she hed put on her bonnet, an' wuz ready. Ez she got in, she sey to me, 'Hev yo' brought him home?' an' we drove 'long, I ridin' behine.

"When we got home, she got out, an' walked up de big walk—up to de poach by herse'f.

"Ole missis hed done fin' de letter in Marse Chan's pocket, wid de love in it, while I wuz 'way, an' she wuz a-waitin' on de poach. Dey sey dat wuz de fust time ole missis cry when she fin' de letter, an' dat she sut'n'y did cry over hit, pintedly.

"Well, seh, Miss Anne she walks right up de steps, mos' up to ole missis stan'in' dyah on de poach, an' jes' falls right down mos' to her, on her knees fust, an' den flat on her face right on de flo', ketchin' at ole missis' dress wid her two han's—so.

"Ole missis stood for 'bout a minit lookin' down at her, an' den she drapt down on de flo' by her, an' took her in bofe her arms.

"I couldn' see, I wuz cryin' so myse'f, an' ev'ybody wuz cryin'. But dey went in arfter a while in de parlor, an' shet de do'; an' I heahd 'em say, Miss Anne she tuk de coffin in her arms an' kissed it, an' kissed Marse Chan, an' call' 'im by his name, an' her darlin', an'

ole missis lef' her cryin' in dyah tell some on 'em went in, an' found her done faint on de flo'.

"Judy she tell me she heah Miss Anne when she axed ole missis mout she wear mo'nin' fur 'im. I don' know how dat is; but when we buried 'im nex' day, she wuz de one whar walked arfter de coffin, holdin' ole marster, an' ole missis she walked next to 'em.

"Well, we buried Marse Chan dyah in de ole grabeyard, wid de fleg wrapped roun' 'im, an' he face lookin' like it did dat mawnin' down in de low groun's, wid de new sun shinin' on it so peaceful.

"Miss Anne she nuver went home to stay arfter dat; she stay wid ole marster an' ole missis ez long ez dey lived. Dat warn' so mighty long, 'cause ole marster he died dat Fall, when dey wuz fallerin' fur wheat—I had jes' married den—an' ole missis she warn' long behine him. We buried her by him next summer. Miss Anne she went in de hospitals to-reckly after ole missis died; an' jes' b'fo Richmond fall she come home sick wid de fever. Yo' nuver wud 'a' knowed her fur de same ole Miss Anne. She wuz light ez a piece o' peth, an' so white, 'cep' her eyes an' her sorrel hyah, an' she kep' on gittin' whiter an' weaker. Judy she sut'n'y did nuss her faithful. But she nuver got no betterment! De fever an' Marse Chan's bein' kilt dataway hed done strain her, an' she died jes' fo' de folks wuz sot free.

"So we buried Miss Anne right by Marse Chan, in a place whar ole missis hed tole us to leave, an' dey's bofe on 'em sleep side by side over in de ole grabeyard at home now.

"An' will yo' please tell me, marster? Dey tells me dat de Bible sey dyah won' be marry in' nor givin' in marriage in heaven, but I don' b'lieve it signifies dat—does you?"

I gave him the comfort of my earnest belief in some other interpretation, together with several spare "eighteen-pences," as he called them, for which he seemed humbly grateful. And as I rode away I heard him calling across the fence to his wife, who was standing in the door of a small whitewashed cabin, near which we had been standing for some time:

"Judy, have Marse Chan's dawg got home?"

SARAH ORNE JEWETT (1849-1909)
MARSH ROSEMARY
(1886)

I

One hot afternoon in August, a single moving figure might have been seen following a straight road that crossed the salt marshes of Walpole. Everybody else had either stayed at home or crept into such shade as could be found near at hand. The thermometer marked at least ninety degrees. There was hardly a fishing-boat to be seen on the glistening sea, only far away on the hazy horizon two or three coasting schooners looked like ghostly Flying Dutchmen, becalmed for once and motionless.

Ashore, the flaring light of the sun brought out the fine, clear colors of the level landscape. The marsh grasses were a more vivid green than usual, the brown tops of those that were beginning to go to seed looked almost red, and the soil at the edges of the tide inlets seemed to be melting into a black, pitchy substance like the dark pigments on a painter's palette. Where the land was higher the hot air flickered above it dizzily. This was not an afternoon that one would naturally choose for a long walk, yet Mr. Jerry Lane stepped briskly forward, and appeared to have more than usual energy. His big boots trod down the soft carpet of pussy-clover that bordered the dusty, whitish road. He struck at the stationary procession of thistles with a little stick as he went by. Flight after flight of yellow butterflies fluttered up as he passed, and then wavered down again to their thistle flowers, while on the shiny cambric back of Jerry's Sunday waistcoat basked at least eight large greenheaded flies in complete security.

It was difficult to decide why the Sunday waistcoat should have been put on that Saturday afternoon. Jerry had not thought it important to wear his best boots or best trousers, and had left his coat at home altogether. He smiled as he walked along, and once when he took off his hat, as a light breeze came that way, he waved it triumphantly before he put it on again. Evidently this was no common errand that led him due west, and him forget the hot weather, and caused him to shade his eyes with his hand, as he looked eagerly at a clump of trees and the chimney of a small house a littleway beyond the boundary of the marshes, where the higher ground began.

Miss Ann Floyd sat by her favorite window, sewing, twitching her thread less decidedly than usual, and casting a wistful glance now and then down the road, or at the bees in her gay little garden outside. There was a grim expression overshadowing her firmly-set, angular face, and the frown that always appeared on her forehead when she sewed or read the newspaper was deeper and straighter than usual. She did not look as if she were conscious of the heat, though she had dressed herself in an old-fashioned skirt of sprigged lawn and a loose jacket of thin white dimity with out-of-date flowing sleeves. Her sandy hair was smoothly brushed; one lock betrayed a slight crinkle at its edge, but it owed nothing to any encouragement of Nancy Floyd's. A hard, honest, kindly face this was, of a woman whom everybody trusted, who might be expected to give of whatever she had to give, good measure, pressed down and running over. She was a lonely soul; she had no near relatives in the world. It seemed always as if nature had been mistaken in not planting her somewhere in a large and busy household.

The little square room, kitchen in winter and sitting-room in summer, was as clean and bare and thrifty as one would expect the dwelling-place of such a woman to be. She sat in a straight-backed, splint-bottomed kitchen chair, and always put back her spool with a click on the very same spot on the window-sill. You would think she had done with youth and with love affairs, yet you might as well expect the ancient cherry-tree in the corner of her yard to cease adventuring its white blossoms when the May sun shone! No woman in Walpole had more bravely and patiently borne the burden of loneliness and lack of love. Even now her outward behavior gave no hint of the new excitement and delight that filled her heart.

"Land sakes alive!" she says to herself presently, "there comes Jerry Lane. I expect, if he sees me settin' to the winder, he'll come in an' dawdle round till supper-time!" But good Nancy Floyd smooths her hair hastily as she rises and drops her work, and steps back toward the middle of the room, watching the gate anxiously all the time. Now, Jerry, with a crestfallen look at the vacant window, makes believe that he is going by, and takes a loitering step or two onward, and then stops short; with a somewhat sheepish smile he leans over the neat picket fence and examines the blue and white and pink larkspur that covers most of the space in the little garden. He takes off his hat again to cool his forehead, and replaces it, without a grand gesture this time, and looks again at the window hopefully. There is a pause. The woman knows that the man is sure she is there; a little blush colors her thin cheeks as she comes boldly to the wide-open front door.

"What do you think of this kind of weather?" asks Jerry Lane complacently, as he leans over the fence, and surrounds himself with an air of self-sacrifice.

"I call it hot," responds the Juliet from her balcony, with deliberate assurance, "but the corn needs sun, everybody says. I shouldn't have wanted to toil up from the shore under such a glare, if I had been you. Better come in and set awhile, and cool off," she added, without any apparent enthusiasm. Jerry was sure to come, anyway. She would rather make the suggestion than have him.

Mr. Lane sauntered in, and seated himself opposite his hostess, beside the other small window, and watched her admiringly as she took up her sewing and worked at it with great spirit and purpose. He clasped his hands together and leaned forward a little. The shaded kitchen was very comfortable, after the glaring light outside, and the clean orderliness of the few chairs, and the braided rugs, and the table under the clock, with some larkspur and asparagus in a china vase for decoration, seemed to please him unexpectedly. "Now just see what ways you women folks have of fixing things up smart!" he ventured gallantly.

Nancy's countenance did not forbid further compliment; she looked at the flowers herself, quickly, and explained that she had gathered them a while ago to send to the minister's sister, who kept house for him. "I saw him going by, and expected he'd be back this same road. Mis' Elton 's be'n havin' another o' her dyin' spells this noon, and the deacon went by after him hot foot. I'd souse her well with stone-cold water. She never sent for me to set up with her; she knows better. Poor man, 'twas likely he was right into the middle of to-morrow's sermon. 'Tain't considerate of the deacon, and when he knows he's got a fool for a wife, he needn't go round persuading other folks she's so suffering as she makes out. They ain't got no larkspur this year to the parsonage, and I was going to let the minister take this over to Amandy; but I see his wagon over on the other road, going towards the village, about an hour after he went by here."

It seemed to be a relief to tell somebody all these things after such a season of forced repression, and Jerry listened with gratifying interest. "How you do see through folks!" he exclaimed in a mild voice. Jerry could be very soft spoken if he thought best. "Mis' Elton's a die-away lookin' creatur'. I heard of her saying last Sunday, comin' out o' meetin', that she made an effort to git there once more, but she expected 't would be the last time. Looks as if she eat well, don't she?" he concluded in a meditative tone.

"Eat!" exclaimed the hostess, with snapping eyes. "There ain't no woman in town, sick or well, can lay aside the food that she does. 'Tain't to the table afore folks, but she goes seeking round in the cupboards half a dozen times a day. An' I've heard her remark 'twas the last time she ever expected to visit the sanctuary as much as a dozen times within five years."

"Some places I've sailed to they'd have hit her over the head with a club long ago," said Jerry, with an utter lack of sympathy that was startling. "Well, I must be gettin' back again. Talkin' of eatin' makes us think o' supper-time. Must be past five, ain't it? I thought I'd just step up to see if there wa'n't anything I could lend a hand about, this hot day."

Sensible Ann Floyd folded her hands over her sewing, as it lay in her lap, and looked straight before her without seeing the pleading face of the guest. This moment was a great crisis in her life. She was conscious of it, and knew well enough that upon her next words would depend the course of future events. The man who waited to hear what she had to say was indeed many years younger than she, was shiftless and vacillating. He had drifted to Walpole from nobody knew where, and possessed many qualities which she had openly rebuked and despised in other men. True enough, he was good-looking, but that did not atone for the lacks of his character and reputation. Yet she knew herself to be the better man of the two, and since she had surmounted many obstacles already she was confident that, with a push here and a pull there to steady him, she could keep him in good trim. The winters were so long and lonely; her life was in many ways hungry and desolate in spite of its thrift and conformity. She had laughed scornfully when he stopped, one day in the spring, and offered to help her weed her garden; she had even joked with one of the neighbors about it. Jerry had been growing more and more friendly and pleasant ever since. His ease-loving, careless nature was like a comfortable cushion for hers, with its angles, its melancholy anticipations and self-questionings. But Jerry liked her, and if she liked him and married him, and took him home, it was nobody's business, and in that moment of surrender to Jerry's cause she arrayed herself at his right hand against the rest of the world, ready for warfare with any and all of its opinions.

She was suddenly aware of the sunburnt face and light, curling hair of her undeclared lover, at the other end of the painted table with its folded leaf. She smiled at him vacantly across the larkspur; then she gave a little start, and was afraid that her thoughts had wandered longer than was seemly. The kitchen clock was ticking faster than usual, as if it were trying to attract attention.

"I guess I'll be getting home," repeated the visitor ruefully, and rose from his chair, but hesitated again at an unfamiliar expression upon his companion's face.

"I don't know as I've got anything extra for supper, but you stop," she said, "an' take what there is. I wouldn't go back across them marshes right in this heat."

Jerry Lane had a lively sense of humor, and a queer feeling of merriment stole over him now, as he watched the mistress of the house. She had risen, too; she looked so simple and so frankly sentimental, there was such an incongruous coyness added to her usually straightforward, angular appearance, that his instinctive laughter nearly got the better of him, and might have lost him the prize for which he had been waiting these many months. But Jerry behaved like a man: he stepped forward and kissed Ann Floyd; he held her fast with one arm as he stood beside her, and kissed her again and again. She was a dear good woman. She had a fresh young heart, in spite of the straight wrinkle in her forehead and her work-worn hands. She had waited all her days for this joy of having a lover.

II

Even Mrs. Elton revived for a day or two under the tonic of such a piece of news. That was what Jerry Lane had hung round for all summer, everybody knew at last. Now he would strike work and live at his ease, the men grumbled to each other; but all the women of Walpole deplored most the weakness and foolishness of the elderly bride. Ann Floyd was comfortably off, and had something laid by for a rainy day; she would have done vastly better to deny herself such an expensive and utterly worthless luxury as the kind of husband Jerry

Lane would make. He had idled away his life. He earned a little money now and then in seafaring pursuits, but was too lazy, in the shore parlance, to tend lobster-pots. What was energetic Ann Floyd going to do with him? She was always at work, always equal to emergencies, and entirely opposed to dullness and idleness and even placidity. She often avowed scornfully that she liked people who had some snap to them, and now she had chosen for a husband the laziest man in Walpole. "Dear sakes," one woman said to another, as they heard the news, "there's no fool like an old fool!"

The days went quickly by, while Miss Ann made her plain wedding clothes. If people expected her to put on airs of youth they were disappointed. Her wedding bonnet was the same sort of bonnet she had worn for a dozen years, and one disappointed critic deplored the fact that she had spruced up so little, and kept on dressing old enough to look like Jerry Lane's mother. As her acquaintances met her they looked at her with close scrutiny, expecting to see some outward trace of such a silly, uncharacteristic departure from good sense and discretion. But Miss Floyd, while she was still Miss Floyd, displayed no silliness and behaved with dignity, while on the Sunday after a quiet marriage at the parsonage she and Jerry Lane walked up the side aisle together to their pew, the picture of middle-aged sobriety and respectability. Their fellow-parishioners, having recovered from their first astonishment and amusement, settled down to the belief that the newly married pair understood their own business best, and that if anybody could make the best of Jerry and get any work out of him, it was his capable wife.

"And if she undertakes to drive him too hard he can slip off to sea, and they'll be rid of each other," commented one of Jerry's 'longshore companions, as if it were only reasonable that some refuge should be afforded to those who make mistakes in matrimony.

There did not seem to be any mistake at first, or for a good many months afterward. The husband liked the comfort that came from such good housekeeping, and enjoyed a deep sense of having made a good anchorage in a well-sheltered harbor, after many years of thriftless improvidence and drifting to and fro. There were some hindrances to perfect happiness: he had to forego long seasons of gossip with his particular friends, and the outdoor work which was expected of him, though by no means heavy for a person of his strength, fettered his freedom not a little. To chop wood, and take care of a cow, and bring a pail of water now and then, did not weary him so much as it made him practically understand the truth of weakly Sister Elton's remark, that life was a constant chore. And when poor Jerry, for lack of other interest, fancied that his health was giving way mysteriously, and brought home a bottle of strong liquor to be used in case of sickness, and placed it conveniently in the shed, Mrs. Lane locked it up in the small chimney cupboard where she kept her camphor bottle and her opodeldoc and the other family medicines. She was not harsh with her husband. She cherished him tenderly, and worked diligently at her trade of tailoress, singing her hymns gayly in summer weather; for she never had been so happy as now, when there was somebody to please beside herself, to cook for and sew for, and to live with and love. But Jerry complained more and more in his inmost heart that his wife expected too much of him. Presently he resumed an old habit of resorting to the least respected of the two country stores of that neighborhood, and sat in the row of loafers on the outer steps. "Sakes alive," said a shrewd observer one day, "the fools set there and talk and talk about what they went through when they follered the sea, and when the women-folks comes tradin' they are obleeged to climb right over 'em."

Things grew worse and worse, until one day Jerry Lane came home a little late to dinner, and found his wife unusually grim-faced and impatient. He took his seat with an amiable smile, and showed in every way a fine determination not to lose his temper because somebody else had. It was one of the days when he looked almost boyish and entirely irresponsible. His hair was bright and curly from the dampness of the east wind, and his wife was forced to remember how, in the days of their courtship, she used to wish that she could pull one of the curling locks straight, for the pleasure of seeing it fly back. Nancy felt old and tired, and was hurt in her very soul by the contrast between herself and her husband. "No wonder I am aging, having to lug everything on my shoulders," she thought. Jerry had forgotten to do whatever she had asked him for a day or two. He had started out that morning to go lobstering, but returned from the direction of the village.

"Nancy," he said pleasantly, after he had begun his dinner, a silent and solitary meal, while his wife stitched busily by the window, and refused to look at him,—"Nancy, I've been thinking a good deal about a project."

"I hope it ain't going to cost so much and bring in so little as your other notions have, then," she responded quickly; though somehow a memory of the hot day when Jerry came and stood outside the fence, and kissed her when it was settled he should stay to supper, —a memory of that day would keep fading and brightening in her mind.

"Yes," said Jerry humbly, "I ain't done right, Nancy. I ain't done my part for our livin'. I've let it sag right on to you, most ever since we was married. There was that spell when I was kind of weakly, and had a pain acrost me. I tell you what it is: I never was good for nothin' ashore, but now I've got my strength up I'm going to show ye what I can do. I'm promised to ship with Cap'n Low's brother, Skipper Nathan, that sails out o' Eastport in the coasting trade, lumber a nd so on. I shall get good wages, and you shall keep the whole on't 'cept what I need for clothes."

"You needn't be so plaintive," said Ann in a sharp voice. "You can go if you want to. I have always been able to take care of myself, but when it comes to maintainin' two, 'tain't so easy. When be you goin'?"

"I expected you would be distressed," mourned Jerry, his face falling at this outbreak. "Nancy, you needn't be so quick. 'Tain't as if I hadn't always set consid'able by ye, if I be wuthless."

Nancy's eyes flashed fire as she turned hastily away. Hardly knowing where she went, she passed through the open doorway, and crossed the clean green turf of the narrow side yard, and leaned over the garden fence. The young cabbages and cucumbers were nearly buried in weeds, and the currant bushes were fast being turned into skeletons by the ravaging worms. Jerry had forgotten to sprinkle them with hellebore, after all, though she had put the watering-pot into his very hand the evening before. She did not like to have the whole town laugh at her for hiring a man to do his work; she was busy from early morning until late night, but she could not do everything herself. She had been a fool to marry this man, she told herself at last, and a sullen discontent and rage, that had been of slow but certain growth, made her long to free herself from this unprofitable hindrance for a time, at any rate. Go to sea? Yes, that was the best thing that could happen. Perhaps when he had worked hard a while on schooner fare, he would come home and be good for something!

Jerry finished his dinner in the course cf time, and then sought his wife. It was not like her to go away in this silent fashion. Of late her gift of speech had been proved sufficiently formidable, and yet she had never looked so resolutely angry as to-day.

"Nancy," he began,—"Nancy, girl! I ain't goin' off to leave you, if your heart's set against it. I'll spudge up and take right holt."

But the wife turned slowly from the fence and faced him. Her eyes looked as if she had been crying. "You needn't stay on my account," she said. "I'll go right to work an' fit ye out. I'm sick of your meechin' talk, and I don't want to hear no more of it. Ef *I* was a man"—

Jerry Lane looked crestfallen for a minute or two; but when his stern partner in life had disappeared within the house, he slunk away among the apple-trees of the little orchard, and sat down on the grass in a shady spot. It was getting to be warm weather, but he would go round and hoe the old girl's garden stuff by and by. There would be something going on aboard the schooner, and with delicious anticipation of future pleasure the delinquent Jerry struck his knee with his hand, as if he were clapping a crony on the shoulder. He also winked several times at the same fancied companion. Then, with a comfortable chuckle, he laid himself down, and pulled his old hat over his eyes, and went to sleep, while the weeds grew at their own sweet will, and the currant worms went looping and devouring from twig to twig.

III

Summer went by, and winter began, and Mr. Jerry Lane did not reappear. He had promised to return in September when he parted from his wife early in June, for Nancy had relented a little at the last, and sorrowed at the prospect of so long a separation. She had already learned the vacillations and uncertainties of her husband's character; but though she accepted the truth that her marriage had been in every way a piece of foolishness, she still clung affectionately to his assumed fondness for her. She could not believe that this marriage was only one of his makeshifts, and that as soon as he grew tired of the constraint he would be ready to throw the benefits of respectable home life to the four winds. A little sentimental speech-making and a few kisses the morning he went away, and the gratitude he might well have shown for her generous care-taking and provision for his voyage won her soft heart back again, and made poor, elderly, simple-hearted Nancy watch him cross the marshes with tears and foreboding.

If she could have called him back that day, she would have done so and been thankful. And all summer and winter, whenever the wind blew and thrashed the drooping elm boughs against the low roof over her head, she was as full of fears and anxieties as if Jerry were her only son and making his first voyage at sea. The neighbors pitied her for her disappointment. They liked Nancy; but they could not help saying, "I told you so." It would have been impossible not to respect the brave way in which she met the world's eye, and carried herself with innocent unconsciousness of having committed so laughable and unrewarding a folly. The loafers on the store steps had been unwontedly diverted one day, when Jerry, who was their chief wit and spokesman, rose slowly from his place, and said in pious tones, "Boys, I must go this minute. Grandma will keep dinner waiting." Mrs. Ann Lane did not show in her aging face how young her heart was, and after the schooner Susan Barnes had departed she seemed to pass swiftly from middle life and an almost youthful vigor to early age and a look of spent strength and dissatisfaction. "I suppose he did find it stupid," she assured herself, with wistful yearning for his rough words of praise, when she sat down alone to her dinner, or looked up sadly from her work, and missed the amusing though unedifying conversation he was wont to offer on stormy winter nights. How many of his marvelous tales were true she never cared to ask. He had come and gone, and she forgave him his shortcomings, and longed for his society with a heavy heart.

One spring day there was news in the Boston paper of the loss of the schooner Susan Barnes with all on board, and Nancy Lane's best friends shook their sage heads, and declared that as far as regarded that idle vagabond, Jerry Lane, it was all for the best. Nobody was interested in any other member of the crew, so the misfortune of the Susan Barnes seemed of but slight consequence in Walpole, she having passed out of her former owners' hands the autumn before. Jerry had stuck by the ship; at least, so he had sent word then to his wife by Skipper Nathan Low. The Susan Barnes was to sail regularly between Shediac and Newfoundland, and Jerry sent five dollars to Nancy, and promised to pay her a visit soon. "Tell her I'm layin' up somethin' handsome," he told the skipper with a grin, "and I've got some folks in Newfoundland I'll visit with on this voyage, and then I'll come ashore for good and farm it."

Mrs. Lane took the five dollars from the

skipper as proudly as if Jerry had done the same thing so many times before that she hardly noticed it. The skipper gave the messages from Jerry, and felt that he had done the proper thing. When the news came long afterward that the schooner was lost, that was the next thing that Nancy knew about her wandering mate; and after the minister had come solemnly to inform her of her bereavement, and had gone away again, and she sat down and looked her widowhood in the face, there was not a sadder nor a lonelier woman in the town of Walpole.

All the neighbors came to condole with our heroine, and, though nobody was aware of it, from that time she was really happier and better satisfied with life than she had ever been before. Now that she had an ideal Jerry Lane to mourn over and think about, to cherish and admire, she was day by day slowly forgetting the trouble he had been and the bitter shame of him, and exalting his memory to something near saintliness. "He meant well," she told herself again and again. She thought nobody could tell so good a story; she felt that with her own bustling, capable ways he had no chance to do much that he might have done. She had been too quick with him, and alas, alas! how much better she would know how to treat him if she could only see him again! A sense of relief at his absence made her continually assure herself of her great loss, and, false even to herself, she mourned her sometime lover diligently, and tried to think herself a broken-hearted woman. It was thought among those who knew Nancy Lane best that she would recover her spirits in time, but Jerry's wildest anticipations of a proper respect to his memory were more than realized in the first two years after the schooner Susan Barnes went to the bottom of the sea. His wife mourned for the man he ought to have been, not for the real Jerry, but she had loved him enough in the beginning to make her own love a precious possession for all time to come. It did not matter much, after all, what manner of man he was; she had found in him something on which to spend her hoarded affection.

IV

Nancy Lane was a peaceable woman and a good neighbor, but she never had been able to get on with one fellow townswoman, and that was Mrs. Deacon Elton. They managed to keep each other provoked and teased from one year's end to the other, and each good soul felt herself under a moral microscope, and understood that she was judged by a not very lenient criticism and discussion. Mrs. Lane clad herself in simple black after the news came of her husband's timely death, and Mrs. Elton made one of her farewell pilgrimages to church to see the new-made widow walk up the aisle.

"She needn't tell me she lays that affliction so much to heart," the deacon's wife sniffed faintly, after her exhaustion had been met by proper treatment of camphor and a glass of currant wine, at the parsonage, where she rested a while after service. "Nancy Floyd knows she's well through with such a piece of nonsense. If I had had my health, I should have spoken with her and urged her not to take the step in the first place. She hasn't spoken six beholden words to me since that vagabond come to Walpole. I dare say she may have heard something I said at the time she married. I declare for't, I never was so outdone as when the deacon came home and informed me Nancy Floyd was going to be married. She let herself down too low to ever hold the place again that she used to hold in folks' minds. And it's my opinion," said the sharp-eyed little woman, "she ain't got through with her pay yet."

But Mrs. Elton did not half comprehend the unconscious prophecy with which her words were freighted.

The months passed by: summer and winter came and went, and even those few persons who were misled by Nancy Lane's stern visage and forbidding exterior into forgetting her kind heart were at last won over to friendliness by her renewed devotion to the sick and old people of the rural community. She was so tender to little children that they all loved her dearly. She was ready to go to any household that needed help, and in spite of her ceaseless industry with her needle she found many a chance to do good, and help her neighbors to lift and carry the burdens of their lives. She blossomed out suddenly into a lovely, painstaking eagerness to be of use; it seemed as if her affectionate heart, once made generous, must go on spending its wealth wherever it could find an excuse. Even Mrs. Elton herself was touched by her old enemy's evident wish to be friends, and said nothing more about poor Nancy's looking as savage as a hawk. The only thing to admit was the truth that her affliction had proved a blessing to her. And it was in a truly kind and compassionate spirit that, after hearing a shocking piece of news, the deacon's hysterical wife forbore to spread it far and wide through the town first, and went down to the Widow Lane's one September afternoon. Nancy was stitching busily upon the deacon's new coat, and looked up with a friendly smile as her guest came in, in spite of an instinctive shrug as she had seen her coming up the yard. The dislike of the poor souls for each other was deeper than their philosophy could reach.

Mrs. Elton spent some minutes in the unnecessary endeavor to regain her breath, and to her surprise found she must make a real effort before she could tell her unwelcome news. She had been so full of it all the way from home that she had rehearsed the whole interview; now she hardly knew how to begin. Nancy looked serener than usual, but there was something wistful about her face as she glanced across the room, presently, as if to understand the reason of the long pause. The clock ticked loudly; the kitten clattered a spool against the table-leg, and had begun to snarl the thread round her busy paws, and Nancy looked down and saw her; then the instant consciousness of there being some unhappy reason for Mrs. Elton's call made her forget the creature's mischief, and anxiously lay down her work to listen.

"Capt'in Nathan Low was to our house to dinner," the guest began. "He's bargaining with the deacon about some hay. He's got a new schooner, Capt'in Nathan has, and is going to build up a regular business of freighting hay to Boston by sea. There's no market to speak of about here, unless you haul it way over to Downer, and you can't make but one turn a day."

"'Twould be a good thing," replied Nancy, trying to think that this was all, and perhaps the deacon wanted to hire her own field another year. He had underpaid her once, and they had not been on particularly good terms ever since. She would make her own bargains with Skipper Low, she thanked him and his wife!

"He's been down to the provinces these two or three years back, you know," the whining voice went on, and straightforward Ann Lane felt the old animosity rising within her. "At dinner-time I wa'n't able to eat much of anything, and so I was talking with Capt'in Nathan, and asking him some questions about them parts; and I expressed something about the mercy 'twas his life should ha' been spared when that schooner, the Susan Barnes, was lost so quick after he sold out his part of her. And I put in a word, bein' 's we were neighbors, about how edifyin' your course had be'n under affliction. I noticed then he'd looked sort o' queer whilst I was talkin', but there was

all the folks to the table, and you know he's a very cautious man, so he spoke of somethin' else. 'Twa'n't half an hour after dinner, I was comin' in with some plates and cups, tryin' to help what my stren'th would let me, and says he, 'Step out a little ways into the piece with me, Mis' Elton. I want to have a word with ye.' I went, too, spite o' my neuralgy, for I saw he'd got somethin' on his mind. 'Look here,' says he, 'I gathered from the way you spoke that Jerry Lane's wife expects he's dead.' Certain, says I, his name was in the list o' the Susan Barnes's crew, and we read it in the paper. 'No,' says he to me, 'he ran away the day they sailed; he wa'n't aboard, and he's livin' with another woman down to Shediac.' Them was his very words."

Nancy Lane sank back in her chair, and covered her horror-stricken eyes with her hands. "'Tain't pleasant news to have to tell," Sister Elton went on mildly, yet with evident relish and full command of the occasion. "He said he seen Jerry the morning he came away. I thought you ought to know it. I'll tell you one thing, Nancy: I told the skipper to keep still about it, and now I've told you, I won't spread t no further to set folks a-talking. I'll keep it secret till you say the word. There ain't much trafficking betwixt here and there, and he's dead to you, certain, as much as if he laid up here in the burying-ground."

Nancy had bowed her head upon the table; the thin sandy hair was streaked with gray. She did not answer one word; this was the hardest blow of all.

"I'm much obliged to you for being so friendly," she said after a few minutes, looking straight before her now in a dazed sort of way, and lifting the new coat from the floor, where it had fallen. "Yes, he's dead to me,—worse than dead, a good deal," and her lip quivered. "I can't seem to bring my thoughts to bear. I've got so used to thinkin'— No, don't you say nothin' to the folks yet. I'd do as much for you." And Mrs. Elton knew that the smitten fellow-creature before her spoke the truth, and forbore.

Two or three days came and went, and with every hour the quiet, simple-hearted woman felt more grieved and unsteady in mind and body. Such a shattering thunderbolt of news rarely falls into a human life. She could not sleep; she wandered to and fro in the little house, and cried until she could cry no longer. Then a great rage spurred and excited her. She would go to Shediac, and call Jerry Lane to account. She would accuse him face to face; and the woman whom he was deceiving, as perhaps he had deceived her, should know the baseness and cowardice of this miserable man. So, dressed in her respectable Sunday clothes, in the gray bonnet and shawl that never had known any journeys except to meeting, or to a country funeral or quiet holiday-making, Nancy Lane trusted herself for the first time to the bewildering railway, to the temptations and dangers of the wide world outside the bounds of Walpole.

Two or three days later still, the quaint, thin figure familiar in Walpole highways flitted down the street of a provincial town. In the most primitive region of China this woman could hardly have felt a greater sense of foreign life and strangeness. At another time her native good sense and shrewd observation would have delighted in the experiences of this first week of travel, but she was too sternly angry and aggrieved, too deeply plunged in a survey of her own calamity, to take much notice of what was going on about her. Later she condemned the unworthy folly of the whole errand, but in these days the impulse to seek the culprit and confront him was irresistible.

The innkeeper's wife, a kindly creature, urged this puzzling guest to wait and rest and eat some supper, but Nancy refused, and without asking her way left the brightly lighted, flaring little public room, where curious eyes already offended her, and went out into the damp twilight. The voices of the street boys sounded outlandish, and she felt more and more lonely. She longed for Jerry to appear for protection's sake; she forgot why she sought him, and was eager to shelter herself behind the flimsy bulwark of his manhood. She rebuked herself presently with terrible bitterness for a womanish wonder whether he would say, "Why, Nancy, girl!" and be glad to see her. Poor woman, it was a work-laden, serious girlhood that had been hers, at any rate. The power of giving her whole self in unselfish, enthusiastic, patient devotion had not belonged to her youth only; it had sprung fresh and blossoming in her heart as every new year came and went.

One might have seen her stealing through the shadows, skirting the edge of a lumber-yard, stepping among the refuse of the harbor side, asking a question timidly now and then of some passer-by. Yes, they knew Jerry Lane, —his house was only a little way off; and one curious and compassionate Scotchman, divining by some inner sense the exciting nature of the errand, turned back, and offered fruitlessly

to go with the stranger. "You know the man?" he asked. "He is his own enemy, but doing better now that he is married. He minds his work, I know that well; and he's taken a good wife." Nancy's heart beat faster with honest pride for a moment, until the shadow of the ugly truth and reality made it sink back to heaviness, and the fire of her smouldering rage was again kindled. She would speak to Jerry face to face before she slept, and a horrible contempt and scorn were ready for him, as with a glance either way along the road she entered the narrow yard, and went noiselessly toward the window of a low, poor-looking house, from whence a bright light was shining out into the night.

Yes, there was Jerry, and it seemed as if she must faint and fall at the sight of him. How young he looked still! The thought smote her like a blow. They never were mates for each other, Jerry and she. Her own life was waning; she was an old woman.

He never had been so thrifty and respectable before; the other woman ought to know the savage truth about him, for all that! But at that moment the other woman stooped beside the supper table, and lifted a baby from its cradle, and put the dear, live little thing into its father's arms. The baby was wide-awake, and laughed at Jerry, who laughed back again, and it reached up to catch at a handful of the curly hair which had been poor Nancy's delight.

The other woman stood there looking at them, full of pride and love. She was young, and trig, and neat. She looked a brisk, efficient little creature. Perhaps Jerry would make something of himself now; he always had it in him. The tears were running down Nancy's cheeks; the rain, too, had begun to fall. She stood there watching the little household sit down to supper, and noticed with eager envy how well cooked the food was, and how hungrily the master of the house ate what was put before him. All thoughts of ending the new wife's sin and folly vanished away. She could not enter in and break another heart; hers was broken already, and it would not matter. And Nancy Lane, a widow indeed, crept away again, as silently as she had come, to think what was best to be done, to find alternate woe and comfort in the memory of the sight she had seen.

The little house at the edge of the Walpole marshes seemed full of blessed shelter and comfort the evening that its forsaken mistress came back to it. Her strength was spent; she felt much more desolate now that she had seen with her own eyes that Jerry Lane was alive than when she had counted him among the dead. An uncharacteristic disregard of the laws of the land filled this good woman's mind. Jerry had his life to live, and she wished him no harm. She wondered often how the baby grew, and fancied again and again the changes and conditions of the far-away household. Alas! she knew only too well the weakness of the man, and once she exclaimed, in a grim outburst of impatience, "I'd rather others should have to cope with him than me!"

But that evening, when she came back from Shediac, and sat in the dark for a long time, lest Mrs. Elton should see the light and risk her life in the evening air to bring unwelcome sympathy,—that evening, I say, came the hardest moment of all, when Ann Floyd, tailor-ess, of so many virtuous, self-respecting years, whose idol had turned to clay, who was shamed, disgraced, and wronged, sat down alone to supper in the little kitchen.

She had put one cup and saucer on the table and then stood and looked at them through bitter tears. Somehow a consciousness of her solitary age, her uncompanioned future, rushed through her mind; the failure of her best earthly hope was enough to break a stronger woman's heart.

Who can laugh at my Marsh Rosemary, or who can cry, for that matter? The gray primness of the plant is made up from a hundred colors if you look close enough to find them. This Marsh Rosemary stands in her own place, and holds her dry leaves and tiny blossoms steadily toward the same sun that the pink lotus blooms for and the white rose.

SILAS WEIR MITCHELL (1829-1914)

A CONSULTATION

(1902)

Both men were physicians. The older of the two was far on in a life of success. The man he bade be seated had blue eyes, and was the owner of forty well-used years.

"Glad to see you, John," said the older man. He was about to add, "You look worried," but, on second thought, said only:

"What can I do for you?"

"You can listen to me for ten minutes."

"As long as you like; you know we do that all day. Don't hurry."

"You know, doctor, that I was once engaged to Helen Daunton. That was ten years ago."

"Yes—I know. Quite so; yes—yes—remember it well—yes."

The younger man said: "No, you do not know, and don't say 'Yes—yes' that way."

The gray head turned with a quick side glance of questioning observation, and knew at once that this was a man to be taken with care. He said: "Go on, John; I interrupted you."

"I fell ill; I went to India and Australia. When I came back she was married, the wife of—of all men—Wanfell, the banker. He was thirty years older than she. What! what was I saying? I mean, she was thirty years younger than he. I did not know why she did it. Now I know."

The older man said: "I remember her well. She was beautiful—but—"

John interrupted hastily: "That's unnecessary. I wish you would listen."

Here he rose and bent over his friend, who remained seated, a hand on his cheek, intent and a little anxious.

"This fellow Wanfell was my father's partner, and—ruined him."

"Yes—yes."

"Oh, damn it! Don't say 'Yes—yes' that way."

The hazel eyes below the gray hair became more tenderly attentive.

"Pardon me, John. I sometimes forget how to listen."

"Well, don't do that again; I—I—can't bear it. I have hoped the years would give me a chance—I mean,—I hoped that man would some day be in my power. He is! He was—and now—now—" Here he paused, and then went on: "What was it I was saying? Oh, that woman!"

The older physician laid a hand on his arm. "You were saying, John, I think—"

"No—no; you asked me why she married that scoundrel."

"No, my dear fellow, I did not ask—"

"But your eyes asked."

"You must excuse them. The curiosity of the eyes is not to be governed. But—go on. What else is there? Tell me quietly."

John sat down.

"Quietly! My God! You know, sir, I have never cared for any other woman. She has always had my—love. I have kept away from her. We have met but twice in a chance way, and once for a mad moment. Now, sir, now—oh, that woman, that woman! I—knew she could not help it—and she is—she is—"

"Drop her, John, and tell me what you want of me."

"I will—I will. It is just this: A week ago, late, about eleven at night, a servant came in haste with a note from her. Would I come instantly to see—Wanfell. He had had a fit. I went; of course I went. She said I must keep —the case. God help and pardon me, I did— I did!"

"Why did you?"

"Why do you ask me? You know—well enough."

"Are you still in charge?"

"Yes. He is very ill; half conscious; a decayed beast. He may die any moment—*any* moment, or drag on for years—*years*."

"I see."

"No, you do not. Every day she says: 'How long will he last? Will he die soon? It is cruel to try to keep him alive!'"

"People often say that," said the older physician.

"I know; but you understand. Don't trifle with me. I told you what she said, and you should not want me to say more. I will not—"

"Whatever I can do for you I will do."

"Then take this case off my hands. You or some one must—take it."

"Very well, John; I—"

"It isn't well at all! Help me now—at once. Can't you see my—my trouble?"

"Yes; I saw it all along. I will help you. It is easy—"

"Easy! Nothing is easy. I say, I cannot stand it! That half-dead dog—and that—that woman!"

He stood up and went on: "Now do you think I was right to yield—to stay on—stay on? Pity me! I had two good—I mean two bad—reasons—the man and the woman. I am plain, you see."

He laughed, and it was not a laugh good to hear.

"I shall be frank with you, my friend. You were wrong; you hate him, and you love—"

John broke in: "Don't say that kind of thing! Don't hint it!"

"But, my dear fellow—"

"We won't discuss it. I am the person concerned. You let him alone—and her, too. You

never were in the hell of a marriage like that. What must I do. I want to be made to do something—forced—"

"Be quiet a moment. Sit down and I will answer you."

He took out his watch and laid a finger on his friend's pulse. Presently he looked up, and said, smiling:

"You have consulted me, and now, as your doctor, I say, my dear fellow, that you are in no state to practise medicine."

"That is so."

"Neither are you fit to have the charge of a man who may die at any moment—"

"And who ought to die, damn him!"

"Yes; but it must not be while he is in your care. Go out of town—at once, to-day. Do not write to her. I will call and explain it all to her—to Mrs. Wanfell."

"Yes—you will do that—and I am ill, very ill. Thank you. Don't you think I ought to see her before I go?"

"I do not. Promise me that you will not."

"I will not—see her. Oh, never, never!"

"Stay away three weeks."

"How can I?"

"You must. Now go."

"Where is my hat?"

"Here. Now I have your word. In a day or two you will be glad you went."

John left him, saying: "Thank you. Yes, I am sick enough—soul sick."

The older man went with him to the door. Returning, he sat down and, playing with his watch-guard, was still a little while, and then spoke aloud the final conclusion of his reflections, which was a way he had:

"It is very easy to let a man die. I was wise to make him run away from it. If he had done his best and that rascal died, he would have lived in the shadow of remorse, where no crime had been; and if—" Here he ceased to speak. But by and by he murmured, as he rose: "What of the woman? A touch and a look may say, 'Do it!' He has told but half."

The younger man went to Aiken and played golf. At the close of a fortnight he received two telegrams; one was from the doctor. He went home the next day, but did not go to the funeral of Wanfell.

As the years went by, some of his friends wondered why he did not marry the woman he had once loved. When the old doctor's wife was thus curious, her husband said that he believed he knew why, but would never tell.

When urged to explain himself, he stated, at last, that it was all clearly set forth in the New Testament.

FRANCIS MARION CRAWFORD (1854-1909)

THE UPPER BERTH

(1894)

Somebody asked for the cigars. We had talked long, and the conversation was beginning to languish; the tobacco smoke had got into the heavy curtains, the wine had got into those brains which were liable to become heavy, and it was already perfectly evident that, unless somebody did something to rouse our oppressed spirits, the meeting would soon come to its natural conclusion, and we, the guests, would speedily go home to bed, and most certainly to sleep. No one had said anything very remarkable; it may be that no one had anything very remarkable to say. Jones had given us every particular of his last hunting adventure in Yorkshire. Mr. Tompkins, of Boston, had explained at elaborate length those working principles, by the due and careful maintenance of which the Atchison, Topeka, and Santa Fé Railroad not only extended its territory, increased its departmental influence, and transported live stock without starving them to death before the day of actual delivery, but also, had for years succeeded in deceiving those passengers who bought its tickets into the fallacious belief that the corporation aforesaid was really able to transport human life without destroying it. Signor Tombola had endeavoured to persuade us, by arguments which we took no trouble to oppose, that the unity of his country in no way resembled the average modern torpedo, carefully planned, constructed with all the skill of the greatest European arsenals, but, when constructed, destined to be directed by feeble hands into a region where it must undoubtedly explode, unseen, unfeared, and unheard, into the illimitable wastes of political chaos.

It is unnecessary to go into further details. The conversation had assumed proportions which would have bored Prometheus on his rock, which would have driven Tantalus to distraction, and which would have impelled Ixion to seek relaxation in the simple but instructive dialogue of Herr Ollendorff, rather than submit to the greater evil of listening to our talk. We had sat at table for hours; we were bored, we were tired, and nobody showed signs of moving.

Somebody called for cigars. We all instinctively looked towards the speaker. Brisbane was a man of five-and-thirty years of age, and remarkable for those gifts which chiefly attract the attention of men. He was a strong man. The external proportions of his figure presented nothing extraordinary to the common eye, though his size was above the average. He was a little over six feet in height, and moderately broad in the shoulder; he did not appear to be stout, but, on the other hand, he was certainly not thin; his small head was supported by a strong and sinewy neck; his broad muscular hands appeared to possess a peculiar skill in breaking walnuts without the assistance of the ordinary cracker, and, seeing him in profile, one could not help remarking the extraordinary breadth of his sleeves, and the unusual thickness of his chest. He was one of those men who are commonly spoken of among men as deceptive; that is to say, that though he looked exceedingly strong he was in reality very much stronger than he looked. Of his features I need say little. His head is small, his hair is thin, his eyes are blue, his nose is large, he has a small moustache, and a square jaw. Everybody knows Brisbane, and when he asked for a cigar everybody looked at him.

"It is a very singular thing," said Brisbane.

Everybody stopped talking. Brisbane's voice was not loud, but possessed a peculiar quality of penetrating general conversation, and cutting it like a knife. Everybody listened. Brisbane, perceiving that he had attracted their general attention, lit his cigar with great equanimity.

"It is very singular," he continued, "that thing about ghosts. People are always asking whether anybody has seen a ghost. I have."

"Bosh! What, you? You don't mean to say so, Brisbane? Well, for a man of his intelligence!"

A chorus of exclamations greeted Brisbane's remarkable statement. Everybody called for cigars, and Stubbs the butler suddenly appeared from the depths of nowhere with a fresh bottle of dry champagne. The situation was saved; Brisbane was going to tell a story.

"I am an old sailor," said Brisbane, "and as I have to cross the Atlantic pretty often, I have my favourites. Most men have their favourites. I have seen a man wait in a Broadway bar for three-quarters of an hour for a particular car which he liked. I believe the barkeeper made at least one-third of his living by that man's preference. I have a habit of waiting for certain ships when I am obliged to cross that duck-pond. It may be a prejudice, but I was never cheated out of a good passage but once in my life. I remember it very well; it was a warm morning in June, and the Custom House officials, who were hanging about waiting for a steamer already on her way up from the Quarantine, presented a peculiarly hazy and thoughtful appearance. I had not much luggage—I never have. I mingled with the crowd of passengers, porters, and officious individuals in blue coats and brass buttons, who seemed to spring up like mushrooms from the deck of a moored steamer to obtrude their unnecessary services upon the independent passenger. I have often noticed with a certain interest the spontaneous evolution of these fellows. They are not there when you arrive; five minutes after the pilot has called "Go ahead!" they, or at least their blue coats and brass buttons, have disappeared from deck and gangway as completely as though they had been consigned to that locker which tradition unanimously ascribes to Davy Jones. But, at the moment of starting, they are there, clean-shaved, blue-coated, and ravenous for fees. I hastened on board. The *Kamtschatka* was one of my favourite ships. I say was, because she emphatically no longer is. I cannot conceive of any inducement which could entice me to make another voyage in her. Yes, I know what you are going to say. She is uncommonly clean in the run aft, she has enough bluffing off in the bows to keep her dry, and the lower berths are most of them double. She has a lot of advantages, but I won't cross in her again. Excuse the digression. I got on board. I hailed a steward, whose red nose and redder whiskers were equally familiar to me.

"One hundred and five, lower berth," said I, in the businesslike tone peculiar to men who think no more of crossing the Atlantic than taking a whisky cocktail at downtown Delmonico's.

The steward took my portmanteau, great coat, and rug. I shall never forget the expression of his face. Not that he turned pale. It is maintained by the most eminent divines that even miracles cannot change the course of nature. I have no hesitation in saying that he did not turn pale; but, from his expression, I judged that he was either about to shed tears, to sneeze, or to drop my portmanteau. As the latter contained two bottles of particularly fine old sherry presented to me for my voyage by my old friend Snigginson van Pickyns, I felt extremely nervous. But the steward did none of these things.

"Well, I'm d——d!" said he in a low voice, and led the way.

I supposed my Hermes, as he led me to the lower regions, had had a little grog, but I said nothing, and followed him. One hundred and five was on the port side, well aft. There was nothing remarkable about the state-room. The lower berth, like most of those upon the *Kamtschatka*, was double. There was plenty of room; there was the usual washing apparatus, calculated to convey an idea of luxury to the mind of a North-American Indian; there were the usual inefficient racks of brown wood, in which it is more easy to hang a large-sized umbrella than the common tooth-brush of commerce. Upon the uninviting mattresses were carefully folded together those blankets which a great modern humorist has aptly compared to cold buckwheat cakes. The question of towels was left entirely to the imagination. The glass decanters were filled with a transparent liquid faintly tinged with brown, but from which an odor less faint, but not more pleasing, ascended to the nostrils, like a far-off sea-sick reminiscence of oily machinery. Sad-coloured curtains half-closed the upper berth. The hazy June daylight shed a faint illumination upon the desolate little scene. Ugh! how I hate that state-room.

The steward deposited my traps and looked at me, as though he wanted to get away—probably in search of more passengers and more fees. It is always a good plan to start in favour with those functionaries, and I accordingly gave him certain coins there and then.

"I'll try and make yer comfortable all I can," he remarked, as he put the coins in his pocket. Nevertheless, there was a doubtful intonation in his voice which surprised me. Possibly his scale of fees had gone up, and he was not satisfied; but on the whole I was inclined to think that, as he himself would have expressed it, he was "the better for a glass." I was wrong, however, and did the man injustice.

II

Nothing especially worthy of mention occurred during that day. We left the pier punctually, and it was very pleasant to be fairly under way, for the weather was warm and sultry, and the motion of the steamer produced a refreshing breeze. Everybody knows what the first day at sea is like. People pace the decks and stare at each other, and occasionally meet acquaintances whom they did not know to be on board. There is the usual uncertainty as to whether the food will be good, bad, or indifferent, until the first two meals have put the matter beyond a doubt; there is the usual uncertainty about the weather, until the ship is fairly off Fire Island. The tables are crowded at first, and then suddenly thinned. Pale-faced people spring from their seats and precipitate themselves towards the door, and each old sailor breathes more freely as his sea-sick neighbour rushes from his side, leaving him plenty of elbow room and an unlimited command over the mustard.

One passage across the Atlantic is very much like another, and we who cross very often do not make the voyage for the sake of novelty. Whales and icebergs are indeed always objects of interest, but, after all, one whale is very much like another whale, and one rarely sees an iceberg at close quarters. To the majority of us the most delightful moment of the day on board an ocean steamer is when we have taken our last turn on deck, have smoked our last cigar, and having succeeded in tiring ourselves, feel at liberty to turn in with a clear conscience. On that first night of the voyage I felt particularly lazy, and went to bed in one hundred and five rather earlier than I usually do. As I turned in, I was amazed to see that I was to have a companion. A portmanteau, very like my own, lay in the opposite corner, and in the upper berth had been deposited a neatly folded rug with a stick and umbrella. I had hoped to be alone, and I was disappointed; but I wondered who my room-mate was to be, and I determined to have a look at him.

Before I had been long in bed he entered. He was, as far as I could see, a very tall man, very thin, very pale, with sandy hair and whiskers and colourless grey eyes. He had about him, I thought, an air of rather dubious fashion; the sort of man you might see in Wall Street, without being able precisely to say what he was doing there—the sort of man who frequents the Café Anglais, who always seems to be alone and who drinks champagne; you might meet him on a race-course, but he would never appear to be doing anything there either. A little over-dressed—a little odd. There are three or four of his kind on every ocean steamer. I made up my mind that I did not care to make his acquaintance, and I went to sleep saying to myself that I would study his habits in order to avoid him. If he rose early, I would rise late; if he went to bed late, I would go to bed early. I did not care to know him. If you once know people of that kind they are always turning up. Poor fellow! I need not have taken the trouble to come to so many decisions about him, for I never saw him again after that first night in one hundred and five.

I was sleeping soundly when I was suddenly waked by a loud noise. To judge from the sound, my room-mate must have sprung with a single leap from the upper berth to the floor. I heard him fumbling with the latch and bolt of the door, which opened almost immediately, and then I heard his footsteps as he ran at full speed down the passage, leaving the door open behind him. The ship was rolling a little, and I expected to hear him stumble or fall, but he ran as though he were running for his life. The door swung on its hinges with the motion of the vessel, and the sound annoyed me. I got up and shut it, and groped my way back to my berth in the darkness. I went to sleep again; but I have no idea how long I slept.

When I awoke it was still quite dark, but I felt a disagreeable sensation of cold, and it seemed to me that the air was damp. You know the peculiar smell of a cabin which has been wet with sea water. I covered myself up as well as I could and dozed off again, framing complaints to be made the next day, and selecting the most powerful epithets in the language. I could hear my room-mate turn over in the upper berth. He had probably returned while I was asleep. Once I thought I heard him groan, and I argued that he was sea-sick. That is particularly unpleasant when one is below. Nevertheless I dozed off and slept till early daylight.

The ship was rolling heavily, much more than on the previous evening, and the grey light which came in through the porthole changed in tint with every movement according as the angle of the vessel's side turned the glass seawards or skywards. It was very cold—unaccountably so for the month of June. I turned my head and looked at the porthole, and saw to my surprise that it was wide open and hooked back. I believe I swore audibly. Then I got up and shut it. As I turned back I glanced at the upper berth. The curtains were drawn close together; my companion had probably felt cold as well as I. It struck me that I had slept enough. The state-room was uncomfortable, though, strange to say, I could not smell the dampness which had annoyed me in the night. My room-mate was still asleep—excellent opportunity for avoiding him, so I dressed at once and went on deck. The day was warm and cloudy, with an oily smell on the water. It was seven o'clock as I came out—much later than I had imagined. I came across the doctor, who was taking his first sniff of the morning air. He was a young man from the West of Ireland—a tremendous fellow, with black hair and blue eyes, already inclined to be stout; he had a happy-go-lucky, healthy look about him which was rather attractive.

"Fine morning," I remarked, by way of introduction.

"Well," said he, eying me with an air of ready interest, "it's a fine morning and it's not a fine morning. I don't think it's much of a morning."

"Well, no—it is not so very fine," said I.

"It's just what I call fuggly weather," replied the doctor.

"It was very cold last night, I thought," I remarked. "However, when I looked about, I found that the porthole was wide open. I had not noticed it when I went to bed. And the state-room was damp, too."

"Damp!" said he. "Whereabout are you?"

"One hundred and five—"

To my surprise the doctor started visibly, and stared at me.

"What is the matter?" I asked.

"Oh—nothing," he answered; "only everybody has complained of that state-room for the last three trips."

"I shall complain too," I said. "It has certainly not been properly aired. It is a shame!"

"I don't believe it can be helped," answered the doctor. "I believe there is something—well, it is not my business to frighten passengers."

"You need not be afraid of frightening me," I replied. "I can stand any amount of damp. If I should get a bad cold I will come to you."

I offered the doctor a cigar, which he took and examined very critically.

"It is not so much the damp," he remarked. "However, I dare say you will get on very well. Have you a room-mate?"

"Yes; a deuce of a fellow, who bolts out in the middle of the night and leaves the door open."

Again the doctor glanced curiously at me. Then he lit the cigar and looked grave.

"Did he come back?" he asked presently.

"Yes. I was asleep, but I waked up and heard him moving. Then I felt cold and went to sleep again. This morning I found the porthole open."

"Look here," said the doctor, quietly, "I don't care much for this ship. I don't care a rap for her reputation. I tell you what I will do. I have a good-sized place up here. I will share it with you, though I don't know you from Adam."

I was very much surprised at the proposition. I could not imagine why he should take such a sudden interest in my welfare. However, his manner as he spoke of the ship was peculiar.

"You are very good, doctor," I said. "But really, I believe even now the cabin could be aired, or cleaned out, or something. Why do you not care for the ship?"

"We are not superstitious in our profession, sir," replied the doctor. "But the sea makes people so. I don't want to prejudice you, and I don't want to frighten you, but if you will take my advice you will move in here. I would as soon see you overboard," he added, "as know that you or any other man was to sleep in one hundred and five."

"Good gracious! Why?" I asked.

"Just because on the last three trips the people who have slept there actually have gone overboard," he answered, gravely.

The intelligence was startling and exceedingly unpleasant, I confess. I looked hard at the doctor to see whether he was making game of me, but he looked perfectly serious. I thanked him warmly for his offer, but told him I intended to be the exception to the rule by which every one who slept in that particular state-room went overboard. He did not say much, but looked as grave as ever, and hinted that before we got across I should probably reconsider his proposal. In the course of time we went to breakfast, at which only an inconsiderable number of passengers assembled. I noticed that one or two of the officers who breakfasted with us looked grave. After breakfast I went into my state-room in order to get a book. The curtains of the upper berth were still closely drawn. Not a word was to be heard. My room-mate was probably still asleep.

As I came out I met the steward whose business it was to look after me. He whispered that the captain wanted to see me, and then scuttled away down the passage as if very anxious to avoid any questions. I went toward the captain's cabin, and found him waiting for me.

"Sir," said he, "I want to ask a favour of you."

I answered that I would do anything to oblige him.

"Your room-mate has disappeared," he said. "He is known to have turned in early last night. Did you notice anything extraordinary in his manner?"

The question coming, as it did, in exact confirmation of the fears the doctor had expressed half an hour earlier, staggered me.

"You don't mean to say he has gone overboard?" I asked.

"I fear he has," answered the captain.

"This is the most extraordinary thing—" I began.

"Why?" he asked.

"He is the fourth, then?" I explained. In answer to another question from the captain, I explained, without mentioning the doctor, that I had heard the story concerning one hundred and five. He seemed very much annoyed at hearing that I knew of it. I told him what had occurred in the night.

"What you say," he replied, "coincides almost exactly with what was told me by the room-mates of two of the other three. They bolt out of bed and run down the passage. Two of them were seen to go overboard by the watch; we stopped and lowered boats, but they were not found. Nobody, however, saw or heard the man who was lost last night—if he is really lost. The steward, who is a superstitious fellow, perhaps, and expected something to go wrong, went to look for him this morning, and found his berth empty, but his clothes lying about, just as he had left them. The steward was the only man on board who knew him by sight, and he has been searching everywhere for him. He has disappeared! Now, sir, I want to beg you not to mention the circumstance to any of the passengers; I don't want the ship to get a bad name, and nothing hangs about an ocean-goer like stories of suicides. You shall have your choice of any one of the officers' cabins you like, including my own, for the rest of the passage. Is that a fair bargain?"

"Very," said I; "and I am much obliged to you. But since I am alone, and have the state-room to myself, I would rather not move. If the steward will take out that unfortunate man's things, I would as lief stay where I am. I will not say anything about the matter, and I think I can promise you that I will not follow my room-mate."

The captain tried to dissuade me from my intention, but I preferred having a state-room alone to being the chum of any officer on board. I do not know whether I acted foolishly, but if I had taken his advice I should have had nothing more to tell. There would have remained the disagreeable coincidence of several suicides occurring among men who had slept in the same cabin, but that would have been all.

That was not the end of the matter, however, by any means. I obstinately made up my mind that I would not be disturbed by such tales, and I even went so far as to argue the question with the captain. There was something wrong about the state-room, I said. It was rather damp. The porthole had been left open last night. My room-mate might have been ill when he came on board, and he might have become delirious after he went to bed. He might even now be hiding somewhere on board, and might be found later. The place ought to be aired and the fastening of the port looked to. If the captain would give me leave, I would see that what I thought necessary were done immediately.

"Of course you have a right to stay where you are if you please," he replied, rather petulantly; "but I wish you would turn out and let me lock the place up, and be done with it."

I did not see it in the same light, and left the captain, after promising to be silent concerning the disappearance of my companion. The latter had had no acquaintances on board, and was not missed in the course of the day. Towards evening I met the doctor again, and he asked me whether I had changed my mind. I told him I had not.

"Then you will before long," he said, very gravely.

III

We played whist in the evening, and I went to bed late. I will confess now that I felt a disagreeable sensation when I entered my stateroom. I could not help thinking of the tall man I had seen on the previous night, who was now dead, drowned, tossing about in the long swell, two or three hundred miles astern. His face rose very distinctly before me as I undressed, and I even went so far as to draw back the curtains of the upper berth, as though to persuade myself that he was actually gone. I also bolted the door of the state-room. Suddenly I became aware that the porthole was open, and fastened back. This was more than I could stand. I hastily threw on my dressing-gown and went in search of Robert, the steward of my passage. I was very angry, I remember, and when I found him I dragged him roughly to the door of one hundred and five, and pushed him towards the open porthole.

"What the deuce do you mean, you scoundrel, by leaving that port open every night? Don't you know it is against the regulations? Don't you know that if the ship heeled and the water began to come in, ten men could not shut it? I will report you to the captain, you blackguard, for endangering the ship!"

I was exceedingly wroth. The man trembled and turned pale, and then began to shut the round glass plate with the heavy brass fittings.

"Why don't you answer me?" I said, roughly.

"If you please, sir," faltered Robert, "there's nobody on board as can keep this 'ere port shut at night. You can try it yourself, sir. I ain't a-going to stop hany longer on board o' this vessel, sir; I ain't, indeed. But if I was you, sir, I'd just clear out and go and sleep with the surgeon, or something, I would. Look 'ere, sir, is that fastened what you may call securely, or not, sir? Try it, sir, see if it will move a hinch."

I tried the port, and found it perfectly tight.

"Well, sir," continued Robert, triumphantly, "I wager my reputation as a A 1 steward, that in 'arf an hour it will be open again; fastened back, too, sir, that's the horful thing—fastened back!"

I examined the great screw and the looped nut that ran on it.

"If I find it open in the night, Robert, I will give you a sovereign. It is not possible. You may go."

"Soverin' did you say, sir? Very good, sir. Very good, sir. Thank ye, sir. Good-night, sir. Pleasant reepose, sir, and all manner of hinchantin' dreams, sir."

Robert scuttled away, delighted at being released. Of course, I thought he was trying to account for his negligence by a silly story, intended to frighten me, and I disbelieved him. The consequence was that he got his sovereign, and I spent a very peculiarly unpleasant night.

I went to bed, and five minutes after I had rolled myself up in my blankets the inexorable Robert extinguished the light that burned steadily behind the ground-glass pane near the door. I lay quite still in the dark trying to go to sleep, but I soon found that impossible. It had been some satisfaction to be angry with the steward, and the diversion had banished that unpleasant sensation I had at first experienced when I thought of the drowned man who had been my chum; but I was no longer sleepy, and I lay awake for some time, occasionally glancing at the porthole, which I could just see from where I lay, and which, in the darkness, looked like a faintly-luminous soup-plate suspended in blackness. I believed I must have lain there for an hour, and, as I remember, I was just dozing into sleep when I was roused by a draught of cold air and by distinctly feeling the spray of the sea blown upon my face. I started to my feet, and not having allowed in the dark for the motion of the ship, I was instantly thrown violently across the state-room upon the couch which was placed beneath the porthole. I recovered myself immediately, however, and climbed upon my knees. The porthole was again wide open and fastened back!

Now these things are facts. I was wide awake when I got up, and I should certainly have been waked by the fall had I still been dozing. Moreover, I bruised my elbows and knees badly, and the bruises were there on the following morning to testify to the fact, if I myself had doubted it. The porthole was wide open and fastened back—a thing so unaccountable that I remember very well feeling astonishment rather than fear when I discovered it. I at once closed the plate again and screwed down the loop nut with all my strength. It was very dark in the state-room. I reflected that the port had certainly been opened within an hour after Robert had at first shut it in my presence, and I determined to watch it and see whether it would open again. Those brass fittings are very heavy and by no means easy to move; I could not believe that the clump had been turned by the shaking of the screw. I stood peering out through the thick glass at the alternate white and grey streaks of the sea that foamed beneath the ship's side. I must have remained there a quarter of an hour.

Suddenly, as I stood, I distinctly heard something moving behind me in one of the berths, and a moment afterwards, just as I turned instinctively to look—though I could, of course, see nothing in the darkness—I heard a very faint groan. I sprang across the state-room, and tore the curtains of the upper berth aside, thrusting in my hands to discover if there were any one there. There was some one.

I remember that the sensation as I put my hands forward was as though I were plunging them into the air of a damp cellar, and from behind the curtain came a gust of wind that smelled horribly of stagnant sea-water. I laid hold of something that had the shape of a man's arm, but was smooth, and wet, and icy cold. But suddenly, as I pulled, the creature sprang violently forward against me, a clammy, oozy mass, as it seemed to me, heavy and wet, yet endowed with a sort of supernatural strength. I reeled across the state-room, and in an instant the door opened and the thing rushed out. I had not had time to be frightened, and quickly recovering myself, I sprang through the door and gave chase at the top of my speed, but I was too late. Ten yards before me I could see—I am sure I saw it—a dark shadow moving in the dimly lighted passage, quickly as the shadow of a fast horse thrown before a dog-cart by the lamp on a dark night. But in a moment it had disappeared, and I found myself holding on to the polished rail that ran along the bulkhead where the passage turned towards the companion. My hair stood on end, and the cold perspiration rolled down my face. I am not ashamed of it in the least: I was very badly frightened.

Still I doubted my senses, and pulled myself together. It was absurd, I thought. The Welsh rare-bit I had eaten had disagreed with me. I had been in a nightmare. I made my way back to my state-room, and entered it with an effort. The whole place smelled of stagnant sea-water, as it had when I had waked on the previous evening. It required my utmost strength to go in and grope among my things for a box of wax lights. As I lighted a railway reading lantern which I always carry in case I want to read after the lamps are out, I perceived that the porthole was again open, and a sort of creeping horror began to take possession of me which I never felt before, nor wish to feel again. But I got a light and proceeded to examine the upper berth, expecting to find it drenched with sea-water.

But I was disappointed. The bed had been slept in, and the smell of the sea was strong; but the bedding was as dry as a bone. I fancied that Robert had not had the courage to make the bed after the accident of the previous night—it had all been a hideous dream. I drew the curtains back as far as I could and examined the place very carefully. It was perfectly dry. But the porthole was open again. With a sort of dull bewilderment of horror, I closed it and screwed it down, and thrusting my heavy stick through the brass loop, wrenched it with all my might, till the thick metal began to bend under the pressure. Then I hooked my reading lantern into the red velvet at the head of the couch, and sat down to recover my senses if I could. I sat there all night, unable to think of rest—hardly able to think at all. But the porthole remained closed, and I did not believe it would now open again without the application of a considerable force.

The morning dawned at last, and I dressed myself slowly, thinking over all that had happened in the night. It was a beautiful day and I went on deck, glad to get out in the early, pure sunshine, and to smell the breeze from the blue water, so different from the noisome, stagnant odour from my state-room. Instinctively I turned aft, towards the surgeon's cabin. There he stood, with a pipe in his mouth, taking his morning airing precisely as on the preceding day.

"Good-morning," said he, quietly, but looking at me with evident curiosity.

"Doctor, you were quite right," said I. "There is something wrong about that place."

"I thought you would change your mind," he answered, rather triumphantly. "You have had a bad night, eh? Shall I make you a pick-me-up? I have a capital recipe."

"No, thanks," I cried. "But I would like to tell you what happened."

I then tried to explain as clearly as possible precisely what had occurred, not omitting to state that I had been scared as I had never been scared in my whole life before. I dwelt particularly on the phenomenon of the porthole, which was a fact to which I could testify, even if the rest had been an illusion. I had closed it twice in the night, and the second time I had actually bent the brass in wrenching it with my stick. I believe I insisted a good deal on this point.

"You seem to think I am likely to doubt the story," said the doctor, smiling at the detailed account of the state of the porthole. "I do not doubt it in the least. I renew my invitation to you. Bring your traps here, and take half my cabin."

"Come and take half of mine for one night," I said. "Help me get at the bottom of this thing."

"You will get to the bottom of something else if you try," answered the doctor.

"What?" I asked.

"The bottom of the sea. I am going to leave the ship. It is not canny."

"Then you will not help me to find out—"

"Not I," said the doctor, quickly. "It is my business to keep my wits about me—not to go fiddling about with ghosts and things."

"Do you really believe it is a ghost?" I inquired, rather contemptuously. But as I spoke I remembered very well the horrible sensation of the supernatural which had got possession of me during the night. The doctor turned sharply on me—

"Have you any reasonable explanation of these things to offer?" he asked. "No; you have not. Well, you say you will find an explanation. I say that you won't, sir, simply because there is not any."

"But, my dear sir," I retorted, "do you, a man of science, mean to tell me that such things cannot be explained?"

"I do," he answered, stoutly. "And, if they could, I would not be concerned in the explanation."

I did not care to spend another night alone in the state-room, and yet I was obstinately determined to get at the root of the disturbances. I do not believe there are many men who would have slept there alone, after passing two such nights. But I made up my mind to try it, if I could not get any one to share a watch with me. The doctor was evidently not inclined for such an experiment. He said he was a surgeon, and that in case any accident occurred on board he must always be in readiness. He could not afford to have his nerves unsettled. Perhaps he was quite right, but I am inclined to think that his precaution was prompted by his inclination. On inquiry, he informed me that there was no one on board who would be likely to join me in my investigations, and after a little more conversation I left him. A little later I met the captain, and told him my story. I said that if no one would spend the night with me I would ask leave to have the light burning all night, and would try it alone.

"Look here," said he, "I will tell you what I will do. I will share your watch myself, and we will see what happens. It is my belief that we can find out between us. There may be some fellow skulking on board, who steals a passage by frightening the passengers. It is just possible that there may be something queer in the carpentering of that berth."

I suggested taking the ship's carpenter below and examining the place; but I was overjoyed at the captain's offer to spend the night with me. He accordingly sent for the workman and ordered him to do anything I required. We went below at once. I had all the bedding cleared out of the upper berth, and we examined the place thoroughly to see if there was a board loose anywhere, or a panel which could be opened or pushed aside. We tried the planks everywhere, tapped the flooring, unscrewed the fittings of the lower berth and took it to pieces —in short, there was not a square inch of the state-room which was not searched and tested. Everything was in perfect order, and we put everything back in its place. As we were finishing our work, Robert came to the door and looked in.

"Well, sir—find anything, sir?" he asked with a ghastly grin.

"You were right about the porthole, Robert," I said, and I gave him the promised sovereign. The carpenter did his work silently and skilfully, following my directions. When he had done he spoke.

"I'm a plain man, sir," he said. "But it's my belief you had better just turn out your things and let me run half a dozen four inch screws through the door of this cabin. There's no good never came o' this cabin yet, sir, and

that's all about it. There's been four lives lost out o' here to my own remembrance, and that in four trips. Better give it up, sir—better give it up!"

"I will try it for one night more," I said.

"Better give it up, sir—better give it up! It's precious bad job," repeated the workman, putting his tools in his bag and leaving the cabin.

But my spirits had risen considerably at the prospect of having the captain's company, and I made up my mind not to be prevented from going to the end of the strange business. I abstained from Welsh rare-bits and grog that evening, and did not even join in the customary game of whist. I wanted to be quite sure of my nerves, and my vanity made me anxious to make a good figure in the captain's eyes.

IV

The captain was one of those splendidly tough and cheerful specimens of seafaring humanity whose combined courage, hardihood, and calmness in difficulty leads them naturally into high positions of trust. He was not the man to be led away by an idle tale, and the mere fact that he was willing to join me in the investigation was proof that he thought there was something seriously wrong, which could not be accounted for on ordinary theories, nor laughed down as a common superstition. To some extent, too, his reputation was at stake, as well as the reputation of the ship. It is no light thing to lose passengers overboard, and he knew it.

About ten o'clock that evening, as I was smoking a last cigar, he came up to me and drew me aside from the beat of the other passengers who were patrolling the deck in the warm darkness.

"This is a serious matter, Mr. Brisbane," he said. "We must make up our minds either way—to be disappointed or to have a pretty rough time of it. You see, I cannot afford to laugh at the affair, and I will ask you to sign your name to a statement of whatever occurs. If nothing happens to-night we will try it again to-morrow and next day. Are you ready?"

So we went below, and entered the state-room. As we went in I could see Robert the steward, who stood a little further down the passage, watching us, with his usual grin, as though certain that something dreadful was about to happen. The captain closed the door behind us and bolted it.

"Supposing we put your portmanteau before the door," he suggested. "One of us can sit on it. Nothing can get out then. Is the port screwed down?"

I found it as I had left it in the morning. Indeed, without using a lever, as I had done, no one could have opened it. I drew back the curtains of the upper berth so that I could see well into it. By the captain's advice I lighted my reading-lantern, and placed it so that it shone upon the white sheets above. He insisted upon sitting on the portmanteau, declaring that he wished to be able to swear that he had sat before the door.

Then he requested me to search the state-room thoroughly, an operation very soon accomplished, as it consisted merely in looking beneath the lower berth and under the couch below the porthole. The spaces were quite empty.

"It is impossible for any human being to get in," I said, "or for any human being to open the port."

"Very good," said the captain, calmly. "If we see anything now, it must be either imagination or something supernatural."

I sat down on the edge of the lower berth.

"The first time it happened," said the captain, crossing his legs and leaning back against the door, "was in March. The passenger who slept here, in the upper berth, turned out to have been a lunatic—at all events, he was known to have been a little touched, and he had taken his passage without the knowledge of his friends. He rushed out in the middle of the night, and threw himself overboard, before the officer who had the watch could stop him. We stopped and lowered a boat; it was a quiet night, just before that heavy weather came on; but we could not find him. Of course his suicide was afterwards accounted for on the ground of his insanity."

"I suppose that often happens?" I remarked, rather absently.

"Not often—no," said the captain; "never before in my experience, though I have heard of it happening on board of other ships. Well, as I was saying, that occurred in March. On the very next trip—What are you looking at?" he asked, stopping suddenly in his narration.

I believe I gave no answer. My eyes were riveted upon the porthole. It seemed to me that the brass loop-nut was beginning to turn very slowly upon the screw—so slowly, however, that I was not sure it moved at all. I watched it intently, fixing its position in my mind, and trying to ascertain whether it changed. Seeing where I was looking, the captain looked too.

"It moves!" he exclaimed, in a tone of conviction. "No, it does not," he added, after a minute.

"If it were the jarring of the screw," said I, "it would have opened during the day; but I found it this evening jammed tight as I left it this morning."

I rose and tried the nut. It was certainly loosened, for by an effort I could move it with my hands.

"The queer thing," said the captain, "is that the second man who was lost is supposed to have got through that very port. We had a terrible time over it. It was in the middle of the night, and the weather was very heavy; there was an alarm that one of the ports was open and the sea running in. I came below and found everything flooded, the water pouring in every time she rolled, and the whole port swinging from the top bolts—not the porthole in the middle. Well, we managed to shut it, but the water did some damage. Ever since that the place smells of sea-water from time to time. We supposed the passenger had thrown himself out, though the Lord only knows how he did it. The steward kept telling me that he could not keep anything shut here. Upon my word—I can smell it now, cannot you?" he inquired, sniffing the air suspiciously.

"Yes—distinctly," I said, and I shuddered as that same odour of stagnant sea-water grew stronger in the cabin. "Now, to smell like this, the place must be damp," I continued, "and yet when I examined it with the carpenter this morning everything was perfectly dry. It is most extraordinary—hallo!"

My reading-lantern, which had been placed in the upper berth, was suddenly extinguished. There was still a good deal of light from the pane of ground glass near the door, behind which loomed the regulation lamp. The ship rolled heavily, and the curtain of the upper berth swung far out into the state-room and back again. I rose quickly from my seat on the edge of the bed, and the captain at the same moment started to his feet with a loud cry of surprise. I had turned with the intention of taking down the lantern to examine it, when I heard his exclamation, and immediately afterwards his call for help. I sprang towards him. He was wrestling with all his might, with the brass loop of the port. It seemed to turn against his hands in spite of all his efforts. I caught up my cane, a heavy oak stick I always used to carry, and thrust it through the ring and bore on it with all my strength. But the strong wood snapped suddenly, and I fell upon the couch. When I rose again the port was wide open, and the captain was standing with his back against the door, pale to the lips.

"There is something in that berth!" he

cried, in a strange voice, his eyes almost starting from his head. "Hold the door, while I look—it shall not escape us, whatever it is!"

But instead of taking his place, I sprang upon the lower bed, and seized something which lay in the upper berth.

It was something ghostly, horrible beyond words, and it moved in my grip. It was like the body of a man long drowned, and yet it moved, and had the strength of ten men living; but I gripped it with all my might—the slippery, oozy, horrible thing. The dead white eyes seemed to stare at me out of the dusk; the putrid odour of rank sea-water was about it, and its shiny hair hung in foul wet curls over its dead face. I wrestled with the dead thing; it thrust itself upon me and forced me back and nearly broke my arms; it wound its corpse's arms about my neck, the living death, and overpowered me, so that I, at last, cried aloud and fell, and left my hold.

As I fell the thing sprang across me, and seemed to throw itself upon the captain. When I last saw him on his feet his face was white and his lips set. It seemed to me that he struck a violent blow at the dead being, and then he, too, fell forward upon his face, with an inarticulate cry of horror.

The thing paused an instant, seeming to hover over his prostrate body, and I could have screamed again from very fright, but I had no voice left. The thing vanished suddenly, and it seemed to my disturbed senses that it made its exit through the open port, though how that was possible, considering the smallness of the aperture, is more than any one can tell. I lay a long time upon the floor, and the captain lay beside me. At last I partially recovered my senses and moved, and I instantly knew that my arm was broken—the small bone of the left forearm near the wrist.

I got upon my feet somehow, and with my remaining hand I tried to raise the captain. He groaned and moved, and at last came to himself. He was not hurt, but he seemed badly stunned.

Well, do you want to hear any more? There is nothing more. That is the end of my story. The carpenter carried out his scheme of running half a dozen four-inch screws through the door of one hundred and five; and if ever you take a passage in the *Kamtschatka*, you may ask for a berth in that state-room. You will be told that it is engaged—yes—it is engaged by that dead thing.

I finished the trip in the surgeon's cabin. He doctored my broken arm, and advised me not to "fiddle about with ghosts and things" any more. The captain was very silent, and never sailed again in that ship, though it is still running. And I will not sail in her either. It was a very disagreeable experience, and I was very badly frightened, which is a thing I do not like. That is all. That is how I saw a ghost— if it was a ghost. It was dead, anyhow.

F. HOPKINSON SMITH (1838–1915)
MISS JENNINGS'S COMPANION
(1907)

The big Liner slowed down and dropped anchor inside the Breakwater. Sweeping toward her, pushing the white foam in long lines from her bow, her flag of black smoke trailing behind, came the company's tender—out from Cherbourg with passengers.

Under the big Liner's upper deck, along its top rail, was strung a row of heads watching the tender's approach—old heads—young heads—middle-aged heads—Miss Jennings's among these last—their eyes taking in the grim Breakwater with its beacon light, the frowning casemates specked with sentinels, and the line of the distant city blurred with masts and spent steam. They saw, too, from their height (they could look down the tender's smokestack) the sturdy figure of her captain, his white cap in relief against the green sea, and below him the flat mass of people, their upturned faces so many pats of color on a dark canvas.

With the hauling taut and making fast of the fore and aft hawsers, a group of sailors broke away from the flat mass and began tugging at the gang-plank, lifting it into position, the boatswain's orders ringing clear. Another group stripped off the tarpaulins from the piles of luggage, and a third—the gang-plank in place—swarmed about the heaps of trunks, shouldering the separate pieces as ants shoulder grains of sand, then scurrying toward the tender's rail, where other ants reached down and relieved them of their loads.

The mass of people below now took on the shape of a funnel, its spout resting on the edge of the gang-plank, from out which poured a steady stream of people up and over the Liner's side.

Two decks below, where Miss Jennings and her fellow-travellers were leaning over the steamer's rail craning their necks, other sights came into view. Here not only the funnel-shaped mass could be seen, but the faces of the individuals composing it, as well as their nationality and class; whether first, second or steerage. Here, too, was the line of stewards reaching out with open hands, relieving the passengers of their small belongings; here, too, stood the first officer in white gloves and gold lace bowing to those he knew and smiling at others; and here, too, was a smooth-shaven closely knit young man in dark clothes and derby hat, who had taken up his position just behind the first officer, and whose steady steel-gray eyes followed the movements of each and every one of the passengers from the moment their feet touched the gang-plank until they had disappeared in charge of the stewards.

These passengers made a motley group: first came a stout American with two pretty daughters; then a young Frenchman and his valet; then a Sister of Charity draped in black, her close-fitting, white, starched cap and broad white collar framing her face, one hand clutching the rope rail as she stepped feebly toward the steamer, the other grasping a bandbox, her only luggage; next wriggled some college boys in twos and threes, and then the rest of the hurrying mass, followed close by a herd of emigrants crowding and stumbling like sheep, the men with pillow-case bundles over their backs, the women with babies muffled in shawls.

When the last passenger was aboard, the closely knit young man with the steel-gray eyes leaned forward and said in a low voice to the first officer:—

"He's not in this bunch."

"Sure?"

"Yes—dead sure."

"Where will you look for him now, Hobson?" continued the officer.

"Paris, maybe. I told the chief we wouldn't get anywhere on this lead. Well, so long"— and the closely knit young man swung himself down the gang-plank and disappeared into the cabin of the tender.

The scenes on the gang-plank were now repeated on the steamer. The old travellers, whose hand luggage had been properly numbered, gave themselves no concern—the stewards would look after their belongings. The new travellers—the Sister of Charity among them—wandered about asking questions that

for the moment no one had time to answer. She, poor soul, had spent her life in restful places, and the inrush of passengers and their proper bestowal seemed to have completely dazed her.

"Can I help you?" asked the first officer— everybody is ready to help a Sister, no matter what his rank or how pressing his duties.

"Yes, please—I want to know where my room is. It is Number 49, so my ticket says."

Here the purser came up—he, too, would help a Sister.

"Sister Teresa, is it not—from the Convent of the Sacred Heart? Yes, we knew you would get on at Cherbourg. You are on the lower deck in the same stateroom with Miss Jennings. Steward—take the Sister to"—

"With whom?" she cried, with a look of blank amazement. "But I thought I was alone! They told me so at the office. Oh, I cannot share my room with anybody. Please let—— "

"Yes, but we had to double up. We would willingly give you a room alone, but there isn't an empty berth on board." He was telling the truth and showed it in his voice.

"But I have the money to pay for a whole room. I would have paid for it at the office in Paris, but they told me it was not necessary."

"I know, Sister, and I'm very sorry, but it can't be helped now. Steward, take Sister Teresa to Number 49." This last came as an order, and ended the discussion.

When the steward pushed open the door Miss Jennings was sitting on the sofa berth reading, a long gray cloak about her shoulders. She had a quiet, calm face and steady eyes framed in gold spectacles. She looked to be a woman of fifty who had seen life and understood it.

"The officer says I am to share your room," began Sister Teresa in a trembling voice. "Don't think me rude, please, but I don't want to share your room. I want to be alone, and so do you. Can't you help me?"

"But I don't mind it, and you won't after you get used to it." The voice was poised and well modulated—evidently a woman without nerves—a direct, masterful sort of woman, who looked you straight in the eyes, was without guile, hated any lie and believed in human nature. "And we ought to get on together," she continued simply, as if it were a matter of course. "You are a Sister, and from one of the French institutions—I recognize your dress. I'm a nurse from the London Hospital. The first officer told me you had the other berth and I was looking for you abroad the Cherbourg tender, but I couldn't see you for the smoke, you were so far below me. We'll get on together, never fear. Which bed will you have —this one or the one curtained off?"

"Oh, do you take the one curtained off," she answered in a hopeless tone, as if further resistance was useless. "The sofa is easier perhaps for me, for I always undress in the dark."

"No, turn on the light. It won't wake me— I'm used to sleeping anywhere—sometimes bolt upright in my chair with my hand on my patient."

"But it is one of the rules of our order to dress and undress in the dark," the Sister pleaded; "candles are luxuries only used for the sick, and so we do without them."

"All right—just as you say," rejoined Miss Jennings cheerily. "My only desire was to make you comfortable."

That night at dinner Sister Teresa and Nurse Jennings found themselves seated next to each other, the chief steward, who had special orders from the first officer to show Miss Jennings and her companion every courtesy, having conducted them to their seats.

Before the repast was half over, the two had attracted the attention of all about them. What was particularly noticed was the abstemious self-denying life of the Sister so plainly shown in the lines of her grave, almost hard, face, framed close in the tight bands of white linen concealing every vestige of her hair, the whole in strong contrast to the kind, sympathetic face of the nurse, whose soft gray locks hung loosely about her temples. Their history, gleaned at the first officer's table, had also become public property. Nurse Jennings had served two years in South Africa, where she had charge of a ward in one of the largest field hospitals outside of Pretoria; on her return to England, she had been placed over an important case in one of the London hospitals—that of a gallant Canadian officer who had been shipped home convalescent, and who had now sent for her to come to him in Montreal. The good Sister was one of those unfortunate women who had been expelled from France under the new law, and who was now on her way to Quebec, there to take up her life work again. This had been the fifth refugee, the officer added, whom the Line had cared for.

When the hour for retiring came, Sister Teresa, with the remark that she would wait until Miss Jennings was in bed before she sought her own berth, followed her companion to the stateroom, bade her good-night, and then, with her hand on the knob, lingered for a moment as if there was still some further word on her lips.

"What is it?" asked the nurse, with one of her direct, searching glances. "Speak out— I'm a woman like yourself, and can understand."

"Well, it's about the Hour of Silence. I must have one hour every day when I can be alone. It has been the custom of my life and I cannot omit it. It will be many days before we reach the land, and there is no other place for me to pray except in here. Would you object if I——"

"Object! Of course not! I will help you to keep it, and I will see, too, that the stewardess does not disturb you. Now, is there anything else? Tell me—I love people who speak right out what they mean."

"No—except that I always rise at dawn, and will be gone when you wake. Goodnight."

The morning after this first night the two lay in their steamer chairs on the upper deck. The first officer, noticing them together, paused for a moment on his way to the bridge.

"You knew, of course, Miss Jennings, that Hobson went back to Cherbourg on the tender. He left good-by for you."

"Hunting for somebody, as usual, I suppose?" she rejoined.

"Yes"—and he passed on.

"A wretched life, isn't it," said Nurse Jennings, "this hunting for criminals? This same man, Mr. Hobson, after a hunt of months, found one in my ward with a bullet through his chest."

"You know him then?" asked Sister Teresa, with a tremor in her voice.

"Yes—he's a Scotland Yard man."

"And you say he was looking for some one on board and didn't find him?"

"No, not yet, but he will find him, he always does; that's the pity of it. Some of these poor hunted people would lead a different life if they had another chance. I tried to save the one Hobson found in my ward. He was quite frank with me, and told me everything. When people trust me my heart always goes out to them—so much so that I often do very foolish things that are apt to get me into trouble. It's when they lie to me—and so many do—making one excuse after another for their being in the ward—that I lose all interest in them. I pleaded with Hobson to give the man another chance, but I could do nothing. Thief as he was, he had told the truth. He had that quality left, and I liked him for it. If I had known

Hobson was on his track I'd have helped him in some way to get off. He stole to help his old mother, and wasn't a criminal in any sense—only weak-hearted. The law is cruel—it never makes allowances—that's where it is wrong."

"Cruel!—it's brutal. It is more brutal often than the crime," answered Sister Teresa in a voice full of emotion. "Do you think the man your friend was looking for here on board will escape?"

"No, I'm afraid not. There is very little chance of any criminal escaping when they once get on his track, so Mr. Hobson has told me. If he is on this steamer he must run another gauntlet in New York, even if he is among the emigrants. You know we have over a thousand on board. If he is not aboard they will track him down. Dreadful, isn't it?"

"Poor fellow," said Sister Teresa, a sob in her voice, "how sorry I am for him. If men only knew how much wiser mercy is than justice in the redemption of the world." Here she rose from her chair, and gathering her black cloak about her crossed to the rail and looked out to sea. In a few minutes she returned. "Let us walk out to the bow where we can talk undisturbed," she said. "The constant movement of the passengers on deck, passing backward and forward, disturbs my head. I see so few people, you know."

When they reached the bow, she made a place beside her for the nurse.

"Don't misunderstand what I said about the brutality of the law," she began. "There must be laws, and brutal men who commit brutal crimes must be punished. But there are so many men who are not brutal, although the crimes may be. I knew of one once. We had educated his little daughter—such a sweet child! The man himself was a scene-painter and worked in the theatres in London. Sometimes he would take part in the play himself, making up for the minor characters, although most of his time was spent in painting scenery. He had married a woman who was on the stage, and she had deserted him for one of the actors, and left her child behind. Her faithlessness nearly broke his heart. Through one of our own people in London he found us and sent the child to the convent where we have a school for just such cases. When the girl got to be seventeen years old he sent for her and she went to London to see him. He remembered her mother's career, and guarded her like a little plant. He never allowed her to come to the theatre except in the middle of the day. Then she would come where he was at work up on the top of the painting platform high above

the stage. There he and she would be alone. One morning while he was at work one of the scene-shifters—a man with whom he had had some difficulty—met the girl as she was crossing the high platform. He had never seen her before and, thinking she was one of the chorus girls, threw his arm about her. The girl screamed, the scene-painter dropped his brushes, ran to her side, hit the man in the face—the scene-shifter lost his balance and fell to the stage. Before he died in the hospital he told who had struck him; he told why, too; that the scene-painter hated him; and that the two had had an altercation the day before—about some colors; which was not true, there only having been a difference of opinion. The man fled to Paris with his daughter. The girl to-day is at one of our institutions at Rouen. The detectives, suspecting that he would try to see her, have been watching that place for the last five months. All that time he has been employed in the garden of a convent out of Paris. Last week we heard from a Sister in London that some one had recognized him, although he had shaved off his beard—some visitor or parent of one of the children, perhaps, who had come upon him suddenly while at work in the garden beds. He is now a fugitive, hunted like an animal. He never intended to harm this man—he only tried to save his daughter—and yet he knew that because of the difficulty that he had had with the dead man and the fact that his daughter's testimony would not help him—she being an interested person—he would be made to suffer for a crime he had not intended to commit. Now, would you hand this poor father over to the police? In a year his daughter must leave the convent. She then has no earthly protection."

Miss Jennings gazed out over the sea, her brow knit in deep thought. Her mind went back to the wounded criminal in the hospital cot and to the look of fear and agony that came into his eyes when Hobson stood over him and called him by name. Sister Teresa sat watching her companion's face. Her whole life had been one of mercy and she never lost an opportunity to plead its cause.

The nurse's answer came slowly:—

"No, I would not. There is misery enough in the world without my adding to it."

"Would you help him to escape?"

"Yes, if what you tell me is true and he trusted me."

Sister Teresa rose to her feet, crossed herself, and said in a voice that seemed to come through pent-up tears:—

"Thank God! I go now to pray. It is my Hour of Silence."

When she returned, Nurse Jennings was still in her seat in the bow. The sun shone bright and warm, and the sea had become calm.

"You look rested, Sister," she said, looking up into her face. "Your color is fresher and the dark rings have gone from your eyes. Did you sleep?"

"No, I wait for the night to sleep. It is hard enough then."

"What did you do?"

"I prayed for you and for myself. Come to the stateroom—I have something to tell you."

"Tell it here," said Nurse Jennings in a more positive tone.

"No, it might hurt you, and others will notice. Come quick, please, or my courage will fail."

"Can't I hear it to-night"— She was comfortable where she was and remembered the narrow, steep steps to the lower deck.

"No! come now—and *quick*."

At the tone of agony in the Sister's voice Miss Jennings scrutinized her companion's face. Her trained ear had caught an indrawn, fluttering sob which she recognized as belonging to a certain form of hysteria. Brooding over her troubles, combined with the effects of the sea air, had unstrung the dear Sister's nerves.

"Yes, certainly," assented Miss Jennings. "Let me take your arm—step carefully, and lean on me."

On reaching the stateroom, Sister Teresa waited until Miss Jennings had entered, then she locked the door and pulled the curtains close.

"Listen, Miss Jennings, before you judge me. You remember yesterday how I pleaded with you to help me find a bedroom where I could be alone. You would not, and I could do nothing but let matters take their course. Fate has placed me in your hands. When you said that you were on the lookout for me and that you knew Hobson, the detective, I knew that all was lost unless your heart went out to me. I know him, too. I faced his eyes when I came aboard. I staggered with fright and caught at the ropes, but he did not suspect— I saw in his face that he did not. He may still trace me and arrest me when I land. If anybody comes for me, say you met me in the hospital where you work."

Nurse Jennings stood staring into the woman's eyes. Her first impulse was to ring the bell for the steward and send for the ship's doctor. Sudden insanity, the result of acute

hysteria, was not uncommon in women leading sedentary lives who had gone through a heavy strain, and the troubles of this poor Sister had, she saw, unseated her reason.

"Don't talk so—calm yourself. No one is seeking you. You ought to lie down. Come——"

"Yes, I know you think I am crazy—I am crazy—crazy from a horrible fear that stares me in the face—from a spectre that——"

"Sister, you *must* lie down! I'll ring for the doctor and he——"

Sister Teresa sprang forward and caught the hand of the nurse before it touched the bell.

"Stop! *Stop!*—or all will be lost! I am not a Sister—I am the scene-painter—the father of that girl! See!" He threw back his hood, uncovering his head, and exposed his short-cropped hair.

Nurse Jennings turned quickly and looked her companion searchingly in the face. The surprise had been so great that for an instant her breath left her. Then slowly the whole situation rushed over and upon her. This man had made use of her privacy—had imposed upon her—tricked her.

"And you—you have dared to come into this room, making me believe you were a woman—and lied to me about your Hour of Silence and all the"——

"It was the only way I could be safe. You and everybody else would detect me if I did not shave and fix up my face. You said a minute ago the dark rings had gone from my eyes —it is this paint-box that did it. Think of what it would mean to me to be taken—and my little girl! Don't—don't judge me wrongly. When I get to New York I promise never to see you again—no one will ever know. If you had been my own sister I could not have treated you with more respect since I have been in the room. I will do anything you wish —to-night I will sleep on the floor—anything, if——"

"To-night! Not another hour will you stay here. I will go to the purser at once and——"

"You mean to turn me out?"

"Yes."

"Oh, merciful God! Don't! Listen—you *must* listen. Let me stay! What difference should it make to you? You have nursed hundreds of men. You have saved many lives. Save mine—give me back my little girl! She can come to me in Quebec and then we can get away somewhere in America and be safe. I can still pass as a Sister and she as a child in my charge until I can find some place where I can throw off my disguise. See how good the real Sisters are to me; they do not condemn me. Here is a letter from the Mother Superior in Paris to the Mother Superior of a convent in Quebec. It is not forged—it is genuine. If they believe in me, why cannot you? Let me stay here, and you stay, too. You would if you could see my child."

The sound of a heavy step was heard outside in the corridor.

Then came a quick, commanding voice: "Miss Jennings, open the door, please."

The nurse turned quickly and made a step toward the door. The fugitive sank upon the sofa and drew the hood over his face.

Again her name rang out—this time in a way that showed them both that further delay was out of the question.

Nurse Jennings shot back the bolt.

Outside stood the first officer.

"There has been a bad accident in the steerage. I hate to ask you, Miss Jennings, knowing how tired you are—but one of the emigrants has fallen down the forecastle hatch. The doctor wants you to come at once."

During the rest of the voyage Nurse Jennings slept in the steerage; she would send to Number 49 during the day for her several belongings, but she never passed the night there, nor did she see her companion. The case was serious, she told the stewardess, who came in search of her, and she dared not leave.

The fugitive rarely left the stateroom. Some days he pleaded illness and had his meals brought to him; often he ate nothing.

As the day approached for the vessel to arrive in New York a shivering nervousness took possession of him. He would stand behind the door by the hour listening for her lightest footfall, hoping against hope that, after all, her heart would soften toward him. One thought absorbed him: would she betray him, and if so, when and where? Would it be to the first officer—the friend of Hobson—or would she wait until they reached New York and then hand him over to the authorities?

Only one gleam of hope shone out illumining his doubt, and that was that she never sent to the stateroom during the Hour of Silence, thus giving him a chance to continue his disguise. Even this ray was dimmed when he began to realize as they approached their destination that she had steadily avoided him, even choosing another deck for a breath of fresh air whenever she left her patient. That she had

welcomed the accident to the emigrant as an excuse for remaining away from her stateroom was evident. What he could not understand was, if she really pitied and justified him, as she had done his prototype, why she should now treat him with such suspicion. At her request he had opened his heart and had trusted her; why then could she not forgive him for the deceit of that first night—one for which he was not responsible?

Then a new thought chilled him like an icy wind: her avoidance of him was only an evidence of her purpose! Thus far she had not exposed him, because then it would be known aboard that they had shared the stateroom together. He saw it all now. She was waiting until they reached the dock. Then no one would be the wiser.

When the steamer entered her New York slip and the gang-plank was hoisted aboard, another thick-set, closely knit man pushed his way through the crowd at the rail, walked straight to the purser and whispered something in his ear. The next moment he had glided to where the nurse and fugitive were standing.

"This is Miss Jennings, isn't it? I'm from the Central Office," and he opened his coat and displayed the gold shield. "We've just got a cable from Hobson. He said you were on board and might help. I'm looking for a man. We've got no clew—don't know that he's on board, but I thought we'd look the list over. The purser tells me that you helped the doctor in the steerage—says somebody had been smashed up. Got anything to suggest? —anybody that would fit this description: 'Small man, only five-feet-six; blue eyes'"— and he read from a paper in his hand.

"No, I don't think so. I was in the steerage, of course, four or five days, and helped on a bad case, but I didn't notice anybody but the few people immediately about me."

"Perhaps, then, among the first-class passengers? Anybody peculiar there? He's a slick one, we hear, and may be working a stunt in disguise."

"No. To tell you the truth, I was so tired when I came aboard that I hardly spoke to any one—no one, really, except my dear Sister Teresa here, who shared my stateroom. They have driven her out of France and she is on her way to a convent in Quebec. I go with her as far as Montreal."

XIV. THE MODERN ROMANTIC DRAMA

Madame Butterfly represents the dramatization by a master craftsman of the theatre, David Belasco, of a character and a situation created by an imaginative artist, John Luther Long. It illustrates also the love of romance, which was reaching a climax at the turn of the century. In his short story *Madame Butterfly*, Long drew a contrast between the civilization of America represented by Lieutenant Pinkerton and the Japanese Cho-Cho-San, a girl of good family, whose standards of honor, inherited from her father, a soldier of the Imperial army, forbid her to take lightly what to Pinkerton is but an incident. It is this casual quality of their relationship from his point of view, which makes the tragedy so keen, for the love of Madame Butterfly is the great passion of her life, and her love, strong and enduring, has lifted her into a permanent position as one of the great characters in our literature.

Madame Butterfly was first performed at the Herald Square Theatre, New York City, on March 5, 1900. Belasco changed the story at the end, for in the original, Cho-Cho-San did not die but decided to live for her child's sake. This and other less important alterations, made for unity of scene, were justified by their stage effect. Through the opera of *Madame Butterfly*, with music by Giacomo Puccini, first performed in New York in English, November 12, 1906, and later in Italian, in 1907, when Geraldine Farrar sang Cio-Cio-San, Louise Homer, Suzuki and Enrico Caruso, Pinkerton, the character has become universal in its appeal.

DAVID BELASCO (1853-   ) and JOHN LUTHER LONG (1861-1927)

MADAME BUTTERFLY

(1900)

DRAMATIS PERSONÆ

CHO-CHO-SAN (MADAME BUTTERFLY)
SUZUKI, *her servant*
MR. SHARPLESS, *the American Consul*
LIEUTENANT B. F. PINKERTON, *of the war ship Connecticut*
YAMADORI, *a citizen of New York*
THE NAKODO, *a marriage broker*
KATE, *Pinkerton's wife*
"TROUBLE"
ATTENDANT
ATTENDANT

NOTE: During the scene in which MADAME BUTTERFLY waits at the shoji for her lover, a night is supposed to pass and the story is resumed on the morning of the following day.

The play takes place in Japan in MADAME BUTTERFLY's *little house at the foot of Higashi Hill, facing the harbor. Everything in the room is Japanese save the American locks and bolts on the doors and windows and an American flag fastened to a tobacco jar. Cherry blos-*
soms are abloom outside, and inside. A sword rack, a shrine on which lie a sword and a pair of men's slippers, a chest of drawers on top of which is a tray containing two red poppies, rouge, powder and hair ornaments, a stand for the tobacco jar and tea, are the only pieces of furniture in the room. As the curtain rises, MADAME BUTTERFLY *is spraying the growing flowers with a small watering pot. She snips off two little bunches, lays them on a plate of rice which she sets reverently on the shrine, then kneels, putting her hands on the floor, her forehead on them.*

Madame Butterfly. Oh, Shaka! Hail! Hail! Also perceive! Look down! I have brought a sacrifice of flowers and new rice. Also, I am quite clean. I am shivering with cleanness. Therefore grant that Lef-ten-ant B. F. Pikker-ton may come back soon.

(*She rises, clasps her hands, comes down to a floor cushion, and sits, fanning herself.*)

Suzuki. (*Entering with a low bow.*) Madame Butterfly's wish?

Madame Butterfly. Suzuki, inform me, if it

please you, how much more nearer beggary we are today than yesterday?

Suzuki. Aye. (*She takes some coins from a small box in her sleeve, and lays them in three piles on her palm, touching them as she speaks.*) Rin, yen, sen . . .

Madame Butterfly. (*Reprovingly.*) Suzuki, how many time I tellin' you—no one shall speak anythin' but those Unite' State' languages in these Lef-ten-ant Pik-ker-ton's house? (*She pronounces his name with much difficulty.*) Once more—an' I put you outside shoji! . . . That's one thin' aeverbody got recomlec' account it's 'Merican house—his wife, his maid.

Suzuki. (*Mouthing to herself, making no sound, counting on her fingers.*) Two dollar.

(*She drops the money into the box, giving it to* MADAME BUTTERFLY.)

Madame Butterfly. O, how we waste my husban's be-autiful moaneys! Tha's shame! Mos' gone.

Suzuki. This moaney hav' kep' us two year . . . Wha's happen to us now, if he don' come back?

Madame Butterfly. (*Scoffing, putting the money in her sleeve.*) O, if he don' come back! . . . Course he come back! He's gone so long accoun' he's got business in those his large country. If he's not come back to his house, why he sign Japanese lease for nine hundred and ninety nine year for me to live? Why he put 'Merican lock to bolt it door, to shut it window? Answer me those question.

Suzuki. (*Doubtfully.*) I dunno.

Madame Butterfly. Of course you dunno! You don' know whichaever. Wael I goin' tell you: to keep out those which are out, and in, those which are in. Tha's me.

(*She rises, goes to the window and looks out.*)

Suzuki. But he don't writin' no ledder.

Madame Butterfly. 'Merican men don' naever write ledder—no time.

Suzuki. (*Cynically.*) Aye . . . I don' naever know 'Merica navy man with Japanese wive come back.

Madame Butterfly. (*Impassively, her eyes narrowing.*) Speak concerning marriage once more, you die! (*She fans herself.* SUZUKI *salaams and backs quickly towards the door.* MADAME BUTTERFLY *claps her hands and* SUZUKI *pauses.*) Don' come back! Lef-ten-ant B. F. Pik-ker-ton don' come back! Ha! Me! I know w'en he comes back—he told me. W'en he goin' 'way, he say in tha's doors: "Madame Butterfly, I have had ver' nice times with my Japanese sweets heart, so now I goin' back to

my own country and here's moaney—an' don' worry 'bout me—I come back w'en 'Robins nes' again!'" Ha-ha! Tha's w'en he come back—w'en robins nes' again.

(*She sways her head triumphantly from side to side, fanning herself.*)

Suzuki. (*Not impressed.*) Yaes, I didn't like ways he said it—like those . . .

(*She imitates a flippant gesture of farewell.*)

Madame Butterfly. (*Laughing.*) Aha, that's 'Merican way sayin' good-bye to girl. Yaes, he come back w'en robins nes' again. Shu'h! Shu'h! (*She claps her hands with delight.* SUZUKI, *with a look of unbelief, starts to go.*) Sa-ey! Why no "shu'h" on you face for? Such a fools! (*Looking towards the window.*) O look! Suzuki—a robins. The firs' these Spring! Go, see if he's stay for nes'.

Suzuki. (*Looking.*) It *is* a robins, O Cho-Cho-San!

Madame Butterfly. (*Running to the window.*) O! O!

Suzuki. But he's fly away.

Madame Butterfly. O! How they are slow this year! Sa-ey, see if you don' fin' one tha's more in-dus-trial an' domestics.

Suzuki. (*Looking out.*) There are none yet.

Madame Butterfly. But soon they nes' now. Suzuki, w'en we see that ship comin' in—sa-ey—then we goin' put flowers aevery where, an' if it's night, we goin' hang up mos' one thousan' lanterns—eh-ha?

Suzuki. No got moaney for thousan'.

Madame Butterfly. Wael, twenty, mebby; an' sa-ey, w'en we see him comin' quick up path—(*imitates*) so—so—so—(*lifts her kimono and strides in a masculine fashion*) to look for liddle wive—me—me jus' goin' hide behind shoji (*making two holes with her wet finger in the low paper shoji and peeking through*) an' watch an' make believe me gone 'way; leave liddle note—sayin': "Goon-bye, sayonara, Butterfly." . . . Now he come in. . . . (*Hides.*) Ah! An' then he get angry! An' he say all kinds of 'Merican languages—debbils—hells! But before he get too angry, me run out an' flew aroun' his neck! (*She illustrates with* SUZUKI, *who is carried away and embraces her with fervor.*) Sa-ey! *You* no flew roun' his neck—jus' me. (*They laugh in each other's arms.*) Then he'll sit down an' sing tha's liddle 'Merican song—O, how he'll laugh. . . . (*She sings as though not understanding a word of it.*)

"I call her the belle of Japan—of Japan
Her name it is O Cho-Cho-San, Cho-Cho-San!
Such tenderness lies in her soft almond eyes,
I tell you, she's just 'ichi ban.'"

(*Laughs.*) Then I'll dance like w'en I was Geisha girl.

(*She dances as* SHARPLESS, *the American consul, appears in the doorway, followed by the* NAKODO.)

Nakodo. This is the house, your Excellency.

Sharpless. (*Removing his clogs outside.*) You may wait.

(NAKODO *bows and* SHARPLESS *enters.*)

I beg pardon. . . .

(MADAME BUTTERFLY, *still dancing, begins the song again.* SHARPLESS *goes to the door and knocks to attract her attention.*)

Madame Butterfly. Ah!

(SUZUKI, *bowing low, leaves the room.*)

Sharpless. This is Madame Cho-Cho-San?

Madame Butterfly. No, I am Mrs. Lef-ten-ant B. F. Pik-ker-ton.

Sharpless. I see. . . . Pardon my interruption. . . . I am Mr. Sharpless, the American consul.

Madame Butterfly. (*Once more salaaming to the ground, drawing in her breath between her teeth to express pleasure.*) O, your honorable excellency, goon night,—no, not night yaet: aexcuse me, I'm liddle raddle',—I mean goon mornin', goon evenin'. Welcome to 'Merican house, mos' welcome to 'Merican girl! (*Pointing to herself. They both bow.*) Be seat. (SHARPLESS *sits on a cushion on the floor, and* MADAME BUTTERFLY *sits at a little distance. There is a slight pause.*) How are those health? You sleepin' good? How are that honorable ancestors—are they well? And those parens'? That grandmother—how are she?

Sharpless. Thanks. They're all doing well, I hope.

Madame Butterfly. (*She claps her hands;* SUZUKI *enters and puts the little stand between them and leaves the room.*) Accep' pipe, your excellency. O, I forgettin'—I have still of those large American cigarette.

(MADAME BUTTERFLY *gestures towards* PINKERTON'S *tobacco jar decorated with the flag of his country.*)

Sharpless. (*Accepting a cigarette while she fills her pipe.*) Thanks. I'm on a little visit of inquiry, Madame Butterfly,—your name, I believe in our language. Lieutenant Pinkerton wrote me to find out—

Madame Butterfly. (*Almost breathless.*) Ah, you have hear from him? He is well?

Sharpless. O, he's all right.

Madame Butterfly. (*Relieved.*) Ah! Tha's mak' me mos' bes' happy female woman in Japan—mebby in that whole worl'—w'at you thing?

Sharpless. Ha-ha! (*Puffing at the cigarette.*) Sawdust. Pinkerton must have left these!

Madame Butterfly. O! I so glad you came. . . . I goin' as' you a liddle question.

Sharpless. Well?

Madame Butterfly. You know 'bout birds in those your country?

Sharpless. Something.

Madame Butterfly. Tha's what I thing—you know aeverything. Tha's why your country sen' you here.

Sharpless. You flatter me.

Madame Butterfly. O, no, you got big head.

Sharpless. Pinkerton again—I can hear him!

Madame Butterfly. O, aexcuse me: I forgettin' my manners. I got liddle more raddle. (*She offers him her pipe which he gravely touches, returning it. She touches it again, then puts it down.* Now, what you know 'bout jus' robins?

Sharpless. What?

Madame Butterfly. 'Bout when do they nes' again? Me, I thing it mus' be mor' early in Japan as in America, accoun' they nestin' here now.

Sharpless. O, at the same time I fancy.

Madame Butterfly. (*Disappointed.*) Yaes? . . . then they's nestin' there. (*Then taking hope again.*) Sa-ey, I tell you—perhaps some time sooner, some time later, jus' how they feel like.

Sharpless. Possibly. Why do you ask?

Madame Butterfly. Because Lef-ten-ant B. F. Pik-ker-ton say he will come back to me w'en the robins nes' again.

Sharpless. (*To himself.*) Poor devil! One of his infernal jokes.

Madame Butterfly. (*Clapping her hands.*) Me, I thing it's time. . . . I've wait so long.

(SUZUKI *enters with a tea-pot.* MADAME BUTTERFLY *gives* SHARPLESS *a cup of tea.*)

Nakodo. (*Appearing at the door.*) Tea, most illustrious?

Madame Butterfly. Ah! Enter, Nakodo. Your presence lights up my entire house. (*She gives him a cup. Accepting it, he goes up to a cushion and sits.*) Tha's bad man. W'en my husban's gone 'way, he try for get me marry again.

Nakodo. The rich Yamadori. Madame Cho-Cho-San is very poor.

Madame Butterfly. (*Bowing politely.*) O, liddle ol' frien'; those are my business.

Nakodo. Rejected advice makes the heart sad.

Madame Butterfly. We-el, if those heart hurt you so much, you better not arrive here no more.

Sharpless. Madame Butterfly; may I ask —er—where are your people?

Nakodo. They have outcasted her!

Madame Butterfly. Sa-ey, tha's foanny! My people make me marry when I don' want; now I am marry, they don' want. Before I marry Lef-ten-ant B. F. Pik-ker-ton, my honorable Father—(*she bows low*—NAKODO *bows*— SHARPLESS *bows*) die—he's officer. These are his sword . . . (*pointing to an inscription*) 'tis written . . .

(*She holds out the sword that the inscription may be read.*)

Nakodo. (*Reading.*) "To die with honor, when one can no longer live with honor."

(*He bows, then turns and bows towards the shrine and goes back to his cushion where he sits.*)

Madame Butterfly. He's kill' himself accoun' he soldier of Emporer an' defeat in battle. Then we get—O—ver' poor. Me? I go dance liddle. Also I thing if some rich man wish me, I gettin' marry for while, accoun' my grandmother, (*she bows respectfully*—NAKODO *bows*—SHARPLESS *politely nods*) don' got no food, no obi. Then ol' Nakodo, he say a (NAKODO *picks up his cushion and moves down to join in the conversation*) man's jus' as' him for nice wive for three monse. Nakodo tell him he don' know none more nizer as me.

Nakodo. (*Salaaming.*) Nizer as you.

Madame Butterfly. (*Salaaming.*) Nizer as me.

SHARPLESS. (*Looking from one to the other.*) Couldn't be nicer! . . .

(*He salaams profoundly—then all salaam.*)

Madame Butterfly. Then Nakodo say—

Nakodo. I say—I don' lig him account he 'Merica—jin.

Madame Butterfly. He also remark with me that he is barbarian an' beas'. But aeveryone say: "Yaes, take him—take him beas'—he's got moaneys." So I say for jus' liddle while, perhaps I can stan'. So Nakodo bring him. . . .

Nakodo . . . For look-at meeting.

Madame Butterfly. (*Laughing.*) Me? Well, I thing that day Lef-ten-ant B. F. Pik-ker-ton is jus' a god! Gold button—lace on his unicorn. At firs', I frightened—he hol' my hans' so close—like—(*she illustrates by giving both hands to* SHARPLESS) and kizz. Japanese girl no lig' kizz; but when Lef-ten-ant B. F. Pik-ker-ton kizz me, I like ver' much. . . . What's use lie? It's not inside of me. (*Noticing that*

her hands are still in SHARPLESS'.) O, I beg your honorable pardon. (*She tucks her hands in her sleeves.*) So we's gettin' marry and then his ship order away an' me—I am jus' waitin' —sometimes cryin', sometimes watchin', but always waitin'.

Nakodo. (*In the doorway—bowing with servility.*) My client, the prosperous Yamadori, approaches for the third time today.

Madame Butterfly. Now I have my liddle joke again. You watch, he comes all time to make smash with me.

SHARPLESS. Pinkerton's slang.

(YAMADORI *enters attended by two servants.* SHARPLESS *rises and bows ceremoniously.* MADAME BUTTERFLY *does not rise, but bends her head and fans herself coquettishly. The two servants squat.*)

Yamadori. Mr. Sharpless: always a pleasure to meet you here or in New York.

Sharpless. Thanks, Mr. Yamadori.

Madame Butterfly. (*Coquettishly.*) You have somethin' nize say to me again today?

Yamadori. Perseverance shall be the religion of my life until the capricious Butterfly deigns to believe me.

Madame Butterfly. You goin' tell me 'gain you kill yourself I don' make kizz with you?

Yamadori. (*Very much embarrassed—looking at consul.*) O!

Madame Butterfly. You can speak—consul know—I been tellin' him 'bout your liddle foolishness.

Yamadori. Such treatment, Mr. Sharpless, is one of the penalties we incur when madly in love with a charming woman.

Madame Butterfly. Tha's ver' nize. Ha-ha! (*Winks behind her fan at* SHARPLESS.)

Sharpless. Heavens! Pinkerton's very wink.

(MADAME BUTTERFLY *gives a cup of tea to* YAMADORI *who drinks it and rolls a cigarette.*)

Yamadori. (*To* SHARPLESS.) I am in Japan for two months—a pleasure trip. Do you blame me?

(*Pointing to* MADAME BUTTERFLY.)

Madame Butterfly. Aevery time he come home, get 'nother woman: must have mor'en eight now.

Yamadori. But I *married* them all . . .

Madame Butterfly. O *he!* He jus' marry whenaever he thing 'bout it.

Yamadori. You shall be different. I will bury *you* with my ancestors. (*To* SHARPLESS.) I offered her a thousand servants.

Nakodo. (*Stunned.*) Thousan'!

Madame Butterfly. Ha! (*Fans.*)

Yamadori. And a palace to live in.

(*The* NAKODO *is overcome by such generosity.*)

Madame Butterfly. He!

Yamadori. Everything her heart can wish.

Madame Butterfly. Ha! Ha!

Yamadori. Is that not enough? (*She shakes her head.*) Then in the presence of this statesman of integrity, I will give you a solemn writing. (SHARPLESS *gives him a quizzical glance.*) Is *that* enough?

Madame Butterfly. Wha's good of that to married womans? (*Pointing to herself.*)

Yamadori. According to the laws of Japan, when a woman is deserted, she is divorced. (MADAME BUTTERFLY *stops fanning and listens.*) Though I have travelled much abroad, I know the laws of my own country.

Madame Butterfly. An' I know laws of my *husban's* country.

Yamadori. (*To* SHARPLESS.) She still fancies herself married to the young officer. If your excellency would explain. . . .

Madame Butterfly. (*To* SHARPLESS.) Sa-ey, when some one gettin' married in America, don' he stay marry?

Sharpless. Usually—yes.

Madame Butterfly. Well, tha's all right. I'm marry to Lef-ten-ant B. F. Pik-ker-ton.

Yamadori. Yes, but a Japanese marriage!

Sharpless. Matrimony is a serious thing in America, not a temporary affair as it often is here.

Madame Butterfly. Yaes, an' you can't like 'Merican mans. Japanese got too many wive, eh?

Sharpless. (*Laughing.*) We are not allowed more than one at a time.

Madame Butterfly. Yaes, an' you can't divorce wive like here, by sayin': "walk it back to parent"—eh?

Sharpless. O, no.

Madame Butterfly. Tha's right, aexactly. When I as' Lef-ten-ant B. F. Pik-ker-ton, he explain those law to me of gettin' divorce in those Unite' State'. He say no one can get aexcept he stan' up before Judge 2—3—4—7—year. Ver' tiresome. Firs' the man he got tell those Judge all he know 'bout womans; then womans, she got tell; then some lawyer quarrel with those Judge; the Judge get jury an' as' wha' they thing—an' if they don' know, they'll all get put in jails. Tha's all right! (*Folds hands.*)

Yamadori. Your friend has told her everything she wanted him to tell her.

Madame Butterfly. (*Who has paid no attention.*) Tha's ver' nize, too, that 'Merican God.

SHARPLESS. I beg your pardon?

Madame Butterfly. Once times, Lef-ten-ant B. F. Pik-ker-ton—

Yamadori. (*Aside to* SHARPLESS.) Pinkerton again!

Madame Butterfly. He's in great troubles, an' he said "God he'p me"; an' sunshine *came right out*—and God he did! Tha's ver' quick—Japanese gods take more time. Aeverything quick in America. Ha—me—sometime I thing I pray large American God to get him back soon; but no use,—he don' know me where *I* live. (*Attracted by a sound.*) Wha's that? . . . You hear?

Sharpless. No. (MADAME BUTTERFLY *runs to the window and listens; then takes up the glasses while* SHARPLESS *speaks in a low voice to* YAMADORI.) Lieutenant Pinkerton's ship was due yesterday. His young wife from America is waiting here to meet him. (*At the word "wife,"* YAMADORI *smiles—takes his fan from his sleeve and fans himself. The* NAKODO, *who is listening, is struck by an idea and departs in such haste that he tumbles over one of* YAMADORI'S *attendants who jabbers at him.*) I'm devilish sorry for that girl.

Yamadori. Then tell her the truth.

Madame Butterfly. Aexcuse me; but I always hearin' soun' like ship gun—ha—ha—tha's naturels.

Yamadori. (*Preparing to go.*) Good morning, Mr. Sharpless. (*Shaking hands. Turning to* MADAME BUTTERFLY.) I leave you to-day. Tomorrow the gods may prompt you to listen to me! (*He bows.*)

Madame Butterfly. (*Bowing.*) Mebby.

(YAMADORI *and attendants go off, bowing. She turns to* SHARPLESS.) Mebby not. Sa-ey, somehow couldn't you let that Lef-ten-ant B. F. Pik-ker-ton know they's other all crazy 'bout me?

SHARPLESS. Madame Butterfly, sit down. (*While she, struck by his solemn manner, looks at him and obeys, he removes the tea-pot and sits on the stand, to the astonishment of* MADAME BUTTERFLY.) I am going to read you part of a letter I have received from Pinkerton.

(*He takes a letter from his pocket.*)

Madame Butterfly. O, jus' let me look at those ledder! (*She slips it under her kimono on her heart and with an indrawn breath, hands it back.*) Now read quick, you mos' bes' nize man in all the whole worl'.

Sharpless. (*Reads.*) "Find out about that little Jap girl. What has become of her? It might be awkward now. If little Butterfly still remembers me, perhaps you can help me out and make her understand. Let her down gently. You won't believe it, but for two weeks after I sailed, I was dotty in love with her."

(SHARPLESS *is amazed to see* MADAME BUT-TERFLY *convulsed with silent joy.*)

Madame Butterfly. Oh, all the gods how it was sweet!.

Sharpless. Why really—

Madame Butterfly. Tha's what I'm afraid: that he loave' me so much he's goin' desert his country an' get in trouble with American eagle—what you thing? Oh, it's more bedder I wait than those!

Sharpless. (*Folding the letter.*) No use—you can't understand. Madame Butterfly, suppose this waiting should never end; what would become of you?

Madame Butterfly. Me? I could dance, mebby, or—die?

Sharpless. Don't be foolish. I advise you to consider the rich Yamadori's offer.

Madame Butterfly. (*Astonished.*) *You* say those? You, 'Merican consul?—when you know that me, I am marry?

Sharpless. You heard Yamadori: it is not binding.

Madame Butterfly. Yamadori lies!

Sharpless. His offer is an unusual opportunity for a girl who—for any Japanese girl in your circumstances.

Madame Butterfly. (*Enraged—she claps her hands.*) Suzuki! The excellent gentleman—(*bowing sarcastically*) who have done us the honor to call—he wish to go hurriedly. His shoes—hasten them!

(SUZUKI, *who has entered carrying a jar, gets* SHARPLESS' *clogs and gives them to him—then passes off with her jar.*)

Sharpless. (*Holding the clogs awkwardly.*) I'm really very sorry.

Madame Butterfly. No, no, don' be angery. But jus' now you tol' me—O, gods! You mean— (*Looks at him pitifully.*) I not Leften-ant B. F. Pik-ker-ton's wive—Me?

Sharpless. Hardly.

Madame Butterfly. O, I— (*She sways slightly.* SHARPLESS *goes to her assistance, but she recovers and fans herself.*) Tha's all right. I got liddle heart illness. I can't . . . I can't someways give up thinkin' he'll come back to me. You thing tha's all over? All finish? (*Dropping her fan.* SHARPLESS *nods assent.*) Oh, no! Loave don' forget some thin's or wha's use of loave? (*She claps her hands—beckoning off.*) Loave's got remember . . . (*pointing*) some thin's!

(*A child enters.*)

Sharpless. A child. . . . Pinkerton's?. . . .

Madame Butterfly. (*Showing a picture of* PINKERTON'S.) Look! Look! (*Holding it up beside the child's face.*) Tha's jus' his face, same hair, same blue eye. . . .

Sharpless. Does Lieutenant Pinkerton know?

Madame Butterfly. No, he come after he goe. (*Looking at the child with pride.*) You thing fath-er naever comes back—tha's what *you* thing? He do! You write him ledder; tell him 'bout one bes' mos' nize bebby aever seen. . . . Ha—ha! I bed all moaneys he goin' come mos' one million mile for see those chil'. Surely this is tie—bebby. Sa-ey, you didn' mean what you said 'bout me not bein' marry? You make liddle joke? (*Moved,* SHARPLESS *nods his head in assent, to the great relief of* MADAME BUTTERFLY.) (*She lays the baby's hand in* SHARPLESS'.) Shake hand consul 'Merican way.

Sharpless. (*Shaking hands with the child.*) Hm . . . hm . . . what's your name?

Madame Butterfly. Trouble. Japanese bebby always change it name. I was thinkin' some day w'en he come back, change it to Joy.

Sharpless. Yes . . . yes . . . I'll let him know.

(*Glad to escape, he takes an abrupt departure.*)

Suzuki. (*In the distance, wailing.*) Ay . . . ay . . . ay . . .

Madame Butterfly. Tha's wail . . .

Suzuki. (*Nearer.*) O, Cho-Cho-San! (MA-DAME BUTTERFLY *goes to the door to meet* SUZU-KI.) Cho-Cho-San!

Madame Butterfly. Speak!

Suzuki. We are shamed through the town. The Nakodo—

Nakodo. (*Appearing.*) I but said the child—(*he points to the baby, whom* MADAME BUTTERFLY *instinctively shelters in her arms*) was a badge of shame to his father. In his country, there are homes for such unfortunates and they never rise above the stigma of their class. They are shunned and cursed from birth.

Madame Butterfly. (*Who has listened stolidly—now with a savage cry, pushing him away from her until he loses his balance and falls to the floor.*) You lie!

Nakado. (*On the floor.*) But Yamadori—

Madame Butterfly. (*Touching her father's sword.*) Lies! Lies! Lies! Say again, I kill! Go . . . (*The* NAKODO *goes quickly.*) Bebby, he lies. . . . Yaes, it's lie. . . . When your fath-er knows how they speak, he will take us 'way from bad people to his own country. I am finish here. (*Taking the American flag from the tobacco jar and giving it to the child.*) Tha's your country—your flag. Now wave like fath-er say w'en excite—wave like "hell!" (*Waves the child's hand.*) Ha'rh! Ha'rh! (*A ship's gun is heard.*) Ah! (MADAME BUTTERFLY *and* SUZUKI *start for the balcony.* MADAME BUTTERFLY *runs back for the child as the gun is heard again; then returning to the shoji, looks through the glasses.*) Look! Look! Warship! Wait . . . can't see name. . . .

Suzuki. Let me—

Madame Butterfly. No! Ah! Name is "Con-nec-ti-cut"! His ship! He's come back! He's come back! (*Laughing, she embraces* SUZUKI—*then sinks to the floor.*) He's come back! Those robins nes' again an' we didn' know! O, bebby, bebby—your fath-er come back! Your fath-er come back! O! O! (*Shaking a bough of cherry blossoms, which fall on them both.*) This is the bes' nize momen' since you was borned. Now your name's Joy! Suzuki; the Moon Goddess sent that bebby straight from Bridge of Heaven to make me courage to wait so long.

Suzuki. Ah, ship's in. . . .

Madame Butterfly. (*Rising in great excitement.*) Hoarry, Suzuki, his room. (SUZUKI *pulls out a screen to form a little room.*) We mus' hoarry—(*Picking flowers from the pots and decorating the room*) like we got eagle's wings an' thousan' feets. His cigarettes. (*Setting the jar in the room.*) His slipper. (SUZUKI *gets them from the shrine.*) His chair, Suzuki—hustle! (SUZUKI *hastens off.* MADAME BUTTERFLY *shakes a cushion and drops it on the floor.*) His bed. (SUZUKI *enters with a steamer chair, which she places upside down.*) Now his room fixed! (SUZUKI *closes the shoji.* MADAME BUTTERFLY *adjusts the chair and sets the lanterns about the room.*) Bring me my wides' obi, kanzashi for my hair, poppies—mus' look ver' pretty!

Suzuki. Rest is bes' beauty. He not come yet. Sleep liddle firs'. . . .

Madame Butterfly. No, no time. (*Taking up a small mirror and looking critically at herself.*) He mus' see me look mos' pretty ever. You thing I change since he went away—not so beauty? (SUZUKI *is silent.*) W'at? . . . I am! (*Brandishing the mirror.*) Say so!

Suzuki. Perhaps you rest liddle, once more you get so pretty again.

Madame Butterfly. Again? . . .

Suzuki. Trouble, tha's make change. . . .

Madame Butterfly. Moach change. (*Still looking in the glass.*) No, I am no more pretty

—an' he come soon. (*On her knees in front of* SUZUKI—*resting her forehead on the maid's feet.*) Ah, Suzuki, be kin' with me—make me pretty . . . don' say you can't—you moas'. An' tomorrow, the gods will. Ah, yes! You can—you can—you got to! Bring powder, comb, rouge, henna, fix it hair like on wedding day. (SUZUKI *brings the toilet articles and they sit on the floor.* SUZUKI *puts the poppies and pins in* MADAME BUTTERFLY'S *hair, and she, in turn, dresses the baby, enveloping him in an obi, so wide that it almost covers the child.*) Now, bebby, when you cry, he'll sing you those liddle 'Merican song he sing me when I cry—song all 'Merican sing for bebby. (*Sitting with the baby in front of her, swaying it by the arms, she sings.*)

> "Rog' a bye bebby,
> Off in Japan,
> You jus' a picture,
> Off of a fan."

(SUZUKI *has found it very difficult to finish the toilet, but at last she accomplishes it.* MADAME BUTTERFLY *lifts the baby up, gives it a doll, then touches it with rouge and adds a final dash of rouge to her own face.*) Now for watch for pa-pa! (*Putting the flag in the child's hand, she takes it up to the window and makes three holes in the shoji, one low down for the baby. As the three look through the shoji, they form the picture she has already described.*)

(*During the vigil, the night comes on.* SUZUKI *lights the floor lamps, the stars come out, the dawn breaks, the floor lights flicker out one by one, the birds begin to sing, and the day discovers* SUZUKI *and the baby fast asleep on the floor; but* MADAME BUTTERFLY *is awake, still watching, her face white and strained. She reaches out her hands and rouses* SUZUKI.)

Suzuki. (*Starting to her feet, surprised and looking about the room.*) He no come?

Madame Butterfly. No. . . .

Suzuki. (*Pityingly.*) Oh!

Madame Butterfly. (*With an imperious gesture.*) No "Oh"! He will come. . . . Bring fresh flowers. (*She collects the lanterns as* SUZUKI *brings in fresh flowers.* MADAME BUTTERFLY *tears up the roses and throws their leaves in Pinkerton's room. Then pointing to the upper part of the house.*) Now I watch from liddle look out place. (*She picks up the child whose doll drops from its hand.*) Have mos' bes' nize breakfas' ready w'en he come.

(*She leaves the room and* SUZUKI *goes to prepare the breakfast.*)

(*The stage is empty. Very faintly a strain of "I call her the Belle of Japan" is heard.* MADAME BUTTERFLY *is singing that she may not weep. A pause. Some one knocks on the door.* LIEUTENANT PINKERTON'S *voice calls outside the shoji.*)

Lieutenant Pinkerton. Madame Butterfly? Madame Butterfly? (*Coming into the room, he looks about.*) Butterfly?

Sharpless. (*Following him.*) They've seen the ship—these decorations were not here when I called.

Madame Butterfly. (*Singing to hush the baby.*)

"Rog'—a—bye, bebby,
Off in Japan,"

(LIEUTENANT PINKERTON *listens to the song coming from above.*)

"You jus' a picture,
Off of a fan."

Lieutenant Pinkerton. She is watching the ship. (*Noticing the screened off part of the room.*) My room . . . just as it used to look . . . my chair. (*Picking up the doll which the child has dropped.*) Poor kid! Poor little devil! . . . Sharpless, I thought when I left this house, the few tears, sobs, little polite regrets, would be over as I crossed the threshold. I started to come back for a minute, but I said to myself: "Don't do it; by this time she's ringing your gold pieces to make sure they're good." You know that class of Japanese girl and—

Sharpless. (*Seeing* NAKODO *who is at the shoji.*) Look here: I have something to settle with you! (NAKODO *comes in cautiously.*) Why did you seek out my friend's wife at the pier?

Lieutenant Pinkerton. Why did you tell her that story—the child and all? Answer me?

Nakodo. (*To* SHARPLESS.) Your Excellency, I but thought if trouble came between the two women, he would surely break with Cho-Cho-San, and then she would be glad to marry the rich Yamadori and I get big fee.

(*Exit*)

Sharpless. You'll never get it. (*To* PINKERTON.) She'll starve first.

Lieutenant Pinkerton. Sharpless, thank God, that's one thing I can do—money.

(*He takes out an envelope containing some money.*)

Sharpless. What did your wife say, Pinkerton?

Lieutenant Pinkerton. Well, it was rather rough on her,—only married four months. Sharpless, my Kate's an angel,—she offered to take the child . . . made me promise I'd speak of it to Butterfly.

Madame Butterfly. (*Calling from above.*) Suzuki?

Sharpless. She's coming.

(PINKERTON *instinctively draws behind the screen.*)

Madame Butterfly. (*Coming down the stairs with the sleeping baby on her back, calling.*) Suzuki? Come for bebby. (*Kissing the child.*) Nize liddle eye, pick out of blue sky, all shut up.

Lieutenant Pinkerton. (*Aside to* SHARPLESS, *his eyes fixed on the mother and child.*) I can't face it! I'm going. Give her the money.

Suzuki. (*Entering, and seeing* PINKERTON *as he passes out of the door.*) Ah!

(SHARPLESS *gives her a warning gesture.*)

Madame Butterfly. (*Seeing* SUZUKI'S *astonished face.*) Wha'—? (*She puts the baby in* SUZUKI'S *arms.* SUZUKI *goes out quickly.* MADAME BUTTERFLY *sees the Consul.*) You! Oh! (*Joyously.*) You seen him?

Sharpless. Yes.

Madame Butterfly. An' you tole him?

Sharpless. Well . . .

Madame Butterfly. But you tole him . . . of bebby?

Sharpless. Yes.

Madame Butterfly. (*Wiping her dry lips.*) Yaes . . . tha's right. Tha's what I—as' you do . . . an'—an' what he *say?*

Sharpless. Well . . . (*Taking out the envelope, and giving her the money which she takes without looking at it.*) He said—er—he was crazy to see you and—(*Aside*) What the devil can I say! (*To her.*) You know he can't leave the ship just yet. (*Pointing to the package in her hand.*) That is in remembrance of the past. He wishes you to be always happy, to have the best of luck; he hopes to see you soon—and—

(*The lies die out on his lips.*)

Madame Butterfly. (*Bending and kissing his hand.*) All—all the gods in the heavens bless you!

(*Overcome, she staggers.* SHARPLESS *catches her, puts her into the chair—she leans against him—her face upraised, her eyes closed.*)

(KATE, *entering hurriedly.*)

Kate. Has Lieutenant Pinkerton gone? Has my husband been here?

(MADAME BUTTERFLY *hears and opens her eyes.*)

Sharpless. For God's sake—(*He looks at* MADAME BUTTERFLY *whose eyes are fixed on his with a look of despair.*) Come, we can overtake him.

Kate (*In a lower voice.*) Did he speak to her of the—

Sharpless. No.

Kate. Then I will ask. (*For the first time seeing* MADAME BUTTERFLY.) Is this— SHARPLESS *nods and goes. There is a short pause, while the two women look at each other, then* MADAME BUTTERFLY, *still seated, slowly bows her head.*) Why, you poor little thing . . . who in the world could blame you or . . . call you responsible . . . you pretty little plaything.

(*Takes* MADAME BUTTERFLY *in her arms.*)

Madame Butterfly. (*Softly.*) No—playthin' . . . I am Mrs. Lef-ten-ant B. F.—No—no— now I am, only—Cho-Cho-San, but no playthin'. . . . (*She rises, then impassively.*) How long you been marry?

Kate. Four months. . . .

Madame Butterfly. (*Counting on her fingers.*) Oh . . . four.

Kate. Won't you let me do something for the child? Where is he? (MADAME BUTTERFLY *gestures toward the next room.* KATE, *seeing the child.*) Ah! The dear little thing! May I—

Madame Butterfly. No! Can look . . . no can touch. . . .

Kate. Let us think first of the child. For his own good . . . let me take him home to my country. . . . I will do all I would do for my own.

Madame Butterfly. (*Showing no emotion.*) He not know then—me—his mother?

Kate. It's hard, very hard, I know; but would it not be better?

Madame Butterfly. (*Taking the money box from her sleeve, and giving the coins to* KATE.) Tha's his . . . two dollar. All tha's lef' of his moaneys. . . . I shall need no more. . . . (*She hands* KATE *the envelope which* SHARPLESS *has just given.*) I lig if you also say I sawry—no— no—no—glad—glad! I wish him that same happiness lig he wish for me . . . an' tell him . . . I shall be happy . . . mebby. Thang him . . . Mister B. F. Pik-ker-ton for also that kindness he have been unto me . . . an' permit me to thang *you*, augustness, for that same. . . . You—you mos' bes' lucky girl in these whole worl' . . . . Goon-night—

(*She stands stolidly with her eyes closed.*)

Kate. (*Wiping her eyes.*) But the child?

Madame Butterfly. Come back fifteen minute. . . . (*With closed eyes, she bows politely.*) Sayonara. (KATE *reluctantly goes.*) God he'p me, but no sun kin shine. (SUZUKI, *who has listened, sinks at* MADAME BUTTERFLY'S *feet.*) Don' cry, Suzuki, liddle maiden . . . accoun' I dizappoint, a liddle dizappoint'—don' cry . . . . (*Running her hand over* SUZUKI'S *head— as she kneels.*) Tha's short while ago you as' me res'—sleep. . . . (*Wearily.*) Well—go way an' I will res' now. . . . I *wish* res'—sleep . . . long sleep . . . an' when you see me again, I pray you look whether I be not beautiful again . . . as a bride.

Suzuki. (*Understanding, sobbing.*) No— no—no.

Madame Butterfly. So that I suffer no more —goon bye, liddle maiden. (SUZUKI *does not go.* MADAME BUTTERFLY *claps her hands, and sobbing,* SUZUKI *leaves the room.* MADAME BUTTERFLY *bolts the shoji, and the door, lights fresh incense before the shrine, takes down her father's sword and reads the inscription:*) "To die with honor . . . when one can no longer live with honor." . . .

(*She draws her finger across the blade, to test the sharpness of the sword, then picks up the hand glass, puts on more rouge, re-arranges the poppies in her hair, bows to the shrine, and is about to press the blade of the sword against her neck, when the door is opened and the child is pushed into the room by* SUZUKI, *who keeps out of sight.* MADAME BUTTERFLY *drops the sword and takes the baby in her arms. A knocking is heard but she pays no heed. She sets the child on a mat, puts the American flag in its hand, and picking up the sword, goes behind the screen that the child may not see what she is about to do. A short pause—the sword is heard to drop.* MADAME BUTTERFLY *reappears, her face deathly—a scarf about her neck to conceal the wound.* SUZUKI *opens the door, sees the face of her mistress—backs out of the room in horror.* MADAME BUTTERFLY *drops to her knees as she reaches the child, and clasps it to her. A hand is thrust through the shoji and the bolt is drawn.*)

(KATE *enters quickly urging the reluctant* PINKERTON *to follow her.*)

Lieutenant Pinkerton. (*Discerning what she has done.*) Oh! Cho-Cho-San!

(*He draws her to him with the baby pressed to her heart. She waves the child's hand which holds the flag—saying faintly.*)

Madame Butterfly. Too bad those robbins didn' nes' again. (*She dies.*)

XV. THE MODERN ESSAY AND BIOGRAPHY

THE prevailing characteristic of the modern essay and biography in America is the emphasis laid upon personality. This shows itself most clearly of course in the familiar essay of Miss Repplier and Mr. Crothers, where the point of view of the essayist controls his material completely, but even in the nature essay of John Burroughs, it is the personality of the author that is most interesting.

The critical essay, it is true, reaches at times a more objective standard. The crusading spirit of Howells, as he led the fight for realism, gives his work a flavor of its own, but he was establishing general principles of criticism, as Poe, Longfellow, and Lowell had done in the earlier period. His defence of the English and American novelists from the charge of parochialism and his establishment of the fact that they are more true to life in its proper proportion than the Continental writers of fiction is a piece of constructive criticism of the highest order. Henry James was a constructive critic, too, but the essay here selected represents him in his keen analysis of a great literary personality, and in his ability to coin magnificent phrases. The criticism of Brownell reaches a more truly objective quality, but his best work was still largely concerned with the analysis of individuals, and the correction of popular judgments.

That the critical work of Woodrow Wilson and Theodore Roosevelt derives its authority from the personality of the author is obvious. Their essays are significant because of their appreciation of the spiritual significance of literature and its close relation to life and to history. In the same category, yet written from the point of view of a philosopher, the scrutiny of our institutions by George Santayana is illuminating, just as the discussion of our national genius by Bliss Perry and Stuart Sherman derives its importance from their keen insight and their sane yet progressive attitude.

The present wide interest in biography arises from the desire for reality in an age when so much of the fiction is inconsequential. Yet modern biography has taken on a fictional garb, with a resulting gain in popular interest, if not in accuracy. In this sense modern biography, or more correctly modern autobiography, begins with Mark Twain. In his autobiography, better suited for selection than his more unified earlier works, he reveals himself, with that refusal to be taken only as a "funny man" which has secured his place in literature. Totally different in tone, *The Education of Henry Adams* is just as truly the explanation of modern New England as Mark Twain's *Autobiography* is the revelation of the modern middle west, or as Adams' *Mont St. Michel* is a revelation of medievalism.

The contemporary biography, whose main function seems to be the reinterpretation of historical characters, may be represented by the work of Gamaliel Bradford and Carl Sandburg. Like all such attempts, they tend to become one-sided, and to present not the true object of their study but rather a portrait as their authors think it should be drawn.

SAMUEL LANGHORNE CLEMENS (1835-1910)
From MARK TWAIN'S AUTOBIOGRAPHY
(1924)
Early Days
(*Written 1897-8*)

. . . So much for the earlier days, and the New England branch of the Clemenses. The other brother settled in the South and is remotely responsible for me. He has collected his reward generations ago, whatever it was. He went South with his particular friend Fairfax, and settled in Maryland with him, but afterward went further and made his home in Virginia. This is the Fairfax whose descendants were to enjoy a curious distinction—that of being American-born English earls. The founder of the house was the Lord General Fairfax of the Parliamentary arm, in Cromwell's time. The earldom, which is of recent date, came to the American Fairfaxes through the failure of male heirs in England. Old residents of San Francisco will remember "Charley," the American earl of the mid-'sixties—tenth Lord Fairfax according to Burke's Peerage, and holder of a modest public office of some sort or other in the new mining town of Virginia City, Nevada. He was never out of America. I knew him, but not intimately. He had a golden character, and that was all his fortune. He laid his title aside, and gave it a holiday until his circumstances should improve to a degree consonant with its dignity; but that time never came, I think. He was a manly man and had fine generosities in his make-up. A prominent and pestilent creature named Ferguson, who was always picking quarrels with better men than himself, picked one with him one day, and Fairfax knocked him down. Ferguson gathered himself up and went off, mumbling threats. Fairfax carried no arms, and refused to carry any now, though his friends warned him that Ferguson was of a treacherous disposition and would be sure to take revenge by base means, sooner or later. Nothing happened for several days; then Ferguson took the earl by surprise and snapped a revolver at his breast. Fairfax wrenched the pistol from him and was going to shoot him, but the man fell on his knees and begged, and said: "*Don't* kill me. I have a wife and children." Fairfax was in a towering passion, but the appeal reached his heart, and he said, "*They* have done me no harm," and he let the rascal go.

Back of the Virginian Clemenses is a dim procession of ancestors stretching back to Noah's time. According to tradition, some of them were pirates and slavers in Elizabeth's time. But this is no discredit to them, for so were Drake and Hawkins and the others. It was a respectable trade then, and monarchs were partners in it. In my time I have had desires to be a pirate myself. The reader, if he will look deep down in his secret heart, will find—but never mind what he will find there. I am not writing his autobiography, but mine. Later, according to tradition, one of the procession was ambassador to Spain in the time of James I, or of Charles I, and married there and sent down a strain of Spanish blood to warm us up. Also, according to tradition, this one or another—Geoffrey Clement, by name—helped to sentence Charles to death. I have not examined into these traditions myself, partly because I was indolent and partly because I was so busy polishing up this end of the line and trying to make it showy; but the other Clemenses claim that they have made the examination and that it stood the test. Therefore I have always taken for granted that I did help Charles out of his troubles, by ancestral proxy. My instincts have persuaded me, too. Whenever we have a strong and persistent and ineradicable instinct, we may be sure that it is not original with us, but inherited—inherited from way back, and hardened and perfected by the petrifying influence of time. Now I have been always and unchangingly bitter against Charles, and I am quite certain that this feeling trickled down to me through the veins of my forebears from the heart of that judge; for it is not my disposition to be bitter against people on my own personal account. I am not bitter against Jeffreys. I ought to be, but I am not. It indicates that my ancestors of James II's time were indifferent to him; I do not know why; I never could make it out; but that is what it indicates. And I have always felt friendly toward Satan. Of course that is ancestral; it must be in the blood, for I could not have originated it.

. . . And so, by the testimony of instinct, backed by the assertions of Clemenses, who said they had examined the records, I have always been obliged to believe that Geoffrey Clement, the martyr maker, was an ancestor of mine, and to regard him with favor, and in fact, pride. This has not had a good effect upon me, for it has made me vain, and that is a fault. It has made me set myself above people who were less fortunate in their ancestry than I, and has moved me to take them down a peg, upon occasion, and say things to them which hurt them before company.

A case of the kind happened in Berlin several years ago. William Walter Phelps was our minister at the Emperor's court then, and one evening he had me to dinner to meet Count S—, a cabinet minister. This nobleman was of long and illustrious descent. Of course I wanted to let out the fact that I had some ancestors, too; but I did not want to pull them out of their graves by the ears, and I never could seem to get the chance to work them in in a way that would look sufficiently casual. I suppose Phelps was in the same difficulty. In fact, he looked distraught now and then—just as a person looks who wants to uncover an ancestor purely by accident and cannot think of a way that will seem accidental enough. But at last, after dinner, he made a try. He took us about his drawing-room, showing us the pictures, and finally stopped before a rude and ancient engraving. It was a picture of the court that tried Charles I. There was a pyramid of judges in Puritan slouch hats, and below them three bareheaded secretaries seated at a table. Mr. Phelps put his finger upon one of the three and said, with exulting indifference:

"An ancestor of mine."

I put my finger on a judge, and retorted with scathing languidness:

"Ancestor of mine. But it is a small matter. I have others."

It was not noble in me to do it. I have always regretted it since. But it landed him. I wonder how he felt! However, it made no difference in our friendship; which shows that he was fine and high, notwithstanding the humbleness of his origin. And it was also creditable in me, too, that I could overlook it. I made no change in my bearing toward him, but always treated him as an equal.

But it was a hard night for me in one way. Mr. Phelps thought I was the guest of honor, and so did Count S—, but I didn't, for there was nothing in my invitation to indicate it. It was just a friendly offhand note, on a card. By the time dinner was announced Phelps was himself in a state of doubt. Something had to

be done, and it was not a handy time for explanations. He tried to get me to go out with him, but I held back; then he tried S—, but he also declined. There was another guest, but there was no trouble about him. We finally went out in a pile. There was a decorous plunge for seats and I got the one at Mr Phelps's left, the count captured the one facing Phelps, and the other guest had to take the place of honor, since he could not help himself. We returned to the drawing-room in the original disorder. I had new shoes on and they were tight. At eleven I was privately crying; I couldn't help it, the pain was so cruel. Conversation had been dead for an hour. S— had been due at the bedside of a dying official ever since half past nine. At last we all rose by one blessed impulse and went down to the street door without explanations—in a pile, and no precedence; and so parted.

The evening had its defects; still, I got my ancestor in, and was satisfied.

Among the Virginian Clemenses were Jere and Sherrard. Jere Clemens had a wide reputation as a good pistol-shot, and once it enabled him to get on the friendly side of some drummers when they wouldn't have paid any attention to mere smooth words and arguments. He was out stumping the state at the time. The drummers were grouped in front of the stand and had been hired by the opposition to drum while he made his speech. When he was ready to begin he got out his revolver and laid it before him and said, in his soft, silky way:

"I do not wish to hurt anybody and shall try not to, but I have got just a bullet apiece for those six drums, and if you should want to play on them don't stand behind them."

Sherrard Clemens was a Republican Congressman from West Virginia in the war days, and then went out to St. Louis, where the James Clemens branch lived and still lives, and there he became a warm rebel. This was after the war. At the time that he was a Republican I was a rebel; but by the time he had become a rebel I was become (temporarily) a Republican. The Clemenses have always done the best they could to keep the political balances level, no matter how much it might inconvenience them. I did not know what had become of Sherrard Clemens; but once I introduced Senator Hawley to a Republican mass meeting in New England, and then I got a bitter letter from Sherrard from St. Louis. He said that the Republicans of the North—no, the "mudsills of the North"—had swept away the old aristocracy of the South with fire and sword, and it ill became me, an aristocrat by blood, to train with that kind of swine. Did I forget that I was a Lambton?

That was a reference to my mother's side of the house. My mother was a Lambton—Lambton with a p, for some of the American Lamptons could not spell very well in early times, and so the name suffered at their hands. She was a native of Kentucky, and married my father in Lexington in 1823, when she was twenty years old and he twenty-four. Neither of them had an overplus of property. She brought him two or three negroes, but nothing else, I think. They removed to the remote and secluded village of Jamestown, in the mountain solitudes of east Tennessee. There their first crop of children was born, but as I was of a later vintage, I do not remember anything about it. I was postponed—postponed to Missouri. Missouri was an unknown new state and needed attractions.

I think that my eldest brother, Orion, my sisters Pamela and Margaret, and my brother Benjamin were born in Jamestown. There may have been others, but as to that I am not sure. It was a great lift for that little village to have my parents come there. It was hoped that they would stay, so that it would become a city. It was supposed that they would stay. And so there was a boom; but by and by they went away, and prices went down, and it was many years before Jamestown got another start. I have written about Jamestown in the *Gilded Age*, a book of mine, but it was from hearsay, not from personal knowledge. My father left a fine estate behind him in the region roundabout Jamestown—75,000 acres. When he died in 1847 he had owned it about twenty years. The taxes were almost nothing (five dollars a year for the whole), and he had always paid them regularly and kept his title perfect. He had always said that the land would not become valuable in his time, but that it would be a commodious provision for his children some day. It contained coal, copper, iron, and timber, and he said that in the course of time railways would pierce to that region and then the property would be property in fact as well as in name. It also produced a wild grape of a promising sort. He had sent some samples to Nicholas Longworth of Cincinnati to get his judgment upon them, and Mr. Longworth had said that they would make as good wine as his Catawbas. The land contained all these riches; and also oil, but my father did not know that, and of course in those early days he would have cared nothing about it if he had known it. The oil was not

discovered until about 1895. I wish I owned a couple of acres of the land now, in which case I would not be writing autobiographies for a living. My father's dying charge was, "Cling to the land and wait; let nothing beguile it away from you." My mother's favorite cousin, James Lampton, who figures in the *Golden Age* as Colonel Sellers, always said of that land—and said it with blazing enthusiasm, too,—"There's millions in it—millions!" It is true that he always said that about everything—and was always mistaken, too, but this time he was right; which shows that a man who goes around with a prophecy-gun ought never to get discouraged. If he will keep up his heart and fire at everything he sees, he is bound to hit something by and by.

Most persons regarded Colonel Sellers as a fiction, an invention, an extravagant impossibility, and did me the honor to call him a "creation"; but they were mistaken. I merely put him on paper as he was; he was not a person who could be exaggerated. The incidents which looked most extravagant, both in the book and on the stage, were not inventions of mine, but were facts of his life; and I was present when they were developed. John T. Raymond's audiences used to come near to dying with laughter over the turnip-eating scene; but, extravagant as the scene was, it was faithful to the facts, in all its absurd details. The thing happened in Lampton's own house, and I was present. In fact, I was myself the guest who ate the turnips. In the hands of a great actor that piteous scene would have dimmed any manly spectator's eyes with tears, and racked his ribs apart with laughter at the same time. But Raymond was great in humorous portrayal only. In that he was superb, he was wonderful—in a word, great; in all things else he was a pygmy of pygmies. The real Colonel Sellers, as I knew him in James Lampton, was a pathetic and beautiful spirit, a manly man, a straight and honorable man, a man with a big, foolish, unselfish heart in his bosom, a man born to be loved; and he was loved by all his friends, and by his family worshiped. It is the right word. To them he was but little less than a god. The real Colonel Sellers was never on the stage. Only half of him was there. Raymond could not play the other half of him; it was above his level. There was only one man who could have played the whole of Colonel Sellers, and that was Frank Mayo.

It is a world full of surprises. They fall, too, where one is least expecting them. When I introduced Sellers into the book, Charles Dudley Warner, who was writing the story with me, proposed a change of Sellers's Christian name. Ten years before, in a remote corner of the West, he had come across a man named Eschol Sellers, and he thought that Eschol was just the right and fitting name for our Sellers, since it was odd and quaint and all that. I liked the idea, but I said that that man might turn up and object. But Warner said it couldn't happen; that he was doubtless dead by this time and, be he dead or alive, we must have the name; it was exactly the right one and we couldn't do without it. So the change was made. Warner's man was a farmer in a cheap and humble way. When the book had been out a week, a college-bred gentleman of courtly manners and ducal upholstery arrived in Hartford in a sultry state of mind and with a libel suit in his eye, and *his* name was Eschol Sellers! He had never heard of the other one and had never been within a thousand miles of him. This damaged aristocrat's program was quite definite and business-like: the American Publishing Company must suppress the edition as far as printed and change the name in the plates, or stand a suit for $10,000. He carried away the company's promise and many apologies, and we changed the name back to Colonel Mulberry Sellers in the plates. Apparently there is nothing that cannot happen. Even the existence of two unrelated men wearing the impossible name of Eschol Sellers is a possible thing.

James Lampton floated, all his days, in a tinted mist of magnificent dreams, and died at last without seeing one of them realized. I saw him last in 1884, when it had been twenty-six years since I ate the basin of raw turnips and washed them down with a bucket of water in his house. He was become old and white-headed, but he entered to me in the same old breezy way of his earlier life, and he was all there yet—not a detail wanting; the happy light in his eye, the abounding hope in his heart, the persuasive tongue, the miracle-breeding imagination—they were all there; and before I could turn around he was polishing up his Aladdin's lamp and flashing the secret riches of the world before me. I said to myself: "I did not overdraw him by a shade, I set him down as he was; and he is the same man to-day. Cable will recognize him." I asked him to excuse me a moment and ran into the next room, which was Cable's. Cable and I were stumping the Union on a reading tour. I said:

"I am going to leave your door open so that you can listen. There is a man in there who is interesting."

I went back and asked Lampton what he was doing now. He began to tell me of a "small venture" he had begun in New Mexico through his son; "only a little thing—a mere trifle—partly to amuse my leisure, partly to keep my capital from lying idle, but mainly to develop the boy—develop the boy. Fortune's wheel is ever revolving; he may have to work for his living some day—as strange things have happened in this world. But it's only a little thing—a mere trifle, as I said."

And so it was—as he began it. But under his deft hands it grew and blossomed and spread—oh, beyond imagination. At the end of half an hour he finished; finished with the remark, uttered in an adorably languid manner:

"Yes, it is but a trifle, as things go nowadays—a bagatelle—but amusing. It passes the time. The boy thinks great things of it, but he is young, you know, and imaginative; lacks the experience which comes of handling large affairs, and which tempers the fancy and perfects the judgment. I suppose there's a couple of millions in it, possibly three, but no more, I think; still, for a boy, you know, just starting in life, it is not bad. I should not want him to make a fortune—let that come later. It could turn his head, at his time of life, and in many ways be a damage to him."

Then he said something about his having left his pocketbook lying on the table in the main drawing-room at home, and about its being after banking hours, now, and—

I stopped him there and begged him to honor Cable and me by being our guest at the lecture—with as many friends as might be willing to do us the like honor. He accepted. And he thanked me as a prince might who had granted us a grace. The reason I stopped his speech about the tickets was because I saw that he was going to ask me to furnish them to him and let him pay next day; and I knew that if he made the debt he would pay it if he had to pawn his clothes. After a little further chat he shook hands heartily and affectionately and took his leave. Cable put his head in at the door and said:

"That was Colonel Sellers."

As I have said, that vast plot of Tennessee land was held by my father twenty years—intact. When he died in 1847 we began to manage it ourselves. Forty years afterward we had managed it all away except 10,000 acres, and gotten nothing to remember the sales by. About 1887—possibly it was earlier—the 10,000 went. My brother found a chance to trade it for a house and lot in the town of Corry, in the oil regions of Pennsylvania. About 1894 he sold this property for $250. That ended the Tennessee land.

If any penny of cash ever came out of my father's wise investment but that, I have no recollection of it. No, I am overlooking a detail. It furnished me a field for Sellers and a book. Out of my half of the book I got $20,000, perhaps something more; out of the play I got $75,000—just about a dollar an acre. It is curious; I was not alive when my father made the investment, therefore he was not intending any partiality; yet I was the only member of the family that ever profited by it. I shall have occasion to mention this land again now and then, as I go along, for it influenced our life in one way or another during more than a generation. Whenever things grew dark it rose and put out its hopeful Sellers hand and cheered us up, and said, "Do not be afraid—trust in me—wait." It kept us hoping and hoping during forty years, and forsook us at last. It put our energies to sleep and made visionaries of us—dreamers and indolent. We were always going to be rich next year—no occasion to work. It is good to begin life poor; it is good to begin life rich—these are wholesome; but to begin it poor and *prospectively* rich! The man who has not experienced it cannot imagine the curse of it.

My parents removed to Missouri in the early 'thirties; I do not remember just when, for I was not born then and cared nothing for such things. It was a long journey in those days, and must have been a rough and tiresome one. The home was made in the wee village of Florida, in Monroe County, and I was born there in 1835. The village contained a hundred people and I increased the population by 1 per cent. It is more than many of the best men in history could have done for a town. It may not be modest in me to refer to this, but it is true. There is no record of a person doing as much—not even Shakespeare. But I did it for Florida, and it shows that I could have done it for any place—even London, I suppose.

Recently some one in Missouri has sent me a picture of the house I was born in. Heretofore I have always stated that it was a palace, but I shall be more guarded now.

I used to remember my brother Henry walking into a fire outdoors when he was a week old. It was remarkable in me to remember a thing like that, and it was still more remarkable that I should cling to the delusion, for thirty years, that I *did* remember it—for of course it never happened; he would not have been able to walk at that age. If I had stopped to reflect, I should not have burdened my memory with that impossible rubbish so long. It is believed by many people that an impression deposited in a child's memory within the first two years of its life cannot remain there five years, but that is an error. The incident of Benvenuto Cellini and the salamander must be accepted as authentic and trustworthy; and then that remarkable and indisputable instance in the experience of Helen Keller—However, I will speak of that at another time. For many years I believed that I remembered helping my grandfather drink his whisky toddy when I was six weeks old, but I do not tell about that any more, now; I am grown old and my memory is not as active as it used to be. When I was younger I could remember anything, whether it had happened or not; but my faculties are decaying now, and soon I shall be so I cannot remember any but the things that never happened. It is sad to go to pieces like this, but we all have to do it.

My uncle, John A. Quarles, was a farmer, and his place was in the country four miles from Florida. He had eight children and fifteen or twenty negroes, and was also fortunate in other ways, particularly in his character. I have not come across a better man than he was. I was his guest for two or three months every year, from the fourth year after we removed to Hannibal till I was eleven or twelve years old. I have never consciously used him or his wife in a book, but his farm has come very handy to me in literature once or twice. In *Huck Finn* and in *Tom Sawyer, Detective* I moved it down to Arkansas. It was all of six hundred miles, but it was no trouble; it was not a very large farm—five hundred acres, perhaps—but I could have done it if it had been twice as large. And as for the morality of it, I cared nothing for that; I would move a state if the exigencies of literature required it.

It was a heavenly place for a boy, that farm of my Uncle John's. The house was a double log one, with a spacious floor (roofed in) connecting it with the kitchen. In the summer the table was set in the middle of that shady and breezy floor, and the sumptuous meals—well, it makes me cry to think of them. Fried chicken, roast pig; wild and tame turkeys, ducks, and geese; venison just killed; squirrels, rabbits, pheasants, partridges, prairie-chickens; biscuits, hot batter cakes, hot buckwheat cakes, hot "wheat bread," hot rolls, hot corn pone; fresh corn boiled on the ear, succotash, butter-beans, string-beans, tomatoes, peas,

Irish potatoes, sweet potatoes; buttermilk, sweet milk, "clabber"; watermelons, muskmelons, cantaloupes—all fresh from the garden; apple pie, peach pie, pumpkin pie, apple dumplings, peach cobbler—I can't remember the rest. The way that the things were cooked was perhaps the main splendor—particularly a certain few of the dishes. For instance, the corn bread, the hot biscuits and wheat bread, and the fried chicken. These things have never been properly cooked in the North—in fact, no one there is able to learn the art, so far as my experience goes. The North thinks it knows how to make corn bread, but this is a mere superstition. Perhaps no bread in the world is quite so good as Southern corn bread, and perhaps no bread in the world is quite so bad as the Northern imitation for it. The North seldom tries to fry chicken, and this is well; the art cannot be learned north of the line of Mason and Dixon, nor anywhere in Europe. This is not hearsay; it is experience that is speaking. In Europe it is imagined that the custom of serving various kinds of bread blazing hot is "American," but it is too broad a spread; it is custom in the South, but is much less than that in the North. In the North and in Europe hot bread is considered unhealthy. This is probably another fussy superstition, like the European superstition that ice-water is unhealthy. Europe does not need ice-water and does not drink it; and yet, notwithstanding this, its word for it is better than ours, because it describes it, whereas ours doesn't. Europe calls it "iced" water. Our word describes water made from melted ice—a drink which has a characterless taste and which we have but little acquaintance with.

It seems a pity that the world should throw away so many good things merely because they are unwholesome. I doubt if God has given us any refreshment which, taken in moderation, is unwholesome, except microbes. Yet there are people who strictly deprive themselves of each and every eatable, drinkable, and smokable which has in any way acquired a shady reputation. They pay this price for health. And health is all they get for it. How strange it is! It is like paying out your whole fortune for a cow that has gone dry.

The farmhouse stood in the middle of a very large yard, and the yard was fenced on three sides with rails and on the rear side with palings; against these stood the smoke-house; beyond the palings was the orchard; beyond the orchard were the negro quarters and the tobacco fields. The front yard was entered over a stile made of sawed-off logs of graduated heights; I do not remember any gate. In a corner of the front yard were a dozen lofty hickory trees and a dozen black walnuts, and in the nutting season riches were to be gathered there.

Down a piece, abreast the house, stood a little log cabin against the rail fence; and there the woody hill fell sharply away, past the barns, the corn-crib, the stables, and the tobacco-curing house, to a limpid brook which sang along over its gravelly bed and curved and frisked in and out and here and there and yonder in the deep shade of overhanging foliage and vines—a divine place for wading, and it had swimming pools, too, which were forbidden to us and therefore much frequented by us. For we were little Christian children and had early been taught the value of forbidden fruit.

In the little log cabin lived a bedridden white-headed slave woman whom we visited daily and looked upon with awe, for we believed she was upward of a thousand years old and had talked with Moses. The younger negroes credited these statistics and had furnished them to us in good faith. We accommodated all the details which came to us about her; and so we believed that she had lost her health in the long desert trip coming out of Egypt, and had never been able to get it back again. She had a round bald place on the crown of her head, and we used to creep around and gaze at it in reverent silence, and reflect that it was caused by fright through seeing Pharaoh drowned. We called her "Aunt" Hannah, Southern fashion. She was superstitious, like the other negroes; also, like them, she was deeply religious. Like them, she had great faith in prayer and employed it in all ordinary exigencies, but not in cases where a dead certainty of result was urgent. Whenever witches were around she tied up the remnant of her wool in little tufts, with white thread, and this promptly made the witches impotent.

All the negroes were friends of ours, and with those of our own age we were in effect comrades. I say in effect, using the phrase as a modification. We were comrades, and yet not comrades; color and condition interposed a subtle line which both parties were conscious of and which rendered complete fusion impossible. We had a faithful and affectionate good friend, ally, and adviser in "Uncle Dan'l," a middle-aged slave whose head was the best one in the negro quarter, whose sympathies were wide and warm, and whose heart was honest and simple and knew no guile. He has served me well these many, many years. I have not seen him for more than half a century, and yet spiritually I have had his welcome company a good part of that time, and have staged him in books under his own name and as "Jim," and carted him all around—to Hannibal, down the Mississippi on a raft, and even across the Desert of Sahara in a balloon—and he has endured it all with the patience and friendliness and loyalty which were his birthright. It was on the farm that I got my strong liking for his race and my appreciation of certain of its fine qualities. This feeling and this estimate have stood the test of sixty years and more, and have suffered no impairment. The black face is as welcome to me now as it was then.

In my schoolboy days I had no aversion to slavery. I was not aware that there was anything wrong about it. No one arraigned it in my hearing; the local papers said nothing against it; the local pulpit taught us that God approved it, that it was a holy thing, and that the doubter need only look in the Bible if he wished to settle his mind—and then the texts were read aloud to us to make the matter sure; if the slaves themselves had an aversion to slavery, they were wise and said nothing. In Hannibal we seldom saw a slave misused; on the farm, never.

There was, however, one small incident of my boyhood days which touched this matter, and it must have meant a good deal to me or it would not have stayed in my memory, clear and sharp, vivid and shadowless, all these slow-drifting years. We had a little slave boy whom we had hired from some one, there in Hannibal. He was from the eastern shore of Maryland, and had been brought away across the American continent, and sold. He was a cheery spirit, innocent and gentle, and the noisiest creature that ever was, perhaps. All day long he was singing, whistling, yelling, whooping, laughing—it was maddening, devastating, unendurable. At last, one day, I lost all my temper, and went raging to my mother and said Sandy had been singing for an hour without a single break, and I couldn't stand it, and *wouldn't* she please shut him up. The tears came into her eyes and her lip trembled, and she said something like this:

"Poor thing, when he sings it shows that he is not remembering and that comforts me; but when he is still I am afraid he is thinking, and I cannot bear it. He will never see his mother again; if he can sing, I must not hinder it, but be thankful for it. If you were older, you would understand me; then that friendless child's noise would make you glad."

It was a simple speech and made up of small words, but it went home, and Sandy's noise was not a trouble to me any more. She never used large words, but she had a natural gift for making small ones do effective work. She lived to reach the neighborhood of ninety years and was capable with her tongue to the last—especially when a meanness or an injustice roused her spirit. She has come handy to me several times in my books, where she figures as Tom Sawyer's Aunt Polly. I fitted her out with a dialect and tried to think up other improvements for her, but did not find any. I used Sandy once, also; it was in *Tom Sawyer*. I tried to get him to whitewash the fence, but it did not work. I do not remember what name I called him by in the book.

I can see the farm yet, with perfect clearness. I can see all its belongings, all its details; the family room of the house, with a "trundle" bed in one corner and a spinning-wheel in another—a wheel whose rising and falling wail, heard from a distance, was the mournfullest of all sounds to me, and made me homesick and low spirited, and filled my atmosphere with the wandering spirits of the dead; the vast fireplace, piled high, on winter nights, with flaming hickory logs from whose ends a sugary sap bubbled out, but did not go to waste, for we scraped it off and ate it; the lazy cat spread out on the rough hearthstones; the drowsy dogs braced against the jambs and blinking; my aunt in one chimney corner, knitting; my uncle in the other, smoking his corncob pipe; the slick and carpetless oak floor faintly mirroring the dancing flame tongues and freckled with black indentations where fire coals had popped out and died a leisurely death; half a dozen children romping in the background twilight; "split"-bottomed chairs here and there, some with rockers; a cradle—out of service, but waiting, with confidence; in the early cold mornings a snuggle of children in shirts and chemises, occupying the hearthstone and procrastinating—they could not bear to leave that comfortable place and go out on the wind-swept floor space between the house and kitchen where the general tin basin stood, and wash.

Along outside of the front fence ran the country road, dusty in the summertime, and a good place for snakes—they liked to lie in it and sun themselves; when they were rattlesnakes or puff-adders, we killed them; when they were black snakes, or racers or belonged to the fabled "hoop" breed, we fled, without shame; when they were "house snakes," or "garters," we carried them home and put

them in Aunt Patsy's workbasket for a surprise; for she was prejudiced against snakes,
and always when she took the basket in her
lap and they began to climb out of it it disordered her mind. She never could seem to get
used to them; her opportunities went for nothing. And she was always cold toward bats,
too, and could not bear them; and yet I think
a bat is as friendly a bird as there is. My
mother was Aunt Patsy's sister and had the
same wild superstitions. A bat is beautifully
soft and silky; I do not know any creature
that is pleasanter to the touch or is more grateful for caressings, if offered in the right spirit.
I know all about these coleoptera, because our
great cave, three miles below Hannibal, was
multitudinously stocked with them, and often
I brought them home to amuse my mother
with. It was easy to manage if it was a school
day, because then I had ostensibly been to
school and hadn't any bats. She was not a
suspicious person, but full of trust and confidence; and when I said, "There's something in my coat pocket for you," she would
put her hand in. But she always took it out
again, herself; I didn't have to tell her. It
was remarkable, the way she couldn't learn
to like private bats. The more experience
she had, the more she could not change her
views.

I think she was never in the cave in her life;
but everybody else went there. Many excursion parties came from considerable distances
up and down the river to visit the cave. It
was miles in extent and was a tangled wilderness of narrow and lofty clefts and passages.
It was an easy place to get lost in; anybody
could do it—including the bats. I got lost in
it myself, along with a lady, and our last candle burned down to almost nothing before we
glimpsed the search party's lights winding
about in the distance.

"Injun Joe," the half-breed, got lost in
there once, and would have starved to death
if the bats had run short. But there was no
chance of that; there were myriads of them.
He told me all his story. In the book called
Tom Sawyer I starved him entirely to death in
the cave, but that was in the interest of art; it
never happened. "General" Gaines, who was
our first town drunkard before Jimmy Finn
got the place, was lost in there for the space of
a week, and finally pushed his handkerchief
out of a hole in a hilltop near Saverton, several
miles down the river from the cave's mouth,
and somebody saw it and dug him out. There
is nothing the matter with his statistics except
the handkerchief. I knew him for years and

he hadn't any. But it could have been his
nose. That would attract attention.

The cave was an uncanny place, for it contained a corpse—the corpse of a young girl of
fourteen. It was in a glass cylinder inclosed in
a copper one which was suspended from a rail
which bridged a narrow passage. The body
was preserved in alcohol, and it was said that
loafers and rowdies used to drag it up by the
hair and look at the dead face. The girl was
the daughter of a St. Louis surgeon of extraordinary ability and wide celebrity. He was an
eccentric man and did many strange things.
He put the poor thing in that forlorn place
himself.

Beyond the road where the snakes sunned
themselves was a dense young thicket, and
through it a dim-lighted path led a quarter of
a mile; then out of the dimness one emerged
abruptly upon a level great prairie which was
covered with wild strawberry plants, vividly
starred with prairie pinks, and walled in on all
sides by forests. The strawberries were fragrant and fine, and in the season we were generally there in the crisp freshness of the early
morning, while the dew beads still sparkled upon the grass and the woods were ringing with
the first songs of the birds.

Down the forest slopes to the left were the
swings. They were made of bark stripped
from hickory saplings. When they became dry
they were dangerous. They usually broke
when a child was forty feet in the air, and this
was why so many bones had to be mended
every year. I had no ill luck myself, but none
of my cousins escaped. There were eight of
them, and at one time and another they broke
fourteen arms among them. But it cost next
to nothing, for the doctor worked by the year
—twenty-five dollars for the whole family. I
remember two of the Florida doctors, Chow-
ning and Meredith. They not only tended an
entire family for twenty-five dollars a year, but
furnished the medicines themselves. Good
measure, too. Only the largest persons could
hold a whole dose. Castor Oil was the principal beverage. The dose was half a dipperful
with half a dipperful of New Orleans molasses
added to help it down and make it taste good,
which it never did. The next standby was
calomel; the next, rhubarb; and the next, jalap.
Then they bled the patient, and put mustard
plasters on him. It was a dreadful system, and
yet the death rate was not heavy. The calomel
was nearly sure to salivate the patient and
cost him some of his teeth. There were no
dentists. When teeth became touched with

decay or were otherwise ailing, the doctor knew of but one thing to do—he fetched his tongs and dragged them out. If the jaw remained, it was not his fault. Doctors were not called in cases of ordinary illness; the family grandmother attended to those. Every old woman was a doctor, and gathered her own medicines in the woods, and knew how to compound doses that would stir the vitals of a cast-iron dog. And then there was the "Indian doctor"; a grave savage, remnant of his tribe, deeply read in the mysteries of nature and the secret properties of herbs; and most backwoodsmen had high faith in his powers and could tell of wonderful cures achieved by him. In Mauritius, away off yonder in the solitudes of the Indian Ocean, there is a person who answers to our Indian doctor of the old times. He is a negro, and has had no teaching as a doctor, yet there is one disease which he is master of and can cure and the doctors can't. They send for him when they have a case. It is a child's disease of a strange and deadly sort, and the negro cures it with a herb medicine which he makes, himself, from a prescription which has come down to him from his father and grandfather. He will not let anyone see it. He keeps the secret of its components to himself, and it is feared that he will die without divulging it; then there will be consternation in Mauritius. I was told these things by the people there, in 1896.

We had the "faith doctor," too, in those early days—a woman. Her specialty was toothache. She was a farmer's old wife and lived five miles from Hannibal. She would lay her hand on the patient's jaw and say, "Believe"; and the cure was prompt. Mrs. Utterback. I remember her very well. Twice I rode out there behind my mother, horseback, and saw the cure performed. My mother was the patient.

Dr. Meredith removed to Hannibal, by and by, and was our family physician there, and saved my life several times. Still, he was a good man and meant well. Let it go.

I was always told that I was a sickly and precarious and tiresome and uncertain child, and lived mainly on allopathic medicines during the first seven years of my life. I asked my mother about this, in her old age—she was in her eighty-eighth year—and said:

"I suppose that during all that time you were uneasy about me?"

"Yes, the whole time."

"Afraid I wouldn't live?"

After a reflective pause—ostensibly to think out the facts—"No—afraid you would."

The country schoolhouse was three miles from my uncle's farm. It stood in a clearing in the woods and would hold about twenty-five boys and girls. We attended the school with more or less regularity once or twice a week, in summer, walking to it in the cool of the morning by the forest paths, and back in the gloaming at the end of the day. All the pupils brought their dinners in baskets—corn dodger, buttermilk, and other good things—and sat in the shade of the trees at noon and ate them. It is the part of my education which I look back upon with the most satisfaction. My first visit to the school was when I was seven. A strapping girl of fifteen, in the customary sunbonnet and calico dress, asked me if I "used tobacco"—meaning did I chew it. I said no. It roused her scorn. She reported me to all the crowd, and said:

"Here is a boy seven years old who can't chew tobacco."

By the looks and comments which this produced I realized that I was a degraded object, and was cruelly ashamed of myself. I was determined to reform. But I only made myself sick; I was not able to learn to chew tobacco. I learned to smoke fairly well, but that did not conciliate anybody and I remained a poor thing, and characterless. I longed to be respected, but I was never able to rise. Children have but little charity for one another's defects.

As I have said, I spent some part of every year at the farm until I was twelve or thirteen years old. The life which I led there with my cousins was full of charm, and so is the memory of it yet. I can call back the solemn twilight and mystery of the deep woods, the earthy smells, the faint odors of the wild flowers, the sheen of rain-washed foliage, the rattling clatter of drops when the wind shook the trees, the far-off hammering of woodpeckers and the muffled drumming of wood pheasants in the remoteness of the forest, the snapshot glimpses of disturbed wild creatures scurrying through the grass—I can call it all back and make it as real as it ever was, and as blessed. I can call back the prairie, and its loneliness and peace, and a vast hawk hanging motionless in the sky, with his wings spread wide and the blue of the vault showing through the fringe of their end feathers. I can see the woods in their autumn dress, the oaks purple, the hickories washed with gold, the maples and the sumachs luminous with crimson fires, and I can hear the rustle made by the fallen leaves as we plowed through them. I can see the blue clusters of wild grapes hanging among the foliage of the saplings, and I remember the taste of them and the smell. I know how the wild blackberries looked, and how they tasted, and the same with the pawpaws, the hazelnuts, and the persimmons; and I can feel the thumping rain, upon my head, of hickory nuts and walnuts when we were out in the frosty dawn to scramble for them with the pigs, and the gusts of wind loosed them and sent them down. I know the stain of blackberries, and how pretty it is, and I know the stain of walnut hulls, and how little it minds soap and water, also what grudged experience it had of either of them. I know the taste of maple sap, and when to gather it, and how to arrange the troughs and delivery tubes, and how to boil down the juice, and how to hook the sugar after it is made, also how much better hooked sugar tastes than any that is honestly come by, let bigots say what they will. I know how a prize watermelon looks when it is sunning its fat rotundity among pumpkin vines and "simblins"; I know how to tell when it is ripe without "plugging" it; I know how inviting it looks when it is cooling itself in a tub of water under the bed, waiting; I know how it looks when it lies on the table in the sheltered great floor space between house and kitchen, and the children gathered for the sacrifice and their mouths watering; I know the crackling sound it makes when the carving knife enters its end, and I can see the split fly along in front of the blade as the knife cleaves its way to the other end; I can see its halves fall apart and display the rich red meat and the black seeds, and the heart standing up, a luxury fit for the elect; I know how a boy looks behind a yard-long slice of that melon, and I know how he feels; for I have been there. I know the taste of watermelon which has been honestly come by, and I know the taste of the watermelon which has been acquired by art. Both taste good, but the experienced know which tastes best. I know the look of green apples and peaches and pears on the trees, and I know how entertaining they are when they are inside of a person. I know how ripe ones look when they are piled in pyramids under the trees, and how pretty they are and how vivid their colors. I know how a frozen apple looks, in a barrel down cellar in the wintertime, and how hard it is to bite, and how the frost makes the teeth ache, and yet how good it is, notwithstanding. I know the disposition of elderly people to select the specked apples for the children, and I once knew ways to beat the game. I know the look of an apple that is roasting and sizzling on a hearth on a winter's evening, and I know the comfort that comes of eating it hot, along with some sugar and a drench of cream. I know the delicate art and mystery of so cracking hickory nuts and walnuts on a flatiron with a hammer that the kernels will be delivered whole, and I know how the nuts, taken in conjunction with winter apples, cider, and doughnuts, make old people's old tales and old jokes sound fresh and crisp and enchanting, and juggle an evening away before you know what went with the time. I know the look of Uncle Dan'l's kitchen as it was on the privileged nights, when I was a child, and I can see the white and black children grouped on the hearth, with the firelight playing on their faces and the shadows flickering upon the walls, clear back toward the cavernous gloom of the rear, and I can hear Uncle Dan'l telling the immortal tales which Uncle Remus Harris was to gather into his book and charm the world with, by and by; and I can feel again the creepy joy which quivered through me when the time for the ghost story was reached—and the sense of regret, too, which came over me, for it was always the last story of the evening and there was nothing between it and the unwelcome bed.

I can remember the bare wooden stairway in my uncle's house, and the turn to the left above the landing, and the rafters and the slanting roof over my bed, and the squares of moonlight on the floor and the white cold world of snow outside, seen through the curtainless window. I can remember the howling of the wind and the quaking of the house on stormy nights, and how snug and cozy one felt, under the blankets, listening; and how the powdery snow used to sift in, around the sashes, and lie in little ridges on the floor and make the place look chilly in the morning and curb the wild desire to get up—in case there was any. I can remember how very dark that room was, in the dark of the moon, and how packed it was with ghostly stillness when one woke up by accident away in the night, and forgotten sins came flocking out of the secret chambers of the memory and wanted a hearing; and how ill chosen the time seemed for this kind of business; and how dismal was the hoo-hooing of the owl and the wailing of the wolf, sent mourning by on the night wind.

I remember the raging of the rain on that roof, summer nights, and how pleasant it was to lie and listen to it, and enjoy the white splendor of the lightning and the majestic booming and crashing of the thunder. It was a very satisfactory room, and there was a lightning rod which was reachable from the window, an adorable and skittish thing to climb up and down, summer nights, when there were duties on hand of a sort to make privacy desirable.

I remember the 'coon and 'possum hunts, nights, with the negroes, and the long marches through the black gloom of the woods, and the excitement which fired everybody when the distant bay of an experienced dog announced that the game was treed; then the wild scramblings and stumblings through briers and bushes and over roots to get to the spot; then the lighting of a fire and the felling of the tree, the joyful frenzy of the dogs and the negroes, and the weird picture it all made in the red glare—I remember it all well, and the delight that everyone got out of it, except the 'coon.

I remember the pigeon seasons, when the birds would come in millions and cover the trees and by their weight break down the branches. They were clubbed to death with sticks; guns were not necessary and were not used. I remember the squirrel hunts, and prairie-chicken hunts, and wild-turkey hunts, and all that; and how we turned out, mornings, while it was still dark, to go on these expeditions, and how chilly and dismal it was, and how often I regretted that I was well enough to go. A toot on a tin horn brought twice as many dogs as were needed, and in their happiness they raced and scampered about, and knocked small people down, and made no end of unnecessary noise. At the word, they vanished away toward the woods, and we drifted silently after them in the melancholy gloom. But presently the gray dawn stole over the world, the birds piped up, then the sun rose and poured light and comfort all around, everything was fresh and dewy and fragrant, and life was a boon again. After three hours of tramping we arrived back wholesomely tired, overladen with game, very hungry, and just in time for breakfast. . . .

[A Boy's Life]

My mother had a good deal of trouble with me, but I think she enjoyed it. She had none at all with my brother Henry, who was two years younger than I, and I think that the unbroken monotony of his goodness and truthfulness and obedience would have been a burden to her but for the relief and variety which I furnished in the other direction. I was a tonic. I was valuable to her. I never thought of it before, but now I see it. I never knew Henry to do a vicious thing toward me, or toward anyone else—but he frequently did righteous ones that cost me heavily. It was his duty to report me, when I needed reporting and neglected to do it myself, and he was very faithful in discharging that duty. He is Sid in Tom Sawyer. But Sid was not Henry. Henry was a very much finer and better boy than Sid ever was.

It was Henry who called my mother's attention to the fact that the thread with which she had sewed my collar together to keep me from going in swimming had changed color. My mother would not have discovered it but for that, and she was manifestly piqued when she recognized that that prominent bit of circumstantial evidence had escaped her sharp eye. That detail probably added a detail to my punishment. It is human. We generally visit our shortcomings on somebody else when there is a possible excuse for it—but no matter. I took it out of Henry. There is always compensation for such as are unjustly used. I often took it out of him—sometimes as an advance payment for something which I hadn't yet done. These were occasions when the opportunity was too strong a temptation, and I had to draw on the future. I did not need to copy this idea from my mother, and probably didn't. It is most likely that I invented it for myself. Still, she wrought upon that principle upon occasion.

If the incident of the broken sugar bowl is in Tom Sawyer—I don't remember whether it is or not—that is an example of it. Henry never stole sugar. He took it openly from the bowl. His mother knew he wouldn't take sugar when she wasn't looking, but she had her doubts about me. Not exactly doubts, either. She knew very well I would. One day when she was not present Henry took sugar from her prized and precious old-English sugar bowl, which was an heirloom in the family—and he managed to break the bowl. It was the first time I had ever had a chance to tell anything on him, and I was inexpressibly glad. I told him I was going to tell on him, but he was not disturbed. When my mother came in and saw the bowl lying on the floor in fragments, she was speechless for a minute. I allowed that silence to work; I judged it would increase the effect. I was waiting for her to ask, "Who did it?"—so that I could fetch out my news. But it was an error of calculation. When she got through with her silence she didn't ask anything about it—she merely gave me a crack on the skull with her thimble that I felt all the way down to my heels. Then I broke out with my injured innocence, expecting to make her very sorry that she had punished the wrong one. I expected her to do something remorseful and pathetic. I told her that I was not the one—it was Henry. But there was no upheaval. She said, without emotion: "It's all right. It isn't any matter. You deserve it for something you've done that I didn't know about; and if you haven't done it, why then you deserve it for something that you are going to do that I shan't hear about."

There was a stairway outside the house, which led up to the rear part of the second story. One day Henry was sent on an errand, and he took a tin bucket along. I knew he would have to ascend those stairs, so I went up and locked the door on the inside, and came down into the garden, which had been newly ploughed and was rich in choice, firm clods of black mold. I gathered a generous equipment of these and ambushed him. I waited till he had climbed the stairs and was near the landing and couldn't escape. Then I bombarded him with clods, which he warded off with his tin bucket the best he could but without much success, for I was a good marksman. The clods smashing against the weather-boarding fetched my mother out to see what was the matter, and I tried to explain that I was amusing Henry. Both of them were after me in a minute, but I knew the way over that high board fence and escaped for that time. After an hour or two, when I ventured back, there was no one around and I thought the incident was closed. But it was not so. Henry was ambushing me. With an unusually competent aim for him, he landed a stone on the side of my head which raised a bump there which felt like the Matterhorn. I carried it to my mother straightway for sympathy, but she was not strongly moved. It seemed to be her idea that incidents like this would eventually reform me if I harvested enough of them. So the matter was only educational. I had had a sterner view of it than that before.

Whenever my conduct was of such exaggerated impropriety that my mother's extemporary punishments were inadequate, she saved the matter up for Sunday and made me go to church Sunday night—which was a penalty sometimes bearable, perhaps, but as a rule it was not, and I avoided it for the sake of my constitution. She would never believe that I had been to church until she had applied her test. She made me tell her what the text was. That was a simple matter—caused me no

trouble. I didn't have to go to church to get a text. I selected one for myself. This worked very well until one time when my text and the one furnished by a neighbor, who had been to church, didn't tally. After that my mother took other methods. I don't know what they were now.

In those days men and boys wore rather long cloaks in the wintertime. They were black, and were lined with very bright and showy Scotch plaids. One winter's night when I was starting to church to square a crime of some kind committed during the week, I hid my cloak near the gate and went off and played with the other boys until church was over. Then I returned home. But in the dark I put the cloak on wrong side out, entered the room, threw the cloak aside, and then stood the usual examination. I got along very well until the temperature of the church was mentioned. My mother said, "It must have been impossible to keep warm there on such a night."

I didn't see the art of that remark, and was foolish enough to explain that I wore my cloak all the time that I was in church. She asked if I kept it on from church home, too. I didn't see the bearing of that remark. I said that that was what I had done. She said: "You wore it with that red Scotch plaid outside and glaring? Didn't that attract any attention?"

Of course to continue such a dialogue would have been tedious and unprofitable, and I let it go and took the consequences.

That was about 1849. Tom Nash was a boy of my own age—the postmaster's son. The Mississippi was frozen across, and he and I went skating one night, probably without permission. I cannot see why we should go skating in the night unless without permission, for there could be no considerable amusement to be gotten out of skating at midnight if nobody was going to object to it. About midnight, when we were more than half a mile out toward the Illinois shore, we heard some ominous rumbling and grinding and crashing going on between us and the home side of the river, and we knew what it meant—the river was breaking up. We started for home, pretty badly scared. We flew along at full speed whenever the moonlight sifting down between the clouds enabled us to tell which was ice and which was water. In the pauses we waited, started again whenever there was a good bridge of ice, paused again when we came to naked water, and waited in distress until a floating vast cake should bridge the place. It took us an hour to make the trip—a trip which we made in a misery of apprehension all the time. But at last we arrived within a very brief distance of the shore. We waited again. There was another place that needed bridging. All about us the ice was plunging and grinding along and piling itself up in mountains on the shore, and the dangers were increasing, not diminishing. We grew very impatient to get to solid ground, so we started too early and went springing from cake to cake. Tom made a miscalculation and fell short. He got a bitter bath, but he was so close to shore that he only had to swim a stroke or two—then his feet struck hard bottom and he crawled out. I ar-rived a little later, without accident. We had been in a drenching perspiration and Tom's bath was a disaster for him. He took to his bed, sick, and had a procession of diseases. The closing one was scarlet fever, and he came out of it stone deaf. Within a year or two speech departed, of course. But some years later he was taught to talk, after a fashion—one couldn't always make out what it was he was trying to say. Of course he could not modulate his voice, since he couldn't hear him-self talk. When he supposed he was talking low and confidentially, you could hear him in Illinois.

[His Tribute to his Wife]

[New York, February 1, 1906]

To-morrow will be the thirty-sixth anniver-sary of our marriage. My wife passed from this life one year and eight months ago, in Florence, Italy, after an unbroken illness of twenty-two months' duration.

I saw her first in the form of an ivory minia-ture in her brother Charley's stateroom in the steamer *Quaker City* in the Bay of Smyrna, in the summer of 1867, when she was in her twenty-second year. I saw her in the flesh for the first time in New York in the following December. She was slender and beautiful and girlish—and she was both girl and woman. She remained both girl and woman to the last day of her life. Under a grave and gentle ex-terior burned inextinguishable fires of sympa-thy, energy, devotion, enthusiasm, and abso-lutely limitless affection. She was *always* frail in body, and she lived upon her spirit, whose hopefulness and courage were indestructible. Perfect truth, perfect honesty, perfect candor, were qualities of her character which were born with her. Her judgments of people and things were sure and accurate. Her intuitions almost never deceived her. In her judgments of the characters and acts of both friends and stran-gers there was always room for charity, and this charity never failed. I have compared and contrasted her with hundreds of persons, and my conviction remains that hers was the most perfect character I have ever met. And I may add that she was the most winningly dignified person I have ever known. Her character and disposition were of the sort that not only invite worship, but command it. No servant ever left her service who deserved to remain in it. And as she could choose with a glance of her eye, the servants she selected did in almost all cases deserve to remain, and they *did* remain. She was always cheerful; and she was always able to communicate her cheerfulness to others. During the nine years that we spent in pov-erty and debt she was always able to reason me out of my despairs and find a bright side to the clouds and make me see it. In all that time I never knew her to utter a word of regret con-cerning our altered circumstances, nor did I ever know her children to do the like. For she had taught them, and they drew their forti-tude from her. The love which she bestowed upon those whom she loved took the form of worship, and in that form it was returned—re-turned by relatives, friends, and the servants of her household. It was a strange combina-tion which wrought into one individual, so to speak, by marriage—her disposition and char-acter and mine. She poured out her prodigal affections in kisses and caresses, and in a vo-cabulary of endearments whose profusion was always an astonishment to me. I was born *re-served* as to endearments of speech, and caress-es, and hers broke upon me as the summer waves break upon Gibraltar. I was reared in that atmosphere of reserve. As I have already said, I never knew a member of my father's family to kiss another member of it except once, and that at a death bed. And our village was not a kissing community. The kissing and caressing ended with courtship—along with the deadly piano-playing of that day.

She had the heart-free laugh of a girl. It came seldom, but when it broke upon the ear it was as inspiring as music. I heard it for the last time when she had been occupying her sick bed for more than a year, and I made a written note of it at the time—a note not to be repeated. . . .

WILLIAM DEAN HOWELLS (1837-1920)
From CRITICISM AND FICTION[1]
(1886-91)

The question of a final criterion for the appreciation of art is one that perpetually recurs to those interested in any sort of æsthetic endeavor. Mr. John Addington Symonds, in a chapter of *The Rennaissance in Italy* treating of the Bolognese school of painting, which once had so great cry, and was vaunted the supreme exemplar of the grand style, but which he now believes fallen into lasting contempt for its emptiness and soullessness, seeks to determine whether there can be an enduring criterion or not; and his conclusion is applicable to literature as to the other arts. "Our hope," he says, "with regard to the unity of taste in the future then is, that all sentimental or academical seekings after the ideal having been abandoned, momentary theories founded upon idiosyncratic or temporary partialities exploded, and nothing accepted but what is solid and positive, the scientific spirit shall make men progressively more and more conscious of these *bleibende Verhältnisse*, more and more capable of living in the whole; also, that in proportion as we gain a firmer hold upon our own place in the world, we shall come to comprehend with more instinctive certitude what is simple, natural, and honest, welcoming with gladness all artistic products that exhibit these qualities. The perception of the enlightened man will then be the task of a healthy person who has made himself acquainted with the laws of evolution in art and in society, and is able to test the excellence of work in any stage from immaturity to decadence by discerning what there is of truth, sincerity, and natural vigor in it."

I

That is to say, as I understand, that moods and tastes and fashions change; people fancy now this and now that; but what is unpretentious and what is true is always beautiful and good, and nothing else is so. This is not saying that fantastic and monstrous and artificial things do not please; everybody knows that they do please immensely for a time, and then, after the lapse of a much longer time, they have the charm of the rococo. Nothing is more curious than the charm that fashion has.

[1] Copyright 1891 by Harper and Brothers; copyright 1918 by Mildred Howells and John Mead Howells.

Fashion in women's dress, almost every fashion, is somehow delightful, else it would never have been the fashion; but if any one will look through a collection of old fashion plates, he must own that most fashions have been ugly. A few, which could be readily instanced, have been very pretty, and even beautiful, but it is doubtful if these have pleased the greatest number of people. The ugly delights as well as the beautiful, and not merely because the ugly in fashion is associated with the young loveliness of the women who wear the ugly fashions, and wins a grace from them, not because the vast majority of mankind are tasteless, but for some cause that is not perhaps ascertainable. It is quite as likely to return in the fashions of our clothes and houses and furniture, and poetry and fiction and painting, as the beautiful, and it may be from an instinctive or a reasoned sense of this that some of the extreme naturalists have refused to make the old discrimination against it, or to regard the ugly as any less worthy of celebration in art than the beautiful; some of them, in fact, seem to regard it as rather more worthy, if anything. Possibly there is no absolutely ugly, no absolutely beautiful; or possibly the ugly contains always an element of the beautiful better adapted to the general appreciation than the more perfectly beautiful. This is a somewhat discouraging conjecture, but I offer it for no more than it is worth; and I do not pin my faith to the saying of one whom I heard denying, the other day, that a thing of beauty was a joy forever. He contended that Keats's line should have read, "Some things of beauty are sometimes joys forever," and that any assertion beyond this was too hazardous.

II

I should, indeed, prefer another line of Keats's, if I were to profess any formulated creed, and should feel much safer with his "Beauty is Truth, Truth Beauty," than even with my friend's reformation of the more quoted verse. It brings us back to the solid ground taken by Mr. Symonds, which is not essentially different from that taken in the great Mr. Burke's *Essay on the Sublime and the Beautiful*—a singularly modern book, considering how long ago it was wrote (as the great Mr. Steele would have written the participle a little longer ago), and full of certain well-mannered and agreeable instruction. In some things it is of that droll little eighteenth-century world, when philosophy had got the neat little universe into the hollow of its hand, and knew just what it was, and what it was for; but it is quite without arrogance. "As for those called critics," the author says, "they have generally sought the rule of the arts in the wrong place; they have sought among poems, pictures, engravings, statues, and buildings; but art can never give the rules that make an art. This is, I believe, the reason why artists in general, and poets principally, have been confined in so narrow a circle; they have been rather imitators of one another than of nature. Critics follow them, and therefore can do little as guides. I can judge but poorly of anything while I measure it by no other standard than itself. The true standard of the arts is in every man's power; and an easy observation of the most common, sometimes of the meanest things, in nature will give the truest lights, where the greatest sagacity and industry that slights such observation must leave us in the dark, or, what is worse, amuse and mislead us by false lights."

If this should happen to be true—and it certainly commends itself to acceptance—it might portend an immediate danger to the vested interests of criticism, only that it was written a hundred years ago; and we shall probably have the "sagacity and industry that slights the observation" of nature long enough yet to allow most critics the time to learn some more useful trade than criticism as they pursue it. Nevertheless, I am in hopes that the communistic era in taste foreshadowed by Burke is approaching, and that it will occur within the lives of men now overawed by the foolish old superstition that literature and art are anything but the expression of life, and are to be judged by any other test than that of their fidelity to it. The time is coming, I hope, when each new author, each new artist, will be considered, not in his proportion to any other author or artist, but in his relation to the human nature, known to us all, which it is his privilege, his high duty, to interpret. "The true standard of the artist is in every man's power" already, as Burke says; Michelangelo's "light of the piazza," the glance of the common eye, is and always was the best light on a statue; Goethe's "boys and blackbirds" have in all ages been the real connoisseurs of berries; but hitherto the mass of common men have

been afraid to apply their own simplicity, naturalness, and honesty to the appreciation of the beautiful. They have always cast about for the instruction of some one who professed to know better, and who browbeat wholesome common-sense into the self-distrust that ends in sophistication. They have fallen generally to the worst of this bad species, and have been "amused and misled" (how pretty that quaint old use of amuse is!) "by the false lights" of critical vanity and self-righteousness. They have been taught to compare what they see and what they read, not with the things that they have observed and known, but with the things that some other artist or writer has done. Especially if they have themselves the artistic impulse in any direction they are taught to form themselves, not upon life, but upon the masters who became masters only by forming themselves upon life. The seeds of death are planted in them, and they can produce only the still-born, the academic. They are not told to take their work into the public square and see if it seems true to the chance passer, but to test it by the work of the very men who refused and decried any other test of their own work. The young writer who attempts to report the phrase and carriage of every-day life, who tries to tell just how he has heard men talk and seen them look, is made to feel guilty of something low and unworthy by people who would like to have him show how Shakespeare's men talked and looked, or Scott's, or Thackeray's or Balzac's, or Hawthorne's, or Dickens's; he is instructed to idealize his personages, that is, to take the life-likeness out of them, and put the book-likeness into them. He is approached in the spirit of the pedantry into which learning, much or little, always decays when it withdraws itself and stands apart from experience in an attitude of imagined superiority, and which would say with the same confidence to the scientist: "I see that you are looking at a grasshopper there which you have found in the grass, and I suppose you intend to describe it. Now don't waste your time and sin against culture in that way. I've got a grasshopper here, which has been evolved at considerable pains and expense out of the grasshopper in general; in fact, it's a type. It's made up of wire and card-board, very prettily painted in a conventional tint, and it's perfectly indestructible. It isn't very much like a real grasshopper, but it's a great deal nicer, and it's served to represent the notion of a grasshopper ever since man emerged from barbarism. You may say that it's artificial. Well, it is artificial; but then it's ideal too; and what you want to do is to cultivate the ideal. You'll find the books full of my kind of grasshopper, and scarcely a trace of yours in any of them. The thing that you are proposing to do is commonplace; but if you say that it isn't commonplace, for the very reason that it hasn't been done before, you'll have to admit that it's photographic."

As I said, I hope the time is coming when not only the artist, but the common, average man, who always "has the standard of the arts in his power," will have also the courage to apply it, and will reject the ideal grasshopper wherever he finds it, in science, in literature, in art, because it is not "simple, natural, and honest," because it is not like a real grasshopper. But I will own that I think the time is yet far off, and that the people who have been brought up on the ideal grasshopper, the heroic grasshopper, the impassioned grasshopper, the self-devoted, adventureful, good old romantic card-board grasshopper, must die out before the simple, honest, and natural grasshopper can have a fair field. I am in no haste to compass the end of these good people, whom I find in the meantime very amusing. It is delightful to meet one of them, either in print or out of it—some sweet elderly lady or excellent gentleman whose youth was pastured on the literature of thirty or forty years ago—and to witness the confidence with which they preach their favorite authors as all the law and the prophets. They have commonly read little or nothing since, or, if they have, they have judged it by a standard taken from these authors, and never dreamed of judging it by nature; they are destitute of the documents in the case of the later writers; they suppose that Balzac was the beginning of realism, and that Zola is its wicked end; they are quite ignorant, but they are ready to talk you down, if you differ from them, with an assumption of knowledge sufficient for any occasion. The horror, the resentment, with which they receive any question of their literary saints is genuine; you descend at once very far in the moral and social scale, and anything short of offensive personality is too good for you; it is expressed to you that you are one to be avoided, and put down even a little lower than you have naturally fallen.

These worthy persons are not to blame; it is part of their intellectual mission to represent the petrifaction of taste, and to preserve an image of a smaller and cruder and emptier world than we now live in, a world which was feeling its way towards the simple, the natural, the honest, but was a good deal "amused and misled" by lights now no longer mistakable for heavenly luminaries. They belong to a time, just passing away, when certain authors were considered authorities in certain kinds, when they must be accepted entire and not questioned in any particular. Now we are beginning to see and to say that no author is an authority except in those moments when he held his ear close to Nature's lips and caught her very accent. These moments are not continuous with any authors in the past, and they are rare with all. Therefore I am not afraid to say now that the greatest classics are sometimes not at all great, and that we can profit by them only when we hold them, like our meanest contemporaries, to a strict accounting, and verify their work by the standard of the arts which we all have in our power, the simple, the natural, and the honest.

These good people must always have a hero, an idol of some sort, and it is droll to find Balzac, who suffered from their sort such bitter scorn and hate for his realism while he was alive, now become a fetich in his turn, to be shaken in the faces of those who will not blindly worship him. But it is no new thing in the history of literature: whatever is established is sacred with those who do not think. At the beginning of the century, when romance was making the same fight against effete classicism which realism is making to-day against effete romanticism, the Italian poet Monti declared that "the romantic was the cold grave of the Beautiful," just as the realistic is now supposed to be. The romantic of that day and the real of this are in certain degree the same. Romanticism then sought, as realism seeks now, to widen the bounds of sympathy, to level every barrier against æsthetic freedom, to escape from the paralysis of tradition. It exhausted itself in this impulse; and it remained for realism to assert that fidelity to experience and probability of motive are essential conditions of a great imaginative literature. It is not a new theory, but it has never before universally characterized literary endeavor. When realism becomes false to itself, when it heaps up facts merely, and maps life instead of picturing it, realism will perish too. Every true realist instinctively knows this, and it is perhaps the reason why he is careful of every fact, and feels himself bound to express or to indicate its meaning at the risk of overmoralizing. In life he finds nothing insignificant; all tells for destiny and character; nothing that God has made is contemptible. He cannot look upon human life and declare this thing or that thing unworthy of notice, any more than the scientist can declare a fact of the material world beneath the dignity of his inquiry. He feels in every nerve the equality of things and the unity of men; his soul is exalted, not by vain shows and shadows and ideals, but by realities, in which alone the truth lives. In criticism it is his business to break the images of false gods and misshapen heroes, to take away the poor silly toys that many grown people would still like to play with. He cannot keep terms with "Jack the Giant-killer" or "Puss-in-boots," under any name or in any place, even when they reappear as the convict Vautrec, or the Marquis de Montrivaut, or the Sworn Thirteen Noblemen. He must say to himself that Balzac, when he imagined these monsters, was not Balzac, he was Dumas; he was not realistic, he was romanticistic.

IX

I would have my fellow-critics consider what they are really in the world for. The critic must perceive, if he will question himself more carefully, that his office is mainly to ascertain facts and traits of literature, not to invent or denounce them; to discover principles, not to establish them; to report, not to create.

It is so much easier to say that you like this or dislike that, than to tell why one thing is, or where another thing comes from, that many flourishing critics will have to go out of business altogether if the scientific method comes in, for then the critic will have to know something besides his own mind. He will have to know something of the laws of that mind, and of its generic history.

The history of all literature shows that even with the youngest and weakest author criticism is quite powerless against his will to do his own work in his own way; and if this is the case in the green wood, how much more in the dry! It has been thought by the sentimentalist that criticism, if it cannot cure, can at least kill, and Keats was long alleged in proof of its efficacy in this sort. But criticism neither cured nor killed Keats, as we all now very well know. It wounded, it cruelly hurt him, no doubt; and it is always in the power of the critic to give pain to the author—the meanest critic to the greatest author—for no one can help feeling a rudeness. But every literary movement has been violently opposed at the start, and yet never stayed in the least, or arrested, by criticism; every author has been condemned for his virtues, but in no wise changed by it. In the beginning he reads the critics; but presently perceiving that he alone

makes or mars himself, and that they have no instruction for him, he mostly leaves off reading them, though he is always glad of their kindness or grieved by their harshness when he chances upon it. This, I believe, is the general experience, modified, of course, by exceptions.

Then, are we critics of no use in the world? I should not like to think that, though I am not quite ready to define our use. More than one sober thinker is inclining at present to suspect that aesthetically or specifically we are of no use, and that we are only useful historically; that we may register laws, but not enact them. I am not quite prepared to admit that aesthetic criticism is useless, though in view of its futility in any given instance it is hard to deny that it is so. It certainly seems as useless against a book that strikes the popular fancy, and prospers on in spite of condemnation by the best critics, as it is against a book which does not generally please, and which no critical favor can make acceptable. This is so common a phenomenon that I wonder it has never hitherto suggested to criticism that its point of view was altogether mistaken, and that it was really necessary to judge books not as dead things, but as living things—things which have an influence and a power irrespective of beauty and wisdom, and merely as expressions of actuality in thought and feeling. Perhaps criticism has a cumulative and final effect; perhaps it does some good we do not know of. It apparently does not affect the author directly, but it may reach him through the reader. It may in some cases enlarge or diminish his audience for a while, until he has thoroughly measured and tested his own powers. If criticism is to affect literature at all, it must be through the writers who have newly left the starting-point, and are reasonable uncertain of the race, not with those who have won it again and again in their own way.

XVI

"How few materials," says Emerson, "are yet used by our arts! The mass of creatures and of qualities are still hid and expectant," and to break new ground is still one of the uncommonest and most heroic of the virtues. The artists are not alone to blame for the timidity that keeps them in the old furrows of the worn-out fields; most of those whom they live to please, or live by pleasing, prefer to have them remain there; it wants rare virtue to appreciate what is new, as well as to invent it; and the "easy things to understand" are the conventional things. This is why the ordinary

English novel, with its hackneyed plot, scenes, and figures, is more comfortable to the ordinary American than an American novel, which deals, at its worst, with comparatively new interests and motives. To adjust one's self to the enjoyment of these costs an intellectual effort, and an intellectual effort is what no ordinary person likes to make. It is only the extraordinary person who can say, with Emerson: "I ask not for the great, the remote, the romantic. . . . I embrace the common; I sit at the feet of the familiar and the low. . . Man is surprised to find that things near are not less beautiful and wondrous than things remote. . . . The perception of the worth of the vulgar is fruitful in discoveries. . . The foolish man wonders at the unusual, but the wise man at the usual . . . To-day always looks mean to the thoughtless; but to-day is a king in disguise . . . Banks and tariffs, the newspaper and caucus, Methodism and Unitarianism, are flat and dull to dull people, but rest on the same foundations of wonder as the town of Troy and the temple of Delphos."

Perhaps we ought not to deny their town of Troy and their temple of Delphos to the dull people; but if we ought, and if we did, they would still insist upon having them. An English novel, full of titles and rank, is apparently essential to the happiness of such people; their weak and childish imagination is at home in its familiar environment; they know what they are reading; the fact that it is hash many times warmed over reassures them; whereas a story of our own life, honestly studied and faithfully represented, troubles them with varied misgiving. They are not sure that it is literature; they do not feel that it is good society; its characters, so like their own, strike them as commonplace; they say they do not wish to know such people.

Everything in England is appreciable to the literary sense, while the sense of the literary worth of things in America is still faint and weak with most people, with the vast majority who "ask for the great, the remote, the romantic," who cannot "embrace the common," cannot "sit at the feet of the familiar and the low," in the good company of Emerson. We are all, or nearly all, struggling to be distinguished from the mass, and to be set apart in select circles and upper classes like the fine people we have read about. We are really a mixture of the plebeian ingredients of the whole world; but that is not bad; our vulgarity consists in trying to ignore "the worth of the vulgar," in believing that the superfine is better.

XXI

It used to be one of the disadvantages of the practice of romance in America, which Hawthorne more or less whimsically lamented, that there were so few shadows and inequalities in our broad level of prosperity; and it is one of the reflections suggested by Dostoïevsky's novel, *The Crime and the Punishment*, that whoever struck a note so profoundly tragic in American fiction would do a false and mistaken thing—as false and as mistaken in its way as dealing in American fiction with certain nudities which the Latin peoples seem to find edifying. Whatever their deserts, very few American novelists have been led out to be shot, or finally exiled to the rigors of a winter at Duluth; and in a land where journeyman carpenters and plumbers strike for four dollars a day the sum of hunger and cold is comparatively small, and the wrong from class to class has been almost inappreciable, though all this is changing for the worse. Our novelists, therefore, concern themselves with the more smiling aspects of life, which are the more American, and seek the universal in the individual rather than the social interests. It is worth while, even at the risk of being called commonplace, to be true to our well-to-do actualities; the very passions themselves seem to be softened and modified by conditions which formerly at least could not be said to wrong any one, to cramp endeavor, or to cross lawful desire. Sin and suffering and shame there must always be in the world, I suppose, but I believe that in this new world of ours it is still mainly from one to another one, and oftener still from one to one's self. We have death, too, in America, and a great deal of disagreeable and painful disease, which the multiplicity of our patent medicines does not seem to cure; but this is tragedy that comes in the very nature of things, and is not peculiarly American, as the large, cheerful average of health and success and happy life is. It will not do to boast, but it is well to be true to the facts, and to see that, apart from these purely mortal troubles, the race here has enjoyed conditions in which most of the ills that have darkened its annals might be averted by honest work and unselfish behavior.

Fine artists we have among us, and right-minded as far as they go; and we must not forget that at evil moments when it seems as if all the women had taken to writing hysterical improprieties, and some of the men were trying to be at least as hysterical in despair of being as improper. Other traits are much more characteristic of our life and our fiction. In most American novels, vivid and graphic as the best of them are, the people are segregated if not sequestered, and the scene is sparsely populated. The effect may be in instinctive response to the vacancy of our social life, and I shall not make haste to blame it. There are few places, few occasions among us, in which a novelist can get a large number of polite people together, or at least keep them together. Unless he carries a snap-camera his picture of them has no probability; they affect one like the figures perfunctorily associated in such deadly old engravings as that of "Washington Irving and his Friends." Perhaps it is for this reason that we excel in small pieces with three or four figures, or in studies of rustic communities, where there is propinquity if not society. Our grasp of more urbane life is feeble; most attempts to assemble it in our pictures are failures, possibly because it is too transitory, too intangible in its nature with us, to be truthfully represented as really existent.

I am not sure that the Americans have not brought the short story nearer perfection in the all-round sense than almost any other people, and for reasons very simple and near to hand. It might be argued from the national hurry and impatience that it was a literary form peculiarly adapted to the American temperament, but I suspect that its extraordinary development among us is owing much more to more tangible facts. The success of American magazines, which is nothing less than prodigious, is only commensurate with their excellence. Their sort of success is not only from the courage to decide which ought to please, but from the knowledge of what does please; and it is probable that, aside from the pictures, it is the short stories which please the readers of our best magazines. The serial novels they must have, of course; but rather more of course they must have short stories, and by operation of the law of supply and demand, the short stories, abundant in quantity and excellent in quality, are forthcoming because they are wanted. By another operation of the same law, which political economists have more recently taken account of, the demand follows the supply, and short stories are sought for because there is a proven ability to furnish them, and people read them willingly because they are usually very good. The art of writing them is now so disciplined and diffused with us that there is no lack either for the magazines or for the newspaper "syndicates" which deal in them almost to the exclusion of the serials.

An interesting fact in regard to the different varieties of the short story among us is that the sketches and studies by the women seem faithfuller and more realistic than those of the men, in proportion to their number. Their tendency is more distinctly in that direction, and there is a solidity, an honest observation, in the work of such women, which often leaves little to be desired. I should, upon the whole, be disposed to rank American short stories only below those of such Russian writers as I have read, and I should praise rather than blame their free use of our different local parlances, or "dialects," as people call them. I like this because I hope that our inherited English may be constantly freshened and revived from the native sources which our literary decentralization will help to keep open, and I will own that as I turn over novels coming from Philadelphia, from New Mexico, from Boston, from Tennessee, from rural New England, from New York, every local flavor of diction gives me courage and pleasure. Alphonse Daudet, in a conversation with H. H. Boyesen said, speaking of Tourguenief, "What a luxury it must be to have a great big untrodden barbaric language to wade into! We poor fellows who work in the language of an old civilization, we may sit and chisel our little verbal felicities, only to find in the end that it is a borrowed jewel we are polishing. The crown-jewels of our French tongue have passed through the hands of so many generations of monarchs that it seems like presumption on the part of any late-born pretender to attempt to wear them."

This grief is, of course, a little whimsical, yet it has a certain measure of reason in it, and the same regret has been more seriously expressed by the Italian poet Aleardi:

"Muse of an aged people, in the eve
 Of fading civilization, I was born.
 . . . Oh, fortunate,
 My sisters, who in the heroic dawn
 Of races sung! To them did destiny give
 The virgin fire and chaste ingenuousness
 Of their land's speech; and, reverenced, their hands
Ran over potent strings."

It will never do to allow that we are at such a desperate pass in English, but something of this divine despair we may feel too in thinking of "the spacious times of great Elizabeth," when the poets were trying the stops of the young language, and thrilling with the surprises of their own music. We may comfort ourselves, however, unless we prefer a luxury of grief, by remembering that no language is ever old on the lips of those who speak it, no matter how decrepit it drops from the pen. We have only to leave our studies, editorial and other, and go into the shops and fields to find the "spacious times" again; and from the beginning Realism, before she had put on her capital letter, had divined this near-at-hand truth along with the rest. Lowell, almost the greatest and finest realist who ever wrought in verse, showed us that Elizabeth was still Queen where he heard Yankee farmers talk. One need not invite slang into the company of its betters, though perhaps slang has been dropping its "s" and becoming language ever since the world began, and is certainly sometimes delightful and forcible beyond the reach of the dictionary. I would not have any one go about for new words, but if one of them came aptly, not to reject its help. For our novelists to try to write Americanly, from any motive, would be a dismal error, but being born Americans, I would have them use "Americanisms" whenever these serve their turn; and when their characters speak, I should like to hear them speak true American, with all the varying Tennesseean, Philadelphian, Bostonian, and New York accents. If we bother ourselves to write what the critics imagine to be "English," we shall be priggish and artificial, and still more so if we make our Americans talk "English." There is also this serious disadvantage about "English," that if we wrote the best "English" in the world, probably the English themselves would not know it, or, if they did, certainly would not own it. It has always been supposed by grammarians and purists that a language can be kept as they find it; but languages, while they live, are perpetually changing. God apparently meant them for the common people; and the common people will use them freely as they use other gifts of God. On their lips our continental English will differ more and more from the insular English, and I believe that this is not deplorable, but desirable.

In fine, I would have our American novelists be as American as they unconsciously can. Matthew Arnold complained that he found no "distinction" in our life, and I would gladly persuade all artists intending greatness in any kind among us that the recognition of the fact pointed out by Mr. Arnold ought to be a source of inspiration to them, and not discouragement. We have been now some hundred years building up a state on the affirmation of the essential quality of men in their rights and duties, and whether we have been right or been wrong the gods have taken us at our word, and have responded to us with a civilization in which there is no "distinction" perceptible to the eye that loves and values it. Such beauty and grandeur as we have is common beauty, common grandeur, or the beauty and grandeur in which the quality of solidarity so prevails that neither distinguishes itself to the disadvantage of anything else. It seems to me that these conditions invite the artist to the study and the appreciation of the common, and to the portrayal in every art of those finer and higher aspects which unite rather than sever humanity, if he would thrive in our new order of things. The talent that is robust enough to front the every-day world and catch the charm of its work-worn, care-worn, brave, kindly face, need not fear the encounter, though it seems terrible to the sort nurtured in the superstition of the romantic, the bizarre, the heroic, the distinguished, as the things alone worthy of painting or carving or writing. The arts must become democratic, and then we shall have the expression of America in art; and the reproach which Arnold was half right in making us shall have no justice in it any longer; we shall be "distinguished."

XXIII

One of the great newspapers the other day invited the prominent American authors to speak their minds upon a point in the theory and practice of fiction which had already vexed some of them. It was the question of how much or how little the American novel ought to deal with certain facts of life which are not usually talked of before young people, and especially young ladies. Of course the question was not decided, and I forget just how far the balance inclined in favor of a larger freedom in the matter. But it certainly inclined that way; one or two writers of the sex which is somehow supposed to have purity in its keeping (as if purity were a thing that did not practically concern the other sex, preoccupied with serious affairs) gave it a rather vigorous tilt to that side. In view of this fact it would not be the part of prudence to make an effort to dress the balance; and indeed I do not know that I was going to make any such effort. But there are some things to say, around and about the subject, which I should like to have some one else say, and which I may myself possibly be safe in suggesting.

One of the first of these is the fact, generally lost sight of by those who censure the Anglo-Saxon novel for its prudishness, that it is really not such a prude after all; and that if it is sometimes apparently anxious to avoid those experiences of life not spoken of before young people, this may be an appearance only. Sometimes a novel which has this shuffling air, this effect of truckling to propriety, might defend itself, if it could speak for itself, by saying that such experiences happened not to come within its scheme, and that, so far from maiming or mutilating itself in ignoring them, it was all the more faithfully representative of the tone of modern life in dealing with love that was chaste, and with passion so honest that it could be openly spoken of before the tenderest society bud at dinner. It might say that the guilty intrigue, the betrayal, the extreme flirtation even, was the exceptional thing in life, and unless the scheme of the story necessarily involved it, that it would be bad art to lug it in, and as bad taste as to introduce such topics in a mixed company. It could say very justly that the novel in our civilization now always addresses a mixed company, and that the vast majority of the company are ladies, and that very many, if not most, of these ladies are young girls. If the novel were written for men and for married women alone, as in continental Europe, it might be altogether different. But the simple fact is that it is not written for them alone among us, and it is a question of writing, under cover of our universal acceptance, things for young girls to read which you would be put out-of-doors for saying to them, or of frankly giving notice of your intention, and so cutting yourself off from the pleasure—and it is a very high and sweet one—of appealing to these vivid, responsive intelligences, which are none the less brilliant and admirable because they are innocent.

One day a novelist who liked, after the manner of other men, to repine at his hard fate, complained to his friend, a critic, that he was tired of the restriction he had put upon himself in this regard; for it is a mistake, as can be readily shown, to suppose that others impose it. "See how free those French fellows are!" he rebelled. "Shall we always be shut up to our tradition of decency?"

"Do you think it's much worse than being shut up to their tradition of indecency?" said his friend.

Then that novelist began to reflect, and he remembered how sick the invariable motive of the French novel made him. He perceived finally that, convention for convention, ours was not only more tolerable, but on the whole was truer to life, not only to its complexion, but also to its texture. No one will pretend that there is not vicious love beneath the surface of our society; if he did, the fetid explo-

sions of the divorce trials would refute him; but if he pretended that it was in any just sense characteristic of our society, he could be still more easily refuted. Yet it exists, and it is unquestionably the material of tragedy, the stuff from which intense effects are wrought. The question, after owning this fact, is whether these intense effects are not rather cheap effects. I incline to think they are, and I will try to say why I think so, if I may do so without offence. The material itself, the mere mention of it, has an instant fascination; it arrests, it detains, till the last word is said, and while there is anything to be hinted. This is what makes a love intrigue of some sort all but essential to the popularity of any fiction. Without such an intrigue the intellectual equipment of the author must be of the highest, and then he will succeed only with the highest class of readers. But any author who will deal with a guilty love intrigue holds all readers in his hand, the highest with the lowest, as long as he hints the slightest hope of the smallest potential naughtiness. He needs not at all be a great author; he may be a very shabby wretch, if he has but the courage or the trick of that sort of thing. The critics will call him "virile" and "passionate"; decent people will be ashamed to have been limned by him; but the low average will only ask another chance of flocking into his net. If he happens to be an able writer, his really fine and costly work will be unheeded, and the lure to the appetite will be chiefly remembered. There may be other qualities which make reputations for other men, but in his case they will count for nothing. He pays this penalty for his success in that kind; and every one pays some such penalty who deals with some such material

But I do not mean to imply that his case covers the whole ground. So far as it goes, though, it ought to stop the mouths of those who complain that fiction is enslaved to propriety among us. It appears that of a certain kind of impropriety it is free to give us all it will, and more. But this is not what serious men and women writing fiction mean when they rebel against the limitations of their art in our civilization. They have no desire to deal with nakedness, as painters and sculptors freely do in the worship of beauty; or with certain facts of life, as the stage does, in the service of sensation. But they ask why, when the conventions of the plastic and histrionic arts liberate their followers to the portrayal of almost any phase of the physical or of the emotional nature, an American novelist may not write a story on the lines of *Anna Karénina* or *Ma-*

dame Bovary. They wish to touch one of the most serious and sorrowful problems of life in the spirit of Tolstoy and Flaubert, and they ask why they may not. At one time, they remind us, the Anglo-Saxon novelist did deal with such problems—De Foe in his spirit, Richardson in his, Goldsmith in his. At what moment did our fiction lose this privilege? In what fatal hour did the Young Girl arise and seal the lips of Fiction, with a touch of her finger, to some of the most vital interests of life?

Whether I wished to oppose them in their aspiration for greater freedom, or whether I wished to encourage them, I should begin to answer them by saying that the Young Girl has never done anything of the kind. The manners of the novel have been improving with those of its readers; that is all. Gentlemen no longer swear or fall drunk under the table, or abduct young ladies and shut them up in lonely country-houses, or so habitually set about the ruin of their neighbors' wives, as they once did. Generally, people now call a spade an agricultural implement; they have not grown decent without having also grown a little squeamish, but they have grown comparatively decent; there is no doubt about that. They require of a novelist whom they respect unquestionable proof of his seriousness, if he proposes to deal with certain phases of life; they require a sort of scientific decorum. He can no longer expect to be received on the ground of entertainment only; he assumes a higher function, something like that of a physician or a priest, and they expect him to be bound by laws as sacred as those of such professions; they hold him solemnly pledged not to betray them or abuse their confidence. If he will accept the conditions, they give him their confidence, and he may then treat to his greater honor, and not at all to his disadvantage, of such experiences, such relations of men and women as George Eliot treats in *Adam*

Bede, in *Daniel Deronda,* in *Romola,* in almost all her books; such as Hawthorne treats in *The Scarlet Letter;* such as Dickens treats in *David Copperfield;* such as Thackeray treats in *Pendennis,* and glances at in every one of his fictions; such as most of the masters of English fiction have at some time treated more or less openly. It is quite false or quite mistaken to suppose that our novels have left untouched these most important realities of life. They have only not made them their stock in trade; they have kept a true perspective in regard to them; they have relegated them in their pictures of life to the space and place they occupy in life itself, as we know it in England and America. They have kept a correct proportion, knowing perfectly well that unless the novel is to be a map, with everything scrupulously laid down in it, a faithful record of life in far the greater extent could be made to the exclusion of guilty love and all its circumstances and consequences.

I justify them in this view not only because I hate what is cheap and meretricious, and hold in peculiar loathing the cant of the critics who require "passion" as something in itself admirable and desirable in a novel, but because I prize fidelity in the historian of feeling and character. Most of these critics who demand "passion" would seem to have no conception of any passion but one. Yet there are several other passions: the passion of grief, the passion of avarice, the passion of pity, the passion of ambition, the passion of hate, the passion of envy, the passion of devotion, the passion of friendship; and all these have a greater part in the drama of life than the passion of love, and infinitely greater than the passion of guilty love. Wittingly or unwittingly, English fiction and American fiction have recognized this truth, not fully, not in the measure it merits, but in greater degree than most other fiction.

HENRY JAMES (1843-1916)

EMERSON

(1887)

Mr. Elliot Cabot has made a very interesting contribution to a class of books of which our literature more than any other, offers admirable examples: he has given us a biography intelligently and carefully composed. These two volumes are a model of responsible editing —I use that term because they consist largely of letters and extracts from letters: nothing

could resemble less the manner in which the mere bookmaker strings together his frequently questionable pearls and shovels the heap into the presence of the public. Mr. Cabot has selected, compared, discriminated, steered an even course between meagreness and redundancy, and managed to be constantly and happily illustrative. And his work, moreover, strikes us as the better done from the fact that it stands for one of the two things that make an absorbing memoir a good deal more than for the other. If these two things be the conscience of the writer and the career of his hero, it is not difficult to see on which side the biographer of Emerson has found himself strongest. Ralph Waldo Emerson was a man of genius, but he led for nearly eighty years a life in which the sequence of events had little of the rapidity, or the complexity, that a spectator loves. There is something we miss very much as we turn these pages— something that has a kind of accidental, inevitable presence in almost any personal record —something that may be most definitely indicated under the name of color. We lay down the book with a singular impression of paleness—an impression that comes partly from the tone of the biographer and partly from the moral complexion of his subject, but mainly from the vacancy of the page itself. That of Emerson's personal history is condensed into the single word Concord, and all the condensation in the world will not make it look rich. It presents a most continuous surface. Mr. Matthew Arnold, in his *Discourses in America*, contests Emerson's complete right to the title of a man of letters; yet letters surely were the very texture of his history. Passions, alternations, affairs, adventures had absolutely no part in it. It stretched itself out in enviable quiet—a quiet in which we hear the jotting of the pencil in the notebook. It is the very life for literature (I mean for one's own, not that of another): fifty years of residence in the home of one's forefathers, pervaded by reading, by walking in the woods and the daily addition of sentence to sentence.

If the interest of Mr. Cabot's pencilled portrait is incontestable and yet does not spring from variety, it owes nothing either to a source from which it might have borrowed much and it is impossible not to regret a little that he has so completely neglected: I mean a greater reference to the social conditions in which Emerson moved, the company he lived in, the moral air he breathed. If his biographer had allowed himself a little more of the ironic touch, had put himself once in a way under the protection of Sainte-Beuve and had attempted something of a general picture, we should have felt that he only went with the occasion. I may overestimate the latent treasures of the field, but it seems to me there was distinctly an opportunity—an opportunity to make up moreover in some degree for the white tint of Emerson's career considered simply in itself.

We know a man imperfectly until we know his society, and we but half know a society until we know its manners. This is especially true of a man of letters, for manners lie very close to literature. From those of the New England world in which Emerson's character formed itself Mr. Cabot almost averts his lantern, though we feel sure that there would have been delightful glimpses to be had and that he would have been in a position—that is that he has all the knowledge that would enable him—to help us to them. It is as if he could not trust himself, knowing the subject only too well. This adds to the effect of extreme discretion that we find in his volumes, but it is the cause of our not finding certain things, certain figures and scenes, evoked. What is evoked is Emerson's pure spirit, by a copious, sifted series of citations and comments. But we must read as much as possible between the lines, and the picture of the transcendental time (to mention simply one corner) has yet to be painted— the lines have yet to be bitten in. Meanwhile we are held and charmed by the image of Emerson's mind and the extreme appeal which his physiognomy makes to our art of discrimination. It is so fair, so uniform and impersonal, that its features are simply fine shades, the gradations of tone of a surface whose proper quality was of the smoothest and on which nothing was reflected with violence. It is a pleasure of the critical sense to find, with Mr. Cabot's extremely intelligent help, a notation for such delicacies.

We seem to see the circumstances of our author's origin, immediate and remote, in a kind of high, vertical moral light, the brightness of a society at once very simple and very responsible. The rare singleness that was in his nature (so that he was *all* the warning moral voice, without distraction or counter-solicitation), was also in the stock he sprang from, clerical for generations, on both sides, and clerical in the Puritan sense. His ancestors had lived long (for nearly two centuries) in the same corner of New England, and during that period had preached and studied and prayed and practised. It is impossible to imagine a spirit better prepared in advance to be exactly what it was—better educated for its office in its far-away unconscious beginnings. There is an inner satisfaction in seeing so straight, although so patient, a connection between the stem and the flower, and such a proof that when life wishes to produce something exquisite in quality she takes her measures many years in advance. A conscience like Emerson's could not have been turned off, as it were, from one generation to another: a succession of attempts, a long process of refining, was required. His perfection, in his own line, comes largely from the non-interruption of the process.

As most of us are made up of ill-assorted pieces, his reader, and Mr. Cabot's, envies him this transmitted unity, in which there was no mutual hustling or crowding of elements. It must have been a kind of luxury to be—that is to feel—so homogeneous, and it helps to account for his serenity, his power of acceptance, and that absence of personal passion which makes his private correspondence read like a series of beautiful circulars or expanded cards "*pour prendre congé.*" He had the equanimity of a result; nature had taken care of him and he had only to speak. He accepted himself as he accepted others, accepted everything; and his absence of eagerness, or in other words his modesty, was that of a man with whom it is not a question of success, who has nothing invested or at stake. The investment, the stake, was that of the race, of all the past Emersons and Bulkeleys and Waldos. There is much that makes us smile, to-day, in the commotion produced by his secession from the mild Unitarian pulpit: we wonder at a condition of opinion in which any utterance of his should appear to be wanting in superior piety —in the essence of good instruction. All that is changed: the great difference has become the infinitely small, and we admire a state of society in which scandal and schism took on no darker hue; but there is even yet a sort of drollery in the spectacle of a body of people among whom the author of *The American Scholar* and of the Address of 1838 at Harvard Divinity College passed for profane, and who failed to see that he only gave his plea for the spiritual life the advantage of a brilliant expression. They were so provincial as to think that brilliancy came ill-recommended, and they were shocked at his ceasing to care for the prayer and the sermon. They might have perceived that he *was* the prayer and the sermon: not in the least a seculariser, but in his own subtle insinuating way a sanctifier.

Of the three periods into which his life divides itself, the first was (as in the case of most men) that of movement, experiment and selection—that of effort too and painful probation. Emerson had his message, but he was a good while looking for his form—the form which, as he himself would have said, he never completely found and of which it was rather characteristic of him that his later years (with their growing refusal to give him the *word*), wishing

to attack him in his most vulnerable point, where his tenure was least complete, had in some degree the effect of despoiling him. It all sounds rather bare and stern, Mr. Cabot's account of his youth and early manhood, and we get an impression of a terrible paucity of alternatives. If he would be neither a farmer nor a trader he could "teach school"; that was the main resource and a part of the general educative process of the young New Englander who proposed to devote himself to the things of the mind. There was an advantage in the nudity, however, which was that, in Emerson's case at least, the things of the mind did get themselves admirably well considered. If it be his great distinction and his special sign that he had a more vivid conception of the moral life than any one else, it is probably not fanciful to say that he owed it in part to the limited way in which he saw our capacity for living illustrated. The plain, God-fearing, practical society which surrounded him was not fertile in variations: it had great intelligence and energy, but it moved altogether in the straightforward direction. On three occasions later—three journeys to Europe—he was introduced to a more complicated world; but his spirit, his moral taste, as it were, abode always within the undecorated walls of his youth. There he could dwell with that ripe unconsciousness of evil which is one of the most beautiful signs by which we know him. His early writings are full of quaint animadversion upon the vices of the place and time, but there is something charmingly vague, light and general in the arraignment. Almost the worst he can say is that these vices are negative and that his fellow-townsmen are not heroic. We feel that his first impressions were gathered in a community from which misery and extravagance, and either extreme, of any sort, were equally absent. What the life of New England fifty years ago offered to the observer was the common lot, in a kind of achromatic picture, without particular intensifications. It was from this table of the usual, the merely typical joys and sorrows that he proceeded to generalize—a fact that accounts in some degree for a certain inadequacy and thinness in his enumerations. But it helps to account also for his direct, intimate vision of the soul itself—not in its emotions, its contortions and perversions, but in its passive, exposed, yet healthy form. He knows the nature of man and the long tradition of its dangers; but we feel that whereas he can put his finger on the remedies, lying for the most part, as they do, in the deep recesses of virtue, of the spirit, he has only a kind of hearsay, uninformed acquaintance with the disorders. It would require some ingenuity, the reader may say too much, to trace closely this correspondence between his genius and the frugal, dutiful, happy but decidedly lean Boston of the past, where there was a great deal of will but very little fulcrum—like a ministry without an opposition.

The genius itself it seems to me impossible to contest—I mean the genius for seeing character as a real and supreme thing. Other writers have arrived at a more complete expression: Wordsworth and Goethe, for instance, give one a sense of having found their form, whereas with Emerson we never lose the sense that he is still seeking it. But no one has had so steady and constant, and above all so natural, a vision of what we require and what we are capable of in the way of aspiration and independence. With Emerson it is ever the special capacity for moral experience—always that and only that. We have the impression, somehow, that life had never bribed him to look at anything but the soul; and indeed in the world in which he grew up and lived the bribes and lures, the beguilements and prizes, were few. He was in an admirable position for showing, what he constantly endeavoured to show, that the prized was within. Any one who in New England at that time could do that was sure of success, of listeners and sympathy; most of all, of course, when it was a question of doing it with such a divine persuasiveness; and, moreover, the way in which Emerson did it added to the charm—by word of mouth, face to face, with a rare, irresistible voice and a beautiful mild, modest authority. If Mr. Arnold is struck with the limited degree in which he was a man of letters I suppose it is because he is more struck with his having been, as it were, a man of lectures. But the lecture surely was never more purged of its grossness—the quality in it that suggests a strong light and a big brush—than as it issued from Emerson's lips; so far from being a vulgarisation it was simply the esoteric made audible, and instead of treating the few as the many, after the usual fashion of gentlemen on platforms, he treated the many as the few. There was probably no other society at that time in which he would have got so many persons to understand that; for we think the better of his audience as we read him, and wonder where else people would have had so much moral attention to give. It is to be remembered however that during the winter of 1847–48, on the occasion of his second visit to Eng-

land, he found many listeners in London and in provincial cities. Mr. Cabot's volumes are full of evidence of the satisfactions he offered, the delights and revelations he may be said to have promised, to a race which had to seek its entertainment, its rewards and consolations, almost exclusively in the moral world. But his own writings are fuller still; we find an instance almost wherever we open them.

"All these great and transcendent properties are ours. . . . Let us find room for this great guest in our small houses. . . . Where the heart is, there the muses, there the gods sojourn, and not in any geography of fame. Massachusetts, Connecticut River, and Boston Bay, you think paltry places, and the ear loves names of foreign and classic topography. But here we are, and if we will tarry a little we may come to learn that here is best. . . . The Jerseys were handsome enough ground for Washington to tread, and London street for the feet of Milton. . . . That country is fairest which is inhabited by the noblest minds."

We feel, or suspect, that Milton is thrown in as a hint that the London streets are no such great place, and it all sounds like a sort of pleasing consolation against bleakness. The beauty of a hundred passages of this kind in Emerson's pages is that they are effective, that they do come home, that they rest upon insight and not upon ingenuity, and that if they are sometimes obscure it is never with the obscurity of paradox. We seem to see the people turning out into the snow after hearing them, glowing with a finer glow than even the climate could give and fortified for a struggle with overshoes and the east wind.

"Look to it first and only, that fashion, custom, authority, pleasure, and money, are nothing to you, are not as bandages over your eyes, that you cannot see; but live with the privilege of the immeasurable mind. Not too anxious to visit periodically all families and each family in your parish connection, when you meet one of these men or women be to them a divine man; be to them thought and virtue; let their timid aspirations find in you a friend; let their trampled instincts be genially tempted out in your atmosphere; let their doubts know that you have doubted, and their wonder feel that you have wondered." When we set against an exquisite passage like that, or like the familiar sentences that open the essay on History ("He that is admitted to the right of reason is made freeman of the whole estate. What Plato has thought, he may think; what a saint has felt, he may feel; what at any time has befallen any man, he can understand"); when we compare the letters, cited by Mr. Cabot, to his wife from Springfield, Illinois (January 1853), we feel that his spiritual tact needed to be very just, but that if it was so it must have brought a blessing.

"Here I am in the deep mud of the prairies, misled I fear into this bog, not by a will-of-the-wisp, such as shine in bogs, but by a young New Hampshire editor, who over-estimated the strength of both of us, and fancied I should glitter in the prairie and draw the prairie birds and waders. It rains and thaws incessantly, and if we step off the short street we go up to the shoulders, perhaps, in mud. My chamber is a cabin; my fellow-boarders are legislators. . . . Two or three governors or ex-governors live in the house. . . . I cannot command daylight and solitude for study or for more than a scrawl". . .

and another extract:—

"A cold, raw country this, and plenty of night-travelling and arriving at four in the morning to take the last and worst bed in the tavern. Advancing day brings mercy and favor to me, but not the sleep. . . . Mercury 15° below zero. . . . I find well-disposed, kindly people among these sinewy farmers of the North, but in all that is called cultivation they are only ten years old."

He said in another letter (in 1860), "I saw Michigan and its forests and the Wolverines pretty thoroughly"; and on another page Mr. Cabot shows him as speaking of his engagements to lecture in the West as the obligation to "wade, and freeze, and ride, and run, and suffer all manner of indignities." This was not New England, but as regards the country districts throughout, at that time, it was a question of degree. Certainly never was the fine wine of philosophy carried to remoter or queerer corners: never was a more delicate diet offered to "two or three governors, or ex-governors," living in a cabin. It was Mercury, shivering in a mackintosh, bearing nectar and ambrosia to the gods whom he wished those who lived in cabins to endeavour to feel that they might be.

I have hinted that the will, in the old New England society, was a clue without a labyrinth; but it had its use, nevertheless, in helping the young talent to find its mould. There were few or none ready-made: tradition was certainly not so oppressive as might have been inferred from the fact that the air swarmed with reformers and improvers. Of the patient, philosophic manner in which Emerson groped and waited, through teaching the young and

preaching to the adult, for his particular vocation, Mr. Cabot's first volume gives a full and orderly account. His passage from the Unitarian pulpit to the lecture-desk was a step which at this distance of time can hardly help appearing to us short, though he was long in making it, for even after ceasing to have a parish of his own he freely confounded the two, or willingly, at least, treated the pulpit as a platform. "The young people and the mature hint at odium and the aversion of faces, to be presently encountered in society," he writes in his journal in 1838; but in point of fact the quiet drama of his abdication was not to include the note of suffering. The Boston world might feel disapproval, but it was far too kindly to make this sentiment felt as a weight: every element of martyrdom was there but the important ones of the cause and the persecutors. Mr. Cabot marks the lightness of the penalties of dissent; if they were light in somewhat later years for the transcendentalists and fruit-eaters they could press but little on a man of Emerson's distinction, to whom, all his life, people went not to carry but to ask the right word. There was no consideration to give up, he could not have been one of the dingy if he had tried; but what he did renounce in 1838 was a material profession. He was "settled," and his indisposition to administer the communion unsettled him. He calls the whole business, in writing to Carlyle, "a tempest in our washbowl"; but it had the effect of forcing him to seek a new source of income. His wants were few and his view of life severe, and this came to him, little by little, as he was able to extend the field in which he read his discourses. In 1835, upon his second marriage, he took up his habitation at Concord, and his life fell into the shape it was, in a general way, to keep for the next half-century. It is here that we cannot help regretting that Mr. Cabot had not found it possible to treat his career a little more pictorially. Those fifty years of Concord—at least the earlier part of them—would have been a subject bringing into play many odd figures, many human incongruities: they would have abounded in illustrations of the primitive New England character, especially during the time of its queer search for something to expend itself upon. Objects and occupations have multiplied since then, and now there is no lack; but fifty years ago the expanse was wide and free, and we get the impression of a conscience gasping in the void, panting for sensations, with something of the movement of the gills of a landed fish. It would take a very fine point to sketch Emerson's benignant, patient, inscrutable countenance during the various phases of this democratic communion; but the picture, when complete, would be one of the portraits, half a revelation and half an enigma, that suggest and fascinate. Such a striking personage as old Miss Mary Emerson, our author's aunt, whose high intelligence and temper were much of an influence in his earlier years, has a kind of tormenting representative value: we want to see her from head to foot, with her frame and her background; having (for we happen to have it), an impression that she was a very remarkable specimen of the transatlantic Puritan stock, a spirit that would have dared the devil. We miss a more liberal handling, are tempted to add touches of our own, and end by convincing ourselves that Miss Mary Moody Emerson, grim intellectual virgin and daughter of a hundred ministers, with her local traditions and her combined love of empire and of speculation, would have been an inspiration for a novelist. Hardly less so the charming Mrs. Ripley, Emerson's life-long friend and neighbour, most delicate and accomplished of women, devoted to Greek and to her house, studious, simple and dainty—an admirable example of the old-fashioned New England lady. It was a freak of Miss Emerson's somewhat sardonic humour to give her once a broomstick to carry across Boston Common (under the pretext of a "moving"), a task accepted with docility but making of the victim the most benignant witch ever equipped with that utensil. These ladies, however, were very private persons and not in the least of the reforming tribe: there are others who would have peopled Mr. Cabot's page to whom he gives no more than a mention. We must add that it is open to him to say that their features have become faint and indistinguishable to-day without more research than the question is apt to be worth: they are embalmed—in a collective way—the apprehensible part of them, in Mr. Frothingham's clever *History of Transcendentalism in New England*. This must be admitted to be true of even so lively a "factor," as we say nowadays, as the imaginative, talkative, intelligent and finally Italianised and shipwrecked Margaret Fuller: she is now one of the dim, one of Carlyle's "then-celebrated" at most. It seemed indeed as if Mr. Cabot rather grudged her a due place in the record of the company that Emerson kept, until we came across the delightful letter he quotes toward the end of his first volume—a letter interesting both as a specimen of inimitable, imperceptible edging away, and as an illustration

of the curiously generalised way, as if with an implicit protest against personalities, in which his intercourse, epistolary and other, with his friends was conducted. There is an extract from a letter to his aunt on the occasion of the death of a deeply-loved brother (his own) which reads like a passage from some fine old chastened essay on the vanity of earthly hopes: strangely unfamiliar, considering the circumstances. Courteous and humane to the furthest possible point, to the point of an almost profligate surrender of his attention, there was no familiarity in him, no personal avidity. Even his letters to his wife are courtesies, they are not familiarities. He had only one style, one manner, and he had it for everything—even for himself, in his notes, in his journals. But he had it in perfection for Miss Fuller; he retreats, smiling and flattering, on tiptoe, as if he were advancing. "She ever seems to crave," he says in his journal, "something which I have not, or have not for her." What he had was doubtless not what she craved, but the letter in question should be read to see how the modicum was administered. It is only between the lines of such a production that we read that a part of her effect upon him was to bore him; for his system was to practise a kind of universal passive hospitality—he aimed at nothing less. It was only because he was so deferential that he could be so detached; he had polished his aloofness till it reflected the image of his solicitor. And this was not because he was an "uncommunicating egotist," though he amuses himself with saying so to Miss Fuller: egotism is the strongest of passions, and he was altogether passionless. It was because he had no personal, just as he had almost no physical, wants. "Yet I plead not guilty to the malice prepense. 'Tis imbecility, not contumacy, though perhaps somewhat more odious. It seems very just, the irony with which you ask whether you may not be trusted and promise such docility. Alas, we will all promise, but the prophet loiters." He would not say even to himself that she bored him; he had denied himself the luxury of such easy and obvious short cuts. There is a passage in the lecture (1844) called "Man the Reformer," in which he hovers round and round the idea that the practice of trade, in certain conditions likely to beget an underhand competition, does not draw forth the nobler parts of character, till the reader is tempted to interrupt him with, "Say at once that it is impossible for a gentleman!"

So he remained always, reading his lectures in the winter, writing them in the summer, and at all seasons taking wood-walks and looking for hints in old books.

"Delicious summer stroll through the pastures. .... On the steep park of Conantum I have the old regret—is all this beauty to perish? Shall none re-make this sun and wind; the sky-blue river; the river-blue sky; the yellow meadow, spotted with sacks and sheets of cranberry-gatherers; the red bushes; the iron-gray house, just the colour of the granite rocks; the wild orchard?"

His observation of Nature was exquisite—always the direct, irresistible impression.

"The hawking of the wild geese flying by night; the thin note of the companionable titmouse in the winter day; the fall of swarms of flies in autumn, from combats high in the air, pattering down on the leaves like rain; the angry hiss of the wood-birds; the pine throwing out its pollen for the benefit of the next century." . . . . (*Literary Ethics*.)

I have said there was no familiarity in him, but he was familiar with woodland creatures and sounds. Certainly, too, he was on terms of free association with his books, which were numerous and dear to him; though Mr. Cabot says, doubtless with justice, that his dependence on them was slight and that he was not "intimate" with his authors. They did not feed him but they stimulated; they were not his meat but his wine—he took them in sips. But he needed them and liked them; he had volumes of notes from his reading, and he could not have produced his lectures without them. He liked literature as a thing to refer to, liked the very names of which it is full, and used them, especially in his later writings, for purposes of ornament, to dress the dish, sometimes with an unmeasured profusion. I open *The Conduct of Life* and find a dozen on the page. He mentions more authorities than is the fashion to-day. He can easily say, of course, that he follows a better one—that of his well-loved and irrepressibly allusive Montaigne. In his own bookishness there is a certain contradiction, just as there is a latent incompleteness in his whole literary side. Independence, the return to nature, the finding out and doing for one's self, was ever what he most highly recommended; and yet he is constantly reminding his readers of the conventional signs and consecrations—of what other men have done. This was partly because the independence that he had in his eye was an independence without ill-nature, without rudeness (though he likes that word), and full of gentle amiabilities, curiosities and tolerances; and partly it is a simple matter of form, a liter-

ary expedient, confessing its character—on the part of one who had never really mastered the art of composition—of continuous expression. Charming to many a reader, charming yet ever slightly droll, will remain Emerson's frequent invocation of the "scholar": there is such a friendly vagueness and convenience in it. It is of the scholar that he expects all the heroic and uncomfortable things, the concentrations and relinquishments, that make up the noble life. We fancy this personage looking up from his book and arm-chair a little ruefully and saying, "Ah, but why *me* always and only? Why so much of me, and is there no one else to share the responsibility?" "Neither years nor books have yet availed to extirpate a prejudice then rooted in me [when as a boy he first saw the graduates of his college assembled at their anniversary], that a scholar is the favourite of heaven and earth, the excellency of his country, the happiest of men."

In truth, by this term he means simply the cultivated man, the man who has had a liberal education, and there is a voluntary plainness in his use of it—speaking of such people as the rustic, or the vulgar, speak of those who have a tincture of books. This is a characteristic of his humility—that humility which was nine-tenths a plain fact (for it is easy for persons who have at bottom a great fund of indifference to be humble), and the remaining tenth a literary habit. Moreover an American reader may be excused for finding in it a pleasant sign of that prestige, often so quaintly and indeed so extravagantly acknowledged, which a connection with literature carries with it among the people of the United States. There is no country in which it is more freely admitted to be a distinction—*the* distinction; or in which so many persons have become eminent for showing it even in a slight degree. Gentlemen and ladies are celebrated there on this ground who would not on the same ground, though they might on another, be celebrated anywhere else. Emerson's own tone is an echo of that, when he speaks of the scholar—not of the banker, the great merchant, the legislator, the artist—as the most distinguished figure in the society about him. It is because he has most to give up that he is appealed to for efforts and sacrifices. "Meantime I know that a very different estimate of the scholar's profession prevails in this country," he goes on to say in the address from which I last quoted (the *Literary Ethics*), "and the importunity with which society presses its claim upon young men tends to pervert the views of the youth in respect to the culture of the intellect." The manner in which that is said represents, surely, a serious mistake: with the estimate of the scholar's profession which then prevailed in New England Emerson could have had no quarrel; the ground of his lamentation was another side of the matter. It was not a question of estimate, but of accidental practice. In 1838 there were still so many things of prime material necessity to be done that reading was driven to the wall; but the reader was still thought the cleverest, for he found time as well as intelligence. Emerson's own situation sufficiently indicates it. In what other country, on sleety winter nights, would provincial and bucolic populations have gone forth in hundreds for the cold comfort of a literary discourse? The distillation anywhere else would certainly have appeared too thin, the appeal too special. But for many years the American people of the middle regions, outside of a few cities, had in the most rigorous seasons no other recreation. A gentleman, grave or gay, in a bare room, with a manuscript, before a desk, offered the reward of toil, the refreshment of pleasure, to the young, the middle-aged, and the old of both sexes. The hour was brightest, doubtless, when the gentleman was gay, like Doctor Oliver Wendell Holmes. But Emerson's gravity never sapped his career, any more than it chilled the regard in which he was held among those who were particularly his own people. It was impossible to be more honoured and cherished, far and near, than he was during his long residence in Concord, or more looked upon as the principal gentleman in the place. This was conspicuous to the writer of these remarks on the occasion of the curious, sociable, cheerful public funeral made for him in 1883 by all the countryside, arriving, as for the last honours to the first citizen, in trains, in waggons, on foot, in multitudes. It was a popular manifestation, the most striking I have ever seen provoked by the death of a man of letters.

If a picture of that singular and very illustrative institution the old American lecture-system would have constituted a part of the filling-in of the ideal memoir of Emerson, I may further say, returning to the matter for a moment, that such a memoir would also have had a chapter for some of those Concord-haunting figures which are not so much interesting in themselves as interesting because for a season Emerson thought them so. And the pleasure of that would be partly that it would push us to inquire how interesting he did really think them. That is, it would bring up the question of his inner reserves and scepticisms, his secret ennuis and ironies, the way he sympathised for courtesy and then, with his delicacy and generosity, in a world after all given much to the literal, let his courtesy pass for adhesion—a question particularly attractive to those for whom he has, in general, a fascination. Many entertaining problems of that sort present themselves for such readers: there is something indefinable for them in the mixture of which he was made—his fidelity as an interpreter of the so-called transcendental spirit and his freedom from all wish for any personal share in the effect of his ideas. He drops them, sheds them, diffuses them, and we feel as if there would be a grossness in holding him to anything so temporal as a responsibility. He had the advantage, for many years, of having the question of application assumed for him by Thoreau, who took upon himself to be, in the concrete, the sort of person that Emerson's "scholar" was in the abstract, and who paid for it by having a shorter life than that fine adumbration. The application, with Thoreau, was violent and limited (it became a matter of prosaic detail, the non-payment of taxes, the non-wearing of a necktie, the preparation of one's food one's self, the practice of a rude sincerity—all things not of the essence), so that, though he wrote some beautiful pages, which read like a translation of Emerson into the sounds of the field and forest and which no one who has ever loved nature in New England, or indeed anywhere, can fail to love, he suffers something of the *amoindrissement* of eccentricity. His master escapes that reduction altogether. I call it an advantage to have had such a pupil as Thoreau; because for a mind so much made up of reflection as Emerson's everything comes under that head which prolongs and reanimates the process—produces the return, again and yet again, on one's impressions. Thoreau must have had this moderating and even chastening effect. It did not rest, moreover, with him alone; the advantage of which I speak was not confined to Thoreau's case. In 1837 Emerson (in his journal) pronounced Mr. Bronson Alcott the most extraordinary man and the highest genius of his time: the sequence of which was that for more than forty years after that he had the gentleman living but half a mile away. The opportunity for the return, as I have called it, was not wanting.

His detachment is shown in his whole attitude toward the transcendental movement—that remarkable outburst of Romanticism on Puritan ground, as Mr. Cabot very well names it. Nothing can be more ingenious, more sympathetic and charming, than Emerson's account and definition of the matter in his lecture (of 1842) called "The Transcendentalist"; and yet nothing is more apparent from his letters and journals than that he regarded any such label or banner as a mere tiresome flutter. He liked to taste but not to drink—least of all to become intoxicated. He liked to explain the transcendentalists but did not care at all to be explained by them: a doctrine "whereof you know I am wholly guiltless," he says to his wife in 1842, "and which is spoken of as a known and fixed element, like salt or meal. So that I have to begin with endless disclaimers and explanations; 'I am not the man you take me for.'" He was never the man any one took him for, for the simple reason that no one could possibly take him for the elusive, irreducible, merely gustatory spirit for which he took himself.

"It is a sort of maxim with me never to harp on the omnipotence of limitations. Least of all do we need any suggestion of checks and measures; as if New England were anything else. . . . Of so many fine people it is true that being so much they ought to be a little more, and missing that are naught. It is a sort of King René period; there is no doing, but rare thrilling prophecy from bands of competing minstrels."

That is his private expression about a large part of a ferment in regard to which his public judgment was that

"That indeed constitutes a new feature in their portrait, that they are the most exacting and extortionate critics. . . . These exacting children advertise us of our wants. There is no compliment, no smooth speech with them; they pay you only this one compliment of insatiable expectation; they aspire, they severely exact, and if they only stand fast in this watchtower, and stand fast unto the end, and without end, then they are terrible friends, whereof poet and priest cannot but stand in awe; and what if they eat clouds and drink wind, they have not been without service to the race of man."

That was saying the best for them, as he always said it for everything; but it was the sense of their being "bands of competing minstrels" and their camp being only a "measure and check," in a society too sparse for a synthesis, that kept him from wishing to don their uniform. This was after all but a misfitting imitation of his natural wear, and what he would have liked was to put that off—he did not wish to button it tighter. He said the best

for his friends of the Dial, of Fruitlands and Brook Farm, in saying that they were fastidious and critical; but he was conscious in the next breath that what there was around them to be criticised was mainly a negative. Nothing is more perceptible to-day than that their criticism produced no fruit—that it was little else than a very decent and innocent recreation—a kind of Puritan carnival. The New England world was for much the most part very busy, but the Dial and Fruitlands and Brook Farm were the amusement of the leisure-class. Extremes meet, and as in older societies that class is known principally by its connection with castles and carriages, so at Concord it came, with Thoreau and Mr. W. H. Channing, out of the cabin and the wood-lot.

Emerson was not moved to believe in their fastidiousness as a productive principle even when they directed it upon abuses which he abundantly recognized. Mr. Cabot shows that he was by no means one of the professional abolitionists or philanthropists—never an enrolled "humanitarian."

"We talk frigidly of Reform until the walls mock us. It is that of which a man should never speak, but if he have cherished it in his bosom he should steal to it in darkness, as an Indian to his bride. . . . Does he not do more to abolish slavery who works all day steadily in his own garden, than he who goes to the abolition meeting and makes a speech? He who does his own work frees a slave."

I must add that even while I transcribe these words there comes to me the recollection of the great meeting in the Boston Music Hall, on the first day of 1863, to celebrate the signing by Mr. Lincoln of the proclamation freeing the Southern slaves—of the momentousness of the occasion, the vast excited multitude, the crowded platform and the tall, spare figure of Emerson, in the midst, reading out the stanzas that were published under the name of the Boston Hymn. They are not the happiest he produced for an occasion—they do not compare with the verses on the "embattled farmers," read at Concord in 1837, and there is a certain awkwardness in some of them. But I well remember the immense effect with which his beautiful voice pronounced the lines—

"Pay ransom to the owner
And fill the bag to the brim.
Who is the owner? The slave is owner,
And ever was. Pay *him!*"

And Mr. Cabot chronicles the fact that the *gran'rifiuto*—the great backsliding of Mr. Webster when he cast his vote in Congress for the Fugitive Slave Law of 1850—was the one thing that ever moved him to heated denunciation. He felt Webster's apostasy as strongly as he had admired his genius. "Who has not helped to praise him? Simply he was the one American of our time whom we could produce as a finished work of nature." There is a passage in his journal (not a rough jotting, but, like most of the entries in it, a finished piece of writing), which is admirably descriptive of the wonderful orator and is moreover one of the very few portraits, or even personal sketches, yielded by Mr. Cabot's selections. It shows that he could observe the human figure and "render" it to good purpose.

"His splendid wrath, when his eyes become fire, is good to see, so intellectual it is—the wrath of the fact and the cause he espouses, and not at all personal to himself. . . . These village parties must be dish-water to him, yet he shows himself just good-natured, just nonchalant enough; and he has his own way, without offending any one or losing any ground. . . . His expensiveness seems necessary to him; were he too prudent a Yankee it would be a sad deduction from his magnificence. I only wish he would not truckle [to the slave-holders]. I do not care how much he spends."

I doubtless appear to have said more than enough, yet I have passed by many of the passages I had marked for transcription from Mr. Cabot's volumes. There is one, in the first, that makes us stare as we come upon it, to the effect that Emerson "could see nothing in Shelley, Aristophanes, Don Quixote, Miss Austen, Dickens." Mr. Cabot adds that he rarely read a novel, even the famous one (he has a point of contact here as well as, strangely enough, on two or three other sides with that distinguished moralist M. Ernest Renan, who, like Emerson, was originally a dissident priest and cannot imagine why people should write works of fiction); and thought Dante "a man to put into a museum, but not into your house; another Zerah Colburn; a prodigy of imaginative function, executive rather than contemplative or wise." The confession of an insensibility ranging from Shelley to Dickens and from Dante to Miss Austen and taking Don Quixote and Aristophanes on the way, is a large allowance to have to make for a man of letters, and may appear to confirm but slightly any claim of intellectual hospitality and general curiosity put forth for him. The truth was that, sparely constructed as he was and formed not wastefully, not with material left over, as it were, for a special function, there were certain

chords in Emerson that did not vibrate at all. I well remember my impression of this on walking with him in the autumn of 1872 through the galleries of the Louvre and, later that winter, through those of the Vatican: his perception of the objects contained in these collections was of the most general order. I was struck with the anomaly of a man so refined and intelligent being so little spoken to by works of art. It would be more exact to say that certain chords were wholly absent; the tune was played, the tune of life and literature, altogether on those that remained. They had every wish to be equal to their office, but one feels that the number was short—that some notes could not be given. Mr. Cabot makes use of a singular phrase when he says, in speaking of Hawthorne, for several years our author's neighbour at Concord and a little —a very little we gather—his companion, that Emerson was unable to read his novels—he thought them "not worthy of him." This is a judgment odd almost to fascination—we circle round it and turn it over and over; it contains so elusive an ambiguity. How highly he must have esteemed the man of whose genius *The House of the Seven Gables* and *The Scarlet Letter* gave imperfectly the measure, and how strange that he should not have been eager to read almost anything that such a gifted being might have let fall! It was a rare accident that made them live almost side by side so long in the same small New England town, each a fruit of a long Puritan stem, yet with such a difference of taste. Hawthorne's vision was all for the evil and sin of the world; a side of life as to which Emerson's eyes were thickly bandaged. There were points as to which the latter's conception of right could be violated, but he had no great sense of wrong—a strangely limited one, indeed, for a moralist—no sense of the dark, the foul, the base. There were certain complications in life which he never suspected. One asks one's self whether that is why he did not care for Dante and Shelley and Aristophanes and Dickens, their works containing a considerable reflection of human perversity. But that still leaves the indifference to Cervantes and Miss Austen unaccounted for.

It has not, however, been the ambition of these remarks to account for everything, and I have arrived at the end without even pointing to the grounds on which Emerson justifies the honours of biography, discussion and illustration. I have assumed his importance and continuance, and shall probably not be gainsaid by those who read him. Those who do not will hardly rub him out. Such a book as Mr.

Cabot's subjects a reputation to a test—leads people to look it over and hold it up to the light, to see whether it is worth keeping in use or even putting away in a cabinet. Such a revision of Emerson has no relegating consequences. The result of it is once more the impression that he serves and will not wear out, and that indeed we cannot afford to drop him. His instrument makes him precious. He did something better than any one else; he had a particular faculty, which has not been surpassed, for speaking to the soul in a voice of direction and authority. There have been many spiritual voices appealing, consoling, reassuring, exhorting, or even denouncing and terrifying, but none has had just that firmness and just that purity. It penetrates further, it seems to go back to the roots of our feelings, to where conduct and manhood begin; and moreover, to us to-day, there is something in it that says that it is connected somehow with the virtue of the world, has wrought and achieved, lived in thousands of minds, produced a mass of character and life. And there is this further sign of Emerson's singular power, that he is a striking exception to the general rule that writings live in the last resort by their form; that they owe a large part of their fortune to the art with which they have been composed. It is hardly too much, or too little, to say of Emerson' writings in general that they were not composed at all. Many and many things are beautifully said;

he had felicities, inspirations, unforgettable phrases; he had frequently an exquisite eloquence.

"O my friends, there are resources in us on which we have not yet drawn. There are men who rise refreshed on hearing a threat; men to whom a crisis which intimidates and paralyses the majority—demanding not the faculties of prudence and thrift, but comprehension, immovableness, the readiness of sacrifice, come graceful and beloved as a bride. . . . But these are heights that we can scarce look up to and remember without contrition and shame. Let us thank God that such things exist."

None the less we have the impression that that search for a fashion and a manner on which he was always engaged never really came to a conclusion; it draws itself out through his later writings—it drew itself out through his later lectures, like a sort of renunciation of success. It is not on these, however, but on their predecessors, that his reputation will rest. Of course the way he spoke was the way that was on the whole most convenient to him; but he differs from most men of letters of the same degree of credit in failing to strike us as having achieved a style. This achievement is, as I say, usually the bribe or toll-money on the journey to posterity; and if Emerson goes his way, as he clearly appears to be doing, on the strength of his message alone, the case will be rare, the exception striking, and the honour great.

JOHN BURROUGHS (1837-1921)

OUR RURAL DIVINITY

(1877)

I wonder that Wilson Flagg did not include the cow among his "Picturesque Animals," for that is where she belongs. She has not the classic beauty of the horse, but in picture-making qualities she is far ahead of him. Her shaggy, loose-jointed body, her irregular, sketchy outlines, like those of the landscape—the hollows and ridges, the slopes and prominences—her tossing horns, her bushy tail, her swinging gait, her tranquil, ruminating habits—all tend to make her an object upon which the artist eye loves to dwell. The artists are forever putting her into pictures too. In rural landscape scenes she is an important feature. Behold her grazing in the pastures and on the hill-sides, or along banks of streams, or ruminating under wide-spreading trees, or standing belly deep in the creek or pond, or lying upon

the smooth places in the quiet summer afternoon, the day's grazing done, and waiting to be summoned home to be milked; and again in the twilight lying upon the level summit of the hill, or where the sward is thickest and softest; or in winter a herd of them filing along toward the spring to drink, or being "foddered" from the stack in the field upon the new snow—surely the cow is a picturesque animal, and all her goings and comings are pleasant to behold.

I looked into Hamerton's clever book on the domestic animals, also expecting to find my divinity duly celebrated, but he passes her by and contemplates the bovine qualities only as they appear in the ox and the bull.

Neither have the poets made much of the cow, but have rather dwelt upon the steer, or the ox yoked to the plow. I recall this touch from Emerson:—

> "The heifer that lows in the upland farm,
> Far heard, lows not thine ear to charm."

But the ear is charmed, nevertheless, especially if it be not too near, and the air be still and dense, or hollow, as the farmer says. And again, if it be springtime and she task that powerful bellows of hers to its utmost capacity, how round the sound is, and how far it goes over the hills.

The cow has at least four tones or lows. First, there is her alarmed or distressed low, when deprived of her calf, or separated from her mates—her low of affection. Then there is her call of hunger, a petition for food, sometimes full of impatience, or her answer to the farmer's call, full of eagerness. Then there is that peculiar frenzied bawl she utters on smelling blood, which causes every member of the herd to lift its head and hasten to the spot— the native cry of the clan. When she is gored or in great danger she bawls also, but that is different. And lastly, there is the long, sonorous volley she lets off on the hills or in the yard, or along the highway, and which seems to be expressive of a kind of unrest and vague longing—the longing of the imprisoned Io for her lost identity. She sends her voice forth so that every god on Mount Olympus can hear her plaint. She makes this sound in the morning, especially in the spring, as she goes forth to graze.

One of our rural poets, Myron Benton, whose verse often has the flavor of sweet cream, has written some lines called "Rumination," in which the cow is the principal figure, and with which I am permitted to adorn my theme. The poet first gives his attention to a little brook that "breaks its shallow gossip" at his feet and "drowns the oriole's voice":—

"But moveth not that wise and ancient cow,
Who chews her juicy cud so languid now
Beneath her favorite elm, whose drooping bough
Lulls all but inward vision, fast asleep:
But still, her tireless tail a pendulum sweep
Mysterious clock-work guides, and some hid pulley
Her drowsy cud, each moment, raises duly.

"Of this great, wondrous world she has seen more
Than you, my little brook, and cropped its store
Of succulent grass on many a mead and lawn;
And strayed to distant uplands in the dawn,
And she has had some dark experience
Of graceless man's ingratitude; and hence

Her ways have not been ways of pleasantness,
Nor all her paths of peace. But her distress
And grief she has lived past; your giddy round
Disturbs her not, for she is learned profound
In deep brahminical philosophy.
She chews the cud of sweetest revery
Above your wordly prattle, brooklet merry,
Oblivious of all things sublunary."

The cow figures in Grecian mythology, and in the Oriental literature is treated as a sacred animal. "The clouds are cows and the rain milk." I remember what Herodotus says of the Egyptians' worship of heifers and steers; and in the traditions of the Celtic nations the cow is regarded as a divinity. In Norse mythology the milk of the cow Andhumbla afforded nourishment to the Frost giants, and it was she that licked into being and into shape a god, the father of Odin. If anything could lick a god into shape, certainly the cow could do it. You may see her perform this office for young Taurus any spring. She licks him out of the fogs and bewilderments and uncertainties in which he finds himself on first landing upon these shores, and up on to his feet in an incredibly short time. Indeed, that potent tongue of hers can almost make the dead alive any day, and the creative lick of the old Scandinavian mother cow is only a large-lettered rendering of the commonest facts.

The horse belongs to the fiery god Mars. He favors war, and is one of its oldest, most available, and most formidable engines. The steed is clothed with thunder, and smells the battle from afar; but the cattle upon a thousand hills denote that peace and plenty bear sway in the land. The neighing of the horse is a call to battle; but the lowing of old Brockleface in the valley brings the golden age again. The savage tribes are never without the horse; the Scythians are all mounted; but the cow would tame and humanize them. When the Indians will cultivate the cow, I shall think their civilization fairly begun. Recently, when the horses were sick with the epizoötic, and the oxen came to the city and helped to do their work, what an Arcadian air again filled the streets. But the dear old oxen—how awkward and distressed they looked! Juno wept in the face of every one of them. The horse is a true citizen, and is entirely at home in the paved streets; but the ox—what a complete embodiment of all rustic and rural things! Slow, deliberate, thick-skinned, powerful, hulky, ruminating, fragrant-breathed, when he came to town the spirit and suggestion of all Georgics and Bucolics came with him. O citizen, was it only a plodding, unsightly brute that went by?

Was there no chord in your bosom, long silent, that sweetly vibrated at the sight of that patient, Herculean couple? Did you smell no hay or cropped herbage, see no summer pastures with circles of cool shade, hear no voice of herds among the hills? They were very likely the only horses your grandfather ever had. Not much trouble to harness and unharness them. Not much vanity on the road in those days. They did all the work on the early pioneer farm. They were the gods whose rude strength first broke the soil. They could live where the moose and the deer could. If there was no clover or timothy to be had, then the twigs of the basswood and birch would do. Before there were yet fields given up to grass, they found ample pasturage in the woods. Their wide-spreading horns gleamed in the duskiness, and their paths and the paths of the cows became the future roads and highways, or even the streets of great cities.

All the descendants of Odin show a bovine trace, and cherish and cultivate the cow. In Norway she is a great feature. Prof. Boyesen describes what he calls the *Saeter*, the spring migration of the dairy and dairy maids, with all the appurtenances of butter and cheese-making, from the valleys to the distant plains upon the mountains, where the grass keeps fresh and tender till fall. It is the great event of the year in all the rural districts. Nearly the whole family go with the cattle and remain with them. At evening the cows are summoned home with a long horn, called the loor, in the hands of the milk-maid. The whole herd comes winding down the mountain side toward the *Saeter* in obedience to the mellow blast.

What were those old Vikings but thick-hided bulls that delighted in nothing so much as goring each other? And has not the charge of beefiness been brought much nearer home to us than that? But about all the northern races there is something that is kindred to cattle in the best sense—something in their art and literature that is essentially pastoral, sweet-breathed, continent, dispassionate, ruminating, wide-eyed, soft-voiced—a charm of kine, the virtue of brutes.

The cow belongs more especially to the northern peoples, to the region of the good, green grass. She is the true *grazing* animal. That broad, smooth, always dewy nose of hers is just the suggestion of green sward. She caresses the grass; she sweeps off the ends of the leaves; she reaps it with the soft sickle of her tongue. She crops close, but she does not bruise or devour the turf like the horse. She is the

sward's best friend, and will make it thick and smooth as a carpet.

"The turfy mountains where live the nibbling sheep"

are not for her. Her muzzle is too blunt; then she does not *bite* as do the sheep; she has not upper teeth; she *crops*. But on the lower slopes, and margins, and rich bottoms, she is at home. Where the daisy and the buttercup and clover bloom, and where corn will grow, is her proper domain. The agriculture of no country can long thrive without her. Not only a large part of the real, but much of the potential wealth of the land is wrapped up in her.

Then the cow has given us some good words and hints. How could we get along without the parable of the cow that gave a good pail of milk and then kicked it over. One could hardly keep house without it. Or the parable of the cream and the skimmed milk, or of the buttered bread? We know, too, through her aid, what the horns of the dilemma mean, and what comfort there is in the juicy cud of revery.

I have said the cow has not been of much service to the poets, and yet I remember that Jean Ingelow could hardly have managed her "High Tide" without "Whitefoot" and "Lightfoot" and "Cusha! Cusha! Cusha, calling"; or Trowbridge his "Evening at the Farm," in which the real call of the American farmboy, of "Co', boss! Co', boss! Co', Co'," makes a very musical refrain.

Tennyson's charming "Milking Song" is another flower of poesy that has sprung up in my divinity's footsteps.

What a variety of individualities a herd of cows presents when you have come to know them all, not only in form and color, but in manners and disposition. Some are timid and awkward, and the butt of the whole herd. Some remind you of deer. Some have an expression in the face like certain persons you have known. A petted and well-fed cow has a benevolent and gracious look; an ill-used and poorly-fed one a pitiful and forlorn look. Some cows have a masculine or ox expression; others are extremely feminine. The latter are the ones for milk. Some cows will kick like a horse; some jump fences like deer. Every herd has its ringleader, its unruly spirit—one that plans all the mischief and leads the rest through the fences into the grain or into the orchard. This one is usually quite different from the master spirit, the "boss of the yard." The latter is generally the most peaceful and law-abiding cow in the lot, and the least bullying and quarrelsome. But she is not to be trifled with; her will is law; the whole herd give way before her, those that have crossed horns with her, and those that have not, but yielded their allegiance without crossing. I remember such a one among my father's milkers when I was a boy—a slender-horned, deep-shouldered, large-uddered dewlapped old cow that we always put first in the long stable so she could not have a cow on each side of her to forage upon; for the master is yielded to no less in the stanchions than in the yard. She always had the first place anywhere. She had her choice of standing room in the milking yard, and when she wanted to lie down there or in the fields the best and softest spot was hers. When the herd were foddered from the stack or barn, or fed with pumpkins in the fall, she was always first served. Her demeanor was quiet but impressive. She never bullied or gored her mates, but literally ruled them with the breath of her nostrils. If any new-comer or ambitious younger cow, however, chafed under her supremacy, she was ever ready to make good her claims. And with what spirit she would fight when openly challenged! She was a whirlwind of pluck and valor; and not after one defeat or two defeats would she yield the championship. The boss cow, when overcome, seems to brood over her disgrace, and day after day will meet her rival in fierce combat.

A friend of mine, a pastoral philosopher, whom I have consulted in regard to the master cow, thinks it is seldom the case that one rules all the herd, if it number many, but that there is often one that will rule nearly all. "Curiously enough," he says, "a case like this will often occur: No. 1 will whip No. 2; No. 2 whips No. 3, and No. 3 whips No. 1; so around in a circle. This is not a mistake; it is often the case. I remember," he continued, "we once had feeding out of a large bin in the centre of the yard six oxen who mastered right through in succession from No. 1 to No. 6; *but No. 6 paid off the score by whipping No. 1.* I often watched them when they were all trying to feed out of the box, and of course trying, dog-in-the-manger fashion, each to prevent any other he could. They would often get in the order to do it very systematically, since they could keep rotating about the box till the chain happened to get broken somewhere, when there would be confusion. Their master-ship, you know, like that between nations, is constantly changing. But there are always Napoleons who hold their own through many vicissitudes; but the ordinary cow is continually liable to lose her foothold. Some cow she has always despised, and has often sent tossing

across the yard at her horns' ends, some pleasant morning will return the compliment and pay off old scores."

But my own observation has been that in herds in which there have been no important changes for several years, the question of might gets pretty well settled, and some one cow becomes the acknowledged ruler.

The bully of the yard is never the master, but usually a second or third rate pusher that never loses an opportunity to hook those beneath her, or to gore the masters if she can get them in a tight place. If such a one can get loose in the stable, she is quite certain to do mischief. She delights to pause in the open bars and turn and keep those at bay behind her till she sees a pair of threatening horns pressing towards her, when she quickly passes on. As one cow masters all, so there is one cow that is mastered by all. These are the two extremes of the herd, the head and the tail. Between them are all grades of authority, with none so poor but hath some poorer to do her reverence.

The cow has evidently come down to us from a wild or semi-wild state; perhaps is a descendant of those wild, shaggy cattle of which a small band is still preserved in some nobleman's park in Scotland. Cuvier seems to have been of this opinion. One of the ways in which her wild instinct still crops out is the disposition she shows in spring to hide her calf —a common practice among the wild herds. Her wild nature would be likely to come to the surface at this crisis if ever; and I have known cows that practiced great secrecy in dropping their calves. As their time approached they grew restless, a wild and excited look was upon them, and if left free, they generally set out for the woods or for some other secluded spot. After the calf is several hours old, and has got upon its feet and had its first meal, the dam by some sign commands it to lie down and remain quiet while she goes forth to feed. If the calf is approached at such time it plays "possum," assumes to be dead or asleep, till on finding this ruse does not succeed, it mounts to its feet, bleats loudly and fiercely, and charges desperately upon the intruder. But it recovers from this wild scare in a little while, and never shows signs of it again.

The habit of the cow, also, in eating the placenta, looks to me like a vestige of her former wild instincts—the instinct to remove everything that would give the wild beasts a clew or a scent, and so attract them to her helpless young.

How wise and sagacious the cows become

that run upon the street, or pick their living along the highway. The mystery of gates and bars is at last solved to them. They ponder over them by night, they lurk about them by day, till they acquire a new sense—till they become *en rapport* with them and know when they are open and unguarded. The garden gate, if it open into the highway at any point, is never out of the mind of these roadsters, or out of their calculations. They calculate upon the chances of its being left open a certain number of times in the season; and if it be but once and only for five minutes, your cabbage and sweet corn suffer. What villager, or countryman either, has not been awakened at night by the squeaking and crunching of those piratical jaws under the window or in the direction of the vegetable patch? I have had the cows, after they had eaten up my garden, break into the stable where my own milcher was tied, and gore her and devour her meal. Yes, life presents but one absorbing problem to the street cow, and that is how to get into your garden. She catches glimpses of it over the fence or through the pickets, and her imagination or epigastrium is inflamed. When the spot is surrounded by a high board fence, I think I have seen her peeping at the cabbages through a knot-hole. At last she learns to open the gate. It is a great triumph of bovine wit. She does it with her horn or her nose, or may be with her ever ready tongue. I doubt if she has ever yet penetrated the mystery of the newer patent fastenings; but the old-fashioned thumb-latch she can see through, give her time enough.

A large, lank, muley or polled cow used to annoy me in this way when I was a dweller in a certain pastoral city. I more than half suspected she was turned in by some one; so one day I watched. Presently I heard the gate-latch rattle; the gate swung open, and in walked the old buffalo. On seeing me she turned and ran like a horse. I then fastened the gate on the inside and watched again. After long waiting the old cow came quickly round the corner and approached the gate. She lifted the latch with her nose. Then as the gate did not move, she lifted it again and again. Then she gently nudged it. Then, the obtuse gate not taking the hint, she butted it gently, then harder and still harder, till it rattled again. At this juncture I emerged from my hiding place, when the old villain scampered off with great precipitation. She knew that she was trespassing, and she had learned that there were usually some swift penalties attached to this pastime.

I have owned but three cows and loved but one. That was the first one, Chloe, a bright-red, curly-pated, golden-skinned, Devonshire cow, that an ocean steamer landed for me upon the banks of the Potomac one bright May Day many clover summers ago. She came from the north, from the pastoral regions of the Catskills, to graze upon the broad commons of the national capital. I was then the fortunate and happy lessee of an old place with an acre of ground attached, almost within the shadow of the dome of the Capitol. Behind a high but aged and decrepit board fence I indulged my rural and unclerical tastes. I could look up from my homely tasks and cast a potato almost in the midst of that cataract of marble steps that flows out of the north wing of the patriotic pile. Ah, when that creaking and sagging back gate closed behind me in the evening, I was happy; and when it opened for my egress thence in the morning, I was not happy. Inside that gate was a miniature farm redolent of homely, primitive life, a tumble-down house and stables and implements of agriculture and horticulture, broods of chickens and growing pumpkins, and a thousand antidotes to the weariness of an artificial life. Outside of it were the marble and iron palaces, the paved and blistering streets, and the high, vacant mahogany desk of a government clerk. In that ancient inclosure I took an earth bath twice a day. I planted myself as deep in the soil as I could to restore the normal tone and freshness of my system, impaired by the above mentioned government mahogany. I have found there is nothing like the earth to draw the various social distempers out of one. The blue devils take flight at once if they see you mean to bury them and make compost of them. Emerson intimates that the scholar had better not try to have two gardens; but I could never spend an hour hoeing up dock and red-root and twitch grass without in some way getting rid of many weeds and fungus, unwholesome growths that a petty, in-doors life was forever fostering in my own moral and intellectual nature.

But the finishing touch was not given till Chloe came. She was the jewel for which this homely setting waited. My agriculture had some object then. The old gate never opened with such alacrity as when she paused before it. How we waited for her coming! Should I send Drewer, the colored patriarch, for her? No; the master of the house himself should receive Juno at the capital.

"One cask for you," said the clerk, referring to the steamer bill of lading.

"Then I hope it's a cask of milk," I said. "I expected a cow."

"One cask it says here."

"Well, let's see it; I'll warrant it has horns and is led by a rope;" which proved to be the case, for there stood the only object that bore my name, chewing its cud, on the forward deck. How she liked the voyage I could not find out; but she seemed to relish so much the feeling of solid ground beneath her feet once more that she led me a lively step all the way home. She cut capers in front of the White House, and tried twice to wind me up in the rope as we passed the Treasury. She kicked up her heels on the broad avenue and became very coltish as she came under the walls of the Capitol. But that night the long-vacant stall in the old stable was filled, and the next morning the coffee had met with a change of heart. I had to go out twice with the lantern and survey my treasure before I went to bed. Did she not come from the delectable mountains, and did I not have a sort of filial regard for her as toward my foster mother?

This was during the Arcadian age at the capital, before the easy-going southern ways had gone out and the prim new northern ways had come in, and when the domestic animals were treated with distinguished consideration and granted the freedom of the city. There was a charm of cattle in the streets and upon the commons: goats cropped your rose-bushes through the pickets, and nooned upon your front porch, and pigs dreamed Arcadian dreams under your garden fence or languidly frescoed it with pigments from the nearest pool. It was a time of peace; it was the poor man's golden age. Your cow, or your goat, or your pig led a vagrant, wandering life, and picked up a subsistence wherever they could, like the bees, which was almost everywhere. Your cow went forth in the morning and came home fraught with milk at night, and you never troubled yourself where she went or how far she roamed.

Chloe took very naturally to this kind of life. At first I had to go with her a few times and pilot her to the nearest commons, and then left her to her own wit, which never failed her. What adventures she had, what acquaintances she made, how far she wandered, I never knew. I never came across her in my walks or rambles. Indeed, on several occasions I thought I would look her up and see her feeding in national pastures, but I never could find her. There were plenty of cows, but they were all strangers. But punctually, between four and five o'clock in the afternoon, her white

horns would be seen tossing above the gate and her impatient low be heard. Sometimes, when I turned her forth in the morning, she would pause and apparently consider which way she would go. Should she go toward Kendall Green to-day, or follow the Tiber, or over by the Big Spring, or out around Lincoln Hospital? She seldom reached a conclusion till she had stretched forth her neck and blown a blast on her trumpet that awoke echoes in the lantern on the dome of the Capitol. Then, after one or two licks, she would disappear around the corner. Later in the season, when the grass was parched or poor on the commons, and the corn and cabbage tempting in the garden, Chloe was loath to depart in the morning, and her deliberations were longer than ever, and very often I had to aid her in coming to a decision.

For two summers she was a well-spring of pleasure and profit in my farm of one acre, when in an evil moment I resolved to part with her and try another. In an evil moment I say, for from that time my luck in cattle left me. The goddess never forgave me the execution of that rash and cruel resolve.

The day is indelibly stamped on my memory when I exposed my Chloe for sale in the public market-place. It was in November, a bright, dreamy, Indian summer day. A sadness oppressed me, not unmixed with guilt and remorse. An old Irish woman came to the market also with her pets to sell, a sow and five pigs, and took up a position next me. We condoled with each other; we bewailed the fate of our darlings together; we berated in chorus the white-aproned but blood-stained fraternity who prowled about us. When she went away for a moment I minded the pigs, and when I strolled about she minded my cow. How shy the innocent beast was of those carnal market-men. How she would shrink away from them. When they put out a hand to feel her condition she would "scrooch" down her back, or bend this way or that, as if the hand were a branding iron. So long as I stood by her head she felt safe—deluded creature—and chewed the cud of sweet content; but the moment I left her side she seemed filled with apprehension, and followed me with her eyes, lowing softly and entreatingly till I returned.

At last the money was counted out for her, and the rope surrendered to the hand of another. How that last look of alarm and incredulity, which I caught as I turned for a parting glance, went to my heart!

Her stall was soon filled, or partly filled, and this time with a native—a specimen of what may be called the cornstalk breed of Virginia: a slender, furtive, long-geared heifer just verging on cowhood, that in spite of my best efforts would wear a pinched and hungry look. She evidently inherited a humped back. It was a family trait, and evidence of the purity of her blood. For the native blooded cow of Virginia, from shivering over half rations of corn stalks, in the open air, during those bleak and windy winters, and roaming over those parched fields in summer, has come to have some marked features. For one thing, her pedal extremities seem lengthened; for another, her udder does not impede her travelling; for a third, her backbone inclines strongly to the curve; then, she despiseth hay. This last is a sure test. Offer a thorough-bred Virginia cow hay, and she will laugh in your face; but rattle the husks or shucks, and she knows you to be her friend.

The new comer even declined corn meal at first. She eyed it furtively, then sniffed it suspiciously, but finally discovered that it bore some relation to her native "shucks," when she fell to eagerly.

I cherish the memory of this cow, however, as the most affectionate brute I ever knew. Being deprived of her calf, she transferred her affections to her master, and would fain have made a calf of him, lowing in the most piteous and inconsolable manner when he was out of her sight, hardly forgetting her grief long enough to eat her meal, and entirely neglecting her beloved husks. Often in the middle of the night she would set up that sonorous lamentation and continue it till sleep was chased from every eye in the household. This generally had the effect of bringing the object of her affection before her, but in a mood anything but filial or comforting. Still, at such times a kick seemed a comfort to her, and she would gladly have kissed the rod that was the instrument of my midnight wrath.

But her tender star was destined soon to a fatal eclipse. Being tied with too long a rope on one occasion during my temporary absence, she got her head into the meal-barrel, and stopped not till she had devoured nearly half a bushel of dry meal. The singularly placid and benevolent look that beamed from the meal-besmeared face when I discovered her was something to be remembered. For the first time also her spinal column came near assuming a horizontal line.

But the grist proved too much for her frail mill, and her demise took place on the third day, not of course without some attempt to relieve her on my part. I gave her, as is usual in such emergencies, everything I "could think of," and everything my neighbors could think of, besides some fearful prescriptions which I obtained from a German veterinary surgeon, but to no purpose. I imagined her poor maw distended and inflamed with the baking sodden mass which no physic could penetrate or enliven.

Thus ended my second venture in live stock. My third, which followed sharp upon the heels of this disaster, was scarcely more of a success. This time I led to the altar a buffalo cow, as they call the "muley" down South—a large spotted, creamy-skinned cow, with a fine udder, that I persuaded a Jew drover to part with for ninety dollars. "Pag like a dish rack (rag)," said he, pointing to her udder after she had been milked. "You vill come pack and gif me the udder ten tollar" (for he had demanded an even hundred), he continued, "after you have had her a gouple of days." True, I felt like returning to him after a "gouple of days," but not to pay the other ten dollars. The cow proved to be as blind as a bat, though capable of counterfeiting the act of seeing to perfection. For did she not lift up her head and follow with her eyes a dog that scaled the fence and ran through the other end of the lot, and the next moment dash my hopes thus raised by trying to walk over a locust tree thirty feet high? And when I set the bucket before her containing her first mess of meal, she missed it by several inches, and her nose brought up against the ground. Was it a kind of far-sightedness and near blindedness? That was it, I think; she had genius, but not talent; she could see the man in the moon, but was quite oblivious to the man immediately in her front. Her eyes were telescopic and required a long range.

As long as I kept her in the stall, or confined to the inclosure, this strange eclipse of her sight was of little consequence. But when spring came, and it was time for her to go forth and seek her livelihood in the city's waste places, I was embarrassed. Into what remote corners or into what terra incognita might she not wander! There was little doubt but she would drift around home in the course of the summer, or perhaps as often as every week or two; but could she be trusted to find her way back every night? Perhaps she could be taught. Perhaps her other senses were acute enough to in a measure compensate her for her defective vision. So I gave her lessons in the topography of the country. I led her forth to graze for a few hours each day and led her home again. Then I left her to come home alone, which feat she accomplished very encouragingly. She came feeling her way along, stepping very high, but apparently a most diligent and interested sight-seer. But she was not sure of the right house when she got to it, though she stared at it very hard.

Again I turned her forth, and again she came back, her telescopic eyes apparently of some service to her. On the third day there was a fierce thunder-storm late in the afternoon, and old buffalo did not come home. It had evidently scattered and bewildered what little wit she had. Being barely able to navigate those streets on a calm day, what could she be expected to do in a tempest?

After the storm had passed, and near sundown, I set out in quest of her, but could get no clew. I heard that two cows had been struck by lightning about a mile out on the commons. My conscience instantly told me that one of them was mine. It would be a fit closing of the third act of this pastoral drama. Thitherward I bent my steps, and there upon the smooth plain I beheld the scorched and swollen forms of two cows slain by thunderbolts, but neither of them had ever been mine.

The next day I continued the search, and the next, and the next. Finally I hoisted an umbrella over my head, for the weather had become hot, and set out deliberately and systematically to explore every foot of open common on Capitol hill. I tramped many miles, and found every man's cow but my own—some twelve or fifteen hundred, I should think. I saw many vagrant boys and Irish and colored women, nearly all of whom had seen a buffalo cow that very day that answered exactly to my description, but in such diverse and widely separate places that I knew it was no cow of mine. And it was astonishing how many times I was myself deceived; how many rumps or heads, or line backs or white flanks I saw peeping over knolls or from behind fences or other objects that could belong to no cow but mine!

Finally I gave up the search, concluded the cow had been stolen, and advertised her, offering a reward. But days passed, and no tidings were obtained. Hope began to burn pretty low—was indeed on the point of going out altogether, when one afternoon, as I was strolling over the commons (for in my walks I still hovered about the scenes of my lost milcher), I saw the rump of a cow, over a grassy knoll, that looked familiar. Coming nearer, the beast lifted up her head; and, behold! it was she! only a few squares from home, where doubtless she had been most of the time. I had overshot the mark in my search. I had ransacked the far-off, and had neglected the near-at-hand, as we are so apt to do. But she was ruined as a milcher, and her history thenceforward was brief and touching!

WOODROW WILSON (1856-1924)

MERE LITERATURE

(1893)

I

"Mere Literature."

A singular phrase this, "mere literature,"— the irreverent invention of a scientific age. Literature we know, but "mere" literature? We are not to read it as if it meant *sheer* literature, literature in the essence, stripped of all accidental or ephemeral elements, and left with nothing but its immortal charm and power. "Mere literature" is a serious sneer, conceived in all honesty by the scientific mind, which despises things that do not fall within the categories of demonstrable knowledge. It means *nothing but literature*, as who should say, "mere talk," "mere fabrication," "mere pastime." The scientist, with his head comfortably and excusably full of knowable things, takes nothing seriously and with his hat off, except human knowledge. The creations of the human spirit are, from his point of view, incalculable vagaries, irresponsible phenomena, to be regarded only as play, and, for the mind's good, only as recreation,—to be used to while away the tedium of a railway journey, or to amuse a period of rest or convalescence; mere byplay, mere make-believe.

And so very whimsical things sometimes happen, because of this scientific and positivist spirit of the age, when the study of the literature of any language is made part of the curriculum of our colleges. The more delicate and subtle purposes of the study are put quite out of countenance, and literature is commanded to assume the phrases and the methods of science. It would be very painful if it should turn out that schools and universities were agencies of Philistinism; but there are some things which should prepare us for such a discovery. Our present plans for teaching everybody involve certain unpleasant things quite inevitably. It is obvious that you cannot have universal education without restricting your teaching to such things as can be universally understood. It is plain that you cannot impart "university methods" to thousands, or create "investigators" by the score, unless you confine your university education to matters which dull men can investigate, your laboratory training to tasks which mere plodding diligence and submissive patience can compass. Yet, if you do so limit and constrain what you teach, you thrust taste and insight and delicacy of perception out of the schools, exalt the obvious and the merely useful above the things which are only imaginatively or spiritually conceived, make education an affair of tasting and handling and smelling, and so create Philistia, that country in which they speak of "mere literature." I suppose that in Nirvana one would speak in like wise of "mere life."

The fear, at any rate, that such things may happen cannot fail to set us anxiously pondering certain questions about the systematic teaching of literature in our schools and colleges. How are we to impart classical writings to the children of the general public? "Beshrew the general public!" cries Mr. Birrell. "What in the name of the Bodleian has the general public got to do with literature?" Unfortunately, it has a great deal to do with it; for are we not complacently forcing the general public into our universities, and are we not arranging that all its sons shall be instructed how they may themselves master and teach our literature? You have nowadays, it is believed, only to heed the suggestions of pedagogics in order to know how to impart Burke or Browning, Dryden or Swift. There are certain practical difficulties, indeed; but there are ways of overcoming them. You must have strength if you would handle with real mastery the firm fibre of these men; you must have a heart, moreover, to feel their warmth, an eye to see what they see, an imagination to keep them company, a pulse to experience their delights. But if you have none of these things, you may make shift to do without them. You may count the words they use, instead, note the changes of phrase they make in successive revisions, put their rhythm into a scale of feet, run their allusions—particularly their female allusions—to cover, detect them in their previous reading. Or, if none of these things please you, or you find the big authors difficult or dull, you may drag to light all the minor writers of their time, who are easy to

understand. By setting an example in such methods you render great services in certain directions. You make the higher degrees of our universities available for the large number of respectable men who can count, and measure, and search diligently; and that may prove no small matter. You divert attention from thought, which is not always easy to get at, and fix attention upon language, as upon a curious mechanism, which can be perceived with the bodily eye, and which is worthy to be studied for its own sake, quite apart from anything it may mean. You encourage the examination of forms, grammatical and metrical, which can be quite accurately determined and quite exhaustively catalogued. You bring all the visible phenomena of writing to light and into ordered system. You go further, and show how to make careful literal identification of stories somewhere told ill and without art with the same stories told over again by the masters, well and with the transfiguring effect of genius. You thus broaden the area of science; for you rescue the concrete phenomena of the expression of thought—the necessary syllabification which accompanies it, the inevitable juxtaposition of words, the constant use of particles, the habitual display of roots, the inveterate repetition of names, the recurrent employment of meanings heard or read— from their confusion with the otherwise unclassifiable manifestations of what had hitherto been accepted, without critical examination, under the lump term "literature," simply for the pleasure and spiritual edification to be got from it.

An instructive differentiation ensues. In contrast with the orderly phenomena of speech and writing, which are amenable to scientific processes of examination and classification, and which take rank with the orderly successions of change in nature, we have what, for want of a more exact term, we call "mere literature,"—the literature which is not an expression of form, but an expression of spirit. This is a fugitive and troublesome thing, and perhaps does not belong in well-conceived plans of universal instruction; for it offers many embarrassments to pedagogic method. It escapes all scientific categories. It is not pervious to research. It is too wayward to be brought under the discipline of exposition. It is an attribute of so many different substances at one and the same time, that the consistent scientific man must needs put it forth from his company, as without responsible connections. By "mere literature" he means mere evanescent color, wanton trick of phrase, perverse departures from categorical statement,—something *all* personal equation, such stuff as dreams are made of.

We must not all, however, be impatient of this truant child of fancy. When the schools cast her out, she will stand in need of friendly succor, and we must train our spirits for the function. We must be free-hearted in order to make her happy, for she will accept entertainment from no sober, prudent fellow who shall counsel her to mend her ways. She has always made light of hardship, and she has never loved or obeyed any, save those who were of her own mind,—those who were indulgent to her humors, responsive to her ways of thought, attentive to her whims, content with her "mere" charms. She already has her small following of devotees, like all charming, capricious mistresses. There are some still who think that to know her is better than a liberal education.

There is but one way in which you can take mere literature as an education, and that is directly, at first hand. Almost any media except her own language and touch and tone are non-conducting. A descriptive catalogue of a collection of paintings is no substitute for the little areas of color and form themselves. You do not want to hear about a beautiful woman, simply—how she was dressed, how she bore herself, how the fine color flowed sweetly here and there upon her cheeks, how her eyes burned and melted, how her voice thrilled through the ears of those about her. If you have ever seen a woman, these things but tantalize and hurt you, if you cannot see her. You want to be in her presence. You know that only your own eyes can give you direct knowledge of her. Nothing but her presence contains her life. 'Tis the same with the authentic products of literature. You can never get their beauty at second hand, or feel their power except by direct contact with them.

It is a strange and occult thing how this quality of "mere literature" enters into one book, and is absent from another; but no man who has once felt it can mistake it. I was reading the other day a book about Canada. It is written in what the reviewers have pronounced to be an "admirable, spirited style." By this I take them to mean that it is grammatical, orderly, and full of strong adjectives. But these reviewers would have known more about the style in which it is written if they had noted what happens on page 84. There a quotation from Burke occurs. "There is," says Burke, "but one healing, catholic principle of toleration which ought to find favor in this

house. It is wanted not only in our colonies, but here. The thirsty earth of our own country is gasping and gaping and crying out for that healing shower from heaven. The noble lord has told you of the right of those people by treaty; but I consider the right of conquest so little, and the right of human nature so much, that the former has very little consideration with me. I look upon the people of Canada as coming by the dispensation of God under the British government. I would have us govern it in the same manner as the all-wise disposition of Providence would govern it. We know he suffers the sun to shine upon the righteous and the unrighteous; and we ought to suffer all classes to enjoy equally the right of worshiping God according to the light he has been pleased to give them." The peculiarity of such a passage as that is, that it needs no context. Its beauty seems almost independent of its subject matter. It comes on that eighty-fourth page like a burst of music in the midst of small talk,—a tone of sweet harmony heard amidst a rattle of phrases. The mild noise was unobjectionable enough until the music came. There is a breath and stir of life in those sentences of Burke's which is to be perceived in nothing else in that volume. Your pulses catch a quicker movement from them, and are stronger on their account.

It is so with all essential literature. It has a quality to move you, and you can never mistake it, if you have any blood in you. And it has also a power to instruct you which is as effective as it is subtle, and which no research or systematic method can ever rival. 'Tis a sore pity if that power cannot be made available in the classroom. It is not merely that it quickens your thought and fills your imagination with the images that have illuminated the choicer minds of the race. It does indeed exercise the faculties in this wise, bringing them into the best atmosphere, and into the presence of the men of greatest charm and force; but it does a great deal more than that. It acquaints the mind, by direct contact, with the forces which really govern and modify the world from generation to generation. There is more of a nation's politics to be got out of its poetry than out of all its systematic writers upon public affairs and constitutions. Epics are better mirrors of manners than chronicles; dramas oftentimes let you into the secrets of statutes; orations stirred by a deep energy of emotion or resolution, passionate pamphlets that survive their mission because of the direct action of their style along permanent lines of thought, contain more history than parliamentary journals. It is not knowledge that moves the world, but ideals, convictions, the opinions or fancies that have been held or followed; and whoever studies humanity ought to study it alive, practice the vivisection of reading literature, and acquaint himself with something more than anatomies which are no longer in use by spirits.

There are some words of Thibaut, the great jurist, which have long seemed to me singularly penetrative of one of the secrets of the intellectual life. "I told him," he says,—he is speaking of an interview with Niebuhr,— "I told him that I owed my gayety and vigor, in great part, to my love for the classics of all ages, even those outside the domain of jurisprudence." Not only the gayety and vigor of his hale old age, surely, but also his insight into the meaning and purpose of laws and institutions. The jurist who does not love the classics of all ages is like a post-mortem doctor presiding at a birth, a maker of manikins prescribing for a disease of the blood, a student of masks setting up for a connoisseur in smiles and kisses. In narrating history, you are speaking of what was done by men; in discoursing of laws, you are seeking to show what courses of action, and what manner of dealing with one another, men have adopted. You can neither tell the story nor conceive the law till you know how the men you speak of regarded themselves and one another; and I know of no way of learning this but by reading the stories they have told of themselves, the songs they have sung, the heroic adventures they have applauded. I must know what, if anything, they revered; I must hear their sneers and gibes; must learn in what accents they spoke love within the family circle; with what grace they obeyed their superiors in station; how they conceived it politic to live, and wise to die; how they esteemed property, and what they deemed privilege; when they kept holiday, and why; when they were prone to resist oppression, and wherefore,—I must see things with their eyes, before I can comprehend their law books. Their jural relationships are not independent of their way of living, and their way of thinking is the mirror of their way of living.

It is doubtless due to the scientific spirit of the age that these plain, these immemorial truths are in danger of becoming obscured. Science, under the influence of the conception of evolution, devotes itself to the study of forms, of specific differences, of the manner in which the same principle of life manifests itself variously under the compulsions of changes of environment. It is thus that it has become "scientific" to set forth the manner in which man's nature submits to man's circumstances; scientific to disclose morbid moods, and the conditions which produce them; scientific to regard man, not as the center or source of power, but as subject to power, a register of external forces instead of an originative soul, and character as a product of man's circumstances rather than a sign of man's mastery over circumstance. It is thus that it has become "scientific" to analyze language as itself a commanding element in man's life. The history of word-roots, their modification under the influences of changes wrought in the vocal organs by habit or by climate, the laws of phonetic change to which they are obedient, and their persistence under all disguises of dialect, as if they were full of a self-originated life, a self-directed energy of influence, is united with the study of grammatical forms in the construction of scientific conceptions of the evolution and uses of human speech. The impression is created that literature is only the chosen vessel of these forms, disclosing to us their modification in use and structure from age to age. Such vitality as the masterpieces of genius possess comes to seem only a dramatization of the fortunes of words. Great writers construct for the adventures of language their appropriate epics. Or, if it be not the words themselves that are scrutinized, but the style of their use, that style becomes, instead of a fine essence of personality, a matter of cadence merely, or of grammatical and structural relationships. Science is the study of the forces of the world of matter, the adjustments, the apparatus, of the universe; and the scientific study of literature has likewise become a study of apparatus,—of the forms in which men utter thought, and the forces by which those forms have been and still are being modified, rather than of thought itself.

The essences of literature of course remain the same under all forms, and the true study of literature is the study of these essences,—a study, not of forms or of differences, but of likenesses,—likenesses of spirit and intent under whatever varieties of method, running through all forms of speech like the same music along the chords of various instruments. There is a sense in which literature is independent of form, just as there is a sense in which music is independent of its instrument. It is my cherished belief that Apollo's pipe contained as much eloquent music as any modern orchestra. Some books live; many die: wherein is the secret of immortality? Not in beauty of form, nor even in force of passion. We might say of literature what Wordsworth said of poetry, the most easily immortal part of literature: it is "the impassioned expression which is in the countenance of all science; it is the breath of the finer spirit of all knowledge." Poetry has the easier immortality because it has the sweeter accent when it speaks, because its phrases linger in our ears to delight them, because its truths are also melodies. Prose has much to overcome,—its plainness of visage, its less musical accents, its homelier turns of phrase. But it also may contain the immortal essence of truth and seriousness and high thought. It too may clothe conviction with the beauty that must make it shine forever. Let a man but have beauty in his heart, and, believing something with his might, put it forth arrayed as he sees it, the lights and shadows falling upon it on his page as they fall upon it in his heart, and he may die assured that that beauty will not pass away out of the world.

Biographers have often been puzzled by the contrast between certain men as they lived and as they wrote. Schopenhauer's case is one of the most singular. A man of turbulent life, suffering himself to be cut to exasperation by the petty worries of his lot, he was nevertheless calm and wise when he wrote, as if the Muse had rebuked him. He wrote at a still elevation, where small and temporary things did not come to disturb him. 'Tis a pity that for some men this elevation is so far to seek. They lose permanency by not finding it. Could there be a deliberate regimen of life for the author, it is plain enough how he ought to live, not as seeking fame, but as deserving it.

"Fame, like a wayward girl, will still be coy
To those who woo her with too slavish knees;
But makes surrender to some thoughtless boy,
And dotes the more upon a heart at ease.

. . . .

"Ye love-sick bards, repay her scorn with scorn;
Ye love-sick artists, madmen that ye are,
Make your best bow to her and bid adieu;
Then, if she likes it, she will follow you."

It behooves all minor authors to realize the possibility of their being discovered some day, and exposed to the general scrutiny. They ought to live as if conscious of the risk. They ought to purge their hearts of everything that is not genuine and capable of lasting the world a century, at least, if need be. Mere literature is made of spirit. The difficulties of style are the artist's difficulties with his tools. The spirit that is in the eye, in the pose, in mien or gesture, the painter must find in his color-box; as he must find also the spirit that nature displays upon the face of the fields or in the hidden places of the forest. The writer has less obvious means. Word and spirit do not easily consort. The language which the philologists set out before us with such curious erudition is of very little use as a vehicle for the essences of the human spirit. It is too sophisticated and self-conscious. What you need is, not a critical knowledge of language, but a quick feeling for it. You must recognize the affinities between your spirit and its idioms. You must immerse your phrase in your thought, your thought in your phrase, till each becomes saturated with the other. Then what you produce is as necessarily fit for permanency as if it were incarnated spirit.

And you must produce in color, with the touch of imagination which lifts what you write away from the dull levels of mere exposition. Black-and-white sketches may serve some purposes of the artist, but very little of actual nature is in mere black-and-white. The imagination never works thus with satisfaction. Nothing is ever conceived completely when conceived so grayly, without suffusion of real light. The mind creates, as great Nature does, in colors, with deep chiaroscuro and burning lights. This is true not only of poetry and essentially imaginative writing, but also of the writing which seeks nothing more than to penetrate the meaning of actual affairs,— the writing of the greatest historians and philosophers, the utterances of orators and of the great masters of political exposition. Their narratives, their analyses, their appeals, their conceptions of principle, are all dipped deep in the colors of the life they expound. Their minds respond only to realities, their eyes see only actual circumstance. Their sentences quiver and are quick with visions of human affairs,—how minds are bent or governed, how action is shaped or thwarted. The great "constructive" minds, as we call them, are of this sort. They "construct" by seeing what others have not imagination enough to see. They do not always know more, but they always realize more. Let the singular reconstruction of Roman history and institutions by Theodor Mommsen serve as an illustration. Safe men distrust this great master. They cannot find what he finds in the documents. They will draw you truncated figures of the antique Roman state, and tell you the limbs cannot be found, the features of the face have nowhere been unearthed. They will cite you fragments such as remain, and show you how far these can be pieced together toward the making of a complete description of private life and public function in those first times when the Roman commonwealth was young; but what the missing sentences were they can only weakly conjecture. Their eyes cannot descry those distant days with no other aids than these. Only the greatest are dissatisfied, and go on to paint that ancient life with the materials that will render it lifelike,—the materials of the constructive imagination. They have other sources of information. They see living men in the old documents. Give them but the torso, and they will supply head and limbs, bright and animate as they must have been. If Mommsen does not quite do that, another man, with Mommsen's eye and a touch more of color on his brush, might have done it,—may yet do it.

It is in this way that we get some glimpse of the only relations that scholarship bears to literature. Literature can do without exact scholarship, or any scholarship at all, though it may impoverish itself thereby; but scholarship cannot do without literature. It needs literature to float it, to set it current, to authenticate it to the race, to get it out of closets, and into the brains of men who stir abroad. It will adorn literature, no doubt; literature will be the richer for its presence; but it will not, it cannot, of itself create literature. Rich stuffs from the East do not create a king, nor warlike trappings a conqueror. There is, indeed, a natural antagonism, let it be frankly said, between the standards of scholarship and the standards of literature. Exact scholarship values things in direct proportion as they are verifiable; but literature knows nothing of such tests. The truths which it seeks are the truths of self-expression. It is a thing of convictions, of insights, of what is felt and seen and heard and hoped for. Its meanings lurk behind nature, not in the facts of its phenomena. It speaks of things as the man who utters it saw them, not necessarily as God made them. The personality of the speaker runs throughout all the sentences of real literature. That personality may not be the personality of a poet: it may be only the personality of the penetrative seer. It may not have the atmosphere in which visions are seen, but only that in which men and affairs look keenly cut in outline, boldly massed in bulk, consummately grouped in detail, to the reader as to the writer. Sentences of perfectly clarified wisdom may be literature no less than stanzas of inspired song, or the intense utterances of impassioned feeling. The personality of the sunlight is in the keen lines

of light that run along the edges of a sword no less than in the burning splendor of the rose or the radiant kindlings of a woman's eye. You may feel the power of one master of thought playing upon your brain as you may feel that of another playing upon your heart.

Scholarship gets into literature by becoming part of the originating individuality of a master of thought. No man is a master of thought without being also a master of its vehicle and instrument, style, that subtle medium of all its evasive effects of light and shade. Scholarship is material; it is not life. It becomes immortal only when it is worked upon by conviction, by schooled and chastened imagination, by thought that runs alive out of the inner fountains of individual insight and purpose. Colorless, or without suffusion of light from some source of light, it is dead, and will not twice be looked at; but made part of the life of a great mind, subordinated, absorbed, put forth with authentic stamp of currency on it, minted at some definite mint and bearing some sovereign image, it will even outlast the time when it shall have ceased to deserve the acceptance of scholars,—when it shall, in fact, have become "mere literature."

Scholarship is the realm of nicely adjusted opinion. It is the business of scholars to assess evidence and test conclusions, to discriminate values and reckon probabilities. Literature is the realm of conviction and vision. Its points of view are as various as they are oftentimes unverifiable. It speaks individual faiths. Its groundwork is not erudition, but reflection and fancy. Your thorough-going scholar dare not reflect. To reflect is to let himself in on his material; whereas what he wants is to keep himself apart, and view his materials in an air that does not color or refract. To reflect is to throw an atmosphere about what is in your mind,—an atmosphere which holds all the colors of your life. Reflection summons all associations, and they so throng and move that they dominate the mind's stage at once. The plot is in their hands. Scholars, therefore, do not reflect; they label, group kind with kind, set forth in schemes, expound with dispassionate method. Their minds are not stages, but museums; nothing is done there, but very curious and valuable collections are kept there. If literature use scholarship, it is only to fill it with fancies or shape it to new standards, of which of itself it can know nothing.

True, there are books reckoned primarily books of science and of scholarship which have nevertheless won standing as literature; books of science such as Newton wrote, books of scholarship such as Gibbon's. But science was only the vestibule by which such a man as Newton entered the temple of nature, and the art he practiced was not the art of exposition, but the art of divination. He was not only a scientist, but also a seer; and we shall not lose sight of Newton because we value what he was more than what he knew. If we continue Gibbon in his fame, it will be for love of his art, not worship of his scholarship. We some of us, nowadays, know the period of which he wrote better even than he did; but which one of us shall build so admirable a monument to ourselves, as artists, out of what we know? The scholar finds his immortality in the form he gives his work. It is a hard saying, but the truth of it is inexorable: be an artist, or prepare for oblivion. You may write a chronicle, but you will not serve yourself thereby. You will only serve some fellow who shall come after you, possessing, what you did not have, an ear for the words you could not hit upon; an eye for the colors you could not see; a hand for the strokes you missed.

Real literature you can always distinguish by its form, and yet is is not possible to indicate the form it should have. It is easy to say that it should have a form suitable to its matter; but how suitable? Suitable to set the matter off, adorn, embellish it, or suitable simply to bring it directly, quick and potent, to the apprehension of the reader? This is the question of style, about which many masters have had many opinions; upon which you can make up no safe generalization from the practice of those who have unquestionably given to the matter of their thought immortal form, an accent or a countenance never to be forgotten. Who shall say how much of Burke's splendid and impressive imagery is part and stuff of his thought, or tell why even that part of Newman's prose which is devoid of ornament, stripped to its shining skin, and running bare and lithe and athletic to carry its tidings to men, should promise to enjoy as certain an immortality? Why should Lamb go so quaintly and elaborately to work upon his critical essays, taking care to perfume every sentence, if possible, with the fine savor of an old phrase, if the same business could be so effectively done in the plain and even cadences of Mr. Matthew Arnold's prose? Why should Gibbon be so formal, so stately, so elaborate, when he had before his eyes the example of great Tacitus, whose direct, sententious style had outlived by so many hundred years the very language in which he wrote? In poetry, who shall measure the varieties of style lavished upon similar themes? The matter of vital thought is not separable from the thinker; its forms must suit his handling as well as fit his conception. Any style is author's stuff which is suitable to his purpose and his fancy. He may use rich fabrics with which to costume his thoughts, or he may use simple stone from which to sculpture them, and leave them bare. His only limits are those of art. He may not indulge a taste for the merely curious or fantastic. The quaint writers have quaint thoughts; their material is suitable. They do not merely satisfy themselves as virtuosi, with collections of odd phrases and obsolete meanings. They needed twisted words to fit the eccentric patterns of their thought. The great writer has always dignity, restraint, propriety, adequateness; what time he loses these qualities he ceases to be great. His style neither creaks nor breaks under his passion, but carries the strain with unshaken strength. It is not trivial or mean, but speaks what small meanings fall in its way with simplicity, as conscious of their smallness. Its playfulness is within bounds; its laugh never bursts too boisterously into a guffaw. A great style always knows what it would be at, and does the thing appropriately, with the larger sort of taste.

This is the condemnation of tricks of phrase, devices to catch the attention, exaggerations and loud talk to hold it. No writer can afford to strive after effect, if his striving is to be apparent. For just and permanent effect is missed altogether unless it be so completely attained as to seem like some touch of sunlight, perfect, natural, inevitable, wrought without effort and without deliberate purpose to be effective. Mere audacity of attempt can, of course, never win the wished for result; and if the attempt be successful, it is not audacious. What we call audacity in a great writer has no touch of temerity, sauciness, or arrogance in it. It is simply high spirit, a dashing and splendid display of strength. Boldness is ridiculous unless it be impressive, and it can be impressive only when backed by solid forces of character and attainment. Your plebeian hack cannot afford the showy paces; only the full-blooded Arabian has the sinew and proportion to lend them perfect grace and propriety. The art of letters eschews the bizarre as rigidly as does every other fine art. It mixes its colors with brains, and is obedient to great Nature's sane standards of right adjustment in all that it attempts.

You can make no catalogue of these features of great writing; there is no science of literature. Literature in its essence is mere spirit, and you must experience it rather than analyze it too formally. It is the door to nature and to ourselves. It opens our hearts to receive the experiences of great men and the conceptions of great races. It awakens us to the significance of action and to the singular power of mental habit. It airs our souls in the wide atmosphere of contemplation. "In these bad days, when it is thought more educationally useful to know the principle of the common pump than Keats' Ode on a Grecian Urn," as Mr. Birrell says, we cannot afford to let one single precious sentence of "mere literature" go by as unread or unpraised. If this free people to which we belong is to keep its fine spirit, its perfect temper amidst affairs, its high courage in the face of difficulties, its wise temperateness and wide-eyed hope, it must continue to drink deep and often from the old wells of English undefiled, quaff the keen tonic of its best ideals, keep its blood warm with all the great utterances of exalted purpose and pure principle of which its matchless literature is full. The great spirits of the past must command us in the tasks of the future. Mere literature will keep us pure and keep us strong. Even though it puzzle or altogether escape scientific method, it may keep our horizon clear for us, and our eyes glad to look bravely forth upon the world.

HENRY ADAMS (1838-1918)

MONT-SAINT-MICHEL AND CHARTRES
(1904)

CHAPTER I

Saint Michiel de la Mer del Peril

The Archangel loved heights. Standing on the summit of the tower that crowned his church, wings upspread, sword uplifted, the devil crawling beneath, and the cock, symbol of eternal vigilance, perched on his mailed foot, Saint Michael held a place of his own in heaven and on earth which seems, in the eleventh century, to leave hardly room for the Virgin of the Crypt at Chartres, still less for the Beau Christ of the thirteenth century at Amiens. The Archangel stands for Church and State, and both militant. He is the conqueror of Satan, the mightiest of all created spirits, the nearest to God. His place was where the danger was greatest; therefore you find him here. For the same reason he was, while the pagan danger lasted, the patron saint of France. So the Normans, when they were converted to Christianity, put themselves under his powerful protection. So he stood for centuries on his Mount in Peril of the Sea, watching across the tremor of the immense ocean,—*immensi tremor oceani*,—as Louis XI, inspired for once to poetry, inscribed on the collar of the Order of Saint Michael which he created. So soldiers, nobles, and monarchs went on pilgrimage to his shrine; so the common people followed, and still follow, like ourselves.

The church stands high on the summit of this granite rock, and on its west front is the platform, to which the tourist ought first to climb. From the edge of this platform, the eye plunges down, two hundred and thirty-five feet, to the wide sands or the wider ocean, as the tides recede or advance, under an infinite sky, over a restless sea, which even we tourists can understand and feel without books or guides; but when we turn from the western view, and look at the church door, thirty or forty yards from the parapet where we stand, one needs to be eight centuries old to know what this mass of encrusted architecture meant to its builders, and even then one must still learn to feel it. The man who wanders into the twelfth century is lost, unless he can grow prematurely young.

One can do it, as one can play with children. Wordsworth, whose practical sense equalled his intuitive genius, carefully limited us to "a season of calm weather," which is certainly best; but granting a fair frame of mind, one can still "have sight of that immortal sea" which brought us hither from the twelfth century; one can even travel thither and see the children sporting on the shore. Our sense is partially atrophied from disuse, but it is still alive, at least in old people, who alone, as a class, have the time to be young.

One needs only to be old enough in order to be as young as one will. From the top of this Abbey Church one looks across the bay to Avranches, and towards Coutances and the Cotentin,—the *Constantinus pagus*,—whose shore, facing us, recalls the coast of New England. The relation between the granite of one coast and that of the other may be fanciful, but the relation between the people who live on each is as hard and practical a fact as the granite itself. When one enters the church, one notes first the four great triumphal piers or columns, at the intersection of the nave and transepts, and on looking into M. Corroyer's architectural study, which is the chief source of all one's acquaintance with the Mount, one learns that these piers were constructed in 1058. Four out of five American tourists will instantly recall the only date of mediæval history they ever knew, the date of the Norman Conquest. Eight years after these piers were built, in 1066, Duke William of Normandy raised an army of forty thousand men in these parts, and in northern France, whom he took to England, where they mostly stayed. For a hundred and fifty years, until 1204, Normandy and England were united; the Norman peasant went freely to England with his lord, spiritual or temporal; the Norman woman, a very capable person, followed her husband or her parents; Normans held nearly all the English fiefs; filled the English Church; crowded the English Court; created the English law; and we know that French was still currently spoken in England as late as 1400, or thereabouts, "After the scole of Stratford atte bowe." The aristocratic Norman names still survive in part, and if we look up their origin here we shall generally find them in villages so remote and insignificant that their place can hardly be found on any ordinary map; but the common people had no surnames, and cannot be traced, although for every noble whose name or blood survived in England or in Normandy, we must reckon hundreds of peasants. Since the generation which followed William to England in 1066, we can reckon twenty-eight or thirty from father to son, and, if you care to figure up the sum, you will find that you had about two hundred and fifty million arithmetical ancestors living in the middle of the eleventh century. The whole population of England and northern France may then have numbered five million, but if it were fifty it would not much affect the certainty that, if you have any English blood at all, you have also Norman. If we could go back and live again in all our two hundred and fifty million arithmetical ancestors of the eleventh century, we should find ourselves doing many surprising things, but among the rest we should pretty certainly be ploughing most of the fields of Cotentin and Calvados; going to mass in every parish church in Normandy; rendering military service to every lord, spiritual or temporal, in all this region; and helping to build the Abbey Church at Mont-Saint-Michel. From the roof of the Cathedral of Coutances over yonder, one may look away over the hills and woods, the farms and fields of Normandy, and so familiar, so homelike are they, one can almost take oath that in this, or the other, or in all, one knew life once and has never so fully known it since.

Never so fully known it since! For we of the eleventh century, hard-headed, close-fisted, grasping, shrewd, as we were, and as Normans are still said to be, stood more fully in the centre of the world's movement than our English descendants ever did. We were a part, and a great part, of the Church, of France, and of Europe. The Leos and Gregories of the tenth and eleventh centuries leaned on us in their great struggle for reform. Our Duke Richard-Sans-Peur, in 966, turned the old canons out of the Mount in order to bring here the highest influence of the time, the Benedictine monks of Monte Cassino. Richard II, grandfather of William the Conqueror, began this Abbey Church in 1020, and helped Abbot Hildebert to build it. When William the Conqueror in 1066 set out to conquer England, Pope Alexander II stood behind him and blessed his banner. From that moment our Norman Dukes cast the Kings of France into the shade. Our activity was not limited to northern Europe, or even confined by Anjou and Gascony. When we stop at Coutances, we will drive out to Hauteville to see where Tancred came from, whose sons Robert and Roger were conquering Naples and Sicily at the time when the Abbey Church was building on the Mount. Normans were everywhere in 1066, and everywhere in the lead of their age. We were a serious race. If you want other proof of it, besides our record in war and in politics, you have only to look at our art. Religious art is the measure of human depth and sincerity; any triviality, any weakness, cries aloud. If this church on the Mount is not proof enough of Norman character, we will stop at Coutances for a wider view. Then we will go to Caen and Bayeux. From there, it would almost be worth our while to leap at once to Palermo. It was in the year 1131 or thereabouts that Roger began the Cathedral at Cefalu and the Chapel Royal at Palermo; it was about the year 1174 that his grandson William began the Cathedral of Monreale. No art—either Greek or Byzantine, Italian or Arab—has ever created two religious types so beautiful, so serious, so impressive, and yet so different, as Mont-Saint-Michel watching over its northern ocean, and Monreale, looking down over its forests of orange and lemon, on Palermo and the Sicilian seas.

Down nearly to the end of the twelfth century the Norman was fairly master of the world in architecture as in arms, although the thirteenth century belonged to France, and we must look for its glories on the Seine and Marne and Loire; but for the present we are in the eleventh century,—tenants of the Duke or of the Church or of small feudal lords who take their names from the neighbourhood,— Beaumont, Carteret, Gréville, Percy, Pierpont,—who, at the Duke's bidding, will each call out his tenants, perhaps ten men-at-arms with their attendants, to fight in Brittany, or in the Vexin toward Paris, or in the great campaign for the conquest of England which is to come within ten years,—the greatest military effort that has been made in western Europe since Charlemagne and Roland were defeated at Roncesvalles three hundred years ago. For the moment, we are helping to quarry granite for the Abbey Church, and to haul it to the Mount, or load it on our boat. We never fail to make our annual pilgrimage to the Mount on the Archangel's Day, October 16. We expect to be called out for a new campaign which Duke William threatens against Brittany, and we hear stories that Harold the Saxon, the powerful Earl of Wessex in England, is a guest, or, as some say, a prisoner or a hostage, at the Duke's Court, and will go with us on the campaign. The year is 1058.

All this time we have been standing on the *parvis*, looking out over the sea and sands which are as good eleventh-century landscape as they ever were; or turning at times towards the church door which is the *pons seclorum*, the bridge of ages, between us and our ancestors. Now that we have made an attempt, such as it is, to get our minds into a condition to cross the bridge without breaking down in the effort, we enter the church and stand fact to face with eleventh-century architecture; a ground-plan which dates from 1020; a central tower, or its piers, dating from 1058; and a church completed in 1135. France can offer few buildings of this importance equally old, with dates so exact. Perhaps the closest parallel to Mont-Saint-Michel is Saint-Benoît-sur-Loire, above Orléans, which seems to have been a shrine almost as popular as the Mount, at the same time. Chartres was also a famous shrine, but the Virgin, and the west porch of Chartres, which is to be our peculiar pilgrimage, was a hundred years later than the ground-plan of Mont-Saint-Michel, although Chartres porch

is the usual starting-point of northern French art. Queen Matilda's Abbaye-aux-Dames, now the Church of the Trinity, at Caen, dates from 1066. Saint-Sernin at Toulouse, the porch of the Abbey Church at Moissac, Notre-Dame-du-Port at Clermont, the Abbey Church at Vezelay, are all said to be twelfth-century. Even San Marco at Venice was new in 1020.

Yet in 1020 Norman art was already too ambitious. Certainly nine hundred years leave their traces on granite as well as on other material, but the granite of Abbot Hildebert would have stood securely enough, if the Abbot had not asked too much from it. Perhaps he asked too much from the Archangel, for the thought of the Archangel's superiority was clearly the inspiration of his plan. The apex of the granite rock rose like a sugar-loaf two hundred and forty feet (73.6 metres) above mean sea-level. Instead of cutting the summit away to give his church a secure rock foundation, which would have sacrificed about thirty feet of height, the Abbot took the apex of the rock for his level, and on all sides built out foundations of masonry to support the walls of his church. The apex of the rock is the floor of the *croisée*, the intersection of nave and transept. On this solid foundation the Abbot rested the chief weight of the church, which was the central tower, supported by the four great piers which still stand; but from the croisée in the centre westward to the parapet of the platform, the Abbot filled the whole space with masonry, and his successors built out still farther, until some two hundred feet of stonework ends now in a perpendicular wall of eighty feet or more. In this space are several ranges of chambers, but the structure might perhaps have proved strong enough to support the light Romanesque front which was usual in the eleventh century, had not fashions in architecture changed in the great epoch of building, a hundred and fifty years later, when Abbot Robert de Torigny thought proper to reconstruct the west front, and build out two towers on its flanks. The towers were no doubt beautiful, if one may judge from the towers of Bayeux and Coutances, but their weight broke down the vaulting beneath, and one of them fell in 1300. In 1618 the whole façade began to give way, and in 1776 not only the façade but also three of the seven spans of the nave were pulled down. Of Abbot Hildebert's nave, only four arches remain.

Still, the overmastering strength of the eleventh century is stamped on a great scale here, not only in the four spans of the nave, and in the transepts, but chiefly in the triumphal columns of the croisée. No one is likely to forget what Norman architecture was, who takes the trouble to pass once through this fragment of its earliest bloom. The dimensions are not great, though greater than safe construction warranted. Abbot Hildebert's whole church did not exceed two hundred and thirty feet in length in the interior, and the span of the triumphal arch was only about twenty-three feet, if the books can be trusted. The nave of the Abbaye-aux-Dames appears to have about the same width, and probably neither of them was meant to be vaulted. The roof was of timber, and about sixty-three feet high at its apex. Compared with the great churches of the thirteenth century, this building is modest, but its size is not what matters to us. Its style is the starting-point of all our future travels. Here is your first eleventh-century church! How does it affect you?

Serious and simple to excess! is it not? Young people rarely enjoy it. They prefer the Gothic, even as you see it here, looking at us from the choir, through the great Norman arch. No doubt they are right, since they are young: but men and women who have lived long and are tired,—who want rest,—who have done with aspirations and ambition,—whose life has been a broken arch,—feel this repose and self-restraint as they feel nothing else. The quiet strength of these curved lines, the solid support of these heavy columns, the moderate proportions, even the modified lights, the absence of display, of effort, of self-consciousness, satisfy them as no other art does. They come back to it to rest, after a long circle of pilgrimage,—the cradle of rest from which their ancestors started. Even here they find the repose none too deep.

Indeed, when you look longer at it, you begin to doubt whether there is any repose in it at all,—whether it is not the most unreposeful thought ever put into architectural form. Perched on the extreme point of this abrupt rock, the Church Militant with its aspirant Archangel stands high above the world, and seems to threaten heaven itself. The idea is the stronger and more restless because the Church of Saint Michael is surrounded and protected by the world and the society over which it rises, as Duke William rested on his barons and their men. Neither the Saint nor the Duke was troubled by doubts about his mission. Church and State, Soul and Body, God and Man, are all one at Mont-Saint-Michel, and the business of all is to fight, each in his own way, or to stand guard for each other. Neither Church nor State is intellectual, or learned, or even strict in dogma. Here we do not feel the Trinity at all; the Virgin but little; Christ hardly more; we feel only the Archangel and the Unity of God. We have little logic here, and simple faith, but we have energy. We cannot do many things which are done in the centre of civilization, at Byzantium, but we can fight, and we can build a church. No doubt we think first of the church, and next of our temporal lord; only in the last instance do we think of our private affairs, and our private affairs sometimes suffer for it; but we reckon the affairs of Church and State to be ours, too, and we carry this idea very far. Our church on the Mount is ambitious, restless, striving for effect; our conquest of England, with which the Duke is infatuated, is more ambitious still; but all this is a trifle to the outburst which is coming in the next generation; and Saint Michael on his Mount expresses it all.

Taking architecture as an expression of energy, we can some day compare Mont-Saint-Michel with Beauvais, and draw from the comparison whatever moral suits our frame of mind; but you should first note that here, in the eleventh century, the Church, however simple-minded or unschooled, was not cheap. Its self-respect is worth noticing, because it was short-lived in its art. Mont-Saint-Michel, throughout, even up to the delicate and intricate stonework of its cloisters, is built of granite. The crypts and substructures are as well constructed as the surfaces most exposed to view. When we get to Chartres, which is largely a twelfth-century work, you will see that the cathedral there, too, is superbly built, of the hardest and heaviest stone within reach, which has nowhere settled or given way; while, beneath, you will find a crypt that rivals the church above. The thirteenth century did not build so. The great cathedrals after 1200 show economy, and sometimes worse. The world grew cheap, as worlds must.

You may like it all the better for being less serious, less heroic, less militant, and more what the French call *bourgeois*, just as you may like the style of Louis XV better than that of Louis XIV,—Madame du Barry better than Madame de Montespan,—for taste is free, and all styles are good which amuse; but since we are now beginning with the earliest, in order to step down gracefully to the stage, whatever it is, where you prefer to stop, we must try to understand a little of the kind of energy which Norman art expressed, or would have expressed if it had thought in our modes. The only word which describes the Norman style is the French word *naïf*. Littré says that *naïf* comes from *natif*, as *vulgar* comes from *vulgus*, as though native traits must be simple, and commonness must be vulgar. Both these derivative meanings were strange to the eleventh century. Naïveté was simply natural and vulgarity was merely coarse. Norman naïveté was not different in kind from the naïveté of Burgundy or Gascony or Lombardy, but it was slightly different in expression, as you will see when you travel south. Here at Mont-Saint-Michel we have only a mutilated trunk of an eleventh-century church to judge by. We have not even a façade and shall have to stop at some Norman village—at Thaon or Ouistreham—to find a west front which might suit the Abbey here, but wherever we find it we shall find something a little more serious, more military, and more practical than you will meet in other Romanesque work, farther south. So, too, the central tower or lantern—the most striking feature of Norman churches—has fallen here at Mont-Saint-Michel, and we shall have to replace it from Cérisy-la-Forêt, and Lessay, and Falaise. We shall find much to say about the value of the lantern on a Norman church, and the singular power it expresses. We shall have still more to say of the towers which flank the west front of Norman churches, but these are mostly twelfth-century, and will lead us far beyond Coutances and Bayeux, from *flèche* to *flèche*, till we come to the flèche of all flèches, at Chartres.

We shall have a whole chapter of study, too, over the eleventh-century apse, but here at Mont-Saint-Michel, Abbot Hildebert's choir went the way of his nave and tower. He built out even more boldly to the east than to the west, and although the choir stood for some four hundred years, which is a sufficient life for most architecture, the foundations gave way at last, and it fell in 1421, in the midst of the English wars, and remained a ruin until 1450. Then it was rebuilt, a monument of the last days of the Gothic, so that now, standing at the western door, you can look down the church, and see the two limits of mediæval architecture married together,—the earliest Norman and the latest French. Through the Romanesque arches of 1058, you look into the exuberant choir of latest Gothic, finished in 1521. Although the two structures are some five hundred years apart, they live pleasantly together. The Gothic died gracefully in France. The choir is charming,—far more charming than the nave, as the beautiful wom-

an is more charming than the elderly man. One need not quarrel about styles of beauty, as long as the man and woman are evidently satisfied and love and admire each other still, with all the solidity of faith to hold them up; but, at least, one cannot help seeing, as one looks from the older to the younger style, that whatever the woman's sixteenth-century charm may be, it is not the man's eleventh-century trait of naïveté;—far from it! The simple, serious, silent dignity and energy of the eleventh century have gone. Something more complicated stands in their place; graceful, self-conscious, rhetorical, and beautiful as perfect rhetoric, with its clearness, light, and line, and the wealth of tracery that verges on the florid.

The crypt of the same period, beneath, is almost finer still, and even in seriousness stands up boldly by the side of the Romanesque; but we have no time to run off into the sixteenth century: we have still to learn the alphabet of art in France. One must live deep into the eleventh century in order to understand the twelfth, and even after passing years in the twelfth, we shall find the thirteenth in many ways a world of its own, with a beauty not always inherited, and sometimes not bequeathed. At the Mount we can go no farther into the eleventh as far as concerns architecture. We shall have to follow the Romanesque to Caen and so up the Seine to the Ile de France, and across to the Loire and the Rhone, far to the South where its home lay. All the other eleventh-century work has been destroyed here or built over, except at one point, on the level of the splendid crypt we just turned from, called the Gros Piliers, beneath the choir.

There, according to M. Corroyer, in a corner between great constructions of the twelfth century and the vast Merveille of the thirteenth, the old refectory of the eleventh was left as a passage from one group of buildings to the other. Below it is the kitchen of Hildebert. Above, on the level of the church, was the dormitory. These eleventh-century abbatial buildings faced north and west, and are close to the present parvis, opposite the last arch of the nave. The lower levels of Hildebert's plan served as supports or buttresses to the church above, and must therefore be older than the nave; probably older than the triumphal piers of 1058.

Hildebert planned them in 1020, and died after carrying his plans out so far that they could be completed by Abbot Ralph de Beaumont, who was especially selected by Duke

William in 1048, "more for his high birth than for his merits." Ralph de Beaumont died in 1060, and was succeeded by Abbot Ranulph, an especial favorite of Duchess Matilda, and held in high esteem by Duke William. The list of names shows how much social importance was attributed to the place. The Abbot's duties included that of entertainment on a great scale. The Mount was one of the most famous shrines of northern Europe. We are free to take for granted that all the great people of Normandy slept at the Mount and, supposing M. Corroyer to be right, that they dined in this room, between 1050, when the building must have been in use, down to 1122 when the new abbatial quarters were built.

How far the monastic rules restricted social habits is a matter for antiquaries to settle if they can, and how far those rules were observed in the case of great secular princes; but the eleventh century was not very strict, and the rule of the Benedictines was always mild, until the Cistercians and Saint Bernard stiffened its discipline toward 1120. Even then the Church showed strong leanings toward secular poetry and popular tastes. The drama

belonged to it almost exclusively, and the Mysteries and Miracles plays which were acted under its patronage often contained nothing of religion except the miracle. The greatest poem of the eleventh century was the "Chanson de Roland," and of that the Church took a sort of possession. At Chartres we shall find Charlemagne and Roland dear to the Virgin, and at about the same time, as far away as at Assisi in the Perugian country, Saint Francis himself—the nearest approach the Western world ever made to an Oriental incarnation of the divine essence—loved the French *romans*, and typified himself in the "Chanson de Roland." With Mont-Saint-Michel, the "Chanson de Roland" is almost one. The "Chanson" is in poetry what the Mount is in architecture. Without the "Chanson," one cannot approach the feeling which the eleventh century built into the Archangel's church. Probably there was never a day, certainly never a week, during several centuries, when portions of the "Chanson" were not sung, or recited, at the Mount, and if there was one room where it was most at home, this one, supposing it to be the old refectory, claims to be the place.

THE EDUCATION OF HENRY ADAMS
(1907)
CHAPTER I
Quincy (1838–1848)

Under the shadow of Boston State House, turning its back on the house of John Hancock, the little passage called Hancock Avenue runs, or ran, from Beacon Street, skirting the State House grounds, to Mount Vernon Street, on the summit of Beacon Hill; and there, in the third house below Mount Vernon Place, February 16, 1838, a child was born, and christened later by his uncle, the minister of the First Church after the tenets of Boston Unitarianism, as Henry Brooks Adams.

Had he been born in Jerusalem under the shadow of the Temple and circumcised in the Synagogue by his uncle the high priest, under the name of Israel Cohen, he would scarcely have been more distinctly branded, and not much more heavily handicapped in the races of the coming century, in running for such stakes as the century was to offer; but, on the other hand, the ordinary traveller, who does not enter the field of racing, finds advantage in being, so to speak, ticketed through life, with the safeguards of old, established traffic. Safe-

guards are often irksome, but sometimes convenient, and if one needs them at all, one is apt to need them badly. A hundred years earlier, such safeguards as his would have secured any young man's success; and although in 1838 their value was not very great compared with what they would have had in 1738, yet the mere accident of starting a twentieth-century career from a nest of associations so colonial— so troglodytic—as the First Church, the Boston State House, Beacon Hill, John Hancock and John Adams, Mount Vernon Street and Quincy, all crowding on ten pounds of unconscious babyhood, was so queer as to offer a subject of curious speculation to the baby long after he had witnessed the solution. What could become of such a child of the seventeenth and eighteenth centuries, when he should wake up to find himself required to play the game of the twentieth? Had he been consulted, would he have cared to play the game at all, holding such cards as he held, and suspecting that the game was to be one of which neither he nor any one else back to the beginning of time knew the rules or the risks or the stakes? He was not consulted and was not responsible, but had he been taken into the confidence of his parents, he would certainly have told them to change nothing as far as concerned him. He would have been astounded by his own luck. Probably no child, born in the year, held better cards than he. Whether life was an honest game of chance, or whether the cards were marked and forced, he could not refuse to play his excellent hand. He could never make the usual plea of irresponsibility. He accepted the situation as though he had been a party to it, and under the same circumstances would do it again, the more readily for knowing the exact values. To his life as a whole he was a consenting, contracting party and partner from the moment he was born to the moment he died. Only with that understanding—as a consciously assenting member in full partnership with the society of his age—had his education an interest to himself or to others.

As it happened, he never got to the point of playing the game at all; he lost himself in the study of it, watching the errors of the players; but this is the only interest in the story, which otherwise has no moral and little incident. A story of education—seventy years of it—the practical value remains to the end in doubt, like other values about which men have disputed since the birth of Cain and Abel; but the practical value of the universe has never been stated in dollars. Although every one cannot be a Gargantua-Napoleon-Bismark and walk off with the great bells of Notre Dame, every one must bear his own universe, and most persons are moderately interested in learning how their neighbors have managed to carry theirs.

This problem of education, started in 1838, went on for three years, while the baby grew, like other babies, unconsciously, as a vegetable, the outside world working as it never had worked before, to get his new universe ready for him. Often in old age he puzzled over the question whether, on the doctrine of chances, he was at liberty to accept himself or his world as an accident. No such accident had ever happened before in human experience. For him, alone, the old universe was thrown into the ash-heap and a new one created. He and his eighteenth-century, troglodytic Boston were suddenly cut apart—separated forever—in act if not in sentiment, by the opening of the Boston and Albany Railroad; the appearance of the first Cunard steamers in the bay; and the telegraphic messages which carried from Baltimore to Washington the news that Henry Clay and James K. Polk were nominated for the Presidency. This was in May, 1844; he was six years old; his new world was ready for use, and only fragments of the old met his eyes.

Of all this that was being done to complicate his education, he knew only the color of yellow. He first found himself sitting on a yellow kitchen floor in strong sunlight. He was three years old when he took this earliest step in education; a lesson of color. The second followed soon; a lesson of taste. On December 3, 1841, he developed scarlet fever. For several days he was as good as dead, reviving only under the careful nursing of his family. When he began to recover strength, about January 1, 1842, his hunger must have been stronger than any other pleasure or pain, for while in after life he retained not the faintest recollection of his illness, he remembered quite clearly his aunt entering the sick-room bearing in her hand a saucer with a baked apple.

The order of impressions retained by memory might naturally be that of color and taste, although one would rather suppose that the sense of pain would be first to educate. In fact, the third recollection of the child was that of discomfort. The moment he could be removed, he was bundled up in blankets and carried from the little house in Hancock Avenue to a larger one which his parents were to occupy for the rest of their lives in the neighboring Mount Vernon Street. The season was midwinter, January 10, 1842, and he never forgot his acute distress for want of air under his blankets, or the noises of moving furniture.

As a means of variation from a normal type, sickness in childhood ought to have a certain value not to be classed under any fitness or unfitness of natural selection; and especially scarlet fever affected boys seriously, both physically and in character, though they might through life puzzle themselves to decide whether it had fitted or unfitted them for success; but this fever of Henry Adams took greater and greater importance in his eyes, from the point of view of education, the longer he lived. At first, the effect was physical. He fell behind his brothers two or three inches in height, and proportionally in bone and weight. His character and processes of mind seemed to share in this fining-down process of scale. He was not good in a fight, and his nerves were more delicate than boys' nerves ought to be. He exaggerated these weaknesses as he grew older. The habit of doubt; of distrusting his own judgment and of totally rejecting the judgment of the world; the tendency to regard every question as open; the hesitation to act except as a choice of evils; the shirking of responsibility; the love of line, form, quality; the horror of ennui; the passion for companionship and the antipathy to society—all these are well-known qualities of New England character in no way peculiar to individuals but in this instance they seemed to be stimulated by the fever, and Henry Adams could never make up his mind whether, on the whole, the change of character was morbid or healthy, good or bad for his purpose. His brothers were the type; he was the variation.

As far as the boy knew, the sickness did not affect him at all, and he grew up in excellent health, bodily and mental, taking life as it was given; accepting its local standards without a difficulty, and enjoying much of it as keenly as any other boy of his age. He seemed to himself quite normal, and his companions seemed always to think him so. Whatever was peculiar about him was education, not character, and came to him, directly and indirectly, as the result of that eighteenth-century inheritance which he took with his name.

The atmosphere of education in which he lived was colonial, revolutionary, almost Cromwellian, as though he were steeped, from his greatest grandmother's birth, in the odor of political crime. Resistance to something was the law of New England nature; the boy looked out on the world with the instinct of resistance; for numberless generations his predecessors had viewed the world chiefly as a thing to be reformed, filled with evil forces to be abolished, and they saw no reason to suppose that they had wholly succeeded in the abolition; the duty was unchanged. That duty implied not only resistance to evil, but hatred of it. Boys naturally look on all force as an enemy, and generally find it so, but the New Englander, whether boy or man, in his long struggle with a stingy or hostile universe, had learned also to love the pleasure of hating; his joys were few.

Politics, as a practice, whatever its professions, had always been the systematic organization of hatreds, and Massachusetts politics had been as harsh as the climate. The chief charm of New England was harshness of contrasts and extremes of sensibility—a cold that froze the blood, and a heat that boiled it—so that the pleasure of hating—one's self if no better victim offered—was not its rarest amusement; but the charm was a true and natural child of the soil, not a cultivated weed of the ancients. The violence of the contrast

was real and made the strongest motive of education. The double exterior nature gave life its relative values. Winter and summer, cold and heat, town and country, force and freedom, marked two modes of life and thought, balanced like lobes of the brain. Town was winter confinement, school, rule, discipline; straight, gloomy streets, piled with six feet of snow in the middle; frosts that made the snow sing under wheels or runners; thaws when the streets became dangerous to cross; society of uncles, aunts, and cousins who expected children to behave themselves, and who were not always gratified; above all else, winter represented the desire to escape and go free. Town was restraint, law, unity. Country, only seven miles away, was liberty, diversity, outlawry, the endless delight of mere sense impressions given by nature for nothing, and breathed by boys without knowing it.

Boys are wild animals, rich in the treasures of sense, but the New England boy had a wider range of emotions than boys of more equable climates. He felt his nature crudely, as it was meant. To the boy Henry Adams, summer was drunken. Among senses, smell was the strongest—smell of hot pine-woods and sweetfern in the scorching summer noon; of new-mown hay; of ploughed earth; of box hedges; of peaches, lilacs, syringas; of stables, barns, cow-yards; of salt water and low tide on the marshes; nothing came amiss. Next to smell came taste, and the children knew the taste of everything they saw or touched, from pennyroyal and flagroot to the shell of a pignut and the letters of a spelling-book—the taste of A-B, AB, suddenly revived on the boy's tongue sixty years afterwards. Light, line, and color as sensual pleasures, came later and were as crude as the rest. The New England light is glare, and the atmosphere harshens color. The boy was a full man before he ever knew what was meant by atmosphere; his idea of pleasure in light was the blaze of a New England sun. His idea of color was a peony, with the dew of early morning on its petals. The intense blue of the sea, as he saw it a mile or two away, from the Quincy hills; the cumuli in a June afternoon sky; the strong reds and greens and purples of colored prints and children's picture-books, as the American colors then ran; these were ideals. The opposites or antipathies, were the cold grays of November evenings, and the thick, muddy thaws of Boston winter. With such standards, the Bostonian could not but develop a double nature. Life was a double thing. After a January blizzard, the boy who could look with pleasure into the violent snow-glare of the cold white sun-shine, with its intense light and shade, scarcely knew what was meant by tone. He could reach it only by education.

Winter and summer, then, were two hostile lives, and bred two separate natures. Winter was always the effort to live; summer was trop-ical license. Whether the children rolled in the grass, or waded in the brook, or swam in the salt ocean, or sailed in the bay, or fished for smelts in the creeks, or netted minnows in the salt-marshes, or took to the pine-woods and the granite quarries, or chased muskrats and hunted snapping-turtles in the swamps, or mushrooms or nuts on the autumn hills, sum-mer and country were always sensual living, while winter was always compulsory learning. Summer was the multiplicity of nature; winter was school.

The bearing of the two seasons on the edu-cation of Henry Adams was no fancy; it was the most decisive force he ever knew; it ran through life, and made the division between its perplexing, warring, irreconcilable prob-lems, irreducible opposites, with growing em-phasis to the last year of study. From earliest childhood the boy was accustomed to feel that, for him, life was double. Winter and summer, town and country, law and liberty, were hos-tile, and the man who pretended they were not, was in his eyes a schoolmaster—that is, a man employed to tell lies to little boys. Though Quincy was but two hours' walk from Beacon Hill, it belonged in a different world. For two hundred years, every Adams, from father to son, had lived within sight of State Street, and sometimes had lived in it, yet none had ever taken kindly to the town, or been taken kindly by it. The boy inherited his double nature. He knew as yet nothing about his great-grandfather, who had died a dozen years before his own birth: he took for granted that any great-grandfather of his must have always been good, and his enemies wicked; but he divined his great-grandfather's character from his own. Never for a moment did he con-nect the two ideas of Boston and John Adams; they were separate and antagonistic; the idea of John Adams went with Quincy. He knew his grandfather John Quincy Adams only as an old man of seventy-five or eighty who was friendly and gentle with him, but except that he heard his grandfather always called "the President," and his grandmother "the Ma-dam," he had no reason to suppose that his Adams grandfather differed in character from his Brooks grandfather who was equally kind and benevolent. He liked the Adams side

best, but for no other reason than that it re-minded him of the country, the summer, and the absence of restraint. Yet he felt also that Quincy was in a way inferior to Boston, and that socially Boston looked down on Quincy. The reason was clear enough even to a five-year old child. Quincy had no Boston style. Little enough style had either; a simpler man-ner of life and thought could hardly exist, short of cave-dwelling. The flint-and-steel with which his grandfather Adams used to light his own fires in the early morning was still on the mantle-piece of his study. The idea of a livery or even a dress for servants, or of an evening toilette, was next to blasphemy. Bath-rooms, water-supplies, lighting, heating, and the whole array of domestic comforts, were unknown at Quincy. Boston had already a bath-room, a water-supply, a furnace, and gas. The superiority of Boston was evident, but a child liked it no better for that.

The magnificence of his grandfather Brooks's house in Pearl Street or South Street has long ago disappeared, but perhaps his country house at Medford may still remain to show what im-pressed the mind of a boy in 1845 with the idea of city splendor. The President's place at Quincy was the larger and older and far the more interesting of the two; but a boy felt at once its inferiority in fashion. It showed plain-ly enough its want of wealth. It smacked of colonial age, but not of Boston style or plush curtains. To the end of his life he never quite overcame the prejudice thus drawn in with his childish breath. He never could compel him-self to care for nineteenth-century style. He was never able to adopt it, any more than his father or grandfather or great-grandfather had done. Not that he felt it as particularly hos-tile, for he reconciled himself to much that was worse; but because, for some remote reason, he was born an eighteenth-century child. The old house at Quincy was eighteenth century. What style it had was in its Queen Anne ma-hogany panels and its Louis Seize chairs and sofas. The panels belonged to an old colonial Vassall who built the house; the furniture had been brought back from Paris in 1789 or 1801 or 1817, along with porcelain and books and much else of old diplomatic remnants; and neither of the two eighteenth-century styles— neither English Queen Anne nor French Louis Seize—was comfortable for a boy, or for any one else. The dark mahogany had been painted white to suit daily life in winter gloom. Nothing seemed to favor, for a child's objects, the older forms. On the contrary, most boys, as well as grown-up people, preferred the new, with good reason, and the child felt himself distinctly at a disadvantage for the taste.

Nor had personal preference any share in his bias. The Brooks grandfather was as amiable and as sympathetic as the Adams grandfather. Both were born in 1767, and both died in 1848. Both were kind to children, and both belonged rather to the eighteenth than to the nineteenth centuries. The child knew no difference between them except that one was associated with winter and the other with summer; one with Boston, the other with Quincy. Even with Medford, the association was hardly easier. Once as a very young boy he was taken to pass a few days with his grandfather Brooks under charge of his aunt, but became so violently homesick that within twenty-four hours he was brought back in disgrace. Yet he could not remember ever being seriously homesick again.

The attachment to Quincy was not altogether sentimental or wholly sympathetic. Quincy was not a bed of thornless roses. Even there the curse of Cain set its mark. There as elsewhere a cruel universe combined to crush a child. As though three or four vigorous brothers and sisters, with the best will, were not enough to crush any child, every one else conspired towards an education which he hated. From cradle to grave this problem of running order through chaos, direction through space, discipline through freedom, unity through multiplicity, has always been, and must always be, the task of education, as it is the moral of religion, philosophy, science, art, politics, and economy; but a boy's will is his life, and he dies when it is broken, as the colt dies in harness, taking a new nature in becoming tame. Rarely has the boy felt kindly towards his tamers. Between him and his master has always been war. Henry Adams never knew a boy of his generation to like a master, and the task of remaining on friendly terms with one's own family, in such a relation, was never easy.

All the more singular it seemed afterwards to him that his first serious contact with the President should have been a struggle of will, in which the old man almost necessarily defeated the boy, but instead of leaving, as usual in such defeats, a lifelong sting, left rather an impression of as fair treatment as could be expected from a natural enemy. The boy met seldom with such restraint. He could not have been much more than six years old at the time —seven at the utmost—and his mother had taken him to Quincy for a long stay with the President during the summer. What became of the rest of the family he quite forgot; but he distinctly remembered standing at the house door one summer morning in a passionate outburst of rebellion against going to school. Naturally his mother was the immediate victim of his rage; that is what mothers are for, and boys also; but in this case the boy had his mother at unfair disadvantage, for she was a guest, and had no means of enforcing obedience. Henry showed a certain tactical ability by refusing to start, and he met all efforts at compulsion by successful, though too vehement, protest. He was in fair way to win, and was holding his own, with sufficient energy, at the bottom of the long staircase which led up to the door of the President's library, when the door opened, and the old man slowly came down. Putting on his hat, he took the boy's hand without a word, and walked with him, paralyzed by awe, up the road to the town. After the first moments of consternation at this interference in a domestic dispute, the boy reflected that an old gentleman close on eighty would never trouble himself to walk near a mile on a hot summer morning over a shadeless road to take a boy to school, and that it would be strange if a lad imbued with the passion of freedom could not find a corner to dodge around, somewhere before reaching the school door. Then and always, the boy insisted that this reasoning justified his apparent submission; but the old man did not stop, and the boy saw all his strategical points turned, one after another, until he found himself seated inside the school, and obviously the centre of curious if not malevolent criticism. Not till then did the President release his hand and depart.

The point was that this act, contrary to the inalienable rights of boys, and nullifying the social compact, ought to have made him dislike his grandfather for life. He could not recall that it had this effect even for a moment. With a certain maturity of mind, the child must have recognized that the President, though a tool of tyranny, had done his disreputable work with a certain intelligence. He had shown no temper, no irritation, no personal feeling, and had made no display of force. Above all, he had held his tongue. During their long walk he had said nothing; he had uttered no syllable of revolting cant about the duty of obedience and the wickedness of resistance to law; he had shown no concern in the matter; hardly even a consciousness of the boy's existence. Probably his mind at that moment was actually troubling itself little about his grandson's iniquities, and much about the iniquities of President Polk, but the boy could scarcely at that age feel the whole satisfaction of thinking that President Polk was to be the vicarious victim of his own sins, and he gave his grandfather credit for intelligent silence. For this forbearance he felt instinctive respect. He admitted force as a form of right; he admitted even temper, under protest; but the seeds of a moral education would at that moment have fallen on the stoniest soil in Quincy, which is, as every one knows, the stoniest glacial and tidal drift known in any Puritan land.

Neither party to this momentary disagreement can have felt rancor, for during these three or four summers the old President's relations with the boy were friendly and almost intimate. Whether his older brothers and sisters were still more favored he failed to remember, but he was himself admitted to a sort of familiarity which, when in his turn he had reached old age, rather shocked him, for it must have sometimes tried the President's patience. He hung about the library; handled the books; deranged the papers; ransacked the drawers; searched the old purses and pocketbooks for foreign coins; drew the sword-cane; snapped the travelling-pistols; upset everything in the corners, and penetrated the President's dressing-closet where a row of tumblers, inverted on the shelf, covered caterpillars which were supposed to become moths or butterflies, but never did. The Madam bore with fortitude the loss of the tumblers which her husband purloined for these hatcheries; but she made protest when he carried off her best cut-glass bowls to plant with acorns or peach-stones that he might see the roots grow, but which, she said. he commonly forgot like the caterpillars.

At that time the President rode the hobby of tree-culture, and some fine old trees should still remain to witness it, unless they have been improved off the ground; but his was a restless mind, and although he took his hobbies seriously and would have been annoyed had his grandchild asked whether he was bored like an English duke, he probably cared more for the processes than for the results, so that his grandson was saddened by the sight and smell of peaches and pears, the best of their kind, which he brought up from the garden to rot on his shelves for seed. With the inherited virtues of his Puritan ancestors, the little boy Henry conscientiously brought up to him in his study the finest peaches he found in the garden, and ate only the less perfect. Naturally he ate more by way of compensation, but the act showed that he bore no grudge. As for

his grandfather, it is even possible that he may have felt a certain self-reproach for his temporary rôle of schoolmaster—seeing that his own career did not offer proof of the worldly advantages of docile obedience—for there still exists somewhere a little volume of critically edited Nursery Rhymes with the boy's name in full written in the President's trembling hand on the fly-leaf. Of course there was also the Bible, given to each child at birth, with the proper inscription in the President's hand on the fly-leaf; while their grandfather Brooks supplied the silver mugs.

So many Bibles and silver mugs had to be supplied, that a new house, or cottage, was built to hold them. It was "on the hill," five minutes' walk above "the old house," with a far view eastward over Quincy Bay, and northward over Boston. Till his twelfth year, the child passed his summers there, and his pleasures of childhood mostly centred in it. Of education he had as yet little to complain. Country schools were not very serious. Nothing stuck to the mind except home impressions, and the sharpest were those of kindred children; but as influences that warped a mind, none compared with the mere effect of the back of the President's bald head, as he sat in his pew on Sundays, in line with that of President Quincy, who, though some ten years younger, seemed to children about the same age. Before railways entered the New England town, every parish church showed half-a-dozen of these leading citizens, with gray hair, who sat on the main aisle in the best pews, and had sat there, or in some equivalent dignity, since the time of St. Augustine, if not since the glacial epoch. It was unusual for boys to sit behind a President grandfather, and to read over his head the tablet in memory of a President great-grandfather, who had "pledged his life, his fortune, and his sacred honor" to secure the independence of his country and so forth; but boys naturally supposed, without much reasoning, that other boys had the equivalent of President grandfathers, and that churches would always go on, with the bald-headed leading citizens on the main aisle, and Presidents or their equivalents on the walls. The Irish gardener once said to the child: "You'll be thinkin' you'll be President too!" The casualty of the remark made so strong an impression on his mind that he never forgot it. He could not remember ever to have thought on the subject; to him, that there should be a doubt of his being President was a new idea. What had been would continue to be. He doubted neither about Presidents nor about

Churches, and no one suggested at that time a doubt whether a system of society which had lasted since Adam would outlast one Adams more.

The Madam was a little more remote than the President, but more decorative. She stayed much in her own room with the Dutch tiles, looking out on her garden with the box walks, and seemed a fragile creature to a boy who sometimes brought her a note or a message, and took distinct pleasure in looking at her delicate face under what seemed to him very becoming caps. He liked her refined figure; her gentle voice and manner; her vague effect of not belonging there, but to Washington or to Europe, like her furniture, and writing-desk with little glass doors above and little eighteenth-century volumes in old binding, labelled "Peregrine Pickle" or "Tom Jones" or "Hannah More." Try as she might, the Madam could never be Bostonian, and it was her cross in life, but to the boy it was her charm. Even at that age, he felt drawn to it. The Madam's life had been in truth far from Boston. She was born in London in 1775, daughter of Joshua Johnson, an American merchant, brother of Governor Thomas Johnson of Maryland; and Catherine Nuth, of an English family in London. Driven from England by the Revolutionary War, Joshua Johnson took his family to Nantes, where they remained till the peace. The girl Louisa Catherine was nearly ten years old when brought back to London, and her sense of nationality must have been confused; but the influence of the Johnsons and the services of Joshua obtained for him from President Washington the appointment of Consul in London on the organization of the Government in 1790. In 1794 President Washington appointed John Quincy Adams Minister to The Hague. He was twenty-seven years old when he returned to London, and found the Consul's house a very agreeable haunt. Louisa was then twenty.

At that time, and long afterwards, the Consul's house, far more than the Minister's, was the centre of contact for travelling Americans, either official or other. The Legation was a shifting point, between 1785 and 1815; but the Consulate, far down in the City, near the Tower, was convenient and inviting; so inviting that it proved fatal to young Adams. Louisa was charming, like a Romney portrait, but among her many charms that of being a New England woman was not one. The defect was serious. Her future mother-in-law, Abigail, a famous New England woman whose authority over her turbulent husband, the second President, was hardly so great as that which she exercised over her son, the sixth to be, was troubled by fear that Louisa might not be made of stuff stern enough, or brought up in conditions severe enough, to suit a New England climate, or to make an efficient wife for her paragon son, and Abigail was right on that point, as on most others where sound judgment was involved; but sound judgment is sometimes a source of weakness rather than of force, and John Quincy already had reason to think that his mother held sound judgments on the subject of daughters-in-law which human nature, since the fall of Eve, made Adams helpless to realize. Being three thousand miles away from his mother, and equally far in love, he married Louisa in London, July 26, 1797, and took her to Berlin to be the head of the United States Legation. During three or four exciting years, the young bride lived in Berlin; whether she was happy or not, whether she was content or not, whether she was socially successful or not, her descendants did not surely know; but in any case she could by no chance have become educated there for a life in Quincy or Boston. In 1801 the overthrow of the Federalist Party drove her and her husband to America, and she became at last a member of the Quincy household, but by that time her children needed all her attention, and she remained there with occasional winters in Boston and Washington, till 1809. Her husband was made Senator in 1803, and in 1809 was appointed Minister to Russia. She went with him to St. Petersburg, taking her baby, Charles Francis, born in 1807; but brokenhearted at having to leave her two older boys behind. The life at St. Petersburg was hardly gay for her; they were far too poor to shine in that extravagant society; but she survived it, though her little girl baby did not, and in the winter of 1814–15, alone with the boy of seven years old, crossed Europe from St. Petersburg to Paris, in her travelling-carriage, passing through the armies, and reaching Paris in the Cent Jours after Napoleon's return from Elba. Her husband next went to England as Minister, and she was for two years at the Court of the Regent. In 1817 her husband came home to be Secretary of State, and she lived for eight years in F Street, doing her work of entertainer for President Monroe's administration. Next she lived four miserable years in the White House. When that chapter was closed in 1829, she had earned the right to be tired and delicate, but she still had fifteen years to serve as wife of a Member of the

House, after her husband went back to Congress in 1833. Then it was that the little Henry, her grandson, first remembered her, from 1843 to 1848, sitting in her panelled room, at breakfast, with her heavy silver teapot and sugar-bowl and cream-jug, which still exist somewhere as an heirloom of the modern safety-vault. By that time she was seventy years old or more, and thoroughly weary of being beaten about a stormy world. To the boy she seemed singularly peaceful, a vision of silver gray, presiding over her old President and her Queen Anne mahogany; an exotic, like her Sèvres china; an object of deference to every one, and of great affection to her son Charles; but hardly more Bostonian than she had been fifty years before, on her wedding-day, in the shadow of the Tower of London.

Such a figure was even less fitted than that of her old husband, the President, to impress on a boy's mind the standards of the coming century. She was Louis Seize, like the furniture. The boy knew nothing of her interior life, which had been, as the venerable Abigail, long since at peace, foresaw, one of severe stress and little pure satisfaction. He never dreamed that from her might come some of those doubts and self-questionings, those hesitations, those rebellions against law and discipline, which marked more than one of her descendants; but he might even then have felt some vague instinctive suspicion that he was to inherit from her the seeds of the primal sin, the fall from grace, the curse of Abel, that he was not of pure New England stock, but half exotic. As a child of Quincy he was not a true Bostonian, but even as a child of Quincy he inherited a quarter taint of Maryland blood. Charles Francis, half Marylander by birth, had hardly seen Boston till he was ten years old, when his parents left him there at school in 1817, and he never forgot the experience. He was to be nearly as old as his mother had been in 1845, before he quite accepted Boston, or Boston quite accepted him.

A boy who began his education in these surroundings, with physical strength inferior to that of his brothers, and with a certain delicacy of mind and bone, ought rightly to have felt at home in the eighteenth century and should, in proper self-respect, have rebelled against the standards of the nineteenth. The atmosphere of his first ten years must have been very like that of his grandfather at the same age, from 1767 till 1776, barring the battle of Bunker Hill, and even as late as 1846, the battle of Bunker Hill remained actual. The tone of Boston society was colonial. The

true Bostonian always knelt in self-abasement before the majesty of English standards; far from concealing it as a weakness, he was proud of it as his strength. The eighteenth century ruled society long after 1850. Perhaps the boy began to shake it off rather earlier than most of his mates.

Indeed this prehistoric stage of education ended rather abruptly with his tenth year. One winter morning he was conscious of a certain confusion in the house in Mount Vernon Street, and gathered, from such words as he could catch, that the President, who happened to be then staying there, on his way to Washington, had fallen and hurt himself. Then he heard the word paralysis. After that day he came to associate the word with the figure of his grandfather, in a tall-backed, invalid arm-chair, on one side of the spare bedroom fireplace, and one of his old friends, Dr. Parkman or P. P. F. Degrand, on the other side, both dozing.

The end of this first, or ancestral and Revolutionary, chapter came on February 21, 1848 —and the month of February brought life and death as a family habit—when the eighteenth century, as an actual and living companion, vanished. If the scene on the floor of the House, when the old President fell, struck the still simple-minded American public with a sensation unusually dramatic, its effect on a ten-year-old boy, whose boy-life was fading away with the life of his grandfather, could not be slight. One had to pay for Revolutionary patriots; grandfathers and grandmothers; Presidents; diplomats; Queen Anne mahogany and Louis Seize chairs, as well as for Stuart portraits. Such things warp young life. Americans commonly believed that they ruined it, and perhaps the practical common-sense of the American mind judged right. Many a boy might be ruined by much less than the emotions of the funeral service in the Quincy church, with its surroundings of national respect and family pride. By another dramatic chance it happened that the clergyman of the parish, Dr. Lunt, was an unusual pulpit orator, the ideal of a somewhat austere intellectual type, such as the school of Buckminster and Channing inherited from the Old Congregational clergy. His extraordinarily refined appearance, his dignity of manner, his deeply cadenced voice, his remarkable English and his fine appreciation, gave to the funeral service a character that left an overwhelming impression on the boy's mind. He was to see many great functions—funerals and festivals —in after-life, till his only thought was to see no more, but he never again witnessed anything nearly so impressive to him as the last services at Quincy over the body of one President and the ashes of another.

The effect of the Quincy service was deepened by the official ceremony which afterwards took place in Faneuil Hall, when the boy was taken to hear his uncle, Edward Everett, deliver a Eulogy. Like all Mr. Everett's orations, it was an admirable piece of oratory, such as only an admirable orator and scholar could create; too good for a ten-year-old boy to appreciate at its value; but already the boy knew that the dead President could not be in it, and had even learned why he would have been out of place there; for knowledge was beginning to come fast. The shadow of the War of 1812 still hung over State Street; the shadow of the Civil War to come had already begun to darken Faneuil Hall. No rhetoric could have reconciled Mr. Everett's audience to his subject. How could he say there, to an assemblage of Bostonians in the heart of mercantile Boston, that the only distinctive mark of all the Adamses, since old Sam Adams's father a hundred and fifty years before, had been their inherited quarrel with State Street, which had again and again broken out into riot, bloodshed, personal feuds, foreign and civil war, wholesale banishments and confiscations, until the history of Florence was hardly more turbulent than that of Boston? How could he whisper the word Hartford Convention before the men who had made it? What would have been said had he suggested the chance of Secession and Civil War?

Thus already, at ten years old, the boy found himself standing face to face with a dilemma that might have puzzled an early Christian. What was he?—where was he going? Even then he felt that something was wrong, but he concluded that it must be Boston. Quincy had always been right, for Quincy represented a moral principle—the principle of resistance to Boston. His Adams ancestors must have been right, since they were always hostile to State Street. If State Street was wrong, Quincy must be right! Turn the dilemma as he pleased, he still came back on the eighteenth century and the law of Resistance; of Truth; of Duty, and of Freedom. He was a ten-year-old priest and politician. He could under no circumstances have guessed what the next fifty years had in store, and no one could teach him; but sometimes, in his old age, he wondered—and could never decide—whether the most clear and certain knowledge would have helped him. Supposing he had seen a New York stock-list of 1900, and had studied the statistics of railways, telegraphs, coal, and steel—would he have quitted his eighteenth-century, his ancestral prejudices, his abstract ideals, his semi-clerical training, and the rest, in order to perform an expiatory pilgrimage to State Street, and ask for the fatted calf of his grandfather Brooks and a clerkship in the Suffolk Bank?

Sixty years afterwards he was still unable to make up his mind. Each course had its advantages, but the material advantages, looking back, seemed to lie wholly in State Street.

AGNES REPPLIER (1858–   )
THE GAYETY OF LIFE
(1904)

Grief is the sister of doubt and ill-temper, and, beyond all spirits, destroyeth man.
—SHEPHERD OF HERMAS.

In the beginning of the last century an ingenious gentleman, Mr. James Beresford, Fellow of Merton College, Oxford, diverted himself and—let us hope—his friends, by drawing up and publishing an exhaustive list of the minor miseries of life. It is a formidable document, realistic in character, and ill calculated to promote the spirit of content. No one would ever imagine that so many disagreeable things could happen in the ordinary course of existence, until the possibilities of each and every one are plainly and pitilessly defined. Some of these possibilities have passed away in the hundred years that lie between King George's day and ours; but others remain for our better discipline and subjection. Political discussions at the dinner-table rank high among Mr. Beresford's grievances; also weak tea,—"an infusion of balm, sage, and rosemary," he calls it,—and "being expected to be interested in a baby."

A great deal of modern literature, and not a little modern conversation, closely resemble this unhappy gentleman's "black list." There is the same earnest desire to point out what we would rather not observe. Life is so full of miseries, minor and major; they press so close upon us at every step of the way, that it is hardly worth while to call one another's attention to their presence. People who do this thing on a more imposing scale than Mr. Beresford are spoken of respectfully as "unfaltering disciples of truth," or as "incapable of childish self-delusion," or as " looking with clear eyes into life's bitter mysteries "; whereas in reality they are merely dwelling on the obvious, and the obvious is the one thing not worth consideration. We are all painfully aware of the seamy side, because we are scratched by the seams. What we want to contemplate is the beauty and the smoothness of that well-ordered plan which it is so difficult for us to discern. When Burke counselled a grave and anxious gentleman to "live pleasant," he was turning him aside from the ordinary aspects of existence.

There is a charming and gracious dogma of Roman Catholicism which would have us believe that all good deeds and holy prayers make up a spiritual treasury, a public fund, from which are drawn consolation for the church suffering, and strength for the church militant. A similar treasury (be it reverently spoken) holds for us all the stored-up laughter of the world, and from it comes human help in hours of black dejection. Whoever enriches this exchequer should be held a benefactor of his race. Whoever robs it—no matter what heroic motives he may advance in extenuation of the deed—has sinned heavily against his fellow men. For the gayety of life, like the beauty and the moral worth of life, is a saving grace, which to ignore is folly, and to destroy is crime. There is no more than we need,—there is barely enough to go round. If we waste our little share, if we extinguish our little light, the treasury is that much poorer, and our neighbour walks in gloom.

The thinkers of the world should by rights be the guardians of the world's mirth; but thinking is a sorry business, and a period of critical reflection, following a period of vigorous and engrossing activity, is apt to breed the "plaintive pessimist," whose self-satisfaction is disproportionate to his worth. Literature, we are assured by its practitioners, "exists to please"; but it has some doubtful methods of imparting pleasure. If, indeed, we sit down to read books on degeneracy and kindred topics, we have no reason to complain of what we find in them. It is not through such gates as these that we seek an escape from mortality. But why should poets and essayists and novelists be so determinedly depressing? Why should

"the earnest prophetic souls who tear the veil from our illusory national prosperity"—I quote from a recent review—be so warmly praised for their vandalism? Heaven knows they are always tearing the veil from something, until there is hardly a rag left for decency. Yet there are few nudities so objectionable as the naked truth. Granted that our habit of exaggerating the advantages of modern civilization and of modern culture does occasionally provoke and excuse plain speaking, there is no need of a too merciless exposure, a too insulting refutation of these agreeable fallacies. If we think ourselves well off, we *are* well off. If, dancing in chains, we believe ourselves free, we *are* free, and he is not our benefactor who weighs our shackles. Reformers have unswervingly and unpityingly decreased the world's content that they might better the world's condition. The first part of their task is quickly done. The second halts betimes. Count Tolstoi has, with the noblest intentions, made many a light step heavy, and many a gay heart sad.

As for poets and novelists, their sin is unprovoked and unpardonable. Story-telling is not a painful duty. It is an art which, in its best development, adds immeasurably to the conscious pleasure of life. It is an anodyne in hours of suffering, a rest in hours of weariness, and a stimulus in hours of health and joyous activity. It can be made a vehicle for imparting instruction, for destroying illusions, and for dampening high spirits; but these results, though well thought of in our day, are not essential to success. Want and disease are mighty factors in life; but they have never yet inspired a work of art. The late Professor Boyesen has indeed recorded his unqualified delight at the skill with which Russian novelists describe the most unpleasant maladies. He said enthusiastically that, after reading one of these masterpieces, he felt himself developing some of the very symptoms which had been so accurately portrayed; but to many readers this would be scant recommendation. It is not symptoms we seek in stories. The dullest of us have imagination enough to invent them for ourselves.

"Poverty," said old Robert Burton, "is a most odious calling," and it has not grown any more enjoyable in the past three hundred years. Nothing is less worth while than to idealize its discomforts, unless it be to sourly exaggerate them. There is no life so hard as to be without compensations, especially for those who take short views; and the view of poverty seldom goes beyond the needs of the hour and their fulfilment. But there has arisen of late years a school of writers—for the most part English, though we have our representatives—who paint realistically the squalor and wretchedness of penury, without admitting into their pictures one ray of the sunshine that must sometimes gild the dreariest hovel or the meanest street. A notable example of this black art was Mr. George Gissing, whose novels are too powerful to be ignored, and too depressing to be forgotten. The London of the poor is not a cheerful place; it is perhaps the most cheerless place in Christendom; but this is the way it appeared in Mr. Gissing's eyes when he was compelled to take a suburban train:—

"Over the pest-stricken region of East London, sweltering in sunlight which served only to reveal the intimacies of abomination; across miles of a city of the damned, such as thought never conceived before this age of ours; above streets swarming with a nameless populace, cruelly exposed by the unwonted light of heaven; stopping at stations which it crushes the heart to think should be the destination of any mortal,—the train made its way at length beyond the outmost limits of dread, and entered upon a land of level meadows, of hedges and trees, of crops and cattle."

Surely this is a trifle strained. The "nameless populace" would be not a little surprised to hear itself described with such dark eloquence. I remember once encountering in a third-class English railway carriage a butcher-boy—he confided to me his rank and profession—who waxed boastful over the size and wealth of London. "It's the biggest city in the world, that's wot it is; it's got five millions of people in it, that's wot it's got; and I'm a Londoner, that's wot I am," he said, glowing with pride that was not without merit in one of mean estate. The "city of the damned" appeared a city of the gods to this young son of poverty.

Such books sin against the gayety of life.

> All the earth round,
> If a man bear to have it so,
> Things which might vex him shall be found;

and there is no form of sadness more wasteful than that which is bred of a too steadfast consideration of pain. It is not generosity of spirit which feeds this mood. The sorrowful acceptance of life's tragedies is of value only when it prompts us to guard more jealously, or to impart more freely, life's manifold benefactions. Mr. Pater has subtly defined the mental attitude which is often mistaken for

sympathy, but which is a mere ineffectual yielding to depression over the sunless scenes of earth.

"He"—Carl of Rosenmold—"had fits of the gloom of other people, their dull passage through and exit from the world, the threadbare incidents of their lives, their dismal funerals, which, unless he drove them away immediately by strenuous exercise, settled into a gloom more properly his own. Yet, at such times, outward things would seem to concur unkindly in deepening the mental shadows about him."

This is precisely the temper which finds expression in much modern verse. Its perpetrators seem wrapped in endless contemplation of other people's gloom, until, having absorbed all they can hold, they relieve their oppressed souls by unloading it in song. Women are especially prone to mournful measures, and I am not without sympathy for that petulant English critic who declined to read their poetry on the plea that it was "all dirges." But men can be mourners, too, and—

> In all the endless road you tread
> There's nothing but the night,

is too often the burden of their verse, the unsolicited assurance with which they cheer us on our way. We do not believe them, of course, except in moments of dejection; but these are just the moments in which we would like to hear something different. When our share of gayety is running pitifully low, and the sparks of joy are dying on life's hearth, we have no courage to laugh down the voices of those who, "wilfully living in sadness, speak but the truths thereof."

Hazlitt, who was none too happy, but who strove manfully for happiness, used to say that he felt a deeper obligation to Northcote than to any of his other friends who had done him far greater service, because Northcote's conversation was invariably gay and agreeable. "I never ate nor drank with him; but I have lived on his words with undiminished relish ever since I can remember; and when I leave him, I come out into the street with feelings lighter and more ethereal than I have at any other time." Here is a debt of friendship worth recording, and blither hearts than Hazlitt's have treasured similar benefactions. Mr. Robert Louis Stevenson gladly acknowledged his gratitude to people who set him smiling when they came his way, or who smiled themselves from sheer cheerfulness of heart. They never knew—not posing as philanthropists—how far they helped him on his road; but he knew, and has thanked them in words not easily forgotten:—

"There is no duty we so much underrate as the duty of being happy. By being happy we sow anonymous benefits upon the world, which remain unknown even to ourselves, or, when they are disclosed, surprise nobody so much as the benefactor. . . . A happy man or woman is a better thing to find than a five-pound note. He or she is a radiating focus of good-will; and their entrance into a room is as though another candle had been lighted."

There is little doubt that the somewhat indiscriminate admiration lavished upon Mr. Stevenson himself was due less to his literary than to his personal qualities. People loved him, not because he was an admirable writer, but because he was a cheerful consumptive. There has been far too much said about his ill health, and nothing is so painful to contemplate as the lack of reserve on the part of relatives and executors which thrusts every detail of a man's life before the public eye. It provokes maudlin sentiment on the one side, and ungracious asperity on the other. But, in Mr. Stevenson's case, silence is hard to keep. He was a sufferer who for many years increased the gayety of life.

Genius alone can do this on a large scale; but everybody can do it on a little one. Our safest guide is the realization of a hard truth,— that we are not privileged to share our troubles with other people. If we could make up our minds to spare our friends all details of ill health, of money losses, of domestic annoyances, of altercations, of committee work, of grievances, provocations, and anxieties, we should sin less against the world's good-humour. It may not be given us to add to the treasury of mirth; but there is considerable merit in not robbing it. I have read that "the most objectionable thing in the American manner is excessive cheerfulness," and I would like to believe that so pardonable a fault is the worst we have to show. It is not our mission to depress, and one recalls with some satisfaction Saint-Simon's remark anent Madame de Maintenon, whom he certainly did not love. Courtiers less astute wondered at the enduring charm which this middle-aged woman, neither handsome nor witty, had for her royal husband. Saint-Simon held the clue. It was her "decorous gayety" which soothed Louis's tired heart. "She so governed her humours that, at all times and under all circumstances, she preserved her cheerfulness of demeanour."

There is little profit in asking ourselves or others whether life be a desirable possession. It is thrust upon us, without concurrence on our part. Unless we can abolish compulsory birth, our relish for the situation is not a controlling force. "Every child," we are told, "is sent to school a hundred years before he is born"; but he can neither profit by his schooling nor refuse his degree. Here we are in a world which holds much pain and many pleasures, oceans of tears and echoes of laughter. Our position is not without dignity, because we can endure; and not without enjoyment, because we can be merry. Gayety, to be sure, requires as much courage as endurance; but without courage the battle of life is lost. "To reckon dangers too curiously, to hearken too intently for the threat that runs through all the winning music of the world, to hold back the hand from the rose because of the thorn, and from life because of death,—this is to be afraid of Pan."

SAMUEL McCHORD CROTHERS (1857-1927)
THE MERRY DEVIL OF EDUCATION
(1910)

"It takes a newspaper man to get it right," he said, handing me the programme of a play given by an undergraduate fraternity, and a notice of the same in the morning paper. The programme announced the play as "The Merry Devil of Edmonton," while the newspaper stated that the undergraduates had revived the old Elizabethan comedy of "The Merry Devil of Education," once attributed to Shakespeare.

"These youngsters make the most absurd mistakes when dealing with the names of famous people. Perhaps some of them have never heard of me, though they are themselves only one of my pranks. Shakespeare was just the man to write me up."

The Merry Devil balanced himself on the edge of my desk and beamed upon me benevolently. I felt that I had known him all my life. There was nothing of the Mephistopheles about him. The twinkle in his eye was evidence that he had never been disillusioned. He had found it good to be alive. He seemed to be the incarnation of generations of incorrigible truants who were saying to their school-masters, "Educate us if you can."

"I hope you believe in Education," he said.

"Yes," I answered, "I have aways been taught to think highly of it."

"So do I," said the Merry Devil, "if it isn't carried too far. My business is to see that it isn't. By the way, have you ever listened to a commencement address on, The Whole Duty of a Scholar in a Democracy; or something of that sort?"

I replied that I had heard a number of such discourses, and that they impressed me as containing sound advice for youth.

"Precisely so. Every June armies of young men and maidens listen to such advice in regard to the duty they owe to the community, and they go forth resolved to practice it. I suppose they would practice it if they knew how."

"But I thought Education meant the knowing how?"

"Now, you might think so if you hadn't any experience with educated people. Let's see, what is it that a liberal education does for one who has it? It enables him to do whatever he has to do 'justly, skillfully, and magnanimously.' Why, if all your educated young people learned to act in that way there would be a revolution every year. One thoroughly just and magnanimous person can upset a community, if he's skillful. Just imagine what a million such persons would do if they were let loose on the world at the same time! I don't like to think about it."

But soon the countenance of the Merry Devil cleared and he looked up with a sunny smile.

"Things aren't so bad as they might be, are they? You are not troubled with too many just and magnanimous young people down your way? You have to thank me for that. It's not that I do not admire high scholarship. I like to see a great scholar who knows his place and keeps in it. I read an article in one of the magazines about a navy yard that can construct the biggest war vessels, but the authorities had forgotten to make a channel deep enough for them to get out. That is the way it ought to be. I like to see intellectual Dreadnoughts whose draught does not allow them to navigate the home waters. They give the public a respect for scholarship and at the same time do not interfere with any practical interests.

"You see I'm working on conservative lines. All that Our People ask is to be let alone. We want to keep things about as they are, on a sound, healthy, unintelligent basis. We don't believe in removing any fine old abuse, so long as we can get anything out of it. A lot of things are going on for no other reason than that folks don't know any better. Now I'm an optimist and believe that whatever's good for me is the best possible thing for the other fellows who can't help themselves. As long as they don't know any better and don't try to help themselves, affairs run smoothly. The minute they begin to use their minds they make trouble. Haven't you observed the number of 'problems' there are in these days? It's the result of allowing education to go too far. In the good old days there weren't any problems, there were facts. If a hundred people died of a typhoid fever, that was a regrettable fact. And if the next week another hundred died, that was another regrettable fact. But there were no meddlesome persons who made trouble for the water company. I tell you there's too much recrimination in these days. There's a way of educating people that makes them uncharitable. When things go wrong they are likely to blame somebody.

"I actually heard a College President admit, in public, that the aim of his institution was to stimulate intellectual curiosity. Just think of it! If he had said that the aim was to satisfy intellectual curiosity, that would have been all right. Boys will be boys, and college is as good a place as any in which to get over their natural inquisitiveness. If the young fellows are allowed four years in which to sow their intellectual wild oats, they can then settle down as respectable members of society and do no more thinking than other people do.

"But to deliberately stimulate intellectual curiosity! That would be like sending a lot of youngsters with lighted candles to investigate the methods of manufacture in a powder mill. I don't care how much a person knows. I regard that as his misfortune, not his fault. What I object to is that he should want to know. It is an uncomfortable habit of mind. The man who wants to know is never satisfied until he gets at the bottom facts. Now the bottom facts are providentially placed where they are so as not to attract attention. That's where they belong, and they should be kept there. Our People don't like to have unauthorized persons poking about and finding out things that ought not to be known.

"Some of the ablest men of my acquaintance tell me that intellectual curiosity is ruining the country. Curiosity makes a man discover something which he thinks is wrong; and then he tries to do something about it. That's what Our People call hysteria. When people are hysterical, they won't take what we offer them. They want to know whether it's good for them; as if that mattered. It has gone so far that everything is investigated. Now you can't expect able men to give their talents to looking after their own interests if they are meddled with in that way. It distracts their minds. By and by the able men will be discouraged, and instead of developing the great industries they will go to writing books, or painting pictures, or teaching kindergartens, just to pass away the time. And then our industries will go to ruin, and the Japanese will catch us. A great many able men feel that way, and express themselves very strongly.

"I find the same feeling among those who are being interfered with in politics. A gentleman who has been carrying on the affairs of a great city and receiving no pay but such as came 'on the side' showed me the report of a Bureau of Municipal Research. It was positively insulting. The men who got it up didn't even know what a bureau is. A bureau is a device for getting things done by referring them to another bureau that refers them back. But these fellows got up a bureau for finding out why our bureaus don't work, and why they cost so much. The report was full of figures. We had no objection to that, for we can figure too. But the mischief of it was that these figures were arranged so that you could tell what they meant. It was a bare-faced attempt to gratify intellectual curiosity.

"My friend said that if this thing kept up, he would give up politics in disgust, and live on the interest of what he had already got out of it.

"He said that the whole system of government, as he understood it, consisted in getting experts to run it. The public is the owner of a high-powered machine; the professional politician is the chauffeur. If the chauffeur wants to take friends out for a 'joy ride,' the owner oughtn't to complain. He can't get along without the chauffeur, for he doesn't know how to run the machine himself."

"But," I asked, "couldn't he learn how?"

"Yes," said the Merry Devil, "I suppose he might, if he took the trouble."

"Then," said I, "I take it that the kind of education you object to is the kind that makes people take the trouble to look into things."

"Precisely," said the Merry Devil, "I hate to see people take the trouble to look into things. It induces the habit of discrimination. Now that isn't healthy. In a state of nature people take everything for granted. Why

shouldn't they? It shows confidence in human nature. I like to see people respectful to their betters. If they allow themselves to ask, 'Are they really our betters?' that isn't respectful. You can't have an aristocracy—not a good comfortable aristocracy—where people ask questions. By the way, have you ever met a Captain of Industry?"

"Yes," I said, "at least that was what the newspapers called him."

"What struck you as his most interesting characteristic?"

"It struck me that he was very rich."

"That is, he had more money, you think, than was good for him?"

"I don't know about that, but he had more than was good for his children."

"Did it ever occur to you," said the Merry Devil, "that it was curious that a captain got so much out of the service as that? Even a major-general does a good deal of hard work for small pay. He can't lay up much. Are you sure that your friend wasn't an army contractor instead of a captain?"

"Now that you mention it," I said, "I do think he talked more like an army contractor. I thought, at the time, that he wasn't very soldierly, especially when I found that he didn't know anything about his men. He said that all his men are on the other side. He seemed to think that was the normal situation."

The Merry Devil laughed heartily. "Just see where you are coming out, and just because I asked you two or three questions. You have come to the conclusion that the gentleman you admired wasn't a Captain of Industry at all, though the newspapers said he was. It isn't safe to ask questions, unless you are willing to hear the answer.

"When Thomas Carlyle invented that term Captains of Industry, it scared Our People half to death. Carlyle's idea was that the time had come when persons would take up business as one goes into the army. An officer has to think of the army first and himself afterward. If he doesn't, he's cashiered. We were afraid that a large number of youths might be educated in that way. When we saw some of the Captains of Industry who passed without question, we were greatly comforted."

The Merry Devil continued in a more chastened mood. "It isn't merely the person who is looking after his own interests, who should be protected against intellectual curiosity. Disinterested persons who spend their lives in doing good, make the same complaint in regard to certain kinds of education. You know we don't object to people trying to do good, so long as they don't succeed. It serves to keep them busy, and it takes their minds off themselves. We like to see them move in the line of the least resistance. The easier their good work is for them, the less it interferes with our plans. We like to see righteousness moving in ruts. It's only when it breaks out in an unexpected place that it's dangerous. But intellectual curiosity gets people out of their ruts, and sometimes they run wild. Education, if it isn't carefully looked after, is a disturbing influence. It more than doubles the labor, and makes a good man dissatisfied with himself.

"The other day a minister, a worthy man, took me into his confidence, and told me his troubles. He had been gifted with a strong voice and a confident manner, and had acquired a reputation for eloquence. He had by constant practice overcome the timidity which comes to a public speaker when he stops to think whether what he is about to say is worth while. He did not need to stop to think, he was such an easy speaker. He never was at a loss for a word, and would use the words as a life-preserver as he struck out boldly for his next head. He knew that he would always be buoyed up in this way, so that the preparation of his sermons never interfered with his parish calls.

"One day in the midst of a most eloquent passage he observed a man in the back pew with a look of intellectual curiosity in his countenance. He was evidently impressed by the volume of sound, and was trying to find out what it was all about. The minister said that instantly the same thought came to his own mind, and for the life of him he couldn't tell what it was about. Unfortunately the man became a regular attendant and always looked interested.

"The minister said that that one parishioner who insists on thinking while he is in church has caused him more mental disquietude than all the others put together. Sometimes a fine illustration is spoiled by seeing the look of inquiry as to what it illustrates. The man in the back pew has changed sermon-making from a pleasure to hard work.

"Now what do you think of an education which makes life harder for good people? When a man is doing his best, it's taking an unfair advantage of him to raise the standard. It makes him unhappy."

There was such a look of genuine commiseration that for the first time it occurred to me that my visitor was human, and I had been remiss in my attentions.

"Do take a chair," I said, vaguely.

"No, thanks! I'll sit on the curb of your ink-well."

"I'm afraid you may fall in."

"No matter if I do. Ink is my native element."

Then he chatted so pleasantly about the kind of education which he found unobjectionable that I was quite charmed with him. He believed sincerely in what are called "accomplishments," and was willing to have them carried to almost any extent.

"I like," he said, "that good old term 'polite learning.' Now the first rule of politeness is not to contradict. So long as Learning doesn't contradict, Our People are willing to treat it liberally and give it things. We don't make any bargain, but of course we expect it to back us up, or at least not to make any trouble. We don't care how long it takes a learned man to come to his conclusions, we are willing to humor him if he wants to use the scientific method, but his conclusions must be sound."

"But what if the facts point the other way?"

"He should be more careful in selecting his facts," said the Merry Devil.

"Wouldn't it be better," I suggested, "if the learned man didn't come to any conclusion at all?"

"Yes," said the Merry Devil, "and that's the way I work it whenever I can. You see there are two kinds of science, pure science and applied science. Now pure science would be perfectly harmless if we could keep people from finding it out, and applying it. I tell the professors that they should be more careful and use obscure language wherever possible. Otherwise their pupils will draw conclusions. Sciences like Ethics and Sociology and History and Political Economy ought to be kept pure. I hate to see a man interested in affairs teaching such subjects."

"I suppose," I said, "that you are afraid that the students would come to see that these are affairs that they have to deal with."

"It's a real danger," said the Merry Devil. "Now I feel a tender affection for Truth. I don't like to see it exposed."

"It seems," I remarked, "that you do not agree with the pragmatic theory that Truth is something that makes a difference, and that a thing which doesn't make a difference isn't true."

"I don't quarrel about words, and if a thing doesn't make any difference I don't care whether it's true or not. I tell Our People that thay needn't worry about Education so long as I look after it. I know communities that are full of educated men, and they don't make any difference. Now what's the harm in it? I have personally conducted parties through all the branches of learning, and they were not in the least affected by it. What I most enjoy is to experiment with a successful self-made man. He is an easy mark and will pay liberally for an educational gold brick. He has made his own way in the world by force of ability and hard work. But when it comes to his son he is the most credulous creature alive. He is ready to believe that something can be had for nothing. When he sends his son to college the last thing he thinks of is that the lad will have to work for all that he gets. He has an idea that a miracle of some kind is about to be performed in the enchanted castle of the Liberal Arts. The boy will have all sorts of things done for him. He will get Mental Discipline, which is a fine thing to have. Certain studies are rich in discipline. If he doesn't elect these disciplinary studies he will doubtless get all the Mental Discipline he needs by living in the same town with a number of hard-working professors. Every college which has been a long time on the same spot has Ideals. The youth is supposed to get these Ideals, though he is unconscious of them at the time. In after years they will be explained to him at the class reunions and he will be glad that he absorbed them. Towards the end of his college course he will show signs of superiority to his parents, and there will be symptoms of world-weariness. He will be inclined to think that nothing is quite worth while. That tired feeling is diagnosed as 'Culture'. The undergraduate has become acquainted with the best that has been said and known in the world, and sees that it doesn't amount to much after all.

"The fellows who have to work their way have a hard time, but the sons of fortune may be educated with surprisingly little effort. They have so many advantages. I notice the same principle in some of the states where the educational test is pleasantly mitigated by what is called 'the grandfather clause.' A person with the right kind of grandfather doesn't need to labor with the alphabet in order to be allowed to vote. It is assumed that he has certain hereditary qualities which are a good substitute for reading and writing."

"I think that there's a great deal in heredity," I said.

"Yes," answered the Merry Devil, "there's a great deal more in it than seems to come out."

He then explained how he gained the confidence of the student and made his college days one long, bright dream.

"He spends four care-free years without being troubled by a serious thought. When the time is up I make use of the psychological method of suggestion. I suggest to him that now he has an education. And he doesn't know but he has,—he has been exposed to it.

"The very elaboration of our educational scheme makes it easier for me to circumvent the educators. It was different with the ancient Persians, who taught their youth to ride, to shoot, and to speak the truth. It was hard to sophisticate so simple a curriculum. You could tell what an educated man could do. If he habitually tumbled off his horse, and missed the mark, and told lies, you knew that he hadn't been educated. But nowadays you can't tell what turn a man's education may have taken.

"Only the other day I met a man who seemed to me the most unintelligent person I had met in many a month. I tried him on all sorts of subjects of common interest, and could not get the slightest response. There seemed to be a lack of sympathetic imagination and a singular aversion to general ideas. I soon learned the reason. He was about to take the last degree, which was to cut him off forever from the unlearned world. He had passed through a terrible ordeal and had for a year or two been subjected to cruel and unusual knowledge. He had taken a Trappist vow of silence upon all subjects unconnected with his Thesis, 'Some Minor Mistakes in Algonkian Etymology.' He was reduced almost to a shadow because he was afraid that the mistakes he had discovered weren't small enough. He must find some mistakes that everybody else had overlooked, in order to prove his capacity for Original Research."

"That seems reasonable enough," I said. "I suppose that he intends to go into original research as his life work, and that is excellent discipline for him. It is a great thing to have a part in the Advancement of Science."

"Advancement of Science! Fiddlesticks!" said the Merry Devil, "he isn't going in for any more research after he finishes his thesis. What he wants to do is to teach in a good school, and people have the idea that an infallible test is the capacity for Original Research."

"But I should think that teaching half-grown boys was quite different; indeed involved almost exactly the opposite methods and talents. The capacity which the ordinary teacher most needs is that of making the rudiments interesting. He is not intent on finding something new, but it is his business to communicate ideas that are the common property of mankind. I should think that, after spending several years in minute study of some unfrequented bypath, he would not be very well fitted to conduct boys upon the main road, and make them interested in it. It would seem to me that he might lose something of the sense of proportion, which, after all, is quite an essential thing. Wouldn't it have been better to have spent the time in getting a strong grasp upon the most essential things, so that he could thoroughly humanize and idealize what he had to teach?"

"You don't understand," said the Merry Devil. "The important thing is to set a high standard."

Then he began to dance about the room, singing,—

"Hi Diddle Diddle, the cat and the fiddle,
The cow jumped over the moon.

"That was a high standard for the cow. It showed what she could do, even if she never tried to do it again. I suppose you may ask whether it added to her value as a plain family cow. Perhaps not, but it was interesting as a sporting proposition. From my point of view there is a great advantage in having the ambitious scholar avoid the habitable parts of the earth, and spend a few years in some arid spot. A little of this aridity gets into his manner. A schoolmaster who has kept to the main road is likely to seize upon the salient points, and to show the relations of one thing to another. Such a person is likely to have an undue influence over boys. They might become as enthusiastic over scholarship as over football. Before you know it, you would be back to the puritanical ideas of Milton of a school where there are 'such Lectures and Explanations upon every opportunity as may lead and draw them in willing obedience, enflamed with the study of Learning, and the admiration of Virtue, stirred up with high hopes of living to be brave men and worthy Patriots, dear to God and famous to all ages.' All the time the schoolmaster would be 'infusing into their young breasts such an ingenuous and noble ardor as would not fail to make many of them renowned and matchless men.' Doesn't that sound hysterical? Just think of inflaming them with the study of learning! I say it's the business of the teacher to cool them off. It all comes back to the talk about learning to do things, not only skillfully but magnanimously. Is that what you want to encourage in schools that cost good money?"

"Magnanimity," I said, "is an excellent quality."

"There you are wrong," said the Merry Devil. "Magnanimity is not a quality, it's a quantity, as you ought to know. It is, literally, big-minded-ness. There is something vulgar about bigness. A neat little mind is much more pleasing to a person of taste. If a man's mind is bigger than his business, it's awkward for him. It gets him into all sorts of trouble. He's always seeing the other side, and going against his own interests. He gets himself so mixed up with the mass of mankind that sometimes he loses the chance to get ahead. And when he does get an idea into his head it's hard to control him. You can't stop a magnanimous man by telling him that he will probably get hurt if he goes on. It's hard to understand his motives. My business is to keep magnanimity from getting too much of a start. I begin early. There is a great deal of magnanimity in small children. They go about with notions that are several sizes too large for them. Whenever I catch a youngster acting from a magnanimous motive I put a little pusillanimous motive in its place. It acts like a charm. Parents and teachers like it because it makes discipline easier. They see results, and that's what they want. Of course there are other results that they don't see.

"Did you ever see," he continued, "a small boy helping his father in the garden? If the father has a large spade and a wheelbarrow the boy wants a little spade and a tiny wheelbarrow, so that he can help. It's a privilege to be allowed to work for the family. You perhaps know Tennyson's little poem called 'Wages.' He says that all that heroes ask is 'the wages of going on.' That sounds very magnanimous, —in a man. Almost all boys are like that to begin with. All they ask is the wages of going on, with people whom they admire and in something that seems to be worth while. Just think what a state of things there would be if they acted that way when they grew up!

"I suggest to the father that he had better pay the boy for all the little services which he had been doing for the love of it. In a little while the lad loses his magnanimous ways and drives a sharp bargain whenever he is sent on an errand. This pleases the father, for he knows now that his son will be able to hold his own. I work the same plan in school. There are all sorts of ways of taking the spirit out of a child. Nagging is one way, but foolish little rewards are often more effective. He can resent a punishment, but he cannot resent a reward of merit that he doesn't want and that he knows he doesn't deserve. He can only feel morally awkward at what is evidently an anti-climax. How would you feel if you had done a moderately heroic act, and the person whom you had rescued were to put his hand in his pocket and say, 'Here, my good man, is a silver dollar,—it is no more than you deserve.' Children are treated that way all the time—and some of them learn to like it. Even in college you may see the student—a grown man—still working for 'marks.' He has not come to the point where he works for the 'wages of going on.'"

"In that case he doesn't go on," I said.

"No," said the Merry Devil, "not after he gets his diploma."

The conversation drifted from one phase of the subject to another. I noticed that as long as we talked of systems and methods the Merry Devil retained his jaunty air. He was an old hand at finding the weak points in the best inventions. But when we came to mention the names of certain teachers, I thought I detected "a lurking trouble in his nether lip." There was evidently a personal element which he could not easily deal with.

"In spite of all your efforts," I said, "I predict that you will be beaten at last. The business of training citizens for a democracy has just begun. Educational ideals have thus far been largely dominated by aristocratic preconceptions. The aim has been to train the few to rule the many, or at least to escape from vulgar contact with those beneath them. Education has been the badge of a superior class.

"Such education was morally superficial. It invited pedantry. But to those who take democracy seriously education becomes at once the most difficult and the most necessary part of statesmanship. Its aim is to enable the many to govern themselves and to realize the possibilities of their own nature. This is the affair not of the pedant but of the patriot. To me the significant thing is the power that lies in the personality of the teacher and which exerts an influence on the whole character. Now I can tell you of a born teacher who—"

"Oh," said the Merry Devil, holding up his hands, "I never claimed to be a match for a born teacher."

WILLIAM CRARY BROWNELL (1851-1928)

From COOPER

(1906)

I

The literary standard of his countrymen is undoubtedly far higher than it was in Cooper's own day. No writer at present with a tenth of his ability would commit his literary faults—faults for which the standard of his day is largely responsible, since it was oblivious to them and since they are precisely those which any widely accepted standard would automatically correct. In other words, Cooper wrote as well as, and builded better than, any one required of him—and though genius, *ex hypothesi*, escapes the operation of evolutionary law, literary or any other artistic expression is almost as much a matter of supply and demand as railroads or any other means of communication; the demand, that is, produces, controls, and gives its character to the supply. The theory that art is due to artists leaves the origin of artists unexplained.

But it is a depressing phenomenon in current American letters that our standard, though satisfactorily higher, should be applied with so little intelligence and elasticity, so mechanically. It is widely held, and the puniest whipsters flourish it like a falchion

when they play at soldiers—our popular literary game at present, it sometimes seems. It is not to deny that this diversion has its uses to assert that it has its limitations. To have popularized a high literary standard is an accomplishment of which American letters may well be proud. Indeed it is, perhaps, the result of which hitherto—a few eminent names excepted—it has most reason to be proud. And no doubt there is still reason to hope that our high popular standard may become even higher and more popular than it is! Meantime one would like to see its application more elastic, less mechanical. The way in which it has been applied to the detriment of Cooper's fame, has been not merely unintelligent but thoroughly discreditable. For Cooper, from any point of view, is one of the most distinguished of our literary assets, and there is something ludicrous in being before all the world—as, assuredly, we sometimes are—in recognizing our own merit where it is contestable and in neglecting it where it is not.

It is only superficially remarkable that Cooper should have been over thirty when he wrote his first story. Had he possessed the native temperament of the literary artist, he certainly would not have deferred experimentation so long. Nor would he, probably, if he had had to cast about for a livelihood, or if his environment had been other than it was. But to determine the literary vocation of a man of literary genius, yet nevertheless a man who had been occupied in wholly unliterary pursuits until so ripe a maturity as his, the accident of a whim was not only an appropriate but altogether the most natural cause. "Precaution" was the result of such an accident. It has no other merit, but it established the fact, which apparently he had never suspected, that he had the gift of improvisation; and when he found his material, in his next book, he produced a work that established his reputation as a writer of romance. He did much better, as he did far worse, afterward, but "The Spy" is eminently characteristic. It betrays his faults—very nearly all of them, I think—and most of his virtues. It signalized the entrance into the field of romance, in the fulness of untried but uncommon powers, of a born story-teller. This he was first of all. Some of his stories are dull, but they are never not stories. He belongs, accordingly, in the same category with Scott and Dumas and George Sand, and in general the writers whose improvising imagination is a conspicuous if not their preponderant faculty—a faculty which, though it may sometimes weary others, seems itself never to tire.

To be one of the great romancers of the world is, in itself, a distinction. But there is more than one kind of romance, and Cooper's has the additional interest of reality. It is based on very solid substance. It is needless to say that it has no interest of literary form —such as distinguishes, though it may not preserve, the exhilarating sophistication of Stevenson. It quite lacks the spiritual fancy of Hawthorne, the inventive extravagance of Poe, the *verve* of Dumas's opulent irresponsibility, the reach and scope of Scott's massive imaginativeness, the richness and beauty of George Sand's poetic improvisation. It has, however, on its side a certain advantage in being absolutely native to its material. More than any other writer of "tales" Cooper fused romance and realism. His books are flights of the imagination, strictly so-called, and at the same time the human documents which it has been left to a later age thus to label. There is not a character, not an incident, in Cooper that could be accused of exaggeration from the standpoint of rationality. And yet the breeze of adventure blows through his pages as if he

had no care whatever for truth and fact. Second, no doubt, to Scott in romantic imaginativeness, he is even his superior in the illusion which gives his books an unpretentious and convincing air of relating rather than of inventing, of keeping within bounds and essaying no literary flights—of, as Arnold said in eulogy of German poetry, "going near the ground."

II

The circumstances of his life explain the characteristics of his books with even more completeness than circumstances—as has now become a commonplace—explain everything, and constitute as well as alter cases. He had little systematic education. His character was developed and affirmed before his mind was either trained or stored. His taste naturally suffered. Taste is the product of tradition, and of tradition he was quite independent, quite ignorant. Fortunately, he was also ignorant of its value, and when at thirty he began to produce literature his energy was unhampered by diffidence. But it was inevitable that the literature he produced should be extremely unliterary, and noticeably so in proportion to its power. The fact that he was thirty before he took up his pen is proof enough that he was not a literary genius, proof enough, indeed, that his talent was not distinctively a literary talent. He had not even a tincture of bookishness. Of the *art* of literature he had perhaps never heard. It was quite possible in his day —singular as it may seem in ours—not to hear of it. He indulged in no youthful experimentation in it, unlike Irving. He left school early and was a sailor, a man of business, a gentleman of more or less leisure—enough, at all events, to encourage a temperament that was aristocratic and critical, and not in the least speculative, adventurous, and æsthetic.

What encouragement the literary temperament could find, too, in the America of his youth is well known. The conditions drove Irving abroad, and made a recluse of Hawthorne. Cooper throve under them. They suited his genius, and when he had once started he worked freely in them. He was personally interested in life, in people, in social and political phenomena, in American history and promise, American traits as already determined, American ideas and "institutions," in the country itself, its lakes and woods and plains and seashore, its mountains and rivers, as well as its cities and "settlements"—as Leatherstocking calls them. At least until he began "The Spy" he had never thought of all this as "material," if, indeed, he ever did afterward—in the express and æsthetic sense in which, for example, Stevenson would have regarded it. He was its historian, its critic, its painter, in his own view. He classed his books as works of the imagination in the rather conventional and limited sense in virtue of which fiction is necessarily, and by definition, imaginative. His "art" was for him the art of story-telling, in which the characters and incidents are imagined instead of being real. That his fiction was imaginative rather than merely imagined, I mean, probably never occurred to him. He never philosophized about it at all, and as he began it by conscious imitation of convention, continued it conventionally, so far as his procedure was conscious. As he wrote "Precaution" to determine whether or no he "could write a novel," he wrote "The Pilot" to prove that he could write a more seamanlike tale than "The Pirate" of Scott. He continued to write story after story, because he had made a success of story-telling, and demonstrated it to be his vocation.

But story-telling did not absorb his interests. He wrote other things, too. He has decided rank as a publicist. And he spoiled some of his novels by his preoccupations of that kind—although, indeed, he gave value and solidity to others of them in the same way; "The Bravo" is, for example, as strong a story as "The Ways of the Hour" is weak. Distinctly what we should call "unliterary," however, his point of view remained as it had been at the outset. Without the poetic or artistic temperament—at least in sufficiently controlling force to stimulate self-expression before almost middle life—he subsisted in an environment, both personal and national, so hostile to the æsthetic and academic as to color what manifestations of these it suffered at all with a decidedly provincial tinge. The conjunction was fortunate. If it was responsible for a long list of the most unliterary works by any writer of eminence in any literature—as I suppose Cooper's may be called—it nevertheless produced an author of acknowledged power and indisputable originality, whose force and vitality are as markedly native and personal as their various manifestations are at times superficial, careless, and conventional. In a word, Cooper was, if not a great writer, a man of conspicuously large mental and moral stature, of broad vision, of wide horizon, of independent philosophy.

His prolixity is perhaps his worst fault; it is, at all events, the source of the worst fault his novels have, the heaviest handicap a novel can

have—namely, their tedium. To begin with, hardly one of them is without its tiresome character. Not a few have more than one. Few of his best characters avoid tedium at times; at times even Leatherstocking is a bore. Cooper must himself, in actual life, have been fond of bores. Perhaps his irascibility was soothed by studying this particular foible of his fellows. The trait is to be suspected in other writers of fiction; Scott, for example. For my own part, I recall no character in Cooper as tiresome as some of "Scott's bores," as they are proverbially called. Cooper, however, in this respect is, in general, unsurpassed. The Scotch doctor in "The Spy," the Dutch father in "The Water-Witch," the Italian disputants in "Wing-and-Wing," the crack-brained psalmodist in "The Last of the Mohicans"—but it is idle to specify, the list is too long.

It is true that to represent a bore adequately a novelist can hardly avoid making him tiresome. That is his *raison d'être*, and for a novelist *nihil humani* can be *alienum*. But Terence himself would have modified his maxim if he could have foreseen Cooper's addiction to this especial genius. And, as I say, some of the best and most interesting of his personages prose at time interminably; the Pathfinder talking about his own and Killdeer's merits at the prize-shooting, not a few, indeed, of the deliverances of this star character of Cooper's entire company are hard to bear. And both the bores who are—so explicitly and, thus, exhaustively—exhibited as such and the non-bores who nevertheless so frequently bore us have the painful and monotonous family resemblance of all being tiresome in one way—in prolixity. They are really not studied very closely as bores or as occasionally tiresome personages, but are extremely simplified by being represented merely as long-winded. No shades of character, no particular and individual weaknesses are illustrated by their prolixity. Their prolixity is itself the trait that distinguishes them.

The conclusion is inevitable that his characters are often so prolix and often such prolix characters because—which also we know to be the fact—Cooper himself was. Speaking of the unreadable "Mercedes of Castile," Professor Lounsbury truly says that the author is as long getting under way with his story as Columbus himself was in arranging for his voyage. And though this inexplicable novel is probably his dullest, there are few others that do not contain long passages whose redundancy is remorseless. He has no standards. He feels no responsibility. He never thinks of the reader. He follows his own inclination completely, quite without concern for company, one must conclude. There was no tribunal whose judgments he had to consider; there was no censure to be dreaded, no praise he had to try to earn by being other than his own disposition prompted, by being more simple, more concise, more respectful of the reader's intelligence—no ideal of perfection, in short, at which the pressure of current criticism constrained him to aim. And of technical perfection in any but its broadest details—such as general composition and construction—he had no notion. His pace was leisurely, because such was his habit of mind, and there was nothing extraneous to hasten it. He lingered because he liked to, and his public was not impatient. He repeated because he enjoyed repetition, and there was no one to wince at it. He was as elaborate in commonplace as the dilettante can be in paradox because novelty as such did not attract nor familiarity repel either himself or his public. As to literary standards, the times have certainly changed since his day. In literary performance there is perhaps an occasional reminder that the tendency to prolixity still subsists. And in actual life!—but, of course, changes in the macrocosm are naturally more gradual.

Yet even our own time may profitably inquire how it is that Cooper's popularity has triumphed so completely over so grave a fault. Largely, I think, it is due to the fact that the fault is a "literary"—that is to say, a technical —defect, and is counterbalanced by the vitality and largeness of the work of which it, too, is a characteristic. It is far from negligible. On the contrary, it is, however accounted for, the chief obstacle that prevents Cooper from attaining truly classic rank—the rank never quite attained by any one destitute of the sense of form, the feeling for perfection which is what makes art artistic, however inane or insubstantial it may be. But Cooper's technical blemishes are in no danger of being neglected. As Thackeray said impatiently of Macaulay's, "What critic can't point them out?" To point out Cooper's is so easy that his critics are singularly apt to sag into caricature in the process. Nevertheless, though it is indubitable that his prolixity is a grave defect, it is important to remember that it is a formal rather than a substantial one, and that in popular esteem it has been more than counterbalanced by compensations of substance. What is less evident, but what is still more worth indicating, is that there is, speaking somewhat loosely, a certain artis-

tic fitness in his diffuseness, and that this is probably the main reason why it has so slightly diminished not only his popularity, but his legitimate fame. It is, in a word, and except in its excess, an element of his illusion. And in a sense, thus, it is rather a quality than a defect of his work. His illusion is incontestable. No writer of romance has more. It is simply impossible to praise him too highly here. And where the effect is so plainly secured one may properly divine some native felicity in the cause, however, abstractly considered, inadequate to anything such a cause may seem.

III

Cooper is usually called the American Scott in a sense that implies his indebtedness to Scott as a model and a master. His romances are esteemed imitations of the Waverly Novels, differing from their originals as all imitations do in having less energy, less spontaneity —of necessity, therefore, less originality. This is to consider mere surface resemblance. How much or how little Cooper owed to Scott is a question for the literary historian rather than the critic. Doubtless he copied Scott in various practical ways. Romance had received a stamp, a *cachet*, from Scott that, devoted to the same *genre*, it was impossible to ignore. Scott's own derivation may be defined quite as clearly, and the record of it is, like similar studies, one that has its uses. But for other than didactic purposes it is the contrast rather than the resemblance, even, between him and Cooper that is pertinent. It is misleading to compare them—in any sense which implies that Cooper's originality is in any way inferior. It is idle to characterize so voluminous a writer as imitative. Whatever its initial impetus imitation will not furnish the momentum for forty volumes. Cooper's inspiration is as genuine, his zest as great, his genius as individual, as Scott's own. He was less of an artist. He was nothing at all of a poet—at least, in any constructional sense. It is simply impossible to fancy him essaying verse. Even balladry, even rhyming, is beyond him.

"Tunstall lies dead upon the field,
His life-blood stains the spotless shield;"

—there is not a note like that in his equipment. For a writer of romance the defect is grave. Nor did he know the world of society as Scott knew it. Any one who can take literally Scott's generous compliment to Miss Austen must never have read "St. Ronan's Well." Neither did he inhabit the same world of the imagination. If he had far less temperament he had also far less culture. His environment forbade it; and he lived in the present. His conservatism was a rationalized liberalism—nothing akin to the instinctive toryism that made it natural for Scott to poetize history. And consequently his environment and his genius combined to confine him in the main to a field which, however interesting in itself, is incontestably inferior to the grandiose theatre of Scott's fiction. A splendid historical pageant winds its way through the Waverly Novels, with which nothing that the pioneer America of Cooper's day furnished could compare.

It is, indeed, in his material that Cooper presents the greatest possible contrast to Scott. It is vain, I think, for American chauvinism itself to deny that our civilization is less romantic than an older one, than that of Europe. To begin with, it has less background, and, as Stevenson pointed out, romanticism in literature largely consists in consciousness of the background. Nothing, it is true, is more romantic than nature, except nature plus man. But the exception is prodigious. Nature in Cooper counts as romantically as she does in Scott, but it is nature without memories, without monuments, without associations. Man, too, with him, though counting on the whole as romantically, does not count as background. His figures are necessarily foreground figures. They are not relieved against the wonderful tapestry of the past. In a word, there is necessarily little *history* in Cooper. Of course, there is "The Bravo," as admirable a tale as "Mercedes of Castile" is an unprofitable one. But the mass of Cooper's most admirable accomplishment is thoroughly and fortunately American, and compared with Europe America has no history. Scott's material in itself, thus, constitutes an incontestable romantic superiority. For fiction history provides offhand a whole world for the exercise of the imagination.

It may undoubtedly be urged that a romantic situation is such in virtue of its elements and not of its associations; that the escape of Uncas from the Hurons in "The Last of the Mohicans" is as romantic as Edward Waverley's visit to the cave of Donald Bean Lean. Or to consider more profoundly, it may be said that, looking within, Hawthorne found in the spiritual drama of New England Puritanism the very quintessence of the romantic, thrown into all the sharper relief by its excessively austere and arid environment—that is to say, by a featureless and thoroughly *un*romantic background. Still, in considering the mass of a writer's work its romantic interest is not to be admeasured mainly by its situations, or its psychology, but by the texture of its entire fabric. And owing to its wealth of imaginative association, the romance of the Waverly Novels is indubitably deeper, richer, more *important* than that of the Leatherstocking Tales. Bernardin de Saint Pierre passes for the father of French literary romanticism, for instance, but it can be only in a purely poetic or very technical sense that "Paul et Virginie" can be called as romantically important as "The Cloister and the Hearth."

There is a quality in Cooper's romance, however, that gives it as romance an almost unique distinction. I mean its solid alliance with reality. It is thoroughly romantic, and yet—very likely owing to his imaginative deficiency, if anything can be so owing—it produces, for romance, an almost unequalled illusion of life itself. This writer, one says to one's self, who was completely unconscious of either the jargon or the philosophy of "art," and who had but a primitively romantic civilization to deal with, has nevertheless, in this way produced the rarest, the happiest, artistic result. He looked at his material as so much life; it interested him because of the human elements it contained. Scott viewed his through an incontestably more artistic temperament, as romantic material. "Quentin Durward" is, it is true, a masterpiece and, to take an analogous novel of Cooper's, "The Bravo" is not; the presentation of the latter's substance is not masterly enough to answer the requirements of a masterpiece; the substance itself is far less important than the splendid historical picture, with its famous historical portraits, that Scott has painted in his monumental work. But Scott was inspired, precisely, by the epic potentialities for painting and portraiture of the struggle between Louis and Charles and its extraordinarily picturesque accessories. Cooper's theme was the effect of oligarchical tyranny on the social and political life of Venice at the acme of her fame and glory. Humanly speaking, "The Bravo" has more meaning. Historical portraiture aside, I do not think there is in "Quentin Durward" the sense of actual life and its significance that one gets from the tragedy of Jacopo Frontoni's heroic story and the picture of the vicious Venetian state whose sway corrupted "alike the ruler and the ruled" and where "each lived for himself." The gist of the latter book is more serious; it is conceived more in the modern manner; it is not a mere panorama of mediæval panoply and performance, but a romance with a thesis—at least so much of a thesis as any highly concentrated epoch must suggest to a thinking and reflective, instead of a merely seeing and feeling, student of its phenomena.

Cooper's genius was a thinking and reflective one. He was certainly not a meditative philosopher, but it was life that interested him and not story-telling as such, even if he might at times get less life and more convention into his books than a romancer *pur sang*. The essence of his romance is that there is no routine in his substance—only in its presentation. His central theme, his main substance, is, like Scott's, his native land. As a romancer his whole attitude toward the pioneer civilization he depicted was one of sympathetic and intelligent interest. He was an observer, a spectator, sufficiently detached to view his subject in the requisite perspective. Some of it he caricatured, and he was oppressively didactic in some of his poorer books. But that proceeded from his constitutional limitations as an artist. On the whole his general and personal interest in the life he depicted makes his account of it solider art, gives his romance even, as I said, more substance and meaning than Scott's historiography. It is more nearly "criticism of life" than the result of a romantic temperament dealing in a purely romantic way with purely romantic elements can be. It is true that Tory as he was, Scott held the balance very true in his pictures of the Cavalier and Roundhead, the Stuart and Hanoverian, contests. But there is more of the philosophy of the latter struggle in "The Two Admirals" than there is in "Waverley" itself.

In "Waverley" the romantic element of the struggle between the legitimist and the legitimate parties, as we may say, is powerfully set forth, the passionate ardor of the one and the practical good sense of the other effectively contrasted, though largely by indirection and in an accessory way. In "Wyandotte" the antagonism between Tory and patriot, between the British and the American partisan, is given far more relief. It is not used merely as a romantic element, tragically dividing a household as it does, but exhibited as a clash of states of mind, of feeling, of conscience, of tradition. *It* is the subject, or at least a part of the subject, not mainly a contribution to its color. The reader notes the reasons that made Major Willoughby a loyalist and Captain Beekman a patriot. The book is a picture of the times, as well as a story, in presenting not only the action but the thinking of the times. One remarks in it that there were "issues" then as well as events. And, of course, with Cooper's noteworthy largeness they are presented with due impartiality, and in this way,

too, acquire a sense of verisimilitude and a value that treatment of them as solely romantic elements could not secure.

And in the way of pure romance—romance quite independent of any associations of time and place—there *are* novels of Cooper that are unsurpassed. For an example of this element, in virtue of which, after all, Cooper's tales have made the tour of the world, take the introductory book of the famous Leatherstocking Tales. "The Deerslayer" is, indeed, a delightful romance, full of imaginative interest, redolent of the woods, compact of incident, and alive with suspense. How many times has the genuine lover of Cooper paid it the tribute of a rereading? For such a reader every small lake in the woods is a Glimmerglass; around its points might at any moment appear one of old Hutter's canoes; at any moment down on yonder sand-spit Le Loup Cervier might issue from the underbrush; in a clearing beyond the nearer tree-tops the Deerslayer might so easily be bound to the stake, be looking into the rifle barrel of his torturer—reassured by his expert knowledge and *sang-froid* to note its ever so slight deflection from a fatal aim! "Treasure Island?" A literary *tour de force*, not only suspiciously clever (aside from the admirable beginning), but so rigorously romantic, so little illusory! "La Dame de Monsoreau"? Pure melodrama, impossible of realization even on the stage, its unreality certain of exposure even by the friendly histrionic test. Quite without the aid of a "literary" presentation, quite without the supplement of historic suggestion and a monumental background, the romance of "The Deerslayer" is, nevertheless, so intrinsic, so essential, and so pervasive as to give the work commanding rank in its class. No tinsel, literary or other, accentuates its simplicity, and no footlight illumination colors its freshness. Cooper is hardly to be called a poet, as I have said. Yet "The Deerslayer's" romance is, in the net impression it leaves, in the resultant effect of its extraordinary visualization of wild and lovely material, as poetic as Chateaubriand's, and fully as effective as that of any work of Scott.

IV

The verisimilitude of Cooper's Indians has been the main point of attack of his caricaturing critics. None of them has failed to have his fling at this. It is extraordinary what a convention his assumed idealization of the Indian has become. I say extraordinary, because it is the fact that the so-called "noble red man," whom he is popularly supposed to have invented, does not exist in his books at all. Successful or not, his Indians, like his other characters, belong to the realm of attempted portraiture of racial types, and are, in intention, at all events, in no wise purely romantic creations.

If they were they would, of course, be superabundantly justified. Ethnology might be reminded that fiction is, to some extent, at least, outside its jurisdiction. The claims of history are far higher, but only a pedant sneers at "Ivanhoe," in which Freeman asserted there was an error on every page, though this is undeniably regrettable; and in recent times, certainly, the great Dumas is not asked to be otherwise, though a reader here and there may be found who would give him higher rank had he been something other. The introduction into literature of the North American Indian, considered merely as a romantic element, was an important event in the history of fiction. He was an unprecedented and a unique figure—at least on the scale and with the vividness with which he is depicted in Cooper, for the Indians of Mrs. Behn and Voltaire and Chateaubriand can in comparison hardly be said to count at all. They are incarnated abstractions didactically inspired for the most part; L'Ingénu, the virtuous, for example, being no more than an expedient for the contrasted exhibition of civilized vices. But Cooper's Indians, whatever their warrant in truth, were notable actors in the picturesque drama of pioneer storm and stress. They stand out in individual as well as racial relief, like his other personages, American, English, French, and Italian, and discharge their rôles in idiosyncratic, as well as in energetic, fashion. To object to them on the ground that, like Don Quixote and Athos, the Black Knight and Saladin, Uncle Toby and Dalgetty, they are ideal types without actual analogues would be singularly ungracious.

However, they are not ideal types, but depend for their validity in large degree on their reality of portraiture as well as on their romantic interest. As I say, they stand on the same ground as Cooper's other characters, and share with them the seriousness a close correspondence to life gives to fiction that has a realistic basis, however great its romantic interest may also be. They are not in the least "ideal" personages. Cooper does not, to be sure, take quite the cowboy view of the Indian, and people with a smattering of pioneering who regard the cowboy as an expert in Indians and echo his opinion that "the only good Indian is a dead one," may find him unduly discriminating. Still, the cowboy's ethnological experience is, after all, limited, and the frontiersman of recent years has had to deal not with the Indian of the time of Cooper's tales, but with his descendants demoralized by contact with his censors, to say nothing of the "century of dishonor." Cooper's view is certainly that the Indian is human. But the fact which is so generally lost sight of is that the "noble red man"—the fictitious character he is charged with inventing—is a stranger to his pages. In general he endows the Indian with traits that would be approved as authentic even by the ranchman, the rustler, or the army officer. His Indians are in the main epitomized in Magua. And in the mass the race is depicted pretty much as Hawkeye conceived the Mingoes of the Mohawk Valley and Leatherstocking the Sioux of the prairies—"varmints" one and all. The exceptions are few. There are the Delawares, Chingachgook and Uncas, Conanchet, and the Pawnee Hardheart—hardly any others of importance. And the "goodness" of these is always carefully characterized as sui generis. The difference between their moral "gifts," as Leatherstocking often enough points out, and those of the white man is always made to appear as radical. The most "idealized" of them is shown as possessing passions and governed by a code that sharply distinguish him from a white of analogous superiority to his fellows. Nor is his ability exaggerated. In spite of his special senses, developed by his life in peace and war, his woodcraft and physical prowess, when it comes to the pinch in any case his inferiority to the white man is generally marked. So far from being untruthful idealizations Cooper's little group of "good Indians" is in both quality and importance considerably below what a writer not actuated by the truly realistic purpose that was always his would be justified in depicting as representative of the best specimens of the Indian race. The history of this country abounds in figures from Massasoit to Brant, from Osceola to Joseph, of moral and mental stature hardly emulated by any of Cooper's aborigines. The only approach to them is in the sage Tamenund of the Lenni Lenape, who is introduced at a great age, and with failing faculties almost extinct. Chingachgook dies a drunkard as old Indian John. Uncas is slain when a mere youth, before his character is thoroughly developed. Conanchet proves untamable by the best of white influences. Wyandotte preserves his fundamental treachery and vengefulness through years of faithful service to the family to which he is attached. Catlin, who passed his life among the Indians, took a far more favorable view of them.

The truth is that not only is Indian character not misrepresented by Cooper, at least in being idealized, but his Indian characters are as carefully studied and as successfully portrayed as his white ones. Their psychology even is set forth with as much definition. They are as much personalities and differ from each other as much. Representatives of a single tribe have their marked individual differences. The Hurons Rivenoak and Le Renard Subtil have but a family resemblance. With the naturally greater simplicity of the savage they are, nevertheless, not represented without the complexities that constitute and characterize the individual. The Tuscarora who enters the room where a mortal struggle is taking place, extinguishes the light, and, one against a dozen, slays the enemies of the white household he serves, in a fray as dramatic as, and far more credible than, the famous fatal fight of the Chevalier de Bussy, is a genuine hero. Yet he is the same man who, for injustice long since forgotten by all but himself, murders his benefactor in absolute cold blood. And the inconsistency is not an anomaly. It is an Indian trait. In short, Cooper's Indians are at once Indians to the core, and thoroughly indivualized as well. The "stock" Indian is no more to be found in his books than the "ideal" primitive hero. He has added to the traditional material of romance an entire race of human beings, possessing in common the romantic elements of strangeness and savagery, but also illustrating a distinctive and coherent racial character.

VII

There is one aspect of his contribution to literature that makes American neglect of Cooper's merits and his fame incomprehensible on any creditable grounds. That aspect is as varied as it is salient, but from its every facet is reflected *the rational aggrandizement of America.* Quite aside from the service to his country involved in the fact itself of his foreign literary popularity—greater than that of all other American authors combined—it is to be remarked that the patriotic is as prominent as any other element of his work. To him, to be sure, we owe it that immediately on his discovery, the European world set an American author among the classics of its own imaginative literature; through him to this world not only American native treasures of romance, but distinctively American traits, ideas and habits, moral, social, and political, were made known and familiar. He first painted for Europe the portrait of America. And the fact that it is in this likeness that the country is still so generally conceived there eloquently attests the power with which it was executed. The great changes that time has wrought in its lineaments have found no hand to depict them vigorously enough—at least in fiction— to secure the substitution of a later presentment for Cooper's. But in speaking of the patriotic element in his work, I refer only indirectly to its service in exalting American literature in European eyes and acquainting European minds with American character. Mainly I wish to signalize—what indirectly this proceeds from—the truth that in a large sense the subject of Cooper's entire work is America, nothing more, nothing less.

The substance of it, of course, is, materially speaking, preponderantly American. But what I mean is that even when he was writing such books as "The Bravo," "The Headsman," and "The Heidenmauer," he was distinctly thinking about his own country as well as his more immediate theme. In each of these novels the theme is really democracy. The fact has been made a reproach to him, and charged with the assumed "inartistic" intrusion of preachment into his romance. Doubtless a picture of Venice, at the time when her sinister oligarchy was most despotic, painted by a pure literary artist like Théophile Gautier, for example, might be spectacularly more "fetching." Cooper's, however, has the merit of being significant. One gets a little tired of the fetich of art, which is, nowadays, brought out of its shrine on so many occasions and venerated with such articulate inveteracy. Art in any other sense than that of a sound and agreeable way of doing things in accordance with their own law might sometimes, one impatiently reflects, be left to itself, to its practitioners, and to the metaphysicians. One may wish incidentally there were more of it! But to reproach such a work as "The Bravo" with a quality that secures its effectiveness is not at all credibly to assert that it would have been a masterpiece of pure beauty had it lacked this quality. As it is, it is an extremely good story made an extremely effective one by the fact that Cooper's democracy gave him a point of view from which the mockery styled the Republic of Venice appeared in a particularly striking light. These novels show at any rate how good a democrat Cooper was, how firmly grounded were his democratic principles, how sincere were his democratic convictions. They show him also as an American democrat—believing in law as well as liberty, that is to say—and not in the least a visionary. The preface alone of "The Headsman" demonstrates the intelligent enthusiasm with which he held his social and political creed. Europe, which nevertheless he thoroughly appreciated, did not disorient him. Nor on his return, whatever may superficially be inferred from his splenetic expressions of disgust with its defects, did his own country disillusionize him.

The undoubted aristocratic blend of his temperament and his traditions did not in the least conflict with his democracy, his Americanism. There is nothing a priori inconsistent in the holding of democratic convictions by the most aristocratic natures. The history of all religions, for example, is conclusive as to this; and from Pericles to the Gracchi, from Montaigne to Emerson, the phenomenon is common enough in politics and philosophy as well. Nor are Cooper's later American books a posteriori evidence of his defection. The excesses and perversions, the faults, and even the eccentricities of democracy, and the way in which these were illustrated by the democracy of his day, are certainly castigated—caricatured on occasion—with vigor, with zest, with temper, indeed. But the wounds are the faithful ones of a friend—an extremely candid friend, of course—in a period of American evolution when candor of the kind was apt to be confounded with censure. His candor, however, was merely the measure of his discrimination. His censure is always delivered from a patriotic standpoint. The things, the traits, he satirizes and denounces are in his view the excrescences of democracy, and infuriate him as perversions, not as inherent evils. There is not the remotest trace of the snob in him. His often trivial and sometimes absurd excursions into the fields of etiquette and etymology, his rating of his countrymen for their minor crudities and fatuities, are the naïve and sometimes elephantine endeavors of a patriotic censor conscious of the value of elegance to precisely such civilization as our own. We can see readily enough to-day that it is calumny to attribute his democracy in Europe to pure idealism, and his disgust with demagogy after his return to an irascibility that changed his conviction. The discriminating American—Lowell, for a prominent example—is naturally an advocate of democracy abroad and a critic of it at home. And Cooper's temperament was not more irascible than his mind was judicial. There is, apparently, a native relation between irascibility and the judicial quality. Breadth of view, unless it is combined with the indifference of the dilettante, is naturally impatient of narrowness.

Defects of temper, at all events, which were conspicuous in Cooper, certainly coexisted with a fair-mindedness equally characteristic. Not a great, he was distinctly a large, man in all intellectual respects. Professor Trent in his "History of American Literature" recurs to this central trait again and again, one is glad to note, in his exceptionally appreciative characterization. He was peppery, but not petulant, iracund without truculence. His quarrels with his encroaching Cooperstown neighbors, and with the unspeakable press of his day, undoubtedly lacked dignity, but in all cases he was in the right, and his outraged sense of justice was at the bottom of his violence. And his fair-mindedness so penetrated his patriotism as to render it notably intelligent, and therefore beneficent. In his day intelligent patriotism was not thoroughgoing enough to be popular. Partisanship was exacted. The detachment which Cooper owed to his experience and judicial-mindedness was simply not understood. It seemed necessarily inconsistent with patriotic feeling. Such scepticism is, in fact, not unknown in our own time! But in Cooper's, appreciation of foreign, and criticism of native, traits was in itself almost universally suspect. Yet such candor as his in noting excellence in men and things of other nations and civilizations is even nowadays rarely to be encountered. France, Italy, England, the Irish, Swiss, Germans—every nationality, in fact, that figures in his pages—are depicted with absolute sympathy and lack of prejudice. In "Jack Tier," written during the Mexican War, the Mexican character at its best is incarnated in the most polished and high-minded, the most refined and least vulgar of personalities. In the matter of national traits it is still more or less true that, as Stendhal observed, "la différence fait la haine"; but to no writer of the English tongue at all events, even since his time, could the reproach be addressed with less reason than to Cooper. "Wing-and-Wing" is a text-book of true cosmopolitanism, and "Wyandotte" a lesson in non-partisanship at home.

No doubt it is only logical to be cosmopolitan and liberal when one is lecturing one's countrymen on their narrowness and provinciality. But the disposition to lecture them on this particular theme itself witnesses Cooper's genuine fair-mindedness and his desire to communicate it to his readers. Moreover, the quality appears in his writings quite as often instinctively as expressly; it pervades their purely artistic as well as their didactic portions. And there are two manifestations of it that are particularly piquant and certainly to be reckoned among Cooper's patriotic services. One is his treatment of New England, and the other that of the Protestant "sects" as distinguished from the Episcopal "Church."

Upon the New England of his day Cooper turned the vision of a writer who was also a man of the world—a product of civilization at that time extremely rare within its borders. He was himself an eminent example of what used to be called in somewhat esoteric eulogy by those who admired the type, a conservative, and New England was the paradise of the radical, the visionary, the doctrinaire. He had no disposition, accordingly, to view it with a friendly eye or to pass by any of its imperfections. The narrowness, the fanaticism, the absurd self-sufficiency and shallowness, the contempt for the rest of the country, the defects of the great New England qualities of thrift and self-reliance characteristic of the section, were particularly salient to him, and to signalize them was irresistible to an emancipated observer who could contemplate them from a detached standpoint. It would be idle to pretend that he interpreted New England types with the intimate appreciation of Hawthorne. On the other hand, his detachment being more complete, his portrayal of them often gives them the relief which can only be brought out by the colorless white light of cold impartiality. Occasionally, without doubt, he satirizes rather than depicts them—though more rarely than his heavy touch leads the reader to imagine. But from "Wing-and Wing" to "Satanstoe" the New England contingent of his company of characters is portrayed with a searching and self-justifying veracity, at least as to its essential features; and, as was his habit, discriminatingly portrayed. Ithuel Bolt is certainly one of the notable characters of fiction, and yet he could no more have been born and developed outside of New England than Leatherstocking could have hailed from Massachusetts. If the Rev. Meek Wolfe in "The Wept of Wish-ton-Wish" is a caricature, he is fully offset by the fine portrait of the Puritan head of the household.

It is difficult now to recall the New England in Cooper's day. Never, perhaps, in the world's history was so much and so widespread mental activity so intimately associated with such extreme provinciality. For a miniature portrait of it consult the first pages of Lowell's essay on Thoreau. At present we need to have the eminence of the section recalled to us. Professor Barrett Wendell's engaging "Literary History," in which he not only limits American literature of much value to New England, but even tucks it into the confines of Harvard College, is an interesting reminder of days that seem curiously distant. Between 1825 and 1850, at all events, New England, always the apex, had become also the incubus of our civilization, and called loudly for the note-taking of a chiel from beyond its borders. Cooper performed that service. And, as I say, it is to be counted to him for patriotism. To him we owe it that not only American authorship but American literature has been from his day of national rather than sectional character. The world he represented to the Europe of his day was a comprehensively American world, and the country as a whole, with the theretofore false proportion of its different sections duly rectified, first appeared in effective presentation in the domain of art.

His analogous hostility to ecclesiastical sectarianism was, perhaps, a corollary of his view of the New England whence largely this sectarianism came. English non-conformity transplanted added to its own defects those inseparable from an establishment, which practically it enjoyed. Its contentiousness became tyrannous, and its virtual establishment, destitute of traditions, served mainly to crystallize its crudities. Cooper's episcopalianism was in a doctrinal sense, no doubt, equally narrow. And his piety was strongly tinctured with dogma. Some of his polemic is absurd, and when he is absurd he is so to a degree only accounted for by his absolute indifference to appearing ridiculous. "The Crater" is an extraordinary exhibition of denominational fatuity. But in his day his churchmanship gave him in religious matters the same advantage of detachment that his treatment of New England enjoyed. It gave him a standard of taste, of measure, of decorum, of deference to tradition and custom, and made him a useful and unsparing critic of the rawness and irresponsibility so rife around him, in a field of considerably more important mundane concern to the community of that time than—owing largely to its own transformation—it has since become. He knew the difference in the ecclesiastical field, as few in his day did, between "a reading from Milton and a reading from Eliza Cook." The intellectual mediocrity of the Episcopal pulpit did not blind him, as it did others, to "the Church's" distinctive superior-ities, secular and religious. A ritual, a clergy (however triturate as a hierarchy), a sense of historic continuity, the possession of traditions, the spirit of conformity in lieu of self-assertion (a spirit so necessary to "the *communion* of saints"), set off the "Churchmen" of that day somewhat sharply from the immensely larger part of their respective societies. And Cooper's criticism of the more unlovely traits of the descendants of the Puritans and the Scotch-Irish immigration on the whole made for an ideal which, socially considered, must be regarded as superior to that he found defective. His "conservative" spirit, in a word, enabled him to perform a genuine and patriotic service to our civilization in this respect, as it did in the case of its portrayal of New England types of character. And as in the latter case he is not to be charged with a provinciality equivalent to that which he exposed, but really judges it from an open-minded and cosmopolitan standpoint, so, too —though naturally in a distinctly lesser degree, in consequence of his own ecclesiastical and theological rigidities—he exhibits the defectiveness of American non-conformity from a distinctly higher plane than its own. The proof of this and of his large tolerance in religious matters—where his controversial spirit is not aroused—is the fact that Catholicism and Catholics always receive just and appreci-

ative treatment at his hands. Even atheism itself he treats with perfect and comprehending appreciation. In this respect the scene in "Wing-and-Wing" where Raoul Yvard is about to be executed as a spy forms a striking contrast to the somewhat analogous one in "Quentin Durward," where Scott uses the death of the unbelieving Hayraddin Mograbin to point a series of perfunctory commonplaces.

I come back in conclusion to Professor Trent's epithet. Cooper's was above all a *large* nature. Even his littlenesses were those of a large nature. Let us refine and scrutinize, hesitate and distinguish, when we have appropriate material to consider. But in considering Cooper's massive and opulent work it is inexcusable to obscure one's vision of the forest by a study of the trees. His work is in no sense a *jardin des plantes;* it is like the woods and sea that mainly form its subject and substance. Only critical myopia can be blind to the magnificent forest, with its pioneer clearings, its fringe of "settlements," its wood-embosomed lakes, its neighboring prairie on the one side, and on the other the distant ocean with the cities of its farther shore—the splendid panorama of man, of nature, and of human life unrolled for us by this large intelligence and noble imagination, this manly and patriotic American representative in the literary parliament of the world.

THEODORE ROOSEVELT (1858-1919)

HISTORY AS LITERATURE

(1913)

There has been much discussion as to whether history should not henceforth be treated as a branch of science rather than of literature. As with most such discussions, much of the matter in dispute has referred merely to terminology. Moreover, as regards part of the discussion, the minds of the contestants have not met, the propositions advanced by the two sides being neither mutually incompatible nor mutually relevant. There is, however, a real basis for conflict in so far as science claims exclusive possession of the field.

There was a time—we see it in the marvellous dawn of Hellenic life—when history was distinguished neither from poetry, from mythology, nor from the first dim beginnings of science. There was a more recent time, at the opening of Rome's brief period of literary splendor, when poetry was accepted by a

great scientific philosopher as the appropriate vehicle for teaching the lessons of science and philosophy. There was a more recent time still—the time of Holland's leadership in arms and arts—when one of the two or three greatest world painters put his genius at the service of anatomists.

In each case the steady growth of specialization has rendered such combination now impossible. Virgil left history to Livy; and when Tacitus had become possible Lucan was a rather absurd anachronism. The elder Darwin, when he endeavored to combine the functions of scientist and poet, may have thought of Lucretius as a model; but the great Darwin was incapable of such a mistake. The surgeons of to-day would prefer the services of a good photographer to those of Rembrandt—even were those of Rembrandt available. No one would now dream of combining the history of the Trojan War with a poem on the wrath of Achilles. Beowulf's feats against the witch who dwelt under the water would not now be mentioned in the same matter-of-fact way that a Frisian or Frankish raid is mentioned. We are long past the stage when we would accept as parts of the same epic Siegfried's triumphs over dwarf and dragon, and even a distorted memory of the historic Hunnish king in whose feast-hall the Burgundian heroes held their last revel and made their death fight. We read of the loves of the Hound of Muirthemne and Emer the Fair without attributing to the chariot-riding heroes who "fought over the ears of their horses," and to their fierce lady-loves more than a symbolic reality. The Roland of the Norman trouvères, the Roland who blew the ivory horn at Roncesvalles, is to our minds wholly distinct from the actual Warden of the Marches who fell in a rear-guard skirmish with the Pyrenean Basques.

As regards philosophy, as distinguished from material science and from history, the specialization has been incomplete. Poetry is still used as a vehicle for the teaching of philosophy. Goethe was as profound a thinker as Kant. He has influenced the thought of mankind far more deeply than Kant because he was also a great poet. Robert Browning was a real philosopher, and his writings have had a hundredfold the circulation and the effect of those of any similar philosopher who wrote in prose, just because, and only because, what he wrote was not merely philosophy but literature. The form in which he wrote challenged attention and provoked admiration. That part of his work which some of us—which I myself, for instance—most care for is merely poetry. But in that part of his work which has exercised most attraction and has given him the widest reputation, the poetry, the form of expression, bears to the thought expressed much the same relation that the expression of Lucretius bears to the thought of Lucretius. As regards this, the great mass of his product, he is primarily a philosopher, whose writings surpass in value those of other similar philosophers precisely because they are not only philosophy but literature. In other words, Browning the philosopher is read by countless thousands to whom otherwise philosophy would be a sealed book, for exactly the same reason that Macaulay the historian is read by countless thousands to whom otherwise history would be a sealed book; because both Browning's works and Macaulay's works are material additions to the great sum of English literature. Philosophy is a science just as history is a science.

There is need in one case as in the other for vivid and powerful presentation of scientific matter in literary form.

This does not mean that there is the like need in the two cases. History can never be truthfully presented if the presentation is purely emotional. It can never be truthfully or usefully presented unless profound research, patient, laborious, painstaking, has preceded the presentation. No amount of self-communion and of pondering on the soul of mankind, no gorgeousness of literary imagery, can take the place of cool, serious, widely extended study. The vision of the great historian must be both wide and lofty. But it must be sane, clear, and based on full knowledge of the facts and of their interrelations. Otherwise we get merely a splendid bit of serious romance-writing, like Carlyle's "French Revolution." Many hard-working students, alive to the deficiences of this kind of romance-writing, have grown to distrust not only all historical writing that is romantic, but all historical writing that is vivid. They feel that complete truthfulness must never be sacrificed to color. In this they are right. They also feel that complete truthfulness is incompatible with color. In this they are wrong. The immense importance of full knowledge of a mass of dry facts and gray details has so impressed them as to make them feel that the dryness and the grayness are in themselves meritorious.

These students have rendered invaluable service to history. They are right in many of their contentions. They see how literature and science have specialized. They realize that scientific methods are as necessary to the proper study of history as to the proper study of astronomy or zoology. They know that in many, perhaps in most, of its forms, literary ability is divorced from the restrained devotion to the actual fact which is as essential to the historian as to the scientist. They know that nowadays science ostentatiously disclaims any connection with literature. They feel that if this is essential for science, it is no less essential for history.

There is much truth in all these contentions. Nevertheless, taking them all together, they do not indicate what these hard-working students believed that they indicate. Because history, science, and literature have all become specialized, the theory now is that science is definitely severed from literature and that history must follow suit. Not only do I refuse to accept this as true for history, but I do not even accept it as true for science.

Literature may be defined as that which has

permanent interest because both of its substance and its form, aside from the mere technical value that inheres in a special treatise for specialists. For a great work of literature there is the same demand now that there always has been; and in any great work of literature the first element is great imaginative power. The imaginative power demanded for a great historian is different from that demanded for a great poet; but it is no less marked. Such imaginative power is in no sense incompatible with minute accuracy. On the contrary, very accurate, very real and vivid, presentation of the past can come only from one in whom the imaginative gift is strong. The industrious collector of dead facts bears to such a man precisely the relation that a photographer bears to Rembrandt. There are innumerable books, that is, innumerable volumes of printed matter between covers, which are excellent for their own purposes, but in which imagination would be as wholly out of place as in the blueprints of a sewer system or in the photographs taken to illustrate a work on comparative osteology. But the vitally necessary sewer system does not take the place of the cathedral of Rheims or of the Parthenon; no quantity of photographs will ever be equivalent to one Rembrandt; and the greatest mass of data, although indispensable to the work of a great historian, is in no shape or way a substitute for that work.

History, taught for a directly and immediately useful purpose to pupils and the teachers of pupils, is one of the necessary features of a sound education in democratic citizenship. A book containing such sound teaching, even if without any literary quality, may be as useful to the student and as creditable to the writer as a similar book on medicine. I am not slighting such a book when I say that, once it has achieved its worthy purpose, it can be permitted to lapse from human memory as a good book on medicine, which has outlived its usefulness, lapses from memory. But the historical work which does possess literary quality may be a permanent contribution to the sum of man's wisdom, enjoyment and inspiration. The writer of such a book must add wisdom to knowledge, and the gift of expression to the gift of imagination.

It is a shallow criticism to assert that imagination tends to inaccuracy. Only a distorted imagination tends to inaccuracy. Vast and fundamental truths can be discerned and interpreted only by one whose imagination is as lofty as the soul of a Hebrew prophet. When we say that the great historian must be a man

of imagination, we use the word as we use it when we say that the great statesman must be a man of imagination. Moreover, together with imagination must go the power of expression. The great speeches of statesmen and the great writings of historians can live only if they possess the deathless quality that inheres in all great literature. The greatest literary historian must of necessity be a master of the science of history, a man who has at his finger-tips all the accumulated facts from the treasure-houses of the dead past. But he must also possess the power to marshal what is dead so that before our eyes it lives again.

Many learned people seem to feel that the quality of readableness in a book is one which warrants suspicion. Indeed, not a few learned people seem to feel that the fact that a book is interesting is proof that it is shallow. This is particularly apt to be the attitude of scientific men. Very few great scientists have written interestingly, and these few have usually felt apologetic about it. Yet sooner or later the time will come when the mighty sweep of modern scientific discovery will be placed, by scientific men with the gift of expression, at the service of intelligent and cultivated laymen. Such service will be inestimable. Another writer of "Canterbury Tales," another singer of "Paradise Lost," could not add more to the sum of literary achievement than the man who may picture to us the phases of the age-long history of life on this globe, or make vivid before our eyes the tremendous march of the worlds through space.

Indeed, I believe that already science has owed more than it suspects to the unconscious literary power of some of its representatives. Scientific writers of note had grasped the fact of evolution long before Darwin and Huxley; and the theories advanced by these men to explain evolution were not much more unsatisfactory, as full explanations, than the theory of natural selection itself. Yet, where their predecessors had created hardly a ripple, Darwin and Huxley succeeded in effecting a complete revolution in the thought of the age, a revolution as great as that caused by the discovery of the truth about the solar system. I believe that the chief explanation of the difference was the very simple one that what Darwin and Huxley wrote was interesting to read. Every cultivated man soon had their volumes in his library, and they still keep their places on our bookshelves. But Lamarck and Cope are only to be found in the libraries of a few special students. If they had possessed a gift of expression akin to Darwin's, the doctrine of evolution would not in the popular mind have been confounded with the doctrine of natural selection and a juster estimate than at present would obtain as to the relative merits of the explanations of evolution championed by the different scientific schools.

Do not misunderstand me. In the field of historical research an immense amount can be done by men who have no literary power whatever. Moreover, the most painstaking and laborious research, covering long periods of years, is necessary in order to accumulate the material for any history worth writing at all. There are important bypaths of history, moreover, which hardly admit of treatment that would make them of interest to any but specialists. All this I fully admit. In particular I pay high honor to the patient and truthful investigator. He does an indispensable work. My claim is merely that such work should not exclude the work of the great master who can use the materials gathered, who has the gift of vision, the quality of the seer, the power himself to see what has happened and to make what he has seen clear to the vision of others. My only protest is against those who believe that the extension of the activities of the most competent mason and most energetic contractor will supply the lack of great architects. If, as in the Middle Ages, the journeymen builders are themselves artists, why this is the best possible solution of the problem. But if they are not artists, then their work, however much it represents of praiseworthy industry, and of positive usefulness, does not take the place of the work of a great artist.

Take a concrete example. It is only of recent years that the importance of inscriptions has been realized. To the present-day scholar they are invaluable. Even to the layman, some of them turn the past into the present with startling clearness. The least imaginative is moved by the simple inscription on the Etruscan sarcophagus, "I, the great lady"; a lady so haughty that no other human being was allowed to rest near her; and yet now nothing remains but this proof of the pride of the nameless one. Or the inscription in which Queen Hatshepsut recounts her feats and her magnificence, and ends by adjuring the onlooker, when overcome by the recital, not to say "how wonderful" but "how like her!"— could any picture of a living queen be more intimately vivid. With such inscriptions before us the wonder is that it took us so long to realize their worth. Not unnaturally this realization, when it did come, was followed by the belief that inscriptions would enable us to dis-

pense with the great historians of antiquity. This error is worse than the former. Where the inscriptions give us light on what would otherwise be darkness, we must be profoundly grateful; but we must not confound the lesser light with the greater. We could better afford to lose every Greek inscription that has ever been found than the chapter in which Thucydides tells of the Athenian failure before Syracuse. Indeed, few inscriptions teach us as much history as certain forms of literature that do not consciously aim at teaching history at all. The inscriptions of Hellenistic Greece in the third century before our era do not, all told, give us so lifelike a view of the ordinary life of the ordinary men and women who dwelt in the great Hellenistic cities of the time, as does the fifteenth idyl of Theocritus.

This does not mean that good history can be unscientific. So far from ignoring science, the great historian of the future can do nothing unless he is steeped in science. He can never equal what has been done by the great historians of the past unless he writes not merely with full knowledge, but with an intensely vivid consciousness, of all that of which they were necessarily ignorant. He must accept what we now know to be man's place in nature. He must realize that man has been on this earth for a period of such incalculable length that, from the standpoint of the student of his development through time, what our ancestors used to call "antiquity" is almost indistinguishable from the present day. If our conception of history takes in the beast-like man whose sole tool and weapon was the stone fist-hatchet, and his advanced successors, the man who etched on bone pictures of the mammoth, the reindeer, and the wild horse, in what is now France, and the man who painted pictures of bison in the burial-caves of what is now Spain; if we also conceive in their true position our "contemporaneous ancestors," the savages who are now no more advanced than the cave-dwellers of a hundred thousand or two hundred thousand years back, then we shall accept Thutmose and Cæsar, Alfred and Washington, Timoleon and Lincoln, Homer and Shakespeare, Pythagoras and Emerson, as all nearly contemporaneous in time and in culture.

The great historian of the future will have easy access to innumerable facts patiently gathered by tens of thousands of investigators, whereas the great historian of the past had very few facts, and often had to gather most of these himself. The great historian of the future cannot be excused if he fails to draw on the vast storehouses of knowledge that have been accumulated, if he fails to profit by the wisdom and work of other men, which are now the common property of all intelligent men. He must use the instruments which the historians of the past did not have ready to hand. Yet even with these instruments he cannot do as good work as the best of the elder historians unless he has vision and imagination, the power to grasp what is essential and to reject the infinitely more numerous non-essentials, the power to embody ghosts, to put flesh and blood on dry bones, to make dead men living before our eyes. In short, he must have the power to take the science of history and turn it into literature.

Those who wish history to be treated as a purely utilitarian science often decry the recital of the mighty deeds of the past, the deeds which always have aroused, and for a long period to come are likely to arouse, most interest. These men say that we should study not the unusual but the usual. They say that we profit most by laborious research into the drab monotony of the ordinary, rather than by fixing our eyes on the purple patches that break it. Beyond all question the great historian of the future must keep ever in mind the relative importance of the usual and the unusual. If he is a really great historian, if he possesses the highest imaginative and literary quality, he will be able to interest us in the gray tints of the general landscape no less than in the flame hues of the jutting peaks. It is even more essential to have such quality in writing of the commonplace than in writing of the exceptional. Otherwise no profit will come from study of the ordinary; for writings are useless unless they are read, and they cannot be read unless they are readable. Furthermore, while doing full justice to the importance of the usual, of the commonplace, the great historian will not lose sight of the importance of the heroic.

It is hard to tell just what it is that is most important to know. The wisdom of one generation may seem the folly of the next. This is just as true of the wisdom of the dry-as-dusts as of the wisdom of those who write interestingly. Moreover, while the value of the by-products of knowledge does not readily yield itself to quantitative expression, it is none the less real. A utilitarian education should undoubtedly be the foundation of all education. But it is far from advisable, it is far from wise, to have it the end of all education. Technical training will more and more be accepted as the prime factor in our educational system, a fac-tor as essential for the farmer, the blacksmith, the seamstress, and the cook, as for the lawyer, the doctor, the engineer, and the stenographer. For similar reasons the purely practical and technical lessons of history, the lessons that help us to grapple with our immediate social and industrial problems, will also receive greater emphasis than ever before. But if we are wise we will no more permit this practical training to exclude knowledge of that part of literature which is history than of that part of literature which is poetry. Side by side with the need for the perfection of the individual in the technic of his special calling goes the need of broad human sympathy, and the need of lofty and generous emotion in that individual. Only thus can the citizenship of the modern state rise level to the complex modern social needs.

No technical training, no narrowly utilitarian study of any kind will meet this second class of needs. In part they can best be met by a training that will fit men and women to appreciate, and therefore to profit by, great poetry and those great expressions of the historian and the statesman which rivet our interest and stir our souls. Great thoughts match and inspire heroic deeds. The same reasons that make the Gettysburg speech and the Second Inaugural impress themselves on men's minds far more deeply than technical treatises on the constitutional justification of slavery or of secession, apply to fitting descriptions of the great battle and the great contest which occasioned the two speeches. The tense epic of the Gettysburg fight, the larger epic of the whole Civil War, when truthfully and vividly portrayed, will always have, and ought always to have, an attraction, an interest, that cannot be roused by the description of the same number of hours or years of ordinary existence. There are supreme moments in which intensity and not duration is the all-important element. History which is not professedly utilitarian, history which is didactic only as great poetry is unconsciously didactic, may yet possess that highest form of usefulness, the power to thrill the souls of men with stories of strength and craft and daring, and to lift them out of their common selves to the heights of high endeavor.

The greatest historian should also be a great moralist. It is no proof of impartiality to treat wickedness and goodness as on the same level. But of course the obsession of purposeful moral teaching may utterly defeat its own aim. Moreover, unfortunately, the avowed teacher of morality, when he writes history, sometimes goes very far wrong indeed. It often happens that the man who can be of real help in inspiring others by his utterances on abstract principles is wholly unable to apply his own principles to concrete cases. Carlyle offers an instance in point. Very few men have ever been a greater source of inspiration to other ardent souls than was Carlyle when he confined himself to preaching morality in the abstract. Moreover, his theory bade him treat history as offering material to support that theory. But not only was he utterly unable to distinguish either great virtues or great vices when he looked abroad on contemporary life—as witness his attitude toward our own Civil War—but he was utterly unable to apply his own principles concretely in history. His "Frederick the Great" is literature of a high order. It may, with reservations, even be accepted as history. But the "morality" therein jubilantly upheld is shocking to any man who takes seriously Carlyle's other writings in which he lays down principles of conduct. In his "Frederick the Great" he was not content to tell the facts. He was not content to announce his admiration. He wished to square himself with his theories, and to reconcile what he admired, both with the actual fact and with his previously expressed convictions on morality. He could only do so by refusing to face the facts and by using words with meanings that shifted to meet his own mental emergencies. He pretended to discern morality where no vestige of it existed. He tortured the facts to support his views. The "morality" he praised had no connection with morality as understood in the New Testament. It was the kind of archaic morality observed by the Danites in their dealings with the people of Laish. The sermon of the Mormon bishop in Owen Wister's "Pilgrim on the Gila" sets forth the only moral lessons which it was possible for Carlyle truthfully to draw from the successes he described.

History must not be treated as something set off by itself. It should not be treated as a branch of learning bound to the past by the shackles of an iron conservatism. It is neither necessary rigidly to mark the limits of the province of history, nor to treat of all that is within that province, nor to exclude any subject within that province from treatment, nor yet to treat different methods of dealing with the same subject as mutually exclusive. Every writer and every reader has his own needs, to meet himself or to be met by others. Among a great multitude of thoughtful people there is room for the widest possible variety of appeals. Let each man fearlessly choose what is of real importance and interest to him personally, reverencing authority, but not in a superstitious spirit, because he must needs reverence liberty even more.

There is an infinite variety of subjects to treat, and no need to estimate their relative importance. Because one man is interested in the history of finance, it does not mean that another is wrong in being interested in the history of war. One man's need is met by exhaustive tables of statistics; another's by the study of the influence exerted on national life by the great orators, the Websters and Burkes, or by the poets, the Tyrtæuses and Körners, who in crisis utter what is in the nation's heart. There is need of the study of the historical workings of representative government. There is no less need of the study of the economic changes produced by the factory system. Because we study with profit what Thorold Rogers wrote of prices we are not debarred from also profiting by Mahan's studies of naval strategy. One man finds what is of most importance to his own mind and heart in tracing the effect upon humanity of the spread of malaria along the shores of the Ægean; or the effect of the Black Death on the labor market of mediæval Europe; or the profound influence upon the development of the African continent of the fatal diseases borne by the bites of insects, which close some districts to human life and others to the beasts without which humanity rests at the lowest stage of savagery. One man sees the events from one viewpoint, one from another. Yet another can combine both. We can be stirred by Thayer's study of Cavour without abating our pleasure in the younger Trevelyan's volumes on Garibaldi. Because we revel in Froissart, or Joinville, or Villehardouin, there is no need that we should lack interest in the books that attempt the more difficult task of tracing the economic changes in the status of peasant, mechanic and burgher during the thirteenth and fourteenth centuries.

History must welcome the entrance upon its domain of every science. As James Harvey Robinson in his "New History" has said:

"The bounds of all departments of human research and speculation are inherently provisional, indefinite, and fluctuating; moreover, the lines of demarcation are hopelessly interlaced, for real men and the real universe in which they live are so intricate as to defy all attempts even of the most patient and subtle German to establish satisfactorily and permanently the *Begriff und Wesen* of any artificially delimited set of natural phenomena, whether words, thoughts, deeds, forces, animals, plants, or stars. Each so-called science or discipline is ever and always dependent on other sciences and disciplines. It draws its life from them, and to them it owes, consciously or unconsciously, a great part of its chances of progress."

Elsewhere this writer dwells on the need of understanding the genetic side of history, if we are to grasp the real meaning of, and grapple most effectively with, the phenomena of our present-day lives; for that which is can be dealt with best if we realize at least in part from what a tangled web of causation it has sprung.

The work of the archæologist, the work of the anthropologist, the work of the palæo-ethnologist—out of all these a great literary historian may gather material indispensable for his use. He, and we, ought fully to acknowledge our debt to the collectors of these indispensable facts. The investigator in any line may do work which puts us all under lasting obligation to him, even though he be totally deficient in the art of literary expression, that is, totally deficient in the ability to convey vivid and lifelike pictures to others of the past whose secrets he has laid bare. I would give no scanty or grudging acknowledgment to the deeds of such a man. He does a lasting service; whereas the man who tries to make literary expression cover his ignorance or misreading of facts renders less than no service. But the service done is immeasurably increased in value when the man arises who from his study of a myriad dead fragments is able to paint some living picture of the past.

This is why the record as great writers preserve it has a value immeasurably beyond what is merely lifeless. Such a record pulses with immortal life. It may recount the deed or the thought of a hero at some supreme moment. It may be merely the portrayal of homely every-day life. This matters not, so long as in either event the genius of the historian enables him to paint in colors that do not fade. The cry of the Ten Thousand when they first saw the sea still stirs the hearts of men. The ruthless death-scene between Jehu and Jezebel; wicked Ahab, smitten by the chance arrow, and propped in his chariot until he died at sundown; Josiah, losing his life because he would not heed the prophet's solemn warning, and mourned by all the singing men and all the singing women—the fates of these kings and of this king's daughter, are part of the common stock of knowledge of mankind. They were petty rulers of petty principalities; yet, compared with them, mighty conquerors, who added empire to empire, Shalmaneser and

Sargon, Amenhotep and Rameses, are but shadows; for the deeds and the deaths of the kings of Judah and Israel are written in words that, once read, cannot be forgotten. The Peloponnesian War bulks of unreal size to-day because it once seemed thus to bulk to a master mind. Only a great historian can fittingly deal with a very great subject; yet because the qualities of chief interest in human history can be shown on a small field no less than on a large one, some of the greatest historians have treated subjects that only their own genius rendered great.

So true is this that if great events lack a great historian, and a great poet writes about them, it is the poet who fixes them in the mind of mankind, so that in after-time importance the real has become the shadow and the shadow the reality. Shakespeare has definitely fixed the character of the Richard III of whom ordinary men think and speak. Keats forgot even the right name of the man who first saw the Pacific Ocean; yet it is his lines which leap to our minds when we think of the "wild surmise" felt by the indomitable explorer-conqueror from Spain when the vast new sea burst on his vision.

When, however, the historian has spoken, his work will never be undone. No poet can ever supersede what Napier wrote of the storming of Badajoz, of the British infantry at Albuera, and of the light artillery at Fuentes d'Oñoro. After Parkman had written of Montcalm and Wolfe there was left for other writers only what FitzGerald left for other translators of Omar Khayyám. Much new light has been thrown on the history of the Byzantine Empire by the many men who have studied it of recent years; we read each new writer with pleasure and profit; and after reading each we take down a volume of Gibbon, with renewed thankfulness that a great writer was moved to do a great task.

The greatest of future archæologists will be the great historian who instead of being a mere antiquarian delver in dust-heaps has the genius to reconstruct for us the immense panorama of the past. He must possess knowledge. He must possess that without which knowledge is of so little use, wisdom. What he brings from the charnel-house he must use with such potent wizardry that we shall see the life that was and not the death that is. For remember that the past was life just as much as the present is life. Whether it be Egypt, or Mesopotamia, or Scandinavia with which he deals, the great historian, if the facts permit him, will put before us the men and women as they actually lived so that we shall recognize them for what they were, living beings. Men like Maspero, Breasted, and Weigall have already begun this work for the countries of the Nile and the Euphrates. For Scandinavia the groundwork was laid long ago in the "Heimskringla" and in such sagas as those of Burnt Njal and Gisli Soursop. Minute descriptions of mummies and of the furniture of tombs help us as little to understand the Egypt of the mighty days, as to sit inside the tomb of Mount Vernon would help us to see Washington the soldier leading to battle his scarred and tattered veterans, or Washington the statesman, by his serene strength of character, rendering it possible for his countrymen to establish themselves as one great nation.

The great historian must be able to paint for us the life of the plain people, the ordinary men and women, of the time of which he writes. He can do this only if he possesses the highest kind of imagination. Collections of figures no more give us a picture of the past than the reading of a tariff report on hides or woolens gives us an idea of the actual lives of the men and women who live on ranches or work in factories. The great historian will in as full measure as possible present to us the every-day life of the men and women of the age which he describes. Nothing that tells of this life will come amiss to him. The instruments of their labor and the weapons of their warfare, the wills that they wrote, the bargains that they made, and the songs that they sang when they feasted and made love: he must use them all. He must tell us of the toil of the ordinary times, and of the play by which that ordinary toil was broken. He must never forget that no event stands out entirely isolated. He must trace from its obscure and humble beginnings each of the movements that in its hour of triumph has shaken the world.

Yet he must not forget that the times that are extraordinary need especial portrayal. In the revolt against the old tendency of historians to deal exclusively with the spectacular and the exceptional, to treat only of war and oratory and government, many modern writers have gone to the opposite extreme. They fail to realize that in the lives of nations as in the lives of men there are hours so fraught with weighty achievement, with triumph or defeat, with joy or sorrow, that each such hour may determine all the years that are to come thereafter, or may outweigh all the years that have gone before. In the writings of our historians, as in the lives of our ordinary citizens, we can neither afford to forget that it is the ordinary every-day life which counts most; nor yet that seasons come when ordinary qualities count for but little in the face of great contending forces of good and of evil, the outcome of whose strife determines whether the nation shall walk in the glory of the morning or in the gloom of spiritual death.

The historian must deal with the days of common things, and deal with them so that they shall interest us in reading of them as our own common things interest us as we live among them. He must trace the changes that come almost unseen, the slow and gradual growth that transforms for good or for evil the children and grandchildren so that they stand high above or far below the level on which their forefathers stood. He must also trace the great cataclysms that interrupt and divert this gradual development. He can no more afford to be blind to one class of phenomena than to the other. He must ever remember that while the worst offense of which he can be guilty is to write vividly and inaccurately, yet that unless he writes vividly he cannot write truthfully; for no amount of dull, painstaking detail will sum up as the whole truth unless the genius is there to paint the truth.

There can be no better illustration of what I mean than is afforded by the history of Russia during the last thousand years. The historian must trace the growth of the earliest Slav communities of the forest and the steppe, the infiltration of Scandinavian invaders who gave them their first power of mass action, and the slow, chaotic development of the little communes into barbarous cities and savage princedoms. In later Russian history he must show us priest and noble, merchant and serf, changing slowly from the days when Ivan the Terrible warred against Bátory, the Magyar king of Poland, until the present moment, when with half suspicious eyes the people of the Czar watch their remote Bulgarian kinsmen standing before the last European stronghold of the Turk. During all these centuries there were multitudes of wars, foreign and domestic, any or all of which were of little moment compared to the slow working of the various forces that wrought in the times of peace. But there was one period of storm and overthrow so terrible that it affected profoundly for all time the whole growth of the Russian people, in inmost character no less than in external dominion. Early in the thirteenth century the genius of Genghis Khan stirred the Mongol horsemen of the mid-Asian pastures to a movement as terrible to civilization as the lava flow of a volcano to the lands around the volcano's foot. When that century opened, the Mongols were of no more weight in the world than the Touaregs of the Sahara are to-day. Long before the century had closed they had ridden from the Yellow Sea to the Adriatic and the Persian Gulf. They had crushed Christian and Moslem and Buddhist alike beneath the iron cruelty of their sway. They sacked Baghdad, the seat of the Caliph. In mid-Europe their presence for a moment caused the same horror to fall on the warring adherents of the Pope and the Kaiser. To Europe they were a scourge so frightful, so irresistible, that the people cowered before them as if they had been demons. No European army of that day, of any nation, was able to look them in the face on a stricken field. Bestial in their lives, irresistible in battle, merciless in victory, they trampled the lands over which they rode into bloody mire beneath the hoofs of their horses. The squat, slit-eyed, brawny horse-bowmen drew a red furrow across Hungary, devastated Poland, and in Silesia overthrew the banded chivalry of Germany. But it was in Russia that they did their worst. They not merely conquered Russia, but held the Russians as cowering and abject serfs for two centuries. Every feeble effort at resistance was visited with such bloodthirsty vengeance that finally no Russian ventured ever to oppose them at all. But the princes of the cities soon found that the beast-like fury of the conquerors when their own desires were thwarted was only equalled by their beast-like indifference to all that was done among the conquered people themselves, and that they were ever ready to hire themselves out to aid each Russian against his brother. Under this régime the Russian who rose was the Russian who with cringing servility to his Tartar overlords combined ferocious and conscienceless greed in the treatment to his fellow Russians. Moscow came to the front by using the Tartar to help conquer the other Russian cities, paying as a price abject obedience to all Tartar demands. In the long run the fierce and pliant cunning of the conquered people proved too much for the short-sighted and arrogant brutality of the conquerors. The Tartar power, the Mongolian power, waned. Russia became united, threw off the yoke, and herself began a career of aggression at the expense of her former conquerors. But the reconquest of racial independence, vitally necessary though it was to Russia, had been paid for by the establishment of a despotism Asiatic rather than European in its spirit and working.

The true historian will bring the past before our eyes as if it were the present. He will make us see as living men the hard-faced archers of Agincourt, and the war-worn spearmen who followed Alexander down beyond the rim of the known world. We shall hear grate on the coast of Britain the keels of the Low-Dutch sea-thieves whose children's children were to inherit unknown continents. We shall thrill to the triumphs of Hannibal. Gorgeous in our sight will rise the splendor of dead cities, and the might of the elder empires of which the very ruins crumbled to dust ages ago. Along ancient trade-routes, across the world's waste spaces, the caravans shall move; and the admirals of uncharted seas shall furrow the oceans with their lonely prows. Beyond the dim centuries we shall see the banners float above armed hosts. We shall see conquerors riding forward to victories that have changed the course of time. We shall listen to the prophecies of forgotten seers. Ours shall be the dreams of dreamers who dreamed greatly, and who saw in their vision peaks so lofty that never yet have they been reached by the sons and daughters of men. Dead poets shall sing to us the deeds of men of might and the love and the beauty of women. We shall see the dancing girls of Memphis. The scent of the flowers in the Hanging Gardens of Babylon will be heavy to our senses. We shall sit at feast with the kings of Nineveh when they drink from ivory and gold. With Queen Meave in her sun-parlor we shall watch the nearing chariots of the champions. For us the war-horns of King Olaf shall wail across the flood, and the harps sound high at festivals in forgotten halls. The frowning strongholds of the barons of old shall rise before us, and the white palace-castles from whose windows Syrian princes once looked across the blue Ægean. We shall know the valor of the two-sworded Samurai. Ours shall be the hoary wisdom and the strange, crooked folly of the immemorial civilizations which tottered to a living death in India and in China. We shall see the terrible horsemen of Timour the Lame ride over the roof of the world; we shall hear the drums beat as the armies of Gustavus and Frederick and Napoleon drive forward to victory. Ours shall be the woe of burgher and peasant, and ours the stern joy when freemen triumph and justice comes to her own. The agony of the galley-slaves shall be ours, and the rejoicing when the wicked are brought low and the men of evil days have their reward. We shall see the glory of triumphant violence, and the revel of those who do wrong in high places; and the broken-hearted despair that lies beneath the glory and the revel. We shall also see the supreme righteousness of the wars for freedom and justice, and know that the men who fell in these wars made all mankind their debtors.

Some day the historians will tell us of these things. Some day, too, they will tell our children of the age and the land in which we now live. They will portray the conquest of the continent. They will show the slow beginnings of settlement, the growth of the fishing and trading towns on the seacoast, the hesitating early ventures into the Indian-haunted forest. Then they will show the backwoodsmen, with their long rifles and their light axes, making their way with labor and peril through the wooded wilderness to the Mississippi; and then the endless march of the white-topped wagon-trains across plain and mountain to the coast of the greatest of the five great oceans. They will show how the land which the pioneers won slowly and with incredible hardship was filled in two generations by the overflow from the countries of western and central Europe. The portentous growth of the cities will be shown, and the change from a nation of farmers to a nation of business men and artisans, and all the far-reaching consequences of the rise of the new industrialism. The formation of a new ethnic type in this melting-pot of the nations will be told. The hard materialism of our age will appear, and also the strange capacity for lofty idealism which must be reckoned with by all who would understand the American character. A people whose heroes are Washington and Lincoln, a peaceful people who fought to a finish one of the bloodiest of wars, waged solely for the sake of a great principle and a noble idea, surely possess an emergency-standard far above mere money-getting.

Those who tell the Americans of the future what the Americans of to-day and of yesterday have done will perforce tell much that is unpleasant. This is but saying that they will describe the arch-typical civilization of this age. Nevertheless, when the tale is finally told, I believe that it will show that the forces working for good in our national life outweigh the forces working for evil, and that, with many blunders and shortcomings, with much halting and turning aside from the path, we shall yet in the end prove our faith by our works, and show in our lives our belief that righteousness exalteth a nation.

GEORGE SANTAYANA (1863-   )
MATERIALISM AND IDEALISM IN AMERICAN LIFE
(1919)

The language and traditions common to England and America are like other family bonds: they draw kindred together at the greater crises in life, but they also occasion at times a little friction and fault-finding. The groundwork of the two societies is so similar, that each nation, feeling almost at home with the other, and almost able to understand its speech, may instinctively resent what hinders it from feeling at home altogether. Differences will tend to seem anomalies that have slipped in by mistake and through somebody's fault. Each will judge the other by his own standards, not feeling, as in the presence of complete foreigners, that he must make an effort of imagination and put himself in another man's shoes.

In matters of morals, manners, and art, the danger of comparisons is not merely that they may prove invidious, by ranging qualities in an order of merit which might wound somebody's vanity; the danger is rather that comparisons may distort comprehension, because in truth good qualities are all different in kind, and free lives are different in spirit. Comparison is the expedient of those who cannot reach the heart of the things compared; and no philosophy is more external and egotistical than that which places the essence of a thing in its relation to something else. In reality, at the centre of every natural being there is something individual and incommensurable, a seed with its native impulses and aspirations, shaping themselves as best they can in their given environment. Variation is a consequence of freedom, and the slight but radical diversity of souls in turn makes freedom requisite. Instead of instituting in his mind any comparisons between the United States and other nations, I would accordingly urge the reader to forget himself and, in so far as such a thing may be possible for him or for me, to transport himself ideally with me into the outer circumstances of American life, the better to feel its inner temper, and to see how inevitably the American shapes his feelings and judgments, honestly reporting all things as they appear from his new and unobstructed station.

I speak of the American in the singular, as if there were not millions of them, north and south, east and west, of both sexes, of all ages, and of various races, professions, and religions. Of course the one American I speak of is mythical; but to speak in parables is inevitable in such a subject, and it is perhaps as well to do so frankly. There is a sort of poetic ineptitude in all human discourse when it tries to deal with natural and existing things. Practical men may not notice it, but in fact human discourse is intrinsically addressed not to natural existing things but to ideal essences, poetic or logical terms which thought may define and play with. When fortune or necessity diverts our attention from this congenial ideal sport to crude facts and pressing issues, we turn our frail poetic ideas into symbols for those terrible irruptive things. In that paper money of our own stamping, the legal tender of the mind, we are obliged to reckon all the movements and values of the world. The universal American I speak of is one of these symbols; and I should be still speaking in symbols and creating moral units and a false simplicity, if I spoke of classes pedantically subdivided, or individuals ideally integrated and defined. As it happens, the symbolic American can be made largely adequate to the facts; because, if there are immense differences between individual Americans—for some Americans are black—yet there is a great uniformity in their environment, customs, temper, and thoughts. They have all been uprooted from their several soils and ancestries and plunged together into one vortex, whirling irresistibly in a space otherwise quite empty. To be an American is of itself almost a moral condition, an education, and a career. Hence a single ideal figment can cover a large part of what each American is in his character, and almost the whole of what most Americans are in their social outlook and political judgments.

The discovery of the new world exercised a sort of selection among the inhabitants of Europe. All the colonists, except the negroes, were voluntary exiles. The fortunate, the deeply rooted, and the lazy remained at home; the wilder instincts or dissatisfaction of others tempted them beyond the horizon. The American is accordingly the most adventurous, or the descendant of the most adventurous, of Europeans. It is in his blood to be socially a radical, though perhaps not intellectually. What has existed in the past, especially in the remote past, seems to him not only authoritative, but irrelevant, inferior, and outworn. He finds it rather a sorry waste of time to think about the past at all. But his enthusiasm for the future is profound; he can conceive of no more decisive way of recommending an opinion or a practice than to say that it is what everybody is coming to adopt. This expectation of what he approves, or approval of what he expects, makes up his optimism. It is the necessary faith of the pioneer.

Such a temperament is, of course, not maintained in the nation merely by inheritance. Inheritance notoriously tends to restore the average of a race, and plays incidentally many a trick of atavism. What maintains this temperament and makes it national is social contagion or pressure—something immensely strong in democracies. The luckless American who is born a conservative, or who is drawn to poetic subtlety, pious retreats, or gay passions, nevertheless has the categorical excellence of work, growth, enterprise, reform, and prosperity dinned into his ears: every door is open in this direction and shut in the other; so that he either folds up his heart and withers in a corner—in remote places you sometimes find such a solitary gaunt idealist—or else he flies to Oxford or Florence or Montmartre to save his soul—or perhaps not to save it.

The optimism of the pioneer is not limited to his view of himself and his own future: it starts from that; but feeling assured, safe, and cheery within, he looks with smiling and most kindly eyes on everything and everybody about him. Individualism, roughness, and self-trust are supposed to go with selfishness and a cold heart; but I suspect that is a prejudice. It is rather dependence, insecurity, and mutual jóstling that poison our placid gregarious brotherhood; and fanciful passionate demands upon people's affections, when they are disappointed, as they soon must be, breed ill-will and a final meanness. The milk of human kindness is less apt to turn sour if the vessel that holds it stands steady, cool, and separate, and is not too often uncorked. In his affections the American is seldom passionate, often deep, and always kindly. If it were given me to look into the depths of a man's heart, and I did not find goodwill at the bottom, I should say without any hesitation, You are not an American. But as the American is an individualist his goodwill is not officious. His instinct is to think well of everybody, and to wish everybody well, but in a spirit of rough comradeship, expecting every man to stand on his own legs and be helpful in his turn. When he has given his neighbour a chance he thinks he has done enough for him; but he feels it is an absolute duty to do that. It will take some hammering to drive a coddling socialism into America.

As self-trust may pass into self-sufficiency, so optimism, kindness, and goodwill may grow into a habit of doting on everything. To the good American many subjects are sacred: sex is sacred, women are sacred, children are sacred, business is sacred, America is sacred, Masonic lodges and college clubs are sacred. This feeling grows out of the good opinion he wishes to have of these things, and serves to maintain it. If he did not regard all these things as sacred he might come to doubt sometimes if they were wholly good. Of this kind, too, is the idealism of single ladies in reduced circumstances who can see the soul of beauty in ugly things, and are perfectly happy because their old dog has such pathetic eyes, their minister is so eloquent, their garden with its three sunflowers is so pleasant, their dead friends were so devoted, and their distant relations are so rich.

Consider now the great emptiness of America: not merely the primitive physical emptiness, surviving in some regions, and the continental spacing of the chief natural features, but also the moral emptiness of a settlement where men and even houses are easily moved about, and no one, almost, lives where he was born or believes what he has been taught. Not that the American has jettisoned these impedimenta in anger; they have simply slipped from him as he moves. Great empty spaces bring a sort of freedom to both soul and body. You may pitch your tent where you will; or if ever you decide to build anything, it can be in a style of your own devising. You have room, fresh materials, few models, and no critics. You trust your own experience, not only because you must, but because you find you may do so safely and prosperously; the forces that determine fortune are not yet too complicated for one man to explore. Your detachable condition makes you lavish with money and cheerfully experimental; you lose little if you lose all, since you remain completely yourself. At the same time your absolute initiative gives you practice in coping with novel situations, and in being original; it teaches you shrewd management. Your life and mind will become dry and direct, with few decorative flourishes. In your works everything will be stark and pragmatic; you will not understand why anybody should make those little sacrifices to instinct or custom which we call grace. The fine arts will seem to you academic luxuries, fit to amuse the ladies, like Greek and Sanskrit; for while you will perfectly appreciate generosity

in men's purposes, you will not admit that the execution of these purposes can be anything but business. Unfortunately the essence of the fine arts is that the execution should be generous too, and delightful in itself; therefore the fine arts will suffer, not so much in their express professional pursuit—for then they become practical tasks and a kind of business—as in that diffused charm which qualifies all human action when men are artists by nature. Elaboration, which is something to accomplish, will be preferred to simplicity, which is something to rest in; manners will suffer somewhat; speech will suffer horribly. For the American the urgency of his novel attack upon matter, his zeal in gathering its fruits, precludes meanderings in primrose paths; devices must be short cuts, and symbols must be mere symbols. If his wife wants luxuries, of course she may have them; and if he has vices, that can be provided for too; but they must all be set down under those headings in his ledgers.

At the same time, the American is imaginative; for where life is intense, imagination is intense also. Were he not imaginative he would not live so much in the future. But his imagination is practical, and the future it forecasts is immediate; it works with the clearest and least ambiguous terms known to his experience, in terms of number, measure, contrivance, economy, and speed. He is an idealist working on matter. Understanding as he does the material potentialities of things, he is successful in invention, conservative in reform, and quick in emergencies. All his life he jumps into the train after it has started and jumps out before it has stopped; and he never once gets left behind, or breaks a leg. There is an enthusiasm in his sympathetic handling of material forces which goes far to cancel the illiberal character which it might otherwise assume. The good workman hardly distinguishes his artistic intention from the potency in himself and in things which is about to realise that intention. Accordingly his ideals fall into the form of premonitions and prophecies; and his studious prophecies often come true. So do the happy workmanlike ideals of the American. When a poor boy, perhaps, he dreams of an education, and presently he gets an education, or at least a degree; he dreams of growing rich, and he grows rich—only more slowly and modestly, perhaps, than he expected; he dreams of marrying his Rebecca and, even if he marries a Leah instead, he ultimately finds in Leah his Rebecca after all. He dreams of helping to carry on and to accelerate the movement of a vast, seething, progressive society, and he actually does so. Ideals clinging so close to nature are almost sure of fulfilment; the American beams with a certain self-confidence and sense of mastery; he feels that God and nature are working with him.

Idealism in the American accordingly goes hand in hand with present contentment and with foresight of what the future very likely will actually bring. He is not a revolutionist; he believes he is already on the right track and moving towards an excellent destiny. In revolutionists, on the contrary, idealism is founded on dissatisfaction and expresses it. What exists seems to them an absurd jumble of irrational accidents and bad habits, and they want the future to be based on reason and to be the pellucid embodiment of all their maxims. All their zeal is for something radically different from the actual and (if they only knew it) from the possible; it is ideally simple, and they love it and believe in it because their nature craves it. They think life would be set free by the destruction of all its organs. They are therefore extreme idealists in the region of hope, but not at all, as poets and artists are, in the region of perception and memory. In the atmosphere of civilised life they miss all the refraction and all the fragrance; so that in their conception of actual things they are apt to be crude realists; and their ignorance and inexperience of the moral world, unless it comes of ill-luck, indicates their incapacity for education. Now incapacity for education, when united with great inner vitality, is one root of idealism. It is what condemns us all, in the region of sense, to substitute perpetually what we are capable of imagining for what things may be in themselves; it is what condemns us, wherever it extends, to think a priori; it is what keeps us bravely and incorrigibly pursuing what we call the good—that is, what would fulfil the demands of our nature—however little provision the fates may have made for it. But the want of insight on the part of revolutionists touching the past and the present infects in an important particular their idealism about the future; it renders their dreams of the future unrealisable. For in human beings—this may not be true of other animals, more perfectly performed—experience is necessary to pertinent and concrete thinking; even our primitive instincts are blind until they stumble upon some occasion that solicits them; and they can be much transformed or deranged by their first partial satisfactions. Therefore a man who does not idealise his experience, but idealises a priori, is incapable of true prophecy; when he dreams he

raves, and the more he criticises the less he helps. American idealism, on the contrary, is nothing if not helpful, nothing if not pertinent to practicable transformations; and when the American frets, it is because whatever is useless and impertinent, be it idealism or inertia, irritates him; for it frustrates the good results which he sees might so easily have been obtained.

The American is wonderfully alive; and his vitality, not having often found a suitable outlet, makes him appear agitated on the surface; he is always letting off an unnecessarily loud blast of incidental steam. Yet his vitality is not superficial; it is inwardly prompted, and as sensitive and quick as a magnetic needle. He is inquisitive, and ready with an answer to any question that he may put to himself of his own accord; but if you try to pour instruction into him, on matters that do not touch his own spontaneous life, he shows the most extraordinary powers of resistance and oblivescence; so that he often is remarkably expert in some directions and surprisingly obtuse in others. He seems to bear lightly the sorrowful burden of human knowledge. In a word, he is young.

What sense is there in this feeling, which we all have, that the American is young? His country is blessed with as many elderly people as any other, and his descent from Adam, or from the Darwinian rival of Adam, cannot be shorter than that of his European cousins. Nor are his ideas always very fresh. Trite and rigid bits of morality and religion, with much seemly and antique political lore, remain axiomatic in him, as in the mind of a child; he may carry all this about with an unquestioning familiarity which does not comport understanding. To keep traditional sentiments in this way insulated and uncriticised is itself a sign of youth. A good young man is naturally conservative and loyal on all those subjects which his experience has not brought to a test; advanced opinions on politics, marriage, or literature are comparatively rare in America; they are left for the ladies to discuss, and usually to condemn, while the men get on with their work. In spite of what is old-fashioned in his more general ideas, the American is unmistakably young; and this, I should say, for two reasons: one, that he is chiefly occupied with his immediate environment, and the other, that his reactions upon it are inwardly prompted, spontaneous, and full of vivacity and self-trust. His views are not yet lengthened; his will is not yet broken or transformed. The present moment, however, in this, as in other things, may mark a great change in him;

he is perhaps now reaching his majority, and all I say may hardly apply to-day, and may not apply at all to-morrow. I speak of him as I have known him; and whatever moral strength may accrue to him later, I am not sorry to have known him in his youth. The charm of youth, even when it is a little boisterous, lies in nearness to the impulses of nature, in a quicker and more obvious obedience to that pure, seminal principle which, having formed the body and its organs, always directs their movements, unless it is forced by vice or necessity to make them crooked, or to suspend them. Even under the inevitable crust of age the soul remains young, and, wherever it is able to break through, sprouts into something green and tender. We are all as young at heart as the most youthful American, but the seed in his case has fallen upon virgin soil, where it may spring up more bravely and with less respect for the giants of the wood. Peoples seem older when their perennial natural youth is encumbered with more possessions and prepossessions, and they are mindful of the many things they have lost or missed. The American is not mindful of them.

In America there is a tacit optimistic assumption about existence, to the effect that the more existence the better. The soulless critic might urge that quantity is only a physical category, implying no excellence, but at best an abundance of opportunities both for good and for evil. Yet the young soul, being curious and hungry, views existence a priori under the form of the good; its instincts to live implies a faith that most things it can become or see or do will be worth while. Respect for quantity is accordingly something more than the childish joy and wonder at bigness; it is the fisherman's joy in a big haul, the good uses of which he can take for granted. Such optimism is amiable. Nature cannot afford that we should begin by being too calculating or wise, and she encourages us by the pleasure she attaches to our functions in advance of their fruits, and often in excess of them; as the angler enjoys catching his fish more than eating it, and often, waiting patiently for the fish to bite, misses his own supper. The pioneer must devote himself to preparations; he must work for the future, and it is healthy and dutiful of him to love his work for its own sake. At the same time, unless reference to an ultimate purpose is at least virtual in all his activities, he runs the danger of becoming a living automaton, vain and ignominious in its mechanical constancy. Idealism about work can hide an intense materialism about life. Man, if he is a

rational being, cannot live by bread alone nor be a labourer merely; he must eat and work in view of an ideal harmony which overarches all his days, and which is realised in the way they hang together, or in some ideal issue which they have in common. Otherwise, though his technical philosophy may call itself idealism, he is a materialist in morals; he esteems things, and esteems himself, for mechanical uses and energies. Even sensualists, artists, and pleasure-lovers are wiser than that, for though their idealism may be desultory or corrupt, they attain something ideal, and prize things only for their living effects, moral though perhaps fugitive. Sensation, when we do not take it as a signal for action, but arrest and peruse what it positively brings before us, reveals something ideal—a colour, shape, or sound; and to dwell on these presences, with no thought of their material significance, is an æsthetic or dreamful idealism. To pass from this idealism to the knowledge of matter is a great intellectual advance, and goes with dominion over the world; for in the practical arts the mind is adjusted to a larger object, with more depth and potentiality in it; which is what makes people feel that the material world is real, as they call it, and that the ideal world is not. Certainly the material world is real; for the philosophers who deny the existence of matter are like the critics who deny the existence of Homer. If there was never any Homer, there must have been a lot of other poets no less Homeric than he; and if matter does not exist, a combination of other things exists which is just as material. But the intense reality of the material world would not prevent it from being a dreary waste in our eyes, or even an abyss of horror, if it brought forth no spiritual fruits. In fact, it does bring forth spiritual fruits, for otherwise we should not be here to find fault with it, and to set up our ideals over against it. Nature is material, but not materialistic; it issues in life, and breeds all sorts of warm passions and idle beauties. And just as sympathy with the mechanical travail and turmoil of nature, apart from its spiritual fruits, is moral materialism, so the continual perception and love of these fruits is moral idealism—happiness in the presence of immaterial objects and harmonies, such as we envisage in affection, speculation, religion, and all the forms of the beautiful.

The circumstances of his life hitherto have necessarily driven the American into moral materialism; for in his dealings with material things he can hardly stop to enjoy their sensible aspects, which are ideal, nor proceed at once to their ultimate uses, which are ideal too. He is practical as against the poet, and worldly as against the clear philosopher or the saint. The most striking expression of this materialism is usually supposed to be his love of the almighty dollar; but that is a foreign and unintelligent view. The American talks about money, because that is the symbol and measure he has at hand for success, intelligence, and power; but as to money itself he makes, loses, spends, and gives it away with a very light heart. To my mind the most striking expression of his materialism is his singular preoccupation with quantity. If, for instance, you visit Niagara Falls, you may expect to hear how many cubic feet or metric tons of water are precipitated per second over the cataract; how many cities and towns (with the number of their inhabitants) derive light and motive power from it; and the annual value of the further industries that might very well be carried on by the same means, without visibly depleting the world's greatest wonder or injuring the tourist trade. That is what I confidently expected to hear on arriving at the adjoining town of Buffalo; but I was deceived. The first thing I heard instead was that there are more miles of asphalt pavement in Buffalo than in any city in the world. Nor is this insistence on quantity confined to men of business. The President of Harvard College, seeing me once by chance soon after the beginning of a term, inquired how my classes were getting on; and when I replied that I thought they were getting on well, that my men seemed to be keen and intelligent, he stopped me as if I was about to waste his time. "I meant," said he, "*what is the number* of students in your classes."

Here I think we may perceive that this love of quantity often has a silent partner, which is diffidence as to quality. The democratic conscience recoils before anything that savours of privilege; and lest it should concede an unmerited privilege to any pursuit or person, it reduces all things as far as possible to the common denominator of quantity. Numbers cannot lie: but if it came to comparing the ideal beauties of philosophy with those of Anglo-Saxon, who should decide? All studies are good—why else have universities?—but those must be most encouraged which attract the greatest number of students. Hence the President's question. Democratic faith, in its diffidence about quality, throws the reins of education upon the pupil's neck, as Don Quixote threw the reins on the neck of Rocinante, and bids his divine instinct choose its own way.

The American has never yet had to face the trials of Job. Great crises, like the Civil War, he has known how to surmount victoriously; and now that he has surmounted a second great crisis victoriously, it is possible that he may relapse, as he did in the other case, into an apparently complete absorption in material enterprise and prosperity. But if serious and irremediable tribulation ever overtook him, what would his attitude be? It is then that we should be able to discover whether materialism or idealism lies at the base of his character. Meantime his working mind is not without its holiday. He spreads humour pretty thick and even over the surface of conversation, and humour is one form of moral emancipation. He loves landscape, he loves mankind, and he loves knowledge; and in music he finds an art which he unfeignedly enjoys. In music and landscape, in humour and kindness, he touches the ideal more truly, perhaps, than in his ponderous academic idealisms and busy religions; for it is astonishing how much even religion in America (can it possibly be so in England?) is a matter of meetings, building-funds, schools, charities, clubs, and picnics. To be poor in order to be simple, to produce less in order that the product may be more choice and beautiful, and may leave us less burdened with unnecessary duties and useless possessions— that is an ideal not articulate in the American mind; yet here and there I seem to have heard a sigh after it, a groan at the perpetual incubus of business and shrill society. Significant witness to such aspirations is borne by those new forms of popular religion, not mere variations on tradition, which have sprung up from the soil—revivalism, spiritualism, Christian Science, the New Thought. Whether or no we can tap, through these or other channels, some cosmic or inner energy not hitherto at the disposal of man (and there is nothing incredible in that), we certainly may try to remove friction and waste in the mere process of living; we may relax morbid strains, loosen suppressed instincts, iron out the creases of the soul, discipline ourselves into simplicity, sweetness, and peace. These religious movements are efforts toward such physiological economy and hygiene; and while they are thoroughly plebeian, with no great lights, and no idea of raising men from the most vulgar and humdrum worldly existence, yet they see the possibility of physical and moral health on that common plane, and pursue it. That is true morality. The dignities of various types of life or mind, like the gifts of various animals, are relative. The snob adores one type only, and the creatures supposed by him to illustrate it perfectly;

or envies and hates them, which is just as snobbish. Veritable lovers of life, on the contrary, like Saint Francis or like Dickens, know that in every tenement of clay, with no matter what endowment or station, happiness and perfection are possible to the soul. There must be no brow-beating, with shouts of work or progress or revolution, any more than with threats of hell-fire. What does it profit a man to free the whole world if his soul is not free? Moral freedom is not an artificial condition, because the ideal is the mother tongue of both the heart and the senses. All that is requisite is that we should pause in living to enjoy life,

and should lift up our hearts to things that are pure goods in themselves, so that once to have found and loved them, whatever else may betide, may remain a happiness that nothing can sully. This natural idealism does not imply that we are immaterial, but only that we are animate and truly alive. When the senses are sharp, as they are in the American, they are already half liberated, already a joy in themselves; and when the heart is warm, like his, and eager to be just, its ideal destiny can hardly be doubtful. It will not be always merely pumping and working; time and its own pulses will lend it wings.

STUART PRATT SHERMAN (1881-1926)
THE GENIUS OF AMERICA
(1921)

Some people have one hobby and some another. Mine is studying the utterances of the Intelligentsia—a word by which those who think that they exhibit the latest aspect of mind designate themselves. I like to hear what our "young people" say, and to read what they write; for, though they are not meek, they will, at least in a temporal sense, inherit the earth—and one is always interested in heirs. So much depends upon them.

Not long ago, progressive thinkers organized a public dinner in order to consult together for the welfare of the Republic. The marks of a progressive thinker are profound pessimism with regard to the past and infinite hope with regard to the future. Such a thinker was the toastmaster. Now, a thoughtful and progressive pessimist is a joy forever. He says for the rest of us those bitter things about history and society which we all feel at times, but hesitate to utter, not being so certain that we possess the antidote. I had long surmised that this was not the best possible of worlds, whether one considered it in its present drunken and reeling state, or whether one peered backward, through stratum after stratum of wrecked enterprises, into its iniquitous and catastrophic antiquity. Accordingly, I felt a kind of rich, tragic satisfaction when this toastmaster, in a ten-minute introduction, reviewed the entire history of the world from the time of the Cave Man to the time of the Treaty of Versailles, and concluded with a delightfully cheerful smile:—

'Up to date civilization has been a failure. Life is tolerable only as a preparation for a state which neither we nor our sons shall enter.

We shall all die in the desert,' he continued, as the gloom thickened to emit the perorational flash; 'but let us die like Moses, with a look into the Promised Land.'

Then he began to call upon his associates in the organization of progress.

Nine-tenths of the speakers were, as is customary on such occasions, of the sort that editors include when they arrange a series of articles called "Builders of Contemporary Civilization." They were the men who get cathedrals begun, and make universities expand, legislatures vote, armies fight, money circulate, commodities exchange, and grass grow two blades for one. They spoke in a businesslike way of eliminating waste and introducing efficiency, of tapping unused resources here, of speeding up production there, of facilitating communications somewhere else. Except for the speeches of the bishop and the university president, the discourses had to my ear a somewhat mechanical twang. Yet one could not but approve and feel braced by the leading idea running through them all, which was to extend the control of man over nature and the control of a creative reason over man. All the speakers—engineer, banker, and farmer, no less than clergyman and educator—seemed to have their eyes fixed on some standard, which some internal passion for improvement urged them to approximate, or to attain. I couldn't help thinking how Franklin would have applauded the spirit of his posterity.

When, as I thought, the programme was completed, they had substituted for the present machinery of society a new outfit of the 1950 model, or perhaps of a still later date.

The country, under intensive cultivation, looked like a Chinese garden. The roads, even in the spring of the year, were not merely navigable but Fordable. Something had happened to the great smoke-producing cities; so that Chicago, for instance, shone like a jewel in clear air and sunlight. High in the heavens, innumerable merchant vessels, guarded by aerial dreadnaughts, were passing in continuous flight across the Gulf to South America. Production had been so enormously increased by the increased expertness, health, and sobriety of the producers, that a man could go to market with only a handful of silver in his pocket and return with bread and butter enough for himself and his wife, and perhaps a couple of biscuits for his dog. Every one of the teeming population, alow and aloft, male and female, was at work in uniform, a rifle and a wireless field-telephone within easy reach; for every one was both an expert workman and a soldier. But no one was fighting. Under the shield of that profound "preparedness," the land enjoyed uninterrupted peace and prosperity.

Perhaps I dreamed some of this. The speeches were long.

When I returned to a condition of critical consciousness, the toastmaster was introducing the last speaker as follows: 'We have now provided for all matters of first-rate importance. But we have with us one of the literary leaders of the younger generation. I am going to call upon him to say a word for the way the man of the new Republic will express himself after he has been fed and clothed and housed. I shall ask him to sketch a place in our programme of democratic progress for art, music, literature, and the like—in short, for the superfluous things.'

That phrase, "The superfluous things," rang in my ear like a gong: not because it was new, but because it was old; because it struck a nerve sensitive from repeated striking; because it really summed up the values of art for this representative group of builders; because it linked itself up with a series of popularly contrasted terms—practical and liberal studies, business English and literary English, useful and ornamental arts, valuable and graceful accomplishments, necessaries and luxuries of life, chemists and professors of English, and so on *ad infinitum*. I myself was a professor of superfluous things, and therefore, a superfluous professor. As I turned this uncomfortable thought over in my mind, it occurred to me that things are superfluous only with reference to particular ends; and that, in a comprehensive plan

of preparation for a satisfactory national life, we might be compelled to revise the epithets conventionally applied to the arts which express our craving for beauty, harmony, happiness.

Before I had gone far in this train of thought, the literary artist was addressing the business men. His discourse was so remarkable, and yet so representative of our most conspicuous group of "young people," that I reproduce the substance of it here.

'The young men of my generation,' he began, 'propose the emancipation of the arts in America. Before our time, such third-rate talents as the country produced were infected, by our institutions, and by the multitude, with a sense of their Messianic mission. Dominated by the twin incubi of Puritanism and Democracy, they servilely associated themselves with political, moral, and social programmes, and made beauty a prostitute to utility. Our generation of artists has seen through all the solemn humbug of your plans for the "welfare of the Republic." With a clearer-eyed pessimism than that of our toastmaster, we have not merely envisaged the failure of civilization in the past: we have also foreseen its failure in the future.

'We have talked with wiser counselors than those pious Philistines, our naïve Revolutionary Fathers. George Moore, our great contemporary, tells us that " Humanity is a pig-sty, where liars, hypocrites, and the obscene in spirit congregate: and it has been so since the great Jew conceived it, and it will be so till the end." Leopardi, who in this respect was our pioneer, declares that " all things else being vain, disgust of life represents all that is substantial and real in the life of man." Theodore Dreiser, our profound philosophical novelist, views the matter, however, with a bit of creative hopefulness. Though God, as he has assured us, cares nothing for the pure in heart, yet God does offer a " universe-eating career to the giant," recking not how the life-force manifests itself, " so long as it achieves avid, forceful, artistic expression." From serving the middle-class American, Flaubert frees us, saying, " Hatred of the bourgeois is the beginning of virtue." Mr. Spingarn, our learned theorist, brushes away the critical cobwebs of antique poetic doctrine, and gives us a clean æsthetic basis, by his revelation that " beauty aims neither at morals nor at truth "; and that " it is not the purpose of poetry to further the cause of democracy, or any other practical 'cause,' any more than it is the purpose of bridge-building to further the cause of Esperanto."

We have had to import our philosophy in fragments from beyond the borders of Anglo-Saxonia, from Ireland, Germany, France, and Italy; and we have had to call in the quick Semitic intelligence to piece it together. But here it is; and you will recognize that it liberates us from Puritanism and from Democracy. It emancipates us from you!

'You ask me, perhaps,' continued the young representative of American letters, 'what we intend to do with this new freedom, which, as Mr. Ludwig Lewisohn truly says, is our "central passion." Well, we intend *to let ourselves out*. If you press me as to what I mean by that, I can refer you to the new psychology. This invaluable science, developed by great German investigators, has recently announced, as you possibly know, an epoch-making discovery—namely, that most of the evil in the world is due to self-control. To modern inquiry, it appears that what all the moralists, especially in Anglo-Saxon countries, have tried to curb or to suppress is precisely what they should have striven to release. If you wish corroboration, let me quote the words of our talented English colleague, Mr. W. L. George, the novelist, who says, "I suspect that it does a people no good if its preoccupations find no outlet."

'In passing I will remark that Mr. George, being an Englishman, shows a certain taint of inherited English Puritanism in defending letting the people out *in order to do them good*. From the point of view of the new philosophy, letting one's self out completely and perfectly is art, which has no purpose and therefore requires no defense.

'But to return: what are the "preoccupations" of the ordinary man? Once more Mr. George shall answer for us. "A large proportion of his thoughts run on sex if he is a live man." French literature proves the point abundantly; American literature, as yet, very imperfectly and scantily. Consequently, a young American desiring to enlarge his sex-consciousness must import his fiction from overseas. But our own Mr. Cabell has also begun to prove the point as well as a foreigner. His release of the suppressed life is very precious. If he were encouraged, instead of being nipped by the frost of a Puritanical censorship; if a taste were developed to support him, he might do for us what George Moore is trying, subterraneously, to do for England.

'Our own Mr. Dreiser has been so preoccupied with this subject that he has been obliged to neglect a little his logic and his grammar. His thinking, however, runs none the less sure-footedly to the conclusion reached by Mr. George. What does that remorseless artist-thinker, Mr. Dreiser, say? He says: "It is the desire to enthrone and enhance, by every possible detail of ornamentation, comfort, and color,—love, sensual gratification,—that man in the main moves, and by that alone." We do not maintain that Mr. Dreiser is a flawless writer. But if, at your leisure, you will study that sentence from his latest and ripest book, till you discover its subject, predicate, and object, and can bridge its anacoluthon, and reconcile "in the main" with "by that alone," then you will be in a position to grasp our leading idea for the future of the arts in America.'

When the young man resumed his seat, there was a ripple of applause among the ladies, one of whom told me later that she thought the speaker's voice 'delicious' and his eyes 'soulful.' But I noticed that the bishop was purple with suppressed wrath; that the university president had withdrawn; while the other builders of civilization, notably the business men, were nodding with a kind of patient and puzzled resignation.

In my neighborhood there was a quick little buzz of questions: 'Will you tell me what all that has to do with a programme of democratic progress?'—'What is George Moore trying subterraneously to do for England? Is he interested in the collieries? I thought he was a novelist.'—'He has downright insulted them,' said my neighbor on the right, 'don't you think?'

'Why, no,' I replied, 'not exactly. He was asked to speak on the superfluous things; and he has really demonstrated that they are superfluous. After this, don't you see, the builders of civilization can go on with their work and not worry about the arts. He has told them that beauty is not for them; and they will swiftly conclude that they are not for beauty. I think he has very honestly expressed what our radical young people are thinking. They are in revolt. They wish by all means to widen the traditional breach between the artist and the Puritan.'

'What do you mean by Puritan?' inquired my friend, as we made our way out of the hall together.

He is a simple-hearted old gentleman who doesn't follow the new literature, but still reads Hawthorne and George Eliot.

'It isn't,' I explained, 'what I mean by Puritan that signifies. It is what the young people mean. A Puritan for them is any man who believes it possible to distinguish between good and evil, and who also believes that, having made the distinction, his welfare depends upon his furthering the one and curbing the other.'

'But,' cried the old gentleman in some heat, 'in that sense, we are all Puritans. That isn't theological Puritanism. That is scarcely even moral Puritanism. It's just—it's just ordinary horse sense. In that sense, for God's sake, who isn't a Puritan?'

I recalled an old case that I thought would illustrate the present situation. 'There was Judge Keeling,' I said, 'in Charles the Second's time. Judge Keeling put Bunyan in jail for failing to use the Book of Common Prayer, and similar misdemeanors. In the reign of the same Defender of the Faith, two merry wits and poets of his court became flown with wine and, stripping themselves naked, ran through the streets, giving a healthy outlet to their suppressed selves in songs of a certain sort. The constable, an ordinary English Puritan, so far misunderstood the spiritual autonomy which the artist should enjoy, that he arrested the two liberators of art. When, however, the news reached Judge Keeling, he released the young men and laid the constable by the heels; which, as Pepys,—himself a patron of the arts, yet a bit of a Puritan,—as Pepys remarked, was a "horrid shame." Now Judge Keeling, I think our own young people would admit, was not a Puritan, even in the latest sense of the term.'

'But those Restoration fellows,' replied my friend,—'Keeling and the wits and the rest of them,—they were opposing the sense of the whole English nation. They made no headway. No one took them seriously. They all disappeared like gnats in a snowstorm. When the central current of English life had done its scouring work, people thought of your two poets as mere stable-boys of the Restoration. Surely you don't think our democratic young people are so silly as to imitate them? We have no merry monarch to reward them. What do they gain by setting themselves against the common sense?'

'Notoriety,' I said, 'which is as sweet under a republican as under a monarchical form of government. I used to think that to insult the common sense and always to be speaking contemptuously of the "bourgeoisie," implied sycophancy, either to a corrupt and degenerate aristocracy, or to a peculiarly arrogant and atheistical lowest class. But our "democratic young people," as you call them, preserve and foster this artistic snobbishness as a form of self-expression.

'When Mr. Dreiser declares that God cares nothing for the Ten Commandments or for the pure in heart, he really means that inanimate nature cares nothing for them, and that the animal kingdom and he and the heroes of his books follow nature. But he denies a faith which in some fifty millions of native Americans survives the decay of dogma, and somehow in attenuated form, keeps the country from going wholly to the dogs. For, of course, if it were demonstrable that God had abandoned a charge so important, plain men of sense would quietly assume responsibility and "carry on" in his stead.'

'I quite agree with you,' said the old gentleman; 'but as I am not acquainted with the author you mention and am just completing my third reading of *Middlemarch*, I will turn in here. Good-night.'

I went on down the street, resuming, unaccompanied, the more difficult part of my meditation on the place of the fine arts in a programme of democratic progress, and internally debating with the young man who had caused such a sensation at dinner. Having made this general acknowledgment of his inspiration, I shall not attempt to reproduce our dialogue; for I found that he simply repeated the main points of his speech, and interrupted my comment upon it.

When Mr. Spingarn, who, as a man, is concerned with truth, morals, and democracy, and has a personal record of civil and military service—when Mr. Spingarn, as an æsthetic theorist, declares that beauty is not concerned with truth or morals or democracy, he makes a philosophical distinction which I have no doubt that Charles the Second would have understood, approved, and could, at need, have illustrated. But he says what the American schoolboy knows to be false to the history of beauty in this country. By divorcing, in his super-subtle Italian fashion, form from substance, he has separated beauty from her traditional associates in American letters, and so has left her open to seduction.

Beauty, whether we like it or not, has a heart full of service. Emancipated, she will still be seeking some vital activity. You have heard how the new writers propose to employ her new leisure: in extending the ordinary man's preoccupation with sex. We don't, you will observe, by the emancipation of the arts from service to truth, morals, and democracy —we don't obtain a 'disinterested' beauty. We obtain merely a beauty with different interests—serving 'sensual gratification' and propagating the curiously related doctrine that

God cares nothing for the Ten Commandments or for the pure in heart.

We arrive finally at some such comprehensive formulation of relationships as this: It is the main function of art to deny what it is the main function of truth, morals, and democracy to affirm. Our speaker for the younger generation has made all this so clear that I suspect the bishop is going home resolved to take music out of his churches. The university president is perhaps deciding to replace his professor of Italian painting by an additional professor of soil-fertility. As for the captains of industry, they can hardly be blamed if they mutter among themselves: 'May the devil fly away with the fine arts! Let's get back to business.'

It is to be hoped, nevertheless, that the devil will not fly away with the fine arts or the fine artists, or with our freshly foot-loose and wandering beauty; for the builders of civilization have need of them. If the young people were not misled by more or less alien-spirited guides, the national genius itself would lead them into a larger life.

When our forefathers, whom it is now customary to speak of as 'grim,' outlined their programme for a new republic, though they had many more immediately pressing matters on their minds, they included among objects to be safeguarded, indeed, among the inalienable rights of mankind, 'the pursuit of happiness.' It appears that they, like ourselves, had some dim idea that the ultimate end of their preparation was, not to fight the English or the savages or the wilderness, but to enjoy, they or their posterity, some hitherto unexperienced felicity. That, at heart, was what sustained them under the burdens and heats of a pioneering civilization, through those years when they dispensed with such ingredients of happiness as musical comedy and moving pictures, and when the most notable piece of imagist verse was Franklin's proverb, 'It is hard for an empty sack to stand upright'—a one-line poem of humor, morality, insight, and imagination all compact.

We, too, entertain, we ordinary puritanical Americans, some shadowy notions of a time, when, at more frequent intervals than now, men shall draw in a delighted breath and cry, 'Oh, that this moment might endure forever!' We believe in this far-off time, because, at least once or twice in a lifetime, each of us experiences such a moment, or, feeling the wind of its retreating wing, knows that it has just gone by. It may have been in the spell-bound glow of some magical sunset, or at the sound of a solemn music, or in the sudden apprehension of a long-sought truth, or at the thrill and tightening of resolution in some crisis, or in the presence of some fair marble image of a thought that keeps its beauty and serenity while we fret and fade. It may even have been at some vision, seen in the multitude of business, of a new republic revealed to the traveling imagination, like a shining city set on a hill in the flash of a midnight storm. Till life itself yields such moments less charily, it is incumbent upon the artist to send them as often as he can.

There came among us in war time an English poet whose face was as sad as his who from the Judecca climbed to see again *delle cose belle che porta il ciel*—the sky-borne beauty of the stars. He had been where his countrymen, fighting with incredible heroism, had suffered one of the most heart-breaking and bloody defeats in English history. His memory was seared with remembrance of the filth, waste, wounds, and screaming lunacy of the battle-front to which he was about to return. When someone asked him to write his name in a volume of his poems, he inscribed below it this line of his own verse:—

The days that make us happy make us wise.

Why these days? Because in them we learn the final object of all our preparation. These days serve us as measures of the success of our civilization.

The ultimate reason for including the 'superfluous things'—art, music, literature—in a plan of national preparation is that, rightly used, they are both causes and consequences of happiness. They are the seed and the fruit of that fine and gracious and finished national life towards which we aspire. When the body is fed and sheltered, there remain to be satisfied—as what Puritan does not know?—the inarticulate hungers of the heart, to which all the arts are merely some of the ministers. Other ministers are religion, morality, patriotism, science, truth. It is only by harmonious coöperation that they can ever hope to satisfy the whole heart, the modern heart, with its ever-widening range of wakened hungers. It is certainly not by banishing or ignoring the austerer ministers, and making poetry, painting, and music perform a Franco-Turkish dance of sensual invitation—it is not thus that the artist should expect to satisfy a heart as religious, as moral, and as democratic as the American heart is, by its bitterest critics, declared to be.

'Art is expression,' says the learned theorist of the young people, 'and poets succeed or fail by their success or failure in completely expressing themselves.' Let us concede that the poet who expresses completely what is in him by a hymn to the devil is as perfect an artist as a poet who expresses what is in him by the Iliad. Then let us remark that the poet who hymns the devil, the devil is likely to fly away with. And let us add as rapidly as possible a little series of neglected truisms. An artist is a man living in society. A great artist is a great man living in a great society. When a great artist expresses himself completely, it is found invariably that he has expressed, not merely himself, but also the dominant thought and feeling of the men with whom he lives. Mr. Spingarn, indeed, indirectly admits the point when he says: 'If the ideals they [the poets] express are not the ideals we admire most, we must blame, not the poets, but ourselves; in the world where morals count, *we have failed to give them the proper materials out of which to rear a nobler edifice.*' (Italics mine.) This seems to mean that society is responsible for the artist, even if the artist is not responsible to society. Society gives him, as a man, what, as an artist, he expresses.

I have perhaps hinted here and elsewhere my suspicion that Mr. Dreiser, a capital illustrative example, is not a great novelist, because, though living in a great society, he does not express or represent its human characteristics, but confines himself to an exhibition of the habits and traits of animals. Is it that we have not given him materials to rear a nobler edifice? That which we—that is, society—can give to a novelist is the moulding and formative influence of the national temper and character. What have we given to Mr. Dreiser? What, in short, are the dominant traits of the national genius? I am delighted to discover in Mr. Dreiser's latest book that he himself knows pretty well what the national genius is, how it has manifested itself in religion and politics, and how it is nourished and sustained by ancient traditions and strong racial proclivities. I like to agree with our young people when I can. When I find one of them testifying, contrary to their custom, that America does now possess a powerful national culture, I like to applaud his discernment. It is a pleasure to make amends for my disparagement of Mr. Dreiser as a novelist, by illustrating his critical ability with these words of his on the national genius:—

'No country in the world (at least, none that I know anything about) has such a peculiar, such a seemingly fierce determination to make the Ten Commandments work. It would be amusing, if it were not pitiful, their faith in these binding religious ideals. I have never been able to make up my mind whether this springs from the zealotry of the Puritans who landed at Plymouth Rock, or whether it is rooted in the soil . . . or whether it is a product of the Federal Constitution, compounded by such idealists as Paine and Jefferson and Franklin and the more or less religious and political dreamers of the preconstitutional days. *Certain it is that no such profound moral idealism animated the French in Canada, the Dutch in New York, the Swedes in New Jersey, or the mixed French and English in the extreme South and New Orleans.*' (Italics mine.)

I know how differently our young people feel; but, to my thinking, a national genius animated by an incomparably profound moral idealism does not seem such a contemptible moulding and formative influence for an artist to undergo. English-speaking poets, from Spenser to Walt Whitman, have grown great under the influence of such an environing spirit. At any rate, if the great artist, in expressing himself, expresses also the society of which he is a part, it should seem to follow, like a conclusion in geometry, that a great American artist must express the 'profound moral idealism' of America. To rail against it, to lead an insurrection against it, is to repeat the folly of the Restoration wits. If in this connection one may use a bit of the American language, it is to 'buck' the national genius; and this is an enterprise comparable with bucking a stone wall. On the other hand to acknowledge the leadership of the national genius, to subject one's self to its influence, to serve it according to one's talents, to find beautiful and potent forms to express its working—this is to ally one's self with the general creative effort of the country in all fields of activity; this is to be in a benign conspiracy with one's time and place, and to be upborne by the central stream of tendency.

There is small place for Bohemia in democratic art. I sometimes wonder with what spiritual refugees, under what rafters, those poets and novelists live who are so anxious to secede from the major effort of their countrymen. For their own sakes one wishes that they might cultivate acquaintance with our eminent 'builders of civilization.' The good that I should expect from this contact is a vision of the national life, a sense of the national will, which are usually possessed in some degree by those Americans, whatever their æsthetic deficiencies, who bear the burden of the state, or are widely conversant with its business, or preside over its religious, moral, or educational undertakings. I do not intend in the least to suggest that the artist should become propagandist or reformer, or that he should go to the bishop or the statesman for a commission, though I believe that Leonardo and Michael Angelo did some very tolerable things under direct inspiration of that nature. What one feels is rather that intercourse with such men might finally create in our artistic secessionists a consciousness of the ignobility of their aims. For in America it will be found more and more that the artist who does not in some fashion concern himself with truth, morals, and democracy, is unimportant, is ignoble.

In an unfinished world, where religion has become so largely a matter of traditional sentiments and observances, poetry has a work to do, poetry of any high seriousness. Our critics and poets of vision have long since recognized what that work is. 'I said to Bryant and to these young people,' wrote Emerson in his journal many years ago, 'that the high poetry of the world from the beginning has been ethical, and it is the tendency of the ripe modern mind to produce it.'—'I hate literature,' said Whitman, perhaps over-emphatically expressing the traditional American disdain for art in its merely decorative and recreative aspects. 'Literature is big only in one way, when used as an aid in the growth of the humanities.' Our young people, of course, will exclaim that these are typical utterances of our New England Puritanism, fatal to the arts; but, as a matter of fact, this Puritanism is of a sort that the New Englanders shared with Plato and Aristotle, who have not been fatal to the arts. When Emerson said, 'Honor every truth by use,' he expressed, I think, what Socrates would have approved, and at the same time he spoke in fullest accord with the national genius, ever driving at practice, ever pressing towards the fulfillment of its vision.

Why should a spokesman for belles-lettres, bred in the national tradition, hesitate to go before a group of 'practical' men and talk to them, unashamed, of the 'utilities' of artistic expression? He may borrow a figure from the economist, and declare that the poet 'socializes' the spiritual wealth of the country. Art is rooted in social instinct, in a desire to communicate goods to others, to share one's private experience and anticipations. It is the spontaneous overflow of thoughts and feelings which one cannot consume alone. 'Full of the common joy,' says Donne, 'I uttered some.'

This is your true and unassailable communism. When Saint Gaudens, having conceived his heroic and inspiring image of Colonel Shaw leading his colored troops, sets it up on Boston Common, it becomes common property; and the loafer in the park, the student, the hurrying merchant, the newsboy, are equal sharers in its commemoration and inspiration. A village poet with an ethical bent makes his thought sing:—

When duty whispers low, 'Thou must,'
The youth replies, 'I can,'—

and he has slipped a spiritual gold-piece into the palm of each of his fellow countrymen. This is wealth really distributed. It would be of advantage to both bards and business men if some spiritual economist would remind them more frequently that the wealth of a community is in proportion to the number of such ideas that it has in common.

Among builders of American civilization, many means are now discussed for awakening national pride and attaching the affections of the people to the state; conspicuous among them are, or were, Liberty Bonds, nationalization of the railroads, and universal military service. Robert Burns and Sir Walter did the work more simply and cheaply for Scotland. It has never been hard for the native-born American to hold America 'first' in political affairs; but musicians as such, painters as such, men of letters as such, cannot, without straining the meaning of the word, hold her first till her national genius expresses itself as adequately, as nobly, in music, painting, and literature, as it has, on the whole, in the great political crises. Irving, at the beginning of the last century, worked with a clear understanding of our deficiencies when he wrote his Rip Van Winkle and other legends of the Hudson Valley, with the avowed purpose 'to clothe home scenes and places and familiar names with those imaginative and whimsical associations so seldom met with in our new country, but which live like charms and spells about the cities of the Old World, binding the heart of the native inhabitant to his home.'

You may persuade all men to buy Liberty Bonds or to invest in the stock of nationalized railroads, or you may legislate them into the army; but you cannot dragoon them into crying, 'O beautiful, my country!' That is the work of the poets, who have entwined their loyalty with their heart-strings. That is the work of the artists, who have made their Americanism vital, devout, affectionate. 'How can our love increase,' asks Thoreau, 'unless our loveliness increases also?' A good question for 'Americanizers' to meditate upon. It would benefit both public men and artists if someone reminded them more frequently that one of the really important tasks of national preparation is to draw out and express in forms of appealing beauty, audible as poetry or music, visible as painting or sculpture, the purpose and meaning of this vast half-articulate land, so that our hosts of new and unlearned citizens may come to understand her as they understand the divine compassion—by often kneeling before some shrine of the Virgin.

When art becomes thus informed with the larger life of the country, it vitalizes and gives permanency to the national ideals. It transmits the hope and courage and aspiration of one generation to the next, with the emotional glow and color undiminished and unimpaired. If we receive and cherish the tradition, our imaginative experience transcends the span of our natural lives. We live in the presence, as Burke declared, of our 'canonized' forefathers and in a kind of reverent apprehension of our posterity, happily conscious of a noble and distinguished national thought and feeling, 'above the vulgar practice of the hour.'

Precisely because Lincoln had communed intimately with the national genius and obeyed devoutly its promptings, America ceases, in some passages of his letters and speeches, to be a body politic and becomes a living soul. Who was it wrote that letter to Mrs. Bixby on the loss of her five sons in battle? 'I cannot refrain from tendering to you the consolation that may be found in the thanks of the Republic that they died to save. I pray that our Heavenly Father may assuage the anguish of your bereavement, and leave you only the cherished memory of the loved and lost, and the solemn pride that must be yours to have laid so costly a sacrifice upon the altar of freedom.'

The words are thrilling still with the pathos and splendor of patriotic death. They seem charged with the tears and valor of the whole Civil War. To speak like that of death is to unfold the meaning of the Latin verse: *Dulce et decorum est pro patria mori*. It is to hallow the altar on which the sacrifice is made. One can hardly read the letter through with dry eyes; and yet reading it makes one very happy. It makes one happy because it renders one in imagination a sharer of that splendid sacrifice, that solemn pride, that divine consolation. It makes one happy because it uplifts the heart and purges it of private interests, and admits one into the higher, and more spacious, and grander life of the nation. For my purposes I am not writing an anti-climax when I say that it makes one happy because it is the perfect expression of a deep, grave, and noble emotion, which is the supreme triumph of the expressive arts. It is the work of a great artist. Was it Lincoln? Or was it the America of our dreams? It was the voice of the true emancipator of our art, who will always understand that his task is not to set Beauty and Puritanism at loggerheads, but to make Puritanism beautiful.

GAMALIEL BRADFORD (1863–   )

THOMAS PAINE

(1923)

I

Oh, what fun it is to be a rebel: to shatter, scatter, tear down, and destroy, and let others worry about building up again; or, if you like, to frame cloud fancies of possible utopias and then brand the dull things of earth who will not let you make such fancies real.

The first half of the eighteenth century was an age of convention, in both good and bad senses, convention in politics, in manners, in thought, in art, in morals. There is nothing like convention to breed rebels, and the last half of the eighteenth century, with the first years of the nineteenth, is a fruitful time for studying the type. The rebel hates control, restraint, limit, demands and delights in the free, abundant exercise of his own will, his own ardent sense of initiative and personality. He likes to assert himself, to make others feel that there is something there to assert: it affords him a concrete assurance of the fact, which is comforting; and it appears that nothing gives us more evidence of our own stability and reality than to destroy something else. The rebel has a splendid, joyous confidence in his own convictions, believes that his bright, glittering reason was given him to hew and cut and thrust through all that seems to him sham, pretense, and old, worm-eaten, time-consecrated falsity. He pursues his triumphant, disastrous way, untroubled by the criticism and abuse of spite and malice, indeed rather stimulated by them; and his royal self-assurance is rarely disturbed by the subtle intrusion of sceptical humor: if he has humor, it turns him from a rebel into something else. Finally, the rebel, at his best, is saved by a passionate enthusiasm for humanity. He wants to make the world over. Of course the way to do this is to begin by turning it upside down. The great ideal rebels are Satan and Prometheus, though perhaps the human enthusiasm was a little more evident in the latter.

Thomas Paine was essentially a rebel. As Mr. Sedgwick puts it, "Wherever revolution was, there was Paine also," and Mr. Sedgwick elsewhere quotes Paine's noble reply to Franklin, who said, "Where liberty is not, there is mine." It is true that Paine had not the dignity of Prometheus, nor the picturesqueness of Satan; neither had he the piquant, romantic cynicism of Voltaire, Iago, and Mephistopheles, who perhaps were not rebels, but critics; he was just a commonplace rebel, entirely practical, a trifle sordid, and altogether English.

Paine was born at Thetford, England, in 1737. His father was a Quaker, of rather humble station, and the boy was but slightly educated. Up to middle life his existence was humdrum and insignificant: two wives lost, by death and separation, little means, little comfort, and no glory. In 1774 he came to America, at the prompting of Franklin, and made his pen a vigorous agent in the American Revolution. He returned to England, wrote "The Rights of Man" and stirred up this world, went to France, mingled in the French Revolution as a member of the Convention, was shut up in prison by fiercer rebels than himself, and there wrote "The Age of Reason" and stirred up the other world. Monroe got him out of his difficulties, he was reinstated in the Convention, but achieved little further in France. In 1802 he returned to America, found himself, to his surprise and disgust, at odds with American respectability, and died in 1809, practically unfriended and forlorn, though by no means forgotten.

Paine's enthusiasm, when he arrived in America, after being drenched for nearly forty years in English obscurity and penury, reminds one of Matthew Arnold's remark: "When the dissenter first lands in America, he thinks he is in heaven." Curiously enough, Paine himself quotes a similar saying by "one of the richest manufacturers in England": "England, Sir, is not a country for a dissenter to live in,—we must go to France." The man's delight, his ecstasy over this new-found paradise are really touching: "The scene which that country presents to the eye of a spectator, has something in it which generates and encourages great ideas." The natural surroundings are inexhaustible in richness, incomparable in beauty. The people are comfortable, contented, happy, untrammeled by old traditions, unvexed by old exactions. They have shaken off the past, they look forward, and when they look forward, every prospect pleases with the promise of a world which may be shaped and moulded to all the dream perfections that any rebel ever imagined.

Though he had made only a few unimportant attempts at writing in England, the charm of this outlook and his gratitude for being offered a share in it made Paine an author, and his pamphlet, "Common Sense," printed early in 1776 and followed at intervals by the various numbers of "The American Crisis," stirred and spurred his new fellow-countrymen far more actively on the road to freedom than any other words produced by tongue or pen, unless the actual Declaration of Independence. Neither these writings nor anything in Paine's later life indicate a gift for practical statesmanship or concrete administration; but his words burn everywhere with a large and splendid ardor for democratic ideals, for liberty, equality, and opportunity for every one, and he was especially happy in insisting upon just the points that were essential in that critical stage of American affairs. When all men were hesitating over the audacity of final separation from Britain, he spoke right out: why palter? why delay? Be free, set up for yourselves, a great destiny is before you, show yourselves worthy of it. He preached nationality, coördination, coöperation, that the people should feel that they were a people and should grow strong in that consciousness. He preached federal union, that petty jealousies and local narrowness should be forgotten, "Our great title is Americans—our inferior one varies with the place." It was Thomas Paine who first used the words that now echo over the whole world, "The United States of America."

For he had a wonderful power of building phrases, of shaping swift, sharp sentences that should pierce dull ears and dead hearts and make them throb and thrill and work and live. He began his first Crisis paper, "These are the times that try men's souls," and few words have been oftener or more aptly repeated. He had a surprising, startling vigor of intense, direct utterance that made the most inert feel that he must do something. And of course he sometimes overshot himself, let the fury of his pen betray him into violence and unnecessary insult. England? He was said to hate England. He did not hate England, but he did hate some English ways of doing things: "It was equally as much from her manners as from her injustice that she lost the colonies," he remarks shrewdly. King George? He was a "Royal Brute," which disposes of him. Tories? "Every Tory is a coward."

But, human nature being what it is, it must be admitted that even these extravagances added to the effect of Paine's pamphlets. And the effect was enormous. "Common Sense" was sold by the hundred thousand. "Every living man in America in 1776, who could read, read 'Common Sense,'" wrote Theodore Parker. Even the discreet Trevelyan is hurried into superlatives on the subject: "It would be difficult to name any human composition which has had an effect at once so instant, so extended, and so lasting."

The consequence of all this was at first naturally an immense admiration and enthusiasm for Thomas Paine, a general applause that might have turned any man's head. He was given the degree of Master of Arts by the University of Pennsylvania, which to an English mechanic must have meant something. The sober and judicious Franklin spoke of "Common Sense" as having "prodigious effects." Washington, whose opinions were always moderate and well-weighed, commented on "the sound doctrine and unanswerable reasoning contained in the pamphlet," and found it "working a powerful change there in the minds of many men"; and he was so impressed with the trumpet exhortation of the first "Crisis" that he ordered it generally read to his dispirited army. Paine's merit was also practically recognized by Congress, which elected him secretary of its Committee of Foreign Affairs, an office which he held for nearly two years. When he returned to England, he was almost equally admired in the more liberal English circles. He dined with dukes and visited them. He was lauded and, what was perhaps even more complimentary, he was feared. When he crossed to France, then in the earlier agonies of the Revolution, he was welcomed as a divine messenger. Here was the man who had established liberty in the new world; why could he not do as much in the old? And as a later but overwhelming climax, Napoleon told him "that a statue of gold ought to be erected to him *in every city in the universe;* he also assured Paine that he always slept with a copy of 'The Rights of Man' under his pillow, and conjured him to honor him with his counsel and advice."

II

Which was all rather too smooth sailing for a rebel. But by the time Napoleon came to praise, Paine's popularity in America had greatly fallen off. His well-meant but indiscreet interference, during his secretaryship, in the financial tangle of Silas Deane first somewhat shook public confidence in him. And as he went on with his later political and finally with his religious writings, the general attitude changed from extreme enthusiasm to a bitterness, a contempt, a hearty repudiation, which lasted for a century at least, is hardly now forgotten, and would be difficult to surpass in the history of human prejudice. With a prophetic instinct he himself described the possibility of this change in general, "It so often happens that men live to forfeit the reputation at one time they gained at another"; but he could hardly have foreseen how complete the reversal would be in his own case. In England he was tried for sedition. In America, bitterest irony of all, he was refused the right to vote as an American citizen. And the fierce invective of Corbett will serve as an illustration of the abuse which the world long heaped upon one who supposed he had done it service: "There he lies, manacled, besmirched with filth, crawling with vermin, loaded with years and infamy. . . . Like Judas he will be remembered by posterity; men will learn to express all that is base, malignant, treacherous, unnatural, and blasphemous by the single monosyllable, Paine."

When one examines Paine's writings in the light of the changes that have taken place since his time, it is difficult to find anything in his general principles that accounts for all this storm of obloquy. As regards politics, he seems to have urged many of the reforms, generally considered beneficial, which are now so much accepted that we cannot imagine the world without them. It is the hard fate of rebels to be sooner or later looked upon as mere conservatives by those who succeeded them in the same line of activity, and even Paine did not entirely escape this misfortune. He was unwilling to go the later lengths of the French Revolution. He reiterates his firm adherence to the principle of private property. In many of his political ideas he is nobly and broadly constructive; and though there is a great deal of vague talk about "rights," such as always tickled eighteenth-century ears, the rights that are asserted are such as one must sympathize with, whether one considers them wholly practical or not. How much of this talk Paine got from Rousseau and others, and how much he spun out of his own brain, will never be settled. He himself insisted on his originality, and in some points, like finance, his independence of view is evident. But it is probable that the ideas that were so widely spread around him had permeated his thought more than he imagined. The immense, insinuating influence of Rousseau is apparent here as elsewhere.

Yet, though the construction in Paine is obvious and undeniable, the destruction is more obvious still, indulged in with even more relish and carried on at all times with all the rebel's intense and unremitting vigor. Construction is so difficult, involves such painful thought, is at best so pervious to criticism. Destruction is so easy. You have only to flourish your pen, and kings and crowns totter—on paper, at any rate. Let us throw over those old relics, get rid of tyranny, get rid of aristocracy, get rid of government, if you push us. What is government anyway, but a device of the devil to override the sacred natural instincts and the lovely primitive kindliness of man?

And this dangerous, treacherous pen does slip so easily into violence and abuse. Paine could frame noble compliment and eulogy; but he could also write bitter, savage, cruel, contemptible sentences, sentences the bitterness of which was sure to damage their author more than any one else. This tendency to bitterness grew with age, perhaps naturally. There was plenty of such writing in the last years of the eighteenth century, and others may have been much worse than Paine; but Paine was bad enough. The "Letters to American Citizens" are brutal and disgusting. The "Letter to Washington," written after Paine's release from the French prison, from which he thought Washington should have extricated him earlier, is inexcusable, in spite of all efforts to excuse it. "You commenced your Presidential career by encouraging and swallowing the grossest adulation, and you traveled America from one end to the other to put yourself in the way of receiving it." This sort of thing could not hurt Washington: it damned Paine.

So much for politics. But, not content with drawing down upon himself the odium of abusing Washington, this light-hearted, quick-tongued iconoclast also set himself to abuse God. The task was even easier, but at the same time a good deal more dangerous. Not that he ever quarreled with God directly. On the contrary, he always treated the Deity with a tenderness not exempt from patronage. But

for those things—whether of religious or social convention—that in his day were chiefly associated with God he had little regard, and he handled them with a fierce sincerity that sent icy shivers down all correct and orthodox backs.

Even here he was not wholly destructive. Indeed he advocated many social reforms that scandalized his own age but are realized, or soon to be realized, in ours. I am not aware that he favored prohibition: he had personal reasons for not doing so. Marriage he respected, and he thought wealth would soon be so harmless that it was not worth bothering with. But he anticipated the abolition of slavery, he anticipated the Society for the Prevention of Cruelty to Animals, he anticipated old age pensions, he anticipated the Shepard-Towner Bill, and he ardently resented the inferior status of women.

Moreover, Paine's religion was constructive enough as regards essentials. He affirmed and reaffirmed, with obvious honesty, his belief in God and his abiding and comforting hope of a future life, though it is interesting to note that his idea of heaven is thoroughly aristocratic: "There is still another description [of men] who are so very insignificant, both in character and conduct, as not to be worth the trouble of damning or saving, or of raising from the dead." Surely these are the very persons whose rights in this world he had been fighting so fiercely to assert. But in general the positive side of "The Age of Reason" and Paine's similar writings is normal, cheerful, and hopeful. There are occasional noble touches, like the saying: "Infidelity does not consist in believing, or in disbelieving; it consists in profession to believe what he does not believe," while no one can question Paine's sincere intent to inspire in his fellow-man "a spirit of trust, confidence, and consolation in his creator." To accomplish this laudable object Paine founded in Paris that pretty dream of an eighteenth-century pedant, the church of Theophilanthropy.

Only he was not a profound thinker. He was shrewd, keen, acute, and his very preoccupation with the surface of things often puts him in the position of modern objective Biblical criticism, without regard to theological subtleties, as Conway justly points out. But the depths of philosophical discussion are utterly beyond him. Above all, he was a rebel: he had no awe, no reverence, and he did like to pull down, cut up, and tear to pieces. When he was eight years old, he made up his mind that "any system of religion that has anything in it that shocks the mind of a child cannot be a true system." When he was nearly sixty, he wrote "The Age of Reason" and knocked the Bible into a cocked hat. The prophets and the disciples, the miracles and the mysteries, the odd adventure of Jonah and the sweet adventure of Ruth, the Virgin and the Magdalen, the Virgin Birth of Christ and the Resurrection, all alike were game for him. He tossed them about and turned them over and worried them like a frolicsome puppy, and when he got through, there was very little left. His object may have been to inculcate "a spirit of trust, confidence, and consolation in the creator"; but what sold his book in huge numbers and made millions read it, as thousands read it still, was something very different and much less edifying.

And though Paine's formal creed was definite and positive enough, there was not an atom of religion in him, no longing, no craving, no aspiration, nothing whatever of the mystic's high emotion and all-absorbing love. Mystery? He abhorred mystery, liked daylight and common sense, and the surface of things. Religion, he expressly explains, cannot have any connection with mystery. As to such matters we know all we need to know, all we ought to know, all we were meant to know.

Which does not imply that the man was not by nature a believer. Indeed, what perpetually astonishes me is the number of things he believed and his happy faculty of doing it. Perhaps it will be found that the rebel is always a believer, whereas the true conservative is the sceptic, who is afraid to lift his foot, lest he should not know where to set it down. At any rate, Thomas Paine was a believer. He had such a luxuriant faculty of believing that he could afford to throw away an odd belief here and there. Why should anybody mind the loss of a belief or two, when they could be had like cherries for picking from the trees? He believed in man, the honesty of man, the future of man, the rights of man, an endless catalogue, above all he performed the superb logical feat of believing in Thomas Paine. After that, who could call him a sceptic?

The truth is, he had a splendid confidence in human reason. That which, to some of us, seems only an alluring, deceiving will-o'-the-wisp, to be used, since we have nothing better, but never to be trusted, was to Paine a clear light, a sure guide, a sharp, unerring instrument which could be relied on to penetrate to the heart of everything. As bearing on others, this is not quite so certain. They may need a word of caution occasionally: "Alas! nothing is so easy as to deceive one's self." But Thomas Paine's reason—"My own line of reasoning is to myself as straight and clear as a ray of light," he says in one case and it applies in most cases; for does he not himself tell us that God "has given me a large share of that divine gift?"

You sometimes meet a shrewd, thoughtful, uneducated mechanic who in half an hour will afflict you with reasons, old as the world, but perfectly new and perfectly convincing to him, reasons that smother you like a heap of feathers, as light and as suffocating. Such was Thomas Paine. He had no faintest conception of the huge, involving, shadowing night of ignorance which descends upon the mind that knows something of past and present and honestly and profoundly begins to think. Perhaps he was better off without such conception. The sense of one's own ignorance does little positive good in the world, shatters no idols, rights no wrongs. But it has some pale and negative merits, such as tolerance, patience, humility. It would have done Paine good, if he could have remembered the saying of the great Jefferson, whom he admired, and who was something of a rebel himself: "Error is the stuff of which the web of life is woven and he who lives longest and wisest is only able to weave out the more of it." And ignorance has also the merit of tranquillity. I have "reposed my head on that pillow of ignorance which a benevolent Creator has made so soft for us, knowing how much we should be forced to use it," says Jefferson again. Or, in the words with which a poet of to-day addresses the indulgent, night-enveloped, all-suffusing, all-enfolding goddess,

> "Grant me thy supreme repose,
>   Medicine my vast despairs
> With the calm that never knows,
>   And the peace that never cares."

III

Repose, humility, and the recognition of ignorance were not distinguishing features of the character of Thomas Paine. Still, though he was mainly rebel, he was not all so: it is interesting to look for the non-rebel traits in him, however one may be impressed by their insignificance. Even in his wandering, unsettled, Bohemian career there came gleams of longing for quiet, tranquillity, domestic peace. When he is in the thick of European excitement, he writes to Jefferson, "I feel like a bird from its nest, and wishing most anxiously to return." Of home, of family surroundings, of the staid continuity of daily routine he knew little, at least in later years. Perhaps he did not much care for them. Yet he wrote to a young lady friend: "Though I appear a sort of wanderer, the married state has not a sincerer friend than I am. It is a harbor of human life, and is, with respect to the things of this world, what the next world is to this. It is *home;* and that one word conveys more than any other word can express."

Of his relations with women we know little, but enough to be sure that they did not play any considerable part in his life. Although he cared for his mother in her old age, she described him in a letter—possibly not authentic —as "the worst of husbands." His first wife died early. His second left him soon after marriage and it is affirmed that they never had any conjugal relation. After this no woman was closely connected with him except Madame Bonneville, who cared for him in his old age, but without any admissible suggestion of scandal. "His relations with ladies were as chaste as affectionate" is the charming expression of his biographer. I accept the chastity, but doubt whether the affection went very deep. He had no children, but was kind to the children of others and took a moderate interest in them.

As regards men, I find no trace of very near intimacy. Paine of course met all sorts in all places. Some liked him and some detested him, but I do not know that any made a way into his heart. Socially he could be very attractive, when he was in the mood and the company pleased him. He liked to play an occasional game of chess or dominoes, but never cards. To any one who has read his writings it is hardly necessary to say that he had no humor in the sense of irony, no subtle, detached appreciation of the strange, unhinging contrasts of the world. But he had quick, vivid thrusts of wit, his memory was stored with all sorts of apt anecdotes, and he was ready to argue without end. Rickman says of him: "In private company and among friends his conversation had every fascination that anecdote, novelty and truth could give it. In mixed company and among strangers he said little, and was no public speaker."

Of the various æsthetic and intellectual diversions that might afford relief from the strenuous career of rebellion Paine knew little or nothing. It does not appear that he had ever heard of painting or sculpture. He had an ear for music, and liked to take part in a chorus; but his ordinary preoccupations did not leave much place for the finer ecstasies of harmony.

One or two passages in his books suggest a certain sensitiveness to the natural world: "Everything conspired to hush me into a pleasing kind of melancholy—the trees seemed to sleep—and the air hung round me with such unbreathing silence, as if listening to my very thoughts." But these notes are rare, and whatever he learned from Rousseau, it was not his intense passion for the beauty of nature. Nor did he read for the pure delight of it. He had little education in youth and little desire in age to make up for the deficiency. "Indeed," says one who talked with him, "he seems to have a contemptuous opinion not only of books, but of their authors." Even in science, in which he took a constant interest, what attracted him was the purely practical. The fascination of knowing for itself was quite omitted from his composition.

Nor did Paine have any great taste for the enjoyment of life, either in simple amusements or in costly and luxurious ones. His wants were moderate and his way of living frugal, sometimes to the point of privation. For a short period in Paris he had means and kept up a certain establishment. But in the main his surroundings were humble and he knew little of ease or comfort. As he expresses it with his unfailing energy of language, "I have confined myself so much of late, taken so little exercise, and lived so very sparingly, that unless I alter my way of life, it will alter me."

Such a mode of existence did not involve the spending of money, and Paine did not need it, and consequently had no great desire to get it. He constantly proclaimed that his writings were meant to benefit mankind, with no thought of profit, and in spite of their immense circulation, they yielded him practically nothing. When one remembers the sums paid to Byron, Moore, and Scott a few years later, one cannot but admire Paine's disinterestedness, though bare need sometimes drove him to appeals for public assistance that are not entirely prepossessing. Bare need seems to have been all that made him think of money through the greater part of his life. He was free in giving what he had for public and private causes. And never at any time, even in the bitterest attacks on him, was any charge of dishonesty proved or seriously maintained. In his later years it admitted that he became a trifle parsimonious, but that would appear to have been no more than the dread of a weakening age when the dearest ideal of life has been independence.

Disregard of money is apt to bring disregard of work, and Paine was sometimes accused of indolence, though others insist upon his enormous capacity for labor. J. J. Henry, with whose family he boarded during the Crisis years, remembers him chiefly as eating, sleeping, and dawdling. This is absurd in a man who accomplished so much. The truth is probably that his whole soul toiled by impulse and then rested and relaxed again by impulse, without much thought for order or system, such not being rebel characteristics.

And the same essential disorder of temperament will account for what truth there is in the exaggerated stories of his untidiness. Roosevelt called him a "filthy little atheist," and his hostile biographers, Oldys and Cheetham, give a disgusting picture of his later years. Untended, wandering widowerhood is not always neat, and it may be conceded that Paine's quarters might not have suited a tidy housekeeper. But he was neither filthy, little, nor an atheist. He was of good height and dignified in appearance, with a quick and piercing black eye, and impartial observers describe him as careless and indifferent as to his dress, but by no means unpresentable.

The same deductions must be made from the accounts of his drinking. It was a drinking period and Paine was no exception. He himself confessed to Rickman that when he was overcome by discouragement in Paris, he drank heavily, and his drinking was probably not light at other times. His ardent biographer, Conway, whose zeal sometimes overweighs his obvious desire for truth, insists on his idol's sobriety perhaps a little more than it will bear, and I cannot forget the testimony of the printer Chapman at the trial connected with "The Rights of Man," that religion was "a favorite subject with him when intoxicated." But here again the grosser stories are manifestly absurd.

In short, what impresses me most in all these attacks on Paine is their futility. The bitterest enemies, hunting every flaw in a character always exposed to the largest public view, could establish nothing but that he sometimes drank and that he was not clean. These are serious objections to a housemate. No doubt it is good to be clean and sober and conservative and do what your fathers did and shun ideals. But some of us occasionally like to think new thoughts and step out of the beaten track, and we like one who makes us do these things, even if he is a trifle untidy in his person. Here is a man who upset the world and you say he did not brush his clothes. Here is a man who beat and shook conventions, who stirred up dusty and old titles, till he showed their rotten vanity, and you complain because some of the dust got on himself. This is childishness.

IV

For, whatever else Paine was, he was a rebel, delighted in change, delighted in novelty, believed the old order doomed and that he and his like could make the world over and better. "We live to improve, or we live in vain," he wrote, in his swift, incisive fashion, and he meant it. Even his untidiness was in a way a protest against the tiresome formality of life. "Let those dress who need it," he said to a friend. He was interested in innovations of all sorts, theoretical and practical. One of the most useful things he ever did was his invention and designing of iron bridges. He fully shared Franklin's passion for discoveries that would benefit mankind. He tried to contrive the steam engine. He tried to conquer yellow fever. He even added a fine touch to his friend Jefferson's precious gunboats.

He had the rebel's restlessness, could not keep still, did not wish to keep still. When he was sixteen, he began life on a privateer, and from then on he kept moving, moving, always. After the American Revolution he thought he should settle down. But the movement possessed him more than ever. He never settled down.

He had the rebel's essential virtue, pugnacity. His Quaker antecedents had instilled into him the love of peace; but that did not prevent a perfect readiness to fight, when fighting was called for. How admirable is his utterance as to this nice Quaker distinction: "I am thus far a Quaker, that I would gladly agree with all the world to lay aside the use of arms, and settle matters by negotiation; but unless the whole will, the matter ends, and I take up my musket and thank heaven he has put it in my power." He did take up his musket, literally, and figured in the revolutionary armies, perhaps with no especial glory, but certainly with no discredit. He had a good, live word for his own physical courage, when addressing Lord Howe, not being given to hiding any of his merits: "I knew the time when I thought that the whistling of a cannon ball would have frightened me almost to death; but I have since tried it, and find that I can stand it with as little discomposure, and, I believe, with a much easier conscience than your lordship." And his moral courage, besides many other proofs, is solidly established by his fine stand for the king's life in the French Convention. No doubt there were other motives mixed with this, as well as mere humanity; but, whatever the motive, it required splendid pluck to vote for clemency in the face of the wolves who were howling for blood.

Also Paine was absolutely sincere. He adopted his principles on what he considered sufficient reasons, and he stuck to them through all abuse and animosity, perhaps with more relish, the greater the abuse. He was not only persistent, he was fiercely obstinate, even in little things, refusing to change what he had written for any one. No threat and no discouragement deterred him. William Duane, who was no conservative, endeavored to dissuade him from religious controversy: "I have fairly told him that he will be deserted by the only party that respects or does not hate him, that all his political writings will be rendered useless, and even his fame destroyed." It was quite unavailing. And the persistency did not falter in the presence of death, though religious partisanship sought to misrepresent this, as with Voltaire and many others. Paine admitted no terror as to the future and no doubt as to the goodness of God. When a benevolent and intrusive old lady in a scarlet cloak visited him in his last illness, insisting that she had a special message from the Almighty urging him to repent, he turned her out, with the apt though petulant comment: "You were not sent with any such impertinent message. . . . He would not send such a foolish ugly old woman as you about with his messages. Go away. Go back—shut the door." The old lady went, dissatisfied. He was persistent because he had an immense ardor and enthusiasm, a belief in his cause, in its justice, its nobility, its ultimate triumph, and a determination to live and die serving it.

Not, I think, that Paine had the pure intellectual passion which inspired men like Spinoza or Lucretius and puts them in an altogether different class from Paine's. He did not spend his days and nights in tortured anxiety to arrive at abstract truth. The principles that interested him were those that led to the direct, practical benefit of humanity. He did not concern himself deeply with their philosophical foundations. Though he liked mathematics, he was not an elaborately logical systematic thinker. His intelligence was keen, alert, shrewd, attentive to the surfaces of things and darting rather than delving into the hidden places.

What he did have supremely was the gift of words, and there is no more shining and convenient—and dangerous—weapon in all the rebel's armory. Really the man was an astonishing writer. Critics have been fooled by his ignorance of grammar. Shakespeare was ignorant of grammar, yet some think he could write. Paine was ignorant of everything, though his remarkable memory made him appear to know a great deal. But he certainly was a master of words. They would glow and glitter at his bidding, and fire men's hearts, and turn a small spark into a great flame. They would bite too, and dart and sting and lash, till his victims writhed and were forced to take refuge in ignoble and usually in dull retaliation. I think Paine's secret, like Swift's, lies more in rhythm than in anything else. His diction is clear and simple and direct; but above all his phrases snap and crack like whips, with a firm and vigorous movement that every daily journalist must envy. How far he understood his own style is a question. He was too busy to study it. That some of the strange problems connected with words interested him is evident from his charming remark: "I have often observed that by lending words for my thoughts I understand my thoughts the better." That he appreciated all the terrible dangers of words is unlikely: rebels seldom do appreciate them. But that he luxuriated in his own verbal power is clear enough.

For he was not a man to miss any of his powers or let any one else miss them. On the contrary, he enjoyed them thoroughly. He himself tells us that he was not ambitious: "I never courted either fame or interest." Many other persons make the same boast, and perhaps in Paine's case it was true, in the larger, deeper sense. But he had a huge, simple, naïve vanity, which is obvious everywhere, and much increased as life went on. He liked to be prominent socially, liked to be "in as elegant style of acquaintance here as any American that ever came over." He liked to be prominent politically, thought that Washington "did not perform his part in the Revolution better . . . than I did mine, and the one part was as necessary as the other," and he wished others to think so. He enjoyed his literary success, and his candor in asserting it is almost unbelievable: "I have not only contributed to raise a new empire in the world founded on a new system of government, but I have arrived at an eminence in political literature, the most difficult of all lines to succeed and excel in, which aristocracy with all its aids has not been able to reach or to rival."

But even greater than his delight in his own verbal achievements, was his true rebel's delight in destruction. Of course he would have denied this, and maintained that construction was his only true pleasure. Well, construction is pleasant; but it is laborious and uncertain. And destruction is so simple. The enthusiastic biographer betrays the whole secret when he says, "The force of Paine's negations was not broken by any weakness for speculations of his own." It was not, and his infinite, riotous glee in knocking over what antiquity consecrated and ages had revered is so evident as hardly to need confirmation. His gay doings with the Bible were just pure fun. He tells us that when he wrote the first part of "The Age of Reason," he had no Bible to refresh his mind, and consequently proceeded with some caution; but when he got hold of a copy, he found things so much worse than he thought, that he regretted his former leniency. He made up for it. When he finished, he was able to say: "I have now gone through the Bible, as a man would go through a wood with an axe on his shoulder, and fell trees." Can't you hear his chuckle of real rebel's exultation? The game was so easy to play. As the man says in the French comedy: "*Quel joli métier, et si facile!*" It was such an endless delight to shatter the miracles and overturn the prophets, a cheap and ready amusement that can no longer be enjoyed, since few people to-day take either prophets or miracles seriously enough to be scandalized. But Paine could carry on the merry revel to his heart's content, could smash idols, and grind up crowns, and blast conventions, and turn society topsy-turvy, making one grand climax in the toast which he gave at a public dinner, with gorgeous satisfaction, to "the Revolution of the world."

All which exposure of the weaker side that Paine insisted on exposing so copiously himself should not make us overlook the finer elements in the man's nature. Whatever vanity and self-assertion there may have been in his constant and energetic efforts, and however unpractical and misdirected some may consider them, they were steadily aimed at what he believed to be a lofty object. Through discomfort, through penury, through obloquy he toiled for an ideal. Such a life has a far nobler

strain in it than the self-seeking and self-indulgent career of a man like Aaron Burr.

And Paine's work was inspired by the love of humanity. This love is perhaps less manifested in particular instances, though during the French Revolution he labored to save lives rather than to destroy them, and such labor was quite out of fashion. But in the larger sympathy for the poor and downtrodden Paine's merits were real and his accomplishment substantial. His own noble words are absolutely just: "I defend the cause of the poor, of the manufacturers, of the tradesmen, of the farmer, and of all those on whom the real burden of taxes fall—but above all, I defend the cause of humanity." He looked forward, he looked upward, with courage and cheerfulness and hope. He anticipated the large benevolence and benign aspiration of the League of Nations, preached the common interest of all peoples in the pursuit of peaceful progress and democratic advancement, the abolition of war and the cultivation of universal understanding, and it is only just to say that the toast given above to "the Revolution of the World" was transformed a few months later into a similar toast to "the Republic of the World."

So it must be recognized that if Paine, like most rebels, did a considerable amount of harm to mankind, he also did a great amount of good. He taught men to think by his very turbulence, and when you remember how averse they are to that process, he deserves some credit for doing so. He taught them the value of liberty, even if he was not a very sure guide as to the use of it. He taught the worth of a high ideal and the lasting, increasing value of the largest human sympathy. And every American ought to be grateful to him as one of the active founders of the United States of America.

As for the rebels, it must be admitted that, though they are occasionally foul-mouthed and slovenly, and often vain, noisy, and altogether distasteful, they are the power that moves the world. I sometimes wish I had the courage and the character to be a rebel myself.

BLISS PERRY (1860-)

EMERSON'S MOST FAMOUS SPEECH

(1923)

I

Let us go upon a literary pilgrimage. The shrine which we are to visit is sacred in the memory of scholars, although Mr. Howells, with dispassionate candor, once described it as

the ugliest spot in the universe of God. It is Harvard Square. Eighty-six years ago—or, to be precise, on August 31, 1837, Phi Beta Kappa day—it was not without a certain tranquil, rural beauty. Great elms shadowed the little green, in whose center stood a town pump quite after the taste of Hawthorne—although very few Phi Beta Kappa men chose to utilize it on anniversary days, to the scandal of the water-drinking minority. Northwestward from the Square runs the broad road to Lexington and Concord, and on the left, opposite the low-fenced Harvard Yard, is the meeting-house of the First Parish. This edifice, completed in 1834, was the successor of that log meeting-house where just two hundred years before, in the summer of 1637, Anne Hutchinson had been brought to trial by the New England Theocracy, and condemned to exile. If any ghosts of the past are hovering in the First Parish Church on this August morning of 1837, surely among them is the amused ghost of that clever woman, waiting to see what will happen to a new champion of rebellion.

Here, then, is our shrine, a plain wooden meeting-house in a country village, built big enough for the modest needs of Harvard University on its anniversary occasions. Let us march toward it in the procession of our Phi Beta Kappa brethren, two hundred and fifteen strong, starting at twelve o'clock precisely from University Hall, in the middle of the Harvard Yard. Preceded by a band of music and the dark-gowned undergraduate members, the black-coated double file of graduate members emerge from the Yard, cross the road—the dust has been laid by the unwonted rain of the previous day—and halt in front of the meeting-house. The undergraduates open to the right and left, and the President of Phi Beta Kappa, the secretary, chaplain, orator, and poet enter in that order, followed by the members, two and two, according to seniority. Brother John Pierce, D.D., of Brookline (Harvard, 1793), indefatigable attendant and note-taker of Harvard anniversaries, will describe the occasion—an epoch-making occasion, although he did not suspect it.

For, let me warn you, before quoting his record of Phi Beta Kappa's most famous day, that the excellent Brother Pierce has a blind spot in those shrewd old eyes of his, and that his mind is beautifully fortified against doctrines which he disapproves. In that unhappy division of the Congregational churches which had absorbed so much of the attention of New England for thirty years, Dr. Pierce stands for Orthodoxy, and year by year, at Harvard Commencements, he has found himself in an ever-diminishing minority. He computes the reckoning annually, and only yesterday, on August 30, 1837, he has discovered that among Harvard graduates in the active ministry there are one hundred and twelve Liberals to but fifty-one of the Orthodox. Like every true New Englander, no doubt, he felt that the growing unpopularity of his opinions was the best confirmation of their soundness. His passion for oratory never abated, though he lived to attend sixty-four Commencements, but from the beginning to the end of his career, Brother Pierce was suspicious of every intellectual or spiritual novelty.

Aside from this air-tight characteristic of the good man's mind, he is an admirable critic. He sums up Brother Pipon's Phi Beta Kappa Oration of 1803 in one line: it "consisted of miscellaneous and severely critical remarks on Man." I seem to have heard Brother Pipon's oration myself! Dr. Pierce usually characterizes the prayers with which the Phi Beta Kappa ceremonies opened. They are "appropriate," or "pertinent," or "pertinent and judicious," or, at least, "4 minutes" long, or "12½ minutes" long; but I regret to say that, in 1804, when Emerson's father—a well-known Liberal—acted as chaplain, Brother Pierce contented himself by recording: "Dr. Emerson then prayed." In 1836 he is still watching the chaplain with the ear of a heresy-hunter: "The Rev. George Ripley [Harvard, 1823] offered an elaborate prayer of 13 minutes, elegantly composed and expressed. In my mind it was deficient in not giving sufficient prominence to the name which is above every name." Dr. Pierce's instinct was justified by the event: two years later, George Ripley will be found defending Emerson's "Divinity School Address"!

The good Doctor, in short, had, like all of us, the defects of his qualities, as a listener to poetry and oratory. He confesses it with admirable frankness. In 1811 he notes: "John Stickney, Esquire, delivered an oration, of three quarters of an hour, on The Qualifications of a Statesman. Through the course of it I reproached myself with the obtuseness of my faculties, as there was so large a portion of it of which I could not form the trace of a conception. But upon mentioning my difficulty to intelligent men, I found that I was not alone. In short, I could compare it to nothing more striking than a dark night now and then enlightened by flashes of lightning."

In 1818, according to Brother Pierce, Caleb Cushing delivers a Phi Beta Kappa poem "on I cannot tell what." In 1821 the poem by William C. Bryant, Esq., "was in Spenserian measure and contained some fine passages. But I was unable to discern a unity of design or precision of subject. It was 25 minutes long." Brother Pierce had, at any rate, an excellent watch! In 1833 he notes: "Prof. Longfellow, of Bowdoin College, gave a poem, I know not on what subject, of 28 minutes. He is a young, handsome man, son of Hon. Stephen Longfellow, Portland, Harvard University, 1798."

II

But while you and I have thus been lingering over the mental peculiarities of the Reverend Doctor John Pierce, the black-coated procession is pushing steadily into the crowded church, and up the aisles to the seats of honor. As the band plays its opening voluntary, you may look, if you like, upon the captains of Israel in their high places. There is President Josiah Quincy (Harvard, 1790), a vigorous gentleman of sixty-five; the fire of his youthful congressional eloquence already half forgotten.

Among the Fellows of the Harvard Corporation, you will note two of the foremost lawyers of the Commonwealth, Joseph Story and Lemuel Shaw. Among the Overseers one seeks instinctively for the well-known faces of John Quincy Adams, and the great Dr. Channing and the "Godlike" Daniel Webster. No need to point out the last, in any assembly of New Englanders; you have but to follow the eyes of the crowd. But perhaps these Overseers are absent today—since the Phi Beta Kappa orator is only a stickit-minister from Concord, author of an anonymous, unintelligible, and unsold little book on "Nature"!

The Faculty of Harvard College are no doubt in their places, as in duty bound, unwearied by the prolonged Commencement exercises of the previous day. The last name upon the Faculty list this year is that of the half-crazed, half-inspired tutor of Greek, Jones Very, of Salem, poet, who is known to idolize the orator. There are "the stern old war gods" of the Divinity School, the Henry Wares, father and son, and J. G. Palfrey, who a year later are to shake their heads in awful but belated protest against Waldo Emerson's astounding utterance to their own pupils, in their very chapel. There is Andrews Norton, now retired from his professorship to the watchful leisure of Shady Hill. Just twenty years ago, as Librarian of Harvard College, he had allowed "Emerson 4th" of the Freshman class, "President Kirkland's Freshman"—a sedate, silent youth—to draw the books of Hume and Priestley and other eighteenth-century thinkers; and here is that very Freshman ready now to utter doctrines which Andrews Norton is soon to characterize as "The Latest Form of Infidelity." Let the Wares and the Nortons listen closely this noon; if they do, they will at least be qualified to say in 1838: "I told you so! I knew it, when I heard his Phi Beta Kappa address!"

But amid all the learning and fashion and beauty which throng the meeting-house, do not overlook the eager boys—for their ears catch overtones and undertones which are unperceived by their elders. You will find two or three Cambridge boys whom you know; one a handsome dreamy Senior who had made an eloquent Coleridgian graduating speech the day before, young Richard H. Dana, home for a year now after his "Two Years Before the Mast"; the other is a reckless, irreverent Junior—not yet exiled to Concord by the Faculty—James Russell Lowell. One Concord boy, we may be sure, is here: grave David Henry Thoreau, graduated yesterday, and fairly certain to celebrate his new liberty by going blackberrying to-day, were it not for his desire to hear a fellow townsman speak. You will recognize, perhaps, among the alumni members of Phi Beta Kappa, the high-bred face of a young Boston lawyer, without clients and reputed to be without ambition, who, nevertheless, within four months of this day and by a single inpromptu speech will win his place in the front rank of American orators—Brother Wendell Phillips, of the class of 1831. And there is a garrulous Boston Sophomore who ought to be here—Edward Everett Hale; yet if he had been there he would surely have talked about it to the end of his days, and I cannot remember that he ever mentioned it. Probably he was swapping stories outside the church.

And now the music of the brass band blares out into silence at last, and the great audience hushes itself. The Reverend Mr. Rogers of Boston offers a prayer which wins the full approval of Brother Pierce, being "singularly devout, short and appropriate." Then, introduced by the President of the Society, rises the speaker of the day.

Let us look at him as he was then—and with the eyes of that audience—not as we know him now in marble and bronze, gleaming with the serene light of earthly immortality. He is a tall, thin man of thirty-four, with sloping shoulders, a man born, you would say, like his ancestors for seven generations, to wear black. His face is asymmetrical. Seen from one side, it is that of a shrewd New England farmer; from the other, it is a face of a seer, a

"Prophetic soul of the wide world
Dreaming on things to come."

The cheeks are fresh-colored, like those of all the Emersons. The thin hair is brown. The eyes are deep blue, with violet lights. He stoops a trifle as he arranges his manuscript upon the pulpit. His manner, though slightly constrained, is suave and courteous. No one in that church, as the Reverend Mr. Emerson pronounced the conventional words "Mr. President and Gentlemen," doubts for a moment his ability to deliver an acceptable discourse. Indeed, he had delivered the Phi Beta Kappa poem, three years before. He belonged, as Dr. Holmes said afterward, to the academic races. This is no amateur, but a professional.

As his clear sweet voice enunciates decorously his opening sentences, the elder Bostonians present are reminded, no doubt, of his father, the gifted minister of the First Church, whose premature death in 1811 had left his boys for a while to the charity of the parish. Chief Justice Shaw, there among the Overseers, had boarded with the widow Emerson on Beacon Street, while she was trying to educate her boys in the Latin School, and perhaps the Justice remembers at this moment the clever poem on Liberty which little Waldo had written in that winter of 1815. Judge Shaw has kept it, and the manuscript is in the Harvard Library to-day.

Possibly the memories of the still older generation go back to the speaker's grandfather, the Reverend William Emerson of Concord, patriot chaplain in the Revolution, and a beautiful pulpit orator, like all that tribe. One listener, I am sure, is thinking of the grandfather, namely, old Dr. Ezra Ripley, of Concord (Harvard, 1776), who has married the chaplain's widow and succeeded him as master of the Old Manse, where the little Emerson boys had spent their vacations with their grandmother. Tough old Ezra Ripley is eighty-six now, but he can still drive himself to Cambridge in his sulky, and it will be some years yet before Waldo Emerson will write his obituary and Hawthorne move into the empty Manse. We know now what Emerson thought of him, but I wish I knew what the old champion of Orthodoxy thinks of Emerson as he sits there in the front pew, revolving many things in his kindly heart.

I fancy that the Harvard professors watch the speaker with a curious and perhaps patronizing interest. He owed them little enough. Kirkland, who had been so kind to him in Wadsworth House, is gone, broken before the time. But there sits Professor Edward Tyrrel Channing ("Ned Channing"), who had corrected Emerson's college themes, and Professor Everett, who had set him an elaborate, and for a while a compelling, pattern for public utterance. And, indeed, the boy had won Bowdoin prizes for essays and a Boylston prize for declamation. But he had otherwise gained no distinction in College, had been the seventh choice of his classmates for the position of Class Poet, and was graduated with a rank of thirtieth in a class of fifty-nine. He was not even, in College, a member of Phi Beta Kappa! His younger brothers, Edward and Charles, won that honor easily. Perhaps there are born candidates for Phi Beta Kappa —as some boys are born to bring flowers to the school-teacher; indeed, the "Harvard Advocate" suggested not long ago that the boy who brings flowers to the teacher becomes naturally a Phi Beta Kappa man. It is the old story: Christopher Wordsworth wins all the prizes at Trinity College, Cambridge, while William Wordsworth reads "Clarissa" during the week preceding the examination, and barely gets a degree. Both Christopher and William have their reward.

If the professors in Harvard College looked askance at Emerson that day, surely the professors of the Divinity School could have done no less. Ask Professor Henry Ware, Senior, who had "approbated" Emerson to preach, at the end of a broken and disappointing career in the Divinity School. "If they had examined me," said Emerson afterward, "they never would have passed me." Professor Henry Ware the younger had been Emerson's colleague in the pastorate of the Second Church in Boston. There, too, had been failure—as the world counts failure: a decorous performance of duty for a brief period, ending in an irreconcilable difference of opinion between pastor and people regarding the celebration of the communion, and in the pastor's resignation. Illness and private sorrow had been added to professional chagrin: his young wife had died; he had sought change and rest in Europe; he had returned and settled down in Concord to make a scanty living by lecturing and occasional preaching. Sorrow still waylaid him; robbed him of these two brilliant prize-winning brothers, Edward and Charles. But he had pulled himself together, being of the old unbeatable Puritan stuff; he had married again, and bought a house, had published a little book, had backed himself to win against his generation—against the world; and here he is, a sweet-faced, tranquil-voiced man, facing the most distinguished audience that could then be gathered in America, to annunciate his new vision of the eternal Truth. What are his chances of triumphing? I do not believe that his friend Henry Ware, Jr., much as he liked Emerson personally, thought that he had one chance in a thousand. But we talk too much about chances: one chance is enough, if you have the right moment and the man. "All that a man ought to ask for in life," said the French etcher Méryon, "is the chance to put himself into his plates." That supreme felicity was Emerson's, in that August noontide of long ago. He put himself into the oration on "The American Scholar."

I do not say that he won everybody in that packed meeting-house. Certainly he did not convince our hard-headed Brother John Pierce, sitting there on a front seat immovable and unconvincible—watch in hand. Listen to his impression of the address; but listen respectfully, for he is an honest man, and he utters the verdict of the older generation:

Rev. Ralph Waldo Emerson gave an oration, of 1¼ hour, on The American Scholar. It was to me in the misty, dreamy, unintelligible style of Swedenborg, Coleridge, and Carlyle. He professed to have method; but I could not trace it, except in his own annunciation. It was well spoken, and all seemed to attend, but how many were in my own predicament of making little of it I have no means of ascertaining. Toward the close, and indeed in many parts of his discourse, he spoke severely of our dependence on British literature. Notwithstanding, I much question whether he himself would have written such an apparently incoherent and unintelligible address, had he not been familiar with the writings of the authors above named. He had already, in 1834, delivered a poem before the Society.

And now farewell to Brother Pierce—though he lives to attend eleven more meetings of the Society. The good man had his chance, too!

III

I must call three other witnesses to the effect of the oration, familiar to many of you as their testimony may be. Let us hear first a clever young Boston doctor, son of the minister of the First Church in Cambridge and brought up in its gambrel-roofed parsonage. He was the pet and the glory of the class of 1829. He had delighted the Phi Beta Kappa Society with his poem in 1836. He is not yet the "Autocrat," but he knows his own mind and the mind of the younger generation. Oliver Wendell Holmes testifies:

The grand Oration was our intellectual Declaration of Independence. Nothing like it had been heard in the halls of Harvard since Samuel Adams

supported the affirmative of the question, "Whether it be lawful to resist the chief magistrate, if the commonwealth cannot otherwise be preserved." It was easy to find fault with an expression here and there. The dignity, not to say the formality of an Academic assembly was startled by the realism that looked for the infinite in "the meal in the firkin; the milk in the pan." They could understand the deep thoughts suggested by "the meanest flower that blows," but these domestic illustrations had a kind of nursery homeliness about them which the grave professors and sedate clergymen were unused to expect on so stately an occasion. But the young men went out from it as if a prophet had been proclaiming to them "Thus saith the Lord." No listener ever forgot that Address, and among all the noble utterances of the speaker it may be questioned if one ever contained more truth in language more like that of immediate inspiration. . . .

Let us next call to the witness stand that other Cambridge boy whom we have already noted in the audience—the reckless, irreverent "Jamie" Lowell of 1837; sober enough now, when he gives his testimony, and it is the testimony, you will remember, of one of the few genuine critics whom America has produced:

The Puritan revolt had made us ecclesiastically and the Revolution politically independent, but we were socially and intellectually moored to English thought, till Emerson cut the cable and gave us a chance at the dangers and glories of blue water. No man young enough to have felt it can forget or cease to be grateful for the mental and moral *nudge* which he received from the writings of his high-minded and brave-spirited countryman. . . . His oration before the Phi Beta Kappa Society at Cambridge, some thirty years ago, was an event without any former parallel in our literary annals, a scene to be always treasured in the memory for its picturesqueness and its inspiration. What crowded and breathless aisles, what windows clustering with eager heads, what enthusiasm of approval, what grim silence of foregone dissent! It was our Yankee version of a lecture by Abélard, our Harvard parallel to the last public appearances of Schelling. . . .

Finally, lest you may think that the mere spell of the orator's spoken word charmed such hearers as Holmes and Lowell into an unreasoning discipleship, listen to an opinion from across the water, by a Scotchman who called no man, save Goethe, master, and who read Emerson's speech in the vast solitude of London town. Thomas Carlyle wrote:

My friend! You know not what you have done for me there. It was long decades of years that I heard nothing but the infinite jangling and jabbering, and inarticulate twittering and screeching, and my soul had sunk down sorrowful, and said there is no articulate speaking then any more, and thou art solitary among stranger-creatures? and lo, out of the West comes a clear utterance, clearly recognizable as a *man's* voice, and I *have* a kinsman and brother: God be thanked for it! I could have *wept* to read that speech; the clear high melody of it went tingling through my heart; I said to my wife, "There, woman!" She read; and returned, and charges me to return for answer, "that there has been nothing met with like it since Schiller went silent." My brave Emerson! And all this has been lying silent, quite tranquil in him, these seven years, and the "vociferous platitude," dinning his ears on all sides, and he quietly answering no word; and a whole world of Thought has silently built itself in these calm depths, and, the day being come, says quite softly, as if it were a common thing, "Yes, I *am* here too." Miss Martineau tells me, "Some say it is inspired, some say it is mad." Exactly so; no *say* could be suitabler. But for you, my dear friend, I say and pray heartily: may God grant you strength; for you have a *fearful* work to do! Fearful I call it; and yet it is great, and the greatest.

IV

Many readers still imagine that Emerson's address had the advantage of a new theme. It did not. His subject, "The American Scholar," had been a conventional theme of Phi Beta Kappa orations ever since he was a boy. The records of the Harvard Chapter prove this fact, beyond dispute. In 1809, for example, the eloquent Dr. J. S. Buckminster, of Boston, had spoken on the "Dangers and Duties of Men of Letters"; an admirable moralistic discussion of the infirmities and temptations of the scholastic life, closing with a plea for increased endowments for Harvard. That was his solution of the difficulty!

In 1815, William Tudor, the editor of the newly founded "North American Review," had discussed the "subjects which America would furnish for future poets." This was a favorite topic for Tudor and his associate Walter Channing in the early volumes of the "North American"; and the burden of their argument was that the remedy for American deficiencies lay in a more vigorous exertion of our own minds.

In 1818, at the end of Emerson's Freshman year, Edward Tyrrel Channing, then commencing his long and fruitful career as a Harvard teacher of rhetoric, took for his Phi Beta Kappa theme, "Independence in Literary Pursuits."

In 1822, William J. Spooner, addressing the Society on "The Prospects of American Literature," admitted that all our literature, up to that date, was an English literature, and yet claimed that our literary destiny was to be as independent of England's as was our political and moral destiny. America, he maintains, has already given proofs of "the unconquerable mind"; now, "let our writers learn to think for themselves." Yet Mr. Spooner's peroration, like Dr. Buckminster's, emphasizes the necessity of enlarging the means of education and of raising the standards of scholarship— the old appeal, you will perceive, to Harvard men.

In 1824 came Edward Everett's oration, delivered in the presence of Lafayette and dedicated to him, on "The Peculiar Motives to Intellectual Exertion in America." Those of you to whom Everett's name has not become as shadowy as the names of Tudor and Buckminster will still read this speech with admiration. He uses the very words, "American scholar"; he pleads nobly for popular institutions, for "the manifold brotherhood which unites and will unite the growing millions of America." He sees in vision the vast populations of the Mississippi and Missouri valleys, waiting to be stirred and inspired by the American idea; and his peroration is not a plea for endowments for Harvard, but a welcome to Lafayette. Thus the years come and go with the Harvard Chapter, but the orators pound imperturbably away on the same note! In 1831, it is James T. Austen, on "The Character and Duties of Educated Men." In 1835, we have Judge Theophilus Parsons, "On the Duties of Educated Men in a Republic"—and an excellent standpat speech it is: pleading for the sovereignty of Truth, the sacredness of Law, the security of Property; and President Wayland, of Brown University, the orator of 1836, made much the same plea under another title. In fact, such discussions of the duties and opportunities of the American Scholar were not confined to academic occasions. In 1831, Dr. William Ellery Channing had printed in the "Christian Examiner" his famous article on "National Literature." "In an age of great intellectual activity," he maintains, "we rely chiefly for intellectual excitement and enjoyment on foreign minds; nor is our own mind felt abroad. . . . We believe that a literature springing up in this new soil would bear new fruits. . . . Juster and profounder views of man may be expected here than elsewhere. In Europe political and artificial distinctions have, more or less, triumphed over and obscured our common nature. . . . Man is not hidden from us by so many disguises as in the Old World. . . ." Yet, as a means toward securing this new and native literature, Dr. Channing recommends "to our educated men a more extensive acquaintance with the intellectual labors of Continental Europe. Our reading is confined too much to English books, and especially to the more recent publications of Great Britain." Quickened by this contact with the Continental mind, power will pass increasingly, not into the hands of government, but into the hands of those who think and write. Thomas Carlyle, in that very year was dreaming the same flattering dream.

You will thus perceive that when the Reverend R. W. Emerson announced in 1837 that his subject was to be "The American Scholar," the Cambridge audience could settle back comfortably in their seats, knowing pretty well what was coming—as you and I do when we listen to a Christmas or an Easter sermon. And I do not need to add that the comfortable Cambridge audience guessed wrong.

V

What was it, after all, that Emerson said, upon his hackneyed theme? What was it that puzzled the elders, and entranced the youth, and sowed the seeds of division? At the Phi Beta Kappa dinner in University Hall, following the exercises in the church—a dinner too Bacchanalian, alas, for the taste of Brother John Pierce—Emerson was toasted in these words: "Mr. President, I suppose you all know where the orator came from; and I suppose all know what he said. I give you—the Spirit of Concord—*it makes us all of one mind.*" The pun was clever enough—as Phi Beta Kappa dinners go—but the well-meant compliment went very wide of the truth. Far from making them all of one mind, the man from Concord had sowed discord—and Emerson, at least, knew it. At the Phi Beta Kappa dinner of the next year, he is aware, his Journal tells us, of the "averted faces," and the aversion dated from this very 31st of August, 1837 —it had only ripened by the summer of 1838 and the "Divinity School Address." What had he really uttered in this speech, which was no loving-cup, but a sword?

He had begun with decorous sentences, quiet and clear as the daylight. His very subject, he admits, is prescribed by the occasion. But before one knows it, he is making his first distinction, namely, that Man, in being divided into Men, has suffered, has become a thing—a farmer, let us say, instead of Man on the farm. Now the Scholar should be *Man Thinking,* not a mere thinker, or, still worse,

the parrot of other men's thinking. What are the influences which the scholar receives?

There are three main influences: Nature, the Past—typified by Books—and Action.

First, then, Nature. "Every day, the sun; and, after sunset, Night and her stars. Ever the winds blow; ever the grass grows." But the scholar must ask what all this means. What *is* Nature? And then comes the puzzling Emersonian answer, already expressed in that little blue-covered unsold book of the year before: Nature is the opposite of the soul, answering to it part for part. (I can fancy Brother John Pierce looking at his watch. Ten minutes gone, and is this nonsense about Nature what we came into the meeting-house to hear?)

But the orator, after these cryptic paragraphs about Nature, is already touching the second influence upon the spirit of the scholar —namely, the Past, or, let us say for convenience, Books. (I imagine that Brother Pierce looks relieved. Books? He has been hearing Phi Beta Kappa talk about books for forty years. It is a safe subject. And yet what is it that the minister from Concord seems to be saying now?) The theory of books is noble, but each age must write its own books. It is the act of creation that is sacred, not the record. The poet chanting was felt to be a divine man: henceforth the chant is divine also. Instantly the book becomes noxious; the guide is a tyrant, though colleges are built on it. (Can he mean the Bible, wonders Professor Ware? Yes, Professor Ware, he does mean the Bible, and he will say so in your own Divinity School upon the invitation of your own students, on the fifteenth of July next! Listen to him as he goes on!) The one thing in the world, of value, is the active soul. The book, the college, the institution of any kind, stop with some past utterance of genius. This is good, say they—let us hold by this. *They pin me down.* They look backward and not forward. Books are for the scholar's idle times. They serve us best when they aim, not to drill, but to create—when they set the hearts of youth on flame. (I should like to watch Professor Ned Channing's sarcastic face, as Waldo Emerson proclaims this doctrine: Waldo Emerson, who had proved himself in college neither drillable nor inflammable!)

But the imperturbable orator of the day has now reached the third section of his address— a plea for Action. Remember that we are in the golden and serious age of American Rhetoric, and do not smile when Emerson argues that action enriches the scholar's vocabulary!

It is pearls and rubies to his discourse! Life is our dictionary. But action is after all better than books. Character is higher than intellect. Thinking is a partial act. The scholar loses no hour which the man lives. Labor is sacred. There is virtue yet in the hoe and the spade even in unlearned hands. (I catch grave young Henry Thoreau smiling a little as Mr. Emerson utters this wholesome New England doctrine of manual labor;—for he has watched the minister trying to spade his new Concord garden, and making but a sorry job of it!)

It remains, concludes the speaker, to say something of the scholar's duties. They may all be comprised in self-trust. Let him not quit his belief that a pop-gun is a pop-gun, though the ancient and honorable of the earth affirm it to be the crack of doom. Let him be free and brave. The world is still fluid, still alive. *Men* count—not "the mass"—"the herd." The private life is the true kingdom. Act for yourself: the man has never lived that can feed us ever. (Professor Ware—stout old war-horse—pricks up his ears again!) But now the orator is sweeping on to his climax: This age of Revolution in which we are living is a very good age. Accept it: embrace the common, the familiar, the low. Burns and Wordsworth and Carlyle are right. Give me insight into to-day, and you may have the antique and future worlds. The important thing is the *single person. The man is all.*

Then follows the wonderful peroration, which you would never forgive me for not quoting word for word:

. . . Mr. President and Gentlemen, this confidence in the unsearched might of man belongs, by all motives, by all prophecy, by all preparation, to the American Scholar. We have listened too long to the courtly muses of Europe. The spirit of the American freeman is already suspected to be timid, imitative, tame: Public and private avarice make the air we breathe thick and fat. The scholar is decent, indolent, complaisant. See already the tragic consequence. The mind of this country, taught to aim at low objects, eats upon itself. There is no work for any but the decorous and the complaisant. Young men of the fairest promise, who begin life upon our shores, inflated by the mountain winds, shined upon by all the stars of God, find the earth below not in unison with these, but are hindered from action by the disgust which the principles on which business is managed inspire, and turn drudges, or die of disgust, some of them suicides. What is the remedy? They did not yet see, and thousands of young men as hopeful now crowding to the barriers for the career do not yet see, that if the single man plant himself indomitably on his instincts, and there abide, the huge world will come round to him. Patience—

patience; with the shades of all the good and great for company; and for solace the perspective of your own infinite life; and for work the study and the communication of principles, the making those instincts prevalent, the conversion of the world. Is it not the chief disgrace in the world, not to be an unit;—not to be reckoned one character;—not to yield that peculiar fruit which each man was created to bear, but to be reckoned in the gross, in the hundred, or the thousand, of the party, the section, to which we belong; and our opinion predicted geographically, as the north, or the south? Not so, brothers and friends—please God, ours shall not be so. We will walk on our own feet; we will work with our own hands; we will speak our own minds. The study of letters shall be no longer a name for pity, for doubt, and for sensual indulgence. The dread of man and the love of man shall be a wall of defense and a wreath of joy around all. A nation of men will for the first time exist, because each believes himself inspired by the Divine Soul which also inspires all men.

VI

That, then, is what Emerson said, eighty-six years ago. What do we think of it? We know what Brother Pierce thought of it, and what was the verdict of Holmes and Lowell and Carlyle. I have amused myself—though I may have wearied you—by intimating what this hearer and that, among the long-vanished audience, may have surmised or hoped or resolved in his own heart, as those beautiful cadences ceased at last, and the great hour was over. I might tell what was said in the newspapers and in the Reviews, and how the entire edition of the address was sold out in one month, whereas it took thirteen years to sell the first five hundred copies of the orator's book on "Nature." Yet all such evidence, interesting as it may be to one's antiquarian curiosity, does not fully explain the meaning or the power of Emerson's address.

The words of Emerson's speech are still legible upon the printed page, but how small a portion of any speech are the mere words! Boys declaim them in school, "meek young men in libraries" study the sources, literary historians endeavor to reconstruct the time and place of utterance. Yet the magic has fled with the magical hour, and the words seem only the garments of a soul that has escaped. The chemical formula for a great speech seems simple enough, but it is mysterious, like all simple things; it is *a Man plus the atmosphere of a given epoch.* The speech falls flat if it be uttered a year, a month, a day earlier or later than its appointed hour. See young Wendell Phillips fighting his way to the platform of Faneuil Hall on December 8th of that very year, 1837, to defend the memory of Lovejoy from the attack of the Attorney-General of Massachusetts. It is now or never for what Phillips has to say, and Phillips knows it. See him forty-four years later, in Sanders Theater, as the Phi Beta Kappa orator of 1881, defending Russian Nihilism; some of us can remember the tense excitement of the American public in that hour over the question of freedom in Russia. Almost no one in Sanders Theater knew what Phillips was to say. Official Harvard, as always, distrusted him. His flashing eloquence, that noon, was the electric discharge, through him, of forces greater than the orator. If you will read that address of 1881 to-day, you cannot withhold your admiration for the cunning art of the consummate craftsman. The right words are all there in their right places. But the spell is broken; "the image of the God is gone."

Now, it is a part of the genius and the glory of Emerson that his spoken words have the accent of literature. Their specific form is, indeed, shaped by the heat and pressure of an occasion. But their substance is perdurable. His phrases are final phrases. His aim is Truth, and not mere eloquence. He has, indeed, learned the art of rhetoric from Everett and Webster, but he has also learned, by watching them, to distrust rhetoric—to keep it in its place. He would like to win his immediate audience, no doubt, but he is forever saying to himself, as Lincoln said of his debates with Douglas in 1858, "there is bigger game than this." Lincoln's ultimate object was to justify the fundamental principles of free government. Emerson's goal was the Truth that sets men free. His words are literature because the Truth that he perceived could be revealed only through Beauty. The revealing phrase is lovely, and the uncovered face of Truth is lovelier still. As Emerson discourses of Nature and Books and Action, he lays bare his own mind, as an athlete strips himself for the race. Exquisite perception of external beauty, ripened wisdom, high courage—these were the man, and by their perfect expression of the man's qualities Emerson's addresses win their place as literature. We read them to-day as we read Montaigne or Bacon, as something forever alive.

I remarked to a friend the other day that I was trying to imagine what Emerson would say if he had to make his Phi Beta Kappa speech over again in the present hour. "If Emerson were living to-day," was the reply, "he would be a very different Emerson." In one sense, of course, my friend was right. If

Emerson had been born seventy-five years later, he would have read Tolstoy and Ibsen, he would have studied under William James, and he would use a somewhat different vocabulary. It is likely that he would have written no journals. He would have missed the discipline and support of the Lyceum audiences. But he would certainly be giving Lowell Institute lectures, as of old, and writing for the "Atlantic Monthly," and lunching with the Saturday Club. It is certain that he would be making Phi Beta Kappa speeches, and I think we may be allowed to guess what he would say. He would still, I believe, have a message for you and me, a message for our academic communities, and a counsel of perfection for the United States.

To the private person he would announce, with the old serenity: "The sun shines to-day also"—"and, after sunset, Night and her stars." In uttering this gospel of Nature he would use new terms, for his mind would have been fascinated by the new discoveries. But while the illustrations would be novel, he would still assert the universality of Law. He would still say: Books are good, but the living soul is better. "Do not teach me out of Leibnitz and Schelling, and I shall find it all out myself." He would still preach to us the gospel of the will, or, in William James's phrase, "the will to believe." "When you renounce your early visions, then dies the man in you." Be a unit. In this whirring social machinery of the twentieth century, in this over-organized, sentimentalized, and easily stampeded age, possess your own soul. By and by the snowstorm of illusions will cease, and you will be left alone with the moral laws of the universe, you alone and they alone. When that supreme hour comes, meet it without fear.

Emerson's message to the academic community would have, I think, a note of yearning. The historic Emerson always wished to be one of us. There was no time in his long career, his biographer says, when he would not gladly have accepted a professorship of rhetoric in any college. If he were of our generation, but still, as of old, outside of our own immediate circle, would he not say: "O you who are cramped in costly buildings, clogged with routine, preoccupied with administrative machinery, how can you see the sun whether it be shining? Where is your free hour for Night and her stars? You are learned in bibliographies, expert in card catalogues, masters of a thousand specialties. You are documented, certificated, sophisticated. But have you the old eager reverence for the great books? And where, by the way, are your own books? From these thousands of American colleges and universities, how many vital, creative books are born? The university of Walden Pond had 'Whim' written above its doorposts, but it bred literature. There was once a type of productive scholar who may be described as 'he that scattereth, and yet increaseth,' but your amazing and multifarious activity, is not much of it wastage rather than growth? Simplify! Coördinate! Find yourselves, and then lift up your hearts!"

And finally I am sure that the spirit of Emerson, if he were revisiting this "great sensual avaricious America," as the historic Emerson once called it, would have a message for the United States in this hour of cowardice, disillusionment, and inhibition. Unless Emerson came back from the under-world with a changed soul, he would assert the supremacy of moral obligations. He would perceive, as in his lifetime, that a "diffidence in the soul was creeping over the American mind." But he would shame that diffidence. He would rally the distrustful. Can we not hear once more his clear and quiet voice: The gods are forever in their places: first, Righteousness, Justice, and Liberty, and after these, Fellowship and Peace. The Law holds. The foundations of human society are moral foundations. They cannot be shaken, even though whole empires should lose their senses and debauch their souls and go toppling down. Be steady. "This time, like all times, is a very good one, if we but know what to do with it." Behold the Law: "God is, not was; He speaketh, not spake." The world is very wide, very strange, it terrifies us, it seems plunging from its orbit. But it cannot plunge from its orbit; that was fixed before the foundation of the world. Patience—patience. Our earth is whirling on its way from God and to God, and the law of its being is the same law of obedience and of faith which is written in the heart of the obscurest scholar.

CARL SANDBURG (1878-   )

From ABRAHAM LINCOLN: THE PRAIRIE YEARS (1926)

[Lincoln and Douglas]

Around the public square of Springfield every day in 1854 came "movers." They drove in covered wagons, heading west for homesteads. They were pioneers. But to speak of them as "pioneers" was considered highfalutin. They were movers.

A Peoria newspaper that year counted 1,473 wagons in one month, movers going to Iowa. Twelve thousand emigrants arrived on railroad trains at Chicago in one week of that year. Three hundred houses were built in Davenport in a year. Though a building boom was on in Bloomington, its hotels sometimes could not accommodate all comers, and Lincoln one evening in that city went canvassing among private houses for a furnished room.

"How's things?" was a query. "Booming," was a reply. Flush times were on. Those incessant westbound wagons were a sign.

Cyrus H. McCormick, the farm-reaper man, had come up from Virginia, with letters of introduction from Stephen A. Douglas; McCormick located in Chicago, having decided it was to be the farm-machinery centre of the world. He said: "I made and sold 1,558 machines in 1854 with less than one-half of one per cent of returned machines. Three-fourths of these were combined reaping and mowing machines. I shall manufacture as near 3,000 machines for 1855 as I can."

That year the Illinois Central made the grade from Chicago to Galena. Six new states for the Union would be carved out in the Northwest, newspapers were saying. On the Great Plains north of the Missouri River, east of the Rockies, and west of the Great Lakes would come fifteen million people in forty years.

Millions of dollars were passing in money orders from America to Europe, the poor people of a new country trying to help the poorer people of the old countries. Edward Everett, of the Department of State, said on December 1, 1851, that official inquiry showed, "The emigrants to the United States, from Ireland alone, besides having subsisted themselves, have sent back to their kindred, for the last three years, nearly five million dollars each year."

In that flush year and those boom times, the Midwest prairie state of Illinois was holding its annual state fair in Springfield, in the harvest month of October.

Shorthorn cattle were feeding in sheds where farmers by hundreds passed through, discussing whether it would pay to try to raise these high-class, high-bred cattle instead of scrubs without pedigree. A shorthorn bull drew particular attention; he had crossed the Atlantic Ocean and the Great Lakes on steamboats; his owner had a tent near by with tables, chairs, whisky, cigars, where farmers could sit and take cheer while they talked about the bull; some of the farmers had heard a caretaker of the bull say: "Thet bull's wuth his weight in gold. Ever sence he left old England, Queen Victoree's been cryin' her eyes out on account o' the loss o' thet calf, fer he was jist a calf then. Now you kin go up and down these sheds and see what a fambly he's got. All the gold in Californy couldn't buy his childern and grandchildern."

Of course the bull was not the only topic. There were sows, boars, stallions, mares, rams, ewes, hens, roosters, geese, ganders, ducks, drakes, turkeys, gobblers; peaches, apples, crab apples, pears, picked from sunny orchards and canned by farmers' wives; also jellies, jams, apple butter, peach marmalade; and wheat, oats, rye, each with its ticket naming the farmer who had raised the grain. And there was keen interest in the farmers named as receiving blue ribbons for the long yellow or golden red ears of corn they had raised.

To walk around among these exhibits, to see the horse races where runners, trotters, and pacers with Kentucky and Tennessee pedigrees competed on a mile track, and then to listen to the political speakers discussing "purr-ins-a-pulls" and "the Const-ti-too-shun"—this made a holiday for the farmers and city people who came.

For many a young couple who came riding on a farm work-horse, the young man in front holding the bridle, the young woman behind him, the two straddling a blanket on the horse's back—it was one of the high holidays of the year. They went home to talk for a year about what they had seen at the state fair in Springfield.

The hero of the holiday came, Stephen A. Douglas, formerly of Springfield, once land commissioner, then supreme-court judge, later a congressman, and then United States senator from Illinois, at forty-three years of age a national leader of the Democratic party and the nearest of any man in Congress to filling the shoes of Clay, Calhoun, or Webster as an orator and parliamentary whip. He had been an active official in the Masonic order; he had carried the bulk of the Irish Catholic vote of the State; a large block of votes in both church and saloon elements were with him.

Blue-eyed, magnetic, chin drawn in, with a lionlike head, pivoting, elusive, with a face that drew men as Napoleon at Austerlitz or Nelson at Trafalgar, he was the most daring and forthright personal political force that had held the American stage since Andrew Jackson stepped off. His hero was Jackson; he was known as the foremost "whole-hog Jackson man." He was spokesman for what he called Young America as against what he called Old Fogyism.

Though he stood a short five feet, two inches, his head was shapely, balanced, large, and with its big shock of a black pompadour swept back in curly waves, and his deep bass voice dramatically calling for an ocean-to-ocean American republic, he was a figure that captured the imaginations of people and led them as Napoleon led; they were willing to go anywhere he said, without asking why; he embodied drama, politics, and a picturesque conduct of life; men wondered about him, tried to solve his personality and had no sooner done so to their satisfaction than he was on the stage in a new rôle with a new play.

He had come close to taking the Democratic nomination for President; Caleb Cushing and the wheelhorses who pulled the nomination for Franklin Pierce were not yet sure that blind luck had not been the chief factor. To be decisive, to be positive, to win men his way by grand acting, was the sport of Douglas's life; political life was to his nostrils what the military was to Napoleon; he had an instinct for the grand manner, the sweeping and absolute jerk of the head or the defiant brandish of clenched fists or the contemplative and majestic pause of the man who knows how and can tell.

When he was leaving for Europe, with his sister managing his Washington house, she told him, "I don't know how to entertain senators and such big men." He asked, "You never have been afraid of me, have you?" "Of course not; I'm older than you and I've managed you." "Well, then, they say I'm the biggest toad in the puddle, and you needn't be afraid of them."

While telling the United States Senate what was right and wrong with the country, he could at times double his fists and shake them at imaginary enemies in the name of the Constitution and Andrew Jackson. He spoke the dedicatory oration for the Jackson equestrian statue in Washington, himself of a piece with the horse rearing on its hind legs with forefeet in the air. "He lashed himself into such a heat," wrote an observer, "that if his body had been made of combustible matter, it would have burnt out."

When the city council of Chicago in 1850 voted with only two dissenting members that the Fugitive Slave Law was cruel, unjust, unconstitutional, and that the city police should not be required to help arrest fugitive slaves, Douglas went to a mass meeting in Chicago where he was hissed to begin with, but in the end his arguments won a vote for the repudiation of the action of the city council. When his bill in Congress for Federal land grants to the proposed Illinois Central Railroad was beaten by southern votes, he won those votes solidly by routing the proposed railroad through southern territory with similar land grants. On his head in that year of 1854 had fallen such a storm of epithets and ridicule as probably no other public man in American history had known.

As the representative friend of Chicago business interests allied with New York and Boston interests, he had set out to open the vast stretch of territory west of Iowa to the Pacific Ocean and make it ready for transportation and trade tributary to Chicago. Toward the south in St. Louis other business interests planned a "National Central Highway" from that city to San Francisco; the plans of Jefferson Davis, the Secretary of War, favored a railway to the Pacific with Memphis as its eastern terminus. The slavery question, land grants, Indian tribal reservations, railroad routes, territorial government for Nebraska, were snarled in what seemed to be a hopeless tangle.

Douglas cut through the tangle and won support for a bill which would make two territories, Nebraska on the north, Kansas on the south, in each of which the ballots of its voters would decide whether it should be free or slave territory. "They could vote slavery up or down" under the principle of "popular sovereignty," also called "squatter sovereignty." Southern votes in Congress came to this measure, with its provision that the Missouri Compromise was expressly repealed.

He had accepted from Senator Dixon of Kentucky a rider to his territorial bill; it was the only way to get required southern support. Dixon quoted Douglas as saying, "By God, sir, you are right, and I will incorporate it in my bill, though I know it will raise a hell of a storm."

On his way from Washington to Illinois, Douglas had looked from car windows to see the burning of dummies rigged out to look like himself, labeled with his name; in Ohio women had presented him with thirty pieces of silver; newspapers declared his middle name of Arnold derived from Benedict Arnold. In Chicago on a Saturday night a crowd had yelled "meow" and "boo" at him for two hours while he tried to explain his Missouri Compromise Bill; he was howled down.

The mob sang, "We won't go home till morning, we won't go home till morning." Douglas faced it, and, "The spirit of a dictator flashed out from his eye, curled upon his lip, and mingled its cold irony in every tone of his voice and every gesture of his body," according to the Chicago *Daily Democratic Press*. At midnight he looked at his watch, shook a fist at the crowd, and shouted, "It is now Sunday morning—I'll go to church, and you may go to hell!"

The opening up of the territory west of the Missouri River for settlement and transportation and trade tributary to Chicago had come at a higher price than he expected.

So he was the central figure of attraction at the state fair. Thousands who hated his face and the very breath of him wanted a look at him. Other thousands who loved him and would go to war and bloody battles for his sake, who would answer his call as the boys of France answered the call of Napoleon, were ready to stand in the frosty night air of mid-October to hear him deliver a speech.

He registered at the Chenery House in Springfield on arriving; a brass band, men with torches, and a street black with people serenaded the senator; there were calls for "the Judge," "Judge Douglas," the "Little Giant"; he came out on the porch of the Chenery House, torches were held up so that the people could see his face; around him stood Lieutenant Governor McMurtry, John A. McClernand, Sam Buckmaster, John A. Logan, William R. Morrison.

And how should a United States senator, accused of wrong, speak to his home people when they came with a brass band and torches to serenade him? Douglas knew how. He should speak slowly, measuredly, distinctly. Each word should come forth from his lips as a piece of money from a deep casket. So he spoke. "Neither—to legislate—slavery—into —a territory—nor to exclude it—therefrom— but—to leave—the peo-ple—perfectly free— to form—and regulate—their—domestic institutions—in their own way—subject—only—to the—Constitution—of—the United States: that is—all—there is—of the Nebraska Bill. That is 'popular sovereignty'—upon which—I

am to speak—tomorrow at the Statehouse."
This was the voice in which he spoke for them,
for Illinois, in Washington, the national capital.

Then he became a little familiar, as befitted
a speech to the home people; the words came
faster, as the torches flickered and the black
mass of people in the street listened amid huge
shadows. "I have come home, as I have done
so many times before, to give an account of my
stewardship. I know the Democrats of Illinois. I know they always do their duty. I
know, Democrats, that you will stand by me
as you have always done. I am not afraid that
you will be led off by those renegades from the
party, Trumbull, Palmer, Judd, and Cook,
who have formed an unholy alliance to turn
the glorious old Democratic party over to the
black Abolitionists. Democrats of Illinois, will
you permit it?" And the street shook with
voices en masse: "No! no! never! never!"
Between the torches his blue eyes flashed,
his lips trembled. "I tell you the time has not
yet come when a handful of traitors in our
camp can turn the great State of Illinois, with
all her glorious history and traditions, into a
negro-worshiping, negro-equality community. Illinois has always been, and always will
be, true to the Constitution and the Union."
And he gracefully wished them good night; the
torches, the brass band, the crowd, vanished;
the street was empty.

On the afternoon of the next day Douglas
spoke for nearly three hours in the Statehouse.
Had not the Missouri Compromise been practically wiped out by the Omnibus Bill of 1850?
Was not the real question whether the people
should rule, whether the voters in a Territory
should control their own affairs? If the people
of Kansas and Nebraska were able to govern
themselves, they were able to govern a few
miserable negroes. The crowd enjoyed it;
cries came, "That's so!" "Hit 'em again,"
and, the speech over, three ringing cheers were
given for the "Little Giant."

Lincoln had a seat up front; he whispered
occasionally in the ears of friends, and they
chuckled and grinned. He walked down the
main aisle at Douglas's elbow, joking the senator. It was only a few years back that Douglas
had loaned Lincoln a hundred dollars and Lincoln had signed a note and later paid it. They
had argued on the stump, in courtrooms,
churches, grocery stores. To a pretty young
woman Abolitionist who told Douglas she
didn't like the speech, Lincoln said: "Don't
bother, young lady. We'll hang the judge's
hide on the fence tomorrow."

When the young woman later insisted to

Lincoln that he had no business laughing and
joking during such a brutal speech, Lincoln
answered that maybe he ought to feel a little
guilty. As to the slaveholder's way of looking
at slavery, it didn't hurt him so very much.
"I have heard it all my life," he said, "and as
the boy said about skinning eels, it don't hurt
'em so very much; it has always been done,
they're used to it." Dick Oglesby hinted to the
young woman that she had been unfair to Lincoln: "He knows how to manage us sap-
suckers; just let him alone."

There had been a saying around court-
houses, "With a good case Lincoln is the best
lawyer in the state, but in a bad case Douglas
is the best lawyer the state ever produced."

The next afternoon Lincoln stood before
the same crowd that Douglas had spoken to.
Judge Douglas had arrived at the Statehouse
in an open carriage, standing with his hat in
his hand bowing to a crowd that cheered him.
In the carriage also were the governor of the
state, Joel A. Matteson, and Douglas's colleague in the United States Senate, General
James T. Shields, who had one time gone with
Lincoln to a sand-bar in the Mississippi River
to fight a duel. Douglas took a seat on the
platform.

Lincoln came in, pushing and squirming his
way to the platform where he was to reply to
Douglas's speech of the day before. After being introduced, he questioned whether he was
just the man who should be selected to reply
to the senator, mentioned the world-wide fame
of Senator Douglas, the high position in the
United States Senate and the power Douglas
held as a debater. He was going to discuss the
Missouri Compromise, presenting his own connected view of it, and in that sense his remarks
would not be specifically an answer to Judge
Douglas, though the main points of Judge
Douglas's address would receive respectful attention. "I do not propose to question the
patriotism or to assail the motives of any man
or class of men, but rather to confine myself
strictly to the naked merits of the question."
With these apologies and explanations out of
the way he was set for his main speech.

He began with a short history of the United
States and slavery. He dug back into beginnings and traced out the growth of slavery:
"Wherever slavery is it has been first introduced without law. The oldest laws we find
concerning it are not laws introducing it, but
regulating it as an already existing thing."

He gave five burning reasons for hating it as
a "monstrous injustice." And he added: "Let
me say I think I have no prejudice against the

southern people. They are just what we would be in their situation. If slavery did not now exist among them, they would not introduce it. If it did now exist among us, we should not instantly give it up. This I believe of the masses North and South. Doubtless there are individuals on both sides who would not hold slaves under any circumstances, and others who would gladly introduce slavery anew if it were out of existence.

"We know that some southern men do free their slaves, go North and become tiptop Abolitionists, while some northern ones go South and become most cruel slave-masters. When southern people tell us they are no more responsible for the origin of slavery than we are, I acknowledge the fact. When it is said that the institution exists, and that it is very difficult to get rid of in any satisfactory way, I can understand and appreciate the saying. I surely will not blame them for not doing what I should not know how to do myself."

Was this oratory? debating? The man, Abraham Lincoln, was speaking to thousands of people as if he and another man were driving in a buggy across the prairie, exchanging their thoughts. He was saying that if all earthly power were given him he wouldn't know what to do as to slavery.

There are not ships and money to send the slaves anywhere else; and when shipped anywhere else outside of America they might all die. "What then? Free them all, and keep them among us as underlings? Is it quite certain that this betters their condition? I think I would not hold one in slavery at any rate, yet the point is not clear enough for me to denounce people upon.

"What next? Free them, and make them politically and socially our equals? My own feelings will not admit of this, and if mine would, we well know that those of the great mass of the whites will not. Whether this feeling accords with justice and sound judgment is not the sole question, if indeed it is any part of it. A universal feeling, whether well or ill founded, cannot be safely disregarded. We cannot then make them equals. It does seem to me that systems of gradual emancipation might be adopted, but for their tardiness in this I will not undertake to judge our brethren of the South."

And yet, while he could not say what should be done about slavery where it was already established and operating, he was sure it would be wrong to let it spread North. "Inasmuch as you do not object to my taking my hog to Nebraska, therefore I must not object

to your taking your slave. Now, I admit that this is perfectly logical, if there is no difference between hogs and negroes."

The South had joined the North in making the law that classified African slave traders as pirates and provided hanging as the punishment. "If you did not feel that it was wrong, why did you join in providing that men should be hung for it? The practice was no more than bringing wild negroes from Africa to such as would buy them. But you never thought of hanging men for catching and selling wild horses, wild buffaloes, or wild bears."

The speaker at times was in a way lost from his audience, as though language had not been invented for what he was trying to say. He referred to the man whose business was to operate "a sort of negro livery stable," buying and selling slaves. "He watches your necessities, and crawls up to buy your slave, at a speculating price. If you cannot help it, you sell to him; but if you can help it, you drive him from your door. You despise him utterly. You do not recognize him as a friend, or even as an honest man. Your children must not play with his; they may rollick freely with the little negroes, but not with the slave dealer's children. If you are obliged to deal with him, you try to get through the job without so much as touching him, instinctively shrinking from the snaky contact. If he grows rich and retires from business, you still remember him, and still keep up the ban of nonintercourse upon him and his family. Now why is this? You do not so treat the man who deals in corn, cotton, or tobacco."

Over the country were 433,643 free black men, at $500.00 a head worth over $200,000,-000.00. "How comes this vast amount of property to be running about without owners? We do not see free horses or free cattle running at large. How is this? All these free blacks are the descendants of slaves or have been slaves themselves; and they would be slaves now but for something which has operated on their white owners. What is that something? Is there any mistaking it? In all these cases it is your sense of justice and human sympathy continually telling you that the poor negro has some natural right to himself—that those who deny it and make mere merchandise of him deserve kickings, contempt, and death. And now why will you ask us to deny the humanity of the slave, and estimate him as only the equal of the hog? Why ask us to do what you will not do yourselves? Why ask us to do nothing that two hundred millions of dollars could not induce you to do?"

He drew a line between his position and that of the Abolitionists. "Let it not be said I am contending for the establishment of political [and social equality between the whites and blacks. I have already said the contrary."

He reasoned that the application of what Douglas called "the sacred right of self-government" depended on whether a negro was a man. "If he is not a man, in that case he who is a man may as a matter of self-government do just what he pleases with him. But if the negro is a man, is it not to that extent a total destruction of self-government to say that he too shall not govern himself? When the white man governs himself, that is self-government; but when he governs himself and also governs another man, that is more than self-government—that is despotism. If the negro is a man, why, then my ancient faith teaches me that 'all men are created equal,' and that there can be no moral right in connection with one's man's making a slave of another. What I do say is that no man is good enough to govern another man without that other's consent. I say this is the leading principle, the sheet anchor of American republicanism."

He referred to bowie knives and six-shooters ruling the border between Missouri and Kansas, with "never a glimpse of the ballot box," analyzed the Nebraska Bill to show that while the people were supposed to decide the slavery question for themselves, no time or place or manner of voting was named in the bill. "Could there be a more apt invention to bring about collision and violence on the slavery question than this Nebraska project is? I do not charge or believe that such was intended by Congress; but if they had literally formed a ring and placed champions within it to fight out the controversy, the fight could be no more likely to come off than it is. And if this fight should begin, is it likely to take a very peaceful, Union-saving turn? Will not the first drop of blood so shed be the real knell of the Union?"

And what should be done first of all? "The Missouri Compromise ought to be restored. For the sake of the Union, it ought to be restored. We ought to elect a House of Representatives which will vote its restoration." If it should not be restored, what would the country see? "The South flushed with triumph and tempted to excess; the North, betrayed as they believe, brooding on wrong and burning for revenge. One side will provoke, the other resent. The one will taunt, the other

defy. Already a few in the North defy all constitutional restraints, resist the execution of the Fugitive Slave Law, and even menace the institution of slavery in the states where it exists. Already a few in the South claim the constitutional right to take and to hold slaves in the free states—demand the revival of the slave trade—and demand a treaty with Great Britain by which fugitive slaves may be reclaimed from Canada."

The speech was three hours long. Through most of it Lincoln spoke as though he were not debating, trying to beat and crush an opponent, but rather as though he were examining his own mind, his own facts and views, his own propositions and the demonstrations of them.

And again he was no philosopher at all; he was a sad, lost man chanting a rhythm of the sad and lost. "Little by little, but steadily as man's march to the grave, we have been giving up the old for the new faith. Near eighty years ago we began by declaring that all men are created equal; but now from that beginning we have run down to the other declaration that for some men to enslave others is a 'sacred right of self-government.' These principles cannot stand together. They are as opposite as God and Mammon; whoever holds to the one must despise the other."

He pointed to "the liberal party throughout the world," watching slavery "fatally violating the noblest political system the world ever saw." And he intimated his knowledge of the movement on foot to extend slavery from the black race to certain lower grades of white labor, in saying: "Is there no danger to liberty itself in discarding the earliest practice and first precept of our ancient faith? In our greed-chase to make profit of the negro, let us beware lest we 'cancel and tear to pieces' even the white man's charter of freedom."

He stood among neighbors, in his shirtsleeves, on a warm October day. The words came slow, hesitating, to begin with, and he spoke often in the tang of his childhood speech. "Just" sounded a little like "jist," and "such" suspiciously like "sich." As his body loosened and swayed to the cadence of his address, and the thoughts unfolded, drops of sweat stood out on his forehead; he was speaking not only with his tongue but with every blood-drop of his body.

A scholarly man said: "His manner was impassioned and he seemed transfigured; his listeners felt that he believed every word he said, and that, like Martin Luther, he would go to the stake rather than abate one jot or tittle of it." A farmer said: "I don't keer fur them great orators. I want to hear jist a plain common feller like the rest on us, thet I kin foller an' know where he's drivin'. Abe Linkern fills the bill."

And the *Springfield Journal* account, written by Bill Herndon: "Lincoln quivered with feeling and emotion. The whole house was as still as death. And the house approved the glorious triumph of truth by loud and continued huzzas. Women waved their white handkerchiefs in token of woman's silent but heartfelt assent. Douglas felt the sting. He frequently interrupted Mr. Lincoln. The Nebraska Bill was shivered, and like a tree of the forest, was torn and rent asunder by the hot bolts of truth. It was a proud day for Mr. Lincoln. His friends will never forget it."

The speech came to an end. The crowd that heard it scattered out of the Statehouse to their homes. But in Peoria twelve days later, Lincoln gave the same speech again to a crowd of thousands and then went home to Springfield and wrote it out for publication.

Now among many politicians and people in Illinois it was seen there was one man in the state who could grapple and hold his own with Stephen A. Douglas. Among Whig and anti-Nebraska politicians it was recognized that a mind was among them that could strip a political issue to what he called its "naked merits." And among thousands of plain people was an instinct, perhaps a hope, that this voice was their voice.

Douglas came to Lincoln after the Peoria speech and told him that he (Lincoln) had been more troublesome than all the opposition he had met in the United States Senate; he made the offer that he would go home and speak no more during the campaign if Lincoln would do the same. Lincoln took the offer. And one friend said, "This was certainly running Douglas into his hole and making him holler 'Enough.'"

XVI. THE CONTEMPORARY SHORT STORY

By the end of the ninth decade of the nineteenth century, when the vogue of the short story of local color seemed established in permanent favor, there were already indications of a new spirit in American fiction. With the work of James Lane Allen, of Mary Wilkins, of Hamlin Garland, and of Margaret Deland, the selection of picturesque incident and setting became less important and the insight into character and realism of portrayal brought the short story into agreement with similar currents in the novel and the drama.

James Lane Allen wrote of Kentucky, it is true, just as Mary Wilkins wrote of New England, or Garland of the Middle West, or Mrs. Deland of Western Pennsylvania, but the locality became relegated to the background. Allen began with an ideal picture of life, but soon passed into a more realistic manner; the other leaders in this movement were from the first uncompromising realists. With them characters were no longer intensifications of good or evil traits; they were people very often of unpromising exterior, whose spiritual or emotional conflicts made them significant. Allen and Garland left short story writing for the novel, though Allen returned to it at the end of his career. Miss Wilkins kept largely to the shorter form. Mrs. Deland, beginning with the novel, turned later to the short story and, perhaps because of this larger fictional conception, has created in Dr. Lavender one of our most permanent characterizations. The great change that came over our fiction can hardly be better illustrated than by comparison between Bret Harte and Mrs. Deland. Both deal with moral contrasts. Harte employs them for their picturesque quality; in Mrs. Deland's hands they become the means by which she incarnates ethical motives. Unrelated to this group, Stephen Crane represents the newspaper man relating the experiences of war from a realistic point of view. He lived in the nineteenth century but his manner was that of the twentieth.

Mrs. Wharton began with the short story and her success with the novel has not interrupted her cultivation of the briefer form. For the two phases she has touched with supreme distinction, the study of social values and the establishment of the supernatural, the short story is especially well suited. With her the story of character came to its height in America, and her marvellous sense of structure, as well as her inimitable style, has made her work a standard during the twentieth century. Most nearly akin to Mrs. Wharton, Miss Sedgwick has represented the American point of view in contact and in conflict with that of the European. This phase cannot be represented so well by her short stories as by her novels, but even in the former her easy superiority to most Americans who have sought to interpret the European scene is apparent.

Already the twentieth century has seen many modes of fiction. Booth Tarkington began with romance, but, even amid the costumes and accessories of *Monsieur Beaucaire*, it is the character of the French nobleman that attracts us. Miss Cather has confined herself largely to the novel, and in it as well as in her short stories, she represents the contrast of the temperament of the artist with the surroundings that tend to stifle the creative spirit. Mrs. Fisher presents in her fiction realistic treatment of character with moral issues kept sufficiently in the background but nearly always present. From the point of view of form, and for his sympathetic if somewhat sardonic interpretation of the life of the swarming crowds of the large cities, O. Henry demands consideration. He has been hailed as the creator of a new species, but in his use of suspense and sudden climax, Aldrich and even Franklin had been before him and his work has often a mere journalistic cleverness.

Dreiser, like Crane and "O. Henry," uses the methods of the newspaper with his fiction. More serious than most of his fellow reporters of life, he has represented the hapless struggle of the unfortunate or the unfit, and at times succeeded, especially at the beginning of his career, in stirring the depths of character. That he has often seemed to stir them only to muddy them, is a criticism he must share with many a writer of to-day, who has not Dreiser's power. With more sense of artistry, Joseph Hergesheimer has contributed a number of studies of native conditions, both past and present, with a real understanding of racial origins and sectional characteristics. Steele represents the short story of situation, often dramatic in intensity.

The short story in America has suffered, so far as its permanent worth is concerned, from a vast overproduction and from the temptations offered by the popular magazines. The earlier standards of magazine literature, for a story of "not more than six thousand words," which, while often embarrassing, nevertheless demanded unity, have given way to a demand for stories of ten thousand words which trickle through the advertising pages. The result has been a general level of mediocrity and a facility which leaves out of consideration the distinction of form which alone preserves the short story in literature.

MARY WILKINS FREEMAN (1862-   )

A HUMBLE ROMANCE
(1884)

She was stooping over the great kitchen sink, washing the breakfast dishes. Under fostering circumstances, her slenderness of build might have resulted in delicacy or daintiness; now the harmony between strength and task had been repeatedly broken, and the result was ugliness. Her finger joints and wrist bones were knotty and out of proportion, her elbows, which her rolled-up sleeves displayed, were pointed and knobby, her shoulders bent, her feet spread beyond their natural bounds—from head to foot she was a little discordant note. She had a pale, peaked face, her scanty fair hair was strained tightly back, and twisted into a tiny knot, and her expression was at once passive and eager.

There came a ringing knock at the kitchen door, and a face of another description, large, strong-featured, and assured, peered out of the pantry, which was over against the sink. "Who is it, Sally?"

"I don' know, Mis' King."

"Well, go to the door, can't you, an' not stan' thar gapin'. I can't; my hands are in the butter."

Sally shook the dish-water off her red, sodden fingers, and shuffled to the door.

A tall man with a scraggy sandy mustache stood there. He had some scales in his hand. "Good-mornin', marm," he said. "Hev you got any rags?"

"I'll see," said the girl. Then she went over to the pantry, and whispered to her mistress that it was the tin-peddler.

"Botheration!" cried Mrs. King, impatiently; "why couldn't he hev come another day? Here I am right in the midst of butter, an' I've got lots of rags, an' I've got to hev some new milk-pails right away."

All of this reached the ears of the tin-peddler, but he merely stood waiting, the corners of his large mouth curving up good-naturedly, and scrutinized with pleasant blue eyes the belongings of the kitchen, and especially the slight, slouching figure at the sink, to which Sally had returned.

"I s'pose," said Mrs. King, approaching the peddler at length, with decision thinly veiled by doubt, "that I shall hev to trade with you, though I don' know how to stop this mornin', for I'm right in the midst of butter-making. I wish you'd 'a happened along some other day."

"Wa'al," replied the peddler, laughing, "an' so I would, marm, ef I'd only known. But I don't see jest how I could hev, unless you'd 'a pasted it up on the fences, or had it put in the newspaper, or mebbe in the almanac."

He lounged smilingly against the door-casing, jingling his scales, and waiting for the woman to make up her mind.

She smiled unwillingly, with knitted brows. "Well," said she, "of course you ain't to blame. I guess I'll go an' pick up my rags, up in the garret. There's quite a lot of 'em, an'

it'll take some time. I don't know as you'll
want to wait."

"Lor', I don't keer," answered the peddler.
"I'd jest as soon rest a leetle as not. It's a
powerful hot mornin' for this time o' year, an'
I've got all the day afore me."

He came in and seated himself, with a loose-
jointed sprawl, on a chair near the door.

After Mrs. King had gone out, he sat a few
minutes eying the girl at the sink intently.
She kept steadily on with her work, though
there was a little embarrassment and uncertainty in her face.

"Would it be too much trouble ef I should
ask you to give me a tumbler of water, miss?"

She filled one of her hot, newly-washed
glasses with water from a pail standing on a
shelf at one end of the sink, and brought it
over to him. "It's cold," she said. "I drawed
it myself jest a few minutes ago, or I'd get
some right out of the well for you."

"This is all right, an' thanky kindly, miss;
it's proper good water."

He drained the glass, and carried it back to
her at the sink, where she had returned. She
did not seem to dare absent herself from her
dish-washing task an instant.

He set the empty glass down beside the pail;
then he caught hold of the girl by her slender
shoulders and faced her round towards him.
She turned pale, and gave a smothered scream.

"Thar! thar! don't you go to being afeard of
me," said the peddler. "I wouldn't hurt you
for the whole world. I jest want to take a
squar look at you. You're the worst-off-
lookin' little cretur I ever set my eyes on."

She looked up at him pitifully, still only
half reassured. There were inflamed circles
around her dilated blue eyes.

"You've been cryin', ain't you?"

The girl nodded meekly. "Please let me
go," she said.

"Yes, I'll let you go; but I'm a-goin' to ask
you a few questions first, an' I want you to
answer 'em, for I'll be hanged ef I ever see—
Ain't she good to you?"—indicating Mrs.
King with a wave of his hand towards the door
through which she had departed.

"Yes, she's good enough, I guess."

"Don't ever scold you, hey?"

"I don' know; I guess so, sometimes."

"Did this mornin', didn't she?"

"A little. I was kinder behind with the
work."

"Keeps you workin' pretty stiddy, don't
she?"

"Yes; thar's consider'ble to do this time o'
year."

"Cookin' for hired men, I s'pose, and butter
an' milk?"

"Yes."

"How long hev you been livin' here?"

"She took me when I was little."

"Do you do anything besides work?—go
round like other gals?—hev any good times?"

"Sometimes." She said it doubtfully, as if
casting about in her mind for reminiscences to
prove the truth of it.

"Git good wages?"

"A dollar a week sence I was eighteen. I
worked for my board an' close afore."

"Got any folks?"

"I guess I've got some brothers and sisters
somewhar. I don' know jest whar. Two of
'em went West, an' one is married somewhar
in York State. We was scattered when father
died. Thar was ten of us, an' we was awful
poor. Mis' King took me. I was the youngest;
'bout four, they said I was. I 'ain't never
known any folks but Mis' King."

The peddler walked up and down the kitchen floor twice; Sally kept on with her dishes;
then he came back to her.

"Look a-here," he said; "leave your dish-
washin' alone a minute. I want you to give me
a good look in the face, an' tell me what you
think of me."

She looked up shyly in his florid, freckled
face, with its high cheek-bones and scraggy
sandy mustache; then she plunged her hands
into the dish-tub again.

"I don' know," she said, bashfully.

"Well, mebbe you do know, only you can't
put it into words. Now jest take a look out the
window at my tin cart thar. That's all my
own, a private consarn. I ain't runnin' for no
company. I owns the cart an' horse, an' disposes of the rags, an' sells the tin, all on my
own hook. An' I'm a-doin' pretty well at it;
I'm a-layin' up a leetle money. I ain't got no
family. Now this was what I was a-comin' at:
s'pose you should jest leave the dishes, an' the
scoldin' woman, an' the butter, an' everything,
an' go a-ridin' off with me on my tin-cart. I
wouldn't know you, an' she wouldn't know
you, an' you wouldn't know yourself, in a
week. You wouldn't hev a bit of work to do,
but jest set up thar like a queen, a-ridin' and
seein' the country. For that's the way we'd
live, you know. I wouldn't hev you keepin'
house an' slavin'. We'd stop along the road
for vittles, and bring up at taverns nights.
What d'ye say to it?"

She stopped her dish-washing now, and
stood staring at him, her lips slightly parted
and her cheeks flushed.

"I know I ain't much in the way of looks," the peddler went on, "an' I'm older than you —I'm near forty—an' I've been merried afore. I don't s'pose you kin take a likin' to me right off, but you might arter a while. An' I'd take keer of you, you poor leetle thing. An' I don't b'lieve you know anything about how nice it is to be taken keer of, an' hev the hard, rough things kep' off by somebody that likes yer."

Still she said nothing, but stood staring at him.

"You ain't got no beau, hev you?" asked the peddler, as a sudden thought struck him.

"No." She shook her head, and her cheeks flushed redder.

"Well, what do you say to goin' with me? You'll hev to hurry up an' make up your mind, or the old lady'll be back."

The girl was almost foolishly ignorant of the world, but her instincts were as brave and innocent as an angel's. Tainted with the shiftless weariness and phlegm of her parents, in one direction she was vigorous enough.

Whether it was by the grace of God, or an inheritance from some far-off Puritan ancestor, the fire in whose veins had not burned low, she could see, if she saw nothing else, the distinction between right and wrong with awful plainness. Nobody had ever called her anything but a *good* girl. It was said with a disparagement, maybe, but it was always "a good girl."

She looked up at the man before her, her cheeks burning painfully hot, her eyes at once drooping and searching. "I—don't know jest —how you mean," she stammered. "I wouldn't go with a king, if—it wasn't to—go honest—"

The peddler's face flushed as red as hers. "Now, look a-here, little un," he said, "You jest listen, an' it's God's own truth; ef I hadn't 'a meant all right I wouldn't 'a come to you, but to some other gal, hansumer, an' pearter, an'—but, O Lord! I ain't that kind, anyway. What I want is to merry you honest, an' take keer of you, an' git that look off your face. I know it's awful sudden, an' it's askin' a good deal of a gal to trust so much in a fellow she never set eyes on afore. Ef you can't do it, I'll never blame you; but ef you kin, well, I don't b'lieve you'll ever be sorry. Most folks would think I was a fool, too, an' mebbe I am, but I wanted to take keer on you the minute I set eyes on you; an' afore I know it the wantin' to take keer on you will be growin' into lovin' you. Now you hurry and make up your mind, or she will be back."

Sally had little imagination, and a loving nature. In her heart, as in all girls' hearts, the shy, secret longing for a lover had strengthened with her growth, but she had never dreamed definitely of one. Now she surveyed the homely, scrawny, good-natured visage before her, and it filled well enough the longing nature had placed in her helpless heart. His appearance dispelled no previous illusion, for previous illusion there had been none. No one had ever spoken to her in this way. Rough and precipitate though it was, it was skilful wooing; for it made its sincerity felt, and a girl more sophisticated than this one could not have listened to it wholly untouched.

The erratic nature of the whole proceeding did not dismay her. She had no conscience for conventionalities; she was too simple; hers only provided for pure right and wrong. Strange to say, the possible injury she would do her mistress by leaving her in this way did not occur to her till afterwards. Now she looked at her lover, and began to believe in him, and as soon as she began to believe in him—poor, unattractive, ignorant little thing that she was!—she began to love just like other girls. All over her crimson face flashed the signs of yielding. The peddler saw and understood them.

"You will—won't you, little un?" he cried. Then, as her eyes drooped more before his, and her mouth quivered between a sob and a smile, he took a step forward and stretched out his arms towards her. Then he stepped back, and his arms fell.

"No," he cried, "I won't; I'd like to give you a hug, but I won't; I won't so much as touch that little lean hand of yours till you're my wife. You shall see I mean honest. But come along now, little un, or she will be back. I declar' ef I don't more'n half believe she's fell in a fit, or she'd ha' been back afore now. Come now, dear, be spry!"

"Now?" said Sally, in turn.

"Now! why, of course now: what's the use of waitin'? Mebbe you want to make some weddin' cake, but I reckon we'd better buy some over in Derby, for it might put the old lady out"; and the peddler chuckled. "Why, I'm jest a-goin' to stow you away in that 'ere tin-cart of mine—there's plenty of room, for I've been on the road a-sellin' nigh a week. An' then I'm a-goin' to drive out of this yard, arter I've traded with your missis, as innocent as the very innocentest lamb you ever see, an' I'm a-goin' to drive along a piece till it's safe; an' then you're a-goin' to git out an' set up on the seat alongside of me, an' we're goin' to keep on till we git to Derby, an' then we'll git married, jest as soon as we kin find a minister as wants to airn a ten-dollar bill."

"But," gasped Sally, "she'll ask whar I am."

"I'll fix that. You lay there in the cart an' hear what I say. Lor', I'd jest as soon tell her to her face, myself, what we was goin' to do, an' set you right up on the seat aside of me, afore her eyes; but she'd talk hard, most likely, an' you look scared enough now, an' you'd cry, an' your eyes would git redder; an' she might sass you so you'd be ready to back out, too. Women kin say hard things to other women, an' they ain't likely to understan' any woman but themselves trustin' a man overmuch. I reckon this is the best way." He went towards the door, and motioned her to come.

"But I want my bonnet."

"Never mind the bunnit; I'll buy you one in Derby."

"But I don't want to ride into Derby bareheaded," said Sally, almost crying.

"Well, I don't know as you do, little un, that's a fact; but hurry an' git the bunnit or she *will* be here. I thought I heard her a minute ago."

"Thar's a leetle money I've saved, too."

"Well, git that; we don't want to make the old lady vallyble presents, an' you kin buy yourself sugar-plums with it. But be spry."

She gave him one more scared glance, and hastened out of the room, her limp calico accommodating itself to every ungraceful hitch of her thin limbs and sharp hips.

"I'll git her a gown with puckers in the back," mused the peddler, gazing after her. Then he hastened out to his tin-cart, and arranged a vacant space in the body of it. He had a great-coat, which he spread over the floor.

"Thar, little un, let me put you right in," he whispered, when Sally emerged, her bonnet on, a figured green delaine shawl over her shoulders, and her little hoard in an old stocking dangling from her hand.

She turned round and faced him once more, her eyes like a child's peering into a dark room. "You mean *honest?*"

"Before God, I do, little un. Now git in quick, for she *is* comin'!"

He had to lift her in, for her poor little limbs were too weak to support her. They were not a moment too soon, for Mrs. King stood in the kitchen door a second later.

"Here! you ain't goin', air you?" she called out.

"No, marm; I jest stepped out to look arter my hoss; he was a trifle uneasy with the flies, an' thar was a yallar wasp buzzin' round." And the peddler stepped up to the door with an open and artless visage.

"Well, I didn't know but you'd git tired waitin'. You spoke so about not bein' in a hurry that I stopped to pick my white rags out from the colored ones. I knew they'd bring more ef I did. I'd been meanin' to hev 'em all sorted out afore a peddler come along. I thought I'd hev Sally pick 'em over last week, but she was sick. Why whar is Sally?"

"Who?"

"Sally—the girl that was washin' dishes when you come—she went to the door."

"Oh, the gal! I b'lieve I saw her go out the door a minute afore I went out to see to my hoss."

"Well, I'll call her, for she'll never git the dishes done, I guess, an' then we'll see about the rags."

Mrs. King strode towards the door, but the peddler stopped her.

"Now, marm, ef you please," said he, "I'd a leetle rayther you'd attend to business first, and call Sally arterwards, ef it's jest the same to you, for I am gittin' in a leetle of a hurry, and don't feel as ef I could afford to wait much longer."

"Well," said Mrs. King, reluctantly, "I don't suppose I orter ask you to, but I do hev such discouragin' times with help. I declare it don't seem to me as ef Sally ever would git them dishes done."

"Wa'al, it don't seem to me, from what I've see, that she ever will, either," said the peddler, as he gathered up Mrs. King's rag-bags and started for the cart.

"Anybody wouldn't need to watch her for more'n two minutes to see how slow she was," assented Mrs. King, following. "She's a girl I took when she was a baby to bring up, an' I've wished more'n fifty times I hadn't. She's a good girl enough, but she's awful slow—no snap to her. How much is them milk pans?"

Mrs. King was reputedly a sharp woman at a bargain. To trade with her was ordinarily a long job for any peddler, but to-day it was shortened through skilful management. The tinman came down with astonishing alacrity from his first price, at the merest suggestion from his customer, and, in a much shorter time than usual, she bustled into the house, her arms full of pans, and the radiant and triumphant conviction of a good bargain in her face.

The peddler whirled rapidly into his seat, and snatched up the lines; but even then he heard Mrs. King calling the girl as he rattled around the corner.

A quarter of a mile from Mrs. King's there was a house; a little beyond, the road ran through a considerable stretch of woods. This was a very thinly settled neighborhood. The peddler drove rapidly until he reached the woods; then he stopped, got down, and peered into the cart.

Sally's white face and round eyes peered piteously back at him.

"How're you gittin' along, little un?"

"Oh, let me git out an' go back?"

"Lor', no, little un, you don't want to go back now! Bless your heart, she's all primed for an awful sassin'. I tell you what 'tis, you sha'n't ride cooped up in thar any longer; you shall git out an' set up here with me. We'll keep our ears pricked up, an' ef we hear anybody comin', I'll stow you in the box under the seat afore you kin say Jack Robinson, an' thar ain't any houses for three mile."

He helped the poor shivering little thing out, and lifted her up to the high seat. When he had seated himself beside her, and gathered up the lines, he looked down at her curiously. Her bonnet the severe taste of Mrs. King had regulated. It was a brown straw, trimmed with brown ribbon. He eyed it disapprovingly. "I'll git you a white bunnit, sich as brides wear, in Derby," said he.

She blushed a little at that, and glanced up at him, a little grateful light over her face.

"You poor little thing!" said the peddler, and put out his hand towards her, then drew it back again.

Derby was a town with the prestige of a city. It was the centre of trade for a large circle of little country towns; its main street was crowded on a fair day, when the roads were good, with any quantity of nondescript and antediluvian-looking vehicles, and the owners thereof presented a wide variety of quaintness in person and attire.

So this eloping pair, the tall, bony, shambling man, and the thin, cowed-looking girl, her scant skirts slipping too far below her waist-line in the back, and following the movements of her awkward heels, excited no particular attention.

After the tin-cart had been put up in the hotel stable, and the two had been legally pronounced man and wife, or, specifically, Mr. and Mrs. Jake Russell, they proceeded on foot down the principal street, in which all the shops were congregated, in search of some amendments to the bride's attire.

If it was comparatively unnoticed, Sally was fully alive to the unsuitableness of her costume. She turned around, and followed with wistful eyes the prettily dressed girls they met. There was a great regret in her heart over her best gown, a brown delaine, with a flounce on the bottom, and a shiny back. She had so confidently believed in its grandeur so long, that now, seen by her mental vision, it hardly paled before these splendors of pleating and draping. It compared, advantageously, in her mind, with a brown velvet suit whose wearer looked with amusement in her eyes at Sally's forlorn figure. If she only had on her brown delaine, she felt that she could walk more confidently through this strangeness. But, nervously snatching her bonnet and her money, she had, in fact, heard Mrs. King's tread on the attic stairs, and had not dared to stop longer to secure it.

She knew they were out on a search for a new dress for her now, but she felt a sorrowful conviction that nothing could be found which could fully make up for the loss of her own beloved best gown. And then Sally was not very quick with her needle; she thought with dismay of the making up; the possibility of being aided by a dressmaker, or a ready-made costume, never entered her simple mind.

Jake shambled loosely down the street, and she followed meekly after him, a pace or two behind.

At length the peddler stopped before a large establishment, in whose windows some ready-made ladies' garments were displayed. "Here we air," said he, triumphantly.

Sally stepped weakly after him up the broad steps.

One particular dress in the window had excited the peddler's warm admiration. It was a trifle florid in design, with dashes of red here and there.

Sally eyed it a little doubtfully, when the clerk, at Jake's request, had taken it down to show them. Untutored as her taste was, she turned as naturally to quiet plumage as a wood-pigeon. The red slashes rather alarmed her. However, she said nothing against her husband's decision to purchase the dress. She turned pale at the price; it was nearly the whole of her precious store. But she took up her stocking-purse determinedly when Jake began examining his pocket-book.

"I pays for this," said she to the clerk, lifting up her little face to him with scared resolve.

"Why, no you don't, little un!" cried Jake, catching hold of her arm. "I'm a-goin' to pay for it, o' course. It's a pity ef I can't buy my own wife a dress."

Sally flushed all over her lean throat, but she resolutely held out the money.

"No," she said again, shaking her head obstinately, "*I* pays for it."

The peddler let her have her way then, though he bit his scraggy mustache with amaze and vexation as he watched her pay the bill, and stare with a sort of frightened wistfulness after her beloved money as it disappeared in the clerk's grasp.

When they emerged from the store, the new dress under his arm, he burst out, "What on airth made you do that, little un?"

"Other folks does that way. When they gits married they buys their own close, ef they kin."

"But it took pretty nearly all you'd got, didn't it?"

"That ain't no matter."

The peddler stared at her, half in consternation, half in admiration.

"Well," said he, "I guess you've got a little will o' your own, arter all, little un, an' I'm glad on't. A woman'd orter hev a little will to back her sweetness; it's all too soft an' slushly otherways. But I'll git even with you about the dress."

Which he proceeded to do by ushering his startled bride into the next dry-goods establishment, and purchasing a dress pattern of robin's-egg blue silk, and a delicate white bonnet. Sally, however, insisted on buying a plain sun-hat with the remainder of her own money. She was keenly alive to the absurdity and peril of that airy white structure on the top of a tin-cart.

The pair remained in Derby about a week; then they started forth on their travels, the blue silk, which a Derby dressmaker had made up after the prevailing mode, and the white bonnet, stowed away in a little new trunk in the body of the cart.

The peddler, having only himself to consult as to his motions, struck a new route now. Sally wished to keep away from her late mistress's vicinity. She had always a nervous dread of meeting her in some unlikely fashion. She wrote a curious little ill-spelled note to her, at the first town where they stopped after leaving Derby. Whether or not Mrs. King was consoled and mollified by it she never knew.

Their way still lay through a thinly settled country. The tin-peddler found readier customers in those farmers' wives who were far from stores. It was late spring. Often they rode for a mile or two through the lovely fresh woods, without coming to a single house.

The girl had never heard of Arcadia, but, all

unexpressed to herself, she was riding through it under gold-green boughs, to the sweet, broken jangling of tin-ware.

When they stopped to trade at the farmhouses, how proudly she sat, a new erectness in her slender back, and held her husband's horse tightly while he talked with the woman of the house, with now and then a careful glance towards her to see if she were safe. They always contrived to bring up, on a Sabbath-day, at some town where there was a place of worship. Then the blue silk and the white bonnet were taken reverently from their hiding-place, and Sally, full of happy consciousness, went to church with her husband in all her bridal bravery.

These two simple pilgrims, with all the beauty and grace in either of them turned only towards each other, and seen rightly only in each other's untutored, uncritical eyes, had journeyed together blissfully for about three months, when one afternoon Jake came out of a little country tavern, where they had proposed stopping for the night, with a pale face. Sally had been waiting on the cart outside until he should see if they could be accommodated. He jumped up beside her and took the lines.

"We'll go on to Ware," he said, in a dry voice; "it's only three mile further. They're full here."

Jake drove rapidly along, an awful look on his homely face, giving it the beauty of tragedy.

Sally kept looking up at him with pathetic wonder, but he never looked at her or spoke till they reached the last stretch of woods before Ware village. Then, just before they left the leafy cover, he slackened his speed a little, and threw his arm around her.

"See her, little un," he said, brokenly. "You've—got—consider'ble backbone, 'ain't you? Ef anything awful should happen, it wouldn't—kill you—you'd bear up?"

"Ef you told me to."

He caught at her words eagerly. "I would tell you to, little un—I do tell you to," he cried. "Ef anything awful ever should—happen—you'll remember that I told you to bear up."

"Yes, I'll bear up." Then she clung to him, trembling. "Oh, what is it, Jake?"

"Never mind now, little un," he answered; "perhaps nothin' awful's goin' to happen; I didn't say thar was. Chirk up an' give us a kiss, an' look at that 'ere sky thar, all pink an' yaller."

He tried to be cheerful, and comfort her with

joking endearments then, but the awful lines in his face stayed rigid and unchanged under the smiles.

Sally, however, had not much discernment, and little of the sensitiveness of temperament which takes impressions of coming evil. She soon recovered her spirits, and was unusually merry, for her, the whole evening, making, out of the excess of her innocence and happiness, several little jokes, which made Jake laugh loyally, and set his stricken face harder the next minute.

In the course of the evening he took out his pocket-book and displayed his money, and counted it jokingly. Then he spoke, in a careless, casual manner, of a certain sum he had deposited in a country bank, and how, if he were taken sick and needed it, Sally could draw it out as well as he. Then he spoke of the value of his stock in trade and horse and cart. When they went to bed that night he had told his wife, without her suspecting he was telling her, all about his affairs.

She fell asleep as easily as a child. Jake lay rigid and motionless till he had listened an hour to her regular breathing. Then he rose softly, lighted a candle, which he shaded from her face, and sat down at a little table with a pen and paper. He wrote painfully, with cramped muscles, his head bent on one side, following every movement of his pen, yet with a confident steadiness which seemed to show that all the subject-matter had been learned by heart beforehand. Then he folded the paper carefully around a little book which he took from his pocket, and approached the bed, keeping his face turned away from his sleeping wife. He laid the little package on his vacant pillow, still keeping his face aside.

Then he got into his clothes quickly, his head turned persistently from the bed, and opened the door softly, and went out, never once looking back.

When Sally awoke the next morning she found her husband gone, and the little package on the pillow. She opened it, more curious than frightened. There was a note folded around a bank-book. Sally spelled out the note laboriously, with whitening lips and dilating eyes. It was a singular composition, its deep feeling pricking through its illiterate stiffness.

"DEAR WIFE,—I've got to go and leve you. It's the only way. Ef I kin ever come back, I will. I told you bout my bizness last night. You'd better drive the cart to Derby to that Mister Arms I told you bout, an' he'll help you

sell it an' the hoss. Tell him your husband had to go away, an' left them orders. I've left you my bank-book, so you can git the money out of the bank the way I told you, an' my watch an' pocketbook is under the pillow. I left you all the money, cept what little I couldn't git long without. You'd better git boarded somewhar in Derby. You'll hev enough money to keep you awhile, an' I'll send you some more when thet's gone, ef I hev to work my fingers to the bone. Don't ye go to worryin' an' workin' hard. An' bear up. Don't forgit thet you promised me to bear up. When you gits to feelin' awful bad, an' you will, jest say it over to yourself—'He told me to bear up, an' I said as I would bear up.' Scuse poor writin' an' a bad pen.   "Yours till death,
                        JAKE RUSSELL."

When Sally had read the letter quite through, she sat still a few minutes on the edge of the bed, her lean, round-shouldered figure showing painfully through her clinging night-dress, her eyes staring straight before her.

Then she rose, dressed herself, put the bank-book, with the letter folded around it, and her husband's pocket-book, in her bosom, and went down-stairs quietly. Just before she went out her room door she paused with her hand on the latch, and muttered to herself, "He told me to bear up, an' I said as I would bear up."

She sought the landlord to pay her bill, and found that it was already paid, and that her recreant husband had smoothed over matters in one direction for her by telling the landlord that he was called away on urgent business, and that his wife was to take the tin-cart next morning, and meet him at a certain point.

So she drove away on her tin-cart in solitary state without exciting any of the wondering comments which would have been agony to her.

When she gathered up the lines and went rattling down the country road, if ever there was a zealous disciple of a new religion, she was one. Her prophet was her raw-boned peddler husband, and her creed and whole confession of faith his parting words to her.

She did not take the road to Derby; she had made up her mind about that as she sat on the edge of the bed after reading the letter. She drove straight along the originally prescribed route, stopping at the farmhouses, taking rags and selling tin, just as she had seen her husband do. There were much astonishment and many curious questions among her customers.

A woman running a tin-cart was an unprecedented spectacle, but she explained matters, with meek dignity, to all who questioned her. Her husband had gone away, and she was to attend to his customers until he should return. She could not always quite allay the suspicion that there must needs be something wrong, but she managed the trading satisfactorily, and gave good bargains, and so went on her way unmolested. But not a farmyard did she enter or leave without the words sounding in her beating little heart, like a strong, encouraging chant, "He told me to bear up, an' I said as I would bear up."

When her stock ran low, she drove to Derby to replenish it. Here she had opposition from the dealers, but her almost abnormal persistence overcame it.

She showed Jake's letter to Mr. Arms, the tin-dealer with whom she traded, and he urged her to take up with the advice in it, promising her a good bargain; but she was resolute.

Soon she found that she was doing as well as her husband had done, if not better. Her customers, after they had grown used to the novelty of a tinwoman, instead of a tinman, liked her. In addition to the regular stock, she carried various little notions needed frequently by housewives, such as pins, needles, thread, etc.

She oftener stayed at a farmhouse overnight than a tavern, and frequently stopped over at one a few days in severe weather.

After her trip to Derby she always carried a little pistol, probably more to guard Jake's watch and property than herself.

Whatever money she did not absolutely require for current expenses went to swell Jake's little hoard in the Derby bank. During the three years she kept up her lonely travelling little remittances came directed to her from time to time, in the care of Mr. Arms. When one came, Sally cried pitifully, and put it into the bank with the rest.

She never gave up expecting her husband. She never woke up one morning without the hope in her heart that he would come that day. Every golden dawn showed a fair possibility to her, and so did every red sunset. She scanned every distant, approaching figure in the sweet country roads with the half conviction in her heart that it was he, and when nearness dispelled the illusion, her heart bounded bravely back from its momentary sinking, and she looked ahead for another traveller.

Still he did not come for three years from the spring he went away. Except through the

money remittances, which gave no clew but the New York postmark on the envelope, she had not heard from him.

One June afternoon she, a poor lonely pilgrim, now without her beloved swain, driving through her old Arcadian solitudes, whose enchanted meaning was lost to her, heard a voice from behind her calling to her, above the jangling of tin, "Sally! Sally! Sally!"

She turned, and there he was, running after her. She turned her head quickly, and, stopping the horse, sat perfectly still, her breath almost gone with suspense. She did not dare look again for fear she had not seen aright.

The hurrying steps came nearer and nearer; she looked when they came abreast the cart. It was he. It always seemed to her that she would have died if it had not been, that time.

"Jake! Jake!"

"Oh, Sally!"

He was up on the seat before she could breathe again, and his arms around her.

"Jake, I did—bear up—I did."

"I know you did, little un. Mr. Arms told me all about it. Oh, you dear little un, you poor little un, a-drivin' round on this cart all alone!"

Jake laid his cheek against Sally's and sobbed.

"Don't cry, Jake. I've airned money, I hev, an' it's in the bank for you."

"Oh, you blessed little un! Sally, they said hard things 'bout me to you in Derby, didn't they?"

She started violently at that. There was one thing which had been said to her in Derby, and the memory of it had been a repressed terror ever since.

"Yes: they said as how you'd run off with— another woman."

"What did you say?"

"I didn't believe it."

"I did, Sally."

"Well, you've come back."

"Afore I married you I'd been married afore. By all that's good an' great, little un, I thought my wife was dead. Her folks said she was. When I come home from peddlin' one time, she was gone, an' they said she was off on a visit. I found out in a few weeks she'd run off with another fellow. I went off peddlin' agin without carin' much what become of me. 'Bout a year arterwards I saw her death in a paper, an' I wrote to her folks, an' they said 'twas true. They were a bad lot, the whole of 'em. I got took in. But she had a mighty pretty face, an' a tongue like honey, an' I s'pose I was green. Three year ago, when I went into that 'ere tavern in Grover, thar she was in the kitchen a-cookin'. The fellow she run off with had left her, an' she'd been trying to hunt me up. She was awful poor, an' had come across this place an' took it. She was allers a good cook, an' she suited the customers fust-rate. I guess they liked to see her pretty face 'round too, confound her!

"Well, little un, she knew me right off, an' hung on to me, an' cried, an' begged me to forgive her; and when she spied you a-settin' thar on the cart, she tore. I hed to hold her to keep her from goin' out an' tellin' you the whole story. I thought you'd die ef she did. I didn't know then how you could bear up, little un. *Ef* you 'ain't got backbone!"

"Jake, I did bear up."

"I know you did, you blessed little cretur. Well, she said ef I didn't leave you, an' go with her, she'd expose me. As soon as she found she'd got the weapons in her own hands, an' could hev me up for bigamy, she didn't cry so much, an' wa'n't quite so humble.

"Well, little un, then I run off an' left you. I couldn't stay with you ef you wa'n't my wife, an' 'twas all the way to stop her tongue. I met her that night, an' we went to New York. I got lodgin's for her; then I went to work in a box factory, an' supported her. I never went nigh her from one week's end to the other; I

couldn't do it without hevin' murder in my heart; but I kep' her in money. Every scrap I could save I sent to you, but I used to lay awake nights, worryin' for fear you'd want things. Well, it's all over. She died a month ago, an' I saw her buried."

"I knowed she was dead when you begun to tell about her, because you'd come."

"Yes, she's dead this time, an' I'm glad. Don't you look scared, little un. I hope the Lord'll forgive me, but *I'm glad*. She was a bad un, you know, Sally."

"Was she sorry?"

"I don' know, little un."

Sally's head was resting peacefully on Jake's shoulder; golden flecks of light sifted down on them through the rustling maple and locust boughs; the horse, with bent head, was cropping the tender young grass at the side of the road.

"Now we'll start up the horse, an' go to Derby an' git married over agin, Sally."

She raised her head suddenly, and looked up at him with eager eyes.

"Jake."

"Well, little un?"

"Oh, Jake, my blue silk dress an' the white bonnet is in the trunk in the cart jest the same, an' I can git 'em out, an' put 'em on under the trees thar, an' wear 'em to be married in!"

JAMES LANE ALLEN (1849–1925)

TWO GENTLEMEN OF KENTUCKY

(1888)

"The woods are hushed, their music is no more:
  The leaf is dead, the yearning passed away:
New leaf, new life—the days of frost are o'er:
  New life, new love, to suit the newer day."

THE WOODS ARE HUSHED

It was near the middle of the afternoon of an autumnal day, on the wide, grassy plateau of Central Kentucky.

The Eternal Power seemed to have quitted the universe and left all nature folded in the calm of the Eternal Peace. Around the pale-blue dome of the heavens a few pearl-colored clouds hung motionless, as though the wind had been withdrawn to other skies. Not a crimson leaf floated downward through the soft, silvery light that filled the atmosphere and created the sense of lonely, unimaginable spaces. This light overhung the far-rolling landscape of field and meadow and wood, crowning with faint radiance the remoter low-

swelling hill-tops and deepening into dreamy half-shadows on their eastern slopes. Nearer, it fell in a white flake on an unstirred sheet of water which lay along the edge of a mass of sombre-hued woodland, and nearer still it touched to spring-like brilliancy a level, green meadow on the hither edge of the water, where a group of Durham cattle stood with reversed flanks near the gleaming trunks of some leafless sycamores. Still nearer, it caught the top of the brown foliage of a little bent oak-tree and burned it into a silvery flame. It lit on the back and the wings of a crow flying heavily in the path of its rays, and made his blackness as white as the breast of a swan. In the immediate foreground, it sparkled in minute gleams along the stalks of the coarse, dead weeds that fell away from the legs and the flanks of a white horse, and slanted across the face of the rider and through the ends of his gray hair, which straggled from beneath his soft black hat.

The horse, old and patient and gentle, stood with low-stretched neck and closed eyes half asleep in the faint glow of the waning heat; and the rider, the sole human presence in all the field, sat looking across the silent autumnal landscape, sunk in reverie. Both horse and rider seemed but harmonious elements in the panorama of still-life, and completed the picture of a closing scene.

To the man it was a closing scene. From the rank, fallow field through which he had been riding he was now surveying, for the last time, the many features of a landscape that had been familiar to him from the beginning of memory. In the afternoon and the autumn of his age he was about to rend the last ties that bound him to his former life, and, like one who had survived his own destiny, turn his face towards a future that was void of everything he held significant or dear.

The Civil War had only the year before reached its ever-memorable close. From where he sat there was not a home in sight, as there was not one beyond the reach of his vision, but had felt its influence. Some of his neighbors had come home from its camps and prisons, aged or altered as though by half a lifetime of years. The bones of some lay whitening on its battlefields. Families, reassembled around their hearth-stones, spoke in low tones unceasingly of defeat and victory, heroism and death. Suspicion and distrust and estrangement prevailed. Former friends met each other on the turnpikes without speaking; brothers avoided each other in the streets of the neighboring town. The rich had grown poor; the poor had become rich. Many of the latter were preparing to move West. The negroes were drifting blindly hither and thither, deserting the country and flocking to the towns. Even the once united church of his neighborhood was jarred by the unstrung and discordant spirit of the times. At affecting passages in the sermons men grew pale and set their teeth fiercely; women suddenly lowered their black veils and rocked to and fro in their pews; for it is always at the bar of Conscience and before the very altar of God that the human heart is most wrung by a sense of its losses and the memory of its wrongs. The war had divided the people of Kentucky as the false mother would have severed the child.

It had not left the old man unscathed. His younger brother had fallen early in the conflict, borne to the end of his brief warfare by his impetuous valor; his aged mother had sunk under the tidings of the death of her latest-born; his sister was estranged from him by his political differences with her husband; his old family servants, men and women, had left him, and grass and weeds had already grown over the door-steps of the shut, noiseless cabins. Nay, the whole vast social system of the old régime had fallen, and he was henceforth but a useless fragment of the ruins.

All at once his mind turned from the cracked and smoky mirror of the times and dwelt fondly upon the scenes of the past. The silent fields around him seemed again alive with the negroes, singing as they followed the ploughs down the corn-rows or swung the cradles through the bearded wheat. Again, in a frenzy of merriment, the strains of the old fiddles issued from crevices of cabin-doors to the rhythmic beat of hands and feet that shook the rafters and the roof. Now he was sitting on his porch, and one little negro was blacking his shoes, another leading his saddle-horse to the stiles, a third bringing his hat, and a fourth handing him a glass of ice-cold sangaree; or now he lay under the locust-trees in his yard, falling asleep in the drowsy heat of the summer afternoon, while one waved over him a bough of pungent walnut leaves, until he lost consciousness and by-and-by awoke to find that they both had fallen asleep side by side on the grass and that the abandoned fly-brush lay full across his face.

From where he sat also were seen slopes on which picnics were danced under the broad shade of maples and elms in June by those whom death and war had scattered like the transitory leaves that once had sheltered them. In this direction lay the district schoolhouse where on Friday evenings there were wont to be speeches and debates; in that, lay the blacksmith's shop where of old he and his neighbors had met on horseback of Saturday afternoons to hear the news, get the mails, discuss elections, and pitch quoits. In the valley beyond stood the church at which all had assembled on calm Sunday mornings like the members of one united family. Along with these scenes went many a chastened reminiscence of bridal and funeral and simpler events that had made up the annals of his country life.

The reader will have a clearer insight into the character and past career of Colonel Romulus Fields by remembering that he represented a fair type of that social order which had existed in rank perfection over the bluegrass plains of Kentucky during the final decades of the old régime. Perhaps of all agriculturists in the United States the inhabitants of that region had spent the most nearly idyllic life, on account of the beauty of the climate, the richness of the land, the spacious comfort of their homes, the efficiency of their negroes, and the characteristic contentedess of their dispositions. Thus nature and history combined to make them a peculiar class, a cross between the aristocratic and the bucolic, being as simple as shepherds and as proud as kings, and not seldom exhibiting among both men and women types of character which were as remarkable for pure, tender, noble states of feeling as they were commonplace in powers and cultivation of mind.

It was upon this luxurious social growth that the war naturally fell as a killing frost, and upon no single specimen with more blighting power than upon Colonel Fields. For destiny had quarried and chiselled him, to serve as an ornament in the barbaric temple of human bondage. There *were* ornaments in that temple, and he was one. A slave-holder with Southern sympathies, a man educated not beyond the ideas of his generation, convinced that slavery was an evil, yet seeing no present way of removing it, he had of all things been a model master. As such he had gone on record in Kentucky, and no doubt in a Higher Court; and as such his efforts had been put forth to secure the passage of many of those milder laws for which his State was distinguished. Often, in those dark days, his face, ânxious and sad, was to be seen amid the throng that surrounded the blocks on which slaves were sold at auction; and more than one poor wretch he had bought to save him from separation from his family or from being sold into the Southern plantations—afterwards riding far and near to find him a home on one of the neighboring farms.

But all those days were over. He had but to place the whole picture of the present beside the whole picture of the past to realize what the contrast meant for him.

At length he gathered the bridle reins from the neck of his old horse and turned his head homeward. As he rode slowly on, every spot gave up its memories. He dismounted when he came to the cattle and walked among them, stroking their soft flanks and feeling in the palm of his hand the rasp of their salt-loving tongues; on his sideboard at home was many a silver cup which told of premiums on cattle at the great fairs. It was in this very pond that as a boy he had learned to swim on a cherry rail. When he entered the woods, the sight of the walnut-trees and the hickory-nut trees, loaded on the topmost branches, gave him a sudden pang.

Beyond the woods he came upon the garden, which he had kept as his mother had left it— an old-fashioned garden with an arbor in the centre, covered with Isabella grape-vines on one side and Catawba on the other; with walks branching thence in four directions, and along them beds of jump-up-johnnies, sweet williams, daffodils, sweet-peas, larkspur, and thyme, flags and the sensitive-plant, celestial and maiden's-blush roses. He stopped and looked over the fence at the very spot where he had found his mother on the day when the news of the battle came.

She had been kneeling, trowel in hand, driving away vigorously at the loamy earth, and, as she saw him coming, had risen and turned towards him her face with the ancient pink bloom on her clear cheeks and the light of a pure, strong soul in her gentle eyes. Overcome by his emotions, he had blindly faltered out the words, "Mother, John was among the killed!" For a moment she had looked at him as though stunned by a blow. Then a violent flush had overspread her features, and then an ashen pallor; after which, with a sudden proud dilating of her form as though with joy, she had sunk down like the tenderest of her lily-stalks, cut from its root.

Beyond the garden he came to the empty cabin and the great wood-pile. At this hour it used to be a scene of hilarious activity—the little negroes sitting perched in chattering groups on the topmost logs or playing leap-frog in the dust, while some picked up baskets of chips or dragged a back-log into the cabins.

At last he drew near the wooden stiles and saw the large house of which he was the solitary occupant. What darkened rooms and noiseless halls! What beds, all ready, that nobody now came to sleep in, and cushioned old chairs that nobody rocked! The house and the contents of its attic, presses, and drawers could have told much of the history of Kentucky from almost its beginning; for its foundations had been laid by his father near the beginning of the century, and through its doors had passed a long train of forms, from the veterans of the Revolution to the soldiers of the Civil War. Old coats hung up in closets; old dresses folded away in drawers; saddle-bags and buckskin-leggins; hunting-jackets, powder-horns, and militiamen hats; looms and knitting-needles; snuffboxes and reticules—what a treasure-house of the past it was! And now the only thing that had the springs of life within its bosom was the great, sweet-voiced clock, whose faithful face had kept unchanged amid all the swift pageantry of changes.

He dismounted at the stiles and handed the

reins to a gray-haired negro, who had hobbled
up to receive them with a smile and a gesture
of the deepest respect.

"Peter," he said, very simply, "I am going
to sell the place and move to town. I can't live
here any longer."

With these words he passed through the
yard-gate, walked slowly up the broad pavement, and entered the house.

MUSIC NO MORE

On the disappearing form of the colonel was
fixed an ancient pair of eyes that looked out at
him from behind a still more ancient pair of
silver-rimmed spectacles with an expression of
indescribable solicitude and love.

These eyes were set in the head of an old
gentleman—for such he was—named Peter
Cotton, who was the only one of the colonel's
former slaves that had remained inseparable
from his person and his altered fortunes. In
early manhood Peter had been a wood-chop-
per; but he had one day had his leg broken by
the limb of a falling tree, and afterwards, out
of consideration for his limp, had been made
supervisor of the wood-pile, gardener, and a
sort of nondescript servitor of his master's
luxurious needs.

Nay, in larger and deeper characters must
his history be writ, he having been, in days
gone by, one of those ministers of the gospel
whom conscientious Kentucky masters often
urged to the exercise of spiritual functions in
behalf of their benighted people. In the course
of preparation for this august work, Peter had
learned to read and had come to possess a well-
chosen library of three several volumes—*Webster's Spelling-Book*, *The Pilgrim's Progress*,
and the Bible. But even these unusual acquisitions he deemed not enough; for being
touched with a spark of poetic fire from heav-
en, and fired by the African's fondness for all
that is conspicuous in dress, he had conceived
for himself the creation of a unique garment
which should symbolize in perfection the
claims and consolations of his apostolic office.
This was nothing less than a sacred blue-jeans
coat that he had had his old mistress make
him, with very long and spacious tails, whereon, at his further direction, she embroidered
sundry texts of Scripture which it pleased him
to regard as the fit visible annunciations of his
holy calling. And inasmuch as his mistress,
who had had the coat woven on her own looms
from the wool of her finest sheep, was, like
other gentlewomen of her time, rarely skilled
in the accomplishments of the needle, and was
moreover in full sympathy with the piety of

his intent, she wrought of these passages a
border enriched with such intricate curves,
marvellous flourishes, and harmonious letter-
ings, that Solomon never reflected the glory in
which Peter was arrayed whenever he put it
on. For after much prayer that the Almighty
wisdom would aid his reason in the difficult
task of selecting the most appropriate texts,
Peter had chosen seven—one for each day in
the week—with such tact, and no doubt heavenly guidance, that when braided together
they did truly constitute an eloquent epitome
of Christian duty, hope, and pleading.

From first to last they were as follows:
"Woe is unto me if I preach not the gospel";
"Servants, be obedient to them that are your
masters according to the flesh"; "Come unto
me, all ye that labour and are heavy laden";
"Consider the lilies of the field, how they
grow; they toil not, neither do they spin";
"Now abideth faith, hope, and charity, these
three; but the greatest of these is charity";
"I would not have you to be ignorant, brethren, concerning them which are asleep"; "For
as in Adam all die, even so in Christ shall all
be made alive." This concatenation of texts
Peter wished to have duly solemnized, and
therefore, when the work was finished, he further requested his mistress to close the entire
chain with the word "Amen," introduced in
some suitable place.

But the only spot now left vacant was one
of a few square inches, located just where the
coat-tails hung over the end of Peter's spine;
so that when any one stood full in Peter's
rear, he could but marvel at the sight of so
solemn a word emblazoned in so unusual a
locality.

Panoplied in this robe of righteousness, and
with a worn leathern Bible in his hand, Peter
used to go around of Sundays, and during the
week, by night, preaching from cabin to cabin
the gospel of his heavenly Master.

The angriest lightnings of the sultriest skies
often played amid the darkness upon those
sacred coat-tails and around that girdle of
everlasting texts, as though the evil spirits of
the air would fain have burned them and
scattered their ashes on the roaring winds.
The slow-sifting snows of winter whitened
them as though to chill their spiritual fires;
but winter and summer, year after year, in
weariness of body, often in sore distress of
mind, for miles along this lonely road and for
miles across that rugged way, Peter trudged
on and on, withal perhaps as meek a spirit as
ever grew foot-sore in the paths of its Master.
Many a poor over-burdened slave took fresh

heart and strength from the sight of that celestial raiment; many a stubborn, rebellious spirit, whose flesh but lately quivered under the lash, was brought low by its humble teaching; many a worn-out old frame, racked with pain in its last illness, pressed a fevered lip to its hopeful hem; and many a dying eye closed in death peacefully fixed on its immortal pledges.

When Peter started abroad, if a storm threatened, he carried an old cotton umbrella of immense size; and as the storm burst, he gathered the tails of his coat carefully up under his armpits that they might be kept dry. Or if caught by a tempest without his umbrella, he would take his coat off and roll it up inside out, leaving his body exposed to the fury of the elements. No care, however, could keep it from growing old and worn and faded; and when the slaves were set free and he was called upon by the interposition of Providence to lay it finally aside, it was covered by many a patch and stain as proofs of its devoted usage.

One after another the colonel's old servants, gathering their children about them, had left him, to begin their new life. He bade them all a kind good-bye, and into the palm of each silently pressed some gift that he knew would soon be needed. But no inducement could make Peter or Phillis, his wife, budge from their cabin. "Go, Peter! Go, Phillis!" the colonel had said time and again. "No one is happier that you are free than I am; and you can call on me for what you need to set you up in business." But Peter and Phillis asked to stay with him. Then suddenly, several months before the time at which this sketch opens, Phillis had died, leaving the colonel and Peter as the only relics of that populous life which had once filled the house and the cabins. The colonel had succeeded in hiring a woman to do Phillis's work; but her presence was a strange note of discord in the old domestic harmony, and only saddened the recollections of its vanished peace.

Peter had a short, stout figure, dark-brown skin, smooth-shaven face, eyes round, deep-set and wide apart, and a short, stub nose which dipped suddenly into his head, making it easy for him to wear the silver-rimmed spectacles left him by his old mistress. A peculiar conformation of the muscles between the eyes and the nose gave him the quizzical expression of one who is about to sneeze, and this was heightened by a twinkle in the eyes which seemed caught from the shining of the inner sun upon his tranquil heart.

Sometimes, however, his face grew sad enough. It was sad on this afternoon while he watched the colonel walk slowly up the pavement, well overgrown with weeds, and enter the house, which the setting sun touched with the last radiance of the finished day.

NEW LIFE

About two years after the close of the war, therefore, the colonel and Peter were to be found in Lexington, ready to turn over a new leaf in the volumes of their lives, which already had an old-fashioned binding, a somewhat musty odor, and but a few unwritten leaves remaining.

After a long, dry summer you may have seen two gnarled old apple-trees, that stood with interlocked arms on the western slope of some quiet hill-side, make a melancholy show of blooming out again in the autumn of the year and dallying with the idle buds that mock their sapless branches. Much the same was the belated, fruitless efflorescence of the colonel and Peter.

The colonel had no business habits, no political ambition, no wish to grow richer. He was too old for society, and without near family ties. For some time he wandered through the streets like one lost—sick with yearning for the fields and woods, for his cattle, for familiar faces. He haunted Cheapside and the court-house square, where the farmers always assembled when they came to town; and if his eye lighted on one, he would button-hole him on the street-corner and lead him into a grocery and sit down for a quiet chat. Sometimes he would meet an aimless, melancholy wanderer like himself, and the two would go off and discuss over and over again their departed days; and several times he came unexpectedly upon some of his old servants who had fallen into bitter want, and who more than repaid him for the help he gave by contrasting the hardships of a life of freedom with the ease of their shackled years.

In the course of time, he could but observe that human life in the town was reshaping itself slowly and painfully, but with resolute energy. The colossal structure of slavery had fallen, scattering its ruins far and wide over the State; but out of the very débris was being taken the material to lay the deeper foundations of the new social edifice. Men and women as old as he were beginning life over and trying to fit themselves for it by changing the whole attitude and habit of their minds—by taking on a new heart and spirit. But when a great building falls, there is always some rubbish, and the colonel and others like him were part of this. Henceforth they possessed only an antiquarian sort of interest, like the stamped bricks of Nebuchadnezzar.

Nevertheless he made a show of doing something, and in a year or two opened on Cheapside a store for the sale of hardware and agricultural implements. He knew more about the latter than anything else; and, furthermore, he secretly felt that a business of this kind would enable him to establish in town a kind of headquarters for the farmers. His account-books were to be kept on a system of twelve months' credit; and he resolved that if one of his customers couldn't pay then, it would make no difference.

Business began slowly. The farmers dropped in and found a good lounging-place. On county-court days, which were great market-days for the sale of sheep, horses, mules, and cattle in front of the colonel's door, they swarmed in from the hot sun and sat around on the counter and the ploughs and machines till the entrance was blocked to other customers.

When a customer did come in, the colonel, who was probably talking with some old acquaintance, would tell him just to look around and pick out what he wanted and the price would be all right. If one of those acquaintances asked for a pound of nails, the colonel would scoop up some ten pounds and say, "I reckon that's about a pound, Tom." He had never seen a pound of nails in his life; and if one had been weighed on his scales, he would have said the scales were wrong.

He had no great idea of commercial despatch. One morning a lady came in for some carpet-tacks, an article that he had forgotten to lay in. But he at once sent off an order for enough to have tacked a carpet pretty well all over Kentucky; and when they came, two weeks later, he told Peter to take her up a dozen papers with his compliments. He had laid in, however, an ample and especially fine assortment of pocket-knives, for that instrument had always been to him one of gracious and very winning qualities. Then when a friend dropped in he would say, "General, don't you need a new pocket-knife?" and, taking out one, would open all the blades and commend the metal and the handle. The "general" would inquire the price, and the colonel, having shut the blades, would hand it to him, saying in a careless, fond way, "I reckon I won't charge you anything for that." His mind could not come down to the low level of such ignoble barter, and he gave away the whole case of knives.

These were the pleasanter aspects of his business life, which did not lack as well its tedium and crosses. Thus there were many dark stormy days when no one he cared to see came in; and he then became rather a pathetic figure, wandering absently around amid the symbols of his past activity, and stroking the ploughs, like dumb companions. Or he would stand at the door and look across at the old court-house, where he had seen many a slave sold and had listened to the great Kentucky orators.

But what hurt him most was the talk of the new farming and the abuse of the old which he was forced to hear; and he generally refused to handle the improved implements and mechanical devices by which labor and waste were to be saved.

Altogether he grew tired of "the thing," and sold out at the end of the year with a loss of over a thousand dollars, though he insisted he had done a good business.

As he was then seen much on the streets again and several times heard to make remarks in regard to the sidewalks, gutters, and crossings, when they happened to be in bad condition, the *Daily Press* one morning published a card stating that if Colonel Romulus Fields would consent to make the race for mayor he would receive the support of many Democrats, adding a tribute to his virtues and his influential past. It touched the colonel, and he walked down-town with a rather commanding figure the next morning. But it pained him to see how many of his acquaintances returned his salutations very coldly; and just as he was passing the Northern Bank he met the young opposition candidate—a little red-haired fellow, walking between two ladies, with a rose-bud in his button-hole—who refused to speak at all, but made the ladies laugh by some remark he uttered as the colonel passed. The card had been inserted humorously, but he took it seriously; and when his friends found this out, they rallied round him. The day of election drew near. They told him he must buy votes. He said he wouldn't buy a vote to be mayor of the New Jerusalem. They told him he must "mix" and "treat." He refused. Foreseeing he had no chance, they besought him to withdraw. He said he would not. They told him he wouldn't poll twenty votes. He replied that *one* would satisfy him, provided it was neither begged nor bought. When his defeat was announced, he accepted it as another evidence that he had no part in the present— no chance of redeeming his idleness.

A sense of this weighed heavily on him at times; but it is not likely that he realized how pitifully he was undergoing a moral shrinkage in consequence of mere disuse. Actually, extinction had set in with him long prior to dissolution, and he was dead years before his heart ceased beating. The very basic virtues on which had rested his once spacious and stately character were now but the mouldy corner-stones of a crumbling ruin.

It was a subtle evidence of deterioration in manliness that he had taken to dress. When he had lived in the country, he had never dressed up unless he came to town. When he had moved to town, he thought he must remain dressed up all the time; and this fact first fixed his attention on a matter which afterwards began to be loved for its own sake. Usually he wore a Derby hat, a black diagonal coat, gray trousers, and a white necktie. But the article of attire in which he took chief pleasure was hose; and the better to show the gay colors of these, he wore low-cut shoes of the finest calf-skin, turned up at the toes. Thus his feet kept pace with the present, however far his head may have lagged in the past; and it may be that this stream of fresh fashions, flowing perennially over his lower extremities like water about the roots of a tree, kept him from drying up altogether.

Peter always polished his shoes with too much blacking, perhaps thinking that the more the blacking the greater the proof of love. He wore his clothes about a season and a half —having several suits—and then passed them on to Peter, who, foreseeing the joy of such an inheritance, bought no new ones. In the act of transferring them the colonel made no comment until he came to the hose, from which he seemed unable to part without a final tribute of esteem, as: "These are fine, Peter;" or, "Peter, these are nearly as good as new." Thus, Peter, too, was dragged through the whims of fashion. To have seen the colonel walking about his grounds and garden followed by Peter, just a year and a half behind in dress and a yard and a half behind in space, one might well have taken the rear figure for the colonel's double, slightly the worse for wear, somewhat shrunken, and cast into a heavy shadow.

Time hung so heavily on his hands at night that with a happy inspiration he added a dress suit to his wardrobe, and accepted the first invitation to an evening party.

He grew excited as the hour approached, and dressed in a great fidget for fear he should be too late.

"How do I look, Peter?" he inquired at length, surprised at his own appearance.

"Splendid, Marse Rom," replied Peter, bringing in the shoes with more blacking on them than ever before.

"I think," said the colonel, apologetically— "I think I'd look better if I'd put a little powder on. I don't know what makes me so red in the face."

But his heart began to sink before he reached his hostess's, and he had a fearful sense of being the observed of all observers as he slipped through the hall and passed rapidly up to the gentlemen's room. He stayed there after the others had gone down, bewildered and lonely, dreading to go down himself. By-and-by the musicians struck up a waltz, and with a little cracked laugh at his own performance he cut a few shines of an unremembered pattern; but his ankles snapped audibly, and he suddenly stopped with the thought of what Peter would say if he should catch him at these antics. Then he boldly went down-stairs.

He had touched the new human life around him at various points: as he now stretched out his arms towards its society, for the first time he completely realized how far removed it was from him. Here he saw a younger generation —the flowers of the new social order—sprung from the very soil of fraternal battlefields, but blooming together as the emblems of oblivious peace. He saw fathers, who had fought madly on opposite sides, talking quietly in corners as they watched their children dancing, or heard them toasting their old generals and their campaigns over their champagne in the supper-room. He was glad of it; but it made him feel, at the same time, that, instead of treading the velvety floors, he ought to step up and take his place among the canvases of old-time portraits that looked down from the walls.

The dancing he had done had been not under the blinding glare of gaslight, but by the glimmer of tallow-dips and star-candles and the ruddy glow of cavernous firesides—not to the accompaniment of an orchestra of wind-instruments and strings, but to a chorus of girls' sweet voices, as they trod simpler measures, or to the maddening sway of a gray-haired negro fiddler standing on a chair in the chimney-corner. Still, it is significant to note that his saddest thought, long after leaving, was that his shirt bosom had not lain down smooth, but stuck out like a huge cracked egg-shell; and that when, in imitation of the others, he had laid his white silk handkerchief across his bosom inside his vest, it had slipped out during the evening, and had been found by him, on confronting a mirror, flapping over his stomach like a little white masonic apron.

"Did you have a nice time, Marse Rom?" inquired Peter, as they drove home through the darkness.

"Splendid time, Peter, splendid time," replied the colonel, nervously.

"Did you dance any, Marse Rom?"

"I didn't *dance*. Oh, I *could* have danced if I'd *wanted* to; but I didn't."

Peter helped the colonel out of the carriage with pitying gentleness when they reached home. It was the first and only party.

Peter also had been finding out that his occupation was gone.

Soon after moving to town, he had tendered his pastoral services to one of the fashionable churches of the city—not because it was fashionable, but because it was made up of his brethren. In reply he was invited to preach a trial sermon, which he did with gracious unction.

It was a strange scene, as one calm Sunday morning he stood on the edge of the pulpit, dressed in a suit of the colonel's old clothes, with one hand in his trousers-pocket, and his lame leg set a little forward at an angle familiar to those who know the statues of Henry Clay.

How self-possessed he seemed, yet with what a rush of memories did he pass his eyes slowly over that vast assemblage of his emancipated people! With what feelings must he have contrasted those silk hats, and walking-canes, and broadcloths; those gloves and satins, laces and feathers, jewelry and fans—that whole many-colored panorama of life—with the weary, sad, and sullen audiences that had often heard him of old under the forest trees or by the banks of some turbulent stream!

In a voice husky, but heard beyond the flirtation of the uttermost pew, he took his text: "Consider the lilies of the field, how they grow; they toil not, neither do they spin." From this he tried to preach a new sermon, suited to the newer day. But several times the thoughts of the past were too much for him, and he broke down with emotion.

The next day a grave committee waited on him and reported that the sense of the congregation was to call a colored gentleman from Louisville. Private objections to Peter were that he had a broken leg, wore Colonel Fields's second-hand clothes, which were too big for him, preached in the old-fashioned way, and lacked self-control and repose of manner.

Peter accepted his rebuff as sweetly as Socrates might have done. Humming the burden of an old hymn, he took his righteous coat from a nail in the wall and folded it away in a little brass-nailed deer-skin trunk, laying over it the spelling-book and the *Pilgrim's Progress*, which he had ceased to read. Thenceforth his relations to his people were never intimate, and even from the other servants of the colonel's household he stood apart. But the colonel took Peter's rejection greatly to heart, and the next morning gave him the new silk socks he had worn at the party. In paying his servants the colonel would sometimes say, "Peter, I reckon I'd better begin to pay you a salary; that's the style now." But Peter would turn off, saying he didn't "have no use fur no salary."

Thus both of them dropped more and more out of life, but as they did so drew more and more closely to each other. The colonel had bought a home on the edge of the town, with some ten acres of beautiful ground surrounding. A high osage-orange hedge shut it in, and forest trees, chiefly maples and elms, gave to the lawn and house abundant shade. Wild-grape vines, the Virginia-creeper, and the climbing-oak swung their long festoons from summit to summit, while honeysuckles, clematis, and the Mexican-vine clambered over arbors and trellises, or along the chipped stone of the low, old-fashioned house. Just outside the door of the colonel's bedroom slept an ancient, broken sundial.

The place seemed always in half-shadow, with hedgerows of box, clumps of dark holly, darker firs half a century old, and aged, crape-like cedars.

It was in the seclusion of this retreat, which looked almost like a wild bit of country set down on the edge of the town, that the colonel and Peter spent more of their time as they fell farther in the rear of onward events. There were no such flower-gardens in the city, and pretty much the whole town went thither for its flowers, preferring them to those that were to be had for a price at the nurseries.

There was, perhaps, a suggestion of pathetic humor in the fact that it should have called on the colonel and Peter, themselves so nearly defunct, to furnish the flowers for so many funerals; but, it is certain, almost weekly the two old gentlemen received this chastening admonition of their all-but-spent mortality. The colonel cultivated the rarest fruits also, and had under glass varieties that were not friendly to the climate; so that by means of the fruits and flowers there was established a pleasant social bond with many who otherwise would never have sought them out.

But others came for better reasons. To a few deep-seeing eyes the colonel and Peter were ruined landmarks on a fading historic landscape, and their devoted friendship was the last steady burning-down of that pure flame of love which can never again shine out in the future of the two races. Hence a softened charm invested the drowsy quietude of that shadowy paradise in which the old master without a slave and the old slave without a master still kept up a brave pantomime of their obsolete relations. No one ever saw in their intercourse aught but the finest courtesy, the most delicate consideration. The very tones of their voices in addressing each other were as good as sermons on gentleness, their antiquated playfulness as melodious as the babble of distant water. To be near them was to be exorcised of evil passions.

The sun of their day had indeed long since set, but like twin clouds lifted high and motionless into some far quarter of the gray twilight skies, they were still radiant with the glow of the invisible orb.

Henceforth the colonel's appearances in public were few and regular. He went to church on Sundays, where he sat on the edge of the choir in the centre of the building, and sang an ancient bass of his own improvisation to the older hymns, and glanced furtively around to see whether any one noticed that he could not sing the new ones. At the Sunday-school picnics the committee of arrangements allowed him to carve the mutton, and after dinner to swing the smallest children gently beneath the trees. He was seen on Commencement Day at Morrison Chapel, where he always gave his bouquet to the valedictorian. It was the speech of that young gentleman that always touched him, consisting as it did of farewells.

In the autumn he might sometimes be noticed sitting high up in the amphitheatre at the fair, a little blue around the nose, and looking absently over into the ring where the judges were grouped around the music-stand. Once he had strutted around as a judge himself, with a blue ribbon in his button-hole, while the band played "Sweet Alice, Ben Bolt," and "Gentle Annie." The ring seemed full of young men now, and no one even thought of offering him the privileges of the grounds. In his day the great feature of the exhibition had been cattle; now everything was turned into a horse-show. He was always glad to get home again to Peter, his true yoke-fellow. For just as two old oxen—one white and one black— that have long toiled under the same yoke will, when turned out to graze at last in the wildest pasture, come and put themselves horn to horn and flank to flank, so the colonel and Peter were never so happy as when ruminating side by side.

NEW LOVE

In their eventless life the slightest incident acquired the importance of a history. Thus, one day in June, Peter discovered a young couple love-making in the shrubbery, and with deepest agitation reported the fact to the colonel.

Never before, probably, had the fluttering of the dear god's wings brought more dismay than to these ancient involuntary guardsmen of his hiding-place. The colonel was at first for breaking up what he considered a piece of underhand proceedings, but Peter reasoned stoutly that if the pair were driven out they would simply go to some other retreat; and without getting the approval of his conscience to this view, the colonel contented himself with merely repeating that they ought to go straight and tell the girl's parents. Those parents lived just across the street outside his grounds. The young lady he knew very well himself, having a few years before given her the privilege of making herself at home among his flowers. It certainly looked hard to drive her out now, just when she was making the best possible use of his kindness and her opportunity. Moreover, Peter walked down street and ascertained that the young fellow was an energetic farmer living a few miles from town, and son of one of the colonel's former friends; on both of which accounts the latter's heart went out to him. So when, a few days later, the colonel, followed by Peter, crept up breathlessly and peeped through the bushes at the pair strolling along the shady perfumed walks, and so plainly happy in that happiness which comes but once in a lifetime, they not only abandoned the idea of betraying the secret, but afterwards kept away from that part of the grounds, lest they should be an interruption.

"Peter," stammered the colonel, who had been trying to get the words out for three days, "do you suppose he has already—*asked* her?"

"Some's pow'ful quick on de trigger, en some's mighty slow," replied Peter, neutrally. "En some," he added, exhaustively, "don't use de trigger 't all!"

"I always thought there had to be asking done by *somebody*," remarked the colonel, a little vaguely.

"I nuver axed Phillis!" exclaimed Peter, with a certain air of triumph.

"Did Phillis ask *you*, Peter?" inquired the colonel, blushing and confidential.

"No, no, Marse Rom! I couldn't er stood dat from no 'oman!" replied Peter, laughing and shaking his head.

The colonel was sitting on the stone steps in front of the house, and Peter stood below, leaning against a Corinthian column, hat in hand, as he went on to tell his love-story.

"Hit all happ'n dis way, Marse Rom. We wuz gwine have pra'r-meetin', en I 'lowed to walk home wid Phillis en ax 'er on de road. I been 'lowin' to ax 'er heap o' times befo', but I ain' jes nuver done so. So I says to myse'f, says I, 'I jes mek my sermon to-night kiner lead up to whut I gwine tell Phillis on de road home.' So I tuk my tex' from de *lef'* tail o' my coat: 'De greates' o' dese is charity'; caze I knowed charity wuz same ez love. En all de time I wuz preachin' an' glorifyin' charity en identifyin' charity wid love, I couldn' he'p thinkin' 'bout what I gwine say to Phillis on de road home. Dat mek me feel better; en de better I *feel*, de better I *preach*, so hit boun' to mek my *heahehs* feel better likewise—Phillis 'mong um. So Phillis she jes sot dah listenin' en listenin' en lookin' like we wuz a'ready on de road home, till I got so wuked up in my feelin's I jes knowed de time wuz come. By-en-by, I had n' mo' 'n done preachin' en wuz lookin' roun' to git my Bible en my hat, 'fo' up popped dat big Charity Green, who been settin' 'longside o' Phillis en tekin' ev'y las' thing I said to *her*se'f. En she tuk hole o' my han' en squeeze 'it, en say she felt mos' like shoutin'. En 'fo' I knowed it, I jes see Phillis wrap 'er shawl roun' 'er head en tu'n 'er nose up at me right quick en flip out de dooh. De dogs howl mighty mou'nful when I walk home by myse'f *dat* night," added Peter, laughing to himself, "en I ain' preach dat sermon no mo' tell atter me en Phillis wuz married.

"Hit wuz long time," he continued, "fo' Phillis come to heah me preach any mo'. But 'long 'bout de nex' fall we had big meetin', en heap mo' um j'ined. But Phillis, she ain't nuver j'ined yit. I preached mighty nigh all roun' my coat-tails till I say to myse'f, D' ain't but one tex' lef', en I jes got to fetch 'er wid dat! De tex' wuz on de *right* tail o' my coat: 'Come unto me, all ye dat labor en is heavy laden.' Hit wuz a ve'y momentous sermon, en all 'long I jes see Phillis wras'lin' wid 'erse'f, en I say, 'She *got* to come *dis* night, de Lohd he'pin' me.' En I had n' mo' 'n said de word, 'fo' she jes walked down en guv me 'er han'.

"Den we had de baptizin' in Elkhorn Creek,

en de watter wuz deep en de curren' tol'ble swif'. Hit look to me like dere wuz five hundred uv um on de creek side. By-en-by I stood on de edge o' de watter, en Phillis she come down to let me baptize 'er. En me en 'er j'ined han's en waded out in de creek, mighty slow, caze Phillis didn't have no shot roun' de bottom uv 'er dress, en it kep' bobbin' on top de watter till I pushed it down. But by-en-by we got 'way out in de creek, en bof uv us wuz tremblin'. En I says to 'er ve'y kin'ly, 'When I put you un'er de watter, Phillis, you mus' try en hole yo'se'f stiff, so I can lif' you up easy.' But I hadn't mo' 'n jes got 'er laid back over de watter ready to souze 'er un'er when 'er feet flew up off de bottom uv de creek, en when I retched out to fetch 'er up, I stepped in a hole; en 'fo' I knowed it, we wuz flounderin' roun' in de watter, en de hymn dey was singin' on de bank sounded mighty confused-like. En Phillis she swallowed some watter, en all 't oncet she jes grap me right tight roun' de neck, en say mighty quick, says she, 'I gwine marry whoever gits me out'n dis yere watter!'

"En by-en-by, when me en 'er wuz walkin' up de bank o' de creek, drippin' all over, I says to 'er, says I:

"'Does you 'member what you said back yon'er in de watter, Phillis?'

"'I ain' out'n no watter yit,' says she, ve'y contemptuous.

"'When does you consider yo'se'f out'n de watter?' says I, ve'y humble.

"'When I git dese soakin' clo'es off'n my back,' says she.

"Hit wuz good dark when we got home, en atter a while I crope up to de dooh o' Phillis's cabin en put my eye down to de key-hole, en see Phillis jes settin' 'fo' dem blazin' walnut logs dressed up in 'er new red linsey dress, en 'er eyes shinin'. En I shuk so I 'mos' faint. Den I tap easy on de dooh, en say in a mighty tremblin' tone, says I:

"'Is you out'n de watter yit, Phillis?'

"'I got on dry dress,' says she.

"'Does you 'member what you said back yon'er in de watter, Phillis?' says I.

"'De latch-string on de outside de dooh,' says she, mighty sof'.

"En I walked in."

As Peter drew near the end of this reminiscence, his voice sank to a key of inimitable tenderness; and when it was ended he stood a few minutes, scraping the gravel with the toe of his boot, his head dropped forward. Then he added, huskily:

"Phillis been dead heap o' years now;" and turned away.

This recalling of the scenes of a time long gone by may have awakened in the breast of the colonel some gentle memory; for after Peter was gone he continued to sit a while in silent musing. Then getting up, he walked in the falling twilight across the yard and through the gardens until he came to a secluded spot in the most distant corner. There he stooped or rather knelt down and passed his hands, as though with mute benediction, over a little bed of old-fashioned China pinks. When he had moved in from the country he had brought nothing away from his mother's garden but these, and in all the years since no one had ever pulled them, as Peter well knew; for one day the colonel had said, with his face turned away:

"Let them have all the flowers they want; but leave the pinks."

He continued kneeling over them now, touching them softly with his fingers, as though they were the fragrant, never-changing symbols of voiceless communion with his past. Still it may have been only the early dew of the evening that glistened on them when he rose and slowly walked away, leaving the pale moonbeams to haunt the spot.

Certainly after this day he showed increasing concern in the young lovers who were holding clandestine meetings in his grounds.

"Peter," he would say, "why, if they love each other, don't they get married? Something may happen."

"I been spectin' some'n' to happ'n fur some time, ez dey been quar'lin' right smart lately," replied Peter, laughing.

Whether or not he was justified in this prediction, before the end of another week the colonel read a notice of their elopement and marriage; and several days later he came up from down-town and told Peter that everything had been forgiven the young pair, who had gone to house-keeping in the country. It gave him pleasure to think he had helped to perpetuate the race of blue-grass farmers.

THE YEARNING PASSED AWAY

It was in the twilight of a late autumn day in the same year that nature gave the colonel the first direct intimation to prepare for the last summons. They had been passing along the garden walks, where a few pale flowers were trying to flourish up to the very winter's edge, and where the dry leaves had gathered unswept and rustled beneath their feet. All at once the colonel turned to Peter, who was a yard and a half behind, as usual, and said:

"Give me your arm, Peter, I feel tired;" and thus the two, for the first time in all their lifetime walking abreast, passed slowly on.

"Peter," said the colonel, gravely, a minute or two later, "we are like two dried-up stalks of fodder. I wonder the Lord lets us live any longer."

"I reck'n He's managin' to use us *some* way, or we wouldn' be heah," said Peter.

"Well, all I have to say is, that if He's using me, He can't be in much of a hurry for his work," replied the colonel.

"He uses snails, en I *know* we ain' ez slow ez *dem*," argued Peter, composedly.

"I don't know. I think a snail must have made more progress since the war than I have."

The idea of his uselessness seemed to weigh on him, for a little later he remarked, with a sort of mortified smile:

"Do you think, Peter, that we would pass for what they call representative men of the New South?"

"We done *had* ou' day, Marse Rom," replied Peter. "We got to pass fur what we *wuz*. Mebbe de *Lohd's* got mo' use fur us yit 'n *people* has," he added, after a pause.

From this time on the colonel's strength gradually failed him; but it was not until the following spring that the end came.

A night or two before his death his mind wandered backward, after the familiar manner of the dying, and his delirious dreams showed the shifting, faded pictures that renewed themselves for the last time on his wasting memory. It must have been that he was once more amid the scenes of his active farm life, for his broken snatches of talk ran thus:

"Come, boys, get your cradles! Look where the sun is! You are late getting to work this morning. That is the finest field of wheat in the county. Be careful about the bundles! Make them the same size and tie them tight. That swath is too wide, and you don't hold your cradle right, Tom. . . .

"Sell *Peter!* Sell *Peter Cotton!* No, sir! You might buy *me* some day and work *me* in your cotton-field; but as long as he's mine, you can't buy Peter, and you can't buy any of *my* negroes. . . .

"Boys! boys! If you don't work faster, you won't finish this field to-day. . . . You'd better go in the shade and rest now. The sun's very hot. Don't drink too much ice-water. There's a jug of whisky in the fence-corner. Give them a good dram around, and tell them to work slow till the sun gets lower." . . .

Once during the night a sweet smile played

over his features as he repeated a few words that were part of an old rustic song and dance. Arranged, not as they came broken and incoherent from his lips, but as he once had sung them, they were as follows:

"O Sister Phœbe! How merry were we
When we sat under the juniper-tree,
     The juniper-tree, heigho!
Put this hat on your head! Keep your head warm;
Take a sweet kiss! It will do you no harm,
     Do you no harm, I know!"

After this he sank into a quieter sleep, but soon stirred with a look of intense pain. "Helen! Helen!" he murmured. "Will you break your promise? Have you changed in your feelings towards me? I have brought you the pinks. Won't you take the pinks, Helen?" Then he sighed as he added, "It wasn't her fault. If she had only known——"

Who was the Helen of that far-away time? Was this the colonel's love-story?

But during all the night, whithersoever his mind wandered, at intervals it returned to the burden of a single strain—the harvesting. Towards daybreak he took it up again for the last time:

"O boys, boys, *boys!* If you don't work faster you won't finish the field to-day. Look how low the sun is! . . . I am going to the house. They can't finish the field to-day. Let them do what they can, but don't let them work late. I want Peter to go to the house with me. Tell him to come on." . . .

In the faint gray of the morning, Peter, who had been watching by the bedside all night, stole out of the room, and going into the garden pulled a handful of pinks—a thing he had never done before—and, re-entering the colonel's bedroom, put them in a vase near his sleeping face. Soon afterwards the colonel opened his eyes and looked around him. At the foot of the bed stood Peter, and on one side sat the physician and a friend. The night-lamp burned low, and through the folds of the curtains came the white light of early day. "Put out the lamp and open the curtains," he said, feebly. "It's day." When they had drawn the curtains aside, his eyes fell on the pinks, sweet and fresh with the dew on them. He stretched out his hand and touched them caressingly, and his eyes sought Peter's with a look of grateful understanding.

"I want to be alone with Peter for a while," he said, turning his face towards the others.

When they were left alone, it was some minutes before anything was said. Peter, not knowing what he did, but knowing what was coming, had gone to the window and hid himself behind the curtains, drawing them tightly around his form as though to shroud himself from sorrow.

At length the colonel said, "Come here!"

Peter, almost staggering forward, fell at the foot of the bed, and, clasping the colonel's feet with one arm, pressed his cheek against them. "Come closer!"

Peter crept on his knees and buried his head on the colonel's thigh.

"Come up here—*closer*"; and putting one arm around Peter's neck he laid the other hand softly on his head, and looked long and tenderly into his eyes. "I've got to leave you, Peter. Don't you feel sorry for me?"

"Oh, Marse Rom!" cried Peter, hiding his face, his whole form shaken by sobs.

"Peter," added the colonel with ineffable gentleness, "if I had served my Master as faithfully as you have served yours, I should not feel ashamed to stand in his presence."

"If my Marseter is ez mussiful to me ez you have been——"

"I have fixed things so that you will be comfortable after I am gone. When your time comes, I should like you to be laid close to me. We can take the long sleep together. Are you willing?"

"That's whar I want to be laid."

The colonel stretched out his hand to the vase, and taking the bunch of pinks, said very calmly:

"Leave these in my hand; I'll carry them with me." A moment more, and he added: "If I shouldn't wake up any more, good-bye, Peter!"

"Good-bye, Marse Rom!"

And they shook hands a long time. After this the colonel lay back on the pillows. His soft, silvery hair contrasted strongly with his child-like, unspoiled, open face. To the day of his death, as is apt to be true of those who have lived pure lives but never married, he had a boyish strain in him—a softness of nature, showing itself even now in the gentle expression of his mouth. His brown eyes had in them the same boyish look when, just as he was falling asleep, he scarcely opened them to say: "Pray, Peter."

Peter, on his knees, and looking across the colonel's face towards the open door, through which the rays of the rising sun streamed in upon his hoary head, prayed, while the colonel fell asleep, adding a few words for himself now left alone.

Several hours later, memory led the colonel

back again through the dim gate-way of the past, and out of that gate-way his spirit finally took flight into the future.

Peter lingered a year. The place went to the colonel's sister, but he was allowed to remain in his quarters. With much thinking of the past, his mind fell into a lightness and a weakness. Sometimes he would be heard crooning the burden of old hymns, or sometimes seen sitting beside the old brass-nailed trunk, fumbling with the spelling-book and *The Pilgrim's Progress*. Often, too, he walked out to the cemetery on the edge of the town, and each time could hardly find the colonel's grave amid the multitude of the dead.

One gusty day in spring, the Scotch sexton, busy with the blades of blue-grass springing from the animated mould, saw his familiar figure standing motionless beside the colonel's resting-place. He had taken off his hat—one of the colonel's last bequests—and laid it on the colonel's head-stone. On his body he wore a strange coat of faded blue, patched and weather-stained, and so moth-eaten that parts of the curious tails had dropped entirely away. In one hand he held an open Bible, and on a much-soiled page he was pointing with his finger to the following words:

"I would not have you ignorant, brethren, concerning them which are asleep."

It would seem that, impelled by love and faith, and guided by his wandering reason, he had come forth to preach his last sermon on the immortality of the soul over the dust of his dead master.

The sexton led him home, and soon afterwards a friend, who had loved them both, laid him beside the colonel.

It was perhaps fitting that his winding-sheet should be the vestment in which, years agone, he had preached to his fellow-slaves in bondage; for if it so be that the dead of this planet shall come forth from their graves clad in the trappings of mortality, then Peter should arise on the Resurrection Day wearing his old jeans coat.

HAMLIN GARLAND (1860-   )

THE RETURN OF A PRIVATE

(1890)

The nearer the train drew toward La Crosse, the soberer the little group of "vets" became. On the long way from New Orleans they had beguiled tedium with jokes and friendly chaff; or with planning with elaborate detail what they were going to do now, after the war. A long journey, slowly, irregularly, yet persistently pushing northward. When they entered on Wisconsin territory they gave a cheer, and another when they reached Madison, but after that they sank into a dumb expectancy. Comrades dropped off at one or two points beyond, until there were only four or five left who were bound for La Crosse County.

Three of them were gaunt and brown, the fourth was gaunt and pale, with signs of fever and ague upon him. One had a great scar down his temple, one limped, and they all had unnaturally large, bright eyes, showing emaciation. There were no bands greeting them at the station, no banks of gayly dressed ladies waving handkerchiefs and shouting "Bravo!" as they came in on the caboose of a freight train into the towns that had cheered and blared at them on their way to war. As they looked out or stepped upon the platform for a moment, while the train stood at the station, the loafers looked at them indifferently. Their blue coats, dusty and grimy, were too familiar now to excite notice, much less a friendly word. They were the last of the army to return, and the loafers were surfeited with such sights.

The train jogged forward so slowly that it seemed likely to be midnight before they should reach La Crosse. The little squad grumbled and swore, but it was no use; the train would not hurry, and, as a matter of fact, it was nearly two o'clock when the engine whistled "down brakes."

All of the group were farmers, living in districts several miles out of the town, and were poor.

"Now, boys," said Private Smith, he of the fever and ague, "we are landed in La Crosse in the night. We've got to stay somewhere till mornin'. Now I ain't got no two dollars to waste on a hotel. I've got a wife and children, so I'm goin' to roost on a bench and take the cost of a bed out of my hide."

"Same here," put in one of the other men. "Hide'll grow on again, dollars'll come hard. It's goin' to be mighty hot skirmishin' to find a dollar these days."

"Don't think they'll be a deputation of citizens waitin' to 'scort us to a hotel, eh?" said another. His sarcasm was too obvious to require an answer.

Smith went on, "Then at daybreak we'll start for home—at least, I will."

"Well, I'll be dummed if I'll take two dollars out o' *my* hide," one of the younger men said. "I'm goin' to a hotel, ef I don't never lay up a cent."

"That'll do f'r you," said Smith; "but if you had a wife an' three young uns dependin' on yeh——"

"Which I ain't, thank the Lord! and don't intend havin' while the court knows itself."

The station was deserted, chill, and dark, as they came into it at exactly a quarter to two in the morning. Lit by the oil lamps that flared a dull red light over the dingy benches, the waiting room was not an inviting place. The younger man went off to look up a hotel, while the rest remained and prepared to camp down on the floor and benches. Smith was attended to tenderly by the other men, who spread their blankets on the bench for him, and, by robbing themselves, made quite a comfortable bed, though the narrowness of the bench made his sleeping precarious.

It was chill, though August, and the two men, sitting with bowed heads, grew stiff with cold and weariness, and were forced to rise now and again and walk about to warm their stiffened limbs. It did not occur to them, probably, to contrast their coming home with their going forth, or with the coming home of the generals, colonels, or even captains—but to Private Smith, at any rate, there came a sickness at heart almost deadly as he lay there on his hard bed and went over his situation.

In the deep of the night, lying on a board in the town where he had enlisted three years ago, all elation and enthusiasm gone out of him, he faced the fact that with the joy of home-coming was already mingled the bitter juice of care. He saw himself sick, worn out, taking up the work on his half-cleared farm, the inevitable mortgage standing ready with open jaw to swallow half his earnings. He had given three years of his life for a mere pittance of pay, and now!——

Morning dawned at last, slowly, with a pale yellow dome of light rising silently above the bluffs, which stand like some huge storm-devastated castle, just east of the city. Out to the left the great river swept on its massive yet silent way to the south. Bluejays called across the water from hillside to hillside through the clear, beautiful air, and hawks began to skim the tops of the hills. The older men were astir

early, but Private Smith had fallen at last into a sleep, and they went out without waking him. He lay on his knapsack, his gaunt face turned toward the ceiling, his hands clasped on his breast, with a curious pathetic effect of weakness and appeal.

An engine switching near woke him at last, and he slowly sat up and stared about. He looked out of the window and saw that the sun was lightening the hills across the river. He rose and brushed his hair as well as he could, folded his blankets up, and went out to find his companions. They stood gazing silently at the river and at the hills.

"Looks natcher'l, don't it?" they said, as he came out.

"That's what it does," he replied. "An' it looks good. D' yeh see that peak?" He pointed at a beautiful symmetrical peak, rising like a slightly truncated cone, so high that it seemed the very highest of them all. It was touched by the morning sun and it glowed like a beacon, and a light scarf of gray morning fog was rolling up its shadowed side.

"My farm's just beyond that. Now, if I can only ketch a ride, we'll be home by dinnertime."

"I'm talkin' about breakfast," said one of the others.

"I guess it's one more meal o' hardtack f'r me," said Smith.

They foraged around, and finally found a restaurant with a sleepy old German behind the counter, and procured some coffee, which they drank to wash down their hardtack.

"Time'll come," said Smith, holding up a piece by the corner, "when this'll be a curiosity."

"I hope to God it will! I bet I've chawed hardtack enough to shingle every house in the coolly. I've chawed it when my lampers was down, and when they wasn't. I've took it dry, soaked, and mashed. I've had it wormy, musty, sour, and blue-mouldy. I've had it in little bits and big bits; 'fore coffee an' after coffee. I'm ready f'r a change. I'd like t' git holt jest about now o' some of the hot biscuits my wife c'n make when she lays herself out f'r company."

"Well, if you set there gabblin', you'll never *see* yer wife."

"Come on," said Private Smith. "Wait a moment, boys; less take suthin'. It's on me." He led them to the rusty tin dipper which hung on a nail beside the wooden water-pail, and they grinned and drank. Then shouldering their blankets and muskets, which they were "takin' home to the boys," they struck out on their last march.

"They called that coffee Jayvy," grumbled one of them, but it never went by the road where government Jayvy resides. I reckon I know coffee from peas."

They kept together on the road along the turnpike, and up the winding road by the river, which they followed for some miles. The river was very lovely, curving down along its sandy beds, pausing now and then under broad basswood trees, or running in dark, swift, silent currents under tangles of wild grapevines, and drooping alders, and haw trees. At one of these lovely spots the three vets sat down on the thick green sward to rest, "on Smith's account." The leaves of the trees were as fresh and green as in June, the jays called cheery greetings to them, and king-fishers darted to and fro with swooping, noise-less flight.

"I tell yeh, boys, this knocks the swamps of Loueesiana into kingdom come."

"You bet. All they c'n raise down there is snakes, niggers, and p'rticler hell."

"An' fightin' men," put in the older man.

"An' fightin' men. If I had a good hook an' line I'd sneak a pick'rel out o' that pond. Say, remember that time I shot that alligator—"

"I guess we'd better be crawlin' along," interrupted Smith, rising and shouldering his knapsack, with considerable effort, which he tried to hide.

"Say, Smith, lemme give you a lift on that."

"I guess I c'n manage," said Smith, grimly.

"Course. But, yo' see, I may not have a chance right off to pay yeh back for the times you've carried my gun and hull caboodle. Say, now, gimme that gun, anyway."

"All right, if yeh feel like it, Jim," Smith replied, and they trudged along doggedly in the sun, which was getting higher and hotter each half-mile.

"Ain't it queer there ain't no teams comin' along," said Smith, after a long silence.

"Well, no, seein's it's Sunday."

"By jinks, that's a fact. It is Sunday. I'll git home in time f'r dinner, sure!" he exulted. "She don't hev dinner usially till about one on Sundays." And he fell into a muse, in which he smiled.

"Well, I'll git home jest about six o'clock, jest about when the boys are milkin' the cows," said old Jim Cranby. "I'll step into the barn, an' then I'll say: 'Heah! why ain't this milkin' done before this time o' day?' An' then won't they yell!" he added, slapping his thigh in great glee.

Smith went on. "I'll jest go up the path. Old Rover'll come down the road to meet me.

He won't bark; he'll know me, an' he'll come down waggin' his tail an' showin' his teeth. That's his way of laughin'. An' so I'll walk up to the kitchen door, an' I'll say, 'Dinner f'r a hungry man!' An' then she'll jump up, an'—"

He couldn't go on. His voice choked at the thought of it. Saunders, the third man, hardly uttered a word, but walked silently behind the others. He had lost his wife the first year he was in the army. She died of pneumonia, caught in the autumn rains while working in the fields in his place.

They plodded along till at last they came to a parting of the ways. To the right the road continued up the main valley; to the left it went over the big ridge.

"Well, boys," began Smith, as they grounded their muskets and looked away up the valley, "here's where we shake hands. We've marched together a good many miles, an' now I s'pose we're done."

"Yes, I don't think we'll do any more of it f'r a while. I don't want to, I know."

"I hope I'll see yeh once in a while, boys, to talk over old times."

"Of course," said Saunders, whose voice trembled a little, too. "It ain't exactly like dyin'." They all found it hard to look at each other.

"But we'd ought'r go home with you," said Cranby. "You'll never climb that ridge with all them things on yer back."

"Oh, I'm all right! Don't worry about me. Every step takes me nearer home, yeh see. Well, good-by, boys."

They shook hands. "Good-by. Good luck!"

"Same to you. Lemme know how you find things at home."

"Good-by."

"Good-by."

He turned once before they passed out of sight, and waved his cap, and they did the same, and all yelled. Then all marched away with their long, steady, loping, veteran step. The solitary climber in blue walked on for a time, with his mind filled with the kindness of his comrades, and musing upon the many wonderful days they had had together in camp and field.

He thought of his chum, Billy Tripp. Poor Billy! A "minie" ball fell into his breast one day, fell wailing like a cat, and tore a great ragged hole in his heart. He looked forward to a sad scene with Billy's mother and sweet-heart. They would want to know all about it. He tried to recall all that Billy had said, and the particulars of it, but there was little to remember, just that wild wailing sound high in the air, a dull slap, a short, quick, expulsive groan, and the boy lay with his face in the dirt in the ploughed field they were marching across.

That was all. But all the scenes he had since been through had not dimmed the horror, the terror of that moment, when his boy comrade fell, with only a breath between a laugh and a death-groan. Poor handsome Billy! Worth millions of dollars was his young life.

These sombre recollections gave way at length to more cheerful feelings as he began to approach his home coolly. The fields and houses grew familiar, and in one or two he was greeted by people seated in the doorways. But he was in no mood to talk, and pushed on steadily, though he stopped and accepted a drink of milk once at the well-side of a neighbor.

The sun was burning hot on that slope, and his step grew slower, in spite of his iron resolution. He sat down several times to rest. Slowly he crawled up the rough, reddish-brown road, which wound along the hillside, under great trees, through dense groves of jack oaks, with tree-tops far below him on his left hand, and the hills far above him on his right. He crawled along like some minute, wingless variety of fly.

He ate some hardtack, sauced with wild berries, when he reached the summit of the ridge, and sat there for some time, looking down into his home coolly.

Sombre, pathetic figure! His wide, round, gray eyes gazing down into the beautiful valley, seeing and not seeing, the splendid cloud-shadows sweeping over the western hills and across the green and yellow wheat far below. His head drooped forward on his palm, his shoulders took on a tired stoop, his cheek-bones showed painfully. An observer might have said, "He is looking down upon his own grave."

II

Sunday comes in a Western wheat harvest with such sweet and sudden relaxation to man and beast that it would be holy for that reason, if for no other, and Sundays are usually fair in harvest-time. As one goes out into the field in the hot morning sunshine, with no sound abroad save the crickets and the indescribably pleasant silken rustling of the ripened grain, the reaper and the very sheaves in the stubble seem to be resting, dreaming.

Around the house, in the shade of the trees, the men sit, smoking, dozing, or reading the papers, while the women, never resting, move about at the housework. The men eat on Sundays about the same as on other days, and breakfast is no sooner over and out of the way than dinner begins.

But at the Smith farm there were no men dozing or reading. Mrs. Smith was alone with her three children, Mary, nine, Tommy, six, and little Ted, just past four. Her farm, rented to a neighbor, lay at the head of a coolly or narrow gully, made at some far-off post-glacial period by the vast and angry floods of water which gullied these tremendous furrows in the level prairie—furrows so deep that undisturbed portions of the original level rose like hills on either side, rose to quite considerable mountains.

The chickens awakened her as usual that Sabbath morning from dreams of her absent husband, from whom she had not heard for weeks. The shadows drifted over the hills, down the slopes, across the wheat, and up the opposite wall in leisurely way, as if, being Sunday, they could take it easy also. The fowls clustered about the housewife as she went out into the yard. Fuzzy little chickens swarmed out from the coops, where their clucking and perpetually disgruntled mothers tramped about, petulantly thrusting their heads through the spaces between the slats.

A cow called in a deep, musical bass, and a calf answered from a little pen near by, and a pig scurried guiltily out of the cabbages. Seeing all this, seeing the pig in the cabbages, the tangle of grass in the garden, the broken fence which she had mended again and again—the little woman, hardly more than a girl, sat down and cried. The bright Sabbath morning was only a mockery without him!

A few years ago they had bought this farm, paying part, mortgaging the rest in the usual way. Edward Smith was a man of terrible energy. He worked "nights and Sundays," as the saying goes, to clear the farm of its brush and of its insatiate mortgage! In the midst of his Herculean struggle came the call for volunteers, and with the grim and unselfish devotion to his country which made the Eagle Brigade able to "whip its weight in wild-cats," he threw down his scythe and grub-axe, turned his cattle loose, and became a blue-coated cog in a vast machine for killing men, and not thistles. While the millionaire sent his money to England for safe-keeping, this man, with his girl-wife and three babies, left them on a mortgaged farm, and went away to fight for an idea. It was foolish, but it was sublime for all that.

That was three years before, and the young

wife, sitting on the well-curb on this bright Sabbath harvest morning, was righteously rebellious. It seemed to her that she had borne her share of the country's sorrow. Two brothers had been killed, the renter in whose hands her husband had left the farm had proved a villain; one year the farm had been without crops, and now the over-ripe grain was waiting the tardy hand of the neighbor who had rented it, and who was cutting his own grain first.

About six weeks before, she had received a letter saying, "We'll be discharged in a little while." But no other word had come from him. She had seen by the papers that his army was being discharged, and from day to day other soldiers slowly percolated in blue streams back into the State and county, but still *her* hero did not return.

Each week she had told the children that he was coming, and she had watched the road so long that it had become unconscious; and as she stood at the well, or by the kitchen door, her eyes were fixed unthinkingly on the road that wound down the coolly.

Nothing wears on the human soul like waiting. If the stranded mariner, searching the sun-bright seas, could once give up hope of a ship, that horrible grinding on his brain would cease. It was this waiting, hoping, on the edge of despair, that gave Emma Smith no rest.

Neighbors said, with kind intentions: "He's sick, maybe, an' can't start north just yet. He'll come along one o' these days."

"Why don't he write?" was her question, which silenced them all. This Sunday morning it seemed to her as if she could not stand it longer. The house seemed intolerably lonely. So she dressed the little ones in their best calico dresses and home-made jackets, and, closing up the house, set off down the coolly to old Mother Gray's.

"Old Widder Gray" lived at the "mouth of the coolly." She was a widow woman with a large family of stalwart boys and laughing girls. She was the visible incarnation of hospitality and optimistic poverty. With Western open-heartedness she fed every mouth that asked food of her, and worked herself to death as cheerfully as her girls danced in the neighborhood harvest dances.

She waddled down the path to meet Mrs. Smith with a broad smile on her face.

"Oh, you little dears! Come right to your granny. Gimme a kiss! Come right in, Mis' Smith. How are yeh, anyway? Nice mornin', ain't it? Come in an' set down. Everything's in a clutter, but that won't scare you any."

She led the way into the best room, a sunny, square room, carpeted with a faded and patched rag carpet, and papered with white-and-green-striped wall-paper, where a few faded effigies of dead members of the family hung in variously sized oval walnut frames. The house resounded with singing, laughter, whistling, tramping of heavy boots, and riotous scufflings. Half-grown boys came to the door and crooked their fingers at the children, who ran out, and were soon heard in the midst of fun.

"Don't s'pose you've heard from Ed?" Mrs. Smith shook her head. "He'll turn up some day, when you ain't lookin' for 'm." The good old soul had said that so many times that poor Mrs. Smith derived no comfort from it any longer.

"Liz heard from Al the other day. He's comin' some day this week. Anyhow, they expect him."

"Did he say anything of——?"

"No, he didn't," Mrs. Gray admitted. "But then it was only a short letter, anyhow. Al ain't much for writin', anyhow.—But come out and see my new cheese. I tell yeh, I don't believe I ever had better luck in my life. If Ed should come, I want you should take him up a piece of this cheese."

It was beyond human nature to resist the influence of that noisy, hearty, loving household, and in the midst of the singing and laughing the wife forgot her anxiety, for the time at least, and laughed and sang with the rest.

About eleven o'clock a wagon-load more drove up to the door, and Bill Gray, the widow's oldest son, and his whole family, from Sand Lake Coolly, piled out amid a good-natured uproar. Every one talked at once, except Bill, who sat in the wagon with his wrists on his knees, a straw in his mouth, and an amused twinkle in his blue eyes.

"Ain't heard nothin' o' Ed, I s'pose?" he asked in a kind of bellow. Mrs. Smith shook her head. Bill, with a delicacy very striking in such a great giant, rolled his quid in his mouth, and said:

"Didn't know but you had. I hear two or three of the Sand Lake boys are comin'. Left New Orleenes some time this week. Didn't write nothin' about Ed, but no news is good news in such cases, mother always says."

"Well, go put out yer team," said Mrs. Gray, "an' go 'n bring me in some taters, an', Sim, you go see if you c'n find some corn. Sadie, you put on the water to bile. Come now, hustle yer boots, all o' yeh. If I feed this yer crowd, we've got to have some raw materials. If y' think I'm goin' to feed yeh on pie—you're jest mightily mistaken."

The children went off into the fields, the girls put dinner on to boil, and then went to change their dresses and fix their hair. "Somebody might come," they said.

"Land sakes, I hope not! I don't know where in time I'd set 'em, 'less they'd eat at the second table," Mrs. Gray laughed, in pretended dismay.

The two older boys, who had served their time in the army, lay out on the grass before the house, and whittled and talked desultorily about the war and the crops, and planned buying a threshing-machine. The older girls and Mrs. Smith helped enlarge the table and put on the dishes, talking all the time in that cheery, incoherent, and meaningful way a group of such women have,—a conversation to be taken for its spirit rather than for its letter, though Mrs. Gray at last got the ear of them all and dissertated at length on girls.

"Girls in love ain't no use in the whole blessed week," she said. "Sundays they're a-lookin' down the road, expectin' he'll come. Sunday afternoons they can't think o' nothin' else, 'cause he's here. Monday mornin's they're sleepy and kind o' dreamy and slimpsy, and good f'r nothin' on Tuesday and Wednesday. Thursday they git absent-minded, an' begin to look off toward Sunday agin, an' mope aroun' and let the dishwater git cold, right under their noses. Friday they break dishes, an' go off in the best room an' snivel, an' look out o' the winder. Saturdays they have queer spurts o' workin' like all p'ssessed, an' spurts o' frizzin' their hair. An' Sunday they begin it all over agin."

The girls giggled and blushed, all through this tirade from their mother, their broad faces and powerful frames anything but suggestive of lackadaisical sentiment. But Mrs. Smith said:

"Now, Mrs. Gray, I hadn't ought to stay to dinner. You've got——"

"Now you set right down! If any of them girls' beaus comes, they'll have to take what's left, that's all. They ain't s'posed to have much appetite, nohow. No, you're goin' to stay if they starve, an' they ain't no danger o' that."

At one o'clock the long table was piled with boiled potatoes, cords of boiled corn on the cob, squash and pumpkin pies, hot biscuit, sweet pickles, bread and butter, and honey. Then one of the girls took down a conch-shell from a nail, and going to the door, blew a long,

fine, free blast, that showed there was no weakness of lungs in her ample chest.

Then the children came out of the forest of corn, out of the creek, out of the loft of the barn, and out of the garden.

"They come to their feed f'r all the world jest like the pigs when y' holler 'poo-ee!' See 'em scoot!" laughed Mrs. Gray, every wrinkle on her face shining with delight.

The men shut up their jack-knives, and surrounded the horse-trough to souse their faces in the cold, hard water, and in a few moments the table was filled with a merry crowd, and a row of wistful-eyed youngsters circled the kitchen wall, where they stood first on one leg and then on the other, in impatient hunger.

"Now pitch in, Mrs. Smith," said Mrs. Gray, presiding over the table. "You know these men critters. They'll eat every grain of it, if yeh give 'em a chance. I swan, they're made o' India-rubber, their stomachs is, I know it."

"Haf to eat to work," said Bill, gnawing a cob with a swift, circular motion that rivalled a corn-sheller in results.

"More like workin' to eat," put in one of the girls, with a giggle. "More eat 'n work with you."

"You needn't say anything, Net. Any one that'll eat seven ears——"

"I didn't, no such thing. You piled your cobs on my plate."

"That'll do to tell Ed Varney. It won't go down here where we know yeh."

"Good land! Eat all yeh want! They's plenty more in the fiel's, but I can't afford to give you young uns tea. The tea is for us women-folks, and 'specially f'r Mis' Smith an' Bill's wife. We're a-goin' to tell fortunes by it."

One by one the men filled up and shoved back, and one by one the children slipped into their places, and by two o'clock the women alone remained around the débris-covered table, sipping their tea and telling fortunes.

As they got well down to the grounds in the cup, they shook them with a circular motion in the hand, and then turned them bottom-side-up quickly in the saucer, then twirled them three or four times one way, and three or four times the other, during a breathless pause. Then Mrs. Gray lifted the cup, and, gazing into it with profound gravity, pronounced the impending fate.

It must be admitted that, to a critical observer, she had abundant preparation for hitting close to the mark, as when she told the girls that "somebody was comin'." "It's a man," she went on gravely. "He is cross-eyed——"

"Oh, you hush!" cried Nettie.

"He has red hair, and is death on b'iled corn and hot biscuit."

The others shrieked with delight.

"But he's goin' to get the mitten, that red-headed feller is, for I see another feller comin' up behind him."

"Oh, lemme see, lemme see!" cried Nettie.

"Keep off," said the priestess, with a lofty gesture. "His hair is black. He don't eat so much, and he works more."

The girls exploded in a shriek of laughter, and pounded their sister on the back.

At last came Mrs. Smith's turn, and she was trembling with excitement as Mrs. Gray again composed her jolly face to what she considered a proper solemnity of expression.

"Somebody is comin' to *you*," she said, after a long pause. "He's got a musket on his back. He's a soldier. He's almost here. See?"

She pointed at two little tea-stems, which really formed a faint suggestion of a man with a musket on his back. He had climbed nearly to the edge of the cup. Mrs. Smith grew pale with excitement. She trembled so she could hardly hold the cup in her hand as she gazed into it.

"It's Ed," cried the old woman. "He's on the way home. Heavens an' earth! There he is now!" She turned and waved her hand out toward the road. They rushed to the door to look where she pointed.

A man in a blue coat, with a musket on his back, was toiling slowly up the hill on the sun-bright, dusty road, toiling slowly, with bent head half hidden by a heavy knapsack. So tired it seemed that walking was indeed a process of falling. So eager to get home he would not stop, would not look aside, but plodded on, amid the cries of the locusts, the welcome of the crickets, and the rustle of the yellow wheat. Getting back to God's country, and his wife and babies!

Laughing, crying, trying to call him and the children at the same time, the little wife, al-most hysterical, snatched her hat and ran out into the yard. But the soldier had disappeared over the hill into the hollow beyond, and, by the time she had found the children, he was too far away for her voice to reach him. And, be-sides, she was not sure it was her husband, for he had not turned his head at their shouts. This seemed so strange. Why didn't he stop to rest at his old neighbor's house? Tortured by hope and doubt, she hurried up the coolly as fast as she could push the baby wagon, the blue-coated figure just ahead pushing steadily, silently forward up the coolly.

When the excited, panting little group came in sight of the gate they saw the blue-coated figure standing, leaning upon the rough rail fence, his chin on his palms, gazing at the empty house. His knapsack, canteen, blan-kets, and musket lay upon the dusty grass at his feet.

He was like a man lost in a dream. His wide, hungry eyes devoured the scene. The rough lawn, the little unpainted house, the field of clear yellow wheat behind it, down across which streamed the sun, now almost ready to touch the high hill to the west, the crickets crying merrily, a cat on the fence near by, dreaming, unmindful of the stranger in blue—

How peaceful it all was. O God! How far removed from all camps, hospitals, battle lines. A little cabin in a Wisconsin coolly, but it was majestic in its peace. How did he ever leave it for those years of tramping, thirsting, kill-ing?

Trembling, weak with emotion, her eyes on the silent figure, Mrs. Smith hurried up to the fence. Her feet made no noise in the dust and grass, and they were close upon him before he knew of them. The oldest boy ran a little ahead. He will never forget that figure, that face. It will always remain as something epic, that return of the private. He fixed his eyes on the pale face covered with a ragged beard.

"Who *are* you, sir?" asked the wife, or, rather, started to ask, for he turned, stood a moment, and then cried:

"Emma!"

"Edward!"

The children stood in a curious row to see their mother kiss this bearded, strange man, the elder girl sobbing sympathetically with her mother. Illness had left the soldier partly deaf, and this added to the strangeness of his manner.

But the youngest child stood away, even after the girl had recognized her father and kissed him. The man turned then to the baby, and said in a curiously unpaternal tone:

"Come here, my little man; don't you know me?" But the baby backed away under the fence and stood peering at him critically.

"My little man!" What meaning in those words! This baby seemed like some other woman's child, and not the infant he had left in his wife's arms. The war had come between him and his baby—he was only a strange man to him, with big eyes; a soldier, with mother hanging to his arm, and talking in a loud voice.

"And this is Tom," the private said, drawing the oldest boy to him. "*He'll* come and see me. *He* knows his poor old pap when he comes home from the war."

The mother heard the pain and reproach in his voice and hastened to apologize. "You've changed so, Ed. He can't know yeh. This is papa, Teddy; come and kiss him —Tom and Mary do. Come, won't you?" But Teddy still peered through the fence with solemn eyes, well out of reach. He resembled a half-wild kitten that hesitates, studying the tones of one's voice.

"I'll fix him," said the soldier, and sat down to undo his knapsack, out of which he drew three enormous and very red apples. After giving one to each of the older children, he said: "*Now* I guess he'll come. Eh, my little man? Now come see your pap."

Teddy crept slowly under the fence, assisted by the overzealous Tommy, and a moment later was kicking and squalling in his father's arms. Then they entered the house, into the sitting room, poor, bare, art-forsaken little room, too, with its rag carpet, its square clock, and its two or three chromos and pictures from *Harper's Weekly* pinned about.

"Emma, I'm all tired out," said Private Smith, as he flung himself down on the carpet as he used to do, while his wife brought a pillow to put under his head, and the children stood about munching their apples.

"Tommy, you run and get me a pan of chips, and Mary, you get the tea-kettle on, and I'll go and make some biscuit."

And the soldier talked. Question after question he poured forth about the crops, the cattle, the renter, the neighbors. He slipped his heavy government brogan shoes off his poor, tired, blistered feet, and lay out with utter, sweet relaxation. He was a free man again, no longer a soldier under command. At supper he stopped once, listened and smiled. "That's old Spot. I know her voice. I s'pose that's her calf out there in the pen. I can't milk her tonight, though. I'm too tired. But I tell you, I'd like a drink o' her milk. What's become of old Rove?"

"He died last winter. Poisoned, I guess." There was a moment of sadness for them all. It was some time before the husband spoke again, in a voice that trembled a little.

"Poor old feller! He'd 'a' known me half a mile away. I expected him to come down the hill to meet me. It 'ud 'a' been more like comin' home if I could 'a' seen him comin' down the road an' waggin' his tail, an' laughin' that way he has. I tell yeh, it kind o' took hold o'

me to see the blinds down an' the house shut up."

"But, yeh see, we—we expected you'd write again 'fore you started. And then we thought we'd see you if you *did* come," she hastened to explain.

"Well, I ain't worth a cent on writin'. Besides, it's just as well yeh didn't know when I was comin'. I tell you, it sounds good to hear them chickens out there, an' turkeys, an' the crickets. Do you know they don't have just the same kind o' crickets down South? Who's Sam hired t' help cut yer grain?"

"The Ramsey boys."

"Looks like a good crop; but I'm afraid I won't do much gettin' it cut. This cussed fever an' ague has got me down pretty low. I don't know when I'll get rid of it. I'll bet I've took twenty-five pounds of quinine if I've taken a bit. Gimme another biscuit. I tell yeh, they taste good, Emma. I ain't had anything like it—— Say, if you'd 'a' hear'd me braggin' to th' boys about your butter 'n' biscuits I'll bet your ears 'ud 'a' burnt."

The private's wife colored with pleasure. "Oh, you're always a-braggin' about your things. Everybody makes good butter."

"Yes; old lady Snyder, for instance."

"Oh, well, she ain't to be mentioned. She's Dutch."

"Or old Mis' Snively. One more cup o' tea, Mary. That's my girl! I'm feeling better already. I just b'lieve the matter with me is, I'm *starved*."

This was a delicious hour, one long to be remembered. They were like lovers again. But their tenderness, like that of a typical American family, found utterance in tones, rather than in words. He was praising her when praising her biscuit, and she knew it. They grew soberer when he showed where he had been struck, one ball burning the back of his hand, one cutting away a lock of hair from his temple, and one passing through the calf of his leg. The wife shuddered to think how near she had come to being a soldier's widow. Her waiting no longer seemed hard. This sweet, glorious hour effaced it all.

Then they rose, and all went out into the garden and down to the barn. He stood beside her while she milked old Spot. They began to plan fields and crops for next year.

His farm was weedy and encumbered, a rascally renter had run away with his machinery (departing between two days), his children needed clothing, the years were coming upon him, he was sick and emaciated, but his heroic soul did not quail. With the same courage with which he had faced his Southern march he entered upon a still more hazardous future.

Oh, that mystic hour! The pale man with big eyes standing there by the well, with his young wife by his side. The vast moon swinging above the eastern peaks, the cattle winding down the pasture slopes with jangling bells, the crickets singing, the stars blooming out sweet and far and serene; the katydids rhythmically calling, the little turkeys crying

querulously, as they settled to roost in the poplar tree near the open gate. The voices at the well drop lower, the little ones nestle in their father's arms at last, and Teddy falls asleep there.

The common soldier of the American volunteer army had returned. His war with the South was over, and his fight, his daily running fight with nature and against the injustice of his fellow-men, was begun again.

STEPHEN CRANE (1871-1900)

A MYSTERY OF HEROISM
(1896)

The dark uniforms of the men were so coated with dust from the incessant wrestling of the two armies that the regiment almost seemed a part of the clay bank which shielded them from the shells. On the top of the hill a battery was arguing in tremendous roars with some other guns, and to the eye of the infantry, the artillerymen, the guns, the caissons, the horses, were distinctly outlined upon the blue sky. When a piece was fired, a red streak as round as a log flashed low in the heavens, like a monstrous bolt of lightning. The men of the battery wore white duck trousers, which somehow emphasized their legs; and when they ran and crowded in little groups at the bidding of the shouting officers, it was more impressive than usual to the infantry.

Fred Collins, of A Company, was saying: "Thunder! I wisht I had a drink. Ain't there any water round here?" Then somebody yelled, "There goes th' bugler!"

As the eyes of half the regiment swept in one machinelike movement there was an instant's picture of a horse in a great convulsive leap of a death wound and a rider leaning back with a crooked arm and spread fingers before his face. On the ground was the crimson terror of an exploding shell, with fibres of flame that seemed like lances. A glittering bugle swung clear of the rider's back as fell headlong the horse and the man. In the air was an odor as from a conflagration.

Sometimes they of the infantry looked down at a fair little meadow which spread at their feet. Its long, green grass was rippling gently in a breeze. Beyond it was the gray form of a house half torn to pieces by shells and by the busy axes of soldiers who had pursued firewood. The line of an old fence was now dimly marked by long weeds and by an occasional

post. A shell had blown the well-house to fragments. Little lines of gray smoke ribboning upward from some embers indicated the place where had stood the barn.

From beyond a curtain of green woods came the sound of some stupendous scuffle, as if two animals of the size of islands were fighting. At a distance there were occasional appearances of swift-moving men, horses, batteries, flags, and, with the crashing of infantry volleys were heard, often, wild and frenzied cheers. In the midst of it all Smith and Ferguson, two privates of A Company, were engaged in a heated discussion, which involved the greatest questions of the national existence.

The battery on the hill presently engaged in a frightful duel. The white legs of the gunners scampered this way and that way, and the officers redoubled their shouts. The guns, with their demeanors of stolidity and courage, were typical of something infinitely self-possessed in this clamor of death that swirled around the hill.

One of a "swing" team was suddenly smitten quivering to the ground, and his maddened brethren dragged his torn body in their struggle to escape from this turmoil and danger. A young soldier astride one of the leaders swore and fumed in his saddle, and furiously jerked at the bridle. An officer screamed out an order so violently that his voice broke and ended the sentence in a falsetto shriek.

The leading company of the infantry regiment was somewhat exposed, and the colonel ordered it moved more fully under the shelter of the hill. There was the clank of steel against steel.

A lieutenant of the battery rode down and passed them, holding his right arm carefully in his left hand. And it was as if this arm was not at all a part of him, but belonged to another man. His sober and reflective charger went slowly. The officer's face was grimy and perspiring, and his uniform was tousled as if he had been in direct grapple with an enemy. He smiled grimly when the men stared at him. He turned his horse toward the meadow.

Collins, of A Company, said: "I wisht I had a drink. I bet there's water in that there ol' well yonder!"

"Yes; but how you goin' to git it?"

For the little meadow which intervened was now suffering a terrible onslaught of shells. Its green and beautiful calm had vanished utterly. Brown earth was being flung in monstrous handfuls. And there was a massacre of the young blades of grass. They were being torn, burned, obliterated. Some curious fortune of the battle had made this gentle little meadow the object of the red hate of the shells, and each one as it exploded seemed like an imprecation in the face of a maiden.

The wounded officer who was riding across this expanse said to himself, "Why, they couldn't shoot any harder if the whole army was massed here!"

A shell struck the gray ruins of the house, and as, after the roar, the shattered wall fell in fragments, there was a noise which resembled the flapping of shutters during a wild gale of winter. Indeed, the infantry paused in the shelter of the bank appeared as men standing upon a shore contemplating a madness of the sea. The angel of calamity had under its glance the battery upon the hill. Fewer white-legged men laboured about the guns. A shell had smitten one of the pieces, and after the flare, the smoke, the dust, the wrath of this blow were gone, it was possible to see white legs stretched horizontally upon the ground. And at that interval to the rear, where it is the business of battery horses to stand with their noses to the fight awaiting the command to drag their guns out of the destruction or into it or wheresoever these incomprehensible humans demanded with whip and spur—in this line of passive and dumb spectators, whose fluttering hearts yet would not let them forget the iron laws of man's control of them—in this rank of brute-soldiers there had been relentless and hideous carnage. From the ruck of bleeding and prostrate horses, the men of the infantry could see one animal raising its stricken body with its fore legs, and turning its nose with mystic and profound eloquence toward the sky.

Some comrades joked Collins about his thirst. "Well, if yeh want a drink so bad, why don't yeh go git it!"

"Well, I will in a minnet, if yeh don't shut up!"

A lieutenant of artillery floundered his horse straight down the hill with as great concern as if it were level ground. As he galloped past the colonel of the infantry, he threw up his hand in swift salute. "We've got to get out of that," he roared angrily. He was a black-bearded officer, and his eyes, which resembled beads, sparkled like those of an insane man. His jumping horse sped along the column of infantry.

The fat major, standing carelessly with his sword held horizontally behind him and with his legs far apart, looked after the receding horseman and laughed. "He wants to get back with orders pretty quick, or there'll be no bat-t'ry left," he observed.

The wise young captain of the second company hazarded to the lieutenant colonel that the enemy's infantry would probably soon attack the hill, and the lieutenant colonel snubbed him.

A private in one of the rear companies looked out over the meadow, and then turned to a companion and said, "Look there, Jim!" It was the wounded officer from the battery, who some time before had started to ride across the meadow, supporting his right arm carefully with his left hand. This man had encountered a shell apparently at a time when no one perceived him, and he could now be seen lying face downward with a stirruped foot stretched across the body of his dead horse. A leg of the charger extended slantingly upward precisely as stiff as a stake. Around this motionless pair the shells still howled.

There was a quarrel in A Company. Collins was shaking his fist in the faces of some laughing comrades. "Dern yeh! I ain't afraid t' go. If yeh say much, I will go!"

"Of course, yeh will! You'll run through that there medder, won't yeh?"

Collins said, in a terrible voice, "You see now!" At this ominous threat his comrades broke into renewed jeers.

Collins gave them a dark scowl and went to find his captain. The latter was conversing with the colonel of the regiment.

"Captain," said Collins, saluting and standing at attention—in those days all trousers bagged at the knees—"captain, I want t' get permission to go git some water from that there well over yonder!"

The colonel and the captain swung about simultaneously and stared across the meadow.

The captain laughed. "You must be pretty thirsty, Collins?"

"Yes, sir, I am."

"Well—ah," said the captain. After a moment, he asked, "Can't you wait?"

"No, sir."

The colonel was watching Collins's face. "Look here, my lad," he said, in a pious sort of a voice—"look here, my lad"—Collins was not a lad—"don't you think that's taking pretty big risks for a little drink of water?"

"I dunno," said Collins uncomfortably. Some of the resentment toward his companions, which perhaps had forced him into this affair, was beginning to fade. "I dunno wether 'tis."

The colonel and the captain contemplated him for a time.

"Well," said the captain finally.

"Well," said the colonel, "if you want to go, why, go."

Collins saluted. "Much obliged t' yeh."

As he moved away the colonel called after him. "Take some of the other boys' canteens with you an' hurry back now."

"Yes, sir, I will."

The colonel and the captain looked at each other then, for it had suddenly occurred that they could not for the life of them tell whether Collins wanted to go or whether he did not.

They turned to regard Collins, and as they perceived him surrounded by gesticulating comrades, the colonel said: "Well, by thunder! I guess he's going."

Collins appeared as a man dreaming. In the midst of the questions, the advice, the warnings, all the excited talk of his company mates, he maintained a curious silence.

They were very busy in preparing him for his ordeal. When they inspected him carefully it was somewhat like the examination that grooms give a horse before a race; and they were amazed, staggered by the whole affair. Their astonishment found vent in strange repetitions.

"Are yeh sure a-goin'?" they demanded again and again.

"Certainly I am," cried Collins, at last furiously.

He strode sullenly away from them. He was swinging five or six canteens by their cords. It seemed that his cap would not remain firmly on his head, and often he reached and pulled it down over his brow.

There was a general movement in the compact column. The long animal-like thing moved slightly. Its four hundred eyes were turned upon the figure of Collins.

"Well, sir, if that ain't th' derndest thing! I never thought Fred Collins had the blood in him for that kind of business."

"What's he goin' to do, anyhow?"

"He's goin' to that well there after water."

"We ain't dyin' of thirst, are we? That's foolishness."

"Well, somebody put him up to it, an' he's doin' it."

"Say, he must be a desperate cuss."

When Collins faced the meadow and walked away from the regiment, he was vaguely conscious that a chasm, the deep valley of all prides, was suddenly between him and his comrades. It was provisional, but the provision was that he return as a victor. He had blindly been led by quaint emotions, and laid himself under an obligation to walk squarely up to the face of death.

But he was not sure that he wished to make a retraction, even if he could do so without shame. As a matter of truth, he was sure of very little. He was mainly surprised.

It seemed to him supernaturally strange that he had allowed his mind to manœuvre his body into such a situation. He understood that it might be called dramatically great.

However, he had no full appreciation of anything, excepting that he was actually conscious of being dazed. He could feel his dulled mind groping after the form and color of this incident. He wondered why he did not feel some keen agony of fear cutting his sense like a knife. He wondered at this, because human expression had said loudly for centuries that men should feel afraid of certain things, and that all men who did not feel this fear were phenomena—heroes.

He was, then, a hero. He suffered that disappointment which we would all have if we discovered that we were ourselves capable of those deeds which we most admire in history and legend. This, then, was a hero. After all, heroes were not much.

No, it could not be true. He was not a hero. Heroes had no shames in their lives, and, as for him, he remembered borrowing fifteen dollars from a friend and promising to pay it back the next day, and then avoiding that friend for ten months. When at home his mother had aroused him for the early labor of his life on the farm, it had often been his fashion to be irritable, childish, diabolical; and his mother had died since he had come to the war.

He saw that, in this matter of the well, the canteens, the shells, he was an intruder in the land of fine deeds.

He was now about thirty paces from his

comrades. The regiment had just turned its many faces toward him.

From the forest of terrific noises there suddenly emerged a little uneven line of men. They fired fiercely and rapidly at distant foliage on which appeared little puffs of white smoke. The spatter of skirmish firing was added to the thunder of the guns on the hill. The little line of men ran forward. A color sergeant fell flat with his flag as if he had slipped on ice. There was hoarse cheering from this distant field.

Collins suddenly felt that two demon fingers were pressed into his ears. He could see nothing but flying arrows, flaming red. He lurched from the shock of this explosion, but he made a mad rush for the house, which he viewed as a man submerged to the neck in a boiling surf might view the shore. In the air, little pieces of shell howled and the earthquake explosions drove him insane with the menace of their roar. As he ran the canteens knocked together with a rhythmical tinkling.

As he neared the house, each detail of the scene became vivid to him. He was aware of some bricks of the vanished chimney lying on the sod. There was a door which hung by one hinge.

Rifle bullets called forth by the insistent skirmishers came from the far-off bank of foliage. They mingled with the shells and the pieces of shells until the air was torn in all directions by hootings, yells, howls. The sky was full of fiends who directed all their wild rage at his head.

When he came to the well, he flung himself face downward and peered into its darkness. There were furtive silver glintings some feet from the surface. He grabbed one of the canteens and, unfastening its cap, swung it down by the cord. The water flowed slowly in with an indolent gurgle.

And now as he lay with his face turned away he was suddenly smitten with the terror. It came upon his heart like the grasp of claws. All the power faded from his muscles. For an instant he was no more than a dead man.

The canteen filled with a maddening slowness, in the manner of all bottles. Presently he recovered his strength and addressed a screaming oath to it. He leaned over until it seemed as if he intended to try to push water into it with his hands. His eyes as he gazed down into the well shone like two pieces of metal and in their expression was a great appeal and a great curse. The stupid water derided him.

There was the blaring thunder of a shell. Crimson light shone through the swift-boiling smoke and made a pink reflection on part of the wall of the well. Collins jerked out his arm and canteen with the same motion that a man would use in withdrawing his head from a furnace.

He scrambled erect and glared and hesitated. On the ground near him lay the old well bucket, with a length of rusty chain. He lowered it swiftly into the well. The bucket struck the water and then, turning lazily over, sank. When, with hand reaching tremblingly over hand, he hauled it out, it knocked often against the walls of the well and spilled some of its contents.

In running with a filled bucket, a man can adopt but one kind of gait. So through this terrible field over which screamed practical angels of death Collins ran in the manner of a farmer chased out of a dairy by a bull.

His face went staring white with anticipation—anticipation of a blow that would whirl him around and down. He would fall as he had seen other men fall, the life knocked out of them so suddenly that their knees were no more quick to touch the ground than their heads. He saw the long blue line of the regiment, but his comrades were standing looking at him from the edge of an impossible star. He was aware of some deep wheel ruts and hoofprints in the sod beneath his feet.

The artillery officer who had fallen in this meadow had been making groans in the teeth of the tempest of sound. These futile cries, wrenched from him by his agony, were heard only by shells, bullets. When wild-eyed Collins came running, this officer raised himself. His face contorted and blanched from pain, he was about to utter some great beseeching cry. But suddenly his face straightened and he called: "Say, young man, give me a drink of water, will you?"

Collins had no room amid his emotions for surprise. He was mad from the threats of destruction.

"I can't!" he screamed, and in his reply was a full description of his quaking apprehension. His cap was gone and his hair was riotous. His clothes made it appear that he had been dragged over the ground by the heels. He ran on.

The officer's head sank down and one elbow crooked. His foot in its brass-bound stirrup still stretched over the body of his horse and the other leg was under the steed.

But Collins turned. He came dashing back. His face had now turned gray and in his eyes was all terror. "Here it is! here it is!"

The officer was as a man gone in drink. His arm bent like a twig. His head drooped as if his neck were of willow. He was sinking to the ground to lie face downward.

Collins grabbed him by the shoulder. "Here it is. Here's your drink. Turn over. Turn over, man, for God's sake!"

With Collins hauling at his shoulder, the officer twisted his body and fell with his face turned toward that region where lived the unspeakable noises of the swirling missiles. There was the faintest shadow of a smile on his lips as he looked at Collins. He gave a sigh, a little primitive breath like that from a child.

Collins tried to hold the bucket steadily, but his shaking hands caused the water to splash all over the face of the dying man. Then he jerked it away and ran on.

The regiment gave him a welcoming roar. The grimed faces were wrinkled in laughter.

His captain waved the bucket away. "Give it to the men!"

The two genial, skylarking young lieutenants were the first to gain possession of it. They played over it in their fashion.

When one tried to drink the other teasingly knocked his elbow. "Don't, Billie! You'll make me spill it," said the one. The other laughed.

Suddenly there was an oath, the thud of wood on the ground, and a swift murmur of astonishment among the ranks. The two lieutenants glared at each other. The bucket lay on the ground empty.

MARGARET DELAND (1857-)

"AN EXCEEDING HIGH MOUNTAIN"
(1903)

I

Robert Gray's first wife, Alys (Old Chester had hard work to swallow her name; "but it's better than any of your silly 'ie's,'" said Old Chester)—this first Mrs. Gray was a good deal of a trial to everybody. She was not only "new," but foreign; not only foreign, but indifferent to Old Chester. Indeed, it took all Old Chester's politeness and Christian forbearance to invite Mrs. Robert Gray to tea—with the certainty that the invitation would be declined. She was an English girl whom Robert met somewhere in Switzerland—a heavy-eyed, silent creature, certainly a very beautiful woman, but most inefficient and sickly; and there were so many nice, sensible girls in Old Chester! (However, there is no use saying things like that: as if a man ever married a girl because she was sensible!)

Yet young Gray certainly needed a sensible wife; his wealth was limited to character and good manners, plus a slender income as tutor in the Female Academy in Upper Chester. Excellent things, all; but a wife with sense (and money) would have been an agreeable addition to his circumstances. Whereas, this very beautiful English girl was a penniless governess, left stranded in Germany by an employer, who had, apparently, got tired of her. Robert Gray had met the poor, frightened creature, who was taking her wandering way back to England, and married her, frantic with rage at the way she had been treated. When he brought her home, he was so madly in love that he probably did not half appreciate Old Chester's patience with her queer ways. But

the fact was, that for the few months she lived, she was so miserable that Old Chester could not help being patient, and forgiving her her half-sullen indifference, and her silence, and her distaste for life—even in Old Chester!

For in spite of Robert's adoration, in spite of all the ready friendliness about her, in spite of the birth of a baby girl, she seemed, as it were, to turn her face to the wall. She died when the child was about a week old. Died, the doctor said, only because, so far as he could see, she did not care to live.

"You ought to try to get better for the baby's sake," said Miss Rebecca Jones, who had come in to help nurse her. And the poor girl frowned and shook her head, the heavy, white lids falling over her dark eyes.

"I don't like it."

And Rebecca (who had too much good sense to be shocked by the vagaries of a sick woman) said, decidedly: "Oh, you'll learn to like her. Come, now, just try!"

But she did not seem to try; even though Robert, kneeling with his arm under her pillow, holding her languid hand to his lips, said, sobbing, "Oh, Alys, Alys, Alys—for God's sake—don't leave me——"

Then she opened her beautiful eyes and looked at him solemnly. "Robert," she said, "I am sorry. I am—sorry. I—am——"

"What for, precious?" he entreated; "sorry for what? to leave me? "Oh, Alys, then live, live, dear!"

"I—am——" she began; and then her voice trailed into eternity.

Miss Rebecca Jones hung about the house

for a few days, to make the poor gentleman comfortable; then he was left alone with the child (purchased at so dreadful a cost) and one servant, and his daily work of teaching the polite languages at the Female Academy. Miss Rebecca's hard face softened whenever she thought of him; but all she could do for him was to go often to see the poor seven-months baby—which seemed for a time inclined to follow its mother.

Now it must be understood at once that Rebecca Jones was not a schemer, or a mean or vulgar woman. She was merely a hard-headed, honest-hearted product of years of public-school teaching, with a passion for truth and no grace in telling it. She was sorry for Mr. Gray, and sorry for the poor baby, who was being allowed, she said to herself, to grow up every which way; and sorry for the comfortless house left to the care of what she called "an uneducated servant-girl." So, after school, and on Saturday mornings, she used to go over to Mr. Gray's house and bustle about to the bettering of several things. Indeed, old Mr. Jones told her more than once that he didn't know what that there widower would do without her. And Rebecca said, truthfully enough, that she didn't know, either. And when she said it her heart warmed with something more than pity.

As for Robert Gray, dazed and absent, trying to do his duty at the Academy during the day, and coming home at night to look blankly at his child, he, too, did not know what he would have done that first year without Miss Rebecca's efficient kindness. He was so centred in his grief, and also of so gentle a nature, that he took the kindness as simply as a child might have done. Like many another sweet-minded man, he had not the dimmest idea of the possible effect of his rather courtly manner and his very delicate courtesy upon a woman of slightly different class, whose life had been starved of everything romantic or beautiful. He became to sharp-tongued Miss Rebecca Jones a vision of romance; and, somehow, quite suddenly, about eighteen months after his wife's death, he discovered that he was going to marry her. In his startled astonishment, he realized that he had himself led up to her avowal of willingness by some talk about her kindness. Perhaps she had misunderstood his words; if she had, Robert Gray was not the man to offer an explanation. . . . However, after the first shock of being accepted, he was gently explicit:

"I realize that the child ought to have the care of a good woman, and therefore I——"

"I'll do my duty by her," Rebecca said.

"I want her brought up to love and reverence her mother. I want her brought up to be like her. It is for the child's sake that I—I marry again. I speak thus frankly, Miss Rebecca, because I so entirely respect you that I could not be anything but frank."

Rebecca's square face flushed over the high cheek-bones to the gaunt forehead and the sparse hair; then her eyes looked passionately into his. "I understand. Yes; I understand. And I will be good to your child, Mr. Gray."

And so he married her; and, when you come to think of it, it was a very sensible thing to do. Even Old Chester said he was very sensible. A man of thirty, with a baby—of course he ought to marry again! "But why on earth," said Old Chester, "when there are so many girls of his own class!—not but what Rebecca Jones is a very worthy person."

Meanwhile, Rebecca, with hard conscientiousness, set herself to bring the child up. She trained her, and disciplined her, and made a painful point of talking to her about the first Mrs. Gray, according to her promise to teach her to "love and reverence her mother." The discipline sometimes made Robert Gray wince; but it was wise, and never unkind; so he never interfered;—but he left the room when it was going on. Once he said, nervously:

"I scarcely think, Mrs. Gray, that it is necessary to be quite so severe?"

"She must be made a good child," Rebecca answered.

"I am not afraid that she will not be a good child," Robert Gray said; "she is her mother's daughter."

"Well, she is her father's daughter, too," Rebecca declared, briefly. And her husband, shrinking, said:

"Light is stronger than darkness; Alice's mother was a creature of light. I am not afraid of her inheritance of darkness."

As for Rebecca, she went away and shut herself up in the garret. " 'Creature of light!' " she said, sitting on the floor under the rafters, and leaning her head on an old horsehair-covered trunk wherein were packed away Mr. Gray's winter flannels—"well, I am a good wife to him, if I ain't a 'creature of light.' "

Yes, she was a good wife. . . . How carefully she put his flannels away in May; how prudently she planned his food; how she managed to make the two ends of his little income meet—yes, and lap over, so that every summer he could go away from her for a two months' vacation in the woods! Not once did he find a button lacking; not once had he put on a clean pair of stockings and then pulled them off because of a hole in the heel. Can our lords say as much, my mistresses? I trow not! Yes, a good wife: that lovely being who left the world with a faint, unfinished regret upon her pitiful lips could never have made him so comfortable.

Indeed, the whole household revolved upon Robert's comfort. Every domestic arrangement had reference to his well-being. That he did not become intolerably selfish was not Rebecca's fault, for, like many good wives, she was absolutely without conscience in the matter of self-sacrifice; but Robert escaped spiritual corruption, thanks to his own very gentle nature and his absolute unconsciousness of the situation. Perhaps, too, Rebecca's tongue mitigated the spoiling process. She never spared him what she considered to be the truth about himself or Alice. But her truthfulness stopped here; she spared the dead, perforce. For what could she say ill of that beautiful creature whose only wrong-doing lay in dying? But she knew, with shame, that she would have liked to speak ill of her—in which reprehensible impulse to remove a fellow-being from a pedestal, Rebecca showed herself singularly like the rest of us.

In this bleak air of unselfishness and truth-telling, Robert Gray became more and more aloof. Gradually he retreated quite into the past, doing his daily work at the Academy—where successive classes of young ladies adored him for his gentle manners and his mild, brown eyes—and living very harmlessly with his memories, which he kept fresh and fragrant by sharing them with Alys's daughter, who, it must be admitted, being young and human, was not always intensely interested; but Rebecca had trained her too well for Alice ever to show any weariness. Robert kept his little collection of pictures and photographs of his first wife shut behind the curtained doors of an old secretary. If his second wife found him standing, his hands clasped behind him, his eyes wandering from one lovely presentment to another, he never displayed an embarrassed consciousness, but he shut the doors. He accepted Rebecca's devotion respectfully; he was never impolite, still less unkind; in fact, in all their married life he had never, she used to tell herself, spoken unkindly save once; and then his words were nothing more dreadful than, "We will not discuss it, if you please, Mrs. Gray." At first he had, very gently, made some grammatical suggestions; and she had profited by them, though, being a true Pennsylvanian, she never mastered "shall" and "will," nor did she lose the Pennsylvania love for the word 'just'; to the end of her days, Rebecca was 'just tired out'; or 'just real glad'; or 'just as busy as could be.' Grammar, however, was as far as Robert Gray went in any personal relation. He addressed her, in his courteous voice (always a little timidly), as "Mrs. Gray"; and he kept as much as possible out of her way. Meantime, Rebecca (remembering why he had married her) did her duty by the child, and never failed to mention, in her hard voice, that Alice must try to grow up like her mother.

"Make me a good girl," Alice used to say in her sleepy prayers every night—"make me a good girl, like my dear mother." Once, of her own accord, the child added, "And make me pretty like her, too." Rebecca, listening to the little figure at her knee, said, sternly, when Alice got up and began to climb into the big four-poster:

"Don't be vain. Don't ask God for foolish things. Beauty is foolish and favor is deceitful. Just ask Him to make you as good as your mother was."

And, indeed, it must be admitted that the child did not inherit her mother's wonderful beauty. At first her father had expected it; he used to take liberties with his Horace, and say:

"O filia pulchra matre pulchriore."

But as Alice grew older, Robert Gray had to admit that the dead woman had taken her beauty away with her. The child had just a pleasant face; eyes that were gray or blue, as it happened; a commonplace nose, and uncompromisingly red hair. In those days red hair was thought to be a mortifying affliction, and poor, plain Alice shed many tears over the rough, handsome shock of hair that broke into curls about her forehead and all around the nape of her pretty, white neck.

II

But in spite of red hair, and what Old Chester religiously believed to be its accompanying temper, Alice Gray was a lovable girl, and at twenty, behold, she had a lover; indeed, she had more than one (not counting Dr. Lavendar); but Alice never gave a thought to anybody but Luther Metcalf. Luther was a good boy, Old Chester said; but added that he would never set the river on fire.

Certainly he did not use his incendiary opportunity; he had a small printing-office, and he owned and edited Old Chester's weekly newspaper, the *Globe*; but neither the news nor the editorial page ever startled or displeased the oldest or the youngest inhabitant. The *Globe* confined itself to carefully accredited cuttings from exchanges; it had a Poet's Corner, and it gave, politely, any Old Chester news that could be found; besides this, it devoted the inner sheet to discreet advertisements, widely spaced to take up room. All Old Chester subscribed for it, and spoke of it respectfully, because it was a newspaper; and snubbed its editor, because he was one of its own boys—and without snubbing boys are so apt to put on airs! Poor Luther was never tempted to put on airs; he was too hard-worked and too anxious about his prospects. He and Alice were to get married when he and the *Globe* were out of debt; for his father had left him a mortgage on the office building, as well as an unpaid-for press. When Luther was particularly low-spirited, he used to tell Alice it would take him five years to pay his debts; and, to tell the truth, that was an optimistic estimate, for the *Globe* and the printing-office together did very little more than pay the interest on the notes and Luther's board.

So, when they became engaged, waiting was what they looked forward to, for, of course, Robert Gray could not help them; it was all Rebecca could do to stretch his salary to cover the expenses of their own household. But the two young people were happy enough, except when Luther talked about five years of waiting.

"We've been engaged two years already," he said, moodily; "I don't want to be another case of Andrew Steele."

"I'm not afraid," Alice said. "Why, if you get the new job press, and get that Mercer work, think how much that will help!"

"Well," Luther said, "yes; but if I get the press, there's another debt. And if I don't get it, I can't get the work; so there it is. A vicious circle."

This question of the purchase of a new press, before the old press had been paid for, was a very serious and anxious one. "I wish father could help," Alice said—they were walking home from Wednesday-evening lecture, loitering in the moonlight, and wishing the way were twice as long.

"Oh, I wouldn't think of such a thing," the young man declared; "we'll pull out somehow. He's gone off to the woods, hasn't he?"

"Yes, he went this morning; he's so pleased to get away! He won't be back till the Academy opens."

"I suppose he hates to leave you, though," Lute said.

"Yes, but I can see that the getting away is a great relief. I keep his pictures dusted, and take the flowers up to the cemetery for him; so he knows things are not neglected."

"But," Luther said, thoughtfully, "I think she's sorry to have him go?"

"Oh yes; sorry, I suppose," Alice admitted "She's fond of him—in her way."

"Then why——" Luther began.

"My dear, she's *jealous* of my mother."

"Oh, Alice!"

"Well, you know," Alice explained, "my mother was so beautiful—and poor Mrs. Gray! But I must say, Lute, she's the justest person I know. She's always told me that my mother was perfect. And of course she was; but when you're jealous, it isn't so easy to acknowledge things like that."

"But I don't see how you can be jealous of the dead," Luther ruminated.

"Oh, *I* do! I could be jealous of some girl who was dead, if you'd loved her, Lute." And then the boy put his arm round her, and they kissed each other there in the shadows of the locust-trees overhanging a garden wall. "I'm so glad there isn't anybody, dead or alive," Alice said, happily; "though I'd rather have her alive than dead. If she were alive, you'd have quarrelled with her, and stopped loving her. But if she were dead, she would keep on being perfect. Yes; I'd rather marry a man who had been—been *divorced*," said Alice, lowering her voice, because the word was hardly considered proper in Old Chester, "than a man whose wife was dead, because he would always be thinking what an angel she was and what a sinner I was."

"He would think you were an angel," the boy told her, blushing at his own fervency.

But the fervency died on his ardent young lips when they got into the house and sat decorously in the parlor with Mrs. Gray. Rebecca was sewing, her hard, square face a little harder than usual. Mr. Gray had gone away on that annual fishing-trip—gone, with a look of relief growing in his eyes even as he stepped into the stage and pulled the door to behind him; pulled it hurriedly, as though he feared she would follow. Then, baring his head politely, he had looked out of the window and said:

"Good-bye. You will send for me should you, by any chance, need me. I trust you will be very well."

"I don't know that I have ever had to interrupt your fishing-trip with any of my needs," Rebecca had answered, briefly. She spoke only the truth; she never had interfered with any pleasure of his; and yet Robert Gray had winced, as if he had not liked her words. Now, alone, in the parlor, darning his stockings, she wondered why. She never said anything but the simple truth; but he looked at her sometimes as a dog looks who expects a blow. He was truthful himself, but he never seemed to care much to hear the truth, she thought, heavily. Once he told her that truth was something more than a statement of fact. The statement of a fact may be a lie, he had said, smiling whimsically; and Rebecca used to wonder how a fact could be a lie? She recalled the time when, with brief accuracy, she had mentioned to him in what condition of ragged neglect she had found his wardrobe after the "creature of light" had left him; and how he had seemed to shrink not from the shiftless dead, but from her. And she remembered painfully that one unkindness: She had told him that, to her mind, not even the weakness of death was quite an excuse for saying you didn't like your own baby; and he had said with a terrible look, "We will not discuss it, if you please, Mrs. Gray." She had never spoken of it again; but his look had burned into her poor, narrow, sore mind; she thought of it now, moodily, as she sat alone, her heart following him on his journey. If his first wife had only not been so perfect, she said to herself, she could have borne it better; if she had had a bad temper, even, it would have been something. But she had often heard Robert tell Alice that her mother had an "angelic temper." Rebecca wished humbly she herself could be pleasanter. "I don't feel unpleasant inside; but I seem to talk so," she thought, helplessly. She was thinking of this when the two young people came in; and looking up over her spectacles, she said, coldly:

"Did you remember to wipe your feet, Luther? You are careless about that. Alice, I found a flower on my daphne; you can carry the pot up to the cemetery when you go."

"Yes, ma'am," Alice said. She took up her sewing (for Rebecca would not have idle hands about); sometimes she glanced at Luther, sitting primly in the corner of the sofa, and once caught his eye and smiled; but there were no sheep's-eyes or sweet speeches. They were Old Chester young people, and such things would have been considered improper; just as sitting by themselves would have been thought not only indecorous, but selfish.

"Oh, Alice," Luther said, suddenly, "I meant to ask you; wasn't your mother's name spelled 'Alys'?"

"Yes. Why?"

"Well, it's such an unusual name that it struck my attention when I saw it in the paper."

"What about it?" Alice asked. "Oh, dear, why didn't father spell me 'Alys' instead of 'Alice'? It's so much prettier!"

"Prettiness isn't everything; and 'Alice' is a sensible name," Rebecca said. "Don't criticise your father."

"It was an advertisement in one of the *Globe's* exchanges," Luther explained. "I was scissoring things, and the name caught my eye. It was information wanted. Of course it's just a coincidence, but it's queer, because—here it is," said the editor of the *Globe*, fumbling in his pocket. "I cut it out and meant to show it to you, but I forgot. Then he read, slowly, "*Information wanted of one Alys Winton———*"

"Why, but Winton was my mother's name!" cried Alice.

"*—one Alys Winton, who married sometime in 1845; husband thought to be an American, name unknown. She (or a child of hers, born in 1846) is requested to communicate with Amos Hughes, Attorney at Law,*" etc.

Alice stared, open-mouthed. "Why, Lute!" she said—"why, but that must be my mother!"

Lute shook his head. "I don't think there's anything in it. Do you, Mrs. Gray?"

"Might be," she said, briefly.

Alice took the crumpled cutting, and holding it under the lamp, read it through to herself. "But, Lute, really and truly," she said, "it is queer. Perhaps some of my mother's rich relations have left her a fortune! Then we could pay off the mortgage. Only I'm afraid my mother hadn't any rich relations—or poor ones, either. I never heard of any. Did you, Mrs. Gray?"

"No," Rebecca said.

"She was a governess, you know, Lute, in some horrid English family; the wife didn't like her, and she discharged my poor little mother; then the family went off and left her all alone in Germany. Perfectly abominable!"

"Don't be unjust, Alice; you don't know anything about it," Mrs. Gray said. "She was very young. Perhaps she couldn't teach the children to suit their parents. Though it was unkind to leave her unprovided for," she added, with painful fairness.

"I guess it was!" cried Alice. "Oh, how angry father gets when he talks about it! He says she was in such terror, poor little thing, when he met her. And yet she was very forgiving, father says. He says she wrote and told the gentleman that she was married. *I* wouldn't have. I'd have let him think I'd starved, so he would have suffered remorse—the wretch!"

"I hope you would not have been so foolish or so selfish," her step-mother said.

"You see, she had no relations to turn to," Alice explained to Luther; "if father hadn't come, dear knows what would have become of her."

"I suppose she could have earned an honest living, like anybody else," Mrs. Gray said.

"Well, anyway," Alice said, thoughtfully, "this advertisement is queer. She had no relations that father ever heard of; but there might be some one. What do you think, Mrs. Gray?"

"There might be," Rebecca said. She thought to herself that it was very probable; that first wife had brought Robert Gray beauty and love; it only needed that she should bring him money to make it all perfect. In her bleak mind a window of imagination suddenly opened, and she had a vision of what wealth would mean to her husband, coming as a gift from those dead hands. She set her lips, and said: "Better find out about it, Luther. Write to the man and say that a person of that name before her marriage, died here in Old Chester, leaving a child—and don't keep your hands in your pockets; it's bad manners."

"Do you really think it is worth while, ma'am?" Luther said, incredulously.

"Of course it is," said Alice. "Suppose it should be some inheritance? Such things do happen."

"In story-books," Lute said.

"Well, then I'd like to be in a story-book," Alice said, sighing. "Just think, Lute, we might pay for the press and pay off the mortgage!"

"Golly!" said Lute.

Then they fell to making all sorts of plans, gayly, each tripping the other up with the prosaic reminder of improbability.

"Or, if it *should* be anything," Luther said, "it won't be more than $100."

"Well, that's something; it will meet two monthly payments on the press."

"It will pay for a diamond-ring for you," Lute said.

"Nonsense! We'll buy father a horse."

"And who will buy the oats?" Rebecca said.

"I could give you a big oleander, Mrs. Gray," Alice told her, smiling.

"You could put the money in the bank, like a sensible girl," Rebecca said, severely. "Don't speak of this outside, either of you.

Mr. Gray wouldn't wish his wife's name talked about."

"And don't let's write anything about it to him," Alice said; "let's have it a surprise!—if there is anything in it; only, of course, there isn't anything," she ended, sighing. "But you might write to the man, Lute."

"Of course there isn't anything," Lute agreed, sensibly. "I'll write if you want me to; but I wouldn't build on it, Ally," he said, as he got up to go. And when he paused a minute in the darkness on the porch, he added, softly, "If you get rich, maybe you won't want a poor printer?"

And she laughed, and said, "Maybe I won't!"

Then he kissed her just under her left ear, and said, "Money isn't everything, Ally."

III

Money isn't everything, but it has so much to do with most things that even a dim, story-book vision of it stirred Alice's imagination. Luther, having no imagination, dismissed the vision from his mind after writing a letter to "Amos Hughes, Attorney at Law." Indeed, Luther had more practical things to think of than possible legacies, poor fellow. His balance-sheet for that month of June was very dark. More than once, after the office was closed for the day, he sat at his desk in his shirt-sleeves, hot and tired and grimy, poring over his ledger by the light of a swinging lamp. Alice grew worried about his pallor and the hollows in his cheeks; but there was nothing she could do, though she chafed against her helplessness to help, and revolved all sorts of schemes in her impractical girl-mind. Indeed, she went so far as to pour out her heart to Dr. Lavendar, in the hope that he could make some suggestion. She found the old man sitting in the wistaria arbor near his beehives, smoking peacefully, and throwing sticks to Danny, who needed exercise and scrambled after them into the tall grass, bringing them back with fatiguing alacrity.

"Look here, sir," said Dr. Lavendar, "don't find 'em so quick. I'm worn out pitching them."

Then Alice Gray came down between the box borders and said she wanted his advice; and Dr. Lavendar, glancing up at her, saw an uncertain lip and heard a catch in her voice; whereupon he told her to give Danny a run. "The scoundrel has kept me working for the last half-hour," he complained.

When she came back, flushed and laughing, and sat down on the arbor step, her voice was quite steady; so he listened placidly to her story.

"You want to get some work to help Lute, do you, good-for-nothing?"

"Yes," Alice said, eagerly. "Oh, Dr. Lavendar, *can* you think of anything? I wanted to go into the office and learn to set type, but Mrs. Gray——"

"Well?"

"Mrs. Gray said I had better learn to keep house economically. She said father wouldn't like it."

"Mrs. Gray would always think first of what your father would like."

Alice scratched lines in the gravel with one of Danny's sticks. "I suppose she would," she admitted.

"And what did Lute say?"

"Oh, he wouldn't listen to it. But I thought maybe you could make him, Dr. Lavendar?"

"I?" said Dr. Lavendar. "No, thank you. Do you think I'd rob the boy?"

"Rob him?"

"Of his self-respect; a boy wants to stand on his own legs; he doesn't want a girl propping him up. You let Lute alone. He'll manage. And you're young yet, anyhow. It won't hurt ye to wait. Mrs. Gray is right. You learn to be as good a housekeeper as she is; and though you mayn't put money into Lute's pocket before you're married, you'll not be taking it out after you're married."

Alice sighed. "Oh, I wish I could help Lute; I wish I had a lot of money."

"A lot of sense is better," Dr. Lavendar said, chuckling. "Oh, you women! You steal a man's unselfishness and self-respect, and you put it down to *love*. Love? You're a pack of thieves, the lot of you. You ought to be prosecuted. I'd do it, if I had time. Hey, Danny! bite her; she's like all the rest of 'em."

Alice hugged him, and defended herself. "You're just an old bachelor; you don't appreciate us."

"Appreciate ye? I appreciate you. Maybe that's why I'm an old bachelor."

But though he discouraged Alice's projects for assisting Luther, Dr. Lavendar went plodding up the printing-office stairs the next morning. Luther, emerging from behind a press, brightened at the sight of his caller, and ushered him into a small closet which he called his private office; and when Dr. Lavendar asked him to print some more missionary-meeting notices, he said he would put them in at cost price.

"Don't you do it!" said Dr. Lavendar, thumping the floor with his umbrella. "Look

here; I'll have to teach you the first principles of business: make your profit—and don't go to 'pauperizing the Church,' sir. There's too much of that sort of thing," he added, with reminiscent crossness. "Some scalawag of a bookseller wrote and offered to sell me books at thirty-three per cent. discount because I was a *parson*. There's no more reason why a parson should get a discount than a policeman. I told him so. I tell you so. Print those slips, and *print 'em better than you did the last lot!* Do you hear that? You forgot a comma on the second line. How's business, Lute?"

Lute's face fell. Then they talked things over, to the boy's great comfort; and at the end of the talk Lute straightened his shoulders and drew a good breath.

"By George! sir, if hanging on does it, I'll hang on——" he stopped, and looked round, in answer to a knock. "Well?" he said, impatiently. But the gentleman who stood in the doorway was not rebuffed.

"Are you Mr. Metcalf, the editor of the *Globe?*"

"Yes, sir," said Luther.

"I called in relation to an advertisement"— Luther was instantly alert, and Dr. Lavendar, scenting a customer, was about to withdraw— "an advertisement in a New York paper, requesting information of a certain person——"

"What!" cried Luther. "I had forgotten all about it."

"My name is Carter. I am from the office of Mr. Amos Hughes. Messrs. Pritchett, Carver, and Pritchett, Solicitors at Law, of London, are our principals. The advertisement was in relation to a person called Alys Winton."

Luther, stumbling in his astonishment over his words, began to explain. "Mrs. Gray is dead," he ended. "And Alice is her daughter; isn't she, Dr. Lavendar? She asked me to write to you."

"Well, well; this is very interesting," said Dr. Lavendar. "I hope your object in seeking to obtain information is to benefit this young lady? She's one of my children."

Mr. Carter, still standing in the doorway, smiled, and said, "Do I understand that this Miss Alice is the daughter of the person named Alys Winton?"

"Yes," said Dr. Lavendar. "You can easily satisfy yourself on that point by consulting my parish records."

"And her mother is the lady you advertised for!" cried Luther. The boy was red with excitement. It was just as Alice said—a story-book. And they could get married right away!

For it would be a lot of money—perhaps $5000; people in England didn't advertise for information of a person dead for twenty-two years for any small amount; well, even if it were $4000, they could get married; even if it were $3000. "How m——" he began, and stopped; of course that was not a proper question. "Alice's mother is the lady you advertised about," he said, lamely.

"Well, that does not follow, young gentleman; but the coincidence of the name was of sufficient interest for our firm to feel that I might, perhaps, just look into it. There may be dozens of Alys Wintons, you know."

"Oh," said Luther, so blankly that Dr. Lavendar laughed.

"Perhaps before beginning at the beginning you might save time by looking at the end," he said to the lawyer. "If you will step over to my church, you will see that our little Alice here is the daughter of Mr. Robert Gray and a lady named Alys Winton."

"A very good idea, sir. You, I infer, are a clergyman in this place? Ah, yes; just so. Lavendar? Ah, yes. I shall be pleased to look at the records, as you suggest, sir."

Luther, rather abashed, longing to accompany them, stood waiting for an invitation. But none came. Dr. Lavendar went pounding down the stairs, followed by Mr. Carter, and Lute heard them talking about the roughness of the road from Mercer over which Mr. Carter had come on the morning stage.

"Confound the road!" said Lute to himself. "Hi! Davidson! I'm going out. The first page is all made up; you can close up the fourth." Then he dashed down the creaking stairs and out into the hot sunshine. He had a glimpse up the street of the church, and Dr. Lavendar bending down fumbling with the key of the vestry door; it was evident that Luther's presence was not considered necessary. "I don't care," the boy said to himself, joyously, and started at a swinging pace over the hill. "I'll be the one to tell her, anyhow!" His face was all aglow. As he hurried along he made calculations as to the rent of the little house. To be sure, he was reckoning on Alice's money; but the boy was so honest, and so in love, that he had no mean self-consciousness of that kind. "We can get married!" He had no room for any other thought.

Mrs. Gray was sitting on the back porch shelling pease; there was a grape trellis running out from the porch roof, and under it the shadows lay cool and pleasant on the damp flagstones. Rebecca, absorbed in the lulling snap of pods, looked up, frowning, at the noisy interruption, for the young man burst in, breathless, swinging his cap, his eyes shining. "Oh, Mrs. Gray, where's Alice? Oh, my, such news! I never was so excited in my life!"

"That is not saying much," Rebecca told him; "you've not had a very exciting life. Alice is in the dining-room. Alice! come out here. Here's Luther. He says he never was so excited in his life; and I hope he won't be again, for he has upset my bucket of pods."

Luther, full of apologies, began to pick them up. "I'm so sorry, but I was so dreadfully excited——"

"Dreadful is a large word," Rebecca said. "I doubt whether either you or I have ever seen anything 'dreadful' in our lives. Don't exaggerate, Luther."

"Yes, ma'am," Lute said. "Oh, there's Alice! Alice!" He stood up, his hands full of pods, his face red. "Oh, Alice, what do you suppose has happened? You'll never guess!"

"The advertisement man!" cried Alice. Luther's face fell a little, and he laughed. "Well, you're pretty smart. Yes, it is——"

"What?" said Rebecca Gray. As for Alice, she whirled out on the cool flags and jumped up and down.

"Oh, Lute, tell us—tell us! What does he say? Has he sent some money? Oh, how much is it? Oh, Lute, we'll pay for the press. Lute, is it—is it $1000? Tell us; hurry, hurry!"

Upon which Lute began to subside. "Well, it isn't quite—I mean, he didn't—he hasn't said just exactly how much. I mean, of course, I suppose, it isn't certain; but I'm sure there isn't a particle of doubt; only——"

"Now, Lute, begin at the beginning and tell us." Alice sat down breathlessly beside her step-mother, and began mechanically to shell the peas.

"Don't," Rebecca said; "I will do my own work. You'd better get your table-cloth and finish that darning." Her face had grown quite pale; she saw the fabric of her life crumbling at the base; if, through that first wife, money should come into the family, what use for her patient economies? What use for her existence? That first wife, yet more perfect, would crowd her further from her husband's life. In her heart, used to the long, dull ache of unloved years, rose up a murderous hatred of the dead woman. At first she hardly heard Luther's story, but as it went on she began to listen and the pain in her tightened throat of unshed tears lessened. It might not be. As this Mr. Carter said, there might be dozens of Alys Wintons. Her hands, motionless after the first shock, went at their work again.

"You're the daughter of a lady of that name," she said, coldly; "but she may not be the lady they want. Better not count on it." Alice looked rather blank for a moment; and then she burst into even more than Luther's confidence.

"Do you suppose it will be $2000? Oh, Lute, just think, we'll pay for the new press right down!"

"No, we won't, either," Lute said, stoutly. "I'm not going to let you spend your money on printing-presses."

"Nonsense!" Alice cried, laughing and stamping her foot.

Rebecca frowned and looked at her over her glasses. "Don't be unlady-like, Alice."

"No, 'm," Alice said; and then she laughed at her own excitement; "it may be only $100."

"It may be nothing at all," Rebecca Gray said, and got up and took her pan and bucket and went into the house. It seemed to her that if she had to hear any more of Alys Winton she would speak out and say some dreadful thing about her. But what could she say with any kind of truth? What could she say ill of that poor creature, so beloved and so harmless? For, after all, though a woman ought to see that a man's buttons are sewed on, you can't say that mere shiftlessness is a sin. Besides, she was sick for those few months. "Perhaps if my health hadn't been good, I would have been careless myself," Rebecca thought, with painful justice. But she went up-stairs to her own room and locked the door. She felt sure that it was as Alice and Luther said: there would be money, and she would be of still less consequence to her husband; for what did Robert Gray, nervously polite, really care for her economies and her good housekeeping?

"Not *that!*" she said to herself, bitterly.

IV

"You will stay and have dinner with me," Dr. Lavendar had told the lawyer, hospitably, "and then Goliath and I will take you up the hill to Mr. Gray's house."

And so, in the early afternoon, Goliath brought Mr. Carter to the Grays' door. Alice, who was on the porch, insisted that Dr. Lavendar should come in, too; she leaned into the buggy to whisper, joyously, "If it is anything nice, I want you to hear it."

But for once Dr. Lavendar did not laugh and give her a kiss and call her his good-for-nothing; he got out silently, and followed Mr. Carter into the parlor, where Luther and Mrs. Gray were awaiting them. There was a tense feeling of expectation in the air. The two

young people were together on the sofa, smiling and laughing, with small, whispered jokes of presses and diamond-rings and mortgages. Rebecca sat by the table, her worn hands in a trembling grip in her lap; she sat very upright, and was briefer and curter than ever, and she looked most of the time at the floor.

"You have been informed of my errand, madam?" said Mr. Carter. "It is unfortunate that Mr. Gray is not at home, but perhaps you may be able to give us some information on certain points, which will at least instruct me as to whether the facts in the case warrant further reference to him for confirmation. I will ask a few questions, if you please?"

"Go on," Rebecca said.

"The late Mrs. Gray, the mother of this young lady," said Mr. Carter—"do you happen to know her nationality?"

"English."

"Ah, yes. Just so. And do you know the date of her marriage to Mr. Gray?"

Rebecca gave it.

"If any facts in regard to her occur to you——" the lawyer began.

"I've heard Mr. Gray say that she was a governess in the family of a Mr. Urquhart," Rebecca said; and added, "They discharged her in Berlin."

Mr. Carter, glancing at a memorandum, his face keen with interest, said, eagerly, "Pray proceed, madam."

"I don't know much more; Mr. Gray met her in Interlaken. They were married three weeks afterwards."

"Ah, Switzerland? That explains; there was no record of a marriage at the Embassy. Can you tell me anything of the parentage of the lady?"

"Her father's name was George Winton," Alice broke in, "and they lived in a place called Medfield. He was a clergyman. Her mother's name was Alys, too. Father has a prayer-book belonging to my grandmother; it has her name in it, and my mother's. Would you like to see it, sir?"

"Exceedingly," Mr. Carter said; and while Alice ran to get the book, he studied his memorandum so closely that no one dared to ask him a question, if, indeed, any one wanted to. Rebecca had answered him dully, looking out of the window part of the time, part of the time at the floor. Dr. Lavendar, on the other side of the room, his hands on the head of his cane, sat silently staring down at the carpet, his face heavy and rather stern. Lute, radiant, twirled his cap in his hands, and resolutely held his tongue.

Alice, as she handed the prayer-book to Mr. Carter, stopped on her way back to Luther and squeezed Dr. Lavendar's hand. "Isn't it wonderful?" she whispered; and he shook his head a little impatiently.

"Go and sit down, my dear," he said.

Mr. Carter, glancing at the name on the fly-leaf, looked at his notes again and then at Alice. "And this young lady—can she give me the date of her birth?"

There was a little laugh, and Luther and Alice gave it together, eagerly.

There were two or three more questions, and then Mr. Carter folded his memorandum and slipped it within its rubber band with a snap; then he smiled. Rebecca looked at him drearily. "Of course," he said, addressing himself to her, "a question of identity cannot be decided offhand; it is necessary to have certain affidavits which the surviving husband of the deceased (who is asserted to be the person in question) would be obliged, legally, to furnish. I think, however, that I am not going beyond the line of discretion and propriety if I say that *if* Mr. Robert Gray can produce such proofs (which I think I am not unwarranted in saying I believe he can)—*if* he can, then this young lady is the heir to a very considerable fortune. I think, in point of fact, I have the right to say that, *if* (as I have said before) these proofs are forthcoming, the amount to be paid to the daughter of Alys Winton is £5000."

Rebecca Gray put her hand to her mouth and stared blindly at the floor. Dr. Lavendar thrust out his lower lip and frowned. As for Alice, she laughed aloud, then burst out crying.

"Oh, *Lute!*" she said, tremulously; and, somehow, the two children found themselves holding hands. "It's—it's so much!" she faltered.

"Five thousand pounds is—is $25,000!" the boy said, turning pale. There was a pause; no one seemed to know just what to say. Then Lute, suddenly: "Is it your mother's father that left it to you, Alice?"

She turned to Mr. Carter, drawing in her breath like a child. "Is it?"

"Ah—no," he answered, briefly.

"But I didn't know my mother had any relations?" Alice said, in a dazed way; "I thought father said—I'm sure he said—she hadn't any relations? Perhaps—perhaps it is a mistake, after all?"

"The testator was not a relative of the Alys Winton in question," Mr. Carter said. He glanced uneasily at Dr. Lavendar, who lifted his head and looked at him searchingly. "It

will be best to make further explanations to Mr. Gray," Mr. Carter said, hurriedly.

"But who has left the money to me—if it is to me?" Alice said, bewildered. "Can't I ask that? What is the name of the kind person? I think I might ask that."

"The name of the testator was Urquhart," Mr. Carter said, "but—but, you know, my dear young lady, the identity is not yet legally authenticated; so—therefore—perhaps—I think, Dr. Lavendar, I had best go now? I think you mentioned that the stage leaves at four?"

"Urquhart?" Alice said; "the man who was so unkind? Oh, Lute, I suppose he repented. Oh, how astonished father will be! He'll have to forgive him now."

"It's a pretty late repentance," Luther said, with a chuckle; "and how did he know about you, Alice? I don't see why he should leave you money, even if he was a brute to your mother. Still," said the boy, gayly, "I guess we won't complain?"

"Gracious!" cried Alice, "that is queer. Well, he *was* a kind person!"

Rebecca Gray stared, frowning, at the lawyer. "He knew—this Urquhart—that she had a child?" she said, slowly.

Mr. Carter was gathering up his papers. "Yes," he said—"yes; he—knew it."

"What?" said Rebecca, in a very low voice —*what?*"

"In view of the fact that, legally, the matter is still undecided," Mr. Carter said, hurriedly, "perhaps we need not take this point up? At all events, not here."

"Sir," said Rebecca, "why does Mr. Urquhart leave £5000 to Robert Gray's daughter?"

"He was sorry he was unkind to my mother," Alice said, her voice quivering. ("Oh, Lute, $25,000!")

"Alice," her step-mother said, in a loud, harsh voice, "you had better leave the room. Luther, go with Alice, please."

The two young people, bewildered, got up with blank faces, and with obvious reluctance obeyed. "But why should I be sent out, Lute?" Alice said, hotly, when they were in the hall. "It's my money—if I'm the person."

Luther stopped, and stood, frowning. On the boy's open, honest face came a perplexed look. But Alice said again, in injured tones, that she didn't know what Mrs. Gray meant.

In the parlor the three elders looked at each other in silence. Mrs. Gray had risen, and stood leaning forward, her trembling hands flat on the table.

"I don't—understand," she said.

"Mr. Carter," said Dr. Lavendar, "certain remarks of yours on our way up here made me apprehensive. I see that my friend, Mrs. Gray, is also—apprehensive. I would suggest that you have a few words with her alone. I will leave you."

"No," Rebecca said; "hear the end of it." Her hard face was red and hot. "Why does Mr. Urquhart leave the child of Robert Gray £5000? Why?"

"It is as I think you surmise, madam," John Carter said, gravely.

Rebecca recoiled, with a broken exclamation of horror.

Dr. Lavendar drew in his breath. "Oh, my poor Robert!" he said.

"It is so stated in the will," the lawyer went on; "there is no disguising it; nor, as far as I can see, can it be hidden from the legatee. The directions for finding this heir make the thing explicit. The testator states that he received information of the expected birth of his child *after* the marriage of the person in question, who did not mention her married name—hence our difficulty in tracing her."

Rebecca, her eyes narrowing into a cruel smile, sat down and rocked backward and forward in her chair.

"Dreadful—dreadful—dreadful!" she said, aloud, exultantly.

V

The last quarter of an hour, packed with tragic revelation, lost Mr. Carter the stage.

"I hope you will put up at the Rectory, sir," Dr. Lavendar said, as they drove away from Robert Gray's door.

"I thank you, sir," said Mr. Carter.

Then they fell into silence—Mr. Carter from politeness, Dr. Lavendar from horror. He was going back in his memory with painful effort; but it was all very vague. . . . He had hardly known her; she had been ill for those months that she had been in Old Chester, and she had made it very clear that she did not care to see people. He thought of her beautiful, sullen face; of Robert Gray's passionate devotion; of Old Chester's silent disapproval. . . . He groaned to himself, and John Carter looked at him sidewise.

After supper at the Rectory, they sat down to smoke in heavy silence; Mr. Carter respected the old man's distress, but wondered if he should not have been more comfortable with Van Horn at the Tavern. The glowing July day had darkened into rainy night, with a grumble of thunder back among the hills; but in the midst of a sudden downpour they heard footsteps on the path, and then some one pushed open the hall door, and flapped a wet umbrella on the steps before entering. A minute later Luther Metcalf stood, hesitating, on the study threshold.

"Dr. Lavendar——"

The old man got up hurriedly. "Yes, Lute. Come into the dining-room. You will excuse me, sir?" he said to Mr. Carter. He put his hand on Lute's arm, in a friendly grip, for there was a break in the boy's voice.

"I know about it," Lute said. They sat down at the dining-room table; Lute swallowed hard, and pulled with trembling fingers at his hatband; he did not lift his eyes. "And —and I want you to tell her not to take it."

"How is she, Lute?"

"I haven't seen her. She wouldn't come down-stairs. She sent me a little note," Luther said, taking it out of his breast-pocket, and then putting it back again tenderly. "'Course I won't pay any attention to it.'"

"Saying she'd release you, I suppose?"

"Yes; but that's nothing. I'll make her understand the minute I see her. But, Dr. Lavendar, I don't want that—that money!" the boy ended, almost with a sob. "I want you to tell her not to take it."

Dr. Lavendar was silent.

"At first I thought—I couldn't help thinking—we could get married right off. We could get married and have a home of our own; you know, we'd be rich people with all that money. And I suppose, honestly, that as things are now, there's no chance of our getting married for a good while. But I—I tell you what, sir. I'd rather never get married than—than touch that money!"

Dr. Lavendar nodded.

"You won't let her, sir? You'll make her give it back?"

"My dear boy, I can't 'make' Alice do anything. The money is hers."

"Oh, but Dr. Lavendar, won't you go and talk to her? It may be a temptation to her, just as it was to me, for a minute. We could just make the office hum, sir. We could put it right on its feet; we could have a real Daily. I know she'll think of that. *I* just thought we could get married. But Alice will think about helping the office, and me."

"Of course the money would bring ease to her father——" Dr. Lavendar stopped abruptly.

"Oh, my *God!*" Lute said, and dropped his head on his arms.

"Bring ease to—to the family," Dr. Lavendar ended lamely.

"You know Mr. Gray won't touch it," Lute burst out; "and I can't let Alice, either. Dr. Lavendar, I thought maybe you'd let me hitch Goliath up and drive you out to the house?"

"Not to-night, Lute. Alice has got to be alone. Poor child, poor child! Yes; we've all of us got to meet the devil alone. Temptation is a lonely business, Lute. To-morrow I'll go, of course. Did you answer her note?"

"Oh yes; right off. I just said, 'Don't be foolish,' and—and some other things. I didn't tell her we mustn't take the money, because I hadn't thought of it then. Mrs. Gray said she wouldn't come out of her room. Oh, just think of her, all by herself!" Luther bent over and fumbled with his shoelace; when he looked up, Dr. Lavendar pretended not to see his eyes.

When the boy went away, Dr. Lavendar went back to the study and asked John Carter some legal questions: Suppose he had not found this child, what would have become of the money? Suppose the child should now decline to take it, what then?

"Well," said Mr. Carter, smiling, "as a remote contingency, I suppose I might reply that it would revert to the residuary estate. But did you ever know anybody decline £5000, Dr. Lavendar?"

"Never knew anybody who had the chance," Dr. Lavendar said; "but there's no telling what human critters will do."

"They won't do that," said John Carter.

What a long night it was, of rain and wind and dreadful thought! . . . Rebecca had told Alice, with kindness, but with such a grip upon herself lest exultation should tremble in her voice, that she seemed harsher than ever. Then she told Lute. He pleaded that Alice would speak to him, and Mrs. Gray had gone to the girl's room and bidden her come downstairs.

"Come, Alice. You must control yourself. Come down and talk to Luther."

Alice shook her head. "I'll—write him a note."

Mrs. Gray carried the note back to Lute, and brought up the answer, which Alice read silently. Rebecca watched her; and then, with an effort, she said:

"Alice, remember we are not to judge. We don't understand. We must not judge. Good-night." She opened the door, and then looked at the child, seated, speechless, with blank eyes, on the edge of the bed. "Good-night, Alice. I—I'm sorry for you, poor girl!" and she came back hastily and kissed her.

At that, even in her daze of horror, a glimmer of astonishment came into Alice's face. But she did not look up or speak. When it grew dark, she began mechanically to get ready for bed; she knelt down, as usual, at the big chintz-covered winged chair and began to say her prayers, her mind blind as to her own words: "Bless dear father——" Then she cried out, suddenly and dreadfully, and covered her poor, shamed head with her arms, and prayed no more. Then came a long fit of crying, and then a dreary calm. Afterwards, as the night shut in with rain and rumble of thunder, the shame lightened a little, for, though she could not read it in the darkness, she held Lute's little note against her lips and kissed it, and cried over it, and said his words over to herself, and felt that at any rate there was one bright spot in it all: Lute would never have any more anxieties. Of Robert Gray she thought pitifully, but with not much understanding. Oh, dreadful, dreadful! But he had loved his wife so much (so the child thought) he would surely forgive her. Not knowing how little forgiveness counts for when a star goes out. Sometimes, sitting there on the floor, listening to the rain, she slept; then woke, with a numb wonder, which darkened into cruel understanding. *Shame; shame*—but Lute wouldn't be worried any more; Lute would be rich.

So the night passed. . . .

Rebecca Gray did not sleep. When the house was still she went up-stairs, eager to be alone. She shut her bedroom door softly; then she put her brass candlestick on the high bureau and looked about her. . . . Everything seemed strange. Here was her old-fashioned bed with its four mahogany posts like four slender obelisks; there was the fine darn in the valance of the tester; the worn strip of carpet on which she had knelt every night for all these twenty years; it was all the same, but it was all different, all unfamiliar. The room was suddenly the room where that woman had died; the old four-poster was the bed of that heartbreaking night, with sheets rumpling under a wandering hand and pillows piled beneath a beautiful, dying head; not her own bed, smooth and decorous and neat, with her own fine darn in the tester valance. She did not know the room as it was now; she did not know herself; nor Robert; nor that—that— *that woman*. She sat down, suddenly a little faint with the effort of readjusting a belief of twenty-two years. "She was a wicked woman," she said, out loud; and her astounded face stared back at her from the dim mirror over the mantel-piece. After a while she got up and began to walk back and forth; sometimes she drew a deep breath; once she laughed. "A wicked woman!" . . . Now he would know. Now he would see. And he would loathe her. He would hate her. He would—her lip drooped suddenly from its fierce, unconscious smile; he would—suffer. Yes; suffer, of course. But that couldn't be helped. Just at first he would suffer. Then he would hate her so much that he would not suffer. Not suffer? It came over her with a pang that there is no suffering so dreadful as that which comes with hating. However, she could not help that. Truth was truth! All the years of her hungry wifehood rose up, eager for revenge; her mind went hurriedly, with ecstasy, over the contrast; her painful, patient, conscientious endeavor to do her best for him. Her self-sacrifice, her actual deprivations—"I haven't had a new bonnet for —for four years!" she thought; and her lip quivered at the pitifulness of so slight a thing. But it was the whole tenor of her life. *She* had no vacations in the mountains; she would have liked new valances, but she spent hours in darning her old ones to save his money; she had turned her black silk twice; she had only had two black silks in twenty years. All the great things she had done, all the petty things she had suffered, rose up in a great wave of merit before her; and against it—what? Hideous deceit! Oh, how he would despise the creature! Then she winced; he would—suffer? Well, she couldn't help that. It was the truth, and he had got to face it. She was walking up and down, whispering to herself, a sobbing laugh on her lips, when suddenly, as she passed the mirror, she had a dim, crazy vision of herself that struck her motionless. A moment later she took the candle, and with one hand clutching for support at the high mantel-shelf —for her knees were shaking under her—held it close to the glass and peered into the back depths. Her pale, quivering face, ravaged with tears, stared back at her, like some poor ghost more ugly even than in life. "*A wicked woman.*" Yes—yes—yes; and he would have to know it. But when he knew it, what then? If his eyes opened to sin, would they open to——

"I have tried to make him comfortable," she said, faintly.

Suddenly she put the candle down and sank into a chair, covering her face with her poor, gaunt hands. . . .

And so the night passed. . . . The dawn was dim and rainy. It was about four o'clock that Alice, sitting on the floor, sleeping heavily, her head on the cushion of the chair, started, bewildered, at the noise of the opening door. Rebecca, in her gray dressing-gown, one hand shielding the flare of her candle, came abruptly into the room.

"Alice," she said, harshly, and stopped by the empty bed; then her eyes found the figure on the floor ("you ought to be in bed"), she said, in a brief aside; then: "Alice, I've been thinking it over. You can't take that money."

"I don't understand," Alice said, confused with sleep and tears.

"You can't take that money. If you do, your father would have to know. And he never must—he never must."

Alice pulled herself up from the floor and sat down in her big chair. "Not take the money?" she said, in a dazed way; "but it's mine."

"That's why you needn't take it. Thank God it was left to you, not just to 'her heirs.' Alice, I've gone all over it. I—I wanted you to take it"—Rebecca's voice broke; "yes, I—did."

"Well, it's mine," Alice repeated, bewildered.

Rebecca struck her hands together. "Yours not to take! Don't you see? You can save your father."

Alice, cringing, dropped her head on her breast with a broken word.

"Don't be a fool," the older woman said, trembling. "He's been your father ever since you were born. And it would be a pretty return for his love to tell him——"

Alice burst out crying; her step-mother softened.

"I am sorry for you, you poor girl. But, oh, Alice, think, *think* of your father!" She clasped her hands and stood, trembling; she took a step forward, almost as if she would kneel.

"If he would feel so dreadfully," Alice said, at last, "why—we needn't tell him where the money comes from."

"Now, Alice, that is absurd. Of course he would know. He would have to know. A girl doesn't inherit £5000 without her father's knowing where it comes from. And, anyway, Mr. Carter said that Mr. Gray would have to make a statement and swear to it. Of course he would—know."

"Do you mean you don't want me to have it at all?" Alice said, blankly.

"I've just explained it to you," Rebecca said, her voice harsh with anxiety. "You *can't* have it."

"But it's my money; I have a right to it. And it would make all the difference in the world to Lute. If he is going to take a girl—

like me, he ought to have the money, anyhow."

"And kill your father?" Rebecca said.

"Alice! Don't you see, he must go on believing that she is"—her voice grew suddenly tender—"that she is 'a creature of light?'"

"I want Lute to have the money," Alice said.

"Alice!" the other exclaimed, with dismay, "don't you think of your father at all? And—for your mother's sake."

Alice was silent; then, in a hard voice, "I don't like her."

"Oh!" Rebecca cried, and shivered. There was a pause; then she said, faintly, "For your own sake?"

Alice looked up sullenly. "Nobody need know; we would only say it had been left to —her. Nobody would know."

Suddenly, as she spoke, despite the plain face and the red hair, Alice looked like her mother. Rebecca stepped back with a sort of shock. Alice, crying a little, got up and began to pull down her hair and braid it, with unsteady fingers. Her step-mother watched her silently; then she turned to go away; then came back swiftly, the tears running down her face.

"Oh, Alice, it is my fault! I've had you twenty-two years, and yet you are like——See, Alice, child; give her a chance to be kind to him, in you. Oh, I—I don't know how to say it; I mean, let her have a chance! Oh—don't you see what I mean? She said she was sorry!" All the harshness had melted out of Rebecca's face; she was nothing but gentleness, the tears falling down her cheeks, her voice broken with love. "Alice, be good, dear. Be good. Be good. And I—I *will* be pleasanter, Alice; I'll try, indeed; I'll try——"

VI

"Well," said Mr. Amos Hughes, a week later, in the cool dusk of Dr. Lavendar's study, just before tea, "this is a most extraordinary situation, sir!"

"Will ye have a pipe?" said Dr. Lavendar, hospitably.

John Carter, his feet well apart, his back to the fireless grate, his hands thrust down into his pockets, said, looking over at his partner:

"Amos, Dr. Lavendar once remarked to me that there was no telling what human critters would do."

Dr. Lavendar chuckled.

"Very true," Amos Hughes admitted, putting one fat knee over the other; "but I must say that I never before knew a human critter throw away £5000."

"I'm sorry you haven't had better acquaintances," said Dr. Lavendar. "I have. I'm not in the least surprised at this child's behavior. Mr. Carter, are you looking for anything? You'll find a decanter on the sideboard in the next room, sir. This is a pretty good world, Mr. Amos Hughes; I've lived in it longer than you have, so you'll take my word for it. It's a pretty good old world, and Miss Alice Gray has simply decided to do the natural and proper thing. Why, what else could she do?"

"I could mention at least one other thing," said Mr. Carter.

"Extraordinary situation! but I suppose the residuary legatees won't make any objection," murmured Amos Hughes.

Dr. Lavendar rapped on the table with the bowl of his pipe. "My dear sir, would you have a girl, for a paltry £5000, break her father's heart?"

"Her father?"

"Mr. Gray would not, in my judgment, survive such a revelation," said Dr. Lavendar, stiffly.

"May I ask one question?" John Carter said.

"G' on," said Dr. Lavendar.

"What I would like to know is: How did you bring Miss Gray to look at the thing in this way?"

"I didn't bring her," said Dr. Lavendar, indignantly; "her Heavenly Father brought her. Look here, sir; this business of the law is all very well, and necessary, I suppose, in its way, but let me tell you, it's a dangerous business. You see so much of the sin of human nature that you get to thinking human nature has got to sin. You are mistaken, sir; it has got to be decent. We are the children of God, sir. I beg that you'll remember that—and then you won't be surprised when a child like our Alice does the right thing. Surprise is confession, Mr. Carter."

Mr. Carter laughed, and apologized as best he could for his view of human nature; and Dr. Lavendar was instantly amicable and forgiving. He took Mr. Amos Hughes's warning, that he should, as a matter of duty, lay very clearly before the young lady the seriousness of what she proposed to do, and not until he had exhausted every argument would he permit her to sign the papers of release which (as a matter of precaution) he had prepared. "She's of age," said Amos Hughes, "and nobody can say that she has not a right to refuse to proceed further in the matter. But I shall warn her."

" 'Course, man," said Dr. Lavendar; "that's your trade."

And so the evening came, and the three men went up to Robert Gray's house.

It was a long evening. More than once Dr. Lavendar trembled as he saw the kingdoms of the world and the glory of them spread before his child's eyes. But he said no word, and once, sternly, he laid his hand on Rebecca's arm to check some word of hers.

"Let her alone," he said.

It was eleven o'clock before there came a moment of solemn silence. Alice bent over a paper, which John Carter had read aloud to her, and signed her name. Luther and Rebecca and Dr. Lavendar witnessed the signature. Then Rebecca Gray took the girl in her arms.

"That young man has got something to him," Mr. Amos Hughes said, as they went back to the Rectory.

"If you could put some printing in his way, it would be a favor to me," said Dr. Lavendar.

"I shouldn't wonder if I could," the lawyer said.

"The girl is a fine creature, poor child," said Mr. Carter.

"Gentlemen," said Dr. Lavendar, "they are both good children, and they have behaved well; but there's somebody else, let me tell you!"

However, he did not tell them. Perhaps he kept his opinion for Robert Gray's ears, for once he said, smiling, in Rebecca's presence: "Robert, this wife of yours is a noble woman."

Mr. Gray, a little surprised, said, politely, looking with kind eyes at Rebecca, "Mrs. Gray is a very good wife, sir."

And Rebecca went up and hid herself in the garret and cried with joy.

BOOTH TARKINGTON (1869-   )
MONSIEUR BEAUCAIRE
(1899-1900)

I

The young Frenchman did very well what he had planned to do. His guess that the Duke would cheat proved good. As the unshod half-dozen figures that had been standing noiselessly in the entryway stole softly into the shadows of the chamber, he leaned across the table and smilingly plucked a card out of the big Englishman's sleeve.

"Merci, M. le Duc!" he laughed, rising and stepping back from the table.

The Englishman cried out, "It means the dirty work of silencing you with my bare hands!" and came at him.

"Do not move," said M. Beaucaire, so sharply that the other paused. "Observe behind you."

The Englishman turned, and saw what trap he had blundered into; then stood transfixed, impotent, alternately scarlet with rage and white with the vital shame of discovery. M. Beaucaire remarked, indicating the silent figures by a polite wave of the hand, "Is it not a compliment to monsieur that I procure six large men to subdue him? They are quite devote' to me, and monsieur is alone. Could it be that he did not wish even his lackeys to know he play with the yo'ng Frenchman who Meestaire Nash does not like in the pomp-room? Monsieur is unfortunate to have come on foot and alone to my apartment."

The Duke's mouth foamed over with chaotic revilement. His captor smiled brightly, and made a slight gesture, as one who brushes aside a boisterous insect. With the same motion he quelled to stony quiet a resentful impetus of his servants toward the Englishman.

"It's murder, is it, you carrion!" finished the Duke.

M. Beaucaire lifted his shoulders in a mock shiver. "What words! No, no, no! No killing! A such word to a such host! No, no, not mur-r-der; only disgrace!" He laughed a clear, light laugh with a rising inflection, seeming to launch himself upon an adventurous quest for sympathy.

"You little devilish scullion!" spat out the Duke.

"Tut, tut! But I forget. Monsieur has pursue' his studies of deportment, amongs' his fellow-countrymen."

"Do you dream a soul in Bath will take your word that I—that I——"

"That M. le Duc de Winterset had a card up his sleeve?"

"You pitiful stroller, you stable-boy, born in a stable——"

"Is it not an honor to be born where monsieur must have been bred?"

"You scurvy foot-boy, you greasy barber, you cutthroat groom——"

"Overwhelm'!" The young man bowed with imperturbable elation. "M. le Duc appoint' me to all the office' of his household'."

"You mustachioed fool, there are not five people of quality in Bath will speak to you——"

"No, monsieur, not on the parade; but how many come to play with me here? Because I will play always, night or day, for what one will, for any long, and al—ways fair, monsieur."

"You outrageous varlet! Every one knows you came to England as the French Ambassador's barber. What man of fashion will listen to you? Who will believe you?"

"All people, monsieur. Do you think I have not calculate', that I shall make a failure of my little enterprise?"

"Bah!"

"Will monsieur not reseat himself?" M. Beaucaire made a low bow. "So. We must not be too tire' for Lady Malbourne's rout. Ha, ha! And you, Jean, Victor, and you others, retire; go in the hallway. Attend at the entrance, Francois. So; now we shall talk. Monsieur, I wish you to think very cool. Then listen; I will be briefly. It is that I am well known to be all, entire' hones'. Gamblist? Ah, yes; true and mos' profitable; but fair, al—ways fair; every one say that. Is it not so? Think of it. And—is there never a w'isper come to M. le Duc that not all people belief him to play al—ways hones'? Ha, ha! Did it almos' be *said* to him las' year, after when he play' with Milor' Tappin'ford at the chocolate-house——"

"You dirty scandal-monger!" the Duke burst out. "I'll——"

"Monsieur, monsieur!" said the Frenchman. "It is a poor valor to insult a helpless captor. Can he retort upon his own victim? But it is for you to think of what I say. True, I am not reco'nize on the parade; that my frien's who come here do not present me to their ladies; that Meestaire Nash has reboff' me in the pomp-room; still, am I not known for being hones' and fair in my play, and will I *not* be belief', even I, when I lif' my voice and charge you aloud with what is already w'isper'? Think of it! You are a noble, and there will be some hang-dogs who might not fall away from you. Only such would be lef' to you. Do you want it tol'? And you can keep out of France, monsieur? I have lef' his service, but I have still the ear of M. de Mirepoix, and he know' I never lie. Not a gentleman will play you when you come to Paris."

The Englishman's white lip showed a row of scarlet dots upon it. "How much do you want?" he said.

The room rang with the gay laughter of Beaucaire. "I hol' your note' for sevenhunder' pound'. You can have them, monsieur. Why does a such great man come to play M. Beaucaire? Because no one else will-in' to play M. le Duc—he cannot pay. Ha, ha! So he come' to good Monsieur Beaucaire. Money, ha, ha! What I want with money?"

His Grace of Winterset's features were set awry to a sinister pattern. He sat glaring at his companion in a snarling silence.

"Money? Pouf!" snapped the little gambler. "No, no, no! It is that M. le Duc, impoverish', somewhat in a bad odor as he is, yet command, the *entrée* any-where—onless I—Ha, ha! Eh, monsieur?"

"Ha! You dare think to force *me*——"

M. Beaucaire twirled the tip of his slender mustache around the end of his white forefinger. Then he said: "Monsieur and me goin' to Lady Malbourne's ball to-night—M. le Duc and me!"

The Englishman roared, "Curse your impudence!"

"Sit quiet. Oh, yes, that's all; we goin' together."

"No!"

"Certain. I make all my little plan'. 'Tis all arrange'." He paused, and then said gravely, "You goin' present me to Lady Mary Carlisle."

The other laughed in utter scorn. "Lady Mary Carlisle, of all women alive, would be the first to prefer the devil to a man of no birth, barber."

"'Tis all arrange'; have no fear; nobody question monsieur's guest. You goin' take me to-night——"

"No!"

"Yes. And after—then *I* have the *entrée*. Is it much I ask? This one little favor, and I never w'isper, never breathe that—it is to say, I am always forever silent of monsieur's misfortune."

"*You* have the *entrée*!" sneered the other. "Go to a lackeys' rout and dance with the kitchen maids. If I would, I could not present you to Bath society. I should have cartels from the fathers, brothers, and lovers of every wench and madam in the place, even I. You would be thrust from Lady Malbourne's door five minutes after you entered it."

"No, no, no!"

"Half the gentlemen in Bath have been here to play. They would know you, wouldn't they, fool? You've had thousands out of Bantison, Rakell, Guilford, and Townbrake. They would have you lashed by the grooms as your ugly deserts are. *You* to speak to Lady Mary Carlisle! 'Od's blood! You! Also, dolt, she would know you if you escaped the others. She stood within a yard of you when Nash expelled you from the pump-room."

M. Beaucaire flushed slightly. "You think I did not see?" he asked.

"Do you dream that because Winterset introduces a low fellow he will be tolerated—that Bath will receive a barber?"

"I have the distinction to call monsieur's attention," replied the young man gayly, "I have renounce' that profession."

"Fool!"

"I am now a man of honor!"

"Faugh!"

"A man of the parts," continued the young Frenchman, "and of deportment; is it not so? Have you seen me of a fluster, or gross ever, or, what shall I say—*bourgeois?* Shall you be shame' for your guest' manner? No, no! And my appearance, is it of the people? Clearly, no. Do I not compare in taste of apparel with your yo'ng Englishman? Ha, ha! To be hope'. Ha, ha! So I am goin' talk with Lady Mary Carlisle."

"Bah!" The Duke made a savage burlesque. "'Lady Mary Carlisle, may I assume the honor of presenting the barber of the Marquis de Mirepoix?' So, is it?"

"No, monsieur," smiled the young man. "Quite not so. You shall have nothing to worry you, nothing in the worl'. I am goin' to assassinate my poor mustachio—also remove this horrible black peruke, and emerge in my own hair. Behol'!" He swept the heavy, curled mass from his head as he spoke, and his hair, coiled under the great wig, fell to his shoulders, and sparkled yellow in the candle-light. He tossed his head to shake the hair back from his cheeks. "When it is dress', I am transform'; nobody can know me; you shall observe. See how little I ask of you, how very little bit. No one shall reco'nize 'M. Beaucaire' or 'Victor.' Ha, ha! 'Tis all arrange'; you have nothing to fear."

"Curse you," said the Duke, "do you think I'm going to be saddled with you wherever I go as long as you choose?"

"A mistake. No. All I requi—all I beg—is this one evening. 'Tis all shall be necessary. *After*, I shall not need monsieur."

"Take heed to yourself—after!" vouch-safed the Englishman between his teeth.

"Conquered!" cried M. Beaucaire, and clapped his hands gleefully. "Conquered for the night! Aha, it is riz'nable! I shall meet what you send—after. One cannot hope too much of your patience. It is but natural you should attem' a little avengement for the rascal trap I was such a wicked fellow as to set for you. I shall meet some strange frien's of yours after to-night; not so? I must try to be not too much frighten'." He looked at the Duke curiously. "You want to know why I create this tragedy, why I am so unkind as to entrap monsieur?"

His Grace of Winterset replied with a chill glance; a pulse in the nobleman's cheek beat less relentlessly; his eye raged not so bitterly; the steady purple of his own color was returning; his voice was less hoarse; he was regaining his habit. "'Tis ever the manner of the vulgar," he observed, "to wish to be seen with people of fashion."

"Oh, no, no, no!" The Frenchman laughed. "'Tis not that. Am I not already one of these 'men of fashion'? I lack only the reputation of birth. Monsieur is goin' supply that. Ha, ha! I shall be noble from to-night. 'Victor,' the artis', is condemn' to death; his throat shall be cut with his own razor. 'M. Beaucaire'——" Here the young man sprang to his feet, caught up the black wig, clapped into it a dice-box from the table, and hurled it violently through the open door. "'M. Beaucaire' shall be choke' with his own dice-box. Who is the Phœnix to remain? What advantage have I not over other men of rank who are merely born to it? I may choose my own. No! Choose for me, monsieur. Shall I be chevalier, comte, vicomte, marquis, what? None. Out of compliment to monsieur can I wish to be anything he is not? No, no! I shall be M. le Duc, M. le Duc de—de Chateaurien. Ha, ha! You see? You are my *confrere.*"

M. Beaucaire trod a dainty step or two, waving his hand politely to the Duke, as though in invitation to join the celebration of his rank. The Englishman watched, his eye still and harsh, already gathering in craftiness. Beaucaire stopped suddenly. "But how I forget my age! I am twenty-three," he said, with a sigh. "I rejoice too much to be of the quality. It has been too great for me, and I had always belief' myself free of such ambition. I thought it was enough to behol' the opera without wishing to sing; but no, England have teach' me I have those vulgar desire'. Monsieur, I am goin' tell you a secret; the ladies of your country are very diff'runt than ours. One may adore the demoiselle, one must worship the lady of England. Our ladies have the—it is the beauty of youth; yours remain comely at thirty. Ours are flowers, yours are stars! See, I betray myself, I am so poor a patriot. And there is one among these stars—ah, yes, there is one—the poor Frenchman has observe' from his humble distance; even there he could bask in the glowing!" M. Beaucaire turned 'to the window, and looked out into the dark. He did not see the lights of the town. When he turned again, he had half forgotten his prisoner; other pictures were before him.

"Ah, what radiance!" he cried. "Those people up over the sky, they want to show they wish the earth to be happy, so they smile, and make this day. Gold-haired, an angel of heaven, and yet a Diana of the chase! I see her fly by me on her great horse one day; she touch' his mane with her fingers. I buy that clipping from the groom. I have it here with my dear brother's picture. Ah, *you!* Oh, yes, you laugh! What do you know! 'Twas all I could get. But I have heard of the endeavor of M. le Duc to recoup his fortunes. This alliance shall fail. It is not the way—that heritage shall be safe' from him! It is you and me, monsieur! You can laugh! The war is open', and by *me!* There is one great step taken: until to-night there was nothing for you to ruin, to-morrow you have got a noble of France—your own *protege*—to besiege and sack. And you are to lose, because you think such ruin easy, and because you understand nothing—far less—of divinity. How could you know? You have not the fiber; the heart of a lady is a blank to you; you know nothing of the vibration. There are some words that were made only to tell of Lady Mary, for her alone—*bellissima*, divine, *glorieuse!* Ah, how I have watch' her! It is sad to me when I see her surround' by your yo'ng captains, your nobles, your rattles, your beaux—ha, ha!—and I mus' hol' far aloof. It is sad for me—but oh, jus' to watch her and to wonder! Strange it is, but I have almos' cry out with rapture at a look I have see' her give another man, so beautiful it was, so tender, so dazzling of the eyes and so mirthful of the lips. Ah, divine coquetry! A look for another, *ab-i-me!* for many others; and even to you, one day, a rose, while I—I, monsieur, could not even be so blessed as to be the groun' beneath her little shoe! But *to-night*, monsieur—ha, ha!—*to-night*, monsieur, you and me, two princes, M. le Duc de Winterset and M. le Duc de Chateaurien—ha, ha! you see?—we are goin' arm-in-arm to that

ball, and *I* am goin' have one of those looks, *I!* And a rose! *I!* It is time. But ten minute', monsieur. I make my apology to keep you waitin' so long while I go in the nex' room and execute my poor mustachio—that will be only murder for jus' this one evening—and inves' myself in white satin. Ha, ha! I shall be very gran', monsieur. Francois, send Louis to me; Victor, to order two chairs for monsieur and me; we are goin' out in the worl' to-night!"

II

The chairmen swarmed in the street at Lady Malbourne's door, where the joyous vulgar fought with muddled footmen and tipsy link-boys for places of vantage whence to catch a glimpse of quality and of raiment at its utmost. Dawn was in the east, and the guests were departing. Singly or in pairs, glittering in finery, they came mincing down the steps, the ghost of the night's smirk fading to jadedness as they sought the dark recesses of their chairs. From within sounded the twang of fiddles still swinging manfully at it, and the windows were bright with the light of many candles. When the door was flung open to call the chair of Lady Mary Carlisle, there was an eager pressure of the throng to see.

A small, fair gentleman in white satin came out upon the steps, turned and bowed before a lady who appeared in the doorway, a lady whose royal loveliness was given to view for a moment in that glowing frame. The crowd sent up a hearty English cheer for the Beauty of Bath.

The gentleman smiled upon them delightedly. "What enchanting people!" he cried. "Why did I not know, so I might have shout' with them?" The lady noticed the people not at all; whereat, being pleased, the people cheered again. The gentleman offered her his hand; she made a slow courtesy; placed the tips of her fingers upon his own. "I am honored, M. de Chateaurien," she said.

"No, no!" he cried earnestly. "Behol' a poor Frenchman whom emperors should envy." Then reverently and with the pride of his gallant office vibrant in every line of his light figure, invested in white satin and very grand, as he had prophesied, M. le Duc de Chateaurien handed Lady Mary Carlisle down the steps, an achievement which had figured in the ambitions of seven other gentlemen during the evening.

"Am I to be lef' in such onhappiness?" he said in a low voice. "That rose I have beg' for so long——"

"Never!" said Lady Mary.

"Ah, I do not deserve it, I know so well! But——"

"Never!"

"It is the greatness of my onworthiness that alone can claim your charity; let your kin' heart give this little red rose, this great alms, to the poor beggar."

"Never!"

She was seated in the chair. "Ah, give the rose," he whispered. Her beauty shone dazzlingly on him out of the dimness.

"Never!" she flashed defiantly as she was closed in. "Never!"

"Ah!"

"Never!"

The rose fell at his feet.

"A rose lasts till morning," said a voice behind him.

Turning, M. de Chateaurien looked beamingly upon the face of the Duke of Winterset.

"'Tis already the daylight," he replied, pointing to the east. "Monsieur, was it not enough honor for you to han' out madame, the aunt of Lady Mary? Lady Rellerton retain' much trace of beauty. 'Tis strange you did not appear more happy."

"The rose is of an unlucky color, I think," observed the Duke.

"The color of a blush, my brother."

"Unlucky, I still maintain," said the other calmly.

"The color of the veins of a Frenchman. Ha, ha!" cried the young man. "What price would be too high? A rose is a rose! A good-night, my brother, a good-night. I wish you dreams of roses, red roses, only beautiful red, red roses!"

"Stay! Did you see the look she gave these street folk when they shouted for her? And how are you higher than they, when she knows? As high as yonder horse-boy!"

"Red roses, my brother, only roses. I wish you dreams of red, red roses!"

III

'Twas well agreed by the fashion of Bath that M. le Duc de Chateaurien was a person of sensibility and *haut ton;* that his retinue and equipage surpassed in elegance; that his person was exquisite, his manner engaging. In the company of gentlemen his ease was slightly tinged with graciousness (his single equal in Bath being his Grace of Winterset); but it was remarked that when he bowed over a lady's hand, his air bespoke only a gay and tender reverence.

He was the idol of the dowagers within a week after his appearance; matrons warmed to him; young belles looked sweetly on him, while the gentlemen were won to admiration or envy. He was of prodigious wealth: old Mr. Bicksit, who dared not, for his fame's sake, fail to have seen all things, had visited Chateaurien under the present Duke's father, and descanted to the curious upon its grandeurs. The young noble had one fault, he was so poor a gambler. He cared nothing for the hazards of a die or the turn of a card. Gayly admitting that he had been born with no spirit of adventure in him, he was sure, he declared, that he failed of much happiness by his lack of taste in such matters.

But he was not long wanting the occasion to prove his taste in the matter of handling a weapon. A certain led-captain, Rohrer by name, notorious, amongst other things, for bearing a dexterous and bloodthirsty blade, came to Bath post-haste, one night, and jostled heartily against him in the pump-room on the following morning. M. de Chateaurien bowed, and turned aside without offense, continuing a conversation with some gentlemen near by. Captain Rohrer jostled against him a second time. M. de Chateaurien looked him in the eye, and apologized pleasantly for being so much in the way. Thereupon Rohrer procured an introduction to him, and made some observations derogatory to the valor and virtue of the French.

There was current a curious piece of gossip of the French court: a prince of the blood royal, grandson of the late Regent and second in the line of succession to the throne of France, had rebelled against the authority of Louis XV., who had commanded him to marry the Princess Henriette, cousin to both of them. The princess was reported to be openly devoted to the cousin who refused to accept her hand at the bidding of the king; and, as rumor ran, the prince's caprice elected in preference the discipline of Vincennes, to which retirement the furious king had consigned him. The story was the staple gossip of all polite Europe; and Captain Rohrer, having in his mind a purpose to make use of it in leading up to a statement that should be general to the damage of all Frenchwomen, and which a Frenchman might not pass over as he might a jog of the elbow, repeated it with garbled truths to make a scandal of a story which bore none on a plain relation.

He did not reach his deduction. M. de Chateaurien, breaking into his narrative, addressed him very quietly. "Monsieur," he said, "none but swine deny the nobleness of that good and gentle lady, Mademoiselle la Princesse de Bourbon-Conti. Every Frenchman know' that her cousin is a bad rebel and ingrate, who had only honor and rispec' for her, but was so wilful he could not let even the king say, 'You shall marry here, you shall marry there.' My frien's," the young man turned to the others, "may I ask you to close roun' in a circle for one moment? It is clearly shown that the Duke of Orleans is a scurvy fellow, but not——" he wheeled about and touched Captain Rohrer on the brow with the back of his gloved hand—"but not so scurvy as thou, thou swine of the gutter!"

Two hours later, with perfect ease, he ran Captain Rohrer through the left shoulder—after which he sent a basket of red roses to the Duke of Winterset. In a few days he had another captain to fight. This was a ruffling buck who had the astounding indiscretion to proclaim M. de Chateaurien an imposter. There was no Chateaurien, he swore. The Frenchman laughed in his face, and, at twilight of the same day, pinked him carefully through the right shoulder. It was not that he could not put aside the insult to himself, he declared to Mr. Molyneux, his second, and the few witnesses, as he handed his wet sword to his lackey—one of his station could not be insulted by a doubt of that station—but he fought in the quarrel of his friend Winterset. This rascal had asserted that M. le Duc had introduced an imposter. Could he overlook the insult to a friend, one to whom he owed his kind reception in Bath? Then, bending over his fallen adversary, he whispered: "Naughty man, tell your master find some better quarrel for the nex' he sen' agains' me."

The conduct of M. de Chateaurien was pronounced admirable.

There was no surprise when the young foreigner fell naturally into the long train of followers of the beautiful Lady Mary Carlisle, nor was there great astonishment that he should obtain marked favor in her eyes, shown so plainly that my Lord Townbrake, Sir Hugh Guilford, and the rich Squire Bantison, all of whom had followed her through three seasons, swore with rage, and his Grace of Winterset stalked from her aunt's house with black brows.

Meeting the Duke there on the evening after his second encounter, de Chateaurien smiled upon him brilliantly. "It was badly done; oh, so badly!" he whispered. "Can you afford to have me strip' of my mask by any but yourself? You, who introduce' me? They will say

there is some bad scandal that I could force you to be my god-father. You mus' get the courage yourself."

"I told you a rose had a short life," was the answer.

"Oh, those roses! 'Tis the very greates' rizzon to gather each day a fresh one." He took a red bud from his breast for an instant, and touched it to his lips.

"M. de Chateaurien!" It was Lady Mary's voice; she stood at a table where a vacant place had been left beside her. "M. de Chateaurien, we have been waiting very long for you."

The Duke saw the look she did not know she gave the Frenchman, and he lost countenance for a moment.

"We approach a climax, eh, monsieur?" said M. de Chateaurien.

IV

There fell a clear September night, when the moon was radiant over town and country, over cobbled streets and winding roads. From the fields the mists rose slowly, and the air was mild and fragrant, while distances were white and full of mystery. All of Bath that pretended to fashion or condition was present that evening at a *fête* at the house of a country gentleman of the neighborhood. When the stately junket was concluded, it was the pleasure of M. de Chateaurien to form one of the escort of Lady Mary's carriage for the return. As they took the road, Sir Hugh Guilford and Mr. Bantison, engaging in indistinct but vigorous remonstrance with Mr. Molyneux over some matter, fell fifty or more paces behind, where they continued to ride, keeping up their argument. Half a dozen other gallants rode in advance, muttering among themselves, or attended laxly upon Lady Mary's aunt on the other side of the coach, while the happy Frenchman was permitted to ride close to that adorable window which framed the fairest face in England.

He sang for her a little French song, a song of the *voyageur* who dreamed of home. The lady, listening, looking up at the bright moon, felt a warm drop upon her cheek, and he saw the tears sparkling upon her lashes.

"Mademoiselle," he whispered then, "I, too, have been a wanderer, but my dreams were not of France; no, I do not dream of that home, of that dear country. It is of a dearer country, a dream country—a country of gold and snow," he cried softly, looking at her white brow and the fair, lightly powdered hair above it. "Gold and snow, and the blue sky of a lady's eyes!"

"I had thought the ladies of France were dark, sir."

"Cruel! It is that she will not understan'! Have I speak of the ladies of France? No, no, no! It is of the faires' country; yes, 'tis a province of heaven, mademoiselle. Do I not renounce my allegiance to France? Oh, yes! I am subjec'—no, content to be slave—in the lan' of the blue sky, the gold, and the snow."

"A very pretty figure," answered Lady Mary, her eyes downcast. "But does it not hint a notable experience in the making of such speeches?"

"Tormentress! No. It prove' only the inspiration it is to know you."

"We English ladies hear plenty of the like, sir; and we even grow brilliant enough to detect the assurance that lies beneath the courtesies of our own gallants."

"Merci! I should believe so!" ejaculated M. de Chateaurien; but he smothered the words upon his lips.

Her eyes were not lifted. She went on: "We come, in time, to believe that true feeling comes faltering forth, not glibly; that smoothness betokens the adept in the art, sir, rather than your true—your true——" She was herself faltering; more, blushing deeply, and halting to a full stop in terror of a word. There was a silence.

"Your—true—lover," he said huskily. When he had said that word both trembled. She turned half way into the darkness of the coach.

"I know what make' you to doubt me," he said, faltering himself, though it was not his art that prompted him. "They have tol' you the French do nothing al—ways but make love, is it not so? Yes, you think I am like that. You think I am like that now!"

She made no sign.

"I suppose," he sighed, "I am unriz'nable; I would have the snow not so col'—for jus' me."

She did not answer.

"Turn to me," he said.

The fragrance of the fields came to them, and from the distance the faint, clear note of a hunting-horn.

"Turn to me," he said.

The lovely head was bent very low. Her little gloved hand lay upon the narrow window ledge. He laid his own gently upon it. The two hands were shaking like twin leaves in the breeze. Hers was not drawn away. After a pause, neither knew how long, he felt the warm fingers turn and clasp themselves tremulously about his own. At last she looked up bravely and met his eyes. The horn was wound again—nearer.

"All the cold was gone from the snows—long ago," she said.

"My beautiful!" he whispered; it was all he could say. "My beautiful!" But she clutched his arm, startled.

"'Ware the road!" A wild halloo sounded ahead. The horn wound loudly. "'Ware the road!" There sprang up out of the night a flying thunder of hoofbeats. The gentlemen riding idly in front of the coach scattered to the hedge-sides; and, with drawn swords flashing in the moon, a party of horsemen charged down the highway, their cries blasting the night.

"Barber! Kill the barber!" they screamed. "Barber! Kill the barber!"

Beaucaire had but time to draw his sword when they were upon him.

"A moi!" his voice rang out clearly as he rose in his stirrups. "A moi, Francois, Louis, Berquin! A moi, Francois!"

The cavaliers came straight at him. He parried the thrust of the first, but the shock of collision hurled his horse against the side of the coach.

"Sacred swine!" he cried bitterly. "To endanger a lady, to make this brawl in a lady's presence! Drive on!" he shouted.

"No!" cried Lady Mary.

The Frenchman's assailants were masked, but they were not highwaymen. "Barber! Barber!" they shouted hoarsely, and closed in on him in a circle.

"See how he use his steel!" laughed M. Beaucaire, as his point passed through a tawdry waistcoat. For a moment he cut through the ring and cleared a space about him, and Lady Mary saw his face shining in the moonlight. "Canaille!" he hissed, as his horse sank beneath him; and, though guarding his head from the rain of blows from above, he managed to drag headlong from his saddle the man who had hamstrung the poor brute. The fellow came suddenly to the ground, and lay there.

"Is it not a compliment," said a heavy voice, "to bring six large men to subdue monsieur?"

"Oh, you are there, my frien'! In the rear—a little in the rear, I think. Ha, ha!"

The Frenchman's play with his weapon was a revelation of skill, the more extraordinary as he held in his hand only a light dress sword. But the ring closed about him, and his keen defense could not avail him for more than a few moments. Lady Mary's outriders, the gallants of her escort, rode up close to the coach and encircled it, not interfering.

"Sir Hugh Guilford!" cried Lady Mary wildly, "if you will not help him, give me your sword!" She would have leaped to the ground, but Sir Hugh held the door.

"Sit quiet, madam," he said to her; then, to the man on the box, "Drive on."

"If he does, I'll kill him!" she said fiercely. "Ah, what cowards! Will you see the Duke murdered?"

"The Duke!" laughed Guilford. "They will not kill him, unless—be easy, dear madam, 'twill be explained. Gad's life!" he muttered to Molyneux, "'Twere time the varlet had his lashing! D'ye hear her?"

"Barber or no barber," answered Molyneux, "I wish I had warned him. He fights as few gentlemen could. Ah—ah! Look at that! 'Tis a shame!"

On foot, his hat gone, his white coat sadly rent and gashed, flecked, too, with red, M. Beaucaire, wary, alert, brilliant, seemed to transform himself into a dozen fencing-masters; and, though his skill appeared to lie in delicacy and quickness, his play being continually with the point, sheer strength failed to beat him down. The young man was laughing like a child.

"Believe me," said Molyneux, "he's no barber! No, and never was!"

For a moment there was even a chance that M. Beaucaire might have the best of it. Two of his adversaries were prostrate, more than one were groaning, and the indomitable Frenchman had actually almost beaten off the ruffians, when, by a trick, he was overcome. One of them, dismounting, ran in suddenly from behind, and seized his blade in a thick leather gauntlet. Before Beaucaire could disengage the weapon, two others threw themselves from their horses and hurled him to the earth. "*A moi! A moi*, Francois!" he cried as he went down, his sword in fragments, but his voice unbroken and clear.

"Shame!" muttered one or two of the gentlemen about the coach.

"'Twas dastardly to take him so," said Molyneux. "Whatever his deservings, I'm nigh of a mind to offer him a rescue in the Duke's face."

"Truss him up, lads," said the heavy voice. "Clear the way in front of the coach. There sit those whom we avenge upon a presumptuous lackey. Now, Whiffen, you have a fair audience, lay on and baste him."

Two men began to drag M. Beaucaire toward a great oak by the roadside. Another took from his saddle a heavy whip with three thongs.

"*A moi, Francois!*"

There was borne on the breeze an answer— "*Monseigneur! Monseigneur!*" The cry grew louder suddenly. The clatter of hoofs urged to an anguish of speed sounded on the night. M. Beaucaire's servants had lagged sorely behind, but they made up for it now. Almost before the noise of their own steeds they came riding down the moonlit aisle between the mists. Chosen men, these servants of Beaucaire, and like a thunderbolt they fell upon the astounded cavaliers.

"Chateaurien! Chateaurien!" they shouted, and smote so swiftly that, through lack of time, they showed no proper judgment, discriminating nothing between non-combatants and their master's foes. They charged first into the group about M. Beaucaire, and broke and routed it utterly. Two of them leaped to the young man's side, while the other four, swerving, scarce losing the momentum of their onset, bore on upon the gentlemen near the coach, who went down beneath the fierceness of the onslaught, cursing manfully.

"Our just deserts," said Mr. Molyneux, his mouth full of dust and philosophy.

Sir Hugh Guilford's horse fell with him, being literally ridden over, and the baronet's leg was pinned under the saddle. In less than ten minutes from the first attack on M. Beaucaire, the attacking party had fled in disorder, and the patrician non-combatants, choking with expletives, consumed with wrath, were prisoners, disarmed by the Frenchman's lackeys.

Guilford's discomfiture had freed the doors of the coach; so it was that when M. Beaucaire, struggling to rise, assisted by his servants, threw out one hand to balance himself, he found it seized between two small, cold palms, and he looked into two warm, dilating eyes, that were doubly beautiful because of the fright and rage that found room in them, too.

M. le Duc Chateaurien sprang to his feet without the aid of his lackeys, and bowed low before Lady Mary.

"I make ten thousan' apology to be the cause of a such *mêlee* in your presence," he said; and then, turning to Francois, he spoke in French: "Ah, thou scoundrel! A little, and it had been too late."

Francois knelt in the dust before him. "Pardon!" he said. "Monseigneur commanded us to follow far in the rear, to remain unobserved. The wind malignantly blew against monseigneur's voice."

"See what it might have cost, my children," said his master, pointing to the ropes with which they would have bound him and to the whip lying beside them. A shudder passed over the lackey's frame; the utter horror in his face echoed in the eyes of his fellows.

"Oh, monseigneur!" Francois sprang back, and tossed his arms to heaven.

"But it did not happen," said M. Beaucaire.

"It could not!" exclaimed Francois.

"No. And you did very well, my children —" the young man smiled benevolently— "very well. And now," he continued, turning to Lady Mary and speaking in English, "let me be asking of our gallants yonder what make' them to be in cabal with highwaymen. One should come to a polite understanding with them, you think? Not so?"

He bowed, offering his hand to conduct her to the coach, where Molyneux and his companions, having drawn Sir Hugh from under his horse, were engaged in reviving and reassuring Lady Rellerton, who had fainted. But Lady Mary stayed Beaucaire with a gesture, and the two stood where they were.

"Monseigneur!" she said, with a note of raillery in her voice, but raillery so tender that he started with happiness. His movement brought him a hot spasm of pain, and he clapped his hand to a red stain on his waistcoat.

"You are hurt!"

"It is nothing," smiled M. Beaucaire. Then, that she might not see the stain spreading, he held his handkerchief over the spot. "I am a little—but jus' a trifling—bruise'; 'tis all."

"You shall ride in the coach," she whispered. "Will you be pleased, M. de Chateaurien?"

"Ah, my beautiful!" She seemed to wave before him like a shining mist. "I wish that ride might las' for al—ways! Can you say that, mademoiselle?"

"Monseigneur," she cried in a passion of admiration, "I would what you would have be, should be. What do you not deserve? You are the bravest man in the world!"

"Ha, ha! I am jus' a poor Frenchman."

"Would that a few Englishmen had shown themselves as 'poor' to-night. The vile cowards, not to help you!" With that, suddenly possessed by her anger, she swept away from him to the coach.

Sir Hugh, groaning loudly, was being assisted into the vehicle.

"My little poltroons," she said, "what are you doing with your fellow-craven, Sir Hugh Guilford, there?"

"Madam," replied Molyneux humbly, "Sir Hugh's leg is broken. Lady Rellerton graciously permits him to be taken in."

"*I* do not permit it! M. de Chateaurien rides with us."

"But——"

"Sir! Leave the wretch to groan by the roadside," she cried fiercely, "which plight I would were that of all of you! But there will be a pretty story for the gossips to-morrow! And I could almost find pity for you when I think of the wits when you return to town. Fine gentlemen you; hardy bravoes, by heaven! to leave one man to meet a troop of horse single-handed, while you huddle in shelter until you are overthrown and disarmed by servants! Oh, the wits! Heaven save you from the wits!"

"Madam."

"Address me no more! M. de Chateaurien, Lady Rellerton and I will greatly esteem the honor of your company. Will you come?"

She stepped quickly into the coach, and was gathering her skirts to make room for the Frenchman, when a heavy voice spoke from the shadows of the tree by the wayside.

"Lady Mary Carlisle will, no doubt, listen to a word of counsel on this point."

The Duke of Winterset rode out into the moonlight, composedly untieing a mask from about his head. He had not shared the flight of his followers, but had retired into the shade of the oak, whence he now made his presence known with the utmost coolness.

"Gracious heavens, 'tis Winterset!" exclaimed Lady Rellerton.

"Turned highwayman and cutthroat," cried Lady Mary.

"No, no," laughed M. Beaucaire, somewhat unsteadily, as he stood, swaying a little, with one hand on the coach-door, the other pressed hard on his side, "he only oversee'; he is jus' a little bashful, sometime.' He is a great man, but he don' want *all* the glory!"

"Barber," replied the Duke, "I must tell you that I gladly descend to bandy words with you; your monstrous impudence is a claim to rank I cannot ignore. But a lackey who has himself followed by six other lackeys——"

"Ha, ha! Has not M. le Duc been busy all this evening to justify me? And I think mine mus' be the bes' six. Ha, ha! You think?"

"M. de Chateaurien," said Lady Mary, "we are waiting for you."

"Pardon," he replied. "He has something to say; maybe it is bes' if you hear it now."

"I wish to hear nothing from him—ever!"

"My faith, madam," cried the Duke, "this saucy fellow has paid you the last insult! He is so sure of you he does not fear you will believe the truth. When all is told, if you do not agree he deserved the lashing we planned to——"

"I'll hear no more!"

"You will bitterly repent it, madam. For your own sake I entreat——"

"And I also," broke in M. Beaucaire. "Permit me, mademoiselle; let him speak."

"Then let him be brief," said Lady Mary, "for I am earnest to be quit of him. His explanation of an attack on my friend and on my carriage should be made to my brother."

"Alas that he was not here," said the Duke, "to aid me! Madam, was your carriage threatened? I have endeavored only to expunge a debt I owed to Bath and to avenge an insult offered to yourself through——"

"Sir, sir, my patience will bear little more!"

"A thousan' apology," said M. Beaucaire. "You will listen, I only beg, Lady Mary?" She made an angry gesture of assent.

"Madam, I will be brief as I may. Two months ago there came to Bath a French gambler calling himself Beaucaire, a desperate fellow with the cards or dice, and all the men of fashion went to play at his lodging, where he won considerable sums. He was small, wore a black wig and mustachio. He had the insolence to show himself everywhere until the Master of Ceremonies rebuffed him in the pump-room, as you know, and after that he forebore his visits to the rooms. Mr. Nash explained (and was confirmed, madam, by indubitable information) that this Beaucaire was a man of unspeakable, vile, low birth, being, in fact, no other than a lackey of the French king's ambassador, Victor by name, de Mirepoix's barber. Although his condition was known, the hideous impudence of the fellow did not desert him, and he remained in Bath, where none would speak to him."

"Is your farrago nigh done, sir?"

"A few moments, madam. One evening, three weeks gone, I observed a very elegant equipage draw up to my door, and the Duke of Chateaurien was announced. The young man's manners were worthy—according to the French acceptance—and 'twere idle to deny him the most monstrous assurance. He declared himself a noble traveling for pleasure. He had taken lodgings in Bath for a season, he said, and called at once to pay his respects to me. His tone was so candid—in truth, I am the simplest of men, very easily gulled—and

his stroke so bold, that I did not for one moment suspect him; and, to my poignant regret —though in the humblest spirit I have shown myself eager to atone—that very evening I had the shame of presenting him to yourself."

"The shame, sir!"

"Have patience, pray, madam. Ay, the shame! You know what figure he hath cut in Bath since that evening. All ran merrily with him until several days ago Captain Badger denounced him as an impostor, vowing that Chateaurien was nothing."

"Pardon," interrupted M. Beaucaire. "'Castle Nowhere' would have been so much better. Why did you not make him say it that way, monsieur?"

Lady Mary started; she was looking at the Duke, and her face was white. He continued: "Poor Captain Badger was stabbed that same day——"

"Most befitting poor Captain Badger," muttered Molyneux.

"—And his adversary had the marvelous insolence to declare that he fought in *my* quarrel! This afternoon the wounded man sent for me, and imparted a very horrifying intelligence. He had discovered a lackey whom he had seen waiting upon Beaucaire in attendance at the door of this Chateaurien's lodging. Beaucaire had disappeared the day before Chateaurien's arrival. Captain Badger looked closely at Chateaurien at their next meeting, and identified him with the missing Beaucaire beyond the faintest doubt. Overcome with indignation, he immediately proclaimed the impostor. Out of regard for me, he did not charge him with being Beaucaire; the poor soul was unwilling to put upon me the humiliation of having introduced a barber; but the secret weighed upon him till he sent for me and put everything in my hands. I accepted the odium; thinking only of atonement. I went to Sir John Wimpledon's *fête*. I took poor Sir Hugh, there, and these other gentlemen aside, and told them my news. We narrowly observed this man, and were shocked at our simplicity in not having discovered him before. These are men of honor and cool judgment, madam. Mr. Molyneux had acted for him in the affair of Captain Badger, and was strongly prejudiced in his favor; but Mr. Molyneux, Sir Hugh, Mr. Bantison, every one of them, in short, recognized him. In spite of his smooth face and his light hair, the adventurer Beaucaire was writ upon him amazing plain. Look at him, madam, if he will dare the inspection. You saw this Beaucaire well, the day of his expulsion from the rooms. Is not this he?"

M. Beaucaire stepped close to her. Her pale face twitched.

"Look!" he said.

"Oh, oh!" she whispered with a dry throat, and fell back in the carriage.

"Is it so?" cried the Duke.

"I do not know—I—cannot tell."

"One moment more. I begged these gentlemen to allow me to wipe out the insult I had unhappily offered to Bath, but particularly to you. They agreed not to forestall me or to interfere. I left Sir John Wimpledon's early, and arranged to give the sorry rascal a lashing under your own eyes, a satisfaction due the lady into whose presence he had dared to force himself."

"'*Noblesse oblige*'?" said M. Beaucaire in a tone of gentle inquiry.

"And now, madam," said the Duke, "I will detain you not one second longer. I plead the good purpose of my intentions, begging you to believe that the desire to avenge a hateful outrage, next to the wish to serve you, forms the dearest motive in the heart of Winterset."

"Bravo!" cried Beaucaire softly.

Lady Mary leaned toward him, a thriving terror in her eyes. "It is false?" she faltered.

"Monsieur should not have been born so high. He could have made little book'."

"You mean it is false?" she cried breathlessly.

"'Od's blood, is she not convinced?" broke out Mr. Bantison. "Fellow, were you not the ambassador's barber?"

"It is all false?" she whispered.

"The mos' fine art, mademoiselle. How long you think it take M. de Winterset to learn that speech after he write it out? It is a mix of what is true and the mos' chaste art. Monsieur has become a man of letters. Perhaps he may enjoy that more than the wars. Ha, ha!"

Mr. Bantison burst into a roar of laughter. "Do French gentlemen fight lackeys? Ho, ho, ho! A pretty country! We English do as was done to-night, have our servants beat them."

"And attend ourselves," added M. Beaucaire, looking at the Duke, "somewhat in the background? But, pardon," he mocked, "that remind' me. Francois, return to Mr. Bantison and these gentlemen their weapons."

"Will you answer a question?" said Molyneux mildly.

"Oh, with pleasure, monsieur."

"Were you ever a barber?"

"No, monsieur," laughed the young man.

"Pah!" exclaimed Bantison. "Let me question him. Now, fellow, a confession may save you from jail. Do you deny you are Beaucaire?"

"Deny to such a judge?"

"Ha!" said Bantison. "What more do you want, Molyneux? Fellow, do you deny that you came to London in the ambassador's suite?"

"No, I do not deny."

"He admits it! Didn't you come as his barber?"

"Yes, my frien', as his barber."

Lady Mary cried out faintly, and, shuddering, put both hands over her eyes.

"I'm sorry," said Molyneux. "You fight like a gentleman."

"I thank you, monsieur."

"You called yourself Beaucaire?"

"Yes, monsieur." He was swaying to and fro; his servants ran to support him.

"I wish——" continued Molyneux, hesitating. "Evil take me!—but I'm sorry you're hurt."

"Assist Sir Hugh into my carriage," said Lady Mary.

"Farewell, mademoiselle!" M. Beaucaire's voice was very faint. His eyes were fixed upon her face. She did not look toward him.

They were propping Sir Hugh on the cushions. The Duke rode up close to Beaucaire, but Francois seized his bridle fiercely, and forced the horse back on its haunches.

"The man's servants worship him," said Molyneux.

"Curse your insolence!" exclaimed the Duke. "How much am I to bear from this varlet and his varlets? Beaucaire, if you have not left Bath by to-morrow noon, you will be clapped into jail, and the lashing you escaped to-night shall be given you thrice tenfold!"

"I shall be—in the—Assembly—Room' at nine—o'clock, one week—from—to-night," answered the young man, smiling jauntily, though his lips were colorless. The words cost him nearly all his breath and strength. "You mus' keep—in the—backgroun', monsieur. Ha, ha!"

The door of the coach closed with a slam.

"Mademoiselle—fare—well!"

"Drive on!" said Lady Mary.

M. Beaucaire followed the carriage with his eyes. As the noise of the wheels and the hoofbeats of the accompanying cavalcade grew fainter in the distance, the handkerchief he had held against his side dropped into the white dust, a heavy red splotch.

"Only—roses," he gasped, and fell back in the arms of his servants.

V

Beau Nash stood at the door of the rooms, smiling blandly upon a dainty throng in the pink of its finery and gay furbelows. The great exquisite bent his body constantly in a series of consummately adjusted bows: before a great dowager, seeming to sweep the floor in august deference; somewhat stately to the young bucks; greeting the wits with gracious friendliness and a twinkle of raillery; inclining with fatherly gallantry before the beauties; the degree of his inclination measured the altitude of the recipient as accurately as a nicely calculated sand-glass measures the hours.

The King of Bath was happy, for wit, beauty, fashion—to speak more concretely: nobles, belles, gamesters, beaux, statesmen, and poets—made fairyland (or opera bouffe, at least) in his dominions; play ran higher and higher, and Mr. Nash's coffers filled up with gold. To crown his pleasure, a prince of the French blood, the young Comte de Beaujolais, just arrived from Paris, had reached Bath at noon in state, accompanied by the Marquis de Mirepoix, the ambassador of Louis XV. The Beau dearly prized the society of the lofty, and the present visit was an honor to Bath: hence to the Master of Ceremonies. What was better, there would be some profitable hours with the cards and dice. So it was that Mr. Nash smiled never more benignly than on that bright evening. The rooms rang with the silvery voices of women and delightful laughter, while the fiddles went merrily, their melodies chiming sweetly with the joyance of his mood.

The skill and brazen effrontery of the ambassador's scoundrelly servant in passing himself off for a man of condition formed the point of departure for every conversation. It was discovered that there were but three persons present who had not suspected him from the first; and, by a singular paradox, the most astute of all proved to be old Mr. Bicksit, the traveler, once a visitor at Chateaurien; for he, according to report, had by a coup of diplomacy entrapped the impostor into an admission that there was no such place. However, like poor Captain Badger, the worthy old man had held his peace out of regard for the Duke of Winterset. This nobleman, heretofore secretly disliked, suspected of irregular devices at play, and never admired, had won admiration and popularity by his remorse for the mistake, and by the modesty of his attitude in endeavoring to atone for it, without presuming upon the privilege of his rank to

laugh at the indignation of society; an action the more praiseworthy because his exposure of the impostor entailed the disclosure of his own culpability in having stood the villain's sponsor. To-night, the happy gentleman, with Lady Mary Carlisle upon his arm, went grandly about the rooms, sowing and reaping a harvest of smiles. 'Twas said work would be begun at once to rebuild the Duke's country seat, while several ruined Jews might be paid out of prison. People gazing on the beauty and the stately but modest hero by her side, said they would make a noble pair. She had long been distinguished by his attentions, and he had come brilliantly out of the episode of the Frenchman, who had been his only real rival. Wherever they went, there arose a buzz of pleasing gossip and adulation.

Mr. Nash, seeing them near him, came forward with greetings. A word on the side passed between the nobleman and the exquisite.

"I had news of the rascal to-night," whispered Nash. "He lay at a farm till yesterday, when he disappeared; his ruffians, too."

"You have arranged?" asked the Duke.

"Fourteen bailiffs are watching without. He could not come within gunshot. If they clap eyes on him, they will hustle him to jail, and his cutthroats shall not avail him a hair's weight. The impertinent swore he'd be here by nine, did he?"

"He said so; and 'tis a rash dog, sir."

"It is just nine now."

"Send out to see if they have taken him."

"Gladly." The Beau beckoned an attendant, and whispered in his ear.

Many of the crowd had edged up to the two gentlemen with apparent carelessness, to overhear their conversation. Those who did overhear repeated it in covert asides, and this circulating undertone, confirming a vague rumor that Beaucaire would attempt the entrance that night, lent a pleasurable color of excitement to the evening. The French prince, the ambassador, and their suites were announced. Polite as the assembly was, it was also curious, and there occurred a mannerly rush to see the newcomers. Lady Mary, already pale, grew whiter as the throng closed round her; she looked pathetically at the Duke, who lost no time in extricating her from the pressure.

"Wait here," he said; "I will fetch you a glass of negus," and disappeared. He had not thought to bring a chair, and she, looking about with an increasing faintness and finding none, saw that she was standing by the door of a small side-room. The crowd swerved back for the passage of the legate of France, and pressed upon her. She opened the door, and went in.

The room was empty save for two gentlemen, who were quietly playing cards at a table. They looked up as she entered. They were M. Beaucaire and Mr. Molyneux.

She uttered a quick cry and leaned against the wall, her hand to her breast. Beaucaire, though white and weak, had brought her a chair before Molyneux could stir.

"Mademoiselle——"

"Do not touch me!" she cried, with such frozen abhorrence in her voice that he stopped short. "Mr. Molyneux, you seek strange company!"

"Madam," replied Molyneux, bowing deeply, as much to Beaucaire as to herself, "I am honored by the presence of both of you."

"Oh, are you mad!" she exclaimed, contemptuously.

"This gentleman has exalted me with his confidence, madam," he replied.

"Will you add your ruin to the scandal of this fellow's presence here? How he obtained entrance——"

"Pardon, mademoiselle," interrupted Beaucaire. "Did I not say I should come? M. Molyneux was so obliging as to answer for me to the fourteen frien's of M. de Winterset and *Meestaire* Nash."

"Do you not know," she turned vehemently upon Molyneux, "that he will be removed the moment I leave this room? Do you wish to be dragged out with him? For your sake, sir, because I have always thought you a man of heart, I give you a chance to save yourself from disgrace—and—your companion from jail. Let him slip out by some retired way, and you may give me your arm and we will enter the next room as if nothing had happened. Come, sir——"

"Mademoiselle——"

"Mr. Molyneux, I desire to hear nothing from your companion. Had I not seen you at cards with him I should have supposed him in attendance as your lackey. Do you desire to take advantage of my offer, sir?"

"Mademoiselle, I could not tell you, on that night——"

"You may inform your high-born friend, Mr. Molyneux, that I heard everything he had to say; that my pride once had the pleasure of listening to his high-born confession!"

"Ah, it is gentle to taunt one with his birth, mademoiselle? Ah, no! There is a man in my country who say strange things of that—that a man is not his father, but *himself*."

"You may inform your friend, Mr. Moly-

neux, that he had a chance to defend himself against accusation; that he said all——"

"That I did say all I could have strength to say. Mademoiselle, you did not see—as it was right—that I had been stung by a big wasp. It was nothing, a scratch; but, mademoiselle, the sky went round and the moon dance' on the earth. I could not wish that big wasp to see he had stung me; so I mus' only say what I can have strength for, and stan' straight till he is gone. Beside', there are other rizzons. Ah, you mus' belief! My Molyneux I sen' for, and tell him all, because he show courtesy to the yo'ng Frenchman, and I can trus' him. I trus' you, mademoiselle—long ago—and would have tol' you ev'rything, excep' jus' because—well, for the romance, the fon! You belief? It is so clearly so; you do belief, mademoiselle?"

She did not even look at him. M. Beaucaire lifted his hand appealingly toward her. "Can there be no faith in—in——" he said timidly, and paused. She was silent, a statue, my Lady Disdain.

"If you had not belief' me to be an imposter; if I had never said I was Chateaurien; if I had been jus' that Monsieur Beaucaire of the story they tol' you, but never with the *heart* of a lackey, an hones' man, a *man*, the man you knew, *himself*, could you—would you——" He was trying to speak firmly; yet, as he gazed upon her splendid beauty, he choked slightly, and fumbled in the lace at his throat with unsteady fingers—"Would you—have let me ride by your side in the autumn moonlight?" Her glance passed by him as it might have passed by a footman or a piece of furniture. He was dressed magnificently, a multitude of orders glittering on his breast. Her eye took no knowledge of him.

"Mademoiselle—I have the honor to ask you; if you had known this Beaucaire was hones', though of peasant birth, would you——"

Involuntarily, controlled as her icy presence was, she shuddered. There was a moment of silence.

"Mr. Molyneux," said Lady Mary, "in spite of your discourtesy in allowing a servant to address me, I offer you a last chance to leave this room undisgraced. Will you give me your arm?"

"Pardon me, madam," said Mr. Molyneux.

Beaucaire dropped into a chair with his head bent low and his arm outstretched on the table; his eyes filled slowly in spite of himself, and two tears rolled down the young man's cheeks.

"An' live men are jus'—*names!*" said M. Beaucaire.

VI

In the outer room, Winterset, unable to find Lady Mary, and supposing her to have joined Lady Rellerton, disposed of his negus, then approached the two visitors to pay his respects to the young prince, whom he discovered to be a stripling of seventeen, arrogant-looking, but pretty as a girl. Standing beside the Marquis de Mirepoix—a man of quiet bearing—he was surrounded by a group of the great, among whom Mr. Nash naturally counted himself. The Beau was felicitating himself that the foreigners had not arrived a week earlier, in which case he and Bath would have been detected in a piece of gross ignorance concerning the French nobility—making much of de Mirepoix's ex-barber.

"'Tis a lucky thing that fellow was got out of the way," he ejaculated, under cover.

"Thank me for it," rejoined Winterset.

An attendant begged Mr. Nash's notice. The head bailiff sent word that Beaucaire had long since entered the building by a side door. It was supposed Mr. Nash had known of it, and the Frenchman was not arrested, as Mr. Molyneux was in his company, and said he would be answerable for him. Consternation was so plain on the Beau's trained face that the Duke leaned toward him anxiously.

"The villain's in, and Molyneux hath gone mad!"

Mr. Bantison, who had been fiercely elbowing his way toward them, joined heads with them. "You may well say he is in," he exclaimed, "and if you want to know where, why, in yonder card-room. I saw him through the half-open door."

"What's to be done?" asked the Beau.

"Send the bailiffs——"

"Fie, fie! A file of bailiffs? The scandal!"

"Then listen to me," said the Duke. "I'll select half-a-dozen gentlemen, explain the matter, and we'll put him in the center of us and take him out to the bailiffs. 'Twill appear nothing. Do you remain here and keep the attention of Beaujolais and de Mirepoix. Come, Bantison, fetch Townbrake and Harry Rakell yonder; I'll bring the others."

Three minutes later, his Grace of Winterset flung wide the card-room door, and, after his friends had entered, closed it.

"Ah!" remarked M. Beaucaire quietly. "Six more large men."

The Duke, seeing Lady Mary, started; but the angry signs of her interview had not left her face, and reassured him. He offered his hand to conduct her to the door. "May I have the honor?"

"If this is to be known, 'twill be better if I leave after; I should be observed if I went now."

"As you will, madam," he answered, not displeased. "And now, you impudent villain," he began, turning to M. Beaucaire, but to fall back astounded. "'Od's blood, the dog hath murdered and robbed some royal prince!" He forgot Lady Mary's presence in his excitement. "Lay hands on him!" he shouted. "Tear those orders from him!"

Molyneux threw himself between. "One word!" he cried. "One word before you offer an outrage you will repent all your lives!"

"Or let M. de Winterset come alone," laughed M. Beaucaire.

"Do you expect me to fight a cutthroat barber, and with bare hands?"

"I think one does not expec' monsieur to fight anybody. Would I fight you, you think? That was why I had my servants, that evening we play. I would gladly fight almos' any one in the worl'; but I did not wish to soil my hand with a——"

"Stuff his lying mouth with his orders!" shouted the Duke.

But Molyneux still held the gentlemen back. "One moment," he cried.

"M. de Winterset," said Beaucaire, "of what are you afraid? You calculate well. Beaucaire might have been belief'—an impostor that you yourself expose'? Never! But I was not goin' reveal that secret. You have not absolve me of my promise."

"Tell what you like," answered the Duke. "Tell all the wild lies you have time for. You have five minutes to make up your mind to go quietly."

"Now you absolve me, then? Ha, ha! Oh, yes! Mademoiselle," he bowed to Lady Mary, "I have the honor to reques' you leave the room. You shall miss no details if these frien's of yours kill me, on the honor of a French gentleman."

"A French what?" laughed Bantison.

"Do you dare keep up the pretense?" cried Lord Townbrake. "Know, you villain barber, that your master, the Marquis de Mirepoix, is in the next room."

Molyneux heaved a great sigh of relief. "Shall I——" He turned to M. Beaucaire.

The young man laughed, and said: "Tell him come here at once."

"Impudent to the last!" cried Bantison, as Molyneux hurried from the room.

"Now you goin' to see M. Beaucaire's master," said Beaucaire to Lady Mary. "'Tis true what I say, the other night. I cross from France in his suite; my passport say as his barber. Then to pass the *ennui* of exile, I come to Bath and play for what one will. It kill the time. But when the people hear I have been a servant they come only secretly; and there is one of them—he has absolve' me of a promise not to speak—of him I learn something he cannot wish to be tol'. I make some trouble to learn this thing. Why I should do this? Well—that is my own rizzon. So I make this man help me in a masque, the unmasking it was, for, as there is no one to know me, I throw off my black wig and become myself—and so I am 'Chateaurien,' Castle Nowhere. Then this man I use', this Winterset, he——"

"I have great need to deny these accusations?" said the Duke.

"Nay," said Lady Mary wearily.

"Shall I tell you why I mus' be 'Victor' and 'Beaucaire' and 'Chateaurien,' and not myself?"

"To escape from the bailiffs for debts for razors and soap," gibed Lord Townbrake.

"No, monsieur. In France I have got a cousin who is a man with a very bad temper at some time', and he will never enjoy his relatives to do what he does not wish——"

He was interrupted by a loud commotion from without. The door was flung open, and the young Count of Beaujolais bounded in and threw his arms about the neck of M. Beaucaire. "Philippe!" he cried. "My brother, I have come to take you back with me."

M. de Mirepoix followed him, bowing as a courtier, in deference; but M. Beaucaire took both his hands heartily. Molyneux came after, with Mr. Nash, and closed the door.

"My warmest felicitations," said the Marquis. "There is no longer need for your incognito."

"Thou best of masters!" said Beaucaire, touching him fondly on the shoulder. "I know. Your courier came safely. And so I am forgiven! But I forget." He turned to the lady. She had begun to tremble exceedingly. "Faires' of all the English fair," he said, as the gentlemen bowed low to her deep courtesy, "I beg the honor to presen' to Lady Mary Carlisle, M. le Comte de Beaujolais. M. de Mirepoix has already the honor. Lady Mary has been very kind to me, my frien's; you mus' help me make my acknowledgment. Madenoiselle and gentlemen, will you give me that favor to detain you one instan'?"

"Henri," he turned to the young Beaujolais, "I wish you had shared my masque—I have been so gay!" The surface of his tone was merry, but there was an undercurrent, weary-

sad, to speak of what was the mood, not the manner. He made the effect of addressing every one present, but he looked steadily at Lady Mary. Her eyes were fixed upon him, with a silent and frightened fascination, and she trembled more and more. "I am a great actor, Henri. These gentlemen are yet scarce convince' I am not a lackey! And I mus' tell you that I was jus' now to be expelled for having been a barber!"

"Oh, no!" the ambassador cried out. "He would not be content with me; he would wander over a strange country."

"Ha, ha, my Mirepoix! And what is better, one evening I am oblige' to fight some frien's of M. de Winterset there, and some ladies and cavaliers look on, and they still think me a servant. Oh, I am a great actor! 'Tis true there is not a peasant in France who would not have then known one 'born'; but they are wonderful, this English people, holding by an idea once it is in their heads—a mos' worthy quality. But my good Molyneux here, he had speak to me with courtesy, jus' because I am a man an' jus' because he is al—ways kind. (I have learn' that his great-grandfather was a Frenchman.) So I sen' to him and tell him ev'rything, and he gain admittance for me here to-night to await my frien's.

"I was speaking to messieurs about my cousin, who will meddle in the affair' of his relativ'. Well, that gentleman, he make a marriage for me with a good and accomplish' lady, very noble and very beautiful—and amiable." (The young count at his elbow started slightly at this, but immediately appeared to wrap himself in a mantle of solemn thought.) "Unfortunately, when my cousin arrange' so, I was a dolt, a little blockhead; I swear to marry for myself and when I please, or never if I like. That lady is all things charming and gentle, and, in truth, she is—very much attach' to me —why should I not say it? I am so proud of it. She is very beautiful and forgiving and sweet; she would be the same, I think, if I—were even —a lackey. But I? I was a dolt, a little unsensible brute; I did not value such thing' then; I was too yo'ng, las' June. So I say to my cousin. 'No, I make my own choosing!' 'Little fool,' he answer, 'she is the one for you. Am I not wiser than you?' And he was very angry, and, as he has influence in France, word come' that he will get me put in Vincennes, so I mus' run away quick till his anger is gone. My good frien' Mirepoix is jus' leaving for London; he take' many risk' for my sake; his hairdresser die before he start', so I travel as that poor barber. But my cousin is a man to be afraid of when he is angry, even in England, and I mus' not get my Mirepoix in trouble. I mus' not be discover' till my cousin is ready to laugh about it all and make it a joke. And there may be spies; so I change my name again, and come to Bath to amuse my retreat with a little gaming—I am al—ways fond of that. But three day' ago M. le Marquis send me a courier to say that my brother, who know where I had run away, is come from France to say that my cousin is appease'; he need me for his little theatre, the play cannot go on. I do not need to espouse mademoiselle. All shall be forgiven if I return, and my brother and M. de Mirepoix will meet me in Bath to felicitate.

"There is one more thing to say, that is all. I have said I learn' a secret, and use it to make a man introduce me if I will not tell. He has absolve' me of that promise. My fren's, I had not the wish to ruin that man. I was not receive'; *Meestaire* Nash had reboff me; I had no other way excep' to use this fellow. So I say, 'Take me to Lady Malbourne's ball as "Chateaurien."' I throw off my wig, and shave, and behol', I am M. le Duc de Castle Nowhere. Ha, ha! You see?"

The young man's manner suddenly changed. He became haughty, menacing. He stretched out his arm, and pointed at Winterset. "Now I am no 'Beaucaire,' messieurs. I am a French gentleman. The man who introduce' me at the price of his honor, and then betray' me to redeem it, is that coward, that card-cheat there!"

Winterset made a horrible effort to laugh. The gentlemen who surrounded him fell away as from pestilence. "A French gentleman!" he sneered savagely, and yet fearfully. "I don't know who you are. Hide behind as many toys and ribbons as you like; I'll know the name of the man who dares bring such a charge!"

"Sir!" cried de Mirepoix sharply, advancing a step towards him; but he checked himself at once. He made a low bow of state, first to the young Frenchman, then to Lady Mary and the company. "Permit me, Lady Mary and gentlemen," he said, "to assume the honor of presenting you to His Highness, Prince Louis-Philippe de Valois, Duke of Orleans, Duke of Chartres, Duke of Nemours, Duke of Montpensier, First Prince of the Blood Royal, First Peer of France, Lieutenant-General of French Infantry, Governor of Dauphiné, Knight of the Golden Fleece, Grand Master of the Order of Notre Dame, of Mount Carmel, and of St. Lazarus in Jerusalem; and cousin to

His most Christian Majesty, Louis the Fifteenth, King of France."

"Those are a few of my brother's names," whispered Henri of Beaujolais to Molyneux. "Old Mirepoix has the long breath, but it take' a strong man two day' to say all of them. I can suppose this Winterset know' now who bring the charge!"

"Castle Nowhere!" gasped Beau Nash, falling back upon the burly prop of Mr. Bantison's shoulder.

"The Duke of Orleans will receive a message from me within the hour!" said Winterset, as he made his way to the door. His face was black with rage and shame.

"I tol' you that I would not soil my hand with you," answered the young man. "If you send a message no gentleman will bring it. Whoever shall bear it will receive a little beating from Francois."

He stepped to Lady Mary's side. Her head was bent low, her face averted. She seemed to breathe with difficulty, and leaned heavily upon a chair. "Monseigneur," she faltered in a half whisper, "can you—forgive me? It is a bitter—mistake—I have made. Forgive."

"Forgive?" he answered, and his voice was as broken as hers; but he went on, more firmly: "It is—nothing—less than nothing. There is—only jus' one—in the—whole worl' who would not have treat' me the way that you treat' me. It is to her that I am goin' to make reparation. You know something, Henri? I am not goin' back only because the king forgive' me. I am goin' to *please* him; I am goin' to espouse mademoiselle, our cousin. My frien's, I ask your felicitations."

"And the king does not compel him!" exclaimed young Henri.

"Henri, you want to fight me?" cried his brother sharply. "Don' you think the King of France is a wiser man than me?"

He offered his hand to Lady Mary.

"Mademoiselle is fatigue'. Will she honor me?"

He walked with her to the door, her hand fluttering faintly in his. From somewhere about the garments of one of them a little cloud of faded roseleaves fell, and lay strewn on the floor behind them. He opened the door, and the lights shone on a multitude of eager faces turned toward it. There was a great hum of voices, and, over all, the fiddles wove a wandering air, a sweet French song of the *voyageur*.

He bowed very low, as, with fixed and glistening eyes, Lady Mary Carlisle, the Beauty of Bath, passed slowly by him and went out of the room.

EDITH WHARTON (1862-   )

THE LADY'S MAID'S BELL

(1902)

I

It was the autumn after I had the typhoid. I'd been three months in hospital, and when I came out I looked so weak and tottery that the two or three ladies I applied to were afraid to engage me. Most of my money was gone, and after I'd boarded for two months, hanging about the employment-agencies, and answering any advertisement that looked any way respectable, I pretty nearly lost heart, for fretting hadn't made me fatter, and I didn't see why my luck should ever turn. It did though —or I thought so at the time. A Mrs. Railton, a friend of the lady that first brought me out to the States, met me one day and stopped to speak to me: she was one that had always a friendly way with her. She asked me what ailed me to look so white, and when I told her, "Why, Hartley," says she, "I believe I've got the very place for you. Come in to-morrow and we'll talk about it."

The next day, when I called, she told me the lady she'd in mind was a niece of hers, a Mrs. Brympton, a youngish lady, but something of an invalid, who lived all the year round at her country-place on the Hudson, owing to not being able to stand the fatigue of town life.

"Now, Hartley," Mrs. Railton said, in that cheery way that always made me feel things must be going to take a turn for the better— "now understand me; it's not a cheerful place I'm sending you to. The house is big and gloomy; my niece is nervous, vapourish; her husband—well, he's generally away; and the two children are dead. A year ago I would as soon have thought of shutting a rosy active girl like you into a vault; but you're not particularly brisk yourself just now, are you? and a quiet place, with country air and wholesome food and early hours, ought to be the very thing for you. Don't mistake me," she added, for I suppose I looked a trifle downcast; "you may find it dull but you wont be unhappy. My niece is an angel. Her former maid, who died last spring, had been with her twenty years and worshipped the ground she walked on. She's a kind mistress to all, and where the mistress is kind, as you know, the servants are generally good-humoured, so you'll probably get on well enough with the rest of the household. And you're the very woman I want for

my niece: quiet, well-mannered, and educated above your station. You read aloud well, I think? That's a good thing; my niece likes to be read to. She wants a maid that can be something of a companion: her last was, and I can't say how she misses her. It's a lonely life . . . Well, have you decided?"

"Why, ma'am," I said, "I'm not afraid of solitude."

"Well, then, go; my niece will take you on my recommendation. I'll telegraph her at once and you can take the afternoon train. She has no one to wait on her at present, and I don't want you to lose any time."

I was ready enough to start, yet something in me hung back; and to gain time I asked, "And the gentleman, ma'am?"

"The gentleman's almost always away, I tell you," said Mrs. Railton, quick-like—"and when he's there," says she suddenly, "you've only to keep out of his way."

I took the afternoon train and got out at D—— station at about four o'clock. A groom in a dog-cart was waiting, and we drove off at a smart pace. It was a dull October day, with rain hanging close overhead, and by the time we turned into Brympton Place woods the daylight was almost gone. The drive wound through the woods for a mile or two, and came out on a gravel court shut in with thickets of tall black-looking shrubs. There were no lights in the windows, and the house *did* look a bit gloomy.

I had asked no questions of the groom, for I never was one to get my notion of new masters from their other servants: I prefer to wait and see for myself. But I could tell by the look of everything that I had got into the right kind of house, and that things were done handsomely. A pleasant-faced cook met me at the back door and called the house-maid to show me up to my room. "You'll see madam later," she said. "Mrs. Brympton has a visitor."

I hadn't fancied Mrs. Brympton was a lady to have many visitors, and somehow the words cheered me. I followed the house-maid upstairs, and saw, through a door on the upper landing, that the main part of the house seemed well furnished, with dark panelling and a number of old portraits. Another flight of stairs led us up to the servants' wing. It was almost dark now, and the house-maid excused herself for not having brought a light. "But there's matches in your room," she said, "and if you go careful you'll be all right. Mind the step at the end of the passage. Your room is just beyond."

I looked ahead as she spoke, and half-way down the passage I saw a woman standing. She drew back into a doorway as we passed and the house-maid didn't appear to notice her. She was a thin woman with a white face, and a darkish stuff gown and apron. I took her for the housekeeper and thought it odd that she didn't speak, but just gave me a long look as she went by. My room opened into a square hall at the end of the passage. Facing my door was another which stood open: the house-maid exclaimed when she saw it:

"There—Mrs. Blinder's left that door open again!" said she, closing it.

"Is Mrs. Blinder the housekeeper?"

"There's no housekeeper: Mrs. Blinder's the cook."

"And is that her room?"

"Laws, no," said the house-maid, cross-like. "That's nobody's room. It's empty, I mean, and the door hadn't ought to be open. Mrs. Brympton wants it kept locked."

She opened my door and led me into a neat room, nicely furnished, with a picture or two on the walls; and having lit a candle she took leave, telling me that the servants'-hall tea was at six, and that Mrs. Brympton would see me afterward.

I found them a pleasant-spoken set in the servants' hall, and by what they let fall I gathered that, as Mrs. Railton had said, Mrs. Brympton was the kindest of ladies; but I didn't take much notice of their talk, for I was watching to see the pale woman in the dark gown come in. She didn't show herself, however, and I wondered if she ate apart; but if she wasn't the housekeeper, why should she? Suddenly it struck me that she might be a trained nurse, and in that case her meals would of course be served in her room. If Mrs. Brympton was an invalid it was likely enough she had a nurse. The idea annoyed me, I own, for they're not always the easiest to get on with, and if I'd known I shouldn't have taken the place. But there I was and there was no use pulling a long face over it; and not being one to ask questions I waited to see what would turn up.

When tea was over the house-maid said to the footman: "Has Mr. Ranford gone?" and when he said yes, she told me to come up with her to Mrs. Brympton.

Mrs. Brympton was lying down in her bedroom. Her lounge stood near the fire and beside it was a shaded lamp. She was a delicate-looking lady, but when she smiled I felt there was nothing I wouldn't do for her. She spoke very pleasantly, in a low voice, asking me my name and age and so on, and if I had everything I wanted, and if I wasn't afraid of feeling lonely in the country.

"Not with you I wouldn't be, madam," I said, and the words surprised me when I'd spoken them, for I'm not an impulsive person; but it was just as if I'd thought aloud.

She seemed pleased at that, and said she hoped I'd continue in the same mind; then she gave me a few directions about her toilet, and said Agnes the house-maid would show me next morning where things were kept.

"I am tired to-night, and shall dine upstairs," she said. "Agnes will bring me my tray, that you may have time to unpack and settle yourself; and later you may come and undress me."

"Very well, ma'am," I said. "You'll ring, I suppose?"

I thought she looked odd.

"No—Agnes will fetch you," says she quickly, and took up her book again.

Well—that was certainly strange: a lady's-maid having to be fetched by the house-maid whenever her lady wanted her! I wondered if there were no bells in the house; but the next day I satisfied myself that there was one in every room, and a special one ringing from my mistress's room to mine; and after that it did strike me as queer that, whenever Mrs. Brympton wanted anything, she rang for Agnes, who had to walk the whole length of the servants' wing to call me.

But that wasn't the only queer thing in the house. The very next day I found out that Mrs. Brympton had no nurse; and then I asked Agnes about the woman I had seen in the passage the afternoon before. Agnes said she had seen no one, and I saw that she thought I was dreaming. To be sure, it was dusk when we went down the passage, and she had excused herself for not bringing a light; but I had seen the woman plain enough to know her again if we should meet. I decided that she must have been a friend of the cook's, or of one of the other women-servants; perhaps she had come down from town for a night's visit, and the servants wanted it kept secret. Some ladies are very stiff about having their servants' friends in the house overnight. At any rate, I made up my mind to ask no more questions.

In a day or two another odd thing happened. I was chatting one afternoon with Mrs. Blinder, who was a friendly disposed woman, and had been longer in the house than the other servants, and she asked me if I was quite comfortable and had everything I needed. I said I had no fault to find with my place or with my mistress, but I thought it odd that in so large a house there was no sewing-room for the lady's maid.

"Why," says she, "there *is* one: the room you're in is the old sewing-room."

"Oh," said I; "and where did the other lady's maid sleep?"

At that she grew confused, and said hurriedly that the servants' rooms had all been changed about last year, and she didn't rightly remember.

That struck me as peculiar, but I went on as if I hadn't noticed: "Well, there's a vacant room opposite mine, and I mean to ask Mrs. Brympton if I mayn't use that as a sewing-room."

To my astonishment, Mrs. Blinder went white, and gave my hand a kind of squeeze. "Don't do that, my dear," said she, trembling-like. "To tell you the truth, that was Emma Saxon's room, and my mistress has kept it closed ever since her death."

"And who was Emma Saxon?"

"Mrs. Brympton's former maid."

"The one that was with her so many years?" said I, remembering what Mrs. Railton had told me.

Mrs. Blinder nodded.

"What sort of woman was she?"

"No better walked the earth," said Mrs. Blinder. "My mistress loved her like a sister."

"But I mean—what did she look like?"

Mrs. Blinder got up and gave me a kind of angry stare. "I'm no great hand at describing," she said; "and I believe my pastry's rising." And she walked off into the kitchen and shut the door after her.

II

I had been near a week at Brympton before I saw my master. Word came that he was arriving one afternoon, and a change passed over the whole household. It was plain that nobody loved him below stairs. Mrs. Blinder took uncommon care with the dinner that night, but she snapped at the kitchen-maid in a way quite unusual with her; and Mr. Wace, the butler, a serious, slow-spoken man, went about his duties as if he'd been getting ready for a funeral. He was a great Bible-reader,

Mr. Wace was, and had a beautiful assortment of texts at his command; but that day he used such dreadful language, that I was about to leave the table, when he assured me it was all out of Isaiah; and I noticed that whenever the master came Mr. Wace took to the prophets.

About seven, Agnes called me to my mistress's room; and there I found Mr. Brympton. He was standing on the hearth; a big fair bull-necked man, with a red face and little bad-tempered blue eyes: the kind of a man a young simpleton might have thought handsome, and would have been like to pay dear for thinking it.

He swung about when I came in, and looked me over in a trice. I knew what the look meant, from having experienced it once or twice in my former places. Then he turned his back on me, and went on talking to his wife; and I knew what *that* meant, too. I was not the kind of a morsel he was after. The typhoid had served me well enough in one way: it kept that kind of gentleman at arm's-length.

"This is my new maid, Hartley," says Mrs. Brympton in her kind voice; and he nodded and went on with what he was saying.

In a minute or two he went off, and left my mistress to dress for dinner, and I noticed as I waited on her that she was white, and chill to the touch.

Mr. Brympton took himself off the next morning, and the whole house drew a long breath when he drove away. As for my mistress, she put on her hat and furs (for it was a fine winter morning) and went out for a walk in the gardens, coming back quite fresh and rosy, so that for a minute, before her colour faded, I could guess what a pretty young lady she must have been, and not so long ago, either.

She had met Mr. Ranford in the grounds, and the two came back together, I remember, smiling and talking as they walked along the terrace under my window. That was the first time I saw Mr. Ranford, though I had often heard his name mentioned in the hall. He was a neighbour, it appeared, living a mile or two beyond Brympton, at the end of the village; and as he was in the habit of spending his winters in the country he was almost the only company my mistress had at that season. He was a slight tall gentleman of about thirty, and I thought him rather melancholy-looking till I saw his smile, which had a kind of surprise in it, like the first warm day in spring. He was a great reader, I heard, like my mistress, and the two were for ever borrowing books of one another, and sometimes (Mr. Wace told me) he would read aloud to Mrs. Brympton by the hour, in the big dark library where she sat in the winter afternoons. The servants all liked him, and perhaps that's more of a compliment than the masters suspect. He had a friendly word for every one of us, and we were all glad to think that Mrs. Brympton had a pleasant companionable gentleman like that to keep her company when the master was away. Mr. Ranford seemed on excellent terms with Mr. Brympton too; though I couldn't but wonder that two gentlemen so unlike each other should be so friendly. But then I knew how the real quality can keep their feelings to themselves.

As for Mr. Brympton, he came and went, never staying more than a day or two, cursing the dulness and the solitude, grumbling at everything, and (as I soon found out) drinking a deal more than was good for him. After Mrs. Brympton left the table he would sit half the night over the old Brympton port and madeira, and once, as I was leaving my mistress's room rather later than usual, I met him coming up the stairs in such a state that I turned sick to think of what some ladies have to endure and hold their tongues about.

The servants said very little about their master; but from what they let drop I could see it had been an unhappy match from the beginning. Mr. Brympton was coarse, loud and pleasure-loving; my mistress quiet, retiring, and perhaps a trifle cold. Not that she was not always pleasant-spoken to him: I thought her wonderfully forbearing; but to a gentleman as free as Mr. Brympton I daresay she seemed a little offish.

Well, things went on quietly for several weeks. My mistress was kind, my duties were light, and I got on well with the other servants. In short, I had nothing to complain of; yet there was always a weight on me. I can't say why it was so, but I know it was not the loneliness that I felt. I soon got used to that; and being still languid from the fever, I was thankful for the quiet and the good country air. Nevertheless, I was never quite easy in my mind. My mistress, knowing I had been ill, insisted that I should take my walk regular, and often invented errands for me:—a yard of ribbon to be fetched from the village, a letter posted, or a book returned to Mr. Ranford. As soon as I was out of doors my spirits rose, and I looked forward to my walks through the bare moist-smelling woods; but the moment I caught sight of the house again my heart dropped down like a stone in a well. It was not a gloomy house exactly, yet I never entered it but a feeling of gloom came over me.

Mrs. Brympton seldom went out in winter; only on the finest days did she walk an hour at noon on the south terrace. Excepting Mr. Ranford, we had no visitors but the doctor, who drove over from D—— about once a week. He sent for me once or twice to give me some trifling direction about my mistress, and though he never told me what her illness was, I thought, from a waxy look she had now and then of a morning, that it might be the heart that ailed her. The season was soft and unwholesome, and in January we had a long spell of rain. That was a sore trial to me, I own, for I couldn't go out, and sitting over my sewing all day, listening to the drip, drip of the eaves, I grew so nervous that the least sound made me jump. Somehow, the thought of that locked room across the passage began to weigh on me. Once or twice, in the long rainy nights, I fancied I heard noises there; but that was nonsense, of course, and the daylight drove such notions out of my head. Well, one morning Mrs. Brympton gave me quite a start of pleasure by telling me she wished me to go to town for some shopping. I hadn't known till then how low my spirits had fallen. I set off in high glee, and my first sight of the crowded streets and the cheerful-looking shops quite took me out of myself. Toward afternoon, however, the noise and confusion began to tire me, and I was actually looking forward to the quiet of Brympton, and thinking how I should enjoy the drive home through the dark woods, when I ran across an old acquaintance, a maid I had once been in service with. We had lost sight of each other for a number of years, and I had to stop and tell her what had happened to me in the interval. When I mentioned where I was living she rolled up her eyes and pulled a long face.

"What! The Mrs. Brympton that lives all the year at her place on the Hudson? My dear, you won't stay there three months."

"Oh, but I don't mind the country," says I, offended somehow at her tone. "Since the fever I'm glad to be quiet."

She shook her head. "It's not the country I'm thinking of. All I know is she's had four maids in the last six months, and the last one, who was a friend of mine, told me nobody could stay in the house."

"Did she say why?" I asked.

"No—she wouldn't give me her reason. But she says to me, *Mrs. Ansey*, she says, *if ever a young woman as you know of thinks of going there, you tell her it's not worth while to unpack her boxes.*"

"Is she young and handsome?" said I, thinking of Mr. Brympton.

"Not her! She's the kind that mothers engage when they've gay young gentlemen at college."

Well, though I knew the woman was an idle gossip, the words stuck in my head, and my heart sank lower than ever as I drove up to Brympton in the dusk. There *was* something about the house—I was sure of it now . . .

When I went in to tea I heard that Mr. Brympton had arrived, and I saw at a glance that there had been a disturbance of some kind. Mrs. Blinder's hand shook so that she could hardly pour the tea, and Mr. Wace quoted the most dreadful texts full of brimstone. Nobody said a word to me then, but when I went up to my room Mrs. Blinder followed me.

"Oh, my dear," says she, taking my hand, "I'm so glad and thankful you've come back to us!"

That struck me, as you may imagine. "Why," said I, "did you think I was leaving for good?"

"No, no, to be sure," said she, a little confused, "but I can't a-bear to have madam left alone for a day even." She pressed my hand hard, and, "Oh, Miss Hartley," says she, "be good to your mistress, as you're a Christian woman." And with that she hurried away, and left me staring.

A moment later Agnes called me to Mrs. Brympton. Hearing Mr. Brympton's voice in her room, I went round by the dressing-room, thinking I would lay out her dinner-gown before going in. The dressing-room is a large room with a window over the portico that looks toward the gardens. Mr. Brympton's apartments are beyond. When I went in, the door into the bedroom was ajar, and I heard Mr. Brympton saying angrily:—"One would suppose he was the only person fit for you to talk to."

"I don't have many visitors in winter," Mrs. Brympton answered quietly.

"You have *me!*" he flung at her, sneeringly.

"You are here so seldom," said she.

"Well—whose fault is that? You make the place about as lively as the family vault——"

With that I rattled the toilet-things, to give my mistress warning, and she rose and called me in.

The two dined alone, as usual, and I knew by Mr. Wace's manner at supper that things must be going badly. He quoted the prophets something terrible, and worked on the kitchen-maid so that she declared she wouldn't go down alone to put the cold meat in the ice-box. I felt nervous myself, and after I had put my

mistress to bed I was half-tempted to go down again and persuade Mrs. Blinder to sit up awhile over a game of cards. But I heard her door closing for the night and so I went on to my own room. The rain had begun again, and the drip, drip, drip seemed to be dropping into my brain. I lay awake listening to it, and turning over what my friend in town had said. What puzzled me was that it was always the maids who left . . .

After a while I slept; but suddenly a loud noise wakened me. My bell had rung. I sat up, terrified by the unusual sound, which seemed to go on jangling through the darkness. My hands shook so that I couldn't find the matches. At length I struck a light and jumped out of bed. I began to think I must have been dreaming; but I looked at the bell against the wall, and there was the little hammer still quivering.

I was just beginning to huddle on my clothes when I heard another sound. This time it was the door of the locked room opposite mine softly opening and closing. I heard the sound distinctly, and it frightened me so that I stood stock still. Then I heard a footstep hurrying down the passage toward the main house. The floor being carpeted, the sound was very faint, but I was quite sure it was a woman's step. I turned cold with the thought of it, and for a minute or two I dursn't breathe or move. Then I came to my senses.

"Alice Hartley," says I to myself, "someone left that room just now and ran down the passage ahead of you. The idea isn't pleasant, but you may as well face it. Your mistress has rung for you, and to answer her bell you've got to go the way that other woman has gone."

Well—I did it. I never walked faster in my life, yet I thought I should never get to the end of the passage or reach Mrs. Brympton's room. On the way I heard nothing and saw nothing: all was dark and quiet as the grave. When I reached my mistress's door the silence was so deep that I began to think I must be dreaming, and was half-minded to turn back. Then a panic seized me, and I knocked.

There was no answer, and I knocked again, loudly. To my astonishment the door was opened by Mr. Brympton. He started back when he saw me, and in the light of my candle his face looked red and savage.

"*You?*" he said, in a queer voice. "*How many of you are there, in God's name?*"

At that I felt the ground give under me; but I said to myself that he had been drinking, and answered as steadily as I could: "May I go in, sir? Mrs. Brympton has rung for me."

"You may all go in, for what I care," says he, and, pushing by me, walked down the hall to his own bedroom. I looked after him as he went, and to my surprise I saw that he walked as straight as a sober man.

I found my mistress lying very weak and still, but she forced a smile when she saw me, and signed to me to pour out some drops for her. After that she lay without speaking, her breath coming quick, and her eyes closed. Suddenly she groped out with her hand, and "*Emma*," says she, faintly.

"It's Hartley, madam," I said. "Do you want anything?"

She opened her eyes wide and gave me a startled look.

"I was dreaming," she said. "You may go, now, Hartley, and thank you kindly. I'm quite well again, you see." And she turned her face away from me.

III

There was no more sleep for me that night, and I was thankful when daylight came.

Soon afterward, Agnes called me to Mrs. Brympton. I was afraid she was ill again, for she seldom sent for me before nine, but I found her sitting up in bed, pale and drawn-looking, but quite herself.

"Hartley," says she quickly, "will you put on your things at once and go down to the village for me? I want this prescription made up—" here she hesitated a minute and blushed— "and I should like you to be back again before Mr. Brympton is up."

"Certainly, madam," I said.

"And—stay a moment—" she called me back as if an idea had just struck her—"while you're waiting for the mixture, you'll have time to go on to Mr. Ranford's with this note."

It was a two-mile walk to the village, and on my way I had time to turn things over in my mind. It struck me as peculiar that my mistress should wish the prescription made up without Mr. Brympton's knowledge; and, putting this together with the scene of the night before, and with much else that I had noticed and suspected, I began to wonder if the poor lady was weary of her life, and had come to the mad resolve of ending it. The idea took such hold on me that I reached the village on a run, and dropped breathless into a chair before the chemist's counter. The good man, who was just taking down his shutters, stared at me so hard that it brought me to myself.

"Mr. Limmel," I says, trying to speak indifferent, "will you run your eye over this, and tell me if it's quite right?"

He put on his spectacles and studied the prescription.

"Why, it's one of Dr. Walton's," says he. "What should be wrong with it?"

"Well—is it dangerous to take?"

"Dangerous—how do you mean?"

I could have shaken the man for his stupidity.

"I mean—if a person was to take too much of it—by mistake of course—" says I, my heart in my throat.

"Lord bless you, no. It's only lime-water. You might feed it to a baby by the bottleful."

I gave a great sigh of relief and hurried on to Mr. Ranford's. But on the way another thought struck me. If there was nothing to conceal about my visit to the chemist's, was it my other errand that Mrs. Brympton wished me to keep private? Somehow, that thought frightened me worse than the other. Yet the two gentlemen seemed fast friends, and I would have staked my head on my mistress's goodness. I felt ashamed of my suspicions, and concluded that I was still disturbed by the strange events of the night. I left the note at Mr. Ranford's, and hurrying back to Brympton, slipped in by a side door without being seen, as I thought.

An hour later, however, as I was carrying in my mistress's breakfast, I was stopped in the hall by Mr. Brympton.

"What were you doing out so early?" he says, looking hard at me.

"Early—me, sir?" I said, in a tremble.

"Come, come," he says, an angry red spot coming out on his forehead, "didn't I see you scuttling home through the shrubbery an hour or more ago?"

I'm a truthful woman by nature, but at that a lie popped out ready-made. "No, sir, you didn't," said I and looked straight back at him.

He shrugged his shoulders and gave a sullen laugh. "I suppose you think I was drunk last night?" he asked suddenly.

"No, sir, I don't," I answered, this time truthfully enough.

He turned away with another shrug. "A pretty notion my servants have of me!" I heard him mutter as he walked off.

Not till I had settled down to my afternoon's sewing did I realise how the events of the night had shaken me. I couldn't pass that locked door without a shiver. I knew I had heard someone come out of it, and walk down the passage ahead of me. I thought of speaking to Mrs. Blinder or to Mr. Wace, the only two in the house who appeared to have an inkling of what was going on, but I had a feeling that if I questioned them they would deny every-thing, and that I might learn more by holding my tongue and keeping my eyes open. The idea of spending another night opposite the locked room sickened me, and once I was seized with the notion of packing my trunk and taking the first train to town; but it wasn't in me to throw over a kind mistress in that manner, and I tried to go on with my sewing as if nothing had happened. I hadn't worked ten minutes before the sewing machine broke down. It was one I had found in the house, a good machine but a trifle out of order: Mrs. Blinder said it had never been used since Emma Saxon's death. I stopped to see what was wrong, and as I was working at the machine a drawer which I had never been able to open slid forward and a photograph fell out. I picked it up and sat looking at it in a maze. It was a woman's likeness, and I knew I had seen the face somewhere—the eyes had an ask-ing look that I had felt on me before. And suddenly I remembered the pale woman in the passage.

I stood up, cold all over, and ran out of the room. My heart seemed to be thumping in the top of my head, and I felt as if I should never get away from the look in those eyes. I went straight to Mrs. Blinder. She was taking her afternoon nap, and sat up with a jump when I came in.

"Mrs. Blinder," said I, "who is that?" And I held out the photograph.

She rubbed her eyes and stared.

"Why, Emma Saxon," says she. "Where did you find it?"

I looked hard at her for a minute. "Mrs. Blinder," I said, "I've seen that face before."

Mrs. Blinder got up and walked over to the looking-glass. "Dear me! I must have been asleep," she says. "My front is all over one ear. And now do run along, Miss Hartley, dear, for I hear the clock striking four, and I must go down this very minute and put on the Virginia ham for Mr. Brympton's dinner."

IV

To all appearances, things went on as usual for a week or two. The only difference was that Mr. Brympton stayed on, instead of go-ing off as he usually did, and that Mr. Ranford never showed himself. I heard Mr. Brympton remark on this one afternoon when he was sit-ting in my mistress's room before dinner:

"Where's Ranford?" says he. "He hasn't been near the house for a week. Does he keep away because I'm here?"

Mrs. Brympton spoke so low that I couldn't catch her answer.

"Well," he went on, "two's company and three's trumpery; I'm sorry to be in Ranford's way, and I suppose I shall have to take myself off again in a day or two and give him a show." And he laughed at his own joke.

The very next day, as it happened, Mr. Ran-ford called. The footman said the three were very merry over their tea in the library, and Mr. Brympton strolled down to the gate with Mr. Ranford when he left.

I have said that things went on as usual; and so they did with the rest of the household; but as for myself, I had never been the same since the night my bell had rung. Night after night I used to lie awake, listening for it to ring again, and for the door of the locked room to open stealthily. But the bell never rang, and I heard no sound across the passage. At last the silence began to be more dreadful to me than the most mysterious sounds. I felt that *someone* was cowering there, behind the locked door, watching and listening as I watched and listened, and I could almost have cried out, "Whoever you are, come out and let me see you face to face, but don't lurk there and spy on me in the darkness!"

Feeling as I did, you may wonder I didn't give warning. Once I very nearly did so; but at the last moment something held me back. Whether it was compassion for my mistress, who had grown more and more dependent on me, or unwillingness to try a new place, or some other feeling that I couldn't put a name to, I lingered on as if spell-bound, though every night was dreadful to me, and the days but little better.

For one thing, I didn't like Mrs. Brympton's looks. She had never been the same since that night, no more than I had. I thought she would brighten up after Mr. Brympton left, but though she seemed easier in her mind, her spirits didn't revive, nor her strength either. She had grown attached to me, and seemed to like to have me about; and Agnes told me one day that, since Emma Saxon's death, I was the only maid her mistress had taken to. This gave me a warm feeling for the poor lady, though after all there was little I could do to help her.

After Mr. Brympton's departure, Mr. Ran-ford took to coming again, though less often than formerly. I met him once or twice in the grounds, or in the village, and I couldn't but think there was a change in him too; but I set it down to my disordered fancy.

The weeks passed, and Mr. Brympton had

now been a month absent. We heard he was cruising with a friend in the West Indies, and Mr. Wace said that was a long way off, but though you had the wings of a dove and went to the uttermost parts of the earth, you couldn't get away from the Almighty. Agnes said that as long as he stayed away from Brympton the Almighty might have him and welcome; and this raised a laugh, though Mrs. Blinder tried to look shocked, and Mr. Wace said the bears would eat us.

We were all glad to hear that the West Indies were a long way off, and I remember that, in spite of Mr. Wace's solemn looks, we had a very merry dinner that day in the hall. I don't know if it was because of my being in better spirits, but I fancied Mrs. Brympton looked better too, and seemed more cheerful in her manner. She had been for a walk in the morning, and after luncheon she lay down in her room, and I read aloud to her. When she dismissed me I went to my own room feeling quite bright and happy, and for the first time in weeks walked past the locked door without thinking of it. As I sat down to my work I looked out and saw a few snow-flakes falling. The sight was pleasanter than the eternal rain, and I pictured to myself how pretty the bare gardens would look in their white mantle. It seemed to me as if the snow would cover up all the dreariness, indoors as well as out.

The fancy had hardly crossed my mind when I heard a step at my side. I looked up, thinking it was Agnes.

"Well, Agnes——" said I, and the words froze on my tongue; for there, in the door, stood Emma Saxon.

I don't know how long she stood there. I only know I couldn't stir or take my eyes from her. Afterward I was terribly frightened, but at the time it wasn't fear I felt, but something deeper and quieter. She looked at me long and long, and her face was just one dumb prayer to me—but how in the world was I to help her? Suddenly she turned, and I heard her walk down the passage. This time I wasn't afraid to follow—I felt that I must know what she wanted. I sprang up and ran out. She was at the other end of the passage, and I expected her to take the turn toward my mistress's room; but instead of that she pushed open the door that led to the backstairs. I followed her down the stairs, and across the passageway to the back door. The kitchen and hall were empty at that hour, the servants being off duty, except for the footman, who was in the pantry. At the door she stood still a moment, with another look at me; then she turned the handle, and stepped out. For a minute I hesitated. Where was she leading me to? The door had closed softly after her, and I opened it and looked out, half-expecting to find that she had disappeared. But I saw her a few yards off hurrying across the courtyard to the path through the woods. Her figure looked black and lonely in the snow, and for a second my heart failed me and I thought of turning back. But all the while she was drawing me after her; and catching up an old shawl of Mrs. Blinder's I ran out into the open.

Emma Saxon was in the wood-path now. She walked on steadily, and I followed at the same pace, till we passed out of the gates and reached the highroad. Then she struck across the open fields to the village. By this time the ground was white, and as she climbed the slope of a bare hill ahead of me I noticed that she left no foot-prints behind her. At sight of that my heart shrivelled up within me, and my knees were water. Somehow, it was worse here than indoors. She made the whole countryside seem lonely as the grave, with none but us two in it, and no help in the wide world.

Once I tried to go back; but she turned and looked at me, and it was as if she had dragged me with ropes. After that I followed her like a dog. We came to the village and she led me through it, past the church and the blacksmith's shop, and down the lane to Mr. Ranford's. Mr. Ranford's house stands close to the road: a plain old-fashioned building, with a flagged path leading to the door between box-borders. The lane was deserted, and as I turned into it I saw Emma Saxon pause under the old elm by the gate. And now another fear came over me. I saw that we had reached the end of our journey, and that it was my turn to act. All the way from Brympton I had been asking myself what she wanted of me, but I had followed in a trance, as it were, and not till I saw her stop at Mr. Ranford's gate did my brain begin to clear itself. I stood a little way off in the snow, my heart beating fit to strangle me, and my feet frozen to the ground; and she stood under the elm and watched me.

I knew well enough that she hadn't led me there for nothing. I felt there was something I ought to say or do—but how was I to guess what it was? I had never thought harm of my mistress and Mr. Ranford; but I was sure now that, from one cause or another, some dreadful thing hung over them. *She* knew what it was; she would tell me if she could; perhaps she would answer if I questioned her.

It turned me faint to think of speaking to

her; but I plucked up heart and dragged myself across the few yards between us. As I did so, I heard the house-door open and saw Mr. Ranford approaching. He looked handsome and cheerful, as my mistress had looked that morning, and at sight of him the blood began to flow again in my veins.

"Why, Hartley," said he, "what's the matter? I saw you coming down the lane just now, and came out to see if you had taken root in the snow." He stopped and stared at me. "What are you looking at?" he says.

I turned toward the elm as he spoke, and his eyes followed me; but there was no one there. The lane was empty as far as the eye could reach.

A sense of helplessness came over me. She was gone, and I had not been able to guess what she wanted. Her last look had pierced me to the marrow; and yet it had not told me! All at once, I felt more desolate than when she had stood there watching me. It seemed as if she had left me all alone to carry the weight of the secret I couldn't guess. The snow went round me in great circles, and the ground fell away from me. . . .

A drop of brandy and the warmth of Mr. Ranford's fire soon brought me to, and I insisted on being driven back at once to Brympton. It was nearly dark, and I was afraid my mistress might be wanting me. I explained to Mr. Ranford that I had been out for a walk and had been taken with a fit of giddiness as I passed his gate. This was true enough; yet I never felt more like a liar than when I said it.

When I dressed Mrs. Brympton for dinner she remarked on my pale looks and asked what ailed me. I told her I had a headache, and she said she would not require me again that evening, and advised me to go to bed.

It was a fact that I could scarcely keep on my feet; yet I had no fancy to spend a solitary evening in my room. I sat downstairs in the hall as long as I could hold my head up; but by nine I crept upstairs, too weary to care what happened if I could but get my head on a pillow. The rest of the household went to bed soon afterward; they kept early hours when the master was away, and before ten I heard Mrs. Blinder's door close, and Mr. Wace's soon after.

It was a very still night, earth and air all muffled in snow. Once in bed I felt easier, and lay quiet, listening to the strange noises that come out in a house after dark. Once I thought I heard a door open and close again below: it might have been the glass door that led to the gardens. I got up and peered out of the window; but it was in the dark of the moon, and nothing visible outside but the streaking of snow against the panes.

I went back to bed and must have dozed, for I jumped awake to the furious ringing of my bell. Before my head was clear I had sprung out of bed, and was dragging on my clothes. *It is going to happen now*, I heard myself saying; but what I meant I had no notion. My hands seemed to be covered with glue—I thought I should never get into my clothes. At last I opened my door and peered down the passage. As far as my candle-flame carried, I could see nothing unusual ahead of me. I hurried on, breathless; but as I pushed open the baize door leading to the main hall my heart stood still, for there at the head of the stairs was Emma Saxon, peering dreadfully down into the darkness.

For a second I couldn't stir; but my hand slipped from the door, and as it swung shut the figure vanished. At the same instant there came another sound from below stairs—a stealthy mysterious sound, as of a latch-key turning in the house-door. I ran to Mrs. Brympton's room and knocked.

There was no answer, and I knocked again. This time I heard someone moving in the room; the bolt slipped back and my mistress stood before me. To my surprise I saw that she had not undressed for the night. She gave me a startled look.

"What is this, Hartley?" she says in a whisper. "Are you ill? What are you doing here at this hour?"

"I am not ill, madam; but my bell rang."

At that she turned pale, and seemed about to fall.

"You are mistaken," she said harshly; "I didn't ring. You must have been dreaming." I had never heard her speak in such a tone. "Go back to bed," she said, closing the door on me.

But as she spoke I heard sounds again in the hall below: a man's step this time; and the truth leaped out on me.

"Madam," I said, pushing past her, "there is someone in the house——"

"Someone——?"

"Mr. Brympton, I think—I hear his step below——"

A dreadful look came over her, and without a word, she dropped flat at my feet. I fell on my knees and tried to lift her: by the way she breathed I saw it was no common faint. But as I raised her head there came quick steps on the stairs and across the hall: the door was flung open, and there stood Mr. Brympton, in his travelling-clothes, the snow dripping from him. He drew back with a start as he saw me kneeling by my mistress.

"What the devil is this?" he shouted. He was less high-coloured than usual, and the red spot came out on his forehead.

"Mrs. Brympton has fainted, sir," said I.

He laughed unsteadily and pushed by me. "It's a pity she didn't choose a more convenient moment. I'm sorry to disturb her, but——"

I raised myself up aghast at the man's action.

"Sir," said I, "are you mad? What are you doing?"

"Going to meet a friend," said he, and seemed to make for the dressing-room.

At that my heart turned over. I don't know what I thought or feared; but I sprang up and caught him by the sleeve.

"Sir, sir," said I, "for pity's sake look at your wife!"

He shook me off furiously.

"It seems that's done for me," says he, and caught hold of the dressing-room door.

At that moment I heard a slight noise inside. Slight as it was, he heard it too, and tore the door open; but as he did so he dropped back. On the threshold stood Emma Saxon. All was dark behind her, but I saw her plainly, and so did he. He threw up his hands as if to hide his

face from her; and when I looked again she was gone.

He stood motionless, as if the strength had run out of him; and in the stillness my mistress suddenly raised herself, and opening her eyes fixed a look on him. Then she fell back, and I saw the death-flutter pass over her. . . .

We buried her on the third day, in a driving snow-storm. There were few people in the church, for it was bad weather to come from town, and I've a notion my mistress was one that hadn't many near friends. Mr. Ranford was among the last to come, just before they carried her up the aisle. He was in black, of course, being such a friend of the family, and I never saw a gentleman so pale. As he passed me, I noticed that he leaned a trifle on a stick he carried; and I fancy Mr. Brympton noticed it too, for the red spot came out sharp on his forehead, and all through the service he kept staring across the church at Mr. Ranford, instead of following the prayers as a mourner should.

When it was over and we went out to the graveyard, Mr. Ranford had disappeared, and as soon as my poor mistress's body was underground, Mr. Brympton jumped into the carriage nearest the gate and drove off without a word to any of us. I heard him call out, "To the station," and we servants went back alone to the house.

AUTRES TEMPS . . .
(1916)

I

Mrs. Lidcote, as the huge menacing mass of New York defined itself far off across the waters, shrank back into her corner of the deck and sat listening with a kind of unreasoning terror to the steady onward drive of the screws. She had set out on the voyage quietly enough,—in what she called her "reasonable" mood,—but the week at sea had given her too much time to think of things and had left her too long alone with the past.

When she was alone, it was always the past that occupied her. She couldn't get away from it, and she didn't any longer care to. During her long years of exile she had made her terms with it, had learned to accept the fact that it would always be there, huge, obstructing, encumbering, bigger and more dominant than anything the future could ever conjure up. And, at any rate, she was sure of it, she understood it, knew how to reckon with it; she had

learned to screen and manage and protect it as one does an afflicted member of one's family.

There had never been any danger of her being allowed to forget the past. It looked out at her from the face of every acquaintance, it appeared suddenly in the eyes of strangers when a word enlightened them: "Yes, the Mrs. Lidcote, don't you know?" It had sprung at her the first day out, when, across the dining-room, from the captain's table, she had seen Mrs. Lorin Boulger's revolving eye-glass pause and the eye behind it grow as blank as a dropped blind. The next day, of course, the captain had asked: "You know your ambassadress, Mrs. Boulger?" and she had replied that, No, she seldom left Florence, and hadn't been to Rome for more than a day since the Boulgers had been sent to Italy. She was so used to these phrases that it cost her no effort to repeat them. And the captain had promptly changed the subject.

No, she didn't, as a rule, mind the past, because she was used to it and understood it. It was a great concrete fact in her path that she had to walk around every time she moved in any direction. But now, in the light of the unhappy event that had summoned her from Italy,—the sudden unanticipated news of her daughter's divorce from Horace Pursh and remarriage with Wilbur Barkley—the past, her own poor miserable past, started up at her with eyes of accusation, became, to her disordered fancy, like the afflicted relative suddenly breaking away from nurses and keepers and publicly parading the horror and misery she had, all the long years, so patiently screened and secluded.

Yes, there it had stood before her through the agitated weeks since the news had come— during her interminable journey from India, where Leila's letter had overtaken her, and the feverish halt in her apartment in Florence, where she had had to stop and gather up her possessions for a fresh start—there it had stood grinning at her with a new balefulness which seemed to say: "Oh, but you've got to look at me *now*, because I'm not only your own past but Leila's present."

Certainly it was a master-stroke of those arch-ironists of the shears and spindle to duplicate her own story in her daughter's. Mrs. Lidcote had always somewhat grimly fancied that, having so signally failed to be of use to Leila in other ways, she would at least serve her as a warning. She had even abstained from defending herself, from making the best of her case, had stoically refused to plead extenuating circumstances, lest Leila's impulsive sympathy should lead to deductions that might react disastrously on her own life. And now that very thing had happened, and Mrs. Lidcote could hear the whole of New York saying with one voice: "Yes, Leila's done just what her mother did. With such an example what could you expect?"

Yet if she had been an example, poor woman, she had been an awful one; she had been, she would have supposed, of more use as a deterrent than a hundred blameless mothers as incentives. For how could any one who had seen anything of her life in the last eighteen years have had the courage to repeat so disastrous an experiment?

Well, logic in such cases didn't count, example didn't count, nothing probably counted but having the same impulses in the blood; and that was the dark inheritance she had bestowed upon her daughter. Leila hadn't consciously copied her; she had simply "taken

after" her, had been a projection of her own long-past rebellion.

Mrs. Lidcote had deplored, when she started, that the *Utopia* was a slow steamer, and would take eight full days to bring her to her unhappy daughter; but now, as the moment of reunion approached, she would willingly have turned the boat about and fled back to the high seas. It was not only because she felt still so unprepared to face what New York had in store for her, but because she needed more time to dispose of what the *Utopia* had already given her. The past was bad enough, but the present and future were worse, because they were less comprehensible, and because, as she grew older, surprises and inconsequences troubled her more than the worst certainties.

There was Mrs. Boulger, for instance. In the light, or rather the darkness, of new developments, it might really be that Mrs. Boulger had not meant to cut her, but had simply failed to recognize her. Mrs. Lidcote had arrived at this hypothesis simply by listening to the conversation of the persons sitting next to her on deck—two lively young women with the latest Paris hats on their heads and the latest New York ideas in them. These ladies, as to whom it would have been impossible for a person with Mrs. Lidcote's old-fashioned categories to determine whether they were married or unmarried, "nice" or "horrid," or any one or other of the definite things which young women, in her youth and her society, were conveniently assumed to be, had revealed a familiarity with the world of New York that, again according to Mrs. Lidcote's traditions, should have implied a recognized place in it. But in the present fluid state of manners what did anything imply except what their hats implied—that no one could tell what was coming next?

They seemed, at any rate, to frequent a group of idle and opulent people who executed the same gestures and revolved on the same pivots as Mrs. Lidcote's daughter and her friends: their Coras, Matties and Mabels seemed at any moment likely to reveal familiar patronymics, and once one of the speakers, summing up a discussion of which Mrs. Lidcote had missed the beginning, had affirmed with headlong confidence: "Leila? Oh, *Leila's* all right."

Could it be *her* Leila, the mother had wondered, with a sharp thrill of apprehension? If only they would mention surnames! But their talk leaped elliptically from allusion to allusion, their unfinished sentences dangled over bottomless pits of conjecture, and they gave their bewildered hearer the impression not so much of talking only of their intimates, as of being intimate with every one alive.

Her old friend Franklin Ide could have told her, perhaps; but here was the last day of the voyage, and she hadn't yet found courage to ask him. Great as had been the joy of discovering his name on the passenger-list and seeing his friendly bearded face in the throng against the taffrail at Cherbourg, she had as yet said nothing to him except, when they had met: "Of course I'm going out to Leila."

She had said nothing to Franklin Ide because she had always instinctively shrunk from taking him into her confidence. She was sure he felt sorry for her, sorrier perhaps than any one had ever felt; but he had always paid her the supreme tribute of not showing it. His attitude allowed her to imagine that compassion was not the basis of his feeling for her, and it was part of her joy in his friendship that it was the one relation seemingly unconditioned by her state, the only one in which she could think and feel and behave like any other woman.

Now, however, as the problem of New York looked nearer, she began to regret that she had not spoken, had not at least questioned him about the hints she had gathered on the way. He did not know the two ladies next to her, he did not even, as it chanced, know Mrs. Lorin Boulger; but he knew New York, and New York was the sphinx whose riddle she must read or perish.

Almost as the thought passed through her mind his stooping shoulders and grizzled head detached themselves against the blaze of light in the west, and he sauntered down the empty deck and dropped into the chair at her side.

"You're expecting the Barkleys to meet you, I suppose?" he asked.

It was the first time she had heard any one pronounce her daughter's new name, and it occurred to her that her friend, who was shy and inarticulate, had been trying to say it all the way over and had at last shot it out at her only because he felt it must be now or never.

"I don't know. I cabled, of course. But I believe she's at—they're at—his place somewhere."

"Oh, Barkley's; yes, near Lenox, isn't it? But she's sure to come to town to meet you."

He said it so easily and naturally that her own constraint was relieved, and suddenly, before she knew what she meant to do, she had burst out: "She may dislike the idea of seeing people."

Ide, whose absent short-sighted gaze had been fixed on the slowly gliding water, turned in his seat to stare at his companion.

"Who? Leila?" he said with an incredulous laugh.

Mrs. Lidcote flushed to her faded hair and grew pale again. "It took *me* a long time—to get used to it," she said.

His look grew gently commiserating. "I think you'll find—" he paused for a word— "that things are different now—altogether easier."

"That's what I've been wondering—ever since we started." She was determined now to speak. She moved nearer, so that their arms touched, and she could drop her voice to a murmur. "You see, it all came on me in a flash. My going off to India and Siam on that long trip kept me away from letters for weeks at a time; and she didn't want to tell me beforehand—oh, I understand *that*, poor child! You know how good she's always been to me; how she's tried to spare me. And she knew, of course, what a state of horror I'd be in. She knew I'd rush off to her at once and try to stop it. So she never gave me a hint of anything, and she even managed to muzzle Susy Suffern —you know Susy is the one of the family who keeps me informed about things at home. I don't yet see how she prevented Susy's telling me; but she did. And her first letter, the one I got at Bangkok, simply said the thing was over—the divorce, I mean—and that the very next day she'd—well, I suppose there was no use waiting; and *he* seems to have behaved as well as possible, to have wanted to marry her as much as——"

"Who? Barkley?" he helped her out. "I should say so! Why what do you suppose——" He interrupted himself. "He'll be devoted to her, I assure you."

"Oh, of course; I'm sure he will. He's written me—really beautifully. But it's a terrible strain on a man's devotion. I'm not sure that Leila realizes——"

Ide sounded again his little reassuring laugh. "I'm not sure that you realize. *They're* all right."

It was the very phrase that the young lady in the next seat had applied to the unknown "Leila," and its recurrence on Ide's lips flushed Mrs. Lidcote with fresh courage.

"I wish I knew just what you mean. The two young women next to me—the ones with the wonderful hats—have been talking in the same way."

"What? About Leila?"

"About *a* Leila; I fancied it might be mine. And about society in general. All their friends

seem to be divorced; some of them seem to announce their engagements before they get
their decree. One of them—*her* name was
Mabel—as far as I could make out, her husband found out that she meant to divorce him
by noticing that she wore a new engagement-
ring."

"Well, you see Leila did everything 'regularly,' as the French say," Ide rejoined.

"Yes; but are these people in society? The
people my neighbours talk about?"

He shrugged his shoulders. "It would take
an arbitration commission a good many sit-
tings to define the boundaries of society nowadays. But at any rate they're in New York;
and I assure you you're *not*; you're farther and
farther from it."

" But I've been back there several times to
see Leila." She hesitated and looked away
from him. Then she brought out slowly:
" And I've never noticed—the least change
—in—in my own case——"

"Oh," he sounded deprecatingly, and she
trembled with the fear of having gone too far.
But the hour was past when such scruples
could restrain her. She must know where she
was and where Leila was. "Mrs. Boulger still
cuts me," she brought out with an embarrassed
laugh.

"Are you sure? You've probably cut *her*;
if not now, at least in the past. And in a cut if
you're not first you're nowhere. That's what
keeps up so many quarrels."

The word roused Mrs. Lidcote to a renewed sense of realities. "But the Purshes,"
she said—"the Purshes are so strong! There
are so many of them, and they all back each
other up, just as my husband's family did. I
know what it means to have a clan against one.
They're stronger than any number of separate
friends. The Purshes will *never* forgive Leila
for leaving Horace. Why, his mother opposed
his marrying her because of—of me. She tried
to get Leila to promise that she wouldn't see
me when they went to Europe on their honey-
moon. And now she'll say it was my example."

Her companion, vaguely stroking his beard,
mused a moment upon this; then he asked,
with seeming irrelevance, "What did Leila
say when you wrote that you were coming?"

"She said it wasn't the least necessary, but
that I'd better come, because it was the only
way to convince me that it wasn't."

"Well, then, that proves she's not afraid of
the Purshes."

She breathed a long sigh of remembrance.
"Oh, just at first, you know—one never is."

He laid his hand on hers with a gesture of in-

telligence and pity. "You'll see, you'll see,"
he said.

A shadow lengthened down the deck before
them, and a steward stood there, proffering a
Marconigram.

"Oh, now I shall know!" she exclaimed.

She tore the message open, and then let it
fall on her knees, dropping her hands on it in
silence.

Ide's enquiry roused her: "It's all right?"

"Oh, quite right. Perfectly. She can't
come; but she's sending Susy Suffern. She
says Susy will explain." After another silence
she added, with a sudden gush of bitterness:
"As if I needed any explanation!"

She felt Ide's hesitating glance upon her.
"She's in the country?"

"Yes. 'Prevented last moment. Longing
for you, expecting you. Love from both.'
Don't you *see*, the poor darling, that she
couldn't face it?"

"No, I don't." He waited. "Do you mean
to go to her immediately?"

"It will be too late to catch a train this
evening; but I shall take the first to-morrow
morning." She considered a moment. "Perhaps it's better. I need a talk with Susy first.
She's to meet me at the dock, and I'll take her
straight back to the hotel with me."

As she developed this plan, she had the sense
that Ide was still thoughtfully, even gravely,
considering her. When she ceased, he remained silent a moment; then he said almost
ceremoniously: "If your talk with Miss Suffern doesn't last too late, may I come and see
you when it's over? I shall be dining at my
club, and I'll call you up at about ten, if I may.
I'm off to Chicago on business to-morrow
morning, and it would be a satisfaction to
know, before I start, that your cousin's been
able to reassure you, as I know she will."

He spoke with a shy deliberateness that,
even to Mrs. Lidcote's troubled perceptions,
sounded a long-silenced note of feeling. Perhaps the breaking down of the barrier of reticence between them had released unsuspected
emotions in both. The tone of his appeal
moved her curiously and loosened the tight
strain of her fears.

"Oh, yes, come—do come," she said, rising.
The huge threat of New York was imminent
now, dwarfing, under long reaches of embattled masonry, the great deck she stood on
and all the little specks of life it carried. One of
them, drifting nearer, took the shape of her
maid, followed by luggage-laden stewards, and
signing to her that it was time to go below. As
they descended to the main deck, the throng

swept her against Mrs. Lorin Boulger's shoulder, and she heard the ambassadress call out to some one, over the vexed sea of hats: "So sorry! I should have been delighted, but I've promised to spend Sunday with some friends at Lenox."

II

Susy Suffern's explanation did not end till after ten o'clock, and she had just gone when Franklin Ide, who, complying with an old New York tradition, had caused himself to be preceded by a long white box of roses, was shown into Mrs. Lidcote's sitting-room.

He came forward with his shy half-humorous smile and, taking her hand, looked at her for a moment without speaking.

"It's all right," he then pronounced.

Mrs. Lidcote returned his smile. "It's extraordinary. Everything's changed. Even Susy has changed; and you know the extent to which Susy used to represent the old New York. There's no old New York left, it seems. She talked in the most amazing way. She snaps her fingers at the Purshes. She told me —me, that every woman had a right to happiness and that self-expression was the highest duty. She accused me of misunderstanding Leila; she said my point of view was conventional! She was bursting with pride at having been in the secret, and wearing a brooch that Wilbour Barkley'd given her!"

Franklin Ide had seated himself in the armchair she had pushed forward for him under the electric chandelier. He threw back his head and laughed. "What did I tell you?"

"Yes; but I can't believe that Susy's not mistaken. Poor dear, she has the habit of lost causes; and she may feel that, having stuck to me, she can do no less than stick to Leila."

"But she didn't—did she?—openly defy the world for you? She didn't snap her fingers at the Lidcotes?"

Mrs. Lidcote shook her head, still smiling. "No. It was enough to defy my family. It was doubtful at one time if they would tolerate her seeing me, and she almost had to disinfect herself after each visit. I believe that at first my sister-in-law wouldn't let the girls come down when Susy dined with her."

"Well, isn't your cousin's present attitude the best possible proof that times have changed?"

"Yes, yes; I know." She leaned forward from her sofa-corner, fixing her eyes on his thin kindly face, which gleamed on her indistinctly through her tears. "If it's true, it's—it's dazzling. She says Leila's perfectly happy. It's

as if an angel had gone about lifting gravestones, and the buried people walked again, and the living didn't shrink from them."

"That's about it," he assented.

She drew a deep breath, and sat looking away from him down the long perspective of lamp-fringed streets over which her windows hung.

"I can understand how happy you must be," he began at length.

She turned to him impetuously. "Yes, yes; I'm happy. But I'm lonely, too—lonelier than ever. I didn't take up much room in the world before; but now—where is there a corner for me? Oh, since I've begun to confess myself, why shouldn't I go on? Telling you this lifts a gravestone from me! You see, before this, Leila needed me. She was unhappy, and I knew it, and though we hardly ever talked of it I felt that, in a way, the thought that I'd been through the same thing, and down to the dregs of it, helped her. And her needing me helped me. And when the news of her marriage came my first thought was that now she'd need me more than ever, that she'd have no one but me to turn to. Yes, under all my distress there was a fierce joy in that. It was so new and wonderful to feel again that there was one person who wouldn't be able to get on without me! And now what you and Susy tell me seems to have taken my child from me; and just at first that's all I can feel."

"Of course it's all you feel." He looked at her musingly. "Why didn't Leila come to meet you?"

"That was really my fault. You see, I'd cabled that I was not sure of being able to get off on the Utopia, and apparently my second cable was delayed, and when she received it she'd already asked some people over Sunday —one or two of her old friends, Susy says. I'm so glad they should have wanted to go to her at once; but naturally I'd rather have been alone with her."

"You still mean to go, then?"

"Oh, I must. Susy wanted to drag me off to Ridgefield with her over Sunday, and Leila sent me word that of course I might go if I wanted to, and that I was not to think of her; but I know how disappointed she would be. Susy said she was afraid I might be upset at her having people to stay, and that, if I minded, she wouldn't urge me to come. But if they don't mind, why should I? And of course, if they're willing to go to Leila it must mean——"

"Of course. I'm glad you recognize that," Franklin Ide exclaimed abruptly. He stood up and went over to her, taking her hand with one of his quick gestures. "There's something I want to say to you," he began——

The next morning, in the train, through all the other contending thoughts in Mrs. Lidcote's mind there ran the warm undercurrent of what Franklin Ide had wanted to say to her.

He had wanted, she knew, to say it once before, when, nearly eight years earlier, the hazard of meeting at the end of a rainy autumn in a deserted Swiss hotel had thrown them for a fortnight into unwonted propinquity. They had walked and talked together, borrowed each other's books and newspapers, spent the long chill evenings over the fire in the dim lamplight of her little pitch-pine sitting-room; and she had been wonderfully comforted by his presence, and hard frozen places in her had melted, and she had known that she would be desperately sorry when he went. And then, just at the end, in his odd indirect way, he had let her see that it rested with her to have him stay. She could still relive the sleepless night she had given to that discovery. It was preposterous, of course, to think of repaying his devotion by accepting such a sacrifice; but how find reasons to convince him? She could not bear to let him think her less touched, less inclined to him than she was: the generosity of his love deserved that she should repay it with the truth. Yet how let him see what she felt, and yet refuse what he offered? How confess to him what had been on her lips when he made the offer: "I've seen what it did to one man; and there must never, never be another"? The tacit ignoring of her past had been the element in which their friendship lived, and she could not suddenly, to him of all men, begin to talk of herself like a guilty woman in a play. Somehow, in the end, she had managed it, had averted a direct explanation, had made him understand that her life was over, that she existed only for her daughter, and that a more definite word from him would have been almost a breach of delicacy. She was so used to behaving as if her life were over! And, at any rate, he had taken her hint, and she had been able to spare her sensitiveness and his. The next year, when he came to Florence to see her, they met again in the old friendly way; and that till now had continued to be the tenor of their intimacy.

And now, suddenly and unexpectedly, he had brought up the question again, directly this time, and in such a form that she could not evade it: putting the renewal of his plea, after so long an interval, on the ground

that, on her own showing, her chief argument against it no longer existed.

"You tell me Leila's happy. If she's happy, she doesn't need you—need you, that is, in the same way as before. You wanted, I know, to be always in reach, always free and available if she should suddenly call you to her or take refuge with you. I understood that—I respected it. I didn't urge my case because I saw it was useless. You couldn't, I understood well enough, have felt free to take such happiness as life with me might give you while she was unhappy, and, as you imagined, with no hope of release. Even then I didn't feel as you did about it; I understood better the trend of things here. But ten years ago the change hadn't really come; and I had no way of convincing you that it was coming. Still, I always fancied that Leila might not think her case was closed, and so I chose to think that ours wasn't either. Let me go on thinking so, at any rate, till you've seen her, and confirmed with your own eyes what Susy Suffern tells you."

III

All through what Susy Suffern told and retold her during their four-hours' flight to the hills this plea of Ide's kept coming back to Mrs. Lidcote. She did not yet know what she felt as to its bearing on her own fate, but it was something on which her confused thoughts could stay themselves amid the welter of new impressions, and she was inexpressibly glad that he had said what he had, and said it at that particular moment. It helped her to hold fast to her identity in the rush of strange names and new categories that her cousin's talk poured out on her.

With the progress of the journey Miss Suffern's communications grew more and more amazing. She was like a cicerone preparing the mind of an inexperienced traveller for the marvels about to burst on it.

"You won't know Leila. She's had her pearls reset. Sargent's to paint her. Oh, and I was to tell you that she hopes you won't mind being the least bit squeezed over Sunday. The house was built by Wilbour's father, you know, and it's rather old-fashioned—only ten spare bedrooms. Of course that's small for what they mean to do, and she'll show you the new plans they've had made. Their idea is to keep the present house as a wing. She told me to explain—she's so dreadfully sorry not to be able to give you a sitting-room just at first. They're thinking of Egypt for next winter, unless, of course, Wilbour gets his appointment. Oh, didn't she write you about that? Why, he

wants Rome, you know—the second secretaryship. Or, rather, he wanted England; but
Leila insisted that if they went abroad she
must be near you. And of course what she
says is law. Oh, they quite hope they'll get it.
You see Horace's uncle is in the Cabinet,—one
of the assistant secretaries,—and I believe he
has a good deal of pull——"

"Horace's uncle? You mean Wilbour's, I
suppose," Mrs. Lidcote interjected, with a
gasp of which a fraction was given to Miss Suffern's flippant use of the language.

"Wilbour's? No, I don't. I mean Horace's.
There's no bad feeling between them, I assure
you. Since Horace's engagement was announced—you didn't know Horace was engaged? Why, he's marrying one of Bishop
Thorbury's girls: the red-haired one who wrote
the novel that every one's talking about, 'This
Flesh of Mine.' They're to be married in the
cathedral. Of course Horace *can*, because it
was Leila who—but, as I say, there's not the
least feeling, and Horace wrote himself to his
uncle about Wilbour."

Mrs. Lidcote's thoughts fled back to what
she had said to Ide the day before on the deck
of the *Utopia*. "I didn't take up much room
before, but now where is there a corner for
me?" Where indeed in this crowded, topsy-
turvey world, with its headlong changes and
helter-skelter readjustments, its new tolerances and indifferences and accommodations,
was there room for a character fashioned by
slower sterner processes and a life broken under their inexorable pressure? And then, in a
flash, she viewed the chaos from a new angle,
and order seemed to move upon the void. If
the old processes were changed, her case was
changed with them; she, too, was a part of the
general readjustment, a tiny fragment of the
new pattern worked out in bolder freer harmonies. Since her daughter had no penalty to
pay, was not she herself released by the same
stroke? The rich arrears of youth and joy were
gone; but was there not time enough left to
accumulate new stores of happiness? That, of
course, was what Franklin Ide had felt and had
meant her to feel. He had seen at once what
the change in her daughter's situation would
make in her view of her own. It was almost—
wondrously enough!—as if Leila's folly had
been the means of vindicating hers.

Everything else for the moment faded for
Mrs. Lidcote in the glow of her daughter's embrace. It was unnatural, it was almost terrifying, to find herself standing on a strange
threshold, under an unknown roof, in a big

hall full of pictures, flowers, firelight, and
hurrying servants, and in this spacious unfamiliar confusion to discover Leila, bareheaded, laughing, authoritative, with a strange
young man jovially echoing her welcome and
transmitting her orders; but once Mrs. Lidcote had her child on her breast, and her child's
"It's all right, you old darling!" in her ears,
every other feeling was lost in the deep sense of
well-being that only Leila's hug could give.

The sense was still with her, warming her
veins and pleasantly fluttering her heart, as
she went up to her room after luncheon. A
little constrained by the presence of visitors,
and not altogether sorry to defer for a few
hours the "long talk" with her daughter for
which she somehow felt herself tremulously
unready, she had withdrawn, on the plea of
fatigue, to the bright luxurious bedroom into
which Leila had again and again apologized
for having been obliged to squeeze her. The
room was bigger and finer than any in her
small apartment in Florence; but it was not
the standard of affluence implied in her daughter's tone about it that chiefly struck her, nor
yet the finish and complexity of its appointments. It was the look it shared with the rest
of the house, and with the perspective of the
gardens beneath its windows, of being part
of an "establishment"—of something solid,
avowed, founded on sacraments and precedents and principles. There was nothing about
the place, or about Leila and Wilbour, that
suggested either passion or peril: their relation
seemed as comfortable as their furniture and
as respectable as their balance at the bank.

This was, in the whole confusing experience,
the thing that confused Mrs. Lidcote most,
that gave her at once the deepest feeling of
security for Leila and the strongest sense of
apprehension for herself. Yes, there was something oppressive in the completeness and com-
pactness of Leila's well-being. Ide had been
right: her daughter did not need her. Leila
with her first embrace, had unconsciously at-
tested the fact in the same phrase as Ide himself and as the two young women with the
hats. "It's all right, you old darling!" she had
said: and her mother sat alone, trying to fit
herself into the new scheme of things which
such a certainty betokened.

Her first distinct feeling was one of irrational resentment. If such a change was to
come, why had it not come sooner? Here was
she, a woman not yet old, who had paid with
the best years of her life for the theft of the
happiness that her daughter's contemporaries
were taking as their due. There was no sense

no sequence, in it. She had had what she
wanted, but she had had to pay too much for
t. She had had to pay the last bitterest price
of learning that love has a price: that it is
worth so much and no more. She had known
he anguish of watching the man she loved dis-
over this first, and of reading the discovery in
iis eyes. It was a part of her history that she
iad not trusted herself to think of for a long
ime past: she always took a big turn about
chat haunted corner. But now, at the sight of
che young man downstairs, so openly and
iovially Leila's, she was overwhelmed at the
senseless waste of her own adventure, and
wrung with the irony of perceiving that the
success or failure of the deepest human experiences may hang on a matter of chronology.

Then gradually the thought of Ide returned
to her. "I chose to think that our case wasn't
closed," he had said. She had been deeply
touched by that. To every one else her case
had been closed so long! *Finis* was scrawled
all over her. But here was one man who had
believed and waited, and what if what he believed in and waited for were coming true? If
Leila's "all right" should really foreshadow
hers?

As yet, of course, it was impossible to tell.
She had fancied, indeed, when she entered the
drawing-room before luncheon, that a too-
sudden hush had fallen on the assembled group
of Leila's friends, on the slender vociferous
young women and the lounging golf-stockinged
young men. They had all received her politely,
with the kind of petrified politeness that may
be either a tribute to age or a protest at
laxity; but to them, of course, she must be an
old woman because she was Leila's mother,
and in a society so dominated by youth the
mere presence of maturity was a constraint.

One of the young girls, however, had presently emerged from the group, and, attaching
herself to Mrs. Lidcote, had listened to her
with a blue gaze of admiration which gave the
older woman a sudden happy consciousness of
her long-forgotten social graces. It was agreeable to find herself attracting this young Charlotte Wynn, whose mother had been among
her closest friends, and in whom something of
the soberness and softness of the earlier manners had survived. But the little colloquy,
broken up by the announcement of luncheon,
could of course result in nothing more definite
than this reminiscent emotion.

No, she could not yet tell how her own case
was to be fitted into the new order of things;
but there were more people—"older people"
Leila had put it—arriving by the afternoon

train, and that evening at dinner she would
doubtless be able to judge. She began to wonder nervously who the new-comers might be.
Probably she would be spared the embarrassment of finding old acquaintances among
them; but it was odd that her daughter had
mentioned no names.

Leila had proposed that, later in the afternoon, Wilbour should take her mother for a
drive: she said she wanted them to have a
"nice, quiet talk." But Mrs. Lidcote wished
her talk with Leila to come first, and had,
moreover, at luncheon, caught stray allusions
to an impending tennis-match in which her
son-in-law was engaged. Her fatigue had been
a sufficient pretext for declining the drive, and
she had begged Leila to think of her as peacefully resting in her room till such time as they
could snatch their quiet moment.

"Before tea, then, you duck!" Leila with a
last kiss had decided; and presently Mrs. Lidcote, through her open window, had heard the
fresh loud voices of her daughter's visitors
chiming across the gardens from the tennis-
court.

IV

Leila had come and gone, and they had had
their talk. It had not lasted as long as Mrs.
Lidcote wished, for in the middle of it Leila
had been summoned to the telephone to receive an important message from town, and
had sent word to her mother that she couldn't
come back just then, as one of the young ladies
had been called away unexpectedly and arrangements had to be made for her departure.
But the mother and daughter had had almost
an hour together, and Mrs. Lidcote was happy.
She had never seen Leila so tender, so solici-
tous. The only thing that troubled her was
the very excess of this solicitude, the exaggerated expression of her daughter's annoyance that their first moments together should
have been marred by the presence of strangers.

"Not strangers to me, darling, since they're
friends of yours," her mother had assured her.

"Yes; but I know your feeling, you queer
wild mother. I know how you've always
hated people." (*Hated people!* Had Leila forgotten why?) "And that's why I told Susy
that if you preferred to go with her to Ridgefield on Sunday I should perfectly understand,
and patiently wait for our good hug. But you
didn't really mind them at luncheon, did you,
dearest?"

Mrs. Lidcote, at that, had suddenly thrown
a startled look at her daughter. "I don't
mind things of that kind any longer," she had
simply answered.

"But that doesn't console me for having exposed you to the bother of it, for having let you come here when I ought to have *ordered* you off to Ridgefield with Susy. If Susy hadn't been stupid she'd have made you go there with her. I hate to think of you up here all alone."

Again Mrs. Lidcote tried to read something more than a rather obtuse devotion in her daughter's radiant gaze. "I'm glad to have had a rest this afternoon, dear; and later—"

"Oh, yes, later, when all this fuss is over, we'll more than make up for it, sha'n't we, you precious darling?" And at this point Leila had been summoned to the telephone, leaving Mrs. Lidcote to her conjectures.

These were still floating before her in cloudy uncertainty when Miss Suffern tapped at the door.

"You've come to take me down to tea? I'd forgotten how late it was," Mrs. Lidcote exclaimed.

Miss Suffern, a plump peering little woman, with prim hair and a conciliatory smile, nervously adjusted the pendent bugles of her elaborate black dress. Miss Suffern was always in mourning, and always commemorating the demise of distant relatives by wearing the discarded wardrobe of their next of kin. "It isn't *exactly* mourning," she would say; "but it's the only stitch of black poor Julia had—and of course George was only my mother's step-cousin."

As she came forward Mrs. Lidcote found herself humorously wondering whether she were mourning Horace Pursh's divorce in one of his mother's old black satins.

"Oh, *did* you mean to go down for tea?" Susy Suffern peered at her, a little fluttered. "Leila sent me up to keep you company. She thought it would be cozier for you to stay here. She was afraid you were feeling rather tired."

"I was; but I've had the whole afternoon to rest in. And this wonderful sofa to help me."

"Leila told me to tell you that she'd rush up for a minute before dinner, after everybody had arrived; but the train is always dreadfully late. She's in despair at not giving you a sitting-room; she wanted to know if I thought you really minded."

"Of course I don't mind. It's not like Leila to think I should." Mrs. Lidcote drew aside to make way for the housemaid, who appeared in the doorway bearing a table spread with a bewildering variety of tea-cakes.

"Leila saw to it herself," Miss Suffern murmured as the door closed. "Her one idea is that you should feel happy here."

It struck Mrs. Lidcote as one more mark of the subverted state of things that her daughter's solicitude should find expression in the multiplicity of sandwiches and the piping-hot ness of muffins; but then everything that had happened since her arrival seemed to increase her confusion.

The note of a motor-horn down the drive gave another turn to her thoughts. "Are those the new arrivals already?" she asked.

"Oh, dear, no; they won't be here till after seven." Miss Suffern craned her head from the window to catch a glimpse of the motor. "It must be Charlotte leaving."

"Was it the little Wynn girl who was called away in a hurry? I hope it's not on account of illness."

"Oh, no; I believe there was some mistake about dates. Her mother telephoned her that she was expected at the Stepleys, at Fishkill, and she had to be rushed over to Albany to catch a train."

Mrs. Lidcote meditated. "I'm sorry. She's a charming young thing. I hoped I should have another talk with her this evening after dinner."

"Yes; it's too bad." Miss Suffern's gaze grew vague. "You *do* look tired, you know," she continued, seating herself at the tea-table and preparing to dispense its delicacies. "You must go straight back to your sofa and let me wait on you. The excitement has told on you more than you think, and you mustn't fight against it any longer. Just stay quietly up here and let yourself go. You'll have Leila to yourself on Monday."

Mrs. Lidcote received the tea-cup which her cousin proffered, but showed no other disposition to obey her injunctions. For a moment she stirred her tea in silence; then she asked: "Is it your idea that I should stay quietly up here till Monday?"

Miss Suffern set down her cup with a gesture so sudden that it endangered an adjacent plate of scones. When she had assured herself of the safety of the scones she looked up with a fluttered laugh. "Perhaps, dear, by to-morrow you'll be feeling differently. The air here, you know—"

"Yes, I know." Mrs. Lidcote bent forward to help herself to a scone. "Who's arriving this evening?" she asked.

Miss Suffern frowned and peered. "You know my wretched head for names. Leila told me—but there are so many—"

"So many? She didn't tell me she expected a big party."

"Oh, not big: but rather outside of her little group. And of course, as it's the first time, she's a little excited at having the older set."

"The older set? Our contemporaries, you mean?"

"Why—yes." Miss Suffern paused as if to gather herself up for a leap. "The Ashton Gileses," she brought out.

"The Ashton Gileses? Really? I shall be glad to see Mary Giles again. It must be eighteen years," said Mrs. Lidcote steadily.

"Yes," Miss Suffern gasped, precipitately refilling her cup.

"The Ashton Gileses; and who else?"

"Well, the Sam Fresbies. But the most important person, of course, is Mrs. Lorin Boulger."

"Mrs. Boulger? Leila didn't tell me she was coming."

"Didn't she? I suppose she forgot everything when she saw you. But the party was got up for Mrs. Boulger. You see, it's very important that she should—well, take a fancy to Leila and Wilbour; his being appointed to Rome virtually depends on it. And you know Leila insists on Rome in order to be near you. So she asked Mary Giles, who's intimate with the Boulgers, if the visit couldn't possibly be arranged; and Mary's cable caught Mrs. Boulger at Cherbourg. She's to be only a fortnight in America; and getting her to come directly here was rather a triumph."

"Yes; I see it was," said Mrs. Lidcote.

"You know, she's rather—rather fussy; and Mary was a little doubtful if—"

"If she would, on account of Leila?" Mrs. Lidcote murmured.

"Well, yes. In her official position. But luckily she's a friend of the Barkleys. And finding the Gileses and Fresbies here will make it all right. The times have changed!" Susy Suffern indulgently summed up.

Mrs. Lidcote smiled. "Yes; a few years ago it would have seemed improbable that I should ever again be dining with Mary Giles and Harriet Fresbie and Mrs. Lorin Boulger."

Miss Suffern did not at the moment seem disposed to enlarge upon this theme; and after an interval of silence Mrs. Lidcote suddenly resumed: "Do they know I'm here, by the way?"

The effect of her question was to produce in Miss Suffern an exaggerated access of peering and frowning. She twitched the tea-things about, fingered her bugles, and, looking at the clock, exclaimed amazedly: "Mercy! Is it seven already?"

"Not that it can make any difference, I suppose," Mrs. Lidcote continued. "But did Leila tell them I was coming?"

Miss Suffern looked at her with pain. "Why, you don't suppose, dearest, that Leila would do anything—"

Mrs. Lidcote went on: "For, of course, it's of the first importance, as you say, that Mrs. Lorin Boulger should be favorably impressed, in order that Wilbour may have the best possible chance of getting Rome."

"I *told* Leila you'd feel that, dear. You see, it's actually on *your* account—so that they may get a post near you—that Leila invited Mrs. Boulger."

"Yes, I see that." Mrs. Lidcote, abruptly rising from her seat, turned her eyes to the clock. "But, as you say, it's getting late. Oughtn't we to dress for dinner?"

Miss Suffern, at the suggestion, stood up also, an agitated hand among her bugles. "I do wish I could persuade you to stay up here this evening. I'm sure Leila'd be happier if you would. Really, you're much too tired to come down."

"What nonsense, Susy!" Mrs. Lidcote spoke with a sudden sharpness, her hand stretched to the bell. "When do we dine? At half-past eight? Then I must really send you packing. At my age it takes time to dress."

Miss Suffern, thus projected toward the threshold, lingered there to repeat: "Leila'll never forgive herself if you make an effort you're not up to." But Mrs. Lidcote smiled on her without answering, and the icy light-wave propelled her through the door.

V

Mrs. Lidcote, though she had made the gesture of ringing for her maid, had not done so.

When the door closed, she continued to stand motionless in the middle of her soft spacious room. The fire which had been kindled at twilight danced on the brightness of silver and mirrors and sober gilding; and the sofa toward which she had been urged by Miss Suffern heaped up its cushions in inviting proximity to a table laden with new books and papers. She could not recall having ever been more luxuriously housed, or having ever had so strange a sense of being out alone, under the night, in a wind-beaten plain. She sat down by the fire and thought.

A knock on the door made her lift her head, and she saw her daughter on the threshold. The intricate ordering of Leila's fair hair and the flying folds of her dressing-gown showed that she had interrupted her dressing to hasten to her mother; but once in the room she paused a moment, smiling uncertainly, as though she had forgotten the object of her haste.

Mrs. Lidcote rose to her feet. "Time to dress, dearest? Don't scold! I sha'n't be late."

"To dress?" Leila stood before her with a puzzled look. "Why, I thought, dear—I mean, I hoped you'd decided just to stay here quietly and rest."

Her mother smiled. "But I've been resting all the afternoon!"

"Yes, but—you know you *do* look tired. And when Susy told me just now that you meant to make the effort—"

"You came to stop me?"

"I came to tell you that you needn't feel in the least obliged—"

"Of course. I understand that."

There was a pause during which Leila, vaguely averting herself from her mother's scrutiny, drifted toward the dressing-table and began to disturb the symmetry of the brushes and bottles laid out on it.

"Do your visitors know that I'm here?" Mrs. Lidcote suddenly went on.

"Do they— Of course—why, naturally," Laila rejoined, absorbed in trying to turn the stopper of a salts-bottle.

"Then won't they think it odd if I don't appear?"

"Oh, not in the least, dearest. I assure you they'll *all* understand." Leila laid down the bottle and turned back to her mother, her face alight with reassurance.

Mrs. Lidcote stood motionless, her head erect, her smiling eyes on her daughter's. "Will they think it odd if I *do?*"

Leila stopped short, her lips half parted to reply. As she paused, the color stole over her bare neck, swept up to her throat, and burst into flame in her cheeks. Thence it sent its devastating crimson up to her very temples, to the lobes of her ears, to the edges of her eyelids, beating all over her in fiery waves, as if fanned by some imperceptible wind.

Mrs. Lidcote silently watched the conflagration; then she turned away her eyes with a slight laugh. "I only meant that I was afraid it might upset the arrangement of your dinner-table if I didn't come down. If you can assure me that it won't, I believe I'll take you at your word and go back to this irresistible sofa." She paused, as if waiting for her daughter to speak; then she held out her arms. "Run off and dress, dearest; and don't have me on your mind." She clasped Leila close, pressing a long kiss on the last afterglow of her subsiding blush. "I do feel the least bit overdone, and if it won't inconvenience you to have me drop out of things, I believe I'll basely take to my bed and stay there till your party scatters. And now run off, or you'll be late; and make my excuses to them all."

VI

The Barkleys' visitors had dispersed, and Mrs. Lidcote, completely restored by her two days' rest, found herself, on the following Monday alone with her children and Miss Suffern.

There was a note of jubilation in the air, for the party had "gone off" so extraordinarily well, and so completely, as it appeared, to the satisfaction of Mrs. Lorin Boulger, that Wilbour's early appointment to Rome was almost to be counted on. So certain did this seem that the prospect of a prompt reunion mitigated the distress with which Leila learned of her mother's decision to return almost immediately to Italy. No one understood this decision it seemed to Leila absolutely unintelligible that Mrs. Lidcote should not stay on with them till their own fate was fixed, and Wilbour echoed her astonishment.

"Why shouldn't you, as Leila says, wait here till we can all pack up and go together?"

Mrs. Lidcote smiled her gratitude with her refusal. "After all, it's not yet sure that you'll be packing up."

"Oh, you ought to have seen Wilbour with Mrs. Boulger," Leila triumphed.

"No, you ought to have seen Leila with her," Leila's husband exulted.

Miss Suffern enthusiastically appended: "I *do* think inviting Harriet Fresbie was a stroke of genius!"

"Oh, we'll be with you soon," Leila laughed "So soon that it's really foolish to separate."

But Mrs. Lidcote held out with the quiet firmness which her daughter knew it was useless to oppose. After her long months in India it was really imperative, she declared, that she should get back to Florence and see what was happening to her little place there; and she had been so comfortable on the *Utopia* that she had a fancy to return by the same ship. There was nothing for it, therefore, but to acquiesce in her decision and keep her with them till the afternoon before the day of the *Utopia's* sailing. This arrangement fitted in with certain projects which, during her two days' seclusion Mrs. Lidcote had silently matured. It had become to her of the first importance to get away as soon as she could, and the little place in Florence, which held her past in every fold of ts curtains and between every page of its books, seemed now to her the one spot where that past would be endurable to look upon.

She was not unhappy during the intervening days. The sight of Leila's well-being, the sense of Leila's tenderness, were, after all, what she had come for; and of these she had had full measure. Leila had never been happier or more tender; and the contemplation of her bliss, and the enjoyment of her affection, were an absorbing occupation for her mother. But they were also a sharp strain on certain overtightened chords, and Mrs. Lidcote, when at last she found herself alone in the New York hotel to which she had returned the night before embarking, had the feeling that she had just escaped with her life from the clutch of a giant hand.

She had refused to let her daughter come to town with her; she had even rejected Susy Suffern's company. She wanted no viaticum but that of her own thoughts; and she let these come to her without shrinking from them as she sat in the same high-hung sitting-room in which, just a week before, she and Franklin Ide had had their memorable talk.

She had promised her friend to let him hear from her, but she had not kept her promise. She knew that he had probably come back from Chicago, and that if he learned of her sudden decision to return to Italy it would be impossible for her not to see him before sailing; and as she wished above all things not to see him she had kept silent, intending to send him a letter from the steamer.

There was no reason why she should wait till then to write it. The actual moment was more favorable, and the task, though not agreeable, would at least bridge over an hour of her lonely evening. She went up to the writing-table, drew out a sheet of paper and began to write his name. And as she did so, the door opened and he came in.

The words she met him with were the last she could have imagined herself saying when they had parted. "How in the world did you know that I was here?"

He caught her meaning in a flash. "You didn't want me to, then?" He stood looking at her. "I suppose I ought to have taken your silence as meaning that. But I happened to meet Mrs. Wynn, who is stopping here, and she asked me to dine with her and Charlotte, and Charlotte's young man. They told me they'd seen you arriving this afternoon, and I couldn't help coming up."

There was a pause between them, which Mrs. Lidcote at last surprisingly broke with the exclamation: "Ah, she *did* recognize me, then!"

"Recognize you?" He stared. "Why—"

"Oh, I saw she did, though she never moved an eyelid. I saw it by Charlotte's blush. The child has the prettiest blush. I saw that her mother wouldn't let her speak to me."

Ide put down his hat with an impatient laugh. "Hasn't Leila cured you of your delusions?"

She looked at him intently. "Then you don't think Margaret Wynn meant to cut me?"

"I think your ideas are absurd."

She paused for a perceptible moment without taking this up; then she said, at a tangent: "I'm sailing to-morrow early. I meant to write to you—there's the letter I'd begun."

Ide followed her gesture, and then turned his eyes back to her face. "You didn't mean to see me, then, or even to let me know that you were going till you'd left?"

"I felt it would be easier to explain to you in a letter—"

"What in God's name is there to explain?" She made no reply, and he pressed on: "It can't be that you're worried about Leila, for Charlotte Wynn told me she'd been there last week, and there was a big party arriving when she left: Fresbies and Gileses, and Mrs. Lorin Boulger—all the board of examiners! If Leila has passed *that*, she's got her degree."

Mrs. Lidcote had dropped down into a corner of the sofa where she had sat during their talk of the week before. "I was stupid," she began abruptly. "I ought to have gone to Ridgefield with Susy. I didn't see till afterward that I was expected to."

"You were expected to?"

"Yes. Oh, it wasn't Leila's fault. She suffered—poor darling; she was distracted. But she'd asked her party before she knew I was arriving."

"Oh, as to that—" Ide drew a deep breath of relief. "I can understand that it must have been a disappointment not to have you to herself just at first. But, after all, you were among old friends or their children: the Gileses and Fresbies—and little Charlotte Wynn." He paused a moment before the last name, and scrutinized her hesitatingly. "Even if they came at the wrong time, you must have been glad to see them all at Leila's."

She gave him back his look with a faint smile. "I didn't see them."

"You didn't see them?"

"No. That is, excepting little Charlotte Wynn. That child is exquisite. We had a talk before luncheon the day I arrived. But when her mother found out that I was staying in the house she telephoned her to leave immediately, and so I didn't see her again."

The colour rushed to Ide's sallow face. "I don't know where you get such ideas!"

She pursued, as if she had not heard him: "Oh, and I saw Mary Giles for a minute too. Susy Suffern brought her up to my room the last evening, after dinner, when all the others were at bridge. She meant it kindly—but it wasn't much use."

"But what were you doing in your room in the evening after dinner?"

"Why, you see, when I found out my mistake in coming,—how embarrassing it was for Leila, I mean—I simply told her I was very tired, and preferred to stay upstairs till the party was over."

Ide, with a groan, struck his hand against the arm of his chair. "I wonder how much of all this you simply imagined!"

"I didn't imagine the fact of Harriet Fresbie's not even asking if she might see me when she knew I was in the house. Nor of Mary Giles's getting Susy, at the eleventh hour, to smuggle her up to my room when the others wouldn't know where she'd gone; nor poor Leila's ghastly fear lest Mrs. Lorin Boulger, for whom the party was given, should guess I was in the house, and prevent her husband's giving Wilbour the second secretaryship because she'd be obliged to spend a night under the same roof with his mother-in-law!"

Ide continued to drum on his chair-arm with exasperated fingers. "You don't *know* that any of the acts you describe are due to the causes you suppose."

Mrs. Lidcote paused before replying, as if honestly trying to measure the weight of this argument. Then she said in a low tone: "I know that Leila was in an agony lest I should come down to dinner the first night. And it was for me she was afraid, not for herself. Leila is never afraid for herself."

"But the conclusions you draw are simply preposterous. There are narrow-minded women everywhere, but the women who were at Leila's knew perfectly well that their going there would give her a sort of social sanction, and if they were willing that she should have it, why on earth should they want to withhold it from you?"

"That's what I told myself a week ago, in this very room, after my first talk with Susy Suffern." She lifted a misty smile to his anxious eyes. "That's why I listened to what you said to me the same evening, and why your arguments half convinced me, and made me

think that what had been possible for Leila might not be impossible for me. If the new dispensation had come, why not for me as well as for the others? I can't tell you the flight my imagination took!"

Franklin Ide rose from his seat and crossed the room to a chair near her sofa-corner. "All I cared about was that it seemed—for the moment—to be carrying you toward me," he said.

"I cared about that, too. That's why I meant to go away without seeing you." They gave each other grave look for look. "Because, you see, I was mistaken," she went on. "We were both mistaken. You say it's preposterous that the women who didn't object to accepting Leila's hospitality should have objected to meeting me under her roof. And so it is; but I begin to understand why. It's simply that society is much too busy to revise its own judgments. Probably no one in the house with me stopped to consider that my case and Leila's were identical. They only remembered that I'd done something which, at the time I did it, was condemned by society. My case has been passed on and classified: I'm the woman who has been cut for nearly twenty years. The older people have half forgotten why, and the younger ones have never really known: it's simply become a tradition to cut me. And traditions that have lost their meaning are the hardest of all to destroy."

Ide sat motionless while she spoke. As she ended, he stood up with a short laugh and walked across the room to the window. Outside, the immense black prospect of New York, strung with its myriad lines of light, stretched away into the smoky edges of the night. He showed it to her with a gesture.

"What do you suppose such words as you've been using—'society,' 'tradition,' and the rest —mean to all the life out there?"

She came and stood by him in the window. "Less than nothing, of course. But you and I are not out there. We're shut up in a little tight round of habit and association, just as we're shut up in this room. Remember, I thought I'd got out of it once; but what really happened was that the other people went out, and left me in the same little room. The only difference was that I was there alone. Oh, I've made it habitable now, I'm used to it; but I've lost any illusions I may have had as to an angel's opening the door."

Ide again laughed impatiently. "Well, if the door won't open, why not let another prisoner in? At least it would be less of a solitude—"

She turned from the dark window back into the vividly lighted room.

"It would be more of a prison. You forget that I know all about that. We're all imprisoned, of course—all of us middling people, who don't carry our freedom in our brains. But we've accommodated ourselves to our different cells, and if we're moved suddenly into new ones we're likely to find a stone wall where we thought there was thin air, and to knock ourselves senseless against it. I saw a man do that once."

Ide, leaning with folded arms against the window-frame, watched her in silence as she moved restlessly about the room, gathering together some scattered books and tossing a handful of torn letters into the paper-basket. When she ceased, he rejoined: "All you say is based on preconceived theories. Why didn't you put them to the test by coming down to meet your old friends? Don't you see the inference they would naturally draw from your hiding yourself when they arrived? It looked as though you were afraid of them—or as though you hadn't forgiven them. Either way, you put them in the wrong instead of waiting to let them put you in the right. If Leila had buried herself in a desert do you suppose society would have gone to fetch her out? You say you were afraid for Leila and that she was afraid for you. Don't you see what all these complications of feeling mean? Simply that you were too nervous at the moment to let things happen naturally, just as you're too nervous now to judge them rationally." He paused and turned his eyes to her face. "Don't try to just yet. Give yourself a little more time. Give me a little more time. I've always known it would take time."

He moved nearer, and she let him have her hand. With a grave kindness of his face so close above her she felt like a child roused out of frightened dreams and finding a light in the room.

"Perhaps you're right—" she heard herself begin; then something within her clutched her back, and her hand fell away from him.

"I know I'm right: trust me," he urged. "We'll talk of this in Florence soon."

She stood before him, feeling with despair his kindness, his patience and his unreality. Everything he said seemed like a painted gauze let down between herself and the real facts of life; and a sudden desire seized her to tear the gauze into shreds.

She drew back and looked at him with a smile of superficial reassurance. "You are right—about not talking any longer now. I'm nervous and tired, and it would do no good. I brood over things too much. As you say, I must try not to shrink from people." She turned away and glanced at the clock. "Why, it's only ten! If I send you off I shall begin to brood again; and if you stay we shall go on talking about the same thing. Why shouldn't we go down and see Margaret Wynn for half an hour?"

She spoke lightly and rapidly, her brilliant eyes on his face. As she watched him, she saw it change, as if her smile had thrown a too vivid light upon it.

"Oh, no—not to-night!" he exclaimed.

"Not to-night? Why, what other night have I, when I'm off at dawn? Besides, I want to show you at once that I mean to be more sensible—that I'm not going to be afraid of people any more. And I should really like another glimpse at little Charlotte." He stood before her, his hand in his beard, with the gesture he had in moments of perplexity. "Come!" she ordered him gaily, turning to the door.

He followed her and laid his hand on her arm. "Don't you think—hadn't you better let me go first and see? They told me they'd had a tiring day at the dressmaker's. I daresay they have gone to bed."

"But you said they'd a young man of Charlotte's dining with them. Surely he wouldn't have left by ten? At any rate, I'll go down with you and see. It takes so long if one sends a servant first." She put him gently aside, and then paused as a new thought struck her. "Or wait; my maid's in the next room. I'll tell her to go and ask if Margaret will receive me. Yes, that's much the best way."

She turned back and went toward the door that led to her bedroom; but before she could open it she felt Ide's quick touch again.

"I believe—I remember now—Charlotte's young man was suggesting that they should all go out—to a music-hall or something of the sort. I'm sure—I'm positively sure that you won't find them."

Her hand dropped from the door, his dropped from her arm, and as they drew back and faced each other she saw the blood rise slowly through his sallow skin, redden his neck and ears, encroach upon the edges of his beard, and settle in dull patches under his kind troubled eyes. She had seen the same blush on another face, and the same impulse of compassion she had then felt made her turn her gaze away again.

A knock on the door broke the silence, and a porter put his head into the room.

"It's only just to know how many pieces there'll be to go down to the steamer in the morning."

With the words she felt that the veil of

painted gauze was torn in tatters, and that she was moving again among the grim edges of reality.

"Oh, dear," she exclaimed, "I never *can* re-member! Wait a minute; I shall have to ask my maid."

She opened her bedroom door and called out: "Annette!"

WILLIAM SIDNEY PORTER (O. HENRY) (1862-1910)

THE GIFT OF THE MAGI

(1905)

One dollar and eighty-seven cents. That was all. And sixty cents of it was in pennies. Pennies saved one and two at a time by bull-dozing the grocer and the vegetable man and the butcher until one's cheeks burned with the silent imputation of parsimony that such close dealing implied. Three times Della counted it. One dollar and eighty-seven cents. And the next day would be Christmas.

There was clearly nothing to do but flop down on the shabby little couch and howl. So Della did it. Which instigates the moral reflection that life is made up of sobs, sniffles, and smiles, with sniffles predominating.

While the mistress of the home is gradually subsiding from the first stage to the second, take a look at the home. A furnished flat at $8 per week. It did not exactly beggar description, but it certainly had that word on the lookout for the mendicancy squad.

In the vestibule below was a letter-box into which no letter would go, and an electric button from which no mortal finger could coax a ring. Also appertaining thereunto was a card bearing the name "Mr. James Dillingham Young."

The "Dillingham" had been flung to the breeze during a former period of prosperity when its possessor was being paid $30 per week. Now, when the income was shrunk to $20, the letters of "Dillingham" looked blurred, as though they were thinking seriously of contracting to a modest and unassuming D. But whenever Mr. James Dillingham Young came home and reached his flat above he was called "Jim" and greatly hugged by Mrs. James Dillingham Young, already introduced to you as Della. Which is all very good.

Della finished her cry and attended to her cheeks with the powder rag. She stood by the window and looked out dully at a gray cat walking a gray fence in a gray backyard. To-morrow would be Christmas Day, and she had only $1.87 with which to buy Jim a present. She had been saving every penny she could for

months, with this result. Twenty dollars a week doesn't go far. Expenses had been greater than she had calculated. They always are. Only $1.87 to buy a present for Jim. Her Jim. Many a happy hour she had spent planning for something nice for him. Something fine and rare and sterling—something just a little bit near to being worthy of the honor of being owned by Jim.

There was a pier-glass between the windows of the room. Perhaps you have seen a pier-glass in an $8 flat. A very thin and very agile person may, by observing his reflection in a rapid sequence of longitudinal strips, obtain a fairly accurate conception of his looks. Della, being slender, had mastered the art.

Suddenly she whirled from the window and stood before the glass. Her eyes were shining brilliantly, but her face had lost its color within twenty seconds. Rapidly she pulled down her hair and let it fall to its full length.

Now, there were two possessions of the James Dillingham Youngs in which they both took a mighty pride. One was Jim's gold watch that had been his father's and his grandfather's. The other was Della's hair. Had the Queen of Sheba lived in the flat across the airshaft, Della would have let her hair hang out the window some day to dry, just to depreciate Her Majesty's jewels and gifts. Had King Solomon been the janitor, with all his treasures piled up in the basement, Jim would have pulled out his watch every time he passed, just to see him pluck at his beard from envy.

So now Della's beautiful hair fell about her, rippling and shining like a cascade of brown waters. It reached below her knee and made itself almost a garment for her. And then she did it up again nervously and quickly. Once she faltered for a minute and stood still while a tear or two splashed on the worn red carpet.

On went her old brown jacket; on went her old brown hat. With a whirl of skirts and with the brilliant sparkle still in her eyes, she fluttered out the door and down the stairs to the street.

Where she stopped the sign read: "Mme. Sofronie. Hair Goods of all Kinds." One flight up Della ran, and collected herself, panting. Madame, large, too white, chilly, hardly looked the "Sofronie."

"Will you buy my hair?" asked Della.

"I buy hair," said Madame. "Take yer hat off and let's have a sight at the looks of it."

Down rippled the brown cascade.

"Twenty dollars," said Madame, lifting the mass with a practised hand.

"Give it to me quick," said Della.

Oh, and the next two hours tripped by on rosy wings. Forget the hashed metaphor. She was ransacking the stores for Jim's present.

She found it at last. It surely had been made for Jim and no one else. There was no other like it in any of the stores, and she had turned all of them inside out. It was a platinum fob chain simple and chaste in design, properly proclaiming its value by substance alone and not by meretricious ornamentation —as all good things should do. It was even worthy of The Watch. As soon as she saw it she knew that it must be Jim's. It was like him. Quietness and value—the description applied to both. Twenty-one dollars they took from her for it, and she hurried home with the 87 cents. With that chain on his watch Jim might be properly anxious about the time in any company. Grand as the watch was, he sometimes looked at it on the sly on account of the old leather strap that he used in place of a chain.

When Della reached home her intoxication gave way a little to prudence and reason. She got out her curling irons and lighted the gas and went to work repairing the ravages made by generosity added to love. Which is always a tremendous task, dear friends—a mammoth task.

Within forty minutes her head was covered with tiny, close-lying curls that made her look wonderfully like a truant schoolboy. She looked at her reflection in the mirror long, carefully, and critically.

"If Jim doesn't kill me," she said to herself, "before he takes a second look at me, he'll say I look like a Coney Island chorus girl. But what could I do—oh! what could I do with a dollar and eighty-seven cents?"

At 7 o'clock the coffee was made and the frying-pan was on the back of the stove hot and ready to cook the chops.

Jim was never late. Della doubled the fob chain in her hand and sat on the corner of the table near the door that he always entered. Then she heard his step on the stair away down

on the first flight, and she turned white for just a moment. She had a habit of saying little silent prayers about the simplest everyday things, and now she whispered: "Please God, make him think I am still pretty."

The door opened and Jim stepped in and closed it. He looked thin and very serious. Poor fellow, he was only twenty-two—and to be burdened with a family! He needed a new overcoat and he was without gloves.

Jim stopped inside the door, as immovable as a setter at the scent of quail. His eyes were fixed upon Della, and there was an expression in them that she could not read, and it terrified her. It was not anger, nor surprise, nor disapproval, nor horror, nor any of the sentiments that she had been prepared for. He simply stared at her fixedly with that peculiar expression on his face.

Della wriggled off the table and went for him.

"Jim, darling," she cried, "don't look at me that way. I had my hair cut off and sold it because I couldn't have lived through Christmas without giving you a present. It'll grow out again—you won't mind, will you? I just had to do it. My hair grows awfully fast. Say 'Merry Christmas!' Jim, and let's be happy. You don't know what a nice—what a beautiful, nice gift I've got for you."

"You've cut off your hair?" asked Jim, laboriously, as if he had not arrived at that patent fact yet even after the hardest mental labor.

"Cut it off and sold it," said Della. "Don't you like me just as well, anyhow? I'm me without my hair, ain't I?"

Jim looked about the room curiously.

"You say your hair is gone?" he said, with an air almost of idiocy.

"You needn't look for it," said Della. "It's sold, I tell you—sold and gone, too. It's Christmas Eve, boy. Be good to me, for it went for you. Maybe the hairs of my head were numbered," she went on with a sudden serious sweetness, "but nobody could ever count my love for you. Shall I put the chops on, Jim?"

Out of his trance Jim seemed quickly to wake. He enfolded his Della. For ten seconds let us regard with discreet scrutiny some inconsequential object in the other direction. Eight dollars a week or a million a year—what is the difference? A mathematician or a wit would give you the wrong answer. The magi brought valuable gifts, but that was not among them. This dark assertion will be illuminated later on.

Jim drew a package from his overcoat pocket and threw it upon the table.

"Don't make any mistake, Dell," he said, "about me. I don't think there's anything in the way of a haircut or a shave or a shampoo that could make me like my girl any less. But if you'll unwrap that package you may see why you had me going a while at first."

White fingers and nimble tore at the string and paper. And then an ecstatic scream of joy; and then, alas! a quick feminine change to hysterical tears and wails, necessitating the immediate employment of all the comforting powers of the lord of the flat.

For there lay The Combs—the set of combs, side and back, that Della had worshipped for long in a Broadway window. Beautiful combs, pure tortoise shell, with jewelled rims—just the shade to wear in the beautiful vanished hair. They were expensive combs, she knew, and her heart had simply craved and yearned over them without the least hope of possession. And now, they were hers, but the tresses that should have adorned the coveted adornments were gone.

But she hugged them to her bosom, and at length she was able to look up with dim eyes and a smile and say: "My hair grows so fast, Jim!"

And then Della leaped up like a little singed cat and cried, "Oh, oh!"

Jim had not yet seen his beautiful present. She held it out to him eagerly upon her open palm. The dull precious metal seemed to flash with a reflection of her bright and ardent spirit.

"Isn't it a dandy, Jim? I hunted all over town to find it. You'll have to look at the time a hundred times a day now. Give me your watch. I want to see how it looks on it."

Instead of obeying, Jim tumbled down on the couch and put his hands under the back of his head and smiled.

"Dell," said he, "let's put our Christmas presents away and keep 'em a while. They're too nice to use just at present. I sold the watch to get the money to buy your combs. And now suppose you put the chops on."

The magi, as you know, were wise men—wonderfully wise men—who brought gifts to the Babe in the manger. They invented the art of giving Christmas presents. Being wise, their gifts were no doubt wise ones, possibly bearing the privilege of exchange in case of duplication. And here I have lamely related to you the uneventful chronicle of two foolish children in a flat who most unwisely sacrificed for each other the greatest treasures of their house. But in a last word to the wise of these days let it be said that of all who give gifts these two were the wisest. Of all who give and receive gifts, such as they are wisest. Everywhere they are wisest. They are the magi.

WILLA SIBERT CATHER (1876-   )
THE SCULPTOR'S FUNERAL
(1905)

A group of the townspeople stood on the station siding of a little Kansas town, awaiting the coming of the night train, which was already twenty minutes overdue. The snow had fallen thick over everything; in the pale starlight the line of bluffs across the wide, white meadows south of the town made soft, smoke-coloured curves against the clear sky. The men on the siding stood first on one foot and then on the other, their hands thrust deep into their trousers pockets, their overcoats open, their shoulders screwed up with the cold; and they glanced from time to time toward the southeast, where the railroad track wound along the river shore. They conversed in low tones and moved about restlessly, seeming uncertain as to what was expected of them. There was but one of the company who looked as if he knew exactly why he was there, and he kept conspicuously apart; walking to the far end of the platform, returning to the station door, then pacing up the track again, his chin sunk in the high collar of his overcoat, his burly shoulders drooping forward, his gait heavy and dogged. Presently he was approached by a tall, spare, grizzled man clad in a faded Grand Army suit, who shuffled out from the group and advanced with a certain deference, craning his neck forward until his back made the angle of a jack-knife three-quarters open.

"I reckon she's a-goin' to be pretty late agin to-night, Jim," he remarked in a squeaky falsetto. "S'pose it's the snow?"

"I don't know," responded the other man with a shade of annoyance, speaking from out an astonishing cataract of red beard that grew fiercely and thickly in all directions.

The spare man shifted the quill toothpick he was chewing to the other side of his mouth.

"It ain't likely that anybody from the East will come with the corpse, I s'pose," he went on reflectively.

"I don't know," responded the other, more curtly than before.

"It's too bad he didn't belong to some lodge or other. I like an order funeral myself. They seem more appropriate for people of some reputation," the spare man continued, with an ingratiating concession in his shrill voice, as he carefully placed his toothpick in his vest pocket. He always carried the flag at the G. A. R. funerals in the town.

The heavy man turned on his heel, without replying, and walked up the siding. The spare man rejoined the uneasy group. "Jim's ez full ez a tick, ez ushel," he commented commiseratingly.

Just then a distant whistle sounded, and there was a shuffling of feet on the platform. A number of lanky boys, of all ages, appeared as suddenly and slimily as eels wakened by the crack of thunder; some came from the waiting-room, where they had been warming themselves by the red stove, or half asleep on the slat benches; others uncoiled themselves from baggage trucks or slid out of express wagons. Two clambered down from the driver's seat of a hearse that stood backed up against the siding. They straightened their stooping shoulders and lifted their heads, and a flash of momentary animation kindled their dull eyes at that cold, vibrant scream, the world-wide call for men. It stirred them like the note of a trumpet; just as it had often stirred the man who was coming home tonight, in his boyhood.

The night express shot, red as a rocket, from out the eastward marsh lands and wound along the river shore under the long lines of shivering poplars that sentinelled the meadows, the escaping steam hanging in grey masses against the pale sky and blotting out the Milky Way. In a moment the red glare from the headlight streamed up the snow-covered track before the siding and glittered on the wet, black rails. The burly man with the dishevelled red beard walked swiftly up the platform toward the approaching train, uncovering his head as he went. The group of men behind him hesitated, glanced questioningly at one another, and awkwardly followed his example. The train stopped, and the crowd shuffled up to the express car just as the door was thrown open, the man in the G. A. R. suit thrusting his head forward with curiosity. The express messenger appeared in the doorway, accompanied by a young man in a long ulster and travelling cap.

"Are Mr. Merrick's friends here?" inquired the young man.

The group on the platform swayed uneasily. Philip Phelps, the banker, responded with dignity: "We have come to take charge of the body. Mr. Merrick's father is very feeble and can't be about."

"Send the agent out here," growled the express messenger, "and tell the operator to lend a hand."

The coffin was got out of its rough-box and down on the snowy platform. The townspeople drew back enough to make room for it and then formed a close semicircle about it, looking curiously at the palm leaf which lay across the black cover. No one said anything. The baggage man stood by his truck, waiting to get at the trunks. The engine panted heavily, and the fireman dodged in and out among the wheels with his yellow torch and long oil-can, snapping the spindle boxes. The young Bostonian, one of the dead sculptor's pupils who had come with the body, looked about him helplessly. He turned to the banker, the only one of that black, uneasy, stoop-shouldered group who seemed enough of an individual to be addressed.

"None of Mr. Merrick's brothers are here?" he asked uncertainly.

The man with the red beard for the first time stepped up and joined the others. "No, they have not come yet; the family is scattered. The body will be taken directly to the house." He stooped and took hold of one of the handles of the coffin.

"Take the long hill road up, Thompson, it will be easier on the horses," called the liveryman as the undertaker snapped the door of the hearse and prepared to mount to the driver's seat.

Laird, the red-bearded lawyer, turned again to the stranger: "We didn't know whether there would be any one with him or not," he explained. "It's a long walk, so you'd better go up in the hack." He pointed to a single battered conveyance, but the young man replied stiffly: "Thank you, but I think I will go up with the hearse. If you don't object," turning to the undertaker, "I'll ride with you."

They clambered up over the wheels and drove off in the starlight up the long, white hill toward the town. The lamps in the still village were shining from under the low, snow-burdened roofs; and beyond, on every side, the plains reached out into emptiness, peaceful and wide as the soft sky itself, and wrapped in a tangible, white silence.

When the hearse backed up to a wooden

sidewalk before a naked, weather-beaten frame house, the same composite, ill-defined group that had stood upon the station siding was huddled about the gate. The front yard was an icy swamp, and a couple of warped planks, extending from the sidewalk to the door, made a sort of rickety foot-bridge. The gate hung on one hinge, and was opened wide with difficulty. Steavens, the young stranger, noticed that something black was tied to the knob of the front door.

The grating sound made by the casket, as it was drawn from the hearse, was answered by a scream from the house; the front door was wrenched open, and a tall, corpulent woman rushed out bareheaded into the snow and flung herself upon the coffin, shrieking: "My boy, my boy! And this is how you've come home to me!"

As Steavens turned away and closed his eyes with a shudder of unutterable repulsion, another woman, also tall, but flat and angular, dressed entirely in black, darted out of the house and caught Mrs. Merrick by the shoulders, crying sharply: "Come, come, mother; you mustn't go on like this!" Her tone changed to one of obsequious solemnity as she turned to the banker: "The parlour is ready, Mr. Phelps."

The bearers carried the coffin along the narrow boards, while the undertaker ran ahead with the coffin-rests. They bore it into a large, unheated room that smelled of dampness and disuse and furniture polish, and set it down under a hanging lamp ornamented with jingling glass prisms and before a "Rogers group" of John Alden and Priscilla, wreathed with smilax. Henry Steavens stared about him with the sickening conviction that there had been a mistake, and that he had somehow arrived at the wrong destination. He looked at the clover-green Brussels, the fat plush upholstery, among the hand-painted china placques and panels and vases, for some mark of identification,—for something that might once conceivably have belonged to Harvey Merrick. It was not until he recognized his friend in the crayon portrait of a little boy in kilts and curls, hanging above the piano, that he felt willing to let any of these people approach the coffin.

"Take the lid off, Mr. Thompson; let me see my boy's face," wailed the elder woman between her sobs. This time Steavens looked fearfully, almost beseechingly into her face, red and swollen under its masses of strong, black, shiny hair. He flushed, dropped his eyes, and then, almost incredulously, looked

again. There was a kind of power about her face—a kind of brutal handsomeness, even; but it was scarred and furrowed by violence, and so coloured and coarsened by fiercer passions that grief seemed never to have laid a gentle finger there. The long nose was distended and knobbed at the end, and there were deep lines on either side of it; her heavy, black brows almost met across her forehead, her teeth were large and square, and set far apart—teeth that could tear. She filled the room; the men were obliterated, seemed tossed about like twigs in an angry water, and even Steavens felt himself being drawn into the whirlpool.

The daughter—the tall, raw-boned woman in crêpe, with a mourning comb in her hair which curiously lengthened her long face—sat stiffly upon the sofa, her hands, conspicuous for their large knuckles, folded in her lap, her mouth and eyes drawn down, solemnly awaiting the opening of the coffin. Near the door stood a mulatto woman, evidently a servant in the house, with a timid bearing and an emaciated face pitifully sad and gentle. She was weeping silently, the corner of her calico apron lifted to her eyes, occasionally suppressing a long, quivering sob. Steavens walked over and stood beside her.

Feeble steps were heard on the stairs, and an old man, tall and frail, odorous of pipe smoke, with shaggy, unkempt grey hair and a dingy beard, tobacco stained about the mouth, entered uncertainly. He went slowly up to the coffin and stood rolling a blue cotton handkerchief between his hands, seeming so pained and embarrassed by his wife's orgy of grief that he had no consciousness of anything else.

"There, there, Annie, dear, don't take on so," he quavered timidly, putting out a shaking hand and awkwardly patting her elbow. She turned and sank upon his shoulder with such violence that he tottered a little. He did not even glance toward the coffin, but continued to look at her with a dull, frightened, appealing expression, as a spaniel looks at the whip. His sunken cheeks slowly reddened and burned with miserable shame. When his wife rushed from the room, her daughter strode after her with set lips. The servant stole up to the coffin, bent over it for a moment, and then slipped away to the kitchen, leaving Steavens, the lawyer, and the father to themselves. The old man stood looking down at his dead son's face. The sculptor's splendid head seemed even more noble in its rigid stillness than in life. The dark hair had crept down upon the wide forehead; the face seemed strangely long, but in it there was not that repose we expect to find in the faces of the dead. The brows were so drawn that there were two deep lines above the beaked nose, and the chin was thrust forward defiantly. It was as though the strain of life had been so sharp and bitter that death could not at once relax the tension and smooth the countenance into perfect peace—as though he were still guarding something precious, which might even yet be wrested from him.

The old man's lips were working under his stained beard. He turned to the lawyer with timid deference: "Phelps and the rest are comin' back to set up with Harve, ain't they?" he asked. "Thank 'ee, Jim, thank 'ee." He brushed the hair back gently from his son's forehead. "He was a good boy, Jim; always a good boy. He was ez gentle ez a child and the kindest of 'em all—only we didn't none of us ever onderstand him." The tears trickled slowly down his beard and dropped upon the sculptor's coat.

"Martin, Martin! Oh, Martin! come here," his wife wailed from the top of the stairs. The old man started timorously: "Yes, Annie, I'm coming." He turned away, hesitated, stood for a moment in miserable indecision; then reached back and patted the dead man's hair softly, and stumbled from the room.

"Poor old man, I didn't think he had any tears left. Seems as if his eyes would have gone dry long ago. At his age nothing cuts very deep," remarked the lawyer.

Something in his tone made Steavens glance up. While the mother had been in the room, the young man had scarcely seen any one else; but now, from the moment he first glanced into Jim Laird's florid face and blood-shot eyes, he knew that he had found what he had been heartsick at not finding before—the feeling, the understanding, that must exist in some one, even here.

The man was red as his beard, with features swollen and blurred by dissipation, and a hot, blazing blue eye. His face was strained—that of a man who is controlling himself with difficulty—and he kept plucking at his beard with a sort of fierce resentment. Steavens, sitting by the window, watched him turn down the glaring lamp, still its jangling pendants with an angry gesture, and then stand with his hands locked behind him, staring down into the master's face. He could not help wondering what link there had been between the porcelain vessel and so sooty a lump of potter's clay.

From the kitchen an uproar was sounding; when the dining-room door opened, the import of it was clear. The mother was abusing the maid for having forgotten to make the dressing for the chicken salad which had been prepared for the watchers. Steavens had never heard anything in the least like it; it was injured, emotional, dramatic abuse, unique and masterly in its excruciating cruelty, as violent and unrestrained as had been her grief of twenty minutes before. With a shudder of disgust the lawyer went into the dining-room and closed the door into the kitchen.

"Poor Roxy's getting it now," he remarked when he came back. "The Merricks took her out of the poor-house years ago; and if her loyalty would let her, I guess the poor old thing could tell tales that would curdle your blood. She's the mulatto woman who was standing in here a while ago, with her apron to her eyes. The old woman is a fury; there never was anybody like her. She made Harvey's life a hell for him when he lived at home; he was so sick ashamed of it. I never could see how he kept himself sweet."

"He was wonderful," said Steavens slowly, "wonderful; but until tonight I have never known how wonderful."

"That is the eternal wonder of it, anyway; that it can come even from such a dung heap as this," the lawyer cried, with a sweeping gesture which seemed to indicate much more than the four walls within which they stood.

"I think I'll see whether I can get a little air. The room is so close I am beginning to feel rather faint," murmured Steavens, struggling with one of the windows. The sash was stuck, however, and would not yield, so he sat down dejectedly and began pulling at his collar. The lawyer came over, loosened the sash with one blow of his red fist and sent the window up a few inches. Steavens thanked him, but the nausea which had been gradually climbing into his throat for the last half hour left him with but one desire—a desperate feeling that he must get away from this place with what was left of Harvey Merrick. Oh, he comprehended well enough now the quiet bitterness of the smile that he had seen so often on his master's lips!

Once when Merrick returned from a visit home, he brought with him a singularly feeling and suggestive bas-relief of a thin, faded old woman, sitting and sewing something pinned to her knee; while a full-lipped, full-blooded little urchin, his trousers held up by a single gallows, stood beside her, impatiently twitching her gown to call her attention to a butterfly he had caught. Steavens, impressed by the tender and delicate modelling of the thin, tired face, had asked him if it were his mother. He remembered the dull flush that had burned up in the sculptor's face.

The lawyer was sitting in a rocking-chair beside the coffin, his head thrown back and his eyes closed. Steavens looked at him earnestly, puzzled at the line of the chin, and wondering why a man should conceal a feature of such distinction under that disfiguring shock of beard. Suddenly, as though he felt the young sculptor's keen glance, Jim Laird opened his eyes.

"Was he always a good deal of an oyster?" he asked abruptly. "He was terribly shy as a boy."

"Yes, he was an oyster, since you put it so," rejoined Steavens. "Although he could be very fond of people, he always gave one the impression of being detached. He disliked violent emotion; he was reflective, and rather distrustful of himself—except, of course, as regarded his work. He was sure enough there. He distrusted men pretty thoroughly and women even more, yet somehow without believing ill of them. He was determined, indeed, to believe the best; but he seemed afraid to investigate."

"A burnt dog dreads the fire," said the lawyer grimly, and closed his eyes.

Steavens went on and on, reconstructing that whole miserable boyhood. All this raw, biting ugliness had been the portion of the man whose mind was to become an exhaustless gallery of beautiful impressions—so sensitive that the mere shadow of a poplar leaf flickering against a sunny wall would be etched and held there for ever. Surely, if ever a man had the magic word in his finger tips, it was Merrick. Whatever he touched, he revealed its holiest secret; liberated it from enchantment and restored it to its pristine loveliness. Upon whatever he had come in contact with, he had left a beautiful record of the experience—a sort of ethereal signature; a scent, a sound, a colour that was his own.

Steavens understood now the real tragedy of his master's life; neither love nor wine, as many had conjectured; but a blow which had fallen earlier and cut deeper than anything else could have done—a shame not his, and yet so unescapably his, to hide in his heart from his very boyhood. And without—the frontier warfare; the yearning of a boy, cast ashore upon a desert of newness and ugliness and sordidness, for all that is chastened and old, and noble with traditions.

At eleven o'clock the tall, flat woman in black announced that the watchers were arriving, and asked them to "step into the dining-room." As Steavens rose, the lawyer said dryly: "You go on—it'll be a good experience for you. I'm not equal to that crowd tonight; I've had twenty years of them."

As Steavens closed the door after him he glanced back at the lawyer, sitting by the coffin in the dim light, with his chin resting on his hand.

The same misty group that had stood before the door of the express car shuffled into the dining-room. In the light of the kerosene lamp they separated and became individuals. The minister, a pale, feeble-looking man with white hair and blond chin-whiskers, took his seat beside a small side table and placed his Bible upon it. The Grand Army man sat down behind the stove and tilted his chair back comfortably against the wall, fishing his quill toothpick from his waistcoat pocket. The two bankers, Phelps and Elder, sat off in a corner behind the dinner-table, where they could finish their discussion of the new usury law and its effect on chattel security loans. The real estate agent, an old man with a smiling, hypocritical face, soon joined them. The coal and lumber dealer and the cattle shipper sat on opposite sides of the hard coal-burner, their feet on the nickel-work. Steavens took a book from his pocket and began to read. The talk around him ranged through various topics of local interest while the house was quieting down. When it was clear that the members of the family were in bed, the Grand Army man hitched his shoulders and, untangling his long legs, caught his heels on the rounds of his chair.

"S'pose there'll be a will, Phelps?" he queried in his weak falsetto.

The banker laughed disagreeably, and began trimming his nails with a pearl-handled pocket-knife.

"There'll scarcely be any need for one, will there?" he queried in his turn.

The restless Grand Army man shifted his position again, getting his knees still nearer his chin. "Why, the ole man says Harve's done right well lately," he chirped.

The other banker spoke up. "I reckon he means by that Harve ain't asked him to mortgage any more farms lately, so as he could go on with his education."

"Seems like my mind don't reach back to a time when Harve wasn't bein' edycated," tittered the Grand Army man.

There was a general chuckle. The minister took out his handkerchief and blew his nose sonorously. Banker Phelps closed his knife with a snap. "It's too bad the old man's sons didn't turn out better," he remarked with reflective authority. "They never hung together. He spent money enough on Harve to stock a dozen cattle-farms, and he might as well have poured it into Sand Creek. If Harve had stayed at home and helped nurse what little they had, and gone into stock on the old man's bottom farm, they might all have been well fixed. But the old man had to trust everything to tenants and was cheated right and left."

"Harve never could have handled stock none," interposed the cattleman. "He hadn't it in him to be sharp. Do you remember when he bought Sander's mules for eight-year olds, when everybody in town knew that Sander's father-in-law give 'em to his wife for a wedding present eighteen years before, an' they was full-grown mules then?"

The company laughed discreetly, and the Grand Army man rubbed his knees with a spasm of childish delight.

"Harve never was much account for anything practical, and he shore was never fond of work," began the coal and lumber dealer. "I mind the last time he was home; the day he left, when the ole man was out to the barn helpin' his hand hitch up to take Harve to the train, and Cal Moots was patchin' up the fence; Harve, he come out on the step and sings out, in his ladylike voice: 'Cal Moots, Cal Moots! please come cord my trunk.'"

"That's Harve for you," approved the Grand Army man. "I kin hear him howlin' yet, when he was a big feller in long pants and his mother used to whale him with a rawhide in the barn for lettin' the cows git foundered in the cornfield when he was drivin' 'em home from pasture. He killed a cow of mine that-a-way onct—a pure Jersey and the best milker I had, an' the ole man had to put up for her. Harve, he was watchin' the sun set acrost the marshes when the anamile got away."

"Where the old man made his mistake was in sending the boy East to school," said Phelps, stroking his goatee and speaking in a deliberate, judicial tone. "There was where he got his head full of nonsense. What Harve needed, of all people, was a course in some first-class Kansas City business college."

The letters were swimming before Steavens's eyes. Was it possible that these men did not understand, that the palm on the coffin meant nothing to them? The very name of their town would have remained for ever buried in the postal guide had it not been now and again mentioned in the world in connection with Harvey Merrick's. He remembered what his master had said to him on the day of his death, after the congestion of both lungs had shut off any probability of recovery, and the sculptor had asked his pupil to send his body home. "It's not a pleasant place to be lying while the world is moving and doing and bettering," he had said with a feeble smile, "but it rather seems as though we ought to go back to the place we came from, in the end. The townspeople will come in for a look at me; and after they have had their say, I shan't have much to fear from the judgment of God!"

The cattleman took up the comment. "Forty's young for a Merrick to cash in; they usually hang on pretty well. Probably he helped it along with whisky."

"His mother's people were not long lived, and Harvey never had a robust constitution," said the minister mildly. He would have liked to say more. He had been the boy's Sunday-school teacher, and had been fond of him; but he felt that he was not in a position to speak. His own sons had turned out badly, and it was not a year since one of them had made his last trip home in the express car, shot in a gambling-house in the Black Hills.

"Nevertheless, there is no disputin' that Harve frequently looked upon the wine when it was red, also variegated, and it shore made an oncommon fool of him," moralized the cattleman.

Just then the door leading into the parlour rattled loudly and every one started involuntarily, looking relieved when only Jim Laird came out. The Grand Army man ducked his head when he saw the spark in his blue, blood-shot eye. They were all afraid of Jim; he was a drunkard, but he could twist the law to suit his client's needs as no other man in all western Kansas could do, and there were many who tried. The lawyer closed the door behind him, leaned back against it and folded his arms, cocking his head a little to one side. When he assumed this attitude in the court-room, ears were always pricked up, as it usually foretold a flood of withering sarcasm.

"I've been with you gentlemen before," he began in a dry, even tone, "when you've sat by the coffins of boys born and raised in this town; and, if I remember rightly, you were never any too well satisfied when you checked them up. What's the matter, anyhow? Why is it that reputable young men are as scarce as millionaires in Sand City? It might almost seem to a stranger that there was some way something the matter with your progressive town. Why did Ruben Sayer, the brightest young lawyer you ever turned out, after he had come home from the university as straight as a die, take to drinking and forge a check and shoot himself? Why did Bill Merrit's son die of the shakes in a saloon in Omaha? Why was Mr. Thomas's son, here, shot in a gambling-house? Why did young Adams burn his mill to beat the insurance companies and go to the pen?"

The lawyer paused and unfolded his arms, laying one clenched fist quietly on the table. "I'll tell you why. Because you drummed nothing but money and knavery into their ears from the time they wore knickerbockers; because you carped away at them as you've been carping here tonight, holding our friends Phelps and Elder up to them for their models, as our grandfathers held up George Washington and John Adams. But the boys were young, and raw at the business you put them to, and how could they match coppers with such artists as Phelps and Elder? You wanted them to be successful rascals; they were only unsuccessful ones—that's all the difference. There was only one boy ever raised in this borderland between ruffianism and civilization who didn't come to grief, and you hated Harvey Merrick more for winning out than you hated all the other boys who got under the wheels. Lord, Lord, how you did hate him! Phelps, here, is fond of saying that he could buy and sell us all out any time he's a mind to; but he knew Harve wouldn't have given a tinker's damn for his bank and all his cattle-farms put together; and a lack of appreciation, that way, goes hard with Phelps.

"Old Nimrod thinks Harve drank too much; and this from such as Nimrod and me!

"Brother Elder says Harve was too free with the old man's money—fell short in filial consideration, maybe. Well, we can all remember the very tone in which brother Elder swore his own father was a liar, in the county court; and we all know that the old man came out of that partnership with his son as bare as a sheared lamb. But maybe I'm getting personal, and I'd better be driving ahead at what I want to say."

The lawyer paused a moment, squared his heavy shoulders, and went on: "Harvey Merrick and I went to school together, back East. We were dead in earnest, and we wanted you all to be proud of us some day. We meant to be great men. Even I, and I haven't lost my sense of humor, gentlemen, I meant to be a great man. I came back here to practise, and I found you didn't in the least want me to be a great man. You wanted me to be a shrewd lawyer—oh, yes! Our veteran here wanted me to get him an increase of pension, because he had dyspepsia; Phelps wanted a new county survey that would put the widow Wilson's little bottom farm inside his south line; Elder wanted to lend money at 5 per cent. a month, and get it collected; and Stark here wanted to wheedle old women up in Vermont into investing their annuities in real-estate mortgages that are not worth the paper they are written on. Oh, you needed me hard enough, and you'll go on needing me!

"Well, I came back here and became the damned shyster you wanted me to be. You pretend to have some sort of respect for me; and yet you'll stand up and throw mud at Harvey Merrick, whose soul you couldn't dirty and whose hands you couldn't tie. Oh, you're a discriminating lot of Christians! There have been times when the sight of Harvey's name in some Eastern paper has made me hang my head like a whipped dog; and, again, times when I liked to think of him off there in the world, away from all this hog-wallow, climbing the big, clean up-grade he'd set for himself.

"And we? Now that we've fought and lied and sweated and stolen, and hated as only the disappointed strugglers in a bitter, dead little Western town know how to do, what have we got to show for it? Harvey Merrick wouldn't have given one sunset over your marshes for all you've got put together, and you know it. It's not for me to say why, in the inscrutable wisdom of God, a genius should ever have been called from this place of hatred and bitter waters; but I want this Boston man to know that the drivel he's been hearing here tonight is the only tribute any truly great man could have from such a lot of sick, side-tracked, burnt-dog, land-poor sharks as the here-present financiers of Sand City—upon which town may God have mercy!"

The lawyer thrust out his hand to Steavens as he passed him, caught up his overcoat in the hall, and had left the house before the Grand Army man had had time to lift his ducked head and crane his long neck about at his fellows.

Next day Jim Laird was drunk and unable to attend the funeral services. Steavens called twice at his office, but was compelled to start East without seeing him. He had a presentiment that he would hear from him again, and left his address on the lawyer's table; but if Laird found it, he never acknowledged it. The thing in him that Harvey Merrick had loved must have gone under ground with Harvey Merrick's coffin; for it never spoke again, and Jim got the cold he died of driving across the Colorado mountains to defend one of Phelps's sons who had got into trouble out there by cutting government timber.

ANNE DOUGLAS SEDGWICK (1873-   )

DAFFODILS
(1918)

I

Though he knew that he was going to die, Marmaduke Follett as he lay in the hospital on the French coast had never in his life been so happy. Until these last days he had not been able to feel it in its completeness. Of the great engagement where he had fallen he remembered only the overwhelming uproar, the blood and mud; and after that, torments, apathies, dim awakenings to the smell of ether and relapses to acquiescent sleep. Now the last operation had failed—or rather, he had failed to recover from it—and there was no more hope for him; but he hardly suffered and his thoughts were emerging into a world of cleanliness, kindness, and repose.

The hospital before the war had been a big hotel, and his was one of the bedrooms on the second floor, its windows crossed by two broad blue bands of sea and sky. As an officer he had a room to himself. The men were in the wards downstairs.

One of his nurses—both were pleasant girls but this was the one who with a wing of black hair curving under her cap reminded him of his cousin Victoria—had put a glass of daffodils beside his bed, but the wild ones that grow in woods; and if she made him think of Victoria how much more they made him think of the woods in spring at Channerley!

He was dying after a gallant deed. It was a fitting death for a Follett and so little in his life had been at all fitted to that initial privilege: it was only in the manner of his death that his life matched at all those thoughts of Victoria and Channerley.

He did not remember much of the manner; it still remained cloaked in the overwhelming uproar; but as he lay there he seemed to read in the columns of the London papers what all the Folletts were so soon to read—because of him:—

"His Majesty the King has been graciously pleased to award the Victoria Cross to the undermentioned officers, non-commissioned officers and men:—

"Sec. Lt. Marmaduke Everard Follett. For most conspicuous bravery.

"He was directed with 50 men to drive the enemy from their trench and under intense shell- and machine-gun fire he personally led three separate parties of bombers against a captured 325 yards of trench; attacking the machine gun, shooting the firer with his revolver, and destroying gun and *personnel* with bombs. This very brave act saved many lives and ensured the success of the attack. In carrying one of his men back to safety Sec. Lt. Follett was mortally wounded."

He felt himself smile, as he soberly spaced it out, to remember that the youths at the office used to call him Marmalade. It was curious that he most felt his present and his present transfigured self, when he thought of Cauldwell's office, where so many years of his past had been spent. When he thought of that, of the jocund youths, of the weary hours and wasted years, it was to feel himself transfigured; when he thought of the Folletts and of Channerley, to feel that he matched them; to feel at last as if he had come home. What to the grimy, everyday world counted as transfiguration, counted as the normal, the expected, to the world of Channerley.

He wondered, lying there and looking out past the daffodils, where Victoria was; he had heard that she was nursing, too, somewhere in France; and again, as he had smiled over the contrast of "Sec. Lt. Marmaduke Everard Follett" and the "Marmalade" of Cauldwell's office, he smiled in thinking of the difference between Victoria and the nice young nurse who, for all her resembling curve of hair, was also second-rate. It would have been very wonderful to have been nursed by Victoria, and yet his thought turned from that. There had never been any sweetness, never even any kindness for him, in Victoria's clear young gaze; when it came to nursing, he could imagine her being kind to a Tommy, but not to him, the dull, submerged cousin; and the nice though second-rate nurse was very kind. He would rather die under her eyes than under Victoria's.

And he would rather think of Victoria as he had last seen her at the big London dance to which, most unexpectedly, he had found himself asked last spring—the spring before the war. He had decided, as with nervous fingers he tied his white cravat,—how rarely disturbed had been that neat sheaf lying in his upper drawer!—that he must have been confused with some other Follett, for he was so seldom asked anywhere, where he would be likely to meet Victoria. However, it was a delight to see her in her snowy dress, her beautiful hair bound with silver, and to feel, as he watched her dancing, that she belonged, in a sense, to him; for he, too, was a Follett.

How much more did she belong to him now! And not only Victoria, but all of them, these Folletts of his and the Folletts of past generations; and Channerley, centre of all his aching, wistful memories. It had been for him, always, part of the very structure of his nature, that beautiful old house where he had spent his boyhood. Perhaps it was because he had been turned out of the nest so early that he never ceased to miss it. His thought, like a maimed fledgling, had fluttered round and round it, longing, exiled, helpless.

If, now, he could have survived, his eldest brother, he felt sure, must have asked him oftener to stay at Channerley. It still gave him a pang, or, rather, the memory of many pangs, to recall that Robert had not asked him for two years, and had seemed to forget all about him after that. They had all seemed to forget about him,—that was the trouble of it,—and almost from the very beginning: Robert, who had Channerly; Austin, who had gone into the army and was now in Mesopotamia; Griselda, married so splendidly up in her northern estate; and Amy, the artistic bachelor-girl of the family, whom he associated with irony and cigarette-smoke and prolonged absences in Paris. Even cheerful Sylvia, of South Kensington, with her many babies and K. C. husband, whom he always thought of, for all her well-being, as very nearly as submerged as himself,—even Sylvia saw little of him and asked him only to family dinners,—Mr. Shillington's family, not hers,—at depressingly punctual intervals.

But Sylvia, the one nearest him in years, was the one who had forgotten least, and she had, after her fashion, done her best for him. Confused at study, clumsy at games, shy and tongue-tied, he had not in any way distinguished himself at a rather second-rate public school; and to distinguish himself had been the only hope for him. The Folletts had never had any money to spare, and Eton and Oxford for Robert and Sandhurst for Austin fulfilled a tradition that became detached and terse

where younger sons who could not distinguish themselves were concerned. Still, he had always felt that, had his father lived, something better would have been found for him than to be bundled, through the instrumentality of Mr. Shillington, into a solicitor's office. There he had been bundled, and there he had stuck for all these years, as clumsy, as confused as ever; a pallid, insignificant little fellow (oh, he had no illusions about himself!) with the yellow hair and small yellow moustache which, together with his name, had earned for him his sobriquet.

They had not disliked him, those direfully facetious companions of his. *Noblesse oblige* was an integral part of his conception of himself, however little they might be aware of his unvarying courtesy towards them as its exercise. He suspected that they thought of him as merely inoffensive and rather piteous; but shyness might give that impression; they could not guess at the quiet aversion that it covered. He was aware sometimes, suddenly, that in the aloofness and contemplative disdain of his pale sidelong glance at them, he most felt himself a Follett. If his mind, for most practical purposes, was slow and clumsy, it was sharp and swift in its preceptions. He judged the young men in Cauldwell's office as a Follett must judge them. In the accurate applying of that standard he was as instinctively gifted as any of his race; and if he knew, from his first look at her, that the nice young nurse was second-rate, how coldly and calmly, all these years, he had known that the young men who called him Marmalade were third-rate. And yet they none of them disliked him, and he wondered whether it was because, when he most felt disdain, he most looked merely timid, or because they recognized in him, all dimly as it might be, the first-rateness that was his inherently and inalienably.

Just as the third-rate young men might recognize the first-rate but dimly, he was aware that to the world the Folletts, too, were not important. It was not one of the names, in spite of centuries of local lustre, to conjure with; and he liked it all the better because of that. They had never, it was true, distinguished themselves; but they were people of distinction, and that was, to his quiet, reflective, savouring, an even higher state. He sometimes wondered if, in any of them, the centring of family consciousness was as intense as in himself. If they were aloof about third-rate people, it was not because they were really very conscious about themselves. They took themselves for granted, as they took

Channerley and the family history; and only Amy was aware that some of the family portraits were good.

The history—it was not of course accurate to call it that, yet it seemed more spacious and significant than mere annals—pored over during long evenings, in faded parchments, deeds, and letters, was known in every least detail to him. How the Folletts had begun, very soberly but very decorously, in the fifteenth century, and how they had gone on: rooting more deeply into their pleasant woodlands and meadows; flowering, down the centuries, now in a type of grace—that charming Antonia who had married so well at James the First's court; and of gallantry—a Follett had fallen at Naseby, and a Follett had fought at Waterloo; or of good-humored efficiency, as in the eighteenth-century judge and the nineteenth-century bishop. And he, who was neither graceful nor gallant nor good-humored (sour and sad he felt himself), never could resist the warming, revivifying influence of these recognitions, stretching himself, sighing, smiling happily before his Bloomsbury fire on a winter's evening, as he laid down the thick pile of yellowed manuscripts to think it all over and feel himself, in spite of everything, a link with it all.

Robert had always been very decent about letting him have and keep the documents for as long as he liked.

It was strange to think that he was never to see his Bloomsbury lodgings again, and stranger, really, that a certain tinge of regret was in the thought; for how, for years, he had hated them, place of exile, of relegation, as he had always felt them! Yet he had come to be fond of his little sitting-room, just because, to his eye, with its mingled comfort and austerity, it was so significant of exile. If a Follett couldn't have what he wanted, that was all he would have—his rack of pipes, his shelves of books, his little collection of mostly marginless mezzotints ranged along the dark, green walls. The room was a refuge and did not pretent to be an achievement, and in that very fact might, to an eye as sharp as his for such significance, suggest the tastes that it relinquished. He had indeed all the tastes and none of the satisfactions of Channerley.

There it was; he had come back to it again, as, indeed, he had, in spirit, never left it—never for a moment. He felt himself, lying there in the hospital on the French coast, with the soft spring sea lapping upon the beach under his window—he felt himself drop, drop, softly, sweetly, deeply, back to his childhood.

From his high nursery-window he saw the dewy tree-tops,—the old hawthorn that grew so near the house, and the old mulberry,—and the rooks wheeling on a spring sky so many years ago. The dogs, at that early hour, just released, might be racing over the lawns: idle, jovial Peter, the spaniel, and Jack, the plucky, hot-tempered little Dandy-Dinmont.

Below the lawns were the high grey garden walls, and above, rising a little from the flagged rose-garden, were the woods where the daffodils grew, daffodils like those beside him now, tall and small, their pale, bright pennons set among warrior spears of green. Little bands of them ran out upon the lawn from under the great trees, and one saw their gold glimmering far, far along the woodlands. Oh, the beauty of it, and the stillness; the age and youth; the smile and the security! How he had always loved it, shambling about the woods and gardens; creeping rather—he always saw himself as creeping somehow—about the dear, gay, faded house! Always such an awkward, insignificant little boy; even his dear old Nanna had felt dissatisfied with his appearance, and he had always known it, when she sent him down with the others to the drawing-room; and his mother, she had made it very apparent, had found him only that.

He shrank from the thought of his mother; perhaps it was because of her, of her vexed and averted eyes, her silken rustle of indifference as she passed him by, that he saw himself as creeping anywhere where she might come. He only remembered her in glimpses: languidly and ironically smiling at her tea-table (Amy had her smile), the artificial tone of her voice had even then struck his boyish ear; reading on a summer afternoon, with bored brows and dissatisfied lips, as she lay on a garden chair in the shade of the mulberry tree; querulously arguing with his father, who, good-humoured and very indifferent, strolled about the hall in his pink coat on a winter morning, waiting for the horses to be brought round; his mother's yellow braids shining under her neatly tilted riding-hat, her booted foot held to the blaze of the great log-fire. A hard, selfish, sentimental woman; and—wasn't it really the only word for what he felt in her?—just a little shoddy. He distinguished it from the second-rate nicely: it was a more personal matter; for his mother, though certainly not a Follett, was of good stock; he knew, of course, all about her stock. It always grieved him to think that it was from her he had his yellow hair and the pale grey of his eyes; his stature, too, for she had been a small woman; all the other Folletts were tall; but she had given him nothing more: not a trace of her beauty was his, and he was glad of it.

It was curious, since he had really had so little to do with him, as little, almost, as with his mother, how blissfully his sense of his father's presence pervaded his childish memories. He was so kind. The kindest thing he remembered at Channerley, except his dear old Nanna and Peter the spaniel. It used to give him a thrill of purest joy when, meeting him, his father, his hands clasped behind his back after his strolling wont, would stop and bend amused and affectionate eyes upon him; rather the eyes, to be sure, that he bent upon his dogs; but Marmaduke always felt of him that he looked upon his children, and upon himself, too, as parts of the pack; and it was delightful to be one of the pack, with him.

"Well, old fellow, and how goes the world with you to-day?" his father would say.

And after that question the world would go in sunshine.

He had always believed that, had his father lived, he would never have been so forgotten; just as he had always believed that his father would never have allowed one of his pack to be bundled into the solicitor's office. For that he had to thank, he felt sure, not only Sylvia's negative solicitude, but his mother's active indifference. Between them both they had done it to him.

And he never felt so to the full his dispossession as in thinking of Robert. He had always intensely feared and admired Robert. He did not know what he feared, for Robert was never unkind. But Robert was everything that he was not: tall and gay and competent, and possessing everything needful, from the very beginning, for the perfect fulfilment of his type. The difference between them had been far more than the ten years that had made of Robert a man when he was still only a little boy. There had been, after all, a time when they had been a very big and a very little boy together, with Austin in between; yet the link had seemed always to break down after Austin. Robert, in this retrospect, had always the air of strolling away from him—for Robert, too, was a stroller. Not that he himself had had the air of pursuit; he had never, he felt sure, from the earliest age, lacked tact; tact and reticence and self-effacement had been bred into him. But his relationship with Robert had seemed always to consist in standing there, hiding ruefulness, and gazing at Robert's strolling back.

The difference from Austin had perhaps

been as great, but it had never hurt so much, for Austin, though with his share of the Follett charm, had never had the charm of Robert. A clear-voiced and clear-eyed, masterful boy, Austin's main contact with others was in doing things with them, and that sort of contact did not mean congeniality. Austin had made use of him; had let him hold his ferrets and field for him at cricket; and a person whom you found useful did not, for the time being, bore you.

But he had bored Robert always—that was apparent; and beautiful Griselda, who was older than either of them, and Amy, who was younger. Griselda had gazed rather sadly over his head; and Amy had smiled and teased him so that he had seldom ventured on a remark in her presence. Even fat little Sylvia, the baby, had always preferred any of the others to him as she grew up; had only not been bored because, while she was good-humored, she was also rather dull. And at the bottom of his heart, rueful always, sore, and still patiently surprised, he knew that, while he found them all a little brutal, he could not admire them the less because of it. It was part of the Follett inheritance to be able to be brutal, unconsciously, and therefore with no loss of bloom.

And now, at last, he was not to bore them any longer; at last, he was not to be forgotten. How could he not be happy,—it brought back every blissful thrill of boyhood, his father's smile, the daffodil woods in spring, heightened to ecstasy,—when he had at last made of himself one of the Folletts who were remembered. He would have his place in the history beside the Follett who fell at Naseby. No family but is glad of a V.C. in its annals. They could no longer stroll away. They would be proud of him; he had done something for all the Folletts forever.

II

The nice young nurse came in. She closed the door gently, and, with her smile, calm before accustomed death, and always, as it were, a little proud of him,—that was because they were both English,—she took his wrist and felt his pulse, holding her watch in the other hand, and asked him, presently, how he felt. Only after that did she say, contemplating him for a moment,—Marmaduke wondered how many hours—or was it perhaps days?—she was giving him to live,—

"A gentleman has come to see you. You may see him if you like. But I've told him that he is only to stay for half an hour."

The blood flowed up to Marmaduke's forehead. He felt it beating hard in his neck and behind his ears, and his heart thumped down there under the neatly drawn bed-clothes.

"A gentleman? What's his name?" Was it Robert?

"Here is his card," said the nurse.

She drew it from her pocket and gave it to him. It couldn't have been Robert, of course. Robert would only have had to come up. Yet he was dizzy with the disappointment. It was as if he saw Robert strolling away for the last time. He would never see Robert again.

Mr. Guy Thorpe was the name. The address was a London club that Marmaduke placed at once as second-rate, and "The Beeches, Arlington Road," in a London suburb. On the card was written in a neat scholarly hand: "May I see you? We are friends."

It was difficult for a moment to feel anything but the receding tide of his hope. The next thing that came was a sense of dislike for Mr. Guy Thorpe and for the words that he had written. Friends? By what right since he did not know his name?

"Is he a soldier?" he asked. "How did he come? I don't know him."

"You needn't see him unless you want to," said the nurse. "No; he's not a soldier. An elderly man. He's driving a motor for the French Wounded Emergency Fund, and came on from the Alliance because he heard that you were here. Perhaps he's some old family friend. He spoke as if he were."

Marmaduke smiled a little. "That's hardly likely. But I'll see him, yes; since he came for that."

When she had gone, he lay looking again at the blue bands across the window. A flock of sea-gulls flew past—proud, swift, and leisurely, glittering in the sun. They seemed to embody the splendor and exultation of his thoughts, and, when they had disappeared, he was sorry, almost desolate.

Mr. Guy Thorpe. He took up the card again in his feeble hand and looked at it. And now, dimly, it seemed to remind him of something.

Steps approached along the passage, the nurse's light footfall and the heavier, careful tread of a man. An oddly polite, almost a deprecating tread. He had gone about a great many hospitals and was cautious not to disturb wounded men. Yet Marmaduke felt again that he did not like Mr. Guy Thorpe, and, as they came in, he was conscious of feeling a little frightened.

There was nothing to frighten one in Mr. Thorpe's appearance. He was a tall, thin, ageing man, travel-worn, in civilian clothes, with a dingy Red-Cross badge on the sleeve of

his waterproof overcoat. Baldish and apparently near-sighted, he seemed to blink towards the bed, and, as if with motoring in the wind, his eyelids were moist and reddened. He sat down, murmuring some words of thanks to the nurse.

A very insignificant man, for all his height and his big forehead. Altogether of The Beeches, Arlington Road. Had he turned grey, he might have looked less shabby, but dark thin locks still clustered above his high crown and behind his long-lobed ears. His eyes were dark, his moustache drooped, and he had a small, straight nose. Marmaduke saw that he was the sort of man who, in youth, might have been considered very handsome. He looked like a seedy poet and some sort of minor civil servant mingled, the civil servant having got the better of the poet. Marmaduke also imagined that he would have a large family and a harassed but ambitious wife, with a genteel accent—a wife a little below himself. His tie was of a dull red silk. Marmaduke did not like him.

Mr. Thorpe glanced round, as if cautiously, to see if the nurse had closed the door, and then, it was really as if more cautiously still, looked at Marmaduke, slightly moving back his chair.

"I'm very grateful to you, very grateful indeed," he said in a low voice, "for seeing me."

"You've come a long way," said Marmaduke.

"Yes. A long way. I had heard of your being here. I hoped to get here. I felt that I must see you. We are all proud of you; more proud than I can say."

He looked down now at the motoring-cap he held, and Marmaduke became aware that the reddened eyes were still more suffused and that the mouth under the drooping moustache twitched and trembled. He could think of nothing to say, except to murmur something about being very glad—though he didn't want to say that; and he supposed, to account for Mr. Thorpe's emotion, that he must be a moving sight, lying there, wasted, bandaged, and dying.

"You don't remember my name, I suppose," said Mr. Thorpe after a moment, in which he frankly got out his handkerchief and wiped his eyes.

"No, I'm afraid I don't," said Marmaduke very politely. He was glad to say this. It was the sort of thing he did want to say.

"Yet I know yours very, very well," said Mr. Thorpe, with a curious watery smile. "I lived at Channerley once. I was tutor there for some time—to Robert, your brother, and

Griselda. Yes," Mr. Thorpe nodded, "I know the Folletts well; and Channerley, the dear old place."

Now the dim something in memory pressed forward, almost with a physical advance, and revealed itself as sundry words scratched on the schoolroom window-panes and sundry succinct drawings in battered old Greek and Latin grammars. Robert had always been very clever at drawing, catching with equal facility and accuracy the swiftness of a galloping horse and the absurdities of a human profile. What returned to Marmaduke now, and as clearly as if he had the fly-leaf before him, was a tiny thumb-nail sketch of such a galloping horse unseating a lank, crouching figure, of whom the main indications were the angles of acute uncertainty taken by the knees and elbows; and a more elaborate portrait, dashed and dotted as if with a ruthless boyish grin— such an erect and melancholy head it was, so dark the tossed-back locks, so classical the nose and unclassical the moustache, and a brooding eye indicated in a triangular sweep of shadow. Beneath was written in Robert's clear, boyish hand, "Mr. Guy Thorpe, Poet, Philosopher, and Friend. Vale." Even the date flashed before him, 1880; and with it—strange, inappropriate association—the daffodils running out upon the lawn, as no doubt he had seen them as he leaned from the schoolroom window, with the Greek grammar under his elbow on the sill.

So that was it. Mr. Guy Thorpe, placed, explained, disposed of—poor dear! He felt suddenly quite kindly towards him, quite touched by his act of loyalty to the old allegiance in coming; and flattered, too,—yes, even by Mr. Thorpe,—that he should be recognized as a Follett who had done something for the name; and smiling very benevolently upon him, he said:—

"Oh, of course; I remember perfectly now— your name, and drawings of you in old schoolbooks, you know. All tutors and governesses get those tributes from their pupils, don't they? But I myself couldn't remember, could I? for it was before I was born that you were at Channerley."

There was a moment of silence after this, and in it Marmaduke felt that Mr. Thorpe did not like being so placed. He had no doubt imagined that there would be less ambiguous tributes, and that his old pupils would have talked of him to the younger generation.

And something of this chagrin certainly came out in his next words as, nodding and looking round at the daffodils, he said:—

"Yes, yes. Quite true. No, of course you couldn't yourself remember. I was more though, I think I may fairly say, than the usual tutor or governess. I came, rather, at Sir Robert's instance."—Sir Robert was Marmaduke's father.— "We had met, made friends, at Oxford; his former tutor there was an uncle of mine, and Sir Robert, in my undergraduate days, used to visit him sometimes. He was very keen on getting me to come. Young Robert wanted something of a firm hand. I was the friend rather than the mere man of books in the family."

"Poet, Philosopher and Friend"—Marmaduke had it almost on his lips, and almost with a laugh, his benevolence deepened for poor Mr. Thorpe, so self-revealed, so entirely Robert's portrait of him. Amusing to think that even the quite immature first-rate can so relegate the third. But perhaps it was a little unfair to call poor Mr. Thorpe third. The Folletts would not be likely to choose a third-rate man for a tutor; second was kinder, and truer. He had, obviously, come down in the world.

"I see. It's natural I never heard, though: there's such a chasm between the elders and the youngers in a big family, isn't there?" he said. "Griselda is twelve years older than I am, and Robert ten, you remember. She was married by the time I began my Greek. You never came back to Channerley, did you? I hope things have gone well with you since those days?"

He questioned, wanting to be very kind; wanting to give something of the genial impression of his father smiling, with his "And how goes the world with you to-day?" But he saw that, while Mr. Thorpe's evident emotion deepened, it was with a sense of present grief as well as of retrospective pathos.

"No; I never came,—that is—. No; I passed by: I never came to stay. I went abroad; I travelled, with a pupil, for some years before my marriage." Grief and confusion were oddly mingled in his drooping face. "And after that—life had changed too much. My dear old friend Sir Robert had died. I could not have faced it all. No, no; when some chapters are read, it is better to close the book; better to close the book. But I have never forgotten Channerley, nor the Folletts of Channerley; that will always remain for me the golden page; the page," said Mr. Thorpe, glancing round again at the daffodils, "of friendship, of youth, of daffodils in springtime. I saw you there," he added suddenly, "once, when you were a very little lad. I saw you. I was passing by; bicycling; no time to stop. You remember the high road skirts the woods to the north. I came and looked over the wall; and there you were—in your holland pinafore and white socks—digging up the daffodils and putting them into your little red-and-yellow cart. A beautiful spring morning. The woods full of sunshine. You wouldn't remember."

But he did remember—perfectly. Not having been seen; but the day; the woods; the daffodils. He had dug them up to plant in his own little garden, down below. He had always been stupid with his garden; had always failed where the other succeeded. And he had wanted to be sure of daffodils. And they had all laughed at him for wanting the wild daffodils like that for himself, and for going to get them in the wood. And why had Mr. Thorpe looked over the wall and not come in? He hated to think that he had been watched on that spring morning—hated it. And, curiously, that sense of fear with which he had heard the approaching footsteps returned to him. It frightened him that Mr. Thorpe had watched him over the wall.

His distaste and shrinking were perhaps apparent in his face, for it was with a change of tone and hastiness of utterance, as though hurrying away from something, that Mr. Thorpe went on:—

"You see,—it's been my romance, always, Channerley—and all of you. I've always followed your lives—always—from a distance—known what you were up to. I've made excuses to myself—in the days when I used to go a good deal about the country—to pass by Channerley and just have a glimpse of you. And when I heard that you had done this noble deed,—when I heard what you had done for England, for Channerley, for us all,—I felt I had to come and see you. You must forgive me if I seem a mere intruder. I can't seem that to myself. I've cared too much. And what I came for, really, was to thank you,—to thank you, my dear boy,—and to tell you that because of you, life must be nobler, always, for all of us."

His words had effaced the silly, groping fear. It was indeed, since his colonel's visit, the first congratulation he had had from the outer world. The nurses, of course, had congratulated him, and the surgeons; but no one who knew him outside; the kindly telegrams from Robert and Sylvia did not count as congratulations. And in a way poor Mr. Thorpe did know him, and though it was only from him, it had its sweetness. He felt himself flush as he answered, "That's very kind of you."

"Oh, no!" said Mr. Thorpe, shaking his head and swinging his foot—Marmaduke

knew that from the queer movement of his body as he sat with very tightly folded arms. "Not kind! That's not the word—from us to you! Not the word at all!"

"I'm very happy, as you may imagine," said Marmaduke. And he was happy again, and glad to share his happiness with poor Mr. Thorpe. "It makes everything worth while, doesn't it, to have brought it off at all?"

"Everything, everything—it would; it would, to you. So heroes feel," said Mr. Thorpe. "To give your life for England. I know it all—in every detail. Yes, you are happy in dying that England may live. Brave boy! Splendid boy!"

Now he was weeping. He had out his handkerchief and his shoulders shook. It made Marmaduke want to cry, too, and he wondered confusedly if the nurse would soon come back. Had not the half hour passed?

"Really—it's too good of you. You mustn't, you know; you mustn't," he murmured, while the word, "boy—boy," repeated, made tangled images in his mind, and he saw himself in the white socks and with the little red-and-yellow cart, and then as he had been the other day, leading his men, his revolver in his hand and the bullets flying about him. "And I'm not a boy," he said; "I'm thirty-four; absurdly old to be only a second lieutenant. And there are so many of us. Why,"—the thought came fantastically, but he seized it, because Mr. Thorpe was crying so and he must seize something,—"we're as common as daffodils!"

"Ah! not for me! not for me!" Mr. Thorpe gulped quickly. Something had given way in him—as if the word "daffodils" had pressed a spring. He was sobbing aloud, and he had fallen on his knees by the bed and put up his hand for Marmaduke's. "I cannot keep it from you! Not at this last hour! Not when you are leaving me forever!— My son! My brave son! I am your father, Marmaduke! I am your father, my dear, dear boy!"

III

It was the stillest room. The two calm bands of blue crossed the window. In the sunlight the gulls came flying back. Marmaduke looked out at them. Were they the same seagulls or another flock? Then quietly he closed his eyes. Stillness—calm. But something else was rising to him from them. Darkness; darkness; a darkness worse than death. Oh! death was sweet compared to this. Compared to this all his life had been sweet; and something far dearer than life was being taken from him. He only knew the terrible confusion of his whole nature.

He opened his eyes again with an instinct of escape. There were the bands of blue, and, still passing in their multitudes, leaving him forever, the proud, exultant sea-gulls. The man still knelt beside him. He heard his own voice come:—

"What do you mean?"

"I never meant to tell you! I never meant to tell you!" a moan answered him. "But— seeing you lying there!—dying!—my son!— who has given his life for England!—And how I have longed for you all these years!—My romance, Marmaduke—How could I be silent? Forgive me! Forgive me, my boy. Yes, mine. My known children are dear to me, but how far dearer the unknown son, seen only by stealth, in snatched glimpses! It is true, Marmaduke, true. We were lovers. She loved me. Do not ask. Do not question. We were young. She was very beautiful. It was springtime; daffodils were in the woods. She said that she had never known any one like me. She said that her life was hollow, meaningless. I opened doors to her, I read to her. Browning—I read Browning," he muttered on, "in the woods; among the daffodils. It was a new life to her— and to me. And we were swept away. Don't blame us, Marmaduke. If there was wrong, there was great beauty—then. Only then; for after, she was cruel—very cruel. She turned from me; she crushed and tore my heart. Oh! —I have suffered! But no one knew. No one ever dreamed of it. Only she and I. My God! —I see her in your hair and eyes!"

It was true. It was absolutely true. Through his whole being he felt its inevitability. Everything was clear, with a strange, black, infernal clearness. His life lay open before him, open from beginning to end: that beginning of tawdry sentiment and shame—with daffodils; and this end, with daffodils again, and again with tawdry sentiment and shame.

He was not a Follett. He had no part in the Folletts. He had no part in Channerley. He was an interloper, a thief. He was the son of this wretched man, in whose very grief he could detect the satisfaction—oh, who more fitted to detect such satisfaction!—of his claim upon a status above his own. He was all that he had always most despised, a second-rate, a third-rate little creature; the anxious, civil, shrinking Marmalade of Cauldwell's office. Why (as the hideous moments led him on, point by point, his old lucidity, sharpened to a needle fineness, seemed to etch the truth in lines of fire upon the blackness), hadn't he always been a pitiful little snob? Wasn't it of the essence of a snob to over-value the things one hadn't and to fear the things one was? It hadn't been other people, it had been himself, what he really was, of whom he had always been afraid. He saw himself reduced to the heretofore unrecognized, yet always operative, element in his own nature—a timid, watchful humility.

Oh, Channerley! Channerley! The wail rose in his heart and it filled the world. Oh, his woods, his daffodils, his father's smile—gone— lost forever! Worse than that—smirched, withered, desecrated!

A hideous gibbering of laughter seemed to rise around him, and pointing fingers. Amy's eyes passed with another malice in their mockery; and Robert would never turn to him now, and Griselda would never look at him. He saw it all, as they would never see it. He was not one of them, and they had always felt it; and oh,—above all,—he had always felt it. And now, quite close it seemed, softly rustling, falsely smiling, moved his loathsome mother: not only as he remembered her in youth, but in her elegant middle years, as he had last seen her, with hard eyes and alien lips and air of brittle, untouched exquisiteness.

Suddenly fury so mounted in him that he saw himself rising in bed, rending his dressings, to seize the kneeling man by the throat and throttle him. He could see his fingers sinking in on either side among the clustered hair, and hear himself say, "How dare you! How dare you! You hound! You snivelling, sneaking hound! You look for pity from me, do you!— and tenderness! Well, take this, this! Everything, everything I am and have that's worth being and having, I owe to them. I've hated you and all you mean, always—yes, your fear and your caution and your admiration and your great high forehead. Oh, I see it! I see it!—it's my own! And though I am only that in myself, then take it from me that I hate myself along with you and curse myself with you!"

It came to him that he was slowly panting, and that after the fever-fury an icy chill crept over him. And a slow, cold smile came with it, and he saw Jephson, the wit of the office, wagging his head and saying, "Little Marmalade take a man by the throat! Ask me another!"

No; little Marmalade might win the V. C.; but only when he thought he was a Follett. Was that what it all came to, really? Something broke and stopped in his mind.

He heard his father's voice. How long ago it had all happened. He had known for years, hadn't he, that this was his father?

"Marmaduke! Mr. Follett! What have I done? Shall I call somebody? Oh, forgive me!"

His father was standing now beside him and bending over him. He looked up at him and shook his head. He did not want any one to come.

"Oh, what have I done?" the man repeated.

"I was dying anyway, you know," he heard himself say.

What a pitiful face it was, this weary, loosened, futureless old face above him! What a frightened face! What long years of slow disgarnishing lay behind it: youth, romance, high hopes, all dropped away. He had come to-day with their last vestiges, still the sentimental, romancing fool, self-centred and craving; but nothing of that was left. He was beaten, at last, down into the very ground. It was a haggard, humiliated, frightened face, and miserable. As he himself had been. But not even death lay before this face. For how many years must it go on sinking down until the earth covered it? Marmaduke seemed to understand all about him, as well as if he had been himself.

"Sit down," he said. He heard that his voice was gentle, though he was not aware of feeling anything, only of understanding. "I was rather upset. No; I don't want any one. Of course I forgive you. Don't bother about it, I beg."

His father sat down, keeping his swollen eyes on the motoring-cap which, unseeingly, he turned and turned in his hands.

"Tell me about yourself a little," said Marmaduke, with slow, spaced breaths. "Where do you live? How? Are you fairly happy?"

He knew that he was not happy; but he might, like most people with whom life had not succeeded, often imagine himself so, and Marmaduke wanted to help him, if possible, to imagine it.

"I live near London. I used to do a good deal of University Extension lecturing. I've a clerkship in the Education Office now." Mr. Thorpe spoke in a dead obedient voice. "A small salary, not much hope of advance; and I've a large family. It's rather up-hill, of course. But I've good children; clever children. My eldest boy's at Oxford; he took a scholarship at Westminster; and my eldest girl's at Girton. The second girl, Winnie, has a very marked gift for painting; she is our artist; we're going to send her to the Slade next year when she leaves the High School. Good children. I've nothing to complain of."

"So you're fairly happy?" Marmaduke repeated. Oddly, he felt himself comforted in hearing about the good and happy children, in hearing about Winnie, her father's favorite.

"Happy? Well, just now, with this terrible war, one can't be that, can one? It is a great adventure for me, however, this work of mine, motoring about France. I don't think I've ever done anything I cared so much about since—for years," said Mr. Thorpe. "It's a beautiful country, isn't it? and the soldiers are such splendid fellows! One gets a lot out of it. But happy? No, I don't suppose I am. I'm pretty much of a failure, and I started life with great imaginings about myself. One doesn't get over that sort of disappointment; one never really gets over it in a way." Mr. Thorpe was looking at him now, and it was as if there were a kindliness between them. "Things have been rather grey and disagreeable on the whole," he said.

"They can be very grey and disagreeable, can't they?" said Marmaduke, closing his eyes.

He was very tired, and as he lay there quietly, having nothing further to know or to suffer, having reached the very limits of conscious dissolution, something else began to come to him. It seemed born of the abolition of self and of the acceptance of the fact that he was dead to all that had given life worth or beauty. It would have been very good to be a Follett; though, he saw it now, he had over-prized that special sort of goodness—with so much else from which he had been, as really, shut out; but he was not a Follett; nor was he merely this poor, insignificant father. He did not quite make out in what the difference lay and he did not rejoice in it, for there was no rejoicing left in him. But, even if the difference were only an acquired instinct (dimly, the terms of his complacent readings in biology and sociology returned to him), even if it were only that, not anything inherent and transmissible, it was, all the same, his own possession; something that he and the Folletts had made together; so that it was as true to say he had won the V. C. as to say that they had. The lessened self that was left to him had still its worth. To see the truth, even if it undid you, was worthy; to see so unwaveringly that it was good to be a Follett even when you weren't one, had the elements of magnanimity; and to accept the fact of being second-rate proved, did it now?—if you still cared to prove it; he felt himself smile as gently at the relinquished self as he had smiled at his father,—that you were not merely second-rate.

There was now a sound of stumbling movement; doors opening and shutting; nurses, surgeons in the room; and his father's face, far away, against the blue bands, looking at him, still so frightened and so miserable that he tried again to smile at him and to say, "It's all right. Quite all right."

At all events he had been decent to the poor old fellow. His thoughts came brokenly, but he was still seeing something, finding something; it was like a soft light growing. At all events, he had behaved as a Follett would wish to behave even when brought to such a pass. No—but it wasn't quite that, either; it was something new. He had behaved as any one decent should wish to behave. And the daffodils glimmering to his vision seemed to light him further still. "We are as common as daffodils," came back to him. Daffodils were for everybody. Foolish little boy who, on the distant spring morning in the woods of Channer-

ley, dug them up to take them to his own garden!

He was there among them with his little red-and-yellow cart, and the thrush was singing high above him, in the rosy topmost branches of an elm.

Beautiful woods. Beautiful flowers of light and chivalry. How the sunshine streamed among them!

"Dear Channerley," he thought. For again he seemed to belong there.

Gentle hands were tending him and, as he turned his cheek on the pilow, it was with the comfort—almost that of the little boy at Channerley being tucked up in the warm nursery to go to sleep—of knowing that he was dying, and that, in spite of everything, he had given something to the name.

DOROTHY CANFIELD (1879-   )

PORTRAIT OF A PHILOSOPHER

(1911)

I

The news of Professor Gridley's death filled Middletown College with consternation. Its one claim to distinction was gone, for in spite of the excessive quiet of his private life, he had always cast about the obscure little college the shimmering aura of greatness. There had been no fondness possible for the austere old thinker, but Middletown village, as well as the college, had been touched by his fidelity to the very moderate attractions of his birthplace. When, as often happened, some famous figure was seen on the streets, people used to say first, "Here to see old Grid, I suppose," and then, "Funny how he sticks here. They say he was offered seven thousand at the University of California." In the absence of any known motive for this steadfastness, the village legend-making instinct had evolved a theory that he did not wish to move away from a State of which his father had been Governor, and where the name of Gridley was like a patent of nobility.

And now he was gone, the last of the race. His disappearance caused the usual amount of reminiscent talk among his neighbors. The older people recalled the bygone scandals connected with his notorious and popular father and intimated with knowing nods that there were plenty of other descendants of the old Governor who were not entitled legally to bear the name; but the younger ones, who had

known only the severely ascetic life and cold personality of the celebrated scholar, found it difficult to connect him with such a father. In their talk they brought to mind the man himself, his queer shabby clothes, his big stooping frame, his sad black eyes, absent almost to vacancy as though always fixed on high and distant thoughts; and those who had lived near him told laughing stories about the crude and countrified simplicity of his old aunt's housekeeping—it was said that the president of Harvard had been invited to join them once in a Sunday evening meal of crackers and milk—but the general tenor of feeling was, as it had been during his life, of pride in his great fame and in the celebrated people who had come to see him.

This pride warmed into something like affection when, the day after his death, came the tidings that he had bequeathed to his college the Gino Sprague Fallères portrait of himself. Of course, at that time, no one in Middletown had seen the picture, for the philosopher's sudden death had occurred, very dramatically, actually during the last sitting. He had, in fact, had barely one glimpse of it himself, as, according to Fallères's invariable rule, no one, not even the subject of the portrait, had been allowed to examine an unfinished piece of work. But, though Middletown had no first-hand knowledge of the picture, there could be no doubt about the value of the canvas. As soon as it was put on exhibition in London, from every art-critic in the three nations who claimed Fallères for their own there rose a wail that this masterpiece was to be buried in an unknown college in an obscure village in barbarous America. It was confidently stated that it would be saved from such an unfitting resting-place by strong action on the part of an International Committee of Artists; but Middletown, though startled by its own good fortune, clung with Yankee tenacity to its rights. Raphael Collin, of Paris, commenting on this in the *Revue des Deux Mondes*, cried out whimsically upon the woes of an art-critic's life, "as if there were not already enough wearisome pilgrimages necessary to remote and uncomfortable places with jaw-breaking names, which must nevertheless be visited for the sake of a single picture!" And a burlesque resolution to carry off the picture by force was adopted at the dinner in London given in honor of Fallères the evening before he set off for America to attend the dedicatory exercises with which Middletown planned to install its new treasure.

For the little rustic college rose to its one great occasion. Bold in their confidence in their dead colleague's fame, the college authorities sent out invitations to all the great ones of the country. Those to whom Gridley was no more than a name on volumes one never read came because the portrait was by Fallères, and those who had no interest in the world of art came to honor the moralist whose noble clear-thinking had simplified the intimate problems of modern life. There was the usual residuum of those who came because the others did, and, also as usual, they were among the most brilliant figures in the procession which filed along, one October morning, under the old maples of Middletown campus.

It was a notable celebration. A bishop opened the exercises with prayer, a United States senator delivered the eulogy of the dead philosopher, the veil uncovering the portrait was drawn away by the mayor of one of America's largest cities, himself an ardent Gridley-ite, and among those who spoke afterward were the presidents of three great universities. The professor's family were represented but scantily. He had had one brother, who had disappeared many years ago under a black cloud of ill report, and one sister who had married and gone West to live. Her two sons, middle-aged merchants from Ohio, gave the only personal note to the occasion by their somewhat tongue-tied and embarrassed presence, for Gridley's aunt was too aged and in-firm to walk with the procession from the Gymnasium, where it formed, to the Library building, where the portrait was installed.

After the inevitable photographers had made their records of the memorable gathering, the procession began to wind its many-colored way back to the Assembly Hall, where it was to lunch. Everyone was feeling relieved that the unveiling had gone off so smoothly, and cheerful at the prospect of food. The undergraduates began lustily to shout their college song, which was caught up by the holiday mood of the older ones. This cheerful tumult gradually died away in the distance, leaving the room of the portrait deserted in an echoing silence. A janitor began to remove the rows of folding chairs. The celebration was over.

Into the empty room there now limped forward a small, shabby old woman with a crutch. "I'm his aunt, that lived with him," she explained apologetically, "and I want to see the picture."

She advanced, peering nearsightedly at the canvas. The janitor continued stacking up chairs until he was stopped by a cry from the newcomer. She was a great deal paler than when she came in. She was staring hard at the portrait and now beckoned him wildly to do the same. "Look at it! Look at it!"

Surprised, he followed the direction of her shaking hand. "Sure, it's Professor Grid to the life!" he said admiringly.

"Look at it! Look at it!" She seemed not to be able to find any other words.

After a prolonged scrutiny he turned to her with a puzzled line between his eyebrows. "Since you've spoken of it, ma'am, I will say that there's a something about the expression of the eyes . . . and mouth, maybe . . . that ain't just the professor. He was more absent-like. It reminds me of somebody else . . . of some face I've seen. . . ."

She hung on his answer, her mild, timid old face drawn like a mask of tragedy. "Who? Who?" she prompted him.

For a time he could not remember, staring at the new portrait and scratching his head. Then it came to him suddenly: "Why, sure, I ought to ha' known without thinkin', seeing the other picture as often as every time I've swep' out the president's office. And Professor Grid always looked like him some, anyhow."

The old woman leaned against the wall, her crutch trembling in her hand. Her eyes questioned him mutely.

"Why, ma'am, who but his own father, to be sure . . . the old Governor."

II

While they had been duly sensible of the luster reflected upon them by the celebration in honor of their distinguished uncle, Professor Gridley's two nephews could scarcely have said truthfully that they enjoyed the occasion. As one of them did say to the other, the whole show was rather out of their line. Their line was wholesale hardware and, being eager to return to it, it was with a distinct feeling of relief that they waited for the train at the station. They were therefore as much displeased as surprised by the sudden appearance to them of their great-aunt, very haggard, her usual extreme timidity swept away by overmastering emotion. She clutched at the two merchants with a great sob of relief: "Stephen! Eli! Come back to the house," she cried, and before they could stop her was hobbling away. They hurried after her, divided between the fear of losing their train and the hope that some inheritance from their uncle had been found. They were not mercenary men, but they felt a not unnatural disappointment that Professor Gridley had left not a penny, not even to his aunt, his one intimate.

They overtook her, scuttling along like some frightened and wounded little animal. "What's the matter, Aunt Amelia?" they asked shortly. "We've got to catch this train."

She faced them. "You can't go now. You've got to make them take that picture away."

"Away!" Their blankness was stupefaction.

She raged at them, the timid, harmless little thing, like a creature distraught. "Didn't you see it? Didn't you *see* it?"

Stephen answered: "Well, no, not to have a good square look at it. The man in front of me kept getting in the way."

Eli admitted: "If you mean you don't see anything in it to make all this hurrah about, I'm with you. It don't look half finished. I don't like that slap-dash style."

She was in a frenzy at their denseness. "Who did it look like?" she challenged them.

"Why, like Uncle Grid, of course. Who else?"

"Yes, yes," she cried, "who else? Who else?"

They looked at each other, afraid that she was crazed, and spoke more gently: "Why, I don't know, I'm sure, who else. Like Grandfather Gridley, of course; but then Uncle Grid always did look like his father."

At this she quite definitely put it out of their power to leave her by fainting away.

They carried her home and laid her on her own bed, where one of them stayed to attend her while the other went back to rescue their deserted baggage. As the door closed behind him the old woman came to herself. "Oh, Stephen," she moaned, "I wish it had killed me, the way it did your uncle."

"What *is* the matter?" asked her great-nephew wonderingly. "What do you think killed him?"

"That awful, awful picture! I know it now as plain as if I'd been there. He hadn't seen it all the time he was sitting for it, though he'd already put in his will that he wanted the college to have it, and when he did see it—" she turned on the merchant with a sudden fury: "How *dare* you say those are your uncle's eyes!"

He put his hand soothingly on hers. "Now, now, Aunt 'Melia, maybe the expression isn't just right, but the color is *fine* . . . just that jet-black his were . . . and the artist has got in exact that funny stiff way uncle's hair stood up over his forehead."

The old woman fixed outraged eyes upon him. "Color!" she said. "And hair! Oh, Lord, help me!"

She sat up on the bed, clutching her nephew's hand, and began to talk rapidly. When, a half-hour later, the other brother returned, neither of them heard him enter the house. It was only when he called at the foot of the stairs that they both started and Stephen ran down to join him.

"You'll see the president . . . you'll fix it?" the old woman cried after him.

"I'll see, Aunt 'Melia," he answered pacifyingly, as he drew his brother out of doors. He looked quite pale and moved, and drew a long breath before he could begin. "Aunt Amelia's been telling me a lot of things I never knew, Eli. It seems that . . . say, did you ever hear that Grandfather Gridley, the Governor, was such a bad lot?"

"Why, mother never said much about her father one way or the other, but I always sort of guessed he wasn't all he might have been from her never bringing us on to visit here until after he died. She used to look queer, too, when folks congratulated her on having such a famous man for father. All the big politicians of his day thought a lot of him. He *was* as smart as chain-lightning!"

"He was a disreputable old scalawag!" cried his other grandson. "Some of the things Aunt Amelia has been telling me make me never want to come back to this part of the country again. Do you know why Uncle Grid lived so poor and scrimped and yet left no money? He'd been taking care of a whole family grandfather had beside ours; and paying back some people grandfather did out of a lot of money on a timber deal fifty years ago; and making it up to a little village in the backwoods that grandfather persuaded to bond itself for a railroad that he knew wouldn't go near it."

The two men stared at each other an instant, reviewing in a new light the life that had just closed. "That's why he never married," said Eli finally.

"No, that's what I said, but Aunt Amelia just went wild when I did. She said . . . gee!" he passed his hand over his eyes with a gesture of mental confusion. "Ain't it strange what can go on under your eyes and you never know it? Why, she says Uncle Grid was just like his father."

The words were not out of his mouth before the other's face of horror made him aware of his mistake. "No! No! Not that! Heavens no! I mean . . . made like him . . . *wanted* to be that kind, 'specially drink . . ." His tongue, unused to phrasing abstractions, stumbled and tripped in his haste to correct the other's impression. "You know how much Uncle Grid used to look like grandfather . . . the same black hair and broad face and thick red lips and a kind of knob on the end of his nose? Well, it seems he had his father's insides, too . . . *but his mother's conscience!* I guess, from what Aunt Amelia says, that the combination made life about as near Tophet for him . . . ! She's the only one to know anything about it, because she's lived with him always, you know, took him when grandmother died and he was a child. She says when he was younger he was like a man fighting a wild beast . . . he didn't dare let up or rest. Some days he wouldn't stop working at his desk all day long, not even to eat, and then he'd grab up a piece of bread and go off for a long tearing tramp that'd last 'most all night. You know what a tremendous physique all the Gridley men have had. Well, Uncle Grid turned into work all the energy the rest of them spent in deviltry. Aunt Amelia said he'd go on like that day after day for a month, and then he'd bring out one of those essays folks are so crazy about. She said she never could bear to *look* at his books . . . seemed to her they were written in his blood. She told him so once and he said it was the only thing to do with blood like his."

He was silent, while his listener made a clucking noise of astonishment. "My! My! I'd have said that there never was anybody more different from grandfather than uncle. Why, as he got on in years he didn't even look like him any more."

This reference gave Stephen a start. "Oh, yes, that's what all this came out for. Aunt Amelia is just wild about this portrait. It's just a notion of hers, of course, but after what she told me I could see, easy, how the idea would come to her. It looks this way, she says, as though Uncle Grid inherited his father's physical make-up complete, and spent all his life fighting it . . . and won out! And here's this picture making him look the way he would if he'd been the worst old . . . as if he'd been like the Governor. She says she feels as though she was the only one to defend uncle . . . as if it could make any difference to him! I guess the poor old lady is a little touched. Likely it's harder for her, losing uncle, than we realized. She just about worshiped him. Queer business, anyhow, wasn't it? Who'd ha' thought he was like that?"

He had talked his unwonted emotion quite out, and now looked at his brother with his usual matter-of-fact eye. "Did you tell the station agent to hold the trunk?"

The other, who was the younger, looked a little abashed. "Well, no; I found the train was so late I thought maybe we could . . . you know there's that business to-morrow . . . !"

His senior relieved him of embarrassment. "That's a good idea. Sure we can. There's nothing we could do if we stayed. It's just a notion of Aunt 'Melia's, anyhow. I agree with her that it don't look so awfully like Uncle Grid, but, then, oil-portraits are never any good. Give me a photograph!"

"It's out of our line, anyhow," agreed the younger, looking at his watch.

III

The president of Middletown College had been as much relieved as pleased by the success of the rather pretentious celebration he had planned. His annoyance was correspondingly keen at the disturbing appearance, in the afternoon reception before the new portrait, of the late professor's aunt, "an entirely insignificant old country woman," he hastily assured M. Fallères after she had been half forced, half persuaded to retire, "whose criticisms were as negligible as her personality."

The tall, Jove-like artist concealed a smile by stroking his great brown beard. When it came to insignificant country people, he told himself, it was hard to draw lines in his present company. He was wondering whether he might not escape by an earlier train.

To the president's remark he answered that no portrait-painter escaped unreasonable relatives of his sitters. "It is an axiom with our guild," he went on, not, perhaps, averse to giving his provincial hosts a new sensation, "that the family is never satisfied, and also that the family has no rights. A sitter is a subject only, like a slice of fish. The only question is how it's done. What difference does it make a century from now, if the likeness is good? It's a work of art or it's nothing." He announced this principle with a regal absence of explanation and turned away; but his thesis was taken up by another guest, a New York art-critic.

"By Jove, it's inconceivable, the ignorance of art in America!" he told the little group before the portrait. "You find everyone so incurably personal in his point of view . . . always objecting to a masterpiece because the watch-chain isn't the kind usually worn by the dear departed."

Someone else chimed in. "Yes, it's incredible that anyone, even an old village granny, should be able to look at that canvas and not be struck speechless by its quality."

The critic was in Middletown to report on the portrait and he now began marshaling his adjectives for that purpose. "I never saw such use of pigment in my life . . . it makes the Whistler 'Carlyle' look like burnt-out ashes . . . the luminous richness of the blacks in the academic gown, the masterly generalization in the treatment of the hair, the placing of those great talons of hands on the canvas carrying out the vigorous lines of the composition, and the unforgettable felicity of those brutally red lips as the one ringing note of color. As for life-likeness, what's the old dame talking about! I never saw such eyes! Not a hint of meretricious emphasis on their luster and yet they fairly flame."

The conversation spread to a less technical discussion as the group was joined by the professor of rhetoric, an ambitious young man with an insatiable craving for sophistication, who felt himself for once entirely in his element in the crowd of celebrities. "It's incredibly good luck that our little two-for-a-cent college should have so fine a thing," he said knowingly. "I've been wondering how such an old skinflint as Gridley ever got the money loose to have his portrait done by—"

A laugh went around the group at the idea. "It was Mackintosh, the sugar king, who put

up for it. He's a great Gridleyite, and persuaded him to sit."

"*Persuade* a man to sit to Falleres!" The rhetoric professor was outraged at the idea.

"Yes, so they say. The professor was dead against it from the first. Falleres himself had to beg him to sit. Falleres said he felt a real inspiration at the sight of the old fellow . . . knew he could make a good thing out of him. He *was* a good subject!"

The little group turned and stared appraisingly at the portrait hanging so close to them that it seemed another living being in their midst. The rhetoric professor was asked what kind of a man the philosopher had been personally, and answered briskly: "Oh, nobody knew him personally . . . the silent old codger. He was a dry-as-dust, bloodless, secular monk—"

He was interrupted by a laugh from the art-critic, whose eyes were still on the portrait.

"Excuse me for any cynical mirth," he said, "but I must say he doesn't look it. I was prepared for any characterization but that. He looks like a powerful son of the Renaissance, who might have lived in that one little vacation of the soul after medievalism stopped hagriding us, and before the modern conscience got its claws on us. And you say he was a blue-nosed Puritan!"

The professor of rhetoric looked an uneasy fear that he was being ridiculed. "I only repeated the village notion of him," he said airily. "He may have been anything. All I know is that he was as secretive as a clam, and about as interesting personally."

"Look at the picture," said the critic, still laughing; "you'll know all about him."

The professor of rhetoric nodded. "You're right, he doesn't look much like my character of him. I never seem to have had a good, square look at him before. I've heard several people say the same thing, that they seemed to understand him better from the portrait than from his living face. There was something about his eyes that kept you from thinking of anything but what he was saying."

The critic agreed. "The eyes are wonderful . . . ruthless in their power . . . fires of hell." He laughed a deprecating apology for his overemphatic metaphor and suggested: "It's possible that there was more to the professorial life than met the eye. Had he a wife?"

"No; it was always a joke in the village that he would never look at a woman."

The critic glanced up at the smoldering eyes of the portrait and smiled. "I've heard of that kind of a man before," he said. "Never known to drink, either, I suppose?"

"Cold-water teetotaler," laughed the professor, catching the spirit of the occasion.

"Look at the color in that nose!" said the critic. "I fancy that the ascetic moralist——"

A very young man, an undergraduate who had been introduced as the junior usher, nodded his head. "Yep, a lot of us fellows always thought old Grid a little too good to be true."

An older man with the flexible mouth of a politician now ventured a contribution to a conversation no longer baffling esthetic: "His father, old Governor Gridley, wasn't he . . . Well, I guess you're right about the son. No halos were handed down in *that* family!"

The laugh which followed this speech was stopped by the approach of Fallères, his commanding presence dwarfing the president beside him. He was listening with a good-natured contempt to the apparently rather anxious murmurs of the latter.

"Of course I know, Mr. Fallères, it is a great deal to ask, but she is so insistent . . . she won't go away and continues to make the most distressing spectacle of herself . . . and several people, since she has said so much about it, are saying that the expression is not that of the late professor. Much against my will I promised to speak to you——"

His mortified uneasiness was so great that the artist gave him a rescuing hand. "Well, Mr. President, what can I do in the matter? The man is dead. I cannot paint him over again, and if I could I would only do again as I did this time, choose that aspect which my judgment told me would make the best portrait. If his habitual vacant expression was not so interesting as another not so permanent a habit of his face . . . why, the poor artist must be allowed some choice. I did not know I was to please his grandmother, and not posterity."

"His aunt," corrected the president automatically.

The portrait-painter accepted the correction with his tolerant smile. "His aunt," he repeated. "The difference is considerable. May I ask what it was you promised her?"

The president summoned his courage. It was easy to gather from his infinitely reluctant insistence how painful and compelling had been the scene which forced him to action. "She wants you to change it . . . to make the expression of the——"

For the first time the artist's equanimity was shaken. He took a step backward.

"Change it!" he said, and although his voice was low the casual chat all over the room stopped short as though a pistol had been fired.

"It's not *my* idea!" The president confounded himself in self-exoneration. "I merely promised, to pacify her, to ask you if you could not do some little thing that would——"

The critic assumed the rôle of conciliator. "My dear sir, I don't believe you quite understand what you are asking. It's as though you asked a priest to make just a little change in the church service and leave out the 'not' in the Commandments."

"I only wish to know Mr. Fallères's attitude," said the president stiffly, a little nettled by the other's note of condescension. "I presume he will be willing to take the responsibility of it himself and explain to the professor's aunt that *I* have done——"

The artist had recovered from his lapse from Olympian calm and now nodded, smiling: "Dear me, yes, Mr. President, I'm used to irate relatives."

The president hastened away and the knots of talkers in other parts of the room, who had been looking with expectant curiosity at the group before the portrait, resumed their loud-toned chatter. When their attention was next drawn in the same direction, it was by a shaky old treble, breaking, quavering with weakness. A small, shabby old woman, leaning on a crutch, stood looking up imploringly at the tall painter.

"My dear madam," he broke in on her with a kindly impatience, "all that you say about Professor Gridley is much to his credit, but what has it to do with me?"

"You painted his portrait," she said with a simplicity that was like stupidity. "And I am his aunt. You made a picture of a bad man. I know he was a good man."

"I painted what I saw," sighed the artist wearily. He looked furtively at his watch.

The old woman seemed dazed by the extremity of her emotion. She looked about her silently, keeping her eyes averted from the portrait that stood so vividly like a living man beside her. "I don't know what to do!" she murmured with a little moan. "I can't *bear* it to have it stay here—people forget so. Everybody'll think that Gridley looked like *that!* And there isn't anybody but me. He never had anybody but me."

The critic tried to clear the air by a roundly declaratory statement of principles. "You'll pardon my bluntness, madam; but you must remember that none but the members of Professor Gridley's family are concerned in the exact details of his appearance. Fifty years from now nobody will remember how he looked, one way or the other. The world is only concerned with portraits as works of art."

She followed his reasoning with a strained and docile attention and now spoke eagerly as though struck by an unexpected hope: "If that's all, why put his name to it? Just hang it up, and call it anything."

She shrank together timidly and her eyes reddened at the laughter which greeted this naïve suggestion.

Fallères looked annoyed and called his defender off. "Oh, never mind explaining me," he said, snapping his watch shut. "You'll never get the rights of it through anybody's head who hasn't himself sweat blood over a composition only to be told that the other side of the sitter's profile is usually considered the prettier. After all, we have the last word, since the sitter dies and the portrait lives."

The old woman started and looked at him attentively.

"Yes," said the critic, laughing, "immortality's not a bad balm for pin-pricks."

The old woman turned very pale and for the first time looked again at the portrait. An electric thrill seemed to pass through her as her eyes encountered the bold, evil ones fixed on her. She stood erect with a rigid face, and "Immortality!" she said, under her breath.

Fallères moved away to make his adieux to the president, and the little group of his satellites straggled after him to the other end of the room. For a moment there was no one near the old woman to see the crutch furiously upraised, hammer-like, or to stop her sudden passionate rush upon the picture.

At the sound of cracking cloth, they turned back, horrified. They saw her, with an insane violence, thrust her hands into the gaping hole that had been the portrait's face and, tearing the canvas from end to end, fall upon the shreds with teeth and talon.

All but Fallères flung themselves toward her, dragging her away. With a movement as instinctive he rushed for the picture, and it was to him, as he stood aghast before the ruined canvas, that the old woman's shrill treble was directed, above the loud shocked voices of those about her: "There ain't anything immortal but souls!" she cried.

THEODORE DREISER (1871-   )

SANCTUARY

(1918)

I

Primarily, there were the conditions under which she was brought to fifteen years of age: the crowded, scummy tenements; the narrow green-painted halls with their dim gas-jets, making the entrance look more like that of a morgue than a dwelling-place; the dirty halls and rooms with their green or blue or brown walls painted to save the cost of paper; the bare wooden floors, long since saturated with every type of grease and filth from oleomargarine and suet leaked from cheap fats or meats, to beer and whiskey and tobacco-juice. A little occasional scrubbing by some would-be hygienic tenant was presumed to keep or make clean some of the chambers and halls.

And then the streets outside—any of the streets by which she had ever been surrounded—block upon block of other red, bare, commonplace tenements crowded to the doors with human life, the space before them sped over by noisy, gassy trucks and vehicles of all kinds. And stifling in summer, dusty and icy in winter; decorated on occasion by stray cats and dogs, pawing in ashcans, watched over by lordly policemen, and always running with people, people, people—who made their living heaven only knows how, existing in such a manner as their surroundings suggested.

In this atmosphere were always longshoremen, wagon-drivers, sweepers of floors, washers of dishes, waiters, janitors, workers in laundries, factories—mostly in indifferent or decadent or despairing conditions. And all of these people existed, in so far as she ever knew, upon that mysterious, evanescent and fluctuating something known as the weekly wage. Always about her there had been drunkenness, fighting, complaining, sickness or death; the police coming in, and arresting one and another; the gas man, the rent man, the furniture man, hammering at doors for their due—and not getting it—in due time the undertaker also arriving amid a great clamor, as though lives were the most precious things imaginable.

It is entirely conceivable that in viewing or in meditating upon an atmosphere such as this, one might conclude that no good could come out of it. What! a dung-heap grow a flower? Exactly, and often, a flower—but not to grow to any glorious maturity probably. Nevertheless a flower of the spirit at least might have its beginnings there. And if it shrank or withered in the miasmatic atmosphere—well, conceivably, that might be normal, although in reality all flowers thus embedded in infancy do not so wither. There are flowers and flowers.

Viewing Madeleine Kinsella at the ages of five, seven, eleven and thirteen even, it might have been conceded that she was a flower of sorts—admittedly not a brave, lustrous one of the orchid or gardenia persuasion, but a flower nevertheless. Her charm was simpler, more retiring, less vivid than is usually accorded the compliment of beauty. She was never rosy, never colorful in the high sense, never daring or aggressive. Always, from her infancy on, she seemed to herself and others to be slipping about the corners and out-of-the-way places of life, avoiding it, staring at it with wide, lamblike eyes, wondering at things, often fearfully.

Her face, always delicately oval and pale, was not of the force which attracted. Her eyes, a milkish blue-gray with a suggestion of black in the iris, her hair black, her hands long-fingered and slim, were not of a type which would appeal to the raw youth of her world. Unconsciously, and ever, her slender, longish body sank into graceful poses. Beside the hard, garish, colorful, strident types of her neighborhoods—the girls whom the boys liked—she was not fascinating, and yet, contemplated at odd moments as she grew, she was appealing enough—at times beautiful.

What most affected her youth and her life was the internal condition of her family, the poverty and general worthlessness of her parents. They were as poor as their poorest neighbors, and quarrelsome, unhappy and mean-spirited into the bargain. Her father came dimly into her understanding at somewhere near her seventh or eighth year as an undersized, contentious and drunken and wordy man, always more or less out of a job, irritated with her mother and her sister and brother, and always, as her mother seemed to think, a little the worse for drink.

"You're a liar! You're a liar! You're a liar! You're a liar!"—how well she remembered this sing-song echoing reiteration of his, in whatever basement or hole they were living at the time! "You're a liar! I never did it! You're a liar! I wasn't there!"

Her mother, often partially intoxicated or morose because of her own ills, was only too willing to rejoin in kind. Her elder sister and brother, much more agreeable in their way and as much put upon as herself, were always coming in or running out somewhere and staying while the storm lasted; while she, shy and always a little frightened, seemed to look upon it all as unavoidable, possibly even essential. The world was always so stern, so mysterious, so non-understandable to Madeleine.

Again it might be, and often was, "Here, you, you brat, go an' get me a can o' beer! Gwan, now!" which she did quickly and fearfully enough, running to the nearest wretched corner saloon with the "can" or "growler," her slim little fingers closed tightly over the five-cent piece or dime entrusted to her, her eyes taking in the wonders and joys of the street even as she ran. She was so small at the time that her little arms were unable to reach quite the level of the bar, and she had to accept the aid of the bartender or some drinker. Then she would patiently wait while one of them teased her as to her size or until the beer was handed down.

Once, and once only, three "bad boys," knowing what she was going for and how wretched and shabby was her father, not able to revenge himself on any one outside his family, had seized her en route, forced open her hand and run away with the dime, leaving her to return fearsomely to her father, rubbing her eyes, and to be struck and abused soundly and told to fight—"Blank-blank you, what the hell are you good for if you can't do that?"

Only the vile language and the defensive soberness of her mother at the time saved her from a worse fate. As for the boys who had stolen the money, they only received curses and awful imprecations, which harmed no one.

Wretched variations of this same existence were endured by the other two members of the family, her brother Frank and her sister Tina. The former was a slim and nervous youth, given to fits of savage temper like his father and not to be ordered and controlled exactly as his father would have him. At times, as Madeleine recalled, he appeared terribly resentful of the conditions that surrounded him and cursed and swore and even threatened to leave; at other times he was placid enough, at least not inclined to share the dreadful scenes which no one could avoid where her father was. At the age of twelve or thirteen he secured work in a box-factory somewhere and for a while brought his wages home. But often there was no breakfast or dinner for him, and when his father and mother were deep in their cups or quarreling things were so generally neglected that even where home ties were strong no one of any worldly experience could have endured them, and he ran away.

His mother was always complaining of "the lumbago" and of not being able to get up, even when he and Tina were working and bringing home a portion of their weekly wage or all of it. If she did, it was only to hover over the wretched cookstove and brew herself a little tea and complain as before.

Madeleine had early, in her ignorant and fearsome way, tried to help, but she did not always know how and her mother was either too ill or too disgruntled with life to permit her to assist, had she been able.

As it had been with Frank so it was with Tina, only it came sooner.

When Madeleine was only five Tina was a grown girl of ten, with yellow hair and a pretty, often smiling face, and was already working somewhere—in a candy store—for a dollar and a half a week. Later, when Madeleine was eight and Tina thirteen, the latter had graduated to a button-works and was earning three.

There was something rather admirable and yet disturbing connected dimly with Tina in Madeleine's mind, an atmosphere of rebelliousness and courage which she could not have described, lacking as she did a mind that registered the facts of life clearly. She only saw Tina, pretty and strong, coming and going from her ninth to her thirteenth year, refusing to go for beer at her father's order and being cursed for it, even struck at or thrown at by him, sometimes by her mother, and often standing at the foot of the stairs after work hours or on a Sunday afternoon or evening, looking at the crowded street or walking up and down with other girls and boys, when her mother wanted her to be doing things in the house—sweeping, washing dishes, making beds —dreary, gray tasks all.

"Fixin' your hair again! Fixin' your hair again! Fixin' your hair again!" she could hear her father screaming whenever she paused before the one cracked mirror to arrange her hair. "Always in front of that blank-blank mirror fixin' her hair! If you don't get away from in front of it I'll throw you an' the mirror in the street! What the hell are you always fixin' your hair for? Say? What're you always fixin' your hair for? Say! What? What're you always fixin' your hair for?"

But Tina was never cast down apparently, only silent. At times she sang and walked with

an air. She dressed herself as attractively as possible, as if with the few things she had she was attempting to cast off the burden of the life by which she was surrounded. Always she was hiding things away from the others, never wanting them to touch anything of hers. And how she had hated her father as she grew, in bitter moments calling him a "sot" and a "fool."

Tina had never been very obedient, refusing to go to church or to do much of anything about the house. Whenever her father and mother were drinking or fighting she would slip away and stay with some girl in the neighborhood that she knew. And in spite of all this squalor and misery and the fact that they moved often and the food was bad, Tina, once she was twelve or thirteen, always seemed able to achieve an agreeable appearance.

Madeleine often remembered her in a plaid skirt she had got somewhere, which looked beautiful on her, and a little gilt pin which she wore at her neck. And she had a way of doing her yellow hair high on her head, which had stuck in Madeleine's mind perhaps because of her father's rude comments on it.

II

It is not surprising that Madeleine came to her twelfth and thirteenth years without any real understanding of the great world about her and without any definite knowledge or skill. Her drunken mother was now more or less dependent upon her, her father having died of pneumonia and her brother and sister having disappeared to do for themselves.

Aside from petty beginners' tasks in shops or stores, or assisting her mother at washing or cleaning, there was little that she could do at first. Mrs. Kinsella, actually compelled by the need for rent or food or fuel after a time, would get occasional work in a laundry or kitchen or at scrubbing or window-cleaning, but not for long. The pleasure of drink would soon rob her of that.

At these tasks Madeleine helped until she secured work in a candy factory in her thirteenth year at the wage of three-thirty a week. But even with this little money paid in regularly there was no assurance that her mother would add sufficient to it to provide either food or warmth. Betimes, and when Madeleine was working, her mother cheered her all too obvious sorrows with the bottle, and at nights or week-ends rewarded Madeleine with a gabble which was all the more painful because no material comfort came with it.

The child actually went hungry at times. Usually, after a few drinks, her mother would begin to weep and recite her past ills: a process which reduced her timorous and very sympathetic daughter to complete misery. In sheer desperation the child sought for some new way in her own mind. A reduction in the working-force of the candy factory, putting her back in the ranks of the work-seekers once more, and a neighbor perceiving her wretched state and suggesting that some extra helpers were wanted in a department store at Christmas-time, she applied there, but so wretched were her clothes by now that she was not even considered.

Then a man who had a restaurant in a near-by street gave her mother and Madeleine positions as dishwashers, but he was compelled to discharge her mother, although he wished to retain Madeleine. From this last, however, because of the frightening attentions of the cook, she had to flee, and without obtaining a part of the small pittance which was due her. Again, and because in times past she had aided her mother to clean in one place and another, she was able to get a place as servant in a family.

Those who know anything of the life of a domestic know how thoroughly unsatisfactory it is—the leanness, the lack of hope. As a domestic, wherever she was—and she obtained no superior places for the time being—she had only the kitchen for her chief chamber or a cubby-hole under the roof. Here, unless she was working elsewhere in the house or chose to visit her mother occasionally, she was expected to remain. Pots and pans and scrubbing and cleaning and bed-making were her world. If any one aside from her mother ever wanted to see her (which was rare) he or she could only come into the kitchen, an ugly and by day inconvenient realm.

She had, as she soon came to see, no privileges whatsoever. In the morning she was expected to be up before any one else, possibly after working late the night before. Breakfast had to be served for others before she herself could eat—what was left. Then came the sweeping and cleaning. In one place which she obtained in her fifteenth year the husband annoyed her so, when his wife was not looking, that she had to leave; in another it was the son. By now she was becoming more attractive, although by no means beautiful or daring.

But wherever she was and whatever she was doing, she could not help thinking of her mother and Tina and Frank and her father, and of the grim necessities and errors and

vices which had seemed to dominate them. Neither her brother nor her sister did she ever see again. Her mother, she felt (and this was due to a sensitiveness and a sympathy which she could not possibly overcome), she would have with her for the rest of her days unless, like the others, she chose to run away.

Daily her mother was growing more inadequate and less given to restraint or consideration. As "bad" as she was, Madeleine could not help thinking what a "hard" time she had had. From whatever places she obtained work in these days (and it was not often any more) she was soon discharged, and then she would come inquiring after Madeleine, asking to be permitted to see her. Naturally, her shabby dress and shawl and rag of a hat, as well as her wastrel appearance, were an affront to any well-ordered household. Once in her presence, whenever Madeleine was permitted to see her, she would begin either a cozening or a lachrymose account of her great needs. "It's out o' oil I am, me dear," or "Wurra, I have no wood" or "bread" or "meat"—never drink. "Ye won't let yer pore old mother go cold or hungry, now, will ye? That's the good girl now. Fifty cents now, if ye have it, me darlin', or a quarter, an' I'll not be troublin' ye soon again. Even a dime, if ye can spare me no more. God'll reward ye. I'll have work o' me own tomorra. That's the good girl now—ye won't let me go away without anything."

Oscillating between shame and sympathy, her daughter would take from the little she had and give it to her, tremulous for fear the disturbing figure would prove her undoing. Then the old woman would go out, lurching sometimes in her cups, and disappear, while an observant fellow servant was probably seeing and reporting to the mistress, who, of course, did not want her to come there and so told the girl, or more practical still, discharged her.

Thus from her fourteenth to her sixteenth year she was shunted from house to house and from shop to shop, always in the vain hope that this time her mother might let her alone.

And at the very same time, life, sweetened by the harmonies of youth in the blood, was calling—that exterior life which promised everything because so far it had given nothing. The little simple things of existence, the very ordinary necessities of clothing and ornament, with which the heart of youth and the inherent pride of appearance are gratified, had a value entirely disproportionate to their worth. Yes, already she had turned the age wherein the chemic harmonies in youth began to sing, thought to thought, color to color, dream to dream. She was being touched by the promise of life itself.

And then, as was natural, love in the guise of youth, a rather sophisticated gallant somewhat above the world in which she was moving, appeared and paid his all but worthless court to her. He was physically charming, the son of a grocer of some means in the vicinity in which she was working, a handsome youth with pink cheeks and light hair and blue eyes, and vanity enough for ten. Because she was shy and pretty he became passingly interested in her.

"Oh, I saw you cleaning the windows yesterday," this with a radiant, winning smile; or "You must live down toward Blake Street. I see you going down that way once in a while."

Madeleine acknowledged rather shamefacedly that it was true. That so dashing a boy should be interested in her was too marvelous.

In the evenings, or at any time, it was easy for a youth of his skill and *savoir-faire* to pick her out of the bobbing stream of humanity in which she occasionally did errands or visited her mother in her shabby room, and to suggest that he be permitted to call upon her. Or, failing that, because of her mother's shabby quarters and her mother herself, that the following Sunday would be ideal for an outing to one of those tawdry, noisy beaches to which he liked to go with other boys and girls in a car.

A single trip to Wonderland, a single visit to one of its halls where music sounded to the splash of the waves and where he did his best to teach her to dance, a single meal in one of its gaudy, noisy restaurants, a taste of its whirly pleasures, and a new color and fillip were given to hope, a new and seemingly realizable dream of happiness implanted in her young mind. The world was happier than she had thought, or could be made so; not all people fought and screamed at each other. There were such things as tenderness, soft words, sweet words.

But the way of so sophisticated a youth with a maid was brief and direct. His mind was of that order which finds in the freshness of womankind a mere passing delight, something to be deflowered and then put aside. He was a part of a group that secured its happiness in rifling youth, the youth of those whose lives were so dull and bleak that a few words of kindness, a little change of scene, the mere proximity of experience and force such as

they had never known, were pay ample for anything which they might give or do.

And of these Madeleine was one.

Never having had anything in her own life, the mere thought of a man so vigorous and handsome, one with knowledge enough to show her more of life than she had ever dreamed of, to take her to places of color and light, to assure her that she was fitted for better things even though they were not immediately forthcoming, was sufficient to cause her to place faith where it was least worthy of being placed. To win his way there was even talk of marriage later on, that love should be generous and have faith—and then—

III

Plain-clothesman Amundsen, patrolling hawk-like the region of Fourteenth and K streets, not so far from Blake, where Madeleine had lived for a time, was becoming interested in and slightly suspicious of a new face.

For several days at odd hours, he had seen a girl half-slinking, half-brazening her way through a region the very atmosphere of which was blemishing to virtue. To be sure, he had not yet seen her speak to any one; nor was there that in her glance or manner which caused him to feel that she might.

Still—with the assurance of his authority and his past skill in trapping many he followed discreetly, seeing where she went, how she lingered for awhile nervously, then returned as she had come. She was very young, not more than seventeen.

He adjusted his tie and collar and decided to attempt his skill.

"Excuse me, Miss. Out for a little stroll? So am I. Mind my walking along with you a little way? Wouldn't like to come and have a drink, would you? I work in an automobile place over here in Grey Street, and I'm just off for the afternoon. Live here in the neighborhood?"

Madeleine surveyed this stranger with troubled eyes. Since the day her youthful lover had deserted her, and after facing every conceivable type of ill, but never being willing to confess or fall back upon her drunken, dreaming mother for aid, she had tested every device. The necessities and expenses incident to a prospective, and to her degrading state, as well as the continued care of her mother, had compelled her, as she had finally seen it, to come to this—for a time anyhow. A street girl, finding her wandering and crying, had taken her in hand and shown her, after aiding her for weeks, how to make her way.

Her burden that she feared so much was artificially if ruthlessly and criminally disposed of. Then she was shown the way of the streets until she could gain a new foothold in life; only, as she had since learned, it was difficult for her to accommodate herself to this fell traffic. She was not of it spiritually. She really did not intend to continue in it; it was just a temporary makeshift, born of fear and a dumb despair.

But neither Detective Amundsen nor the law was ready to believe that. To the former she seemed as worthless as any—one of those curious, uncared-for flowers never understood by the dull.

In a nearby café she had listened to his inquiries, the fact that he had a room in a nearby hotel, or could secure one. Contemning a fate which drove her to such favors, and fully resolved to leave it soon, to make something better of her life in the future, she went with him.

Then came the scarring realization that he was an officer of the law, a cynical, contemptuous hawk smirking over her tears and her explanations. It was absolutely nothing to him that she was so young and could scarcely have been as hardened as he pretended. She was compelled to walk through the streets with him to the nearest police station, while he nodded to or stopped to explain to passing brothers of the cloth the nature of his latest conquest.

There was the registering of her under the false name that she chose, rather than be exposed under her true one, before a brusque and staring sergeant in shirtsleeves; a cell with a wooden bench, the first she had ever known; a matron who searched her; then a ride somewhere in a closed vehicle, and the usual swift and confusing arraignment before a judge whose glance was seemingly so cold that it was frightening.

"Nellie Fitzpatrick; Officer Amundsen, Eighth Precinct."

The friend who had taught her the ways of the streets had warned her that if caught and arrested it might mean months of incarceration in some institution, the processes or corrective meaning of which she did not quite comprehend. All that she had grasped fully was that it meant a severance from her freedom, the few little things, pitiful as they were, that she could call her own. And now here she was, in the clutches of the law, and with no one to defend her.

The testimony of the officer was as it had been in hundreds of cases before this; he had been walking his beat and she had accosted him, as usual.

There being no legal alternative, the magistrate had held her for sentence, pending investigation, and the investigation proving, as it only could, that her life would be better were some corrective measures applied to it, she was sent away. She had never had any training worthy the name. Her mother was an irresponsible inebriate. A few months in some institution where she could be taught some trade or craft would be best.

And so it was that for a period of a year she was turned over to the care of the Sisterhood of the Good Shepherd.

IV

The gray and bony walls of that institution starkly dominated one of the barest and most unprepossessing regions of the city. Its northern façade fronted a stone-yard, beyond which were the rocks of the racing Sound and a lighthouse. To the east, rocks and the river, a gray expanse in winter picked over by gulls, mourned over by the horns of endless craft. To the south, bare coal-yards, wagon-yards, tenements.

Twice weekly, sentenced delinquents of various ages—the "children," of whom Madeleine was one; the "girls," ranging from eighteen to thirty; the "women," ranging from thirty to fifty; and the old people, ranging from fifty until the last years of life—were brought here in an all but air-tight cage, boxed like a great circus van, and with only small barred air-holes at the top. Inside the van were bare, hard benches, one against either wall. A representative of the probation and control system of the city, a gaunt female of many years, sat within; also an officer of such prodigious proportions that the mere sight of him might well raise the inquiry of why so much unnecessary luggage. For amusement in dull hours he smoothed his broad mouth with the back of his red, hairy hand, and dreamed of bygone days.

The institution itself was operated by a Mother Superior and thirty nuns, all of the order mentioned, all expert in their separate ways in cooking, housekeeping, laundering, buying, lace-making, teaching, and a half dozen other practical or applied arts.

Within the institution were separate wings or sections for each of the four groups before mentioned, sections in which each had its separate working, eating, sleeping and playing rooms. Only one thing was shared in common: the daily, and often twice or thrice daily, religious ceremonies in the great chapel, a lofty, magi-decorated and be-altared and be-candled chamber, whose tall, thin spire surmounted with a cross might easily be seen from many of the chambers in which the different groups worked. There were masses in the mornings, vespers and late prayers in the afternoons, often late prayers at night or on holidays, when additional services of one kind and another were held. To the religious-minded these were of course consoling. To the contrary-minded they became at times a strain.

Always, and over all the work and all the routine relaxations or pleasures of the institution, there hung the grim insistence of the law, its executive arm, upon order, seemliness, and, if not penance, at least a servility of mind which was the equivalent thereof. Let the voices of the nuns be never so soft, their footfalls light, their manners courteous, their ways gentle, persuasive, sympathetic, their mood tender; back of it all lay the shadow of the force which could forthwith return any or all to the rough hands of the police, the stern and not-to-be-evaded dictum of the courts.

This, much more than any look of disappointment or displeasure, if such were ever necessary, spoke to these delinquents or victims, whatever their mood, and quieted them in their most rebellious hours. Try as they would, they could not but remember that it was the law that had placed them here and now detained them. That there reigned here peace, order, sweetness and harmony, was well enough, comforting in cases, yet and always the life here had obviously a two-fold base: one the power of the law itself, the other the gentle, appealing, beautiful suasion of the nuns.

But to so inexperienced and as yet unreasoning a child as Madeleine all of this savored at this time of but one thing: the sharp, crude, inconsiderate and uninquiring forces of law or life, which seemed never to stop and inquire how or why, but only to order how, and that without mercy. Like some frightened animal faced by a terrifying enemy, she had thus far been able to think only of some darksome corner into which she might slip and hide, a secret place so inconspicuous and minute that the great savage world without would not trouble or care to follow.

And well enough the majority of the Sisterhood, especially those in immediate authority over her, understood the probable direction and ramifications of her present thoughts.

They knew her mood, for had they not during years past dealt with many such? And stern as was the law, they were not unmindful of her welfare. So long as she was willing and obedient there was but one thing more: that somehow her troubled or resentful or congealed and probably cruelly injured mind should be wooed from its blind belief in the essential injustice of life, to be made to feel, as they themselves were ready to believe, that all paths were not closed, all forces not essentially dark or evil.

For them there was hope of sorts for all, a way out, and many—even she—might find ways and means of facing life, better possibly than any she had ever known.

V

Sister St. Agnes, for instance, who controlled the spotlessly clean but barnlike and bleak room in which were a hundred machines for the sewing of shirtwaists, was a creature of none too fortunate a history herself.

Returning at the age of eighteen and at the death of her father from a convent in which she had been placed by him in order to escape the atmosphere of a home which he himself had found unsatisfactory, she had found a fashionable mother leading a life of which she could scarcely conceive, let alone accept. The taint, the subterfuge, the self-indulgent waste, had as soon sickened her as had the streets Madeleine.

Disappointed, she felt herself after a time incapable of enduring it and had fled, seeking first to make her way in a world which offered only meagre wages and a barren life to those incapable of enduring its rugged and often shameless devices; later, again wearied of her own trials, she had returned to the convent in which she had been trained and asked to be schooled for service there. Finding the life too simple for a nature grown more rugged, she had asked to be, and had been, transferred to the House of the Good Shepherd, finding there for the first time, in this institution, duties and opportunities which somehow matched her ideals.

And by the same token the Mother Superior of this same institution, Mother St. Bertha, who often came through and inquired into the story of each one, was of a history and of an order of mind which was not unlike that of Sister St. Agnes, only it had even more of genuine pathos and suffering in it. The daughter of a shoe manufacturer, she had seen her father fail, her mother die of consumption, a favorite brother drink and carouse until he finally fell under the blight of disease and died. The subsequent death of her father, to whom she had devoted her years, and the failing of her own dreams of a personal love, had saddened her, and she sought out and was admitted to this order in the hope that she, too, might still make especial use of a life that promised all too little in the world outside.

Her great comfort was in having some one or something to love, the satisfaction of feeling that lives which otherwise might have come to nothing had by some service of hers been lifted to a better state. And in that thought she worked here daily, going about among those incarcerated in different quarters, seeing to it that their tasks were not too severe, their comforts and hopes, where hope still remained, in nowise betrayed.

But to Madeleine at first the solemn habits of the nuns, as well as the gray gingham apron she had to don, the grayer woolen dress, the severe manner in which she had to dress her hair, her very plain shoes, the fact that she had to rise at six-thirty, attend mass and then breakfast at eight, work from eight-thirty to twelve-thirty, and again from one-thirty to four; lunch regularly at twelve-thirty and sup at six, attend a form of prayer service at four-thirty, play at simple games with her new companions between five and six and again between seven and nine, and then promptly retire to a huge sleeping-ward set with small white iron beds in long rows, and lit, after the retiring bell had sounded, by small oil cups or candles burning faintly before various images, all smacked of penance, the more disturbing because it was strange, a form of personal control which she had not sought and could not at once accept.

Nor could she help thinking that some severer form of punishment was yet to be meted out to her, or might ensue by reason of one unavoidable error or another. Life had always been so with her. But, once here a time, things proved not so bad.

The large workroom with its hundred machines and its tall windows, which afforded a stark view of the coal-pockets to the south, and the river with its boats and gulls, proved not unpleasing. The clean, bright windows, polished floors and walls—washed and cleaned by the inmates themselves, the nuns not disdaining to do their share—and the habits of the Sisters, their white-fringed hoods, black robes and clinking beads and their silent tread and low speech, impressed her greatly.

The fact that there was no severe reproof for any failure to comprehend at first, but only slow and patient explanations of simple things, not difficult in themselves to do; that aside from the routine duties, the marching in line with hands crossed over breast and head up, as well as genuflections at mass, prayers before and after meals, at rising and on retiring and at the peal of the Angelus, morning, noon and night, there was no real oppression, finally caused her to like it.

The girls who were here with her, shy or silent or cold or indifferent at first, and each with her world of past experiences, contacts, and relationships locked in her heart, were still, placed as they were elbow to elbow at work, at meals, at prayer, at retiring, incapable of not achieving some kind of remote fellowship which eventually led to speech and confidences.

Thus the young girl who sat next at her right in the sewing-room—Viola Patters by name, a brave, blonde, cheerful little thing—although she had endured much that might be called ill-fortune, was still intensely interested in life.

By degrees and as they worked the two reached an understanding. Viola confessed that her father, who was a non-union painter by trade, had always worked well enough when he could get work, but that he managed badly and could not always get it. Her mother was sickly and they were very poor and there were many children.

Viola had first worked in a box-factory, where she had been able to earn only three dollars or less at piece work—"pasting corners," as she described it—and once she had been sworn at and even thrown away from a table at which she had been working because she didn't do it right, and then she quit. Then her father in turn swearing at her for her "uppishness," she had got work in a five-and-ten-cent store, where she had received three dollars a week and a commission of one per cent on her sales, which were not sufficient to yield more than a dollar more. Then she had secured a better place in a department store at five dollars a week, and there it was that she had come by the handsome boy who had caused her so much trouble.

He was a taxi-driver, who always had a car at his disposal when he worked, only it was very seldom that he cared to work. Although he married her swiftly enough and took her away from her family, still he had not supported her very well, and shortly after they were married he was arrested and accused with two others of stealing a machine and selling it, and after months and months of jail life he had been sentenced to three years in the penitentiary.

In the meantime he had called upon her to aid him, pressed her to raise sums of which she had never previously dreamed—and by ways of which she had never previously dreamed—was pleaded with, all but ordered—and still she loved him. And then in executing the "how" of it she had been picked up by the police and sent here, as had Madeleine, only she never told, not even to Madeleine, what the police had never discovered—that at the suggestion of her first love she had included robbery among her arts.

"But I don't care," she had whispered finally as they worked. "He was good to me, anyhow, when he had work. He was crazy about me, and he liked to go places and dance and eat and see shows when he had money, and he always took me. Gee, the times we've had! And if he wants me to stick to him when he gets out, I will. He ain't half as bad as some. Gee, you oughta hear some of the girls talk!"

And so it was finally that Madeleine was induced to tell her story.

There were other girls here who, once this bond of sympathy was struck, were keen enough to tell their tales—sad, unfortunate, harried lives all—and somehow the mere telling of them restored to Madeleine some of her earlier faint confidence or interest in life. It was "bad," but it was vivid. For in spite of their unfortunate beginnings, the slime in which primarily and without any willing of their own they had been embedded and from which nearly all were seeking to crawl upwards, and bravely enough, they had heart for and faith in life.

In all cases, apparently, love was their star as well as their bane. They thought chiefly of the joy that might be had in joining their lives with some man or being out in the free world, working again possibly, at least in touch in some feeble way with the beauty and gayety of life, as beauty and gayety manifested themselves to them.

And so by degrees, the crash of her own original hopes echoing less and less loudly in the distance, the pain of her great shame and rude awakening passed farther and farther from her. The smoothness and regularity of this austere life, indifferent as it seemed at times, consoled her by its very security and remoteness from the world. It was lean and spare, to be sure, but it offered safety and rest to the mind and heart. Now, rising in her dim, silent ward of a morning, repeating her instructed prayers, marching in silence to chapel, to breakfast, to work, hearing only the soft hum of the machines, marching again to chapel, playing each day, but not too noisily, and finally retiring in the same ordered and silent way to her tiny bed, she was soothed and healed.

And yet, or perhaps because of this, she could not help thinking of the clangor and crash of the world without. It had been grim and painful to her, but in its rude, brutal way it had been alive. The lighted streets at night! The cars! That dancing pavilion in which once she had been taught to dance by the great blue sea! The vanished touches of her faithless lover's hands—his kisses—brief, so soon over! Where was he now in the great strange world outside? With whom? What was she like? And would he tire of her as quickly? Treat her as badly? Where was Tina? Frank? Her mother? What had happened to her mother? Not a word had she heard.

To Sister St. Agnes, after a time, sensing her to be generous, faithful, patient, she had confided all concerning herself and her mother, crying on her shoulder, and the Sister had promised to learn what she could. But the investigation proving that her mother had been sent to the work-house, she deemed it best to say nothing for the present. Madeleine would find her quickly enough on returning to the world. Why cloud the new budding life with so shameful a memory?

VI

And then once more, in due time, and with the memory of these things clinging fast to her, she was sent forth into the world, not quite as poorly-armed as before, perhaps, but still with the limited equipment which her own innate disposition compelled.

After many serious and presumably wise injunctions as to the snares and pitfalls of this world, and accompanied by a black-habited nun, who took her direct to one of those moral and religious families whose strict adherence to the tenets of this particular faith was held to provide an ideal example, she was left to her own devices and the type of work she had previously followed, the nuns themselves being hard put to it to discover anything above the most menial forms of employment for their various charges. Theirs was a type of schooling and training which did not rise above a theory of morality requiring not so much skill as faith and blind obedience.

And again, here, as in the institution itself, the idea of a faith, a religion, a benign power above that of man and seeking his welfare, surrounded her as the very air itself or as an aura, although she personally was by no means ready to accept it, never having given it serious thought.

Everywhere here, as in the institution itself, were little images or colored pictures of saints, their brows circled by stars or crowns, their hands holding sceptres or lilies, their bodies arrayed in graceful and soothing robes of white, blue, pink and gold. Their faces were serene, their eyes benignly contemplative, yet to Madeleine they were still images only, pretty and graceful, even comforting, but at so great variance to life as she knew it as to be little more than pretty pictures.

In the great church which they attended, and to which they persuaded her to accompany them, were more of these same candle-lit pictures of saints, images and altars starred with candles, many or few, at which she was wont to stare in wonder and awe. The vestments of the priest and the acolytes, the white-and-gold and red-and-gold of the chasuble and the stole and the cope, the gold and silver crosses, chalices and winecups, overawed her inexperienced and somewhat impressionable mind without convincing it of the immanence of superior forces whose significance or import she could in nowise guess. God, God, God— she heard of Him and the passion and death of the self-sacrificing Lord Jesus.

And here, as there, the silence, the order, the cleanliness and regularity, as well as simplicity, were the things which most invested her reason and offered the greatest contrasts to her old life.

She had not known or sensed the significance of these things before. Now, day by day, like the dripping of water, the ticking of time, they made an impression, however slight. Routine, routine, routine, and the habit and order and color of a vast and autocratic religion, made their lasting impression upon her.

And yet, in spite of an occasional supervisory visit on the part of one or other of the nuns of the probation department, she was not only permitted but compelled to work out her life as best she might, and upon such wages as she could command or devise. For all the prayers and the good-will of the nuns, life was as insistent and driving as ever. It did not appear to be so involved with religion. In spite of the admonitions of the church, the family for whom she was working saw little more in its religious obligation than that she should be housed and fed according to her material merits. If she wished to better herself, as she soon very clearly saw she must, she would have to develop a skill which she did not now have and which, once developed, would make her of small use here. At the same time, if the months spent in the institution had conveyed to her the reasonableness of making something better of her life than hitherto she had been able to do, the world, pleasure, hope, clanged as insistently and as wooingly as ever before. But how? How? was the great problem. Hers was no resourceful, valiant soul, capable of making its own interesting way alone. Think as she would, and try, love, and love only, the admiration and ministering care of some capable and affectionate man was the only thing that seemed likely to solve for her the various earthly difficulties which beset her.

But even as to this, how, in what saving or perfect way, was love to come to her? She had made one mistake which in the development of any honest relationship with another would have to be confessed. And how would it be then? Would love, admiration, forgive? Love, love, love, and the peace and comfort of that happy routine home life which she imagined she saw operative in the lives of others— how it glimmered afar, like a star!

And again there was her mother.

It was not long after she had come from the institution that sheer loneliness, as well as a sense of daughterly responsibility and pity, had urged her to look up her mother, in order that she might restore to herself some little trace of a home, however wretched it might be. She had no one, as she proceeded to argue. At least in her own lonely life her mother provided, or would, an ear and a voice, sympathetic if begging, a place to go.

She had learned on returning to their last living-place on one of her afternoons off, that her mother had been sent away to the "Island," but had come back and since had been sent to the city poor-farm. This last inquiry led eventually to her mother's discovery of her and of her fixing herself upon her once more as a dependent, until her death somewhat over a year later.

But in the meantime, and after all, life continued to call and call and to drive her on, for she was still full of the hope and fever of youth.

Once, before leaving the institution in which they had worked together, Viola Patters had said to her in one of those bursts of confidence based on attraction:

"Once you're outa here an' I am, too, I'd like to see you again, only there ain't no use your writin' me here, for I don't believe they'd give it to me. I don't believe they'd want us to run together. I don't believe they like me as well as they do you. But you write me, wherever you are, care of—," and here she gave a definite address—"an' I'll get it when I get out."

She assured Madeleine that she would probably be able to get a good place, once she was free of the control of the Sisters, and then she might be able to do something for her.

Often during these dark new days she thought of this, and being hard-pressed for diverting interests in her life she finally wrote her, receiving in due time a request to come and see her.

But, as it proved, Viola was no avenue of improvement for her in her new mood. She was, as Madeleine soon discovered, part of a small group which was making its way along a path which she had promised herself henceforth to avoid. Viola was more comfortably placed in quarters of her own than Madeleine had ever been, but the method by which she was forwarding her life she could not as readily accept.

Yet her own life, move about as she might and did after a time from one small position to another, in store or factory, in the hope of bettering herself, held nothing either. Day by day as she worked she sensed all the more clearly that the meagre tasks at which she toiled could bring her nothing of permanent value. Her mother was dead now, and she more alone than ever. During a period of several years, in which she worked and dreamed, leading a thin, underpaid life, her mind was ever on love and what it might do for her—the pressure of a seeking hand, the sanctuary of an enveloping heart.

And then, for the second time in her brief life, love came, or seemed to—at least in her own heart if nowhere else.

She had by now, and through her own efforts, attained to a clerkship in one of the great stores at the salary of seven dollars a week, on which she was trying to live. And then, behold, one day among her customers one of those suave and artful masters of the art of living by one's wits, with a fortune of looks, to whom womanhood is a thing to be taken by an upward curl of a pair of mustachios, the vain placement of ringed locks, spotless and conspicuous linen, and clothes and shoes of a newness and lustre all but disturbing to a very work-a-day world. His manners and glances were of a winsomeness which only the feminine heart—and that unschooled in the valuelessness of veneer—fully appreciates.

Yes, the sheer grace of the seeking male, his shallow and heartless courtesy, the lustre of his

eye and skin, a certain something of shabby-grand manner, such as she had never known in the particularly narrow world in which she moved, was sufficient to arrest and fix her interest.

He leaned over and examined the stationery and pencils which she sold, commenting on prices, the routine of her work, smiled archly and suggested by his manner entire that she was one in whom he could be deeply interested. At the same time a certain animal magnetism, of the workings of which she was no more conscious than might be any stick or stone, took her in its tow.

Here was one out of many, a handsome beau, who was interested in her and her little life. The oiled and curled hair became the crown of a god; the mustachios and the sharp, cruel nose harmonies of exquisite beauty. Even the muscular, prehensile hands were rhythmic, musical in their movements. She had time only to sense the wonder of his perfect self before he went away. But it was to return another day, with an even more familiar and insinuating grace.

He was interested in her, as he frankly said the next time, and she must be his friend. At lunch-time one day he was waiting to take her to a better restaurant than she would ever have dreamed of entering; on another day it was to dinner that she accompanied him.

According to him, she was beautiful, wonderful. Her flower-like life was being wasted on so rude a task. She should marry him, and then her difficulties would be solved. He was one who, when fortune was with him, so he said, made much, much money. He might even take her from the city at times to see strange places and interesting scenes.

As for her own stunted life, from most of the details of which she forbore, he seemed in nowise interested. It was not due to any lack on her part in the past that her life had been so ill. . . .

Love, love love. . . . The old story. In a final burst of admiration and love for his generosity she told him of her one great error, which caused him a few moments of solemn cogitation and was then dismissed as nothing of importance, a pathetic, childish mistake. Then there followed one of those swift and seemingly unguarded unions, a common-place of the tangled self-preserving underworld of poverty. A clergyman was found whose moral assurances seemed to make the union ideal. Then a room in a commonplace boarding-house, and the newer and better life which eventually was to realize all was begun.

VII

To those familiar with the brazen and relentless methods of a certain type of hawk of the underworld, which picks fledglings from the nest and springlings from the fields and finds life itself only a hunting-ground in which those mentally or physically weaker than itself may be enslaved, this description will seem neither strained nor inadequate. Fagins of sex, creatures who change their women as they would their coats, they make an easy if reprehensible bed of their lives, and such of their victims as have known them well testify that for a while at least in their care or custody they were not unhappy.

So it was with Madeleine and her lover. With amused and laughing tolerance toward her natural if witless efforts to build up a home atmosphere about their presumably joint lives, to build for a future in which they should jointly share, he saw in them only something trivial or ridiculous, whereas to her it was as though the heavens had opened and she was surveying a new world. For in his love and care there was to be peace. Latterly, if not now—for already he complained of conditions which made it impossible for him to work— the results of their several labors were to be pooled in order to prepare for that something better which would soon be achieved—a home, an ideally happy state somewhere. Even children were in her mind.

The mere fact that he shortly complained of other temporary reverses which made it necessary for him and her to keep close watch over their resources, and that for the time being, until he "could arrange his affairs," she must find some employment which would pay much better than her old one, gave her no shock.

Indeed, it was an indescribable joy for her to do for her love, for love had come, that great solvent of all other earthly difficulties, that leveler of all but insurmountable barriers. Even now love was to make her life flower at last. There was an end to loneliness and the oppressive indifference of the great sea of life.

But, as in the first instance, so now the awakening was swift and disconcerting. Realizing the abject adoration in which she held his surface charms and that his thin, tricky soul was the beginning and the end of things for her, it was all the easier to assure her, and soon insist, that the easiest and swiftest way of making money, of which she was unfortunately aware, must be resorted to, for a great necessity had come upon him. The usual tale

of a threatening disaster, a sudden loss at cards which might end in imprisonment for him and their enforced separation, was enough.

Swiftly he filled her ears with tales of rescues by women of many of his men friends similarly circumstanced, of the "fools" and "marks" that filled the thoroughfares to be captured and preyed upon by women. Why hesitate? Consider the meagre, beggarly wages she had previously earned, the nothingness of her life before. Why jeopardize their future now? Why be foolish, dull? Plainly it was nothing to love, as he saw it. Should it be so much to her? In this wise she was persuaded.

But now it was not the shame and the fear of arrest that troubled her, but the injury which love had done and was doing to her, that cut and burned and seared and scarred.

Love, as she now began dimly to realize once more, should not be so. More than anything else, if love was what she had always dreamed, should it not protect and save and keep her for itself? And now see. Love was sending her out again to loiter in doorways and before windows and to "make eyes."

It was this that turned like a wheel in her brain and heart. For in spite of the roughness of her emotional experiences thus far, she had faith to believe that love should not be so, should not do so.

Those features which to this hour, and long after, like those features of her first love, seemed so worship-worth, those eyes that had seemed to beam on her with love, the lips that had smiled so graciously and kissed hers, the hands and arms that had petted and held her, should not be part of the compulsion that sent her here.

No, love should be better than than. He himself had told her so at first—that she was worth more than all else to him — and now see!

And then one night, fully a year and a half later, the climax. Being particularly irritated by some money losses and the need of enduring her at all, even though she might still prove of some value as a slave, he turned on her with a savage fury.

"What, only . . . ! Get to hell outa here! What do you think I am—a sucker? And let go my arm. Don't come that stuff on me. I'm sick of it. Don't hang on my arm, I tell yah! I'm tired, damned tired! Get out! Go on— beat it, an' don't come back, see? I'm through —through—yuh hear me? I mean what I say. I'm through, once an' fer all. Beat it, an' fer good. Don't come back. I've said that before, but this time it *goes!* Go on, now quick—

Scat!—an' don't ever let me see yah around here any more, yah hear?—yah damned piece o' mush, yah!"

He pushed her away, throwing open the door as he did so, and, finding her still pleading and clinging, threw her out with such force that she cut her left eye and the back of her left hand against the jamb of the door.

There was a cry of "Fred! Fred! Please! Please!"—and then the door was slammed and she was left leaning disconsolately and brokenly against the stair-rail outside.

And now, as before, the cruelty and inscrutability of life weighed on her, only now, less than before, had she hope wherewith to buoy herself. It was all so dark, so hopeless. Often in this hour she thought of the swift, icy waters of the river, glistening under a winter moon, and then again of the peace and quiet of the House of the Good Shepherd, its shielding remoteness from life, the only true home or sanctuary she had ever known. And so, brooding and repressing occasional sobs, she made her way toward it, down the long streets, thinking of the pathetically debasing love-life that was now over—the dream of love that never, never could be again, for her.

VIII

The stark red walls of the institution stood as before, only dim and gray and cold under a frosty winter moon. It was three of a chill, cold morning. She had come a long way, drooping, brooding, half-freezing and crying. More than once on the way the hopelessness of her life and her dreams had given her pause, causing her to turn again with renewed determination toward the river—only the vivid and reassuring picture she had retained of this same grim and homely place, its restricted peace and quiet, the sympathy of Sister St. Agnes and Mother St. Bertha, had carried her on.

En route she speculated as to whether they would receive her now, so objectionable and grim was her tale. And yet she could not resist continuing toward it, so reassuring was its memory, only to find it silent, not a single light burning. But, after all, there was one, at a side door—not the great cold gate by which she had first been admitted but another to one side, to her an all but unknown entrance; and to it after some brooding hesitation she made her way, ringing a bell and being admitted by a drowsy nun, who ushered her into the warmth and quiet of the inner hallway. Once in she mechanically followed to the bronze grille which, as prison bars, obstructed the way, and here on one of the two plain chairs placed a small aperture she now sank wearily and looked through.

Her cut eye was hurting her and her bruised hands. On the somewhat faded jacket and crumpled hat, pulled on indifferently because she was too hurt to think or care, there was some blown snow. And when the Sister Secretary in charge of the room after midnight, hearing footsteps, came to the grille, she looked up wanly, her little red, rough hands crossed on her lap.

"Mother," she said beseechingly, "may I come in?"

Then remembering that only Mother St. Bertha could admit her, added wearily:

"Is Mother St. Bertha here? I was here before. She will know me."

The Sister Secretary surveyed her curiously, sensing more of the endless misery that was ever here, but seeing that she was sick or in despair hastened to call her superior, whose rule it was that all such requests for admission should be referred to her. There was no stir in the room in her absence. Presently pattened feet were heard, and the face of Mother St. Bertha, wrinkled and a-weary, appeared at the square opening.

"What is it, my child?" she asked curiously if softly, wondering at the crumpled presence at this hour.

"Mother," began Madeleine tremulously, looking up and recognizing her, "don't you remember me? It is Madeleine. I was here four years ago. I was in the girls' ward. I worked in the sewing-room."

She was so beaten by life, the perpetual endings to her never more than tremulous hopes, that even now and here she expected little more than an indifference which would send her away again.

"Why, yes, of course I remember you, my child. But what is it that brings you now, dear? Your eye is cut, and your hand."

"Yes, mother, but please don't ask—just now. Oh, please let me come in! I am so tired! I've had such a hard time!"

"Of course, my child," said the Mother, moving to the door and opening it. "You may come in. But what has happened, child? How is it that your cheek is cut, and your hands?"

"Mother," pleaded Madeleine wearily, "must I answer now? I am so unhappy! Can't I just have my old dress and my bed for to-night—that little bed under the lamp?"

"Why, yes, dear, you may have them, of course," said the nun, tactfully sensing a great grief. "And you need not talk now. I think I know how it is. Come with me."

She led the way along bare, dimly lit corridors and up cold solid iron stairs, echoing to the feet, until once more, as in the old days, the severe but spotless room in which were the baths and the hampers for soiled clothes was reached.

"Now, my child," she said, "you may undress and bathe. I will get something for your eye."

And so here at last, once more, Madeleine put aside the pathetic if showy finery that for a time had adorned and shamed her: a twilled skirt she had only recently bought in the pale hope of interesting *him*, the commonplace little hat for which she had paid ten dollars, the striped shirtwaist, once a pleasure to her in the hope that it would please *him*.

In a kind of dumbness of despair she took off her shoes and stockings and, as the Mother left, entered the warm, clean bath which had been provided. She stifled a sob as she did so, and others as she bathed. Then she stepped out and dried her body and covered it with the clean, simple slip of white which had been laid on a chair, brushing her hair and touching her eye, until the Mother Sister returned with an unguent wherewith to dress it.

Then she was led along other silent passages, once dreary enough but now healing in their sense of peace and rest, and so into the great room set with row upon row of simple white iron beds, covered with their snowy linen and illuminated only by the minute red lamps or the small candles burning before their idealistic images here and there, beneath which so many like herself were sleeping. Over the bed which she had once occupied, and which by chance was then vacant, burned the one little lamp which she recognized as of old—her lamp, as she had always thought of it—a thin and flickering flame, before an image of the Virgin. At sight of it she repressed a sob.

"You see, my child," said the Mother Superior poetically, "it must have been waiting for you. Anyhow it is empty. Perhaps it may have known you were coming."

She spoke softly so that the long rows of sleepers might not be disturbed, then proceeded to turn down the coverlets.

"Oh, Mother," Madeleine suddenly whispered softly as she stood by the bed, "won't you let me stay always? I never want to go out any more. I have had such a hard time. I will work so hard for you if you will let me stay!"

The experienced Sister looked at her curiously. Never before had she heard such a plea.

"Why, yes, my child," she said. "If you wish to stay I'm sure it can be arranged. It is not as we usually do, but you are not the only one who has gone out in the past and come back to us. I am sure God and the Blessed Virgin will hear your prayer for whatever is right. But now go to bed and sleep. You need rest. I can see that. And tomorrow, or any time, or never, as you choose, you may tell me what has happened."

She urged her very gently to enter and then tucked the covers about her, laying finally a cool, wrinkled hand on her forehead. For answer Madeleine seized and put it to her lips, holding it so.

"Oh, Mother," she sobbed as the Sister bent over her, "don't ever make me go out in the world again, will you? You won't, will you? I'm so tired! I'm so tired!"

"No dear, no," soothed the Sister, "not unless you wish it. And now rest. You need never go out into the world again unless you wish."

And withdrawing the hand from the kissing lips, she tiptoed silently from the room.

JOSEPH HERGESHEIMER (1880–   )

CHARLESTON

(1927)

At Broad Street and East Bay the ranks of the Carolina Rifle Club broke and its members gathered about the entrance of the Trenholm banking building. Their companions in parade, the older Schutzenfest, continued in marching order toward the Battery. The officers of the Carolina Rifle Club carried canes and bouquets of violets; the bouquets became a difficulty, and they were temporarily left in a fragrant heap by the door. All the men wore black felt hats turned up with green rosettes, grey coats of Kentucky jeans, hunting-shirts with green braid, and black trousers; but John Fearnes, who was rifle master, had a horn in green worsted on his arm. The occasion had been under the command of Walker Irvine, the first Vice-President; and, addressing Fearnes, he directed him to attend a special meeting in the club rooms above. John Fearnes had kept his violets, and, going slowly up the long dark stairway, he had a feeling that he was partly sustained by their sweetness. He loved flowers. And peace, he reminded himself. The truth was that he loved everything flowers suggested —quiet gardens and hours; the pastoral poetry of Thomson's Seasons; drawing-rooms with yellow roses; and low charming voices:

But the charming voices, he further realized, were all in the background: perhaps the one really fortunate circumstance in the tragic present was the fact that he owned no attachment to a woman. None was dependent on him. However, he was not concerned by that. Women had never very strongly attracted him. Through all the forty years of life he could remember he had been equally retiring. Indifferent. His vitality, and for that reason his desires, had never been intense. If—before the war, of course—he had been poor he would have been a teacher of literature or philosophy; as it was he had become, he had always been, a dreamer. A man who hated noise and contention; who was actually frightened by brutality; who was frightened by mere ugliness.

Physically he was slight, with a pale thin face, slightly drawn as though by the memory of pain, and fragile hands. Hands for the brittle pages of old books. His hesitating manner and mobile expression remained those of a boy; he had a sensitive boy's questioning candor; and his voice was as gentle as his air. He contrived, when it was possible, even in the Carolina Rifle Club, to stay unnoticed. It was strange, Fearnes thought, that he had been elected rifle master. There were twenty men in the club better fitted for that responsibility. In fact, he had protested against accepting it, but no one had listened to him. He didn't, for one thing, like rifles. They, too, filled him with a vague dread; and yet he was in charge of them. A serious position. It was enveloped, like all life now, with an unpleasant, a mocking, aspect of humor.

Walker Irvine had reached the club rooms before him; Rondelet was there and Dobbs Fenwicke; when the meeting was called to order ten men were present. Irvine spoke. "I was sorry to ask you to parade today, it's troublesome and dangerous, and looked particularly useless now. I did it for the reason we always show ourselves publicly. For effect. But that, I must admit, was small enough in the election. With Moses successful. Franklin J. Moses Governor of South Carolina! We can hardly add anything to that. But he isn't the business of this meeting. Gentlemen, we are

completely in the hands of the North. We thought it was bad under Scott; it will be worse with Moses. God knows what will happen to the State debt. Last year it was over twenty-two million dollars. Gleaves, one of the worst niggers in South Carolina, is Lieutenant-Governor. Beverley Nash, the Republican leader in the State Senate, blacked boots at the Pavilion Hotel. He was respectable compared with the Senator from Georgetown. The President of the Senate is a negro. The Speaker of the House is a negro. So is the State Treasurer. Wright, a nigger, is a justice of the Supreme Court. The Attorney-General, Elliott, is black, and Grant has put a black postmaster in Charleston. Our degradation is almost complete."

Why, Fearnes wondered, irritably, did Walker Irvine repeat what they all knew? It was clear that the State, that Charleston, woulf be accumulatively worse under Moses than it had been when Scott was Governor. Everything in South Carolina was worse. "It's no good going on with that," Irvine admitted. "We are only too familiar with it. Charleston has been under nigger rule for six years. But now our position is more serious." He paused. "Mingo Harth is back. Openly." Ashton Charville asked sharply: "Do you mean the Postle?" Yes, Irvine replied, he did. Charville thought he had been executed. "After the conspiracy with the Haiti slaves. I remember he was proved guilty." Irvine replied shortly: "He escaped. That was the last time he was in Charleston until yesterday. He says the Union Republicans are going to elect him mayor." There was a general stir of incredulity. "Why," Holt Gaddens declared, "the Postle would cut a Yankee throat just as soon as mine or yours. Sooner, because there would be money in a Yankee's pocket. The negroes know him. They ought to make it impossible." Irvine continued:

"He was with Banks Knell and later with Simril. The two most political negroes in the state. There was a meeting of some sort. I was assured Harth was truthful. For the moment. If he is, we have had no trouble at all yet. None. I know him better than anyone else does here. The blacks won't, as Holt suggests, finish him among themselves because they are afraid of him. He isn't an ordinary nigger. His name shows that: the Postle. He got most of his influence selling charms. The last time he was beaten for it he insisted they were love charms. But there was a healthy doubt. I ought to say an unhealthy doubt. Juju, I was told. But I paid no attention to that. Thank

God, I haven't got a black mind. We are here to discuss reality and not superstitions. The reality is bad enough."

"It seems to me our duty is clear," Charville spoke again. "The Carolina Rifle Club was not organized for parades." Irvine answered decidedly: "Harth is too cunning. He won't expose himself. If he's nominated he will have an escort: Soldiers at the door. No, it would have to be stopped at Columbia. If possible. I needn't point out the consequences if he was elected. He hates us all generally and some of us very much in particular. By name, I might say. That isn't specially important. I mean what he could do to us individually. We face that every day. It's other things. I couldn't even suggest them. I don't know what they'd be. He has imagination. But we are getting nowhere. Do any of you remember Beverley Nash?"

John Fearnes unhappily admitted that he had encountered Nash at the Pavilion and on the sloop Annie. Walker Irvine was obviously relieved. "Then, Colonel Fearnes, it is my suggestion you go to the capitol and see Nash privately. Point out to him that the present condition can't last forever. His carpet-bagger friends have left already. Tell him he will soon need the support of his own state. Promise it to him, in reason, if the Postle isn't nominated." Fearnes agreed. "Very well, if that is your decision. I will do what I can, Walker, but I have no confidence in my success. You won't think I am trying to avoid a disagreeable duty." Irvine smiled. "Hardly," he said; "not after your record in the war. Under fire. John, I am going to be even more unfeeling and turn Mingo Harth over to you personally. You can exercise your ingenuity on him. The resources of the club are back of you, of course, but there is no need to spread that on the minutes. We can't, unhappily, wear our bays publicly. Draw, when you have to, on the special fund, and remember we are only a sentimental rifle club . . . with bouquets."

John Fearnes walked slowly past Elliott and Tradd Streets to the East Battery; the paving and tracks were broken and the openings choked with weeds; the wharves, Boyce's, the Adgers', and Vanderhorst Wharf, were empty and dilapidated; the Cotton Press opposite and a house on Stoll's Alley had been hit by shells. Beyond, the water of Charleston Harbor was an idyllic blue. The city itself, Fearnes thought, was stagnant; there was no movement in the air; it seemed to lie thick and dead on the roofs. He had been away from Charles-

ton through the last three years of the war, with the Nineteenth South Carolina infantry; but he could imagine that it had been better during the siege, heroic and unfallen, than it was now. The tonic smell of gunpowder in place of the smell of negroes. It was curious—in the past he had liked negroes; he had liked to think that he knew them . . . a little. No one who was white could know more than a little about negroes. Vague perceptions. Guesses. Fantastic deductions:

He remembered Walker Irvine's disdain for juju. His own feeling was different; he wasn't as certain about it as Walker. In the past—the incredibly happy past—the truth was, he had been interested in such black magic. Only he had called it primitive religion. Obviously its right description. But opportunities for finding out about it practically didn't exist. Aside from a price he had been congenitally unwilling to face. The fact that it even occurred to him had frozen him with fear. Yet, together with the horror, it held an undeniable fascination. And so—with enormous relief—he had given the whole affair up. Except for things he accidentally saw and heard. He had, at times, been able to put scattered hints and words together. But, he realized, to no reputable result. He had denied himself the further study of primitive powers.

But he had, Fearnes insisted, liked negroes. Until now. And what had happened was not their fault. They were bad at present because they were neither slaves nor free. That, he saw, might with equal justice be said of himself. However! Slavery was gone, the old serene days were gone. A new and shameful time, with its corruption, was everywhere evident about him. Fearnes reached the South Battery walk and turned to the right. Ahead the White Point Garden, its crape myrtles set against the blue tide, was seductive with a false appearance of peace. The walks were cool in shade, the iron benches commanded tranquil reaches of foliage and water. But it was all, the truth was, treacherous; the retreat of vileness and imminent danger. The open Battery walk, in reality, was not safe. He never unnecessarily went out alone at night.

Yes, the air—now that it was no longer purified by fire—was stagnant; it was debased like mixed blood. There were, occasionally, muskets discharged into it, but they were muffled and surreptitious. The dull sounds of murder. It would be no better, he realized, in Columbia. Sherman, as usual, had been effective there. Utter destruction. Useless. The Union General had engaged himself to preserve the city, but burned it at the signal of three rockets. Soldiers hacking at the fire-hose. Breaking the water-tanks. Still, that, John Fearnes remembered, was war. Frightful. He didn't, now, see how he had lived through it—three years without a conscious moment free from horror. Actual and mental. Not, though, that one was less real than the other. Less destructive. Well, he had survived; only to come upon something more devastating. This business of Mingo Harth. The Postle. Walker Irvine hadn't exaggerated Harth's possibilities as mayor of Charleston. Harth, of course, was insane with the peculiar insanity of the jungle. Murder would be a commonplace, but it wouldn't be commonplace murder.

John Fearnes stopped, beyond King Street, at a dignified house of yellow brick separated from the walk by a high iron grille. Curved stone steps rose from the shallow inclosed garden to the front door; it had an iron handrail, and it was massed with blooming Cherokee roses. The roses were the only reassuring things he had seen in the whole city. Within, the high hall was empty and cold; a single chair stood by a tall dusty mirror and there were fragments of paper on the floor. John Fearnes went up to the second floor, to an impressive drawing-room with its length open in long windows on the Battery. There was a China carpet, with a design in rose and indigo-blue and dull orange on a white ground; the walls were painted terra-cotta red, and there were two great cut-glass chandeliers. At the farther end an old man looked up from a table deep in papers. It was Allds Fearnes, John Fearnes's father. He was engaged in making a register of St. Philip's Parish. The younger asked: "How are you getting along?"

"I am having the devil of a time with the Greens and the Greenes," he replied. "There is no difference observed in the spelling at all. It was like that, perhaps you will remember, with the Faulkners. Looking ahead, I can see it will be the same with the Lees. I may have to index them all as Leas. Then on September second, Seventeen thirty-two, Childermus, the son of Abraham Croft and Ann Maria, was born; and in Seventeen thirty-two Ann the daughter of Childermus Croft and Catherine his wife was born; but I can't make out that month. It is blurred. I must know when it was." His voice and brow were worried, and John Fearnes put a hand on his shoulder. "The light is fading," he explained. "Put the records away until tomorrow and then it will all be clear."

"I thought of ordering candles," his father replied. "But where the servants are I can't make out. You might pull on the bell-cord until your arm dropped off."

There was no one to hear a bell, a fact Allds Fearnes constantly forgot. "The servants are all gone," the younger man patiently explained. "We have had none since the war began." His father said: "That's so, the rascals. It won't stay in my mind. I hope the woman still comes in to cook. A gentleman may cook on a military campaign, but not in his own house. Where were you all afternoon?" John Fearnes told him that the Carolina Rifles had been parading with the Schutzenfest. "You did say that," he admitted. "John, I'm tired; and I'm not a third through the register. If I don't live to finish it you must take it up." They were seated on a balcony at the back of the house. Below, a garden had grown into confusion. There was the heavy scent of a banana shrub. A musical cry came from Legaré Street: "Sweet rose tomaytoes!" There was another, far off: "She craib, she craib, she craib." The elder Fearnes repeated hardly above his breath:

"Load my gun
Wid sweet sugar-plum
An' shoot dem nung gal."

"I shall have to go to Columbia tomorrow," John Fearnes said suddenly. "I must be away two or perhaps three days. I hope you will be all right. I will give you some money, only you must be careful with it. Let Saby in by the side door. I don't like to leave you, but it can't be helped." Why, his father demanded querulously. "I can take care of myself. I always keep a pair of loaded pistols by me. It's safe to kill almost anyone now." His hands, on the arms of his chair, were remarkably like his son's; but the skin was like the rind of a lemon; the veins were indigo. A mocking-bird sang with a sustained liquid sweetness. "You never hear a chuck-will's-widow any more," Allds Fearnes complained. "They used to come with the dusk."

The rebuilding of Columbia, Fearnes saw, was confined to the main street: the heaps of fire-blackened bricks and charred rafters were being hauled away and new stores were in course of construction. Columbia, like Charleston, was sunk in a careless and exhausted lethargy. Walking toward the State House, he passed imposing and dilapidated mansions set back in melancholy neglected gardens. Urns and statues were overthrown and broken, paths were unraked and lost, the porticoes were empty. Soon, however, he was caught in an increasing activity of negroes. A rough fence inclosed the littered and barren grounds of the State House. Near by a white officer, from the Army of the North, was drilling a black company; there were groups of negroes in serious consultation; others—legislators—slept sprawled on the grass; a solitary statesman in an old black frock-coat, with a rusty high silk hat and a torn woolen scarf about his throat, paced muttering loudly to himself. There were shouts of laughter, high calls, even a wail of song.

Where, John Fearnes asked a decent-appearing negro, could he find Beverley Nash? It was hard to say about Mr. Nash, he was informed. Mr. Nash was busy with near everything and everybody. He might be in the Senate Chamber, and then he might be in one of the committee rooms. Sometimes he stopped next to the office of the Clerk of the Senate. That retreat, Fearnes discovered, was completely furnished with senators and representatives, wines and liquors, cold dishes and cigars. There was no formality in the frankest satisfaction of personal appetites—there were negroes with champagne and corncob pipes, negroes with whisky and Havana cigars, negroes happy with beer and sliced chicken, negroes with unrestricted gin and Virginia ham. They were neither sober nor drunk, but united in a spirit of amazed and noisy pleasure. They were not only continuously eating and drinking, but begging one another to drink and eat just a little more.

Where, Fearnes asked again, was Beverley Nash? Beverley had been in that very room not a minute ago. Probably now he was back in the Senate. A white friend of Senator Nash's was looking for him. "Here, boy!" A ragged negro child was captured. "You're one of the Senate pages. Take this gentleman where he can find Mr. Beverley Nash." In the Senate Chamber Nash was discovered to have gone to the House. There the floor was in an uproar. A dozen members were on their feet at once in a shouted confusion of parliamentary terms. A point of order! A point of personal privilege. The gentleman from Laurens County. The chair please and I was talking first. The gavel fell in a sustained minor thunder of warning. The confusion slowly subsided. There were scattered laughs. The members, in every variety of dress, were seated in every possible attitude; pairs of incredible feet were elevated on the desks. There was a general eating of bananas and peanuts. Banana skins, peanut shells, were dropped over the floor.

A Representative was speaking. "Congress has passed the Force Bills. The Ku Klux trials came to the right end they came to. For one I am not in favor of delving into the past. The present is what this honorable body is engaged with. For that reason I am opposed to devoting any large sum of money on the Ku Klux and our scattered country brothers. Let us concentrate our money and our power. There is too much personal talk here. Take it to Captain Hubbard and the State Constabulary. See the Committee on Contingencies. Don't burden us with your aches and pains and troubles——" He was interrupted by a second lawmaker. The honorable gentleman forgot that he was once a scattered country brother. Did he ever have the Ku Klux wang in his door? Did the honorable gentleman ever see a Ku Klux in the middle of the night with red horns a foot long?

The gavel fell. Speeches on the floor were limited to five minutes. In a corner, silent and bewildered and grim, sat the few white Democratic members of the House. They were from the mountains—a useless sacrifice in the magnified black chatter. John Fearnes identified the seven white men who supported the negro party. They, rather than the negroes, were growing rich in the universal stealing. The entire appropriation for the State Insane Asylum had disappeared. There was a new issue of fraudulent State bonds at every session. He approached a small group of white men at the rail. "I am looking for Beverley Nash," he explained. There was no answer. John Fearnes repeated his words. An individual in a wide battered hat, his lips brown with tobacco, replied that he was damned if he cared who anyone was looking for.

"Nash is over there," another member of the group said. "You can just see his head. Now, Crews," he returned to a confidential discussion. That, then, was Joe Crews, the ex-nigger-trader. He had been in the Legislature, a commissioner of elections and a trial justice, and military aide to Governor Scott. Crews had armed the negroes of Columbia with six or seven hundred stands of improved Springfield rifles and ammunition. The taller man, with the patriarchal beard, Fearnes decided, was Whittemore. The Reverend B. F. Whittemore of Boston, who had owned slaves, and, carpetbagging, risen to power in South Carolina by marrying negroes for small fees. He had been expelled from Congress for selling cadetships to Annapolis and West Point, and, in recognition of so much, he was the State Senator from Darlington. Fearnes recognized Beverley Nash.

"Nash," he said, "I am Colonel Fearnes, of Charleston." Nash, who was a tall and handsome negro, carefully dressed, looked down on John Fearnes. He didn't, he replied, appear to remember him. He hoped, however, Fearnes had been colonel on the right side. "In the sacred cause of liberty." Fearnes ignored that. "I came to Columbia to see you about a rumor in Charleston." Nash interrupted him. He wasn't, he said, interested in Charleston rumors. Charleston, it was known, was disloyal to the Union, and as far as he, Beverley Nash, was concerned, the city might be excised from the map. Things seemed as if it might be. That, too, John Fearnes overlooked. "I want to talk to you," he replied more decidedly; "and this doesn't seem to be the place." Nash, it appeared, couldn't talk to him now in this place or any other. He had three committees that afternoon. This was Tuesday—he might see him on Friday. Yes, it was barely possible he would be at liberty, for a very little while, on Friday. Fearnes said: "Today or tomorrow." His voice was low and cold and quiet. Beverley Nash started to speak more loudly; it was possible that in a moment more he would be shouting; but suddenly his manner changed; it dissolved before Fearnes's level stare.

The best Nash could do was that night, and then it would be very inconvenient. Governor Moses was having a ball, and, if Colonel Fearnes would come to the Governor's mansion at about eleven o'clock, he would contrive to see him. That, Fearnes realized, was final. He agreed shortly. "Very well." He left the State House as quickly as possible. His face was whiter than usual and his knees were weak. His lips were pinched. From the United States barracks, on the outskirts of the town, came the strains of a military band playing John Brown's Body. The street was full of negroes on foot and in gigs going out for the parade and sunset music. Even war had been corrupted. John Fearnes thought with envy of all men killed in action. His mind was haunted by the insane spectacle of government in the negro House of Representatives, by the greed, the political malice, of the North. Mingo Harth was the symbol of Union, a black seal on the fate of South Carolina.

Seated in an alcove of the mansion lately acquired by Governor Franklin J. Moses, waiting for the social activities of Beverley Nash to reach a pause, John Fearnes's faint constant sense of horror was increased by the grotesque unreality of his surroundings. The Governor, in a florid version of evening dress, passed accompanied by his aides, negro and white, in uniforms brilliant with looped scarlet cords and gilt buttons; the Lieutenant-Governor, Gleaves, wore a violet coat and his hair pasted across a black forehead. The orchestra, in a farther room, played a triumphal march, and the dancers crowded respectfully forward to view the imposing cortège. It was followed by exclamations of satisfaction and wonder. Most of those present were negroes, negroes of every conceivable shade—there were girls so pale, so gracefully lovely, that even Fearnes was in doubt about them; and men with the dry blackness of charcoal. The girls wore bright colors, green and primitive red and sunflower yellow, their light or dark bare shoulders were grey with powder. Their necks and wrists were hung with gold and barbaric stones, and they were drenched with heavy perfume. Waves of hot scent alternated with the acrid odor of black bodies. The men were more variously garbed: there was an extravagant elegance and bright shabby makeshift. Against a background of music a continuous bass and treble laughter rose in an eager stammering pressure of pleasure, with a constant undertone of hysteria. None of this would have caused John Fearnes the slightest uneasiness; it was familiar and merely distasteful; but as the body of a ball in the Executive Mansion of the State it was, briefly, monstrous.

The degraded white element, he decided again, was what gave the occasion its air of corruption. He was repelled by the animal vigor of the negroes; but, following with a cold curiosity the white figures in the throng, his face was bitter. He saw a woman in pink tulle, unmistakably blonde, dancing with Cardoza, the mulatto State Treasurer. A northern captain in uniform was dancing with a young girl with the rich negro whiteness of a gardenia. She wore a honey-colored dress and long earrings of topaz and pale Spanish gold. A Gulla nigger of the Fifty-seventh Massachusetts Regiment roughly shoved aside a carefully dressed and apologetic white man. Beverley Nash stopped in front of Fearnes. He referred to John Fearnes as his Nemesis, and doubted if, after all, he had time to confer with him.

"It will only need a few minutes," Fearnes proceeded. "There is a rumor in Charleston Mingo Harth is to be nominated for mayor on the Union Republican ticket. If he is elected it will be fatal for the negro cause in South Carolina. At last. There is a limit, Washington will discover, we can't go beyond. I'll remind you that none of this was Mr. Lincoln's plan, but U. S. Grant's. The Union League and Freedmen's Bureau, the North, are only interested in your vote. In separating you from the Democratic party. Before the war no respectable negro would recognize Mingo Harth." Nash interrupted him to say that if he had known what the Colonel was after he would not have granted him an interview. Beverley Nash repeated that he had no concern with Charleston. Mingo might be bad, but he couldn't be bad enough for that white sepulcher. Besides, times had changed, what was low had become high, and Mingo Harth had gone up. He would, today, get a big vote. For several reasons. John Fearnes saw that it was useless to continue. Probably Mingo Harth would be mayor of Charleston . . . for a little. However, the damage in that short period must be incalculable.

He was sorry, Nash said, but he could wait no longer. Governor Moses wanted to consult with him, and there were others. Very different. But there was no reason for the Colonel to hurry away. He had better stay and enjoy himself. If he took a fancy to anyone in particular, say that he was Beverley Nash's guest. John Fearnes made no reply; his face was set like a death mask; and Nash, suddenly uneasy, withdrew. He must go at once, Fearnes realized, but for the moment he was incapable of movement. He was crushed into his seat by the whole weight of present tragic misfortunes. The dance continued. The music and voices grew louder. Joe Crews, his planter's hat arrogantly across his eyes, passed. Fearnes saw the bearded and reverend-appearing Mr. Whittemore. Cardoza, who was from Charleston, stopped and spoke civilly; he presented the woman with him. She was a Mrs. Dembo. She came, Cardoza proceeded, from New Orleans. John Fearnes acknowledged this adequately. He was standing, turning finally away, when he happened to see an artificial blue mark in the palm of the woman's right hand.

She was slight, graceful, and pale; her skin was uncommonly bright, almost orange, in color; and her eyes, no more than half opened, were amber. Somnolent. She spoke in a low and indifferent voice with a trace of Spanish. Her whole bearing was indifferent, supported by the insolence of some hidden pride or power. Perhaps Mrs. Dembo would like to talk to Colonel Fearnes, Cardoza proceeded. He bowed ceremoniously and turned away. He didn't, she said, like the party or the people around them. The men had the manners of

field hands, the women were frightfully dressed, and the music horrible. In New Orleans such an occasion would be very different. Did he know the Calinda? "I have never been to Louisiana," Fearnes acknowledged. There was a fine gold chain about her neck, its ends disappeared into the lace at her breast, and he speculated upon what was hidden. He had given up the intention, neglected the need, of leaving immediately.

Mrs. Dembo fell into a silent remoteness. In repose her face was haggard; her mouth was bloodless and malign. She was, in reality, curiously hideous. Her grace, her bright and surprising color, ordinarily hid that. It was impossible to guess her age. At first John Fearnes would have said thirty; now he saw that she might be fifty. She wasn't, of course. He asked her, formally, if she cared to dance.

He found that she danced better than well, with a complicated perverse rhythm within the time of the music. She was extraordinarily light and cold in his arms. A wave of giddiness swept over John Fearnes; the weakness in his knees returned; his breath, he thought, had turned solid, choking him. The room was packed with dancers, hot beyond support. The music had become horrible. He turned sharply to avoid collision, and the object at the end of her chain swung into view; it was a small crucifix of black lava; every carved agonized detail was perfect, but it was attached to the chain at the bottom. It hung upside down. The time had come to speak. His parched lips were close to her ear. "It is the Mama who speaks the will of one whose tongue was split. Others who know this wait."

She signed faintly. There was no other evidence that Mrs. Dembo had heard him. The music tore at him with a feverish and destructive intensity. He had failed again. Mrs. Dembo's fingers tightened on his wrist. She was replying. "In the darkness it is dangerous to light the candle of wisdom." Fearnes continued: "The light is guarded from eyes that see and are blind." There was an amber glimmer between her eyelids. "A fire without sticks cannot warm the eggs that have no shells." The crucifix had vanished. His giddiness changed to an acute sickness; it was absolutely necessary for him to get out into the air. John Fearnes led Mrs. Dembo to a side door, and they stood at the top of a narrow flight of steps leading into a darkness of massed and neglected shrubbery. The noise behind him lost all sense; it became an inarticulate and savage jabber; at intervals he heard the low boom of a drum. "I must speak to you," Fearnes said. He was shocked by the inappropriate and futile sanity of his words.

Returned to Charleston he found the iron gate and doors of his dwelling unceremoniously open. There were negro soldiers in the hall. The old man, they casually informed him, had been killed last night. They knew nothing more than that and sullenly resented further questioning. John Fearnes saw Saby and cried at her: "What has happened to my father?" She, too, was ignorant; half insolent in manner. There were negroes in the drawing-room above, rifles and belts in the corners; but Allds Fearnes, incredibly emaciated, was alone. When his body had been carried away, under a guard of honor from the Carolina Rifle Club, John Fearnes began an existence of complete solitude. Saby had gone and he conducted all the practical details of living. The negroes continued to inhabit the lower floor; he drove them out, but they returned; a formal request to have them moved brought no reply. They gambled and slept and argued —turning his hall into a kind of guard-room— and, except for stealing his food and clothes, paid very little attention to him. Fearnes, against urgent advice, stubbornly remained. He sat mostly on the rear balcony, listening to the mocking-birds and the musical cries of the Charleston streets. He kept his father's papers together—if Beverley Nash and the black Republicans were successful in totally obliterating Charleston the register of St. Philip's Parish might be valuable.

The spirit of Charleston, however, was not entirely dead. There was, for example, a changeless love for it in himself, for its wharves and water and tranquil streets, its single houses and walled gardens. It was closer to him, more actual, than any abstraction of union. South Carolina was a reality, its history was his history, its annals were the names of his ancestors. Charleston was the evidence of its pride and richness, and of its fall. It had fallen. Oh, very decidedly. It could never be born again; not in its past image. Grant had seen to that; reaching for a second term, he had made it impossible. None of Fearnes's associates agreed with him; they insisted the state would survive, glorious; Charleston, they contended, would be built again. Never, he knew, in the old form and mold. The very shape of life had changed. The cotton warehouses on East Bay Street would never be filled again—cotton had moved south and west. There could be no plantations without slaves. Without plantations the familiar cherished facts of South Carolina would become a tradition.

That, though, would live forever; Charleston would be deathless in the history of lovely cities. Its tradition was as tangible as stone and brick. He had fought, a last act of veneration, to leave it perfect. John Fearnes hadn't, through the years of the war, realized that. He saw now that success was never for a moment possible. It wasn't the North but the present which had conquered him. He didn't, at the last, very greatly mind. He preferred to belong to the past. There was a noise in the room behind him, and he found three negroes in uniform bending over an opened drawer. They were visibly confused and, muttering they had thought he was out, left quickly.

There was a long-drawn call outside. Fresh whiting! The fishermen had returned from the bay. Later he encountered a negro soldier, a captain, of a different spirit, on the stairs. He wasn't a colonel, Fearnes was told; Fearnes was nothing. If he got in the way he would be less. The Captain's sword was bare. There was no one else near, the hall was darkening with evening, and John Fearnes said rapidly: "When the rooster sings the Ave Maria it is then time for the crows to end their chatter." The sword fell and slid clattering down the bare steps. The negro flattened himself against the railing for Fearnes to go by.

His feeling of sickness returned, accompanied by self-hatred. John Fearnes told himself that he had betrayed his birth; he was sinking deeper and deeper into infamy. He was tormented by what he knew. Yet the reason for his interest in—in primitive religion, his plans, justified it. He recalled Walker Irvine's command, his assertion that the Carolina Rifle Club must be obviously innocent. He was, therefore, proceeding in the best way open to him. What frightened him were the dark implications of the world he had entered. He opposed against them—for the escape of his soul—the serene and familiar phrases of the Book of Common Prayer, but its beauty was remote from him like its heaven. That region, spun of gold and blue, was hidden by an imminent pall. John Fearnes had a destructive illusion that his skin was turning darker; it was, of course, nonsense, but it persisted at the back of his mind. He woke suddenly at night and, hearing the negroes below, lost all sense of his identity; he might be black or white, living or dead. He didn't immediately know. He fought off an impulse to make a light and, getting the yellow chalk he kept hidden, draw an indicated pat-

ring in his ears, the temple gongs calling blindly to the blind, the alluring and incomprehensible accents of the boatmen's tongue which he was to have made his own and lightened with the fierce sweet name of the Cross—and now could not.

Poor young Minister Malden, he turned his face away. He gave up "the field" for the bride, and when the bride went out in mid-ocean, he had neither bride nor field. He drifted back to New England, somehow or other, and found Yen Sin.

He found another bride too; Minister Malden was human. It was a mercy of justice, folks said, when Widow Gibbs got a man like Minister Malden. Heaven knows she had had bad enough luck with Gibbs, a sallow devil of a whaler who never did a fine act in his life till he went down with his vessel and all hands in the Arctic one year and left Sympathy Gibbs, sitting alone in the Pillar House on Lovett's Court, pretty, plump, and rather well-to-do as Urkey goes.

Everybody in the island was glad enough when those two undertook to mend each other's blasted life—everybody but Mate Snow. He had been thinking of Sympathy Gibbs himself, they said; and they said he stood behind the prescription screen in his drugstore far into the night, after the betrothal was given out in Center Church, his eyes half-closed, his thin lips bluish white, and hell-fire smoldering out of sight in him. And they said Mate was the kind that never forgets. That was what made it so queer.

It seems to me that I must remember the time when the minister lived in the Pillar House with Sympathy Gibbs.

Back there in the mists of youth I seem to see them walking home together after the Sunday morning preaching, arm in arm and full of a sedate joy; turning in between the tubbed box-trees at Lovett's Court, loitering for a moment to gaze out over the smooth harbor and nod to the stragglers of the congregation before they entered the big green door flanked by lilac panes.

Perhaps it was told me. There can be no question, though, that I remember the night when Minister Malden came home from the Infield Conference, a father of two days' standing. Urkey village made a festival of that homecoming to the tiny daughter he had never seen, and to Sympathy Gibbs, weak and waiting and radiant. Yes, I remember.

We were all at the landing, making a racket. The minister looked ill when he came over the packet's side, followed by Mate Snow,

who had gone to Conference with him as lay delegate from Center Church. Our welcome touched him in a strange and shocking way; he staggered and would have fallen had it not been for Mate's quick hand. He had not a word to say to us; he walked up the shore street between the wondering lines till he came to the Pillar House, and there he stood for a moment, silhouetted against the open door, a drooping, hunted figure, afraid to go in.

We saw his shadow later, moving uncertainly across the shades in the upper chamber where Sympathy Gibbs lay with her baby, his hand lifted once with the fingers crooked in mysterious agony. Some one started a hymn in the street below and people took it up, bawling desperately for comfort to their souls. Mate Snow didn't sing. He stood motionless between the box-trees, staring up at the lighted window shades, as if waiting. By-and-by Minister Malden came down the steps, and moving away beside him like a drunken man, went to live in the two rooms over the drugstore. And that was the beginning of it.

Folks said Mate Snow was not the kind to forget an injury, and yet it was Mate who stood behind the minister through those first days of shock and scandal, who out-faced the congregation with his stubborn, tight lips, and who shut off the whisperings of the Dorcas Guild with the sentence which was destined to become a sort of formula on his tongue through the ensuing years:

"You don't know what's wrong, and neither do I; but we can all see the man's a saint, can't we?"

"But the woman?" some still persisted.

"Sympathy Gibbs? You ought to know Sympathy Gibbs by this time."

And if there was a faint curling at the corners of his lips, they were all too dull to wonder at it. As for me, the boy, I took the changing phenomena of life pretty well for granted, and wasted little of my golden time speculating about such things. But as I look back now on the blunt end of those Urkey days, I seem to see Minister Malden growing smaller as he comes nearer, and Mate Snow growing larger —Mate Snow browbeating the congregation with a more and more menacing righteousness —Minister Malden, in his protecting shadow, leaner, grayer, his eyes burning with an ever fiercer zeal, escaping Center Church and slipping away to redeem the Chinaman.

"There is more joy in heaven over one sinner," was his inspiration, his justification, and, I suspect, his blessed opiate.

But it must have been hard on Yen Sin. I

remember him now, a steam-blurred silhouette, earlier than the earliest, later than the latest, swaying over his tubs and sad-irons in the shanty on the stranded scow by Pickett's wharf, dreaming perhaps of the populous rivers of his birth, or of the rats he ate, or of the opium he smoked at dead of night, or of those weird, heathen idols before which he bowed down his shining head—familiar and inscrutable alien.

An evening comes back to me when I sat in Yen Sin's shop and waited for my first "stand up" collar to be ironed, listening with a kind of awe to the tide making up the flats, muffled and unfamiliar, and inhaling the perfume compounded of steam, soap, hot linen, rats, opium, tea, idols and what-not, peculiar to Yen Sin's shop and to a thousand lone shops in a thousand lone villages scattered across the mainland. When the precious collar was at last in my hands, still limp and hot from its ordeal, Yen Sin hung over me in the yellow nimbus of the lamp, smiling at my wonder. I stared with a growing mistrust at the flock of tiny bird-scratches inked on the band.

"What," I demanded suspiciously, "is *that?*"

"Lat's Mista You," he said, nodding his head and summoning another hundred of wrinkles to his damp, polished face.

"That ain't my name. You don't know my name," I accused him.

"Mista Yen Sin gottee name, allee light."

The thing fascinated me, like a serpent.

"Whose name is *that*, then?" I demanded, pointing to a collar on the counter between us. The band was half-covered with the cryptic characters, done finely and as if with the loving hand of an artist.

Yen Sin held it up before his eyes in the full glow of the lamp. His face seemed incredibly old; not senile, like our white-beards, mumbling on the wharves, but as if it had been a long, long time in the making and was still young. I thought he had forgotten me, he was so engrossed in his handiwork.

"Lat colla?" he mused by-and-by. "Lat's Mista Minista, boy."

"Mister Minister *Malden?*"

And there both of us started a little, for there was a voice at the door.

"Yes? Yes? What is it?"

Minister Malden stood with his head and shoulders bent, wary of the low door-frame, and his eyes blinking in the new light. I am sure he did not see me on the bench; he was looking at Yen Sin.

"How is it with you tonight, my brother?"

The Chinaman straightened up and faced him, grave, watchful.

"Fine," he said. "Mista Yen Sin fine. Mista Minista fine, yes?"

He bowed and motioned his visitor to a rocker, upholstered with a worn piece of Axminster and a bit of yellow silk with half a dragon on it. The ceremony, one could see, was not new. Vanishing into the further mysteries of the rear, he brought out a bowl of tea, steaming, a small dish of heathenish things, nuts perhaps, or preserves, deposited the offering on the minister's pointed knees, and retired behind the counter to watch and wait.

An amazing change had come over the minister. Accustomed to seeing him gentle, shrinking, illusively non-resisting, I scarcely knew this white flame of a man, burning over the tea-bowl.

"You are kind to me," he cried, "and yet your heart is not touched. I would give up my life gladly, brother, if I could only go up to the Throne and say to Jesus, 'Behold, Lord, Thy son, Yen Sin, kneeling at the foot of the Cross. Thou gavest me the power, Lord, and the glory is thine!' If I could say that, brother, I—I——"

His voice trailed off, though his lips continued to move uncertainly. His face was transfigured, his eyes filmed with dreams. He was looking beyond Yen Sin now, and on the lost yellow millions. The tea, untasted, smoked upward into his face, an insidious, narcotic cloud. I can think of him now as he sat there, wresting out of his easeless years one moment of those seminary dreams; the color of far-away, the sweet shock of the alien and the bizarre, the enormous odds, the Game. The walls of Yen Sin's shop were the margins of the world, and for a moment the missionary lived.

"He would soften your heart," he murmured, "in a wondrous way. Have you never thought, Yen Sin, 'I would like to be a good man?'"

The other spread his right hand across his breast.

"Mista Yen Sin velly humble dog. Mista Yen Sin no good. Mista Yen Sin's head on le glound. Mista Yen Sin velly good man. Washy colla fine."

It was evidently an old point, an established score for the heathen.

"Yes, I must say, you do do your work. I've brought you that collar for five years now, and it still seems new." The minister's face fell a little. Yen Sin continued grave and alert.

"Howsoever like no other be the mode you may employ,
There's an order in the ages for the ages to enjoy;
Though the temples you are shaping and the passions you are singing
Are a long way from Athens and a longer way from Troy.   20

"When we promise more than ever of what never shall arrive,
And you seem a little more than ordinarily alive,
Make a note that you are sure you understand our obligations—
For there's grief always auditing where two and two are five.

"There was this for us to say and there was this for you to know,
Though it humbles and it hurts us when we have to tell you so.
If you doubt the only truth in all our perjured composition,
May the True Gods attend you and forget us when we go."
                                                        1920

From TRISTRAM

V

Griffon, the giant scourge of Brittany,
Threatened while Tristram was appraising it,
In his anticipation, all the peace
Awaiting him across the foaming waves
That were to wash, in Gouvernail's invention,
Time out of life. And there King Howel's
      child,
Isolt of the white hands, living on hope,
Which in all seeming had itself alone
To live on, was for love and safety now
A prisoner in that castle by the sea   10
Where Tristram once, not thinking twice of it,
Had said that he would some day come again,
And more as a gay plaything than a pledge
Had left with her an agate which had been
For long her father's just. It was her heart,
Which she had taken out of her white bosom,
He said, and in the forest or in the sea
Would presently be lost and never found
Again—not even for Tristram when he came.
But when he came there was no time for talk
Of hearts and agates. Welcome and wonder-
      ment   21
Appeased, and the still whiteness of Isolt
Regarded once and then at once forgotten,
Tristram, like one athirst with wine before
      him,
Heard the King's talk of a marauding host
That neither force nor craft had yet subdued
Or more than scattered, like an obscene flock
Of rooks alert around a living quarry
That might not have a longer while to live 29
Than a few days would hold, or not so many.

"Praise be to God, I could almost have said
For your ill fortune, sir, and for your danger,"
Was Tristram's answer to the King's grim
      news.
"I have been groping slowly out of life

Into a slough of darkness and disuse—
A place too far from either for life or death
To share with me. Yes, I have had too much
Of what a fool, not knowing its right name,
Would call the joy of life. If that be joy,
Give me a draught out of your cup of trouble,
And let it be seen then what's left of me   41
To deal with your bad neighbor. For tonight,
Let me have rest before tomorrow's work,
Which may be early."

                     "Early and late, I fear,"
The King said, and eyed Tristram cautiously,
And with a melancholy questioning
Of much that was for him no more a question.
"If it be God that brings you here today,
I praise him in my thanks given to you,
Tristram, for this. Sleep, and forget tomorrow
Until tomorrow calls you. If ill comes   51
To you for this, I shall not wish to live—
But for my child. And if ill comes to her,
It will be death to live."

                          "Tomorrow, sir,
These ills may be the dregs in empty cups
With all the bitterness drunk out of them.
No ill shall come to her till you and I
And all your men go down defending her;
And I can figure no such havoc as that.
I'm not a thousand men, or more than one,
Yet a new mind and eye, and a new arm   61
At work with yours, may not combine for
      ruin."

Uncertain afterwards in a foreseen
Achievement unachieved, Tristram rejoiced
At last when he saw Griffon at his feet
And saw the last of his pernicious minions
Dispatched or disappearing. And that night,
Having espied Isolt's forgotten harp,

He plucked and sang the shadow of himself,
To her his only self, unwittingly   70
Into the soul and fabric of her life,
Till death should find it there. So day by day
He fostered in his heart a tenderness
Unrecognized for more than a kind fear
For what imaginable small white pawn
Her candor and her flame-white loveliness
Could yet become for the cold game of kings,
Who might not always, if they would, play
     quite
Their game as others do.

            Once by the shore
They lingered while a summer sun went down
Beyond the shining sea; and it was then   81
That sorrow's witchcraft, long at work in him,
Made pity out of sorrow, and of pity
Made the pale wine of love that is not love,
Yet steals from love a name. And while he felt
Within her candor and her artlessness
The still white fire of her necessity,
He asked in vain if this were the same fate
That for so long had played with him so
     darkly—
With him and with Isolt, Isolt of Ireland.   90
Isolt of the wild frightened violet eyes
That once had given him that last look of hers
Above the moaning call of those cold waves
On those cold Cornish rocks. This new Isolt,
This new and white Isolt, was nothing real
To him until he found her in his arms,
And, scarcely knowing how he found her there,
Kissed her and felt the sting of happy tears
On his bewildered lips. Her whiteness burned
Against him till he trembled with regret;   100
For hope so long unrealized real at last
To her, was perilously real to him.
He knew that while his life was in Cornwall,
Something of this white fire and loneliness
In Brittany must be his whereon to lavish
The comfort of kind lies while he should live.
There were some words that he would have
     been saying
When her eyes told him with a still reproof
That silence would say more; and Tristram
     wished
That silence might say all.

            For a long time   110
They sat there, looking off across the water
Between them and Tintagel to the north,
Where Tristram saw himself chained to a stake
With flames around him and Isolt of Ireland
Held forcibly to see. King Mark, he knew,
Would in his carnal rage cling to his word
And feast his eyes and hate insatiably
On his fulfilment of it—in itself

The least of Tristram's fear. It was her eyes,
Held open to behold him, that he saw,   120
More than it was himself, or any torture
That would be only torture worse than his
For her. He turned himself away from that,
And saw beside him two gray silent eyes
Searching in his with quaint solemnity
For some unspoken answer to a thought
Unspoken.

         "When I told my father first
That you would come, he only smiled at me,"
She said. "But I believe by saying always
That you were coming, he believed you would,
Just as I knew you would."   131

            "And why was that,
My child?" he asked, a captive once again
To her gray eyes and her white need of him.
"You might have told your father I was
     coming
Till the world's end, and I might not have
     come."

"You would have come, because I knew you
     would,"
She said, with a smile shaking on her lips
And fading in her eyes. "And you said that,
Because you knew, or because you knew noth-
     ing,
Or cared less than you know. Because you
     knew,   140
I like to fancy. It will do no harm."

"Were I so sure of that," he thought, "as you
     are,
There would be no infection of regret
In my remembrance of a usefulness
That Brittany will say was mine. Isolt
Of Brittany? Why were two names like that
Written for me by fate upon my heart
In red and white? Is this white fire of pity,
If pity it be, to burn deeper than love?"   149
Isolt of Ireland's dark wild eyes before him
In the moonlight, and that last look of hers,
Appeared in answer. Tristram gazed away
Into the north, and having seen enough,
He turned again to find the same gray light
In the same eyes that searched in his before
For an unspoken answer to a thought
Unspoken. They came silently away,
And Tristram sang again to her that night.

And he sang many a time to her thereafter
Songs of old warriors, and old songs of love   160
Triumphant over wars that were forgotten;
And many a time he found in her gray eyes,
And in the rose-white warmth of her attention,

Dominion of a sure necessity
Beyond experience and the need of reason,
Which had at first amused him and at last
Had made him wonder why there should be
    tears
In a man's eyes for such a mild white thing
That had so quaint a wisdom in its mildness,
Unless because he watched it going slowly 170
Its mild white way out of the world without
    him.
"Can she see farther into time, by chance,
Than I do?" he would ask, observing her:
"She might do so, and still see little farther
Than to the patient ends of her white fingers
That are so much alive, like all of her."
She found him smiling, but in her large eyes
There was no smile. There was a need of him
That made him cold, as if a ghost had risen
Before him with a wordless admonition 180
That he must go or stay. And many a time
He would have gone, if he had not perforce
As many a time remained to sing for her
Those old songs over, and as many a time
Found in her gaze that sure necessity
Which held him with a wisdom beyond
    thought,
Or with an innocence beyond all wisdom,
Until he sang one night for the last time
To the King's child. For she was his child
    now,
And for as long as there was life in him 190
Was his to cherish and to wonder at,
That he should have this white wise fiery
    thing
To call his wife.

           "Magicians might have done it"
He pondered once, alone, "but in so far
As I'm aware of them, there are none left
In Brittany so adept as to achieve it.
Stars may have done it." Then King Howel,
    pleased,
Though in his pleasure as incredulous
As if he were somehow a little injured,
Appearing out of silence from behind him, 200
Took Tristram's hands approvingly in his,
And said, "You have a child that was a woman
Before she was a child, and is today
Woman and child, and something not of either,
For you to keep or crush—without a sound
Of pain from her to tell you so. Beware
Somewhat of that, Tristram; and may you
    both
Be wise enough not to ask more of life
Than to be life, and fate." The last word fell
Like a last coin released unwillingly 210
By caution giving all. And while the King
Said what he said, Tristram was seeing only

A last look in two dark and frightened eyes
That always in the moonlight would be shin-
    ing,
Alone above the sound of Cornish waves
That always in the moonlight would be break-
    ing,
Cold upon Cornish rocks.

                        But occupation,
Like a neglected and insistent hound
Leaping upon his master's inattention,
Soon found him wearing on his younger shoul-
    ders 220
The yoke of a too mild and easy-trusting
And easy-futured king. He shaped and trained
An army that in time before would soon
Have made of Griffon a small anecdote
Hardly worth telling over after supper;
He built new ships and wharves, and razed old
    houses,
And so distressed a realm with renovation
Unsought and frowned on by slow denizens
For decades undisturbed, that many of them,
Viewing the visioned waste of a new hand, 230
Had wished him dead, or far from Brittany;
And for the flower of his activities,
He built a royal garden for Isolt
Of the white hands to bloom in, a white rose
Fairer than all fair roses in the world
Elsewhere—save one that was not white but
    dark,
Dark and love-red for ever, and not there,
Where the white rose was queen.

                              So for two years
She reigned and waited, and there in her gar-
    den
Let rumor's noise, like thunder heard far off,
Rumble itself to silence and as nigh 241
To nothing as might be. But near the end
Of a long afternoon, alone with him,
She sat there watching Tristram, who in turn,
Still mystified at having in his care
To keep or crush, even as her father said,
So brave and frail a flower, sat watching her
With eyes that always had at least been kind,
If they had not said always everything
She would have had them say. Staring at him,
Like someone suddenly afraid of life, 251
She chilled him slowly with a question: "Tris-
    tram,"
She said, "what should I do were you to die?"

"Are there no prettier notions in your head
Than that?" said he, and made a task of
    laughing.
"There are no mortal purposes in me
Today, yet I may say what you would do:

Were I to die, you would live on without me.
But I would rather sing you an old song   259
Than die, and even for you, this afternoon."

"Yes, presently you will sing me an old song,"
She said. "It was a wonder seized me then
And made me ask like that what I should do
Were you to die. Were you to tire of me,
And go away from me and stay some time,
I should not die, for then you would come back.
You came back once, and you would come
    again;
For you would learn at last you needed me
More than all other creatures. But if you
    died,
Then you would not come back. What should
    I do   270
If you should go away and never come back?
I see almost a shadow on you sometimes,
As if there were some fearful thing behind you,
Not to be felt or seen—while you are here."

"I can feel only the sun behind me now—
Which is a fearful thing if we consider it
Too long, or look too long into its face."
Saying that, he smiled at her, not happily,
But rather as one who has left something out,
And gazed away over a vine-hung wall,   280
And over the still ocean where one ship
Was coming slowly in.

                        "If I lost you
For a long time," she said, with her insistence,
"I should not cry for what had come between,
For I should have you here with me again.
I am not one who must have everything.
I was not fated to have everything.
One may be wise enough, not having all,
Still to be found among the fortunate."

She stood beside him now and felt his arm
Closing around her like an arm afraid.   291
"Little you know, my child," he thought, in
    anguish
A moment for the fear and innocence
That he was holding and was his to hold,
"What ashes of all this wisdom might be left
    you

After one blast of sick reality
To tell the wise what words are to the heart."
And then aloud: "There's a ship coming in
From somewhere north of us."

                          "There are no ships
From the north now that are worth looking
    at,"   300
She said; and he could feel her trembling warm
Against him till he felt his scorching him
With an unconscious and accusing fire.
"There was a time when I was always gazing
North for a ship, but nothing is there now;
Or ships are all alike that are there now."

"They are not all like this one," Tristram
    said,
More to himself than to the white Isolt
Arming herself with blindness against fate,
"For there are trumpets blowing, as if a king
Were coming—and there's a dragon on the
    sail.   311
One of King Arthur's barges—by the Lord
In heaven, it is—comes here to Brittany,
And for a cause that lives outside my knowl-
    edge.
Were this the King, we should have known of
    him."

"What does it mean?" she whispered; and her
    words
Wavered as if a terror not yet revealed
Had flown already inland from that ship.

"God knows," he said, "but it will not be
    long
Before we shall all know." She followed him
Into her father's castle, where the new   321
Looked ancient now; and slowly, after silence,
He left her waiting there at the same window
Where she had waited for so long before,
When she was looking always to the north;
And having left her there, alone with wonder,
He went alone with wonder to the shore,
Where a gay ship was coming gaily in,
And saw descending from it soon, and gaily,
As always, Sir Gawaine from Camelot.   330
                                              1927

EDGAR LEE MASTERS (1869–   )

From the SPOON RIVER ANTHOLOGY

Louise Smith

Herbert broke our engagement of eight years
When Annabelle returned to the village
From the Seminary, ah me!

If I had let my love for him alone
It might have grown into a beautiful sorrow—
Who knows?—filling my life with healing
    fragrance.
But I tortured it, I poisoned it,

I blinded its eyes, and it became hatred—
Deadly ivy instead of clematis.
And my soul fell from its support,   10
Its tendrils tangled in decay.
Do not let the will play gardener to your soul
Unless you are sure
It is wiser than your soul's nature.

1914

John Hancock Otis

As to democracy, fellow citizens,
Are you not prepared to admit
That I, who inherited riches and was to the
    manor born,
Was second to none in Spoon River
In my devotion to the cause of Liberty?
While my contemporary, Anthony Findlay,
Born in a shanty and beginning life
As a water carrier to the section hands,
Then becoming a section hand when he was
    grown,
Afterwards foreman of the gang, until he rose
To the superintendency of the railroad,   11
Living in Chicago,
Was a veritable slave driver,
Grinding the faces of labor,
And a bitter enemy of democracy.
And I say to you, Spoon River,
And to you, O republic,
Beware of the man who rises to power
From one suspender.

1914

Alexander Throckmorton

In youth my wings were strong and tireless,
But I did not know the mountains.
In age I knew the mountains
But my weary wings could not follow my
    vision—
Genius is wisdom and youth.

1914

Abel Melveny

I bought every kind of machine that's known—
Grinders, shellers, planters, mowers,
Mills and rakes and ploughs and threshers—
And all of them stood in the rain and sun,
Getting rusted, warped and battered,
For I had no sheds to store them in,
And no use for most of them.
And toward the last, when I thought it over,
There by my window, growing clearer
About myself, as my pulse slowed down,   10
And looked at one of the mills I bought—
Which I didn't have the slightest need of,

As things turned out, and I never ran—
A fine machine, once brightly varnished,
And eager to do its work,
Now with its paint washed off—
I saw myself as a good machine
That Life had never used.

1914

Rutherford McDowell

They brought me ambrotypes
Of the old pioneers to enlarge.
And sometimes one sat for me—
Some one who was in being
When giant hands from the womb of the world
Tore the republic.
What was it in their eyes?—
For I could never fathom
That mystical pathos of drooped eyelids,
And the serene sorrow of their eyes.   10
It was like a pool of water,
Amid oak trees at the edge of a forest,
Where the leaves fall,
As you hear the crow of a cock
From a far-off farm house, seen near the hills
Where the third generation lives, and the
    strong men
And the strong women are gone and forgotten.
And these grand-children and great-grand-
    children
Of the pioneers!
Truly did my camera record their faces, too,
With so much of the old strength gone,   21
And the old faith gone,
And the old mastery of life gone,
And the old courage gone,
Which labors and loves and suffers and sings
Under the sun!

1914

SIMON SURNAMED PETER

Time that has lifted you over them all—
O'er John and o'er Paul;
Writ you in capitals, made you the chief
Word on the leaf—
How did you, Peter, when ne'er on His breast
You leaned and were blest,
And none except Judas and you broke the faith
To the day of His death,—
You, Peter, the fisherman, worthy of blame,
Arise to this fame?   10

'Twas you in the garden who fell into sleep
And the watch failed to keep,
When Jesus was praying and pressed with the
    weight
Of the oncoming fate.

'Twas you in the court of the palace who
　　warmed
Your hands as you stormed
At the damsel, denying Him thrice, when she
　　cried:
"He walked at his side!"
You, Peter, a wave, a star among clouds, a
　　reed in the wind,
A guide of the blind,　　　　　　　　　20
Both smiter and flyer, but human alway, I
　　protest,
Beyond all the rest.

When at night by the boat on the sea He ap-
　　peared
Did you wait till he neared?
You leaped in the water, not dreading the
　　worst
In your joy to be first
To greet Him and tell Him of all that had
　　passed
Since you saw Him the last.
You had slept while He watched, but fierce
　　were you, fierce and awake
When they sought Him to take,　　　　30
And cursing, no doubt, as you smote off, as
　　one of the least,
The ear of the priest.
Then Andrew and all of them fled, but you
　　followed Him, hoping for strength
To save him at length,
Till you lied to the damsel, oh penitent Peter,
　　and crept
Into hiding and wept.

Oh well! But he asked all the twelve, "Who
　　am I?"
And who made reply?
As you leaped in the sea, so you spoke as you
　　smote with the sword;
"Thou art Christ, even Lord!"　　　　40
John leaned on His breast, but He asked you,
　　your strength to foresee,
"Nay, lovest thou me?"
Thrice over, as thrice you denied Him, and
　　chose you to lead
His sheep and to feed;
And gave you, He said, the keys of the den
　　and the fold
To have and to hold.
You were a poor jailer, oh Peter, the dreamer,
　　who saw
The death of the law
In the dream of the vessel that held all the
　　four-footed beasts,
Unclean for the priests;　　　　　　50
And heard in the vision a trumpet that all
　　men are worth

The peace of the earth
And rapture of heaven hereafter,—oh Peter,
　　what power
Was yours in that hour:
You warder and jailer and sealer of fates and
　　decrees,
To use the big keys
With which to reveal and fling wide all the
　　soul and the scheme
Of the Galilee dream,
When you flashed in a trice, as later you smote
　　with the sword:
"Thou art Christ, even Lord!"　　　60
We men, Simon Peter, we men also give you
　　the crown
O'er Paul and o'er John.
We write you in capitals, make you the chief
　　Word on the leaf.
We know you as one of our flesh, and 'tis well
You are warder of hell,
And heaven's gatekeeper forever to bind and
　　to loose—
Keep the keys if you choose.
Not rock of you, fire of you make you sublime
In the annals of time.　　　　　　70
You were called by Him, Peter, a rock, but we
　　give you the name
Of Peter the Flame.
For you struck a spark, as the spark from the
　　shock
Of steel upon rock.
The rock has his use but the flame gives the
　　light
In the way in the night:—
Oh Peter, the dreamer, impetuous, human,
　　divine,
Gnarled branch of the vine!
　　　　　　　　　　　　　　　1915

SO WE GREW TOGETHER

Reading over your letters I find you wrote
　　me
"My dear boy," or at times "dear boy," and
　　the envelope
Said "master"—all as I had been your very
　　son,
And not the orphan whom you adopted.
Well, you were father to me! And I can recall
The things you did for me or gave me:
One time we rode in a box car to Springfield
To see the greatest show on earth;
And one time you gave me redtop boots,
And one time a watch, and one time a gun.
Well, I grew to gawkiness with a voice　　11
Like a rooster trying to crow in August
Hatched in April, we'll say.

And you went about wrapped up in silence
With eyes aflame, and I heard little rumors
Of what they were doing to you, and how
They wronged you—and we were poor—so
    poor!
And I could not understand why you failed,
And why if you did good things for the people
The people did not sustain you.   20
And why you loved another woman than Aunt
    Susan,
So it was whispered at school, and what could
    be baser,
Or so little to be forgiven? . . .

      They crowded you hard in those days.
But you fought like a wounded lion
For yourself I know, but for us, for me.
At last you fell ill, and for months you tottered
Around the streets as thin as death,
Trying to earn our bread, your great eyes
    glowing
And the silence around you like a shawl!   30
But something in you kept you up.
You grew well again and rosy with cheeks
Like an Indian peach almost, and eyes
Full of moonlight and sunlight, and a voice
That sang, and a humor that warded
The arrows off. But still between us
There was reticence; you kept me away
With a glittering hardness; perhaps you
    thought
I kept you away—for I was moving
In spheres you knew not, living through   40
Beliefs you believed in no more, and ideals
That were just mirrors of unrealities.
As a boy can be I was critical of you
And reasons for your failures began to arise
In my mind—I saw specific facts here and
    there
With no philosophy at hand to weld them,
And synthesize them into one truth.
And a rush of the strength of youth
Deluded me into thinking the world
Was something so easily understood and man-
    aged,   50
While I knew it not at all in truth.
And an adolescent egotism
Made me feel you did not know me,
Or comprehend the all that I was.
All this you divined. . . .

      So it went. And when I left you and
          passed
To the world, the city—still I see you
With eyes averted, and feel your hand
Limp with sorrow—you could not speak.   59
You thought of what I might be, and where
Life would take me, and how it would end—

There was longer silence. A year or two
Brought me closer to you. I saw the play now,
And the game somewhat and understood your
    fights
And enmities, and hardnesses and silences,
And wild humor that had kept you whole—
For your soul had made it as an antitoxin
To the world's infections. And you swung to
    me
Closer than before—and a chumship began
Between us. . . .   70

      What vital power was yours!
You never tired, or needed sleep, or had a pain,
Or refused a delight. I loved the things now
You had always loved, a winning horse,
A roulette wheel, a contest of skill
In games or sports . . . long talks on the
    corner
With men who have lived and tell you
Things with a rich flavor of old wisdom or
    humor;
A woman, a glass of whisky at a table
Where the fatigue of life falls, and our reserves
That wait for happiness come up in smiles,   81
Laughter, gentle confidences. Here you were
A man with youth, and I a youth was a man,
Exulting in your braveries and delight in life.
How you knocked that scamp over at Harry
    Varnell's
When he tried to take your chips! And how I,
Who had thought the devil in cards as a boy,
Loved to play with you now and watch you
    play;
And watch the subtle mathematics of your
    mind
Prophesy, divine the plays. Who was it   90
In your ancestry that you harked back to
And reproduced with such various gifts
Of flesh and spirit, Anglo-Saxon, Celt?—
You with such rapid wit and powerful skill
For catching illogic and whipping Error's
Fangèd head from the body? . . .

      I was really ahead of you
At this stage, with more self-consciousness
Of what man is, and what life is at last,   99
And how the spirit works, and by what laws,
With what inevitable force. But still I was
Behind you in that strength which in our
    youth,
If ever we have it, squeezes all the nectar
From the grapes. It seemed you'd never lose
This power and sense of joy, but yet at times
I saw another phase of you. . . .

      There was the day
We rode together north of the old town,

Past the old farm houses that I knew—
Past maple groves, and fields of corn in the
shock, 110
And fields of wheat with the fall green.
It was October, but the clouds were summer's,
Lazily floating in a sky of June;
And a few crows flying here and there,
And a quail's call, and around us a great silence
That held at its core old memories
Of pioneers, and dead days, forgotten things!
I'll never forget how you looked that day.
Your hair
Was turning silver now, but still your eyes
Burned as of old, and the rich olive glow 120
In your cheeks shone, with not a line or
wrinkle!—
You seemed to me perfection—a youth, a
man!
And now you talked of the world with the old
wit,
And now of the soul—how such a man went
down
Through folly or wrong done by him, and how
Man's death cannot end all,
There must be life hereafter! . . .

As you were that day, as you looked and
spoke,
As the earth was, I hear as the soul of it all
Godard's *Dawn*, Dvorák's *Humoresque*, 130
The Morris Dances, Mendelssohn's *Barcarole*,
And old Scotch songs, *When the Kye Come
Hame*,
And *The Moon Had Climbed the Highest Hill*,
The Musetta Waltz and Rudolph's Narrative;
Your great brow seemed Beethoven's
And the lust of life in your face Cellini's,
And your riotous fancy like Dumas.
I was nearer you now than ever before,
And finding each other thus I see to-day
How the human soul seeks the human soul
And finds the one it seeks at last. 141
For you know you can open a window
That looks upon embowered darkness,
When the flowers sleep and the trees are still
At Midnight, and no light burns in the room;
And you can hide your butterfly
Somewhere in the room, but soon you will see
A host of butterfly mates
Fluttering through the window to join
Your butterfly hid in the room. 150
It is somehow thus with souls. . . .

This day then I understood it all:
Your vital democracy and love of men
And tolerance of life; and how the excess of
these
Had wrought your sorrows in the days

When we were so poor, and the small of mind
Spoke of your sins and your connivance
With sinful men. You had lived it down,
Had triumphed over them, and you had grown
Prosperous in the world and had passed 160
Into an easy mastery of life and beyond the
thought
Of further conquests for things.
As the Brahmins say, no more you worshiped
matter,
Or scarcely ghosts, or even the gods
With singleness of heart.
This day you worshiped Eternal Peace,
Or Eternal Flame, with scarce a laugh or jest
To hide your worship; and I understood,
Seeing so many facets of you, why it was
Blind Condon always smiled to hear your
voice, 170
And why it was in a greenroom years ago
Booth turned to you, marking your face
From all the rest, and said, "There is a man
Who might play Hamlet—better still Othel-
lo";
And why it was the women loved you; and the
priest
Could feed his body and soul together drinking
A glass of beer and visiting with you. . . .

Then something happened:
Your face grew smaller, your brow more nar-
row,
Dull fires burned in your eyes, 180
Your body shriveled, you walked with a cyni-
cal shuffle,
Your hands mixed the keys of life,
You had become a discord.
A monstrous hatred consumed you—
You had suffered the greatest wrong of all,
I knew and granted the wrong.
You had mounted up to sixty years, now
breathing hard,
And just at the time that honor belonged to
you
You were dishonored at the hands of a friend.
I wept for you, and still I wondered 190
If all I had grown to see in you and find in you
And love in you was just a fond illusion—
If after all I had not seen you aright as a boy:
Barbaric, hard, suspicious, cruel, redeemed
Alone by bubbling animal spirits—
Even these gone now, all of you smoke
Laden with stinging gas and lethal vapor . . .
Then you came forth again like the sun after
storm—
The deadly uric acid driven out at last
Which had poisoned you and dwarfed your
soul— 200
So much for soul!

The last time I saw you
Your face was full of golden light,
Something between flame and the richness of
    flesh.
You were yourself again, wholly yourself.
And oh, to find you again and resume
Our understanding we had worked so long to
    reach—
You calm and luminant and rich in thought!
This time it seemed we said but "yes" or
    "no"—
That was enough; we smoked together   210
And drank a glass of wine and watched
The leaves fall sitting on the porch . . .
Then life whirled me away like a leaf,
And I went about the crowded ways of New
    York.

And one night Alberta and I took dinner
At a place near Fourteenth Street where the
    music
Was like the sun on a breeze-swept lake
When every wave is a patine of fire,
And I thought of you not at all
Looking at Alberta and watching her white
    teeth   220
Bite off bits of Italian bread;
And watching her smile and the wide pupils
Of her eyes, electrified by wine
And music and the touch of our hands

Now and then across the table.
We went to her house at last.
And through a languorous evening,
Where no light was but a single candle,
We circled about and about a pending theme,
Till at last we solved it suddenly in rapture
Almost by chance; and when I left   231
She followed me to the hall and leaned above
The railing about the stair for the farewell
    kiss.
And I went into the open air ecstatically,
With the stars in the spaces of sky between
The towering buildings, and the rush
Of wheels and clang of bells,
Still with the fragrance of her lips and cheeks,
And glinting hair about me, delicate
And keen in spite of the open air.   240
And just as I entered the brilliant car
Something said to me you were dead—
I had not thought of you, was not thinking of
    you.
But I knew it was true, as it was,
For the telegram waited me at my room . . .
                    I didn't come back.
I could not bear to see the breathless breath
Over your brow—nor look at your face—
However you fared or where,
To what victories soever—   250
Vanquished or seemingly vanquished!
                    1916

EDWIN MARKHAM (1852–   )

THE MAN WITH THE HOE

Bowed by the weight of centuries he leans
Upon his hoe and gazes on the ground,
The emptiness of ages in his face,
And on his back the burden of the world.
Who made him dead to rapture and de-
    spair,
A thing that grieves not and that never hopes,
Stolid and stunned, a brother to the ox?
Who loosened and let down this brutal jaw?
Whose was the hand that slanted back this
    brow?
Whose breath blew out the light within this
    brain?   10

Is this the Thing the Lord God made and gave
To have dominion over sea and land;
To trace the stars and search the heavens for
    power;
To feel the passion of Eternity?
Is this the dream He dreamed who shaped the
    suns
And marked their ways upon the ancient deep?
Down all the caverns of Hell to their last gulf

There is no shape more terrible than this—
More tongued with cries against the world's
    blind greed—
More filled with signs and portents for the
    soul—   20
More packt with danger to the universe.

What gulfs between him and the seraphim!
Slave of the wheel of labor, what to him
Are Plato and the swing of Pleiades?
What the long reaches of the peaks of song,
The rift of dawn, the reddening of the rose?
Through this dread shape the suffering ages
    look;
Time's tragedy is in that aching stoop;
Thru this dread shape humanity betrayed,
Plundered, profaned and disinherited,   30
Cries protest to the Powers that made the
    world,
A protest that is also prophecy.

O masters, lords and rulers in all lands,
Is this the handiwork you give to God,

This monstrous thing distorted and soul-
quencht?
How will you ever straighten up this shape;
Touch it again with immortality;
Give back the upward looking and the light;
Rebuild in it the music and the dream;
Make right the immemorial infamies, 40
Perfidious wrongs, immedicable woes?

O masters, lords and rulers in all lands,

How will the future reckon with this Man?
How answer his brute question in that hour
When whirlwinds of rebellion shake all shores?
How will it be with kingdoms and with kings—
With those who shaped him to the thing he
is—
When this dumb Terror shall rise to judge the
world,
After the silence of the centuries?
                                    1899, 1924

LINCOLN, THE MAN OF THE PEOPLE

When the Norn Mother saw the Whirlwind
Hour
Greatening and darkening as it hurried on,
She left the Heaven of Heroes and came down
To make a man to meet the mortal need.
She took the tried clay of the common road—
Clay warm yet with the genial heat of Earth,
Dasht through it all a strain of prophecy,
Tempered the heap with thrill of human tears
Then mixt a laughter with the serious stuff.
Into the shape she breathed a flame to light
That tender, tragic, ever-changing face; 11
And laid on him a sense of the Mystic Powers,
Moving—all husht—behind the mortal vail.
Here was a man to hold against the world,
A man to match the mountains and the sea.

The color of the ground was in him, the red
earth,
The smack and tang of elemental things:
The rectitude and patience of the cliff,
The good-will of the rain that loves all leaves,
The friendly welcome of the wayside well, 20
The courage of the bird that dares the sea,
The gladness of the wind that shakes the corn,
The pity of the snow that hides all scars,
The secrecy of streams that makes their way
Under the mountain to the rifted rock,
The tolerance and equity of light
That gives as freely to the shrinking flower
As to the great oak flaring to the wind—
To the grave's low hill as to the Matterhorn
That shoulders out the sky. Sprung from the
West, 30

He drank the valorous youth of a new world.
The strength of virgin forests braced his mind,
The hush of spacious prairies stilled his soul.
His words were oaks in acorns; and his
thoughts
Were roots that firmly gript the granite truth.

Up from log cabin to the Capitol,
One fire was on his spirit, one resolve—
To send the keen ax to the root of wrong,
Clearing a free way for the feet of God,
The eyes of conscience testing every stroke,
To make his deed the measure of a man. 41
He built the rail-pile as he built the State,
Pouring his splendid strength through every
blow:
The grip that swung the ax in Illinois
Was on the pen that set a people free.

So came the Captain with the mighty heart;
And when the judgment thunders split the
house,
Wrenching the rafters from their ancient rest,
He held the ridgepole up, and spikt again 49
The rafters of the Home. He held his place—
Held the long purpose like a growing tree—
Held on through blame and faltered not at
praise—
Towering in calm rough-hewn sublimity.
And when he fell in whirlwind, he went down
As when a lordly cedar, green with boughs,
Goes down with a great shout upon the hills,
And leaves a lonesome place against the sky.
                                    1900, 1919

JOSEPHINE PRESTON PEABODY (1874-1922)

CANONIZED

There by the wayside, so she ever stood,
  Shadowed and small, unwitting of the sky,
Nought but a little lorn beatitude
  To pray to and pass by.

So young she was, not all the grievous rain
  That wept to her had ever taught her tears;
Yet no May morning kindled blue again
  Her wide eyes, dulled with years.

So cold she was with vigil—the one care
  To be a steadfast saint, she did not know   10
Vines called to her; her hands held unaware
  The mocking gift of snow.

Life was not life to her: she dimly saw
  Dim flocks gone by, and herdsmen weary-
      dull,
And loitering children, to whose brimming awe
  She seemed all-beautiful.

Time was not time to her: she heard, content,
  The hour, like one more prayer-bead,
      slipped along
A rosary of vigil never spent,
  Matins and even-song.   20

Was it because she knew not how to stir
  An empty hand, and beckon gladness
      come,—
The wingèd secret spread its wings to her
  And took her heart for home?

For close as silence, rounded as a song,
  Built sure within the quiet of her breast,—
Shy sanctuary, all the year has clung
  A brown deserted nest.

Surely she woke to find the world at spring,
  And all her sainthood quickened with the
      rime;   30
Surely there came to her on rain-soft wing,
  Love, for a summer-time.

Query, and heart-beat, and the eager stress
  Of sunward wings made wise her solitude;
Love, and the warm content of littleness
  With her maid-motherhood.

Since when she stands as patiently adream
  With empty hands outheld, that make no
      stir,—
All in a long last-year: it well may seem
  Time is not time to her.   40

And yet she knows the plea of vines that call,
  The weariness of folk that pass, with eyes
Outlooking on the burden of them all,
  Awakened, warm, and wise.

O wind of summer, blow her songs of thine;
  O wind of winter, look ye spare alone
One nest, not now too lordly for a shrine,
  —Since all the birds are flown.
                                        1898

UNSAID

Ah, lad, if I could only say
  The smiles are not for you!
But since your eyes are turned this way,
  What is there I can do?
It's one I see beyond, beyond,
  My heart is leaning to.

I know, I know, the whole hour long
  I have been dull and sad,
And answered not the word at all
  I meant to answer, lad;   10
Because my wits were gone astray
  With all the heart I had.

And now the latest ones are come,
  And he is coming too;
And I would keep the starlight back,
  But oh, it will shine through!
And since you never turn to see,
  You take it all to you.
                                        1903

THOMAS AUGUSTINE DALY (1871–   )

LEETLA JOE

Leetla Joe he always say:
"W'en I am beeg man som' day,
  Eef so be I gona grow
Strong an' fat so like my Pop,
I weell go for be a cop,
  Mebbe so."
Soocha talk for four-year-old!
Dough he brag so beeg an' bold
Een wan handa you could hold
  Leetla Joe.   10

Leetla Joe he lay hees cheek
On my breast w'en he ees seeck,
  Squeeze my arm an' tal me: "Oh!

Pretta soon I gona gat
Granda muscle lika dat.
  W'en I grow
Like my Pop how proud I be!
Justa wait an' you weell see."
Ah! so sweet to hug to me
  Leetla Joe!   20

But, baycause I'm 'fraid dat he
Wan day would be 'shame' of me,—
  'Shame for call me "Pop" an' know,
W'en he's fina 'Merican,
I'm so poor old Dagoman—
  W'en I go
Where hees grave ees on da heell,
Dere ees joy for me to feel

Dat my heart can keep heem steell
Leetla Joe.   30

1908

PADRE ANGELO

Padre Angelo he say:
"Why you no gat married, eh?
You are maka playnta mon'
For gon' taka wife, my son."
"No; I am too beeza man
'Tandin' dees peanutta stan'.
I no gatta time for play
Fooleeshness weeth girls," I say.
"My! you don'ta tal me so?"
Ees say Padre Angelo.   10

Bimeby, Mebbe two, t'ree day,
Younga girl she com' an' say:
"Padre Angelo ees here?
No? Eet eesa vera queer!
Heesa housakeepa say
I gon' find heem deesa way."
While she eesa speaka so
Ees com' Padre Angelo.
"Rosa! you are look for me?"
He ees say to her, an' she   20
Say: "Oh, pleass, go homa, queeck,
You are want' for som' wan seeck.
I am sand for find you here."
"Ah! da seecka-call, my dear.
Com'," say Padre Angelo,
"Deesa younga man ees Joe;
Shaka han's bayfore we go."
So I am shak' han's weeth her—
Leetla han' so sof' like fur—
Den she bow to me an' go   30
Weetha Padre Angelo.

Bimeby, s'pose two, t'ree day more,
She ees com' jus' like bayfore,
An' she aska me: "You know
Where ees Padre Angelo?
Housakeep' she tal me wait
Eef he don't be vera late."
So I tal her taka seat
An' to hav' som' fruit for eat.
Den I talk to her an' she   40
Smila sweet an' talk to me;
How long time I donta know.
Den com' Padre Angelo.
"Oh," she say, "go homa queeck,
You are want' for som' wan seeck."
"My!" he say, "dese seecka-call!
I am gat no peace at all."
"Oh, wal, com', my dear," he say,
An' he takin' her way.
I am sad for see her go   50
Weetha Padre Angelo.

Many times ees lika dat.
Peopla always seem for gat
Seecka when he ees away.
Rosa com' mos' evra day.
An' som' time she gatta stay
Pretta longa time, you know,
Teel com' Padre Angelo.
Steel I no gat any keeck
How mooch peopla gatta seeck;   60
I am feela glad dey do—
Rosa, she no keeckin', too.
Lasta night my Rosa she
Go to Padre weetha me,
An' I tal heem: "Pretta soon—
Mebbe so da firsta June—
Rosa gona be my wife!"
He ees s'prise', you bat my life!
"W'at?" he say, an' rub hees eyes,
"Dees ees soocha glada s'prise!   70
My! you don'ta tal me so?"
Ees say Padre Angelo.   1909

BETWEEN TWO LOVES

I gotta love for Angela,
    I love Carlotta, too.
I no can marry both o' dem,
    So w'at I gona do?

Oh, Angela ees pretta girl,
She gotta hair so black, so curl,
An' teeth so white as anytheeng.
An' oh, she gotta voice to seeng,
Dat mak' your hearta feel eet must
Jomp up an' dance or eet weell bust.   10
An' alla time she seeng, her eyes
Dey smila like Italia's skies,
An' makin' flirtin' looks at you—
But dat ees all w'at she can do.

Carlotta ees no gotta song,
But she ees twice so big an' strong
As Angela, an' she no look
So beautiful—but she can cook.
You oughta see her carry wood!
I tal you w'at, eet do you good.   20
W'en she ees be som'body's wife
She worka hard, you bat my life!
She nevva gattin' tired, too—
But dat ees all w'at she can do.

Oh, my! I weesh dat Angela
    Was strong for carry wood,
Or else Carlotta gotta song
    An' looka pretta good.
I gotta love for Angela,
    I love Carlotta, too.   30

I no can marry both o' dem,
So w'at I gona do?
1909

THE SONG OF THE THRUSH

Ah! the May was grand this mornin'!
Shure, how could I feel forlorn in
Such a land, when tree and flower tossed their
kisses to the breeze?
Could an Irish heart be quiet
While the Spring was runnin' riot,
An' the birds of free America were singin' in
the trees?
In the songs that they were singin'
No familiar note was ringin',
But I strove to imitate them an' I whistled
like a lad.
Oh, my heart was warm to love them   10
For the very newness of them—

For the ould songs that they helped me to
forget—an' I was glad.

So I mocked the feathered choir
To my hungry heart's desire,
An' I gloried in the comradeship that made
their joy my own,
Till a new note sounded, stillin'
All the rest. A thrush was trillin'!
Ah! the thrush I left behind me in the fields
about Athlone!
Where, upon the whitethorn swayin',
He was minstrel of the Mayin',   20
In my days of love an' laughter that the years
have laid at rest;
Here again his notes were ringin'!
But I'd lost the heart for singin'—
Ah! the song I could not answer was the one I
knew the best.
1909

ROBERT FROST (1875–   )

MY NOVEMBER GUEST

My Sorrow, when she's here with me,
Thinks these dark days of autumn rain
Are beautiful as days can be;
She loves the bare, the withered tree;
She walks the sodden pasture lane.

Her pleasure will not let me stay.
She talks and I am fain to list:
She's glad the birds are gone away,
She's glad her simple worsted grey
Is silver now with clinging mist.   10

The desolate, deserted trees,
The faded earth, the heavy sky,
The beauties she so truly sees,
She thinks I have no eye for these,
And vexes me for reason why.

Not yesterday I learned to know
The love of bare November days
Before the coming of the snow,
But it were vain to tell her so,
And they are better for her praise.   20
1912

MENDING WALL

Something there is that doesn't love a wall,
That sends the frozen-ground-swell under it,
And spills the upper boulders in the sun;
And makes gaps even two can pass abreast.
The work of hunters is another thing:
I have come after them and made repair
Where they have left not one stone on a stone,
But they would have the rabbit out of hiding,
To please the yelping dogs. The gaps I mean,
No one has seen them made or heard them
made,   10
But at spring mending-time we find them
there.
I let my neighbor know beyond the hill;
And on a day we meet to walk the line
And set the wall between us once again.
And keep the wall between us as we go.

To each the boulders that have fallen to each.
And some are loaves and some so nearly balls
We have to use a spell to make them balance:
"Stay where you are until our backs are
turned!"
We wear our fingers rough with handling
them.   20
Oh, just another kind of out-door game,
One on a side. It comes to little more:
There where it is we do not need the wall:
He is all pine and I am apple orchard.
My apple trees will never get across
And eat the cones under his pines, I tell
him.
He only says, "Good fences make good neigh-
bours."
Spring is the mischief in me, and I wonder

If I could put a notion in his head:
"*Why* do they make good neighbours?
     Isn't it   30
Where there are cows? But here there are no
     cows.
Before I built a wall I'd ask to know
What I was walling in or walling out,
And to whom I was like to give offence.
Something there is that doesn't love a wall,
That wants it down." I could say "Elves"
     to him,

But it's not elves exactly, and I'd rather
He said it for himself. I see him there
Bringing a stone grasped firmly by the top
In each hand, like an old-stone savage armed.
He moves in darkness as it seems to me,   41
Not of woods only and the shade of trees.
He will not go behind his father's saying,
And he likes having thought of it so well
He says again, "Good fences make good
     neighbours."

1914

THE BLACK COTTAGE

We chanced in passing by that afternoon
To catch it in a sort of special picture
Among tar-banded ancient cherry trees,
Set well back from the road in rank lodged
     grass,
The little cottage we were speaking of,
A front with just a door between two windows,
Fresh painted by the shower a velvet black.
We paused, the minister and I, to look.
He made as if to hold it at arm's length
Or put the leaves aside that framed it in.   10
"Pretty," he said. "Come in. No one will
     care."
The path was a vague parting in the grass
That led us to a weathered window-sill.
We pressed our faces to the pane. "You see,"
     he said,
"Everything's as she left it when she died.
Her sons won't sell the house or the things in
     it.
They say they mean to come and summer here
Where they were boys. They haven't come
     this year.
They live so far away—one is out west—
It will be hard for them to keep their word. 20
Anyway they won't have the place disturbed."
A buttoned hair-cloth lounge spread scrolling
     arms
Under a crayon portrait on the wall
Done sadly from an old daguerreotype.
"That was the father as he went to war.
She always, when she talked about war,
Sooner or later came and leaned, half knelt
Against the lounge beside it, though I doubt
If such unlifelike lines kept power to stir
Anything in her after all the years.   30
He fell at Gettysburg or Fredericksburg,
I ought to know—it makes a difference which:
Fredericksburg wasn't Gettysburg, of course.
But what I'm getting to is how forsaken
A little cottage this has always seemed;
Since she went more than ever, but before—
I don't mean altogether by the lives
That had gone out of it, the father first,

Then the two sons, till she was left alone.
(Nothing could draw her after those two sons.
She valued the considerate neglect   41
She had at some cost taught them after years.)
I mean by the world's having passed it by—
As we almost got by this afternoon.
It always seems to me a sort of mark
To measure how far fifty years have brought
     us.
Why not sit down if you are in no haste?
These doorsteps seldom have a visitor.
The warping boards pull out their own old
     nails
With none to tread and put them in their
     place.   50
She had her own idea of things, the old lady.
And she liked talk. She had seen Garrison
And Whittier, and had her story of them.
One wasn't long in learning that she thought
Whatever else the Civil War was for
It wasn't just to keep the States together,
Nor just to free the slaves, though it did both.
She wouldn't have believed those ends enough
To have given outright for them all she gave.
Her giving somehow touched the principle   60
That all men are created free and equal.
And to hear her quaint phrases—so removed
From the world's view to-day of all those
     things.
That's a hard mystery of Jefferson's.
What did he mean? Of course the easy way
Is to decide it simply isn't true.
It may not be. I heard a fellow say so.
But never mind, the Welshman got it planted
Where it will trouble us a thousand years.
Each age will have to reconsider it.   70
You couldn't tell her what the West was
     saying,
And what the South to her serene belief.
She had some art of hearing and yet not
Hearing the latter wisdom of the world.
White was the only race she ever knew.
Black she had scarcely seen, and yellow never.
But how could they be made so very unlike

By the same hand working in the same stuff?
She had supposed the war decided that.
What are you going to do with such a person?
Strange how such innocence gets its own
    way. 81
I shouldn't be surprised if in this world
It were the force that would at last prevail.
Do you know but for her there was a time
When to please younger members of the
    church,
Or rather say non-members in the church,
Whom we all have to think of nowadays,
I would have changed the Creed a very little?
Not that she ever had to ask me not to;
It never got so far as that; but the bare
    thought 90
Of her old tremulous bonnet in the pew,
And of her half asleep was too much for me.
Why, I might wake her up and startle her.
It was the words 'descended into Hades'
That seemed too pagan to our liberal youth.
You know they suffered from a general on-
    slaught.
And well, if they weren't true why keep right
    on
Saying them like the heathen? We could drop
    them.
Only—there was the bonnet in the pew.
Such a phrase couldn't have meant much to
    her. 100
But suppose she had missed it from the Creed

As a child misses the unsaid Good-night,
And falls asleep with heartache—how should
    I feel?
I'm just as glad she made me keep hands off,
For, dear me, why abandon a belief
Merely because it ceases to be true.
Cling to it long enough, and not a doubt
It will turn true again, for so it goes.
Most of the change we think we see in life
Is due to truths being in and out of favour. 110
As I sit here, and oftentimes, I wish
I could be monarch of a desert land
I could devote and dedicate forever
To the truths we keep coming back and back
    to.
So desert it would have to be, so walled
By mountain ranges half in summer snow,
No one would covet it or think it worth
The pains of conquering to force change on.
Scattered oases where men dwelt, but mostly
Sand dunes held loosely in tamarisk 120
Blown over and over themselves in idleness.
Sand grains should sugar in the natal dew
The babe born to the desert, the sand storm
Retard mid-waste my cowering caravans—

"There are bees in this wall." He struck the
    clapboards,
Fierce heads looked out; small bodies pivoted.
We rose to go. Sunset blazed on the windows.
                   1914

BIRCHES

When I see birches bend to left and right
Across the lines of straighter darker trees,
I like to think some boy's been swinging them.
But swinging doesn't bend them down to stay.
Ice-storms do that. Often you must have seen
    them
Loaded with ice a sunny winter morning
After a rain. They click upon themselves
As the breeze rises, and turn many-colored
As the stir cracks and crazes their enamel.
Soon the sun's warmth makes them shed crys-
    tal shells 10
Shattering and avalanching on the snow-
    crust—
Such heaps of broken glass to sweep away
You'd think the inner dome of heaven had
    fallen.
They are dragged to the withered bracken by
    the load,
And they seem not to break; though once they
    are bowed
So low for long, they never right themselves:
You may see their trunks arching in the woods

Years afterwards, trailing their leaves on the
    ground
Like girls on hands and knees that throw their
    hair
Before them over their heads to dry in the sun.
But I was going to say when Truth broke in 21
With all her matter-of-fact about the ice-storm
(Now am I free to be poetical?)
I should prefer to have some boy bend them
As he went out and in to fetch the cows—
Some boy too far from town to learn baseball,
Whose only play was what he found himself,
Summer or winter, and could play alone.
One by one he subdued his father's trees
By riding them down over and over again 30
Until he took the stiffness out of them,
And not one but hung limp, not one was left
For him to conquer. He learned all there was
To learn about not launching out too soon
And so not carrying the tree away
Clear to the ground. He always kept his poise
To the top branches, climbing carefully
With the same pains you use to fill a cup

Up to the brim, and even above the brim.
Then he flung outward, feet first, with a swish,
Kicking his way down through the air to the
　ground.　　　　　　　　　　　　　　　41
So was I once myself a swinger of birches.
And so I dream of going back to be.
It's when I'm weary of considerations,
And life is too much like a pathless wood
Where your face burns and tickles with the
　cobwebs
Broken across it, and one eye is weeping
From a twig's having lashed across it open.
I'd like to get away from earth awhile
And then come back to it and begin over.　50
May no fate willfully misunderstand me

And half grant what I wish and snatch me
　away
Not to return. Earth's the right place for love:
I don't know where it's likely to go better.
I'd like to go by climbing a birch tree,
And climb black branches up a snow-white
　trunk
Toward heaven, till the tree could bear no
　more,
But dipped its top and set me down again.
That would be good both going and coming
　back.
One could do worse than be a swinger of
　birches.　　　　　　　　　　　　　　　60
　　　　　　　　　　　　　　　　1915

THE ROAD NOT TAKEN

Two roads diverged in a yellow wood,
And sorry I could not travel both
And be one traveler, long I stood
And looked down one as far as I could
To where it bent in the undergrowth;

Then took the other, as just as fair,
And having perhaps the better claim,
Because it was grassy and wanted wear;
Though as for that the passing there
Had worn them really about the same,　10

And both that morning equally lay
In leaves no step had trodden black.
Oh, I kept the first for another day!
Yet knowing how way leads on to way,
I doubted if I should ever come back.

I shall be telling this with a sigh
Somewhere ages and ages hence:
Two roads diverged in a wood, and I—
I took the one less traveled by,
And that has made all the difference.　20
　　　　　　　　　　　　　　　　1915

PLACE FOR A THIRD

Nothing to say to all those marriages!
She had made three herself to three of his.
The score was even for them, three to three.
But come to die she found she cared so much:
She thought of children in a burial row;
Three children in a burial row were sad.
One man's three women in a burial row
Somehow made her impatient with the man.
And so she said to Laban, "You have done
A good deal right; don't do the last thing
　wrong.　　　　　　　　　　　　　　　10
Don't make me lie with those two other
　women."

Laban said, No, he would not make her lie
With anyone but that she had a mind to,
If that was how she felt, of course, he said.
She went her way. But Laban having caught
This glimpse of lingering person in Eliza,
And anxious to make all he could of it
With something he remembered in himself,
Tried to think how he could exceed his
　promise,
And give good measure to the dead, though
　thankless.　　　　　　　　　　　　　20

If that was how she felt, he kept repeating.
His first thought under pressure was a grave
In a new boughten grave plot by herself,
Under he didn't care how great a stone:
He'd sell a yoke of steers to pay for it.
And weren't there special cemetery flowers,
That, once grief sets to growing, grief may
　rest:
The flowers will go on with grief awhile,
And no one seem neglecting or neglected?
A prudent grief will not despise such aids.　30
He thought of evergreen and everlasting.
And then he had a thought worth many of
　these.
Somewhere must be the grave of the young
　boy
Who married her for playmate more than
　helpmate,
And sometimes laughed at what it was be-
　tween them.
How would she like to sleep her last with him?
Where was his grave? Did Laban know his
　name?
He found the grave a town or two away.

The headstone cut with *John, Beloved Husband*,
Beside it room reserved, they say a sister's, 40
A never-married sister's of that husband,
Whether Eliza would be welcome there.
The dead was bound to silence: ask the sister.
So Laban saw the sister, and, saying nothing
Of where Eliza wanted *not* to lie,
And who had thought to lay her with her first
    love,
Begged simply for the grave. The sister's face
Fell all in wrinkles of responsibility.
She wanted to do right. She'd have to think.
Laban was old and poor, yet seemed to care; 50
And she was old and poor—but she cared, too.
They sat. She cast one dull, old look at him,
Then turned him out to go on other errands
She said he might attend to in the village,
While she made up her mind how much she
    cared—
And how much Laban cared—and why he
    cared,
(She made shrewd eyes to see where he came
    in.)
She'd looked Eliza up her second time,
A widow at her second husband's grave,
And offered her a home to rest awhile 60
Before she went the poor man's widow's way,

Housekeeping for the next man out of wed-
    lock.
She and Eliza had been friends through all.
Who was she to judge marriage in a world
Whose Bible's so confused in marriage coun-
    sel?
The sister had not come across this Laban;
A decent product of life's ironing-out;
She must not keep him waiting. Time would
    press
Between the death day and the funeral day.
So when she saw him coming in the street 70
She hurried her decision to be ready
To meet him with her answer at the door.
Laban had known about what it would be
From the way she had set her poor old mouth,
To do, as she had put it, what was right.

She gave it through the screen door closed be-
    tween them:
"No, not with John. There wouldn't be no
    sense.
Eliza's had too many other men."
Laban was forced to fall back on his plan
To buy Eliza a plot to lie alone in: 80
Which gives him for himself a choice of lots
When his time comes to die and settle down.

                                    1920

THE CENSUS-TAKER

I came an errand one cloud-blowing evening
To a slab-built, black-paper-covered house
Of one room and one window and one door,
The only dwelling in a waste cut over
A hundred square miles round it in the moun-
    tains:
And that not dwelt in now by men or women
(It never had been dwelt in, though, by
    women,
So what is this I make a sorrow of?)
I came as census-taker to the waste
To count the people in it and found none, 10
None in the hundred miles, none in the house,
Where I came last with some hope, but not
    much
After hours' overlooking from the cliffs
An emptiness flayed to the very stone.
I found no people that dared show themselves,
None not in hiding from the outward eye.
The time was autumn, but how anyone
Could tell the time of year when every tree
That could have dropped a leaf was down
    itself
And nothing but the stump of it was left 20
Now bringing out its rings in sugar of pitch;
And every tree up stood a rotting trunk

Without a single leaf to spend on autumn,
Or branch to whistle after what was spent.
Perhaps the wind the more without the help
Of breathing trees said something of the time
Of year or day the way it swung a door
Forever off the latch, as if rude men
Passed in and slammed it shut each one behind
    him
For the next one to open for himself. 30
I counted nine I had no right to count
(But this was dreamy unofficial counting)
Before I made the tenth across the threshold.
Where was my supper? Where was anyone's?
No lamp was lit. Nothing was on the table.
The stove was cold—the stove was off the
    chimney—
And down by one side where it lacked a leg.
The people that had loudly passed the door
Were people to the ear but not the eye.
They were not on the table with their el-
    bows.
They were not sleeping in the shelves of bunks. 40
I saw no men there and no bones of men there.
I armed myself against such bones as might be
With the pitch-blackened stub of an axe-
    handle

I picked up off the straw-dust covered floor.
Not bones, but the ill-fitted window rattled.
The door was still because I held it shut
While I thought what to do that could be
    done—
About the house—about the people not there.
This house in one year fallen to decay   50
Filled me with no less sorrow than the houses
Fallen to ruin in ten thousand years
Where Asia wedges Africa from Europe.
Nothing was left to do that I could see

THE WITCH OF COÖS

Circa 1922

I staid the night for shelter at a farm
Behind the mountain, with a mother and son,
Two old-believers. They did all the talking.

Mother. Folks think a witch who has
    familiar spirits
She could call up to pass a winter evening,
But won't, should be burned at the stake or
    something.
Summoning spirits isn't "Button, button,
Who's got the button," I would have them
    know.

Son. Mother can make a common table
    rear
And kick with two legs like an army mule.   10

Mother. And when I've done it, what good
    have I done?
Rather than tip a table for you, let me
Tell you what Ralle and Sioux Control once
    told me.
He said the dead had souls, but when I asked
    him
How could that be—I thought the dead were
    souls,
He broke my trance. Don't that make you
    suspicious
That there's something the dead are keeping
    back?
Yes, there's something the dead are keeping
    back.

Son. You wouldn't want to tell him what
    we have
Up attic, mother?   20

Mother. Bones—a skeleton.

Son. But the headboard of mother's bed
    is pushed
Against the attic door; the door is nailed.

Unless to find that there was no one there
And declare to the cliffs too far for echo
"The place is desert and let whoso lurks
In silence, if in this he is aggrieved,
Break silence now or be forever silent.
Let him say why it should not be declared so."
The melancholy of having to count souls   61
Where they grow fewer and fewer every year
Is extreme where they shrink to none at all.
It must be I want life to go on living.   1921

It's harmless. Mother hears it in the night
Halting perplexed behind the barrier
Of door and headboard. Where it wants to get
Is back into the cellar where it came from.

Mother. We'll never let them, will we, son?
    We'll never!

Son. It left the cellar forty years ago
And carried itself like a pile of dishes   30
Up one flight from the cellar to the kitchen,
Another from the kitchen to the bedroom,
Another from the bedroom to the attic,
Right past both father and mother, and
    neither stopped it.
Father had gone upstairs; mother was down-
    stairs.
I was a baby: I don't know where I was.

Mother. The only fault my husband found
    with me—
I went to sleep before I went to bed,
Especially in winter when the bed
Might just as well be ice and the clothes snow.
The night the bones came up the cellar-
    stairs   41
Toffile had gone to bed alone and left me,
But left an open door to cool the room off
So as to sort of turn me out of it.
I was just coming to myself enough
To wonder where the cold was coming from,
When I heard Toffile upstairs in the bedroom
And thought I heard him downstairs in the
    cellar.
The board we had laid down to walk dry-shod
    on
When there was water in the cellar in spring 50
Struck the hard cellar bottom. And then
    someone
Began the stairs, two footsteps for each step,
The way a man with one leg and a crutch,
Or a little child, comes up. It wasn't Toffile:
It wasn't anyone who could be there.

The bulkhead double-doors were double-
    locked
And swollen tight and buried under snow.
The cellar windows were banked up with
    sawdust
And swollen tight and buried under snow.
It was the bones. I knew them—and good
    reason.   60
My first impulse was to get to the knob
And hold the door. But the bones didn't try
The door; they halted helpless on the land-
    ing,
Waiting for things to happen in their favor.
The faintest restless rustling ran all through
    them.
I never could have done the thing I did
If the wish hadn't been too strong in me
To see how they were mounted for this walk.
I had a vision of them put together
Not like a man, but like a chandelier.   70
So suddenly I flung the door wide on him.
A moment he stood balancing with emotion,
And all but lost himself. (A tongue of fire
Flashed out and licked along his upper teeth.
Smoke rolled inside the sockets of his eyes.)
Then he came at me with one hand out-
    stretched,
The way he did in life once; but this time
I struck the hand off brittle on the floor,
And fell back from him on the floor myself.
The finger-pieces slid in all directions.   80
(Where did I see one of those pieces lately?
Hand me my button-box—it must be there.)
I sat up on the floor and shouted, "Toffile,
It's coming up to you." It had its choice
Of the door to the cellar or the hall.
It took the hall door for the novelty,
And set off briskly for so slow a thing,
Still going every which way in the joints,
    though,
So that it looked like lightning or a scribble,
From the slap I had just now given its hand. 90
I listened till it almost climbed the stairs
From the hall to the only finished bedroom,
Before I got up to do anything;
Then ran and shouted, "Shut the bedroom
    door,
Toffile, for my sake!" "Company," he said,
"Don't make me get up; I'm too warm in
    bed."
So lying forward weakly on the handrail
I pushed myself upstairs, and in the light
(The kitchen had been dark) I had to own
I could see nothing. "Toffile, I don't see it. 100
It's with us in the room though. It's the
    bones."
"What bones?" "The cellar bones—out of
    the grave."

That made him throw his bare legs out of bed
And sit up by me and take hold of me.
I wanted to put out the light and see
If I could see it, or else mow the room,
With our arms at the level of our knees,
And bring the chalk-pile down. "I'll tell you
    what—
It's looking for another door to try.
The uncommonly deep snow has made him
    think   110
Of his old song, The Wild Colonial Boy,
He always used to sing along the tote-road.
He's after an open door to get out-doors.
Let's trap him with an open door up attic."
Toffile agreed to that, and sure enough,
Almost the moment he was given an opening,
The steps began to climb the attic stairs.
I heard them. Toffile didn't seem to hear
    them.
"Quick!" I slammed to the door and held the
    knob.
"Toffile, get nails." I made him nail the door
    shut,   120
And push the headboard of the bed against it.
Then we asked was there anything
Up attic that we'd ever want again.
The attic was less to us than the cellar.
If the bones liked the attic, let them have it,
Let them stay in the attic. When they some-
    times
Come down the stairs at night and stand per-
    plexed
Behind the door and headboard of the bed,
Brushing their chalky skull with chalky
    fingers,
With sounds like the dry rattling of a shutter,
That's what I sit up in the dark to say— 131
To no one any more since Toffile died.
Let them stay in the attic since they went
    there.
I promised Toffile to be cruel to them
For helping them be cruel once to him.

    Son. We think they had a grave down in
        the cellar.

    Mother. We know they had a grave down
        in the cellar.

    Son. We never could find out whose bones
        they were.

    Mother. Yes, we could too, son. Tell the
        truth for once.
They were a man's his father killed for me. 140
I mean a man he killed instead of me.
The least I could do was to help dig their
    grave.

We were about it one night in the cellar.
Son knows the story: but 'twas not for him
To tell the truth, suppose the time had come.
Son looks surprised to see me end a lie
We'd kept all these years between ourselves
So as to have it ready for outsiders.
But tonight I don't care enough to lie—
I don't remember why I ever cared.   150

Toffile, if he were here, I don't believe
Could tell you why he ever cared himself . . .
She hadn't found the finger-bone she wanted
Among the buttons poured out in her lap.
I verified the name next morning: Toffile.
The rural letter-box said Toffile Lajway.
                                          1922

NEW HAMPSHIRE

I met a lady from the South who said
(You won't believe she said it, but she said it):
"None of my family ever worked, or had
A thing to sell." I don't suppose the work
Much matters. You may work for all of me.
I've seen the time I've had to work myself.
The having anything to sell is what
Is the disgrace in man or state or nation.

I met a traveller from Arkansas
Who boasted of his state as beautiful   10
For diamonds and apples. "Diamonds
And apples in commercial quantities?"
I asked him, on my guard. "Oh yes," he
answered,
Off his. The time was evening in the Pullman.
"I see the porter's made your bed," I told him.

I met a Californian who would
Talk California—a state so blessed,
He said, in climate none had ever died there
A natural death, and Vigilance Committees
Had had to organize to stock the grave-
yards   20
And vindicate the state's humanity.
"Just the way Steffanson runs on," I mur-
mured,
"About the British Arctic. That's what comes
Of being in the market with a climate."
I met a poet from another state,
A zealot full of fluid inspiration,
Who in the name of fluid inspiration,
But in the best style of bad salesmanship,
Angrily tried to make me me write a protest
(In verse I think) against the Volstead Act.
He didn't even offer me a drink   31
Until I asked for one to steady him.
This is called having an idea to sell.

It never could have happened in New Hampshire.

The only person really soiled with trade
I ever stumbled on in old New Hampshire
Was someone who had just come back
ashamed

From selling things in California.
He'd built a noble mansard roof with balls
On turrets like Constantinople, deep   40
In woods some ten miles from a railroad sta-
tion,
As if to put forever out of mind
The hope of being, as we say, received.
I found him standing at the close of day
Inside the threshold of his open barn,
Like a lone actor on a gloomy stage—
And recognized him through the iron grey
In which his face was muffled to the eyes
As an old boyhood friend, and once indeed
A drover with me on the road to Brighton. 50
His farm was "grounds," and not a farm at all;
His house among the local sheds and shanties
Rose like a factor's at a trading station.
And he was rich, and I was still a rascal.
I couldn't keep from asking impolitely,
Where had he been and what had he been
doing?
How did he get so? (Rich was understood.)
In dealing in "old rags" in San Francisco.
Oh it was terrible as well could be.
We both of us turned over in our graves.   60

Just specimens is all New Hampshire has,
One each of everything as in a show-case
Which naturally she doesn't care to sell.

She had one President (pronounce him Purse,
And make the most of it for better or worse.
He's your one chance to score against the
state).
She had one Daniel Webster. He was all
The Daniel Webster ever was or shall be.
She had the Dartmouth needed to produce
him.

I call her old. She has one family   70
Whose claim is good to being settled here
Before the era of colonization,
And before that of exploration even.
John Smith remarked them as he coasted by
Dangling their legs and fishing off a wharf
At the Isles of Shoals, and satisfied himself

They weren't Red Indians but veritable
Pre-primitives of the white race, dawn people,
Like those who furnished Adam's sons with
    wives;
However uninnocent they may have been 80
In being there so early in our history.
They'd been there then a hundred years or
    more.
Pity he didn't ask what they were up to
At that date with a wharf already built,
And take their name. They've since told me
    their name—
Today an honored one in Nottingham.
As for what they were up to more than fish-
    ing—
Suppose they weren't behaving Puritanly,
The hour had not yet struck for being good,
Mankind had not yet gone on the Sabbatical.
It became an explorer of the deep   91
Not to explore too deep in others' business.

Did you but know of him, New Hampshire has
One real reformer who would change the world
So it would be accepted by two classes,
Artists the minute they set up as artists,
Before, that is, they are themselves accepted,
And boys the minute they get out of college.
I can't help thinking those are tests to go by.

And she has one I don't know what to call
    him,
Who comes from Philadelphia every year 101
With a great flock of chickens of rare breeds
He wants to give the educational
Advantages of growing almost wild
Under the watchful eye of hawk and eagle—
Dorkings because they're spoken of by Chau-
    cer,
Sussex because they're spoken of by Herrick.

She has a touch of gold. New Hampshire
    gold—
You may have heard of it. I had a farm
Offered me not long since up Berlin way 110
With a mine on it that was worked for gold;
But not gold in commercial quantities.
Just enough gold to make the engagement
    rings
And marriage rings of those who owned the
    farm.
What gold more innocent could one have asked
    for?

One of my children ranging after rocks
Lately brought home from Andover or Ca-
    naan
A specimen of beryl with a trace
Of radium. I know with radium

The trace would have to be the merest trace
To be below the threshold of commercial, 121
But trust New Hampshire not to have enough
Of radium or anything to sell.

A specimen of everything, I said.
She has one witch—old style. She lives in
    Colebrook.
(The only other witch I ever met
Was lately at a cut-glass dinner in Boston.
There were four candles and four people pres-
    ent.
The witch was young, and beautiful (new
    style), 129
And open-minded. She was free to question
Her gift for reading letters locked in boxes.
Why was it so much greater when the boxes
Were metal than it was when they were
    wooden?
It made the world seem so mysterious.
The S'ciety for Psychical Research
Was cognizant. Her husband was worth mil-
    lions.
I think he owned some shares in Harvard Col-
    lege.)

New Hampshire *used* to have at Salem
A company we called the White Corpuscles,
Whose duty was at any hour of night 140
To rush in sheets and fool's caps where they
    smelled
A thing the least bit doubtfully perscented
And give someone the Skipper Ireson's Ride.
One each of everything as in a show-case.

More than enough land for a specimen
You'll say she has, but there there enters in
Something else to protect her from herself.
There quality makes up for quantity.
Not even New Hampshire farms are much for
    sale.
The farm I made my home on in the moun-
    tains 150
I had to take by force rather than buy.
I caught the owner outdoors by himself
Raking up after winter, and I said,
"I'm going to put you off this farm: I want
    it."
"Where are you going to put me? In the
    road?"
"I'm going to put you on the farm next to
    it."
"Why won't the farm next to it do for you?"
"I like this better." It was really better.

Apples? New Hampshire has them, but un-
    sprayed,
With no suspicion in stem-end or blossom-end

Of vitriol or arsenate of lead,   161
And so not good for anything but cider.
Her unpruned grapes are flung like lariats
Far up the birches out of reach of man.

A state producing precious metals, stones,
And—writings; none of these except perhaps
The precious literature in quantity
Or quality to worry the producer
About disposing of it. Do you know,
Considering the market, there are more   170
Poems produced than any other thing?
No wonder poets sometimes have to *seem*
So much more business-like than business men.
Their wares are so much harder to get rid of.

She's one of the two best states in the Union.
Vermont's the other. And the two have been
Yoke-fellows in the sap-yoke from of old
In many Marches. And they lie like wedges,
Thick end to thin end and thin end to thick
    end,
And are a figure of the way the strong   180
Of mind and strong of arm should fit together,
One thick where one is thin and vice versa.
New Hampshire raises the Connecticut
In a trout hatchery near Canada,
But soon divides the river with Vermont.
Both are delightful states for their absurdly
Small towns—Lost Nation, Bungey, Muddy
    Boo,
Poplin, Still Corners (so called not because
The place is silent all day long, nor yet
Because it boasts a whisky still—because   190
It set out once to be a city and still
Is only corners, cross-roads in a wood).
And I remember one whose name appeared
Between the pictures on a movie screen
Election night once in Franconia,
When everything had gone Republican
And Democrats were sore in need of comfort:
Easton goes Democratic, Wilson 4
Hughes 2. And everybody to the saddest
Laughed the loud laugh, the big laugh at the
    little.   200
New York (five million) laughs at Manchester,
Manchester (sixty or seventy thousand) laughs
At Littleton (four thousand), Littleton
Laughs at Franconia (seven hundred), and
Franconia laughs, I fear,—did laugh that
    night—
At Easton. What has Easton left to laugh at,
And like the actress exclaim, "Oh my God"
    at?
There's Bungey; and for Bungey there are
    towns,
Whose townships named but without popu-
    lation.

Anything I can say about New Hampshire   210
Will serve almost as well about Vermont,
Excepting that they differ in their mountains.
The Vermont mountains stretch extended
    straight;
New Hampshire mountains curl up in a coil.

I had been coming to New Hampshire moun-
    tains.
And here I am and what am I to say?
Here first my theme becomes embarrassing.
Emerson said, "The God who made New
    Hampshire
Taunted the lofty land with little men."
Another Massachusetts poet said,   220
"I go no more to summer in New Hampshire.
I've given up my summer place in Dublin."
But when I asked to know what ailed New
    Hampshire,
She said she couldn't stand the people in it,
The little men (it's Massachusetts speaking).
And when I asked to know what ailed the
    people,
She said, "Go read your own books and find
    out."
I may as well confess myself the author
Of several books against the world in general.
To take them as against a special state   230
Or even nation's to restrict their meaning.

I'm what is called a sensibilitist,
Or otherwise an environmentalist.
I refuse to adapt myself a mite
To any change from hot to cold, from wet
To dry, from poor to rich, or back again.
I make a virtue of my suffering
From nearly everything that goes on round
    me.
In other words, I know wherever I am,
Being the creature of literature I am,   240
I shall not lack for pain to keep me awake.
Kit Marlowe taught me how to say my prayers:
"Why this is Hell, nor am I out of it."
Samoa, Russia, Ireland I complain of,
No less than England, France and Italy.
Because I wrote my novels in New Hampshire
Is no proof that I aimed them at New Hamp-
    shire.

When I left Massachusetts years ago
Between two days, the reason why I sought
New Hampshire, not Connecticut,   250
Rhode Island, New York, or Vermont was
    this:
Where I was living then, New Hampshire of-
    fered
The nearest boundary to escape across.
I hadn't an illusion in my hand-bag

About the people being better there
Than those I left behind. I thought they
    weren't.
I thought they couldn't be. And yet they
    were.
I'd sure had no such friends in Massachusetts
As Hall of Windham, Gay of Atkinson,
Barlett of Raymond (now of Colorado), 260
Harris of Derry, and Lynch of Bethlehem.
The glorious bards of Massachusetts seem
To want to make New Hampshire people over.
They taunt the lofty land with little men.
I don't know what to say about the people.
For art's sake one could almost wish them
    worse
Rather than better. How are we to write
The Russian novel in America
As long as life goes so unterribly?
There is the pinch from which our only outcry
In literature to date is heard to come. 271
We get what little misery we can
Out of not having cause for misery.
It makes the guild of novel writers sick
To be expected to be Dostoievskis
On nothing worse than too much luck and
    comfort.
This is not sorrow, though; it's just the vapors,
And recognized as such in Russia itself
Under the new régime, and so forbidden.
If well it is with Russia, then feel free 280
To say so or be stood against the wall
And shot. It's Pollyanna now or death.
This, then, is the new freedom we hear tell of;
And very sensible. No state can build
A literature that shall at once be sound
And sad on a foundation of wellbeing.

To show the level of intelligence
Among us; it was just a Warren farmer
Whose horse had pulled him short up in the
    road
By me, a stranger. This is what he said, 290
From nothing but embarrassment and want
Of anything more sociable to say:
"You hear those hound-dogs sing on Moosi-
    lauke?
Well they remind me of the hue and cry
We've heard against the Mid-Victorians
And never rightly understood till Bryan
Retired from politics and joined the chorus.
The matter with the Mid-Victorians
Seems to have been a man named John L.
    Darwin."
"Go 'long," I said to him, he to his horse. 300

I knew a man who failing as a farmer
Burned down his farmhouse for the fire in-
    surance,

And spent the proceeds on a telescope
To satisfy a life-long curiosity
About our place among the infinities.
And how was that for other-worldliness?

If I must choose which I would elevate—
The people or the already lofty mountains,
I'd elevate the already lofty mountains. 309
The only fault I find with Old New Hampshire
Is that her mountains aren't quite high
    enough.
I was not always so; I've come to be so.
How, to my sorrow, how have I attained
A height from which to look down critical
On mountains? What has given me assurance
To say what height becomes New Hampshire
    mountains,
Or any mountains? Can it be some strength
I feel as of an earthquake in my back
To heave them higher to the morning star?
Can it be foreign travel in the Alps? 320
Or having seen and credited a moment
The solid moulding of vast peaks of cloud
Behind the pitiful reality
Of Lincoln, Lafayette and Liberty?
Or some such sense as says how high shall jet
The fountain in proportion to the basin?
No, none of these has raised me to my throne
Of intellectual dissatisfaction,
But the sad accident of having seen
Our actual mountains given in a map 330
Of early times as twice the height they are—
Ten thousand feet instead of only five—
Which shows how sad an accident may be.
Five thousand is no longer high enough.
Whereas I never had a good idea
About improving people in the world,
Here I am over-fertile in suggestion,
And cannot rest from planning day or night
How high I'd thrust the peaks in summer
    snow
To tap the upper sky and draw a flow 340
Of frosty night air on the vale below
Down from the stars to freeze the dew as
    starry.

The more the sensibilitist I am
The more I seem to want my mountains wild;
The way the wiry gang-boss liked the log-jam.
After he'd picked the lock and got it started,
He dodged a log that lifted like an arm
Against the sky to break his back for him,
Then came in dancing, skipping, with his life
Across the roar and chaos, and the words 350
We saw him say along the zigzag journey
Were doubtless as the words we heard him say
On coming nearer: "Wasn't she an *i*-deal
Son-of-a-bitch? You bet she was an *i*-deal."

For all her mountains fall a little short,
Her people not quite short enough for Art,
She's still New Hampshire, a most restful
state.

Lately in converse with a New York alec
About the new school of the pseudo-phallic,
I found myself in a close corner where   360
I had to make an almost funny choice.
"Choose you which you will be—a prude, or
puke,
Mewling and puking in the public arms."
"Me for the hills where I don't have to
choose."
"But if you had to choose, which would you
be?"
I wouldn't be a prude afraid of nature.
I know a man who took a double axe
And went alone against a grove of trees;
But his heart failing him, he dropped the axe
And ran for shelter quoting Matthew Arnold:
"Nature is cruel, man is sick of blood;   371
There's been enough shed without shedding
mine.
Remember Birnam Wood! The wood's in
flux!"
He had a special terror of the flux
That showed itself in dendrophobia.
The only decent tree had been to mill
And educated into boards, he said.
He knew too well for any earthly use
The line where man leaves off and nature
starts,
And never over-stepped it save in dreams.   380
He stood on the safe side of the line talking;
Which is sheer Matthew Arnoldism,
The cult of one who owned himself "a foiled,
Circuitous wanderer," and "took dejectedly

His seat upon the intellectual throne."
Agreed in frowning on these improvised
Altars the woods are full of nowadays,
Again as in the days when Ahaz sinned
By worship under green trees in the open.
Scarcely a mile but that I come on one,   390
A black-cheeked stone and stick of rain-
washed charcoal.
Even to say the groves were God's first tem-
ples
Comes too near to Ahaz' sin for safety.
Nothing not built with hands of course is
sacred.
But here is not a question of what's sacred;
Rather of what to face or run away from.
I'd hate to be a runaway from nature.
And neither would I choose to be a puke
Who cares not what he does in company,   399
And, when he can't do anything, falls back
On words, and tries his worst to make words
speak
Louder than actions, and sometimes achieves
it.
It seems a narrow choice the age insists on.
How about being a good Greek, for instance?
That course, they tell me, isn't offered this
year.
"Come, but this isn't choosing—puke or
prude?"
Well, if I have to choose one or the other,
I choose to be a plain New Hampshire farmer
With an income in cash of say a thousand
(From say a publisher in New York City).
It's restful to arrive at a decision,   411
And restful just to think about New Hamp-
shire.
At present I am living in Vermont.

                                    1923

STOPPING BY WOODS ON A SNOWY EVENING

Whose woods these are I think I know.
His house is in the village though;
He will not see me stopping here
To watch his woods fill up with snow.

My little horse must think it queer
To stop without a farmhouse near
Between the woods and frozen lake
The darkest evening of the year.

He gives his harness bells a shake
To ask if there is some mistake.   10
The only other sound's the sweep
Of easy wind and downy flake.

The woods are lovely, dark and deep.
But I have promises to keep,

And miles to go before I sleep,
And miles to go before I sleep.

                                    1923

SAND DUNES

Sea waves are green and wet,
But up from where they die,
Rise others vaster yet,
And those are brown and dry.

They are the sea made land
To come at the fisher town,
And bury in solid sand
The men she could not drown.

She may know cove and cape,
But she does not know mankind   10

If by any change of shape,
She hopes to cut off mind.

Men left her a ship to sink:
They can leave her a hut as well;
And be but more free to think
For the one more cast off shell.
1926

A SOLDIER

He is that fallen lance that lies as hurled,
That lies unlifted now, come dew, come rust,
But still lies pointed as it plowed the dust.
If we who sight along it round the world,
See nothing worthy to have been its mark,
It is because like men we look too near,
Forgetting that as fitted to the sphere,
Our missiles always make too short an arc.
They fall, they rip the grass, they intersect
The curve of earth, and striking, break their
own;   10

They make us cringe for metal-point on stone.
But this we know, the obstacle that checked
And tripped the body, shot the spirit on
Further than target ever showed or shone.
1928

A MINOR BIRD

I have wished a bird would fly away,
And not sing by my house all day;

Have clapped my hands at him from the door
When it seemed as if I could bear no more.

The fault must partly have been in me.
The bird was not to blame for his key.

And of course there must be something wrong
In wanting to silence any song.
1928

PERCY MACKAYE (1875–   )

ODE ON THE CENTENARY OF ABRAHAM LINCOLN[1]

Yet may we strive to trace
His shadow—where it pulses vast
Upon imagination, cast
By the oft-handtrimm'd lamp of history—
In carvèd breath, or bronze, that we may scan
The imagined child and man
Whose life and death are looms of our own destiny.

I

It was the season bleak
Of silence and long night,
And solemn starshine and large solitude;
Hardly more husht the world when first the
word
Of God creation stirred,
Far steept in wilderness. By the frore creek,
Mute in the moon, the sculptured stag in flight
Paused, panting silver; in her cedarn lair,
Crouched with her starveling litter, the numb
lynx
Winked the keen hoar-frost, quiet as a sphinx;
On the lone forest trail   11
Only the coyote's wail
Quivered, and ceased.
It was the chrisom rude
Of winter and wild beast
That consecrated, by harsh nature's rite,
A meagre cabin crude,
Builded of logs and bark,

[1] Delivered before the Brooklyn Institute of Arts and Sciences at the Academy of Music, Brooklyn, New York, February, 1909.

To be a pilgrim nation's hallow'd ark
And shrine the goal aspiring ages seek.   20
No ceremonial
Of pealèd chime was there, or blarèd horn,
Such as hath blazoned births of lesser kings,
When he—the elder brother of us all,
Lincoln—was born.
At his nativity
Want stood as sponsor, stark Obscurity
Was midwife, and all lonely things
Of nature were unconscious ministers
To endow his spirit meek   30
With their own melancholy. So when he—
An infant king of commoners—
Lay in his mother's arms, of all the earth
[Which now his fame wears for a diadem]
None heeded of his birth;
Only a star burned over Bethlehem
More bright, and, big with prophecy,
A secret gust from that far February
Fills now the organ-reeds that peal his cen-
tenary.

II

Who shall distil in song those epic years?   40
Only the Sibyl of simplicity,
Touched by the light and dew of common
tears,
Might chant that homely native Odyssea.

For there are lives too large in simple truth
For art to limn or elegy to gauge,

And there are men so near to God's own ruth
They are the better angels of their age,
And such was he: beyond the pale of song
His grandeur looms in truth, with awful grace;
He lives where beauty's origins belong   50
Deep in the primal raptures of his race.

Yet may we strive to trace
His shadow—where it pulses vast
Upon imagination, cast
By the oft-handtrimm'd lamp of history—
In carvèd breath, or bronze, that we may scan
The imagined child and man
Whose life and death are looms of our own
      destiny.

III

The loveliness which is reality
Surrounds us, but its glamourous romance   60
We glean afar from heroes of old France,
Or Hellas' arms, or Gothic heraldry,
While Roland and his conquerors
With Sigmund sleep beside our doors,
And Homer's age awaits us at our hearth.

How like a saga of the northern sea
Our own Kentucky hero-tale begins!
      Once on a time, far in a wintry wood,
      A lone hut stood;
      There lived a poor man's son, that was to be
      A master man of earth.   71
And so for us,
Like children in the great hall of his spirit,
The homebred fairy-story spins
Annals whose grace the after-times inherit.

The uncouth homestead by the trail of Boone,
The untitled grant, the needy exodus,
The ox-cart on the Indiana heath,
The log shack by the Sangamon, and soon
The fever'd mother and the forest death—   80
From these the lonely epic wanders on.

The longshank boy, with visage creased by toil
And laughter of the soil,
Cribbing his book of statutes from his chore,
Erelong his nooning fellows of the field
Hail their scrub-orator, or at sundown—
Slouching his gaunt and sallow six-foot-four—
Their native Touchstone of the village store.
Or from the turf, where he has matched his
      build
To throw the county champion in the loam,
Idly he saunters home   91
To rock some mother's cradle in the town;
Or, stretched on counter calico, with Clay
And organ-sounding Webster, dream the night
      away.

But time begins
Slowly to sift the substance from the slag.
And now along the county pike's last lap,
With giant shins
Shut knifewise in his wabbling rattletrap,
The circuit lawyer trots his tired nag   100
Toward the noon tavern, reins up, and unrolls
His awkward length of wrinkled bombazine,
Clutching his tattered green
Umbrella and thin carpetsack,
And flings a joke that makes the rafters roar:
As if, uplooming from of yore,
Some quaint-accoutred king of trolls,
Out-elbowing a sexton's suit of black
In Christmas glee,
Should sudden crack   110
His shrilly jest of shrewd hilarity,
And shake the clambering urchins from his
      back.

IV

How vast the war invisible
When public weal battles with public will!
Proudly the stars of Union hung their wreath
On the young nation's lordly architrave;
Yet underneath
Its girding vaults and groins,
Half the fair fabric rested on the loins
And stooping sinews of a slave,   120
That—raised to the just stature of a man—
Should rend the whole asunder.

And now the million-headed serf began
To stir in wonder,
And from the land, appalled by that low thun-
      der,
"Kansas-Nebraska!" rang
The cry, and with exceeding pang
Out of the earth blood sprang
And out of men's hearts, fire. And that hot
      flame,
Fed by the book that burned in all men's
      homes,   130
Kindled from horizon to horizon
Anguish and shame
And aspiration, by its glow
Ruddying the state-house domes
With monstrous shadows of Dred Scott
And gaunt-limbed effigies of Garrison.

Then in the destined man matured the slow
Strong grandeur of that lot
Which singled him; till soon,
Ushered with lordly train,   140
The champion Douglas met him on the plain,
And the broad prairie moon
Peered through white schooners at the mad
      bonfires

And multitudes astir,
Where—roped like wrestlers in a ring—
The *Little Giant* faced the *Railsplitter;*
And serious crowds harked silently,
With smothered taunts and ires,
While Commonsense grappled with 'Sover-
    eignty,'
Till the lank, long-armed wrestler made his
    fling.   150
And still sublime
With common sympathy, that cool
Sane manfulness survives: *You cannot fool
All of the people all the time.*
No; by that power we misname fate,
'Tis character which moulds the state.
Statutes are dead when men's ideals dissent,
And public will is more than precedent,
And manhood more than constitutions can
    create.
Higher than bar and documental ban,   160
Man's highest court is still the heart of Man.

V

Bold to his country, sick with compromise,
Spoke the plain advocate;
*Half slave, half free, our Union dies,
But it shall live!* And done with sophistries,
The people answered with tempestuous call
That shook the revolutionary dead,
And high on rude rails garlanded
Bore their backwoodsman to the Capitol.
"Who is this common huckster?" sneered the
    great,   170
"This upstart Solon of the Sangamon?"
And chastened Douglas answered: "He is one
Who wrestles well for Truth." But some
Scowled unbelief, and some smiled bitterly;
And so, beneath the derrick'd half-built dome,
While dumb artillery
And guards battalioned the black lonely form,
He took his oath.
We are not enemies, but friends!
Yet scarce the sad rogation ends   180
Ere the warped planks of Union split in storm
Of dark secession.
                    Then, as on a raft
Flood-rended, where by night the Ohio sweeps
Into the Mississippi, 'mid the roil
Of roaring waters with eroded soil
From hills primeval, the strong poleman keeps
Silence, midway the shallows and the rocks,
To steer his shipment safe, while [fore and aft
The scrambling logmen scream at him, or scold
With prayers and malisons, or burst the locks
And loot the precious bales, so—deaf and mute
To sneers and imprecations both—   192
The lone Flatboatman of the Union poled
His country's wreck midstream, and resolute

Held still his goal:
To lash his ballast to the sundered half,
And save the whole.

*"They seek a sign,
But no sign shall be given them,"* he said;
And reaching Godward, with his pilot's gaff 200
Probed in the dark, among the drowning and
    the dead,
And sunk his plummet line
Deep in the people's heart, where still his own
    heart bled,
And fathomed there the inundated shore
Swept by the flood and storm of elemental war.

VI

The war!—Far on the dim verge of To-day
Its rack of livid splendor fades away.
The bane is past;
The awful lightnings, spent,
Have wrought a chastening not a chastisement;
The beauty and the benediction last.   211
And mustering, in season due,
From farthest hill
And hamlet—still
Keeping the morning last but one in May
Proud with great memories—one by one,
Whose young life sank not with the sun
Of Gettysburg or Missionary Ridge,
Buttons his coat of blue,
And from his whitened hair   220
Removes the hat with golden-corded brim
And plants again old colors in old graves;
And groups of simple children fair
And folk of middle age are there
To kneel by him,
And honor, though they cannot share,
His pensive privilege.
Still in the living past we may recall
The war's live tribute. Go to Washington
On New Year's morning of Emancipation,   230
When even from Arlington
Beyond the Capitol
The streets and alleys all
Surge black with singing tides. There creep a
    few
Sweet-visaged, swart and hoary men
To bask them in the sun
That beats on Pennsylvania Avenue,
Or lounge in smiling knots
At drowsier spots,
To listen where one boasts again   240
Of ancient bondage, now his pedigree.
Those are the nation's honored slaves
Knighted of old by the great Proclamation.
For them the empower'd saviour dipt his pen
In blood of equity,
And signed away the curse as old as Ptolemy.

The War! It was a forging blast
From God's own furnace, welding North
And South henceforth
To be one weapon for His hand,   250
Till even that word which once inflamed the
      land
Falls idle at the last:
What need to boast of *union*, being one?
The War is done.

Yet who that, in complacent day
Of peace, invokes the right divine
Of labor to reward itself,
Or vested power to hoard its pelf,
Reaping the enviable embrace
Of joy denied to others,   260
Remembering that dark assay
Our country and our chief withstood,
When fathers sought their sons in blood
And brothers fought with brothers,—
Who then, before the memoried face
Of Lincoln, but must pause, and pray
For love like his, whose larger grace
Outclimbs the individual—
Dreadful, and yet more dear than all—
The love that serves our race.   270

VII

"To sleep, perchance to dream!"—No player,
      rapt
In conscious art's soliloquy, might know
To subtilize the poignant sense so apt
As he, almost in shadow of the end,
Murmured its latent sadness to a friend;
And then he said to him: "Ten nights ago
I watched alone; the hour was very late;
I fell asleep and dreamed;
And in my dreaming, all
The White House lay in deathlike stillness
      round;   280
But soon a sobbing sound,
Subdued, I heard, as of innumerable
Mourners. I rose and went from room to room;
No living being there was visible;
Yet as I passed, unspeakably it seemed
They sobbed again, subdued. In every room
Light was, and all things were familiar:
But who were those once more
Whose hearts were breaking there? What
      heavy gloom
Wrapt their dumb grieving? Last, the east-
      room door   290
I opened, and it lay before me: High
And cold on solemn catafalque it lay,
Draped in funereal vestments, and near by
Mute soldiers guarded it. In black array
A throng of varied race
Stood weeping,

Or gazing on the covered face.
Then to a soldier: 'Who is dead
In the White House?' I asked. He said:
'The President.'   300
And a great moan that through the people went
Waked me from sleeping."

God! that a nation too should have bad
      dreams!
The cities all are still and voiceless all
The valleys and the woods:
But what are these husht sounds insufferable
Of moaning multitudes?
Through the Republic's silent house
From room to room the awful Spirit walks,
Yet all things are familiar; it seems   310
No change has been:
From Maine to Florida
Still flash the blue seas; California
Is quick with April green;
The middle ways are pied
With crocus blooms and river fleur-de-lis;
And the great western rooms are open wide
To greet the northing sun;
In every one   319
Are strewn the Saviour's lilies of white peace
In festival of him who quenched the fiery
      feuds.
What, then, is that which mocks
The victory and grace that were before?
Once more, and now insufferably once more—
The moan of multitudes!
The lofty Spirit knocks
And opening last the door
Into the Capitol, with pensive head,
Stooping his deathless stature o'er the dead,
Looks there on his own image—tenderness,
Pity, on which sad truth has set its seal,   331
Heroic patience, strong humility,
Power, whose human courage shines not less
That humor leavens the shrewd honesty:
Democracy's own brow—the American ideal.

While triumph pealed his consummated task,
And that great theatre
Where late he watched the war's solemnity
Was narrowed to a moment's comedy,
The sudden angel of the tragic mask   340
Flashed on his gaze the blinding sepulchre.

VIII

It was a dream! for that which fell in death,
Seared by the assassin's lightning, and there
      lay
A spectacle for anguish, was a wraith;
The real immortal Lincoln went his way
Back to his only home and native heath—

The common people's common heart. And
    they
Who speak of Lincoln to his countrymen—
Now while one vast communion makes To-day
His temple—speak *to* Lincoln, born again   350
From that perennial earth
Whereof he had his birth,
And estimating him, they estimate
The source of all that made, and yet shall
    make us great.

IX

The loving and the wise
May seek—but seek in vain—to analyze
The individual man, for having caught
The mystic clue of thought,
Sudden they meet the controverting whim,
And fumbling with the enchanted key,   360
Lose it then utterly.

Æsop and old Isaiah held in him
Strange sessions, winked at by Artemus Ward,
Till sudden in their midst bright Seraphim
Stood, summoned by a sad, primeval bard
Who, bearing still no name, has ever borne
Within his heart the music of mankind:
Sometime a lonely singer blind
Beside the Ionian sea;
Sometime, between two thieves in scorn,   370
A face in Calvary.

That was his master soul—
The mystic demi-god of common man—
Who, templed in the steadfast mind,
Hid his shy gold of genius in the bran
Of Hoosier speech and garb, softening the wan
Strong face of shrewdness with strange aureole.

He was the madstone to his country's ire,
Drawing the rancorous blood of envious quar-
    rel
Alike from foe and friend; his pity, stirr'd, 380
Restored to its bough the storm-unnested bird,
Or raised the wallow'd pig from out the mire.
And he who sowed in sweat his boyhood's crop,
And tackled Euclid with a wooden spade,
And excavated Blackstone from a barrel
To hold moot trials in the gloaming, made
By lighted shavings in a cooper's shop,
He is the people's still—their Railsplitter,
Himself a rail, clean-grained, of character
Self-hewn in the dark glades of Circumstance
From that deep-hearted tree   391
Democracy,
Which, by our race's heritage,
Reforests age on age,
Perpetual in strong fecundity.

X

Those are the rails to build republics with,
Their homesteads and their towns. God give
    us more
And ever more of such to build our own,
Enlarging still in manhood, not in stone
And iron merely and in metal ore: 400
Not men, like rails of polish'd steel,
Invoice-begotten breeds, that pour
Stillborn from laboring wombs of stark ma-
    chines
And all alike,
With flange and spike
To couple and dovetail and serve as means
To cart more gold-dust on the commonweal;
Not those: but such as breathe
Yet of the trail, the redwood and the ranch,
The gale-swept mountain and the prairie's
    sheen,   410
And cities where the stars can still look in
And leave their benediction: common men,
Kindled by nature's awe to contemplation,
And by her goads to courage; not too vain
Of self, to show the clean knots in their grain,
Blazed from the same great bole that grew Abe
    Lincoln's branch:
Such be the men of whom we build our nation !

XI

But he is more than ours, as we are more
Than yet the world dares dream. His stature
    grows
With that illimitable state   420
Whose sovereignty ordains no tribute shore
And borderland of hate,
But grounds its justice in the joy it sows.
His spirit is still a power to emancipate
Bondage—more base, being more insidious,
Than serfdom—that cries out in the midst of
    us
For virtue, born of opportunity,
And manhood, weighed in honest human
    worth,
And freedom, based in labor. He stands forth
'Mongst nations old—a new-world Abraham,
The patriarch of people still to be,   431
Blending all visions of the promised land
In one Apocalypse.

                    His voice is heard—
Thrilling the moulder'd lintels of the past—
In Asia; old Thibet is stirred
With warm imaginings;
Ancestral China, 'mid her mysteries,
Unmasks, and flings
Her veils wide to the occident; the wand

Of hope awakes prone Hierapolis;   440
Even by the straits of old that Io swam,
The immemorial sultan, sceptreless,
Stands awed; and heartened by that bold suc-
    cess,
Pale Russia rises from her holocaust.

And still the emancipating influence,
The secret power, the increasing truth, are
    his,
For they are ours: ours by the potencies
Poured in our nation from the founts of time,
Blending in us the mystic seeds of men,
To sow them forth again   450
For harvests more sublime
Throughout the world.

XII

Leave, then, that wonted grief
Which honorably mourns its martyred dead,
And newly hail instead
The birth of him, our hardy shepherd chief,

Who by green paths of old democracy
Leads still his tribes to uplands of glad peace.

As long as—out of blood and passion blind—
Springs the pure justice of the reasoning mind,
And justice, bending, scorns not to obey   461
Pity, that once in a poor manger lay,
As long as, thrall'd by time's imperious will,
Brother hath bitter need of brother, still
His presence shall not cease
To lift the ages toward his human excellence,
And races yet to be
Shall in a rude hut do him reverence
And solemnize a simple man's nativity.[1]
                                        1909.

[1] The dream of Lincoln, recounted in this poem, takes significance from its authenticity. Shortly before his death, Lincoln actually had this dream, and described it to a friend in
words, which the writer has closely followed . . . [in lines 271-
302]. The passage, *To sleep, perchance to dream,* Lincoln himself quoted in this connection. Cf. Norman Hapgood's "Abraham Lincoln, the Man of the People," pages 405-406. It is
perhaps worthy of mention that the words of Lincoln, itali-
cized in the Ode, are also authentic, being usually *verbatim* his
own. The book, referred to at . . . [line 130], is of course "Uncle
Tom's Cabin." (*Author's note*)

URIEL[1]

Stanzas to the Memory of William Vaughn Moody

I

Uriel, you that in the ageless sun
Sit in the awful silences of light,
Singing of vision hid from human sight,—
Prometheus, beautiful rebellious one!
And you, Deucalion,
For whose blind seed was brought the illuming
    spark,
Are you not gathered, now his day is done,
Beside the brink of that relentless dark—
The dark where your dear singer's ghost is
    gone?

II

Imagined beings, who majestic blend   10
Your forms with beauty!—questing, uncon-
    fined,
The mind conceived you, though the quenchèd
    mind
Goes down in dark where you in dawn ascend.
Our songs can but suspend
The ultimate silence: yet could song aspire
The realms of mortal music to extend
And wake a Sibyl's voice or Seraph's lyre—
How should it tell the dearness of a friend?

[1] William Vaughn Moody, poet and dramatist, died October
17, 1910. This poem was written about a year later. Shortly
before his death, he told a friend about a new drama, on the
theme of Saint Paul, the outlines of which had come to him
splendidly as a vision. To this the sixth stanza of *Uriel* refers
symbolically. (*Author's note*)

III

The simplest is the inexpressible;
The heart of music still evades the Muse,   20
And arts of men the heart of man suffuse,
And saddest things are made of silence still.
In vain the senses thrill
To give our sorrows glorious relief
In pyre of verse and pageants volatile,
And I, in vain, to speak for him my grief
Whose spirit of fire invokes my waiting will.

IV

To him the best of friendships needs must be
Uttered no more; yet was he so endowed
That Poetry because of him is proud   30
And he more noble for his poetry,
Wherefore infallibly
I obey the strong compulsion which this verse
Lays on my lips with strange austerity—
Now that his voice is silent—to rehearse
For my own heart how he was dear to me.

V

Not by your gradual sands, elusive Time,
We measure your gray sea, that never rests:
The bleeding hour-glasses in our breasts
Mete with quick pangs the ebbing of our prime,
And drip—like sudden rime   41

In March, that melts to runnels from a pane
The south breathes on—oblivion of sublime
Crystallizations, and the ruthless wave
Of glittering stars, that scarce had range to
    climb.

VI

Darkling those constellations of his soul
Glimmered, while racks of stellar lightnings
    shot
The white, creative meteors of thought
Through that last night, where—clad in cloudy
    stole—
Beside his ebbing shoal   50
Of lifeblood, stood Saint Paul, blazing a theme
Of living drama from a fiery scroll
Across his stretchèd vision as in dream—
When Death, with blind dark, blotted out the
    whole.

VII

And yet not all: though darkly alien
Those uncompleted worlds of work to be
Are waned; still, touched by them, the memory
Gives afterglow; and now that comes again
The mellow season when
Our eyes last met, his kindling currents run 60
Quickening within me gladness and new ken
Of life, that I have shared his prime with one
Who wrought large-minded for the love of men.

VIII

But not alone to share that large estate
Of work and interchange of communings—
The little human paths to heavenly things
Were also ours: the casual, intimate
Vistas, which consecrate—
With laughter and quick tears—the dusty noon
Of days, and by moist beams irradiate   70
Our plodding minds with courage, and attune
The fellowship that bites its thumb at fate.

IX

Where art thou now, mine host Guffanti?—
    where
The iridescence of thy motley troop!
Ah, where the merry, animated group
That snuggled elbows for an extra chair,
When space was none to spare,
To pour the votive Chianti, for a toast
To dramas dark and lyrics debonair,
The while, to *Bella Napoli*, mine host   80
Exhaled his Parmazan, Parnassan air!

X

Thy Parmazan, immortal laird of ease,
Can never mold, thy caviare is blest,
While still our glowing Uriel greets the rest

Around thy royal board of memories,
Where sit, the salt of these,
He of the laughter of a Hundred Lights,
Blithe Eldorado of high poesies,
And he—of enigmatic, gentle knights
The kindly keen—who sings of *Calverly's*.   90

XI

Because he never wore his sentient heart
For crows and jays to peck, ofttimes to such
He seemed a silent fellow, who o'ermuch
Held from the general gossip-ground apart,
Or tersely spoke, and tart:
How should they guess what eagle tore, within,
His quick of sympathy for humblest smart
Of human wretchedness, or probed his spleen
Of scorn against the hypocritic mart!

XII

Sometimes insufferable seemed to come   100
That wrath of sympathy: One windy night,
We watched through squalid panes, forlornly
    white,—
Amid immense machines' incessant hum—
Frail figures, gaunt and dumb,
Of overlabored girls and children, bowed
Above their slavish toil: "O God!—A bomb,
A bomb!" he cried, "and with one fiery cloud
Expunge the horrible Cæsars of this slum!"

XIII

Another night dreams on the Cornish hills: 109
Trembling within the low moon's pallid fires,
The tall corn-tassels lift their fragrant spires;
From filmy spheres, a liquid starlight fills—
Like dew of daffodils—
The fragile dark, where multitudinous
The rhythmic, intermittent silence thrills,
Like song, the valleys.—"Hark!" he mur-
    murs, "Thus
May bards from crickets learn their canticles!"

XIV

Now Morning, not less lavish of her sweets,
Leads us along the woodpaths—in whose hush
The quivering alchemy of the pure thrush   120
Cools from above the balsam-dripping heats—
To find, in green retreats,
'Mid men of clay, the great, quick-hearted
    man
Whose subtle art our human age secretes,
Or him whose brush, tinct with cerulean,
Blooms with soft castle-towers and cloud-
    capped fleets.

XV

Still to the sorcery of August skies
In frillèd crimson flaunt the hollyhocks,

Where, lithely poised along the garden walks,
His little maid enamoured blithe outvies   130
The dipping butterflies
In motion—ah, in grace how grown the while,
Since he was wont to render to her eyes
His knightly court, or touch with flitting smile
Her father's heart by his true flatteries!

XVI

But summer's golden pastures boast no trail
So splendid as our fretted snowshoes blaze
Where, sharp across the amethystine ways,
Iron Ascutney looms in azure mail,
And, like a frozen grail,   140
The frore sun sets, intolerably fair;
Mute, in our homebound snow-tracks, we exhale
The silvery cold, and soon—where bright logs flare—
Talk the long indoor hours, till embers fail.

XVII

Ah, with the smoke what smouldering desires
Waft to the starlight up the swirling flue!—
Thoughts that may never, as the swallows do,
Nest circling homeward to their native fires!
Ardors the soul suspires
The extinct stars drink with the dreamer's breath;   150
The morning-song of Eden's early choirs
Grows dim with Adam; close at the ear of death
Relentless angels tune our earthly lyres!

XVIII

Let it be so: More sweet it is to be
A listener of love's ephemeral song,
And live with beauty though it be not long,
And die enamoured of eternity,
Though in the apogee
Of time there sit no individual
Godhead of life, than to reject the plea   160
Of passionate beauty: loveliness is all,
And love is more divine than memory;

XIX

And love of beauty is the abiding part
Of friendship: by its hallowed beams we char
Away all dead and gross familiar
Disguise, and lay revealed truth's living heart—
The spirit's counterpart,
Which was in him a flaming Uriel
Obscured by chaining flesh, but freed by art
And by the handclasp that his friends knew well,   170
To make from time the imprisoned splendors start.

XX

The splendors start again from common things
At thought of quiet hours of fellowship,
When his shy fancy, like an elfin ship,
On foam of pipe-smoke spread elusive wings,
While subdued carollings
Of viewless fervors followed in her wake,
Till, with swift tack and rhythmic sweep of strings,
She flew before his darkening thought, and strake
On reefs that rolled with solemn thunderings.   180

XXI

The simple and the mighty themes, that keep
Friendship robust and taut the mental tether,
Of these we talked in casual ways together,
Delighting in the shallow and the deep:
Nature, quick or asleep,
And poetry, the fool's anathema,
Plays, and the magic house where passions weep
Or laugh at their own image, America
Our gallant country, and her captainship.

XXII

But special-privileged investitures   190
Of beauty liked him not. To him the fact
Was by its passion only made compact
Of beauty; as, amid the Gloucester moors,
The loveliness, which lures
The artist's eye, for him was nature's prism
To illume his love of country: art which endures
At once is poetry and patriotism,
In spite of jingoists and epicures.

XXIII

So, since his soul contemned thoughts which suborn
Glory from theft, where he stood, unafraid,
"Before the solemn bronze Saint-Gaudens made,"   201
It was his consecration to be torn
Between swift grief and scorn
For the island pillage of our Myrmidons,
And there alone, along of the high born,
He spoke, as the great sculptor spoke in bronze,
From love, whose worth can never be outworn.

XXIV

Long may we heed his voice, though he be mute
As the wan stars to instigate us more!
Long shall we need his voice, in the gross war
Of civic pillagers whose hands pollute   211

But that which shone of all most clear
  Was startled, sadder thought
That I should give her back the fear
  Of life she had forgot.

And I blushed for the world we'd made,
  Putting God's hand aside,
Till for the want of sun and shade
  His little children died;

And blushed that I who every year
  With Spring went up and down,   70
Must greet a soul that ached for her
  With "penny for a bun!"

Struck as a thief in holy place
  Whose sin upon him cries,
I watched the flowers leave her face,
  The song go from her eyes.

Then she, sweet heart, she saw my rout,
  And of her charity
A hand of grace put softly out
  And took the coin from me.   80

A red-cap sang in Bishop's wood,
  A lark o'er Golder's lane;
But I, alone, still glooming stood,
  And April plucked in vain;

Till living words rang in my ears
  And sudden music played:
*Out of such sacred thirst as hers
  The world shall be remade.*

Afar she turned her head and smiled
  As might have smiled the Spring,   90
And humble as a wondering child
  I watched her vanishing.

                                   1914

HOME

He came, her hero crowned.
  Neat as a lily trim,
She put slim arms around
  The hell of him.

The horror with no name
  He looked on night and day,
Though it met her like a flame,
  Her love would slay.

Her soft hands, they should cling;
  Her kisses, they should wean   10
Him from the strange, dark Thing
  That he had seen.

And when his days grew mild,
  And he said "You let me go;
But I forgive you, child;
  You did not know;"

She yet knew not her loss.
  His soul its shore would keep,
And in no world would cross
  To hers asleep.   20

                                   1919

LUTE AND FURROW

I

The winter has grown so still
I can stand at the foot of the hill
Where the stream beneath the bridge
Is dry as a heart after grief,
And hear at the top of the ridge
The wind as it lifts a leaf.

At last there is time, I say;
I will shut out the strife to-day;
I will take up my pen and once more
Meet that stranger, my soul, nor be dumb   10
As when earth was the whirlwind's floor,
And Life at her loom sat numb.

Springs, many as ever have been,
On sandals of moss shall slip in;
There is time for the laugh we would fling,
For the wiping of dust from our stars,

For a bee on his marketing wing,
For the forester wind's wild wares.

Comes the joy and the rushing pulse
That in beauty's beginning exults;   20
Then the weight tied fast to the heart;
The doubt that deadens the dawn;
And the raining sting and the smart
Of invisible whips laid on.

II

What is this sudden gaiety that shakes the
    greyest boughs?
A voice is calling fieldward, 'tis time to start
    the ploughs!
To set the furrows rolling while all the old
    crows nod,
And deep as life, the kernel, to cut the golden
    sod!

The pen, let nations have it,—we'll plough
  awhile for God.

When half the things that must be done are
  greater than our art,   30
And half the things that must be done are
  smaller than our heart,
And poorest gifts are dear to burn on altars
  unrevealed,
Like music comes the summons, the challenge
  from the weald,—
"They tread immortal measure who make a
  mellow field!"

The planet may be pleasant, alluring in its
  way;
But let the ploughs be idle, and none of us can
  stay.
Here's where there is no doubting, no ghosts
  uncertain stalk,
A-travelling with the plough beam, beneath
  the sailing hawk,
Cutting the furrow deep and true where Destiny will walk.

III

The winter has grown so still   40
I can pause and pluck what I will
From the arms of Time as he goes.
All the poems with beauty half-hid,
Yet touching my haste like a rose,
May fall to me now if I bid.

There's the book whose pages shall read
Like the hearts of old friends, who will need
For its quaint flowered paths no guide,
And into the late, sweet night
Will smile as they lay it aside—   50
The book that they once meant to write;

And one that may haunt a strange road,
Like a voice blown low from a wood,
And be song to the wanderer there,
Till the inn is a dark thing and cold,

And the night is a roof-tree dear,
And the moon his hearth of warm gold;

And that other whose music may be
As a flight of birds to the sea;
To the far island beaches made brave   60
With the feet of to-morrows; where strain
The lifters of stone from the grave
Of the world we have dreamed us and slain.

IV

Reproach is dark upon me; I almost grasp the
  pen;
When comes a laugh like daybreak, and "Winter's broke," says Len.
His eye is like a highpriest's as glowingly he
  'lows
He saw a bat by daylight fly roun' the pigeon-
  house.
"Ain't no time now for foolin', we got to start
  the ploughs."

We'll set the furrows rolling, and drop the
  yellow corn;
We'll plough along the universe that babies
  may be born.   70
Ay, no more time for fooling, here's task without a bound;
It's not the tame old earth now that's spinning
  us around;
It's Jupiter and Neptune when the plough is in
  the ground.

How light, how light the heart grows with
  something surely done!
When all the ploughs are going, and all the
  tasks are one!
Then Fame's a lass that smirks too late; the
  sun's a brother lout;
The moon's a lantern in our hand; the stars are
  fieldmen stout.
Oh, luck to die in ploughing time,—'twill be
  just one step out!

                        1922

JOB 31 : 1

The prophet's lips are wan as winds
Whose fury has been spent for long;
His voice is faint as buried sins,
Too faint to sound above a song;
His hand, raised toward the starry coasts,
Thins like a ghost's.

The maiden's eyes are brown as hay,
With edges burnt to tender gold;
Her lips are coals where red life gay
Laughs at the stars so far, so old.   10
And Youth who has no world to lose
Is asked to choose.

                        1922

TWILIGHT UNDER BLACK CAP

It is the month of Spring's full star.
  Now Redwing makes each thicket his,
  And now the apple blossom is
The oriole's honey jar.

The road flows down with bend and whirl;
  (They take it who to market go;)
  Flows, ripples, flies and falls, as though
The mountain wore a curl.

Great shadows drop and darker stare,
  Slow nestling down like giant birds,   10
  And silent worlds with baffled words
Tap at the door of air.

One brown field sleeps, where row to row
  We laid the corn in furrow house
  Before the lighted dogwood boughs
Might drop their stars of snow.

A bullbat measures downily
  His wheeling watch above the wood,
  And a Golden owl drifts down a rood
Beyond her chestnut tree.   20

Yon grim, unpassioned peak where wades
  An early star in swelling night,
  Can reel with berries, drunken bright,
And laugh with lowland raids.

And that ravine where waters sound,
  And hemlock trees cloud duskily,
  Is neither dread nor dark to me,
But sweet as maying ground;

For once a belted kingfisher
  Drew Love and me with sapphire flaunt   30
  Far up the stream, a fairy's jaunt,
On moss as soft as fur.

II

Above the dawn I leaned in fear
  To see him ride the gray mist down.
  Safe be the road to market-town,
My phantom wagoner!

I watched until the sun set high
  His cedar fires on Black-cap Spur;
  Till far below the valley blur
Shone like a tangled sky;   40

Then to the full day, swift and meek,
  I turned, and not alone;
  For safely, softly, half unknown,
Love moved at hide-and-seek.

Against my apple-basket spread,
  The book he loved lay as I pared;
  And the bardic gold again we shared
As goldenly he read.

The spoon he carved,—brown wood inlaid
  With whitest holly—leaf and wren—   50
  Whirred in my bowl and sang again
The song the carver made.

And dipping water from the spring,
  The stone-crop set in mossy cleft
  Held up its stars,—his woodland theft,
There for my wondering.

At last a rifling hour I spent
  By beds in flower, with ruthless knife
  Where blossom clans were saucy rife,
And as I silent bent   60

Thought came of how he said "Let be
  The valley lilies by the door;
  They are the flowers that you wore
The day you came to me."

I rose, with strange remembering;
  Again my heart was high and lone;
  Then stood as quiet as a stone
With eyes upon my ring.

Let Fortune bless as Fortune can,
  Fame show her face nor hide again,   70
  Still is supreme the white hour when
The woman goes to man.

And blithe the way of thorn and furze,
  And royal then a rustic part,
  If he but bear a singing heart,
And all that heart is hers.

III

Now every flower is a bride's
  In Twilight's hair. Soon she will sleep,
  And fingers of the moon will creep
Along her paling sides.   80

And up and up the flowing road
  A sound will greet me as I lean,
  Of wheels that climb and climb between
The dark wings of the wood;

On where the stream strives to the sea,
  A laughing god, in one white leap;
  And blossoms of the bloodroot keep
Their candles milkily.

On by the rhododendrons where
  Gay leaves will touch a cheek for me;   90
On till the height has wrestled free
And night lies blue and bare.

            IV

O Beauty, most you love the Night!
And now you hold her like a mate,

While all her moon-swept mountains wait
As altar waits the rite.

As still as they, for Love grown late,
  Watching the road that like a curl
Drops flowing down with bend and whirl,
As still as they I wait.   100

                          1922

JOHN G. NEIHARDT (1881–   )

From THE SONG OF THREE FRIENDS
(1919)

The Quarrel

                Perceptibly, at length,
The days grew longer, and the winter's strength
Increased to fury. Down across the flat
The blizzards bellowed; and the people sat
Fur-robed about the smoky fires that stung
Their eyes to streaming, when a freak gust flung
The sharp reek back with flaws of powdered
    snow.
And much the old men talked of long ago,
Invoking ghostly Winters from the Past,
Till cold snap after cold snap followed fast, 10
And none might pile his verbal snow so deep
But some athletic memory could heap
The drifts a trifle higher; give the cold
A greater rigor in the story told;
Put bellows to a wind already high.
And ever greater reverence thereby
The old men won from gaping youths, who
    heard,
Like marginalia to the living word,
The howling of the poplars tempest-bent,
The smoke-flap cracking sharply at the vent, 20
The lodge poles creaking eerily. And O!
The happy chance of living long ago,
Of having wrinkles now and being sires
With many tales to tell around the fires
Of days when things were bigger! All night
    long
White hands came plucking at the buckskin
    thong
That bound the door-flap, and the writhing
    dark
Was shrill with spirits. By the snuffling bark
Of dogs men knew that homesick ghosts were
    there.
And often in a whirl of chilling air   30
The weird ones entered, though the flap still
    held,
Built up in smoke the shapes they knew of eld,
Grew thin and long to vanish as they came.

Now had the scandal, like a sudden flame
Fed fat with grasses, perished in the storm.
The fundamental need of keeping warm
Sufficed the keenest gossip for a theme;
And whimsies faded like a warrior's dream
When early in the dawn the foemen cry.

The time when calves are black had blustered
    by—   40
A weary season—since the village saw
The chief's wife pitching for her son-in-law
The nuptial lodge she fashioned. Like a bow
That feels the arrow's head, the moon hung
    low
That evening when they gave the wedding
    gifts;
And men had seen it glaring through the rifts
Of wintry war as up the east it reeled,
A giant warrior's battle-bitten shield—
But now it braved no more the charging air.
Meanwhile the lodge of Carpenter stood there
Beside the chieftain's, huddled in the snows, 51
And, like a story everybody knows,
Was little heeded now.

                But there was one
Who seldom noted what was said or done
Among his comrades; he would sit and look
Upon the fire, as one who reads a book
Of woeful doings, ever on the brink
Of ultimate disaster. It was Fink:
And seeing this, Talbeau was sick at heart
With dreading that his friends might drift
    apart
And he be lost, because he loved them both. 61
But, knowing well Mike's temper, he was
    loath
To broach the matter. Also, knowing well
That silence broods upon the hottest hell,
He prayed that Fink might curse.

So worried past
The days of that estrangement. Then at last
One night when round their tent the blizzard
    roared
And, nestled in their robes, the others snored,
Talbeau could bear the strain no more and
    spoke.
He opened with a random little joke,   70
Like some starved hunter trying out the range
Of precious game where all the land is strange;
And, as the hunter, missing, hears the grim
And spiteful echo-rifles mocking him,
His own unmirthful laughter mocked Talbeau.
He could have touched across the ember-glow
Mike's brooding face—yet Mike was far away.
And O that nothing more than distance lay
Between them—any distance with an end!
How tireless then in running to his friend   80
A man might be! For suddenly he knew
That Mike would have him choose between
    the two.
How could he choose 'twixt Carpenter and
    Fink?
How idle were a choice 'twixt food and drink
When, choosing neither, one were sooner dead!

Thus torn within, and hoarse with tears un-
    shed,
He strove again to find his comrade's heart:
"O damn it, Mike, don't make us drift apart!
Don't do it, Mike! This ain't a killin' fuss,
And hadn't ought to faze the three of us   90
That's weathered many a rough-and-tumble
    fight!
W'y don't you mind that hell-a-poppin' night
At Baton Rouge three years ago last fall—
The time we fit the whole damned dancin' hall
And waded out nigh belly-deep in men?
O who'd have said a girl could part us, then?
And, Mike, that fracas in the Vide Poche dive!
Can you forget it long as you're alive?—
A merry time! Us strollin' arm-in-arm
From drink to drink, not calculatin' harm,
But curious, because St. Louis town   101
Fair boiled with greasy mountain men, come
    down
All brag and beaver, howlin' for a spree!
And then—you mind?—a feller jostled me—
'Twas at the bar—a chap all bones and big.
Says he in French: 'You eater of a pig,
Make room for mountain men!' And then
    says you
In Irish, aimin' where the whiskers grew,
And landin' fair: 'You eater of a dog,
Make room for boatmen!' Like a punky log   110
That's water-soaked, he dropped. What hap-
    pened then?
A cyclone in a woods of mountain men—

That's what! O Mike, you can't forget it now!
And what in hell's a woman, anyhow,
To memories like that?"

                        So spoke Talbeau,
And, pausing, heard the hissing of the snow,
The snoring of the sleepers, and the cries
Of blizzard-beaten poplars. Still Fink's eyes
Upon the crumbling embers pored intent.
Then momently, or so it seemed, there went   120
Across that alien gaze a softer light,
As when bleak windows in a moony night
Flush briefly with a candle borne along.
And suddenly the weary hope grew strong
In him who saw the glimmer, and he said:
"O Mike, I see the good old times ain't dead!
Why don't you fellers shoot the whisky cup
The way you used to do?"

                        Then Fink looked up.
'Twas bad the way the muscles twitched and
    worked
About his mouth, and in his eyes there lurked   130
Some crouchant thing. "To hell wid you!" he
    cried.
So love and hate that night slept side by side;
And hate slept well, but love lay broad awake
And, like a woman, for the other's sake
Eked out the lonely hours with worrying.

Now came a heartsick yearning for the spring
Upon Talbeau; for surely this bad dream
Would vanish with the ice upon the stream,
Old times be resurrected with the grass!
But would the winter ever, ever pass,   140
The howling of the blizzard ever cease?
So often now he dreamed of hearing geese
Remotely honking in the rain-washed blue;
And ever when the blur of dawn broke through
The scudding rack, he raised the flap to see,
By sighting through a certain forkèd tree,
How much the sun made northward.

                        Then, one day,
The curtain of the storm began to fray;
The poplars' howling softened to a croon;
The sun set clear, and dusk revealed the
    moon—   150
A thin-blown bubble in a crystal bowl.
All night, as 'twere the frozen prairie's soul
That voiced a hopeless longing for the spring,
The wolves assailed with mournful questioning
The starry deeps of that tremendous hush.
Dawn wore the mask of May—a rosy flush.
It seemed the magic of a single bird
Might prove the seeing of the eye absurd
And make the heaped-up winter billow green.
On second thought, one knew the air was
    keen—   160

A whetted edge in gauze. The village fires
Serenely builded tenuous gray spires
That vanished in the still blue deeps of awe.
All prophets were agreed upon a thaw.
And when the morning stood a spearlength high,
There grew along the western rim of sky
A bank of cloud that had a rainy look.
It mounted slowly. Then the warm chinook
Began to breathe a melancholy drowse
And sob among the naked poplar boughs, 170
As though the prairie dreamed a dream of June
And knew it for a dream. All afternoon
The gale increased. The sun went down blood-
    red;
The young moon, perilously fragile, fled
To early setting. And the long night roared.

Tempestuously broke the day and poured
An intermittent glory through the rifts
Amid the driven fog. The sodden drifts
Already grooved and withered in the blast; 179
And when the flying noon stared down aghast,
The bluffs behind the village boomed with flood.
What magic in that sound to stir the blood
Of winter-weary men! For now the spring
No longer seemed a visionary thing,
But that which any morning might bestow.
And most of all that magic moved Talbeau;
For, scrutinizing Fink, he thought he saw
Some reflex of that February thaw—
A whit less curling of the upper lip.
O could it be returning comradeship, 190
That April not beholden to the moon
Nor chatteled to the sun?

　　　　　　　　　　That afternoon
They played at euchre. Even Fink sat in;
And though he showed no eagerness to win,
Forgot the trumps and played his bowers wild,
There were not lacking moments when he
    smiled,
A hesitating smile 'twixt wan and grim.
It seemed his stubborn mood embarrassed him
Because regret now troubled it with shame.

The great wind died at midnight. Morning
    came, 200
Serene and almost indolently warm—
As when an early April thunder storm
Has cleansed the night and vanished with the
    gloom;
When one can feel the imminence of bloom
As 'twere a spirit in the orchard trees;
When, credulous of blossom, come the bees
To grumble 'round the seepages of sap.
So mused Talbeau while, pushing back the flap,
Instinctively he listened for a bird
To fill the hush. Then presently he heard— 210

And 'twas the only sound in all the world—
The trickle of the melting snow that purled
And tinkled in the bluffs above the town.
The sight of ragged Winter patched with
    brown,
The golden peace and, palpitant therein,
That water note, spun silverly and thin,
Begot a wild conviction in the man:
The wounded Winter weakened! Now began
The reconciliation! Hate would go
And, even as the water from the snow, 220
Old comradeship come laughing back again!

All morning long he pondered, while the men
Played seven-up. And scarce a trick was
    played
But someone sang a snatch of song or made
A merry jest. And when the game was balked
By one who quite forgot his hand, and talked
Of things in old St. Louis, none demurred.
And thus, by noon, it seemed the lightest word
Of careless salutation would avail
To give a happy ending to the tale 230
Of clouded friendship. So he 'rose and went,
By studied indirection, to the tent
Of Carpenter, as one who takes the air.
And, as he raised the flap and entered there,
A sudden gale of laughter from the men
Blew after him. What music in it then!
What mockery, when memory should raise
So often in the coming nights and days
The ruthless echo of it!

　　　　　　　　　Click on click
Amid the whirlwind finish of a trick 240
The cards fell fast, while King and Queen and
    Ace,
With meaner trumps for hounds, pursued the
    chase
Of wily Knave and lurking Deuce and Ten;
When suddenly the game-enchanted men
Were conscious of a shadow in the place,
And glancing up they saw the smiling face
Of Carpenter, thrust in above Talbeau's.
"How goes it, Boys?" said he; and gaily those
Returned the greeting. "Howdy, Mike!" he
    said;
And with a sullen hanging of the head 250
Fink mumbled "Howdy!" Gruff—but what
    of that?
One can not doff displeasure like a hat—
'Twould dwindle snow-like.

　　　　　　　　　　Nothing else would do
But Carpenter should play. Now Fink played
    too;
And, having brought his cherished ones to-
    gether,

Talbeau surrendered to the languid weather
And, dreamily contented, watched the sport.
All afternoon the pictured royal court
Pursued its quarry in the mimic hunt;
And Carpenter, now gayer than his wont, 260
Lost much; while Fink, with scarce a word to
    say,
His whole attention fixed upon the play,
Won often. So it happened, when the sun
Was near to setting, that the day seemed won
For friendliness, however stood the game.
But even then that Unseen Player came
Who stacks the shuffled deck of circumstance
And, playing wild the Joker men call Chance,
Defeats the Aces of our certainty. 269

The cards were dealt and Carpenter bid three.
The next man passed the bid, and so the next.
Then Fink, a trifle hesitant and vexed.
Bid four on spades. And there was one who
    said
In laughing banter: "Mike, I'll bet my head
As how them spades of your'n 'll dig a hole!"
And in some subtle meaning of the soul
The wag was more a prophet than he knew.

Fink held the Ace and Deuce, and that made
    two:
His black King scored another point with
    Knave.
But Carpenter, to whom the Weird One gave
A band of lesser trumps to guard his Ten, 281
Lay low until the Queen had passed, and then
Swept in a last fat trick for Game, and scored.
And now the players slapped their knees and
    roared:
"You're set! You're in the hole! He set you,
    Mike!"

Then suddenly they saw Fink crouch to strike;
And ere they comprehended what they saw,
There came a thud of knuckles on a jaw
And Carpenter rolled over on the ground.
One moment in a breathless lapse of sound 290
The stricken man strove groggily to 'rise,
The emptiness of wonder in his eyes
Turned dreamily with seeming unconcern
Upon Mike's face, where now began to burn
The livid murder-lust. 'Twixt breath and
    breath
The hush and immobility of death
Made there a timeless picture. Then a yell,
As of a wild beast charging, broke the spell.
Fink sprang to crush, but midway met Talbeau
Who threw him as a collie dog may throw 300
A raging bull. But Mike was up again,
And wielding thrice the might of common men,
He gripped the little man by nape and thigh

And lightly lifted him and swung him high
And flung him; and the smitten tent went
    down.
Then 'rose a roar that roused the teeming town,
And presently a shouting rabble surged
About the wreck, whence tumblingly emerged
A knot of men who grappled Fink and clung.
Prodigiously he rose beneath them, flung 310
His smashing arms, man-laden, forth and back;
But stubbornly they gripped him, like a pack
That takes uncowed the maulings of a bear.
"Let Carpenter get up!" they cried. "Fight
    fair!
Fight fair! Fight fair!"

                                Quite leisurely the while
The stricken man arose, a sleepy smile
About his quiet eyes. Indeed, he seemed
As one but lately wakened, who has dreamed
A pleasing dream. But when he stroked his
    beard
And gazed upon his fingers warmly smeared 320
With crimson from the trickle at his jaw,
His eyes went eagle-keen with what they saw.
The stupor passed. He hastily untied
His buckskin shirt and, casting it aside,
Stood naked to the hips. The tumult ceased
As, panting hard, the *voyageurs* released
Their struggling charge, and, ducking to a
    swing
Of those freed arms, sought safety, scampering.

Fink also stripped his shirt; and as the man
Stood thus revealed, a buzz of wonder ran 330
Amid the jostling rabble. Few there were
Who in that moment envied Carpenter,
Serenely poised and waiting placid browed:
For shall a lonely cedar brave a cloud
Bulged big and shapen to the cyclone's whirl?
Lo, even as the body of a girl,
The body of the blond was smooth and white;
But vaguely, as one guesses at the might
Of silent waters running swift and deep,
One guessed what store of power lay asleep 340
Beneath the long fleet lines of trunk and limb.
Thus God had made experiment with him;
And, groping for the old Adamic dream,
Had found his patterns in the tree and stream,
As Fink's in whirling air and hungry flame.

Now momently the picture there became
A blur of speed. Mike rushed. The tiptoe
    town
Craned eagerly to see a man go down
Before that human thunder gust. But lo!
As bends a sapling when the great winds blow,
The other squatted, deftly swayed aside, 351
And over him the slashing blows went wide.

Fink sprawled. But hardly had a spreading
    roar
O'errun the town, when silence as before
Possessed the scene; for Mike flashed back
    again
With flame-like speed, and suddenly the men
Clenched, leaning neck to neck.

                        Without a word,
Like horn-locked bulls that strive before the
    herd,
They balanced might with might; till Mike's
    hands whipped   359
Beneath the other's arm-pits, met and gripped
Across the broad white shoulders. Then began
The whole prodigious engine of the man
To bulge and roll and darken with the strain.
Like rivulets fed suddenly with rain,
The tall one's thews rose ropily and flowed
Converging might against the growing load
Of those tremendous arms that strove to
    crush.

Their labored breathing whistled in the rush.
One saw the blond man's face go bluish red,
As deeper, deeper sank Fink's shaggy head
Amid his heaped-up shoulder brawn. One
    knew   371
That very soon the taller of the two
Must yield and take that terrible embrace.

A tense hypnotic quiet filled the place.
The men were like two wrestlers in a dream
That holds an endless moment; till a scream
Fell stab-like on the hush. One saw Talbeau,
Jaws set, hands clenched, eyes wild, and bend-
    ing low,
As though he too were struggling, slowly bowed
Beneath Fink's might. And then—

                    What ailed the crowd?   380
Swept over by a flurry of surprise,
They swayed and jostled, shouting battle-cries
And quips and jeers of savage merriment.
One moment they had seen the tall man bent,
About to break: then, falling back a-haunch,
His feet had plunged against the other's
    paunch
And sent Fink somersaulting.

                        Once again
A silence fell as, leaping up, the men
Were mingled briefly in a storm of blows.
Now, tripping like a dancer on his toes,   390
The blond man sparred; while, like a baited
    bear,
Half blinded with the lust to crush and tear,
Fink strove to clutch that something lithe and
    sleek

That stung and fled and stung. Upon his
    cheek
A flying shadow laid a vivid bruise;
Another—and his brow began to ooze
Slow drops that spattered on his bearded jaw.
Again that shadow passed—his mouth went
    raw,
And like a gunshot wound it gaped and bled.

Fink roared with rage and plunged with low-
    ered head   400
Upon this thing that tortured, hurled it back
Amid the crowd. One heard a thud and smack
Of rapid blows on bone and flesh—and then
One saw the tall man stagger clear again
With gushing nostrils and a bloody grin,
And down his front the whiteness of the skin
Was striped with flowing crimson to the waist.
Unsteadily he wheeled about and faced
The headlong hate of his antagonist.
Now toe to toe and fist to flying fist,   410
They played at give and take; and all the while
The blond man smiled that riddle of a smile,
As one who meditates upon a jest.

Yet surely he was losing! Backward pressed,
He strove in vain to check his raging foe.
Fink lunged and straightened to a shoulder
    blow
With force enough to knock a bison down.
The other dodged it, squatting. Then the town
Discovered what a smile might signify.
For, even as the futile blow went by,   420
One saw the lithe white form shoot up close in,
A hooked white arm jab upward to the chin—
Once—twice—and yet again. With eyes
    a-stare,
His hands aloft and clutching at the air,
Fink tottered backward, limply lurched and
    fell.

Then came to pass what stilled the rabble's
    yell,
So strange it was. And 'round the fires that
    night
The wisest warriors, talking of the fight,
Could not explain what happened at the end.
No friend, they said, makes war upon a friend;
Nor does a foe have pity on a foe;   431
And yet the tall white chief had bathed with
    snow
The bloody mouth and battered cheek and
    brow
Of him who fell!

                    Queer people, anyhow,
The Long Knives were—and hard to under-
    stand!   1919

Still planted on in the woods alone.
Ohio and young Indiana—
These were his wide altar-stone,
Where still he burnt out flesh and bone.
Twenty days ahead of the Indian, twenty
    years ahead of the white man,
At last the Indian overtook him, at last the
    Indian hurried past him;   200
At last the white man overtook him, at last
    the white man hurried past him;
At last his own trees overtook him, at last his
    own trees hurried past him.
Many cats were tame again,
Many ponies tame again,
Many pigs were tame again,
Many canaries tame again;
And the real frontier was his sunburnt breast.
From the fiery core of that apple the earth,
Sprang apple-amaranths divine.
Love's orchards climbed to the heavens of the
    West.   210
And snowed the earthly sod with flowers.
Farm hands from the terraces of the blest
Danced on the mists with their ladies fine;
And Johnny Appleseed laughed with his
    dreams,
And swam once more the ice-cold streams.
And the doves of the spirit swept through the
    hours,
With doom-calls, love-calls, death-calls,
    dream-calls;
And Johnny Appleseed, all that year,
Lifted his hands to the farm-filled sky,
To the apple-harvesters busy on high;   220
And so once more his youth began,
And so for us he made great medicine—
Johnny Appleseed, medicine-man.
Then
The sun was his turned-up broken barrel,
Out of which his juicy apples rolled,
Down the repeated terraces,
Thumping across the gold,
An angel in each apple that touched the forest
    mold,
A ballot-box in each apple,   230
A state capital in each apple,

Great high schools, great colleges,
All America in each apple,
Each red, rich, round, and bouncing moon
That touched the forest mold.
Like scrolls and rolled-up flags of silk,
He saw the fruits unfold,
And all our expectations in one wild-flower
    written dream,
Confusion and death sweetness, and a thicket
    of crab-thorns,
Heart of a hundred midnights, heart of the
    merciful morns.   240
Heaven's boughs bent down with their alche-
    my,
Perfumed airs, and thoughts of wonder.
And the dew on the grass and his own cold tears
Were one in brooding mystery,
Though death's loud thunder came upon him,
Though death's loud thunder struck him
    down—
The boughs and the proud thoughts swept
    through the thunder,
Till he saw our wide nation, each State a
    flower,
Each petal a park for holy feet,
With wild fawns merry on every street,   250
With wild fawns merry on every street,
The vista of ten thousand years, flower-lighted
    and complete.

Hear the lazy weeds murmuring, bays and
    rivers whispering,
From Michigan to Texas, California to Maine;
Listen to the eagles screaming, calling,
"Johnny Appleseed, Johnny Appleseed,"
There by the doors of old Fort Wayne.

In the four-poster bed Johnny Appleseed built,
Autumn rains were the curtains, autumn
    leaves were the quilt.
He laid him down sweetly, and slept through
    the night,   260
Like a bump on a log, like a stone washed
    white,
There by the doors of old Fort Wayne.
    1921

CARL SANDBURG (1878-   )

CHICAGO

Hog Butcher for the World,
Tool Maker, Stacker of Wheat,
Player with Railroads and the Nation's Freight Handler;
Stormy, husky, brawling,
City of the Big Shoulders:

They tell me you are wicked and I believe them, for I have seen your painted women under the
    gas lamps luring the farm boys.

And they tell me you are crooked and I answer: Yes, it is true I have seen the gunman kill and
    go free to kill again.
And they tell me you are brutal and my reply is: On the faces of women and children I have
    seen the marks of wanton hunger.
And having answered so I turn once more to those who sneer at this my city, and I give them
    back the sneer and say to them:
Come and show me another city with lifted head singing so proud to be alive and coarse and
    strong and cunning.   10
Flinging magnetic curses amid the toil of piling job on job, here is a tall bold slugger set vivid
    against the little soft cities;
Fierce as a dog with tongue lapping for action, cunning as a savage pitted against the wilderness,
        Bareheaded,
        Shoveling,
        Wrecking,
        Planning,
        Building, breaking, rebuilding,
Under the smoke, dust all over his mouth, laughing with white teeth,
Under the terrible burden of destiny laughing as a young man laughs,
Laughing even as an ignorant fighter laughs who has never lost a battle,   20
Bragging and laughing that under his wrist is the pulse, and under his ribs the heart of the
    people,
        Laughing!
Laughing the stormy, husky, brawling laughter of Youth, half-naked, sweating, proud to be
    Hog-Butcher, Tool Maker, Stacker of Wheat, Player with Railroads and Freight Handler
    to the nation.
                                                                                                        1914

FOG

The fog comes
on little cat feet.
It sits looking
over harbor and city
on silent haunches
and then moves on.
                    1916

WASHINGTON MONUMENT BY NIGHT

1

The stone goes straight.
A lean swimmer dives into night sky,
Into half-moon mist.

2

Two trees are coal black.
This is a great white ghost between.
It is cool to look at.
Strong men, strong women, come here.

3

Eight years is a long time.
To be fighting all the time.

4

The republic is a dream.   10
Nothing happens unless first a dream.

5

The wind bit hard at Valley Forge one Christmas.

Soldiers tied rags on their feet.
Red footprints wrote on the snow . . .
. . . and stone shoots into stars here
. . . into half-moon mist to-night.

6

Tongues wrangle dark at a man.
He buttoned his overcoat and stood alone.
In a snowstorm, red hollyberries, thoughts,
he stood alone.

7

Women said: He is lonely   20
. . . fighting . . . fighting . . . eight years . . .

8

The name of an iron man goes over the world.
It takes a long time to forget an iron man.

9

. . . .
. . . .
                                            1922

BRIAN HOOKER (1880-   )

LILACS IN THE CITY

Amid the rush and fever of the street,
    The snarl and clash of countless quarreling
        bells,
And the sick, heavy heat,
    The hissing footsteps, and the hateful smells,
I found you, speaking quietly
    Of sunlit hill-horizons and clean earth;
    While the pale multitude that may not dare
To pause and live a moment, lest they die,
    Swarmed onward with hot eyes, and left
        you there—
An armful of God's glory, nothing worth.   10

You are more beautiful than I can know.
    Even one loving you might gaze an hour
Nor learn the perfect flow
    Of line and tint in one small, purple flower.
There are no two of you the same,
And every one is wonderful and new—
    Poor baby-blossoms that have died un-
        blown,
    And you that droop yourselves as if for
        shame,
You too are perfect. I had hardly known
    The grace of your glad sisters but for you.   20

You myriad of little litanies!
    Not as our bitter piety, subdued
To cold creed that denies
    Or lying law that severs glad and good;
But like a child's eyes, after sleep
    Uplifted; like a girl's first wordless prayer
Close-held by him who loves her—no dis-
        tress
Nor storm of supplication, but a deep,
    Dear heartache of such utter happiness
As only utter purity can bear.   30

For you are all the robin feels at dawn;
    The meaning of green dimness, and calm
        noons
On high fields far withdrawn,
    Where the haze glimmers and the wild bee
        croons.
You are the soul of a June night:—
    Intimate joy of moon-swept vale and glade,
Warm fragrance breathing upward from the
        ground,
    And eager winds tremulous with sharp de-
        light
Till all the tense-tuned gloom thrills like a
        sound—
    Mystery of sweet passion unafraid.   40

O sweet, sweet, sweet! You are the proof of all
That over-truth our dreams have memory of
That day cannot recall:
    Work without weariness, and tearless love,
And taintless laughter. While we run
To measure dust, and sounding names are
        hurled
    Into the nothingness of days unborn,
You hold your little hearts up to the sun,
    Quietly beautiful amid our scorn—
God's answer to the wisdom of this world.   50
                                        1907

ARS LONGA

Not thy great gifts, O God! I would not be
The prophet honored in an alien clime;
Or send my name trumpeting down through
        time,
Selling my manhood for a memory.
So should I fade into the shows of me:—
My joy become the reason of a rhyme,
My pain, a figure in the pantomime,
My love, a light over an unknown sea.
Give me but that thou givest all mankind:
A little faith in that I labor for,   10
A friend whose name I daily think to bless,
A woman in whose eyes I seek and find,
Children mysteriously mine—no more
Than common, ordinary happiness.
                                        1908

SONG

Dear, though you wander over peace and pas-
        sion,
    Searching the days to prove yourself untrue,
You cannot hide me. Still, in my own fashion,
    I shall come back to you.

In other eyes, on lips that bid you doubt me,
    In music, in the little things we knew,
In your blind prayers for happiness without
        me—
    I shall come back to you.

God keep you safe through all the ache of
        learning,
    Through all the wrong you need to be and
        do,   10
Till in the wise joy of unfearful yearning
    I shall come back—I shall come back to you!
                                        1908

There was a courteous hostler
  (He is in Heaven to-night)
He held Our Lady's bridle
  And helped her to alight;   20
He spread clean straw before her
  Whereon she might lie down,
And Jesus Christ has given him
  An everlasting crown.

Unlock the door this evening
  And let your gate swing wide,
Let all who ask for shelter
  Come speedily inside.
What if your yard be narrow?
  What if your house be small?   30
There is a Guest whose coming
  Will glorify it all.

There was a joyous hostler
  Who knelt on Christmas morn
Beside the radiant manger
  Wherein his Lord was born.
His heart was full of laughter,
  His soul was full of bliss
When Jesus, on His Mother's lap,
  Gave him His hand to kiss.   40

Unbar your heart this evening
  And keep no stranger out,
Take from your soul's great portal
  The barrier of doubt.
To humble folk and weary
  Give hearty welcoming,
Your breast shall be to-morrow
  The cradle of a King.

IN MEMORY OF RUPERT BROOKE

In alien earth, across a troubled sea,
His body lies that was so fair and young.
His mouth is stopped, with half his songs unsung;
His arm is still, that struck to make men free.
But let no cloud of lamentation be
Where, on a warrior's grave, a lyre is hung.
We keep the echoes of his golden tongue,
We keep the vision of his chivalry.
So Israel's joy, the loveliest of kings,
Smote now his harp, and now the hostile horde.
To-day the starry roof of Heaven rings   11
With psalms a soldier made to praise his Lord;
And David rests beneath Eternal wings,
Song on his lips, and in his hand a sword.
                        1915

ROUGE BOUQUET

In a wood they call the Rouge Bouquet
There is a new-made grave to-day,
Built by never a spade nor pick
Yet covered with earth ten metres thick.
There lie many fighting men,
  Dead in their youthful prime,
Never to laugh nor love again
  Nor taste the Summertime.
For Death came flying through the air
And stopped his flight at the dugout stair,   10
Touched his prey and left them there,
  Clay to clay.
He hid their bodies stealthily
In the soil of the land they fought to free
  And fled away.
Now over the grave abrupt and clear
  Three volleys ring;
And perhaps their brave young spirits hear
  The bugle sing:
"Go to sleep!   20
Go to sleep!
Slumber well where the shell screamed and fell.
Let your rifles rest on the muddy floor,
You will not need them any more.
Danger's past;
Now at last,
Go to sleep!"

There is on earth no worthier grave
To hold the bodies of the brave
Than this place of pain and pride   30
Where they nobly fought and nobly died.
Never fear but in the skie
Saints and angels stand
Smiling with their holy eyes
On this new-come band.
St. Michael's sword darts through the air
And touches the aureole on his hair
As he sees them stand saluting there,
  His stalwart sons;
And Patrick, Brigid, Columkill   40
Rejoice that in veins of warriors still
  The Gael's blood runs.
And up to Heaven's doorway floats,
  From the wood called Rouge Bouquet,
A delicate cloud of buglenotes
  That softly say:
"Farewell!
Farewell!
Comrades true, born anew, peace to you!
Your souls shall be where the heroes are   50
And your memory shine like the morning-star.
Brave and dear,
Shield us here.
Farewell!"
  1918   1918

WILLIAM ALEXANDER PERCY (1885–   )

CHORUS
(AFTER THE GREEK)

Surely in no benignant mood
The gods have fashioned us, but craftily
  To send us homing to the sod
Wise only in our own futility.

With hyacinthine brows of youth,
We enter life as to a festival;
  But, ere the feast is spread, the gods
Snatch back the wine, the song, the coronal.

And, lusterless, we turn, afraid,
Turn to the sole vouchsafèd heritage,   10

And in the shaken darkness clutch
The disenchanted ledges of old age.
                                                1915

OVERTONES

I heard a bird at break of day
  Sing from the autumn trees
A song so mystical and calm,
  So full of certainties,
No man, I think, could listen long
  Except upon his knees.
Yet this was but a simple bird
  Alone, among dead trees.
                                                1917

JOHN HALL WHEELOCK (1886–   )

EARTH

Grasshopper, your tiny song
And my poem alike belong
To the dark and silent earth
From which all poetry has birth;
All we say and all we sing
Is but as the murmuring
Of that drowsy heart of hers
When from her deep dream she stirs:
If we sorrow, or rejoice,
You and I are but her voice.   10

Deftly does the dust express
In mind her hidden loveliness,
And from her cool silence stream
The cricket's cry and Dante's dream;
For the earth that breeds the trees
Breeds cities too, and symphonies.
Equally her beauty flows
Into a savior, or a rose—
Looks down in dream, and from above
Smiles at herself in Jesus' love.   20
Christ's love and Homer's art
Are but the workings of her heart;
Through Leonardo's hand she seeks
Herself, and through Beethoven speaks
In holy thunderings around
The awful message of the ground.

The serene and humble mold
Does in herself all selves enfold—
Kingdoms, destinies, and creeds,
Great dreams, and dauntless deeds,   30
Science that metes the firmament,
The high, inflexible intent
Of one for many sacrificed—

Plato's brain, the heart of Christ;
All love, all legend, and all lore
Are in the dust forevermore.

Even as the growing grass
Up from the soil religions pass,
And the field that bears the rye
Bears parables and prophecy.   40
Out of the earth the poem grows
Like the lily, or the rose;
And all man is, or yet may be,
Is but herself in agony
Toiling up the steep ascent
Toward the complete accomplishment
When all dust shall be, the whole
Universe, one conscious soul.

Yea, the quiet and cool sod
Bears in her breast the dream of God. 50

If you would know what earth is, scan
The intricate, proud heart of man,
Which is the earth articulate,
And learn how holy and how great,
How limitless and how profound
Is the nature of the ground—
How without terror or demur
We may entrust ourselves to her
When we are wearied out, and lay
Our faces in the common clay.   60

For she is pity, she is love,
All wisdom, she, all thoughts that move
About her everlasting breast
Till she gathers them to rest:

All tenderness of all the ages,
Seraphic secrets of the sages,
Vision and hope of all the seers,
All prayer, all anguish, and all tears
Are but the dust, that from her dream
Awakes, and knows herself supreme—   70
Are but earth, when she reveals
All that her secret heart conceals

Down in the dark and silent loam,
Which is ourselves, asleep, at home.

Yea, and this, my poem, too,
Is part of her as dust and dew,
Wherein herself she doth declare
Through my lips, and say her prayer.

1917

BE BORN AGAIN!

Who shall lay bare love's inmost meaning, who
Reveal the sovereign splendor on its throne,
Or utter forth in language the unknown!—
Old is all language, but all love is new.
How may I tell you of this love that to
Your bosom draws me from my very own,
And wakes me to one need, and one alone —

O love, the need to be reborn from you!
There is no word whereby love may declare
His holy will; but in the breathless deed   10
Of adoration, in the primal prayer
At the belovèd breast, he tells his need
To the one kind and conquering heart, and she
In the great silence answers silently.

1919

ABSENCE

Moonlight is memory; now the sun
His radiant race in heaven has run,
Backward he sheds from far away
The light of our lost yesterday.

On the pillow where your head
Lay dreaming, on the empty bed
Falls the moonlight, on the walls
The lonely light of memory falls.

Where it rested, your pale hair
Has left its print in moonlight, where   10
Your perfect loveliness did press
Lingers a vanished loveliness.

Gaunt in the moonlight the road lies
That took you from my longing eyes,
And one wide window, drenched with light,
Stares out into the marble night. . . .

1919

THE HOLY EARTH

In the immense cathedral of the holy earth,
    Whose arches are the heavens and the great vault above,
    Groined with its myriad stars—what miracles of birth,
    What sacraments of death, what rituals of love!

Her nave is the wide world and the whole length of it,
    One flame on all her altars kindles her many fires;
Wherever the clear tapers of trembling life are lit
    Resound for joy the old, indomitable choirs.

The holy church of earth with clamorous worshippers
    Is crowded and fierce hungers, faithful every one   10
To the one faith; that stern and simple faith of hers
    Contents the heart that asks no pity, giving none.

Each on the other feeds, and all on each are fed,
    And each for all is offered—a living offering, where
In agony and triumph the ancient feast is spread,
    Life's sacramental supper, that all her sons may share.

They mingle with one another, blend—mingle—merge, and flow
    Body into wild body; in rapture endlessly

Weaving, with intricate motions of being, to and fro,
   The pattern of all Being, one mighty harmony: 20

One Body of all bodies woven and interwrought—
   One Self in many selves, through their communion
In love and death, made perfect; wherein each self is nought
   Save as it serve the many, mysteriously made One.

And all are glad for life's sake, and all have found it good
   From the beginning; all, through many and warring ways,
In savage vigor of life and wanton hardihood
   Live out, like a brave song, the passion of their days.

With music woven of lust and music woven of pain,
   Chapel and aisle and choir, the great cathedral rings—   30
One voice in all her voices chanting the old disdain
   Of pity, the clean hunger of all primal things.

From the trembling of Arcturus even to the tiny nest
   Of the grey mouse the glories of her vast frame extend:
The span of her great arches, stretching from east to west,
   Is endless—the immense reaches are without end.

Evening closes. The light from heaven's high window falls
   Vaguer and softer now. In vain the twilight pleads
With stubborn night, his shadow looms on the massive walls—
   Darkness. The immemorial ritual proceeds.   40

The spider in her quivering web watches and waits;
   The moth flutters entangled, in agony of fear
He beats amid the toils that bind him; she hesitates
   Along the trembling wires—she pauses—she draws near.

She weaves her delicate bondage around him; in the net,
   As in a shroud, he labors—but, labor as he will,
The cunning threads hold fast; her drowsy mouth is set
   Against the body that shivers softly, and is still.

And through the leafy dark the owl with noiseless flight
   Moves, peering craftily among the tangled trees
And thickets of the wood all slumbrous in the night—   50
   The fledgling's bitter cry comes sharp upon the breeze.

With dreadful ceremony all things together move
   To the one end: shrill voices in triumph all around
Prolong deliriously their monotone of love—
   Arches and aisles are heavy with incense and dim sound.

Hush!—the whole world is kneeling! Murmurous is the air—
   The Host is lifted up. Upon the altar lies
The sacramental Body. The wind breathes like a prayer—
   Solemnly is renewed the eternal sacrifice.   60

With mingled moan and might of warring wills made one
   The vast cathedral shudders. From chancel, nave and choir
Sounds the fierce hymn to life: her holy will be done!
   Upon her myriad altars flames the one sacred fire.

Into the Void—we know not why nor where;
Embattled between two oblivions
We stand, for a brief moment, and lift up
Our faces to the light—but in our blood
The voices of the generations past
Strive, and the generations still unborn
Are urgent in us that we play our part,
As actors in a stately tragedy   190

To some triumphant close. Courage and faith,
These are most needful. Surely they shall
     avail!
Surely they have the truth! And as for Him
Whom we have sought beyond the stars in
     vain,
Perhaps He may be nearer than we know.
                                        1927

DU BOSE HEYWARD (1885–   )

THE LAST CREW

I

Spring found us early that eventful year,
Seeming to know in her clairvoyant way
The bitterness of hunger and despair
That lay upon the town.
Out of the sheer
Thin altitudes of day
She drifted down
Over the grim blockade
At the harbor mouth,
Trailing her beauty over the decay   10
That war had made,
Gilding old ruins with her jasmine spray,
Distilling warm moist perfume
From chill winter shade.

Out of the south
She brought the whisperings
Of questing wings.
Then, flame on flame,
The cardinals came,
Blowing like driven brands   20
Up from the sultry lands
Where Summer's happy fires always burn.
Old silences, that pain
Had held too close and long,
Stirred to the mocker's song,
And hope looked out again
From tired eyes.

Down where the White Point Gardens drank
     the sun,
And rippled to the lift of springing grass,
The women came;   30
And after them the aged, and the lame
That war had hurled back at them like a taunt.
And always, as they talked of little things,
How violets were purpling the shade
More early than in all remembered Springs,
And how the tides seemed higher than last
     year,
Their gaze went drifting out across the bay
To where,
Thrusting out of the mists,

Like hostile fists,   40
Waited the close blockade—
Then, dim to left and right,
The curving islands with their shattered
     mounds
That had been forts;
Mounds, which in spite
Of four long years of rending agony
Still held against the light;
Faint wraiths of color
For the breeze to lift
And flatten into faded red and white.   50

These sunny islands were not meant for wars;
See, how they curve away
Before the bay,
Bidding the voyager pause.
Warm with the hoarded suns of centuries,
Young with the garnered youth of many
     Springs,
They laugh like happy bathers, while the seas
Break in their open arms,
And the slow-moving breeze   59
Draws languid fingers down their placid brows.
Even the surly ocean knows their charms,
And under the shrill laughter of the surf,
He booms and sings his heavy monotone.

II

There are rare nights among these waterways
When Spring first treads the meadows of the
     marsh,
Leaving faint footprints of elusive green
To glimmer as she strays,
Breaking the Winter silence with the harsh
Sharp call of waterfowl;
Rubbing dim shifting pastels in the scene   70
With white of moon
And blur of scudding cloud,
Until the myrtle thickets
And the sand,
The silent streams,
And the substantial land

Go drifting down the tide of night
Aswoon.

On such a night as this
I saw the last crew go   80
Out of a world too beautiful to leave.
Only a chosen few
Beside the crew
Were gathered on the pier;
And in the ebb and flow
Of dark and moon, we saw them fare
Straight past the row of coffins
Where the fifth crew lay
Waiting their last short voyage
Across the bay.   90

And, as they went, not one among them
      swerved,
But eyes went homing swiftly to the West,
Where, faint and very few,
The windows of the town called out to them
Yet held them nerved
And ready for the test.
Young every one, they brought life at its best.
In the taut stillness, not a word
Was uttered, but one heard
The deep slow orchestration of the night   100
Swell and relapse; as swiftly, one by one,
Cutting a silhouette against the gray,
They rose, then dropped out softly like a
      dream
Into the rocking shadows of the stream.

A sudden grind of metal scarred the hush;
A marsh-hen threshed the water with her
      wings,
And, for a breath, the marsh life woke and
      throbbed.
Then, down beneath our feet, we caught the
      gleam
Of folded water flaring left and right,
While, with a noiseless rush,   110
A shadow darker than the rest
Drew from its fellows swarming round the
      quay,
Took an oncoming breaker,
Shook its shoulders free,
And faced the sea.

Then came an interval that seemed to be
Part of eternity.
Years might have passed, or seconds;
No one knew!   119
Close in the dark we huddled, each to each,
Too stirred for speech.
Our senses, sharpened to an agony,
Drew out across the water till the ache
Was more than we could bear;

Till eyes could almost see,
Ears almost hear.
And waiting there,
I seemed to feel the beach
Slip from my reach,
While all the stars went blank.   130
The smell of oil and death enveloped me,
And I could feel
The crouching figures straining at a crank,
Knees under chins, and heads drawn sharply
      down,
The heave and sag of shoulders,
Sting of sweat;
An eighth braced figure stooping to a wheel,
Body to body in the stifling gloom,
The sob and gasp of breath against an air
Empty and damp and fetid as a tomb.   140
With them I seemed to reel
Beneath the spin and heel
When combers took them fair,
Bruising their bodies,
Lifting black water where
Their feet clutched desperate at the floor.

And as each body spent out of its ebbing store
Of strength and hope,
I felt the forward thrust,
At first so sure,   150
Fail in its rhythm,
Falter slow,
And slower—
Hang an endless moment—
Till in a rush came fear—
Fear of the sea, that it might win again,
Gathering one crew more,
Making them pay in vain.

Then through the horror of it, like a clear
Sweet wind among the stars,   160
I felt the lift
And drive of heart and will
Working their miracles until
Spent muscles tensed again to offer all
In one transcendent gift.

III

A sudden flood of moonlight drenched the sea,
Pointing the scene in sharp, strong black and
      white.
Sumter came shouldering through the night,
Battered and grim.
The curve of ships shook off their dim   170
Vague outlines of a dream;
And stood, patient as death,
So certain in their pride,
So satisfied
To wait
The slow inevitableness of Fate.

Close, where the channel
Narrowed to the bay,
The *Housatonic* lay
Black on the moonlit tide,   180
Her wide
High sweep of spars
Flaunting their arrogance among the stars.

Darkness again,
Swift-winged and absolute,
Gulping the stars,
Folding the ships and sea,
Holding us waiting, mute.
Then, slowly in the void,
There grew a certainty   190
That silenced fear.
The very air
Was stirring to the march of Destiny.

One blinding second out of endless time
Fell, sundering the night.
I saw the *Housatonic* hurled,
A ship of light,
Out of a molten sea,
Hang an unending pulse-beat,
Glowing, stark;   200
While the hot clouds flung back a sullen roar.
Then all her pride, so confident and sure,
Went reeling down the dark.

Out of the blackness wave on livid wave
Leapt into being—thundered to our feet;
Counting the moments for us, beat by beat,
Until the last and smallest dwindled past,
Trailing its pallor like a winding-sheet
Over the last crew and its chosen grave.

IV

Morning swirled in from the sea,   210
And down by the low river-wall,
In a long unforgettable row,
Man faces tremulous, old;
Terrible faces of youth,
Broken and seared by the war,
Where swift fire kindled and blazed
From embers hot under the years,
While hands gripped a cane or a crutch;
Patient dumb faces of women,
Mothers, sisters, and wives: 220
And the vessel hull-down in the sea,

Where the waters, just stirring from sleep,
Lifted bright hands to the sun,
Hiding their lusty young dead,
Holding them jealously close
Down to the cold harbor floor.

There would be eight of them.
Here in the gathering light
Were waiting eight women or more
Who were destined forever to pay,   230
Who never again would laugh back
Into the eyes of life
In the old glad, confident way.
Each huddled dumbly to each;
But eyes could not lift from the sea,
Only hands touched in the dawn.

"He would have gone, my man;
He was like that. In the night
When I awoke with a start,
And brought his voice up from my dream: 240
That was goodbye and godspeed.
I know he is there with the rest."

Brave, but with quivering lips,
Each alone in the press of the crowd,
Was saying it over and over.

The day flooded all of the sky;
And the ships of the sullen blockade
Weighed anchor and drew down the wind,
Leaving their wreck to the waves.
Hour heaved slowly on hour,   250
Yet how could the city rejoice
With the women out there by the wall!
Night grew under the wharves,
And crept through the listening streets,
Until only the red of the tiles
Seemed warm from the breath of the day;
And the faces that waited and watched
Blurred into a wavering line,
Like foam on the curve of the dark,
Down there by the reticent sea.   260

What if the darkness should bring
The lean blockade-runners across
With food for the hungry and spent . .
Who could joy in the sudden release
While the faces, still-smiling, but wan,
Turned slowly to hallow the town?
                                        1922

HORIZONS

This sun-drugged land of ours,
Huge, tawny-limbed, low-breasted like a man,
Sprawling in indolence among sea-nurtured
        flowers,

Dreaming a dream that started
When the first dawn began;
Impersonal as lust,
As fiercely taking;

Holding us until the last
Sharp awful breaking,
Then closing sleepy fingers on our dust.   10

Why should we give it all!
Why should we bring
Swift pulses, shackled dreams,
White early love!
Wall beyond lifted wall
The Andes swing
Their tilted beauty.
Till Gobi and Sahara pale and flare.
Alaskan stars on snow
Call bitter-clear.   20
And one may know
The transient solace of old, chiseled stone,
And many a girl Madonna,
Many a saint,
Fixed for a heart-beat in a square of paint.

I have said, "I will go.
Another sun will see me freed
Of this old torrid passion.
But, for tonight, I have a need
To rest on warm brown sand,   30
And watch the slow
Dark breaker of the night
Gather and grow,
Topple against the west,
Then break, and race
Under its spray of stars
To beach on space;
Leaving the east behind it
Washed and white."

Then, while I lie, resolved,   40
And wait for day;
Across the low-hung moon
Late curlews sway
The trailing pennant
Of their silent flight.
Slowly they curve,
And then come streaming back
Across the yellow disc,
Low on the water like a riding-light,
Then out to sea along the copper track.   50

That only—nothing more:
Late curlews—and a later moon.
Yet, when the sun

Calls the blue heron out to wade the creek,
While alligators boom a sunrise gun
In the dark swamp,
And many-tongued, the waking marshes
    speak;
I know again that I have been undone.

Undone!
                To dream a whirl of years away
Beneath their tireless spin of suns and moons,
To feel my body drinking, deep and free,   61
Of sky that knows no trammels but the sea:
And a low range of far tide-bitten dunes.

Undone!
                To stumble on a vacant shore
That has been busy with its urgent life,
And given of its wealth to taking hands.
And watch the sea returning for its own,
Trampling earth ramparts into fluid sands,
Heaping a forest skyward, bone on bone,
Until the equinox shall sweep it bare.   70

Undone!
                To feel immensity bend near
And lay its weight on me;
While wind, clean from another sphere,
Blows by like pitying laughter.
Then silence—aching—long—
And after,
The raw irony
Of spending soul and brain upon a song.

Undone!
                And yet I know that I shall stay;
Asking but life outside of city walls,   80
Tides and savannas,
And the aimless sway
Of far curlews,
A solitary heron voyaging south,
The ocean's wide, innumerable blues,
And the sweet bitterness
Of salt upon my mouth.
For these are life,
And when they pass from me,
Leaving me stricken and uncomforted,   90
Although I still may hold the avid ground
Beneath my feet, and thrill to sight and sound,
I shall most surely know that I am dead.
                                                          1924

ENVOY

So, at the last, I think that we must follow,
When Death has struck us free to dream and
    rest;
When the great engines rock the world about us,
And sow bright, bitter cities down the West.

Then we may go, we who have guarded Beauty
Hidden from eyes that were not taught to see,
Out to the city's edge, in the covering night-
    time,
Bearing a ghostly treasure secretly.

And those who meet us in the echoing silence
Will neither challenge us nor stay our pace. 10
For our shimmering store would fetch no silver
Under the sun in any market-place.
Only the sky will know us, and the silence,
And the great cloud-leviathans that spawn
Their sullen young beyond the smoking
   marshes
To range the painted ocean of the dawn.
Time will flow by us then like a wide blue river.
But we will never heed its steady pull,
Nor mourn the tragic freightage that it carries,

Broken, but beautiful.   20
We will hold fast against the crowding shadows,
Late and soon,
Beauties that breath built tenderly at sunrise,
To fade at noon.
These we will hoard, and treasure, and remem-
   ber;
Waiting dead captains who will never come,
Statesmen, and dreamers, workers with taut
   sinews,
Who builded Beauty here, and called it *home*.
                       1924

EDNA ST. VINCENT MILLAY (1892–   )

BLUEBEARD

This door you might not open, and you did;
So enter now, and see for what slight thing
You are betrayed. . . . Here is no treasure hid,
No cauldron, no clear crystal mirroring
The sought-for truth, no heads of women slain
For greed like yours, no writhings of distress,
But only what you see. . . . Look yet again—

An empty room, cobwebbed and comfortless.
Yet this alone out of my life I kept
Unto myself, lest any know me quite   10
And you did so profane me when you crept
Unto the threshold of this room to-night
That I must never more behold your face.
This now is yours. I seek another place.
                       1916

THE SPRING AND THE FALL

In the spring of the year, in the spring of the
   year,
I walked the road beside my dear.
The trees were black where the bark was wet.
I see them yet, in the spring of the year.
He broke me a bough of the blossoming peach
That was out of the way and hard to reach.

In the fall of the year, in the fall of the year,
I walked the road beside my dear.
The rooks went up with a raucous trill.

I hear them still, in the fall of the year.   10
He laughed at all I dared to praise,
And broke my heart, in little ways.

Year be springing or year be falling,
The bark will drip and the birds be calling.
There's much that's fine to see and hear
In the spring of a year, in the fall of a year.
'Tis not love's going hurts my days,
But that it went in little ways.
                       1923

STEPHEN VINCENT BENÉT (1898–   )

THE HEMP

(*A Virginia Legend*)

I. *The Planting of the Hemp*

Captain Hawk scourged clean the seas
(*Black is the gap below the plank*)
From the Great North Bank to the Caribbees.
(*Down by the marsh the hemp grows rank*).

His fear was on the seaport towns,
The weight of his hand held hard the downs.

And the merchants cursed him, bitter and black,
For a red flame in the sea-fog's wrack
Was all of their ships that might come back.

For all he had one word alone,   10
One clod of dirt in their faces thrown,
"*The hemp that shall hang me is not grown!*"

His name bestrode the seas like Death,
The waters trembled at his breath.

This is the tale of how he fell,
Of the long sweep and the heavy swell,
And the rope that dragged him down to hell.

The fight was done, and the gutted ship,
Stripped like a shark the sea-gulls strip,

Lurched blindly, eaten out with flame,   20
Back to the land from whence she came,
A skimming horror, an eyeless shame.

And Hawk stood up on his quarter-deck,
And saw the sky and saw the wreck.

Below, a butt for sailors' jeers,
White as the sky when a white squall nears,
Huddled the crowd of the prisoners.

Over the bridge of the tottering plank,
Where the sea shook and the gulf yawned
blank,
They shrieked and struggled and dropped and
sank.   30

Pinioned arms and hands bound fast.
One girl alone was left at last.

Sir Henry Gaunt was a mighty lord.
He sat in state at the Council board.

The governors were as naught to him
From one rim to the other rim

Of his great plantations, flung out wide
Like a purple cloak, was a full month's ride.

Life and death in his white hands lay,
And his only daughter stood at bay,   40
Trapped like a hare in the toils that day.

He sat at wine in his gold and his lace,
And far away, in a bloody place,
Hawk came near, and she covered her face.

He rode in the fields, and the hunt was brave,
And far away, his daughter gave
A shriek that the seas cried out to hear,
And he could not see and he could not save.

Her white soul withered in the mire
As paper shrivels up in fire,   50
And Hawk laughed, and he kissed her mouth,
And her body he took for his desire.

II. The Growing of the Hemp

Sir Henry stood in the manor room,
And his eyes were hard gems in the gloom.

And he said, "Go, dig me furrows five
Where the green marsh creeps like a thing
alive—
There at its edge where the rushes thrive."

And where the furrows rent the ground
He sowed the seed of hemp around.

And the blacks shrink back and are sore afraid
At the furrows five that rib the glade,   61
And the voodoo work of the master's spade.

For a cold wind blows from the marshland near,
And white things move, and the night grows
drear,
And they chatter and crouch and are sick with
fear.

*But down by the marsh, where the grey slaves
glean,*
The hemp sprouts up, and the earth is seen
Veiled with a tenuous mist of green.

And Hawk still scourges the Caribbees,
And many men kneel at his knees.   70

Sir Henry sits in his house alone,
And his eyes are hard and dull like stone.

And the waves beat, and the winds roar,
And all things are as they were before.

And the days pass, and the weeks pass,
And nothing changes but the grass.

But down where the fireflies are like eyes,
And the damps shudder, and the mists rise,
The hemp-stalks stand up toward the skies.

And down from the poop of the pirate ship   80
A body falls, and the great sharks grip.

Innocent, lovely, go in grace!
At last there is peace upon your face.

And Hawk laughs loud as the corpse is thrown,
"The hemp that shall hang me is not grown!"

Sir Henry's face is iron to mark,
And he gazes ever in the dark.

And the days pass, and the weeks pass,
And the world is as it always was.

But down by the marsh the sickles gleam,   90
Glitter on glitter, gleam on gleam,
And the hemp falls down by the stagnant stream.

And Hawk beats up from the Caribbees,
Swooping to pounce in the Northern seas.

Sir Henry sits sunk deep in his chair,
And white as his hand is grown his hair.

And the days pass, and the weeks pass,
And the sands roll from the hour-glass.

But down by the marsh, in the blazing sun,
The hemp is smoothed and twisted and spun. 100
The rope made, and the work done.

III.   *The Using of the Hemp*

Captain Hawk scourged clean the seas,
(Black is the gap below the plank)
From the Great North Bank to the Caribbees
(Down by the marsh the hemp grows rank)

He sailed in the broad Atlantic track
And the ships that saw him came not back.

Till once again, where the wide tides ran,
He stopped to harry a merchantman.

He bade her stop. Ten guns spake true   110
From her hidden ports, and a hidden crew,
Racking his great ship through and through.

Dazed and dumb with the sudden death,
He scarce had time to draw a breath

Before the grappling-irons bit deep
And the boarders slew his crew like sheep.

Hawk stood up straight, his breast to the
  steel;
His cutlass made a bloody wheel.

His cutlass made a wheel of flame.
They shrank before him as he came.   120

And the bodies fell in a choking crowd,
And still he thundered out aloud.

"The hemp that shall hang me is not grown!"
They fled at last. He was left alone.

Before his foe Sir Henry stood.
"The hemp is grown and my word made good!"

And the cutlass clanged with a hissing whir
On the lashing blade of the rapier.

Hawk roared and charged like a maddened
  buck.
As the cobra strikes, Sir Henry struck,   130

Pouring his life in a single thrust,
And the cutlass shivered to sparks and dust.

Sir Henry stood on the blood-stained deck,
And set his foot on his foe's neck.

Then, from the hatch, where the torn decks
  slope,
Where the dead roll and the wounded grope,
He dragged the serpent of the rope.

The sky was blue and the sea was still,
The waves lapped softly, hill on hill,
And between one wave and another wave   140
The doomed man's cries were little and shrill.

The sea was blue and the sky was calm,
The air dripped with a golden balm.
Like a wind-blown fruit between sea and sun,
A black thing writhed at a yard-arm.

Slowly then, and awesomely,
The ship sank, and the gallows-tree,
And there was nought between sea and sun—
Nought but the sun and the sky and the sea.

But down by the marsh, where the fever breeds, 150
Only the water chuckles and pleads;
For the hemp clings fast to a dead man's throat,
And blind Fate gathers back her seeds.

                                        1916

THE BALLAD OF WILLIAM SYCAMORE
(1790–1871)

My father, he was a mountaineer,
His fist was a knotty hammer;
He was quick on his feet as a running deer,
And he spoke with a Yankee stammer.

My mother, she was merry and brave,
And so she came to her labor,
With a tall green fir for her doctor grave
And a stream for her comforting neighbor.

And some are wrapped in the linen fine,
And some like a godling's scion;   10

But I was cradled on twigs of pine
In the skin of a mountain lion.

And some remember a white, starched lap
And a ewer with silver handles;
But I remember a coonskin cap
And the smell of bayberry candles.

The cabin logs, with the bark still rough,
And my mother who laughed at trifles,
And the tall, lank visitors, brown as snuff,
With their long, straight squirrel-rifles.   20

I can hear them dance, like a foggy song,
Through the deepest one of my slumbers,
The fiddle squeaking the boots along
And my father calling the numbers.

The quick feet shaking the puncheon-floor,
And the fiddle squealing and squealing,
Till the dried herbs rattled above the door
And the dust went up to the ceiling.

There are children lucky from dawn till dusk,
But never a child so lucky!   30
For I cut my teeth on "Money Musk"
In the Bloody Ground of Kentucky!

When I grew tall as the Indian corn,
My father had little to lend me,
But he gave me his great, old powder-horn
And his woodsman's skill to befriend me.

With a leather shirt to cover my back,
And a redskin nose to unravel
Each forest sign, I carried my pack
As far as a scout could travel.   40

Till I lost my boyhood and found my wife,
A girl like a Salem Clipper!
A woman straight as a hunting-knife
With eyes as bright as the Dipper!

We cleared our camp where the buffalo feed,
Unheard-of streams were our flagons,
And I sowed my sons like the apple-seed
On the trail of the Western wagons.

They were right, tight boys, never sulky or
slow,

A fruitful, a goodly muster.   50
The eldest died at the Alamo.
The youngest fell with Custer.

The letter that told it burned my hand.
Yet we smiled and said, "So be it!"
But I could not live when they fenced the
land,
For it broke my heart to see it.

I saddled a red, unbroken colt
And rode him into the day there;
And he threw me down like a thunderbolt
And rolled on me as I lay there.   60

The hunter's whistle hummed in my ear
As the city-men tried to move me,
And I died in my boots like a pioneer
With the whole wide sky above me.

Now I lie in the heart of the fat, black soil,
Like the seed of a prairie-thistle;
It has washed my bones with honey and oil
And picked them clean as a whistle.

And my youth returns, like the rains of Spring,
And my sons, like the wild-geese flying;   70
And I lie and hear the meadow-lark sing
And have much content in my dying.

Go play with the towns you have built of
blocks,
The towns where you would have bound me!
I sleep in my earth like a tired fox,
And my buffalo have found me.
1922

XVIII. THE CONTEMPORARY DRAMA

Lazarus Laughed is the climax, so far, of the work of Eugene O'Neill and the loftiest example of romantic tragedy America has produced since *Francesca da Rimini*. While it is partly in prose, the rhythmic flow is continuous, and the medium as well as the conception lifts it into poetry. *Lazarus Laughed* marks a stage in the development of O'Neill's dramatic achievement. His earliest plays,—the portrayals of his own experiences in the one-act dramas of the forecastle; the revelation of his longing for adventure in *Beyond the Horizon;* the profound study of a woman's nature in *Anna Christie;* and the celebration of the unquenchable hold on hope in *The Straw*—these were cast in a realistic mould. In his next phase, ushered in by *The Emperor Jones*, and continued in *The Hairy Ape*, *All God's Chillun Got Wings*, and *Desire Under the Elms*, he portrayed the struggle of primitive forces, physical and emotional, for fuller expression. In this group of plays he also substituted for the older unities of the stage a unity of impression which permitted the employment of an apparently looser technique.

With *The Fountain*, written in 1921–2, he entered into a phase of romantic symbolism. Both in the rhythmic form and in the theme, that of the search for the "Eternal Becoming which is Beauty," represented symbolically by the Fountain of Eternal Youth, *The Fountain* revealed O'Neill distinctly as a poet. *Marco Millions*, in which the age-long contrast of the East and West is symbolized in the adventures of the arch-trader Marco Polo, came next in order of composition. In *The Great God Brown*, the symbolism was more apparent and the protest of the creative artist against the materialism of the world was expressed through a technique in which O'Neill again revealed his ability to move forward the frontiers of drama.

Lazarus Laughed, published in 1927, and produced at the Pasadena Community Playhouse on April 9, 1928, is the most imaginative, so far, of O'Neill's plays. The life of Lazarus, after he returns from the grave, is represented in a series of scenes, rising in dramatic intensity, in which the power of Lazarus' character and personality triumphs over the scepticism of paganism, over the opposition of the Roman Empire, and finally over the flames of martyrdom. Lazarus is the symbol of the laughter of God, never mocking His creatures but comforting them with the message that "There is no Death; There is only Life! There is only laughter!" Lazarus, the only man who knows what is beyond the grave, is the happiest, and his mission is to banish fear. The discriminating critics of O'Neill's work, who have seen the essential optimism of nearly all his plays, have recognized in *Lazarus Laughed* the supreme expression of an apostle of hope. The presentation at Pasadena was highly successful, and proved again O'Neill's skill as a playwright. But O'Neill is to be considered in our literature not only as a dramatist but preeminently as a poet and a mystic.

In *Strange Interlude* (1928) he seems to have departed from the romantic and poetic play and to have given a profound interpretation of the clutch of one woman upon the lives of five men who love her. The technique was unusual, for the characters uttered aloud thoughts which would have precipitated tragedy if they had been heard by the other characters. This produced a dramatic reaction in the audience, for they were included, in a manner impossible to make clear to those who have not seen the play, in the confidence of the author. In *Dynamo* (1929) O'Neill wrote a drama of ideas, dealing with the conflict of religion and science, in which the latter was symbolized by the generator of electricity, the modern god. But however powerful *Strange Interlude* or *Dynamo* may be, *Lazarus Laughed* still remains a loftier poetic utterance and a greater piece of dramatic art.

EUGENE O'NEILL (1888–   )

LAZARUS LAUGHED

(1927)

ACT ONE:

Scene One: Lazarus' home in Bethany—a short time after the miracle.

Scene Two: Months later. Outside the House of Laughter in Bethany. Late evening.

ACT TWO:

Scene One: A street in Athens. A night months later.

Scene Two: A temple immediately inside the walls of Rome. Midnight. Months later.

ACT THREE:

Scene One: Garden of Tiberius' palace. A night a few days later.

Scene Two: Inside the palace. Immediately after.

ACT FOUR:

Scene One: The same. A while after.

Scene Two: Interior of a Roman theatre. Dawn of the same night.

CHARACTERS

LAZARUS OF BETHANY
HIS FATHER
HIS MOTHER
MARTHA ⎫ *his sisters*
MARY   ⎭
MIRIAM, *his wife*
SEVEN GUESTS, *neighbors of Lazarus*
CHORUS OF OLD MEN
AN ORTHODOX PRIEST
CHORUS OF LAZARUS' FOLLOWERS
A CENTURION
GAIUS CALIGULA
CRASSUS, *a Roman General*
CHORUS OF GREEKS
SEVEN CITIZENS OF ATHENS
CHORUS OF ROMAN SENATORS
SEVEN SENATORS
CHORUS OF LEGIONARIES
FLAVIUS, *a centurion*
MARCELLUS, *a patrician*
CHORUS OF THE GUARD
TIBERIUS CÆSAR
POMPEIA

CHORUS OF YOUTHS AND GIRLS
CHORUS OF THE ROMAN POPULACE
CROWDS

ACT I

SCENE I

SCENE: *Exterior and interior of* LAZARUS' *home at Bethany. The main room at the front end of the house is shown—a long, low-ceilinged, sparely furnished chamber, with white walls gray in the fading daylight that enters from three small windows at the left. To the left of center several long tables placed lengthwise to the width of the room, around which many chairs for guests have been placed. In the rear wall, right, a door leading into the rest of the house. On the left, a doorway opening on a road where a crowd of men has gathered. On the right, another doorway leading to the yard where there is a crowd of women.*

Inside the house, on the men's side, seven male Guests are grouped by the door, watching LAZARUS *with frightened awe, talking hesitantly in low whispers. The Chorus of Old Men, seven in number, is drawn up in a crescent, in the far corner, right, facing* LAZARUS.

[*All of these people are masked in accordance with the following scheme: There are seven periods of life shown: Boyhood (or Girlhood), Youth, Young Manhood (or Womanhood), Manhood (or Womanhood), Middle Age, Maturity and Old Age; and each of these periods is represented by seven different masks of general types of character as follows: The Simple, Ignorant; the Happy, Eager; the Self-Tortured, Introspective; the Proud, Self-Reliant; the Servile, Hypocritical; the Revengeful, Cruel; the Sorrowful, Resigned. Thus in each crowd (this includes among the men the Seven Guests who are composed of one male of each period-type as period one—type one, period two—type two, and so on up to period seven—type seven) there are forty-nine different combinations of period and type. Each type has a distinct predominant color for its costumes which varies in kind according to its period. The masks of the Chorus of Old Men are double the size of the others. They are all seven in the Sorrowful, Resigned type of Old Age.*]

On a raised platform at the middle of the one table placed lengthwise at center sits LAZARUS, *his head haloed and his body illumined by a soft radiance as of tiny phosphorescent flames.*

LAZARUS, *freed now from the fear of death, wears no mask.*

In appearance LAZARUS *is tall and powerful, about fifty years of age, with a mass of gray-black hair and a heavy beard. His face recalls that of a statue of a divinity of Ancient Greece in its general structure and particularly in its quality of detached serenity. It is dark-complected, ruddy and brown, the color of rich earth upturned by the plow, calm but furrowed deep with the marks of former suffering endured with a grim fortitude that had never softened into resignation. His forehead is broad and noble, his eyes black and deep-set. Just now he is staring straight before him as if his vision were still fixed beyond life.*

Kneeling beside him with bowed heads are his wife, MIRIAM, *his sisters,* MARTHA *and* MARY, *and his* FATHER *and* MOTHER.

MIRIAM *is a slender, delicate woman of thirty-five, dressed in deep black, who holds one of his hands in both of hers, and keeps her lips pressed to it. The upper part of her face is covered by a mask which conceals her forehead, eyes and nose, but leaves her mouth revealed. The mask is the pure pallor of marble, the expression that of a statue of Woman, of her eternal acceptance of the compulsion of motherhood, the inevitable cycle of love into pain into joy and new love into separation and pain again and the loneliness of age. The eyes of the mask are almost closed. Their gaze turns within, oblivious to the life outside, as they dream down on the child forever in memory at her breast. The mouth of* MIRIAM *is sensitive and sad, tender with an eager, understanding smile of self-forgetful love, the lips still fresh and young. Her skin, in contrast to the mask, is sun-burned and earth-colored like that of* LAZARUS. MARTHA, MARY *and the two parents all wear full masks which broadly reproduce their own characters.* MARTHA *is a buxom middle-aged housewife, plain and pleasant.* MARY *is young and pretty, nervous and ' high-strung. The* FATHER *is a small, thin, feeble old man of over eighty, meek and pious. The* MOTHER *is tall and stout, over sixty-five, a gentle, simple woman.*

All the masks of these Jews of the first two scenes of the play are pronouncedly Semitic.

A background of twilight sky. A dissolving touch of sunset still lingers on the horizon.

It is some time after the miracle and Jesus has gone away.

Chorus of Old Men. (In a quavering rising and falling chant—their arms outstretched toward LAZARUS)

Jesus wept!
Behold how he loved him!
He that liveth,
He that believeth,
Shall never die!
Crowd. (On either side of house, echo the chant.)
He that believeth
Shall never die!
Lazarus, come forth!
First Guest. (A Simple Boy—in a frightened whisper after a pause of dead silence.) That strange light seems to come from within him! *(With awe.)* Think of it! For four days he lay in the tomb! *(Turns away with a shudder.)*
Second Guest. (A Happy Youth—with reassuring conviction.) It is a holy light. It came from Jesus.
Fifth Guest. (An Envious, Middle-Aged Man.) Maybe if the truth were known, our friend there never really died at all!
Fourth Guest. (A Defiant Man, indignantly.) Do you doubt the miracle? I tell you I was here in this house when Lazarus died!
Seventh Guest. (An Aged, Sorrowful Man.) And I used to visit him every day. He knew himself his hour was near.
Fourth Guest. He wished for death! He said to me one day: "I have known my fill of life and the sorrow of living. Soon I shall know peace." And he smiled. It was the first time I had seen him smile in years.
Third Guest. (A Self-Tortured Man—gloomily.) Yes, of late years his life had been one long misfortune. One after another his children died—
Sixth Guest. (A Mature Man with a cruel face—with a harsh laugh.) They were all girls. Lazarus had no luck.
Seventh Guest. The last was a boy, the one that died at birth. You are forgetting him.
Third Guest. Lazarus could never forget. Not only did his son die but Miriam could never bear him more children.
Fifth Guest. (Practically.) But he could not blame bad luck for everything. Take the loss of his father's wealth since he took over the management. That was his own doing. He was a bad farmer, a poor breeder of sheep, and a bargainer so easy to cheat it hurt one's conscience to trade with him!
Sixth Guest. (With a sneer—maliciously.) You should know best about that! *(A suppressed laugh from those around him.)*
First Guest. (Who has been gazing at LAZARUS—*softly.)* Ssssh! Look at his face! *(They all stare. A pause.)*
Second Guest. (With wondering awe.) Do

you remember him, neighbors, before he died? He used to be pale even when he worked in the fields. Now he seems as brown as one who has labored in the earth all day in a vineyard beneath the hot sun! (*A pause.*)

Fourth Guest. The whole look of his face has changed. He is like a stranger from a far land. There is no longer any sorrow in his eyes. They must have forgotten sorrow in the grave.

Fifth Guest. (*Grumblingly.*) I thought we were invited here to eat—and all we do is stand and gape at him!

Fourth Guest. (*Sternly.*) Be silent! We are waiting for him to speak.

Third Guest. (*Impressively.*) He did speak once. And he laughed!

All the Guests. (*Amazed and incredulous.*) Laughed?

Third Guest. (*Importantly.*) Laughed! I heard him! It was a moment after the miracle—

Miriam. (*Her voice, rich with sorrow, exultant now.*) Jesus cried, "Lazarus, come forth!" (*She kisses his hand. He makes a slight movement, a stirring in his vision. The* GUESTS *stare. A frightened pause.*)

Fifth Guest. (*Nudging the* SECOND—*uneasily.*) Go on with your story!

Third Guest. Just as he appeared in the opening of the tomb, wrapped in his shroud—

Second Guest. (*Excitedly—interrupting.*) My heart stopped! I fell on my face! And all the women screamed! (*Sceptically.*) You must have sharp ears to have heard him laugh in that uproar!

Third Guest. I helped to pry away the stone so I was right beside him. I found myself kneeling, but between my fingers I watched Jesus and Lazarus. Jesus looked into his face for what seemed a long time and suddenly Lazarus said "Yes" as if he were answering a question in Jesus' eyes.

All the Guests. (*Mystified.*) Yes? What could he mean by yes?

Third Guest. Then Jesus smiled sadly but with tenderness, as one who from a distance of years of sorrow remembers happiness. And then Lazarus knelt and kissed Jesus' feet and both of them smiled and Jesus blessed him and called him "My Brother" and went away; and Lazarus, looking after Him, began to laugh softly like a man in love with God! Such a laugh I never heard! It made my ears drunk! It was like wine! And though I was half-dead with fright I found myself laughing, too!

Miriam. (*With a beseeching summons.*) Lazarus, come forth!

Chorus. (*Chanting.*) Lazarus! Come forth!

Crowd. (*On either side of the house—echoing the chant.*) Come forth! Come forth!

Lazarus. (*Suddenly in a deep voice—with a wonderful exultant acceptance in it.*) Yes! (*The* GUESTS *in the room, the* CROWDS *outside all cry out in fear and joy and fall on their knees.*)

Chorus. (*Chanting exultantly.*)
The stone is taken away!
The spirit is loosed!
The soul let go!

Lazarus. (*Rising and looking around him at everyone and everything—with an all-embracing love—gently.*) Yes! (*His family and the* GUESTS *in the room now throng about* LAZARUS *to embrace him. The* CROWDS *of men and women on each side push into the room to stare at him. He is in the arms of his* MOTHER *and* MIRIAM *while his* SISTERS *and* FATHER *kiss and press his hands. The five are half hysterical with relief and joy, sobbing and laughing.*)

Father. My son is reborn to me!

Chorus. Hosannah!

All. (*With a great shout.*) Hosannah!

Father. Let us rejoice! Eat and drink! Draw up your chairs, friends! Music! Bring wine! (*Music begins in the room off right, rear —a festive dance tune. The company sit down in their places, the* FATHER *and* MOTHER *at* LAZARUS' *right and left,* MIRIAM *next to the* MOTHER, MARTHA *and* MARY *beside the* FATHER. *But* LAZARUS *remains standing. And the* CHORUS OF OLD MEN *remain in their formation at the rear. Wine is poured and all raise their goblets toward* LAZARUS—*then suddenly they stop, the music dies out, and an awed and frightened stillness prevails, for* LAZARUS *is a strange, majestic figure whose understanding smile seems terrible and enigmatic to them.*)

Father. (*Pathetically uneasy.*) You frighten us, my son. You are strange—standing there— (*In the midst of a silence more awkward than before he rises to his feet, goblet in hand—forcing his voice, falteringly.*) A toast, neighbors!

Chorus. (*In a forced echo.*) A toast!

All. (*Echoing them.*) A toast!

Father. To my son, Lazarus, whom a blessed miracle has brought back from death!

Lazarus. (*Suddenly laughing softly out of his vision, as if to himself, and speaking with a strange unearthly calm in a voice that is like a loving whisper of hope and confidence.*) No! There is no death! (*A moment's pause. The people remain with goblets uplifted, staring at him. Then all repeat after him questioningly and frightenedly.*)

All. There—is—no—death?

Sixth Guest. (*Suddenly blurts out the question which is in the minds of all.*) What did you find beyond there, Lazarus? (*A pause of silence.*)

Lazarus. (*Smiles gently and speaks as if to a group of inquisitive children.*) O Curious Greedy Ones, is not one world in which you know not how to live enough for you?

Sixth Guest. (*Emboldened.*) Why did you say yes, Lazarus?

Fourth Guest. Why did you laugh?

All the Guests. (*With insistent curiosity but in low awed tones.*) What is beyond there, Lazarus?

Chorus. (*In a low murmur.*) What is beyond there? What is beyond?

Crowd. (*Carrying the question falteringly back into silence.*) What is beyond?

Lazarus. (*Suddenly again—now in a voice of loving exaltation.*) There is only life! I heard the heart of Jesus laughing in my heart; "There is Eternal Life in No," it said, "and there is the same Eternal Life in Yes! Death is the fear between!" And my heart reborn to love of life cried "Yes!" and I laughed in the laughter of God! (*He begins to laugh, softly at first—a laugh so full of a complete acceptance of life, a profound assertion of joy in living, so devoid of all self-consciousness or fear, that it is like a great bird song triumphant in depths of sky, proud and powerful, infectious with love, casting on the listener an enthralling spell. The crowd in the room are caught by it. Glancing sideways at one another, smiling foolishly and self-consciously, at first they hesitate, plainly holding themselves in for fear of what the next one will think.*)

Chorus. (*In a chanting murmur.*)

Lazarus laughs!
Our hearts grow happy!
Laughter like music!
The wind laughs!
The sea laughs!
Spring laughs from the earth!
Summer laughs in the air!
Lazarus laughs!

Lazarus. (*On a final note of compelling exultation.*) Laugh! Laugh with me! Death is dead! Fear is no more! There is only life! There is only laughter!

Chorus. (*Chanting exultingly now.*)

Laugh! Laugh!
Laugh with Lazarus!
Fear is no more!
There is no death!

(*They laugh in a rhythmic cadence dominated by the laughter of* LAZARUS.)

Crowd. (*Who, gradually, joining in by groups or one by one—including* LAZARUS' *family with the exception of* MIRIAM, *who does not laugh but watches and listens to his laughter with a tender smile of being happy in his happiness—have now all begun to laugh in rhythm with the* CHORUS—*in a great, full-throated pæan as the laughter of* LAZARUS *rises higher and higher.*)

Laugh! Laugh!
Fear is no more!
There is no death!

Chorus.

Laugh! Laugh!
There is only life!
There is only laughter!
Fear is no more!
Death is dead!

Crowd. (*In a rhythmic echo.*)

Laugh! Laugh!
Death is dead!
There is only laughter!

(*The room rocks, the air outside throbs with the rhythmic beat of their liberated laughter—still a bit uncertain of its freedom, harsh, discordant, frenzied, desperate and drunken, but dominated and inspired by the high, free, aspiring, exulting laughter of* LAZARUS.)

CURTAIN

SCENE 2

SCENE: *Some months later. Exterior of* LAZARUS' *home in Bethany, now known as the House of Laughter. It is a clear bright night, the sky sparkling with stars. At the extreme front is a road. Between this and the house is a small raised terrace. The house is low, of one story only, its walls white. Four windows are visible with a closed door in the middle of the wall. Steps lead up to this door, and to the left of door a flight of stairs goes up to the balustraded roof. The windows shine brilliantly with the flickering light of many candles which gives them a throbbing star-like effect. From within comes the sound of flutes and dance music. The dancers can be seen whirling swiftly by the windows. There is continually an overtone of singing laughter emphasizing the pulsing rhythm of the dance.*

On the road in the foreground, at left and right, two separate groups of Jews are gathered. They are not divided according to sex as in the previous scene. Each is composed about equally of men and women, forty-nine in each, masked and costumed as before. It is religious belief that now divides them. The adherents of Jesus, the Nazarenes, among whom may be noted MARTHA and MARY, *are on the left; the Orthodox, among whom are* LAZARUS' FATHER *and* MOTHER *and a* PRIEST, *are at right. Between the two hostile groups is the same* CHORUS OF OLD MEN, *in a formation like a spearhead, whose point is placed at the foot of the steps leading to the terrace. All these people are staring fascinatedly at the house, listening entranced, their feet moving, their bodies swaying to the music's beat, stiffly, constrainedly, compelled against their wills. Then the music suddenly stops and the chant of youthful voices is heard:*

Followers of Lazarus. (*From within the house.*)

Laugh! Laugh!
There is only life!
There is only laughter!

Chorus of old men. (*As if they were subjects moved by hypnotic suggestion—miserably and discordantly.*)

Ha-ha-ha-ha!
There is only laughter!
Ha-ha—

Crowd. (*In the same manner.*) Ha-ha—

Mary. Ha— (*Then frantically—half-weeping with indignant rage—to the Nazarenes.*) Stop! Oh, how can we laugh! We are betraying Jesus! My brother Lazarus has become a devil!

The Orthodox Priest. (*His mask is that of a religious fanatic. He is sixty or so.*) Ha—ha— (*Tearing his beard and stamping with rage.*) Stop it, you fools! It is a foul sin in the sight of Jehovah! Why do you come here every night to listen and watch their abominations? The Lord God will punish you!

Mary. (*Echoing him—to her people.*) Jesus will never forgive you!

The Priest. (*Angrily.*) Jesus? (*He turns to look at the Nazarenes disdainfully and spits on the ground insultingly.*) (*The members of the two groups begin to glare at each other. The* CHORUS *falls back, three on each side, leaving one neutral figure before the steps. The* PRIEST *goes on tauntingly.*) Did you hear her, friends? These renegade Nazarenes will soon deny they are Jews at all! They will begin to worship in filthy idolatry the sun and stars and man's body—as LAZARUS in there (*points to the house*), the disciple of their Jesus, has so well set them the example! (*This is followed by an outburst of insulting shouts of accusation and denial from both sides.*)

A Nazarene. (*The* FOURTH GUEST *of Scene One.*) You lie! Lazarus is no disciple! He is a traitor to Jesus! We scorn him!

Priest. (*Sneeringly.*) But your pretended Messiah did not scorn him. According to your stupid lies, he raised him from the dead! And answer me, has your Jesus ever denied Lazarus, or denounced his laughter? No! No doubt he is laughing, too, at all you credulous fools—for if Lazarus is not his disciple, in the matter of the false miracle he was his accomplice! (*This provokes a furious protest from the Nazarenes and insulting hoots and jeers from the Orthodox, penetrated by a piercing scream from* LAZARUS' MOTHER, *who, crushed in the crowd, sinks fainting to the ground. The* FATHER *bends over her. The group of the Orthodox falls back from them. With frightened cries* MARTHA *and* MARY *run from the group of Nazarenes and kneel beside her.*)

Father. (*Pitifully.*) Rachel! Darling! Speak to me!

Martha. (*Practically.*) She has only fainted.

Mary. She is opening her eyes! Mother, dear!

Mother. (*Weakly.*) Did I fall? (*Recognizing* MARTHA *and* MARY.) Martha—and Mary—my dear ones! (*They embrace her, weeping.*) I have not kissed you since you left home to follow that Jesus— Oh, if we were only at home again—and if, also, my poor boy, Lazarus— (*She sobs.*)

Father. (*Gruffly.*) You must not speak of him!

Martha. Do not worry your head about Lazarus. He is not worth it!

Mary. (*With surprising vindictiveness.*) He is accursed! He has betrayed our Lord!

Priest. (*To those around him—mockingly.*) Do you hear? They already call the Nazarene "Lord!" A Lord who is in the common prison at Jerusalem, I heard today! A fine Lord whom our High Priests have had arrested like a thief!

Mary. (*With fanatic fervor.*) He is a king! Whenever He chooses He will gather a great army and He will seize His kingdom and all who deny Him shall be crucified!

Priest. (*Tauntingly.*) Now their jail-bird is a king, no less! Soon they will make him a god, as the Romans do their Cæsars!

Mary. (*Her eyes flashing.*) He is the Messiah!

Priest. (*Furiously.*) The Messiah! May Jehovah smite you in your lies! Step back among your kind! You defile us! (*As she stands defiantly he appeals to the* FATHER.) Have you no authority? She called him the Messiah—that common beggar, that tramp! Curse her!

Father. (*Confused, pitifully harried, collect-*

ing his forces.) Wait! Go back, Mary! You chose to follow that impostor—

Mary. (*Defiantly.*) The Messiah!

Martha. (*Trying to calm her.*) Ssssh! Remember he is our father!

Mary. (*Fanatically.*) I deny him! I deny all who deny Jesus!

Mother. (*Tearfully.*) And me, darling?

Mary. You must come to us, Mother! You must believe in Jesus and leave all to follow Him!

Father. (*Enraged.*) So! You want to steal your mother away, to leave me lonely in my old age! You are an unnatural daughter! I disown you! Go, before I curse—

Mother. (*Beseechingly.*) Father!

Martha. (*Pulling* MARY *away.*) Mary! Jesus teaches to be kind.

Mary. (*Hysterically.*) He teaches to give up all and follow Him! I want to give Him everything! I want my father to curse me!

Father. (*Frenziedly.*) Then I do curse you! No—not you—but the devil in you! And the devil in Martha! And the great mocking devil that dwells in Lazarus and laughs from his mouth! I curse these devils and that Prince of Devils, that false prophet, Jesus! It is he who has brought division to my home and many homes that were happy before. I curse him! I curse the day he called my good son, Lazarus, from the grave to walk again with a devil inside him! It was not my son who came back but a devil! My son is dead! And you, my daughters, are dead! I am the father only of devils! (*His voice has risen to a wailing lament.*) My children are dead!

Lazarus. (*His voice rings from within the house in exultant denial.*) Death is dead! There is only laughter! (*He laughs.*) (*The voices of all his* FOLLOWERS *echo his laughter. They pour in a laughing rout from the doorway onto the terrace. At the same moment the* CHORUS OF FOLLOWERS *appears on the roof and forms along the balustrade, facing front.*)

(*These* FOLLOWERS OF LAZARUS, *forty-nine in number, composed about equally of both sexes, wear a mask that, while recognizably Jewish, is a* LAZARUS *mask, resembling him in its expression of fearless faith in life, the mouth shaped by laughter. The* CHORUS OF FOLLOWERS, *seven in number, all men, have identical masks of double size, as before. The Period of all these masks is anywhere between Youth and Manhood (or Womanhood).*)

(*The music continues to come from within. Laughing, the* FOLLOWERS *dance to it in weaving patterns on the terrace. They are dressed in* bright-colored diaphanous robes. *Their chorused laughter, now high and clear, now dying to a humming murmur, stresses the rhythmic flow of the dance.*)

Chorus of Followers.

Laugh! Laugh!
There is no death!
There is only laughter!

Followers.

There is only laughter!
Death is dead!
Laugh! Laugh!

Crowd. (*The two groups of Nazarenes and Orthodox, on the appearance of the* FOLLOWERS, *immediately forget their differences and form into one mob, led by their Chorus of Old Men, whose jeering howls they echo as one voice.*) Yaah! Yaah! Yaah! (*But they cannot keep it up. The music and laughter rise above their hooting. They fall into silence. Then they again begin to feel impelled by the rhythm and laughter, their feet move, their bodies sway. Their lips quiver, their mouths open as if to laugh. Their Chorus of Old Men are the first to be affected. It is as if this reaction were transmitted through the* CHORUS *to the* CROWD.)

Priest. (*His mouth twitching—fighting against the compulsion in him—stammers.*) Brothers—listen—we must unite—in one cause —to—stamp out—this abomination! (*It is as if he can no longer control his speech. He presses his hand over his mouth convulsively.*)

An Aged Orthodox Jew. (*The* SEVENTH GUEST *of Scene One—starts to harangue the crowd. He fights the spell but cannot control his jerking body nor his ghastly, spasmodic laughter.*) Neighbors! Our young people are corrupted! They are leaving our farms—to dance and sing! To laugh! Ha—! Laugh at everything! Ha-ha—! (*He struggles desperately to control himself.*)

Chorus of Old Men. (*A barking laugh forced from them.*) Ha-ha—!

Crowd. (*Echoing this.*) Ha-ha—!

The Aged Jew. They have no respect for life! When I said in kindness, "You must go back to work," they laughed at me! Ha—! "We desire joy. We go to Lazarus," they said —and left my fields! I begged them to stay —with tears in my eyes! I even offered them more money! They laughed! "What is money? Can the heart eat gold?" They laughed at money! Ha-ha—! (*He chokes with exasperated rage.*)

Chorus of Old Men. (*Echoing him.*) Ha-ha—!

Crowd. (*Echoing the* CHORUS.) Ha-ha—!

Aged Jew. (*Shaking his fist at* LAZARUS' FOLLOWERS.) That loafer taught them that! They come to him and work for nothing! For nothing! And they are glad, these undutiful ones! While they sow, they dance! They sing to the earth when they are plowing! They tend his flocks and laugh toward the sun! Ha-ha-ha—! (*He struggles again.*)

Chorus of Old Men. (*As before.*) Ha-ha-ha—

Crowd. (*As before.*) Ha-ha-ha—

Aged Jew. How can we compete with labor for laughter! We will have no harvest. There will be no food! Our children will starve! Our race will perish! And he will laugh! Ha-ha-ha-ha! (*He howls with furious, uncontained laughter.*)

Chorus of Old Men. (*Echoing his tone.*) Our children will starve! Our race will perish! Lazarus laughs! Ha-ha-ha-ha! Ha-ha-ha-ha!

Crowd. (*As before.*) Ha-ha-ha-ha! Ha-ha-ha-ha! (*Their former distinctions of Nazarenes and Orthodox are now entirely forgotten. The members of* LAZARUS' *family are grouped in the center as if nothing had ever happened to separate them. The* CHORUS OF OLD MEN *is again joined in its spearhead formation at the stairs. Apparent first in this* CHORUS, *a queer excitement begins to pervade this mob. They begin to weave in and out, clasping each other's hands now and then, and moving mechanically in jerky steps to the music in a grotesque sort of marionettes' country dance. At first this is slow but it momentarily becomes more hectic and peculiar. They raise clenched fists or hands distended into threatening talons. Their voices sound thick and harsh and animal-like with anger as they mutter and growl, each one aloud to himself or herself.*)

Chorus of Old Men. (*Threateningly, gradually rising to hatred.*)

Hear them laugh!
See them dance!
Shameless! Wanton!
Dirty! Evil!
Infamous! Bestial!
Madness! Blood!
Adultery! Murder!
We burn!
We kill!
We crucify!
Death! Death!
Beware, Lazarus!

(*This last in a wild frenzy.*)

Crowd. (*Frenziedly.*)
Beware, Lazarus!
We burn! We kill!
We crucify!
Death! Death!

(*They crowd toward the gateway, their arms stretched out as if demanding* LAZARUS *for a sacrificial victim. Meanwhile they never cease to hop up and down, to mill around, to twist their bodies toward and away from each other in bestial parody of the dance of the* FOLLOWERS.)

(*The tall figure of* LAZARUS, *dressed in a white robe, suddenly appears on the roof of the house. He stands at the balustrade in the middle of the* CHORUS. *Beside him, a little behind,* MIRIAM *appears dressed in black, her face upturned, her lips praying. She appears to have grown older, to be forty now.* LAZARUS' *body is softly illumined by its inner light. The change in him is marked. He seems ten years younger, at the prime of forty. His body has become less angular and stiff. His movements are graceful and pliant. The change is even more noticeable in his face, which has filled out, become purer in outline, more distinctly Grecian. His complexion is the red-brown of rich earth, the gray in his black, curly beard has almost disappeared.*)

(*He makes a sign and the music ceases. His* FOLLOWERS *remain fixed in their dancing attitudes like figures in a frieze. Each member of the mob remains frozen in a distorted posture. He stares down at the mob pityingly, his face calm.*)

Lazarus. (*Speaks amid a profound silence. His voice releases his own dancers and the mob from their fixed attitudes. The music begins to play again within the house, very soft and barely audible, swelling up and down like the sound of an organ from a distant church.*) You laugh, but your laughter is guilty! It laughs a hyena laughter, spotted, howling its hungry fear of life! That day I returned did I not tell you your fear was no more, that there is no death? You believed then—for a moment! You laughed—discordantly, hoarsely, but with a groping toward joy. What! Have you so soon forgotten, that now your laughter curses life again as of old? (*He pauses—then sadly.*) That is your tragedy! You forget! You forget the God in you! You wish to forget! Remembrance would imply the high duty to live as a son of God—generously!—with love!—with pride!—with laughter! This is too glorious a victory for you, too terrible a loneliness! Easier to forget, to become only a man, the son of a woman, to hide from life against her breast, to whimper your fear to her resigned heart and be comforted by her resignation! To live by denying life! (*Then exhortingly.*) Why are your eyes always either fixed on the ground in weariness of thought, or watching one another with suspicion? Throw your gaze upward! To Eternal Life! To the fearless and deathless! The everlasting! To the stars! (*He stretches out his arms to the sky—then suddenly points.*) See! A new star has appeared! It is the one that shone over Bethlehem! (*His voice becomes a little bitter and mocking.*) The Master of Peace and Love has departed this earth. Let all stars be for you henceforth symbols of Saviors—Sons of God who appeared on worlds like ours to tell the saving truth to ears like yours, inexorably deaf! (*Then exaltedly.*) But the greatness of Saviors is that they may not save! The greatness of Man is that no god can save him—until he becomes a god! (*He stares up at the stars, rapt in contemplation, oblivious to all around him now.*)

(*Rapidly approaching from the left a man's voice jarring in high-pitched cruel laughter is heard. They all listen, huddled together like sheep.*)

Messenger. (*The* THIRD GUEST *of Scene One rushes in breathlessly, shouting.*) The Nazarene has been crucified!

Priest. (*With fierce triumph.*) Jehovah is avenged! Hosannah!

Orthodox. Hosannah! The false prophet is dead! The pretended Messiah is dead! (*They jump and dance, embracing one another. The* NAZARENES *stand paralyzed and stunned. The two groups mechanically separate to right and left again, the* CHORUS OF OLD MEN *dividing itself as before.*)

Mary. (*In a frenzy of grief.*) Do not believe him! Jesus could not die! (*But at this moment a Nazarene youth, exhausted by grief and tears, staggers in from the left.*)

Messenger. (SECOND GUEST *of Scene One.*) Jesus is dead! Our Lord is murdered! (*He sinks on his knees sobbing. All the* NAZARENES *do likewise, wailing, rending their garments, tearing their hair, some even beating their heads on the ground in the agony of their despair.*)

Mary. (*Insane with rage now.*) They have murdered Him! (*To her followers—savagely.*) An eye for an eye! Avenge the Master! (*Their frenzy of grief turned into rage, the* NAZARENES *leap to their feet threateningly. Concealed swords and knives are brought out by both sides.*)

Miriam. (*Leaning over the balustrade—in a voice of entreaty.*) Mary! Brothers! (*But none heed her or seem to see her.* LAZARUS *and his*

FOLLOWERS *remain oblivious to men, arms upstretched toward the stars, their heads thrown back.*)

Mary. (*Wildly.*) Vengeance! Death to His murderers!

Priest. (*Fiercely to his followers.*) Death to the Nazarenes! (*With cries of rage the two groups rush on one another. There is a confused tumult of yells, groans, curses, the shrieks of women, the sounds of blows as they meet in a pushing, whirling, struggling mass in which individual figures are indistinguishable. Knives and swords flash above the heads of the mass, hands in every tense attitude of striking, clutching, tearing are seen upraised. As the fight is at its height a* ROMAN CENTURION *and a squad of eight* SOLDIERS *come tramping up at the double-quick. They all are masked. These Roman masks now and henceforth in the play are carried out according to the same formula of Seven Periods, Seven Types, as those of the Jews seen previously, except that the basis of each face is Roman—heavy, domineering, self-complacent, the face of a confident dominant race. The* CENTURION *differs from his soldiers only in being more individualized. He is middle-aged, his soldiers belong to the Period of Manhood. All are of the Simple, Ignorant Type.*)

Centurion. (*Shouts commandingly.*) Disperse! (*But no one hears him—with angry disgust to his* SOLDIERS.) Charge! Cut them down! (*The* SOLDIERS *form a wedge and charge with a shout. They soon find it necessary to use their swords, and strike down everyone in their way.*)

Miriam. Mercy, Romans! (*As they pay no attention to her, in desperation she embraces* LAZARUS *beseechingly, forcing his attention back to earth.*) Lazarus! Mercy!

Lazarus. (*Looks down upon the struggling mass and cries in a ringing voice.*) Hold! (*Each person stands transfixed, frozen in the last movement, even the Roman soldiers and the* CENTURION *himself. Ten dead and mortally wounded lie on the ground, trampled by the feet of friend and foe alike.* LAZARUS *looks at the* CROWD. *To each he seems to look at him or her alone. His eyes are accusing and stern. As one head, the heads of all are averted. Even the* CENTURION *stares at the ground humbly, in spite of himself. Finally* LAZARUS *speaks in a voice of infinite disdain.*) Sometimes it is hard to laugh—even at men! (*He turns his eyes from them, staring straight before him. This seems to release them from their fixed positions. The* NAZARENES *and the* ORTHODOX *separate and slink guiltily apart. The* CHORUS OF OLD MEN *forms again, the apex at the center of the steps as before. A low wail of lamentation arises from them. The two crowds of Nazarenes and Orthodox echo this.*)

Chorus of Old Men. (*In a wailing chant.*)

Woe unto Israel!
Woe unto thee, Jerusalem!
O divided house,
Thou shalt crumble to dust,
And swine shall root
Where thy Temple stood!
Woe unto us!

Crowd. (*In a great echoing cry.*) Woe unto us!

Centurion. (*Gruffly to hide his embarrassment at being awed by* LAZARUS.) Here, you! Drag your carcasses away! (*From each side men and women come forward to identify and mourn their dead. The wail of lamentation rises and falls. The* CENTURION *looks up at* LAZARUS —*harshly.*) You, there! Are you he whom they call the Laugher?

Lazarus. (*Without looking at him*—*his voice seeming to come from some dream within him.*) I am Lazarus.

Centurion. Who was brought back from death by enchantment?

Lazarus. (*Looking down at him now*—*with a smile, simply.*) No. There is no death!

Chorus of Followers. (*Chanting joyously.*) There is no death!

Followers. (*Echoing.*) There is no death!

An Orthodox Man. (*Bending beside the body of* LAZARUS' FATHER.) Here is your father, Lazarus. He is dead.

An Orthodox Woman. This is your mother, Lazarus. She is dead.

A Nazarene. Here is your sister, Martha, Lazarus. She is dead.

A Nazarene Woman. And this is Mary, Lazarus. She is dead.

Miriam. (*Suddenly*—*with deep grief.*) And Jesus who was the Son of Man, who loved you and gave you life again has died, Lazarus—has died!

Lazarus. (*In a great triumphant voice.*) Yes! Yes!! Yes!!! Men die! Even a Son of Man must die to show men that Man may live! But there is no death!

Centurion. (*At first in a tone of great awe—to his* SOLDIERS.) Is he a god? (*Then gruffly, ashamed of his question.*) Come down, Jew! I have orders to bring you to Rome to Cæsar!

Lazarus. (*As if he were answering not the* CENTURION *but the command of his fate from the sky.*) Yes! (*He walks down the narrow stairs and,* MIRIAM *following him, comes down the path to the road. He goes and kneels for a moment each beside the bodies of his* FATHER, MOTHER,

and SISTERS *and kisses each in turn on the forehead. For a moment the struggle with his grief can be seen in his face. Then he looks up to the stars and, as if answering a question, again says simply and acceptingly.*) Yes! (*Then exultantly.*) Yes!! (*And begins to laugh from the depths of his exalted spirit. The laughter of his* CHORUS *and then of his* FOLLOWERS *echoes his. The music and dancing begin again.*)

(*The* CENTURION *grins sheepishly. The* SOLDIERS *chuckle. The* CENTURION *laughs awkwardly. The* SOLDIERS *laugh. The music from the house and the laughter of the* FOLLOWERS *grow louder. The infection spreads to the* CHORUS OF OLD MEN *whose swaying grief falls into the rhythm of the laughter and music as does that of the mourners.*)

Lazarus' Followers. (*Led by their* CHORUS.) Laugh! Laugh!

Chorus of Old Men. (*Torn by the conflict—torturedly.*)

Ha-ha-ha—
Woe to us, woe!

Crowd. (*Beside the bodies.*)

Woe to us, woe!
Ha-ha—!

Centurion. (*Laughingly.*) You are brave, you Laugher! Remember Tiberius never laughs! And boast not to Cæsar there is no death, or he will invent a new one for you!

Lazarus. (*With a smile.*) But all death is men's invention! So laugh! (*He laughs and the* CENTURION *and* SOLDIERS *laugh with him, half dancing clumsily now to the beat of the music.*)

Chorus of Lazarus' Followers.

Laugh! Laugh!
Fear is no more!
There is no death!
There is only life!
There is only laughter!

Followers. (*Dancing.*)

Laugh! Laugh!
Fear is no more!
Death is dead!

Chorus of Old Men. (*Forgetting their grief—their eyes on* LAZARUS *now, their arms outstretched to him as are those of the crowd grouped around the bodies but forgetting them.*)

Death is no more!
Death is dead!
Laugh!

Crowd.

Laugh! Laugh!
Death is no more!

Centurion. (*Laughing, to his laughing Sol-diers.*) Forward! (*They tramp, dancing off.*) (*Lazarus and Miriam start to follow.*)

Miriam. (*Suddenly pointing to his Follow-ers who are dancing and laughing obliviously —pityingly.*) But your faithful ones who love you, Lazarus?

Lazarus. (*Simply, with a trace of a sad sternness.*) This is their test. Their love must remember—or it must forget. Come! (*With a last gesture back like a blessing on all he is leaving, he goes. The laughter of the Soldiers recedes. That of the Chorus of Old Men and of the Crowd falters and breaks into lamenting grief again, guilt-stricken because of its laughter.*)

Chorus of Old Men.

Laugh! Laugh!
Death is dead!
Laugh!—But woe!
There lie our dead!
Oh shame and guilt!
We forget our dead!

Crowd. (*With fierce remorseful grief.*)

Woe to us, woe!
There lie our dead!

Chorus of Lazarus' Followers. (*Their voices and the music growing more and more hesitating and faint.*)

Laugh! Laugh!
There is only life!
There is only—
Laugh—

(*Their dance is faltering and slow now.*)

Fear is no—
Death is—
Laugh—

(*The music and dancing and voices cease. The lights in the windows, which have been growing dim, go out. There is a second of complete, death-like silence. The mourning folk in the foreground are frozen figures of grief. Then a sudden swelling chorus of forlorn bewilderment, a cry of lost children comes from the Chorus of Follow-ers and the Followers themselves. They huddle into groups on the roof and on the terrace. They stretch their arms out in every direction supplicatingly.*)

Chorus of Followers.

Oh, Lazarus, laugh!
Do not forsake us!

We forget!
Where is thy love fled?
Give back thy laughter,
Thy fearless laughter!
We forget!

Followers.

Give back thy laughter!
We forget!

Chorus of Followers. (*With dull, resigned terror now.*)

Death slinks out
Of his grave in the heart!
Ghosts of fear
Creep back in the brain!
We remember fear!
We remember death!

Followers.

Death in the heart!
Fear in the brain!
We remember fear!
We remember death!

Chorus of Followers. (*Wailing hopelessly now.*)

Forgotten is laughter!
We remember
Only death!
Fear is God!
Forgotten is laughter!
Life is death!

Followers.

Forgotten is laughter!
Life is death!

All. (*The Chorus of Old Men and the Crowd joining in.*)

Life is a fearing,
A long dying,
From birth to death!
God is a slayer!
Life is death!

CURTAIN

ACT II

SCENE I

Scene: *Some months later. A square in Athens about ten o'clock at night. In the rear, pure and beautiful in the light of a full moon, is the façade of a temple. An excited crowd of Greeks of both sexes is gathered in the square as if for some public festival. They are masked ac-cording to the scheme of Seven Periods in Seven Types of Character for each sex. Here, of course, the foundation of the mask is the Grecian type of face.*

On the left, the CHORUS OF GREEKS *is grouped, seven in number, facing front, in the spearhead formation. As before the* CHORUS *wears masks double the life size of the* CROWD *masks. They are all of the* Proud Self-Reliant *type, in the period of* Young Manhood.

These seven are clad in goat skins, their tanned bodies and masks daubed and stained with wine lees, in imitation of the old followers of Dionysus. Rumor has led them to hope and believe that LAZARUS *may be the reincarnation of this deity.*

The people in the crowd are holding themselves in restraint with difficulty, they stir and push about restlessly with an eager curiosity and impatience. All eyes are fixed off left. A buzz of voices hums in the air.

Acting as police, a number of Roman legionaries (masked like the soldiers of Scene Two) armed with staves, keep back the crowd from the line of the street that runs from left to right, front. They resent this duty, which has already kept them there a long time, and are surly and quick-tempered with the Greeks.

At front, pacing impatiently up and down, is a young Roman noble of twenty-one, clad richly, wearing beautifully wrought armor and helmet. This is GAIUS, *the heir of Tiberius Cæsar, nicknamed* CALIGULA *by the soldiers in whose encampments he was born and where he spent his childhood. His body is bony and angular, almost malformed, with wide, powerful shoulders and long arms and hands, and short, skinny, hairy legs like an ape's. He wears a half-mask of crimson, dark with a purplish tinge, that covers the upper part of his face to below the nose. This mask accentuates his bulging, prematurely wrinkled forehead, his hollow temples and his bulbous, sensual nose. His large troubled eyes, of a glazed greenish-blue, glare out with a shifty feverish suspicion at everyone. Below his mask his own skin is of an œnemic transparent pallor. Above it, his hair is the curly blond hair of a child of six or seven. His mouth also is childish, the red lips soft and feminine in outline. Their expression is spoiled, petulant and self-obsessed, weak but domineering. In combination with the rest of the face there is an appalling morbid significance to his mouth. One feels that its boyish cruelty, encouraged as a manly attribute in the coarse brutality of camps, has long ago become naïvely insensitive to any human suffering but its own.*

Walking with CALIGULA *is* CNEIUS CRASSUS, *a Roman general—a squat, muscular man of sixty, his mask that of a heavy battered face full of coarse humor.*

Chorus of Greeks. (*Intoning solemnly.*)
Soon the God comes!
Redeemer and Savior!
Dionysus, Son of Man and a God!

Greek Crowd. (*Echoing.*)
Soon the God comes
Redeemer and Savior!
Dionysus!

First Greek. They say an unearthly flame burns in this Lazarus!

Second Greek. The sacred fire! He must be the Fire-born, the son of Zeus!

Third Greek. Many who have seen him swear he is Dionysus, rearisen from Hades!

Fourth Greek. (*Importantly.*) I saw Lazarus at Antioch where the galley on which they were taking him to Rome had been thrice blown back by a storm. Fear of this warning omen is why they now march with him by land.

First Greek. Does he truly resemble a god?

Fourth Greek. (*Impressively.*) One look in his eyes while his laughter sings in your ears and you forget sorrow! You dance! You laugh! It is as if a heavy weight you had been carrying all your life without knowing it suddenly were lifted. You are like a cloud, you can fly, your mind reels with laughter, you are drunk with joy! (*Solemnly.*) Take my word for it, he is indeed a god. Everywhere the people have acclaimed him. He heals the sick, he raises the dead, by laughter.

Seventh Greek. But I have heard that when he has gone people cannot remember his laughter, that the dead are dead again and the sick die, and the sad grow more sorrowful.

Fifth Greek. Well, we shall soon see with our own eyes. But why should the God return in the body of a Jew?

Sixth Greek. What better disguise if he wishes to remain unknown? The fools of Romans will never suspect him!

Third Greek. (*Laughing.*) Never! They are beginning to claim he is a Roman!

Fifth Greek. So much the better! He will be in their confidence!

Fourth Greek. He will lead us against Rome! He will laugh our tyrants into the sea! Ha! (*He turns toward the Romans and laughs sneeringly. This is taken up by the* CROWD—*unpleasant, resentful laughter. They push forward aggressively and almost sweep the soldiers from their feet.*)

Crassus. (*Angrily.*) Drive them back!

Caligula. (*Suddenly with a distorted warped smile.*) Order them to use their swords

Cneius. Let the scum look at their dead and learn respect for us!

Soldiers. (*Shoving and whacking.*) Back! Step back! Back there! (*The crowd push back to their former line. There are muttered curses, groans, protests, which subside into the former hum of expectancy.*)

Caligula. (*With the same smile.*) The sword, my old hyena! Corpses are so educational!

Crassus. (*Surlily.*) I would like to, I promise you! When I see how they hate us—!

Caligula. (*Carelessly.*) Let them hate—so long as they fear us! We must keep death dangling (*he makes the gesture of doing so*) before their eyes! (*He gives a soft, cruel laugh.*) Will you not sacrifice in my honor? What are a few Greeks? (*Queerly.*) I like to watch men die.

Crassus. I dare not, Caligula. Cæsar has forbidden bloodshed.

Caligula. Tiberius is a miser. He wants to hoard all of death for his own pleasure! (*He laughs again.*)

Crassus. (*With rough familiarity.*) I wager no one will make that complaint against you when you are Cæsar! (*He chuckles.*)

Caligula. (*With the sudden grandiose posturing of a bad actor unintentionally burlesquing grandeur.*) When I, Gaius Caligula, am Cæsar, I— (*Then superstitiously looking up at the sky with cringing foreboding.*) But it brings bad luck to anticipate fate. (*He takes off his helmet and spits in it—then with a grim smile.*) The heirs of a Cæsar take sick so mysteriously! Even with you who used to ride me on your knee, I do not eat nor drink until you have tasted first.

Crassus. (*Nodding approvingly.*) You are sensible. I suppose I, too, have my price—if they were only clever enough to discover it. (*He laughs hoarsely.*)

Caligula. (*Steps back from him with an uneasy shudder.*) You are honest, at least—too honest, Cneius! (*Grimly.*) If my father Germanicus had had you for his counselor, he might have escaped their poison. (*Then gloomily.*) I must fear everyone. The world is my enemy.

Crassus. Kill it then! (*He laughs again.*)

Chorus. (*Stretching out their arms in the direction from which* LAZARUS *is expected—supplicatingly.*)

Son of the Lightning!
Deadly thy vengeance!
Swift thy deliverance!
Beholding thy Mother,
Greece, our Mother,

Her beauty in bondage,
Her pride in chains!
Hasten, Redeemer!

Crowd. (*As before—echoing the chant.*)
Hasten, Redeemer!
Son of the Lightning!
Deadly thy vengeance!
Swift thy deliverance!

Caligula. (*Disdainfully.*) What clods! Mob is the same everywhere, eager to worship any new charlatan! They have already convinced themselves this Lazarus is a reincarnation of Dionysus! A Jew become a god! By the breasts of Venus that *is* a miracle! (*He laughs.*)

Crassus. (*Seriously.*) But he must be expert in magic. He was buried four days and came out unharmed. Maybe he is not a Jew. Some say his father was really a legionary of our garrison in Judea. And he teaches people to laugh at death. That smacks of Roman blood!

Caligula. (*Ironically.*) Better still! He tells them there is no death at all. Hence the multitude of fools who have acclaimed him everywhere since he left his own country—and why Tiberius has begun to fear his influence.

Crassus. (*Sententiously.*) Whom Cæsar fears—disappears!

Caligula. Yes, the dupes who follow Lazarus will be killed. But Tiberius believes this Lazarus may know a cure for death or for renewing youth, and the old lecher hopes he can worm the secret out of him—before he kills him. (*He laughs ironically, then disgustedly.*) That is why I must escort this Jew to Rome —as a special honor! (*With fierce, haughty resentment.*) I, the heir of Cæsar! (*Savagely.*) Oh, if I were Cæsar—!

Crassus. (*With a coarse, meaning smirk.*) Patience. Tiberius is old.

Caligula. (*Suddenly becoming terribly uneasy at some thought.*) Cneius! What if this Lazarus has really discovered a cure for old age and should reveal it to Tiberius! (*His lips tremble, his eyes are terrified, he shrinks against* CRASSUS *for protection—with boyish pleading.*) Oh, Cneius, what could I do then?

Crassus. (*Matter-of-factly.*) Kill him before Cæsar can talk to him.

Caligula. (*Almost in tears.*) But if he knows a charm against death how could he be slain, old fool?

Crassus. (*Gruffly.*) Bah! (*Then with grim humor.*) Death in bed I suspect, but when men are killed I know they stay dead! (*Dis-*

gustedly.) A moment ago you were laughing at him! (*Scornfully.*) Do you fear him now?

Caligula. (*Rather shamefacedly pulls himself together—then broodingly.*) I fear everyone who lives. Even you. As you advised me. (*He turns away.*)

Crassus. (*Contemptuously.*) Well, maybe he can teach you to laugh at fear. You would welcome him then, eh, cry baby?

Caligula. (*With sudden passionate intensity but only half aloud as if to himself.*) I would love him, Cneius! As a father! As a god! (*He stands staring before him strangely. There is a new stir from the crowd who again push forward.*)

Crassus. (*Pointing off right.*) Look! I see a great crowd! Your Lazarus must be coming at last!

Chorus. (*Chanting in a deep, rhythmic monotone like the rising and falling cadences of waves on a beach.*)

He comes, the Redeemer and Savior!
Laughing along the mountains!
To give back our lost laughter
To raise from the dead our freedom
To free us from Rome!

Crowd. (*Echoing this chant.*)

Fire-born! Redeemer! Savior!
Raise from the dead our freedom!
Give back our lost laughter!
Free us from Rome!

(*They have been pushing forward, more and more fiercely and defiantly. The* ROMAN SOLDIERS *in spite of their efforts are pushed backward step by step.*)

Soldiers. (*Angrily.*) Back! Back!

(*The* SOLDIERS *work with a will, dealing out blows with their staves at everyone in reach. But now these blows seem only to infuriate the* CROWD *which steadily pushes them back into the street. At the same time the distant sound of exultant music, singing and laughter becomes steadily louder. Both* SOLDIERS *and* CROWD *are inspired to battle by these strains without their knowing it.* CALIGULA *is listening spell-bound, his mouth open, his body swaying and twitching. Even* CRASSUS *stares off at the oncomers, forgetful of the growing plight of his* SOLDIERS.)

Crowd. (*Led by their* CHORUS—*angrily.*)

Cowards! Pigs!
Strike! Hit!
Stones! Knives!
Stab! Kill!
Death to the Romans!
Death!

A Soldier. (*Alarmed, calls to* CRASSUS.) General! Let us use our swords!

Soldiers. (*Enraged—eagerly.*) Yes! Swords!

Crowd. Death!

Crassus. (*Turning—uneasy but afraid to give any drastic order.*) Bah! Staves are enough. Crack their skulls!

Crowd. (*Led by the* CHORUS—*defiantly.*)

Death to Crassus!
Drunkard! Coward!
Death to him!

(*They continue to push forward, hooting and jeering.*)

Crassus. (*Exploding for a second.*) By the gods—! (*To the* SOLDIERS.) Draw your swords!

(*The troops do so eagerly. The* CROWD *sag back momentarily with exclamations of fear.*)

Caligula. (*Listening as in a trance to the music and what is going on behind him—in a queer whisper.*) Kill, Cneius! Let me dance! Let me sing! (*The music and crashing of cymbals and the ferment of passions around him cause him to lose all control over himself. He gives a crazy leap in the air and begins to dance grotesquely and chant in a thick voice.*) He is coming! Death, the Deliverer! Kill, soldiers! I command you! I, Caligula! I will be Cæsar! Death!

Crowd. (*Led by the* CHORUS—*savage now.*)

Beast! Cur!
Death to Caligula!

(*They crowd forward.*)

Caligula. (*Drawing his sword and flourishing it drunkenly—his eyes glazed.*) Death!

Crassus. (*Drawing his own sword in a frenzy.*) Strike! Death!

(*His* SOLDIERS *raise their swords. The* CROWD *have raised whatever weapons they have found— knives, clubs, daggers, stones, bare fists.*)

Chorus. (*Chanting fiercely.*)
Death!

All. (ROMANS *and* GREEKS *alike as one great voice.*)
Death!

(*The chorused word beats down all sound into a stricken silence. The wild joyous music ceases. The Romans and Greeks seem to lean back from one another and collect strength to leap forward. At this moment the voice of* LAZARUS *comes ringing through the air like a command from the sky.*)

Lazarus. There is no death!

(*The* SOLDIERS *and* GREEKS *remain frozen in their attitudes of murderous hate. Following his*

words the laughter of LAZARUS *is heard, exultant
and gaily mocking, filling them with the sheepish
shame of children caught in mischief. Their
hands hang, their arms sink to their sides. The
music starts once more with a triumphant clash of
cymbals,* LAZARUS' *laughter is echoed from the
throats of the multitude of his* FOLLOWERS *who
now come dancing into the square, preceded by a
band of masked musicians and by their* CHORUS.

(*This* CHORUS *wears, in double size, the laughing
mask of* LAZARUS' FOLLOWERS *in the same
Period and Type as in the preceding scene, except
that here the mask of each member of the* CHORUS
*has a different racial basis—Egyptian, Syrian,
Cappadocian, Lydian, Phrygian, Cilician,
Parthian. The* FOLLOWERS *are costumed and
masked as in the preceding scene, seven Types in
seven Periods, except that, as in the* CHORUS,
*racially there are many nations represented. All
have wreaths of ivy in their hair and flowers in
their hands which they scatter about. They whirl
in between the* SOLDIERS *and* CROWD, *forcing
them back from each other, teasing them, sifting
into the* CROWD, *their* CHORUS *in a half circle,
confronting the* CHORUS OF GREEKS.)

Chorus of Followers.

Laugh! Laugh!
There is no death!
There is only life!
There is only laughter!

Followers. (*Echoing.*)

Laugh! Laugh!
There is no death!

(CALIGULA *and* CRASSUS *are swept to one side,
left. Then the cries and laughter of all become
mingled into one exclamation.*)

All. Lazarus! Lazarus!

(*The squad of* ROMAN SOLDIERS *led by the* CEN-
TURION, *who had taken* LAZARUS *prisoner,
march in with dancers' steps, like a proud guard
of honor now, laughing, pulling a chariot in
which* LAZARUS *stands dressed in a tunic of
white and gold, his bronzed face and limbs radiant in the halo of his own glowing light.*)

(LAZARUS *now looks less than thirty-five. His
countenance now might well be that of the positive
masculine Dionysus, closest to the soil of the
Grecian Gods, a Son of Man, born of a mortal.
Not the coarse, drunken Dionysus, nor the effemi-
nate God, but Dionysus in his middle period,
more comprehensive in his symbolism, the soul of
the recurring seasons, of living and dying as
processes in eternal growth, of the wine of life
stirring forever in the sap and blood and loam of
things.* MIRIAM *is beside him, dressed in black,*

smiling the same sad tender smile, holding
LAZARUS' *arm as if for protection and in protection. She appears older, a woman over forty-five.*)

Chorus of Greeks. (*Rushing to* LAZARUS'
car.)

Hail, Dionysus!
Iacchus!
Lazarus!
Hail!

(*They surround him, throw over his shoulders
and head the finely dressed hide of a bull with
great gilded horns, force into his right hand the
mystic rod of Dionysus with a pine cone on top,
then prostrate themselves.*)

Hail, Savior!
Redeemer!
Conqueror of Death!

All. (*In a repeated chorus which finally includes even the* ROMAN SOLDIERS, *raising their
arms to him.*)

Hail, Lazarus!
Redeemer!
Hail!

(*They are silent.* LAZARUS *looks at them, seeming to see each and all at the same time, and his
laughter, as if in answer to their greetings, is
heard rising from his lips like a song.*)

Crassus. (*Awed.*) Look! He is more than
man!
Caligula. (*Trembling, in a queer agitation.*)
I dare not look!
Crassus. Do you hear his laughter?
Caligula. (*Chokingly—puts his hands over
his ears.*) I will not hear!
Crassus. But you must welcome him in
Cæsar's name!
Caligula. (*His teeth chattering.*) I must kill
him!
Lazarus. (*Looking directly at him—gaily
mocking.*) Death is dead, Caligula! (*He begins
to laugh again softly.*)
Caligula. (*With an hysterical cry of defiant
terror.*) You lie! (*Sword in hand he whirls to
confront* LAZARUS, *but at the first sight of his
face he stops in his tracks, trembling, held fascinated by* LAZARUS' *eyes, mumbling with a last
pitiful remainder of defiance.*) But—you lie—
whatever you are! I say there must be death!
(*The sword has fallen to his side. He stares open-
mouthed at* LAZARUS. *There is something of a
shy, wondering child about his attitude now.*
LAZARUS *looks at him, laughing with gentle
understanding.* CALIGULA *suddenly drops his
sword and covering his face with his hands weeps
like a boy who has been hurt.*) You have mur-

dered my only friend, Lazarus! Death would have been my slave when I am Cæsar. He would have been my jester and made me laugh at fear! (*He weeps bitterly.*)

Lazarus. (*Gaily.*) Be your own jester instead, O Caligula! Laugh at yourself, O Cæsar-to-be! (*He laughs. The* CROWD *now all join in with him.*)

(CALIGULA *suddenly uncovers his face, grins his warped grin, gives a harsh cackle which cracks through the other laughter with a splitting discord, cuts a hopping caper like some grotesque cripple which takes him to the side of* LAZARUS' *chariot where he squats on his hams and, stretching out his hand, fingers* LAZARUS' *robe inquisitively and stares up into his face in the attitude of a chained monkey.*)

Caligula. (*With a childish, mischievous curiosity.*) Then if there is no death, O Teacher, tell me why I love to kill?

Lazarus. Because you fear to die! (*Then gaily mocking.*) But what do you matter, O Deathly-Important One? Put yourself that question—as a jester! (*Exultantly.*) Are you a speck of dust danced in the wind? Then laugh, dancing! Laugh yes to your insignificance! Thereby will be born your new greatness! As Man, Petty Tyrant of Earth, you are a bubble pricked by death into a void and a mocking silence! But as dust, you are eternal change, and everlasting growth, and a high note of laughter soaring through chaos from the deep heart of God! Be proud, O Dust! Then you may love the stars as equals! (*Then mockingly again.*) And then perhaps you may be brave enough to love even your fellow men without fear of their vengeance!

Caligula. (*Dully.*) I cannot understand. I hate men. I am afraid of their poison and their swords and the cringing envy in their eyes that only yields to fear!

Lazarus. (*Gaily mocking.*) Tragic is the plight of the tragedian whose only audience is himself! Life is for each man a solitary cell whose walls are mirrors. Terrified is Caligula by the faces he makes! But I tell you to laugh in the mirror, that seeing your life gay, you may begin to live as a guest, and not as a condemned one!. (*Raising his hands for silence—with a playful smile.*) Listen! In the dark peace of the grave the man called Lazarus rested. He was still weak, as one who recovers from a long illness—for, living, he had believed his life a sad one! (*He laughs softly, and softly they all echo his laughter.*) He lay dreaming to the croon of silence, feeling as the flow of blood in his own veins the past reënter the heart of God to be renewed by faith into the future. He thought: "Men call this death"—for he had been dead only a little while and he still remembered. Then, of a sudden, a strange gay laughter trembled from his heart as though his life, so long repressed in him by fear, had found at last its voice and a song for singing. "Men call this death," it sang. "Men call life death and fear it. They hide from it in horror. Their lives are spent in hiding. Their fear becomes their living. They worship life as death!"

Chorus of Followers. (*In a chanting echo.*)
Men call life death and fear it.
They hide from it in horror.
Their lives are spent in hiding.
Their fear becomes their living.
They worship life as death!

Lazarus. And here the song of Lazarus' life grew pitiful. "Men must learn to live," it mourned. "Before their fear invented death they knew, but now they have forgotten. They must be taught to laugh again!" And Lazarus answered "Yes!" (*He now addresses the crowd—especially* CALIGULA, *directly, laughingly.*) Thus sang his life to Lazarus while he lay dead! Man must learn to live by laughter! (*He laughs.*)

Chorus of Followers.
Laugh! Laugh!
There is only life!
There is only laughter!
Fear is no more!
Death is dead!

Chorus of Greeks.
Laugh! Laugh!
Hail, Dionysus!
Fear is no more!
Thou hast conquered death!

All. (*Laughing—in a great laughing chorus.*)
Laugh! Laugh!
Fear is no more!
Death is dead!

Lazarus. (*As to a crowd of children—laughingly.*) Out with you! Out into the woods! Upon the hills! Cities are prisons wherein man locks himself from life. Out with you under the sky! Are the stars too pure for your sick passions? Is the warm earth smelling of night too desirous of love for your pale introspective lusts? Out! Let laughter be your new clean lust and sanity! So far man has only learned to snicker meanly at his neighbor! Let a laughing away of self be your new right to live forever! Cry in your pride, "I am Laughter, which is Life, which is the Child of God!" (*He laughs and again his voice leads and dominates the rhythmic chorus of theirs. The music and dancing begin again.*)

The Two Choruses. (*Chanting in unison.*)
Laugh! Laugh!
There is only God!
We are His Laughter!

All. (*Echoing.*)
There is only God!
We are His Laughter!
Laugh! Laugh!

(*They take hold of his chariot traces, and as he had come, in the midst of a happy multitude, now augmented by all the* GREEKS, *and the* ROMAN SOLDIERS *who had awaited him, dancing, playing, singing, laughing, he is escorted off. The noise of their passing recedes.* CALIGULA *and* CRASSUS *are left in the empty square, the former squatting on his hams, monkey-wise, and brooding somberly.*)

Crassus. (*Is swaying and staggering, like a man in a drunken stupor, in a bewildered, stubborn struggle to control himself. He stammers after the* SOLDIERS.) Ha-ha-ha— Halt! Halt, I say! No use—they are gone—mutiny— Halt! (*He continues to stumble toward left.*) Ha-ha— Stop it, curse you! Am I laughing? Where am I going? After Lazarus? Thirty years of discipline and I— Halt, traitor! Remember Cæsar! Remember Rome! Halt, traitor! (*He faints with the violence of his struggle and falls in a limp heap.*)

Caligula. (*Startled by his fall, terrified, hops to his feet and snatches up his sword defensively, glancing over his shoulder and whirling around as if he expected someone to stab him in the back. Then, forcing a twisted grin of self-contempt— harshly.*) Coward! What do I fear—if there is no death? (*As if he had to cut something, he snatches up a handful of flowers—desperately.*) You must laugh, Caligula! (*He starts to lop off the flowers from their stems with a savage intentness.*) Laugh! Laugh! Laugh! (*Finally, impatiently, he cuts off all the remaining with one stroke.*) Laugh! (*He grinds the petals under his feet and breaks out into a terrible hysterical giggle.*) Ha-ha—

CURTAIN

SCENE 2

SCENE: *A midnight, months later. Immediately inside the walls of Rome. In the foreground is the portico of a temple between whose massive*

columns one looks across a street on a lower level to the high wall of Rome at the extreme rear. In the center of the wall is a great metal gate. The night is thick and oppressive. In the sky overhead lightning flashes and thunder rumbles and crashes but there is no rain.

Within the portico on rows of chairs placed on a series of wide steps which are on each side, members of the Senate are seated in their white robes. High hanging lamps cast a wan light over their faces. They are all masked in the Roman mask, refined in them by nobility of blood but at the same time with strength degenerated, corrupted by tyranny and debauchery to an exhausted cynicism. The three periods of Middle Age, Maturity and Old Age are represented in the types of the Self-Tortured, Introspective; Proud, Self-Reliant; the Servile, Hypocritical; the Cruel, Revengeful; and the Resigned, Sorrowful. The SENATORS are divided into two groups on each side, thirty in each. Seated in the middle of the lower of the three high broad stairs that lead to the level from which the columns rise is the CHORUS OF SENATORS, seven in number, facing front, in double-sized masks of the Servile, Hypocritical type of Old Age.

LAZARUS, in his robe of white and gold, the aura of light surrounding his body seeming to glow more brightly than ever, stands in the rear at the edge of the portico, center, gazing upward into the pall of sky beyond the wall. His figure appears in its immobility to be the statue of the god of the temple. Near him, but to the rear and to the left of him, facing right, MIRIAM is kneeling in her black robes, swaying backward and forward, praying silently with moving lips like a nun who asks mercy for the sins of the world. She has grown much older, her hair is gray, her shoulders are bowed.

On the other side, placed similarly in relation to LAZARUS and facing MIRIAM, CALIGULA is squatting on his hams on a sort of throne-chair of ivory and gold. He is dressed with foppish richness in extreme bright colors, a victory wreath around his head. He stares blinkingly and inquisitively at LAZARUS, then at MIRIAM. He is half-drunk. A large figured goblet of gold is in his hand. A slave with an amphora of wine crouches on the steps by his chair. The slave wears a black negroid mask.

At the opening of the scene there is heard the steady tramp of departing troops, whose masks, helmets and armored shoulders can be seen as they pass through the street before LAZARUS to the gate beyond. Finally with a metallic clash the gate is shut behind them and there is a heavy and oppressive silence in which only the murmured prayers of MIRIAM are heard.

Chorus of the Senate. (*Intones wearily, as if under a boring compulsion.*)

The Roman Senate
Is the Roman Senate
The Mighty Voice
Of the Roman People
As long as Rome is Rome.

Caligula. (*As if he hadn't heard—sings hoarsely an old camp song of the Punic Wars, pounding with his goblet.*)

A bold legionary am I!
March, oh march on!
A Roman eagle was my daddy,
My mother was a drunken drabby,
Oh, march on to the wars!

Since lived that lady Leda
March, oh march on!
Women have loved high-fliers
And we are eagles of Rome!
Oh march on to the wars!

Comrades, march to the wars!
There's pretty girls in Carthage
And wine to swill in Carthage,
So we must capture Carthage
And fight for Mother Rome!

(*Holds out his goblet to be refilled. There is silence again. He stares at* LAZARUS *with a somber intentness. He says thickly.*) The legions have gone, Lazarus. (LAZARUS *gives no evidence of having heard him.* CALIGULA *gulps at his wine. The* SENATORS *begin to talk to each other in low voices.*)

First Senator. How does that Jew make that light come from him, I wonder? It is a well-contrived bit of magic.

Second Senator. What are we waiting for? A messenger came to me with Cæsar's command that the Senate meet here at midnight.

Third Senator. (*Bored.*) Some new whim of Tiberius, naturally— (*With a meaning titter*) —or rather I should say, unnaturally!

Fourth Senator. Perhaps Cæsar has decided to abolish our august body by a massacre in mass!

Third Senator. (*Yawning.*) There was a feast at Cinna's last night that lasted until this evening. I could welcome my own murder as an excuse for sleeping!

Fifth Senator. (*Pompously.*) Tiberius would not dare harm the Senate. He may mistreat individual Senators, but the Roman Senate is the Roman Senate!

Chorus of the Senate. (*As before—wearily as if under a boring compulsion—intones.*)

While Rome is Rome
The Senate is the Senate
The Mighty Voice of the Roman People.

First Senator. (*With the ghost of a laugh—wearily.*) The Senate is an empty name—a pack of degenerate cowards with no trace of their ancient nobility or courage remaining—that and no more!

Third Senator. (*Flippantly.*) You are too severe with yourself, Lucius! (*A titter of laughter.*)

First Senator. (*Wearily.*) A degenerate coward. I am, I confess it. So are you too, Sulpicius—a hundred fold!—whether you admit it or not. (SULPICIUS *laughs weakly without taking offense.*)

Sixth Senator. (*After a pause—sighing.*) In truth, the Senate is not what it used to be. I can remember—

First Senator. Let us forget, if we can! (*Then impatiently.*) What are we doing here?

Second Senator. I imagine it has something to do with the followers of this Lazarus encamped outside the wall. Probably the legions are to butcher them in their sleep.

Seventh Senator. And what part do we play —official witnesses? But how can we witness at night and through a wall? (*With bored resignation.*) Ah well, the moods of Tiberius are strange, to say the least. But Cæsar is Cæsar.

Chorus. (*Again with bored weariness as before.*)

Hail!
Cæsar is Cæsar
The August One
Prince of the Senate
Tribune over Tribunes
Consul of Consuls
Supreme Pontiff
Emperor of Rome
God among Gods
Hail!

First Senator. (*After a pause of silence—dryly.*) Cæsar is a beast—and a madman!

Fifth Senator. (*Pompously.*) Respect, sir! More respect for Cæsar!

Third Senator. (*Mockingly.*) Or caution, Lucius. One of us might repeat your opinion to him.

First Senator. You would if it would pay you. But all my money is squandered. My death is worthless to Tiberius. He would not reward you. Moreover, you would not be revenged on me, for I long for death.

he wrote the poem at one sitting, April 26, 1861. It was shortly after published in the New Orleans *Delta*. It was set to the music of *Lauriger Horatius* by Miss Jenny Carey, of Baltimore, and sung for the first time by her to the soldiers under General Beauregard at Fairfax Courthouse, after she and her sister Hetty were exiled from Maryland as Southern sympathizers.

748. Dixie. *Dixie* was composed first by Daniel Decatur Emmett, of Ohio, in 1859, as a "walk-around" for Bryant's Minstrels in New York City. In the fall of 1860 it was sung in New Orleans, in John Brougham's burlesque play of *Pocahontas*, by Mrs. John Wood. Several sets of words were written to the air, but the one which has become established and which has the most truly literary quality is that by General Albert H. Pike, published by him in the Natchez *Courier*, May 30, 1861. General Pike was born in New England, but lived at the outbreak of the war in Arkansas.

Emmett's version, which was never displaced in popular favor, is as follows:

DIXIE

I wish I was in de land ob cotton, old times dar are not forgotten;
  Look away, look away, look away, Dixie land!
In Dixie land whar I was born in, early on one frosty mornin'
  Look away, look away, look away, Dixie land!

(*Chorus*)

Den I wish I was in Dixie, hooray! hooray!
In Dixie land I'll took my stand, to lib and die in Dixie,
Away, away, away down south in Dixie!
Away, away, away down south in Dixie!

740. The Bonnie Blue Flag. The original version was written to the melody of *The Irish Jaunting Car*, by a comedian, Harry McCarthy, at the time a volunteer soldier in the Confederate army. The song was first sung by his sister, Marion McCarthy, at the Varieties Theater in New Orleans, in 1861. General Butler issued an order fining anyone $25.00 who "sang, whistled, or played it on any instrument." He also arrested the publisher and destroyed the manuscript. McCarthy's version began:

"We are a band of brothers and native to the soil,
Fighting for our liberty with treasure, blood and toil."

740. John Brown's Body. There are many accounts of the genesis of *John Brown's Body*. The best authenticated traces the tune to an old camp meeting song, *Say, Brothers, Will You Meet Us?* which seems to have been made the basis of *John Brown's Body* by members of a Massachusetts regiment quartered in Boston Harbor, in April, 1861. The soldiers of this regiment sang it as they marched down Broadway, July 24, 1861, on their way from Boston to the front. The version here given is the one which was actually sung by the soldiers and which has been attributed to a number of authors. Efforts were made to substitute words of a more elevated quality, but the soldiers steadily refused to sing them. It was only after Mrs. Howe had used the melody as a basis for her great *Battle Hymn of the Republic* that a successful rival arose to the original song.

750. The Picket Guard. Many claims arose for the authorship of this poem, which was originally published on November 30, 1861, in *Harper's Weekly*, and which seems certainly to have been written by Mrs. Ethelinda Elliot Beers. She was a prolific writer of war lyrics, under the name of Ethel Lynn Beers.

750. Battle Hymn of the Republic. According to Mrs. Howe's own statement she wrote the *Hymn* while she was in Washington, late in 1861, after witnessing a review of the Union troops. She took as a basis the music of *John Brown's Body* and composed the words while lying in bed. Fearing to lose them, she arose and wrote them down. In the morning, after arising, she tried to recall the lines before looking at them and found that they had completely vanished from her memory. The title, *Battle Hymn of the Republic*, was suggested by James T. Fields, editor of the *Atlantic Monthly*.

751. Ode to America. This poem was written early in 1862. It is one of the earliest expressions of national resentment against the attitude of England and France toward the United States, but its significance lies in its note of courage and optimism during a period of doubt and discouragement.

752. We Are Coming, Father Abraham, Three Hundred Thousand More was published anonymously in the New York *Evening Post*, July 16, 1862, and its authorship was attributed to Bryant, who was then the editor of the paper. James Sloan Gibbons was a Quaker, born July 1, 1810, at Wilmington, Del., who settled in New York City in 1835. In 1830 he had joined the Abolition movement and was for a time one of the editors of *The Antislavery Standard*. During the draft riots in 1863, his house was sacked.

753. "Our Left." This poem, according to Paul Hamilton Hayne, was inspired by the indomitable courage of the Confederate left wing at the first battle of Bull Run. They withstood the attack of MacDowell's division of the Army of the Potomac until they were reinforced by the timely arrival of reinforcements under General Joseph E. Johnston.

753. Dirge for Ashby. At a crucial point in the Peninsular campaign, General McClellan was promised a reinforcement of 40,000 men, under General MacDowell. The United States government, however, being panic-stricken at the rapid movements of Stonewall Jackson in the Shenandoah Valley, became alarmed for the safety of Washington and delayed too long in sending the reinforcements. In preventing the junction of McClellan and MacDowell, the Confederate forces under General Turner Ashby encountered the First New Jersey Cavalry in a skirmish near Harrisburg, Va., immediately preceding the battle of Cedar Keys.

General Ashby was born at Rose Hill, Va., in 1824. At the outbreak of the war he raised a cavalry regiment, becoming brigadier general in the Confederate Army operating in Virginia and Kentucky. He died June 5, 1862.

754. Dirge for a Soldier. *Dirge for a Soldier* was written in memory of General Philip Kearny. Philip Kearny was born in New York City, June 2, 1815, and, after graduating from Columbia College, entered the United States Army. Although he inherited property worth a million dollars, he continued his military career with several intermissions, in one of which he visited France and served on the staff of the Duke of Orléans in Africa. Returning to this country in 1840, he took part in the Mexican War and won his grade of major for valiant service at the battle of Cherubusco, in which his left arm was shattered. In 1859 he returned to France and was made commander of Cavalry of the Guard, under Napoleon III, winning the Cross of the Legion of Honor at Solferino. He returned to military duty at the beginning of the Civil War and became commander of the First New Jersey Brigade in the Army of the Potomac, becoming a major general July 7, 1862. After brilliant service at the second battle of Bull Run, he was mortally wounded while reconnoitering at the battle of Chantilly and died September 1, 1862.

754. Wanted—A Man. *Wanted—A Man* was published September 8, 1862, inspired by public discontent with the failure of the Union armies to capture Richmond. It has usually been spoken of as an attack on McClellan, and there can be little doubt that the second stanza, with the line "Fit to do as well as to plan," refers to him. There is, however, a clear indication in the third stanza that Stedman had in mind other generals also. President Lincoln read the poem, it is said, to his cabinet. The poem appeared, curiously enough, just nine days before McClellan defeated Lee at Antietam.

755. Pelham. Yielding to public demand, Lincoln removed McClellan from the command of the Army of the Potomac. General Hooker, who replaced him, advanced in April, 1863, and

was badly defeated at Chancellorsville. Meanwhile, there had been skirmishing, and General John Pelham was killed, March 17, 1863.

755. "The Brigade Must Not Know, Sir!" The defeat at Chancellorsville was more than counterbalanced by the death of Stonewall Jackson. Dr. Esther P. Ellinger, in her *Southern War Poetry of the Civil War*, records sixteen poems bearing upon Stonewall Jackson's death.

755. The High Tide at Gettysburg. This poem was delivered July 4, 1888, at the twenty-fifth anniversary ceremonies held at Gettysburg. It is included, however, since Thompson was a Confederate soldier and in every sense the poem is a genuine product of the war. Note the successful use of proper names and the personification of the call of one state to another which had always been the characteristics of Southern war poetry. The author was born in Georgia, the son of the Rev. Grigg Thompson. He became an engineer and a lawyer. His death occurred in Seattle, Wash., August 10, 1918.

756. Sheridan's Ride. *Sheridan's Ride* celebrates one of the most popular of the Northern generals. His career, beginning after his graduation from West Point in 1853, was a continued series of promotions, based upon his skill and daring as a cavalry leader. Given command of all the cavalry in the Army of the Potomac, he distinguished himself so that he was put in charge of the Army of the Shenandoah and drove the Confederates, under General Early, out of that valley. But Early returned, reinforced, and on October 19, 1864, surprised the Union forces and drove them back. General Sheridan, who had been at Washington and was stopping at Winchester on his return, hurried to the field and led his troops to victory. He won for this a promotion to be major general in the regular army and continued to direct cavalry operations during Grant's campaigns. After the Civil War he became successively lieutenant general and general, being appointed Commander in Chief of the Army in 1883. He died August 5, 1888.

757. The Battle Cry of Freedom. *The Battle Cry of Freedom* is said to have been sung at the time of the capture of Vicksburg, July 4, 1863. Root was also the author of *Tramp, Tramp, Tramp, the Boys are Marching; Just Before the Battle, Mother*, and other well known songs on the Union side.

758. The Black Regiment. *The Black Regiment* was written to celebrate the charge of the colored troops at Port Hudson, May 27, 1863.

759. Little Giffen. *Little Giffen* first appeared in *The Land We Love*, published at Charlotte, North Carolina, November, 1867. It was inspired by a real incident. Isaac Newton Giffen, the son of a blacksmith in East Tennessee, had been wounded at either Murfreesboro or Chickamauga. He had been given up as a hopeless case by the attending surgeons, but Mrs. Ticknor suggested to Dr. Ticknor that he be brought from the hospital in Columbus to their home at Torch Hill, Georgia, where she nursed him back to health. During his recovery Mrs. Ticknor taught him to read and write. He left Torch Hill in March, 1864, and nothing was afterwards heard from him.

759. Carolina. According to Paul Hamilton Hayne, *Carolina* was written "early in the war."

760. On Board the Cumberland. On March 8, 1862, the Confederate ram "Merrimac" attacked the Union fleet at Hampton Roads. The "Cumberland" refused to surrender and went down with her flag flying. Before the "Merrimac" could complete her work, the "Monitor" arrived and changed the defeat into victory.

762. Charleston. *Charleston* was written before the attack by sea and land, early in 1863.

762. The Sword in the Sea. The "Alabama" was built by Laird and Sons at Birkenhead and was a screw steam sloop of wood. During her construction the United States government protested to the British government that the vessel was intended for Confederate war service, but she was allowed to escape on July 1, 1862. During her career she captured sixty-five vessels, occasioning a loss of about four million dollars directly and an almost incalculable indirect loss to the United States merchant shipping. On June 11, 1864, she entered the harbor of Cherbourg in France to refit, and the American ship "Kearsarge," under Captain Winslow, challenged her to fight. A battle took place on Sunday, June 19, and after one hour's fight, when she was about to sink, Captain Semmes, her captain, surrendered.

The Secretary of State, Mr. Seward, made a claim against the British government for damages, and the Board of Arbitration, consisting of the Queen of England, the President of the United States, the King of Italy, the President of the Swiss Confederation, and the Emperor of Brazil, awarded damages to the amount of £3,229,166.

762. The Bay Fight. Brownell had written and printed anonymously in the *Evening Press*, of Hartford, a rimed version of the "General Orders" of Admiral Farragut, issued to his fleet before the attack upon New Orleans. Farragut had in consequence written to Brownell and finally appointed him, in 1863, to a post upon the Hartford, where he eventually became ensign. According to the introduction by M. A. DeWolfe Howe to his edition of Brownell's *Lines of Battle*, the poet took part in the battle of Mobile Bay, August 5, 1864.

768. Driving Home the Cows. This appeared first in *Harper's Magazine*, March, 1865.

770. South Carolina to the States of the North. *South Carolina to the States of the North* was written as a protest against the horrors of the reconstruction period. It will be noted that the appeal characteristically is made "Especially to Those That Formed a Part of the Original Thirteen." The patrician attitude of the Southerner was intensified by the state pride of the South Carolinian, who declined to make his appeal to any of the States except those who were, in his judgment, on a par with the independent Commonwealth of South Carolina.

772. The Blue and the Gray. This poem, which appeared in the *Atlantic Monthly* in September, 1867, was suggested by an incident occurring at Columbus, Mississippi, where the graves of the Union soldiers were decorated by the Southern women along with those of their own kinsmen who had fallen during the war. Francis Miles Finch, after graduating from Yale College in 1849, had a distinguished career as a lawyer, and, after fifteen years spent as Judge of the Court of Appeals, became Professor of the History of Law and Dean of the Law Faculty at Cornell University.

X. WALT WHITMAN

774. WALT WHITMAN

Walter (Walt) Whitman was born in Suffolk County, Long Island, May 31, 1819. Leaving school at the age of twelve, he acquired his education largely in printing offices. From 1836 to 1838 he taught school on Long Island, tried his hand during the next three years at publishing and editing newspapers, with relapses into school teaching, and from 1841 to 1846 made a living by writing or setting type for newspapers in Brooklyn. In 1846 he became the editor of the Brooklyn *Daily Eagle*, but did not retain the position, partly because of his free soil principles, but also because in this early period he seemed to have little fixity of purpose. He welcomed perhaps in consequence the offer of a position on the *Daily Crescent* of New Orleans, and this experience of the South, short as it was, left a deep impression upon him. Returning to Brooklyn, he prepared for the writing of *Leaves of Grass*, which appeared first in 1855 and which he reissued with alterations and additions in many editions. Going to the front in 1862 in search of his brother, he became a nurse in the hospitals in Washington, remaining through the war. Becoming a clerk in the Indian Bureau in 1865 he was dismissed on account of certain passages in *Leaves of Grass*, but was immediately reappointed by the Attorney General. *Drum Taps* appeared in 1865 and *Democratic Vistas* in 1871. In consequence of a partial paralytic stroke he resigned his position in 1873 and from that time resided in Camden, New Jersey. Besides the constant revisions of *Leaves of Grass*, he published *Specimen Days and Collect* (1882-83), *November Boughs* (1888), and *Goodbye My Fancy* (1891). Whitman died March 26, 1892. For bibliography, see E. Holloway and H. S. Saunders, *CHAL*, II, 551-581; also O. L. Triggs, in *The Complete Writings of Walt Whitman*, X, 139-233. For *Leaves of Grass* and selections from Whitman's prose, the "Inclusive Edition" (1926) is best; for the remainder of his work, *The Complete Writings of Walt Whitman*, 10v., 1902, issued by his literary executors. The best biographies are: Bliss Perry, *Walt Whit-*

man, his Life and Work (Amer. Men of Letters Ser., 1906, revised 1908); G. R. Carpenter, *Walt Whitman* (English Men of Letters Ser., 1909); and Emory Holloway, *Whitman, an Interpretation in Narrative* (1926). A personal view is given by Thomas Donaldson in *Walt Whitman, the Man* (1896), and by Horace Traubel in *With Walt Whitman in Camden* (1908); the foreign point of view is expressed in J. A. Symonds, *Walt Whitman* (1893); John Bailey, *Walt Whitman* (English Men of Letters, New Series, 1926); Léon Bazalgette, *Walt Whitman, the Man and his Work*, translated by Ellen Fitzgerald (1920). The text of the poems and dates are here taken by permission from *Leaves of Grass*, Inclusive Edition, edited by Emory Holloway, New York, Doubleday, Doran and Company, 1926.

XI. THE COMEDY OF MANNERS

819. WILLIAM DEAN HOWELLS

William Dean Howells was born at Martin's Ferry, Ohio, March 1, 1837. In his autobiographical volumes, especially *My Year in a Log Cabin, The Country Printer, Years of My Youth* and *My Literary Friends and Acquaintance*, he gives vivid pictures of his education as a printer, editor, and writer, and of his visit East to meet the New England group of poets. After his first book, *Poems by Two Friends* (1860), and his *Life of Lincoln* (1860), he was appointed Consul at Venice, where he remained until 1865. He became assistant editor of the *Atlantic Monthly* in 1866 and was editor from 1872 to 1880. His first novel, *Their Wedding Journey*, appeared in 1872, and in 1886 he became associated with

Harper's Magazine, conducting *The Editor's Study* and *The Easy Chair* for many years. His most significant period as a novelist began in 1882 with *A Modern Instance*, followed by *A Woman's Reason* (1883), *The Rise of Silas Lapham* (1885), *Indian Summer* (1886), *April Hopes* (1888), and *A Hazard of New Fortunes* (1889). Howells died in 1920. (For his comedies and his criticism, see Introductions to Sections XI and XV.) For bibliography, see *CHAL*, IV, 663-666. For biography see D. G. Cooke, *William Dean Howells: A Critical Study* (1922); O. W. Firkins, *William Dean Howells, A Study* (1924); Mildred Howells, *Life in Letters of William Dean Howells*, 2v., 1928.

XII. THE POETRY OF THE LATER NINETEENTH CENTURY

831. THOMAS BAILEY ALDRICH

Thomas Bailey Aldrich was born at Portsmouth, N. H., November 11, 1836, and has reflected his boyhood life there in his *Story of a Bad Boy* (1869). Aldrich's first volume of verse, *The Bells*, appeared in 1855, and the next year he became assistant editor of the *Home Journal*. After the war, during which he acted as a correspondent, he moved to Boston, in 1865, when he became editor of *Every Saturday*, reaching the climax of his editorial career in the conduct of the *Atlantic Monthly* (1881-1890). Meanwhile he had been writing the charming poetry and prose which gave him his secure position in fiction and in social and narrative verse. His most significant volumes were *Marjorie Daw and other Stories* (1873), *Mercedes and Later Lyrics* (1884), *The Stillwater Tragedy* (1880), and *Judith and Holofernes* (1896). He died March 19, 1907. For bibliography, see *CHAL*, II, 618; III, 644-645; 657. The standard edition of his works is the Riverside Edition, 9v., 1907. The best life is by Ferris Greenslet (1908), with bibliog-

raphy. For a charming personal picture see *Crowding Memories*, by his wife, Lilian W. Aldrich (1920).

838. LOUISE CHANDLER MOULTON

[Ellen] Louise Chandler was born at Pomfret, Conn., April 10, 1835, and married in 1855 William Upham Moulton. Her first volume, containing stories and poems, *This, That and the Other*, appeared in 1853, but her first important volume of poetry was the *Poems* of 1878. For thirty years she made annual visits to England, where she became a close friend of the Brownings. She died August 10, 1908. Her work is best read in the collected edition, *Poems and Sonnets* (1909), edited by Harriet P. Spofford. See for life, Lillian Whiting, *Louise Chandler Moulton, Poet and Friend* (1910).

839. EDMUND CLARENCE STEDMAN

Edmund Clarence Stedman was born at Hartford, Conn., October 8, 1833. He entered Yale College in 1849, but was suspended for a slight infraction of the rules and did not complete his course. After some editorial experience, he went into the banking business in 1855, returning to it after his service as war correspondent for the New York *World*. His first important publication was his *Poems, Lyrical and Idyllic* (1860), and he continued to issue volumes of verse at various intervals. They are now collected in *The Poems of Edmund Clarence Stedman* (1908). Stedman's critical works, *Poets of America* (1885) and *The Nature and Elements of Poetry* (1892), and his anthologies, especially his *American Anthology* (1900) and his *Library of American Literature* (1890), are of great service to the student. He died January 18, 1908.

See Laura Stedman and George M. Gould, *Life and Letters of Edmund Clarence Stedman*, 2v., 1910, for biography and full bibliography.

845. EMILY DICKINSON

Emily Dickinson was born at Amherst, Massachusetts, December 11, 1830, a member of a family which had been for nine generations in New England. She was educated at private schools, read widely, and lived largely in her books and her garden. Returning from a visit to her father in Washington, she met in Philadelphia a clergyman who fell in love with her and to whom she gave her affection. Knowing that he was married, she at once returned to Amherst, and refused to see him when he followed her to her home. The incident shadowed her entire life, however, and strengthened her natural inclination toward a life of seclusion. Indeed, after her father's death, she remained within the limits of her house and garden until her own death, May 16, 1886.

She published nothing during her lifetime, though a few poems found their way into print through friends. They are best read now in *The Complete Poems of Emily Dickinson* (1924) and *Further Poems of Emily Dickinson* (1929), both edited by her niece, Martha Dickinson Bianchi, the author of *The Life and Letters of Emily Dickinson* (1924).

846. EDWARD ROWLAND SILL

Edward Rowland Sill was born at Windsor, Connecticut, April 29, 1841, and graduated from Yale College in 1861. His frail health sent him to California, but he remained Eastern in feeling and his literary work deals with general themes. He taught from 1868 to 1871 at Cuyahoga Falls, Ohio; then in a high school at Oakland, California, from 1871 to 1874, and was Professor of English Literature at the University of California from 1874 to 1882. Resigning on account of ill health, he returned to Ohio, where he lived until his death on February 27, 1887. He published little—*The Hermitage and Other Poems* (London, 1867; New York, 1867) and *The Venus of Milo and Other Poems* (1883). Since his death his poems have been reprinted and are found most conveniently in *Collected Poetical Works* (1906). For life, see W. B. Parker, *Edward Rowland Sill, his Life and Work* (1915).

847. SILAS WEIR MITCHELL

Silas Weir Mitchell was born in Philadelphia, February 15, 1829, and educated at the College of the University of Pennsylvania and the Jefferson Medical School. From 1861 to 1865 he was an army surgeon, unconsciously gathering the material for *In War Time, Roland Blake*, and *Westways*. He became the first specialist in Philadelphia in nervous diseases, and won international fame in that specialty. Owing to the advice of Dr. Holmes, Dr. Mitchell did not publish his first volume of verse, *The Hill of Stones*, until 1882, although he had contributed to magazines since 1864. His first fiction was an anonymous story, "The Case of George Dedlow," in the *Atlantic Monthly*, July, 1866. After two novelettes, he published his first novel, *In War Time* (1884). His most important novels are his historical romances, *Hugh Wynne* (1898), *The Adventures of François* (1899), and *The Red City* (1908); and his psychological studies, *Circumstance* (1901), *Constance Trescott* (1905), and (the union of romance and psychology) *Roland Blake* (1886). "The Consultation" is taken from his volume *Little Stories* (1903), first published serially the year before. Dr. Mitchell died in 1914.

His poetry is best read in *Complete Poems* (1914), forming now one volume of the *Author's Definitive Edition* of Dr. Mitchell's works (1915). No adequate biography exists but a life is in progress.

853. RICHARD WATSON GILDER

Richard Watson Gilder was born February 8, 1844, at Bordentown, New Jersey. After some experience in newspaper work and service in the Civil War in the Philadelphia Battery, he became assistant editor of *Scribner's Monthly* in 1870 and editor in 1881, continuing as editor of *The Century Magazine* when the change occurred. It was due to his discriminating judgment that many of the poets and prose writers of the later nineteenth century found recognition. His first volume of poems, *The New Day*, appeared in 1875, and his last, *The Fire Divine*, in 1907. His *Complete Poems* appeared in 1908. He died November 18, 1909. See *Letters of Richard Watson Gilder*, ed. by Rosamund Gilder (1916), for an account not only of his literary work, but also of his activity in civil service reform, tenement house sanitation, and other civic fields.

854. LLOYD MIFFLIN

Lloyd Mifflin was born at Columbia, Pennsylvania, September 15, 1846. Educated at private schools, he studied painting with Thomas Moran and with Herzog at Düsseldorf, Germany, travelled widely, but later had to abandon painting on account of his health. His first book of verse, *The Hills*, appeared in 1896, but his first important volume, *At the Gates of Song*, containing 150 sonnets, was published in 1897. He wrote about 500 sonnets, the best being contained in *The Collected Sonnets of Lloyd Mifflin* (1905). He died July 16, 1921. For biography see *America's Greatest Sonneteer*, by E. H. Sneath (1928).

855. LOUISE IMOGEN GUINEY

Louise Imogen Guiney was born in Boston, January 17, 1861, daughter of General Patrick Guiney of the United States Army. After her graduation from her convent school at Elmhurst, R. I., in 1879, her life was devoted to her work as poet, essayist, and biographer, interrupted by the necessity of earning her living, from 1894 to 1902, as postmistress at Auburndale and later as a librarian in the Boston Public Library. She had spent two years in England, 1889 to 1891, and after 1903 she made her home there, dying at Chipping Camden, November 2, 1920. She was a devoted student of the Caroline period of English literature and her own work partook of the exquisite finish and delicate imagery of some of her great favorites.

Her earliest volumes, *Songs at the Start* (1884) and *The White Sail and other Poems* (1887), are now rare. Her poetry is best found collected in *Happy Ending* (1909, rev. ed. 1927). Her essays are found in *Goose Quill Papers* (1885) and *Patrins* (1897). *The Letters of Louise Imogen Guiney*, ed. by Grace Guiney, appeared in two volumes in 1926. For biography see a charming estimate by Alice Brown, *Louise Imogen Guiney* (1921), and a more detailed account in *Louise Imogen Guiney*, by E. M. Tenison, London, 1923, with descriptive bibliography.

856. FRANCIS BRET HARTE

[Francis] Bret Harte was born in Albany, New York, in 1836. He read Dickens at six years and wrote verse for publication at eleven, but left school at thirteen years of age. In 1854 he went to California. During the next two years he taught school, was an express messenger for Wells Fargo, and became a printer and editor. Returning to San Francisco in 1857, he joined the staff of the *Golden Era*, helped Mark Twain establish *The Californian*, and became editor of *The Overland Monthly* on its foundation in 1868. Here he published "The Luck of Roaring Camp" and "Plain Language from Truthful James." These made him famous. His first volume of verse, *The Lost Galleon* and his *Condensed Novels* had appeared in 1867. He left for the East in 1871, where his first volume of stories had been published in 1869. In 1878 he was appointed U. S. Commercial Agent at Crefeld, Prussia, and from 1880 to 1884 was Consul at Glasgow, living from then until his death on May 5, 1902, in London.

For bibliography, see *CHAL*, II, 622–625. The standard edition is the Riverside Edition, 19v., 1897–1903. For biography, see H. W. Boynton, *Bret Harte* (1903); T. E. Pemberton, *Life of Bret Harte* (1903); and (the best) H. C. Merwin, *Life of Bret Harte* (1911). *The Letters of Bret Harte*, edited by his son, G. B. Harte (1926), add greatly to an understanding of his personal character.

861. JOHN HAY

John Hay was born at Salem, Indiana, October 8, 1838, graduated from Brown University in 1858, was private secretary to President Lincoln, and then began a distinguished public career which included an ambassadorship to England and the Secretaryship of State under President McKinley. His first volume of poetry, *Jim Bludso and Little Breeches*, appeared in 1871, to be followed by *Pike County Ballads* (1873). A collected edition of his poems appeared in 1890. He died in 1905.

For biography, see J. B. Bishop, *John Hay, Scholar and Statesman* (1906), and W. R. Thayer, *Life and Letters of John Hay*, 2v., 1915.

862. JOAQUIN MILLER

Cincinnatus Hiner (or Heine) Miller was born in 1841 while his father and mother (who, according to his autobiographical sketch, differed as to the year) were crossing the dividing line between Indiana and Ohio. At the age of eleven, he went to Oregon, then to California, returning to study at Columbia College, Oregon, an institution, now extinct, of high school grade. In 1868 he published his first book of verse, *Specimens*, followed by the volume *Joaquin, et al* (1869) which gave him his pen name. Lacking encouragement, he went to London, where in 1871 he brought out *Pacific Poems* at his own expense and was soon lionized. After issuing his *Songs of the Sierras* (1871), he returned by way of the Orient to his own land. After a picturesque career, including variety performances, he died in California, February 17, 1913.

The Bear Edition, 6v., 1909, and 7v., 1917, is based on his own selections. His autobiographical sketch, in this edition, is not trustworthy. F. L. Pattee, in his *History of American Literature Since 1870*, gives a more accurate account, as does S. P. Sherman, in his introduction to the one-volume edition (1923).

865. JAMES WHITCOMB RILEY

James Whitcomb Riley was born at Greenfield, near Indianapolis, October 7, 1849. After studying law and abandoning it, he became a local editor on the *Democrat* at Anderson, Indiana, and was connected with the Indianapolis *Journal* from 1877 to 1885. In 1883 his first volume, *The Old Swimmin' Hole and 'Leven More Poems*, appeared under the pen name of "Benjamin F. Johnson of Boone." He published vo-

sionate Pilgrim and Other Tales (1875). This contained "The Romance of Certain Old Clothes," which appeared originally in the *Atlantic*, February, 1868. While he only occasionally touched the supernatural, it was in this field that he did some of his most striking work, like the novelette *The Turn of the Screw* (1898). During these thirty years he produced his best novels, *The American* (1877), *Confidence* (1879), *The Portrait of a Lady* (1881), *The Tragic Muse* (1890), and novelettes like *The Altar of the Dead* (1895) and his one popular story, *Daisy Miller* (1878). After 1896 his besetting fault of indirectness became more and more definite. His most important critical books are *French Poets and Novelists* (1878), *Partial Portraits* (1888), *Essays in London and Elsewhere* (1893), *The Art of Fiction* (1884), *The Lesson of Balzac* and *The Question of our Speech* (1905).

Bibliographies have been made by Philip Le-Roy (1906), F. A. King [see Cary, below], and Rebecca West (1916). See also *CHAL*, IV, 671–675. The standard edition is the "New York Edition," 26v., 1907–1917. Henry James's autobiographical books, *A Small Boy and Others* (1913), *Notes of a Son and Brother* (1914), *The Middle Years* (1917), are valuable, but indefinite as to facts. See also *The Letters of Henry James*, ed. by Percy Lubbock, 2v., 1920. For criticism, see E. L. Cary, *The Novels of Henry James, a Study* (1905, with bibliography); Rebecca West, *Henry James* (1916); F. M. Hueffer, *Henry James* (1916); J. W. Beach, *The Method of Henry James* (1918); W. B. Cairns, *Character Portrayal in the Work of Henry James*, Univ. of Wisconsin Ser. in Lang. and Lit. No. 2 (1919); Pelham Edgar, *Henry James, Man and Author* (1927); and the articles by W. C. Brownell in *American Prose Masters*, by S. P. Sherman in *Contemporary Literature* (1917), and by Gamaliel Bradford in *American Portraits* (1920).

915.   FRANCIS BRET HARTE

See above, p. N 37.

925.   THOMAS BAILEY ALDRICH

See above, p. N 35.

934.   GEORGE WASHINGTON CABLE

George Washington Cable was born October 12, 1844, in New Orleans, of mingled Virginian and New England ancestry. On account of his diminutive stature, he escaped in boys' clothing from the city after its capture by the Union Army, and enlisted in the Fourth Mississippi Cavalry. He spent some time in the cotton business and surveying, writing stories in such leisure as he had, until his first short story, "Sieur George," was accepted by *Scribner's Monthly* in 1872. With the publication of *Old Creole Days* in 1879, from which "Posson Jone" has been selected for this anthology, his career as a writer really began. Among the novels that

followed, the most significant were *The Grandissimes* (1880), *Madame Delphine* (1881), *Dr. Sevier* (1884), *Bonaventure* (1889) and *Bylow Hill* (1902). Cable's later stories, such as *Gideon's Band* (1914) and *Lovers of Louisiana* (1918), hardly maintained his reputation. In 1884 he moved to Simsbury, Conn., and later to Northampton, Mass. He was a very successful public reader, and took great interest in social work, especially the "Home Study Clubs." He died February 8, 1925.

The standard biography is *George W. Cable, His Life and Letters*, by his daughter, Lucy L. C. Biklé (1928).

942.   JOEL CHANDLER HARRIS

Joel Chandler Harris was born near Eatonton, Putnam Co., Georgia, December 9, 1848. His mother, Mary Harris, was deserted by her husband, and resumed her maiden name. Harris was educated in printing offices and through newspaper work, supplemented by wide reading. After several changes of position, he joined the staff of the Atlanta *Constitution* in 1877, and he made his home in Atlanta until his death, July 3, 1908. The "Uncle Remus" stories were contributed to this paper, the first sketch, "Uncle Remus's Politics," appearing November 28, 1876. In 1880 the first collection, *Uncle Remus, His Songs and His Sayings*, was published, from which selections have been made for this anthology, followed by many others, of which the best are *Nights with Uncle Remus* (1883), *Uncle Remus and His Friends* (1892), *Told by Uncle Remus* (1905), and *Uncle Remus and the Little Boy* (1910). The first stories were told him by a negro, "Uncle George" Terrell, but Harris travelled widely through the South to collect the later tales. The name Uncle Remus was probably suggested by a negro gardener in Forsyth, Georgia, where Harris had worked. In addition to the Uncle Remus stories, Harris wrote two novels, *Sister Jane* (1896) and *Gabriel Tolliver* (1902); three novelettes and seven volumes of short stories, of which the best are found in *Free Joe and Other Sketches* (1887).

For bibliography, see *CHAL*, II, 611–14. For biography see Julia C. Harris, *The Life of Joel Chandler Harris* (1918), and R. L. Wiggins, *The Life of Joel Chandler Harris* (1918), the latter of which contains some of the earlier, unpublished work of Harris.

950.   FRANK R. STOCKTON

Francis Richard Stockton was born in Philadelphia, April 4, 1834. Graduating from the Philadelphia Central High School in 1852, he was first an engraver, but, after some experience in newspaper work, joined the staff of *Scribner's Monthly*, following the fortunes of its successor, the *Century Magazine*, and when *St. Nicholas* was established in 1873 becoming assistant editor. After 1880 he devoted himself entirely to the writing of fiction. His first collection of short stories, *Ting-a-Ling Stories*, was written for children, and for many years his fantastic tales were the feature of *St. Nicholas*. The publication of "The Lady or the Tiger?" in the *Century Magazine* for November, 1882, made a sensation, for the ending is not a mere trick: it is an appeal to human sympathy. This story was published in 1884 with others of his well known tales as *The Lady or the Tiger and Other Stories*. Among his many volumes, the best are *Rudder Grange* (1879), *The Casting Away of Mrs. Lecks and Mrs. Aleshine* (1886), *The Late Mrs. Null* (1886), and *The Hundredth Man* (1887). Stockton died April 20, 1902.

The Shenandoah edition of his works in twenty-three volumes was published in 1904. In Vol. XXIII is to be found a memoir by his wife, Marian E. Stockton, and a bibliographical list of his writings.

953. THOMAS NELSON PAGE

Thomas Nelson Page was born April 23, 1853, at Oakland, Virginia, and was descended from two Virginia governors. He saw the Civil War at first hand as a boy and gathered the material he afterwards used in his stories. He was educated at Washington and Lee University while Robert E. Lee was president, and graduated from the Law School of the University of Virginia in 1874. His first published work was his poem, "Uncle Gabe's White Folks," in *Scribner's Monthly* in 1877, but it was the instant and wide popularity of "Marse Chan," after it appeared in the *Century* in 1884, which established his reputation. Together with "Meh Lady," "Uncle Edinburg's Drowndin'," "Ole 'Stracted, "No Haid Pawn," and others, it was published under the title of *In Ole Virginia* in 1887. Although Page worked on a larger canvas in such a later novel as *Red Rock* (1898), a powerful story of Reconstruction, it is doubtful if he ever did more significant work than in this first volume of stories, in which he pictured the romance of the South before and during the Civil War. He was Ambassador to Italy from 1913 to 1919 and wrote his *Italy and the World War* from first hand knowledge. Page died November 1, 1922.

The Plantation Edition in 18v., 1906–1912, contains Page's most significant stories and his *Life of Robert E. Lee*. For biography see *Thomas Nelson Page, a Memoir of a Virginia Gentleman*, by his brother, Rosewell Page (1923).

964. SARAH ORNE JEWETT

Sarah Orne Jewett was born at Berwick, Maine, September 3, 1849, daughter of Dr. Theodore Jewett, whose character she has drawn in her novel *A Country Doctor* (1884), and whom she accompanied on his round of visits. Her short stories began to appear in the *Atlantic Monthly* in 1869, and in 1877 her first book, *Deephaven*, a series of sketches descriptive of a typical though imagined New England town, was published. European travel with her devoted companion, Mrs. James T. Fields, only made more complete her understanding of the life she could best depict. *The Country of the Pointed Firs* (1896) was perhaps the most distinguished of her longer fiction, but her art is seen at its best in her short stories, found now most availably in such volumes as *Tales of New England*, *A Native of Winby*, or *The Life of Nancy*, in some cases rearrangements of earlier collections. Bowdoin College awarded her a Litt.D. in 1901, the first it had given to a woman. Miss Jewett died June 24, 1909.

A collected edition of Miss Jewett's works in seven vols. was published in 1910, and a selected edition in two vols. with introduction by Willa Cather in 1925. For biography, see the delightful *Letters of Sarah Orne Jewett*, edited by Annie Fields (1911), and *Sarah Orne Jewett*, by Francis O. Matthiessen (1929).

972. SILAS WEIR MITCHELL
See above, p. **N** 36.

974. FRANCIS MARION CRAWFORD

Francis Marion Crawford was born August 2, 1854, at Bagni di Lucca, Italy, the son of Thomas Crawford, an American sculptor. On his mother's side he was descended from General Francis Marion of Revolutionary fame. His education included study in Italy, at St. Paul's School in New Hampshire, the University of Rome, Cambridge University, and Heidelberg University. Intending to become a teacher of language, he studied Sanskrit in India, where for eighteen months he was editor of the Allahabad *Herald*, and then entered Harvard University in 1881. His first novel, *Mr. Isaacs* (1882), was written about a diamond merchant named Jacobs whom he had met in India, and it became vastly popular. He returned to Italy, married, and settled at Sorrento, visiting America on occasions to lecture, and being selected to write the National Ode at the Centennial of the American Constitution, September 17, 1887. He died in April, 1909.

Crawford wrote forty-five novels, of which the best are his studies of Italian life, *Saracinesca* (1887), *Sant' Ilario* (1889), *Don Orsino* (1892), *Pietro Ghisleri* (1893), and *Marzio's Crucifix* (1887); his *A Cigarette Maker's Romance* (1890), laid in Munich; and his historical novels, *Via Crucis* (1898), *In the Palace of the King* (1900), and *Marietta* (1901).

No life of Crawford has been published. Some facts are given in *The Diary of a Diplomatist's Wife* (1910), by his sister, Mrs. Hugh Fraser. See also F. W. Halsey, *Authors of Our Day in Their Homes* (1902).

A publisher's note in the original edition of *The Upper Berth* says: "The two stories by Mr. Crawford, presented in this volume, have been in print before, having been originally written for two Christmas annuals which were issued some years back...." These the present editors have not been able to identify and have therefore given the story the date of its first independent publication.

983.   F. HOPKINSON SMITH

Francis Hopkinson Smith was born in Baltimore, Maryland, October 23, 1838, the great-grandson of Francis Hopkinson. He prepared for Princeton College but did not enter, owing to financial difficulties, and began as a mechanical engineer, learning his profession while working for an iron manufacturing firm in New York. He then became a bridge constructor, building, among other things, the Race Rock Lighthouse and the foundations for the Statue of Liberty in New York Harbor. While engaged in the practice of engineering he also developed his second talent, for painting, in which art he was practically self-taught, having had only the instruction which he received from a painter in Baltimore. Smith did not write for publication until he was forty-five years of age. He was preparing a series of sketches and was asked to provide

text for them. He wrote in consequence "The Church of San Pablo-Seville," which appeared later in his volume *Well-Worn Roads of Spain and Holland* (1886), his first book. This was followed by *A White Umbrella in Mexico* (1889), and then, in 1891, he wrote his masterpiece, *Colonel Carter of Cartersville*. This novelette proved so popular that he wrote a sequel entitled *Colonel Carter's Christmas* (1903). From 1891 until his death on April 8, 1915, Smith published a long series of novels, novelettes, and short stories. Probably the most enduring of his novels will be *Tom Grogan* (1896), *The Fortunes of Oliver Horn* (1902), and *The Tides of Barnegat* (1906). Among his shorter fiction such a novelette as *The Romance of an Old-Fashioned Gentleman* (1897), or his stories dealing with the mountaineers in Kentucky, under the general title of *No Respecter of Persons*, or his frankly romantic fiction, to be found in the volume *The Veiled Lady of Stamboul* (1907), from which the story "Miss Jennings's Companion" has been selected for the present volume, are most characteristic. Smith was widely popular as a reader of his own fiction, and "Miss Jennings's Companion" was among his favorite readings.

XIV. THE MODERN ROMANTIC DRAMA

989   DAVID BELASCO

David Belasco was born in San Francisco, July 25, 1853, and grew up in the theatre. His career as director, author, adapter, and producer of plays since he went to New York in 1882 has brought him into a variety of adventures too complex to be recorded here. As a producer he has become noted for the splendor of his productions, his invention of new stage devices, and for the independence of his attitude. He has written plays since he was twelve years of age, but the best period of his career was that in which he collaborated with John Luther Long in writing *Madame Butterfly* (1900), *The Darling of the Gods* (1902), and *Adrea* (1904). Few of his plays have been printed. A volume, entitled *Six Plays: Madame Butterfly, Du Barry, The Darling of the Gods, Adrea, The Girl of the Golden*

West, and *The Return of Peter Grimm*, appeared in 1928. *The Life of David Belasco*, by William Winter (2v., 1918) is the standard biography.

989.   JOHN LUTHER LONG

John Luther Long was born in Pennsylvania in 1861. He was admitted to the bar and practised law in Philadelphia. He published several volumes of short stories, beginning with *Madame Butterfly* (1898), which first appeared in the *Century* in 1897. In addition to the plays written with David Belasco, he was the author of *The Dragon Fly* (1905), *Dolce* (1907), *Kassa* (1910), *Crowns* (1923) and others. Long died in 1927. A writer of great imaginative power, Long hardly achieved proper recognition in a period turning toward realism.

XV. THE MODERN ESSAY AND BIOGRAPHY

999. SAMUEL LANGHORNE CLEMENS (MARK TWAIN)

Samuel Langhorne Clemens was born at Florida, Missouri, November 30, 1835. In 1839 the family moved to Hannibal, a small town on the Mississippi River, and Clemens grew up among conditions reflected in *Tom Sawyer* (1876) and *Huckleberry Finn* (1884). He learned the trade of printing on his brother Orion's paper and from 1853 to 1857 wandered as a journeyman printer through St. Louis, New York, Philadelphia, Washington, and Cincin-

nati. Going to New Orleans with the idea of a South American voyage, he became instead a pilot on the Mississippi River. Here he met an old pilot, Isaiah Sellers, who used the pen name of "Mark Twain," derived from the custom of heaving the lead, and he parodied Sellers' work so well that the latter ceased writing. Clemens took the name afterwards, he explains, as a kind of reparation. In 1861 he joined Orion in Nevada, and then went to California, where he helped Bret Harte on *The Californian*. Here he published "The Jumping Frog," which he sent to *The Saturday Press* and which, when published in book form with other sketches in 1866, established his reputation. In June, 1867, he set out on his trip around the world, which resulted in *Innocents Abroad* (1869). For a time he was editor of the Buffalo *Express*, then lived in Hartford, Conn., from 1871 to 1891, becoming one of the most popular of American lecturers. Next came *Roughing It* (1872); *The Gilded Age* (1873), a novel written with Charles Dudley Warner; *A Tramp Abroad* (1880), written after another trip to Europe; *The Prince and the Pauper* (1882); and *Life on the Mississippi* (1883), part of which had appeared in 1875 in the *Atlantic Monthly* as "Old Times on the Mississippi." From 1891 to 1900 Clemens spent largely in Europe, from 1900 to 1908 he was in New York City, and from 1908 to his death, April 21, 1910, he lived at Redding, Connecticut. His life was an intensely active one, and his ventures in the publishing field, where he made and lost a fortune, and in which, like Scott, he paid the debts of his firm, can only be indicated. Among his later works, *Pudd'nhead Wilson* (1894), *Joan of Arc* (1896), *Following the Equator* (1897), and his volumes of short stories like *The Man that Corrupted Hadleyburg* (1900), are the most significant.

Of special interest is his *Autobiography*, of which instalments were published in *The North American Review* from September, 1906, to December, 1907, but which appeared first complete in two volumes in 1924. Clemens had begun to write this in 1870, but it was not until 1897, when he was in Vienna, that real composition commenced. Of this portion, A. B. Paine says in his Introduction, "his memory was fresh and eager and in none of his work is there greater charm." Clemens did not arrange his material chronologically, but wrote or dictated as his fancy led him. In this anthology, however, the selections have been arranged so that the events proceed in historical order.

The "Authorized Uniform Edition" of Mark Twain's Writings in 25v., 1899–1910, is the standard. For bibliography, see Merle Johnson, *A Bibliography of the Work of Mark Twain* (1910), and also *Mark Twain*, by Archibald Henderson (1911). Even more useful is the bibliography in the standard life, *Mark Twain, A Biography*, by Albert Bigelow Paine, 3v., 1912. This contains a chronological list from 1851 to 1910. An abridgement of this biography, *A Short Life of Mark Twain*, appeared in 1920. A remarkable personal impression is given in *My Mark Twain*, by W. D. Howells (1910).

1012. WILLIAM DEAN HOWELLS

For biography, see above, p. N 35. *Criticism and Fiction* is made up of contributions to "The Editor's Study," published in *Harper's Magazine* from 1886 to 1891.

1020. HENRY JAMES

For biography, see above, p. N 39.

1030. JOHN BURROUGHS

John Burroughs was born at Roxbury, New York, April 3, 1837, attended country schools until 1854, and taught school for seven years. He had written for publication as early as 1856, but it was through the writing of the "Back Country" series of articles for the New York *Leader* in 1861, and his study of birds that he found his life work. From 1864 to 1872 he served in the Treasury Department at Washington, where he met Whitman (see *Notes on Walt Whitman as Poet and Person*, 1867). In 1871 *Wake Robin* was published, and in 1874 he went to live in Riverby, at West Park on the Hudson. European visits and extended travel in the United States provided him with inspiration for his essays, which have appeared in a growing list of volumes, dealing with birds, animals, and other phases of nature study, literary criticism, the relation of religion and science, and kindred topics. Among the most significant, after *Wake Robin*, are *Birds and Poets* (1877), from which the selection has been made for this anthology, *Locusts and Wild Honey* (1879), *Fresh Fields* (1884), *The Ways of Nature* (1905), *Field and Study* (1919), *Accepting the Universe* (1920).

For biography see *My Boyhood*, by John Burroughs (1923), *John Burroughs, Boy and Man*, by Clara Barrus (1922), and *Life and Letters of John Burroughs* (2v., 1925), by Clara Barrus. Dr. Barrus, who was his literary secretary, has also edited *The Heart of Burroughs' Journals* (1928).

1037. WOODROW WILSON

Woodrow Wilson was born in Staunton, Virginia, December 28, 1856. His early life was spent in Augusta, Georgia, and Columbia, South Carolina, and after one year at Davidson College, North Carolina, he entered Princeton College and graduated in 1879, proceeding to his degree of LL.B. at the University of Virginia in 1882. He practised law only a short time, taking graduate courses at Johns Hopkins and teaching successively at Bryn Mawr College, Wesleyan University, and Princeton University. In 1902 he became President of Princeton and in 1911 Governor of New Jersey. On March 4, 1913, he was inaugurated President of the United States, being re-elected in 1916. Any discussion of his career as the leader of liberal thought in domestic and foreign policies would be out of place here. After the triumph of the Allies, he endeavored to secure the incorporation of his ideals of democracy in the League of Nations, and after being victorious at Paris, returned to find the opponents of his policies in Congress stronger than he. In an effort to carry his message to the people he broke down and, after a lingering illness, died February 3, 1924. President Wilson's achievement as a writer of literature includes his volumes of history, such as *Division and Reunion, 1829–1889* (1893), *A History of the American People* (1902); his essays containing his literary and political philosophy and his study of history as an art, contained in *An Old Master and Other Political Essays* (1893) and *Mere Literature and Other Essays* (1896); his addresses and state papers, such as his first Inaugural Address, his address to Congress, January 8, 1918 (known as the "Fourteen Points Speech"), or that delivered December 2, 1918, before leaving for Paris.

These are found most conveniently in *Selected Literary and Political Papers and Addresses of Woodrow Wilson* (3v., 1926). For bibliography see Harry Clemons, *An Essay Toward a Bibliography of the Published Writings and Addresses of Woodrow Wilson, 1875–1910* (1913); continued under similar title for the period 1910–1917, by George D. Brown (1917), and for the period 1917–1921 by Howard S. Leach (1922), all issued under the auspices of the Library of Princeton University. The standard biography is *Woodrow Wilson : Life and Letters*, by Ray Stannard Baker (Vols. I and II, 1927— other volumes to follow). Among other biographies, the most helpful are *Woodrow Wilson and His Work*, by W. E. Dodd (1922), *Woodrow Wilson as I Knew Him*, by Joseph P. Tumulty (1921), *Eight Years with Wilson's Cabinet*, by David F. Houston (2v., 1926).

1044.   HENRY ADAMS

Henry Brooks Adams was born in Boston, February 16, 1838, the grandson of John Quincy Adams and great-grandson of John Adams, second President of the United States. After graduating from Harvard he went to Berlin for graduate study in civil law, later travelling in Italy and France. On his return he acted as secretary to his father, Charles Francis Adams, first in Washington and later in England. In 1869 he became assistant professor of History at Harvard and at the same time conducted the *North American Review*. Although giving up teaching after a few years, he retained his interest in historical study, and in 1889 published the first two volumes of his *History of the United States*. In nine volumes he covered the administrations of Jefferson and Madison. After extensive travel in the Orient with La Farge the artist) and in Europe and America he returned to the writing of history with *Mont-Saint-Michel and Chartres*, a remarkable interpretation of the spiritual forces that made the twelfth century a genuine renaissance. The work was privately printed in 1904 and issued to the public in 1913. *The Education of Henry Adams* (1906) is practically an autobiography, rich in background and personal philosophy. Adams made two ventures into fiction, *Democracy: An American Novel* (1880), and *Esther* (1884). He died March 27, 1918. For a brief biography see the *D.A.B.* The *Education* may be supple-

mented by *A Cycle of Adams Letters*, edited by W. C. Ford (2v., 1920).

1057.   AGNES REPPLIER

Agnes Repplier was born in Philadelphia, April 1, 1858, and was educated at the Convent of the Sacred Heart, at Torresdale, Pennsylvania. She has received the degree of Litt.D. from the University of Pennsylvania in 1902, Yale in 1925, and Columbia in 1927. Her first volume of essays, *Books and Men*, appeared in 1888. Since then she has been a constant contributor to magazines, and has published fourteen volumes of familiar and critical essays, of which *Points of View* (1891); *In the Dozy Hours* (1894); *Compromises* (1904), from which "The Gayety of Life" has been selected for this anthology; *Americans and Others* (1912); *Counter Currents* (1916); and *Points of Friction* (1920) are the best. Her autobiographical books, *In Our Convent Days* (1905) or *A Happy Half Century* (1908), are charming, and her historical writing, such as *Père Marquette* (1929), is sound as well as entertaining.

1059.   SAMUEL McCHORD CROTHERS

Samuel McChord Crothers was born in Oswego, Illinois, June 7, 1857. He graduated from Wittenberg College in 1873, from Princeton in 1874, from the Union Theological Seminary in 1877, and the Harvard Divinity School in 1882. Harvard also awarded him the degree of D.D. in 1899, and he received the Litt.D. from St. Lawrence University in 1904, Princeton in 1909, and Western Reserve in 1923. He was ordained in the Presbyterian ministry in 1877 and entered the Unitarian ministry in 1882. His charges included churches at Brattleboro, Vermont, and St. Paul, and he was rector of the First Church, Cambridge, Mass., from 1894 until his death, November 9, 1927. He was one of the most charming lecturers of his day and many of his essays were delivered first by him in that form. The best of these are included in the collections known as *The Gentle Reader* (1903), *The Pardoner's Wallet* (1906), *Among Friends* (1910), *Humanly Speaking* (1912), *The Pleasures of an Absentee Landlord* (1916), *The Dame School of Experience* (1920), *The Cheerful Giver* (1923), and *The Thought Broker* (1928). *Oliver Wendell Holmes and His Fellow Boarders* (1909) is a biographical sketch of a man whose successor Dr. Crothers in a sense became. See also his *Ralph Waldo Emerson, How to Know Him* (1920).

1066.   WILLIAM CRARY BROWNELL

William Crary Brownell was born in New York City, August 30, 1851. He received from Amherst College the degree of A.B. in 1871, Litt.D. in 1896, and LL.D. in 1916. Columbia University awarded him a Litt.D. in 1910. He was on the staff of *The Nation* from 1879 to 1881 and for thirty-nine years was literary advisor for Charles Scribner's Sons. His first book of essays, *French Traits, an Essay in Comparative Criticism* (1889), revealed him as a critic of distinction, and his subsequent volumes, *French Art, Classic and Contemporary Painting and Sculpture* (1892); *Newport* (1896); *Victorian Prose Masters* (1901); *American Prose Masters* (1914); *Criticism* (1914); *Standards* (1917); and *The Genius of Style* (1924), won him a secure place among the foremost critics of America. Brownell died July 22, 1928. An appreciative essay by Edith Wharton appeared in *Scribner's Magazine*, LXXXIV (Nov. 1928), 596–602.

1075. *Lowell's essay on Thoreau.* Printed above, pp. 628–634.

1076. THEODORE ROOSEVELT

Theodore Roosevelt was born in New York, October 27, 1858, of an old Knickerbocker family. After graduating from Harvard he sat in the New York legislature and served as President of the New York Police Board, distinguishing himself in both places by his vigorous advocacy of reform. In 1897 he became Assistant Secretary of the Navy. On the outbreak of the Spanish American War he organized the Rough Riders and won high repute by his brilliant command. In 1898 he was elected Governor of New York and in 1900 became Vice-President of the United States. Upon the assassination of President McKinley in 1901 he succeeded to the Presidency, and upon the completion of his term was elected to the office in 1904. After retiring from the White House he went on an extensive hunting trip in Africa and afterwards became a contributing editor of the *Outlook*. When the United States entered the World War he offered his services to the army, but the offer was declined. His death, which occurred January 6, 1919, was hastened by an infection acquired on his trip in the South American jungle and by grief over the loss of a son killed in the war.

In the intervals of a crowded life he found time to write voluminously on hunting, ranching, history, natural history, biography, and politics. He read widely and the range of his interests was unlimited. He wrote with insight on topics as far apart as the old Irish sagas and the history of the British navy. Among his more important works are *The Naval War of 1812* (1882), *Hunting Trips of a Ranchman* (1885), *The Winning of the West* (4v., 1889–96), *African Game Trails* (1910), and his *Autobiography* (1913). His essays and addresses fill a number of volumes, among them *American Ideals* (1897), *The Strenuous Life* (1900), *African and European Addresses* (1910), and *History as Literature and Other Essays* (1913).

The standard edition of his works is the National Edition, 20v., 1926. *A Bibliography of Theodore Roosevelt* by John Hall Wheelock appeared in 1920. For biography see the lives by Jacob A. Riis (1904), W. R. Thayer (1919), W. D. Lewis (1919), J. B. Bishop (2v., 1920), and Lord Charnwood (1923). These should be supplemented by *Selections from the Correspondence of Theodore Roosevelt and Henry Cabot Lodge, 1884–1918* (2v., 1925) and the charming *Letters to his Children* (1919). On his writings see "Roosevelt as a Man of Letters" in H. A. Beers' *Four Americans* (1919).

The essay here printed was delivered as a presidential address before the American Historical Association in December, 1912.

1080. *The Gettysburg Speech and the Second Inaugural.* See above, pp. 744 and 745.

1081. *Tyrtæuses and Körners.* Tyrtæus, a Greek schoolmaster (seventh cent., B. C.), who by his songs inspired the Spartans to victory. Karl Theodore Körner (1791–1813), a German lyric poet, playwright, and soldier.

1085. GEORGE SANTAYANA

George Santayana was born in Madrid, Spain, December 16, 1863, and came to the United States in 1872. He received the degrees of A.B. (1886) and Ph.D. (1889) from Harvard University, and Litt.D. from the University of Wisconsin in 1911. He was appointed instructor in philosophy at Harvard in 1889, becoming assistant professor in 1898 and professor in 1907, resigning in 1911. Since then he has lived mainly abroad. In 1894 he published his *Sonnets and Other Poems*, followed by *The Sense of Beauty* (1896), *Lucifer, a Theological Tragedy* (1898), *Interpretations of Poetry and Religion* (1900), *The Hermit of Carvel and Other Poems* (1901), *The Life of Reason*, (5v., 1905–6, rev. 1922 and 1928), *Three Philosophical Poets* (1910), *Sonnets and Other Verses* (1906), *Winds of Doctrine* (1914), *Character and Opinion in the United States* (1920), from which the present selection has been made, *Soliloquies in England and Later Soliloquies* (1922); *Scepticism and Animal Faith, Introduction to a System to Philosophy* (1923), *Dialogues in Limbo* (1925); *Platonism and the Spiritual Life* (1927); *The Realm of Essence* (1928). His poetry is best read in the selected edition, *Poems* (1923). For criticism, see J. B. Rittenhouse, *The Younger American Poets* (1904), and Carl Van Doren, *Many Minds* (1924).

1091. STUART PRATT SHERMAN

Stuart Pratt Sherman was born at Anita, Iowa, October 1, 1881. He graduated from Williams College in 1903 and received his Ph.D. from Harvard in 1906. After a year as instructor at Northwestern University, he became associate in English at the University of Illinois in 1907, and professor in 1911, resigning in 1924 to become literary editor of the New York *Herald Tribune*, which position he held until his death by drowning, on August 21, 1926. Sherman's essays, which are included in the volumes *On Contemporary Literature* (1917), *Americans* (1922), *The Genius of America* (1923), *My Dear Cornelia* (1924), and *Points of View* (1924), gave him a leading position among the younger generation of critics of liberal tendencies. He was one of the editors of the *Cambridge History of American Literature*, and in his untimely death American scholarship lost one of its most promising contributors. For biography see *The Life and Letters of Stuart P. Sherman* by Jacob Zeitlin and Homer Woodbridge (1929). "The Genius of America" first appeared in the *Atlantic Monthly*, Jan. 1921, under the title "The National Genius."

1098. GAMALIEL BRADFORD

Gamaliel Bradford was born in Boston, Massachusetts, October 9, 1863. He began publication with his *Types of American Character* (1895), but his most significant work came with his *Lee, the American* (1912), followed by his *Confederate Portraits* (1914), *Union Portraits* (1916), *Portraits of Women* (1916), *Portraits o American Women* (1919), *Shadow Verses* (1920), *American Portraits, 1875–1900* (1922), *Damaged Souls* (1923), from which the biography of Paine has been selected, *Bare Souls* (1924), *Wives* (1925), *As God Made Them* (1929).

1100. *Common Sense* and *The Crisis*. See above, pp. 143–156.

1106. BLISS PERRY

Bliss Perry was born at Williamstown, Massachusetts, November 25, 1860. Graduating at Williams College in 1881, he studied at Berlin and Strassburg and has received honorary degrees from Princeton, Virginia, Harvard, Pennsylvania, and other universities. He has

been Professor of English at Williams College (1886–1893), at Princeton (1893–1900), and since 1907 at Harvard. From 1899 to 1909 he was editor of the *Atlantic Monthly*. He has received many honors and is a Fellow of the Royal Society of Literature and a member of the American Academy of Arts and Letters. He began authorship with *The Broughton House* (1890) and *Salem Kittredge and Other Stories* (1894), but soon commenced a series of biographies and critical studies which combine sound scholarship with unusual charm. Among these perhaps the most significant are *The Study of Prose Fiction* (1902); *Walt Whitman* (1906); *Park St. Papers* (1909); *The American Mind* (1912); *Carlyle, How to Know Him* (1915); *The American Spirit in Literature* (1918); *A Study of Poetry* (1920); and *The Praise of Folly* (1923), from which the selection has been made for this anthology.

1112. *The American Scholar.* For the full text of Emerson's address, see above, pp. 541–549.

1115. CARL SANDBURG

Carl Sandburg was born at Galesburg, Illinois, January 6, 1878. He was educated at Lombard College, Illinois, was Secretary to the Mayor of Milwaukee, 1910–1912, and has been connected with various newspapers and magazines, including the Chicago *Daily News*. During the Spanish War he was a private in the Sixth Illinois Volunteers, seeing service in Porto Rico. His writings include *Chicago Poems* (1915), *Corn Huskers* (1918), *Smoke and Steel* (1920), *Slabs of the Sunburnt West* (1922), *Rootabaga Stories* (1922), *Abraham Lincoln: the Prairie Years* (2v., 1926), and *Good Morning, America* (1928).

XVI. THE CONTEMPORARY SHORT STORY

1123. MARY WILKINS FREEMAN

Mary Wilkins was born in Randolph, Massachusetts, in 1862, of Puritan ancestry. She married Dr. Charles M. Freeman in 1902, and has lived since then in Metuchen, New Jersey. She began publication with her short stories of New England life, of which the best representatives are *A Humble Romance and Other Stories* (1887), from which the selection for the present anthology has been made; and *A New England Nun and Other Stories* (1891). Her novelettes, like *Jane Field* (1892), and her novels, like *Pembroke* (1894), while faithfully realistic, hardly rise to the level of her earliest short stories. In *The Wind in the Rosebush* (1903) appeared several effective stories of the supernatural, and in *Edgewater People* (1918) Mrs. Freeman presented stories of New England character almost if not quite as significant as those in her earlier volumes.

1131. JAMES LANE ALLEN

James Lane Allen was born near Lexington, Kentucky, December 21, 1849. He graduated in 1872 at the University of Kentucky, known before his time and since as Transylvania University, and entered Johns Hopkins University, intending to study comparative philology. Financial difficulties forced him, however, into teaching at the Transylvania Academy and Bethany College, West Virginia, and later to become headmaster of the Allen Academy in Lexington. His critical articles began to appear in *The Critic* in 1882, and he left Kentucky for New York City, determined to make his living by writing. The struggle was hard and he was on the point of resuming his teaching when a series of articles on Kentucky life was accepted by the New York *Evening Post* and he returned temporarily to Kentucky to gather material. Other sketches appeared in *Harper's Magazine* and the *Century*, later collected under the title of *The Blue Grass Region of Kentucky*, in 1892. In the meantime the first volume of his short stories had been published, *Flute and Violin* (1891), containing some of his finest studies of Kentucky character. From this volume "Two Gentlemen of Kentucky" has been selected for this anthology. Then came his idyllic stories, *A Kentucky Cardinal* (1894) and *Aftermath* (1895); *The Choir Invisible* (1897), laid in Kentucky in 1795, a revision of his earlier *John Gray*; his realistic studies, the best of which are *The Reign of Law* (1900) and *The Mettle of the Pasture* (1903); and his uncompleted trilogy, *The Bride of the Mistletoe* (1909) and *The Doctor's Christmas Eve* (1910). His later stories are of less significance, although *The Alabaster Box* (1923) and *The Landmark* (1925), a collection of short stories, have some of his distinctive qualities, including the distinguished style of his best period. Allen lived a retired life in New York City and died February 18, 1925.

For biography, see J. W. Townsend, *James Lane Allen* (1927), a sketch, consisting mainly of letters. No adequate life has appeared.

1143. HAMLIN GARLAND

Hamlin Garland was born September 16, 1860, on a farm near West Salem, Wisconsin. In 1869 the family moved into the untamed prairie of Mitchell County, Iowa, where he became familiar with pioneer life and took full share in the labor and drudgery of a frontier farm. He was graduated from Cedar Valley Seminary, Osage, Iowa, in 1881; and after two years spent in tramping and teaching, he took up a claim in Dakota in 1883. To further prepare himself for teaching he went to Boston in 1884, where he became a pupil and then a teacher in the Boston School of Oratory and taught American and English literature to private classes. A visit to his people in Dakota, Iowa, and Wisconsin in 1887 led to his first stories and a determination to tell the truth about farm life. Under the guidance of the Boston *Evening Transcript*, he was given a hearing and further cheered and encouraged by W. D. Howells. These stories, with others, were included in his initial volume, *Main-Travelled Roads* (1890), generally recognized as an artistic and intellectual success and containing interpretations of Middle Western rural types that can be ranked with the best provincial literature in America. "The Return of a Private" has been chosen from these for this anthology. Two other volumes of short stories, *Prairie Folks* (1892) and *Other Main-Travelled Roads* (1892), followed his decision to abandon teaching for writing. The finest of the novels came with *Rose of Dutcher's Coolly* (1895), largely an autobiographical account. The best of the more romantic novels of the Far West, the second period of his work, are *The Captain of the Gray Horse*

Troop (1902) and *Cavanagh, Forest Ranger* (1909). In 1917 with *A Son of the Middle Border* Garland resumed the themes and success of his first realistic phase. Through the autobiographic methods of this and *A Daughter of the Middle Border* (1921), the significance of this latest and third period is equal to the first. After a brief transference of his literary headquarters to Chicago in 1893, he moved to New York, where he lives at the present time. He is a member of the American Academy of Arts and Letters.

1151. STEPHEN CRANE

Stephen Crane was born in Newark, New Jersey, November 1, 1871. He spent one year at Lafayette College, transferring in 1890 to Syracuse University, where he began newspaper work as correspondent for the New York *Tribune*. But his college career ended in 1891 and he had hard work in establishing himself as a writer, his uncompromising realism being ahead of its time. He published his first novel, *Maggie, a Girl of the Streets*, in 1893, under the name of "Johnson Smith," and it was not until *The Red Badge of Courage*, a story of the Civil War, an imaginative picture of the real feeling of the soldier in battle, appeared in 1895 that he became recognized, although Hamlin Garland and W. D. Howells had already encouraged him. In 1896 he was sent to Jacksonville by the Irving Bacheller syndicate, with $7,000 in gold, to report real war among the filibusters in Cuba. Here he was shipwrecked, and his health was permanently affected by exposure and, later, by his experiences in the Greco-Turkish war. For a time he lived at the Brede Place, in England, writing industriously and doing his best work in the field of the short story. His short stories appeared in various collections, such as *The Little Regiment* (1896), from which "A Mystery of Heroism" has been selected as representative of Crane's description of the psychology of war; or *The Open Boat and Other Tales of Adventure* (1898). His longer stories, *George's Mother* (1896), with its grim reality, or the amusing satire on the war correspondent, *Active Service* (1899), are hardly as significant. His verse, found in *War is Kind* (1899), is of uneven merit. Crane went to Cuba at the outbreak of the Spanish-American war as a reporter for the New York *World*. His last years were spent in England, but he died at Badenweiler, Germany, of tuberculosis, June 5, 1900, leaving *The O'Ruddy*, a burlesque romance, to be completed by Robert Barr.

A collected edition of Stephen Crane's works, in 12v., edited by Wilson Follett, was published in 1925–26. *Stephen Crane, A Bibliography*, by Vincent Starrett (1923), and *Stephen Crane, a Study in American Letters*, by Thomas Beer, with an introduction by Joseph Conrad (1923), give the best information in their respective fields.

1155. MARGARET DELAND

Margaretta Wade Campbell was born February 23, 1857, in Manchester, now a part of Allegheny, Pennsylvania, then an attractive small town. It is the origin of "Ashurst" and "Old Chester." In 1873 she entered a drawing class in the Cooper Institute, New York, becoming an instructor in design at the Girls' Normal College, now Hunter College, New York. Here she remained until 1880, when she married Lorin F. Deland, of Boston. During the Great War she was active in relief work in France. At present she lives at Cambridge, Massachusetts.

Mrs. Deland began her work in fiction with *John Ward Preacher* (1888), following this with her novels *Sidney* (1890), *Philip and his Wife* (1894), and her volumes of short stories, *Mr. Tommy Dove and Other Stories* (1893), *The Wisdom of Fools* (1897), *Old Chester Tales* (1898) and *Dr. Lavendar's People* (1903), from which "An Exceeding High Mountain" has been selected for the present anthology. This was the best period of Mrs. Deland's work, for in 1906 came her novel *The Awakening of Helena Richie*, and in 1911 its sequel, *The Iron Woman*. Her later books have not maintained this high level, although *Around Old Chester* (1915) contains some interesting short stories, her last novel, *The Kays* (1926), has one fine character study, and in *New Friends in Old Chester* (1924) at least one story, "Elliott's Katy," has the power of her best period.

1169. BOOTH TARKINGTON

(Newton) Booth Tarkington was born in Indianapolis, Indiana, July 29, 1869. He began his college work at Purdue University, but at the beginning of his Junior Year entered Princeton College, which awarded him the honorary degrees of A.M. in 1899 and Litt.D. in 1918. Tarkington was a member of the Indiana House of Representatives in 1902–1903. He is a member of the American Academy of Arts and Letters. According to Tarkington's autobiographical account, *The World Does Move* (1928), he spent some time in New York City struggling for recognition, then returned to Indianapolis. Recognition came first with the publication of "Monsieur Beaucaire" in *McClure's Magazine* for December, 1899, and January, 1900, and its appearance in book form during the latter year. In some ways Tarkington never surpassed this fine romance, which had also a stage success in the version in which Richard Mansfield played for several years. While "Monsieur Beaucaire" was going the rounds of the magazines, Tarkington had written *The Gentleman from Indiana* (1899), in which he turned from romance to the description of Indiana life. Since then Tarkington has written twenty-six novels or novelettes and seventeen plays. Probably the most significant of the fiction are *Penrod* (1914) and *Seventeen* (1916), studies of adolescence; *The Turmoil* (1915), *The Magnificent Ambersons*, which won the Pulitzer Prize in 1918, *Alice Adams*, Pulitzer Prize winner in 1921, and *The Plutocrat* (1927), in which he pictures American types. His uncanny knowledge of feminine nature is shown in his volume of short stories, *Women* (1925). Tarkington's plays are not as well done as his fiction, although *The Man from Home* (1907–8) and *Clarence* (1919–1921) were popular successes. Tarkington thinks in his dramas in terms of the theatre; in his fiction he thinks more often in terms of real life.

For biography see *Booth Tarkington*, by Robert C. Holliday (1918), and, for bibliography of his fiction, *Booth Tarkington, a Sketch*, by Asa Don Dickinson (1926). For a complete list of his plays see *A History of the American Drama from the Civil War to the Present Day*, by A. H. Quinn (1927).

1185. EDITH WHARTON

Edith Newbold Jones was born in New York in 1862, educated privately, and married Edward Wharton of Boston in 1885. For many years her residence was at Lenox, Massachusetts, but of late years she has lived chiefly in France, where she was active in relief work during the Great War. Among other honors, she has received the degree of Litt.D. from Yale and was made an officer of the Legion of Honor. Mrs. Wharton's first volume of short stories, *The Greater Inclination*, was published in 1899, followed by a novelette, *The Touchstone* (1900), and another volume of short stories, *Crucial Instances* (1901). Her historical novel of Italy in the eighteenth century, *The Valley of Decision* (2v., 1902), and the novelette *Sanctuary* (1903), preceded one of the best of her collections of short fiction, *The Descent of Man* (1904), from which "The Lady's Maid's Bell" has been selected to represent the story of the supernatural, one of the fields in which Mrs. Wharton is supreme. In 1905 *The House of Mirth*, one of the outstanding novels of the century, appeared, and in 1907 *Madame de Trymes*, a subtle international study. A novel, *The Fruit of the Tree* (1907), and two volumes of short stories, *The Hermit and the Wild Woman* (1908) and *Men, Women, and Ghosts* (1910), were followed by *Ethan Frome* (1911), in which she revealed New England character with marvellous skill. *The Reef* (1912) and *The Custom of the Country* (1913), novels laid here and abroad, declined slightly in power, but in *Xingu and Other Stories* (1916), Mrs. Wharton showed that she was still the best representative of the short story dealing with social values. "Autre Temps," selected for this anthology, is a brilliant exposition of the truth that society will not reconstruct its social judgments. Mrs. Wharton's war experience was reflected in her descriptive work, *Fighting France* (1917), the short story, *The Marne* (1918), and her novel *A Son at the Front* (1923). Meanwhile in 1920 one of her greatest novels, *The Age of Innocence*, had appeared, and in *Old New York* (1924) she included four novelettes, of which *The Old Maid* is easily one of the finest of her productions. *Summer* (1917), *The Glimpses of the Moon* (1922), *The Mother's Recompense* (1925), and *Twilight Sleep* (1927), while far above the usual novel, are hardly up to her own high standard. Yet in *Here and Beyond* (1926), she included some of her best stories of the supernatural, and in *The Children* (1928), a study of divorce, she showed no slackening of her power. Among her critical and descriptive works, *French Ways and Their Meaning* (1919) and *The Writing of Fiction* (1925) are the most significant. For a critical study see *Edith Wharton*, by R. M. Lovett (1925).

1208. WILLIAM SYDNEY PORTER (O. HENRY)

William Sydney Porter (O. Henry) was born in Greensboro, Guilford County, North Carolina, September 11, 1862, and was educated by his aunt, Evelina Porter, in her private school in Greensboro. After some years as a clerk in his uncle's drug store, where he exercised his talent for drawing caricatures, he went to Texas in 1882, living first on a ranch and from 1884 to 1895 in Austin, making a living by various occupations from selling drugs to acting as draftsman in the General Land Office (1887–1891). In January, 1891, he became teller in the First National Bank of Austin, resigning in December, 1894. In 1896, the bank having failed, he was charged with embezzlement. Although he claimed to be innocent, he fled to Honduras, Central America, where he remained until, hearing his wife was dying, he returned to Austin in 1897 and on February, 1898, was convicted and remained in the Ohio Penitentiary at Columbus from 1898 to 1901. His first short story, "The Miracle of Lava Cañon," was published in 1898, but it was only after he entered prison that he began seriously to write short stories as distinguished from the humorous sketches of his columnist days. In 1901 he adopted the name "O. Henry" and soon went to New York, where success was rapid. In 1904 his first book, *Cabbages and Kings*, was published, a novel dealing largely with his South American adventures. In 1906 came *The Four Million*, short stories of New York City, and from that time until his death, June 5, 1910, two volumes yearly were issued. *Sixes and Sevens* (1911) and *Rolling Stones* (1913) appeared posthumously, and there are stories in *Waifs and Strays* (1917), which also includes a number of personal and critical appreciations.

The standard life is *O. Henry Biography*, by C. Alphonso Smith (1924). See also *O. Henry Papers*, with an index of his works (1924).

1210. WILLA SIBERT CATHER

Willa Sibert Cather was born in Winchester, Va., December 7, 1876. She graduated from the University of Nebraska in 1895, and received the degree of Litt.D. in 1917. From 1897 to 1901 she was connected with the Pittsburgh *Daily Leader*, and from 1906 to 1912 she was associate editor of *McClure's Magazine*. Miss Cather began her career of authorship in 1903 with a volume of verse, *April Twilights*, followed by a book of short stories, *The Troll Garden* (1905), from which the present selection, "The Sculptor's Funeral," is taken. *Alexander's Bridge* (1912), her first novel, a character study, was followed by novels dealing with the West, such as *O Pioneers* (1913), *My Antonia* (1918), and *A Lost Lady* (1923). Among her other significant stories were *The Song of the Lark* (1915), the story of an opera singer; *One of Ours* (1922), a story of the War, which won the Pulitzer Prize; *The Professor's House* (1925); and a brilliant picture of early Western civilization and the character of the early missionaries in *Death Comes for the Archbishop* (1927).

1217. ANNE DOUGLAS SEDGWICK

Anne Douglas Sedgwick was born at Englewood, New Jersey, March 28, 1873. Since 1882 she has lived in England or France and while in France studied painting for several years. In 1908 she married Basil de Selincourt. At present she lives at Far End, Kingham, Oxon., England. She began her work in fiction in 1898 with *The Dull Miss Archinard*, and has published fifteen novels and two volumes of short stories, besides a charming description of her girlhood, entitled *A Childhood in Brittany* (1918). Her novels are brilliant studies of national or international contrasts, such as *A Fountain Sealed* (1907), *Franklin Winslowe Kane* (1910), *Adrienne Toner* (1922), *The Little French Girl* (1924); or penetrating studies in the psychology of genius, such as *Tante* (1911), *The Encounter* (1914); or studies of the older and newer generations, such as *Dark Hester* (1929). *The Third Window* (1920) is a striking story of the supernatural.

1226. DOROTHY CANFIELD

Dorothea Frances Canfield was born in Lawrence, Kansas, February 17, 1879, daughter of James Hulme Canfield, well known in educational work, especially at Ohio State and Columbia Universities. She graduated from Ohio State University (1899) and took the degree of Ph.D. at Columbia in 1904. From 1902 to 1905 she was secretary of the Horace Mann School. In 1907 she married John R. Fisher of New York. It was shortly after this that she made her home at Arlington, Vermont, and grew to know the people described in her volume, *Hillsboro People*, from which "Portrait of a Philosopher" has been selected to represent her fiction. While she has done distinguished work in her novels, *The Bent Twig* (1915), *The Brimming Cup* (1921), and *Her Son's Wife* (1926), she has not surpassed the fine art of *Hillsboro People* or of *Home Fires in France* (1918), stories which reflected her three years' experience in war work abroad. Her skill in languages is shown in her translation of Papini's *Life of Christ* (1921).

1232. THEODORE DREISER

Theodore Dreiser was born in Terre Haute, Indiana, August 27, 1871. He was educated at Indiana University, and began newspaper work with the Chicago *Globe* in 1892. In 1893 he became dramatic editor and travelling correspondent for the St. Louis *Globe-Democrat*, joining the staff of the St. Louis *Republic* in 1894. From 1895 to 1898 he was editor of *Every Month*; then, after seven years spent in writing for the leading journals, he was made editor of *Smith's Magazine* in 1905 and managing editor of the *Broadway Magazine* in 1906. From 1907 to 1910 he was editor-in-chief of the Butterick publications. His first novel, *Sister Carrie*, appeared in 1900, to be followed in 1911 by *Jennie Gerhardt*; both attracted critical attention by their realism. His later novels, *The Financier* (1912), *The Titan* (1914), *The Genius* (1915), and *An American Tragedy* (1925), grew progressively less important on account of Dreiser's obsession that all details are of equal importance. At times in his shorter fiction, he writes more significant literature, as in *Chains* (1927), from which "Sanctuary" has been selected for this anthology. *A Traveller at Forty* (1913), and *A Book About Myself* (1922), give autobiographical accounts of Dreiser. *A Bibliography of the Writings of Theodore Dreiser*, by E. D. McDonald, was published in 1928. For biography, see *Theodore Dreiser*, by Burton Rascoe (1925).

1245. JOSEPH HERGESHEIMER

Joseph Hergesheimer was born in Philadelphia, February 15, 1880. He was educated in Friends' schools and at the Academy of Fine Arts in Philadelphia. His most important volumes of fiction are *The Lay Anthony* (1914), *Mountain Blood* (1915), *The Three Black Pennys* (1917), *Java Head* (1919), *Linda Condon* (1919), probably his best novel; *Steel* (1920), *Cytherea* (1922), *The Bright Shawl* (1922), *Balisande* (1924), *Tampico* (1926), and *Quiet Cities* (1928), from which "Charleston" has been selected for this anthology. Hergesheimer has also published several descriptive volumes, of which *San Cristobal de Habaña* (1920) is probably the best. *Swords and Roses* (1929), dealing with the South, is too ornate to be effective.

1256. WILBUR DANIEL STEELE

Wilbur Daniel Steele was born at Greensboro, North Carolina, March 17, 1886. After graduating from the University of Denver in 1907, he studied art for several years: at the Museum of Fine Arts, Boston, 1907–08, at the Académie Julian in Paris, 1908–09, and at the Art Students League, New York, 1909–10. His first publication was *Storm* in 1914. Since then he has published several novels, collections of short stories, and a book of one-act plays. His most important novels are: *The Isles of the Blest* (1924), *Taboo* (1925), and *Meat* (1928). His short stories have been issued in collections under the titles, *Land's End* (1918), *Urkey Island* (1926) (from which the story in the present anthology was selected), and *The Man Who Saw Through Heaven* (1927). A book of plays, *The Terrible Woman*, appeared in 1925. Steele won a special award from the O. Henry Prize Committee in 1921 for maintaining the highest degree of merit for three years among American short story writers. In 1925, he won the Harper Short Story Contest. He lives at Nantucket, Mass.

XVII. CONTEMPORARY POETRY

1268. LIZETTE WOODWORTH REESE

Lizette Woodworth Reese was born in Waverly, Baltimore County, Maryland, now a part of Baltimore, January 9, 1856, and educated in Baltimore. For many years, until she retired in 1921, she taught English in the Western High School of Baltimore. She took a leading part in women's organizations in that city, being one of the founders of the Woman's Literary Club of Baltimore.

Her first poem to be published, "The Deserted Home," appeared in the *Southern Magazine* in 1874. Miss Reese's first volume of verse, *A Branch of May* (1887), was reprinted in 1891 with additional poems as *A Handful of Lavender*. These additions were republished sepa-

rately in 1909 as *A Handful of Lavender*, and later reprints of both volumes preserve this distinction. Her later volumes are *A Quiet Road* (1896), *A Wayside Lute* (1909), *Spicewood* (1920), *Wild Cherry* (1923), *Selected Poems* (1926), and *Little Henrietta* (1927). An appreciation of Miss Reese's poetry by Jessie B. Rittenhouse appears as a "Foreword" to the 1920 reprint of *A Branch of May*, and a biographical and critical account by L. H. Wrenshall is included in Vol. X of the *Library of Southern Literature*.

1272. RICHARD HOVEY

Richard Hovey was born at Normal, Illinois, May 4, 1864, and graduated from Dartmouth

College in 1885. He entered the General Theological Seminary in New York but, abandoning the idea of a clerical profession, he became a newspaper man and an actor, and finally Professor of English Literature in Barnard College. Hovey died suddenly, February 24, 1900. His early verses, of which volumes had appeared in 1880, 1889, 1891, and 1893, were collected in *Along the Trail* (1898). His lyrics of the open road, written with Bliss Carman, appeared as *Songs from Vagabondia* (1894), *More Songs from Vagabondia* (1896), and *Last Songs from Vagabondia* (1900). His ambitious *Lancelot and Guenevere* was to have included nine poetic dramas, of which only five were published: *The Quest of Merlin* (1891), *The Marriage of Guenevere* (1895), *The Birth of Gallahad* (1898), *Taliesin, A Masque* (1900), and *The Holy Graal* (1900). His later lyrics were edited by Mrs. Hovey under the title of *To the End of the Trail* (1908).

1273. WILLIAM VAUGHN MOODY

William Vaughn Moody was born at Spencer, Indiana, July 8, 1869. He grew up in Albany, Indiana, and taught in Riverside Academy, New York, while preparing for Harvard College, from which he graduated in 1893. As he had completed the courses for the bachelor's degree in 1892, he spent the year in European travel and then proceeded to his master's degree in 1894. For two years he taught English at Harvard and then became a member of the English Department at the University of Chicago, teaching actively until 1902 and retaining a nominal connection thereafter. The remainder of his life was spent in writing and in travel. Moody died at Colorado Springs, October 17, 1910, the primary cause of his premature death being an attack of typhoid fever in 1908.

Moody's work is found best in *The Poems and Plays of William Vaughn Moody* (2v., 1912), with a valuable introduction, biographical and critical, by John M. Manly. These volumes include his verse dramas, *The Masque of Judgment* (1900) and *The Fire Bringer* (1904), the lyrics in *Poems* (1902), and the prose plays *The Great Divide* (1909) and *The Faith Healer* (1909, rev. 1910). For biography see also *Some Letters of William Vaughn Moody*, edited by Daniel E. Mason (1913). A life of Moody in three volumes is in preparation by his sister, Julia Moody Schmalz.

1278. GEORGE CABOT LODGE

George Cabot Lodge was born in Boston, October 10, 1873, and graduated from Harvard College in 1895. He spent the next three years in Europe, principally in Paris and Berlin, studying Romance philology and German drama. In 1898 his first volume, *A Song of the Wave*, appeared. In January of that year he became secretary to his father, Senator Henry Cabot Lodge, in Washington. On the out-

break of the Spanish War he entered the navy as a cadet on board the "Dixie," seeing service along the Cuban coast and in Porto Rico, and taking part in the capture of Ponce. He then returned to Washington and wrote several novels, which he destroyed. His verse drama *Cain* appeared in 1904, and *The Great Adventure* in 1905. Another verse drama, *Herakles*, was published in 1908. Lodge died August 21, 1909, of heart failure.

Lodge's work may be found most conveniently in *Poems and Dramas of George Cabot Lodge*, with introduction by Theodore Roosevelt (2v., 1911). These include the volumes already mentioned and, in addition, a posthumous volume, *The Soul's Inheritance and Other Poems*. For biography, see *The Life of George Cabot Lodge*, by Henry Adams (1911). An appreciative criticism by Edith Wharton, "Lodge as Man and Poet," appeared in *Scribner's Magazine*, XLVII (February, 1910), 263-9.

1279. EDWIN ARLINGTON ROBINSON

Edwin Arlington Robinson was born December 22, 1869, at Head Tide, Maine, whence his family moved to Gardiner when he was a child of about a year old. Gardiner is probably the origin of "Tilbury Town," so often the scene of his poetry. He entered Harvard College in 1891 but left in 1893 on account of his father's ill health. From 1905 to 1909 he occupied a position in the New York Custom House, to which he had been appointed by President Roosevelt. In 1922 he received a Litt.D. from Yale University. Since 1911 he has lived in New York or at the MacDowell Colony. Robinson's first volume of verse, *The Torrent and the Night Before*, was privately printed in 1896. Then came *The Children of the Night* (1897), *Captain Craig* (1902), and *The Town Down the River* (1910), but though they contained some of his most distinguished work, he had to wait for general recognition until *The Man Against the Sky* appeared in 1916. With *Merlin* (1917) he began his treatment of the Arthurian themes, doing even better work in *Lancelot* (1920) and challenging in *Tristram* (1927) comparison with any earlier rendering of this theme in English. Meanwhile, in 1920, *The Three Taverns*, a volume of narratives and dramatic lyrics, appeared, and a narrative poem, *Avon's Harvest* (1921). In 1923 his work up to this point was brought together in *Collected Poems*, which won the Pulitzer Prize for the year. Since then his verse has been largely narrative, in *Roman Bartholow* (1923), *The Man Who Died Twice* (1924), which also won the Pulitzer Prize, *Dionysus in Doubt* (1925), *Tristram* (1927), and *Cavender's House* (1929).

Robinson's poetry is now found best in the Collected Edition in five volumes (1927) or in the one-volume edition of 1929. *Sonnets 1899-1927* (1928) brought together in one volume eighty-two examples of the form in which Robinson has done such distinctive work. For a brilliant critical estimate of his work see *The Poetry of Edwin Arlington Robinson*, by Lloyd Morris, with a bibliography by W. Van R. Whitall (1923). For biographical and critical treatment see also *Edwin Arlington Robinson*, by B. R. Redman (1926).

1288. EDGAR LEE MASTERS

Edgar Lee Masters was born in Garnet, Kansas, August 23, 1869, of a pioneer family which had come from Virginia to Tennessee, thence to Illinois and Kansas, and then back to Illinois, where he grew up, in Petersburg and later in Lewiston. He attended Knox College for a year, studied law, and then went to Chicago. During this time he was writing plays in blank verse and prose, none of which, however, were successful. His first volumes of poems, which appeared in 1905, 1910, and 1912, were issued under pseudonyms. He then contributed a number of Spoon River poems to *Reedy's Mirror*, and they began to attract attention. They were published in book form in 1915 as *Spoon River Anthology*. His later volumes include *Songs and Satires*, from which "Simon Surnamed Peter" and "So We Grew Together" have been selected for this anthology. Among others of his volumes, perhaps the best is *The Great Valley* (1916). He has recently turned his attention to narrative verse and to the writing of dramatic poems like *Lee* (1926). Of more permanent value, perhaps, are his works in prose, such as *Children of the Market Place* (1923), a fine study of the character of Stephen A. Douglas.

1293.   EDWIN MARKHAM

Edwin Markham was born in Oregon City, Oregon, April 23, 1852, of pioneer parents. Early in his life he went to California, where he herded cattle and sheep. He was educated at Christian College, Santa Rosa, California, and studied law but did not practise. Some years spent in teaching and administrative work in the public school system of California culminated in the headmastership of the Tompkins Observation School at Oakland, California. In 1899 he resigned this position and moved to New York, prompted by the success of "The Man with the Hoe," written upon seeing J. F. Millet's painting. His principal work is included in *The Man with the Hoe and Other Poems* (1899), *Lincoln, and Other Poems* (1901), *The Shoes of Happiness and Other Poems* (1915), *Gates of Paradise* (1920), *California the Wonderful* (1924), and *The Ballad of the Gallowsbird* (1926).

1294. JOSEPHINE PRESTON PEABODY

Josephine Preston Peabody was born in Brooklyn, New York, May 30, 1874. At ten years of age, her father having died, she went to Dorchester, Massachusetts, and was educated at the Girls' Latin School of Boston, which she left before graduation in 1892. As early as 1888 she had written verse which was published, and while she was studying in Radcliffe College as a special student (1894-96) her poetry was appearing in the *Atlantic Monthly* and other leading magazines. At Radcliffe she came under the influence of her teacher, William Vaughn Moody. Her first book of verse, *The Wayfarers* (1898), was followed by *Fortune and Men's Eyes* (1900) and *Marlowe* (1901), verse dramas of distinction. Miss Peabody was a lecturer on poetry at Wellesley College from 1901 to 1903, a book of lyrics, *The Singing Leaves*, appearing in the latter year. In 1906 she married Lionel Marks, of the faculty of Harvard University. In 1910 her verse drama, *The Piper*, published in 1909, won the Stratford Prize Competition of £300 for the best poetic drama in English. It was produced July 26, 1910, and at once took its place as one of the finest verse plays in the language. Her later poetry, including a book of lyrics, *The Singing Man* (1911), and her verse dramas, *The Wolf of Gubbio* (1913) and *The Portrait of Mrs. W.* (1922), show her love of humanity and her protest against selfishness and oppression which made *The Piper* so notable. Mrs. Marks died December 4, 1922. For biography, see *The Diary and Letters of Josephine Preston Peabody*, edited by Christina H. Baker (1925). Her works are found most conveniently in the *Collected Poems* (1927) and the *Collected Plays* (1927).

1295. THOMAS AUGUSTINE DALY

Thomas Augustine Daly was born in Philadelphia, May 28, 1871. He studied at Villanova College and Fordham University, which, although his course was not completed, gave him an honorary M.A. in 1901 and Litt.D. in 1910. Daly joined the staff of the Philadelphia *Record* in 1891, became in 1898 the General Manager of the *Catholic Standard and Times*, and in 1915 Associate Editor of the Philadelphia *Evening Ledger*. He has lectured widely since 1905, being recognized as the foremost representative of the poetry of the immigrant. This popularity has somewhat obscured the lyric quality of his verse in normal English. His first volume was *Canzoni* (1906), followed by *Carmina* (1909), *Madrigali* (1912), *Songs of Wedlock* (1916), and *McAroni Ballads* (1919).

1297.   ROBERT FROST

Robert Frost was born in San Francisco, March 26, 1875, but grew up in the East. He was a student at Dartmouth for a few months in 1892, but he found college irksome and it was only after his marriage that he spent two years at Harvard from 1897 to 1899. Although he did not graduate, he has received several honorary degrees, including a L.H.D. from Yale in 1923. From 1900 to 1905 he was a farmer in Derry, New Hampshire. From 1905 until 1911 he taught English at Pinkerton Academy, and during the next year he was an instructor in psychology at the New Hampshire State Normal School. From 1911 to 1915 he spent in England, and here in 1913 he brought out his first volume, *A Boy's Will*, some of the poems having been written twenty years before. *North of Boston* (1914) also appeared first in London. These volumes were quickly reprinted in the United States, and in 1916 came *Mountain Interval*. In the same year Frost became Professor of English at Amherst College and has maintained a flexible relation with that college from 1916 to 1920, from 1923 to 1925, and since 1926. He was Poet in Residence at the University of Michigan during 1921–23 and Fellow in Letters, 1925–26. He has never lost his interest in farming, however, and his permanent residence is at South Shaftsbury, Vermont. He writes slowly, publishing no volume from 1916 until 1923, when *New Hampshire* won the Pulitzer Prize. His *Selected Poems* appeared in 1928, but Frost is best read in his individual volumes, of which the latest, *West Running Brook*, came in 1928. For a personal and critical account, see *Robert Frost, Original "Ordinary Man,"* by Sidney Cox (1929).

1309. PERCY MACKAYE

Percy (Wallace) MacKaye was born in New York City, March 16, 1875. After graduation from Harvard College in 1897, he spent two years in study in Europe, and then taught school, at the same time writing verse and plays. Since 1904 he has devoted himself entirely to writing, living at Cornish, New Hampshire. MacKaye has written over thirty dramatic works. Among these the most important are *Jeanne d'Arc* (1906), *Sappho and Phaon* (1907), *The Canterbury Pilgrims* (1903–1909), *The Scarecrow* (1908–1910), and his masques, *Saint Louis* (1914), *Caliban* (1916), and *The Evergreen Tree* (1917). His poems are found most conveniently in Vol. I of his *Poems and Plays* (2v., 1916). This contains the poems issued separately as *Poems* (1909, rev. 1915), *The Lincoln Centenary Ode* (1909), *Uriel and Other Poems* (1912), and *The Present Hour* (1914). Since the collected edition appeared, *Dogtown Common* (1921), a narrative of New England, has been published. See *Percy MacKaye, a Sketch of his Life with Bibliography of his Works*, prepared by him for his class at Harvard (1922). Among his latest publications, the most important is *Epoch, the Life of Steele MacKaye* (2v., 1927), a storehouse of information concerning the American theatre.

1315. 90. *The kindly keen*. The reference is to Edwin Arlington Robinson.

1316. 193. *Gloucester moors*. See p. 1277. 201. "*Before the solemn bronze Saint-Gaudens made*." The line is from Moody's *Ode in Time of Hesitation*, printed above, p. 1273.

1317. 228. *Michaelis*. The central character in Moody's *The Faith Healer*.

1317. THEODOSIA GARRISON

Theodosia Pickering was born in Newark, New Jersey, in 1874, and educated in the private schools of Newark. Her first husband was Joseph Garrison, of Newark, whom she married in 1898, and she has retained his surname in her published work. Since 1911 she has been in private life Mrs. Frederic J. Faulks. Her first volume of poetry, *The Joy o' Life*, was published in 1909, followed by *Earth Cry and Other Poems* (1910), *The Dreamers* (1917), and *As The Larks Rise* (1921). Mrs. Garrison has touched with distinction the notes of patriotism, of motherhood, and has written some of the best devotional poetry of the time.

1320. OLIVE TILFORD DARGAN

Olive Tilford was born in Grayson County, Kentucky, and was educated at the University of Nashville and Radcliffe College, Cambridge, Massachusetts. She taught school in Arkansas, Missouri, Texas, and in Canada until her marriage to Pegram Dargan. Since then she has lived in New York, Boston, and in the Carolinas, except for a period of foreign travel from 1910 to 1914. Mrs. Dargan began to publish in the field of the poetic drama, *Semiramis and Other Plays* appearing in 1904, *Lords and Lovers and Other Dramas* in 1906, and *The Mortal Gods and Other Plays* in 1912. Her lyric gift became apparent in *Path Flower and Other Poems* (1914), and in her sonnet sequence, *The Cycle's Rim* (1916), which won the prize offered by the Southern Society of New York for the best book by a Southern writer. Outside of "Path Flower," the selections are made from *Lute and Furrow* (1922), dealing with nature in the mountains, which she has also treated with great understanding in her short stories, *Highland Annals* (1925).

1324. JOHN G. NEIHARDT

John Gneisenau Neihardt was born near Sharpsburg, Illinois, January 8, 1881. He graduated from a course in science at Nebraska Normal College in 1897, and was awarded a Litt.D. by the University of Nebraska in 1917. He lived among the Omaha Indians from 1901 to 1907, studying their history and characteristics. In 1903 he was appointed Professor of Poetry in the University of Nebraska. Since 1926 he has been literary editor of the St. Louis *Post Despatch*. His first volume of verse, *The Divine Enchantment*, appeared in 1900, followed by eight volumes, most of which have been collected in *The Quest* (1916). His most significant work has been the epic recital of the conquest of the West, contained in *The Song of Hugh Glass* (1915), *The Song of Three Friends* (1919), which won the annual prize of the Poetry Society of America and from which the selection has been made for this anthology, and *The Song of the Indian Wars* (1925). These as well as his other poems are found best in *Collected Poems* (1926).

1329. THOMAS S. JONES, JR.

Thomas Samuel Jones, Jr., was born in Booneville, New York, November 6, 1882. He graduated from Cornell University in 1904 and was on the dramatic staff of the New York Times from 1904 to 1907. He became associate editor of The Pathfinder in 1911. His first volume of verse, The Path o' Dreams, appeared in 1905, followed by The Rose Jar (1906), From Quiet Valleys (1908), Interlude (1908), Ave Atque Vale (1909), From the Heart of the Hills (with Clinton Scollard, 1909), The Voice in the Silence (1911), Sonnets of the Cross (1922), Sonnets of the Saints (1925), and Six Sonnets (1926). One of the foremost sonnet writers of today, Mr. Jones has struck with rare distinction the note of regret for the vanished pagan beauty, with the recognition of a faith that conquered superstition.

1330. SARA TEASDALE

Sara Teasdale was born in St. Louis, Missouri, August 8, 1884, and educated in private schools in St. Louis. She married Ernst B. Filsinger of St. Louis, in 1914. Her first volume was Sonnets to Duse and Other Poems (1907), followed by Helen of Troy and Other Poems (1911), Rivers to the Sea (1915), Love Songs (1917), Flame and Shadow (1920), and Dark of the Moon (1926). Her prevailing note is that of the supremacy of love coupled with a doubt of its permanence. Her interest in the theme is reflected in her anthology, The Answering Voice, One Hundred Love Lyrics by Women (1917).

1331. AMY LOWELL

Amy Lowell was born in Brookline, Massachusetts, on February 9, 1874, and was educated in private schools. She received an honorary Litt.D. from Baylor University (1920) and held various lectureships, including the Francis Bergen Foundation at Yale in 1921. She died after a brief illness May 12, 1925. Miss Lowell's first volume of verse, A Dome of Many Colored Glass (1912), revealed her as a skilful painter of pictures such as "The Road to Avignon," which has been selected for this anthology. Sword Blades and Poppy Seeds (1914) hardly maintained this standard, but in Men, Women and Ghosts better work was done, especially in the regular metres or in poems like "Patterns," in which there is a real sense of rhythm. The weakest are the attempts at polyphonic prose. By this time Miss Lowell had become the champion of the so-called "New Poetry," and in 1917 she published her Tendencies in Modern American Poetry, which, like her own verse, is singularly uneven in its merit. In Con Grande's Castle (1918) she continued her "polyphonic prose" with no marked success and since then her volumes, especially the posthumous ones, What o' Clock (1925) and Ballads for Sale (1927), added little to her reputation. Her life of Keats (1925) was the subject, too, of

much dispute. The calmest critical judgment now recognizes that a large portion of her own work is transitory, just as the movement she headed is no longer to be treated as a very significant part of our literary history. For most readers The Selected Poems of Amy Lowell, edited by J. L. Lowes (1928), will prove sufficient.

1333. VACHEL LINDSAY

(Nicholas) Vachel Lindsay was born in Springfield, Illinois, November 10, 1879. He studied at Hiram College, Ohio, 1897–1900, the Chicago Art Institute, 1900–1903, and the New York School of Art, 1904–1905. He became a professional lecturer for Y. M. C. A. and Anti-Saloon activities from 1905 to 1910. In 1912 he walked from Illinois to Mexico, selling his verse and preaching the "Gospel of Beauty." Lindsay's first volume of verse, General William Booth Enters Heaven, was published in 1913. This was followed by The Congo and Other Poems (1914), from which "Abraham Lincoln" has been selected, The Chinese Nightingale and Other Poems (1917), and The Golden Whales of California (1920). His Collected Poems appeared in 1923, rev. 1925. Later volumes include Going to the Sun (1923) and Going to the Stars (1926), The Candle and the Cabin (1926). Lindsay's prose includes Adventures while preaching the Gospel of Beauty (1914), Handy Guide for Beggars (1916), and The Golden Book of Springfield (1920).

1339. CARL SANDBURG

For biography, see above, p. N 46.

1341. BRIAN HOOKER

(William) Brian Hooker was born in New York City, November 2, 1880. He received the degrees of A.B. (1902) and A.M. (1904), from Yale University. He was assistant in English at Columbia University from 1903 to 1905, instructor in rhetoric at Yale from 1905 to 1909, and has been lecturer in Extension Teaching at Columbia since 1915. In 1917 he was literary editor of the New York Sun. His first book, The Right Man, appeared in 1908. In 1911 he wrote the libretto for the opera Mona, which won the Metropolitan Opera prize of $10,000 for the best American opera, the music being composed by Horatio Parker. It was produced March 14, 1912. His opera Fairyland won a prize in the American Opera Association competition in 1915. His lyrics were published in Poems (1915), from which the selections have been made for the present anthology. In 1923 he made a remarkable translation of Cyrano de Bergerac for Walter Hampden, which was at least in part responsible for the great success of the play. He lives at Farmington, Connecticut.

1342. ALAN SEEGER

Alan Seeger was born in New York City, June 22, 1888. He grew up in New York, but spent two years, from 1900 to 1902, in Mexico, and another year in California. Graduating from Harvard College in 1910, he lived for two years in New York City and then went to Paris. His love for France carried him into the Foreign Legion three weeks after war was declared in 1914. His experiences are told vividly in *Letters and Diary of Alan Seeger* (1917). The *Ode in Memory of the American Volunteers Fallen in France* was to have been read before the statue of Washington and Lafayette in Paris, on Decoration Day, May 30, 1916, but his leave came too late. On July 4, 1916, the Legion was ordered to attack the village of Belloy-en Santerre. The first section of the Third Battalion, to which Seeger belonged, was cut to pieces by the German machine guns, and he fell, dying before he knew of the ensuing victory. His *Poems* were first collected and published in 1916, with an introduction by William Archer.

1343.   JOYCE KILMER

(Alfred) Joyce Kilmer was born in New Brunswick, New Jersey, December 6, 1886. He graduated from Rutgers College in 1904 and also received an A.B. from Columbia University in 1906. Shortly after graduation he married Aline Murray, who has herself written verse of distinction. After teaching Latin at the Morristown High School, he became a journalist, was connected with a number of magazines, for a time was literary editor of *The Churchman*, and later a special writer for the New York *Times*. In August, 1913, he published "Trees" in *Poetry* and at once became widely known. In the same year he became a Roman Catholic, and the spiritual struggle through which he went found its record in a number of devotional poems, of which "Gates and Doors" is an example. In May, 1917, he enlisted in the Seventh Regiment of New York, being transferred later to the 165th Infantry, made up of the old "69th" of New York, the so-called "fighting Irish regiment." While in France he became a sergeant. In the five days battle for the hills near the Ourcq River, he volunteered to establish the location of some German machine guns which were doing great damage. When the battalion later reached the spot, Kilmer was found dead, July 30, 1918.

Kilmer's works and biography are found best in *Joyce Kilmer, Edited with a Memoir*, by R. C. Holliday (1918). Vol. I contains the memoir and the poems; Vol. II, Kilmer's prose, including his critical essays and his letters. These include his earlier volumes, such as *Trees and Other Poems* (1914) and *Main Street and Other Poems* (1917).

1345.   WILLIAM ALEXANDER PERCY

William Alexander Percy was born in Greenville, Mississippi, May 14, 1885. He graduated from the University of the South in 1904, and from the Law School of Harvard University in 1908, since when he has practiced law at Greenville. In 1916 he became a member of the Commission for Relief in Belgium, but on our entrance into the war he returned to America and became a First Lieutenant of Infantry in 1917. He served with the 37th Division of the A. E. F. in France, receiving a Captain's commission in 1919. His poetry appears in *Sappho in Levkas* (1915), from which a "chorus" has been selected; in *In April Once* (1920), which contains "Overtones," widely praised for its formal beauty; and in *Enzio's Kingdom* (1924). Percy is editor of the "Yale Series of Younger Poets."

1345.   JOHN HALL WHEELOCK

John Hall Wheelock was born at Far Rockaway, Long Island, New York, in 1886. He graduated from Harvard College in 1908, and studied at Göttingen University in 1909 and at Berlin University in 1910. Since 1911 he has been with Charles Scribner's Sons. His first volume of verse, *The Human Fantasy*, which appeared in 1911, was followed by *The Beloved Adventure* (1912), *Love and Liberation* (1913), *Alan Seeger, the Poet of the Foreign Legion* (1918). In *Dust and Light* (1919), from which "Earth" and "Be Born Again" have been selected, Wheelock took his place as one of the foremost poets of the day. *The Black Panther* (1923) hardly reached this level, but in *The Bright Doom* (1927) Wheelock celebrates the eternal progress of life with a profound searching yet with a note of final optimism.

1350.   DU BOSE HEYWARD

Du Bose Heyward was born in Charleston, South Carolina, August 31, 1885, and educated in the public schools of Charleston. He has been a leader in stimulating literary activity in his native state, being the organizer of the Poetry Society of South Carolina. His first volume of verse, *Carolina Chansons*, which he wrote in collaboration with Hervey Allen, appeared in 1922, and from that volume and from his *Skylines and Horizons* (1924) the present selections have been made. They portray vividly the indomitable spirit of both the patrician and the mountaineer of South Carolina. Heyward's novels have dealt with the negro in *Porgy* (1925), which was dramatized with great success by the author and his wife, Dorothy Heyward, in 1927; with the mountain whites in *Angel* (1926), and with both white and negro in *Mamba's Daughters* (1929). Heyward's sense of artistry makes him one of the most significant writers of the present day.

1350. The Last Crew.

The author supplies the following note: The "Fish-Boat" of the Confederate Navy, which exhaustive research indicates to have been the first submarine vessel to sink an enemy ship in time of war, was designed by Horace L. Hundley in 1863. This boat was twenty feet long, three and one-half feet wide, and five feet deep. Her motive power consisted of eight men whose duty it was to turn the crank of the propeller shaft by hand until the target had been reached. When this primitive craft was closed for diving there was only sufficient air to support life for half an hour. Since the torpedo was attached to the boat itself there was no chance of escape. The only hope was to reach and destroy the enemy vessel before the crew were suffocated or drowned.

Five successive volunteer crews died without reaching their objectives. But the sixth crew was successful in sinking the Federal blockading ship "Housatonic," their own craft being caught and crushed beneath the foundering vessel. These crews went to certain death in the night time, in such secrecy that it was often months before their own families knew the names of the men. And now, with the lapse of scarcely more than half a century, it has been possible to find the names of only sixteen of those who paid the price.

Because no nation of any time can point to a more inspiring example of self-sacrifice, and because now, in a country reunited and indissoluble, the traditions of both the North and the South are a common, glorious heritage, the poem, which presents the final episode in the drama, is written as a memorial to all who gave their lives in the venture.

1354. EDNA ST. VINCENT MILLAY
Edna St. Vincent Millay was born in Rockland, Maine, February 22, 1892. She graduated from Vassar College in 1917. In 1923 she married Eugen Jean Boissevain. She first attracted critical attention with her poem "Renascence," which became the title poem of the volume appearing in 1917, and which was followed by volumes of lyrics, *A Few Figs from Thistles* (1920), *Second April* (1921), *The Harp Weaver and Other Poems* (1923), and *The Buck in the Snow* (1928). Her work in lyric poetry is quite uneven, but her verse plays, *Aria da Capo*, performed at the Provincetown Playhouse (1919), *The Lamp and the Bell* (1921), and especially *The King's Henchman*, which formed the libretto for a grand opera, with music by Deems Taylor, in 1927, showed unusual power. Miss Millay lives at Auster City, New York.

1354. STEPHEN VINCENT BENÉT
Stephen Vincent Benét was born at Bethlehem, Pennsylvania, July 22, 1898. He took his A.B. at Yale in 1919 and A.M. in 1920. Before his graduation he had published *Five Men and Pompey* (1915) and *Young Adventure* (1918), but already in the latter he had shown his ability to write vigorous narrative verse in "The Hemp," selected for the present anthology. In *Heavens and Earth* (1920) and in *Tiger Joy* (1925), in which he reprinted some of his earlier verse, his excellence in writing the modern ballad, such as "The Ballad of William Sycamore," became more evident. His most important work in poetry was his long narrative, *John Brown's Body* (1928), in which he followed the Civil War, with sympathetic if uneven interpretations of the spirit of North and South. It won the Pulitzer Prize for poetry.

XVIII. THE CONTEMPORARY DRAMA

1359. EUGENE O'NEILL
Eugene Gladstone O'Neill was born in New York City, October 16, 1888. His first seven years were spent on tour with his father, James O'Neill, the romantic actor. Thirteen years followed at boarding schools and then one year at Princeton, which ended in suspension for an infraction of the rules. An engineering trip to the Spanish Honduras brought on fever and after some months with his father's company, he sailed for Buenos Aires (1910–11), from which he made a voyage to South Africa and then shipped as seaman on a tramp steamer to New York. His last experience on the sea came as an able seaman on the American line steamers "New York" and "Philadelphia." After acting with his father in the West, he became a reporter on the New London *Telegraph*, until incipient tuberculosis sent him in 1912 to a sanitarium in Connecticut. Soon being discharged, he began to write plays, and in 1914–15 attended Professor Baker's courses at Harvard. In the summer of 1916 he acted with the Provincetown Players, then experimenting in their theatre at Provincetown, Massachusetts, and when they opened in New York in the fall of 1916, his *Bound East for Cardiff* and other one-act plays were produced. Since then his career has been largely concerned with his playwriting, an analysis of which is given in the Introduction to The Contemporary Drama. Of late years he has lived at Ridgefield, Connecticut, or in Bermuda, taking a long trip to Europe and the East in 1928. He is now residing in France.

The standard edition of O'Neill's plays is *The Complete Works of Eugene O'Neill* (2v., 1924) a limited edition, which has been reprinted in 4v., 1925. Plays since 1925 are found in *The Great God Brown, The Fountain, etc.* (1926), *Marco Millions* (1927), *Lazarus Laughed* (1927), *A Play, Strange Interlude* (1928), *Dynamo* (1929). The best biography is *Eugene O'Neill, the Man and His Plays*, by B. H. Clark (1926, rev. 1929), containing bibliography, pp. 200–214. Among many treatments of the plays see Clayton Hamilton, *Conversations on Contemporary Drama* (1924), O. M. Sayler, *Our American Theatre* (1923), T. H. Dickinson, *Playwrights of the New American Theatre* (1924); P. H. Boynton, *Some Contemporary Americans* (1924); and A. H. Quinn, *History of the American Drama from the Civil War to the Present Day*, Vol. II (1927).